Nuclear Weapons Databook

Volume IV
Soviet Nuclear Weapons

Nuclear Weapons Databook

Volume IV
Soviet Nuclear Weapons

by
Thomas B. Cochran, William M. Arkin, Robert S. Norris,
and Jeffrey I. Sands

A book by the
Natural Resources Defense Council, Inc.

1817

Harper & Row, Publishers, New York
BALLINGER DIVISION

Grand Rapids, Philadelphia, St. Louis, San Francisco
London, Singapore, Sydney, Tokyo

Copyright © 1989 by the Natural Resources Defense Council, Inc. All rights reserved. No part of this publication may be reproduced, stored in a retrieval system, or transmitted in any form or by any means, electronic, mechanical, photocopy, recording, or otherwise, without the prior written consent of the publisher.

International Standard Book Number: 0–88730–048–0 (CL)
0–88730–049–9 (PB)

Library of Congress Catalog Card Number: 89–11156

Printed in the United States of America

Library of Congress Cataloging-in-Publication Data

Soviet nuclear weapons / Thomas B. Cochran . . . [et al.].
    p.   cm.—(Nuclear weapons databook; v. 4)
    Bibliography: p. 404.
    Includes index.
    ISBN 0–88730–048–0   ISBN 0–88730–049–9 (pbk.)
    1. Nuclear weapons—Soviet Union. 2. Soviet Union—Armed forces—Weapons systems. I. Cochran, Thomas B. II. Series.
U264.C6   1984 vol. 4
355.8′25119′0947—dc20   89–11156
                                                                          CIP

89 90 91 92 HC 9 8 7 6 5 4 3 2 1

About the Authors

Thomas B. Cochran is a Senior Staff Scientist and Director of the *Nuclear Weapons Databook* Project at the Natural Resources Defense Council, Inc. He is coauthor of the first three volumes of the *Nuclear Weapons Databook*. He has served as a consultant to numerous government agencies and non-government organizations on energy and nuclear non-proliferation matters and was Assistant Professor of Physics at the Naval Postgraduate School in Monterey, California, while on active duty in the Navy. He is the author of *The Liquid Metal Fast Breeder Reactor: An Environmental and Economic Critique* (Washington, DC: Resources for the Future, 1974). He has a Ph.D. in physics from Vanderbilt University.

William M. Arkin is Director of the National Security Program and the Arms Race and Nuclear Weapons Research Project at the Institute for Policy Studies in Washington, DC. He is a consultant to the Natural Resources Defense Council, Inc. and a member of the editorial board of the *Bulletin of the Atomic Scientists*. He has been an intelligence analyst with the U.S. Army in Berlin and a Senior Staff Member of the Center for Defense Information. He is author of *Research Guide to Current Military and Strategic Affairs* (Washington, DC: IPS, 1981), *SIOP: The Secret U.S. Plan for Nuclear War* (with Peter Pringle) (New York: W.W. Norton, 1983), and *Nuclear Battlefields: Global Links in the Arms Race* (with Richard Fieldhouse) (Cambridge, MA: Ballinger, 1985), and is coauthor of the first three volumes of the *Nuclear Weapons Databook*.

Robert S. Norris is a Senior Research Associate at the Natural Resources Defense Council, Inc. and coauthor of Volumes II and III of the *Nuclear Weapons Databook*. He has taught political science and international relations at several universities and has been a Senior Staff Member of the Center for Defense Information. He has a Ph.D. in political science from New York University.

Jeffrey I. Sands was a research assistant at the Natural Resources Defense Council, Inc. and is currently a Ph.D. candidate in political science in the Defense and Arms Control program at the Massachusetts Institute of Technology. He is a member of the Center for International Studies and the Soviet Security Studies Working Group at MIT.

Table of Contents

List of Figures ix
List of Tables xiii
Preface xv
Acknowledgments xvii
Nuclear Weapons Databook Advisory Board xviii

CHAPTER ONE
Soviet Nuclear Weapons: An Overview

Introduction 2
Early History of Soviet Nuclear Weapons
  Development 4
New Capabilities and the Introduction of Nuclear
  Weapons into Soviet Armed Forces 6
Achieving Nuclear Parity 8
Strategic Weapons Developments in the 1980s ... 13
Non-strategic Weapons Developments in the
  1980s 13
The Nuclear Stockpile Today 14
Nuclear Operations and Readiness 15
  Strategic Rocket Forces 17
  Air Forces 18
  Naval Forces 18
Soviet Military Thought: Definitions 20

CHAPTER TWO
The Soviet Nuclear Stockpile

Introduction 22
DOD Estimates of the Size of the Soviet Stockpile 22
Components of the Soviet Nuclear Stockpile 24
Strategic Forces 28
  ICBMs 28
  SLBMs 31
  Bomber Weapons 32
  Strategic Defense 32
Non-strategic Forces 32
  Surface-to-Surface Missiles 33
  Nuclear Artillery 34
  Non-strategic Aviation 35
  Air-to-Surface Missiles 36
  Naval Nuclear Forces 37
    Sea-Launched Cruise and Anti-ship Missiles .. 38
    Anti-Submarine Weapons 39
Soviet Megatonnage 41

CHAPTER THREE
Soviet Military Organization

Overview 46
Communist Party Control of the Soviet Military .. 46
  The Department of Defense Industry 49
  The Defense Council 50
The Supreme High Command 50
Ministry of Defense 51
  Collegium 51
  General Staff 51
Administrative Organization of the Armed Forces 52
  Strategic Rocket Forces 53
  Ground Forces 55
  Air Defense Troops 56
    Radio-Technical Troops 57
    Zenith Rocket Troops 58
    Fighter Aviation 58
  Air Forces 58
    Air Forces of the Military Districts and Groups
      of Soviet Forces 59
    Strategic Air Armies 59
  Navy 61
Wartime Organization of the Armed Forces 63
  Theaters of War 64
  Theaters of Military Operations 65
  Operational Formations 66

CHAPTER FOUR
Design and Production of Nuclear Weapons Systems

Overview 68
Government Organizations 70
  Military-Industrial Commission................. 70
  State Planning Committee 70
Research and Development Organizations 72
  Industrial Ministries 72
    Ministry of Medium Machine Building 72
    Ministry of General Machine Building 73
    Ministry of Machine Building 73
    Ministry of Defense Industry 73
    Ministry of Shipbuilding Industry 73
    Ministry of Aviation Industry 73
    Communications-Electronics Industries 73
  Design Bureaus 74
    Missiles 74
    Aircraft 75
    Ships and Submarines 75
    Artillery and Tracked Vehicles 76
Weapon Systems Production 76
  Missile Production 77
  Aircraft Production 77
  Naval Production 78
Nuclear Warhead Production 78
  Nuclear Weapons Materials Production 79
  Plutonium Production 79
    The Kyshtym Complex 79
    The Siberian Plant 81
    Beloyarsky 81
  Power Reactor Capacity Available for
    Plutonium Production 81

Cumulative Plutonium (Equivalent) Production	86
Heavy Water Production	88
Tritium Production	88
Uranium Production	90
Uranium Mining and Processing	90
Uranium Enrichment	90
The Design Cycle	95

CHAPTER FIVE
Strategic Nuclear Forces

Overview	98
History of Strategic Missiles	98
Land-Based Missiles	98
Sea-Based Missiles	105
Current Strategic Force Structure (mid-1988)	110
Intercontinental Ballistic Missiles	110
Submarine-Launched Ballistic Missile Systems	112
Submarine-Launched Ballistic Missiles	113
Strategic Bomber Force	115
Strategic Defense Nuclear Forces	116
ABM Systems	117
SS-X-16 Sinner Mobile ICBM	118
Surface-to-air Missiles	120
Land-Based Missile Systems	121
SS-11 Sego	121
SS-13 Mod 2 Savage	123
SS-17 Mod 3 Spanker	125
SS-18 Mod 4 Satan	127
SS-19 Mod 3 Stiletto	129
SS-24 Scalpel	131
SS-25 Sickle	133
Ballistic Missile Submarines	136
Golf V and Hotel III Class	136
Yankee Class	137
Delta Class	139
Typhoon Class	141
Naval Strategic Missiles	143
SS-N-6 Serb	143
SS-N-8 Sawfly	145
SS-N-17 Snipe	147
SS-N-18 Stingray	148
SS-N-20 Sturgeon	150
SS-N-23 Skiff	151

CHAPTER SIX
Cruise Missiles and Anti-ship Missiles

Overview	154
History	154
Air-Launched Missiles	157
Sea-Launched Missiles	158
Ground-Launched Cruise Missiles	160
Long-Range Cruise Missile Developments	161
Air-Launched	162
AS-2 Kipper	162
AS-3 Kangaroo	163
AS-4 Kitchen	164
AS-5 Kelt	166
AS-6 Kingfish	168
AS-15 Kent	169
Sea-Launched	171
SS-N-3a/c Shaddock/SS-N-3b Sepal	171
SS-N-7 Starbright	173
SS-N-9 Siren	174
SS-N-12 Sandbox	176
SS-N-19 Shipwreck	178
SS-N-21 Sampson	180
SS-N-22 Sunburn	182
SS-NX-24	184
Ground-Launched Cruise Missiles	185
SSC-1b Sepal	185
SSC-X-4	186

CHAPTER SEVEN
Non-Strategic Missiles, Rockets, and Artillery

Overview	190
History	190
Long-range Missiles	194
Operational-Tactical and Tactical Missiles and Rockets	196
Nuclear Artillery	198
Atomic Demolition Munitions	202
Nuclear-Capable Artillery	203
Ballistic Missile Submarine	206
Golf II SSB	206
Naval Non-strategic Missiles	208
SS-N-5 Sark	208
Missile Systems	209
SS-20 Saber	209
SS-4 Sandal	212
SS-12M Scaleboard B	215
SS-23 Spider	218
SS-1c Scud-B	220
SS-21 Scarab	223
FROG-7	225

CHAPTER EIGHT
Nuclear-Capable Aviation

Overview	228
History	228
Current Nuclear-Capable Aircraft (mid-1988)	231
Strategic Bombers	231
Non-strategic Bombers	232
Tactical Aircraft	234
Soviet Naval Aviation	234
Strategic Bombers	237
Tu-95 Bear A/B/C/G, Tu-142 Bear H	237
Tu-160 Blackjack A	240
Bombers	242
Tu-26 Backfire A/B/C (Tu-22M)	242
Tu-22 Blinder A/B (Tu-105)	245
Tu-16 Badger A/C/G	247
Tactical Aircraft	250
Su-24 Fencer A/B/C/D/E	250

Table of Contents

MiG-27 Flogger D/J 253
MiG-23 Flogger B/G 255
Su-17 Fitter C/D/H 258
MiG-21bis Fishbed L 260
Su-7B Fitter A (BMK Fitter A) 262
Naval Aviation 263
  Tu-142 Bear F 263
  Il-38 May 264
  Be-12 Mail (M-12 Tchaika) (Seagull) 266
Nuclear-Capable ASW Helicopters 268
  Ka-27 Helix A, Ka-25 Hormone A............... 268

CHAPTER NINE
Naval Nuclear Weapons

Overview 272
History 272
Naval Nuclear Weapon Systems 274
  Anti-Submarine Nuclear Weapon Systems 274
  Anti-Air Warfare 275
Non-strategic Submarines 275
  Cruise Missile Submarines 275
  Attack Submarines 276
Surface Ships 278
  Aircraft Carriers 278
  Cruisers 278
  Destroyers 279
  Frigates/Patrol Combatants 279
Nuclear Weapon Support Ships 279
Geographic Constraints 279
Cruise Missile Submarines 280
  Oscar I (SSGN) 280
  Charlie I/II (SSGN) 282
  Cruise Missile Submarines (SSG/N) 284
Yankee Conversions (SSN/SSGN) 287
Attack Submarines 288
  Akula (SSN) 288
  Mike (SSN) 290
  Sierra (SSN) 292
  Alfa (SSN) 294
  Victor (SSN) 296
  Echo I, November, Hotel II 299
  Diesel-Powered Attack Submarines (SS) 302
Aircraft Carriers 305
  Tbilisi 305
  Aviation Ships 307
Cruisers 311
  Kirov (CGN) 311
  Slava (CG) 313
  Kara (CG) 314
  Kresta I/II (CG), Kynda (CG), Sverdlov (CL) 316

Destroyers 319
  Sovremennyy (DDG) 319
  Udaloy (DDG) 321
  Kildin/Mod Kildin (DDG), Kanin (DDG), Kashin/
    Mod Kashin (DDG), Kotlin/Mod Kotlin/SAM
    Kotlin (DDG) 323
Frigates 326
  Krivak I/II (FFG) 326
Nuclear-Capable Patrol Craft (PGG/PGGH) 327
  Nanuchka I/III (PGG), Sarancha (PGGH),
    Tarantul III (PGG) 327
Minor Surface Combatants with 21-inch Torpedo
  Tubes 329
  Skoryy (DD), Grisha (FFL), Riga (FF), Turya
    (PTH) 329

CHAPTER TEN
Soviet Nuclear Testing

Overview 332
Effects of Various Testing Treaties Limiting
  Nuclear Testing 333
Main Areas of Testing in the Soviet Union 333
Atmospheric Testing and Nuclear Weapons
  Design 336
Underground Testing 337
  Calculation of Yields of Soviet Underground
    Explosions 337
  Soviet Underground Nuclear Explosions 340
  Distribution of Soviet Underground Nuclear
    Tests by Time and Yield 341
  Histograms of Soviet Underground Testing as a
    Function of Yield 341
  Concentration of Soviet Testing into Particular
    Yields 343
  Soviet Compliance with the Threshold Test Ban
    Treaty 346
Peaceful Nuclear Explosions 347
Appendices
  A. Short Titles of Frequently Cited
    References 384
  B. Soviet Weapons Designations 387
  C. Gazetteer 394
  D. Conversion Factors 402
Bibliography of Declassified and Partially
  Declassified Documents Obtained Under the
  FOIA 404
Glossary
  Glossary of Abbreviations and Acronyms 410
  Glossary of Terms 416
Index 426

List of Figures

Figure 1.1 Missiles in Cuba, October 1962 8
Figure 1.2 SS-5 Skean IRBM 9
Figure 1.3 SS-8 Sasin ICBM 10
Figure 1.4 SS-9 Scarp ICBM 11
Figure 1.5 SS-9 Scarp ICBM 11
Figure 1.6 SS-9 Scarp ICBM 11
Figure 1.7 SS-X-15 Scrooge missile 12
Figure 1.8 SS-X-14 Scamp MRBM 12
Figure 1.9 Mya-4 Bison bomber 13
Figure 1.10 Victor III and Oscar submarines 16
Figure 1.11 Amga class missile transport ship 19
Figure 2.1 Comparison of Soviet and U.S. Nuclear Weapons Stockpiles, 1956-1982 (from Wohlstetter) 22
Figure 2.2 Comparison of Soviet and U.S. Nuclear Weapons Stockpiles, 1965-1983 (from Wagner) 22
Figure 2.3 Comparison of Soviet and U.S. Nuclear Weapons Stockpiles, 1965-1984 (from Weinberger) 23
Figure 2.4 Comparison of Soviet and U.S. Nuclear Weapons Stockpiles, 1955-1985 (from Iklé/Wohlstetter) 23
Figure 2.5 U.S. Nuclear Weapons Stockpile, 1945-1976 (from JCAE) 23
Figure 2.6 Comparison of U.S. Nuclear Weapons Stockpile Graphs from JCAE, Wagner, and Weinberger 26
Figure 2.7 Comparison of Soviet Nuclear Weapons Stockpile Graphs from Wohlstetter, Wagner, and Iklé/Wohlstetter 27
Figure 2.8 Alexander Brykin submarine tender ... 30
Figure 2.9 FROG-7 resupply vehicle on ZIL-135 chassis 34
Figure 2.10 D-20 152mm howitzer 34
Figure 2.11 Golf II SSB* 34
Figure 2.12 Sverdlov CL* 38
Figure 2.13 Comparison of Soviet and U.S. Megatonnage, 1960-1987 (from Carlucci) 41
Figure 2.14 U.S. Nuclear Weapons Stockpile Yield, 1950-1984 (from DOE-OMA) 41
Figure 2.15 Comparison of DOE-OMA Graph of U.S. Nuclear Weapons Stockpile Yield with Wagner, Weinberger, Carlucci and Iklé/Wohlstetter 42

Figure 2.16 Best Comparison of Soviet and U.S. Megatonnage, 1960-1987 43
Figure 3.1 Peacetime Structure of the Soviet Military 47
Figure 3.2 Operational Chain of Command for Soviet Military Forces 48
Figure 3.3 Soviet ICBM Bases and Test Centers ... 54
Figure 3.4 Launch pad at Tyuratum 55
Figure 3.5 Krasnoyarsk radar 58
Figure 3.6 Moscow Ballistic Missile Defense 59
Figure 3.7 Soviet Bomber Bases and Test Centers 60
Figure 3.8 Northern Fleet attack submarine base 62
Figure 3.9 Submarine tunnels 62
Figure 3.10 Soviet Navy Bases 63
Figure 4.1 Soviet Bureaucracy for Weapons Acquisition 68
Figure 4.2 Soviet Design Bureaus and Military Production Facilities 71
Figure 4.3 Kiev CVHG 76
Figure 4.4 Kirov CGN 78
Figure 4.5 Plutonium Production and Channel Power Reactor Sites 80
Figure 4.6 Kyshtym Area Photos 82
Figure 4.7 Tu-160 Blackjack A bomber 91
Figure 4.8 Oscar SSGN 91
Figure 4.9 Soviet Uranium Deposits and Processing Centers 92
Figure 5.1 Soviet ICBMs 111
Figure 5.2 Soviet Strategic SLBMs 114
Figure 5.3 SA-2 Guideline SAM 117
Figure 5.4 Nuclear-Capable Surface-to-Air Missiles 119
Figure 5.5 ABM-1B Galosh 119
Figure 5.6 SS-11 Sego ICBM 121
Figure 5.7 SS-13 Savage ICBM 123
Figure 5.8 SS-24 Rail-mobile Scalpel ICBM 131
Figure 5.9 SS-25 Road-mobile Sickle ICBM 133
Figure 5.10 SS-25 deployment base 134
Figure 5.11 Yankee I SSBN 137
Figure 5.12 Yankee II SSBN 138
Figure 5.13 Delta I SSBN 140

List of Figures

Figure 5.14 Delta II SSBN 140
Figure 5.15 Delta III SSBN 140
Figure 5.16 Delta IV SSBN 140
Figure 5.17 Typhoon SSBN 141
Figure 5.18 SS-N-6 Serb SLBM 143
Figure 5.19 SS-N-8 Sawfly SLBM 145
Figure 6.1 Soviet Cruise Missile and Anti-ship Missile Development 156
Figure 6.2 Air-Launched Nuclear-Capable Cruise Missiles and Anti-Ship Missiles (mid-1988) 157
Figure 6.3 Nuclear-Capable Sea-Launched Cruise Missiles and Anti-Ship Missiles (mid-1988) 159
Figure 6.4 AS-4 Kitchen missile 164
Figure 6.5 AS-4 Kitchen and Backfire* 165
Figure 6.6 AS-5 Kelt and Badger* 166
Figure 6.7 Bear H bomber 169
Figure 6.8 SS-N-3/Juliett SSG* 171
Figure 6.9 SS-N-9 Siren launcher/Nanuchka I PPG* 174
Figure 6.10 SS-N-12 launcher/Slava CG 176
Figure 6.11 SS-N-12 launcher/Minsk CVHG 177
Figure 6.12 SS-N-19/Kirov CGN 178
Figure 6.13 SS-N-19/Kirov CGN 178
Figure 6.14 SS-N-19/Kirov CGN 179
Figure 6.15 Yankee Notch SSN 180
Figure 6.16 Sovremenyy DDG* 182
Figure 6.17 SSC-X-4 GLCM 186
Figure 6.18 SSC-X-4 GLCM launch canister 187
Figure 6.19 SSC-X-4 GLCM tractor-trailer 187
Figure 7.1 SS-20 Operating Bases (end-1987) 195
Figure 7.2 SS-4 Bases (end-1987) 196
Figure 7.3 SS-12M Bases (end-1987) 198
Figure 7.4 SS-23 Bases (end-1987) 200
Figure 7.5 152mm Nuclear-Capable Artillery 203
Figure 7.6 D20 152mm towed howitzer 203
Figure 7.7 2S3 152mm self-propelled gun/howitzer 203
Figure 7.8 2S5 152mm self-propelled gun/howitzer 204
Figure 7.9 203mm Nuclear-Capable Artillery 204
Figure 7.10 240mm Nuclear-Capable Artillery 205
Figure 7.11 2S7 203mm self-propelled gun 205
Figure 7.12 M-240 240mm towed heavy mortar 205
Figure 7.13 Golf II SSB* 206
Figure 7.14 Golf II SSB* 207
Figure 7.15 SS-20 Saber IRBM 209
Figure 7.16 SS-20 "front end" 209
Figure 7.17 SS-20 canister 210
Figure 7.18 SS-20 missile transport vehicle 210
Figure 7.19 SS-20 TEL 211
Figure 7.20 SS-20 launcher garage 211
Figure 7.21 SS-4 Sandal IRBM 212
Figure 7.22 SS-4 fuel truck 212
Figure 7.23 SS-4 missile launcher 213
Figure 7.24 SS-4 fixed launch platform 214
Figure 7.25 SS-12M Scaleboard SRBM 215
Figure 7.26 SS-12 transport vehicle 216
Figure 7.27 SS-12 mobile launcher 216
Figure 7.28 SS-12 at field site 217
Figure 7.29 SS-23 Spider SRBM 218
Figure 7.30 SS-23 missile transport vehicle 219
Figure 7.31 SS-23 missile launcher 219
Figure 7.32 SS-1c SCUD B SRBM 220
Figure 7.33 SCUD B and transporter vehicle 221
Figure 7.34 SCUD B TEL 221
Figure 7.35 SS-21 Scarab SRBM 223
Figure 7.36 SS-21 TEL 224
Figure 7.37 FROG-7 and TEL 225
Figure 7.38 FROG-7 and TEL 226
Figure 7.39 FROG-7 and TEL 226
Figure 8.1 Soviet Bombers 232
Figure 8.2 Soviet Nuclear Capable Fighters 235
Figure 8.3 Tu-142 Bear H bomber 237
Figure 8.4 Tu-95 Bear G bomber 238
Figure 8.5 Tu-142 Bear H bomber 238
Figure 8.6 Tu-160 Blackjack A bomber 240
Figure 8.7 Tu-26 Backfire bomber* 242
Figure 8.8 Tu-26 Backfire bomber 243
Figure 8.9 Tu-22 Blinder B bomber 245
Figure 8.10 Tu-22 Blinder bomber 246
Figure 8.11 Tu-16 Badger G bomber 247
Figure 8.12 Tu-16 Badger C bomber* 248
Figure 8.13 Tu-16 Badger bombers refueling 248
Figure 8.14 Su-24 Fencer fighter-bomber 250
Figure 8.15 Su-24 Fencer fighter-bomber* 251
Figure 8.16 Su-24 Fencer fighter-bomber* 251

List of Figures

Figure 8.17 MiG-27 Flogger D fighter	253
Figure 8.18 MiG-23 Flogger G fighter*	255
Figure 8.19 MiG-23 Flogger B fighter*	256
Figure 8.20 Su-17 Fitter C fighter	258
Figure 8.21 MiG-21 Fishbed fighter	260
Figure 8.22 MiG-21 Fishbed fighter	261
Figure 8.23 Il-38 May ASW aircraft	264
Figure 8.24 Il-38 May ASW aircraft*	265
Figure 8.25 Be-12 Mail ASW aircraft*	266
Figure 8.26 Ka-27 Helix ASW helicopter	268
Figure 8.27 Ka-25 Hormone A ASW helicopter	268
Figure 8.28 Ka-27 Helix ASW helicopter	269
Figure 8.29 Ka-25 Hormone A ASW helicopter	269
Figure 8.30 Ka-27 Helix A ASW helicopter	269
Figure 9.1 Oscar I SSGN	280
Figure 9.2 Oscar I SSGN	281
Figure 9.3 Charlie I SSGN	282
Figure 9.4 Charlie II SSGN	283
Figure 9.5 Charlie I SSGN	283
Figure 9.6 Papa SSGN	284
Figure 9.7 Echo II SSGN	284
Figure 9.8 Juliett SSG*	286
Figure 9.9 Akula SSN	288
Figure 9.10 Mike SSN	290
Figure 9.11 Sierra SSN	292
Figure 9.12 Sierra SSN	293
Figure 9.13 Alfa SSN	294
Figure 9.14 Victor I SSN	296
Figure 9.15 Victor II SSN	297
Figure 9.16 Victor III SSN	297
Figure 9.17 Echo I SSN	299
Figure 9.18 November SSN	299
Figure 9.19 Hotel II SSN	300
Figure 9.20 Kilo SS	302
Figure 9.21 Tango SS	302
Figure 9.22 Foxtrot SS	303
Figure 9.23 Romeo SS	303
Figure 9.24 Zulu SS	303
Figure 9.25 Whiskey SS*	303
Figure 9.26 Tbilisi CVN	305
Figure 9.27 Tbilisi CVN	305
Figure 9.28 Kiev CVHG*	307
Figure 9.29 Kiev CVHG*	308
Figure 9.30 Kiev CVHG*	308
Figure 9.31 Kiev CVHG/Yak-36 Forger STOL aircraft	308
Figure 9.32 Moskva CHG	309
Figure 9.33 Moskva CHG*	310
Figure 9.34 Kirov CGN	311
Figure 9.35 Kirov CGN	312
Figure 9.36 Slava CG	313
Figure 9.37 Kara CG*	314
Figure 9.38 Kresta I CG*	316
Figure 9.39 Kresta II CG*	316
Figure 9.40 Kynda CG	317
Figure 9.41 Sverdlov CL*	318
Figure 9.42 Sovremennyy DDG*	319
Figure 9.43 Udaloy DDG*	321
Figure 9.44 Udaloy DDG*	322
Figure 9.45 Kildin DDG*	323
Figure 9.46 Kanin DDG	323
Figure 9.47 Mod Kashin DDG*	324
Figure 9.48 Kotlin DDG	324
Figure 9.49 Krivak FFG*	326
Figure 9.50 Nanuchka PPG*	327
Figure 9.51 Tarantul PPG*	327
Figure 9.52 Nanuchka III PPG*	328
Figure 9.53 Skoryy DD	329
Figure 9.54 Riga FF	329
Figure 10.1 Soviet Underground Atomic Weapons Testing Areas, 1963-1987 and Sites of Underground Explosions for Peaceful Purposes	334
Figure 10.2 U-2 Photograph of a Crater From a Nuclear Test at the Kazakh Test Site	335
Figure 10.3 Schematic Diagram of the Seismic Velocity and Seismic Attenuation Structure of the Outer 200 Kilometers of the Earth Beneath the Nevada Test Site and Test Sites in Older, Stable Regions Such as the Central and Eastern United States and the Main Soviet Test Sites	338
Figure 10.4 Calibration Curve for the Magnitude of Seismic Surface Waves (M_s) as a Function of Yield for Explosions of Known Yield at Various Test Sites Throughout the World	338
Figure 10.5 Calibration Curve for Magnitudes (m_b) of Short Period P-waves as Normalized to the Shagan River Area of Kazakh Test Site as a Function of Yield for Contained Underground	

List of Figures

Nuclear Explosions and Two Large Chemical Explosions in the Soviet Union 338

Figure 10.6 Magnitude (m_b) as a Function of Announced Yields of Very Large Explosions at the Nevada Test Site and Amchitka Normalized to Novaya Zemlya 338

Figure 10.7 Histograms of Yields for All Underground Nuclear Explosions Detonated by the Soviet Union for Two Time Intervals 342

Figure 10.8 Histograms of Underground Nuclear Explosions Detonated by the Soviet Union at Novaya Zemlya Test Sites for Two Time Intervals 343

Figure 10.9 Histograms of Underground Nuclear Explosions Detonated by the Soviet Union at the Kazakhstan Test Site for Two Time Intervals 344

Figure 10.10 Histograms of Underground Nuclear Explosions Detonated by the Soviet Union at Western Kazakhstan Sites for Two Time Intervals 344

Figure 10.11 Histograms of Underground Nuclear Explosions Announced by the Soviet Union as Peaceful Explosions or Underground Explosions Away from Main Testing Areas for Two Time Intervals 345

Figure 10.12 Histograms of Underground Nuclear Explosions by the Soviet Union for Time Period 1980 Through 1985 Smoothed Using Standard Deviation of ± 0.1 m_b Units 345

Figure 10.13 Calculated Yields of All Recorded Soviet Nuclear Weapons Tests of Yields Greater than 25 Kilotons from 1963 Through January 1987 346

Figure 10.14 Yields of the Largest Soviet and U.S. Underground Nuclear Explosions Detonated in Any Calendar Year Since the Start of Underground Testing in 1957 347

*Photos courtesy Swedish Ministry of Defense

List of Tables

Table 1.1 Soviet Nuclear Weapons (1953-1988) ... 3
Table 1.2 Milestones in Soviet Nuclear Weapons Developments ... 5
Table 1.3 Soviet Nuclear Weapons Research and Development Programs (1988) ... 15
Table 2.1 DOD/DOE Estimates of the Size of the U.S. and Soviet Stockpiles ... 25
Table 2.2 Soviet Dual-Capable Weapons ... 27
Table 2.3 Soviet Nuclear Stockpile (mid-1988) ... 28
Table 2.4 Intercontinental Ballistic Missile (ICBM) Warheads (mid-1988) ... 29
Table 2.5 Submarine-Launched Ballistic Missile (SLBM) Warheads (mid-1988) ... 29
Table 2.6 Strategic Bomber-Delivered Warheads (mid-1988) ... 31
Table 2.7 Strategic Defense Forces Warheads (mid-1988) ... 32
Table 2.8 Non-strategic Surface-to-Surface Missiles (mid-1988) ... 33
Table 2.9 Non-strategic Land-Based Aircraft Warheads (mid-1988) ... 35
Table 2.10 Air-to-Surface Missiles (mid-1988) ... 36
Table 2.11 Non-strategic Naval Warheads (mid-1988) ... 37
Table 2.12 Soviet Naval Aviation (mid-1988) ... 38
Table 2.13 Sea-Launched Cruise Missile and Anti-ship Missile Warheads (mid-1988) ... 39
Table 2.14 Anti-Submarine Nuclear Warheads (mid-1988) ... 39
Table 2.15 DOD/DOE Estimates of the Cumulative Yield (megatonnage) of the U.S. and Soviet Stockpiles ... 40
Table 3.1 Political Leadership of the Soviet Union ... 49
Table 3.2 Allocation of Nuclear Weapons by Service (1988) ... 53
Table 3.3 Strategic Rocket Forces ICBM Main Operating Bases (1988) ... 55
Table 3.4 Bomber Bases (1988) ... 61
Table 3.5 Naval Bases (1988) ... 64
Table 4.1 Soviet Industrial Ministries That Support the Military ... 69
Table 4.2 Soviet Military Design Bureaus ... 73
Table 4.3 Principal Missile Design Bureaus ... 74
Table 4.4 Principal Aircraft and Engine Design Bureaus ... 75
Table 4.5 Launcher, Tracked Vehicles and Artillery Design Bureaus and Production Facilities ... 76
Table 4.6 Soviet Military Production Plants ... 77
Table 4.7 Soviet Nuclear Power and Plutonium Production Reactors ... 84
Table 4.8 Upper-bound Estimate of Plutonium Produced by the Siberian Plant ... 87
Table 4.9 Estimated Plutonium Produced by Graphite-Moderated Channel-Type Power Reactors ... 89
Table 4.10 Soviet Uranium Deposits and Processing Centers ... 93
Table 5.1 Strategic Offensive Nuclear Forces (mid-1988) ... 99
Table 5.2 Strategic Offensive Force Loadings (1956-1988) ... 100
Table 5.3 Strategic Land-Based Missiles (mid-1988) ... 101
Table 5.4 Soviet ICBM Forces (1960-1988) ... 102
Table 5.5 Soviet Ballistic Missile Submarine Forces (1958-1988) ... 106
Table 5.6 Strategic Submarines (mid-1988) ... 112
Table 5.7 Strategic Submarine Forces (mid-1988) ... 113
Table 5.8 Strategic Bomber Forces (mid-1988) ... 115
Table 5.9 Soviet Strategic Bomber Forces (1956-1988) ... 116
Table 6.1 Soviet Nuclear-Capable Cruise Missiles and Anti-Ship Missiles ... 155
Table 6.2 Soviet Air-launched Nuclear-Capable Cruise Missiles ... 157
Table 6.3 Soviet Nuclear-Capable Sea-launched Cruise and Anti-ship Missiles ... 159
Table 7.1 Soviet Non-strategic Long-range Missiles (1956-1988) ... 191
Table 7.2 Soviet INF Missiles, Launchers, and Bases (1987/mid-1988) ... 193
Table 7.3 SS-20 Saber Missile Deployments (1987/1988) ... 194
Table 7.4 SS-4 Sandal Missile Deployments (1987/1988) ... 197

List of Tables

Table 7.5 SS-12M Scaleboard B Missile Deployments (1987/1988) 199

Table 7.6 SS-23 Spider Missile Deployments (1987/1988) 201

Table 8.1 Nuclear-Capable Aircraft (1988) 233

Table 9.1 Soviet Nuclear-Capable Ships and Submarines (1988) 274

Table 9.2 Soviet Navy Deployments by Fleet (mid-1988) 276

Table 9.3 Major Soviet Submarine and Naval Accidents 277

Table 10.1 Known Soviet Nuclear Explosions, 1949-1962 349

Table 10.2 Known Soviet Underground Nuclear Explosions, 1961-1987 355

Table 10.3 Summary of Known Nuclear Explosions, 1949-1987 373

Table 10.4 Soviet Seismic Events That Have Not Been Identified as Being Earthquakes, Large Chemical Explosions, or Nuclear Explosions 374

Table 10.5 Known Nuclear Explosions in Eastern Kazakhstan (KTS) by Month 375

Table 10.6 Known Nuclear Explosions in Novaya Zemlya by Month 376

Table 10.7 Summary of Explosions in Eastern Kazakhstan (KTS) and Novaya Zemlya (NZ) by Month 377

Table 10.8 Underground Nuclear Explosions in Eastern Kazakhstan (KTS) by Yield Range (1962-1985) 377

Table 10.9 Underground Nuclear Explosions in Novaya Zemlya by Yield Range (1962-1985) 378

Table 10.10 Underground Nuclear Explosions in Western Kazakhstan by Yield Range (1962-1985) 379

Table 10.11 Underground Nuclear Explosions Outside Main Test Areas or Announced as Explosions for Peaceful Purposes by Yield Range (1962-1985) 380

Table 10.12 Known Soviet Underground Nuclear Explosions by Yield Range (1961-1985) 381

Table 10.13 Large Underground Nuclear Explosions at Eastern Kazakhstan (KTS), April 1976 - December 1985 382

Preface

The *Nuclear Weapons Databook* is meant to be a current and accurate encyclopedia of information about nuclear weapons. Information is an essential prerequisite for a democratic society to function. Without it knowledgeable decision-making by the public and its leaders will suffer.

The Natural Resources Defense Council, a private non-profit environmental organization long concerned about the dangers and problems posed by the unleashed atom, initiated work on its *Nuclear Weapons Databook* series in 1980 to provide information and to promote a more enlightened and rational discussion of critical nuclear weapons issues. The series is the result of the most thorough compilation, analysis, and survey of information on nuclear weapons ever undertaken by a non-governmental organization. The NRDC *Databook* staff makes extensive use of the vast information resources of the U.S. government, including careful monitoring of publications, reports, hearings, and statements, as well as the filing of substantial numbers of Freedom of Information requests.

The first volume of the *Databook, U.S. Nuclear Forces and Capabilites* was published in 1984, with a second edition scheduled for publication in 1989. The second and third volumes, *U.S. Nuclear Warhead Production* and *U.S. Nuclear Warhead Facility Profiles*, were published in 1987. Work on a fifth volume, *British, French and Chinese Nuclear Weapons and Nuclear Proliferation*, is well underway. Volumes on the history of nuclear weapons, command and control, nuclear strategy, arms control, and the environmental, health, and safety implications of nuclear weapons are envisioned.

This fourth volume on Soviet nuclear weapons has proven to be the most difficult to prepare. Information about Soviet nuclear weapons is shrouded in secrecy, which makes detailed analyses of nuclear forces, plans, and policies difficult at best. Soviet information sources provide a few clues about possible strategies for the employment of nuclear weapons, but the Soviet government's unfortunate propensity for secrecy and military security means that virtually no official empirical information about nuclear forces is available.

In Volume IV we have assembled the best information from the most reliable sources. We have utilized existing reference works, U.S. government documents, historical extrapolations, intelligence reports, and interviews with government and intelligence officials. As much as possible, we have used primary sources.

The volume relies largely on information collected, analyzed, and made public by the U.S. government and Western intelligence services. This reliance raises three additional problems: the constraints that the intelligence organizations themselves face in obtaining accurate information, the willingness of the U.S. and other governments to make that information public, and the often fragmentary or biased nature of the information that is ultimately made public.

The reader is also cautioned to take into account that there are often significant variations in information from different U.S. government agencies and from agencies of other countries. These differences can most often be attributed to a lack of clarification about the date of information. (Estimates of weapons characteristics change over time.) Also, many descriptions or comparisons of forces fail to specify which systems are being counted.

Within the U.S. intelligence community there is often no empirical "truth" about the composition and characteristics of Soviet forces. Rather, the data bases of the U.S. government—including the Department of Defense, its military services, the Defense Intelligence Agency, the National Security Agency, the Central Intelligence Agency, and the Department of Energy—reflect *estimates* of Soviet capabilities. By necessity we have had to make judgments about what appears to us to be the most accurate information. It is hoped that the extensive footnotes will assist the reader in understanding our assumptions.

Finally, it is crucial to understand that much of the information about Soviet nuclear weapons (even at high levels of security classification) is speculative. "We have only sketchy, usually circumstantial, evidence on their current weapons," Secretary of Energy James Schlesinger stated before Congress in 1979. "With regard to the warheads themselves, we know almost nothing about what capabilities the Soviets have," Richard Wagner, Assistant to the Secretary of Defense for Atomic Energy stated to a congressional committee in 1983. Information in this volume about warhead size, yield, and numbers is highly speculative, as are estimates about the accuracy of nuclear weapons.

The emphasis in this volume is on contemporary Soviet nuclear forces and capabilities. An overview is provided in Chapter One tracing the growth and evolution of Soviet nuclear forces noting the key milestones throughout more than four decades. Chapter Two surveys the Soviet nuclear arsenal and the assumptions used to estimate its size and provides a detailed breakdown of Soviet nuclear weapons by category. Chapter Three describes the political and military organizations that have nuclear weapon responsibilities. Chapter Four describes the research, development, and production facilities and organizations that make special nuclear materials for warheads, and the delivery systems that carry them.

The five subsequent chapters describe the panoply of Soviet nuclear weapons. Chapter Five deals with stra-

Preface

tegic nuclear weapons, such as ballistic missiles and submarines. Chapter Six surveys cruise missiles, air-to-surface missiles, and anti-ship missiles. Chapter Seven discusses non-strategic missiles, rockets and artillery, all land-based "theater" weapons, excluding aircraft. Chapter Eight examines 16 nuclear-capable aircraft types in the Soviet Air Forces and Soviet Naval Aviation. Chapter Nine describes 20 different classes of submarines and 23 different classes of surface ships and the kinds of nuclear weapons they are capable of carrying. Chapter Ten provides an extensive analysis of Soviet nuclear warhead testing, with tables detailing information on more than 600 tests. The appendices include a short-title list of frequently cited references, a comprehensive list of Soviet weapons designations, a gazetteer of locations mentioned in the book, and some useful conversion factors. A bibliography of documents obtained through use of the Freedom of Information Act is included, as are glossaries of terms, abbreviations, and acronyms.

The information in the *Databook* is based, as much as possible, on original documentation, and the sources of information are indicated in the extensive footnotes accompanying the text. The *Databook*, however, is only as useful as the accuracy of the information presented. We therefore strongly encourage the reader to contribute to this effort—to advise us of errors and new information. Please advise us also of other subject areas that should be included in future editions and any changes that could improve the format of the books. We would like to hear from experts willing to serve as contributors or from reviewers of the various sections of the *Databook*, particularly in subject areas not now covered.

Please address all correspondence to *Nuclear Weapons Databook* Project, Natural Resources Defense Council, 1350 New York Avenue, N.W., Suite 300, Washington, DC 20005 (202-783-7800).

---

1 SASC, FY 1980 DOE, p. 225.
2 HASC, FY 1984 DOE, p. 12. See also, HASC, FY 1984 DOE, pp. 27-28; HAC, FY 1984 DOD, Part 6, p. 272.

Acknowledgments

Volume IV of the *Nuclear Weapons Databook* could not have been completed without the invaluable assistance of many individuals and institutions. The Advisory Board to the *Nuclear Weapons Databook* Project, and its Chairman, Dr. Sidney Drell, provided valuable comments and advice. They undertook indepth reviews of draft chapters at three meetings over the course of the preparation of the book (see overleaf).

We are grateful to the U.S. Department of Defense, the Department of Energy, the Arms Control and Disarmament Agency, and the Central Intelligence Agency for their responsiveness to our numerous requests for information. The Air Force, the staffs of the Pentagon library, the Armed Forces News Branch, and the Defense Intelligence Agency were particularly helpful. We would especially like to thank the staff members of the offices that handled our hundreds of requests for information under the Freedom of Information Act.

We are particularly indebted to Peter Almquist of the Institute for Defense Analyses (IDA) for providing valuable assistance and comments on Chapters Three and Four, and to Lynn R. Sykes of Lamont-Doherty Geological Observatory, Columbia University, and Steven Ruggi of Columbia University, for coauthoring most of Chapter Ten. The staff of the Institute for Policy Studies Arms Race and Nuclear Weapons Research Project—Joshua Handler, Julie Morrissey, and Jacquelyn Walsh—made valuable contributions and assisted in research using the extensive files of the Project.

During three special workshops the following individuals provided valuable insights and comments on early manuscript drafts: Michael Deane, Matthew Evangelista, Raymond Garthoff, Howard Stoertz, Andreas Tamberg, Edward Warner, Bob Weinland, and James Westwood. We also wish to thank the following individuals who provided comments on chapter drafts or answered queries for information: Bruce Blair, Julian Cooper, Richard Fieldhouse, David Holloway, William Kelly, Dunbar Lockwood, Thomas Longstroth, and Michael MccGwire.

Photographs were kindly provided by Ken Carter and Bob Bockman of the Office of the Secretary of Defense photo office, Christer Larsson of Space Media Network, and SPOT Image Corp. The Central Intelligence Agency, Defense Intelligence Agency, U.S. Army, Navy, and Air Force, and the Swedish Ministry of Defense also provided photographs.

The Natural Resources Defense Council and the authors with to acknowledge gratefully the support and encouragement given to the *Nuclear Weapons Databook* by the William Bingham Foundation, the Bydale Foundation, the Columbia Foundation, the Field Foundation, the Ford Foundation, the W. Alton Jones Foundation, the J.M. Kaplan Fund, the Joe and Emily Lowe Foundation, the Joyce Mertz-Gilmore Foundation, the New Hope Foundation, the Ploughshares Fund, the Charles H. Revson Foundation, the Rockefeller Family Fund, the Role Foundation, the Samuel Rubin Foundation, the Wallace Genetic Foundation, David B. Arnold, Jr., Charles E. Merrill, Mr. and Mrs. Julius Rosenwald II, Frances Tyson, Mrs. Philip S. Weld, and three anonymous donors.

We appreciate the continuing encouragement and support of the entire Board of Trustees and the staff of the Natural Resources Defense Council. Very special thanks goes to Adrian W. DeWind, Chairman of the Board, for his invaluable guidance and assistance. We also want to recognize James Marshall, a member of the board until his death in August 1986, and Joan K. Davidson, NRDC Honorary Trustee, for their exceptional support and commitment. John H. Adams, Executive Director of NRDC, and S. Jacob Scherr, Senior Staff Attorney, have been enormously helpful. We are deeply indebted to Judy B. Funderburk, who prepared numerous Freedom of Information requests and worked through the countless drafts of this volume. Andrew Burrows and Mathieu Carlson assisted in numerous research tasks, and Bill Christie was unfailingly helpful in his work. Wayne E. Nail designed the *Databook* series and coordinated production. Ron Carnahan prepared the artwork for this volume and Cindy Buck did an excellent job of editing the cumbersome draft. Finally, we would like to thank Carol Franco, former President of Ballinger Publishing Company, for her unfailing support of the entire *Databook* project, and for her patience in the production of this volume.

Advisory Board

Nuclear Weapons Databook Advisory Board

Chairman: Professor Sidney Drell
Deputy Director
Stanford Linear Accelerator Center

Professor Paul Bracken
Yale School of Organization and Management

Hon. Thomas Downey
U.S. House of Representaives

Professor Lawrence Freedman
Department of War Studies
King's College, London

Dr. Richard L. Garwin
IBM Thomas J. Watson Research Center

Admiral Noel Gayler, USN (Ret.)
American Committee on East-West Accord

Professor John Keegan
Soviet Studies Center
Royal Military Academy, Sandhurst

William Kincade
Director, ACCESS

Norman Polmar
Consultant and Author

Thomas Powers
Author

Hon. Walter B. Slocombe, Esq.
Caplin & Drysdale

Cyrus R. Vance, Esq.
Simpson, Thacker & Bartlett

Professor Frank von Hippel
Princeton University

Paul C. Warnke, Esq.
Clifford & Warnke

The authors appreciate the valuable assistance provided by the Advisory Board. We are grateful to the members of the board for their insights and ideas. The members of the board made extensive and very helpful comments on drafts of this volume. However, the selection and analysis of data is the sole responsibility of the authors.

Nuclear Weapons Databook

Volume IV
Soviet Nuclear Weapons

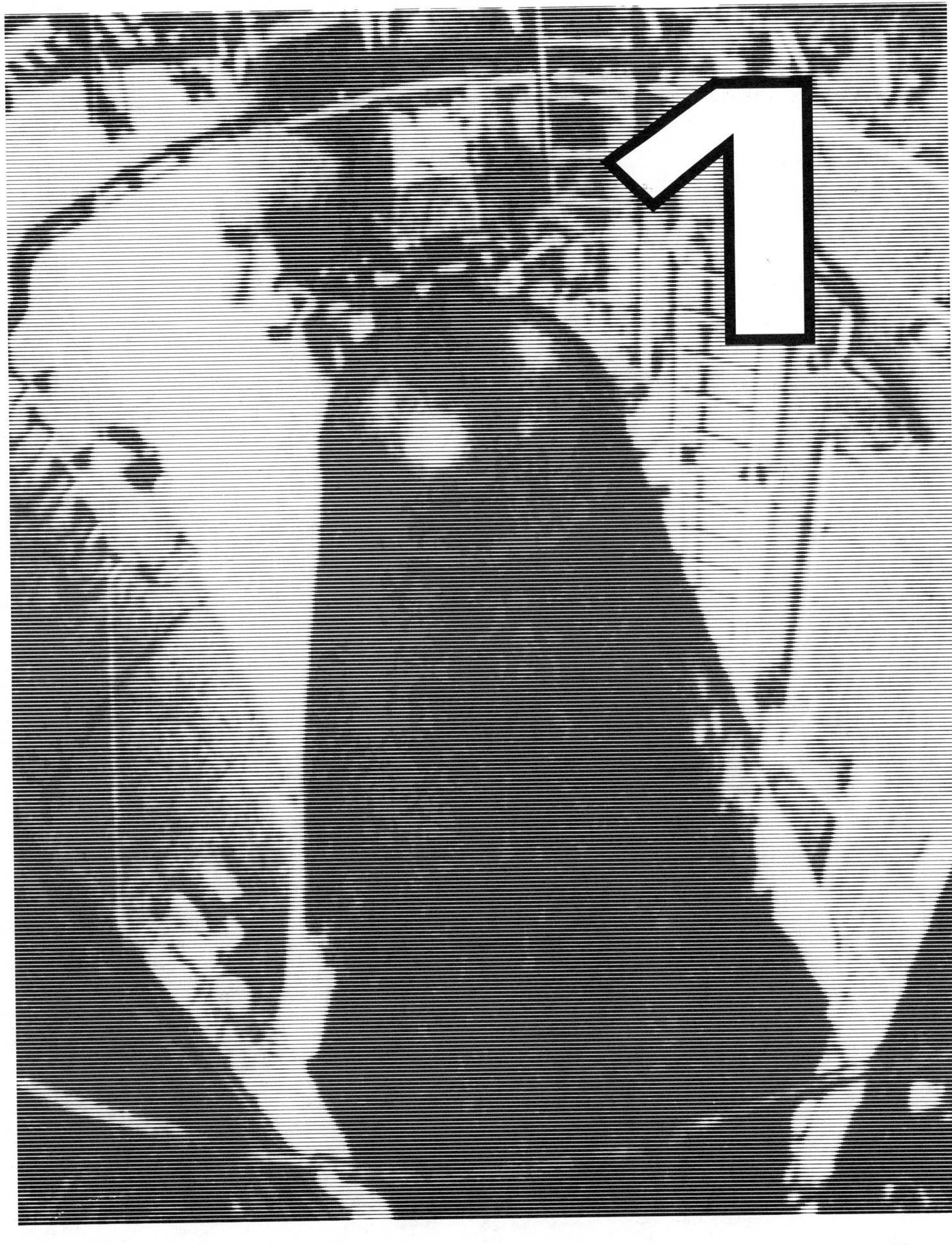

Chapter One
Soviet Nuclear Weapons: An Overview

Introduction

Since the first Soviet nuclear test in August 1949, the Soviet nuclear arsenal has grown from a few dozen fission atomic bombs in the early 1950s to some 33,000 warheads in 1988.[1] Nuclear warheads have been fitted on over 75 different types of weapons, from atomic demolition munitions (ADMs) to intercontinental ballistic missiles (ICBMs), with yields from under one kiloton to many megatons. The warheads have been integrated into over 100 different kinds of delivery systems, which include artillery guns, missiles, rockets, airplanes, ships, and submarines (see Table 1.1). The 60 types of weapons on some 85 delivery systems currently deployed are described in the chapters that follow.

The Soviet Union has adopted nuclear missions for all of its military services: Strategic Rocket Forces, Air Defense Forces, Ground Forces, Air Forces, and Navy. Nuclear-capable systems are integrated into virtually all military formations, at fighter and bomber bases, on ships and submarines, down to the division level in the Ground Forces. A giant and complex nuclear infrastructure has been created, manned by hundreds of thousands of personnel and costing billions of rubles.

The growth and evolution of Soviet nuclear forces has been caused by a variety of factors. Among the more important have been: the perception of how to achieve national security, the advancement of certain foreign policy goals, the desire for recognition as a superpower, domestic political struggles, bureaucratic inertia, and military service rivalry. Defining the purposes of Soviet nuclear force development, and tracing the military doctrine and strategy that has accompanied it, is a matter of intense debate and analysis in the West.[2]

The Soviet Union, like the United States, has basically four kinds of nuclear weapons policies: declaratory, employment, deployment, and acquisition. Soviet *declaratory* policy is embodied in that collection of public statements by political and military officials that address why the Soviets possess nuclear weapons, how they might use them, and how the dangers of living with nuclear weapons might be lessened. *Employment* policy establishes the goals for and determines how the Soviet Union would actually use its present nuclear weapons to fight a war. Employment policy constitutes the real war plans, developed and known to only a few. It may be either somewhat congruent with or quite different from the declaratory policy. *Deployment* policy is reflected in where Soviet forces are located. *Acquisition* policy addresses how the complex bureaucracies allocate resources to research, develop and produce nuclear weapons.

This volume examines in some detail the panoply of Soviet nuclear weapons systems, chiefly their technical characteristics and capabilities. The book also surveys the Soviet military and other government organizations where decisions are made to research, produce, deploy, and possibly use, nuclear weapons.

It is useful to divide up the post-war period into phases that can be demarcated by the key milestones in the growth and increasing sophistication of the Soviet nuclear arsenal (see Table 1.2). At least four periods can be discerned. The first period, from the early 1940s to the mid-1950s, saw the Soviet Union produce the required nuclear materials, successfully test an atomic (fission) device, begin the integration of weapons into its military services, and successfully test a thermonuclear (fusion) device. The second period, from the mid-1950s to the mid-1960s, saw an expansion of the nuclear arsenal, both in number and type, and the development of new delivery capabilities through advancements in ICBMs and submarine-launched ballistic missiles (SLBMs). The third period, from the late 1960s to the early 1980s, saw a still further expansion in numbers, with a growing refinement of capabilities. The weapons introduced during this period had improved accuracies and longer ranges and were more reliable. This was also a time when parity was achieved with the United States and successful arms control limitation agreements introduced some predictability into the arms race and kept the arsenals somewhat smaller than they might have become.[1]

A fourth period appears to have begun in the mid-1980s with the transition from an older generation of political leaders to Mikhail Gorbachev. The Soviet leadership has undertaken a major reevaluation of Soviet soci-

---

1 The basis for this estimate and its uncertainty are discussed in more detail in Chapter Two.
2 These topics are not the focus of this book. A most useful survey of the debate, and the problems that surround the issue, is provided by Benjamin S. Lambeth, *The State of Western Research on Soviet Military Strategy and Policy* (Santa Monica, CA: Rand, October 1984), Note N-2230-AF. For a sample of the extensive literature see, William C. Green, *Soviet Nuclear Weapons Policy: A Research and Bibliographic Guide* (Boulder, CO: Westview Press), 1987; John Baylis and Gerald Segal, eds., *Soviet Strategy* (London: Croom Helm, 1981); Derek Leebaert, ed., *Soviet Military Thinking* (London: George Allen & Unwin, 1981); Michael MccGwire, *Military Objectives in Soviet Foreign Policy* (Washington, DC; The Brookings Institution, 1987); William T. Lee and Richard F. Staar, *Soviet Military Policy Since World War II* (Stanford, CA: Hoover Institution Press, 1986).
3 For a discussion of how large Soviet ICBM forces might have become, without SALT, see MccGwire, *op. cit.*, pp. 237-241.

Table 1.1
Soviet Nuclear Weapons (1953-1988)

Weapon Type/Name	Service[a]	Year deployed	Status
Intercontinental Ballistic Missiles			
SS-6 Sapwood	SRF	1960	Retired in 1968
SS-7 Saddler	SRF	1962-1963	Retired in 1978
SS-8 Sasin	SRF	1963	Retired in 1978
SS-9 Scarp			
Mod 1	SRF	1967	Retired in 1980
Mod 2		1966?	Retired
Mod 3		1969?[1]	Retired
Mod 4		1971	Retired
SS-X-10	SRF	—	Program cancelled in 1968
SS-11 Sego			
Mod 1	SRF	1966	Probably retired
Mod 2		1973	Active
Mod 3		1973	Active
SS-13 Savage			
Mod 1	SRF	1969	Retired circa 1975-1976
Mod 2		1972-1973	Active
SS-X-15 Scrooge	SRF	—	Program cancelled circa 1968[2]
SS-X-16 Sinner	SRF	—	Never deployed[3]
SS-17 Spanker			
Mod 1	SRF	1975	Retired in 1983
Mod 2		1977	Retired in 1984
Mod 3		1979	Being partially retired
SS-18 Satan			
Mod 1	SRF	1974	Retired in 1983
Mod 2		1976	Retired in 1985
Mod 3		1976	Retired in 1983
Mod 4		1979	Active
SS-19 Stiletto			
Mod 1	SRF	1974	Retired in 1984
Mod 2		1977	Retired in 1985
Mod 3		1979	Being partially retired
SS-24 Scalpel			
Mod 1	SRF	1987	Being deployed
SS-25 Sickle	SRF	1985	Being deployed
Submarine-launched Ballistic Missiles			
SS-N-4 Sark	N	1960	Retired in 1980
SS-N-5 Serb	N	1963	Being retired
SS-N-6			
Mod 1	N	1968	
Mod 2		1973	
Mod 3		1973-1974	
SS-N-8 Sawfly			
Mod 1	N	1973	Active
Mod 2		1977-1978	Active
SS-NX-13	N?	—	Cancelled[4]
SS-N-17 Snipe	N	1977	Active
SS-N-18 Stingray			
Mod 1	N	1978	Active
Mod 2		1978	Active
Mod 3		1978?	Active
SS-N-20 Sturgeon	N	1983	Being deployed
SS-N-23 Skiff	N	1986	Being deployed
Anti-ballistic Missiles			
Griffon	PVO	—	Cancelled
Galosh			
ABM-1	PVO	1969	Retired in the mid-1970s
ABM-1B		mid-1970s	Being retired
Mod Galosh		1980s	Being deployed
Gazelle			
ABM-3?	PVO	1980s	Being deployed
Non-strategic Land-based Rockets and Missiles			
FROG-1/2	GF	1957	Retired by about 1970
FROG-3	GF	1960	Retired by about 1970[5]
FROG-4	GF	1964	Retired by the 1980s
FROG-5	GF	1964	May still be active in small numbers
FROG-7	GF	1965	Active
SSC-1A Shaddock	N	1962	Retired in 1970s
B Sepal	N	1962	Active
SSC-X-4	N	—	Eliminated under the INF Treaty
SS-1 Scunner	GF	1947?	Cancelled in early 1950s[6]
SS-1a SCUD	GF	1953-1955	
SS-1b SCUD A	GF	1957-1961	Retired in 1976
SS-1c SCUD B	GF	1965	Active
SS-2 Sibling	GF	late 1940s	Retired in early 1950s
SS-3 Shyster	SRF[7]	1955	Retired in 1968-1969
SS-4 Sandal	SRF	1959	Being retired
SS-5 Skean	SRF	1961	Retired in 1983
SS-12 Scaleboard	SRF	1969	Retired
M Scaleboard B		1979	Eliminated under the INF Treaty
SS-X-14 Scamp		—	Cancelled in 1970[8]
SS-20 Saber	SRF	1977	Eliminated under the INF Treaty
SS-21 Scarab	GF	1976	Being deployed
SS-23 Spider	GF	1986	Eliminated under the INF Treaty
Sea-launched Cruise Missiles			
SS-N-1 Scrubber[9]	N	1958	Retired in 1977[10]
SS-N-3A Shaddock	N	1962	Active
B Sepal		1962	Active
C Shaddock		1960	Retired?
SS-N-7 Starbright	N	1968	Active
SS-N-9 Siren	N	1969	Active
SS-N-12 Sandbox	N	1976	Active
SS-N-19 Shipwreck	N	1980	Active
SS-N-21 Sampson	N	1987	Being deployed
SS-N-22 Sunburn	N	1980	Active
Air-to-surface Missiles			
AS-2 Kipper	SAA,N	1961	Active
AS-3 Kangaroo	SAA	1961-1962	Active
AS-4 Kitchen	SAA,N	1967[11]	Active
AS-5 Kelt	N	1968	Active
AS-6 Kingfish	N	1970	Active
AS-11 Kilter?	AF	1984	Being deployed
AS-15 Kent	SAA	1984	Being deployed
Anti-submarine Weapons/Missiles			
600mm Torpedo?	N	?	Status unknown
Type 65 Torpedo	N	1965?	Active
SS-N-15 Starfish	N	1973	Active
SS-N-16 Stallion	N	1979-1981	Active
FRAS-1	N	1967	Active
Depth bomb	N	1967	Active
ET-80 Torpedo	N	1980?	Active
Depth bomb	N	1960s? 1980s?	Active
Artillery			
M-1955 D-20 152mm	GF	1955	Being retired
M-240 240mm mortar	GF	1955	Active in small numbers
M-1955 (M55) 203mm	GF	1955	Being retired
M-1957 310mm	GF	1957	Limited deployments only
M-1957 420mm mortar	GF	1957	Limited deployments only
M-1960 420mm mortar	GF	1960	Retired in mid-1960s?
152-mm naval gun	N	1962	Active
2S4 M-1975 240mm mortar	GF	1975-1976	Active
2S7 M-1975 203mm	GF	1977	Active
2S3 M-1973 152mm	GF	1978	Active
M-1980? 203mm	GF	1980	Active
2S5 M-1981 152mm	GF	1981	Active
M-1976 152mm	GF	1983	Active
Aircraft			
Be-12 Mail	N	1966	Active
Il-28 Beagle	AF,N	1953	Retired in 1976-1978
Il-38 May	N	1968	Active
Ka-25 Hormone-A	N	1967	Active
Ka-27 Helix-A	N	1982	Active
MiG-21 Fishbed L	AF	1969	Being retired
MiG-23 Flogger B/G	AF	1971-1972	Active
MiG-27 Flogger D/J	AF	1975	Active
Mya-4 Bison A	SAA	1955	Retired in 1986
Su-7 Fitter A	AF	1959	Being retired
Su-17 Fitter C/D	AF,N	1972	Active
Su-24 Fencer	AF,SAA	1974	Active
Tu-4 Bull	LRA,N	1953	Retired in 1964
Tu-16 Badger A	SAA,N	1954	Retired in early 1970s
C		1961	Active

1
Early History

Table 1.1
Soviet Nuclear Weapons (1953-1988) (continued)

Weapon Type/Name	Service*	Year deployed	Status
G		1965	Active
Tu-22 Blinder A	LRA,N	1962	Active
B	SAA	1967	Active
Tu-22M Backfire B	SAA,N	1974	Active
C		1983	Being deployed
Tu-95 Bear A	SAA	1955	Active
B		1962	Active
C		1963	Active
G		1983	Active
Tu-142 Bear H	SAA	1984	Being deployed
F	N	1971	Being deployed

Weapon Type/Name	Service*	Year deployed	Status
Yak-28 Brewer	AF	1961	Retired in 1977
Surface-to-air Missiles			
SA-1 Guild	PVO	1954	Active
SA-2 Guideline	PVO,GF	1958	Active
SA-5 Gammon	PVO	1970	
SA-10 Grumble	PVO	1980-1981	Active
SA-N-1	N		
SA-N-3 Goblet	N	1967	Active
SA-N-6	N	1979	Being deployed

1. Fractional Orbital Bombardment System (FOBS) deployed at Tyuratam.
2. The SS-X-15 program was cancelled after eight test firings. The missile may have been deployed for a brief period in the Far East.
3. The last known test of the SS-X-16 was in 1976.
4. The last known test was in November 1973.
5. Some FROG-3/5 launchers and missiles may still be deployed.
6. The missile, similar to the V-2, may never have been deployed.
7. The SS-3 was under LRA control until the establishment of the SRF in 1959.
8. The SS-X-14 was cancelled after 19 tests, including two crew training tests one in 1969 and one in 1970. The missile may have been deployed for a brief period in the Far East.
9. The SS-N-1 missile is also known as Strela.
10. The SS-N-1 may still be held on reserve on one Kildin class destroyer.
11. First shown in 1961.

* Services are Long Range Aviation (LRA), Strategic Air Armies (SAA), Ground Forces (GF), Air Defense Forces (PVO), Air Forces (AF), and the Navy (N).

---

ety. Major discussions are under way over how to allocate resources to the civilian and military sectors. General Secretary Gorbachev has made many arms control proposals, unilaterally stopped nuclear testing for 19 months, accepted the asymmetrical elimination of intermediate-range nuclear forces (INF), supported a 50 percent strategic force reduction, proposed the entire elimination of nuclear weapons, and called for "general and complete disarmament." Gorbachev has advanced a doctrine of "necessary defensive sufficiency, of the preservation and consolidation of the military-strategic parity between the USA and the USSR."[4] This doctrine of "military equality, or equal security for all,"[5] is based on the assumption that not every military advance by the United States needs to be matched, so long as "reasonably sufficient" nuclear forces are maintained.[6] It is too early to conclude whether these new policies have been translated into appropriate force structures, deployments, and exercises that are consistent with a "defensive" strategy. There has been an assertion that Soviet defense spending is being reduced.[7] There is also an indication that the tempo of certain military activities has been reduced.[8] Perhaps the most important new development is the reassertion by Gorbachev of the primacy and authority of civilian leadership in doctrinal and arms control matters, with the political component of military doctrine granted a more important role in war prevention.[9]

Early History of Soviet Nuclear Weapons Development[10]

During the 1930s the Soviet Union had active research programs in atomic and nuclear physics.[11] In February 1939, when Soviet physicists learned from foreign journals of the discovery of nuclear fission,[12] the military

---

4. V. Varennikov, "Na strazhe mira i bezopasnosti narodov" (On Guard for Peace and Security for All People), *Partinyaya zhizn* (Party Life) No. 5, 1987, pp. 10-12.
5. S. F. Akhromeyev, "Slava i gordost' Sovestskogo naroda" *Sovetskaya Rossiya* 2d ed., 21 February 1987, p. 1.
6. See, for example, Mikhail Gorbachev, Political Report of the CPSU Central Committee to the 27th Congress of the Communist Party of the Soviet Union, 25 February 1986 (Moscow: Novosti, 1986).
7. R. Jeffrey Smith, "Arms Budget Cut, Soviet Says," *Washington Post*, 27 July 1988, p. A1.
8. "Soviet naval deployments overseas in 1987 declined by six percent compared to 1986, continuing a three-year downward trend"; Studeman, USN, Statement before HASC, March 1988, p. 39. According to U.S. Navy figures, the Soviet fleet deployed an average of 46 submarines each day in 1984; in 1987 the average was 25. In 1984 the average deployment of warships was 31 per day; in 1987 the average was 24; Michael R. Gordon, "Soviets Scale Back Naval Deployments and Large Exercises," *New York Times*, 17 July 1988, p. 1.
9. See, for example, Yu. Zhilin, "Faktor vremeni v yadernyy vek", *Kommunist*, No. 11, 1986, pp. 120-122; and V. Serebryannikov, "Zashchita sotsializma v yadernyy vek", *Krasnaya Zvezda*, 19 December 1986, pp. 2-3.
10. The early history of the Soviet nuclear weapons program is presented by David Holloway in *The Soviet Union and the Arms Race*, 2d ed. (1984) and in "Entering the Nuclear Arms Race: The Soviet Decision to Build the Atomic Bomb, 1939-1945," Washington, DC, Wilson Center, Working Paper No. 9, presented at an International Security Studies Program colloquium, 25 July 1979. The first extensive analysis of the military and civilian development of atomic energy in the Soviet Union was by Arnold Kramish, *Atomic Energy in the Soviet Union* (Stanford, CA: Stanford University Press, 1959). Other useful sources include I. N. Golovin, *I. V. Kurchatov: A Socialist-Realist Biography of the Soviet Nuclear Scientist*, translated from the Russian by William H. Dougherty (Bloomington, IN: Selbstverlag Press, 1968); Herbert F. York, *The Advisors: Oppenheimer, Teller, and the Superbomb* (San Francisco: W. H. Freeman and Company, 1976); Peter Pringle and James Spigelman, *The Nuclear Barons* (New York: Holt, Rinehart and Winston, 1981), pp. 57-70.
11. Paul R. Josephson, "Early Years of Soviet Nuclear Physics," *Bulletin of the Atomic Scientists*, December 1987, pp. 36-39.
12. Holloway, "Entering the Nuclear Arms Race," *op. cit.*, p.10. Nuclear fission of uranium was discovered in late 1938 by Otto Hahn and Fritz Strassmann in Berlin. It was left to Lise Meitner, then living in Sweden, and Otto Frisch, working in Copenhagen, to suggest—in a letter to *Nature* on 16 January 1939—what proved to be the correct interpretation of the results of Hahn and Strassmann, namely, the splitting of the uranium nucleus into nuclei of roughly equal size after neutron capture. For further discussion, see Samuel Glasstone, *Sourcebook on Atomic Energy*, 3d ed. (New York: Van Nostrand Reinhold Co., 1967), pp. 473-477; Richard Rhodes, *The Making of the Atomic Bomb* (New York: Simon and Schuster, 1987), pp. 247-275.

significance was immediately recognized.[13] By April 1939 Soviet scientists had independently established that each uranium nucleus fissioned emitted between two and four neutrons and that a chain reaction was therefore possible. By 1940 Soviet physicists had concluded that a chain reaction could be established using either uranium-235 (U-235) or natural uranium, and a moderator such as heavy water.

In June 1940 the Uranium Commission was established by the Presidium of the Soviet Academy of Sciences to conduct research on the "uranium problem." Work was to proceed on a broad front including exploration for uranium deposits (lack of uranium was an important constraint on early Soviet work), production of heavy water, construction of cyclotrons, studies of isotopic separation, and measurements of the nuclear constants.[14]

Research proceeded at a slow pace during the next year, and then was brought to a halt altogether after the German invasion on 22 June 1941.[15] Early in 1942, however, the Soviet leadership began to pursue more seriously the possibility of an atomic bomb as a result of intelligence information about British, American, and German work on the bomb and advice from Soviet scientists.[16] While worried about the high cost of development of an atomic bomb, Stalin nonetheless initiated a small-scale project in 1943 under the scientific direction of Igor Vasil'evich Kurchatov (1903-1960).[17]

Kurchatov drew up a plan of research with three main goals: to achieve a chain reaction in an experimental reactor using natural uranium; to develop methods of isotope separation; and to study the design of both the U-235 and plutonium bombs.[18] Fifty scientists were working in his new laboratory by the end of 1943, a figure which doubled by the end of 1944.[19] By the time of the Potsdam Conference, which began at the same time as the first U.S. nuclear weapon test on 16 July 1945, the Soviet Union had a serious atomic bomb project under way.[20] Eight days after the U.S. test, on 24 July President Truman casually mentioned to Stalin after one conference session that the United States had a "new weapon of unusual destructive force."[21] Stalin told Truman he hoped

Table 1.2
Milestones in Soviet Nuclear Weapons Developments

Date	Event
25 Dec 1946	First Soviet nuclear chain reaction takes place.
1947	SS-1a Scunner, first Soviet rocket, derived from the German V-2 is tested.
29 Aug 1949	Soviets detonate first nuclear device.
12 Aug 1953	Soviets detonate first thermonuclear device.
late 1953	First operational nuclear weapons delivered to the Soviet armed forces.
1955	First Bear A heavy bomber is deployed.
1955	First medium-range ballistic missile (MRBM), the SS-3 Shyster, entered service. This was the first Soviet operational nuclear armed missile.
21 Sep 1955	First underwater explosion of a nuclear device.
22 Nov 1955	First two stage thermonuclear device is exploded.
3 Aug 1957	First launch of a Soviet ICBM, the SS-6 Sapwood.
1958	SS-N-1 Scrubber, first Soviet sea-launched cruise missile is deployed.
1959	SS-4 Sandal MRBM, first Soviet missile to use storable liquid fuel, is deployed.
1960	First Soviet SLBM, the SS-N-4 Sark, is deployed on Golf and Hotel class submarines.
11 Oct 1961	First Soviet underground nuclear test.
30 Oct 1961	A 58 megaton device is exploded, the largest thermonuclear device ever exploded.
1962	First Soviet supersonic bomber, the Tu-22 Blinder, is deployed.
2 Feb 1962	First Soviet underground nuclear explosion reported by the United States.
1969	SS-13 Savage, the first Soviet large missile to have solid propulsion, is deployed.
1969:	Continuous ballistic missile submarine patrols by Yankee class submarines begin in the Atlantic.
1973	SS-11 Mod 2, first Soviet ICBM to carry penetration aids is deployed.
Apr 1973	The SS-19 is the first Soviet ICBM to be tested in a MIRVed configuration.
27 Oct 1973	A 3.5 megaton device is exploded underground, believed to be the largest Soviet underground test.
1974	SS-18 and SS-19 ICBMs, first to be equipped with MIRV warheads, are deployed.
1974	Fencer A, first fighter aircraft designed specifically for ground-attack, and the first to carry a weapons system officer, is deployed.
1977	First Soviet non-strategic missile with multiple warheads, the SS-20 Saber, is deployed.
1978	SS-N-18 Mod 1 Stingray, first MIRVed SLBM, is deployed on Delta III class submarines.
1980	SS-N-17 Snipe, first solid-fuel SLBM, and first with a post boost vehicle, is deployed.
1984	AS-15 Kent, first of a new generation of long-range cruise missiles, is deployed on Bear H bombers.
1985	SS-25 Sickle, first Soviet mobile ICBM, is operationally deployed.
1987	SS-N-21 Sampson, first long-range sea-launched cruise missile, is deployed in the Northern Fleet.
late 1987	SS-24 Scalpel, first Soviet rail mobile ICBM, is operationally deployed.

---

13 According to York, Igor Tamm, a leading Soviet physicist, remarked to a group of students, "Do you know what this new discovery means? It means that a bomb can be built that will destroy a city out to a radius of maybe ten kilometers"; York, *op. cit.*, p. 29; See also, Golovin, op. cit., p. 34.
14 Holloway, *The Soviet Union and the Arms Race*, 1984, p. 16; Holloway, "Entering the Arms Race," *op. cit.*, p. 11.
15 Holloway, "Entering the Arms Race," *op. cit.*, p. 17.
16 Holloway, *The Soviet Union and the Arms Race*, 1984, pp. 17-18. See also, Golovin, op. cit., pp. 39-40. In early 1942 Georgiy N. Flerov (1913–), a young associate of Kurchatov's, noticed that articles on nuclear fission were no longer being published in the West, a sign to him that secret work was under way on an atomic bomb. In May 1942 Flerov wrote to S. V. Kaftanov, who was responsible for science in the State Committee of Defence (GKO), and to Stalin that "we must build the uranium bomb without delay"; David Holloway, "Military Technology," in Ronald Amann, Julian Cooper, and R. W. Davies,eds., *The Technological Level of Soviet Industry* (New Haven, CT: Yale University Press, 1977), pp. 451-452.
17 Holloway, *The Soviet Union and the Arms Race*, 1984, p. 18. Kurchatov had been director of the nuclear laboratory at the Leningrad Physico-Technical Institute. Kurchatov would continue to direct not only the development of the Soviet atomic bomb but the development of thermonuclear weapons as well.
18 *Ibid.*, p. 19.
19 *Ibid.*
20 *Ibid.*
21 Harry S. Truman, *Memoirs: Year of Decisions* (New York, 1955), p. 458; Truman Journal, 25 July 1945, HST Library, cited in Gregg Herken, *The Winning Weapon* (New York: Vintage Books, 1984), p. 19.

1

New Capabilities

the United States would make "good use of it against the Japanese." He also instructed Kurchatov to speed up his work.[22]

Following the bombing of Hiroshima and Nagasaki by the United States in August 1945, Stalin is said to have ordered his deputies and Kurchatov to "[p]rovide us with atomic weapons in the shortest possible time."[23] The day after the United States bombed Hiroshima, Stalin put his secret-police chief Lavrenti P. Beria in charge of a Soviet version of the Manhattan Project.[24] By 1947 the institutional framework was in place to develop nuclear weapons, long-range rockets, and jet propulsion.[25]

In the spring of 1945 Kurchatov ordered work to begin on the design of an industrial reactor for producing plutonium.[26] Kurchatov also supervised the construction of an experimental graphite-moderated natural uranium-fueled pile—called the Fursov Pile or F-1—in his Laboratory No. 2 (formerly the Moscow Institute of Atomic Energy and now the I. V. Kurchatov Institute of Atomic Energy),[27] where the first Soviet chain reaction took place on 25 December 1946.[28]

The first Soviet nuclear test took place on 29 August 1949. Two more tests were conducted in the fall of 1951, and a fourth test was not conducted until 12 August 1953. This test was also the detonation of the first nuclear device incorporating thermonuclear fuel (see Chapter Ten).

The reseach, development, and production of Soviet nuclear weapons remained under Beria's control, administered through a "semi-ministry" called the First Main Administration of the USSR Council of Ministers, from 1946 until he was arrested and killed in 1953. The Ministry of Medium Machine Building was created in July 1953,[29] and the state security apparatus was reorganized, resulting in the 13 March 1954 creation of the Committee for State Security (*Komitet Gosudarstvennoy Bezopasnosti*), (KGB).[30] In 1954 the Ministry of Medium Machine Building assumed responsibility for the research, development, and production of nuclear weapons.[31] The KGB retained custodial and transport responsibilities for nuclear "charges" (i.e., warheads) (see Chapter Four).[32]

Soviet work on the thermonuclear bomb began in 1948 when Kurchatov set up a theoretical group, which included Andrei Sakharov, under Igor Tamm.[33] Sakharov is generally credited with being the "father of the Soviet H-bomb," and he himself says he was "the author or coauthor of several key ideas."[34]

New Capabilities and the Introduction of Nuclear Weapons into Soviet Armed Forces

The Soviet Union's long tradition of rocket development reaches back to the 1920s, and before that to the work of Konstantin E. Tsiolkovsky (1857-1935).[35] This experience was supplemented after World War II by exploitation of the German guided and ballistic missile programs. By the end of 1945 a decision was taken to build versions of the German A-4 (V-2), largely directed and funded by the military. It appears that two groups worked on creating derivatives of the V-2: one drawn from Germans who had not fled to the West, the other a Soviet group under S. P. Korolev.[36] Both teams' rockets were tested in October 1947.[37] The Soviet-designed rocket, designated R-1 (R for *raketa*, "rocket") (SS-1a Scudder), performed better than the 300 kilometer-range German-designed rocket. The R-1 was introduced into

---

22 According to Marshal Zhukov, "after this meeting Stalin in my presence told Molotov about his conversation with Truman. Molotov reacted immediately: 'They are trying to bid up.' Stalin laughed: 'Let them. I'll have to talk it over with Kurchatov today and get him to speed things up.' I understood they were talking about the development of the atomic bomb"; Marshal of the Soviet Union G. Zhukov, *Reminiscences and Reflections*, Vol. 2, 1974. English-language ed. (Moscow: Progress Publishers, 1985), p. 449.
23 Ibid.
24 Nikita S. Khrushchev, *Khrushchev Remembers: The Last Testament*, translated and edited by Strobe Talbott (Boston: Little, Brown, 1974), pp. 58-59.
25 The institutions included scientific-technical councils created for atomic bomb and rocket development, consisting of scientists, engineers, and industrial managers; Holloway, *The Soviet Union and the Arms Race*, 1984, pp. 21-22. See also, Walter A. McDougall, *The Heavens and the Earth: A Political History of the Space Age* (New York: Basic Books, Inc.: 1985), pp. 53-54. Boris L. Vannikov (1897-1962), the People's Commissar of Munitions, headed the atomic council, with Mikhail G. Pervukhin, Deputy Premier and People's Commissar (i.e., minister) of the Chemical Industry, and Kurchatov as his deputies. The rocket council was chaired by D. F. Ustinov, the People's Commissar of Armaments and later Minister of Defense. A special department of government was set up to manage the nuclear program. The secret police had a department for atomic energy; half of all research for nuclear weapons development was done in prison institutes, while most of the construction and mining was done by prison labor; Holloway, *The Soviet Union and the Arms Race*, 1984, p. 22.
26 A. I. Yoriysh, I. D. Morokhov, S. K. Ivanov, *A-Bomba* (Moscow: Nauka, 1980), p. 377, cited by Holloway, *The Soviet Union and the Arms Race*, 1984, p. 19.
27 Golovin, op. cit., p. 51. F-1 stands for *fizicheskii pervyi uranovyi kotel*, "first physics uranium pile."
28 Holloway, *The Soviet Union and the Arms Race*, 1984, p. 26. This low-power air-cooled pile was undoubtedly the prototype for the Soviet's larger water-cooled plutonium production reactors; Golovin, op cit., p. 51. See also, DIA, *Nuclear Power Technology-USSR*, DST-1520S-152-75, 30 September 1975, p. 104; CIA, *Soviet Nuclear Research Reactors*, OSI-SR/64-41, 22 September 1964, p. 2. According to Golovin, it initially achieved 100 watts (p. 55) and was subsequently operated up to a maximum intensity of 1000 kilowatts (p. 57). Kramish, op. cit., p. 112, claims the first Soviet reactor put into operation was a low- power device constructed of graphite and uranium metal, its primary function being the testing of uranium slugs and other material to be used in their production reactors. The Soviet reactor had characteristics like those of the Hanford 305 test reactor, which were: power: 10 watts; diameter: 19 feet; loading: 25-50 tons uranium; lattice spacing: 8 inches; and rod diameter: 1.2-1.6 inches. Richard G. Hewlett and Oscar E. Anderson, Jr., *The New World, 1939-1946* (University Park, PA: Pennsylvania State University Press, 1962), p. 224, place a "small thirty-watt pile in which graphite bars were tested," in the 300 area of Hanford ca. 1943-44.
29 Holloway, *The Soviet Union and the Arms Race*, 1984, p. 117.
30 Jeffrey T. Richelson, *Sword and Shield: Soviet Intelligence and Security Apparatus* (Cambridge, MA: Ballinger Publishing, 1986), p. 16.
31 Those in charge of the Ministry of Medium Machine-Building since 1953 have been: Vyacheslav Aleksandrovich Malyshev (1902-1957), Minister from 1953-1955; Avraamiy Pavlovich Zavenyagin (1901-1956), Minister from 1955 until his sudden death; Mikhail Georgievich Pervukhin (1904- ?), Minister from May-July 1957; Yefrim Pavlovich Slavsky (1898-), Minister from mid-1957 to 1963, Chairman of the State Production Committee for Medium Machine Building from 1963 to 1965, when it was demoted from a ministry to a state committee, then Minister again from 1965 until 21 November 1986, when he was relieved by the Presidium of the Supreme Soviet and replaced by Lev Demitriyevich Ryabev (1928-), the current Minister.
32 Stephen M. Meyer, "Soviet Nuclear Operations," in Ashton B. Carter, John D. Steinbruner, and Charles A. Zraket, eds., *Managing Nuclear Operations* (Washington, DC: The Brookings Institution, 1987), p. 487.
33 Holloway, *The Soviet Union and the Arms Race*, pp. 24-25
34 York, op. cit., p. 88.
35 McDougall, op. cit., pp. 17-40; Milan Kocourrek, "Rocketry: Level of Technology in Launch Vehicles and Manned Space Capsules," in Amann, Cooper, and Davies, op. cit., pp. 490-498; G. A. Tokaty, "Soviet Rocket Technology," in Eugene M. Emme, ed., *The History of Rocket Technology* (Detroit: Wayne State University Press, 1964), pp. 271-284.
36 Holloway, "Military Technology," op. cit., p. 455.
37 The first of the German rockets was launched on 17 October 1947; Harriet Fast Scott, "The Strategic Rocket Forces and Their Five Elites," *Air Force Magazine*, March 1983, p. 60.
38 Holloway, "Military Technology," op. cit., p. 457.

New Capabilities

military service, although it is not clear on what scale.[38] The 600 kilometer R-2 (SS-2 Sibling), an improved SS-1, was successfully tested in 1950.

The decision to build a missile that could serve as an ICBM was taken in principle in 1947, though the specific development decision was made in 1953.[39] The Navy pursued its own versions of the V-2, called Golem I and II, but neither was ever deployed. While weapons development was shifting in the early 1950s from short-range rockets to longer range ballistic missiles, the bomber would be the first to carry nuclear weapons.

The Soviet armed forces reportedly received its first nuclear weapons (nuclear bombs) in 1953[40] or at the beginning of 1954.[41] The first nuclear-capable delivery systems were believed to be the Tu-4 Bull or Il-28 Beagle bombers.[42]

Following an initial spate of articles in 1945 and 1946,[43] nothing appeared in open or restricted military publications on atomic energy and weapons until 1954.[44] Military publications devoted little attention to the implications of nuclear weapons for military operations. Virtually all Soviet military thought was made to conform to Stalin's five "permanently operating factors" issued during the Great Patriotic War.[45] Soon after Stalin's death, however, Minister of Defense Bulganin issued a directive ordering "the study of nuclear weapons and the features of the preparation, conduct and support of operations and battles in conditions of the use of these weapons."[46]

The early years of nuclear integration resulted in an "agonizing reappraisal of the previous [Second World War] experience and, mainly, an adaptation of the new [nuclear] weapons and means of conflict to the old views and concepts."[47] Nuclear weapons were seen "as some new quantitative expression of the chief factor in armed conflict—fire power."[48] Many Soviet writers believed that the stockpiles of nuclear weapons were too small to be "decisive means of the conduct of war, and consequently, [to] accomplish a fundamental transformation in military affairs."[49] The prevailing view was that nuclear war was possible but not inevitable.[50]

In September 1954 the first large-scale military exercise including a live atomic bomb detonation was reportedly conducted.[51] By 1955 small numbers of nuclear weapons were being produced for weapons systems of the Ground Forces, Navy, and Air Forces. Nuclear tests during 1955 included air-delivered fission devices, the first Soviet underwater nuclear detonation, an air-delivered weaponized version of the 12 August 1953 thermonuclear device, and a test of the first Soviet two-stage thermonuclear device.

Soviet concern with growing U.S. bomber capabilities resulted in the establishment in 1954 of an independent Air Defense Forces (PVO) as an armed service. Soviet Air Forces and Naval Aviation forces were cut, and many of the interceptors and fighters were transferred to the PVO. That same year nuclear-capable SA-1 Guild surface-to-air missiles (SAMs) began to ring Moscow, to be supplemented by nuclear-capable SA-2 Guideline SAMs in 1958. ABM research also began in the mid-1950s.

Three new nuclear-capable bombers (the Tu-16 Badger A, the Tu-95 Bear A, and the Mya-4 Bison) and the SS-3 Shyster medium-range ballistic missile (MRBM) entered operational service in 1954-1955.[52] The Tu-16 was the first Soviet aircraft specifically designed for long-range missions, and it replaced the older piston engine Tu-4 Bull. The Tu-95 Bear and the Mya-4 Bison bombers were the first Soviet aircraft able to deliver nu-

---

39 *Ibid.*, p. 458. Tokaty recounts that on 15 March 1947 Stalin said, in his presence, "Such a rocket could change the face of the war.... The problem of the creation of transatlantic rockets is of extreme importance to us." Also on that day, according to Tokaty, a special state commission was formed for the study of the problems of long-range rockets; Tokaty, *op. cit.*, p. 281.

40 Holloway, *The Soviet Union and the Arms Race*, 1984, p. 31, citing Col. Gen. A. Radzievskii, "Thirty Years of the Military Academy of the General Staff," *Voennaya Mysl'*, No. 10, 1966, p. 8.

41 B. V. Panov, *Istoriya voyennogo iskusstva* (History of Military Art) (Moscow: Voyenizdat, 1984), p. 457.

42 The Tu-4 Bull was a Soviet copy of the U.S. B-29. First flown in 1947, its existence was revealed in an air show near Moscow the following year; Prados, *Soviet Estimate*, p. 39. In 1950 USAF Intelligence was reporting that the Tu-4 bomber was capable of delivering the newly developed atomic weapon; HQ USAF, Directorate of Intelligence, and Department of the Navy, Office of Naval Intelligence, *An Estimate of Soviet Air Capabilities and Air Order of Battle*, National Archives Record Group 341, Entry 267, Box 127, File Number 2-18347, 1 October 1950.

43 While working furiously to build the bomb Stalin disingenuously stated in September 1946 that he "did not consider the atomic bomb as serious a force as some politicians are inclined to do. Atomic bombs are meant to frighten those with weak nerves, but they cannot decide the fate of wars since atomic bombs are quite insufficient for that"; quoted in Holloway, *The Soviet Union and the Arms Race*, 1984, p. 27.

44 Raymond Garthoff, *Soviet Strategy in the Nuclear Age* (New York: Praeger, 1958), p. 64. In the two years after Stalin's death, the Army newspaper *Red Star* published over 50 pieces on the implications of nuclear weapons; McDougall, *op. cit.*, p. 265.

45 "Now the fate of the war will be decided not by such transitory aspects as the aspect of surprise, but by the permanently operating factors: the stability of the rear, the morale of the troops, the quantity and quality of divisions, the armaments of the army, and the organizing ability of the command personnel of the army"; Stalin's speech ("Order of the People's Commissar of Defense") on Red Army Day, 23 February 1942, excerpt in Harriet Fast Scott and William F. Scott, eds., *The Soviet Art of War: Doctrine, Strategy and Tactics* (Boulder, CO: Westview Press, 1982), p. 80. All Soviet military thinking during this period conformed with Stalin's views. As General Major Kozlov later noted, "An attempt was made to fit everything new in military affairs into one or another saying of Stalin"; S. N. Kozlov, M. V. Smirnov, I. S. Baz' and P. A. Sidonov, *O Sovetskoy Voyennoy Nauke* (On Soviet Military Science), 2d ed. (Moscow: Voyenizdat, 1964), quoted in Meyer, "Soviet Theatre Nuclear Forces," Part I, pp. 7-8.

46 V. G. Kulikov, ed., *Academiya General'nogo Shtaba* (The Academy of the General Staff) (Moscow: Voyenizdat, 1976), p. 129.

47 S. N. Kozlov, "The Development of Soviet Military Science After World War II," *Voennaya Mysl'* (Military Thought) February 1964, p. 29.

48 *Ibid.*, pp. 39-40. See also Thomas W. Wolfe, *Soviet Strategy at the Crossroads* (Cambridge, MA: Harvard University Press, 1965), pp. 154-155; Garthoff, *op. cit.*, pp. 76-78.

49 M.V. Zakharov, et al., *50 Let Vooruzhennykh Sil SSSR* (50 Years of the USSR Armed Forces) (Moscow: Voyenizdat, 1968), p. 520; Wolfe, *op. cit.*, pp. 154-155; Garthoff, *op. cit.*, pp. 76-78; Kozlov, *op. cit.*, p. 29.

50 In the political struggle for leadership in the aftermath of Stalin's death, Malenkov stated in March 1954 that war in the nuclear age would mean the "destruction of civilization." In contrast, Khrushchev believed there was no absolute weapon and hence no absolute deterrent with nuclear weapons, and that a balanced development of the Soviet armed forces was called for; see Herbert S. Dinerstein, *War and the Soviet Union* (New York: Praeger, 1962), pp. 70-77. The debate was resolved in February 1955 when Khrushchev succeeded in forcing Malenkov to resign his position after a number of policy disagreements; Holloway, *The Soviet Union and the Arms Race*, 1984, p. 32.

51 Zakharov, et al., *op. cit.*, p. 520; S. A. Tyushkevich, *Sovetskiye Vooruzhennyye Sily: Istoriya Stroitel'stva* (The Soviet Armed Forces: The History of Their Development) (Moscow: Voyenizdat, 1978), p. 509. During 1955-1956, a number of command and staff exercises exploring nuclear combat were also held; Kulikov, *op. cit.*, pp. 149-150. These exercises convinced military leaders that "[s]urprise attack, employing atomic and hydrogen weapons and other means of conflicts, now takes on new forms and is capable of leading to singularly greater results than in the past war"; P. Rotmistrov, "On the Role of Surprise in Contemporary War," *Military Thought*, No. 2, February 1955, as quoted by Dinerstein, *op. cit.*, p. 186.

52 The SS-3 was never widely deployed; only 28 missiles were operationally deployed at the peak in the mid-1960s. Newer and more reliable missiles such as the SS-4 Sandal and the SS-12 Scaleboard were pursued instead.

1

Nuclear Parity

clear weapons at intercontinental distances and were for a while the only Soviet nuclear weapon system capable of attacking the United States.

The first of the short-range FROG (Free Rocket Over Ground) and SCUD short-range missiles of the Ground Forces followed in 1957.[53] The first SLBM—the SS-N-4 Sark, which was based on the SCUD—was tested from a modified Zulu class attack submarine in 1955. The Zulu system may have achieved a limited operational status by early 1959, with a first patrol that year. In 1960, the SS-N-4 SLBM reached full operational status on diesel-powered Golf class submarines and on the nuclear-powered Hotel class. The first non-strategic naval nuclear weapons—nuclear torpedoes on attack submarines and the SS-N-1 Scrubber first-generation sea-launched cruise missiles (SLCMs) on surface ships—were deployed in 1958.[54]

The growth of the Soviet nuclear arsenal necessitated a reexamination of the basic questions of military science. The Twentieth Party Congress, best known for Khrushchev's denunciation of Stalin, also led to a rejection of Stalinist military concepts. After the congress, explicit discussions of the role of nuclear weapons in theater conflicts began to appear, and the individual service branches began to reassess their weapons programs, force structures, and force planning concepts in light of new nuclear capabilities.[55] By the end of 1959 military theorists agreed that doctrine and strategy needed revision to take into account the impending availability of nuclear missiles.[56] In contrast to earlier views that nuclear weapons might not be employed in combat, the new belief was the use of nuclear weapons was inevitable in a future war.[57]

On 3 August 1957 a successful launch of the SS-6 Sapwood ICBM took place. On 4 October an SS-6 was used to launch Sputnik 1 into space. The SS-6 ICBM was not deployed until 1960, and then only four would be fielded. Technical difficulties and a highly unstable liquid propellant were the major impediments to reliable operations. The SS-4 was also first tested in 1957 and was initially deployed in 1959. It was the first missile to be deployed in large numbers—over 600 at the peak in the mid-1960s. On 17 December 1959 a new independent service was created, partly out of the Missile and Artillery Troops of the Ground Forces: the Rocket Troops of Strategic Designation (referred to in the West as the Stra-

Figure 1.1 The Cuban Missile Crisis of October 1962 was initiated when it was discovered that the Soviet Union was deploying groups of SS-4 medium-range ballistic missiles (MRBM) and SS-5 intermediate-range ballistic missiles (IRBMs) to Cuba. Twenty of 24 SS-4 launchers were believed to be fully operational at the time the crisis was resolved on 28 October 1962. This photo released by the CIA shows a missile base in Cuba.

tegic Rocket Forces or SRF).[58]

In 1960 a new version of the FROG missile (FROG-3) was also fielded, as was the SS-N-3 Shaddock SLCM, designed for land-attack operations, and deployed on submarines.

Achieving Nuclear Parity

On 14 January 1960 First Secretary Khrushchev outlined a new military doctrine.[59] Its essence was that the

---

53 The SCUD A was derived from the SS-1a Scunner, but had twice the range. Although the first SCUD A missiles were seen in 1957, they were not widely deployed until 1961.
54 As of March 1958, U.S. intelligence analysts believed that the Soviets had conducted tests of nuclear devices associated with naval operations (both surface and underwater), ground-force maneuvers, surface-to-surface missiles, air-to-surface missiles, and air-to-surface defense missiles; CIA, Office of Scientific Intelligence, *Impact of a September 1958 Nuclear Test Moratorium on Soviet Nuclear Weapons Capabilities*, Appendix E, 18 March 1958, pp. 7-8. The original torpedoes were replaced by the Type 65, presumably introduced in the mid-1960s, and the ET-80, introduced in the early 1980s.
55 Scott and Scott, *Armed Forces*, p. 41; Meyer, "Soviet Theatre Nuclear Forces," Part I, pp. 15-16.
56 Holloway, *The Soviet Union and the Arms Race*, 1984, p. 38.
57 G. Pokrovskiy, "Samolety, Mezhkontinental'nyye Rakety i Drugiye Nositeli Termoyadernogo Oruzhiya" (Aircraft, Intercontinental Rockets and Other Carriers of Thermonuclear Weapons, in P. T. Astashenkov, ed., *Atomnaya Energiya v Aviatsii i Raketnoy Tekhnike* (Atomic Energy in Aviation and Rocket Technology) (Moscow: Voyenizdat, 1959), p. 10; V. Ivanov, "The Development of Operational Art," *Military*

 Thought, No. 3, March 1967, p. 13; Meyer, "Soviet Theatre Nuclear Forces," Part I, p. 14.
58 An alternative proposal reportedly was to distribute rocket-missile weapons proportionally among the four services or between the Air Forces and the Navy; V. Tolubko, *Nedelin* (Moscow: Molodaya Gvardiya, 1979), p. 188; V. Tolubko, "Poligon" (Missile Range), interview in *Literaturnaya Gazeta* (Literary Gazette), 8 August 1984, p. 10, as translated in FBIS, *Soviet Union: Daily Report*, 9 August 1984, p. AA4. Other organizational changes included the transformation of the artillery arm of the Ground Forces into the Rocket and Artillery Troops, which would constitute the basic firepower of the Ground Forces.
59 The nuclear-dominant military doctrine was outlined by Khrushchev in a speech given to the Supreme Soviet, entitled "Disarmament—For Durable Peace and Friendship," on 14 January 1960, and elaborated on by Minister of Defense Marshal R. Ya. Malinovskiy the following day. For excerpts of both speeches, see Scott and Scott, *Art of War*, op. cit., pp. 162-166. Knowledge of, and excerpts and notes on the top secret document "Special Collection of Articles," was passed to the West by Colonel Oleg V. Penkovskiy before his arrest on 22 October 1962. The articles by senior Soviet officers were first published in *Military Thought*, beginning in January 1960 and formed the basis for the new doctrine; Oleg Penkovskiy, *The Penkovskiy Papers*, (Garden City, NY: Doubleday & Company, 1965), pp. 251-260; Scott and Scott, *Armed Forces*, p. 42.

1
Nuclear Parity

Figure 1.2 Part of Khrushchev's new military doctrine of the early 1960s was the build-up of the land-based missile force, including the SS-5 Skean intermediate-range ballistic missile (IRBM). At the peak in the mid-1960s almost 100 were deployed, most targeted on Western Europe. All were retired by 1984.

nuclear rocket would be the centerpiece of military strategy[60] and it would be the decisive factor in either European wars or those involving the major powers.[61] War, it was thought, would begin with a massive surprise attack using nuclear weapons.[62] The newly formed SRF became the premier service of the armed forces. This fundamental shift reversed the belief that victory came with success by the Ground Forces in military operations at the tactical and then at the operational levels in cooperation with the other services.

The new doctrine underscored the importance of a civil defense program so that the country as a whole would be prepared for inevitable nuclear war.[63] Hardened bunkers were built for political and military leaders.[64] At the same time, work on developing the Moscow ABM system was begun, and construction continued at a sporadic pace through the early and middle 1960s, until four Galosh nuclear missile sites became operational in 1969-1970. Beginning in 1960 Warsaw Pact military exercises gave principal attention to nuclear weapons and the conduct of military operations under nuclear conditions.

In 1961 flight-testing began on the second generation of long-range missiles. Both the SS-7 Saddler and SS-8 Sasin were two-stage, liquid-propellant missiles with large-yield warheads. In 1962 the SS-7 was deployed, followed a year later by the SS-8. By the end of 1965 some 222 of the missiles were deployed, most of them SS-7s. While the Soviet ICBM threat was exaggerated by U.S. intelligence,[65] SS-4 MRBM and SS-5 Skean intermediate-range ballistic missile (IRBM) (begun in 1961) deployments were substantial. More than 600 SS-4s and nearly 100 SS-5s were operational by the middle of the decade. Both missiles were initially deployed in aboveground soft sites; only 15 percent would ever be placed in semi-hardened launchers.

The dominance of the land-based missile force had the result of preventing or slowing down the development of nuclear weapons for the other services.[66] A nuclear-powered submarine that was intended to deliver the submerged-launch SS-N-5 Serb SLBM was cancelled, and 13 diesel-powered Golf class submarines and seven Hotel class nuclear powered submarines armed with the surface-launched SS-N-4 missiles were subsequently modified to carry the new SS-N-5 instead.

The long-range bomber forces also underwent re-evaluation, as they were no longer seen as the optimum nuclear delivery vehicles.[67] A portion of the Tu-95 Bear and Mya-4 Bison bomber force, originally assigned intercontinental missions, was reassigned to theater missions.[68] Neither was built in large numbers. The Il-28 Beagle remained the only ground-attack fighter with nuclear capability until the late 1950s. And second-generation ground-attack fighters, such as the Su-7 Fitter and the MiG-21 Fishbed, which entered service in the late 1950s, had only a secondary nuclear mission.

The Air Forces, recognizing the increased relevance of the standoff attack and the decreasing importance of the bomber force, began to focus upon cruise missiles, which would have a higher penetration rate and were cheaper to build and operate than bombers.[69] In 1961 the nuclear armed AS-2 Kipper and AS-3 Kangaroo ASMs were deployed for carriage on Tu-16 Badger and Tu-95 Bear bombers, respectively.[70] The Tu-22 Blinder, the first Soviet bomber capable of short supersonic dash, entered

---

60 Penkovskiy, *op. cit.*, p. 259.
61 Scott and Scott, *Armed Forces*, pp. 42-49.
62 Ibid, p. 45; Meyer, "Soviet Theatre Nuclear Forces," Part I, p. 18; Thomas W. Wolfe, *Soviet Power and Europe 1945-1970* (Baltimore, MD: Johns Hopkins University Press, 1970), pp. 197-198; W. R. Kinter and Harriet Fast Scott, *The Nuclear Revolution in Soviet Military Affairs* (Norman: University of Oklahoma Press, 1968).
63 V. D. Sokolovskiy, *Soviet Military Strategy*, 3d ed., Harriet Fast Scott, ed. (New York: Crane, Russak & Company, 1975), pp. xxxi, 11; Scott and Scott, *Armed Forces*, pp. 45-49; Holloway, *The Soviet Union and the Arms Race*, 1984 pp. 39-42.
64 See General Colonel A. I. Gastilovich, "Preparing a Country to Repulse Aggression," in Sokolovskiy, *op. cit.*, pp. 331-333. Soviet civil defense programs, in existence since the 1930s, began to take account of nuclear weapons in 1954. In July 1961 the program was centralized under the Ministry of Defense; Holloway, *The Soviet Union and the Arms Race*, 1984, p. 52.
65 U.S. overestimates of Soviet ICBM deployments resulted from evidence of a strong SS-6 test program, exaggerations by Khrushchev of the size of the program, a lack of adequate surveillance, and the refusal of the U.S. intelligence community to change earlier predictions. The U.S. Air Force in particular continued to insist on a high rate of Soviet deployment despite no actual evidence of SS-6 deployment; Freedman, *U.S. Intelligence*, pp. 67-80; Prados, *Soviet Estimate*, pp. 111-126.
66 Due in part to a limited amount of fissionable material; Khrushchev *op. cit.*, p. 52. "We organized the production of rockets on a fully automated assembly line. We started turning them out like sausages at our aircraft plants. After a while, the manufacture of missiles took priority over that of jet bombers and interceptors" (p. 51).
67 Meyer, "Soviet Theatre Nuclear Forces," Part I, p. 20.
68 *Ibid.*, p. 12.
69 The term *rocket-carrying aircraft* was substituted for *bombers* at this time; see ibid., pp. 16, 20.
70 The AS-1 missile, which was also deployed on Badger B aircraft in 1958, was not nuclear-capable.

1
Nuclear Parity

Figure 1.3 The SS-8 Sasin was a two-stage, liquid-propellant missile with a large yield warhead deployed in 1963.

service with the Air Forces in 1962, and with the Navy in 1964, but was deployed only in small numbers. By the mid-1960s second-generation cruise missiles were beginning to enter operational service; they included the AS-4 Kitchen, AS-5 Kelt, and AS-6 Kingfish ASMs, all deployed in 1967-1968, and the SS-N-7 Starbright and SS-N-9 Siren SLCMs, deployed in 1968-1969.

Even though a variety of nuclear systems were being fielded, the period of rapid nuclearization and transformation of the Soviet armed forces was short-lived. As early as 1963 articles appeared in the military press arguing that the Soviet Union would also need to be able to respond to conventional attacks with conventional means. The "revolution in military affairs" had run its course, at least in terms of its influence on strategy and force structure. By the spring of 1964 forces had mobilized against Khrushchev to resist further reforms. Overall dissatisfaction with Khrushchev's leadership led to his removal from power on 14 October 1964 at the Central Committee Plenum.

The departure of Khrushchev allowed the military leadership to openly criticize the overemphasis on nuclear weapons. While nuclear weapons would continue to have a determining influence on military organizations and methods of waging war in Soviet doctrine, there was recognition that many kinds of war, "world and local, swift and protracted, with the use of the nuclear weapons and without," might be waged.[71]

The shift in NATO strategy to "flexible response" in 1967 led, in part, to the change in Soviet strategy, allowing for an initial conventional phase of a conflict between the major powers. In addition, a long conventional war, while assumed to be unlikely, was considered possible. In 1967 the post of commander-in-chief of the Ground Forces was reestablished and large-scale, non-nuclear maneuvers were held.[72]

The deployment of U.S. Polaris submarines beginning in 1960 provided an impetus for the development of a new generation of Soviet ballistic missile submarines. The resulting Yankee class submarine, under development since the early 1960s, was deployed beginning in 1968. Thirty-four submarines were deployed by 1974, each carrying the third-generation SS-N-6 SLBM, a design derived from the SS-11 ICBM. The SS-N-6 missile was a vast improvement over the SS-N-5; it had over twice the range and greatly improved accuracy and reliability. Nonetheless, the range of the missile still required that Yankee class submarines venture far out into the Atlantic and Pacific Oceans to target the United States. A new, even longer range missile, the two-stage SS-N-8 Sawfly, was deployed beginning in 1973 on the Delta I class submarine, a lengthened modification of the Yankee class. The 4200 kilometer range of the SS-N-8 allowed for Delta submarine deployments in waters contiguous to the Soviet Union.

By the late 1960s the Soviet Union reached parity with the United States in intercontinental nuclear missiles. The Soviet ICBM force surpassed that of the United States in numbers of launchers in 1969, and in numbers of warheads in 1977. Between 1966 and 1974, 288 third-generation SS-9 Scarp ICBMs and more than 1030 third-generation SS-11 Sego ICBMs were deployed.[73] The new

---

[71] Lenin Military-Political Academy, Department of Marxist-Leninist Philosophy, *Methodological Problems of Military Theory and Practice* (Moscow: 1966), p. 127.

[72] In September 1967 the large-scale Dnepr maneuvers in the western Soviet Union focused on non-nuclear operations; Holloway, *The Soviet Union and the Arms Race*, 1984, p. 41.

[73] The global-range SS-X-10 was cancelled after eight tests.

1
Nuclear Parity

Figure 1.4 Between 1966 and 1974, 288 SS-9 Scarp ICBMs were deployed in underground "hardened" silos in widely-separated locations.

Figure 1.5 The SS-9 Scarp ICBM on parade in Red Square in Moscow.

missiles were deployed in underground silos and were more reliable than the SS-7 and SS-8 missiles. The capabilities of both the SS-9 and SS-11 were enhanced with the introduction of multiple reentry vehicles (MRVs) in 1971 and 1973, respectively. The new modifications led to a shift in targeting for the SS-9 from area to hard targets, and for the SS-11 from intercontinental targets in the United States to both intercontinental and theater targets (partially replacing SS-4 and SS-5 missiles).[74] The last of the Soviet third-generation ICBMs to be deployed was the SS-13 Savage in 1969, the Soviet Union's first large solid fuel missile. The SS-13 was originally intended to be a mobile missile, but difficulties ensued and it was deployed in underground silos in limited numbers.

A third generation of nuclear-capable tactical fighters began to enter service in 1969, beginning with the late-model MiG-21 Fishbed J and followed by the MiG-23 Flogger (1971-1972), the Su-17 Fitter C (1972), and the MiG-27 Flogger (1975). The most capable of the third-generation aircraft were the Tu-26 Backfire bomber and the Su-24 Fencer fighter-bomber, both deployed in 1974. These newer aircraft are capable of making a swift transition from conventional to nuclear operations.[75] The first Backfire medium-range bomber squadron was deployed in 1974 with Long Range Aviation, and in 1975 with Soviet Naval Aviation. Backfire development had begun about the time the Blinder B became operational; the Backfire shared the supersonic speed, longer range, greater reliability, and increased weapons-carrying capacity of the Blinder B. The Su-24 Fencer was the first Soviet fighter-bomber specifically designed for long-range ground attack and nuclear delivery, and the first to include a weapons system officer. The Backfire and Fencer, still in production in mid-1988, are replacing older Badger and Fitter A/D aircraft.

The deployment of ships, submarines, and naval aircraft in the late 1960s emphasized anti-submarine operations. Nuclear anti-submarine warfare (ASW) weapons included a new nuclear torpedo, a nuclear depth bomb for delivery by maritime patrol aircraft—the Be-12 Mail short-range (1967), the Il-38 May medium-range (1968), and the Tu-142 Bear F long-range (1971) patrol craft—a submarine-launched ASW rocket that carried a nuclear torpedo (the SS-N-16 Stallion), and a shipboard ASW rocket (the FRAS-1).

After a decade in development, fourth-generation ICBMs, the SS-17 Spanker, SS-18 Satan, and SS-19 Stiletto ICBMs, began deployment in 1974-1975.[76] This new generation of missiles, all silo-deployed, were more accurate and reliable than previous ICBMs, and all had multiple independently targetable reentry vehicles (MIRVs). The largest of the fourth generation, the SS-18, replaced the SS-9, while the SS-17 and SS-19 were developed as follow-ons to the SS-7 and SS-11. With the even-

Figure 1.6 Close-up of a SS-9 Scarp ICBM being lowered into its hardened underground silo.

---

74 The shift in targeting emphasis for the SS-11 was partially related to the failure to develop a long-range mobile theater missile in the 1960s. It was not until the deployment of the SS-12 Scaleboard in 1969 that such a capability was introduced, and even then, only about 100 launchers were deployed.

75 General-Lieutenant I. G. Zav'yalov, "Novoye oruzhiye i voyennoye iskusstvo (The New Weapon and Military Art), *Red Star*, 30 October 1970, pp. 2-3, cited in *Selected Soviet Military Writings 1970-1975* (Washington, DC: GPO, 1977), p. 211.

76 All had improved modifications throughout the 1970s and 1980s. The first available missile of this generation, the SS-16 Sinner, was never operationally deployed.

1

Nuclear Parity

Figure 1.7 The SS-X-15 Scrooge was one of three (the other two were the SS-X-10 and SS-X-14) ballistic missiles cancelled after progressing through certain research and development stages. It was the first attempt to build a fully mobile ballistic missile.

Figure 1.8 The mobile MRBM SS-X-14 Scamp was cancelled in 1970 after 19 tests. It is pictured here on its transporter-erector-launcher (TEL).

tual MIRVing of the fourth-generation missiles between 1979 and 1984, the size of Soviet strategic offensive forces increased considerably.

Four lengthened versions of the Delta I ballistic missile submarine (designated Delta II) entered service from 1976 to 1978, each carrying 16 rather than 12 SS-N-8 SLBMs. In 1978 the Soviet Navy also deployed its first MIRVed SLBM—the SS-N-18 Stingray—aboard Delta III class submarines. The initial deployment of the first solid-fueled SLBM, the SS-N-17 Snipe, took place in 1980 aboard a modified Yankee I class submarine, which was designated Yankee II. Due to difficulties with the solid-fuel propulsion and the short range of the SS-N-17, only one submarine was converted to the Yankee II configuration.

At the theater strategic level, fixed-site SS-4 and SS-5 missiles started to be replaced with the mobile, three warhead SS-20 Saber missile, starting in 1977. The solid-fuel SS-20 was more accurate and had a shorter reaction time than the older missiles. The replacement of the two vintage theater missiles by the SS-20 led to speculation that three other missiles under development—the SS-12M Scaleboard B (earlier designated the SS-22), the SS-23 Spider, and the SS-21 Scarab—were meant to replace the SS-12 Scaleboard, SCUD, and FROG. But the new missiles were never deployed in the quantities expected.[77]

Substantial investments were made in other dual-capable systems. The introduction of self-propelled artillery (152mm and 203mm) and mortars (240mm) during the 1970s increased the number of dispersible, mobile, nuclear-capable systems in the Ground Forces several-fold. While the level of nuclearization of Soviet artillery is still uncertain, the adoption of new self-propelled guns has had a significant impact on both Soviet firepower and the survivability of the Ground Forces.

In the Navy, three new anti-ship cruise missiles—two launched from both ships and submarines (the SS-N-12 Sandbox, operational in 1976, and the SS-N-19 Shipwreck, operational in 1980)—and a ship-launched missile (the SS-N-22 Sunburn, operational in 1980) were deployed. A nuclear ASW missile, the SS-N-15, also entered service on submarines in 1979, the same year the dual-capable SA-N-6 Grumble SAM was introduced.

---

[77] Both the SS-12M and the SS-23 will be eliminated under the INF Treaty; the SS-21 will not be deployed in the same numbers as the FROG.

Weapons Developments

Strategic Weapons Developments in the 1980s

Two new mobile ICBMs have recently been deployed in Soviet strategic forces: the solid-fuel and mobile single-warhead SS-25 Sickle (1985), and the 10 warhead MIRVed SS-24 Scalpel (late 1987). These fifth-generation missiles could represent the beginning of a shift in the land-based missile forces from silo to mobile basing, a shift as significant as the introduction of MIRVing in the late 1970s. With deployment of the two new mobile ICBMs, the Soviet Union has begun withdrawing SS-17 and SS-19 missiles, presumably to stay within SALT limits. SS-11 missiles also continue to be withdrawn as SS-24 and SS-25 missiles are deployed.

In the long term, ICBM developments will include new solid-propellant missiles, both silo-based and mobile, and a liquid-fuel SS-18 follow-on. The SS-18 follow-on, designated the SS-X-26, was first successfully tested in December 1986, after two failures. An SS-24 Mod 2 is also expected to begin flight-testing in the next few years.

Naval forces are undergoing significant improvements as well. Two new MIRVed long-range SLBMs have entered service in the 1980s: the 10 warhead SS-N-20 Sturgeon on the huge Typhoon class (1983), and the four-warhead SS-N-23 Skiff on the Delta IV class (1985). These new missiles provide the Soviet Navy with a survivable, long-range capability to strike the continental United States from waters contiguous to the Soviet Union. Both submarines are designed for under-ice operations.

The Soviet ballistic missile submarine force will shrink in size over the next decade as older Golf, Hotel, Yankee, and Delta class submarines are retired and arms control agreements restrict the size of the force. By the early 1990s, the Soviet Navy could have as many as six Delta IV and eight Typhoon submarines, both types being in production in 1988. It is anticipated that the SS-N-20 and SS-N-23 missiles will be further modified and improved. If the Soviets work out the reliability problems of the SS-N-23 missile, it may also be backfit onto Delta III submarines in place of their SS-N-18 missiles. An SS-N-20 follow-on modification and a completely new SLBM are also thought to be under development. A new class of submarine is reportedly under construction in the Arctic and is likely to enter the force in the early 1990s.

Future strategic bomber improvements include deployment of new or modified long-range bombers and standoff weapons, including air-launched cruise missiles (ALCMs) and ASMs. The Bear bomber force is being upgraded, with Bear B/C bombers being modified (and redesignated Bear G) to launch the dual-capable AS-4 ASM instead of the nuclear only AS-3. A new variant of

Figure 1.9 The Mya-4 Bison bomber, which first went into service in 1956, was retired in 1986.

the Bear bomber—the Bear H—entered service in late 1984 along with the first Soviet long-range ALCM, the AS-15 Kent, which provides greater standoff range and accuracy for the bombers. The Blackjack A bomber, now in advanced flight testing, is likely to enter full service in 1988[78] or 1989 and will carry the AS-15. A new short-range attack missile, designated the AS-X-16, is also under development.

Finally, expansion of the Moscow ABM system to the full 100 launcher limit allowed by the 1972 ABM Treaty is almost completed, with the new Gazelle endo-atmospheric missiles and modified ABM-1b Galosh exo-atmospheric missiles replacing the older Galosh missiles. The SA-X-12B Giant SAM will also have some ABM capabilities, though against precisely what type of missile is unknown.

Non-strategic Weapons Developments in the 1980s

In 1982 then Chief of the General Staff Marshal Nikolai Ogarkov wrote "A profound revolution, in the full meaning of the word, is taking place in military affairs in our time in connection with the development of thermonuclear weapons, rapid advances in electronics, development of weapons based on new principles of physics, as well as extensive qualitative improvement of conventional weapons."[79] At about the same time, Soviet armed forces underwent a number of important reorganizations: resubordination of forces within the Air Forces; centralization of the strategic assets of the Air Defense Forces; the resurrection of intermediate-level strategic leadership in the form of joint theater commands (see Chapter Three); the revival of the World War II mobile group concept with the Operational Maneuver Groups (OMGs);

---

78 In early August General-Colonel Boris F. Korolkov, first deputy commander-in-chief of the Soviet air force, said that the bomber recently became operational; *Aviation Week and Space Technology*, 8 August 1988, p. 14.

79 Marshal N.G. Ogarkov, *Vsegda v gotovnosti k zashchite otechestva* (Always in Readiness to Protect the Fatherland) (Moscow: Voyenizdat, 1982), p. 31. See also, D. A. Volkoganov, ed., *Marksistsko-Leninskopye Ucheniy Voyne i Armii* (Marxist-Leninist Teachings on War and the Army) (Moscow: Voyenizdat, 1984), p. 236.

1
Stockpile Today

and improvements in command and control. While strategic nuclear weapons continue to be the basic factor "that restrains the aggressor," high-technology conventional weapons are seen as increasingly important in determining the outcome of future wars.[80]

As Soviet non-strategic nuclear forces evolve over the next decade, the most important factor will be the elimination, under the terms of the INF Treaty, of missiles with ranges of 500 to 5500 kilometers:

- SS-4 and SS-20 intermediate- and medium-range ballistic missiles
- SS-12M and SS-23 short-range ballistic missiles
- SSC-X-4 ground-launched cruise missiles (GLCMs) and
- Any future missiles in this range, including the follow-on to the SS-20 and the supersonic ground-launched version of the SS-NX-24 SLCM, both currently under development.

The elimination of these weapons will also affect the eventual retirement of the 25-year-old SCUD missile, which was to be replaced by the SS-23.

Nuclear-capable artillery, especially self-propelled guns, has increased over the past decade. Production of these guns is likely to continue into the 1990s. The short-range SS-21 missile will probably continue in production at a modest rate, but it will not replace the FROG-7 missile at the division level; instead, the SS-21 will be assigned to brigades at the Army level.

In 1988 the Soviets have four types of nuclear-capable aircraft in production that could serve to offset INF missile reductions. The Tu-26 Backfire and the Su-24 Fencer are the most significant of these aircraft, and production of both—since they are replacing older medium-range bombers and fighters—is expected to continue into the 1990s. A new nuclear-capable ASM that arms the Fencer—thought to be the AS-11 Kilter—is currently entering the force. The new fourth-generation of Soviet fighters—the MiG-29 Fulcrum, Su-27 Flanker A, MiG-31 Foxhound, and Su-25 Frogfoot—which began introduction in 1983, do not appear to include any nuclear capability. The primary role of the new fighters is conventional ground attack and fighter escort.

In late 1987 the SS-N-21 Sampson long-range SLCM was first deployed on Victor III class attack submarines in the Northern Fleet and on Akula class attack submarines in the Pacific Fleet. Over the next decade a few hundred SS-N-21 missiles are likely to be deployed on attack submarines (and possibly on surface ships). The follow-on to the subsonic SS-N-21 SLCM (the air-launched variant is the AS-15) is a larger supersonic missile designated SS-NX-24 in the sea-launched role, and AS-X-19 in the air-launched role. The SS-NX-24 has been flight-tested from a converted Yankee class ballistic missile submarine, which has been converted to a specialized cruise missile carrier. It is still unclear whether the SS-NX-24 will ever be deployed, at least in large numbers. A new cruise missile submarine (possibly the Oscar II class) for launching the SS-NX-24 is believed to be in production.

Several new classes of attack and cruise missile submarines are in production, including the Oscar class, Victor III class, Akula class, and Sierra class. SS-N-19 cruise missiles for the Oscar class remain in production, and the Victor, Akula, and Sierra classes are being armed with newer SS-N-15 and SS-N-16 ASW missiles and the SS-N-21 SLCM. A new nuclear torpedo introduced in the early 1980s—the ET-80—is also believed to be in production.

The construction programs for several multipurpose surface ships continue, including the Kirov and Slava class cruisers and the Sovremenny and Udaloy class destroyers. Fitting out of the first, and construction of the second large-deck aircraft carrier continues at the Nikolayev Shipyard in the Black Sea. The first ship—the Tbilisi—is expected to begin sea trials in 1989 but not to be fully operational until the mid-1990s.[81]

The Nuclear Stockpile Today

The Soviet nuclear weapons stockpile contains 33,000 warheads of some 60 different weapon types.[82] The oldest weapon still in the stockpile is thought to be the SA-1 Guild, first deployed in 1954. The newest are the SS-N-21 Sampson long-range SLCM and the SS-24 ICBM, both first deployed in late 1987. The stockpile consists of 15 strategic offensive missile types, two types of ABMs, four strategic defensive SAM types, 14 non-strategic missiles, eight cruise missile types, aircraft, artillery, and presumably ADMs (i.e., land mines). Nuclear bombs and depth bombs are deliverable by 16 different kinds of strategic and non-strategic aircraft.

The stockpile is more or less evenly split between strategic and non-strategic weapons, with some 13,000 strategic offensive, 4000 strategic defensive, and 16,000 non-strategic warheads. The largest groups of nuclear weapons are bombs and bomber weapons, and land-based ICBMs, each category with some 7000-7600 nuclear warheads—followed by non-strategic land-based missiles with an estimated 4700 total warheads. The number of air-delivered nuclear weapons and nuclear artillery projectiles is unknown, and the estimates in this volume of the *Databook* are largely a matter of conjecture (see Chapter Two).

Soviet strategic offensive force loadings as of mid-1988 are 6500 warheads on 1414 land-based missiles, another 3400 on 942 SLBMs, and 950 air-delivered weapons. An additional 2200 warheads are also thought to exist beyond these "force loadings" and are used for maintenance spares, testing, or reloads. Four types of

---

80 See, for example, the interview with N. G. Ogarkov, "*Zashchita sotsializma: oryt istorii i Sovremenost*" (The Defense of Socialism: The Lesson of History and the Modern Period), *Krasnaya zvezda*, 9 May 1984, pp. 2-3.
81 Normam Polmar, "The New Carrier," *Proceedings*, August 1988, pp. 66-67.
82 The term *nuclear weapon* is used because virtually nothing is known about the specifics of Soviet nuclear warheads. Throughout this volume, the term nuclear warheads implies mass-produced, reliable, nuclear explosive devices capable of being carried and delivered by missiles, aircraft, or other means. Nuclear weapons are meant to convey a fully integrated nuclear warhead with its delivery system. A nuclear bomb delivered by aircraft is referred to as both a *nuclear warhead* and a *nuclear weapon*.

Operations and Readiness

Table 1.3
Soviet Nuclear Weapons Research and Development Programs (1988)

Program	Status
Strategic Offensive	
SS-18 Mod 5?	Improved accuracy version, late 1988-early 1989
SS-X-26	Replace SS-18, liquid propellant ICBM, with increased accuracy and throw weight, first test flight, 2 April 1986, first successful test flight, December 1986, IOC: 1990s
SS-24 Mod 2	ICBM expected to begin flight-testing in 1991
SS-24 follow-on	Solid propellant ICBM under development, IOC: 1990s
ICBM MaRV	Could begin flight-testing by end of the 1980s
SS-N-23 mod	Technological R&D
SS-N-20 mod SLBM	upgrade SS-N-20s on Typhoon SSBNs, IOC: 1990s
SS-N-20 follow-on	replace SS-N-20s on Typhoon SSBNs,
New class of SSBNs	May be under construction
AS-X-19 ALCM	Supersonic air-launched cruise missile variants for Blackjack A and Bear H, IOC: 1990s
AS-X-16 SRAM	New short-range attack missile for Blackjack and Bear H bombers
Strategic Defense	
Gazelle	Silo-based high-acceleration ABM, augments modified Galosh, IOC: late 1980s
SA-X-12B	Giant Mobile SAM with anti-cruise anti-tactical ballistic missile capabilities, IOC: 1989
Non-strategic Programs	
SS-NX-24 SLCM	New large, supersonic sea-launched cruise missile for modified Yankee-class SSGNs, IOC: 1988-1989
Oscar II SSGN	Upgraded submarine, possibly to launch SS-NX-24
Tbilisi class CVN	New large deck, 65,000 ton aircraft carrier, initial sea trials 1989, IOC: mid-1990s
Utka-class aircraft	New wing-in-ground aircraft, for coastal defense and amphibious operations, armed with up to six SS-N-22 missiles
TAG-D aircraft	New sea plane under development; potential replacement for the Be-12 Mail, with possible ASW, surveillance, and mining roles

SAMs and two types of ABMs are nuclear-capable and are armed with some 4200 nuclear warheads.

Non-strategic nuclear forces include some 1700 warheads for long-range theater ballistic cruise missiles, tactical aircraft, naval anti-submarine, anti-air, and anti-ship weapons, artillery, and possibly land mines.

The Soviet Union deploys three land-based, long-range ballistic missiles, the SS-20, SS-12M, and SS-4, and two sea-based long-range systems, the SS-N-5 ballistic missile and the SS-N-21 SLCM. Two other shorter range SLCMs, the SS-N-3 and SS-N-19, also have land-attack roles. Non-strategic aircraft types with nuclear missions include nine kinds of medium bombers and attack and fighter aircraft. Many, particularly the fleet of medium bombers, have long-range strike missions. The aircraft are armed with some 6400 nuclear warheads (mostly bombs) and some 1600 ASMs.

Shorter range non-strategic nuclear weapons include four types of ballistic missiles (SS-23, SCUD-b, SS-21, and FROG-7) with some 3000 warheads and nine types of nuclear-capable artillery guns, some with 2000 nuclear artillery projectiles. Many fighter and attack aircraft are restricted to short-range strikes because of their limited range. The Soviet Union is also thought to possess ADMs.

Nuclear-capable ships include some 276 surface vessels and 262 attack and cruise missile submarines armed with 2200 nuclear warheads of all types, including nuclear torpedoes, ASW rockets, missiles and depth bombs, SLCMs, and ship-based artillery. Nuclear-capable SLCM types carry some 400 nuclear warheads. Soviet Naval Aviation, which is almost exclusively land-based, has 10 different nuclear-capable aircraft types with some 1700 ASMs or bombs. Some 1000 anti-submarine and anti-surface ship nuclear warheads are deliverable by five different types of torpedoes, rockets, and missiles. Some 400 nuclear depth bombs are deliverable by two types of fixed-wing anti-submarine aircraft and two types of helicopters.

Nuclear Operations and Readiness

Although much has been written about Soviet nuclear doctrine and strategy, little is available in the open literature about actual Soviet nuclear operations and plans.[83] The types of nuclear operations that Soviet forces might undertake in wartime can be deduced from the peacetime force structure, deployment patterns, readiness levels, and military exercises of nuclear capable forces.

---

[83] The most extensive analysis of Soviet nuclear operations, and its relationship to doctrine and strategy is Meyer, "Soviet Nuclear Operations," *op. cit.*, pp. 470-531.

1
Operations and Readiness

Figure 1.10 A Victor III (foreground) and an Oscar submarine are shown during an exercise in the North Atlantic in 1985.

Soviet nuclear forces are assigned to all five military services—Strategic Rocket Forces, Ground Forces, Air Defense Forces, Air Forces, and Navy—and would be centrally controlled in crisis or wartime by the Supreme High Command, which would transmit orders from political authorities to use nuclear weapons through joint theater commands (TVs/TVDs) (see Chapter Three). Strategic offensive nuclear forces assigned to the Strategic Rocket Forces, Air Forces (Strategic Air Armies), and Navy would be assigned directly to the Supreme High Command as the command's reserve. Strategic defensive nuclear forces assigned to the Air Defense Forces would also remain under the centralized control of the Supreme High Command. Other nuclear forces would be assigned to the joint theater commands or regional military districts (MDs) inside the Soviet Union. Theater nuclear forces would include certain weapons assigned to the Strategic Rocket Forces and Air Forces, as well as some ballistic missile submarines of the Navy.[84]

Soviet nuclear forces have multilevel controls that combine physical devices and procedural practices to impede the unauthorized or unintentional use of nuclear weapons. Electromechanical devices, similar to U.S. permissive action links (PALs), are thought to be fitted to individual nuclear weapons.[85] Nuclear warheads also appear to be routinely kept separate from delivery systems.[86] Nuclear warheads are also physically controlled by KGB officers or officers of the Main Political Administration, who are outside of the normal military chain of command. Storage sites appear to be either manned by assigned KGB guard troops or supervised by KGB officers.[87]

Soviet nuclear forces are kept at a low level of peacetime alert. Only 50-60 percent of land-based ICBMs, and 15 percent of ballistic missile submarines are on alert at any time.[88] Soviet bombers, both strategic and non-strategic, are not kept on air or ground nuclear alert, but rely on "generated" alerts instead.[89] There is no evidence, moreover, that Soviet nuclear forces have ever been placed at higher levels of alert in response to crises.[90]

---

84 ICBMs, for instance, have "minimum trajectories of about 500 nautical miles"; DOD, FY 1976 Annual Report, p. III-66.
85 It is unclear which types of Soviet nuclear weapons have devices to impede unauthorized arming and detonation. SRF missiles are launched through a multiple-key system; Meyer, "Soviet Nuclear Operations," op. cit., p. 491.
86 The exception is land-based ICBMs on alert and ballistic missile submarines on patrol. Even so, the warheads for the original SS-7 ICBMs were kept separate from the missiles; Berman and Baker, Soviet Strategic Forces, p. 18.
   According to U.S. naval intelligence, "The Soviet Navy routinely deploys antiship cruise missiles on surface ships and submarines with nuclear warheads"; SASC, FY 1980 DOD, Part 2, p. 282. And in 1980 Secretary of Defense Harold Brown stated, "There has been the introduction of nuclear warhead cruise missile submarines in the Baltic Sea. . . The cruise missile launching submarines certainly have nuclear warheads"; Secretary of Defense Harold Brown, statement following the NATO Nuclear Planning Group Meeting, Bodo, Norway, 4 June 1980. It is not believed, however, that non-strategic nuclear warheads on ships or submarines are actually fitted to weapons on launchers.
87 Private communications with the authors. The number of nuclear weapons storage sites in Eastern Europe, as well as the number distributed to the Ground Forces and the Air Forces, is much lower than in the United States. See also, Meyer, "Soviet Nuclear Operations," op. cit., p. 493. According to Meyer, "Through the 1950s and into the mid-1960s, political control over Soviet nuclear forces was maintained by the physical separation of nuclear charges from missiles and bombers. This separation was enforced by assigning the KGB custody and transport responsibilities for nuclear charges and assigning the military the responsibility for custody and transport of delivery vehicles" (p. 487). Meyer points out that when the incident involving the nuclear-armed Soviet Whiskey class attack submarine occurred in Sweden in 1981, the political officer on the ship, not the captain, seemed to be in charge of communications with Swedish authorities (p. 492).
88 The United States keeps virtually all of its on-line ICBMs on alert, and 60 percent of its on-line strategic submarines and SLBMs.
89 DOD, FY 1980 Annual Report, p. 75; Meyer, "Soviet Theater Nuclear Forces," Part II, p. 17. A multistage alert system is used; Meyer, "Soviet Nuclear Operations," op. cit., p. 506.
90 Desmond Ball, "Soviet Strategic Planning and the Control of Nuclear War," in Roman Kolkowicz and Ellen Propper Mickiewicz, eds., The Soviet Calculus of Nuclear War (Lexington, MA: Lexington Books, 1986), p. 61.

1
Strategic Rocket Forces

After many years of what appeared to be a practice of not stationing nuclear warheads outside of the Soviet Union, in the late 1970s or early 1980s nuclear weapons were deployed to Eastern Europe for the first time. Today, nuclear warheads are believed to be stored in East Germany, Czechoslovakia, Hungary, and Poland.[91] In contrast to the United States, which has formal arrangements to share nuclear weapons with NATO allies, the Soviet Union does not appear to have such arrangements with its Warsaw Pact allies. Non-Soviet Warsaw Pact forces deploy nuclear-capable SCUD, FROG, and SS-21 short-range missiles, nuclear- capable artillery guns, and nuclear-capable fighter aircraft built by the Soviet Union, though it does not appear that they can fire nuclear warheads.[92]

The peacetime readiness level of Soviet nuclear forces appears to be heavily influenced by a belief that mobilization would be possible, even in the case of an intentional nuclear war. "Indeed, to prepare their command and control system the Soviets rely heavily on their ability to exploit a period of mounting tensions—much more heavily than does the United States."[93] The shift to a wartime footing would include changes in the operational control of forces (see Chapter Three) and the activation of new communications and command systems for the direction of military forces.

Given the Soviet belief that there would be a period of mobilization during which nuclear forces could be brought to high levels of readiness and made more survivable against attack, peacetime readiness levels are unrelated to policies of nuclear preemption, launch on warning, or nuclear warfighting. According to *Soviet Military Power*, the preferred Soviet option upon warning of preparations of a U.S. nuclear attack is preemption. If preemption is not possible,

[t]he comprehensive Soviet planning for a nuclear war includes preparing their forces to perform their missions under the most adverse conditions. In the event the Soviets fail to execute their preemptive option, they will depend on their early warning networks to provide them with sufficient response time. . . . Once notified [of an attack], the SRF would have to launch its missiles before enemy warheads hit. To ensure that it can do so, the SRF exercises the procedures involved in such a response.[94]

For the use of nuclear weapons in the midst of a conventional conflict,

the Soviets would hope to preempt an impending enemy escalation to nuclear combat with a massed nuclear strike throughout the TVD [theater of military operations] against air, nuclear, command-and-control, and ground forces targets, with the Soviet Supreme High Command exercising overall control. Nuclear weapons would be delivered by frontal aviation, artillery, missiles, and some naval systems, as well as the Strategic Rocket Forces and Strategic Aviation [the five Strategic Air Armies].[95]

Strategic Rocket Forces

The only element of Soviet strategic forces to be kept on alert—that is, able to respond to a surprise attack—are the land based ICBMs of the Strategic Rocket Forces.[96] Even so, only 50-60 percent of the ICBM force is ready and able to be fired at any time.[97] It is unclear how much the low alert level is related to reliability problems with missiles. With the deployment of the fourth- and fifth-generation ICBMs with greater reliability, the alert rates reportedly increased.[98]

To ensure that the ICBM force is ready, the Soviets conduct a much more active program of live firings throughout the year than the United States does, with many of the missile tests being conducted from operational complexes.[99] The Soviets also practice the refurbishment and reloading of ICBM silos,[100] although it is not believed that there is a large stockpile of reload mis-

---

91 Soviet practice until the late 1970s or early 1980s was evidently to retain non-strategic nuclear warheads in the Soviet Union, with plans to move them to Eastern Europe upon warning of attack or during a conflict. Before the permanent deployment of Su-24 Fencer fighter-bomber to Eastern Europe in August 1981, there was no clear evidence of the actual storage of nuclear warheads in Eastern Europe. Secretary of Defense Harold Brown noted in 1978 that "[i]t is conceivable that they may have deployed some nuclear weapons to Eastern Europe," though Soviet practice was "to retain these weapons in the USSR and to depend on warning to permit their rapid deployment to an essential theater." He also noted that the United States believed that the Soviets had sent nuclear warheads as well as launchers to Cuba in 1962; DOD, FY 1979 *Annual Report*, p. 69. Secretary of Defense Caspar Weinberger stated in June 1983 that deployments of nuclear warheads to Eastern Europe had been occurring "since about 1979"; DOD, Public Affairs Office, Secretary of Defense Caspar W. Weinberger, remarks upon arrival at Evenes, Norway, 2 June 1983. Manfred Woerner, the West German defense minister, agreed with Weinberger's assessment; "Bonn Questioning Soviet Motives on Missiles," *New York Times*, 16 June 1983, p. A7. About 30 nuclear storage sites have been identified in Eastern Europe; see, for example, SASC, FY 1980 DOD, Part 3, p. 847; ACDA, FY 1981 ACIS, p. 235; HASC, FY 1981 DOD, Part 4, Book 2, p. 2297; *Soviet Aerospace*, 13 June 1983, p. 46. The storage sites have been hardened against attack; ACDA, FY 1983 ACIS, p. 149.
92 JCS, FY 1980, p. 53; JCS, FY 1981, p. 83; General Research Corporation, "Theater Nuclear Asymmetries (U)," Vol. I, main report, prepared for the Defense Nuclear Agency (McLean, VA: October 1976) (partially declassified and released under the FOIA), p. 54.
93 Meyer, "Soviet Nuclear Operations," *op. cit.*, p. 476.
94 SMP 1988, p. 44.
95 *Ibid.*, p. 73.
96 Marshal Tolubko recently stated, "Our forces [SRF] are now equipped with the most sophisticated missile complexes with all their operational and combat application processes automated to the maximum degree. They have a high level of combat readiness . . . . In recent years the missile forces' combat readiness has increased immeasurably. Whereas during the period of formation it took many hours to prepare a missile for firing, now it takes just seconds"; Chief Marshal of Artillery V. Tolubko, commander in chief of the Strategic Rocket Forces and USSR deputy defense minister, "Always in Combat Readiness," *Krasnaya Zvezda*, 25 April 1985, 2d ed., p. 2 (translated in FBIS, *Soviet Union: Daily Report*, 2 May 1985, p. V1). The ICBM silos not only have redundant lines of communications to and from silos and SRF headquarters and the Supreme High Command, but can be launched from airborne command posts.
97 Private communications with the authors. Missiles not on alert include those undergoing routine maintenance or modification, or those involved in exercises. A major factor in the alert level of Soviet ICBMs has been the program to harden silos against attack; SMP 1988, p. 46. Meyer claims that 80 percent of Soviet ICBMs "are ready to be launched in minutes from their day-to-day alert status"; Meyer, "Soviet Nuclear Operations," *op. cit.*, p. 494.
98 Reliance on liquid fuel propulsion systems and problems with guidance technology kept the cost of operating the ICBM force much higher prior to the fourth generation; Berman and Baker, *Soviet Strategic Forces*, p. 36. By the mid-1970s, a higher percentage of ICBMs were on day-to-day peacetime alert than previously; DOD, FY 1980 *Annual Report*, p. 75; DOD, FY 1981 *Annual Report*, p. 81.
99 SMP 1988, p. 44; SMP 1986, p. 26; SMP 1985, p. 30; SMP 1984, p. 24. In 1974 the numbers of operational firings were as follows: two SS-7, one SS-8, 54 SS-11, and five SS-13; USAF, *Summary Review*, 1975, p. B-8. The number of live firings from operational complexes may have dropped somewhat since the mid-1970s due to the increase in reliability of the newer missiles. But a significant number of operational firings are still conducted. In 1982 the Soviets conducted about 150 test and training launches of ICBMs; SAC, FY 1984 DOD, Part l, p. 34.
100 SMP 1988, p. 45.

1
Air and Naval Forces

siles (see Chapter Two). Newer Soviet ICBMs can also be rapidly retargeted.[101]

Air Forces

The Soviet bomber force is secondary in importance and status to the land- and sea-based missile force in strategic nuclear warfare, yet it plays a significant role in conventional operations and theater warfare.[102] Although the strategic bomber force has never been maintained on ground or airborne alert,[103] the bombers evidently have alert procedures and are assigned dispersal airfields,[104] and crews are trained for intercontinental operations.[105]

The low peacetime alert rates are probably related to the fact that the bomber force is intended to provide a follow-on strike capability after initial missile strikes.[106] Still, the readiness level and intercontinental strike capability of the force has been increasing. More Bear bombers are being fitted with standoff weapons, and considerable attention has been paid since the mid-1960s to staging exercises at forward Arctic bases and to aerial refueling.[107] Bear G bombers conduct training exercises against naval and land targets in the northern Pacific Ocean and have begun to overfly North Korea on intelligence collection missions into the South China Sea and central Pacific.[108] Bear H bombers, which are based at Dolon in Central Asia, conduct routine intercontinental training to points off the North American coasts, particularly around Alaskan airspace.[109]

The number of fighter aircraft and fighter-bomber aircraft assigned exclusive nuclear missions is limited; the majority of non-strategic aircraft would probably be used in a conventional role.[110] The major limitations for nuclear delivery are the lack of trained and certified pilots for nuclear missions and the lack of nuclear bomb storage facilities at many fighter bases.[111] According to one unofficial estimate, only about seven percent of the fighter and fighter-bomber force, and 25-30 percent of the bomber force, in the Western TVD would be withheld from initial conventional engagements in order to be available for possible nuclear missions.[112] Another source claims that the Department of Defense believes that some 30 percent of 4000 Soviet nuclear capable fighters are "assigned to nuclear delivery roles."[113]

Naval Forces

Only about 12-15 Soviet ballistic missile submarines (about 20 percent of ballistic missile submarines) are normally on patrol or in transit to and from patrol stations, able to respond to nuclear alerts.[114] Four or five Delta class submarines patrol in the Norwegian Sea, Greenland Sea, and Barents Sea areas, sometimes venturing as far south as the Azores. Up to three Delta I/III submarines patrol in the Pacific around the Kamchatka peninsula and in the Sea of Okhotsk. One or two Typhoon class submarines patrol in Arctic waters near the Kola peninsula or in the Barents and Norwegian Seas.[115] Until the end of 1987, up to two Pacific Fleet and three Northern Fleet Yankee I class submarines patrolled within range of the U.S. coasts.[116] These submarines have shifted their patrols to areas closer to the European and Asian landmass.[117]

A number of reasons account for the low percentage of Soviet submarines at sea. The submarines are kept at a lower level of peacetime alert because the majority of the forces would not be called upon to be part of any initial strike. In addition, at least through 1979 there was a high shipyard workload, with an average of 20 submarines per year in overhaul.[118] Unlike the U.S. practice, moreover, the Soviets historically have not maintained a two-crew manning system on all classes of submarines to reduce the turnaround time between deployments.[119] Furthermore, Soviet submarines and missiles experience a much higher accident rate than comparable U.S. systems and have much higher material failure incidence rates.

Since Soviet ballistic missile submarines at sea are the centerpiece of the nuclear reserve force, they are maintained in "bastions" close to Soviet shores. These submarines are protected by land-based aviation, surface combatants, and attack submarines, but can still be

---

101 JCS, FY 1978, p. 85.
102 DIA, *Soviet Air Force, Strategic Bombers*, 1981, p. 3. The JCS has noted that while Bear bombers pose the primary air threat to the continental United States, they could perform conventional and/or theater missions as well; JCS, FY 1983, p. 106. *Soviet Military Power* has noted that the primary mission of the strategic aviation bombers is "to perform intercontinental and peripheral nuclear or conventional strike operations"; SMP 1983, p. 61.
103 Berman and Baker, *Soviet Strategic Forces*, p. 36; DOD, FY 1980 *Annual Report* (class.), p. 75.
104 SMP 1986, p. 24; SMP 1985, p. 84; SMP 1984, p. 21; SMP 1983, p. 17; The 1985 and 1986 editions of SMP note that the bombers are assigned dispersal airfields, but omit the mention of alert procedures that appeared in the 1983 and 1984 editions. On the dispersal basing of aircraft, see Meyer, "Soviet Theatre Nuclear Forces," Part I, p. 46, note 68, citing P. Korobkov, "Dispersed Basing of Aviation Under Conditions of Waging Modern War," *Military Thought*, No. 11, 1973, pp. 62-72.
105 DIA, *Soviet Air Forces, Strategic Bombers*, 1981, p. 10; SMP 1985, p. 84.
106 DIA, *Soviet Air Force, Strategic Bombers*, 1981, p. 3; SASC, Strategic Force Modernization Programs, 1981, pp. 8-9; SMP 1983, p. 61.
107 DOD, FY 1966 *Annual Report* (class.), p. 51; DOD, FY 1968 *Annual Report* (class.), p. 48; DOD, FY 1970 *Annual Report* (class.), pp. 82-83.
108 SMP 1988, pp. 28, 79.
109 *Ibid.*, p. 51; JCS, FY 1987, p. 31.
110 *NATO and the Warsaw Pact*, 1984, p. 10; *NATO and the Warsaw Pact*, 1982, p. 15.
111 In 1976, according to the Defense Intelligence Agency, only 350 pilots were trained for tactical air-to-surface missions; Norbert Hannig, "The End of U.S. Strategic Supremacy and its Consequences for Western Europe," *International Defense Review*, No. 8, 1978, p. 1241.
112 Phillip A. Petersen and Major John R. Clark, "Soviet Air and Antiair Operations," *Air University Review*, March-April 1985, pp. 36-54; see also, SASC, FY 1980 DOD, Part 3, p. 876.
113 *Aviation Week & Space Technology*, 2 May 1988, p. 20.
114 JCS, FY 1978, p. 28; ACDA, FY 1980 ACIS, p. 14. See also, DOD, FY 1979 *Annual Report*, p. 28, noting a figure of 15 percent. A figure of 10-15 percent has also been reported as the percentage of the submarine force deployed outside home waters; JCS, FY 1979, p. 87. Before 1977, an average of nine submarines were at sea continuously; "Soviet's Nuclear Arsenal Continues to Proliferate," *Aviation Week & Space Technology*, 16 June 1980, p. 75. According to a report of a speech by Col. Donald R. Arniaz, Deputy Chief of Staff for Intelligence, Air Force Tactical Air Command, the number of submarines in firing position against the United States is never less than 10; *Soviet Aerospace*, 19 September 1983, Vol. 39, No. 2, p. 9; *Aviation Week & Space Technology*, 28 November 1983, p. 17.
115 As of mid-1988, new Delta IV submarines had not been on operational patrols outside of home waters.
116 These submarines were believed at the time to be intended for use against the U.S. command, control, and communications bases.
117 Studeman, USN, Statement before HASC, March 1988, p. 22.
118 This workload may have been lessened as the number of repair and overhaul facilities were increased and expanded; DOD, FY 1979 *Annual Report*, p. 28.
119 Meyer, "Soviet Nuclear Operations," *op. cit.*, p. 494; John Jordan, "Soviet Ballistic Missile Submarines," Part 2, *Jane's Defence Weekly*, 28 January 1984, p. 122. Admiral James Watkins, then U.S. Chief of Naval Operations, testified before Congress in 1985 that the Soviet Union uses a two-crew system for its SSBNs; HAC, FY 1986 DOD, Part 2, p. 927. It has been suggested that a two-crew system is being used for the Typhoon class; John Jordan, "Leviathan of the Deep," *Jane's Defence Weekly*, 1 March 1986, p. 381.

Naval Forces

within firing range of continental U.S. targets.[120] Protective submarine tunnel complexes have been constructed in the Northern and Pacific Fleets.[121] The Soviets have also enhanced the capabilities of the Typhoon class submarine for under-ice operations. Command and control of the submarine force has been enhanced by an extremely low frequency (ELF) communications system and new Bear J mobile very low frequency (VLF) relay aircraft.[122]

To accomplish its priority mission of protecting ballistic missile submarines forces and countering sea-based strikes against the Soviet mainland, Soviet Navy operations would be likely to attempt in wartime to control all or large portions of the Norwegian and North Seas, as well as the Seas of Japan and Okhotsk and the area off the Kamchatcka peninsula.[123] Soviet anti-submarine operations would involve attack submarines, land-based aircraft, and surface task groups, all of which could be armed with nuclear weapons. Attack submarines with nuclear weapons routinely deploy with strategic missile submarines on patrol.[124]

Despite improvements over the years in individual Soviet ships and submarines, and generally increased forward deployments, not many vessels are available for continuous oceanic operations. The Soviet Navy stresses preparedness to deploy for combat on short notice rather than extended operations at sea on a regular basis.[125] The level of naval activity out of home waters is much lower than for the United States. Only about 10-15 percent of the non-strategic vessels of the Soviet Navy are regularly at sea or located away from home waters,[126] and only about 35 percent of out-of-area ship days are by combatant ships, a figure less than half that of the U.S. Navy.[127] Admiral Gorshkov, former commander-in-chief of the Soviet Navy, reportedly claimed that 70 percent of the Soviet Navy could put to sea within 21 days.[128] Soviet attack submarines have demonstrated a surge deployment capability of 24-48 hours on a number of occasions.[129]

When away from home waters, about 70 percent of Soviet surface combatants spend the vast majority of their time at designated anchorages or in port.[130] The low level of activity is directly related to a desire to maintain and achieve high levels of material readiness. In addition, Soviet at-sea replenishment capabilities of missiles, ordnance, and supplies is very limited.[131]

Figure 1.11 A port side view of the 104 meter long Amga, a ship which transports ballistic missiles for SSBNs.

---

120 SMP 1986, p. 29; USN, *Soviet Naval Developments* (Rev. 4/85), p. 12; ACDA, FY 1987 ACIS, p. 39; HAC, FY 1986 DOD, Part 2, p. 908. According to Meyer, "10 percent to 20 percent of Soviet alert SSBNs are dockside, but possess missiles capable of reaching the United States from port"; Meyer, "Soviet Nuclear Operations," *op. cit.*, p. 494.

121 SASC, FY 1986 DOD, Part 8, p. 4363. Four tunnel complexes have been under construction for over ten years; Ted Agres, "Soviet Navy Completing Four Tunnels to Hide Subs," *Washington Times*, 27 March 1984, p. 1.

122 SMP 1988, p. 48. See also, SMP 1986, p. 31; SMP 1985, p. 33; SMP 1984, p. 26; HASC, FY 1985 DOD, Part 3, p. 3.

123 DIA, *The Soviet Naval Threat Circa 2000*, DST-1200F-597-82, October 1982 (partially declassified and released under the FOIA), p. 3; SASC, FY 1984 DOD, Part 6, p. 2977. In a July 1985 naval exercise in the Atlantic, the North Sea, and the Norwegian Sea, the Soviet Navy practiced sea denial operations farther away from the Soviet Union, but still focused on countering vessels attempting to threaten Soviet forces; SMP 1985, pp. 91-93. In the July 1985 exercise, the Soviet carrier battle group consisted of the Kiev carrier, the Kirov, two Kresta cruisers, two Sovremennyy and two Udaloy destroyers, and a Kashin destroyer; *Jane's Defence Weekly*, 27 July 1985, p. 155.

124 Victor III attack submarines, for example, routinely ride "shotgun" on Soviet SSBNs; HAC, FY 1986 DOD, Part 2, p. 213.

125 In-area training activities are quite active with a much greater expenditure of weapons than of Western navies during exercises; JEC, Allocation of Resources - Part 3, 1977, p. 199; HASC, FY 1985 DOD, Part 3, p. 4; SASC, FY 1984 DOD, Part 6, p. 2935.

126 SMP 1985, p. 108; HASC, FY 1985 DOD, Part 3, p. 4.

127 SASC, FY 1984 DOD, Part 4, p. 46. The figures are for 1980, when 35 percent of Soviet and 78 percent of U.S. out-of-area ship days were by combatants.

128 *Jane's Defence Weekly*, 16 March 1985, p. 442.

129 HAC, FY 1986 DOD, Part 2, p. 927.

130 For example, deployed ships in the Mediterranean spend some 70 percent of their time in an anchorage or port, the majority around the Gulf of Hamamet, rear Tunisia; JEC, Allocation of Resources - Part 3, 1977, p. 199. During the November 1982-January 1983 Caribbean deployment, 52 out of the total 68 days were spent in port; HASC, FY 1984 DOD, Part 4, p. 46.

131 DOD, FY 1985 *Annual Report*, p. 25. A series of explosions and fires at the Severomorsk naval base on 13-18 May 1984 destroyed a portion of the Northern Fleet's stock of SAMs and surface-to-surface cruise missiles—including the complete stock of about 80 of the new SS-N-22 missiles—severely constraining the fleet's resupply capabilities during 1984 and, in some instances for a longer period. For example, the production lines for the SA-N-1 and SA-N-3 missiles were shut down in the 1970s, and the destruction of 65 percent of the fleet's stock of these missiles cannot be fully replenished from stores; Derek Wood, "Soviets' Northern Fleet Disabled...'Not Viable' for Six Months," *Jane's Defence Weekly*, 14 July 1984, p. 3.

1
Soviet Military Thought

Soviet Military Thought: Definitions

The Soviet use of military terminology—such as *military doctrine, military science, strategy, operational art,* and *tactics*—is based on precise meanings that often are the reverse of meanings commonly used in the West. These definitions may at first seem irrelevant to an understanding of Soviet nuclear forces and capabilities. Yet they are important to understanding the Soviet nuclear weapons decisionmaking process because they express the primacy of the political leadership in determining military goals. It is the political leadership that takes account of wider political, economic, institutional, and organizational factors in the Soviet defense planning process, as well as any fundamental changes in the relationship of forces in the world arena.

Military doctrine identifies the policy of the political leadership of the Communist Party of the Soviet Union (CPSU) and the Soviet state in the military field. It is defined as a system of views approved by the political leadership on the goals and nature of possible future wars, on the preparation of the armed forces and the country for war, and also on the methods of waging, as well as preventing wars.[1] Military doctrine has two closely connected, interdependent sides: the sociopolitical, which sets out the purposes and character of war and the scope, direction, and pace of the country's preparation for war; and the military-technical, which is subordinate to the sociopolitical and deals with the structure of the armed forces to prepare the military and the country for war and the likely methods with which future wars will be fought.[2]

In contrast, *military science* is the study of military doctrine for the purpose of establishing factors that would determine victory. Military science is defined as the system of knowledge of the character and laws of war, the preparation of the armed forces and the country for war, and the methods of conducting combat operations.[3] Subordinate to and consistent with military doctrine, military science (or the science of war, as it is sometimes called) is devised by the military leadership and staff. Professional military expertise can play an important part in the formulation of the military-technical aspect of military doctrine through military science,[4] but changes in doctrine affect all aspects of military science, thereby providing the political leadership with the means for directly influencing professional military thinking.[5]

Military art, the basic component of military science, is the theory and practice of preparing and conducting military operations and includes *strategy* and *operational art* and *tactics*.[6] *Strategy* is the highest level of military art and is concerned with the fundamentals of preparing for and waging war as a whole and its campaigns.[7] As the basis for war planning, force structuring, weapons development, and deployment, strategy implements doctrine and is general and common for all service branches and weapons.[8] *Operational art*—what in the West would be called *strategy*—is the theory and practice of preparing for and conducting operations by field forces or major formations of the armed forces to achieve goals specified by strategy. Each of the services and branches has its own operational art.[9] *Tactics*, linked to strategy by operational art, focus upon specific questions of preparing and conducting operations on land, at sea, and in the air by specific small-, medium-, or large-sized units (such as division-level tactics).[10]

---

1 See Holloway, *The Soviet Union and the Arms Race*, 1984 p. 29; *Sovetskaya Voyennaya Entsiklopediya* (Soviet Military Encyclopedia), (hereafter referred to as SVE), Vol. 3 (1977), p. 225; Scott and Scott, *Armed Forces*, p. 37, citing "Doktrina Voyennaya" (Military Doctrine), *Voyennyy Entsiklopedicheskiy Sovar'* (Military Encyclopedic Dictionary) (hereafter referred to as VES) (1983), p. 240; N. V. Ogarkov, *Vsegda v gotovnostik zashchite otechestva* (Always in Readiness to Protect the Fatherland) (Moscow: Voyenizdat, 1982), p. 53; A. A. Grechko, *The Armed Forces of the Soviet Union*, English-language ed. (Moscow: Progress Publishers, 1977) (originally published as *Vooruzhennyye Sily Sovetskogo Gosudarstva* (The Armed Forces of the Soviet State) (Moscow: Voyenizdat, 1975); see also, *Armed Forces of the Soviet State*, U.S. translation (Washington, DC: GPO, 1975), pp. 270-271. The recent changes in the definition of doctrine to include not only the nature of future war but also how to prevent it suggests a possible broadening of the definition of *national security* to include questions of foreign policy and arms control issues; see VES (1986), p. 240.

2 See Scott and Scott, *Armed Forces*, pp. 37-38, citing VES (1983), p. 240; Ogarkov, *op. cit.*, p. 53. See also the discussions in Holloway, *The Soviet Union and the Arms Race*, 1984, pp. 29-30; Meyer, "Soviet Theatre Nuclear Forces," Part I, pp. 3-4.

3 See Scott and Scott, *Armed Forces*, p. 74, citing "Voyennaya Nauka" (Military Science), VES (1983), p. 136; Holloway, *The Soviet Union and the Arms Race*, 1984, p. 30, citing SVE, Vol. 2 (1976), p. 184.

4 See, for example, Meyer, "Soviet Theatre Nuclear Forces," Part I, p. 4, citing Ogarkov, *op. cit.*, pp. 56-58; Holloway, *The Soviet Union and the Arms Race*, 1984, p. 30, citing Col. Gen. N. A. Lomov, "O Sovetskoi voennoi doktrine," and Maj. Gen. S. N. Kozlov, "Voyennaya doktrina i voyennaya nauka" in P. M. Derevyanko, ed., *Problemy resolyutsii i voyennom dele* (Problems of the Revolution in Military Affairs) (Moscow: Voyenizdat, 1965), pp. 40-56 and pp. 57-59.

5 See Meyer, "Soviet Theatre Nuclear Forces," Part I, p. 4; Holloway, *The Soviet Union and the Arms Race*, 1984, p. 30. Holloway notes that Soviet professional military writers emphasize that a military doctrine that is not influenced by professional military advice will be prone to serious error.

6 Holloway, *The Soviet Union and the Arms Race*, 1984, p. 30, citing SVE, Vol. 2 (1976), p. 221; Scott and Scott, *Armed Forces*, p. 75, citing S. P. Ivanov and A.I. Yeseyev, "Voyennoye Iskusstvo" (Military Art), SVE, Vol. 2 (1976), p. 211; A. I. Radzievskii, ed. *Slovar' osnovnikh voyenikh terminov* (Dictionary of Basic Military Terms) (Moscow: Voyenizdat, 1965), from the translation by the USAF, *Dictionary of Basic Military Terms: A Soviet View*, Soviet Military Thought series (Washington, DC: GPO, 1965), p. 39. Other components of military science include the theory of military structuring or organization; the theory of troop training and education; the theory of the rear services of (or the problem of supply for) the armed forces; the theory of military economics; and the knowledge of military historical experience; see Scott and Scott, *Armed Forces*, p. 74, citing VES(1983), p. 136.

7 V. D. Sokolovskiy, *Soviet Military Strategy*, 3d ed., Harriet Fast Scott, ed. (New York: Crane, Russak & Company, 1975, p. xviii, citing S. Kozlov, *The Officer's Handbook* (Moscow: Voyenizdat, 1971), p. 68. See also the discussion in N. G. Ogarkov, "Strategiya Voyennaya" (Military Strategy), SVE, Vol. 7 (1979), pp. 555-565.

8 Meyer, "Soviet Theatre Nuclear Forces," Part I, p. 4; Ogarkov, "Military Strategy," SVE, Vol. 7 (1979), pp. 555-565.

9 Scott and Scott, *Armed Forces*, p. 75, citing V. G. Kulikov, "Operativnoye Iskusstvo" (Operational Art), SVE, Vol. 6 (1978), pp. 53-57; Meyer, "Soviet Theatre Nuclear Forces," Part I, p. 4.

10 Scott and Scott, *Armed Forces*, p. 75, citing I. G. Pavlovskiy, P. V. Kutakhov, S. G. Gorshkov, V. D. Sozinov, and I. G. Borets, "Taktika" (Tactics), SVE, Vol. 7 (1979), pp. 628-634.

Chapter Two
The Soviet Nuclear Stockpile

Introduction

Estimating the size and composition of the Soviet nuclear stockpile is fraught with uncertainty. The Soviet government's own excessive secrecy and the lack of any publicly released U.S. government estimates of Soviet nuclear warhead production and deployment means that virtually no reliable empirical information is available. Our estimates of Soviet nuclear forces are thus derived from two approaches. The first is to take comparative graphs released by the U.S. government of the total size of the U.S. and Soviet nuclear stockpiles, analyze these figures based upon our knowledge of the size of the U.S. nuclear stockpile, and attempt to quantify the size of the Soviet stockpile. The second approach, not completely independent of the first, is to break down the nuclear stockpile by categories of weapons, estimate the level of nuclearization in each category, and aggregate the information to create an overall picture of Soviet nuclear forces for mid-1988.

As can be seen, the two methods produce similar estimates. The various U.S. government estimates extrapolated to 1988 place the size of the Soviet stockpile at between 30,000 and 40,000 nuclear warheads. The composition of the stockpile derived from an analysis of each component of Soviet nuclear forces places the size at some 33,000 warheads. This latter figure is our best estimate of the size of the Soviet nuclear stockpile as of mid-1988.[1] What follows is an analysis of various U.S. government projections—the first approach—followed by detailed calculations for each component of Soviet nuclear forces, presented with the underlying assumptions used in our analysis.

DOD Estimates of the Size of the Soviet Stockpile

In 1984, the U.S. Department of Defense (DOD) released three separate graphic representations of the size of the Soviet nuclear weapons stockpile by year relative to that of the U.S. nuclear stockpile (Figures 2.1, 2.2, and 2.3). A fourth curve was released in 1988 (Figure 2.4). The first of these (Figure 2.1) was published by Albert Wohlstetter (hereafter referred to as the "Wohlstetter" estimates).[2] The second (Figure 2.2) was released in congressional testimony by Richard L. Wagner, Assistant to

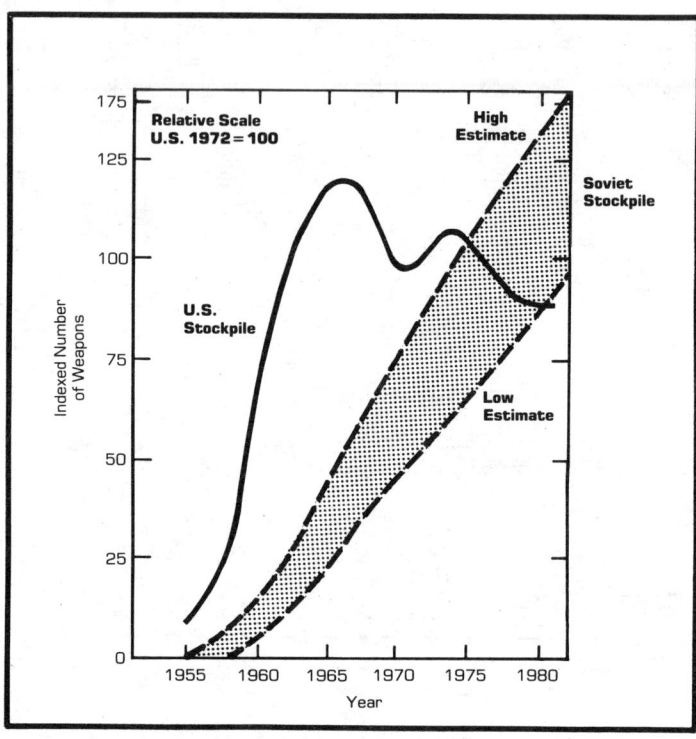

Figure 2.1 Comparison of Soviet and United States nuclear weapons stockpiles, 1956-1982 (from Wohlstetter).

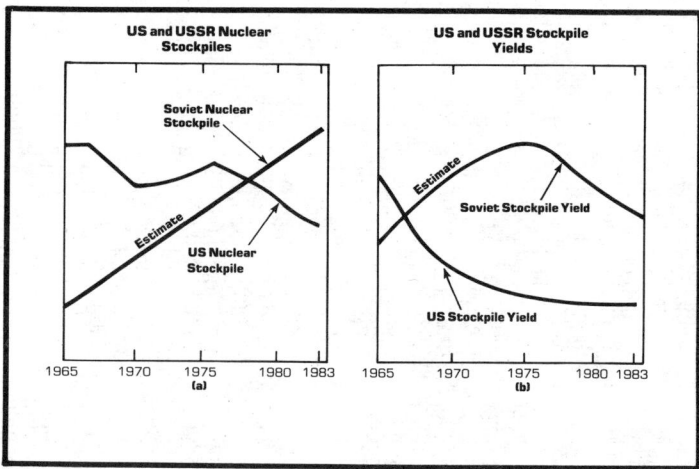

Figure 2.2 Comparison of Soviet and United States nuclear weapons stockpiles, 1965-1983 (from Wagner).
Source: HAC, FY 1985, EWDA, Part 6, p. 118.

---

1 As of mid-1988, the U.S. nuclear stockpile is estimated to contain some 23,400 nuclear warheads; see Thomas B. Cochran, William M. Arkin, and Robert S. Norris, *Nuclear Weapons Databook: Volume I: U.S. Forces and Capabilities*, 2d ed. (Cambridge, MA: Ballinger Publishing Co., 1989).

2 Albert Wohlstetter, "Staatsmaenner, Bischoefe and Sonstige Strategen Ueber Bombenanguffe Auf Unscholdige," in *Pro Pace* (Bonn: Deutsches Strategie-Forum, 1984).

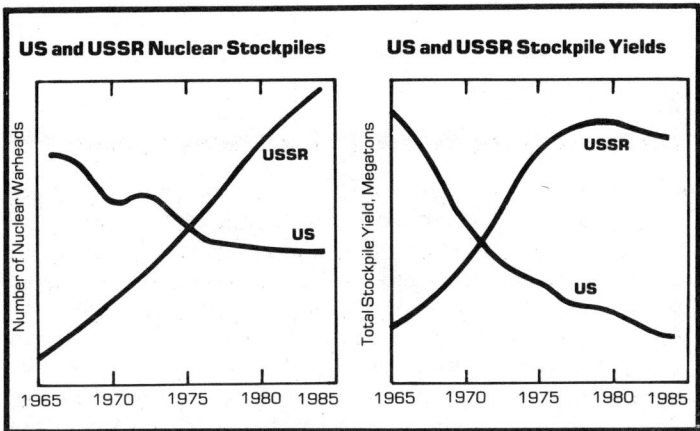

Figure 2.3 Comparison of Soviet and United States nuclear weapons stockpiles, 1965-1984 (from Weinberger).
Source: SASC, FY 1985 DOD, Part 1, p. 123; also reproduced in HAC, FY 1986, EWDA, Part 7, p. 238.

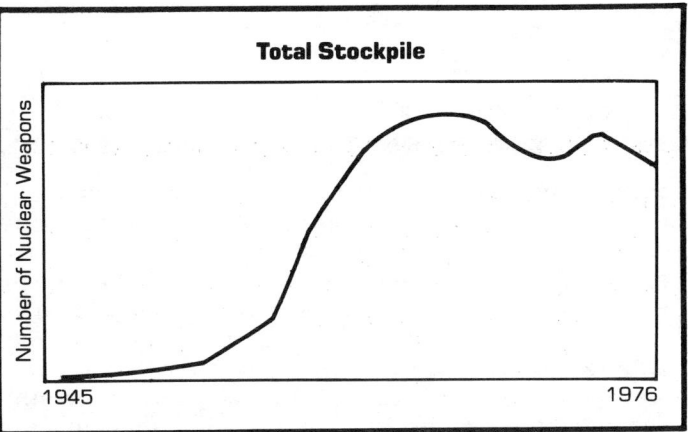

Figure 2.5 United States nuclear weapons stockpile, 1945-1976 (from JCAE).
Source: JCAE, Development, Use and Control of Nuclear Energy for Common Defense and Security and for Peaceful Purposes, Second Annual Report, 30 June 1976, p. 135.

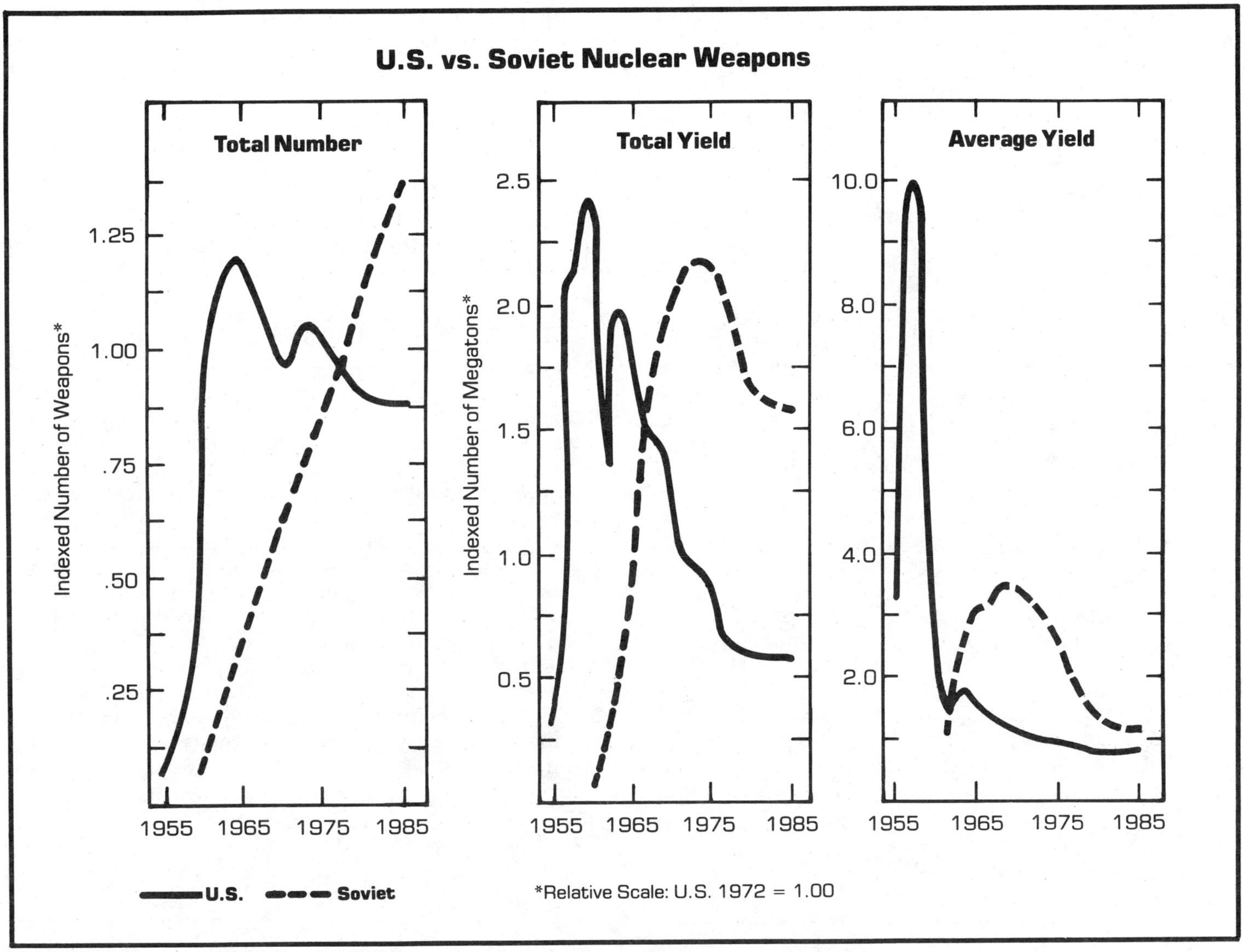

Figure 2.4 Comparison of Soviet and United States nuclear weapons stockpiles, 1955-1985 (from Iklé/Wohlstetter).
Source: *Discriminate Deterrence*, Report of the Commission on Integrated Long-term Strategy, January 1988.

Nuclear Weapons Databook, Volume IV

2

Stockpile Components

the Secretary of Defense (Atomic Energy) (the "Wagner" estimates).[3] The third (Figure 2.3) was released in congressional testimony by Secretary of Defense Caspar Weinberger (the "Weinberger" estimates).[4] The fourth (Figure 2.4) was presented in the report of the Commission on Integrated Long-Term Strategy, chaired by Fred C. Iklé and Albert Wohlstetter (referred to hereafter as the "Iklé/Wohlstetter" estimates).[5] The Wagner and Weinberger stockpile graphs were accompanied by comparative curves of U.S. and Soviet megatonnage (see "Soviet Megatonnage"). In all four cases, quantitative data were not provided. The graphs themselves are smoothed freehand curves and do not purport to be precise representations of the actual numbers used to plot the graphs. As demonstrated below, the Weinberger estimates in Figure 2.3 are inconsistent with the other three, are in error, and should be discarded.

Since each set of figures displays a graph of the U.S. stockpile, the first step in estimating the Soviet values was to compare each of the U.S. stockpile curves against reliable figures for the size of the U.S. stockpile. Next, all curves were plotted to the same scale and assigned quantitative values. The most accurate graph of the relative size of the U.S. stockpile by year was released in 1976 by the former Joint Committee on Atomic Energy (JCAE) of the U.S. Congress (Figure 2.5).[6] So that the Wohlstetter, Wagner, Weinberger and Iklé/Wohlstetter U.S. stockpile curves in Figures 2.1 through 2.4 could be scaled to the respective JCAE curves in Figure 2.5, all of the curves were digitized by machine.[7] The scaling parameters were then calculated by applying a least-squares technique to annual data points for the years in which the data overlapped. Since the size of the U.S. stockpile by year is reasonably well known,[8] the ordinates of each graph were quantified; that is, the actual number of warheads was plotted and compared. The quantitative scale for the JCAE curve is based on a peak of the U.S. stockpile in 1967 at 32,500 warheads.[9] The resulting data are presented in Table 2.1.

Following the above approach, in Figure 2.6a the Wagner curve of the U.S. stockpile size from Figure 2.2a is compared against the more accurate JCAE curve from Figure 2.5. Similarly, in Figure 2.6b, the Weinberger curve of the U.S. stockpile from Figure 2.3a is compared to the more accurate JCAE curve in Figure 2.5. Clearly, the U.S. data in Wagner's Figure 2.2a curve is more accurate than the U.S. data in Weinberger's Figure 2.3a curve,

and consequently Weinberger's Soviet estimate in Figure 2.3a is suspect. The same approach was taken to compare the accuracy of the estimates by Wagner and Weinberger of the U.S. megatonnage (see "Soviet Megatonnage"). Again, Wagner's curve is the better fit and Weinberger's curve is suspect. In conclusion, the Weinberger curves in Figure 2.3 appear to be erroneous and should be discarded.

In Figure 2.7, estimates of the size of the Soviet stockpile from Wohlstetter (Figure 2.1), Wagner (Figures 2.2), and Iklé/Wohlstetter (Figure 2.4) are compared. As seen from Figure 2.7, the Iklé/Wohlstetter curve follows the Wagner curve closely, dropping off in later years. The Wagner and Iklé/Wohlstetter curves track slightly above midway between Wohlstetter's high and low values. The Wohlstetter low estimate is most consistent with our best estimate of 33,000 warheads as of mid-1988 and is taken, therefore, as our best estimate of the growth in the Soviet stockpile.

The reader is cautioned that, for most purposes, the more relevant comparison in the sizes of the Soviet and U.S. stockpiles is in offensive forces. Thus, excluding what could be 4200 strategic defensive warheads on antiballistic and surface-to-air missiles (SAMs), the total Soviet nuclear stockpile is estimated to be 29,000 warheads as of mid-1988.

Components of the Soviet Nuclear Stockpile

A careful analysis of Soviet military equipment, military strategy, plans for the potential use of nuclear weapons, weapons production, force structure, deployment patterns, and nuclear-related training activity can contribute to an assessment of the degree of nuclearization of Soviet forces. The number of delivery platforms (large missiles and launchers, ships and submarines, aircraft, guns, and so on) that are capable of firing nuclear weapons is relatively well known. The number of nuclear warheads in these categories can be deduced from calculations of the number of warheads/reentry vehicles on ballistic missiles, the launcher loads of ships and submarines, and the carrying capacity of aircraft and bombers. For certain categories of weapons there is a much larger number of delivery systems than nuclear warheads (for example, tactical aircraft and artillery guns). For these categories, warhead estimates are based upon assumed

---

3 HAC, FY 1985 EWDA, Part 6, p. 118.
4 SASC, FY 1985 DOD, Part 1, p. 123. Also reproduced in HAC, FY 1986 EWDA, Part 7, p. 238.
5 Fred C. Iklé and Albert Wohlstetter, *Discriminate Deterrence*, Report of the Commission on Integrated Long-Term Strategy (Washington, DC: GPO, January 1988).
6 JCAE, *Development, Use and Control of Nuclear Energy for Common Defense and Security and for Peaceful Purposes*, Second Annual Report, 30 June 1976, p. 135. A notable difference between this and similar graphs released by the U.S. government since then is that the draftsman drew straight-line segments between annual data points. This is a strong indication that actual data was used in drawing the curve.

7 Courtesy of University of Pennsylvania, Department of Landscape Architecture and Regional Planning.
8 See *Nuclear Weapons Databook*, Volume I (2nd edition), Volume II, p. 18.
9 The Iklé/Wohlstetter curve for the U.S. stockpile size is not a good fit to the JCAE curve. To force a better fit, the peak in the U.S. stockpile as projected by Iklé/Wohlstetter was shifted to 1967, and the curve for the 1955-1967 period was stretched out (accounting for the missing data points in Table 2.1, column 10). The Iklé/Wohlstetter curve for the U.S. stockpile was normalized by choosing 32,500 warheads as the U.S. stockpile size when it peaked in 1967. Other than this normalization, no adjustments were made in the Soviet stockpile curve.

Stockpile Estimates

Table 2.1
DOD/DOE Estimates of the Size of the U.S. and Soviet Stockpiles

YEAR	JCAE US	Wohlstetter US	Wohlstetter USSR-High	Wohlstetter USSR-Low	Wagner US	Wagner USSR	Weinberger US	Weinberger USSR	Iklé/Wohlstetter US	Iklé/Wohlstetter USSR
1955	2110	2760	280	0	....	....	....	....	1980	....
1956	3760	4000	900	0	....	....	....	....	2940	....
1957	5420	5800	1590	0	....	....	....	....	4090	....
1958	7520	8190	2440	224	....	....	....	....	6280	....
1959	11,700	13,000	3550	1040	....	....	....	....	10,000	....
1960	18,700	18,900	4520	1710	....	....	....	....	....	3430
1961	23,100	23,300	5770	2430	....	....	....	....	25,100	4850
1962	27,000	26,700	7180	3080	....	....	....	....	....	6280
1963	29,800	29,000	8970	4030	....	....	....	....	29,800	7710
1964	31,600	31,100	10,600	5100	....	....	....	....	31,200	9130
1965	32,200	32,400	12,300	6280	33,200	8400	34,600	4120	....	10,600
1966	32,200	33,000	13,700	7540	33,300	9960	34,600	5350	....	12,000
1967	32,500	32,800	15,500	8840	32,000	11,500	34,400	7000	32,500	13,400
1968	31,600	31,300	17,400	10,000	30,200	13,100	32,200	8980	32,000	14,800
1969	29,700	29,100	19,000	11,300	28,200	14,600	29,600	10,900	29,900	16,300
1970	28,000	27,000	20,800	12,500	27,200	16,200	27,400	12,700	28,200	17,700
1971	27,000	26,700	22,100	13,500	27,500	17,800	27,300	14,500	27,100	19,000
1972	28,000	27,500	23,600	14,600	28,000	19,300	28,400	16,600	27,000	20,300
1973	29,500	28,700	25,400	15,800	28,700	20,900	27,700	18,800	27,800	21,600
1974	29,800	29,500	26,800	16,800	29,600	22,400	25,900	21,100	28,700	22,900
1975	28,300	28,800	28,800	17,900	30,500	24,000	24,000	23,500	28,400	24,300
1976	28,400	27,500	30,500	19,100	29,400	25,600	22,400	25,800	27,700	25,500
1977	....	26,100	32,000	20,200	28,400	27,100	21,200	28,400	27,100	26,700
1978	....	25,100	33,500	21,300	27,000	28,700	20,700	31,400	26,500	28,100
1979	....	24,500	35,000	22,500	25,600	30,300	20,400	34,000	25,900	29,400
1980	....	24,400	36,500	23,700	23,600	31,800	20,000	36,300	25,600	30,800
1981	....	24,400	37,800	24,900	22,300	33,400	19,800	38,700	25,200	32,100
1982	....	24,300	39,400	26,300	21,300	35,000	19,800	40,800	25,000	33,500
1983	....	....	....	....	....	....	19,700	42,600	24,900	34,600
1984	....	....	....	....	....	....	19,800	44,500	24,800	35,700
1985	....	....	....	....	....	....	19,900	46,100	24,800	36,800
1986	....	....	....	....	....	....	....	....	24,700	....
1987	....	....	....	....	....	....	....	....	24,700	....

Relative scales released by DOD and DOE. Quantitative values assigned by the *Databook* staff. All stockpile values have been rounded to three significant figures. This reflects the precision in reproducing the curves and does not reflect the accuracy of DOD and DOE estimates of the Soviet stockpile.

ratios of warheads to delivery systems. Many nuclear weapon systems are nuclear-only, that is, they are not capable of firing conventional warheads. Others are dual-capable (see Table 2.2). Virtually all strategic nuclear weapons are nuclear-only; there are, however, a small number of dual-capable air-to-surface missiles (ASMs) on bombers. For non-strategic forces, a much larger percentage of weapon systems are dual-capable. The nuclear-only non-strategic systems include the SS-N-5 submarine-launched ballistic missile (SLBM), the SS-20 and SS-4 intermediate-range ballistic missiles (IRBMs), nuclear artillery projectiles, nuclear torpedoes, the SS-N-15 nuclear depth bomb, the SS-N-21 sea-launched cruise missiles (SLCMs), nuclear bombs, and nuclear depth bombs.

For each class of weapons, the level of detail and the accuracy of information varies. More information is available on strategic offensive forces than on any other category of the Soviet arsenal. A public database of information exists on the number of warheads on strategic missiles as a result of the SALT and START negotiations. The additional warheads that might exist in the Soviet arsenal for possible reload/refire purposes, maintenance spares, and/or testing, for example, can also be somewhat reliably estimated based upon known practices and comparable ratios of extra warheads in the U.S. arsenal.

2
Stockpile Estimates

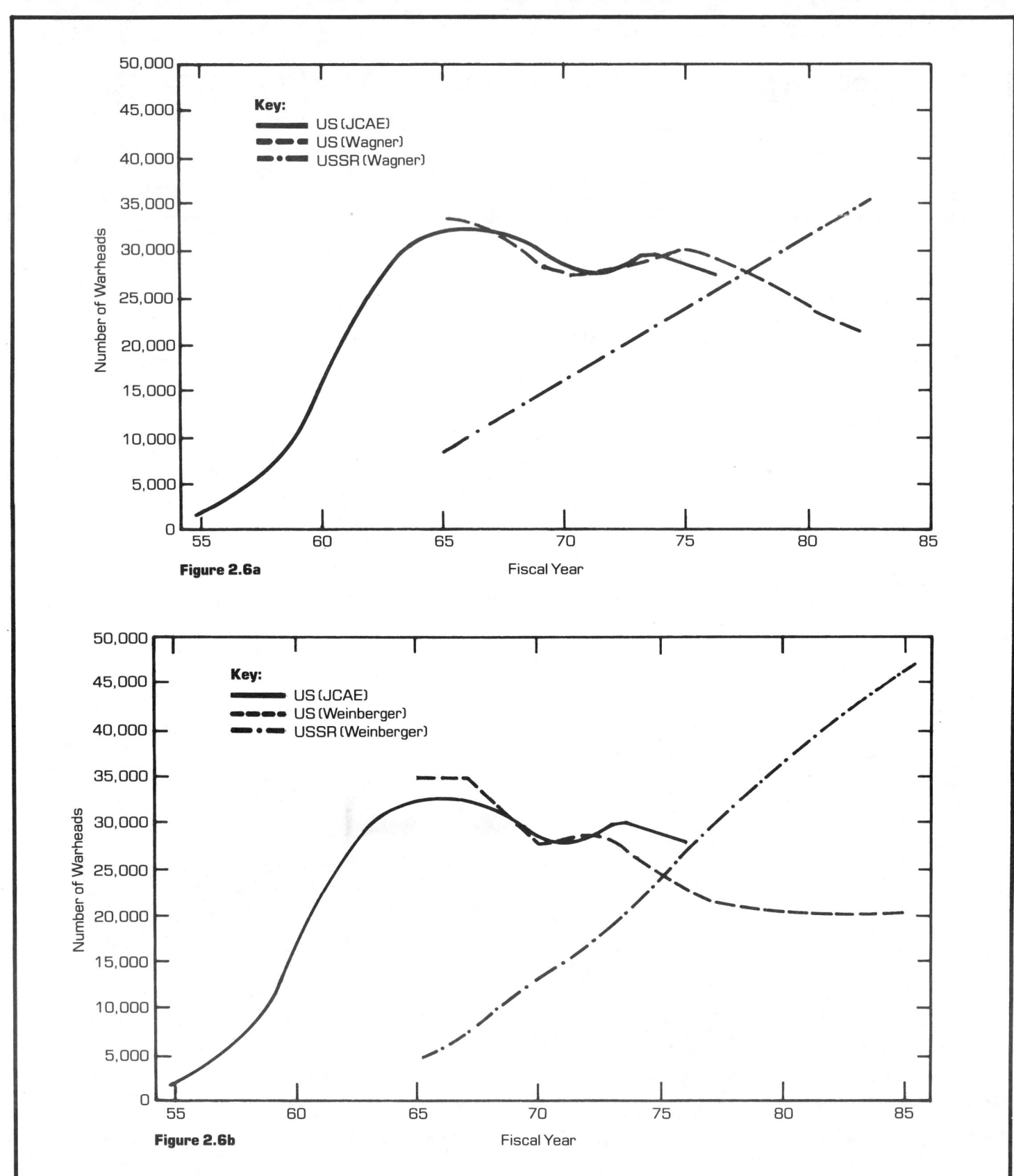

Figure 2.6 Comparison of United States nuclear weapons stockpile graphs from JCAE, Wagner, and Weinberger.

2
Stockpile Estimates

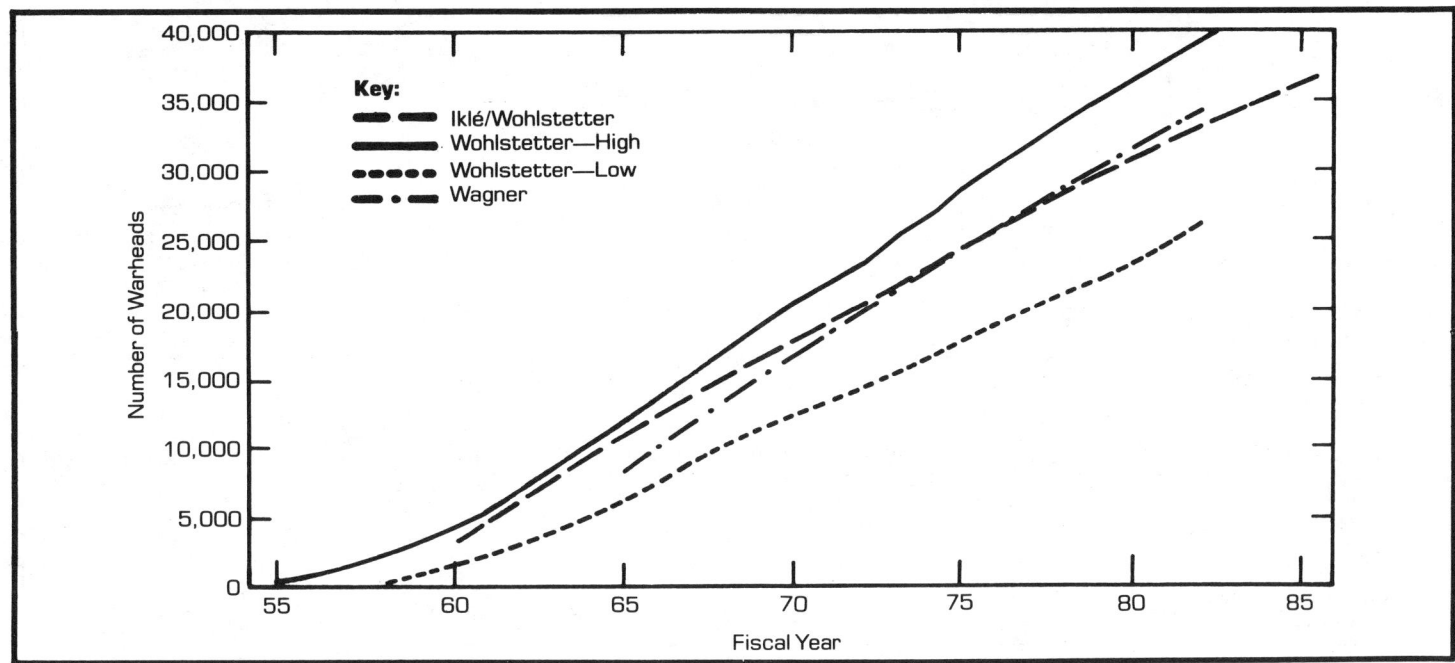

Figure 2.7 Comparison of Soviet nuclear weapons stockpile graphs from Wohlstetter, Wagner, and Iklé/Wohlstetter.

Table 2.2
Soviet Dual-Capable Weapons

Strategic Defense
Surface-to-air Missiles
- SA-1 Guild
- SA-2 Guideline
- SA-5 Gammon
- SA-10 Grumble

Land-based Non-strategic
Missiles
- FROG-3/5/7
- SCUD B
- SS-12M Scaleboard
- SS-21 Scarab
- SS-23 Spider

Air-to-surface missiles
- AS-2 Kipper
- AS-4 Kitchen
- AS-5 Kelt
- AS-6 Kingfish

Naval
Anti-submarine weapons
- FRAS-1
- SS-N-16 Stallion

Coastal Missiles
- SSC-1b Sepal

Anti-ship missiles
- SS-N-3 Shaddock/Sepal
- SS-N-7 Starbright
- SS-N-9 Siren
- SS-N-12 Sandbox
- SS-N-19 Shipwreck
- SS-N-22 Sunburn

All nuclear-capable Soviet artillery guns, bombers, fighters, and anti-submarine aircraft are dual-capable. Soviet nuclear bombs, depth bombs, and torpedoes do not have convertible warheads.

As noted above, most non-strategic delivery systems are dual-capable. Since the non-strategic weapon systems are invariably smaller than strategic intercontinental ballistic missiles (ICBMs), the number of associated nuclear warheads (whether nuclear bombs, warheads on dual-capable missiles, or nuclear torpedoes and artillery projectiles) can be estimated based either upon an analysis of warhead production and storage or upon an assumed level of nuclearization, which is derived from an understanding of a systems delivery capacity (for example, number of launchers) and its assigned conventional and nuclear missions.

Since virtually no information is available on Soviet warhead production or storage, our estimates of non-strategic nuclear forces are based upon delivery and mission assumptions. Even here, there are enormous uncertainties. There are a large number of delivery systems in certain categories, such as short-range missiles or tactical fighter aircraft, for which the number of associated nuclear warheads must logically be less than the total delivery capacity of the systems. For example, in the case of short-range missiles, either the SCUD B or FROG systems, there are over 600 reloadable mobile launchers in each category. In U.S. forces, the ratio of *nuclear warheads* to launchers for comparable short-range Lance missiles is nine to one.[10] If a comparable reload ratio were used to calculate the nuclearization of Soviet short-range missile forces, there would be 11,500 warheads. The number of nuclear bombs for tactical aircraft and nu-

---

10 There are a total of 100 Lance launchers—48 U.S. and 52 Allied—and 915 warheads in the U.S. stockpile.

2
ICBMs

Table 2.3
Soviet Nuclear Stockpile
(mid-1988)

Category/Type	Launchers	Force Loading	Total Stockpile
Strategic Offense			
ICBM	1414	6500	7600
SLBM	942	3400	4000
Bomber	160	950	1400
Subtotal	**2516**	**10,800**	**13,000**
Strategic Defense			
Anti-ballistic missiles	100	100	110
Surface-to-air missiles	7070	n.a.	4100
Subtotal	**7170**	**n.a.**	**4200**
Non-Strategic			
Missiles	2074	2900	4700
Aircraft	4780	unk	5100
Artillery	6760	unk	2000
Atomic demolitions	unk	unk	unk
Subtotal	**13,614**	**n.a.**	**11,800**
Naval			
Attack aviation	470	unk	1270
Missiles (non-strategic)	36	36	50
Cruise/anti-ship missiles	946	n.a.	400
Anti-submarine	1056	n.a.	1400
Anti-air	64	260	260
Artillery	n.a.	100	100
Coastal missiles	100	100	100
Mines	n.a.	unk	unk
Subtotal	**2636**	**n.a.**	**3600**
Total	**n.a.**	**n.a.**	**33,000**

n.a.: not available; unk: unknown
Force loading is defined as the number of deliverable nuclear warheads on operational systems. It does not include warheads that may be available for reloads or spares. The total number of warheads and the subtotals for each category of weapon are rounded.

clear artillery projectiles would be in the thousands as well. In each of these categories, our estimates of levels of nuclearization are assumed to be smaller (Table 2.3). If the Soviet nuclear weapons stockpile is in fact larger than our estimate of some 33,000, its actual size probably includes a larger number of warheads in one or more of these categories.

Strategic Forces

Soviet strategic offensive nuclear forces consist of intercontinental ballistic missiles (ICBMs), submarine-launched ballistic missiles (SLBMs), and intercontinental bombers that carry bombs and air-to-surface missiles (ASMs). As of mid-1988, there were an estimated 13,000 nuclear warheads allocated to weapons in these categories, or 40 percent of the total Soviet stockpile. Some 60 percent are on the land-based ICBM force, 30 percent are on the submarine force, and 10 percent are assigned to the bomber force (see Table 2.3).[11] Of the 13,000 warheads, some 10,800 are part of Soviet on-line forces, referred to as "force loadings." Strategic defensive forces consist of some 4200 warheads on anti-ballistic missiles and surface-to-air missiles (SAMs). Following is the breakdown of strategic forces among ICBMs, SLBMs, bombers, and strategic defensive missiles.

ICBMs

The Soviet ICBM force as of mid-1988 is composed of 1414 missiles armed with 6506 warheads (see Table 2.4). There are seven different types of missiles. The SS-13 and SS-25 missiles have single warheads. The SS-11 is deployed in two different modifications—one with single warheads and one with three warheads in multiple reentry vehicles (MRVs).[12]

---

[11] In 1979, the breakdown was 75 percent ICBM, 25 percent SLBM, and five percent bomber warheads; DOD, FY 1981 *Annual Report*, p. 89.
[12] Multiple reentry vehicles (MRVs) are to be distinguished from multiple independently targetable reentry vehicles (MIRVs), in that the MRV warheads land in close proximity to each other, rather than widely separated, in effect hitting the same target. MIRV warheads are capable of hitting widely dispersed targets. For purposes of counting the nuclear stockpile, each individual MRV warhead is counted separately, although they are most often counted as one in force loading comparisons with the United States.

2
ICBMs and SLBMs

Table 2.4
Intercontinental Ballistic Missile (ICBM) Warheads
(mid-1988)

Missile Type	Launchers	Per Launcher	Warheads Force Loading	Total Stockpile with Spares
SS-11 Sego	420	MRV x 2	420	900
SS-13 Savage	60	1	60	70
SS-17 Spanker	130	MIRV x 4	520	600
SS-18 Satan	308	MIRV x 10	3080	3400
SS-19 Stilletto	350	MIRV x 6	2100	2300
SS-24 Scalpel	20	MIRV x 10	200	220
SS-25 Sickle	126	1	126	140
Total	**1414**		**6500**	**7600**

Launchers are silos at operational ICBM complexes or mobile launchers at main operating bases, exclusive of test ICBM launchers and training launchers of mobile SS-24 and SS-25 missiles. Force loadings represent one warhead per missile for SS-11, SS-13, and SS-25; four warheads for SS-17; six warheads for SS-19; and ten warheads for SS-18 and SS-24. SS-11 Mod 3 carries three MRV, which are counted as one in force loading. Total, counting MRVs individually and including approximately 10 percent additional warheads for spares and reloads, represents authors' rounded estimates.

Table 2.5
Submarine-Launched Ballistic Missile (SLBM) Warheads
(mid-1988)

Missile Type	Submarines	Launchers	Warheads Force Loading	Total Stockpile with Spares
SS-N-6 Serb		256	256	560
Yankee I	16			
SS-N-8 Sawfly		286	286	320
Hotel II[1]	1	(6)	(6)	
Delta I	18	(216)	(216)	
Delta II	4	(64)	(64)	
SS-N-17 Snipe		12	12	15
Yankee II	1			
SS-N-18 Stingray		224	1568	1700
Delta III	14			
SS-N-20 Sturgeon		101	1000	1100
Golf V[2]	1	(1)	(0)	
Typhoon	5	(100)	(1000)	
SS-N-23 Skiff		64	256	280
Delta IV	4			
Total	**63**	**942**	**3400**	**4000**

Launchers are launch tubes on operational strategic missile submarines and those on sea trials.
Force loadings represent one warhead per missile for SS-N-8 and SS-N-17; two warheads for SS-N-6; seven warheads for SS-N-18; ten warheads for SS-N-20; and four warheads for SS-N-23. Total, including approximately 10 percent additional warheads for spares and reloads, represents authors' rounded estimates of the total stockpile.

[1] The Hotel III submarine was not SALT-accountable; but the six launchers were SALT-accountable.

[2] The Golf V test submarine is not counted as carrying nuclear warheads.

2
ICBMs

Figure 2.8 The Soviet Union has only 29 auxiliary naval ships which are capable of nuclear weapons support, a force much smaller than the U.S. Navy. Twelve of these ships are submarine tenders such as the Alexander Brykin, a new Soviet Navy supply ship especially designed to reload SSBNs away from the homeport. This may indicate some reload capability for strategic submarines.

The SS-17, SS-18, SS-19, and SS-24 missiles have more than one warhead in multiple independently targetable reentry vehicles (MIRVs). For these four missiles, the number of warheads on each is assumed to be the number determined by the counting rules under the SALT II and START negotiations: four warheads for the SS-17, six warheads for the SS-19, and ten warheads for the SS-18 and SS-24 missiles. In both negotiations, the MIRVed ICBM launchers have established counting rules irrespective of how many warheads they may actually be carrying.[13] Some modified versions of the SS-17, SS-18, and SS-19 missiles carry a single warhead, but they are thought to be deployed in small numbers if at all.

The total stockpile of nuclear warheads in the ICBM force, beyond force loading, depends on the existence of extra missiles that could be used for reloading ICBM silos or mobile launchers (often called "reload missiles") for follow-on strikes during a protracted nuclear war. Many Soviet launchers can theoretically be reloaded after an initial launch. According to *Soviet Military Power* 1988, "provisions have been made to refurbish and reload SRF [Strategic Rocket Forces] silos"[14] The cold-launch technique used for the SS-17, SS-18, SS-24, and SS-25 missiles minimizes damage to the silos and mobile launchers, and as the U.S. Strategic Air Command (SAC) believes, the launchers "can therefore in principle be reloaded in a relatively short time."[15]

In 1980, Secretary of Defense Harold Brown reported to Congress that there was "no evidence that the Soviets have any capability to use excess missiles as reserves, or refires."[16] That same year, however, an exercise reportedly took place in which Strategic Rocket Forces practiced the reload of SS-18 missile silos.[17] The DOD then stated two years later that the Soviets have contingency

---

13 SFRC, Salt II Treaty, Report 96-14, p. 325.
14 SMP 1988, p. 45.
15 SAC, *Soviet Military Capabilities*, July 1981, p. 17. The SAC 'threat" briefing notes, "should evidence accumulate that the Soviets are testing or training with this capability, the impact on the strategic balance could be significant."

16 DOD, FY 1981 *Annual Report*, p. 80.
17 The exercise took place over a five-day period and included some 25-40 missile silos. No refire missiles were actually tested, but all the hardware from the original missiles in the silos was removed; *Air Force Magazine*, November 1980, p. 22.

2
SLBMs

Table 2.6
Strategic Bomber-Delivered Warheads
(mid-1988)

Bomber Type/Weapon Type	Aircraft	Warheads	
		Force Loading	Total Stockpile with Spares
Tu-95 Bear A	20		
Bombs		40	80
Tu-95 Bear B/C	30		
Bombs		120	240
AS-3 missile		(30)	30
Tu-95 Bear G[1]	45		
Bombs		180	360
AS-4 missile		90	100
Tu-95 Bear H	65		
AS-15 missile		520	570
Total	**160**	**950**	**1400**

Force loading represents two bombs on Bear A; four bombs on Bear B/C/G; one AS-3 on Bear B/C in lieu of bombs; two AS-4 on Bear G; and eight AS-15 on Bear H.

Total includes 100 percent additional spares and reloads for bombs and 10 percent additional warheads for smaller AS-4 and AS-15 missiles. Total stockpile figures are rounded.

1. Bear G bombers are assigned theater roles even though they are counted as part of strategic forces; SMP 1988, p. 79.

---

plans for reloading and refiring ICBMs and have an "in-being wartime reconstitution capability for the strategic missile forces."[18] The DOD has also stated that the Soviets may be able to "reconstitute a portion of their hot-launched missile force—SS-11, SS-13, and SS-19—as well."[19]

The rate of Soviet ICBM production from 1980 to 1986 has averaged some 150 missiles per year.[20] *Soviet Military Power* 1986 states that liquid-propellant ICBMs were being manufactured for "troop training and to sustain the deployed force,"[21] and *Soviet Military Power* 1988 reported that series production of the fourth generation has ended.[22] The rate of production of new missiles during 1980-1986 appears to approximately equal the rate of deployment of new missiles plus the rate of testing.[23] Any Soviet ICBMs in addition to those deployed are likely maintained as a stock of test assets, maintenance spares, and training missiles. While some of these remaining missiles could be used for reload and refire in a protracted nuclear conflict, our assumption is that the Soviets have manufactured no more than the normal complement of about 10 percent additional nuclear warheads for spares and testing.

SLBMs

The Soviet SLBM force as of mid-1988 was estimated to be composed of 942 missiles armed with 3400 warheads (see Table 2.5). There are six different types of missiles. The SS-N-8 and SS-N-17 missiles have single warheads. The SS-N-6 carries two MRV warheads, each of which is counted separately. For the three MIRVed missiles (SS-N-18, SS-N-20, and SS-N-23), the number of warheads is assumed to be the full load as determined by counting rules in the SALT II and START negotiations: four warheads for the SS-N-23, seven warheads for the SS-N-18, and 10 warheads for the SS-N-20 missiles.[24]

As with the ICBMs, some of these extra SLBMs could be used for reload and refire in a protracted nuclear conflict. *Soviet Military Power* 1984 stated that "resupply systems are available to reload Soviet SSBNs in protected waters" and notes that the Soviets are continuing to produce "four SLBMs—the SS-N-6, SS-N-8, SS-N-17 and SS-N-18."[25] The Alexander Brykin, a new Soviet Navy supply ship, "is specially designed to reload Soviet SSBNs away from their homeport"[26] Amga, Lama, and MP 6 class missile tenders can also deliver cruise missiles and ballistic missiles to submarines and could theoretically

---

18. HAC, Hearings on A Resolution to Approve Funding for the MX Missile, S.Con.Res. 24, FY 1984, p. 254. The DOD states that 'it would probably take a few days to refurbish and reload an individual silo, and reloading a significant fraction of the ICBM force might take up to several weeks'; SAC, FY 1984 DOD, Part 1, p. 321.
19. JCS, FY 1982, p. 100.
20. SMP 1987, p. 122; SMP 1986, pp. 113, 120-121; SMP 1985, p. 38.
21. SMP 1986, p. 121. DOD also states that "[t]here is no evidence that production of missiles for which there are existing launchers (SS-17, SS-18, and SS-19) is significantly greater than the number of those launchers'; DOD, FY 1981 *Annual Report*, p. 80.
22. SMP 1988, p. 39.
23. The level of Soviet missile testing has averaged some 378 missile tests per year of all types, during the period 1980-1986; U.S. Space Command, letter to Institute for Policy Studies, 4 March 1988.
24. SFRC, Salt II Treaty, Report 96-14, p. 325. In both negotiations, the MIRVed SLBM launchers are counted at their maximum, no matter how many warheads they are carrying. The SS-N-18 missile also has modified versions that carry a single warhead.
25. SMP 1984, pp. 22, 98.
26. SMP 1988, pp. 49-50.

2

Strategic Defense

supply reload SLBMs to submarines during wartime.[27] *Soviet Military Power* 1988 states that there has been a "lower level of SLBM production since the early 1980s ... due primarily to the production phaseout of older missiles and to the slower production of two new missiles."[28]

The average annual production rate of SLBMs from 1980 to 1986 was about 125 missiles. Given the level of new deployments and missile testing rates, this production rate suggests that the Soviets maintain a level of extra or spare missiles that is about 10 percent over the number of deployed missiles. Our assumption is that the level of extra warheads for the SLBM force is also 10 percent, the same as for the ICBM force.

Bomber Weapons

The long-range bomber force as of mid-1988 consists of some 160 Bear bombers, armed with an estimated 950 nuclear warheads (see Table 2.6). The nuclear warheads are a combination of free-fall nuclear bombs and ASMs. Little information is available on the size or composition of the nuclear bomb stockpile, and the precise number of bombs carried or actually deployed on Soviet aircraft is unknown.[29] The size of the ASM force (see Chapter Six), given the limited carrying capability of the bombers, makes it easier to estimate the stock of nuclear warheads in this category.

Our assumption is that Bear A bombers carry an average of two nuclear bombs. The Bear B/C bombers carry four bombs, or a single large AS-3 Kangaroo nuclear ASM. The Bear G bombers (converted Bear B/C bombers) carry an average of four bombs and two AS-4 Kitchen dual-capable ASMs. The newly deployed Bear H bombers have an average load of eight AS-15 Kent nuclear long-range air-launched cruise missiles (ALCMs). The total stockpile of nuclear bombs allocated to the bomber force is assumed to be twice the force loading.[30] For the smaller AS-4 and AS-15 missiles, 10 percent additional warheads are assumed to exist as spares. A total of 1400 warheads is assumed to be allocated to the bomber force.

Strategic Defense

Defensive nuclear forces include anti-ballistic missiles (ABMs) and surface-to-air missiles (SAMs) and as of mid-1988 total some 100 ABM launchers and warheads and 7070 SAM launchers with an estimated 4100 warheads (see Table 2.7). The ABM force consists of two types of nuclear missiles: the modified Galosh (ABM-1B) and the Gazelle (ABM-2). The SAM force consists of four types of dual-capable missiles: the SA-1 Guild, the SA-2 Guideline, the SA-5 Gammon, and the SA-10 Grumble.[31]

Table 2.7
Strategic Defense Forces Warheads
(mid-1988)

Missile Type	Launchers	Total Warheads
ABM-1B Galosh	32	32
ABM-2 Gazelle	68	68
SA-1 Guild	1600	1600
SA-2 Guideline	2400	800
SA-5 Gammon	1870	1200
SA-10 Grumble	1100[1]	400
Total	**7070**[2]	**4100**

All missile types carry a single warhead. The number of nuclear warheads on long-range SAMs is uncertain. The estimates assume that all SA-1 launchers have missiles with nuclear warheads, some SA-2s and SA-10s (one-third) have them, and most SA-5s (two-thirds) have them. Warhead estimates for SAMs have been rounded.

1. There are 1100 SA-10 launchers with 4400 rails for missiles.
2. Total number of launchers does not count 150 SA-2 and 70 SA-5 launchers in Eastern Europe and Mongolia.

Our assumption for the level of nuclear warheads allocated to the SAM force is based upon interviews with intelligence analysts in the U.S. government. It is assumed that all of the SA-1 launchers have missiles with nuclear warheads, that one-third of the SA-2 and SA-10 launchers have nuclear warheads, and that two-thirds of the SA-5 launchers have nuclear warheads. This only applies to SAMs deployed in the Soviet Union.

The number of strategic SAMs has declined from a level of 9600 in 1985 to 8560 in 1987.[32] The number of nuclear-armed SAMs is declining significantly as SA-1 and SA-2 missiles are being replaced. According to Soviet sources, these missiles are being rapidly denuclearized, and thus the total number of defensive nuclear warheads may be as low as 2500 in the near future, if not already.[33]

Non-strategic Forces

Soviet non-strategic nuclear forces include a wide variety of surface-to-surface missiles (SSMs) assigned to the Strategic Rocket Forces and the Ground Forces, nuclear artillery in the Ground Forces, nuclear-capable aviation assigned to the Air Forces and the Navy, and naval

---

27 Polmar, *Guide to the Soviet Navy*, 1986, pp. 293-296.
28 SMP 1988, p. 40.
29 The range of estimates in the open literature of the number of bombs carried by strategic bombers is from one to four. Berman and Baker, *Soviet Strategic Forces*, p. 38, assumes one warhead per Bear bomber. Collins and Victory, *U.S./Soviet Military Balance*, 1988, p. 21, assumes two warheads per Bear bomber. IISS, *Military Balance*, 1987-1988, p. 207, assumes two to three bombs per Bear bomber. Congressional Budget Office, *An Analysis of Administration Strategic Arms Reduction Proposals*, March 1984, p. 64, assumes four bombs per Bear bomber. DIA, *Force Structure Summary*, November 1987, p. 8, states that the Bear bomber force of 160+ bombers carries 620+ weapons. If the 60 Bear H bombers with AS-15 cruise missiles are assumed to be carrying eight missiles each (480 total weap-

ons), this leaves 140 weapons on 100 bombers, or an average of 1.4 weapons per bomber.
30 There is no information available on the total stockpile of bombs. Based on past U.S. practice, we assume that the total strategic inventory of bombs is about twice the force loading.
31 Some 150 of these "strategic" SAMs are deployed in Eastern Europe with theater forces, and some 70 are deployed in Mongolia; DIA, *Force Structure Summary*, November 1987, pp. 26, 37.
32 JCS, FY 1986, p. 33; DIA, *Force Structure Summary*, November 1987, p. 11. According to intelligence sources, there were 3242 SA-1, 2946 SA-2, and 1908 SA-5 missiles on launchers in 1981; private communications with authors.
33 Private communications with authors.

Surface-to-surface Missiles

Table 2.8
Non-strategic Surface-to-Surface Missiles (SSMs)
(mid-1988)

Missile	Operational Launchers	Total Missiles	Warheads Force Loading	Warheads Total Stockpile with Spares
SS-20 Saber	405	654	1215	1350
SS-4 Sandal	63	149	52	60
SS-12M Scaleboard B	37	718	115	260
SS-23 Spider	64	239	82	90
SS-1c SCUD B	620	~3100	620	1370
SS-21 Scarab	140	~280	140	150
FROG-3/5/7[1]	660	~3300	660	1450
Total	**1989**	**~8440**	**2900**	**4700**

All missiles carry a single warhead except for the SS-20, which carries three MIRV. Launcher totals for SS-20, SS-4, SS-12M, and SS-23 reflect estimated operational launchers. Total launchers (including training, spares, and other non-deployed) given in the *INF Treaty: 1 June 1988 Data Update* are: 523 SS-20, 85 SS-4, 132 SS-12M, and 106 SS-23. Missile total for SS-20, SS-4, SS-12M, and SS-23 reflects numbers provided in *INF Treaty: 1 June 1988 Data Update*. For SCUD B and FROG, total reflects estimate based upon same ratio of missiles to total launchers as for SS-12M. For SS-21 total reflects estimate based upon same ratio of missiles to total launchers as for SS-23.

For comparisons with original data exchange of November 1987, see Table 7.2.
Total stockpile includes no reloads for SS-20, SS-4, SS-23, and SS-21, but an additional 10 percent spares and one reload per launcher for SS-12M, SCUD, and FROG, plus 10 percent spares. Stockpile totals are rounded.
Does not include 360 SSM launchers in non-Soviet Warsaw Pact forces (75 Bulgaria, 65 Czechoslovakia, 70 East Germany, 30 Hungary, 80 Poland, 40 Rumania); DIA, *Force Structure Summary*, November 1987, pp. 14, 27.

1 It is unknown what percentage of these missiles are older FROG-3/5 types.

---

nuclear weapons including non-strategic SLBMs, nuclear torpedoes, anti-submarine warfare (ASW) missiles and rockets, nuclear depth bombs, and nuclear SAMs. In addition, a small number of nuclear warheads are thought to exist for atomic demolition munitions, naval artillery, and coastal missiles. As of mid-1988, there are an estimated 15,400 nuclear warheads allocated to weapons in these categories, or 47 percent of the total Soviet stockpile.[34] Some 31 percent are on the SSM force, 33 percent are on non-strategic aircraft (excluding naval aviation), 13 percent are nuclear artillery projectiles, and 23 percent are assigned to naval forces (including naval aviation).

Surface-to-surface Missiles

Soviet Strategic Rocket Forces and Ground Forces deploy some seven different types of SSMs of less than intercontinental range. Some 2074 operational launchers exist for these missiles, and they are thought to be armed with a total of 4700 nuclear warheads (see Table 2.8). Of the missiles in this class (SS-20, SS-4, SS-12M, SS-23, SCUD B, SS-21, and FROG), only the SS-20 has more than one nuclear warhead. (It is armed with three MIRV.) With the exception of the SS-4 and SS-20, all of the missiles are dual-capable.[35]

The INF Treaty has revealed more information about four of the weapons in this class than about any other types of Soviet nuclear weapons. As of November 1987, there were a total of 85 SS-4, 523 SS-20, 135 SS-12M, and 102 SS-23 launchers.[36] As of November 1987, the number of missiles for these launchers totaled 1746: 650 SS-20, 170 SS-4, 726 SS-12M, and 200 SS-23.[37] The number of SS-4, SS-20, and SS-23 missiles—given a logical number needed for testing, maintenance, and training, as well as the co-location of extra missiles with launchers—seems to indicate a negligible, if not nonexistent, nuclear reload capability.[38] For the SS-12M, it appears that there is a modest nuclear reload capability of one missile and warhead extra per launcher.[39]

---

34 Richard DeLauer, the under secretary of defense for research and engineering, reported in 1984 that the Soviets have an overall advantage in non-strategic land-attack and defensive nuclear warheads of roughly two to one over the United States; DOD, FY 1985 RDA, pp. II-17 to II-18.
35 The SS-12M missile system, though dual-capable, is considered to be "primarily nuclear in mission"; HASC, FY 1984 DOD, Part 5, pp. 1280-1281. The SCUD B is the Ground Forces' "primary nuclear fire support means"; SMP 1988, p. 55.
36 As of 1 June 1988 the launcher figures were 509 SS-20, 72 SS-4, 132 SS-12M, and 106 SS-23; *INF Treaty: 1 June 1988 Update*.
37 As of 1 June 1988 the missile figures were 1760 total: 654 SS-20, 149 SS-4, 633 SS-12M, and 239 SS-23; ibid.
38 Prior to the INF Treaty, the DOD stated on numerous occasions, with great assurance, that these missiles were all reloadable; JCS, FY 1986, p. 35; JCS, FY 1982, p. 102; SMP 1981, p. 26; SASC, Strategic Force Modernization Programs, Hearings, 1981, p. 5. Indeed, a complete set of SS-20s with three warheads each were thought to exist for 441 launchers. After the INF Treaty, in SMP 1988, p. 53, the DIA again stated, "The Soviets have the capability to reload and refire SS-20s."
39 DIA, *Soviet Front Fire Support*, p. 70, and JCS, FY 1986, p. 38, stated that the reload capability for SS-12 launchers was one missile per launcher. See JCS, FY 1987, p. 33, and JCS, FY 1988, p. 48, for other depictions of reload capability.

2

Nuclear Artillery

Figure 2.9 As with other components of the Soviet nuclear stockpile, it is very difficult to estimate the correlation between delivery systems and the actual number of nuclear warheads. For example, a FROG-7 short range missile resupply vehicle, here displayed in the 7 November 1965 parade in Moscow on a ZIL-135 wheeled vehicle, is deployed at the FROG battalion within the division. The number of nuclear warheads is less than the total delivery capacity of the FROG weapon system; many of these missiles are intended to carry conventional or chemical warheads.

Figure 2.10 The Soviet Ground Forces have some 6760 artillery guns of nine different types in three calibers which are thought to be capable of firing nuclear projectiles. This nuclear-capable 152mm D-20 howitzer is one of some 6300 such guns. These older guns are assumed to be nuclear capable, but it is unknown whether they or the newer self-propelled models have the same capabilities and roles.

The ratio of total missiles to total launchers for the shorter range SS-12M and SS-23 missile systems is 5.3:1 and 1.9:1, respectively. Since the SS-23 is newer and was still in production at the time the INF Treaty was concluded, it is assumed that the ratio of total missiles to launchers for the SCUD B and FROG short-range missiles not included in the INF Treaty (with the exception of the SS-21, which has been deployed only in limited numbers) is more in line with the SS-12M. The SCUD-B missile is assumed to have the same number of nuclear reloads per launcher as the SS-12M. The FROG launchers are reloadable and dual-capable, and three "ready-to-fire" missiles are assigned to each missile battalion of four launchers.[40] It is assumed that there is one nuclear reload for each FROG launcher, the remainder being conventional missiles.[41]

Nuclear Artillery

Three calibers of artillery guns in Soviet Ground Forces are thought to be capable of firing nuclear projectiles—152mm, 203mm, and 240mm.[42] There are some 6760 guns of nine different types in these three calibers that are credited with being nuclear-capable (see Chapter Seven). Although no information is available on the number of nuclear warheads deployed for artillery, we estimate that they are supplied with some 2000 nuclear artillery warheads.[43]

Figure 2.11 Thirteen Golf II class submarines were included in SALT II accountability, but not the 39 SS-N-5 SLBMs they carry. The SS-N-5 is one of 22 types of non-strategic naval nuclear weapons; 12 submarines are deployed (1988).

Guns of 203mm and 240mm caliber have traditionally been considered to be nuclear-capable, although it was not until the 1980s that statements about the nuclear capability of Soviet artillery became more definitive. According to the Defense Intelligence Agency (DIA), delivery of nuclear projectiles by the larger caliber artillery

---

40 DIA, *Soviet Front Fire Support*, p. 72. Each motorized rifle and tank division has a missile battalion of four FROG or SS-21 launchers assigned to it.

41 SMP 1988, p. 109, states that increasing numbers of refire missiles are being deployed by the Soviets for their short-range missiles not constrained by the INF Treaty. "The refires for these launchers are estimated to have been increased by between 50 and 100 percent over the past several years. Consequently, the Pact has been able to plan on using these missiles, armed with *non-nuclear warheads*, to strike NATO air defenses, airfields, and command-and-control nodes without sacrificing their ability to plan on using the same missiles, if needed, in theater nuclear strikes" (emphasis added). See also DOD, FY 1988 *Annual Report*, p. 30.

42 A partially declassified 1976 DIA report, *Soviet Self-propelled Artillery*, DDI-1130-6-76, p. 9, states, "We believe that the Soviets have the capability to deploy nuclear rounds for 152mm, 180mm, and 203mm tube artillery weapons and for the 240mm mortar." IISS, *Military Balance*, 1983-1984, p. 121, also credited the SS-23 towed 180mm gun with being nuclear-capable. The gun, however, is not standard in the Ground Forces and is being replaced by newer 203mm self-propelled howitzers. More recently, only three calibers of guns have been referenced by DOD as being nuclear-capable: 152mm, 203mm, and 240mm.

43 The number of nuclear warheads is based upon a similar ratio of warheads to guns for the Soviets as for the United States.

Table 2.9
Non-strategic Land-Based Aircraft Warheads
(mid-1988)

Aircraft Category/Type	Number of Aircraft	Weapons Load	Total Stockpile
Primary Nuclear Aircraft			
Tu-26 Backfire	180	2 bombs or AS-4	360
Tu-22 Blinder A	60	4 bombs	240
Blinder B	60	4 bombs and 1 AS-4	300
Tu-16 Badger	250	4 weapons, including AS-2/5/6	1000
Su-24 Fencer	815	2 bombs	1630
Subtotal	1365		3500
Secondary Nuclear Aircraft			
MiG-27 Flogger D/J	830	nominally 1 bomb	
MiG-23 Flogger B/G	1570	nominally 1 bomb	
Su-17 Fitter D/H	800	nominally 1 bomb	1600
Su-7 Fitter A	80	nominally 1 bomb	
MiG-21bis Fishbed L	135	nominally 1 bomb	
Subtotal	3415		1600
Total	4780		5100

Stockpile total assumes the approximate same ratio of nuclear weapons on tactical aircraft in the Soviet Union and the United States. The actual number of nuclear bombs and warheads on aircraft-delivered weapons is unknown. The primary nuclear-capable aircraft are estimated to have nuclear warheads available for them.

Sufficient nuclear warheads are also thought to exist in the arsenal to arm the MiG-27 and Su-17 nuclear-capable fighters, although they could also be allocated to the other nuclear-capable aircraft. The total and subtotal stockpile numbers are rounded.

guns (240mm or larger) has taken place in testing.[44] There are some 200 203mm guns of three types—M-1980?, 2S7 M-1975, and M-1955 (M55)—and 206 240mm mortars of two types—2S4 M-1975 and 2S4 M-240.[45]

There are some 6300 Soviet nuclear-capable 152mm artillery guns.[46] Most older 152mm howitzers are now considered by the DOD to be nuclear-capable, although before the deployment of the newer self-propelled models, older guns were believed to have only conventional capability.[47]

Non-strategic Aviation

The Soviet Air Force and Navy deploy 14 different types of non-strategic nuclear-capable aircraft (see Tables 2.9 and 2.12). As of mid-1988, these Soviet aircraft are assessed as having some 6800 nuclear warheads assigned to them, including 4900 bombs, 1500 nuclear ASMs, and 400 nuclear depth bombs. (The ASW aircraft and nuclear depth bombs are discussed below.) Little information is available on the actual stockpile of nuclear weapons allocated to these dual-capable aircraft, and our calculations are based upon force loading calculations for each individual plane, assuming that certain planes have a primary nuclear mission and others have a secondary mission.[48] Most non-strategic fighter aircraft, it should be noted, are heavily biased towards conventional, rather than nuclear, missions.[49]

The main nuclear-capable aircraft are the Backfire, Badger, and Blinder medium bombers, as well as the longer range Fencer fighter-bombers assigned mostly to the Air Forces' Strategic Air Armies (SAA) and Soviet Naval Aviation (SNA). The Backfire bomber, the newest of the non-strategic bombers, carries two nuclear weapons—one or two nuclear bombs internally or two AS-4 Kitchen ASMs on the fixed center section panel of each wing, or a single AS-4 ASM on a semi-recessed centerline mount with no internal bomb load.[50] The Blinder has two weapon bays and is thus thought to carry four nuclear weapons. The Blinder B versions can carry one AS-4 Kitchen as well. The Badger A/G/G Modified bombers are

---

44 DIA, *Soviet Artillery Trends and Scientific and Technical Projections*, DST-1130S-027-80, 30 September 1980 (partially declassified and released under the FOIA), p. 205.
45 The M-1955 and M-240 exist in small numbers in the Soviet Union only and have negligible nuclear capabilities.
46 DIA, *Force Structure Summary*, November 1987, p. 15, reports that there are 5760 self-propelled artillery guns and mortars (260 mortars). Subtracting some 3000 2S1 non-nuclear self-propelled 122mm howitzers and 203mm and 240mm guns leaves some 2300 nuclear-capable 152mm self-propelled guns. In addition, there are some 4000 towed nuclear-capable guns: M-1955 (D-20) and M-1976 152mm systems; *NATO and the Warsaw Pact*, 1984, p. 42.
47 JCS, FY 1986, p. 40.
48 The range of estimates in the open literature of the number of bombs carried by non-strategic aircraft is one to four. *NATO and the Warsaw Pact*, 1984, p. 36, assumes that longer range INF aircraft (Backfire, Badger, and Blinder bombers) carry two or three nuclear warheads. DOD, FY 1982 *Annual Report*, p. 66, assumes two warheads. DIA, *Force Structure Summary*, November 1987, p. 8, states that Badger and Blinder bombers carry four nuclear weapons.
49 Meyer, "Soviet Theatre Nuclear Forces," Part II, p. 22; *NATO and the Warsaw Pact*, 1984, p. 10.
50 DOD, FY 1982 *Annual Report*, p. 66, indicated four weapons per Backfire bomber. DIA, *Force Structure Summary*, November 1987, p. 8, states two weapons per plane.

2

Air-to-surface Missiles

Table 2.10
Air-to-Surface Missiles (ASMs)
(mid-1988)

Missile Type	Delivery System	Nuclear Warheads
AS-2 Kipper	Badger C	70
AS-3 Kangaroo	Bear B/C	30
AS-4 Kitchen	Backfire B/C, Blinder B, Bear G	800
AS-5 Kelt	Badger G, Badger C Modified	440
AS-6 Kingfish	Badger G Modified	300
AS-11 Kilter?	Fencer	unk
AS-15 Kent	Bear H	570
Total		**2200**

unk: unknown
All weapons are dual-capable except AS-3 and AS-15.

estimated to carry four nuclear weapons, either bombs in internal bays or AS-2 Kipper, AS-5 Kelt, or AS-6 Kingfish ASMs. The Badger C bomber is assumed to carry two AS-2 or AS-5 missiles, but not to carry bombs. The Fencer fighter-bombers are assessed as having the capability of carrying two nuclear weapons each.[51] The 1730 planes in this category are assessed as being equipped with a stockpile of some 4700 nuclear weapons, or 70 percent of the total non-strategic air-delivered nuclear arsenal.

The remaining Soviet nuclear-capable fighters—MiG-27 Flogger D/J, MiG-23 Flogger B/G, MiG-21 Fishbed L, Su-17 Fitter C/D/H, and Su-7 Fitter A—are believed to have available about 1700 nuclear bombs. Each plane is assessed as being able to carry one nuclear bomb. Some are probably not nuclear-equipped, and some can carry more than one bomb on numerous wing pylons.[52]

Even though they are capable of carrying nuclear weapons, many aircraft in this category would likely be used for conventional missions. The nuclear capability of the aircraft would be determined by the mission in wartime, the availability of nuclear weapons at tactical air bases, and the training of pilots in the delivery of nuclear weapons.[53] Some planes, such as the MiG-21 and the MiG-23, of which some 1700 exist, are thought to have primary air-superiority missions with secondary bombing missions, even though they are commonly credited with being part of the nuclear force.

Air-to-surface Missiles

The Soviet Air Force and Navy operate seven nuclear-capable ASMs (see Table 2.10).[54] Although little information is available on the total inventory of missiles or nuclear warheads, the number of aircraft is well known, and the carrying capacity of those aircraft is also known. The AS-2 Kipper, AS-4 Kitchen, AS-5 Kelt, and AS-6 Kingfish missiles are dual-capable, while the AS-3 Kangaroo and AS-15 Kent missiles (assigned to strategic forces) are nuclear-only. We assume that nuclear warheads exist for one set of ASMs/ALCMs for each delivery aircraft, regardless of the aircraft's specific mission and geographic location. Additional ASMs undoubtedly exist for conventional missions, but they are not counted as having nuclear warheads available. No additional warheads are counted for maintenance spares or reload, as they are considered to be part of the overall force.

The AS-2 Kipper is deployed on the Badger C bomber. The AS-2 is being replaced by the AS-5 Kelt, and the bombers are then redesignated Badger C Modified. It is estimated that a full complement of 70 Badger C bombers are still armed with 70 nuclear AS-2s. The AS-3 Kangaroo is carried only on the Bear B/C strategic bomber. Some 30 Bear B/C bombers still exist. One AS-3 is thought to exist for each bomber. The Bear B/Cs are being modified to Bear G types to carry the AS-4 Kitchen instead of the AS-3. The AS-4 Kitchen is the most common of the ASMs, delivered by the Bear G, Backfire, and Blinder bombers. As of mid-1988, some 800 nuclear missiles are thought to exist. Each of the 45 Bear G bombers and the 335 Backfire bombers carry two AS-4 missiles. Each of the 60 Blinder B bombers carry one AS-4 missile. The AS-5 Kelt is deployed on both Badger C Modified and Badger G bombers. Some 440 AS-5 missiles are thought to exist; 300 on 150 Badger Gs and 140 on 70 Badger C Modified bombers. The AS-6 Kingfish is deployed on Badger G Modified bombers. Half of the total inventory of Badger G bombers, that is, 150 aircraft,

---

51 This may include a new dual-capable ASM, the AS-11 Kilter, which was deployed in 1984.
52 DIA, *Force Structure Summary*, November 1987, p. 18, reports that there are some 2800 ground-attack aircraft in the non-strategic force (not including Backfire, Badger, or Blinder). If some 270 non-nuclear Su-25 Frogfoot fighters are subtracted from this total (IISS, *Military Balance*, 1987-1988, p. 36), some 2530 aircraft are theoretically nuclear-capable. This would largely eliminate the MiG-21 and MiG-23 fighters, leaving some 2475 fighters, as indicated in Table 2.11 (including Fencer, Flogger D/J, and Fitter). See also, *Aviation Week & Space Technology*, 2 May 1988, p. 20.
53 *NATO and the Warsaw Pact*, 1984, pp. 40-41, states, for instance, that not all Soviet pilots flying nuclear-capable aircraft are trained to deliver nuclear weapons.
54 The AS-1 Kennel, AS-7 Kerry, AS-9 Kyle, AS-10 Karen, AS-12 Kegler, and AS-14 Kedge are not nuclear-capable.

2
Naval Nuclear Forces

Table 2.11
Non-strategic Naval Warheads
(mid-1988)

Category	Launchers	Warheads Force Loading	Warheads Total Stockpile
Ballistic Missiles			
SS-N-5 Serb[1]	36	36	50
Attack Aviation			
Bombers	365	1170	1170
Fighters	105	unk	100
Cruise Missiles	946	n.a.	400
Anti-Submarine			
Torpedo	575	575	575
SS-N-15/16	100	400	400
FRAS-1	6	25	25
Depth bombs	375	375	400
Anti-air[2]	64	260	260
Artillery[3]	n.a.	n.a.	100
Coastal Missiles[4]	100	100	100
Mines	n.a.	unk	unk
Total	**2572**		**3600**

n.a.: not available; unk: unknown

Launchers for SS-N-5 ballistic missiles are individual launch tubes on Golf II class submarines, individual bombers and fighters, and individual launchers for cruise missiles aboard submarines and surface vessels (with the exception of the SS-N-21, which is launched from standard 21-inch torpedo tubes). Launchers for torpedoes, SS-N-15/16, FRAS-1, SAMs, and artillery are ship and submarine platforms; for coastal missiles, launchers are ground launchers.

Stockpile total represents two SLCMs per ship, except on Kiev and Kirov class, which get four; four SLCMs per submarine, except Oscar class, which gets 12; SS-N-21-equipped submarines, which are estimated to carry six SLCMs each; four SS-N-15 and SS-N-16 per submarine; one nuclear torpedo average per ship/submarine; one ASW nuclear depth bomb per nuclear-capable ASW aircraft and helicopter; and four SAM nuclear warheads per ship.

1 On 12 Golf II class non-strategic ballistic missile submarines in the Baltic Sea and the Sea of Japan.
2 Includes ship-based nuclear-capable SA-N-1 Goa, SA-N-3 Goblet, and SA-N-6 Grumble SAMs. The SA-N-2 Guideline and the SA-N-7 Gadfly could also be nuclear-capable.
3 Ship-based 152 mm artillery shells reportedly on the older Sverdlovsk class cruisers.
4 Includes the SSC-1b Sepal ground-launched cruise missile assigned to coastal artillery.

are thought to be modified to carry the AS-6, a total of 300 nuclear missiles. The AS-15 Kent ALCM is carried on Bear H strategic bombers.

Naval Nuclear Forces

The Soviet Navy is thought to have a total of 3600 non-strategic naval nuclear weapons of 22 different types (see Table 2.11).[55] Some 276 surface combatants, 60 cruise missile submarines, and 202 attack submarines are nuclear-capable. Some 845 SNA aircraft (discussed above) are armed with some 1700 nuclear warheads, including some 400 nuclear depth bombs (see Table 2.12). Our estimates on naval nuclear capability are largely derived from an analysis of delivery platforms, including the capacity of each platform to deliver weapons.

Nuclear systems in the non-strategic force generally fall into a number of specific categories: land-attack ballistic missiles, air-delivered weapons, SLCMs, and anti-ship missiles, anti-submarine weapons, anti-air weapons, naval artillery, and coastal defense missiles.

A number of these categories contain only small numbers of nuclear weapons. Twelve Golf II class diesel-powered ballistic missile submarines (SSBs) with 36 SS-N-5 Serb missiles are allocated to the non-strategic force. Each missile carries one nuclear warhead. A single coastal defense division is armed with some 100 SSC-1b Sepal nuclear-capable ground-launched cruise missiles (GLCMs).[56] The Soviets may also stockpile nuclear artillery projectiles for 152mm guns carried by five Sverdlov

---

55 The types include SS-N-5 Serb ballistic missiles, two types of nuclear bombs and nuclear depth bombs, two types of nuclear torpedoes, three ASW rockets, three types of SAMs, seven types of SLCMs, one coastal missile, and one type of nuclear artillery projectile.

56 SMP 1984, p. 13; IISS, *Military Balance*, 1983-1984, p. 119. IISS, *Military Balance*, 1984-1985, p. 134, reported that the SSC-1b was armed only with nuclear warheads. The SSC-2 Samlet and SSC-3 Styx ground-launched coastal missiles are not nuclear-capable.

2

Naval Missiles

Table 2.12
Soviet Naval Aviation (SNA)
(mid-1988)

Aircraft Category/Type	Number of Aircraft	Weapons Load	Total Stockpile
Primary Nuclear Aircraft			
Tu-26 Backfire	145	2 bombs or 2 AS-4	290
Tu-22 Blinder A	30	4 bombs	120
Tu-16 Badger	190	4 weapons, including AS-2/5/6	760
Subtotal	365		1200
Secondary Nuclear Aircraft			
Su-24 Fencer E	35	2 bombs	100
Su-17 Fitter C	70	1 bomb	
Subtotal	105		100
Anti-submarine Warfare			
Be-12 Mail	95	1 depth bomb	95
Il-38 May	45	1 depth bomb	45
Tu-142 Bear F	60	1 depth bomb	60
Ka-25 Hormone A	115	1 depth bomb	115
Ka-25 Helix A	60	1 depth bomb	60
Subtotal	375		400
Total	845		1700

The total and subtotal stockpile numbers are rounded.

class cruisers.[57] Some sources also report the existence of Soviet nuclear mines, but we do not assume that they exist in any appreciable numbers (see Chapter Nine).

The Soviet Navy operates three kinds of nuclear-capable SAMs: the SA-N-1 Goa, the SA-N-3 Goblet, and the SA-N-6 Grumble.[58] Some 260 nuclear warheads are estimated to exist for SAMs, calculated at an average of four SAM nuclear warheads per ship. The SA-N-1 is deployed on Kresta I, Kynda, Kanin, Kashin SAM, and Kotlin class cruisers and destroyers. The SA-N-3 is deployed on Moskva and Kiev class carriers and on Kresta II and Kara class cruisers. The SA-N-6 is deployed on one ship of the Kara class and on newer Kirov and Slava class cruisers.

Sea-launched Cruise and Anti-ship Missiles

The Soviet Navy as of mid-1988 had some 942 sea-launched cruise missile (SLCM) and anti-ship missile (ASM) launchers deployed on some 100 surface combatants and 64 submarines. The SLCMs are of seven types—SS-N-3 Shaddock/Sepal, SS-N-7 Starbright, SS-N-9 Siren, SS-N-12 Sandbox, SS-N-19 Shipwreck, SS-N-21 Sampson, and SS-N-22 Sunburn (see Table 2.13).[59] All of the missiles, with the exception of the SS-N-3a Shaddock and the SS-N-21, are dual-capable.[60] All of the missiles

---

[57] Collins and Victory, U.S./Soviet Military Balance, 1988, p. 45, notes that the guns may be nuclear-capable. See also, Polmar, Guide to the Soviet Navy, 1986, p. 412.

[58] The SA-N-6, a derivative of the SA-10, is the only long-range naval SAM deployed. The SA-N-3 is credited with being nuclear-capable despite the fact that it is derived from the non-nuclear SA-6 Gainful. The SA-N-2 Guideline and the SA-N-7 Gadfly could be nuclear-capable as well, but there is not enough evidence to so credit them. The SA-N-4, SA-N-5, SA-N-8, and SA-N-9 are not nuclear-capable.

[59] The short-range SS-N-2 Styx SLCM is not nuclear-capable.

[60] According to SMP 1984, p. 31, the SS-N-21 could be upgraded to carry a conventional warhead in the future. As of mid-1988, it does not appear that the SS-N-21 is dual-capable.

Figure 2.12 152mm artillery guns are deployed aboard the Sverdlov, a guided-missile light cruiser with 12 guns. The ships are credited with having a nuclear capability.

2 Anti-submarine Weapons

Table 2.13
Sea-Launched Cruise Missile and Anti-Ship Missile Warheads
(mid-1988)

Missile Type	Delivery Platform	Launchers	Total Warheads
SS-N-3a/c Shaddock	Echo II, Juliett	148	104
SS-N-3b Sepal	Kresta I, Kynda	80	16
SS-N-7 Starbright	Charlie I, Papa	90	44
SS-N-9 Siren	Charlie II, Papa, Nanuchka, Sarancha	208	78
SS-N-12 Sandbox	Kiev, Slava, Echo II	200	76
SS-N-19 Shipwreck	Kirov, Oscar	136	56
SS-N-21 Sampson	Akula, Victor III, Sierra, Yankee Notch SSN	4	16
SS-N-22 Sunburn	Sovremennyy, Tarantul III	80	24
Total		**946**	**400**

SS-N-1 Scrubber/Strela on single Kilden class destroyer has been retired. Total warheads are rounded.
Stockpile total represents two SLCMs per ship, except on Kiev and Kirov class, which get four; four SLCMs per submarine, except Oscar class, which gets 12. SS-N-21 launcher refers to submarines, not specific launch tubes. Some four SS-N-21 missiles are estimated to be carried in each submarine.

are dedicated to anti-ship missions, with the exception of the SS-N-3a/c and the SS-N-21, which are primarily for land attack. The SS-N-12 and SS-N-19 have secondary land-attack roles. Our estimates for the total stockpile of SLCMs assumes that there are two nuclear missiles per SLCM-capable ship—except on the larger Kiev and Kirov class surface combatants, which are assumed to carry four nuclear missiles—and that there are four nuclear SLCMs per cruise missile-capable submarine—except for the larger Oscar class, which is assumed to carry 12 nuclear missiles.

The newest SLCM, the SS-N-21, similar to the U.S. Tomahawk missile, was first deployed in late 1987. It is launched from standard 21-inch torpedo tubes, unlike other Soviet SLCMs. It is therefore deployed on attack submarines, as opposed to specially configured cruise missile submarines. The likely platforms for the SS-N-21 are the Victor III, Akula, Sierra, and a single, converted, Yankee class attack submarine (designated Yankee Notch SSN). The missile has been flight-tested from Victor III, Akula and the converted Yankee boat.

Anti-submarine Weapons

The Soviet Navy deploys five kinds of nuclear anti-submarine weapons: nuclear torpedoes, SS-N-15 Starfish rocket-delivered nuclear depth bombs, SS-N-16 Stallion ASW missiles, FRAS-1 (Free Rocket Anti-Submarine) rockets, and air-delivered nuclear depth bombs.[61] Since no information is available on the number of these types of weapons produced or in existence (with the exception of the FRAS-1, for which there are only very limited numbers of launchers), our estimations are based on the number of delivery platforms for these missiles. Four SS-N-15 and SS-N-16 nuclear missiles are estimated to be deployed per attack submarine that can deliver these missiles, and one nuclear torpedo and one nuclear depth bomb exists for each appropriate delivery platform (surface ship, submarine, patrol plane, ASW helicopter). This results in a total of some 1400 nuclear ASW weapons (see Table 2.14).

Table 2.14
Anti-Submarine Nuclear Warheads
(mid-1988)

Weapon Type	Delivery Platforms	Total Stockpile
SS-N-15 Starfish	Typhoon, Charlie I/II, Papa, Oscar, Romeo	400
SS-N-16 Stallion	Tango, Victor I/II/III, Alfa, Sierra, Mike, Akula	
FRAS-1	Kiev, Moskva	25
Torpedoes Type 65/ET-80	All surface combatants and submarines	575
Depth bombs	Bear F, Helix A, Hormone A, Mail, May	400
Total		**1400**

Stockpile total represents four SS-N-15 and SS-N-16 per submarine; one nuclear torpedo average per ship/submarine; and one ASW nuclear depth bomb per nuclear-capable ASW aircraft and helicopter. Stockpile total is rounded.

---

[61] Many sources claim that the SS-N-14 Silex rocket-propelled torpedo is nuclear-capable, but it is not.

2

Megatonnage Estimates

Table 2.15
DOD/DOE Estimates of the Cumulative Yield (megatonnage) of the U.S and Soviet Stockpiles

YEAR	OMA US	Wagner US	Wagner USSR	Weinberger US	Weinberger USSR	Iklé/Wohlstetter US	Iklé/Wohlstetter USSR	Carlucci US	Carlucci USSR
1950	77								
1951	103								
1952	128								
1953	154								
1954	386								
1955	2820								
1956	9150					1530			
1957	16,300					3440			
1958	16,100					15,500			
1959	17,800					15,800			
1960	19,000					17,900		19,300	-1000
1961	10,300					18,400		11,400	29
1962	12,200					14,700		2,400	898
1963	14,800					11,400	8801	14,600	1890
1964	15,800					9920	1510	16,000	3040
1965	14,100	16,600	10,900	15,500	3300	14,400	2290	15,400	4900
1966	13,100	14,400	12,300	14,600	3760	14,600	3480	13,000	7350
1967	11,900	12,400	13,500	13,400	4320	14,400	5260	11,100	9190
1968	11,000	10,300	14,800	12,000	4960	13,300	6990	10,100	11,000
1969	10,900	8890	16,100	10,500	5880	11,900	9030	9520	13,200
1970	9110	8260	17,100	9060	6830	11,200	12,200	8810	15,100
1971	7990	7600	17,900	7880	8010	10,700	13,400	8260	16,400
1972	7960	6770	18,600	7080	9220	9910	14,300	8040	17,300
1973	7920	6230	19,300	6520	10,700	8030	15,000	7890	17,800
1974	7800	6070	19,700	6150	12,300	7200	15,600	7540	17,800
1975	6800	5930	19,700	5760	13,400	6920	16,100	6330	17,300
1976	5560	5730	19,200	5090	14,200	6550	15,900	5660	16,400
1977	5480	5480	18,300	4580	14,700	5440	15,400	5440	15,300
1978	5370	5330	17,300	4240	14,900	4950	14,400	5330	13,600
1979	5330	5300	16,300	4080	15,000	4660	13,600	5330	13,600
1980	5290	5270	15,100	3870	15,000	4600	13,000	5240	12,300
1981	5060	5310	14,300	3590	14,800	4570	12,600	5090	10,500
1982	5020	5270	13,600	3180	14,500	4530	12,300	4940	10,700
1983	4900	5110	13,100	2810	14,300	4500	12,200	4790	10,500
1984	4870			2550	14,200	4480	12,100	4680	10,500
1985				2340	14,230	4480	12,100	4650	10,500
1986								4640	

Relative scales released by DOD and DOE. Quantitative values assigned by the *Databook* staff. All megatonnage values have been rounded to three significant figures.

This reflects the precision in reproducing the curves and does not reflect the accuracy of DOD and DOE estimates of the Soviet stockpile.

The most common anti-submarine nuclear weapon is the 21-inch nuclear torpedo, the first Soviet non-strategic naval nuclear weapon (deployed in 1958).[62] At least two different types of nuclear torpedoes currently exist—the Type 65 and the ET-80.[63] The newest nuclear torpedo was deployed in the early 1980s.[64] Virtually all surface combatants and all submarines are thought to be capable of firing nuclear torpedoes, and it is thought that some 575 exist in the Soviet arsenal. Maritime patrol aircraft may also be capable of delivering nuclear torpedoes.

The submarine-launched SS-N-15 Starfish rocket-propelled nuclear depth bomb (similar to the U.S. SUBROC) is deployed on Typhoon class ballistic missile submarines, Charlie I/II and Oscar class cruise missile submarines, and Victor I/II, Alfa, Sierra, Mike, and Akula class attack submarines.[65] The submarine-launched

---

62 The Soviet Navy also deploys a 16-inch torpedo that is not nuclear-capable and a 26-inch torpedo that may be nuclear-capable.

63 JCS, FY 1989, p. 54.
64 SMP 1987, p. 43.
65 Tango class diesel-powered attack submarines may also be capable of firing the SS-N-15.

2
Megatonnage Estimates

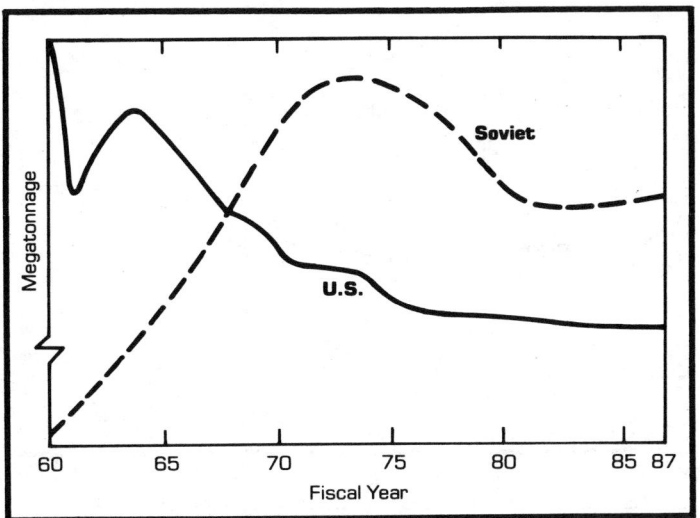

Figure 2.13 Comparison of Soviet and United States megatonnage, 1960-1987 (from Carlucci).

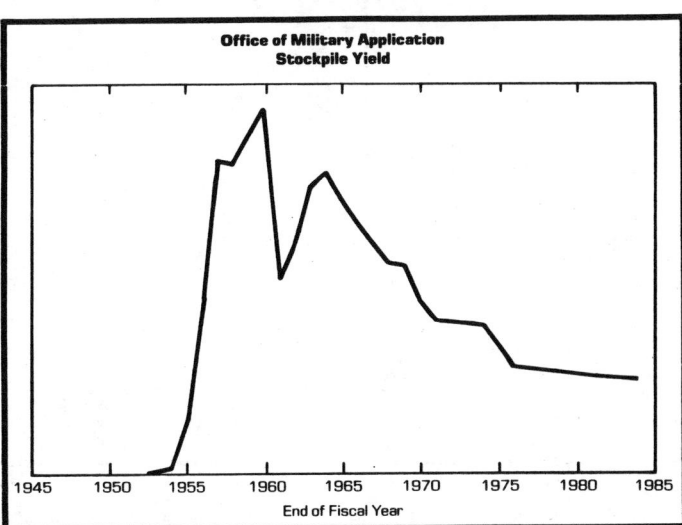

Figure 2.14 United States nuclear weapons stockpile yield, 1950-1984 (from DOE-OMA).
Source: Letter from John E. Rudolph, DOE Office of Military Application, to Thomas B. Cochran, 28 August 1987.

dual-capable SS-N-16 ASW missile (similar to the U.S. ASROC, but longer in range and launching a nuclear torpedo rather than a nuclear depth bomb) is deployed on Typhoon, Oscar, Victor II/III, Sierra, Mike, and Akula classes. It is unclear whether the SS-N-15 and SS-N-16 can be launched from 21-inch torpedo tubes, or perhaps from 26-inch tubes. It is estimated that there are four nuclear missiles of either type for each capable submarine, for a total of 400 SS-N-15 and SS-N-16 nuclear warheads. There are also some 25 nuclear-armed FRAS-1 (Free Rocket Anti-submarine) rockets (a derivative of the FROG-7 SSM) on two Moskva and four Kiev class aircraft carriers.[66]

SNA also deploys some 375 nuclear-capable ASW patrol planes and helicopters (see Table 2.9). It is estimated that there are about 400 nuclear depth bombs in the Soviet nuclear arsenal—or roughly one nuclear depth bomb per nuclear-capable airplane and helicopter. At least two types of nuclear depth bombs exist—the DOD reported in 1987 that a new nuclear depth bomb had entered service "in the early 1980s."[67]

Soviet Megatonnage

The stockpile graphs released by Wagner, Weinberger, and Iklé/Wohlstetter were accompanied by graphs displaying the cumulative yield, or "megatonnage," of the Soviet stockpile by year relative to that of the United States (Figures 2.2b, 2.3b, and 2.4b, respectively). A fourth megatonnage comparison was released by Secretary of Defense Frank Carlucci in the DOD FY 1989 *Annual Report* (see Figure 2.13).[68] The most accurate graph of its cumulative yield (see Figure 2.14) was released by the Department of Energy's Office of Military Application (DOE-OMA) in 1985.[69]

The quantitative scale was chosen to make the DOE-OMA curve of the cumulative yield of the U.S. stockpile peak in 1959 at 19,000 metric tons.

In Figure 2.15a the Wagner curve of U.S. stockpile cumulative yield in Figure 2.2b is compared against the more accurate DOE-OMA curve from Figure 2.14. Similarly, in Figure 2.15b the Weinberger curve from Figure 2.3b, in Figure 2.15c the Carlucci curve from Figure 2.4b, and in Figure 2.15d the Iklé/Wohlstetter curve from Figure 2.13, are compared to the more accurate DOE-OMA curve taken from Figure 2.14. As with the stockpile curves, the U.S. data in Wagner's Figure 2.2b curve is a better fit to the DOE-OMA data than Weinberger's Figure 2.3b curve, and consequently the Soviet estimate in Weinberger's Figure 2.3b curve is again suspect. Also, Secretary Weinberger testified elsewhere that "[b]ecause of the fractionation of payloads that began in the early seventies, the total Soviet megatonnage probably peaked around the mid-seventies and has since, decreased, by as much as 33 percent."[70] A decrease by one-third is consistent with the Wagner graph (Figure 2.2b), but inconsistent with the Weinberger curve (Figure 2.3b). The Weinberger curve should be discarded as erroneous. The Wagner, Iklé/Wohlstetter, and Carlucci curves reproduced in Figure 2.16 appear to represent the DOD's best estimates of Soviet stockpile yield. The reader is cautioned, however, that these estimates of megatonnage may be high by about 20 percent, a consequence of overestimating the yield of Soviet nuclear tests and therefore Soviet nuclear warheads (see Chapter Ten).

---

66 Polmar, *Guide to the Soviet Navy*, 1986, p. 434. Although the Moskva began its first deployment in July 1967, the SUW-N-1/FRAS-1 weapon system may not have been fully operational until 1968; DIA, *ASW Handbook*, 1977, p. 2-2.
67 SMP 1987, p. 43.
68 DOD, FY 1989 *Annual Report*, p. 111.
69 John E. Rudolph, DOE Office of Military Application, letter to Thomas B. Cochran, 28 August 1987, with enclosure: Stockpile Yield Graph. The graph is reproduced in *Nuclear Weapons Databook, Volume II: U.S. Nuclear Warhead Production*, Figure 1.4, p. 17.
70 HAC, FY 1986 DOD, Part 1, p. 98.

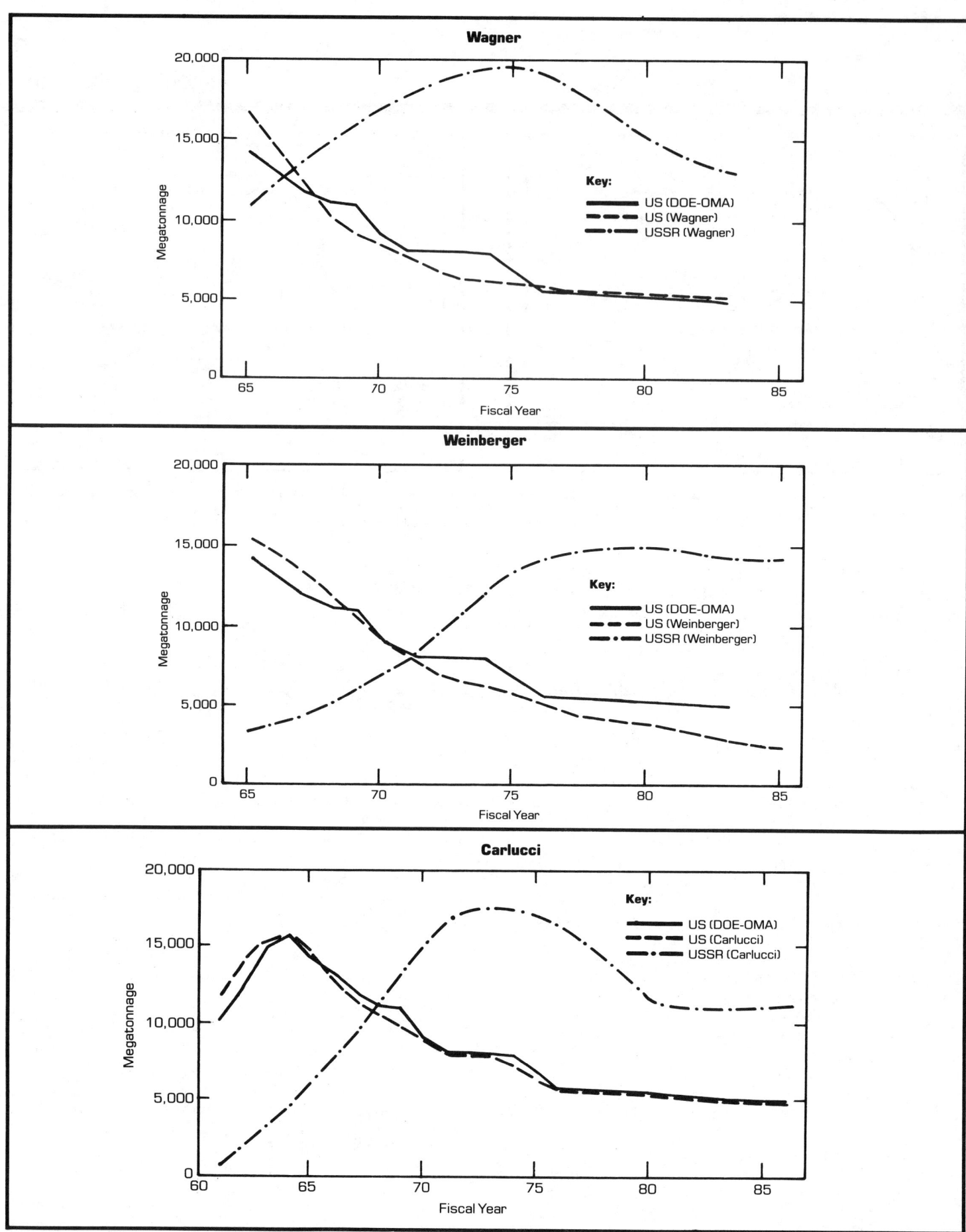

Figure 2.15 United States nuclear weapons stockpile yield graphs comparing DOE-OMA graph with: Wagner (2.15a), Weinberger (2.15b), Carlucci (2.15c), and Iklé/Wohlstetter (2.15d).

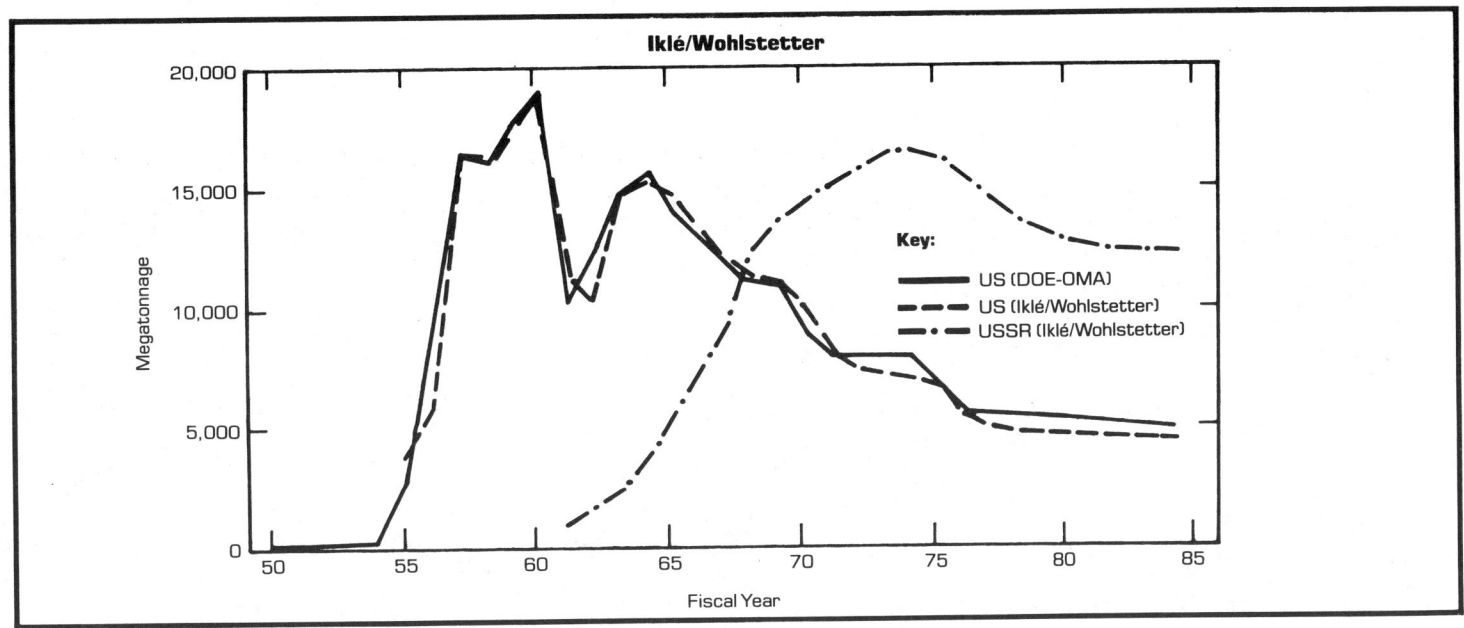

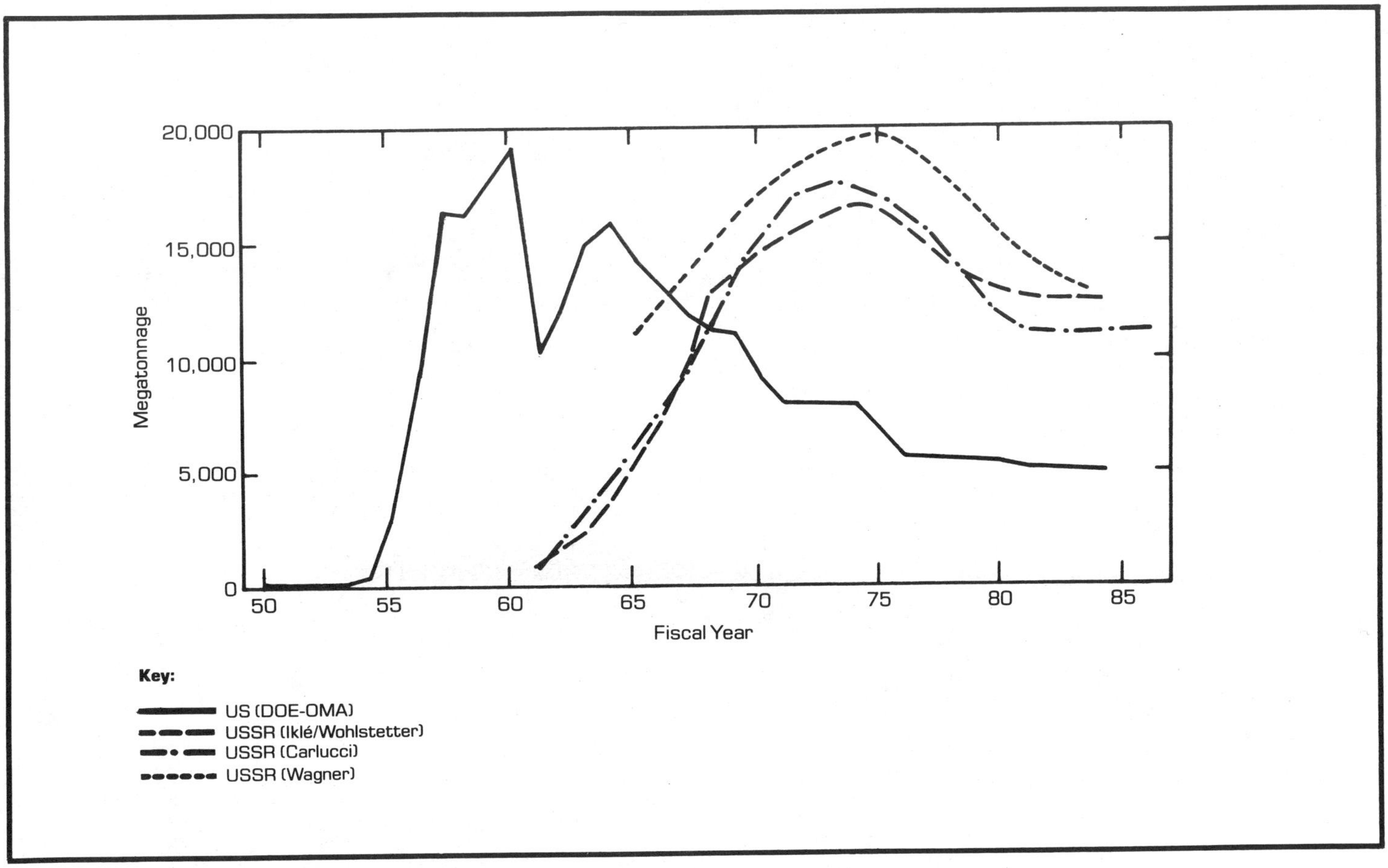

Figure 2.16 Best comparison of Soviet and United States megatonnage, 1960-1987.

3
Soviet Military Organization

Chapter Three
Soviet Military Organization

Overview

Soviet military forces are organized along two lines: one for peacetime administrative support, training, provisioning, and supply, and the other for wartime operational command. Since the late 1970s, the operational command structure has undergone significant reorganization to create the infrastructure necessary for ongoing theater planning and to facilitate a more rapid and orderly transition to wartime footing.

Figure 3.1 shows the peacetime structure of the Soviet military. The chain of command passes from the general secretary of the Communist Party of the Soviet Union (CPSU) to the Defense Council, to the Ministry of Defense (MOD) and the General Staff, to the five military services (Strategic Rocket Forces, Ground Forces, Air Defense Troops, Air Forces, and Navy). Sixteen military districts (MDs) inside the Soviet Union and four groups of Soviet forces (GSFs) in Eastern Europe are responsible for raising and training units in their respective geographic areas.[1]

Figure 3.2 shows the operational chain of command for Soviet military forces. The Defense Council probably would be expanded into a wartime defense council.[2] The MOD and the General Staff would organize into the headquarters (*Stavka*) of the Supreme High Command (VGK).[3] The VGK would incorporate the commanders-in-chief of the five military services. Strategic Rocket Forces, the ballistic missile submarines of the Navy, and the Strategic Air Armies of the Air Forces would fall under the direct operational control of the Supreme High Command. Other military forces, the Ground Forces, Air Forces, Navy, and Air Defense Troops would be placed under the command of unified theaters of war (TVs) and their subordinate theaters of military operations (TVDs).

At present, there are thought to be three TVs (Far East, Western, and Southern), ten continental TVDs, and four oceanic TVDs (OTVDs).[4]

Communist Party Control of the Soviet Military

Control of the Soviet Union's armed forces is vested by the Soviet Constitution in the CPSU and in the highest bodies of the Soviet government, namely, the Presidium of the Supreme Soviet and the Council of Ministers. The party is the ultimate decisionmaking authority, and its dominance is assured by power over personnel appointments.[5] The party's Politburo—led by the general secretary of the CPSU and presently composed of a dozen voting and eight non-voting members—exercises direct political control of the armed forces and authorizes the use of nuclear weapons.[6]

The CPSU general secretary is thus functionally equivalent to the U.S. president, who is commander-in-chief of the U.S. armed forces (see Table 3.1 for a chronology of past leaders of the Soviet Union). Each Politburo member has a personal staff. The party's Central Committee elects the Politburo, but otherwise has no collective voice in military matters.

The Secretariat of the party, chaired by the general secretary and typically made up of about a dozen individuals—some of whom are also members of the Politburo—oversees virtually every sphere of activity on behalf of the party and provides analysis and recommendations for the Politburo.[7] The secretaries of the party, who make up the membership of the Secretariat, are responsible for the development and regulation of broad areas, such as agriculture, ideology, or heavy industry.

---

1. Groups of Forces in Czechoslovakia, and Southern Groups of Forces in Hungary.
2. SMP 1988, p. 16.
3. The Soviets place great stock in their experiences in the "Great Patriotic War" (1941-1945) and have spent much time and effort in drawing conclusions for contemporary organization and management from historical experience. This is true in their general military planning as well as in the organizational specifics of their command structure. There is much disagreement as to the existence of certain organizations. While the Politburo will continue to function, some believe that the Defense Council will be reorganized into the State Defense Committee (GKO), and the Main Military Council into the *Stavka*. Thus, the wartime chain of command would flow from the Politburo and its GKO, to the *Stavka* of the VGK.
4. Peacetime High Commands of Forces (HCOFs) have been established in four of the TVDs: Western, Southwestern, Southern, and Far Eastern; SMP 1988, p. 13. The headquarters for TVs, the other TVDs, and the OTVDs would likely be established during hostilities.
5. Party control is also assured by the KGB's Third Chief Directorate, the directorate responsible for monitoring the military, and the MOD's Main Political Directorate.
6. "It is primarily the political, not the military leaders, who determine the necessity of employing weapons of mass destruction, who specify the principal targets, and when they are to be hit"; Col. M. P. Skirdo, *Narod, armiya, polkovodets*, (The People, the Army, the Commander) (Moscow: Voyenizdat, 1977), pp. 146-147. Custody and control of nuclear warheads, particularly non-strategic nuclear forces in the field, rests with the authority of the KGB, and that limited release authorization would be provided through KGB communications channels; William F. and Harriet Fast Scott, *The Armed Forces of the USSR* (Boulder, CO: Westview, 1982), p. 220. Although little specific information is available on the Soviet system of positive control of nuclear warheads, the Soviet Union appears to have adopted the American concept of national control as a "safety catch" that prevents several thousand nuclear triggers from being pulled; see Paul Bracken, *The Command and Control of Nuclear Forces* (New Haven, CT: Yale University Press, 1983), pp. 196-200. See also, House Committee on International Relations, Subcommittee on International Security and Scientific Affairs, Authority to Order the Use of Nuclear Weapons, 94th Cong., 1st Sess., CRS Report, 1 December 1975, pp. 18-22.
7. Little is known about the internal functioning of the Secretariat and its associated departments. It reportedly meets about once a week, allowing it to prepare questions for discussion at weekly Politburo meetings. It is estimated that the staff of the Secretariat as a whole, including the staffs of the various Central Committee departments overseen by the Secretariat, numbers about 1000-1500. See Elizabeth Teague, "The Foreign Departments of the Central Committee of the CPSU," *RFE-RL Research Bulletin*, Supplement, 27 October 1980, p. 3; Abdurakhman Avtorkhanov, *The Communist Party Apparatus* (Chicago: Henry Regnery Co., 1966), p. 209-210; Jerry Hough and Merle Fainsod, *How the Soviet Union Is Governed* (Cambridge, MA: Harvard University Press, 1979), p. 424. For general information on the Secretariat, see Alexander Rahr, "The Central Committee Secretariat," Radio Liberty Research RL 439/84, 16 November 1984.

3
Soviet Military Organization

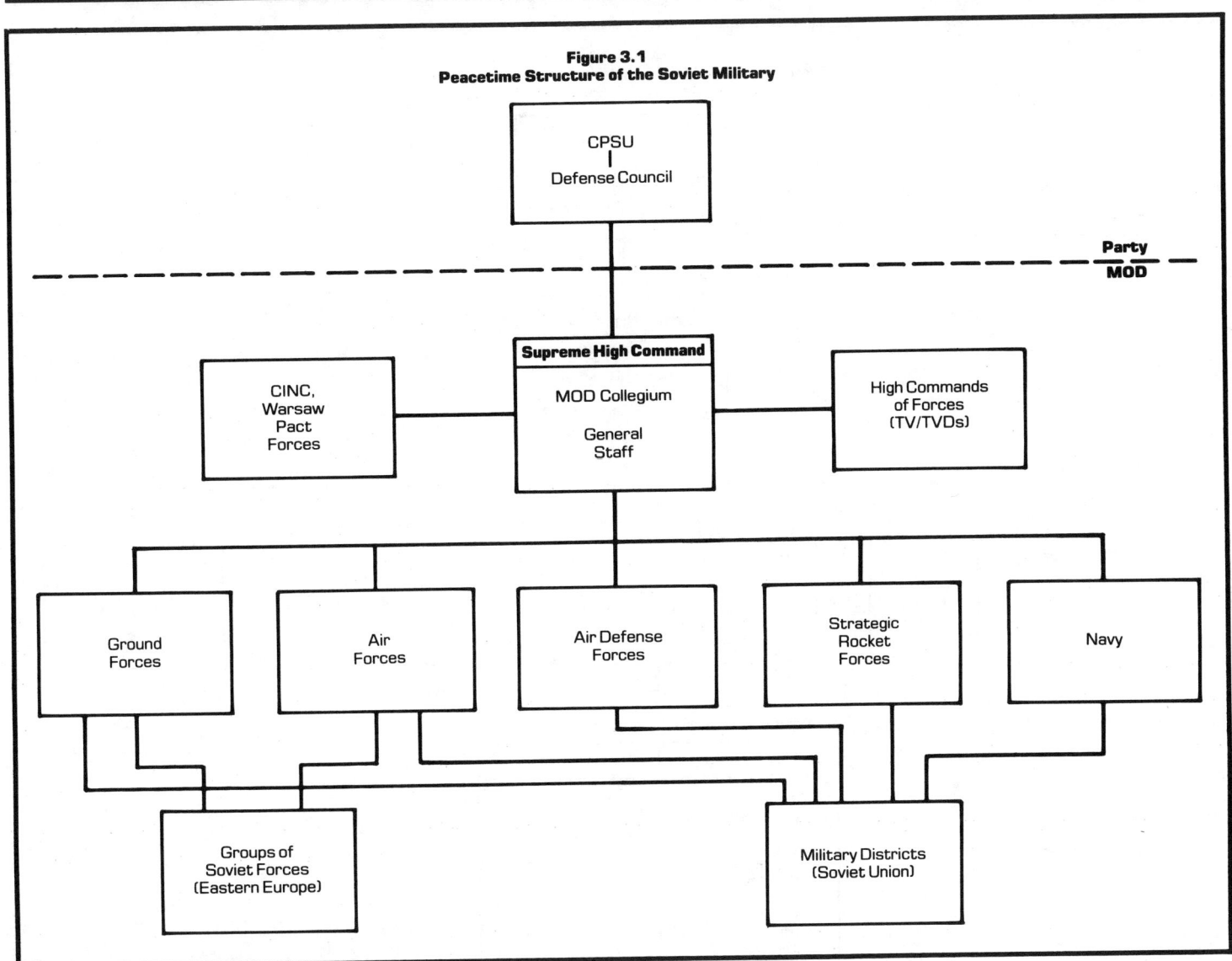

Figure 3.1 Peacetime Structure of the Soviet Military.

Each secretary exercises authority through one or more departments in the Central Committee *apparat*.[8] While there is no secretary holding a general "defense" portfolio, there is a secretary for defense industrial matters.[9]

The secretary for defense industrial matters oversees the military, defense industry, internal security, and space programs.[10] He is responsible for about 20 state organizations (half of them defense-related), which are supervised through the party's Department of Defense Industry (which in turn oversees the nine ministries that have primary responsibility for military preparedness: Defense Industry, Aviation Industry, General Machine Building, Machine Building, Communication Equipment Industry, Medium Machine Building, Radio Industry, Electronics Industry, and Shipbuilding Industry); through the Department of Administrative Organs (which in turn oversees security, police, and justice ministries); and through the Main Political Administration (which ostensibly oversees the military, but focuses on the loyalty of the military rather than military *policy*).[11]

---

8 Each department is under a secretary, and each secretary oversees one or more departments.
9 This post was held by D. F. Ustinov from 1965-1976, when he became minister of defense, and by Yakov P. Ryabov from 1976 to 1979. From 1979 to 1983, there was apparently no single secretary with exclusive defense industry responsibilities. The post was held by G. V. Romanov from 1983 to 1985; from 1985 to February 1988 by Lev N. Zaikov, former director of a major military-electronics research organization in Leningrad and successor to Romanov in the Leningrad party leadership when Romanov was appointed to the Secretariat; and since February 1988 by O. S. Baklanov, former minister of general machine building.
10 Hough and Fainsod, *op. cit.*, pp. 411, 425.
11 *Ibid.*, p. 413. The responsibilities of the secretary for defense industry may have shifted under Gorbachev, emphasizing technology and giving up some responsiblities in the security apparatus.

Nuclear Weapons Databook, Volume IV **47**

3
Soviet Military Organization

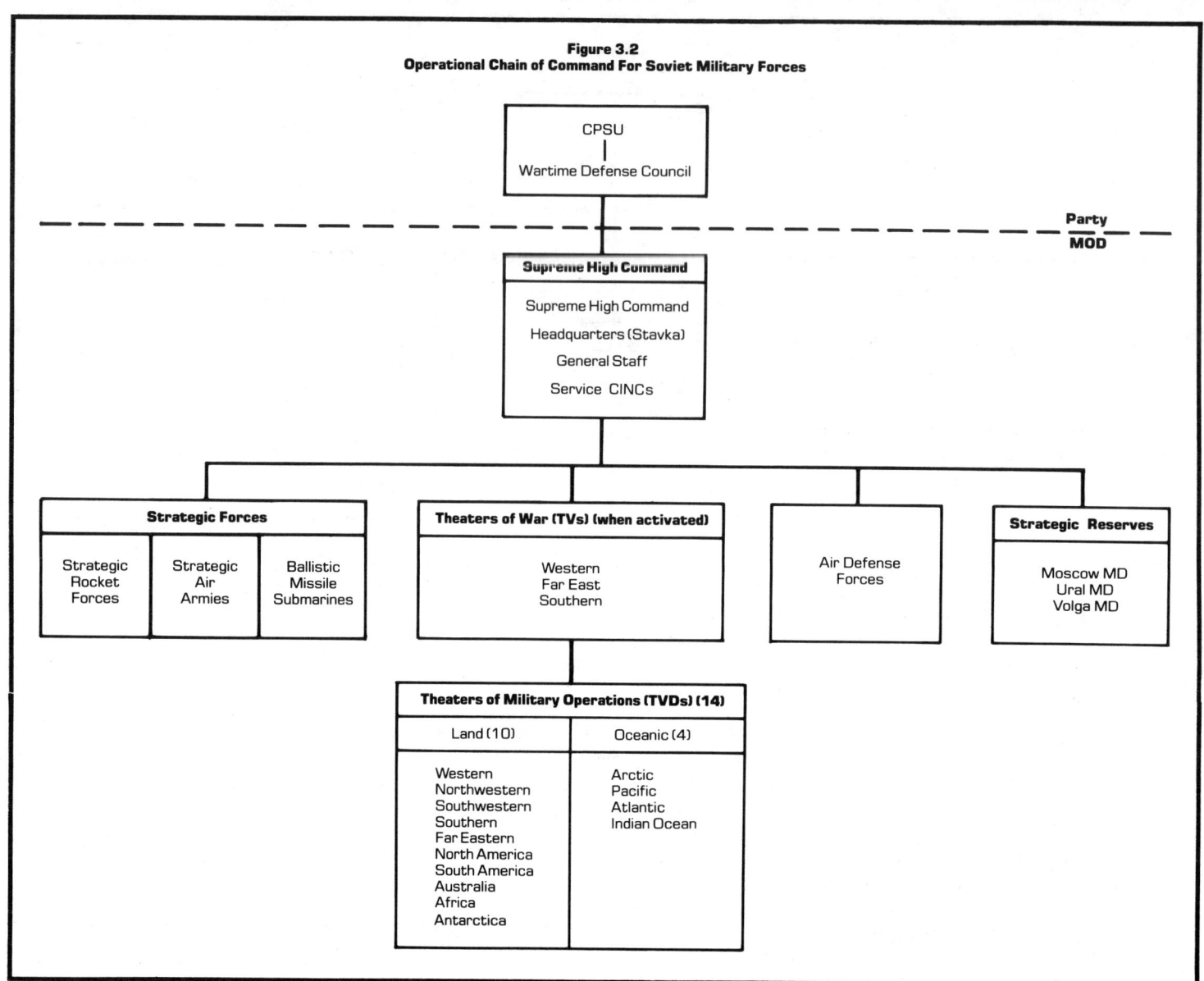

Figure 3.2 Operational Chain of Command for Soviet Military Forces.

Table 3.1
Political Leadership of the Soviet Union

Leader	Period	Official Title
Lenin[1]	07 Nov 1917-21 Jan 1924	Premier
Joseph Stalin[2]	21 Jan 1924-06 Mar 1953	General Secretary CPSU
	06 May 1941-06 Mar 1953	Premier
Nikita S. Khrushchev[3]	06 Mar 1953-15 Oct 1964	First Secretary CPSU
	27 Mar 1958-15 Oct 1964	Premier
Leonid I. Brezhnev[4]	Oct 1964-10 Nov 1982	First Secretary CPSU
	16 Jun 1977-10 Nov 1982	President
Yuri V. Andropov[5]	12 Nov 1982-09 Feb 1984	General Secretary CPSU
Konstantin U. Chernenko[6]	13 Feb 1984-10 Mar 1985	General Secretary CPSU
Mikhail S. Gorbachev	11 Mar 1985-Present	General Secretary CPSU
	01 Oct 1988-Present	President

1. Lenin was the pseudonym taken by Vladimir Ilyich Ulyanov.
2. Stalin was the pseudonym taken by Josef Dzugashvili. Stalin was already General Secretary of the Communist Party at the time of Lenin's death on 21 Jan 1924. He consolidated power through a series of purges in the 1930s and became President of the Council of Ministers (Premier) on 6 May 1941.
3. Following Stalin's death Georgi M. Malenkov became Premier on 7 March 1953. Malenkov resigned on 8 February 1955, became Deputy Premier, and was dropped 3 July 1957. Marshal Nikolai A. Bulganin became Premier on 8 February 1955, and was demoted on 27 March 1958, when Khrushchev assumed the position.
4. Alexei N. Kosygin replaced Khrushchev as Premier on 15 October 1964.
5. By mid-June 1983 Andropov had assumed all of Brezhnev's three titles.
6. By mid-April 1984 Chernenko also assumed the title of President.

The Department of Defense Industry

The Central Committee's Department of Defense Industry (DODI) is responsible for monitoring the implementation of defense research, development, and production. There are about 20 other departments that monitor a range of areas from culture to heavy industry and provide analysis for the Secretariat.

The head of the department oversees the state ministries, state committees, and the departments in the State Planning Committee (*Gosplan*) that fall into its domain.[12] Because the departments are thought to be organized in parallel with the branches and ministries they oversee, it is likely that the Department of Defense Industry includes sections for shipbuilding, ground-forces equipment, electronics, nuclear energy, aviation, and missiles.[13] Space research also falls within its domain. In addition, DODI supervises the defense sections of *Gosplan*.[14]

The central committees of the Soviet republics and the party committees of the regions and cities also have their own departments. These departments are not as large as those of the CPSU Central Committee and generally are less specialized than those on the national level. There are departments of defense industry in some republic and district (*Oblast*) party organizations, such as in Leningrad, a key defense industrial center. Where there are few defense industries, it seems likely that this role is served by the regional central committee's industrial department.

The state government has both an administrative, or executive branch—the Council of Ministers—and a legislative branch—the Supreme Soviet. Unlike the U.S. Congress, the Supreme Soviet as a body has virtually no policymaking role. The president of the USSR presides over the Supreme Soviet.[15] In the past his position was largely ceremonial, as was being a member of the Presidium of the Supreme Soviet, although this is changing with Gorbachev's assumption of the office.

The Council of Ministers is the highest administrative organ of the state government. Because of the unwieldy size of the council (over 100 members), its activities are overseen by its own smaller presidium, whose members are the chairman of the council, his deputies (of which there are 10 to 12, including three or four first deputies), and the heads of several of the state commissions.[16] Real policymaking power in the state government resides with the chairman, his personal staff, and several of his senior deputies.

---

12. The heads (*zaveduyushchii*) of the Department of Defense Industry have been I. D. Serbin (1958-1981), I. F. Dmitriyev (1981-1985), and O. S. Belyakov (1985-). Within the Department of Defense Industry there is a first deputy head, and a number of deputy heads. The latter each typically supervise several sections, with each section responsible for a ministry or other major organization; Hough and Fainsod, op. cit., p. 420. A department typically is made up of 100-150 staff members, known as "instructors"; Michael Voslensky, *Nomenklatura: The Soviet Ruling Class* (Garden City, NY: Doubleday, 1984), p. 94. The Department of Defense Industry may be a bit smaller than average: it has been reported that it has a staff of 90-100; "Ruestungsbeschaffung in der Sowjetunion," *Oesterreichasche Militaerische Zeitschrift*, No. 6, 1982, p. 470. By way of comparison, the Department of Administrative Organs, which is responsible for overseeing police and security functions in the Soviet Union, is estimated to have a staff of fewer than 50, with perhaps 20 of these in its military sectors. See Timothy Colton, *Commissars, Commanders, and Civilian Authority: The Structure of Soviet Military Politics* (Cambridge, MA: Harvard University Press, 1979), p. 29. The International Department, responsible for international affairs and Soviet foreign policy, has an estimated 150 people on its staff. See Lilita Dzirkals, Thane Gustafson, and A. Ross Johnson, *The Media and Intra-Elite Communication in the USSR* (Santa Monica, CA: Rand Corporation, 1982), pp. 14, 20.
13. It should be noted that another department that might play a role, the Department of Science and Education, reportedly has little, if any, impact on those organizations working for the defense industries. See Robert F. Miller, "The Role of the Communist Party in Soviet Research and Development," *Soviet Studies*, Vol. 37, No. 1, January 1985, pp. 31-59.
14. Avtorkhanov, op. cit., p. 203.
15. The president is usually a member of the Politburo. The position is currently held by General Secretary Mikhail S. Gorbachev, who replaced Andrei A. Gromyko on 1 October 1988.
16. The Presidium of the Council of Ministers is somewhat analogous to the Cabinet of the U.S. president.

3

Defense Council

The Defense Council

Soviet national security policy is made by the Defense Council (*Sovet oborony*), a peacetime and wartime organization. The membership of the Defense Council, formally a state organization,[17] is principally made up of Politburo members, and is headed by the CPSU general secretary,[18] creating an interlocking directorate between state military affairs and party leadership. The Minister of Defense is the only military member of the Defense Council, although the chief of the General Staff probably serves as secretary.[19] The remaining membership probably includes the chairman of the Council of Ministers, the foreign minister, the chairman of the KGB, and the chairman of *Gosplan*.[20] The Presidium of the Supreme Soviet officially names Defense Council members, although in all likelihood the Politburo actually selects the membership.[21]

While there has been little Soviet discussion of the role of the Defense Council,[22] it is known that the council serves as the senior state body for decisionmaking in preparing the country's defense, strengthening its military readiness, determining the principles of organization of the armed forces, coordinating defense administrative needs with the economy, and making the senior appointments in the MOD and General Staff.[23] Inasmuch as the Defense Council is made up of the Politburo's leading foreign policy and defense decisionmakers, it is the closest functional equivalent of the U.S. National Command Authority (NCA).[24] It presumably has the exclusive authority to approve the use of nuclear weapons.

The Defense Council apparently does not maintain an independent staff.[25] It relies largely on the General Staff to provide analysis of both its own proposals and those of others.[26] The General Staff also serves as the council's executive arm, implementing Defense Council decisions.[27] Thus, while the Defense Council provides senior party oversight of the MOD and national security in general, the MOD and its General Staff retain considerable influence over policy.

Although the Defense Council is not officially subordinate to the Politburo, it provides the Politburo with national security analysis and recommendations.[28] Of course, since the number of Defense Council members on the Politburo has increased with the promotion to the Politburo of the minister of foreign affairs, the minister of defense,[29] the chairman of the KGB (all in April 1973), and the chairman of *Gosplan* (in October 1985), there may be greater willingness to deal with defense issues in the larger group.

In wartime, the Defense Council would continue to function with an expanded membership. This would include "additional representatives of the highest party, state and military leadership."[30] The wartime Defense Council would function similarly to the State Defense Committee (*Gosudarstvennyy komitet oborony*, or GKO), which existed in World War II and was headed by the general secretary of the CPSU.[31] Soviet writings imply that the wartime Defense Council would order when and where nuclear weapons are to be used.

The Supreme High Command

The Supreme High Command (*Verkhovnoye glavnokomandovaniye*, or VGK), is the "highest organ of strategic leadership for the armed forces."[32] According to *Soviet Military Power*, "General Secretary Gorbachev would function as wartime Defense Council Chairman and exercise direct leadership of the Soviet Armed Forces as Supreme Commander in Chief of the VGK and

---

17 The existence of the Defense Council in 1958 is indicated in V. S. Golubovich, *Marshal R. Ya. Malinovskiy* (Moscow: Voyenizdat, 1984), p. 207. When Brezhnev was promoted to marshal of the Soviet Union on 7 May 1976, the official announcement indicated that he was chairman of the Defense Council. N. V. Ogarkov, ed., *Voennyi entsiklopedicheskiy slovar'* (Military Encyclopedia Dictionary) (hereafter referred to as VES) (Moscow: Voyenizdat, 1983), p. 100, also indicates that Brezhnev had been chairman since 1964, implying that the office is even older. The existence of the Defense Council was only publicly acknowledged in 1976, and it was formally included in the 1977 Soviet Constitution as a *state*(rather than party) organ, although it has apparently existed in other forms since the revolution.

18 "Gorbachev Now Heads Key Defense Committee," *Baltimore Sun*, 2 August 1985, p. 5, (Reuter). Brezhnev assumed the chairmanship in 1964 ('Brezhnev," in VES) and was followed in this post by Andropov, Chernenko, and the current general secretary, Mikhail Gorbachev.

19 SMP 1987, p. 11.

20 Ibid., p. 12. U.S. intelligence sources report that the Defense Council in 1978 consisted of Brezhnev, Kosygin, Ustinov, "and possibly four or five others"; JEC, Allocation of Resources -1978, Part 4, p. 187. In this source, Ustinov is identified as "probably" on the Defense Council (p. 170). See also Jan Sjena and Joseph D. Douglass, Jr., *Decision-Making in Communist Countries: An Inside View* (Cambridge, MA: Institute for Foreign Policy Analysis, Inc., 1986), pp. 30-31; Harriet Fast Scott and William F. Scott, *The Soviet Control Structure: Capabilities for Wartime Survival*, National Strategy Information Center, Inc., Strategy Paper 39 (New York: Crane, Russak, 1983), pp. 47-48; Harry Gelman, *The Brezhnev Politburo and the Decline of Detente* (Ithaca, NY: Cornell University Press, 1984), passim; Michael J. Deane, Ilana Kass, and Andrew G. Porth, "The Soviet Command Structure in Transformation," Strategic Review, Spring 1984, pp. 55-70.

21 *Konstitutsiya (Osnovnoy zakon) Soyuza Sovetskikh Sotsialisticheskikh Respublik* (Constitution [Fundamental Law] of the Union of Soviet Socialist Republics), 1977, Article 121, Clause 14.

22 The Soviets have been willing to discuss the defense councils of their Warsaw Pact allies. The most detailed *Soviet* discussion of a defense council's membership concerns the Rumanian Defense Council, which is made up of the general secretary (chairman and commander-in-chief of the armed forces), the prime minister, the minister of defense, the minister of internal affairs, the chairman of the State Planning Committee, the minister of foreign affairs, the secretary of the Supreme Political Council, the chief of the General Staff, and "others appointed by the Central Committee and approved by decree of the State Council"; see *Armiy stran Varshavskogo Dogovora* [Armies of the Countries of the Warsaw Pact] (Moscow: Voyenizdat, 1985), pp. 131-132.

23 *Armiy Stran Varshavskogo Dogovora*, op. cit., pp. 64, 88, 111, 131, 155, 182. For an interesting "inside" perspective on the role of the Defense Council in pre-1968 Czechoslovakia, see Sjena and Douglass, op. cit., pp. 30-40; SMP 1987, p. 11.

24 The U.S. NCA consists solely of the president and the secretary of defense and their duly deputized successors.

25 It should be noted, however, that each Politburo member has a small personal staff, although there is no evidence that these staffs include civilians with military expertise.

26 General Secretary Gorbachev has apparently opened participation in military decisons to a wider civilian audience than ever before, augmenting the role of the General Staff.

27 Kenneth Currie, "The Soviet General Staff," *Problems of Communism*, March-April 1984, p. 38; Coit Blacker, "Military Forces," in Robert F. Byrnes, ed., *After Brezhnev: Sources of Soviet Conduct in the 1980s*, pp. 125-185 (Bloomington: Indiana University Press, 1983), p. 141; JEC, Allocation of Resources -1981, Part 7, p. 209.

28 For example, Marshall Shulman reported that Politburo members not on the Defense Council were denied access to specific military information; see Richard D. Anderson, "The Defense Council, Succession Politics, and Soviet Military Spending," Subcommittee on International Trade, Finance, and Security Economics of the Joint Economic Committee and the Congressional Research Service in *Soviet Military Economic Relations: Proceedings of a Workshop*, pp. 57-68 (Washington, DC: GPO, 1983), p. 59.

29 Dmitri F. Ustinov was a full Politburo member *before* he was appointed minister of defense. His successor, Sergei L. Sokolov, only reached the status of candidate (or non-voting) member, as has the current minister of defense, Dmitri T. Yazov.

30 SMP 1987, p. 19.

31 The GKO's work in World War II revolved around preparing the state for war, maintaining the war economy, and controlling the consequences of the war. In the event of a major crisis of war, the Defense Council would be organized into a "higher agency of leadership [that] may be given the same power as the State Defense Committee during the Great Patriotic War"; V. D. Sokolovskiy, *Soviet Military Strategy*, 3d ed., Harriet Fast Scott, ed. (New York: Crane, Russak, 1975), p. 361; SMP 1988, p. 16; SMP 1987, p. 19.

32 See "Verkhovnoye glavnokomandovaniye" in VES, p. 125.

head of its General Headquarters (*Stavka*) [of the Supreme High Command]."[33]

The *Stavka* would most likely be organized out of the Ministry of Defense Collegium (see below) and would be chaired by the general secretary of the CPSU.[34] The *Stavka* would probably also include the minister of defense, the chief of the General Staff, the first deputy minister of defense, the chief of the Main Political Directorate of the MOD, and the commanders-in-chief of Soviet forces (Ground Forces, Strategic Rocket Forces, Air Defense Troops, Air Forces, Naval Forces, Warsaw Pact Forces).[35]

The role of the *Stavka* is to provide the strategic leadership and planning required by the VGK and to exercise overall control of Soviet nuclear forces through the directorates of the General Staff. Historical evidence suggests that it would be the most important element in the Soviet wartime chain of command.[36]

Ministry of Defense

The Ministry of Defense[37] is the Soviet equivalent of the U.S. Department of Defense and oversees virtually all Soviet military activities,[38] coordinating the five services and managing a number of support services and special troops (for example, civil defense and chemical troops). The MOD is responsible for direct control of the daily support of the armed forces, as well as for ensuring the peacetime preparedness of the armed forces for transition to wartime footing. The minister of defense is roughly comparable in authority to the U.S. secretary of defense and the chairman of the Joint Chiefs of Staff combined.

Subordinate to the minister of defense are three first deputy ministers: the chief of the General Staff, the commander-in-chief of Warsaw Pact Forces, and a first deputy minister who is responsible for administration of the ministry itself.[39] There are 11 deputy ministers. Five of these deputy ministers are the chiefs of the armed services. Other deputy ministers are responsible for civil defense, rear services and supply, construction and billeting, personnel (or cadres), armaments, and the Main Inspectorate.[40]

The deputy minister for armaments is responsible for research and development; monitoring the various scientific research institutes, design bureaus, and defense plants; delivery of military equipment; and training forces on new equipment. In the early post-war period, this post was held by specialists in missiles, but since the mid-1950s it has been held by specialists in electronics.[41]

Collegium

The Collegium of the MOD functions as its key consultative body and policy review board and would probably provide the foundation for the wartime Supreme High Command.[42] It is chaired by the defense minister and includes the three first deputy defense ministers, the 11 deputy ministers, and the chief of the Main Political Directorate.[43]

The Collegium is primarily responsible for coordinating the various economic plans and requirements of its subordinate organizations—for example, the industrial production associations. In the MOD, these plans and requirements are presumably generated by the staffs of the services and the other MOD administrations, which in turn work with the General Staff. The Collegium probably spends most of its time on day-to-day administrative and economic questions, similar to the Defense Resources Board of the U. S. Department of Defense.

General Staff

While the Collegium is responsible for peacetime administrative management of the armed forces, direct leadership of the military is exercised by the General Staff, which serves as the operational staff and executive agent of the VGK.[44] The General Staff is the most important organization within the MOD and is the heart of military planning and operational command. It is divided into several administrations and directorates responsible

---

33 SMP 1987, pp. 19-20.
34 SMP 1988, p. 16.
35 *Ibid.*, p. 16; SMP 1987, p. 12.
36 During World War II, the *Stavka* directly led the fronts, fleets, and Long-range Aviation, establishing tasks, planning operations, and ensuring the uninterrupted support of the forces. See the discussion under "Stavka" in the *Velikaya Otechestvennaya voyna, 1941-1945: entsiklopediya* (Encyclopedia of the Great Patriotic War, 1941-1945) (Moscow: Sovetskaya entsiklopediya, 1985).
37 The minister of defense in 1988 is General of the Army Dmitri T. Yazov.
38 A small military force of Border Troops is also maintained by the KGB.
39 The first deputy minister serves the same function as the U.S. deputy secretary of defense.
40 SMP 1988, p. 13.
41 The first deputy minister for armaments was apparently M. N. Tukhachevskiy, appointed chief of armaments for the Soviet Army in 1931. After the war, the post was held by Artillery Marshall N. D. Yakolev (1947-1952), then Artillery Marshall M. I. Nedelin (1952-1953), both closely involved with the development of missiles. From 1953 to 1964, there was apparently not a deputy minister for armaments per se, but there was a deputy minister for radar and radioelectronics: A. I. Berg from 1953 to 1957 and A. V. Gerasimov from 1957 to 1964. In 1964, Gerasimov became first deputy chief of the General Staff for armaments. The appointment of N. N. Alekseyev in 1970, who had been from 1960 to 1970 chairman of the General Staff's Scientific-Technical Committee, apparently returned the armaments portfolio to the deputy minister level. He was succeeded in 1980 by V. M. Shabanov. For further information on the post and its occupants, see V. M. Ivanov, *Marshal M. N. Tukhachevskiy* (Moscow: Voyenizdat, 1985), pp. 280-286; David Holloway, "Innovation in the Defence Sector," in Ronald Amann and Julian Cooper, eds., *Industrial Innovation in the Soviet Union* (New Haven, CT: Yale University Press, 1982), pp. 322,

328; V. M. Shabanov, "Marshal voysk svyazi N. N. Alekseyev" *Voyenno-Istoricheskiy Zhurnal*, No. 6, 1984, pp. 88-90; Gerard Smith, *Doubletalk: The Story of SALT I* (Lanham, MD:University Press of America, 1985), p. 48.
42 SMP 1988, p. 13. Some have suggested that the Collegium and another organization, the Main Military Council, are the same. However, while the Soviets acknowledge the continuing existence of the MOD's Collegium (simply the leading officials in any ministry), the Main Military Council has had a convoluted history. The *Soviet Military Encyclopedia* (*Sovetskaya voyennaya entsiklopediya*, (Moscow: Voyenizdat, 1976) (hereafter referred to as SVE), Vol. 2, indicates that the Main Military Council was abolished in 1953, though it may simply have been redesignated with a different name as a body of the Defense Council. Golubovich, *op. cit.*, p. 207, states, "The Military Council *Voyennyy sovet* attached to the USSR Defense Council was renamed in November 1957 the Main Military Council *Glavnyy voyennyy sovet* attached to the USSR Defense Council." The question of these bodies is further clouded by the fact that there are "military councils" in the branches of the armed forces, in military districts, groups of forces, PVO districts, and fleets. These include the region's senior military and party officials, and they are responsible for overseeing peacetime development of armed forces and mobilization. See 'Voyennyy sovet," in VES, 1986; Scott and Scott, *Soviet Control Structure, op. cit.*, pp. 48-53; Deane, et al., *op. cit.*, pp. 55-70 for contrasting discussions of this issue. The high degree of personnel overlap in the upper echelons may make any organizational distinction academic.
43 SMP 1988, p. 19; SMP 1987, p. 18. The Main Political Directorate guides party political work in the Soviet Armed Forces. It is responsible to the CPSU Central Committee and extends throughout the armed forces structure.
44 SMP 1987, p. 20.

3

Administrative Organization

for determining not only military operations but also military art and strategy.[45] Soviet authorities characterize the General Staff as the "brain of the Army."[46]

The General Staff serves as the direct link between the Soviet politico-military leadership and the nuclear forces. In wartime, it becomes the staff of the *Stavka*. It is the rough equivalent of the Joint Chiefs of Staff combined with the Joint Strategic Target Planning Staff and the operations and plans directorates (the offices of the deputy chiefs of staff for operations and plans, or the deputy chief of naval operations) in the four services of the U.S. military.

The chief of the General Staff[47] is generally second only to the minister of defense in protocol listings and is supported by three first deputy chiefs and a number of deputy chiefs.

In peacetime the General Staff ensures the coordinated action of the main staffs of the five services, the staff of Rear Services, the staff of Civil Defense, the main and central administration of the Ministry of Defense, the staffs of military districts, the four groups abroad, air defense districts, and the four fleets.[48]

The most important function of the General Staff is operations planning, a task undertaken by the Main Operations Directorate.[49] Within the Operations Directorate, Soviet "war plans" are developed, including strategic nuclear targeting plans. Thus, the Main Operations Directorate prepares the Soviet equivalent of the U.S. Single Integrated Operational Plan (SIOP)—the strategic nuclear war plan—as well as various theater and tactical nuclear plans and target lists.[50]

In the event of war, the General Staff, through its Operations Directorate,[51] would have operational control of military forces. It would be responsible for ensuring "the Armed Forces leadership by the Supreme High Command and Defense Minister."[52] Presumably, this means placing Soviet nuclear forces on alert, providing the VGK with attack assessment data, and transmitting *Stavka* directives to military commands.[53] The General Staff will exercise command over the Strategic Rocket Forces (SRF), ballistic missile submarines, and the Strategic Air Armies. It can, in fact, bypass the headquarters of the SRF and take control of the SRF directly.[54] The General Staff also probably retains direct control of the "strategic reserve" of forces, including about 17 divisions and an "air army" held in the Moscow, Volga, and Ural military districts.

In addition to the Operations Directorate, the General Staff is supported by a number of other functional administrations with specialized tasks: military intelligence (GRU), which collects military and technical information; communications; organization and mobilization; cryptography; topography; Warsaw Pact Forces; military assistance to other countries; armaments; and military science.[55] There is also a deputy chief of the General Staff responsible for armaments, and it has been suggested that the General Staff's involvement in procurement has increased since the mid-1960s, in an effort to address three "problem areas: the rising cost of modern weapons, the efficient choice of what weapons to produce, and the need for increased flexibility in weapon R&D."[56]

Administrative Organization of the Armed Forces

The MOD military services and military districts provide the military support infrastructure for the purpose of raising and training military forces.[57] This infrastructure does not function in the command structure for the operational subordination of Soviet military forces. The administrative structure, however, would not totally disappear in wartime. Parts of the military services (for example, strategic nuclear forces and air defense forces) would continue to operate intact under direct supervision of the VGK. The rest of the five military services and the military districts would continue to sustain military forces in the field, generate additional forces, and operate in support of aerospace defense, civil defense, and post-

---

45. The General Staff does not formulate doctrine, although its analysis of military art presumably is used by the political leadership in doing so.
46. V. G. Kulikov, "Mozg Armii" (Brain of the Army), *Pravda*, 13 November 1974, p. 2.
47. The Chief of the General Staff in 1988 is Marshall of the Soviet Union Sergei F. Akhromeyev.
48. SMP 1988, p. 13; SMP 1987, p. 19; SVE, Vol. 2, p. 513.
49. The chief of the General Staff "leads all work on preparation for war, including for the future VGK"; M. A. Gareyev, *M. V. Frunze: Voyennyy teoretik* [M. V. Frunze: Military Theoretician] (Moscow: Voyenizdat, 1985), pp. 187-188.
50. During World War II, the plans were assigned to those responsible for the "strategic direction" and the front, with representatives of the *Stavka* coordinating much of the work. Large-scale operations, achieved in World War II through combining fronts, are now the responsibility of theater-level commands; SMP 1988, p.13.
51. The chief of the Operations Directorate is a deputy chief of the General Staff, and its reported chiefs have been M. V. Povaliy (1964-1969), M. M. Kozlov (1969-1974, when he was appointed a first deputy chief of the General Staff), S. F. Akhromeyev (1974-1979, when he was appointed a first deputy chief of the General Staff), and I. A. Gashkov (1985-1987). See Michel Garder, *A History of the Soviet Army* (New York: Praeger, 1966), p. 163; V. G. Kulikov, *Akademiya Generalnogo Shtaba* [Academy of the General Staff] (Moscow: Voyenizdat, 1976), p. 185; John Erickson, "Soviet Military Power," supplement to *Strategic Review*, Vol.1, No.1, p. 29; A. P. Antonov, "Operativnoye upravleniye Generalnogo shtaba v gody Velikoy Otechestvennoy vony" [Operations Administration of the General Staff in the Great Patriotic War], *Voyenno-istoricheskiy zhurnal* (Military Historical Journal), No. 5, 1988, pp. 12-18; Ulrich-Joachim Schulz-Torge, "The Soviet Military High Command," *Military Technology*, No. 8, 1985, pp. 111-121.
52. "General'nyi shtab" (General Staff), in *VES*, p. 186.
53. Kulikov, "Mozg Armii," *op. cit.*, p. 2.
54. SMP 1981, p. 55.
55. Of these, the Military Science Directorate may be the most important, for it provides much of the historical and contemporary analysis that supports the plans of the Operations Directorate. The increasing importance of the Military Science Directorate is reflected in the promotion in 1985 of its chief since 1975, M. A. Gareyev, to the position of deputy chief of the General Staff. Gareyev wrote what is perhaps the most important recent text on Soviet strategic thinking, *M. V. Frunze: Voyennyy teoretik*, under the guise of analyzing the work of M. V. Frunze. In fact, Gareyev provides a wide-ranging critique of outdated Soviet military thinking (including the classic volume edited by V. D. Sokolovskiy, *Soviet Military Strategy*) and discusses several important contemporary issues. The Military Science Directorate also publishes the classified General Staff journal, *Voyennaya Mysl'* (Military Thought), in which various ideas are discussed prior to, and during, their implementation.
56. DIA, *Soviet Weapons Acquisition Process, with Special Emphasis on the Ground Forces*, DST-1830S-336-80 (partially declassified and released under the FOIA), 1980, p. 39.
57. "Territorially, the USSR is divided into 16 military districts (MDs). An MD is a high-level element of military administration with subordinate military units, training institutions, recruitment and mobilization offices, and other military establishments. Aside from supervising combat training, the MD commander is responsible for overseeing draftee registration and induction, mobilization planning, civil defense, and premilitary and reserve training"; SMP 1988, p. 13.

Strategic Rocket Forces

Table 3.2
Allocation of Nuclear Weapons by Service (1988)

Weapon	Strategic Rocket Forces	Ground Forces	Air Defense Forces	Air Forces	Naval Forces
ABMs			X		
Artillery		X			
AS-2				X	X
AS-3				X	X
AS-4				X	X
AS-5					X
AS-6				X	X
AS-15				X	
Bombs				X	X
Depth bombs				X	X
FRAS-1					X
FROG-3/5/7		X			
SA-1			X		
SA-2			X		
SA-5			X		
SA-10			X		
SCUD B		X			
SS-4	X				
SS-11	X				
SS-12M		X			
SS-13	X				
SS-17	X				
SS-18	X				
SS-19	X				
SS-20	X				
SS-21		X			
SS-23		X			
SS-24	X				
SS-25	X				
SSC-1b					X
SS-N-3					X
SS-N-5					X
SS-N-7					X
SS-N-8					X
SS-N-9					X
SS-N-12					X
SS-N-15					X
SS-N-16					X
SS-N-17					X
SS-N-18					X
SS-N-19					X
SS-N-20					X
SS-N-23					X
Torpedoes					X

nuclear reconstitution.[58] Each service commander has a chief of rear services (*Tyl*) who is responsible for maintenance and supply, as well as a political administration chief (MPA) who represents the party.[59]

Strategic Rocket Forces

Soviet military literature refers to the Strategic Rocket Forces (*Raketnye voiyska strategicheskogo naznacheniya*—"rocket troops of strategic designation") as the "primary service" of the Soviet military. The SRF is the newest of the five Soviet military services, having been established in December 1959.[60] All land-based surface-to-surface missiles (SSMs) with a range greater than 1000 kilometers are under the control of the SRF. The SRF operates three categories of missiles:

- intercontinental ballistic missiles (ICBMs), with ranges between 9400 and 13,000 kilometers;
- SS-20 mobile intermediate range ballistic missiles (IRBMs), with a range of 5000 kilometers; and
- SS-4 stationary medium range ballistic missiles (MRBMs), with a range of 2000 kilometers.

In all, the SRF maintains about 9300 nuclear warheads, comprising 28 percent of the Soviet nuclear arsenal. Approximately 298,000 personnel reportedly fill SRF ranks.[61]

The SRF commander-in-chief is also a deputy minister of defense, equal in standing to the other four service chiefs.[62] His Moscow headquarters, like those of the other services, is organized along the lines of the VGK. The commander-in-chief, two first deputy commander-in-chiefs (one of which is also the chief of the Main Staff), six deputy commander-in-chiefs (with responsibilities such as armaments, combat training, military schools, and rear services), and the chief of the Political Administration make up the SRF Collegium, or Military Council.[63]

The chain of command extends to what are believed to be six rocket armies, three independent IRBM theater corps, and 10-12 rocket divisions.[64] ICBM divisions are subdivided into approximately ten regiments (launch groups) of six to ten batteries each, with each battery con-

---

58 LTC John G. Hines and Dr. Phillip A. Petersen, "The Changing Soviet System of Control for Theater War," *Signal*, December 1986, p. 106. The commanders-in-chief of the military services would also be members of the VGK *Stavka* and would therefore be involved in the operational direction of military forces.
59 The commander and MPA representative usually work together closely; see Colton, *op. cit.*, p. 10-11.
60 Kozlov, *Spravochnik ofitsera*, p. 129.
61 IISS, *Military Balance*, 1987-1988, p. 33. According to DIA, *Force Structure Summary*, November 1987, p. 39, strategic attack forces, including personnel assigned to the SRF, SLBMs, and strategic bombers, number 410,500. According to Collins and Victory, *U.S./Soviet Military Balance*, 1988, pp. 3, 6, Soviet strategic nuclear forces involved approximately 180,000 military personnel as of 1 January 1987. Another 105,000 support personnel were involved, and 480,000 personnel released from active duty may provide a ready reserve manpower force.
62 The commander-in-chief of the SRF in 1988 is Yuri P. Maksimov.
63 Scott and Scott, *The Armed Forces of the USSR*, *op. cit.*, p. 136; *Air Force Magazine*, March 1988, p. 62.
64 Private communications with the authors; *Soviet Armed Forces Review Annual 1986*, Vol. 9, p. 104. The six SRF armies are thought to be the Northern, Southern, Moscow, Central, Eastern, and Far Eastern; Berman and Baker, *Soviet Strategic Forces*, pp. 15-21.

3
Strategic Rocket Forces

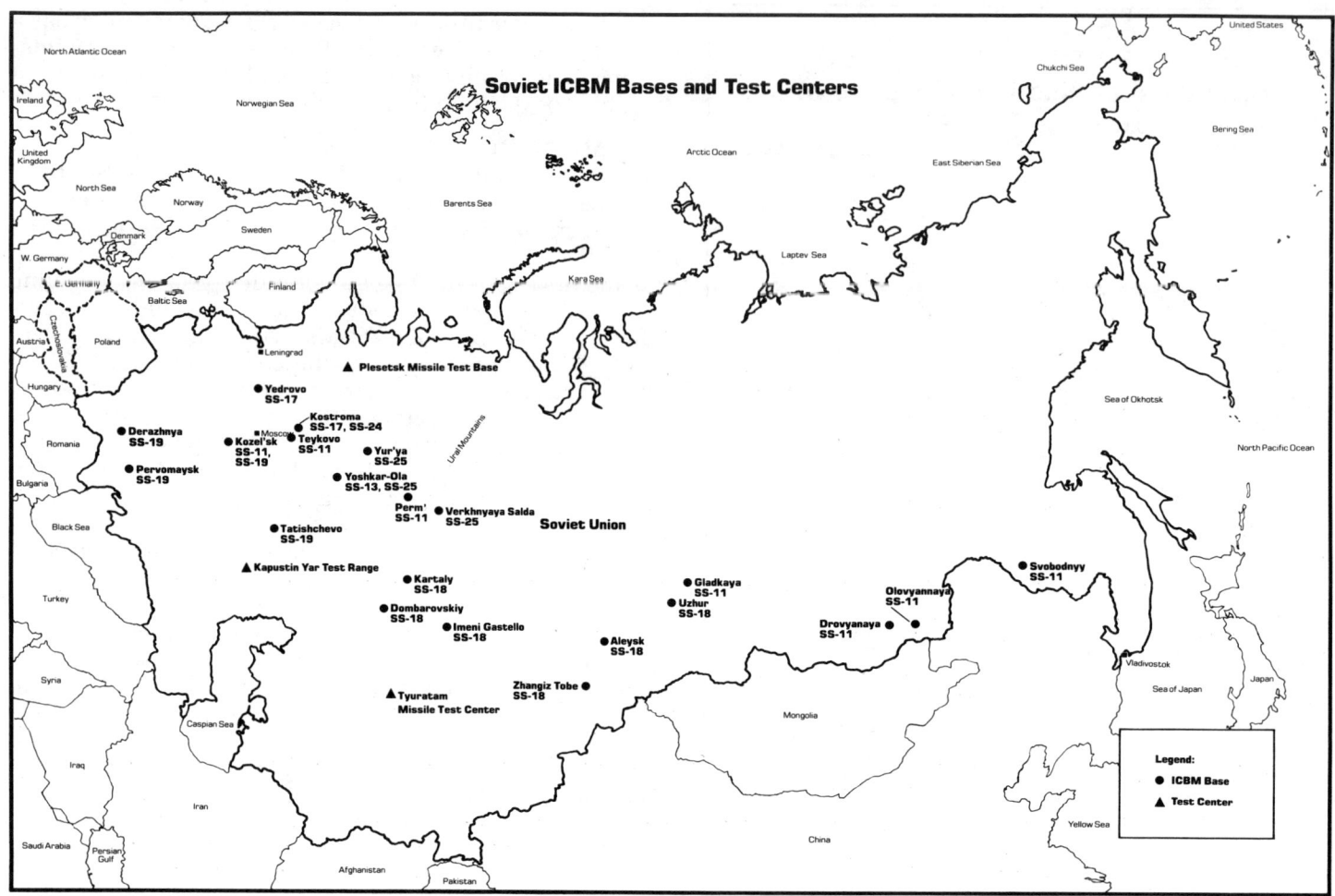

Figure 3.3 Soviet ICBM Bases and Test Centers.

sisting of a single missile launcher.[65] Missiles are dispersed among some 28 fields (centered around main operating bases).[66] Forty-eight SS-20 regiments are operational and accounted for in the INF Treaty, each with two or three battalions of six or nine launchers. At the time the INF Treaty was signed, 65 SS-4 MRBM missiles remained operationally deployed at both soft and hardened sites.

Each rocket army has its own hardened central command post and alternative airborne command post. Fixed or mobile launch control centers control each regiment. In all, there are 300 hardened launch control centers (LCCs) manned by a minimum of two launch control officers.[67]

The Soviets classify targets for Soviet missile attacks as either primary or secondary, depending on their time urgency and military importance.[68] Soviet writings stress three general target types:

- strategic, operational, and tactical means of nuclear attack (primary): ICBMs, SSBN, IRBM launchers, C^3 centers, early-warning radars, aircraft carriers and other nuclear-capable naval vessels, nuclear-capable aircraft and their bases (particularly strategic air command (SAC) bases), cruise missile bases, nuclear artillery, and nuclear storage sites;
- conventional military forces and their means of support (secondary): especially supply dumps, fuel depots, naval bases, and airfields; and
- administrative and economic centers (secondary): major cities.[69]

---

65 Two SS-18 regiments have ten launchers; the remainder of the ICBMs are deployed in batteries of six launchers each; private communications with the authors.
66 IISS, *Military Balance*, 1987-1988, p. 33.
67 JEC, *Allocation of Resources - 1981*, Part 7, p. 199; see also, 'Close-up on ICBM Command and Control," *Jane's Defence Weekly*, 6 February 1988, p. 225.
68 Joseph D. Douglass, Jr., *Soviet Strategy in Europe* (New York: Pergamon, 1980), p. 74; see also, SMP 1988, p. 44.
69 Sokolovskiy, *op. cit.*, passim; V. Zemskov, "Kharakternye cherty sovremennykh voin i vozmozhnye metody ikh vedeniya" (Characteristic Features of Modern Wars and Possible Methods of Conducting Them), *Voyennaya Mysl'* (Military Thought), No. 7, July 1969, p. 20; Berman and Baker, *Soviet Strategic Forces*, p. 19.

3
Ground Forces

Table 3.3
Strategic Rocket Forces ICBM Main Operating Bases (1988)

Base	Missile Type
Aleysk	SS-18
Derazhnya	SS-19
Dombarovskiy	SS-18
Drovyanaya	SS-11
Gladkaya	SS-11
Imeni Gastello	SS-18
Kapustin Yar Test Range	
Kartaly	SS-18
Kostroma	SS-17, SS-24
Kozel'sk	SS-11, SS-19
Olovyannaya	SS-11
Perm'	SS-11
Pervomaysk	SS-19
Plesetsk Missile Test Base	
Svobodnyy	SS-11
Tatischevo	SS-19
Teykovo	SS-11
Tyuratam Missile Test Center	
Uzhur	SS-18
Verkhnyaya Salda	SS-25
Yedrovo	SS-17
Yoshkar Ola	SS-13, SS-25
Yur'ya	SS-25
Zhangiz Tobe	SS-18

Figure 3.4 A CIA photo taken in 1959 by a U-2 aircraft shows A-vehicle launch pad at Tyuratum in south central USSR in Kazahhstan. Tyuratum was the site from which the first Soviet ICBM's were fired, all the early Sputniks, all manned flights, all lunar and planetary flights, all fractional orbit bombardment system flights.

The SRF seems wedded to a war-fighting strategy based on the principles of artillery employment.[70] Its deployment of variable-range ballistic missiles throughout Soviet territory enables each rocket army to cover both theater and intercontinental targets while withholding a portion of its missiles for strategic or theater reserves. Overlapping target assignments provide considerable flexibility of employment. Table 3.3 gives an estimate of the deployment and composition of the six rocket armies.

Ground Forces

The Ground Forces is the largest of the five Soviet military services.[71] Officially, the Soviet Army is called "the Ground Forces" (*Sukhoputnye voiska*). In the Soviet military, the term *army* is often informally used to refer to either the ground forces or all the armed forces exclusive of the navy.

Approximately two million men fill Ground Forces ranks, and about 202 maneuver divisions (airborne, armored, and motorized-rifle) and about 18 artillery divisions are the basic combat formations.[72] Nuclear weapons assigned to the Ground Forces include 152mm, 203mm, and 240mm artillery and short-range SSMs (FROG, SS-21, SCUD B, SS-23, and SS-12M). Nuclear systems are assigned to Ground Forces fronts, armies, and divisions.[73] The Ground Forces have some 5060 nuclear warheads, comprising 15 percent of the Soviet nuclear arsenal. Almost all of the Ground Forces nuclear weapons systems are also capable of firing conventional and chemical munitions.

---

70 The first SRF commander-in-chief, Marshal M. I. Nedelin, was an artillery officer. He organized the service according to the structure and employment principles of Soviet artillery. Two most notably featured concepts are "massed fire" along the enemy's front and "counter-preparation" (*kontrapodgotovka*) of the enemy front and operational depth.

71 SMP 1987, p. 9; IISS, *Military Balance*, 1987-1988, p. 34.

72 Only about 50 front-line divisions are classified as having a Category 1 degree of combat readiness (75-100 percent strength with full equipment). The rest range from 75 percent strength of men and equipment to cadre-level status. It should be noted that in 1964 Khrushchev abolished the post of Ground Forces commander-in-chief as part of his effort to deemphasize conventional military services in favor of the SRF. Brezhnev and Kosygin reestablished the post in 1967 during a major reevaluation of Soviet defense policy.

73 DIA, *Soviet Front Fire Support*, pp. 69-71.

3

Air Defense Troops

Ground Forces units are trained and equipped for fighting in both conventional and nuclear environments. Tanks, armored personnel carriers, and other vehicles are designed with sealed chambers to protect against radioactive fallout, as well as against biological and chemical agents.[74]

Ground Forces nuclear weapons fall under the administrative jurisdiction of the chief of Rocket Troops and Artillery through his subordinates in the 16 MDs and four GSFs.[75] Nuclear warheads are believed to be deployed in Eastern Europe,[76] in the western Soviet Union facing NATO, and in Mongolia and the Far East opposite China. Warheads are held in special storage facilities that, while presumably similar to their NATO counterparts, are reportedly fewer in number.[77] In a crisis, the warheads would be dispersed to various formations and coupled with delivery systems.[78]

Soviet fronts (typically made up of five armies) have an SS-12M Scaleboard B brigade in their order of battle. The SS-12M Scaleboard B carries exclusively nuclear warheads and has a range of approximately 800-900 kilometers. A Scaleboard brigade is made up of three battalions of four to six transporter-erector-launchers (TELs), with a reload missile available for each TEL.[79]

A SCUD or SS-23 short-range missile brigade is organic to Soviet tank and combined-arms armies and may be assigned to fronts. The Scud-B SS-1C SSM has a range of 280-300 kilometers. Its replacement, the SS-23, has a 500 kilometer range. The brigade's organization is similar to that of the Scaleboard brigade: three battalions of four to six TELs each, with one reload apiece.[80]

Soviet tank and motorized infantry divisions have an organic Free-rocket-over-ground (FROG) or SS-21 short-range missile battalion. The FROG-7 dual-capable SSM, which serves as a battlefield support weapon, is now being replaced by the SS-21. The missile battalion normally consists of two firing batteries of two TELs each and support elements, including a resupply vehicle with three reload missiles. Alternatively, the battalion's four TELs may be organized into four separate batteries.[81]

In wartime, the VGK would probably assign a heavy artillery brigade from its own reserve to the various fronts. Heavy artillery brigades are equipped with dual-capable 203mm self-propelled howitzers and 240mm self-propelled mortars. These weapons have estimated ranges of ten and eighteen kilometers, respectively, and would be assigned to divisional sectors.[82] The brigade is probably organized into four battalions, two for each weapon type.

Army-level independent artillery formations—which until recently consisted of two battalions of non-nuclear-capable guns and one battalion of 152mm howitzers—are now being equipped with two artillery brigades, each with two battalions of field guns and howitzers. Additionally, some army-level battalions have had their strength increased from 18 to 24 guns.[83] Since 1978, two 152mm-capable guns, towed and self-propelled, have entered service, and some of the older 152mm guns are now considered nuclear-capable.[84] The S-23 180mm towed gun (30 kilometer range), first introduced in the early 1950s, is still in service and may be capable of firing nuclear weapons.[85]

There have been reports that the Soviet Army possesses nuclear land mines, or atomic demolition munitions (ADMs).[86] These would presumably be used by special forces (*Spetsnaz*) or KGB detachments behind enemy lines. Until recently, Army Air Defense Troops operated the SA-2 SAM, which may be available at the front level. The SA-2, which probably is nuclear-capable,[87] has now been subordinated to the Air Defense Troops.

The basic function of Soviet Ground Forces nuclear weapons in peacetime and in non-nuclear war is to deter NATO or China from using nuclear weapons. In case of nuclear war, the functions are to destroy enemy nuclear weapons, to destroy enemy forces and command structures, and to isolate the battlefield.[88] In addition, "planning focuses on the necessity to counter enemy employment of nuclear . . . weapons, to maintain the initiative and momentum of the offensive, and to maintain fire superiority over the enemy [preempt his strikes]."[89]

In the 1970s, the Soviet Army began to emphasize a trend toward quick-reacting, decentralized fire control.[90] Greater authority over nuclear targeting (nuclear release remains the sole prerogative of the VGK) has reportedly been delegated to TV/TVD commanders.[91] Wartime operational control of nuclear weapons would then be further delegated to front and army commanders.[92]

Air Defense Troops

Since its formal establishment in 1954, the National Air Defense Troops (*Voyska protivovozdushnoy oboronystrany*, PVO or PVO-S) have been responsible for

---

74. Scott and Scott, *The Armed Forces of the USSR, op. cit.*, p. 143.
75. Ibid., pp. 143-144.
76. Deployment of nuclear warheads to Eastern Europe occurred in the late 1970s; private communications with the authors.
77. A "mobile rocket technical base" is responsible for rocket and missile resupply and is presumably the site for nuclear weapons storage and maintenance at the army and front level in the Ground Forces.
78. Bracken, *op. cit.*, p. 167.
79. DIA, *Soviet Front Fire Support*, p. 70; U.S. Department of the Army, *Opposing Forces Europe*, Field Manual 30-102, 18 November 1977 (hereafter referred to as FM 30-102), pp. 14-34.
80. DIA, *Soviet Front Fire Support*, p. 70; FM 30-102, pp. 14-33 to 14-34.
81. DIA, *Soviet Front Fire Support*, p. 71; FM 30-102, p. 14-33. The older FROG-3, FROG-4, and FROG-5 missiles have a range of about 35 kilometers.
82. DIA, *Soviet Front Fire Support*, p. 70.
83. David C. Isby, "Soviets Refurbish Artillery for Deeper Attack Mission," *Defense Week*, 5 December 1983, p. 12.
84. SMP 1984, p. 59; Collins and Victory, *U.S./Soviet Military Balance*, 1988, p. 38.
85. DIA, *Soviet Self-Propelled Artillery*, DDI-1130-6-76, (partially declassified and released under the FOIA), 1976, p. 9.
86. Bracken, *op. cit.*, p. 141; DIA, *A Guide to Foreign Nuclear Weapon Systems Under the Control of Ground Force Commanders*, DST-1040S-541-83 (partially declassified and released under the FOIA), 17 August 1984, Chg. 1, pp. xii, 72.
87. DIA, *Soviet Front Fire Support, op. cit.*, p. 114.
88. Ibid.
89. Ibid., p. 70.
90. U.S. Department of the Army, Operations Field Manual 100-5, 1976 (hereafter referred to as FM 100-5), pp. 2-14.
91. Private communications with the authors.
92. FM 100-5, pp. 2-14; Bracken, *passim*; DIA, *Soviet Front Fire Support, op. cit.*, p. 70.

3
Air Defense Troops

strategic and theater air defense of the Soviet Union. Nuclear weapons assigned to the PVO include Galosh and Gazelle anti-ballistic missiles and SA-1, SA-2, SA-5, and SA-10 surface-to-air missiles (SAMs). In all, some 4100 nuclear warheads are estimated to be assigned to the PVO, or 12 percent of the Soviet nuclear arsenal.

The PVO's chain of command, equipment, and missions historically have overlapped those of the Air Forces and Ground Forces Air Defense Troops. In response to growing U.S. cruise missile and low-level penetration bomber deployments, these air defense forces have undergone at least two major reorganizations since the late 1970s.[93] These reorganizations have attempted to rationalize administrative and operational control of the strategic and tactical components of Soviet armed forces responsible for air defense.

The service reorganization begun in 1978 eliminated the overlap of PVO and tactical air defense assets, allowing the PVO to concentrate exclusively on defense against strategic air attack. Strategic air defense forces (*PVO Strany*) and air defense assets of the ground forces (*PVO Voysk*) were combined into a service officially renamed *Voyska* PVO on 1 January 1981.[94] Control of air defense aircraft, SAMs, and radars was also shifted in 1980 to the 16 MDs.[95] More recently, SAMs and interceptor aircraft have apparently been shifted back under the control of national authorities, probably subordinate to the TVDs.[96]

The Air Defense Troops are believed to be divided into five geographic air defense districts (ADDs) inside the Soviet Union for central operational control of interceptor and SAM forces.[97] According to one analyst,

> Whereas previously these [air defense districts] were part of a national command system, they are now subordinated to the theater headquarters. Each of the TVD commanders now has a deputy for PVO responsible for air defense throughout the theater. The PVO has taken over FA [frontal aviation] fighter division and integrated them into the air-defense system.[98]

Subordinate to the commander-in-chief of PVO are three administrative branches:
- Radio-Technical Troops (RTV), which operate early-warning (EW), anti-ballistic missile (ABM), SAM radars, and attack assessment systems;
- Zenith-Rocket Troops (ZRV), which operate SAMs; and
- Fighter Aviation (IA), which maintain the service's interceptor force.

The PVO's RTV operate the Moscow ABM system and control space- and ground-based anti-satellite (ASAT) systems.[99]

Radio-Technical Troops According to the U.S. Department of Defense, the PVO maintains "the world's most extensive early warning system for both ballistic missile and air defense."[100] Its Radio-Technical Troops provide three layers of satellite warning, including ICBM/SLBM launch-detection satellites, electronic intelligence (ELINT), and photo reconnaissance satellites. In addition, the PVO operates three over-the-horizon Backscatter (OTH-B) radars and nine large phased array radars (LPARs), which provide warning of ICBM firings.[101] The Hen-series large EW radars (including 11 Hen House radars at six near-border sites), linked to the intermediate-range Dog House (2800 kilometer range) and Cat House target-tracking radars, as well as to the Pill Box and Try Add missile guidance and engagement radars for the Moscow-based ABM system, make up the PVO's point defense EW system.[102] These cover most of the Soviet Union's periphery out to 6000 kilometers. Finally, over 7000 ground-based air surveillance, target acquisition, height-finder, and missile control radars, able to track incoming aircraft at medium to high altitudes out to 600 kilometers, make up the PVO's inner EW defense layer.[103] In addition to giving warning of nuclear attack, the RTV would also provide attack assessment data to the VGK (or its successor) following a nuclear attack.

The Soviet Union's single ABM system, operated by the RTV, consists of 32 improved Galosh nuclear ABM (320 kilometer range) launchers and 64 Gazelle launchers, deployed around Moscow (see Figure 3.6).[104] The Soviets are still in the process of modifying and upgrading the entire system to 100 silo-based launchers.

Finally, the PVO controls the Soviet ASAT program.[105] According to the U.S. Department of Defense, "since 1971 the Soviets have had the capability to attack satellites in near-earth orbit with a ground-based orbital interceptor." Several of these non-nuclear ASAT rockets, utilizing pellet blasts for destructive effect, are located at

---

93 Before the reorganizations, the PVO, with 500,000 personnel, was the second largest service in the Soviet armed forces, following the Ground Forces; SMP 1984, p. 31.
94 PVO is a generic term that here will be used in reference to the strategic air defense service of the Soviet Armed Forces. SMP 1987 actually refers throughout to the service of the PVO as Soviet Aerospace Forces.
95 SMP 1987, p. 59; SMP 1984, p. 55.
96 SMP 1987, p. 59.
97 Five PVO air defense district (ADD) headquarters have been disbanded, leaving five still operational which are believed to be at Moscow (the largest), Arkhangelsk, Minsk, Kiev, and Novosibirsk. Each district is divided into two to five air defense zones with their own operational headquarters. In the event of war, PVO air defense district forces would operate under the direct General Staff command in the strategic defense role.
98 Mark L. Urban, "Major Reorganization of Soviet Air Forces," *International Defense Review*, No. 6, 1983, p. 756.
99 Private communications with the authors.
100 SMP 1984, p. 32.
101 SMP 1987, pp. 46-47, 60.
102 A ten-site LPAR (2000 kilometer) system complementing the Hen-series radars, will probably be operational by the late 1980s. Six such radars are now operational or under construction. (A limited low-altitude capability is concentrated in the European USSR and other high-priority areas, and two new air surveillance radars started deployment in 1983 and are expected to provide improved coverage against low-flying cruise missiles and bombers.)
103 SMP 1984, pp. 32-33.
104 Until 1967, the Soviets also reportedly referred to Anti-Rocket Defense (*Protivoraketnay Oborona*, or PRO) troops within the PVO. It is unclear whether such a branch ever existed or still exists.
105 In the mid-1960s, the Soviets reportedly talked about Anti-Space Defense (*Protivokosmicheskaya Oborona*, or PKO) troops as a subordinate branch of the PVO. It is unclear whether such a branch ever existed or still exists.

3
Air Forces

Figure 3.5 The National Air Defense Troops or PVO are divided into three administrative branches, one of which is the Radio-Technical Troops, who operate early-warning (EW), anti-ballistic missile (ABM), and SAM radars and attack assessement systems. One of these is the controversial Krasnoyarsk radar installation shown here.

Tyuratam, where two launch pads are available for use. Two Soviet ground-based test lasers might have an ASAT capability.[106]

Zenith Rocket Troops The Zenith-Rocket Troops of the PVO have over 9000 SAM launchers located at more than 900 sites in the Soviet Union.[107] Nuclear warheads probably are available for SA-1 Guild, SA-2 Guideline, SA-5 Gammon, and SA-10 Grumble launchers in the Soviet Union.

Fighter Aviation PVO Fighter Aviation operates about 2250 interceptors dedicated to strategic air defense. These aircraft, with modification, may be capable of carrying nuclear free-fall bombs.[108] Three new IA assigned interceptors, the MiG-31 Foxhound, MiG-29 Fulcrum, and Su-27 Flanker, all with look-down, shoot-down capabilities, may operate with the new IA Il-76 mainstay airborne warning and control system (AWACS) aircraft, substantially improving Soviet capabilities against low-flying targets.[109]

Air Forces

The Air Forces (*Voyenno vozdushnyye sili*, or VVS) has two distinct wartime tasks: to support Ground Forces operations and to execute theater and intercontinental nuclear strikes. It numbers some 450,000 personnel, with over 5000 fighters, fighter-bombers, reconnaissance, and electronic warfare aircraft.[110] Unlike the PVO, the VVS operates every type of military aircraft—bombers, fighters, and interceptors.

The dual-capable inventory of the VVS includes variants of the Su-7 Fitter, MiG-21 Fishbed, MiG-27 Flogger,

---

106 SMP 1983, p. 65; SMP 1984, pp. 34-35.
107 SMP 1987, p. 9. This does not include Soviet strategic SAMs (SA-2/3/5) in Mongolia or with GSFs in Eastern Europe.
108 Some, but not all, of the approximately 4150 Soviet interceptors have been subordinated to the new Aviation Armies of the Soviet Union. The 2250 interceptor figure represents those interceptors dedicated to strategic air defense; SMP 1987, p. 59.

109 *Ibid.*, p. 60; SMP 1984, pp. 37-38.
110 SMP 1987, p. 77; IISS, *Military Balance*, 1987-1988, p. 36; 'Soviets Reequip Forward Air Forces,' *Aviation Week & Space Technology*, 21 May 1984, p. 65; SMP 1984, p. 55. These figures include 95,000 personnel in the Strategic Air Armies.

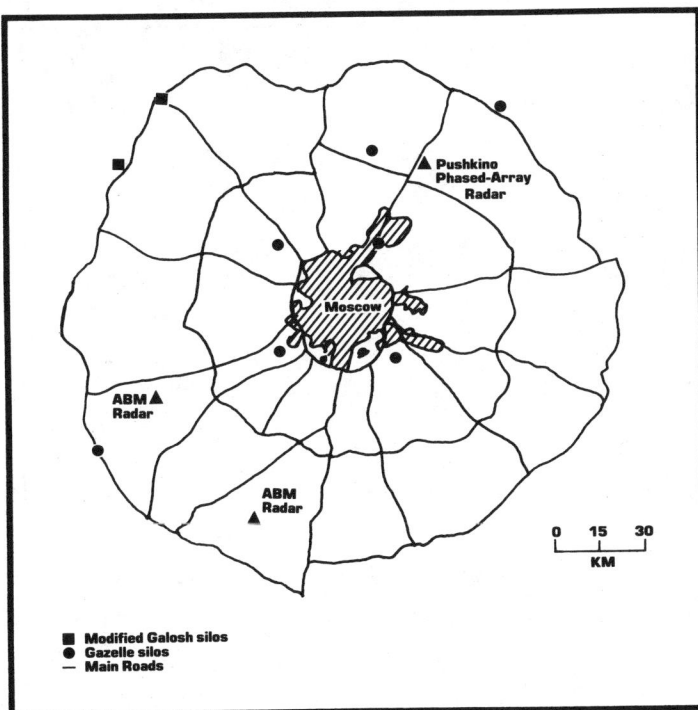

Figure 3.6 Moscow Ballistic Missile Defense.

Su-17 Fitter, and Su-24 Fencer tactical strike aircraft; the Tu-16 Badger, Tu-22 Blinder, and Tu-22M Backfire medium-range bombers; and the Tu-95/142 Bear heavy bombers. A new heavy bomber, the Blackjack, is in advanced stages of flight testing. Some 6500 nuclear warheads are estimated to be assigned to the VVS—including nuclear bombs and ASMs—or some 20 percent of the Soviet nuclear arsenal.

Until about 1980, the commander-in-chief of the VVS was in charge of three service branches:
- Military-Transport Aviation (VTA), controlling transport aircraft;
- Long-range Aviation (*Dalnaya Aviatsiya*, or DA), controlling long- and medium-range strategic bombers; and
- Frontal Aviation (*Frontovaya Aviatsaya*, or FA), controlling tactical and theater aircraft in the European and Asian border areas of the Soviet Union.[111]

In 1980 DA and FA were reorganized into air forces of the military district, groups of forces (AFMD/GOF), and into independent Strategic Air Armies.

Air Forces of the Military Districts and Groups of Soviet Forces Fighter aircraft and interceptors are now organized into commands representing each of the MDs and GSFs.[112] The MD air forces are organized into divisions of three regiments of varying strength, most organized in divisions of three squadrons totaling about 45 aircraft. They are administratively controlled by MD commanders through their chiefs of aviation.[113] In wartime, operational control would be transferred to theater commanders, who would assign air units to front commanders (the so-called Air Forces of the Fronts) for tactical support.[114] The long-range Fencer fighter-bomber is assigned to AFMD/GOF (as well as being assigned to the Strategic Air Armies), but all of the bomber aircraft are assigned to the Strategic Air Armies.[115]

Strategic Air Armies The so-called Aviation Armies of the Soviet Union (also called, in the West, Strategic Air Armies) commanded by the former head of DA, now control bombers (both intercontinental and theater) and strike aircraft.[116] The forces of the Strategic Air Armies are deployed at some 25 airfields in the Soviet Union (see Figure 3.7 and Table 3.4).[117]

Five Strategic Air Armies are subordinate to and under the operational control the VGK:[118]

Smolensk (46th) Air Army: reportedly made up of four bomber divisions of 12 bomber regiments (Backfire, Blinder, Badger),[119] and independent reconnaissance regiments. It is the Western Theater strike force operating out of Poltava (Ukraine) and Sol-Tsio (near Leningrad).

Vinnitsa (24th) Air Army: contains a mix of theater strike forces and tactical assets, including Fencer and Flogger fighters and Fishbed, Flogger, and Flanker escorts.[120] The Vinnitsa Air Army supports the Southwestern Theater.

Legnica (4th) Air Army: contains a mix of theater strike forces and tactical assets, including Fencer and Flogger fighters and Fishbed, Flogger, and Flanker escorts.[121] The Legnica Air Army supports the Western Theater.

Irkutsk (30th) Air Army: contains Bear, Backfire,

---

111 FA was considerably larger than the other two VVS branches, given the Soviet Union's historical concern with air defense against strong NATO air forces and reliance on the SRF as the basis of its nuclear deterrent. Prior to the late 1970s, FA was organized by numbered tactical air armies, divisions, and regiments in the 16 MDs of the Soviet Union and four GSFs in Europe. The air armies were assigned missions essentially limited to intercept/defensive air superiority and ground support; *Soviet Armed Forces Review Annual*, 1981, Vol. 5, pp. 470-471.
112 SMP 1987, p. 76; SMP 1984, p. 55. There would presumably be 20 AFMD/GOFs of the Soviet Union, Mongolia, and Afghanistan if all of the formations had Air Forces, but only 12 MDs and four GSFs are thought to have Air Forces in peacetime.
113 "Soviet Air Force Reequipment," *Jane's Defence Review*, Vol. 4, No. 3, 1983, pp. 250-251.
114 SMP 1987, p. 77; SMP 1984, p. 55; *Soviet Armed Forces Review Annual*, 1981, Vol. 5, p. 463.
115 SMP 1988, p. 79.
116 SMP 1987, p. 77; SMP 1984, p. 55; "Soviets Reequip Forward Air Forces," *Aviation Week & Space Technology*, 21 May 1984, p. 65.
117 Private communications with the authors.
118 SMP 1987, p. 35; "Soviets Reequip Forward Air Forces," *Aviation Week & Space Technology*, 21 May 1984, p. 65.
119 SMP 1988, p. 79.
120 *Ibid.*; Michael Sadykiewicz, *Soviet-Warsaw Pact Western Theater of Military Operations: Organization and Missions* (Santa Monica, CA: Rand Corporation, August 1987), p. 44.
121 SMP 1988, p. 79; Sadykiewicz, *op. cit.*, p. 44.

3
Air Forces

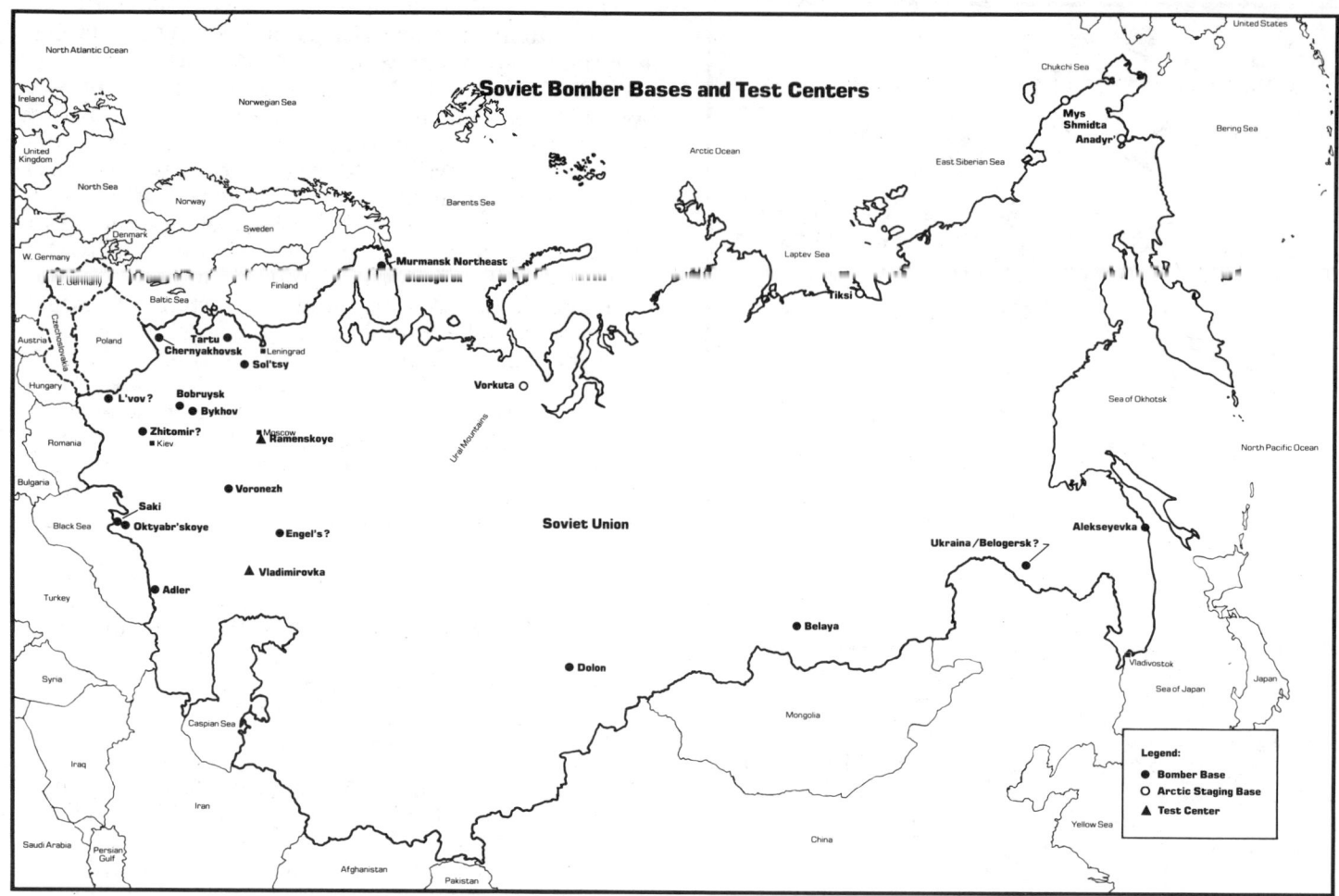

Figure 3.7 Soviet Bomber Bases and Test Centers.

Blinder, Badger, and Fencer bombers and fighters[122] and reconnaissance regiments for Far Eastern Theater operations. About 70 Bear bombers are assigned to the Irkutsk Air Army, including 45 Bear Gs.[123] About 20 percent of the bombers and fighter-bombers in the VVS are assigned to the Irkutsk Air Army.[124] It also maintains some interceptor regiments. Its main base is at Belaya, near Irkutsk.

Moscow (36th) Air Army: contains the strategic Bear B/C/H bombers, as well as tankers and reconnaissance/electronic warfare aircraft. It has four European and one Far Eastern main operating base (Dolon in Central Asia) and reportedly controls five Arctic forward airfields.[125]

The Smolensk, Vinnitsa, and Legnica Air Armies maintain over 700 deep-strike, ground-attack, and reconnaissance aircraft, electronic warfare aircraft, and more than 300 medium bombers facing NATO in Europe.[126] Some 250 Flogger, Fishbed, and Flanker fighters provide escort fighter protection.[127] The Legnica and Vinnitsa Air Armies contain more than 500 Fencers, 200 Fishbed, Flogger, and Flanker fighters of various types, and 120 reconnaissance and electronic warfare aircraft.[128]

---

[122] SMP 1988, p. 79.
[123] Ibid.
[124] SMP 1987, p. 77.
[125] Private communications with the authors.
[126] "Soviets Reequip Forward Air Forces," *Aviation Week & Space Technology*, 21 May 1984, p. 65.
[127] SMP 1987, p. 77.
[128] SMP 1988, p. 79.

3
Navy

Navy

The Soviet Navy is the lowest in precedence of the five military services, but nuclear weapons have given it added prominence within the traditionally land-oriented armed forces. Naval nuclear weapons include a wide variety of strategic and non-strategic submarine-launched ballistic missiles (SLBMs), cruise and anti-ship missiles, SAMS, bombs, depth bombs, artillery, torpedoes, and anti-submarine warfare (ASW) missiles and rockets. Many Soviet naval weapons systems have both conventional and nuclear capability. Some 7600 nuclear warheads, or 23 percent of the nuclear arsenal, are estimated to be assigned to the Navy.

The Soviet Navy is organized administratively into four fleets—Northern (Atlantic Ocean) (NORFLT), Pacific Ocean (PACFLT), Baltic, and Black Sea—and the Caspian Sea Flotilla.[129] Ballistic missile submarine forces, the largest offensive element of the Navy, are assigned to the Northern and Pacific Fleets.[130] Some 477,000 personnel are in the Navy, including about 17,000 assigned to the ballistic missile submarine force. The commander-in-chief of Naval Forces and the Main Naval Staff have administrative control of the four fleets, as well as of the land-based Soviet Naval Aviation (SNA), which is assigned to the fleets. The Main Naval Staff has at its disposal numerous shore-based command posts, two converted Sverdlov class command cruisers, at least one converted Golf class submarine—and a Hotel class—and extensive C³ systems aboard the Kirov class cruisers.[131]

The General Staff maintains operational control over naval forces in peacetime and in crisis. The VGK would control the Navy in wartime, particularly controlling the release of naval nuclear weapons for employment.[132] In wartime, the ballistic missile submarine force could continue to report directly to the VGK, but other naval forces would be assigned to the theater commands.

The nuclear force structures of the Northern and Pacific Fleets differ widely from those of the Baltic and Black Sea Fleets. Due to their relatively unimpeded oceanic access, the former hold a near-monopoly on the ballistic missile submarine force. They also have the largest shares of cruise missile submarines, nuclear-equipped major surface combatants, and nuclear-capable SNA aircraft. In contrast, the restricted-waters Baltic and Black Sea Fleets concentrate on anti-submarine warfare, amphibious operations, and small coastal-patrol craft.[133] Only since 1976 have six old Golf class diesel-powered ballistic missile submarines (SSBs) been assigned to the Baltic Fleet. Four Juliett class cruise missile submarines joined the fleet a short time later in 1982. The Black Sea Fleet has no nuclear ballistic or cruise missile submarines.[134]

Table 3.4
Bomber Bases (1988)

Base	Function
(Adler)	unknown[1]
Alekseyevka	Backfire (SNA)
Anadyr'	Artic staging base, Backfire
Belaya	Backfire (SAA)
Bykhov	Backfire (SNA)
Bobruysk	Badger
Chernyakhovsk	Blinder? (SNA)
Dolon	Bear H (SAA)
(Engel's)	unknown[2]
Murmansk Northeast	Backfire? (SNA)
Mys Shmidta	Artic staging base, Backfire
Oktyabr'skoye	Backfire (SNA)
Olenegorsk	Artic staging area, Backfire
Ramenskoye	bomber test center[3]
Saki	Blinder? (SNA)
Sol'tsy	Backfire? (SAA)
Tartu	unknown
Tiksi	Artic staging base, Backfire
Ukraina	unknown[4]
Vladimirovka	bomber test center[5]
Vorkuta	Artic staging base, Backfire
Voronezh	Backfire? (SAA)

Two additional bases a few hundred kilometers north of the Black Sea are shown on a chart in SMP 1987, p. 25. While their precise locations have not been established, *The Penkovsky Papers*, published in 1965, refers to nuclear bomber bases at, or near, Zhitomir and L'vov.[6]

1. A bomber base in this general location is identified on a chart in SMP 1987, p.25. It is presumed to be the Adler airfield.
2. A bomber base in this general location is identified on a chart in SMP 1987, p.25. It is presumed to be the Engel's airfield.
3. SMP 1987, p. 25.
4. A bomber base in this general location is identified on a chart in SMP 1987, p.25. It is presumed to be either the Ukraina airfield at Svobodnyy or the Vozzhayevka Northeast airfield at Belogersk.
5. SMP 1987, p. 25.
6. Oleg Penkovsky, *The Penkovsky Papers* (New York: Doubleday & Co.: 1965), pp. 343, 345.

---

129 The Caspian Flotilla is a separate command, as is the Leningrad naval base. The flotilla is largely a coastal patrol force, and the latter a training and repair facility. It is unlikely that either have nuclear capability.
130 Six old Golf II class submarines are assigned to the Baltic Fleet as well.
131 Polmar, *Guide to the Soviet Navy*, 1986, p. 40; USN, *Soviet Naval Developments* (Rev. 4/85), p. 55.
132 V. Sokolovskiy and M. Cherednichenko, "Voyennoye iskusstvo na novom etape" (Military Art at a New Stage), *Krasnaya Zvezda*, 28 October 1964.
133 DIA, *Unclassified Communist Naval Orders of Battle*, April 1986, pp. 1-7; see also, Polmar, *Guide to the Soviet Navy*, 1986, pp. 19-23.
134 A single Golf class submarine, deployed in the Black Sea, was modified to test the SS-N-20 (Golf V). It is used exclusively for research and development and is not thought to be armed.

3
Navy

Figure 3.8 There are 23 major shipyards in the Soviet Union, five responsible for submarine production. The Soviet Navy is organized into four fleets—Northern, Pacific, Baltic, and Black Sea. Attack submarines are assigned to each of these fleets and to a base within a fleet, such as the one pictured above in the Northern Fleet.

Figure 3.9 Artist's drawing of a Soviet submarine base including tunnels to protect the submarines against attack.

The Pacific Ocean Fleet is the largest of the four fleets, including, at the end of 1987, two aircraft carriers, 84 principal surface combatants, 121 smaller combatants, 90 auxiliaries, and 120 submarines (including 32 ballistic missile submarines). Some 560 aircraft are assigned to naval aviation in the Pacific. The fleet also maintains a continuous presence in the Indian Ocean. Ships in the Pacific Fleet are homeported on the Kamchatka peninsula and at Far East coastal bases near Vladivostok and around the Sea of Okhotsk. Vladivostok is the Pacific Fleet headquarters.

The Northern Fleet is the second largest fleet, including, at the end of 1987, one aircraft carrier, 75 principal surface combatants, 88 smaller combatants, 95 auxiliaries, and 170 submarines (including 37 ballistic missile submarines). Some 446 aircraft are assigned to naval aviation in the Northern Fleet. The Northern Fleet contributes submarines and surface ships to the Soviet naval forces (Fifth *Eskadra* [squadron]) in the Mediterranean. Ships in the Northern Fleet are homeported on and around the Kola peninsula. Headquarters for the Northern Fleet is located at Severomorsk.

The Baltic Fleet is composed of 44 principal surface combatants, 96 other combatant ships, 45 auxiliaries, and 48 submarines (including six ballistic missile submarines). Naval aviation in the Baltic Fleet is assigned some 282 aircraft. Headquarters for the Baltic Fleet is Kaliningrad.

The Black Sea Fleet/Caspian Flotilla includes one aircraft carrier, 76 principal surface combatants, 74 smaller combatants, and 35 attack submarines.[135] Some 468 aircraft are assigned to the Black Sea Fleet. The secondary mission of the Black Sea Fleet would be to support Soviet naval forces in the Mediterranean. "Soviet Mediterranean forces, backed up by land-based strike air, would also attempt to destroy U.S. and French carriers as well as SLCM [sea-launched cruise missile] platforms outside striking distance of the Crimea."[136] Headquarters for the Black Sea Fleet is Sevastopol.

Nuclear-powered attack submarines participate in all of the main missions of the Soviet Navy: defense of the homeland against attack, protection of Soviet offensive (ballistic missile submarine) forces, and support of offensive naval operations. The diesel submarines support similar missions, but because of their more limited range and more limited ability to operate underwater for long periods of time, they would likely be used in coastal areas and enclosed seas (for example, the Baltic and the Mediterranean), and in support of local ground-force operations.[137]

---

[135] The land-locked Caspian Flotilla is comprised of five principal surface combatants and 29 other combatants.

[136] HASC, FY 1988/1989 DOD Seapower and Strategic and Critical Materials Subcommittee, p. 5.

[137] HAC, FY 1986 DOD, Part 2, p. 910.

3
Wartime Organization

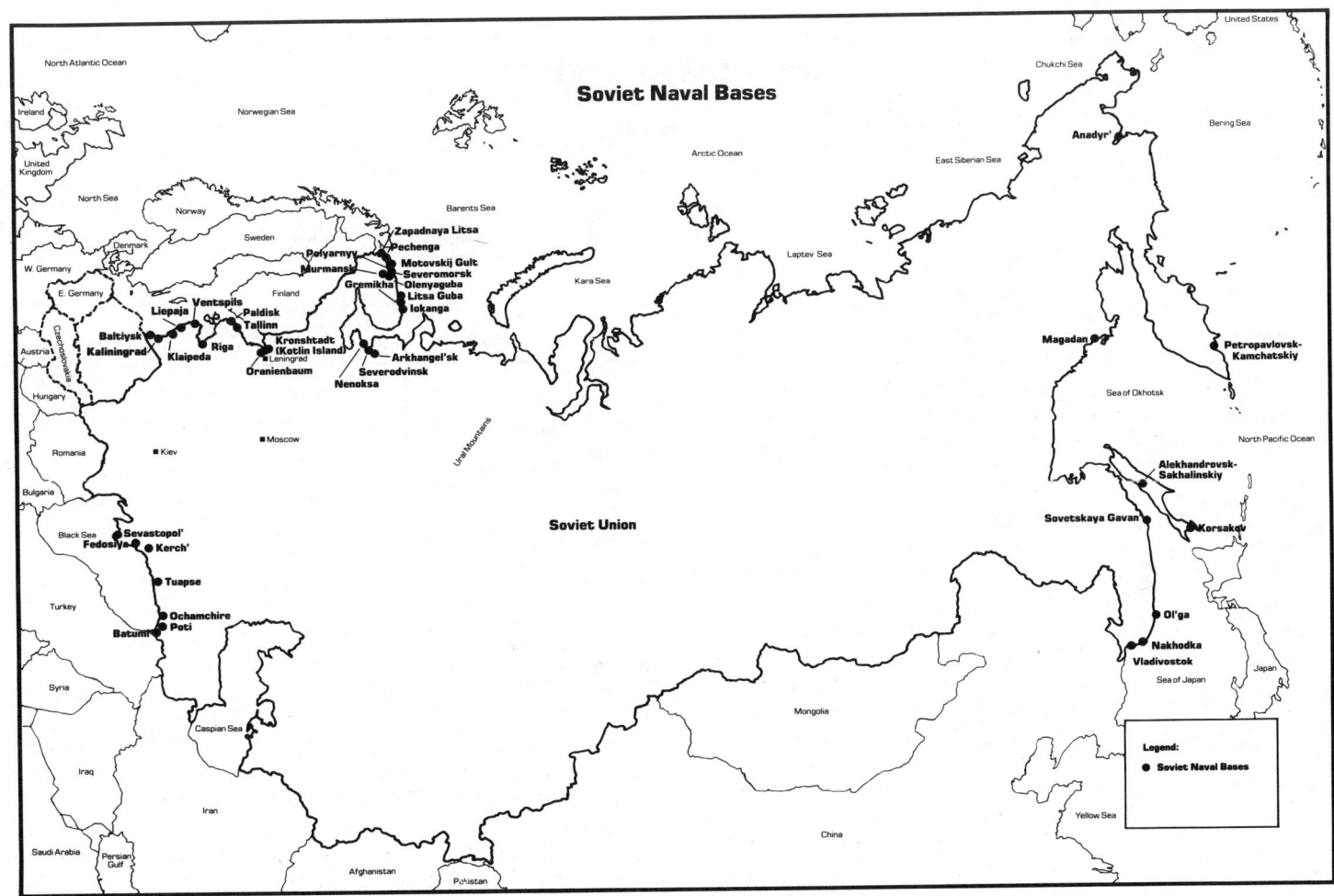

Figure 3.10 Soviet Naval Bases.

The Black and Baltic Sea Fleets have a primary mission of supporting Warsaw Pact ground forces.[138] In both the Baltic and Black Seas, there are active alliance naval establishments. Soviet, East German, and Polish naval units in the Baltic are reportedly under the joint command of the Allied Socialist Fleets in the Baltic (also known as the Joint Baltic Fleet).[139] The Bulgarian Navy is also reportedly integrated into the Soviet Black Sea Fleet for local operations.

Wartime Organization of the Armed Forces

During wartime, Soviet armed forces would be commanded by the VGK, either directly or through regional theater commands. The VGK, through the General Staff Operations Directorate, would directly control strategic nuclear forces (*strategicheskiye yaderniye sili*) (ICBMs, bombers, ballistic missile submarines) of the SRF, VVS, and Navy.[140] According to U.S. naval intelligence, "the bulk of the SSBNs [nuclear-powered ballistic missile submarines] would probably be preserved as a significant component of the Soviet Supreme High Command's strategic nuclear reserve" and would not be directly assigned to the regional commands.[141]

The High Commands of Forces (HCOFs) at the regional commands (TVs or TVDs—see below) represent an intermediate-level command between the VGK and the front, the basic maneuver command in the Soviet armed forces. Instituted to ensure orderly flow of command, flexibility, and coordinated operation of combined forces over large land and sea areas, TVs/TVDs would have operational control of all the armed forces within their theaters. The sole exceptions would be stra-

---

138 HASC, FY 1988/1989 DOD Seapower and Strategic and Critical Materials Subcommittee, p. 6.
139 Milan Vego, "Command and Control of the Warsaw Pact Navies," *Proceedings*, September 1987, pp. 115-117; see also, Sadykiewicz, *op. cit.*, p. 43.
140 SMP 1988, p. 17; N.V. Ogarkov, "Za mir, za nadiozhnuiu oboronu" (For Peace, For Reliable Defense), *Krasnaya Zvezda*, 23 September 1983; see also, Daniel Gouree, "C³ and the New Soviet Nuclear Forces," *Signal*, December 1986, pp. 86-89.
141 HASC, FY 1988/1989 DOD Seapower and Strategic and Critical Materials Subcommittee, p. 4.

3

Theaters of War

Table 3.5
Naval Bases (1988)

Base	Fleet	Function
Alekhandrovsk-Sakhalinskiy	Pacific	minor base; submarine homeport
Anadyr'	Pacific	minor base
Arkhangel'sk	Northern	major base
Baltiysk	Baltic	major base; Cruiser, Destroyer homeport
Batumi	Black Sea	minor base
Fedosiya	Black Sea	minor base; submarine homeport
Iokanga	Northern	minor base
Kaliningrad	Baltic	HQ, Baltic Fleet; Golf II homeport
Kerch'	Black Sea	minor base
Klaipeda	Baltic	minor base
Korsakov	Pacific	minor base; submarine homeport
Kronshtadt (Kotlin Island)	Baltic	major base
Liepāja	Baltic	major base; submarine homeport
Litsa Guba	Northern	minor base
Magadan	Pacific	minor base; submarine homeport
Motovskij Gult	Northern	minor base
Murmansk	Northern	HQ, Northern Fleet; Kiev homeport
Nakhodka	Pacific	minor base; submarine homeport
Nenoksa	Northern	SS-N-20 launch site
Ochamchire	Black Sea	minor submarine base
Olenyaguba	Northern	minor base
Ol'ga	Pacific	minor base
Oranienbaum	Baltic	minor base
Paldisk	Baltic	minor base
Pechenga	Northern	minor base
Petropavlovsk-Kamchatskiy	Pacific	major base; Yankee I and Delta homeport
Polyarnyy	Northern	major base, Yankee I, Delta, Hotel III homeport
Poti	Black Sea	major base; destroyer homeport
Riga	Baltic	minor base
Sevastopol'	Black Sea	HQ, Black Sea Fleet; major base; submarine homeport
Severodvinsk	Northern	minor base
Severomorsk	Northern	major base, Delta IV?
Sovetskaya Gavan'	Pacific	major base; submarine homeport
Tallinn	Baltic	major base; submarine homeport
Tuapse	Black Sea	minor base
Ventspils	Baltic	minor winter base
Vladivostok	Pacific	HQ, Pacific Fleet; major base
Zapadnaya Litsa	Northern	major base; submarine homeport

tegic nuclear forces assigned to the General Staff or nonstrategic nuclear weapons requiring Defense Council release authority. In effect, the HCOFs allow the Soviets to "accommodate centralized strategic leadership with decentralized battle management."[142]

Theaters of War

The military reorganization instituted by former Chief of the General Staff Marshall N. V. Ogarkov[143] resulted in the creation of modern theaters of war (*teatry voyny*, or TVs) and subordinate theaters of military operation (TVDs).[144] The Soviets define the TV as follows:

A theater of war is the land, oceans, and airspace and outer space above them, within the bounds of which the armed forces of states (coalition of states) may conduct war or military operations on a strategic scale. A TV does not have strictly defined boundaries; it usually contains one continent with its surrounding waters or one ocean with its coastal areas, archipelagoes, and islands.[145]

---

142 SMP 1981, p. 18.
143 N.V. Ogarkov, *Vsegda v gotovnosti k zashchite otechestva* [Always in Readiness to Protect the Fatherland] (Moscow: Voyenizdat, 1982), pp. 33-34.
144 The TV is the equivalent of a U.S. unified command, such as European Command; or a NATO command, such as Allied Command Europe. A TVD is the equivalent of a subunified command, such as Allied Forces Northern Europe (AFNORTH) or Allied Forces Central Europe (AFCENT).
145 See "*Teatry voyny*" (Theaters of War), in VES, p. 733.

3
Theaters of Military Operations

Theater commands have been the subject of intense examination and controversy in the West, and their actual status is not altogether clear.[146] The activation of TVs would presumably occur in the event of global war, when numerous TVDs were operating simultaneously.[147]

Although they have not been activated in peacetime, there are three nominal TVs: Western Theater, Far East Theater, and Southern Theater.[148] The Western Theater would have responsibility for all of Europe and North Africa and would command air, ground, and naval forces from the Arctic to the Mediterranean. The Southern Theater would be reponsible for the Middle East and the Indian subcontinent and would command naval forces in the Indian Ocean. The Far East Theater would command forces in Asia, covering the Pacific Arctic as well as the Pacific Ocean and Southeast Asia.

Theaters of Military Operations

Theaters of military operations (*teatry voyennykh deystviy*, or TVDs), sometimes translated as "theaters of strategic military action," are defined as

> an extensive land area of a continent and its coastal seas, or the waters of an ocean (sea), including islands and adjacent continental coastal areas, as well as the airspace and outer space above them, within the bounds of which strategic groupings of armed forces (ground, air, and naval) may deploy and conduct military operations on a strategic scale. The military-political leadership of the states (coalitions of states) determines the borders and forces of the TVD.[149]

Overall, there are believed to be ten land TVDs and four maritime or oceanic (*okeanskiy*) OTVDs:[150]

Land TVDs	Oceanic TVDs
Western TVD	Arctic OTVD
Northwestern TVD	Pacific OTVD
Southwestern TVD	Atlantic OTVD
Southern TVD	Indian Ocean OTVD
Far Eastern TVD	
North America TVD	
South America TVD	
Australia TVD	
Africa TVD	
Antarctic TVD	

Each of these TVDs is in a different stage of activation, with peacetime headquarters (an HCOF) activated in four.[151] In 1979, the Soviets activated the first peacetime HCOF at Chita for the Far Eastern TVD.[152] It is commanded by Army General I. M. Voloshin.[153] An HCOF for the Western TVD was probably established in September 1984.[154] It is headquartered either at Zossen-Wuensdorf, East Germany,[155] or Legnica, Poland, and it is commanded by Marshall N. V. Ogarkov.[156] HCOFs were also established in 1984 for the Southwestern TVD (possibly at Vinnitsa) and for the Southern TVD (possibly at Tashkent).[157] The Southwestern TVD is under Army General I. A. Gerasimov (former commander of the Kiev MD), and the Southern TVD is under Army General M. M. Zaytsev.[158]

Presumably, each TVD has a main staff (similar to the General Staff and having responsibilities for various service "branches" within the TVD).[159]

> The four groups [of forces in Eastern Europe] and most military districts are subordinate to one of four permanent regional high commands. These high commands of forces control the ground, air, and naval forces that would conduct operations.... Acting as regional extensions of the Supreme High Command and General Staff, the four high commands are designed to centralize General Staff control over wartime theater operations.[160]

---

146 Hines and Petersen, op. cit., p. 107, claim that TVs do not exist. IISS, *Military Balance*, 1987-1988, pp. 39-45 state that 'strategic theaters" have been created: Western Strategic Theater, with headquarters in Kiev; Southern Strategic Theater, with headquarters in Tashkent; and Far Eastern Strategic Theater, with headquarters in Irkutsk. These are, in fact, HCOFs for TVDs. As far as can be surmised, peacetime TVs have not been activated.
147 See discussion in Sadykiewicz, op. cit., pp. 6-7.
148 SMP 1988, pp. 14-15.
149 See "*Teatr voyennykh deystviy*" (Theaters of Military Operations), in VES, p. 732. The TVD is also referred to as theater of military operations (TMO), theater of military action, and theater of strategic military action (TSMA). Hines and Petersen, op. cit., p. 99, use the official definition for the TVD as "a particular territory, together with associated airspace and sea areas, including islands (archipelagos), within whose limits a known part of the armed forces ... operates in wartime, engaged in strategic missions which ensue from the war plan. A theater of operations may be ground, maritime, or intercontinental. According to their military-political and economic importance, theaters of operations are classified as main or secondary."
150 SMP 1986, pp. 12-13. See also, Hines and Petersen, op. cit., p. 101.
151 HCOFs have been established in peacetime in four of the ten land TVDs; SMP 1988, p. 13. None of the commanders of the TVDs has, to our knowledge, been identified as *glavnokomanduyushchiy* (commander-in-chief). Instead, they are typically characterized as being engaged in "responsible work in the Ministry of Defense." However, they have been identified by Western sources as the officers in charge of the various TVDs, and that post, according to Soviet writings, is the post of commander-in-chief. This is the same title given to the commanding officers of each of the services and the officer in charge of the Group of Soviet Forces in Germany (GSFG). Interestingly, the *Soviet Military Encyclopedia* (SVE) makes a point that the services and the GSFG were *until 1976* the only organizations with this position.
152 The first commander-in-chief was P. A. Belik. He was succeeded by V. I. Petrov (1979-1980), V. L. Govorov (1980-1984), and I. M. Tret'yak (1984-1986). Govorov was identified at the 26th Party Congress (1981) as "commander-in-chief" of the Troops of the Far East, harkening back to the title held by A. M. Vasilevskiy at the end of World War II. In 1986, Tret'yak was promoted to deputy minister of defense, apparently for civil defense, and replaced by Ivan Makarovich Voloshin. See also, Berman and Baker, *Soviet Strategic Forces*, p. 13.
153 Sadykiewicz, op. cit., p. 8.
154 Some sources believe that Ogarkov was appointed commander of the Western TVD in September 1984, but that it has existed since World War II; see discussion in Sadykiewicz, op. cit., pp. 54-55.
155 Viktor Suvorov, "Strategic Command and Control: The Soviet Approach," *International Defense Review*, No. 12, 1984, p. 1818.
156 It is unclear whether Marshall Ogarkov's command responsibilities as commander of the Western TVD would be limited to the TVD or would include the Western TV upon activation, and therefore encompass the Northwestern and Southwestern TVDs as well.
157 SMP 1988, p. 71; No HCOF has been established for the Northwestern TVD in peacetime.
158 Sadykiewicz, op. cit., p. 7.
159 Nikolaij Nor-Mesek and Wolfgang Rieper claim to identify various officials of the TVDs in their monograph, "Supreme Command of the Soviet Armed Forces, 1986," published as an ISOS Special Edition by the Institut fur Sowjet-Studien, West Germany [n.d.].
160 SMP 1988, p. 13. During wartime, the fleet commanders would become naval component commanders of one of the five land TVDs or the three OTVDs: Arctic, Atlantic, and Pacific.

3

Operational Formations

During wartime, non-Soviet Warsaw Pact forces would come under the HCOFs for the Western and Southwestern TVDs.[161] Operations in OTVDs would, for the most part, be on an equal level with land TVDs, although naval forces would be assigned to both oceanic and land TVDs.[162] North Atlantic operations contiguous to Norway and Iceland would fall under the Northwestern TVD; North Sea and Baltic operations against NATO would fall under the Western TVD; Black Sea and Mediterranean Sea operations would fall under the Southwestern TVD; Persian Gulf operations would fall under the Southwestern TVD; and close-in Pacific Ocean operations would fall under the Far Eastern TVD.

Operational Formations

The ground maneuver portion of Soviet theater operations during wartime would be conducted by "the front."[163] At the beginning of World War II, a front (typically four or five armies) was described as "the highest strategic formation of armed forces"[164] and was considered the main form of combat on an operational (as opposed to strategic) scale. Strategic objectives, defined by the Soviets as those whose accomplishment would change the course or direction of a war, were achieved through a series of operational successes by the front. The operational chain of command went directly from the General Staff to front commanders, rather than through regional commands. During the war, however, it became apparent that coordination problems between fronts jeopardized whatever momentum had been achieved by each front individually. Fronts were frequently insufficient to achieve "large scale political-military objectives," and groups of fronts were required. These were to be "unified" by a common concept and were to be under the unified control of the VGK. Thus "a new form of military action was born, which differed significantly from the Front operation—the operation of a group of Fronts."[165]

Operations by combined fronts were undertaken under the commander-in-chief of a "strategic direction" (*strategicheskoye napravleniye*, sometimes translated as "strategic sector," or "strategic axis"). These strategic directions became the highest level of strategic action,[166] and three such directions were initially established to coordinate the actions of fronts.[167] But with the introduction of nuclear weapons to the Soviet forces in 1954, and perhaps even more important, the subsequent introduction of various long-range delivery systems, the principal operation became "not the Front or even the group of Fronts, but a more contemporary, better, and larger-scale form — the operation in the theater of military actions (teatry voyennykh deystviy or TVD)."[168] The apparent overemphasis of the early 1960s on nuclear weapons and deep strikes provoked something of a backlash in the late 1960s and early 1970s. As a conventional war (or, at least, a longer conventional phase of a war) was again seen as possible, Soviet planners returned to emphasizing "combined arms" military art (strategy, operational art, and tactics). The TVD became potentially important for planning both conventional and nuclear warfare.

As a result of changes in technology and Soviet military thinking, Marshall N. V. Ogarkov emphasized that "previous forms of employing combined units and formations of the different armed services have in large measure ceased to correspond to present day conditions."[169] In the mid-1970s the General Staff Academy began to teach: "The basic form of waging military action will be strategic operations in the TVD, combat action of the *PVO-Strany* [Air Defense Forces], and independent operations of Navy and the Long-Range Air Force [currently Strategic Air Armies]."[170]

Today, the front is defined as:

> an operational-strategic formation of armed forces, usually created on the eve of a war ... to achieve operational-strategic objectives on one strategic or several operational directions of a continental TVD.[171]

In wartime a front would operate in a strategic sector, or axis, within a TVD. Like the TVD, the strategic sector is a flexible, military-geographic division for front operations.[172] A front's first echelon is generally formed from multiservice forces of two MDs. Second and succeeding echelons would be drawn from MDs in the interior of the Soviet Union. A typical European front could contain one or two tank armies, three to four combined arms armies, an air army, fleet elements, and organic nuclear forces at the front, army, fleet, and division levels.[173] There could be three such fronts in the Western TVD: Northern, Central, and Southern, with typical frontages of 200 kilometers (offense) to 400 kilometers (defense) and depths of 400 kilometers.

---

161 SMP 1988, p. 13.
162 Hines and Petersen, *op. cit.*, pp. 100-101.
163 A front is the equivalent of a NATO Army Group (NORTHAG or CENTAG).
164 SVE, "Front," pp. 332-333.
165 N. V. Ogarkov, *Vsegda v gotovnosti k zashchite otechestva*, op.cit., pp. 34-35. Ogarkov's later volume, *Istoriya uchit bditel'nosti* [History Teaches Vigilance] (Moscow: Voyenizdat, 1985), p. 47, says almost the same thing, but it is now the 'representatives of the *Stavka* of the Supreme High Command," rather than the Supreme High Command itself, that oversees the TVD's actions. For a recent discussion of an operation by a group of Fronts, see the article by the former chief of the General Staff's Main Operations Directorate, V. I. Varennikov, "Klassicheskiy primer nastupleniya gruppy frontov" (A Classic Example of an Offensive of a Group of Fronts), *Voyenno-Istoricheskiy Zhurnal*, No. 8, 1987, pp. 12-19.
166 Recall that a Front was the highest level of *operational* action.
167 These were the Northwest, Western, and Southwestern strategic directions, under K. Ye. Voroshilov, S. K. Timoshenko, and S. M. Budennyy, respectively. In 1945, an additional strategic sirection for the Far East was established under A. M. Vasilevskiy. See the discussions in S. M. Shtemenko, *The Soviet General Staff at War: 1941-1945*, Vol. 1 (Moscow: Progress Publishers, 1985), pp. 43, 423.
168 Ogarkov, *Istoriya uchit bditel'nosti, op. cit.*, p. 47. Note that this paragraph is very similar to one that appeared in the 1982 Ogarkov monograph, *Vsegda v gotovnosti k zashchite otechestva, op. cit.*, p. 34. The 1985 work added the phrase, "and groups of Fronts," while the earlier work noted that it would be *strategic* operations that would take place in the TVD.
169 N. V. Ogarkov, "Always in Readiness to Defend the Homeland" (available in translation), 1982, p. 34-35. Three years later, after Ogarkov lost his post as chief of the General Staff and was made commander-in-chief of the Western TVD, he reworked the sentence in a new book, making it even more explicit: "It is customary to view as basic no longer the Frontal operation or even the operation of a group of Fronts, but a more modern, perfected and large-scale form—the operation in a theater of military operations"; Ogarkov, *Isto riya uchit bditel'nosti, op. cit.*, p. 47.
170 V.G. Kulikov, ed., *Akademiya Generalnogo Shtaba, op.cit.*, p. 161.
171 See "Front," in VES, p. 787.
172 Gregory C. Baird, *Soviet Intermediary Strategic C2 Entities—The Historical Experience* (McLean, VA: BDM Corporation, 1979), pp. 31-32; "Strategicheskoe napravlenie," in SOVT.
173 SMP 1988, p. 71; FM 30-102, pp. 13-1 to 13-12.

4
Design and Production

Chapter Four
Design and Production of Nuclear Weapons Systems*

Overview[1]

Nuclear weapons research, development, and production in the Soviet Union is the shared responsibility of party and state organizations (see Figure 4.1):
- the party draws up policy guidelines and monitors their fulfillment;
- the government, through its various ministries, state committees, and commissions, runs the economy and its defense-related industrial activities;
- the Ministry of Defense (MOD), as part of the government, generates requirements for defense industries and is the consumer of their products.

High-level representatives of the party and government, including military personnel, serve on the Defense Council, the highest body advising the Politburo on major defense policy issues (see Chapter Three).

The party sets priorities through the national planning process, allocates resources, and monitors the progress of defense programs. A party secretary has responsibility for defense industrial matters, overseeing the Central Committee's Department of Defense Industry and its subordinates.[2] Government management of the defense industries is centralized in the USSR Council of Ministers. Most of this management is performed by the Council's Military-Industrial Commission (VPK), which coordinates and controls all military-related research, design, development, testing, and production and serves as a primary orchestrator for acquisition and assimilation of foreign technologies. The State Planning Committee (*Gosplan*) serves as the central coordinating body for assigning production goals and allocating raw materials to defense industries. Other key state committees are:
- the State Committee for Science and Technology (GKNT), which plans and implements scientific-technical policy for the entire economy;
- the State Committee for Material-Technical Supply, which distributes supplies to industrial plants; it implements defense priorities by rationing goods in short supply to competing users; and
- the State Committee for Standards, which sets technical specifications and quality standards.

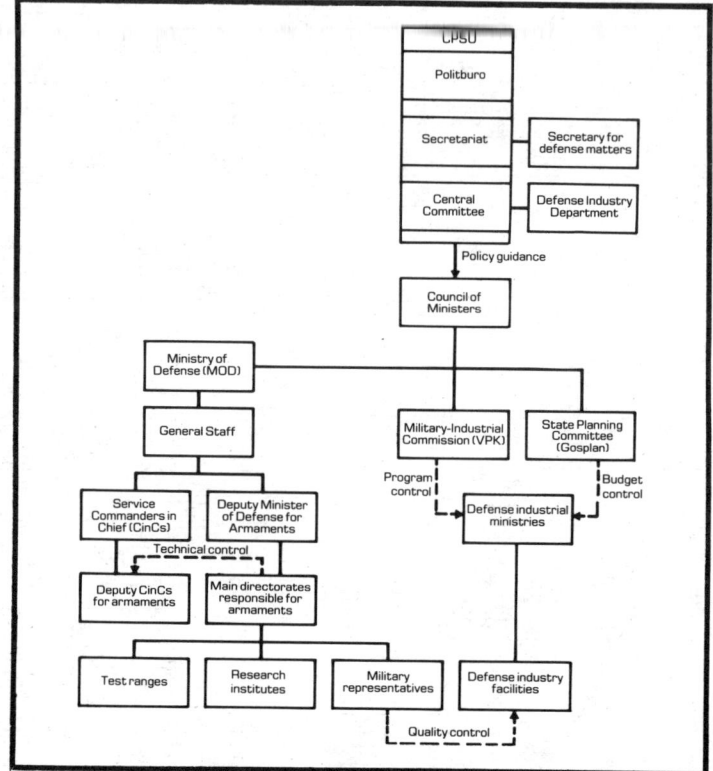

Figure 4.1 Soviet Bureaucracy for Weapons Acquisition.

Research and development is conducted by the Soviet Academies of Sciences, which oversee basic research, higher education institutions undertaking exploratory research, and organizations under the industrial ministries conducting applied research. Each of nine defense industrial ministries—including the Ministry of Medium Machine Building, which is responsible for nuclear weapons and military-related nuclear materials—oversees the work of design bureaus, research facilities, and production plants (See Table 4.1). Various production plants are frequently combined into production associations, which may also include research and experimental facilities. In some cases an intermediate layer of management—a main directorate or all-union in-

---

* Peter Almquist, a research staff member of the Institute for Defense Analyses, Alexandria, Virginia, prepared a major portion of this chapter.
1 The principal source for this overview section is CIA, *Soviet Weapons Industry*, 1986. Three other useful introductions to Soviet military industry and weapons acquisition are John A. McDonnell, "The Soviet Weapons Acquisition Process," in *Soviet Armed Forces Review Annual*, 1979, Vol. 3, pp. 175-203; David Holloway, "The Soviet Union," in Nicole Ball and Milton Leitenberg, eds., *The Structure of the Defense Industry: An International Survey* (New York: St. Martin's, 1983), pp. 50-80; and "The Soviet Union," in Scilla McLean, ed., *How Nuclear Weapons Decisions Are Made* (New York: St. Martin's, 1986), pp. 1-31.
2 The nature and extent of the party's role in supervising the defense industries has varied over time.

4
Soviet Industrial Ministries

Table 4.1
Soviet Industrial Ministries That Support the Military

Ministries with Primary Responsibility to the Military

Ministry	Military Responsibilities	Civilian Responsibilities
Medium Machine Building	Nuclear weapons and high-energy lasers	Civilian nuclear power equipment and nuclear fuel cycle activities
General Machine Building	Liquid- and solid-propellant ballistic missiles, including submarine-launched; SLBM fire-control systems; space launch vehicles, spacecraft, and surface-to-surface cruise missiles	Television sets
Machine Building	Conventional ordnance munitions, fuzing, and solid propellants	Bicycles, refrigerators, electric razors, samovars, and drills
Defense Industry	Conventional ground-force weapons; mobile, solid-propellant ballistic missiles; optical systems, anti-tank guided missiles, tactical SAMS, lasers, and ASW missiles	Fishing equipment, cameras, motorcycles, lasers, and industrial and scientific optical equipment
Shipbuilding Industry	Naval vessels and weaponry, submarine detection systems, naval acoustic systems, and radars	Merchant ships of all types, drilling platforms, and irrigation equipment
Aviation Industry	Aircraft, aerodynamic missiles, spacecraft, AAMs, defensive missiles (tactical and strategic), tactical ASMs, and ASW missiles	Passenger aircraft, cameras, vacuum cleaners, alarm clocks, baby carriages, aluminum kitchen utensils, and snowmobiles
Communications Equipment Industry	Communications equipment, radar components, electronic warfare equipment, military computers, and facsimile equipment	Tape recorders, televisions, intercoms, and facsimile equipment
Electronics Industry	Electronic parts, components, subassemblies, and computers	Consumer radios, television sets, computers, telephone equipment, and lasers
Radio Industry	Radars, communications equipment, special-purpose computers, guidance and control systems, and lasers	Telephone equipment, televisions, radios, tape recorders, and computers

Other Military-Related Ministries

Ministry	Responsibilities
Atomic Power Generation	Operation of civil nuclear power plants
Automotive	Trucks, armored personnel carriers, and heavy equipment transporters
Chemical Industry	Fuels, fiberglass components for rocket motors, and propellants
Civil Aviation	Transport aircraft
Electrical Equipment Industry	Batteries, electrical components, communications equipment, radar components, and biological/chemical warfare detectors
Heavy and Transport Machine Building	Armored vehicles, diesel engines, and generators
Instrument Making, Automation Equipment and Control Systems	Computers and instrumentation control systems
Petroleum Refining and Petrochemical Industry	Tires, rubbers, fuels, and lubricants
Power Machine Building	Generators
Tractor and Agriculture Machine Building	Tanks and tracked vehicles

Source: CIA, *Soviet Weapons Industry*, 1986, pp. viii, 3. The Ministry of Atomic Power Generation (or Nuclear Power) was organized out of the Ministry of Power and Electrification (and other ministries) following the Chernobyl accident.

dustrial association—has direct responsibility for specific functional areas within a ministry.

The MOD exerts considerable influence on the planning and management of the defense industries. As the primary customer, the MOD is involved in all stages of the arms acquisition process, from generating requirements to overseeing the manufacture and acceptance of new weapons. Through the deputy minister of defense for armaments, the MOD wields a vigorous monitoring apparatus. The deputy minister has a number of main armaments directorates that supervise a network of military representatives, who monitor all aspects of the mili-

4

Government Organizations

tary acquisition cycle and ensure that technical specifications and delivery deadlines are met.[3]

Requirements for new or modified weapon systems are formulated by staff organizations of the MOD working in collaboration with the research community. New capabilities are proposed to top echelons of the party and government and, if accepted, are implemented by a joint resolution—a one-time, multiyear commitment by both the party and the government to research, design, test, and produce a weapon. For major new weapons, the Defense Council participates in the decision. The fulfillment of the joint resolution is the responsibility of the appropriate ministry, with constant oversight by MOD representatives. To ensure that weapons development proceeds as efficiently as possible, VPK decrees are apparently given precedence throughout the Soviet industrial sector.[4]

Producing the equipment required by the Soviet military is a massive job. Defense and supporting industries maintain at least 450 military research and development organizations, some 50 major design bureaus, and thousands of weapons production plants (see Figure 4.2).

Government Organizations

Military research, development, and production is conducted primarily by government institutes, design bureaus, test facilities, and production plants. These are organized under various government ministries, with the exception of some basic research institutes that are run by various academies of science. At the highest government level the ministries are overseen by the USSR Council of Ministers. Most of the government's management of the defense industries is performed by the VPK. As noted previously, the VPK serves to coordinate and control all military-related research, design, development, testing, and production of military systems. Gosplan serves as the central coordinating body for assigning production targets and allocating resources to the defense industries.

The Military-Industrial Commission

The Military-Industrial Commission (*Voyenno-promyshlennaya kommissiya*, or VPK) has responsibilities for overseeing and coordinating the defense industrial ministries. Established in 1938,[5] the VPK is made up of representatives of 12 ministries, nine of which have a major role in defense activities. These nine (see Table 4.1) are the Ministries of Defense Industry, Aviation Industry, Shipbuilding Industry, Machine Building, General Machine Building, Medium Machine Building, Electronics Industry, Communications Equipment Industry, and Radio Industry. Those represented on the VPK with a predominantly civilian role are the Ministries of Chemical Industry, Petrochemical Industry, and Electrical Equipment Industry.

The VPK's chief is a deputy chairman of the Council of Ministers.[6] Besides the ministers of the 12 ministries already noted, representatives of *Gosplan*, the party apparatus, the Academy of Sciences, and the MOD are probably involved in its work.[7]

The VPK issues directives to industrial organizations to implement production programs. A proposed program has to be approved by the VPK, which then coordinates the allocation of funds and enforces the allocation of resources. A "VPK Project" is typically given precedence over other projects that might require resources.

A second role of the VPK has become information acquisition and processing. In the early 1970s the decision was reportedly made to emphasize acquiring information and materials from abroad;[8] by the late 1970s and early 1980s the VPK was annually receiving about 3500 requests from its industries, generally for information about foreign military technology. It combines and levies these requests on intelligence collection agencies:[9] the Committee for State Security (KGB), the General Staff's Main Intelligence Directorate (GRU), the State Committee on Science and Technology (GKNT), the State Committee for Foreign Economic Relations (GKES), and the Ministry of Foreign Trade.

The State Planning Committee

The State Planning Committee (*gosudarstvennyy planovyy komitet SSSR*, or *Gosplan*) is responsible for planning, budgeting, and coordinating the economy as a whole, including development of the five-year plan.[10] The military's requirements for weapons production are detailed in a five-year defense plan, which is a subset of the five-year plan for the economy as a whole. This military plan covers such activities as training, logistics, and military assistance and spells out the need for new weaponry and research. Long-term forecasts are incorporated into prospective plans for 15 years or longer.[11]

---

3 These directorates station military officers and civilian technicians at virtually every plant and institute where military items are designed, developed, produced, or delivered (see Box, p. 95). In July 1986, in an attempt to ensure a similar high standard of quality control in the civilian sector, the Soviet leadership created a network of inspectors, subordinate to the USSR State Committee for Standards, to monitor output quality in civilian industries.
4 SMP 1987, p. 108.
5 "O sozdanii voyenno-promyshlennoi komissii pri Komitete Oborony' (On the Formation of the Military Industrial Commission Attached to the Committee of Defense), 31 January 1938, in KPSS o Vooruzhennykh Silakh Sovetskogo Soyuza: Dokumenty 1917-1981 (Moscow: Voyenizdat, 1981), pp. 268-269. Although founded in the late 1930s, the VPK appears to have been reinvigorated in the late 1950s when Ustinov was probably its head.
6 In the late 1950s the VPK chief was probably Ustinov. His successor was L. V. Smirnov (1963-1985), who was replaced by Yuri V. Maslyukov, a former Ministry of Defense Industry official and Gosplan deputy chairman. In 1988, Gorbachev moved Maslyukov from the VPK to head *Gosplan*, continuing the trend of placing key defense industrial officials in critical civilian posts. Maslyukov was replaced as VPK chairman by the former minister of shipbuilding industry, B. S. Belousov.
7 JEC, Allocation of Resources - 1983, Part 9, p. 130; Raymond Garthoff, "SALT and the Soviet Military," Problems of Communism, Vol. XXIV, No. 1, January-February 1975, p. 29.
8 See Henry Eric Firdman, Decision-making in the Soviet Microelectronics Industry (Falls Church, VA: Delphic Associates, 1985).
9 Henri Regnard, "The USSR and Scientific, Technical, and Technological Intelligence," Defense Nationale, December 1983, pp. 107-121, translated in FBIS-SU, pp. U1-U8, 18 January 1984, p. U2. See also Philip Hanson, "Soviet Industrial Espionage: Some New Information," RIIA Discussion Papers No. 1 (London: Royal Institute of Internaional Affairs, 1987); CIA, Soviet Acquisition of Militarily Significant Western Technology: An Update(Washington, DC: GPO, September 1985), p. 6.
10 As a consequence of economic reforms under Gorbachev, Gosplan's responsibility for distribution of material resources in the economy will probably be declining in the future.
11 CIA, Soviet Weapons Industry, 1986, p. 13.

4
State Planning Committee

Figure 4.2 Soviet Design Bureaus and Military Production Facilities.

As a unit, *Gosplan* is supervised by the Central Committee's Department of Planning and Finance Organs, but other Central Committee departments, including the Department of Defense Industry, take an active role in *Gosplan*'s work. Without the approval of the responsible Central Committee department, serious planning decisions cannot be made.[12]

Gosplan has a chairman, as well as several first deputy chairmen and deputy chairmen responsible for overseeing specialized areas within the Central Committee.[13] Since at least 1962, one first deputy chairman has had responsibility for the defense industries.[14] At present, *Gosplan* has three types of departments: summary functional, summary resource, and branch.[15]

The branch departments within *Gosplan* are reportedly organized on the same lines as ministries,[16] which would suggest nine relevant departments overseeing the nine defense-industry ministries (listed in Table 4.1). In fact, branch departments have been identified for instruments, ships and ship-repair, radio, electronics, general machine building, and aircraft.[17] The Summary Department for National Economic Planning for Defense Indus-

---

12 Fyodor I. Kushnirsky, Soviet Economic Planning, 1965-1980 (Boulder, CO: Westview, 1982), p. 83.
13 In February 1988, Yuri D. Maslyukov was made chairman of Gosplan, replacing Nikolai V. Talyzin.
14 Those responsible for defense industries since 1962 have been V. M. Ryabikov (1962-1974), G. A. Titov (1974-1980), L. A. Voronin (1980-1982), Yu. D. Maslyukov (1982-1985), and V. I. Smyslov (from 1985).
15 Kushnirsky, *op. cit.*, p. 55.
16 Jerry Hough and Merle Fainsod, How the Soviet Union is Governed (Cambridge, MA: Harvard University Press, 1979), pp. 390-391. With the Nazi attack on the Soviet Union in 1941, one of the first acts undertaken was the establishment within *Gosplan* of departments for armaments, ammunition, shipbuilding, aviation construction, and tank-building, to parallel the most important defense ministries at the time. See S.A. Tyushkevich, *Sovietskiye Vooruzhennye Sily* (Moscow: Voyenizdat, 1978), pp. 266-267. While the specifics of *Gosplan* organization having certainly changed since the war, this system of parallelling the ministerial structure has apparently continued.
17 CIA, Directory of Soviet Officials of National Organizations (Washington, DC: GPO).

4

Research and Development Organizations

try reportedly exists, supported by the relevant branch departments.[18] The summary functional departments provide aggregation of related branches (for example, the Summary Department of Machine Building coordinates about 20 civilian machine-building departments in *Gosplan*).

Research and Development Organizations

Soviet research and development falls into three organizational categories, depending upon their functions:
- academies of sciences, charged with conducting basic research in the natural and social sciences;
- higher education institutions, subordinate to the Ministry of Higher and Secondary Education, undertaking exploratory research and providing education to all prospective scientists and engineers; and
- research institutes, design bureaus, and test facilities of the industrial ministries, which conduct applied research.

The Soviet Academy of Sciences oversees much of the basic science in the Soviet Union. Much of what results from this oversight feeds into the military system. In addition to the Soviet Academy there are 14 republic academies. Together, the Soviet and republic academies control more than 350 research facilities and 300,000 scientists. Institutes of the academies on occasion perform research tasks for the MOD—for example, research on techniques for measuring the yields of nuclear tests.

Industrial Ministries

There are nine ministries with primary military responsibilities. The ministries oversee the development of some 150 to 200 major weapon systems at any given time. About 150 major plants assemble these weapons. The designers and producers are supported by a network of facilities that extends throughout Soviet academia and industry.

The most important ministry with responsibilities in the area of nuclear weapons is clearly the Ministry of Medium Machine Building. In the production of delivery vehicles, the most important are the Ministries of General Machine Building, Aviation Industry, and Shipbuilding Industry. It should be recognized, however, that each defense industrial ministry is probably involved to some degree in supplying components for nuclear weapons, or in producing material that supports nuclear weapon systems.

Within each ministry, the two basic types of research organizations are the scientific research institutes (*nauchno-issledovatelskiye institut*, or NII) and the design bureaus (*konstruktorskoye byuro*, or KB). The essential difference between the NII and the KB is that the NII is engaged primarily in basic research, rather than in engineering. The NII focus is on theoretical development, rather than on production of a final product.[19] The KBs, on the other hand, emphasize conversion of new principles developed by the NIIs into weapons. Work in the KBs focuses on "draft-design work and work on the manufacture and finishing of prototypes, while experimental-theoretical [work] has secondary significance and relatively less weight than in an NII, and is carried out in so far as it is needed for decisions on this or that draft proposal in the case of the design and manufacture of new equipment."[20]

As is the case in most Soviet industry, defense industrial production is largely concentrated in the more populated and developed areas of the western Soviet Union. Research and development facilities are principally located in Moscow and Leningrad, also the sites of the most prestigious facilities of Soviet higher education and science. "The geographic concentration of the defense industries both reflects and intensifies the firm direction of the Soviet military-industrial complex from the center."[21]

The Ministry of Medium Machine Building

The Ministry of Medium Machine Building (*Obshchesoyuznoye ministerstvo srednogo mashinostroyenlya*, or *Minsredmash*) is responsible for development and production of nuclear weapons and the administration of military-related nuclear programs, including the production of fissionable materials and the fabrication of nuclear devices and warheads. It is also responsible for civilian nuclear power equipment, high-energy lasers, and the production of chemical-biological-radiological protective equipment.[22]

The Minsredmash supervises the entire chain of production for nuclear weapons, from the mining of uranium ore through the fabrication of warheads, and is responsible for the production of all nuclear materials, reactors, and weapons research, development, testing, and production.[23]

---

18 A rare Soviet reference to what appears to be the Summary Department for National Economic Planning for Defense Industry is contained in the obituary of N. P. Marakhovskiy, its apparent chief from 1977 to 1985; *Izvestiya*, 18 October 1985, p. 6. Marakhovskiy worked his way up from being a *Gosplan* sector chief to being the chief of various departments before his promotion in 1977, and he was described as being a "specialist in the area of planning the development of the defense branch of industry" throughout his 31-year career at *Gosplan*. Michael Checinski, extrapolating from his first-hand knowledge of the Polish system, suggests that there is a "mobilization section" within a Military Department, and that "*Gosplan*'s Military Department delegates to the military departments of [military] ministries only that sector of the economic plan dealing exclusively with the projected final and semi-manufactured production that is to be delivered to the military customer"; Michael Checinski, *A Comparison of the Polish and Soviet Armaments Decisionmaking Systems*, (Santa Monica, CA: Rand Corporation, 1981), pp. 52-53.

19 N. D. Tyamshanskiy, *Ekonomika i organizatsiya nauchno-issledovatel'skikh rabot v mashinostroyenii* (Leningrad: Mashinostroitelniye, 1967), p. 17.

20 Tyamshanskiy, *op. cit.*, p. 21.

21 CIA, *Soviet Weapons Industry*, 1986, p. 1.

22 CIA, *Directory of Soviet Officials of National Organizations* (1984); CIA, *Soviet Weapons Industry*, 1986, p. 3; CIA, *Soviet Acquisition, op. cit.*, p. 33; DIA, *Soviet Weapons Acquisition Process, with Special Emphasis on the Ground Forces*, DST-1830S-336-80, (partially declassified and released under FOIA), 12 September 1980, p. 43.

23 Andrew Sheren, "The Structure and Organization of Defense-Related Industries," in US Joint Economic Committee, *Economic Performance and the Military Burden* (Washington, DC: GPO, 1970), p. 130. John McDonnell states flatly that the Minsredmash "handles the mining and refining of uranium and other nuclear fuels, the manufacture of nuclear weapons and reactors for both military and civilian use, and the production of radioisotopes"; John McDonnell, *Soviet Armed Forces Review Annual*, 1978, Vol. 2, p. 95. See also, SMP 1984, p. 44.

4

Research and Development Organizations

The Ministry of General Machine Building

The Ministry of General Machine Building (*Minobshchemash*) is responsible for ballistic missiles and space vehicles, large surface-to-air missiles (SAMs) and cryptographic equipment, and is probably responsible for cruise missiles.[24]

The bulk of the Soviet ballistic missile and space production programs fall within the domain of Minobshchemash, which reportedly has four main administrations: the Main Administration for Ground-based Equipment (such as launch and control facilities), the Main Administration for Rocket Engine Production, the Main Administration for Production of Guidance Systems, and the Main Administration for the Production of Missile Bodies.[25]

The Ministry of Machine Building

In 1968, a new ministry was formed from parts of the Ministry of Defense Industry and named the Ministry of Machine Building (*Minmash*). Its responsibilities are in the areas of conventional munitions, projectiles (including anti-tank missiles), fuzes, solid propellants, anti-submarine weapons, and explosives.[26]

The Ministry of Defense Industry

The Ministry of Defense Industry (*Minoboronprom*, or MOP) is responsible for the design and production of ground-force armament and ammunition (artillery, tanks, vehicles, small arms, fuzes, primers, propellants, explosives, and possibly tactical guided missiles), as well as some civilian products (cameras, optical products, petrochemicals, railroad cars, tractors, and motorcycles).[27]

The Ministry of Shipbuilding Industry

The Ministry of Shipbuilding Industry is responsible for both the military and civilian fleets. In addition to ships, the ministry is also responsible for naval fire-control systems, mines, torpedoes, shipyards, electrical assembly plants, storage tanks, pipes, boilers, barrels, chains, and perhaps large structural assemblies.[28]

The Ministry of Aviation Industry

The Ministry of Aviation Industry (*Minaviaprom*, or MAP) is responsible for aircraft and aircraft components, as well as for air-to-air missiles (AAMs) and air-to-surface missiles (ASMs). It also produces various consumer goods (for example, refrigerators, washers, aluminum kitchenware, medical equipment).[29]

MAP is in many ways prototypical of the defense industrial ministries. It designs and builds aircraft and aerodynamic missiles for all branches of the MOD and the Ministry of Civil Aviation. It supervises a number of research organizations, including the Central Aerodynamic Institute and the Central Scientific Research Institute of Aviation Motor Building. MAP has eight aircraft KBs and seven air-breathing-missile system KBs. These are supported by 16 component and accessory KBs and ten KBs that develop power plants. MAP's test facilities include flight-and static-test capabilities for bombers at Ramenskoye Air Base near Moscow, diversified liquid- and solid-rocket-propellant test stands, rocket sled tracks, and wind tunnels. Reflecting the continuing high priority of its products, MAP's facilities have grown by more than 25 percent during the past decade.[30]

The Communications-Electronics Industries

The Ministry of Radio Industry is responsible for radios and electronics assemblies, television sets and tape recorders, as well as radars and large computers.[31]

The Ministry of Communications Equipment Industry was spun off from the Ministry of Radio Industry in early 1974. It is responsible for electronic systems, radio, televisions, telegraph and telephone equipment, radar, navigation aids, antennae, satellites, and military and space computers.

The Ministry of Electronics Industry is responsible for electronic components and parts (subassemblies, but not final products, which are apparently the domain of the Ministry of Communications Equipment Industry), including solid-state devices and miniature electronic components. Apparently, it is also responsible for at least a portion of the anti-ballisitic missile (ABM) radar development and computer work.[32]

Table 4.2
Soviet Military Design Bureaus

Specialization	Number
Strategic Missiles and Space Boosters	7
Tactical Missiles	9
Aircraft	9
Ships	6
Satellites	6
Tracked Vehicles and Artillery	7
Radars	8
Total	**52**

Source: DOD, FY 1987 RDA, p. II-6. Note that some design bureaus have responsibilities in more than one area.

---

24 CIA, Soviet Acquisition, *op. cit.*, p. 32. Production of cruise missiles could also be the function of the Ministry of Aviation Industry.
25 Michael Agursky, The Research Institute of Machine-Building Technology: A Part of the Soviet Military Industrial Complex, Soviet Institutions Series No. 8 (Jerusalem: Hebrew University of Jerusalem, n.d.), p. 31.
26 DIA, Soviet Weapons Acquisition Process, *op. cit.*, p. 43; CIA, Soviet Acquisition, *op. cit.*, pp. 4, 31.
27 See, for example, CIA, Soviet Acquisition, *op. cit.*, p. 4, 31, in which the Ministry's responsibilities are described as mostly in the areas of armor and electro-optics.
28 DIA, Soviet Weapons Acquisition Process, *op. cit.*, p. 43.
29 Richard D. Ward, "Soviet Practice in Designing and Procuring Military Aircraft," Astronautics and Aeronautics, September 1981, pp. 24-38.
30 SMP 1987, p. 109.
31 CIA, *Directory of Soviet Officials of National Organizations* (1984); CIA, *Soviet Weapons Industry*, 1986, p. 3; CIA, Soviet Acquisition, *op. cit.*, p. 33; DIA, Soviet Weapons Acquisition Process, *op. cit.*, p. 43.
32 See A. Fedoseyev, *Zapadnya: Chelovek i Sotsialism*, 2d ed. (Frankfurt/Main: Posev, 1979); and Firdman, *op. cit.*, p. 15.

4
Design Bureaus

Table 4.3
Principal Missile Design Bureaus

Name[1]	Location	Product
Chelomei[2]	Moscow	ICBMs, SLBMs, cruise missiles
Glushko[3]	Kaliningrad	Rocket engines
Grushin[4]	Moscow/Khimki	SAMs, ABMs
Isayev	Kaliningrad?	Rocket engines
Izotov[5]	Leningrad	Rocket engines
Korolev[6]	Kaliningrad	Space boosters
Lavochkin[7]	Khimki	SAMs, cruise missiles
Lyul'yev	Sverdlovsk	SAMs or cruise missiles?
Makeyev	Chelyabinsk	SLBMs
Nadiradze	Moscow	ICBMs, IRBMs
Pilyugin[8]	Moscow	Guidance systems
Yangel[9]	Dnepropetrovsk	ICBMs

1. Name of founding or leading designer. In some cases, the individual may not head a design bureau but is in charge of a design organization.
2. Vladimir N. Chelomei (17 June 1914–1984).
3. Valentin P. Glushko (20 August 1908-1989).
4. Petr D. Grushin (2 January 1906–?).
5. Izotov is listed in both missile and aircraft engines.
6. Sergei Pavlovich Korolev (1906–1966).
7. Semyon A. Lavochkin.
8. Nikolai A. Pilyugin (5 May 1908–?).
9. Mikhail K. Yangel (?–October 1971).

Design Bureaus

The design of weapon systems takes place mostly in the design bureaus (KBs) of the responsible production ministry.[33] Thus, the Ministry of Aviation Industry is responsible for the design of aircraft to a much greater extent than is the MOD, although the latter has a small number of KBs itself and design work takes place in various military academies.

While the KBs and production facilities are frequently collocated, they have very different functions. As one Soviet writer emphasized, it is necessary to have scientific research organizations separate from the day-to-day concerns of the production enterprise: "The task of the production enterprise is production and the output of products in coordination with the plan, and not scientific-research work."[34]

Soviet military designers have historically been more visible than the basic scientists of the research institutes or the managers responsible for the serial production of the weapons. But for many weapons systems, even identifying the designers is a difficult task.[35]

Missiles

There are three major KBs for intercontinental ballistic missiles (ICBMs) (see Table 4.3). For convenience, these are referred to as the Yangel, Chelomei, and Nadiradze bureaus, after their most important designers.[36] Yangel's bureau, currently headed by V. F. Utkin, is located in Dnepropetrovsk. Chelomei's bureau (the current chief has not been identified) is in Moscow and has been responsible for both ballistic and aerodynamic (cruise) missiles. A. D. Nadiradze's bureau, responsible for solid fueled missiles, is also in Moscow.[37]

While the Chelomei bureau may have been involved with submarine-launched ballistic missiles (SLBMs),[38] the main SLBM bureau is that of V. P. Makeyev, apparently situated in Chelyabinsk.[39]

P. D. Grushin has been involved in missile development for many years, apparently in the area of SAMs and

---

33. According to the DOD, there are 52 major military KBs in the Soviet Union (see Table 4.2 and Figure 4.2).
34. Tyamshanskiy, op. cit., p. 8.
35. While aircraft have the designer's initials in the aircraft's designation (Yakovlev's Yak-series, or Mikoyan and Gureyvich's MiG- series, for example), the designers of other weapons systems are not so apparent; missiles designed by Chelomei or Yangel KBs are not called "Che-1" or "Ya-18."
36. The Korolev bureau (TsKBEM, or Tsentral'noye konstruktorskoye byuro eksperimental'nogo mashinostroyeniya), located in Kaliningrad, north of Moscow, is currently headed by engine designer V. P. Glushko. It is apparently no longer in the missile business, specializing now in rockets for space exploration.
37. There have been conflicting reports about the location of the Nadiradze bureau. Based on what little evidence is available, it seems likely that this bureau is in Moscow. Nadiradze's bureau has also been reported in Biysk, but this is more likely to be the production and test site for its missiles.
38. The submarine association is based in part on the signatures on Chelomei's obituary. The association with aerodynamic missiles is noted in DIA, Estimated Expenditures for Research and Development by the Soviet Ministry of Aviation Industry (MAP), DIA-450-2-6-71-INT, July 1971, p. 185; and Nikita Khrushchev, edited and translated by Strobe Talbott, Khrushchev Remembers: The Last Testament (Boston: Little, Brown, 1974), p. 43.
39. Makeyev died in 1984 and his successor has not been identified. The SLBM association is suggested again by the signatures on Makeyev's obituary. He is also referred to as Mikhail Turetsky, The Introduction of Missile Systems into the Soviet Navy (1945-1962) (Falls Church, VA: Delphic Associates, 1983), p. 21 (where he is referred to as "Nakeyev"), and p. 65 (where he is referred to as 'Makayev').

4
Design Bureaus

Table 4.4
Principal Aircraft and Engine Design Bureaus

Name	Location	Product
Alekseyev[1]	?	Fighters
Antonov[2]	Kiev	Transports
Beriev[3]	Taganrog	Marine aircraft
Bratukhin[4]	?	Helicopters
Dobrynin[5]	?	Engines
Ilyushin[6]	Moscow	Transports, maritime patrol
Isotov[7]	Leningrad	Engines
Kamov[8]	Moscow	Helicopters
Ivchyenko[9]	Zaporozh'ye	Engines
Koliesov[10]	?	Engines
Kuznetsov[11]	Kuybyshev	Engines
Lavochkin[12]	Khimki	Fighters
Lyulka[13]	Moscow	Engines
Mikoyan-Guryevich[14]	Moscow	Fighters, interceptors
Mikulin[15]	?	Engines
Mil'[16]	Moscow	Helicopters
Myasishchyev[17]	Moscow	Bombers
Soloviev[18]	Perm'	Engines
Sukhoi[19]	Moscow	Fighters, interceptors
Tumanskiy[20]	Moscow	Engines
Tupolev[21]	Moscow, Kazan'	Bombers, transports
Yakovlev[22]	Moscow, Kuybyshev	Fighters, bombers, transports

1 Semyon M. Alekseyev, deactivated in 1948.
2 Oleg K. Antonov (7 February 1906–?).
3 Georgii M. Beriev (1902–July 1979).
4 Ivan P. Bratukhin (12 February 1911–?), deactivated in 1951.
5 Vladimir A. Dobrynin (VD).
6 Sergei V. Ilyushin (31 March 1884–9 February 1977).
7 Sergei P. Isotov, listed in both missile and aircraft engines.
8 Nikolai I. Kamov (1902–24 November 1973).
9 Aleksandr G. Ivchyenko (successor Vladimir Lotarev) (AI).
10 Successor to V. A. Dobrynin.
11 Nikolai D. Kuznetsov (NK) (10 June 1911–?).
12 Syemyen A. Lavochkin (11 September 1900–9 June 1960).
13 Arkhip M. Lyulka (AL).
14 Artyem I. Mikoyan (5 August 1905–9 December 1970) Mikhail I. Guryevich (12 January 1893–21 November 1976).
15 Aleksandr A. Mikulin (AM) (1895–?).
16 Mikhail Lentyevich Mil' (22 November 1909–31 January 1970).
17 Vladimir M. Myasishchyev (1902–14 October 1978), deactivated in 1960.
18 P. A. Soloviev.
19 Pavel O. Sukhoi (10 July 1895–September 1975).
20 Sergei K. Tumanskiy.
21 Andrei N. Tupolev (10 September 1888–23 December 1972).
22 Aleksandr S. Yakovlev (19 March 1906–).

ABMs.[40] The KB of S. A. Lavochkin has concentrated on SAMs and cruise missiles.[41] Based on his obituary, it seems that the KB of L. V. Lyul'yev, located in Sverdlovsk, may also have been involved in these fields.

N. A. Pilyugin was one the leading designers of guidance systems for missiles and spacecraft, and V. P. Glushko, A. M. Isayev, and S. P. Izotov headed leading rocket engine KB for many years.

One other individual perhaps worthy of mentioning is V. P. Barmin, a member of the Academy of Sciences and the principal designer of missile and rocket launch facilities.[42]

Aircraft

The KBs of the aircraft industry are much better known than those of other ministries. The designers of Soviet aircraft were considered heroes during the Great Patriotic War, and their names are included in the designation of each aircraft. The design bureaus are listed in Table 4.4.

Ships and Submarines

Ship and submarine KBs and designers are seldom identified, although it seems that the most important are based in Leningrad, the heart of the naval industry. N. N. Isanin is probably chief designer of the Typhoon subma-

---

40 DIA, *Estimated Expenditures for Research and Development, op. cit.*, p. 191.
41 *Ibid.*, p. 201. Lavochkin died in 1960, and the current head of the bureau is not known.
42 Barmin is misidentified by Khrushchev as "Bardin," and by the editor as I. P. Bardin (*Krushchev Remembers, op. cit.*, p. 48), a different member of the Academy. Barmin's recollections of his career are included in an interview with the him, published in *Trud*, 12 April 1987, p. 1.

4
Weapons Systems Production

Table 4.5
Launcher, Tracked Vehicles and Artillery Design Bureaus and Production Facilities

Name[1]	Location	Product
Barrikady Plant	Volgograd	SS-12M, SS-20, SS-23 launcher production
Ivanov	?	Artillery
M. I. Kahnin Machine Building Plant	Sverdlovsk	SSC-X-4 launcher production
Kotin	Leningrad	Armored vehicles
V. I. Lenin Heavy Mathine Building Plant	Petropavlovsk	SS-23 launcher production
Morozov	Khar'kov	Armored vehicles
Petrov	Sverdlovsk	Artillery
Shaposhnik	Minsk	TELs, tracked vehicles

1 Name of founding or leading designer. In some cases, the individual may not head a design bureau but be in charge of a design organization.

Figure 4.3 The four Kiev V/STOL aircraft carriers were built at the 500 acre Nikolayev south shipyard, at the mouth of the Bug River on the Black Sea.

rine, and Z. A. Deribin has also been identified as a submarine designer. The KB affiliations (if any) of these men is unknown. Many shipyards have KBs associated with them (for example, R. Ye. Alekseyev, who died in 1980, was the chief designer at Gor'kiy's Krasnoye Sormovo shipyard for hydrofoils), but few details of their work are known.[43]

Artillery and Tracked Vehicles

The designers of tracked vehicles and artillery are also given some prominence. The most important ones known for the post-war period and continuing in operation through at least the mid-1970s are listed in Table 4.5. As perhaps the leading Soviet artillery designer in the post-war period, Petrov almost certainly was involved in designing artillery for nuclear weapons.[44]

Weapon Systems Production

Since the early 1960s, the Soviets have been forming "production associations," made up of existing production organizations (for example, enterprises, existing associations of enterprises, or research organizations). These associations allow (in theory) closer coordination between various producers of both components and finished products.

In 1970, there were 608 such production associations, and by 1980 there were 4083.[45] By 1984, it was reported that the number had reached more than 4500, and

---

43 Some detail is known about the KBs in the Leningrad area. There are three submarine KBs: TsKB-16 (*Tsentralniy konstruktorskoye byuro*, or Central Design Bureau), TsKB-18, and TsKB-143. There are four surface ship KBs: Nevsky TsKB, Western TsKB, Northern TsKB, and Lyedokol'noye TsKB. Military Unit No. 27177 of the Krylov Naval Academy of Shipbuilding and Armaments designs armaments. The Krylov Central Scientific Institute of Shipbuilding Industry and Leningrad Shipbuilding Institute design ships; Ephraim Suhir, *Soviet Naval Architecture: Theory and Application of Hydrodynamics* (Falls Church, VA: Delphic Associates, 1986), pp. 8, 24.
44 In fact, his obituary was signed by a staff member of the Ministry of Medium Machine Building.
45 I. G. Zhikharevich, et al., *Sovershenstvovabiye organizatsii i upravleniya proizvodstvom v tsvetnoi metallurgii* (Moscow: Metallurgiya, 1984), p. 31.

4
Weapons Systems Production

that these included 18,000 production units and enterprises and more than 575 scientific research and draft-design organizations. Two hundred and fifty of these associations were scientific production associations[46] (*nauchno-proizvodstvennye ob'edineniya*, or NPOs), that is, associations whose lead unit is an NII or KB.[47] As with production associations, the administrative apparatus of the lead unit serves as the administrative apparatus for the association as a whole.[48]

KBs are often collocated with plants responsible for either prototype or series production. In general, however, it appears that once a design has been approved for production, it is farmed out to a plant while the KB begins work on a follow-on system.

Although a number of smaller plants contribute to the defense effort, about 150 major plants or associations produce the bulk of Soviet military equipment (see Table 4.6). These plants are concentrated in a relatively small number of cities. It has also been reported that the Ministry of Medium Machine Building has 47 facilities, although details are unknown.[49]

Missile Production

There are reportedly more than 20 missile production facilities located throughout the Soviet Union, manufacturing various components. Missile production takes place in Krasnoyarsk (SLBMs), Biysk (solid fuel missile engines), Pavlograd Chemical Plant (SS-24 missile engines),[50] Sverdlovsk (SAMs), Zlatoust, Orenburg, Kuybyshev, Leningrad (SAMs), Kiev, Smolensk, Dnepropetrovsk (Dnepropetrovsk Missile Development and Production Center, the largest missile-producing plant in the world—two millions square feet of floor space—where ICBMs designed by the Yangel KB are built), Dubna, Moscow (SAMs and ASMs), Kovrov (SAMs), Kirov (SAMs), Ustinov, and Votkinsk (SS-20, SS-12, SS-23, and SS-25).[51] Others are reportedly located in Gor'kiy, Il'men, Irkutsk, Kalinin, Kazan', Khimki (SAMs), Novosibirsk, Omsk, Plesetsk, Podberesye-Kimli, Riga, Rostov (cruise missiles), Tomsk, Tula (AAMs), Tyumen' (ABMs), and Ufa.[52]

Aircraft Production

There are reportedly two plants producing bombers, at least five plants producing fighter aircraft, seven producing cargo aircraft plants, and five producing helicopters.[53] Aircraft production takes place in Komsomol'sk, Ulan-Ude, Irkutsk, Novosibirsk, Tashkent, Kuybyshev, Saratov, Rostov, Tbilisi, Taganrog, Kiev, Smolensk, Khar'kov, Voronezh, Moscow, Gor'kiy, Ul'yanovsk, Kazan', Arsen'yev, and Zaporozh'ye.

Table 4.6
Soviet Military Production Plants

Missiles and Components	49 plants
Missile systems	(~20)
SAMs	(~5)
Aircraft and Components	37 plants
Bombers	(~2)
Tactical aircraft	(~4+)
Cargo	(~7)
Ground-Force Materiel	24 plants
Tanks	(~4)
Other armored vehicles	(~7)
Artillery	(~2-9)
Helicopters	(~5)
Naval Shipyards	24 yards
Ministry of Medium Machine Building (many of these plants are involved in nuclear weapons production)	47 plants[1]
Total	**181 plants**

1 It is unclear how many are "defense plants."

Sources: JEC, *Allocation of Resources—1981*, Part 7, p. 12; SMP 1984, pp. 95-98; and Phillip Hanson, "Soviet Industrial Espionage: Some New Information," RIIA Discussion Papers No. 1 (London: Royal Institute of International Affairs, 1987), p. 9.

The factory producing the Tupolev Tu-26 (or, by Soviet designation, the Tu-22M) Backfire is located in Kazan' (the S. P. Gorbunov Kazan' Aircraft Production Association). The Tupolev Tu-95 Bear H aircraft are built in Kuybyshev (at the Kuybyshev Aircraft Plant).[54] Series production of another Tupolev bomber, the Blackjack, is also expected to take place in Kazan'. The Myasishchev Mya-4 bomber, developed in the 1950s and now retired, was built in Moscow at the Fili Aircraft Plant No. 23.

The main fighter plants are located at Komsomol'sk (where the Su-27 Flanker is built), Moscow (the MiG-29 Fulcrum), Gor'kiy (MiG-21 Fishbed, MiG-31 Foxhound), Tbilisi (MiG-21 Fishbed, Su-25 Frogfoot, and possibly the MiG-29 Fulcrum), and Irkutsk (MiG-21 Fishbed, MiG-23/27 Flogger).[55] The Su-24 Fencer fighter-bomber may be in production at Komsomol'sk.

---

46. S. Ye. Kamenitser and F. M. Rusinov, eds., *Organizatsiya, planirovaniye, upravleniye deyatel'nost'yu promyshlennykh predpriyatii* (Moscow: Vysshaya Shkola, 1984), p. 13.
47. K. I. Taksir, *Upravleniye promyshlennost'yu SSSR* (Moscow: Vysshaya Shkola, 1985), p. 191.
48. Taksir, op. cit., p. 196.
49. Hanson, op. cit., p. 9.
50. Identified by DOD following an explosion at the plant on 12 May 1988; "Soviet Missile-Motor Plant Shut By Explosion, Pentagon Says," *Washington Post*, 18 May 1988, p. A30.
51. CIA, *Soviet Weapons Industry*, 1986; SMP 1986, p. 112; INF Treaty Memorandum of Understanding for the SS-20, SS-12, SS-23, and SS-25.
52. CIA, *Soviet Weapons Industry*, 1986. Other cities are included in 'Die sowjetische Luftfahrtindustrie (I)," *Oesterreichasche Militaerische Zeitschrift*, No. 6, 1983, pp. 519-528, at p. 526; and Bill Gertz, "Satellite Photos Unearth Radar, Interceptor Sites," *Washington Times*, 10 March 1988, p. 1.
53. SMP 1986, p. 120; CIA, *Soviet Weapons Industry*, 1986; "Die sowjetische Luftfahrtindustrie (I)," op. cit., p. 526.
54. *Soviet Military Power* has given two different locations for production of the Bear H. In SMP 1983, it was reported taking place in Taganrog, presumably at the Dimitrov Airframe Plant. The Kuybyshev reference is contained in the 1986 edition.
55. "Die sowjetische Luftfahrtindustrie (I)," op. cit., p. 526.

4
Nuclear Warhead Production

Figure 4.4 Aerial view of a Kirov class nuclear-powered guided missile cruiser operating in the area east of Bermuda where a Yankee class submarine sank on 6 October 1986.

Naval Production

There are 23 major shipyards in the Soviet Union. The most important are located in Vladivostok, Petropavlovsk-Kamchatskiy, Khabarovsk, Komsomol'sk, Zlatoust, Kerch', Nikolayev, Kaliningrad, Leningrad, Severodvinsk, Kiev, Gor'kiy, and Zelenodol'sk.[56] Five are responsible for submarine production: the Admiralty Yard (No. 194) at Leningrad (SSNs), Krasnoye Sormovo (No. 112) at Gor'kiy (SSGNs), Leninskaya Komsomola (No. 199) at Komsomol'sk (SSBNs), Severodvinsk (No. 402) (SSBNs), and the Sudomekh Yard (No. 196) at Leningrad (SSNs).

Nuclear Warhead Production

Information about current Soviet nuclear weapons design and production is understandably very difficult to obtain. The leading institute for fundamental research on nuclear weapons during the early years of the Soviet weapons program was the Kurchatov Institute of Atomic Energy (*Institut atomnoy energii imeni I. V. Kurchatov*, or IAE) in Moscow.[57] Since the early 1960s research at the IAE has been devoted primarily to civilian nuclear power and general nuclear theory. While nuclear weapons research has been shifted to other facilities, there is still some question as to the extent to which the IAE is involved in weapons activities.[58]

One of the Soviet nuclear weapons research laboratories is probably located at the Kyshtym Complex, or at Kasli nearby. The Sungul Radiological Institute, about 40 kilometers north of the city of Kyshtym, is believed to be a second weapons laboratory.[59] Nuclear weapons research and development facilities are also reportedly located in Sarova, south of Gor'kiy. The Kyshtym Complex is one of the Soviet nuclear materials production sites (see below). Whether Kyshtym was (or is still) the location of Soviet final assembly and disassembly facilities for nuclear warheads, equivalent to the U.S. Pantex plant, is not known. It has also been reported that nuclear weapons design facilities are located in Arzamas, south of Gor'kiy, and at Semipalatinsk, although the latter probably refers to activities at the Kazakh Test Site (see Chapter Ten).

Several warhead research, development, and production facilities have been identified in the Soviet Union; the main ones are located in Novosibirsk (the lo-

---

56 For good discussions of all major Soviet shipyards, see Polmar, *Guide to the Soviet Navy*, 1986, pp. 463-477.
57 See Holloway, *The Soviet Union and the Arms Race*, 1984, pp. 16-20, 144.
58 Sergei Polikanov, *Nuclear Physics in the Soviet Union: Current Status and Future Prospects* (Falls Church, VA: Delphic Associates, 1984); William J. Broad, "Space Arms Projects Ignite Debate on US-Soviet Science Exchanges," *New York Times*, 1 July 1985, p. 1. The IAE developed the first Soviet nuclear weapons under the leadership of Kurchatov.

While the CIA reports that the IAE is subordinate to the civilian State Committee for the Utilization of Atomic Energy, Polikanov states that it is subordinate to, and funded by, both the State Committee and the Ministry of Medium Machine Building; see Polikanov, op. cit., p. 112.

59 The Sungul Radiological Institute was operating at least into the early 1950s. An outer fence almost 7 kilometers by 17 kilometers probably encloses facilities for conducting high explosive experiments, similar to Site 300 at the U.S. Lawrence Livermore National Laboratory.

4
Plutonium Production

tion of the Khimapparat and Khimkonsentrat plants)[60] and Sverdlovsk, with final assembly taking place in Chelyabinsk. Chelyabinsk may be a reference to Chelyabinsk-40, a Soviet reference to the Kyshtym Complex (see discussion below).

Nuclear Weapons Materials Production

Although information in the open literature on Soviet nuclear materials production is quite limited,[61] it is clear that the Soviet Union followed a pattern of nuclear weapons materials production similar to that of the United States. Each began with construction of natural-uranium-fueled, graphite-moderated thermal reactors for plutonium production and development of gaseous diffusion technology for the enrichment of uranium. Today the Soviet Union and the United States both rely on production reactors for plutonium and tritium, and on gaseous diffusion plants for uranium enrichment.

Plutonium Production

According to the U.S. Department of Energy, "the Soviet Union has a plutonium equivalent production capability, both plutonium and tritium dedicated to military needs, that is ... substantially larger than our own."[62] In addition, the Soviets, like the United States, " 'mine' the nuclear materials from retired weapons for later use."[63]

Soviet plutonium production for weapons takes place at at least four sites: the Kyshtym Complex, located about 15 km east of the city of Kyshtym on the east side of the Urals in Chelyabinsk Province; Dodonovo, on the Yenisey River just northeast of Krasnoyarsk in Siberia; the "Siberian plant," reported to be located near Troitsk or Tomsk;[64] and Beloyarskiy, near Sverdlovsk just north of Kyshtym (see Figure 4.5). Kyshtym and Dodonovo are believed to be sites of dedicated plutonium production reactors. The Siberian Plant and Beloyarskiy are dual purpose reactors used for the production of plutonium and electricity. Nothing further is known about the Dodonovo facility other than that it is probably the site of Soviet tritium production.[65]

The Kyshtym Complex. The Kyshtym Complex was reportedly constructed during the 1945-1948 period, using approximately 70,000 inmates of 12 labor camps. At least in the 1950s, the complex covered a restricted area approximately 60 kilometers north-south and 45 kilometers east-west.[66] Referred to by the Soviets as Chelyabinsk-40,[67] it is similar to, and probably fashioned after, the U.S. Hanford Reservation.

The first Soviet plutonium production reactor, constructed at Kyshtym, was referred to by the Soviets as Unit 0 (*Nulevoy Ob'yekt*).[68] This graphite-moderated, natural-uranium-fueled (aluminum-clad or aluminum-alloy) reactor[69] was loaded with all the uranium then available in the country. It achieved criticality on 10 June 1948,[70] and its plutonium was used for the first Soviet atomic bomb exploded in August 1949.[71]

The Kyshtym Complex is located among many large lakes in the upper Techa River drainage and contains numerous smaller lakes with interconnecting watercourses. Unit 0 was cooled using water from Lake Kyzyltash, which was discharged to a large artificial lake or holding pond dug in the northeastern part of the industrial zone of the Kyshtym Complex.[72] Both lakes discharged into the Techa River. In 1950, based on "scanty evidence," the CIA believed that the "Soviets probably had two 250 megawatt graphite-moderated production piles in operation since late 1948."[73] This estimate now appears doubtful, given that the first Siberian reactor, which went on line in 1958, was only 286 megawatts-thermal (Mw$_t$).[74] By 1952 there were thought to be three graphite-moderated production reactors, discharging into the same artificial lake.[75]

All Soviet production reactors are believed to be still in operation. A thermal plume, visible at the southeast

---

60 Avraham Shifrin, *The First Guidebook to Prisons and Concentration Camps of the Soviet Union* (New York: Bantam, 1982).
61 Information in the open literature on Soviet nuclear materials production is primarily confined to the early historical development of technologies for plutonium, highly enriched uranium and heavy-water production, and current nuclear power reactors, uranium deposits, and processing centers. Information in the open literature on the production of the thermonuclear materials, tritium, and lithium is virtually non-existent.
62 HASC, FY 1984 DOE, p. 23. Since this reference is to production *capability*, this quote may be referring to the fact that the Soviets have the capability to produce weapons plutonium at their graphite power reactors, without regard to whether this source is actually used for weapons plutonium.
63 HASC, FY 1984 DOD, Part 2, p. 132.
64 Diane M. Soran and Danny B. Stillman, "An Analysis of the Alleged Kyshtym Disaster," Los Alamos National Laboratory (LANL), LA-9217-MS, January 1982. The city of Kyshtym is located on the railroad linking the industrial cities of Chelyabinsk and Sverdlovsk. The area has a long history of munitions production, dating back to the time of the tsars. Kyshtym (known as Chelyabinsk-40) has been identified by DIA as one of several reactor locations that do not appear on published lists of nuclear electric power reactors; Robert C. Hardzog, FOIA officer, DIA, 13 February 1986 Letter to Thomas B. Cochran. Responding to a request to identify the "locations of all nuclear reactors in the Soviet Union *exclusive* of those reactors believed to be smaller than 100 Mw (thermal) and those reactors listed as nuclear (electric) power reactors in *Nuclear News*, February 1985, pp. 91-92," the DIA listed eight locations: Azerbaijan, Gor'kiy, Kharkov, Kyshtym, Minsk, Volgodonsk, Volgograd, Voronezh. The six locations, other than Kyshtym and Azerbaijan, are sites of reactors known to be under construction and/or used solely, or in part, for district heating. Azerbaijan is believed to be a new power station in the very early stages of construction; see *Elekstricheskie Stantsii*, No. 9, 1985, p. 74. Kyshtym, however, does not appear as the location of a nuclear power station in the CIA's *USSR Energy Atlas*; see CIA, *USSR Energy Atlas*, January 1985, pp. 52-53. 56-57, 68-78.
65 Private communications with the authors.
66 G.F. Wilson, CIA, enclosure 14 attached to 11 November 1977 reply to FOIA request by Richard B. Pollock for information relating to a nuclear disaster alleged to have occurred in the Ural Mountains in the Soviet Union in 1958.
67 Soran and Stillman, *op. cit.*, pp. 1, 3.
68 At the beginning of 1946, Kurchatov invited Nikolai Dollezhal' to participate as chief designer of the first "industrial" reactor (as it is known in Soviet literature) for the production of plutonium. *Pravda*, 12 November 1984; *Bol'shaya Sovetskaya Entsiklopediya, Ezhegodnik*, 1963, p. 577; *Moskva, Entsiklopediya*, Moscow: 1980, p. 242; all cited by Julian Cooper, lecturer in Soviet technology and industry, University of Birmingham, 10 July 1986 letter to Thomas B. Cochran.
69 Soran and Stillman, *op. cit.*, pp. 7-8; John R. Trabalka, L. Dean Eyman, and Stanley I. Auerbach, "Analysis of the 1957-58 Soviet Nuclear Accident," Oak Ridge National Laboratory, ORNL-5613, December 1979, p. 23.
70 I. F. Zhezherun, *Stroitel'stvo i pusk pervogo v Sovetskom Soyuze atomnogo reaktora* (Moscow: Atomizdat, 1978), p. 133, as cited by Holloway, *The Soviet Union and the Arms Race*, 1984, p. 26.
71 For his contribution, Dollezhal' was made a Hero of Socialist Labor and received a Stalin Prize. In 1953 Academician Dollezhal' became director of the Scientific Research and Design Institute of Power Technology (NIKIET) in Moscow; Cooper, 10 July 1986 letter to Thomas B. Cochran, *op. cit.*
72 Soran and Stillman, *op. cit.*, p. 8.
73 CIA, Joint Atomic Energy Intelligence Committee, *Status of the Soviet Atomic Energy Program*, CIA/SCI-2/50, 4 July 1950, pp. 1-2 and p. 2 of accompanying "Facts and Discussion." In the late 1940s and early 1950s, U.S. intelligence estimates of the size of the Soviet nuclear weapons stockpile were based on estimates of the cumulative production of fissile material. The first U.S. production reactors, located at Hanford, were 250 megawatts-thermal (Mw$_t$) graphite-moderated reactors. Thus, this CIA estimate of Soviet production may have been based on the assumption that Soviet development paralleled the U.S. program, with no additional information on the Soviet design.
74 Cooper, 10 July 1986 letter to Thomas B. Cochran, *op. cit.*
75 The three reactors were referred to as Units 0, 301, and 701; Soran and Stillman, op. cit., pp. 7-8.

4
Plutonium Production

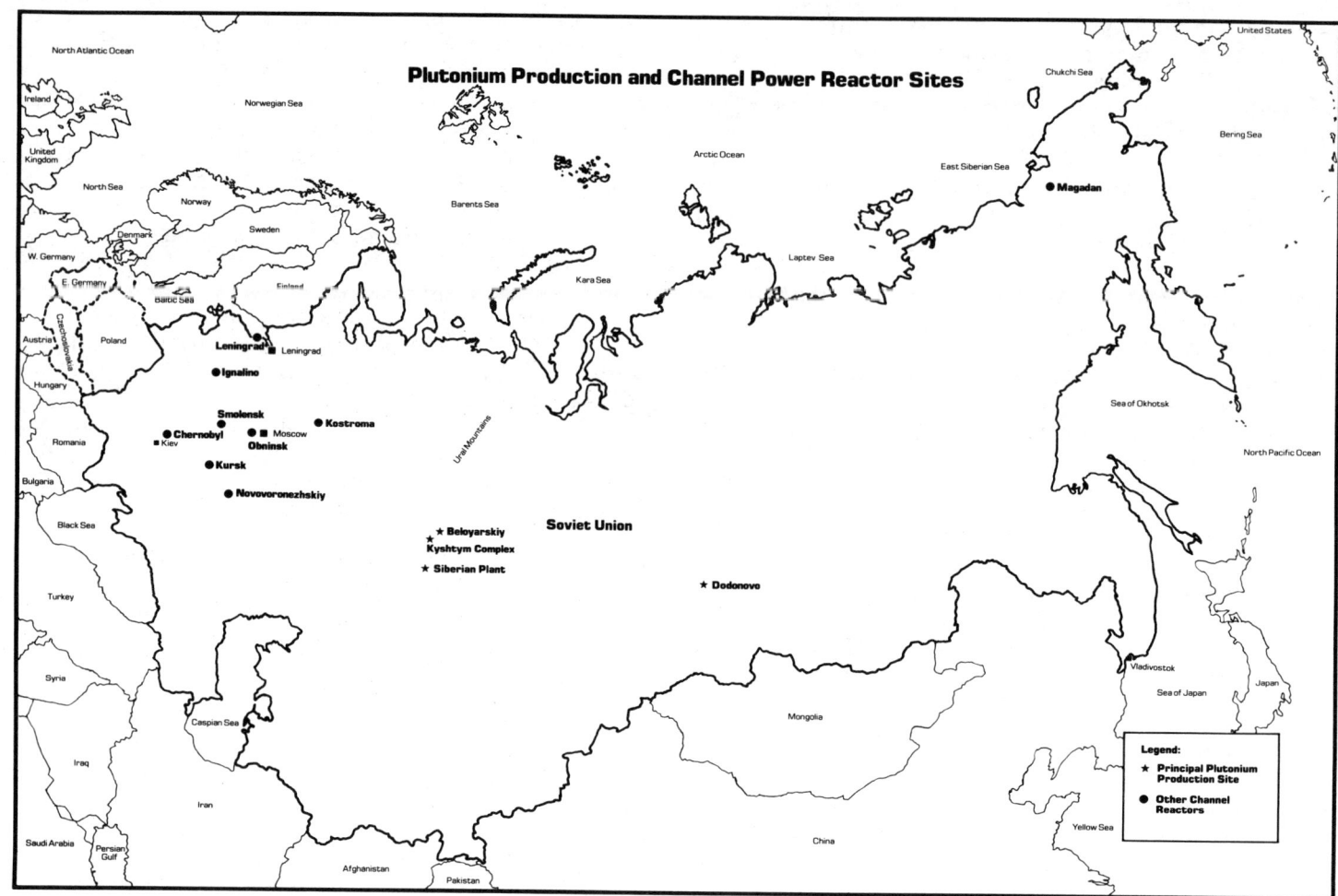

Figure 4.5 Plutonium Production and Channel Power Reactor Sites.

side of Lake Kysyltash in recent Landsat photographs, indicates Kyshtym is still an active production site.

Kyshtym is the site not only of several plutonium production reactors, but also the location for the fuel-reprocessing facilities, used to chemically separate the plutonium from the highly radioactive fission products contained in the irradiated reactor fuel elements, and for facilities for storage of the high-level radioactive waste.[76]

Kyshtym was the site of a major nuclear accident which occurred sometime between 1956 and 1961, most likely in the winter of 1957-1958. The so-called Kyshtym Disaster has been the subject of considerable analysis and speculation.[77] While the precise cause of the accident is not known, it appears to have involved the atmospheric release of reprocessed fission product wastes (cooling time: approximately one to two years).[78] The accident contaminated a large area of some 100 to 1000 square kilometers, with an estimated one million curies of strontium-90 (reference nuclide). The accident resulted in the evacuation and/or resettlement of thousands of people in the area, and in the isolation of Lake Kyzyltash through the construction of a canal and

---

[76] The Soviets appear to have relied upon the sodium uranyl acetate precipitation process for fuel reprocessing in early years and may have continued to use it into the 1960s; Trabalka, et al., op. cit., p. 24.

[77] The first (and most comprehensive) published reports of a Soviet nuclear accident are attributable to Zhores Aleksandrovich Medvedev, *New Scientist*, 1976, p. 264; 1977, p. 761; 1977, p. 352 (see also, *New Scientist*, 1976, p. 692; and *Nuclear Disaster in the Urals* [New York: W.W. Norton, 1979] [paperback edition, New York: Vintage Books, 1980]). The most comprehensive analyses of the Kyshtym Disaster are by Trabalka, et al., op. cit.; John R. Trabalka, L. Dean Eyman, Stanley I. Auerbach, "Analysis of the 1957-1958 Soviet Nuclear Accident," *Science*, 18 July 1980, pp. 345-352; Soran and Stillman, op. cit.; W. Stratton, D. Stillman, S. Barr, and H. Agnew, "Are Portions of the Urals Really Contaminated," *Science*, 26 October 1979, pp. 423-425; and Frank L. Parker, "Search of the Russian Scientific Literature for the Descriptions of the Medical Consequences of the Kyshtym 'Accident,'" Vanderbilt University, Battelle Project Management Division, ONWI-424, March 1983. Additional references are cited in the above documents.

[78] Six possible events within two major categories have been postulated to explain the incident: detonation of a nuclear explosive (weapon test, weapon production accident, or applications for peaceful purposes) and incidents involving aspects of plutonium production technology (reactors, chemical separation plants, and high-level radioactive waste storage sites); Trabalka, et al., ORNL, op. cit., pp. 22-23. According to Parker, op. cit., the best supposition is that there were many releases of waste to the river system over time, plus an explosion in the fuel processing plant. Contrary views also have been advanced by Soran and Stillman, op. cit., who argue that the contamination was not catastrophic but was probably caused by a series of minor incidents and was severely compounded by a history of sloppy practices associated with the complex and a blatant disregard for the people and their surroundings. The work of Soran and Stillman has been criticized by J. R. Trabalka, S. I. Averbach, and L. D. Eyman, "Technical Note: 1957-1958 Soviet Nuclear Accident in the Urals," *Nuclear Safety*, January 1980, pp. 94-99; and S. White and C. Joyce, "Urals Disaster: Explosion or Just Pollution," *New Scientist*, 22 April 1982, p. 200.

4
Plutonium Production

reservoir system, on the Techa River just east of Lake Kyzyltash, to reduce hydrologic transport of radioactive materials down the river.[79]

Photographs of the Kyshtym area were taken by the French SPOT (Satellite Pour l'Observation de la Terre) satellite in 1987. A new reactor complex is clearly shown on the northwestern edge of the artificial lake constructed on the Techa River, immediately downstream from Lake Kyzyltash (see Figure 4.6). There are reportedly two production reactors at this site; however, the SPOT photographic resolution (20 m) is insufficient to confirm this number. No other reactor sites are discernible in the SPOT images, including along the south shore of Lake Kyzyltash where the thermal plume is visible in Landsat photographs and where Soran and Stillman placed the Kyshtym Complex in the 1950s.[80] The reactor complex shown in the recent SPOT photographs does not appear in U. S. Landsat photos taken prior to 1977—evidence that it is a new facility.[81]

The Siberian Plant. By 1958 the Soviet Union had completed construction of its first graphite-moderated channel-reactor, known as the "Siberian plant".[82] While its location was said by Soviets to be in Siberia, Western sources claim that it is at Troitsk, 120 kilometers south of Chelyabinsk in the region of the Urals near the Kazakh border. A more likely location is near Tomsk. In 1964 it was reported that the station had exceeded its design capacity of 600 megawatts-electric (Mw_e), and in 1979 it was reported that "the capacity of this nuclear power station considerably exceeds 600,000 Kw [kilowatts]."[83] Western sources always describe it as now consisting of six 100 w_e units, and this appears to have been the original intention. But according to Aleksandrov, the second unit was 200 Mw_e.[84] Subsequent units were probably even larger, and the power output of all units was probably increased significantly over time.[85]

There can be little doubt that the primary function of the Siberian power station is the production of plutonium for weapons. Writing in 1964, Dollezhal', the chief designer of graphite reactors, revealingly described the Siberian plant as a huge "industrial" atomic power station.[86] In 1976, then chairman of the State Committee for the Utilization of Atomic Energy, Dollezhal', wrote: "The Siberian nuclear power station is a classic example of the use of waste heat in the production of plutonium for the generation of electric power. The principal expenses of this nuclear power station are covered by the cost of the plutonium produced."[87] According to *Nuclear News*, the Siberian power station is operated by the Ministry of Medium Machine Building, not by the Ministry of Power and Electrification.[88] Also, its output is often omitted from figures of total nuclear electric capacity in the Soviet Union. The omission of the Siberian plant from the CIA *USSR Energy Atlas*[89] gives further weight to the proposition that this is one of the principal plutonium production reactor locations in the Soviet Union.

Beloyarskiy. Beloyarskiy is the site of two graphite-moderated, channel reactors which began operations in 1964 and 1967, respectively. These reactors are reportedly used periodically to fulfill shortfalls in plutonium production[90] (see discussion below).

Power Reactor Capacity Available for Plutonium Production

Beyond the Siberian plant and the Beloyarskiy reactors, it is not known to what extent the Soviet Union actually utilizes its power reactors (listed in Table 4.7) as a source of nuclear materials for weapons. According to the U.S. DOD, there is a "large uncertainty associated with production quantities."[91] The Soviets, according to the U.S. Department of Energy, "also have a commercial reactor program that is easily adaptable to plutonium surge capability; as a result the Soviet Union would not be constrained by special nuclear material supply, should they decide to expand rapidly their nuclear weapon stockpile."[92] The Ministry of Medium Machine Building, which manages the research, development, and production of nuclear weapons, also appears to have administrative responsibility for all aspects of the fuel cycle of commercial power reactors, with the exception of the power reactors themselves. Power reactors were under the control of the Ministry of Power and Electrification until shortly after the Chernobyl accident, when management of nuclear power stations was consolidated under the newly created Ministry of Atomic Power Generation.[93] Thus, the Ministry of Medium Machine Building apparently controls the uranium mining, fuel fabrication, and spent-fuel processing and can readily di-

---

79 Trabalka, et al., ORNL, *op. cit.*, pp. 18-21.
80 Soran and Stillman, *op. cit.*, p. 9.
81 Mikael Stern, Space Media Network, private communication with the authors, 7 June 1988.
82 In September 1958, a brief announcement in *Pravda* revealed that the first stage of a second atomic power station (following the 5 megawatts-electric (Mw_e) experimental installation at Obninsk) had entered service, and that its eventual capacity would reach 600 Mw_e. A film of the new station was shown to delegates at the Second Geneva Conference on the Peaceful Uses of Atomic Energy, then in session, and it was disclosed that its location was in Siberia.
83 A. M. Petrosy'ants, *Problems of Nuclear Science and Technology*, 4th ed., translated from the Russian by W. E. Jones (Oxford: Pergamon Press, 1981), p. 103.
84 *Kommunist*, No. 1, 1976, p. 65. Academician Anatolii Aleksandrov was director of the Kurchatov Institute of Atomic Energy from 1960 to 1987 and President of the Academy of Sciences, USSR from 1975 to 1987.
85 By comparison, in the U.S. program at Hanford the first four graphite reactors, B, D, F, and DR, which began operating between 1944 and 1950, had a design power level of 250 Mw_t; the next two, H and C, which came on line in 1948 and 1951, had design power levels of 400 and 600 Mw_t, respectively; and the last two, KE and KW, were initially rated at 1850 Mw_t at startup in 1952 and 1953. By 1964 the rating of these eight reactors had been increased to between 2090 and 4400 Mw_t; see *Nuclear Weapons Databook*, Vol. II, p. 61.
86 As found in *Sovetskaya Rossiya*, 26 June 1964, cited by Cooper 10 July 1986 letter to Dr. Thomas B. Cochran, *op. cit.*
87 A. M. Petrosy'ants, *op. cit.*, p. 103. A. Klimov was probably referring to the Siberian plant when he wrote that "in modern reactors producing conditioned plutonium for military purposes it is justifiable to obtain some amount of electric power so that it could reduce the cost of plutonium," A. Klimov, *Nuclear Physics and Nuclear Reactors*, English-language edition (Moscow: MIR Publishers, 1975), pp. 339-340. On the basis of this, Kramish concluded that "the prevailing concept in the Soviet Union has been, and continues to be, that civilian power subsidizes plutonium and thus military power. . ."; Arnold Kramish, "America's Plutonium Predicament," *Strategic Review*, Summer 1982, p. 50.
88 *Nuclear News*, February 1988, p. 80.
89 CIA, *USSR Energy Atlas*, January 1985, pp. 52-53, 56-57, 68-78.
90 Private communications with the authors.
91 SASC, FY 1984 DOE, p. 39.
92 HASC, FY 1984 DOE, p. 23.
93 According to SMP 1984, p. 44, "the ministry controlling nuclear weapons development and production [the Ministry of Medium Machine Building] is in charge of all nuclear materials, reactors, and weapons research and development as well as production."

4
Plutonium Production

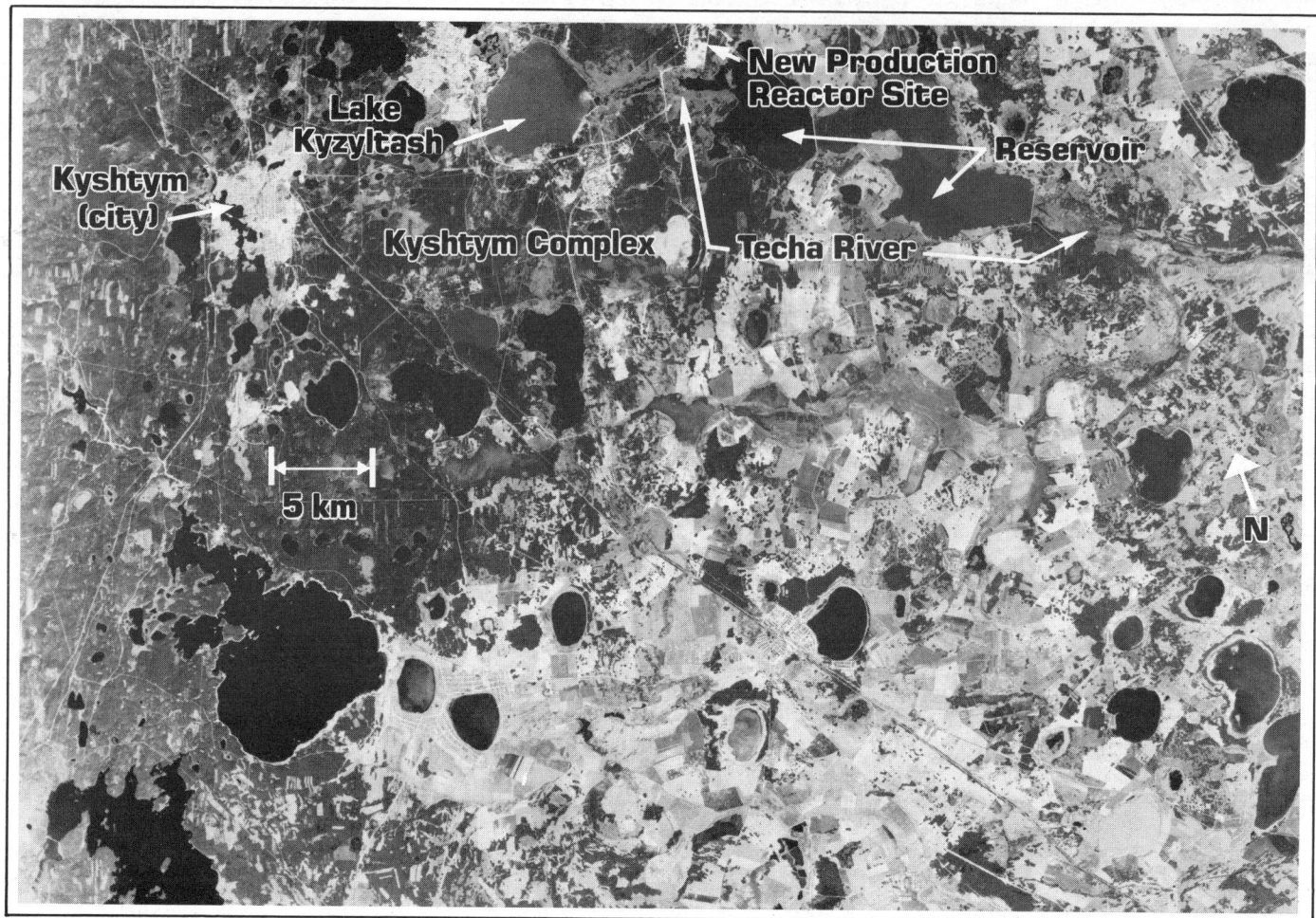

Figure 4.6—Photo 1 This SPOT satellite photograph shows the Kyshtym complex lying approximately 15 kilometers east of the city of Kyshtym on the south and west shore of Lake Kyzyltash. It is here (on the south shore) that the Soviet Union chose to build their first plutonium production reactor in the late 1940s. In the winter of 1957-1958 a huge accidental release of radioactivity occurred at the site leading to the permanent evacuation of many villages north of the site and the construction of a canal and reservoir system along the Techa river downstream from Lake Kyzyltash.

rect which commercial reactors are to be used to supply weapons plutonium. As noted by DOD: "Since the ministry controls virtually all facilities related to the nuclear industry, reactor utilization can be unilaterally altered to satisfy military requirements, regardless of the military or commercial nature of the particular reactor facility."[94]

In the early 1950s, Soviet nuclear power planning focused on the development of the so-called "channel-type" power-and-plutonium production reactors.[95] These light-water-cooled, graphite-moderated thermal reactors offer two important advantages over other reactor types for plutonium production. They are designed for on-line refueling, that is, they can be refueled without shutting down the reactor. This is particularly advantageous in the production of weapon-grade plutonium because frequent refueling is necessary to limit fuel burn-up, which in turn minimizes the buildup of Pu-240 and other undesirable isotopes. These reactors also have a relatively high conversion ratio (the ratio of plutonium produced to uranium fissioned), making them more efficient in the production of plutonium.

The channel-type reactors, according to DOD, "appear to be dual purpose reactors, civilian power reactors that provide power for the civilian grid, but also manufacture plutonium. They are on line refueled. It is just very difficult to monitor or measure what the output

---

[94] SMP 1984, p. 44.
[95] The first Soviet nuclear power reactor, at Obninsk, was reportedly designed by Kurchatov, who directed the Soviet atomic bomb project and the construction of the military production reactors at Kyshtym, which were similar in design.

4
Plutonium Production

Photo 2 This enlargement of the western shore of the first reservoir on the Techa river downstream from Lake Kyzyltash shows a site of several new production reactors. The jetty into the reservoir is assumed to be used to separate the cooling water intake and outfall lines. The canal system around the north shore of the reservoir is clearly seen. A railroad line and high voltage power lines pass through the site. LANDSAT photos indicate that site construction began sometime after 1977. The lack of a thermal plume suggests these reactors are not yet operating.

Photo 3 This enlargement of the southern shore of Lake Kyzyltash is believed to be the location of the first Soviet plutonium production reactors. LANDSAT photographs reportedly indicate thermal discharges into the lake which suggests that production reactors are still operating in the area.
Photos 1-3 Copyright © Space Media Network/CNES SPOT Satellite Image

is."[96] Finally, it is perhaps noteworthy that the Soviet Union has chosen not to export its channel-reactor technology, but does export its VVER reactors.[97] VVERs are pressurized water reactors (PWRs) similar to the U.S. PWRs and are designed for high fuel burn-up and off-line refueling.

The development of graphite-moderated, channel-type power reactors occurred in two stages. The first stage began with the commissioning of the world's first nuclear power plant at Obninsk in 1954. This was the prototype for the six-unit Siberian nuclear power plant reportedly located at Troitsk, the first and second units at Beloyarskiy, and a small four-unit station at Bilibino.

The second stage of development of channel-type reactors in the Soviet Union was the high-power boiling-water reactor (designated RBMK-1000 for "large-capacity boiling-water reactor"), also referred to as a channel-reactor. Plants of this type were placed in operation at Le-

---

96 SASC, FY 1984 DOE, p. 39.
97 This is indicative of a Soviet concern for the proliferation potential of the channel-type reactors.

Table 4.7
Soviet Nuclear Power and Plutonium Production Reactors

Name of Station (by type)	Location (nearby town)	Reactor Type	Operating End-1988	Under Construction	Mw$_t$	Unit Power Mw$_e$ (gross/net)	Date of First Commercial Operation/ Full Power (month/year)
PRODUCTION REACTORS							
Kyshtym Complex	Kyshtym, Urals	LGR	?	2?	?	?6-48 / ?	
Siberian[2]	Troitsk, or Tomsk	LGR	6		286+	100+/200+	9-58 /; /12-59; /12-60; /12-61; /12-62; /12-63
Dodonovo	Dodonovo, East Siberia	LGR	?	?			
Beloyarskiy[3]	Beloyarskiy, Sverdlovsk[4]	LGR	2		293;517	108/102; 194/175	4-64 / 9-67; 12-67/12-69
POWER REACTORS[5]							
APS-1 Obninsk	Obninsk, Kaluga	LGR	1		30	5/	6-54/
Magadan[6]	Bilibino, Magadan, Siberia[7]	LGR	4		62	12/11	1-74/; 12-74/; 12-76/; 12-76/
Leningrad[8]	Sosnovyy Bor	RBMK	4		3200	1000/960	12-73/; 7-75/; 1-76;12-79/ 6-80; 2-81/ 8-81
Kursk', RSFSR[9]	Kursk', RSFSR	RBMK	4	1	3200	1000/960	12-76/10-77; 1-79/ 8-79; 10-83/ 3-84; 12-85/ -94/
Chernobyl	Pripyat, Ukraine	RBMK	3[10]	2	200	1000/960	9-77/ 6-81; 12-78/12-81; 6-82;; 12-83/; -91/; -92/
Smolensk	Desnogorsk, RSFSR	RBMK	3	1	3200	1000/960	12-82/ 7-83; -84/ 5-85; -87/; -90/
Ignalino	Ignalina, Lithuania[11]	RBMK	2		4800	1500/1440	12-83/12-84; -87/
Kostroma	Buy, RSFSR	RBMK	1		4800	1500/1440	12-88/; -89/
Novovoronezhskiy	Novovoronezhskiy, RSFSR		5		760; 1320; 1375x2; 3200	210/196;[12] 365/338; 365/338; 1000/920	9-64/12-64; 12-69/ 4-70; 12-71/6-72; 12-72/ 4-73; 5-80/ 2-81
Kola	Polyannyye Zori, Murmansk	VVER	4		1375	440/420	6-73/12-73; 12-74/ 2-75; 3-81/12-82; 11-84/
Armenian	Oktemberyan, Armenia[13]	VVER	2		1375	440/407.5[14]	12-76/10-77; 1-80/ 5-80
Rovno	Kuznetsovsk, W. Ukraine[15]	VVER	3	1	1375x2; 3200	440/420x2; 1000/960	12-80/ 6-82; 12-81/12-82; 12-86/; -90/
Nikolaev[16]	Konstantinovka, S. Ukraine	VVER	3	1	3200	1000/960	12-82/ 6-84; 12-84/; -87/; -89/
Kalinin	Udomlya, Volga	VVER	2		3200	1000/960	12-84/; 12-86/
Zaporozh'ye	Energodar, Ukraine	VVER	2		3200	1000/960	5-84/11-84; 6-85/12-86; -87/; 12-87/; -87/
Khme'nitskiy[17]	Slavuta, W. Ukraine[18]	VVER	2	1	3200	1000/960	12-87/; -88/; -90/
Balakovo	Balakovo, Saratov	VVER	1		3200	1000/960	6-86/; 10-87/; -90/
Aktask[19]	Kerch, Crimean Penin.[20]	VVER	2	1	3200	1000/960	-87/; 12-87/
Tatar	Koma	VVER		1	3200	1000/960	-89/
Nizhnekamsk[21]	Nizhnekamsk, Bashkir[22]	VVER		1	3200	1000/960	-88/; -89/
Rostov	Rostov-na-Donu[23]	VVER		3	3200	1000/960	-88/; -89/; -90/; -91/
OTHERS							
VK-50 Melekess	Dimitrovgrad, RSFSR	BWR	1		250	62/50	1-66/
BOR-60	Dimitrovgrad, RSFSR	LMFBR	1		60	12/11	2-70/
BN-350	Shevchenko, Kazakh[24]	LMFBR	1		1000	350[23]/	7-73/
BN-600	Beloyarskiy, Sverdlovsk	LMFBR	1		1470	600/570	4-80/12-81

Location	Type	Units	Capacity (MW)	
Odessa, Ukraine[26]	ATET(VVER)[27]	1?		1000/960-89/canceled
Minsk, Belorussiya	ATET	2	3200	1000/960
Gor'kiy, RSFSR	AST	2	500x2	— ?
Voronezh	AST	2	500x2	— ?

1. Dates in the future are subject to slippage or cancellation.
2. The Siberian Nuclear Power Station (NPS) reportedly had a total capacity of 100 MW$_e$ in 1958. In 1976 it was stated that its capacity "significantly exceeds 600 MW$_e$." It is not clear how many reactors the station has, what the designations of these are, nor where the station is located. The station nowadays is often omitted from figures of total capacity in the USSR; Kelly, et al., op. cit., p. 52.
3. Its formal name is the I. V. Kurchatov Nuclear Station.
4. Zarechnyy is also given as the location.
5. The dual purpose Siberian and Beloyarskiy reactors listed under "Production Reactors" are also power reactors.
6. Also referred to as Bilibino.
7. Chukotka is also given as the location.
8. Its formal name is the I. V. Lenin Nuclear Power Station.
9. Kurchatov is also given as the location.
10. The Chernobyl Unit-4 was destroyed in an accident on 26 April 1986. Unit-3, although apparently undamaged, was shut down for several months due to its proximity to Unit-4.
11. Insolianska and Snieckus are also given as the location.
12. This capacity reportedly was raised from 210 MW$_e$ (net)/196 MW$_e$ (gross) in February 1965, and—briefly—to 280 MW$_e$ (gross) in January 1969; Kelly, et al., op. cit.
13. Metsamor is also given as the location.
14. The VVER-440 units have a gross output of 440 MW$_e$ and a net output of 407.5 MW$_e$.
15. Sarny is also given as the location.
16. Also referred to as South Ukraine.
17. Also referred to as West Ukraine.
18. Neteshin is also given as the location.
19. Also referred to as Kerch' or Crimea.
20. Shchelkimo is also given as the location.
21. Also referred to as Bashkir.
22. Agidel is also given as the location.
23. Volgodonsk is also given as the location.
24. The Shevchenko Power Station is located on the eastern coast of the Caspian Sea at Mangyshalk, Fort Shevchenko, about 10 kilometers north of Shevchenko.
25. BN-350 is used to generate electricity and desalinate sea water (150 MW$_e$ output when the reactor is coupled to the desalination plant, which has an output of 120,000 MT of fresh water per day); Fujii, op. cit., p. 605; and V.A. Vasiliev, "Nuclear Power in the USSR," Nuclear Energy 21, April 1982, p. 115.
26. Teplodar is also given as the location.
27. According to Nucleonics Week, 8 November 1984, pp. 10-11 the "ATET is to be based on two VVER-1000 units, each with a capacity of 900-megawatts electric."

Sources: Haruo Fujii, ed., *Directory of Nuclear Power Plants in the World* (Tokyo: Japan Nuclear-Energy Information Center, (1985); *Nuclear News*, February 1988, pp. 80-82; CIA, *USSR Energy Atlas*, January 1985, pp. 52, 56-57; William J. Kelly, Hugh L. Shaffer, and J. Kenneth Thompson, *Energy Research and Development in the USSR* (Durham, NC: Duke University Press, 1986).

Symbols:
- LGR Light-water-cooled, graphite-moderated reactor (channel-type power reactor).
- RBMK Soviet nomenclature for "large capacity boiling-water (or channel) reactor"; a high-power version of the light water-cooled graphite-moderated pressure-type (channel-type) reactor similar to LGR.
- VVER Soviet nomenclature for "water energetics reactor"; a pressurized water reactor similar to U.S. PWR.
- BWR Boiling-water reactor.
- LMFBR Liquid-metal fast-breeder reactor.
- ATET A modification of the VVER-1000 design whereby a portion of the steam, normally used for electricity production in turbines, is diverted and used as a heat source for district heating.
- AST A boiling water reactor used to produce heat only for district heating.

4

Plutonium Production

ningrad, Kursk, Smolensk, and Chernobyl. It was found that the RBMK-1000 design could be modified to increase the power level by 50 percent without changing the size and number of fuel assemblies. The first plant of this type (RBMK-1500) is in operation at Ignalina. The design of larger reactors of this type, RBMK-2000 and RBMK-2400, also have been discussed in the Soviet literature;[98] however, in light of the accident at Chernobyl, the Soviets have decided not to construct any new RBMKs.[99] Each of the operating, graphite-moderated, channel-type power reactors are described more fully in Table 4.7.

Cumulative Plutonium (Equivalent) Production

Since the number and size of the reactors dedicated to the production of plutonium for weapons is not known, their plutonium output cannot be estimated directly.

In the unlikely event that the power levels were not increased over the years, the six Siberian reactors could have produced 7-10 metric tons (MT) of weapon-grade plutonium (6 percent Pu-240) through 1988.[100] As previously indicated, however, there is evidence that the reactor power levels were upgraded, although the amount of upgrade is unknown. Using the original eight graphite production reactors at the U.S. Hanford Reservation as a model, the power level of each of the six reactors could have been increased eightfold over 18 years.[101] Under this rather arbitrary assumption, the Siberian plant could have produced as much as 45 MT of weapon-grade plutonium through 1988.[102] It would not be unreasonable to assume that the cumulative plutonium output of the Kyshtym Complex and Dodonovo could be a comparable amount, totaling roughly 130 MT.

Assuming their capacity has not been upgraded beyond their rated values of 293 Mw_t and 517 Mw_t, respectively, the two Beloyarskiy light-water-cooled, graphite-moderated channel-type reactors (LGRs) could produce only 130 kilograms to 180 kilograms of weapon-grade plutonium (6 percent Pu-240) annually.[103] These reactors could have produced 3-4 MT of weapon-grade plutonium through 1988.[104]

An upper-bound estimate of Soviet plutonium-equivalent (plutonium and tritium) production can be made from the Soviet contribution to the buildup of krypton-85 (Kr-85) in the earth's atmosphere. Kr-85 is a gaseous fission product produced when U-235 or Pu-239 is fissioned. It is ordinarily released to the atmosphere when spent nuclear fuel is chemically processed. Chemically inert and with a radioactive half-life of 10.76 years, Kr-85 accumulates in the atmosphere. The Soviet contribution to the atmosphere's Kr-85 is estimated by subtracting the contributions from known sources outside the Soviet Union from the estimated total releases. The U.S. intelligence community monitors the atmospheric concentrations of Kr-85 and uses these data to estimate the cumulative plutonium-equivalent production over time and from that, the annual production rate. Using a similar approach, and the data on atmospheric concentrations of Kr-85 published in the open literature, von Hippel, et al. have estimated that the Soviets have released some 60 ± 10 megacuries of Kr-85 as of the end of 1983.[105] Assuming the fraction of plutonium-equivalent production for alternative uses (tritium, R&D, and civil use) is similar in the Soviet Union and the United States, the stockpiles of plutonium for weapons use in the Soviet Union is not more than about 115 ± 20 MT.[106]

The plutonium produced by Soviet power reactors can also be estimated more directly. Such an estimate for the graphite-moderated, channel-type power reactors, exclusive of any upgrade in the capacity of the Siberian plant, is given in Table 4.8. The high and low estimates are based on different assumptions regarding the plant capacity factors. Since fuel burn-up also is not known, production estimates have been made for two cases: assuming all reactors are operated to produce weapon-grade plutonium (6 percent Pu-240), and alternatively, reactor-grade plutonium (30 percent Pu-240). These assumptions, which should span the likely operating ranges of the reactors, suggest that the channel-type power reactors have produced between 35 and 85 MT of plutonium through 1988. It is not known how much of this plutonium has been recovered by chemically processing the spent fuel, or what use has been made of the recovered plutonium.

The Chernobyl Unit-4 at the time of the 26 April 1986 accident was operating at an average burn-up of 10.3 gigawatt days per metric ton (Gwd/MT) of uranium and thus produced reactor-grade plutonium (Pu-240 content approximately 30 percent). This suggests that some, if not all, RBMK reactors are optimized for electricity production, rather than for weapon-grade plutonium production. Even if optimized for electricity production, it is unlikely that the higher burn-ups were achieved until recently. Thus a mid-value of about 60 MT is a reasonable estimate for plutonium production from these reactors.

---

98. I. Ya. Emel'yanov, et al., "Increasing the Efficiency of Uranium Utilization in the RBMK-1000 Reactor," translated from *Atomnaya Energiya* 46, March 1979, pp. 139-141, by Plenum Publishing Corporation, 1979, pp. 161-163. These reactors are also referred to as RBMKP, where "P" stands for superheated steam.
99. *New York Times*, 28 January 1988, p. A9.
100. All six reactors are assumed to have a capacity factor of 286 Mw_t and produce 0.86g Pu/Mwd. The low estimate assumes the capacity factor is 0.4 in the first year, 0.5 thereafter; the high estimate assumes 0.4 in the first year, 0.5 in the second, and 0.7 thereafter.
101. Thomas B. Cochran, et al., *Nuclear Weapons Databook*, Vol. II, p. 61.
102. This calculation assumes that the power level of each reactor was doubled after six years of operation, doubled again after 12 years, and doubled a third time after 18 years (see Table 4.9).
103. This calculation assumes the reactors produce 0.86 g Pu/Mwd. The low estimate is based on a capacity factor of 0.5, while the high estimate assumes a capacity factor of 0.7.
104. The low estimate assumes the capapcity factor is 0.4 in the first year and 0.5 thereafter; the high estimate assumes 0.4 in the first year, 0.5 in the second, and 0.7 thereafter.
105. Frank von Hippel, David H. Albright and Barbara G. Levi, 'Quantities of Fissile Materials in the U.S. and Soviet Nuclear Weapons Arsenals," Princeton University, 27 March 1986.
106. *Ibid.* See also, Harold A. Feiveson, Frank von Hippel, and David Albright, *Bulletin of the Atomic Scientists*, March 1986, p. 26. U.S. weapon material inventories are estimated in *Nuclear Weapons Databook*, Vol. II, pp. 74-92.

4
Plutonium Production

Table 4.8
Upper-bound Estimate of Plutonium Produced by the Siberian Plant[1]

YEAR (end CY)	CAPACITY[2] (Mw$_t$)	ANNUAL OUTPUT[3] (1000 Mwd)[5]	CUM. OUTPUT (1000 Mwd)	PU (6%)[4] (kg)	CUMULATIVE PU (6%) (MT)
1958	290	9	9	7	.0
1959	570	46	54	39	.0
1960	860	100	160	86	.1
1961	1100	170	320	150	.3
1962	1400	240	570	210	.5
1963	1700	320	880	270	.8
1964	2000	390	1300	330	.1
1965	2000	490	1800	420	1.5
1966	2000	580	2300	500	2.0
1967	2500	660	3000	570	2.6
1968	2500	730	3700	630	3.2
1969	2500	800	4500	690	3.9
1970	2500	880	5400	750	4.7
1971	2500	1000	6400	980	5.5
1972	2500	1200	7600	1000	6.5
1973	5700	1300	8900	1100	7.7
1974	5800	1500	10,000	1300	8.9
1975	9000	1600	12,000	1400	10
1976	12,000	1800	14,000	1500	12
1977	16,000	2000	16,000	1800	14
1978	19,000	2300	18,000	2000	16
1979	25,000	2600	21,000	2300	18
1980	25,000	2900	24,000	2500	20
1981	28,000	3200	27,000	2800	24
1982	35,000	3500	30,000	3000	26
1983	46,000	3500	34,000	3000	29
1984	49,000	3500	37,000	3000	32
1985	52,000	3500	41,000	3000	35
1986	54,000	3500	44,000	3000	38
1987	57,000	3500	48,000	3000	41
1988	62,000	3500	51,000	3000	44

1. The numbers in this table, which have been rounded to two significant figures, do not reflect the large uncertainty in these estimates, which at best are good to only one significant figure.
2. Without knowledge of the capacity of the Siberian reactors, it has been assumed, based on U.S. Hanford operations, that the power level of each reactor was doubled after six years of operation, doubled again after 12 years, and doubled a third time after 18 years.
3. Assumes capacity factor for each reactor was 40% in the first year, 50% in the second year, and 70% thereafter. The "low" estimate assumes 40% in the first year and 50% thereafter. From 1979 to 1981, the average capacity factor for the Leningrad, Kursk, and Chernobyl reactors was 73.6%; B. A. Semenov, "Nuclear Power in the Soviet Union," IAEA Bulletin 25, June 1983, p. 52.
4. Assumes 0.86 g of Pu produced per Mwd (megawatt-day-thermal) for 6% Pu-240 production.
5. Megawatt day (thermal) (Mwd).

4

Heavy Water and Tritium Production

Heavy Water Production[107]

Prior to the Second World War, the Soviet Union conducted research on heavy water (D_2O), as did every other major power. In 1938 a commission on heavy water was established in the Academy of Sciences (later expanded to the Commission on Isotopes). In 1939 a unit under the Pisarzhevski Institute of Physical Chemistry at Dnepropetrovsk installed research equipment at the Dnepr Dam to produce heavy water by electrolysis on a very small scale. At the Conference on Isotopes in April 1940, it was decided to build a pilot plant capable of producing approximately 15 kilograms of pure D_2O per year, an amount sufficient only for laboratory experimentation. This pilot plant, located at Chirchik Nitrogen Plant near Tashkent, was not yet in operation by 1944. In 1941 the Pisarzhevski Institute was overrun by the German Army and the scientists, together with some minor equipment, were evacuated. Toward the end of the war, the Soviets designed a variation on the Bamag hydrogen electrolyzer specifically for producing by-product heavy water.

Following the war the Soviets showed considerable interest in German research on the production of heavy water. The principal German pilot plant was located in the Leuna Works at Merseberg (now in East Germany). In October 1945, under the auspices of the Ministry of Internal Affairs (MVD), a number of individuals specializing in heavy water were assembled at Leuna. This group drafted the preliminary plans of an H_2S-H_2O exchange plant capable of producing five tons of heavy water per year. Upon the completion of these plans, the Leuna group was evacuated to the Soviet Union on 21 October 1946. These people worked at the Institute of Physical Chemistry until mid-1948, when they were sent to Rubeshnoye in the Ukraine to work on the construction of the Lisichansk nitrogen plant. Whether or not the Soviets constructed an H_2S-H_2O exchange plant is not known.

In the meantime, the Soviets adopted the method of obtaining heavy water as a by-product from the synthetic ammonia industry. Manufacture of electrolyzers commenced in October 1946 at the Urals Chemical Machine Factory near Sverdlovsk. The electrolytic cells at the nitrogen combine in Chirchik were refitted and the plant as a whole was expanded, with heavy-water production commencing sometime in 1948. Electrolytic hydrogen units were installed at the nitrogen plants in Kirovakan, Dneprodzerzhinsk, and Gorlovka, and these plants were put into operation in late 1950 or early 1951. U.S. intelligence estimated that if a process similar to that used at the Canadian Trail plant was employed, a maximum of 50 tons a year of heavy water may have ultimately been recovered as a by-product of the synthetic ammonia industry in these plants by 1952.

The prototype for the heavy-water-moderated and -cooled production reactors was the heavy-water reactor (TVR), which went critical in April 1949 at the Moscow Institute of Theoretical Physics.[108] According to a mid-1950 CIA estimate, sufficient heavy water was available in the Soviet Union to permit the construction of two 50 megawatt heavy-water production piles for plutonium production, one starting to produce in late 1949 and another in late 1950.[109] With respect to current production, the number and location of Soviet heavy-water reactors, other than those used for research, is not known.

Tritium Production

Initial work on tritium production can be dated by Soviet interest in thermonuclear weapons. Soviet work on the thermonuclear bomb began in 1948 when, after reports of a superbomb had been received from the West, Kurchatov set up a theoretical group (which included Andrei Sakharov) under Igor Tamm.[110] This interest may have been aroused by Klaus Fuchs, who told his Soviet case officer about studies of these weapons at Los Alamos.[111] By the time of the first Soviet atomic test on 29 August 1949, Tamm's group had concluded that thermonuclear weapons were possible, and by early November 1949 Kurchatov began to work on the development of a thermonuclear bomb as a matter of priority.[112] In 1951-1952, the Soviet's first isotope reactor (IR) went critical and was the prototype for their tritium-producing reactors.[113] It was a graphite-moderated, water-cooled reactor with an estimated power of 50 Mw_t, indicating that the Fursov Pile and the production reactors served as its predecessors.[114]

With the availability of enriched uranium by early-1951, heavy-water reactors, if they existed, also could have been efficiently used for the production of tritium.[115] Prior to that time, as in the U.S. program, tritium for thermonuclear research could have been obtained, albeit less efficiently, by displacing up to about 10 percent of the plutonium production capacity of existing graphite-moderated reactors.[116]

The first Soviet test of a boosted fission device occurred on 12 August 1953.[117] This device, however, apparently utilized lithium deuteride as a fusion material. The first Soviet two-stage thermonuclear device tested was a shot on 22 November 1955.[118] Ten additional high-yield tests were conducted through 28 February 1958

---

107 The following section is largely derived from CIA, *National Intelligence Survey, USSR*, (Section 73, "Atomic Energy"), NIS-26, January 1951.
108 CIA, *Soviet Nuclear Research Reactors*, Scientific Intelligence Report, OSI-SR/64-41, 22 September 1964, pp. 2-3.
109 CIA, Joint Atomic Energy Intelligence Committee, op. cit., p. 2.
110 Holloway, *The Soviet Union and the Arms Race*, 1984, p. 24.
111 Ibid.
112 Ibid., p. 25.
113 CIA, *Soviet Nuclear Research Reactors*, op. cit., p. 2.
114 Ibid., pp. 2, 4. The Fursov Pile, completed in 1946, was the first Soviet reactor.
115 In the mid-1950s the CIA estimated that a 50 Mw_t heavy-water reactor operating on natural uranium could produce 0.15 g of tritium per pile per day, while a 250 Mw_t graphite pile would produce about 0.05 g per pile per day; CIA, Joint Atomic Energy Intelligence Committee, op. cit., p. 4 of accompanying "Facts and Discussion."
116 In the mid-1950s the CIA estimated that a 50 Mw_t heavy-water reactor operating on natural uranium could produce 0.15 g of tritium per pile per day, while a 250 Mw_t graphite pile would produce about 0.05 g per pile per day; CIA, Joint Atomic Energy Intelligence Committee, op. cit., p. 4 of accompanying "Facts and Discussion."
117 Called Joe 4 (named "Joe" after Joseph Stalin), this fourth Soviet test was a shot with a yield of 200-300 kilotons.
118 Called Joe 19, its yield was 1.6 megatons.

Table 4.9
Estimated Plutonium Produced by Graphite-Moderated Channel-Type Power Reactors

YEAR (end CY)	CAPACITY (MWt)	ANNUAL OUTPUT LOW (1000 Mwd)	ANNUAL OUTPUT HIGH (1000 Mwd)	CUMULATIVE OUTPUT LOW (1000 Mwd)	CUMULATIVE OUTPUT HIGH (1000 Mwd)	ANNUAL PU (6%) LOW (kg)	ANNUAL PU (6%) HIGH (kg)	ANNUAL PU (30%) LOW (kg)	ANNUAL PU (30%) HIGH (kg)	CUMULATIVE PU (6%) LOW (MT)	CUMULATIVE PU (6%) HIGH (MT)	CUMULATIVE PU (30%) LOW (MT)	CUMULATIVE PU (30%) HIGH (MT)
1954	30	2	2	2	2	2	2	1	1	.0	.0	.0	.0
1955	30	5	5	7	7	4	4	2	2	.0	.0	.0	.0
1956	30	5	6	12	13	5	6	3	3	.0	.0	.0	.0
1957	30	5	8	18	21	5	7	3	4	.0	.0	.0	.0
1958	316	5	8	23	29	5	7	3	4	.0	.0	.0	.0
1959	602	5	8	29	36	5	7	3	4	.0	.0	.0	.0
1960	888	5	8	34	44	5	7	3	4	.0	.0	.0	.0
1961	1170	5	8	40	52	5	7	3	4	.0	.0	.0	.0
1962	1460	5	8	45	59	5	7	3	4	.0	.0	.0	.0
1963	1750	5	8	51	67	5	7	3	4	.0	.1	.0	.0
1964	2040	35	37	86	104	30	32	17	19	.1	.1	.0	.1
1965	2040	54	57	140	161	47	49	27	29	.1	.1	.1	.1
1966	2040	57	74	198	235	49	64	29	37	.2	.2	.1	.1
1967	2560	61	84	258	319	52	72	30	42	.2	.3	.1	.2
1968	2560	131	154	389	473	118	133	66	77	.3	.4	.2	.2
1969	2560	149	173	538	646	128	149	74	87	.5	.6	.2	.3
1970	2560	149	208	687	954	128	179	74	104	.6	.7	.3	.4
1971	2560	149	208	836	1060	128	179	74	104	.7	.9	.4	.5
1972	2560	149	208	984	1270	128	179	74	104	.8	1.1	.5	.6
1973	5760	173	232	1160	1500	149	200	86	116	1.0	1.3	.6	.8
1974	5880	632	691	1790	2190	543	594	316	346	1.5	1.9	.9	1.1
1975	9080	976	1040	2770	3240	840	901	488	524	2.4	2.8	1.4	1.6
1976	12400	1290	1590	4060	4830	1110	1370	646	795	3.5	4.2	2.0	2.4
1977	15600	1970	2380	6030	7210	1690	2050	985	1190	5.2	6.2	3.0	3.6
1978	18800	2470	3020	8490	10200	2120	2600	1230	1510	7.3	8.8	4.2	5.1
1979	25200	3470	4320	11960	14500	2980	3710	1740	2160	10	12	6.0	7.0
1980	25200	4170	5190	16100	19700	3580	4460	2080	2590	14	17	8.1	9.9
1981	28400	4690	6170	20800	25900	4030	5310	2340	3080	18	22	10	13
1982	34800	5120	6840	25900	32700	4410	5880	2560	3420	22	28	13	16
1983	46000	6440	8360	32400	41100	5540	7190	3220	4180	28	35	16	21
1984	49200	8050	10130	40400	51200	6920	8710	4020	5060	35	44	20	26
1985	52400	8620	11300	49100	62600	7420	9740	4310	5660	42	54	24	31
1986	49200	8260	11300	57300	73800	7100	9680	4130	5630	49	64	29	36
1987	57200	9010	12300	66300	86100	7750	10500	4510	6130	57	74	33	43
1988	62000	9480	12900	75800	99000	8150	11100	4740	6470	65	85	38	50

1 The reactor startup dates are taken from Table 4.7. It has been assumed that the Obninsk and Siberian reactors are still in operation. No credit has been given for the increase in capacity of the Siberian stations.
2 The "high" estimate assumes the capacity factor for each reactor was 40% in the first year, 50% in the second year, and 70% thereafter. The "low" estimate assumes 40% in the first year and 50% thereafter. From 1979 to 1981 the average capacity factor for the Leningrad, Kursk and Chernobyl reactors was 73.6%. B. A. Semenov, op. cit., p. 52.
3 Assumes 0.85 g of Pu produced per Mwd for 6% Pu-240 production.
4 Assumes 0.5 g of Pu produced per Mwd for 30% Pu-240 production.

4
Uranium Production

(see Chapter Ten). Although the Soviets had some heavy-water-moderated production reactors in existence by 1957,[119] it is not known how much, if any, capacity of this type was (or currently is) utilized for tritium production. The Soviets presumably still use water-cooled, graphite-moderated production reactors patterned after the IR prototype for tritium production.

Uranium Production

Uranium Mining And Processing.[120] According to Soviet geologic literature, almost every type of uranium deposit found elsewhere in the world has been found and exploited in the Soviet Union.[121] In addition, some of the uranium deposits described seem to have no Western counterparts. These include deposits associated with iron ores and albitites in Precambrian metamorphic rocks, and those with phosphates in clays with detrital fishbones.

Uranium exploration and mining methods in the Soviet Union are essentially the same as those applied in the West. Exploration methods include geologic, geophysical, geochemical, aerial radiometric, and magnetic surveys. Mining methods include:

- underground mining to recover high-grade, vein-type deposit at a depth of 200 meters or more;
- open-pit methods applicable for low-grade ores dispersed near the surface in large areas; and
- in situ leaching techniques that use sulfuric-acidified waters to exploit low-grade deposits that cannot be mined economically by open-pit or underground methods.

As elsewhere in the world, uranium milling, leaching, and concentration processes in the Soviet Union are carried out in proximity of mining operations to facilitate the separation of relatively small quantities of a uranium oxide—"yellowcake"—(U_3O_8) from large volumes of ore. There are three distinct stages in processing:[122]

- extraction of U_3O_8 at or near the mining site;
- conversion of U_3O_8 to uranium tetrafluoride (UF_4) by reaction with fluoride; and
- reduction of UF_4 to metal for direct use in weapons or reactor fuel or for conversion to gaseous hexafluoride (UF_6) to permit enrichment in the uranium-235 isotope.

Information is available on the locations of uranium deposits and processing centers (see Figure 4.9). Western estimates of U_3O_8 production for nuclear power, excluding requirements for nuclear weapons, are given in the insert to Figure 4.9.

Uranium Enrichment. Upon entering Berlin in April 1945, the Soviets immediately began to dismantle and ship German industrial equipment to the Soviet Union. They also began to conscript leading German scientists for nuclear research.[123] German nuclear research groups were established in the Soviet Union around mid-1946, in parallel to existing Soviet research groups, to pursue uranium isotope separation. Competing German and Soviet research teams investigated each of the three enrichment technologies pursued by the United States during the Manhattan Project, namely, gaseous diffusion, electromagnetic separation, and gas centrifuge.[124]

By 1948 one of the German researchers, Professor Adolf Thiessen, had developed a laboratory-model gaseous diffusion barrier.[125] In early 1948 Thiessen's model barrier was selected by the Soviets for mass production at the Elektrostal plant south of Noginsk near Moscow.[126] Procurement of barrier material was underway by mid-1949, and by the end of the year small quantities had been delivered.[127] Though delivery of barrier material for 1949 did not meet schedules, no great concern over this was apparent until the fall of that year, at which time there was a definite increase in the priority for barrier material, together with a demand for more than double the annual production.[128]

Thiessen's barrier was completed sometime around 1949. It was the first of the various isotope separation methods in the Soviet Union to yield satisfactory results.[129] The Soviets, who had previously regarded the isotope separation race as an open one, decided henceforth to put all available resources into the gaseous diffusion method.[130] In 1949 the Soviet's first gaseous diffusion cascade was constructed in Kefirstadt (now called Verkhniy-Neyvinskiy).[131] Corrosion problems were en-

---

119 R. E. Tomlinson, ed., *Radioactive Wastes from the Nuclear Fuel Cycle*, AICE Symposium Series No. 154 (New York: American Institute of Chemical Engineers, 1956).
120 This section is largely derived from CIA, *USSR Energy Atlas*, January 1985, pp. 42-43.
121 Only limited data on uranium occurrences in the Soviet Union, and minor details on reserves, mining, and processing operations, have been published. Uranium deposits in the Soviet Union are generally classified as either vein-type ores associated with metamorphic and intrusive-extrusive igneous rocks or hydrothermal deposits emplaced in sedimentary rocks. These two geologically distinct types, which seldom occur together, are of roughly equal importance as uranium resources.
122 Information about Soviet uranium processing is even less available than that on the distribution and production of uranium.
123 CIA, *The Problem of Uranium Isotope Separation by Means of Ultracentrifuge*, Report No. DB-0-3-633-414, 8 October 1957, p. 6. The Soviets apparently stopped short of using German scientists to assist in construction of the atomic bomb itself.
124 CIA, "Isotope Separation by Ultracentrifuge," *op. cit.*, p. 8. Two groups of German scientists were located at Sinop and Agudzeri, respectively. These research centers were near Sukhumi on the Caucasian coast of the Black Sea, one about 5 km southeast of Sukhumi. A German research group also worked on the Troepfchen Method, a countercurrent diffusion technique whereby a thin vertical liquid stream enters a tube in which it breaks up into drops. These drops evaporate, and the heavy and light fractions of the fluid evaporate at different rates. The model gases that were used for this method were either chlorine or bromine; *Ibid.*, p. 15. The competition between the Soviet and German research groups was one-sided. While the Soviets received the technical reports of their German counterparts, the Germans, with rare exceptions, received no reports from their Soviet counterparts, and no information as to their actual progress and accomplishments; *Ibid.*, pp. 8, 9, 12.
125 *Ibid.*, p. 9. Thiessen's research group was working at the German research institute set up at Sinop in the Soviet Union; *Ibid.*, p. 7.
126 *Ibid.*, pp. 9, 12. The location of the Elektrostal plant south of Noginsk is given in USAF, Air Intelligence Division, *A Strategic Vulnerability Study of the Soviet Atomic Energy Program*, Study No. 218, 1 February 1949. In separate tables, conflicting coordinates are given: 55°47'N 38°27'E and 54°47'25"N 38°27'37"E. The latitude of the latter is a typographical error and should read 55°47'25"N. Elektrostal is described as a large-scale uranium-smelting plant that produces uranium metal; *Ibid.*, p. 4. "In or near the Elektrostal Steel Plant, the first large scale smelting of uranium took place in the spring of 1947 under the direction of German scientists specializing in the metallurgy of uranium"; *Ibid.*, Annex III.
127 CIA, Joint Atomic Energy Intelligence Committee, *op. cit.*, p. 3 of accompanying "Facts and Discussion." About 300,000 square feet of barrier material were ordered for 1949.
128 *Ibid.* Some 750,000 square feet of barrier material were ordered for 1950.
129 CIA, "Isotope Separation by Ultracentrifuge," *op. cit.*, p. 12.
130 *Ibid.* The Smyth Report, published 12 August 1945, had confirmed that this was the method used by the United States.
131 *Ibid.*, pp. 12, 26. The compressors for the gaseous diffusion plant were constructed in the Kirov plant in Leningrad; *Ibid.*, p. 36.

Figure 4.7 A Tu-160 Blackjack A bomber, shown here at Kubinka Air Base during Secretary of Defense Carlucci's visit to the Soviet Union in August 1988. The plane is built at the Kazan Airframe Plant and was first observed at the Ramenskoye test center on 25 November 1981.

Figure 4.8 Oscar submarines are built at the Severodvinsk shipyard on the Dvina Gulf, 35 kilometers west of the city of Arkangel'sk. Located near the Artic Circle, beyond the warming waters of the North Atlantic Drift, the area is normally ice-locked from mid-November to mid-May.

4
Uranium Production

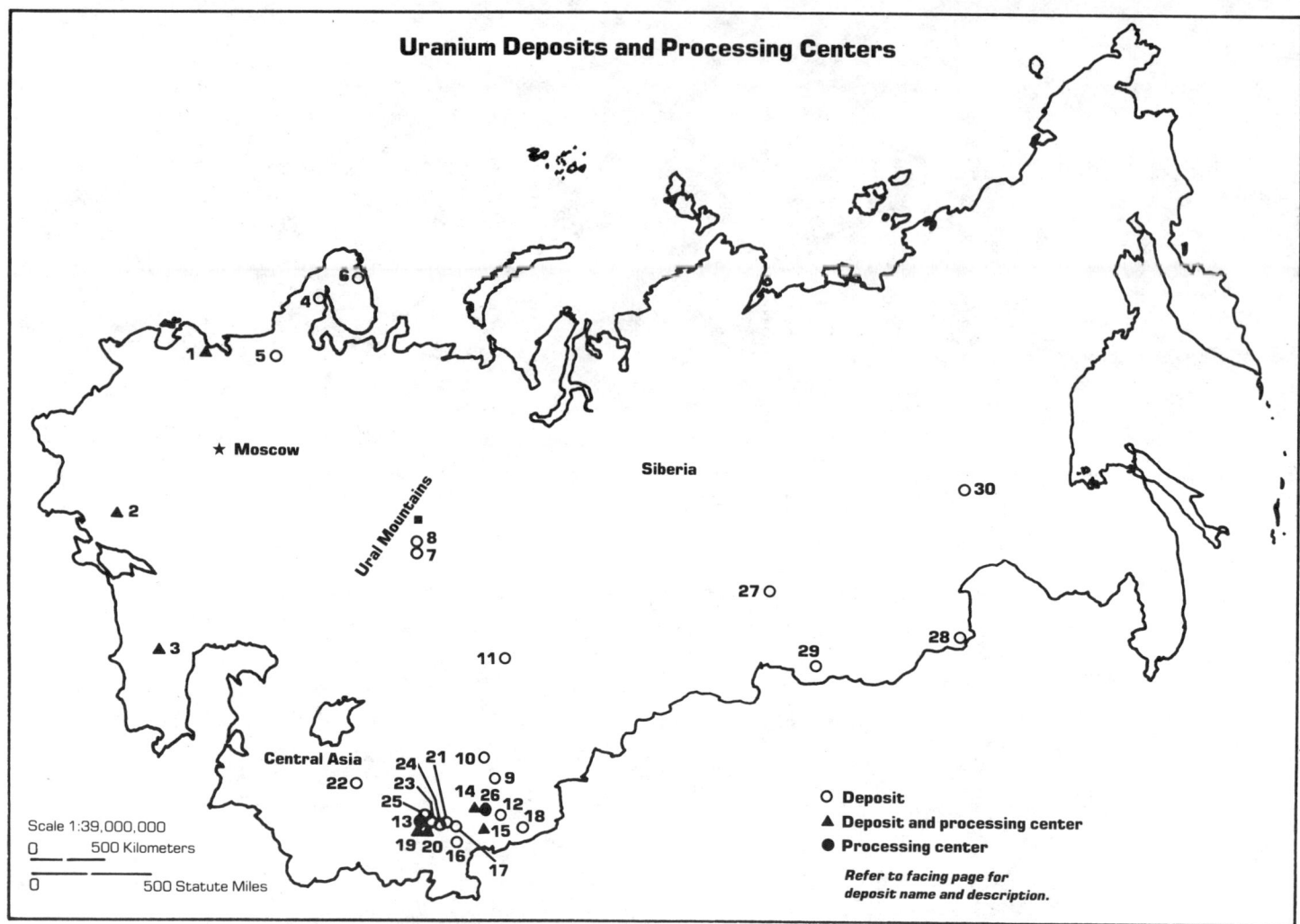

Figure 4.9 Uranium Deposits and Processing Centers.

countered in the barrier, rendering the plant incapable of producing weapon-grade uranium, that is, a U-235 concentration above 90 percent.[132]

Dr. Max Steenbeck, a former Siemens Company official in Germany, was conscripted by the Soviets to lead the German gas centrifuge research effort at Sinop (a suburb of Sukhumi on the Black Sea coast). In 1949 he proposed and received permission to begin construction of a centrifuge topping plant to enrich the output of the diffusion cascade from 50 percent to 90 percent U-235.[133] During this same period Thiessen began investigating means to correct the corrosion problem in the diffusion barrier.[134] By late 1950 or early 1951 the Soviets had solved the diffusion plant corrosion problem, and the centrifuge research project ceased to be of great importance.[135] On 18 October 1951 the Soviets tested their first nuclear device utilizing highly enriched uranium. Thus, the gaseous diffusion plant at Kefirstadt was presumably producing kilogram quantities per day of highly enriched uranium by early 1951.[136]

Despite the success of the gaseous diffusion technology, the Soviets continued research on the gas centrifuge method. The centrifuge topping plant project under Steenbeck was redirected to pursue development of a centrifuge plant capable of taking natural uranium to 96 percent U-235, with an output of one kilogram of metal a day.[137] This research effort was shifted from Sinop to the Kirov plant in Leningrad on 15 September 1951.[138] Be-

---

132 *Ibid.*, pp. 12, 26-27.
133 *Ibid.*, pp. 26-27. Steenbeck's group was formed during June 1946, when its principal members (including Steenbeck) were separated from Soviet prisoners of war.
134 *Ibid.*, p. 12.
135 *Ibid.*, p. 32.
136 CIA, Joint Atomic Energy Intelligence Committee, *Status of the Soviet Atomic Energy Program*, NSIE-1, CIA/SI 13-52, 8 January 1953, p. 11. Joe 3 utilized a composite core design; in other words, the fissile material was a composite of plutonium and highly enriched uranium.
137 CIA, "Isotope Separation by Ultracentrifuge," *op. cit.*, pp. 34, 44.
138 *Ibid.*, p. 34.

Table 4.10
Soviet Uranium Deposits and Processing Centers

Deposit	Description
European USSR	
1. Sillamäe	Uranium-phosphate rare earth association in clays with dentrital fishbones.
	Uranium mining and milling operations.
2. Zheltyye Vody-Terny	Precambrian uranium-iron ore formation.
	Irregular stratiform albitized uranium bodies.
	Uranium in association with conglomerates. uranium minerals include uraninite, pitchblende and nenadkevite.
	Uranium mining and milling.
3. Lermontov	Uranium-molybdenum associated with volcanic rocks.
	Uranium mining and milling operations.
4. Chupa District	Uraniferous pegmatites in Precambrian gneisses.
	Uranium mineralization in paleovolcanic and intrusive rocks of Baltic shields.
5. Lake Onega	Uranium and vanadium mineral in association with black graphitic marine shales, peat, and asphaltite.
6. Lovozero Tundra	Uranium with thorium minerals in alkalic rocks.
Urals	
7. Vishnevogorsk	Uranium mineralization in nepheline syenite intrusions.
8. Novogornyy	Uranium mineralization in nepheline syenite.
■ Verkhniy-Neyvinskiy	Gaseous diffusion uranium enrichment plant.
Kazakhstan and Central Asia	
9. Aksuyek-Kiyakhty	Uranium mining.
10. Koktas	Uranium associated with copper mining.
11. Stepnogorsk	Possible in situ leaching of deep-seated uranium deposit.
	Uranium extraction as part of the "Tselinnyy Mining Complex."
12. Ak-Tyuz-Bordunskiy	Uranium, thorium, and rare earths associated with lead mining.
13. Chigirik	Uranium milling and processing facilities.
14. Granitogorsk	Uranium possibly associated with lead mining, milling, and concentration center.
15. Min-Kush	Uranium mining and milling operations associated with lignite in 1960s.
16. Tyuya-Muyun	Uranium-vanadium association in metamorphic limestone interlayered with volcanic tuffs and breccia.
	Tyuyamuyunite, a uranium-vanadium mineral species that was named after this locality.
17. Kyzyl-Dzhar	Uranium mining associated with gold production.
18. Kadzhi-Say	Uranium associated with lignite mining.
19. Taboshar	Uranium vanadium mining.
	U_3O_8 extraction plant.
20. Chkalovsk	Possible uranium extraction and hexafluoride conversion site for Taboshar mine ore.
21. Sumsar	Possible uranium mining.
22. Uchkuduk	Uranium associated with gold mining at Kokpatas gold mine.
	Possible uranium extraction at Navoi Mining and Metallurgical Complex.
	Ore genetically similar to South African deposits.
23. Naugarzan	Uranium-flurite mining. Ore milling at Chigirik.
24. Charkesar	Site of former uranium mining.
25. Chavlisay-Krasnogorskiy-Yangiabad	Site of uranium mining operation.
26. Kara-Balta	Uranium processing center.
Siberia	
27. Vikhorevka	Possible uranium-thorium mining of vein-type deposits in ultrametamorphic Archean rocks.
28. Krasnokamensk	Uranium-fluorspar association in mesozoic volcanic basins.
29. Slyudyanka	Pegmatites-uranium and rare earths.
	Mining reported in 1958 from Precambrian crystalline limestone.
30. Aldan	Uranium, thorium, and rare earths associated with gold mining.

Source: CIA, *USSR Energy Atlas* (Washington, DC: USGPO, January 1985), p. 42.

4
Uranium Production

tween 1951 and mid-1953, the Germans were gradually being eased out of the project, and by September 1953 the Soviets had assumed total control.[139] It is not known whether a centrifuge plant was ever constructed during this early period.

As in the United States, the Soviets have relied on gaseous diffusion technology for essentially all of their weapon-grade uranium production to date.[140] The enrichment plant at Verkhniy-Neyvinskiy (formerly Kefirstadt) has been expanded and continues to operate today. Whether there are other gaseous diffusion plant sites in the Soviet Union is not known. A Soviet nuclear engineer told one of the authors that an enrichment plant was located within 20 kilometers of Kansk, probably west of Kansk toward Krasnoyarsk.[141] This is consistent with a recent reference to uranium enrichment sites at Krasnoyarsk and Achinsk.[142] Also, a former International Atomic Energy Agency (IAEA) official was told that Soviet uranium was enriched near Lake Baikal. While none of these references have been confirmed, they are each near large sources of electricity, which would be needed to operate a gaseous diffusion plant.[143]

Several alternatives to the gaseous diffusion method of uranium enrichment have received attention in the Soviet Union, including experimentation with photochemical technology using lasers (laser isotope separation).[144]

Figures for highly enriched uranium production in the Soviet Union are not available. A 1979 estimate of the capacity of a Soviet gaseous diffusion plant "located somewhere in Siberia"—perhaps referring to the Krasnoyarsk plant—was 7-10 million kilogram separative work units (SWUs) per year.[145] The number and size of the gaseous diffusion plants in the Soviet Union is not known. If the Soviet Union had one to three plants of 7-10 million SWUs/yr each—a reasonable estimate of the total Soviet enrichment capacity—they would yield 7-30 million SWUs/yr or one-fourth to one times the peak U.S. capacity of 27.3 million SWUs/yr. In the early 1980s, the Soviets were reported to have 3 million SWUs/yr available for export, and through its marketing agent Techsnabexport, held contracts for export of between 0.6 and 3 million SWUs/yr.[146]

It has been reported that between 1946 and 1977, the Soviets had built up a 200,000-ton stockpile of uranium.[147] While the reliability of this estimate is unknown, it is perhaps noteworthy that this would be sufficient to manufacture some 600 to 700 MT of weapon-grade uranium using current gaseous diffusion technology. Moreover, it has been estimated that out of an annual supply of 17,500 tons in the mid-1970s, the Soviet Union consumed (including exports) only about 1800 tons for "civilian" nuclear power use.[148] The remainder would have been available for weapons use.

In conclusion, the above figures suggest that the Soviet stockpile of highly enriched uranium for weapons is probably comparable to the U.S. stockpile of 500 MT. The uncertainty in this estimate is large—at least 50 percent. It is reasonable, nevertheless, to assume, as is the case in the United States, that highly enriched uranium production is not a constraint on Soviet nuclear weapons production.

---

139 *Ibid.*, pp. 44, 46.
140 See B. A. Semenov, "Nuclear Power in the Soviet Union," IAEA Bulletin, 25, June 1983, p. 55; House Committee on Energy and Commerce, Uranium Enrichment Policy, 98 Cong. 1st sess., 21 October 1983, p. 120. The Soviets assisted China in the construction of a gaseous diffusion plant in the mid-1950s. The Soviets suspended atomic aid and stopped work on the plant sometime between the summer of 1958 and August 1959; Gloria Duffy, "Soviet Nuclear Energy: Domestic and International Policies," RAND Corporation, R-2362-DOE, December 1979, p. 3.
141 Private communications with the authors.
142 Avraham Shifrin, *The First Guidebook to Prisons and Concentration Camps of the Soviet Union* (New York: Bantam, 1982), pp. 34, 347. The enrichment plant at Achinsk is called Glinozemnyi. Krasnoyarsk is referred to as an "old Siberian city [that] has a uranium enrichment plant, no. P/Ia 26, as well as other military construction sites."
143 CIA, *USSR Energy Atlas*, January 1985, pp. 56-57.
144 *Ibid.*, p. 43.
145 Congressional Research Service, *West European Nuclear Energy Development: Implications for the United States*, No. 46-183 (Washington, DC: GPO, 1979), p. 8, as referenced in Allan S. Krass, Peter Boskma, Boelie Elzen, and Wim A. Smit, *Uranium Enrichment and Nuclear Weapons Proliferation* (London: Taylor & Francis Ltd, 1983), p. 214.
146 House Committee on Energy and Commerce, "Uranium Enrichment Policy," *op. cit.*, pp. 120, 123; HAC, FY 1983 EWDA, Part 5, pp. 563, 575; Congressional Budget Office, *Uranium Enrichment: Investment Options for the Long Term*, October 1983, p. 16. By comparison, the United States produced some 500-600 MT of highly enriched uranium for weapons between 1944 and 1964, with annual enrichment production peaking in FY 1961 at 16.5 million SWUs (see *Nuclear Weapons Databook*, Vol. II, Chapter Three).
147 *Newsweek*, 14 March 1977, p. 13, as quoted by Duffy, "Soviet Nuclear Energy," *op. cit.*, p. 68, and insert in Figure 4.8.
148 Duffy, *op. cit.*, pp. 67-69.

The Design Cycle

The weapons design cycle consists of a number of stages, which have been codified in the Unified System of Design Documentation (YeSKD), including the assignment of a technical task, the presentation of a technical proposal, a draft project, and finally a technical project. After this design work has been completed, testing series production takes place.[1]

Weapons systems have two basic origins: requirements by the military services and developments by weapons designers. Military requirements are formulated by the services (each service has a technical administration and at least one research institute), which submit them to the Council of Ministers and the CPSU Central Committee (presumably through the Department of Defense Industry) for approval. Upon approval (based on both the expressed objectives and the availability of resources), a design request is submitted through the VPK to the responsible production ministry as a technical task (*taktiko-tekhnicheskii zadaniye*, or TTZ).[2] The ministry passes it on to at least one (and more likely two or more) of its design organizations. The TTZ states the required characteristics (*taktiko-tekhnicheskiye kharak-teristicheski*, or TTKhs) of the new system.[3]

Once established and approved (by the designer, the ministry, the military, and the VPK), these characteristics become part of the documentation and standards with which prototypes and finished products will be compared. The approval process can take two years or more.[4] In the aircraft industry, these specifications are submitted for review to an expert commission made up of about 20 representatives of various staff organizations, the Soviet air forces, and/or Aeroflot.

While the establishment of the TTZ by the service is probably the more common route in developing new weapons systems, the designers also develop and submit proposals to the responsible service. Presumably, the proposal is then formalized and submitted, as described above, back to the designer.

Designers work closely with the representatives of the services (typically military engineers, known as *voyenpredy*).[5] There are *voyenpredy* at each step of the process—from design to series production at different plants—in an effort to ensure quality control.

Each participating design bureau (KB) prepares at least one technical proposal (*tekhnicheskoye predlozheniye*, or TP), detailing both their design and the resources needed for its development. This is presented and defended before an expert commission and the customer. The commission selects one or two designs for further development as draft projects.[6] A draft project (*eskiznyy proyekt*) tests how well the design can be put into production, the interaction of various subcomponents, and so on. The draft project sets the course for all subsequent stages.[7] Again, the customer and the ministry must approve the draft project before moving on to the prototype stage.

KBs are usually collocated with prototype production plants, and a number of prototypes are prepared for testing.[8] These are tested by a commission made up of representatives of the designers, the producers, and the service customer. The commission helps uncover hidden flaws prior to the next stage, that of approval and state tests.

Also at this (or any other) stage, it may become apparent that one of the systems being considered is not satisfactory and must be dropped. At the same time the prototypes are being prepared, the design documentation that will be sent to the plants responsible for serial production is prepared.

After successful testing at the plant level, prototypes are turned over to the service for the State Acceptance Trials, which are conducted with an eye towards both technical and *tactical* employment capabilities. These tests are typically conducted by a commission—headed by an officer—of representatives of the service and the producers. The commission recommends acceptance, improvements, or rejection. Only with acceptance can the weapon begin series production.[9]

Series production is assigned to production plants in the form of a technical agreement (*tekhnicheskiye usloviye*, or TU), which lays out the technical data, methods of quality control, the nature of future testing (which is conducted periodically on the series-production models), how to transport the finished product, and so on. Again, the military engineer monitors each stage.

All of these documents are given to the responsible plant. Resources for the weapon's production come from the ministry and the customer.

---

1. For a relatively detailed discussion of the sequence of steps, see the article by N. N. Alekseyev, "Ispytaniya voyennoy tekhniki,' *Sovetskaya voyennaya entsiklopediya*, Vol. 3 (Moscow: Voyenizdat, 1977), pp. 616-618. See also, CIA, *Soviet Weapons Industry*, 1986.
2. Non-military products also have technical tasks (*tekhnicheskiye zadniya*, or TZs). In addition, it appears that each KB may develop two approaches to satisfying the requirements. See V. P. Mishin, ed., *Osnovy proyektirovaniya letatel'nykh apparatov (transportnyye sistemy)* (Moscow: Mashinostroyeniye, 1985), p. 294; Lev Chaiko, 'Helicopter Construction in the USSR," (Falls Church, VA: Delphic Associates, 1985), p. 23; Richard D. Ward, "Soviet Practice in Designing and Procuring Military Aircraft," *Astronautics and Aeronautics*, September 1981, pp. 24-38.
3. See Yu. V. Chuyev, "Taktiko-tekhnicheskiye dannyye" *Sovetskaya voyennaya entsiklopediya*, Vol. 7 (1979), pp. 636-637. See also, S. A. Sarkisiyan and D. E. Starik, *Ekonomika Aviatsionnoy Promyshlennosti* 2d ed. (Moscow: Vysshaya Shkola, 1985), p. 283.
4. DIA, *Estimated Expenditures for Research and Development by the Soviet Ministry of Aviation Industry (MAP)*, DIA-450-2-6-71-INT, July 1971, pp. 10-11.
5. Chaiko, *op. cit.*, p. 20; Mikhail Turetskiy, "The Introduction of Missile Systems into the Soviet Navy," (Falls Church, VA: Delphic Associates, 1983), pp. 5-6; V. A. Silinskiy, "Voyennyy predstavitel," *Sovetskaya voyennaya entsiklopediya*, Vol. 2 (1976), pp. 271-272; DIA, *op. cit.*, p. 11; BDM Corporation, *The Role of the Military Representatives in the Soviet Defense Industry—A Case Study of the 3896th Military Representative Group (MRG) in Riga* (McLean, VA: BDM Corporation, May 1981).
6. Sarkisiyan and Starik, *op. cit.*, p. 287.
7. *Sovetskaya voyennaya entsiklopediya*, Vol. 3 (1977), p. 616.
8. *Ibid.*
9. *Ibid.*

5

Chapter Five
Strategic Nuclear Forces

Overview

Soviet strategic offensive nuclear force loadings as of mid-1988 consist of about 10,800 nuclear warheads delivered by land-based intercontinental ballistic missiles (ICBMs), submarine-launched ballistic missiles (SLBMs), and long-range bombers (see Table 5.1). Strategic nuclear defensive capabilities consist of some 4200 warheads of the anti-ballistic missile (ABM) and surface-to-air missile (SAM) forces.

The land-based ICBM force of 1414 missiles is armed with 6500 warheads and comprises 60 percent of the strategic offensive force, and about 20 percent of the total nuclear arsenal. Deployment of multiple independently targetable reentry vehicles (MIRVs) starting in December 1974 resulted in increases in the number of warheads of 300 percent (four times as many) over a ten-year period. The fourth- and fifth-generation ICBMs have improved guidance systems and are more reliable, which results in greatly increased targeting flexibility and alert rates.[1]

The SLBM force consists of 64 submarines carrying 942 missiles and 3400 warheads.[2] This represents 30 percent of the strategic offensive force, and about 10 percent of the total nuclear arsenal. Submarine missiles began to receive multiple warheads (MIRVs) in 1977; the number of warheads increased from 1500 to 3400 in ten years. Although there has been an increase in the number of warheads and in missile accuracy, at least one of the newer missiles is experiencing reliability problems that constrain submarine operations.[3]

The strategic bomber force—160 Bear bombers that carry an estimated 950 nuclear weapons—is the smallest component of Soviet strategic forces (some 10 percent). (The history and capabilities of the strategic bombers are discussed in Chapter Eight). Bomber forces, nonetheless, are expanding through deployment of long-range air-launched cruise missiles (ALCMs) and other air-to-surface missiles (ASMs), spurred in part by stricter arms control constraints that will be placed on ballistic missiles under the INF and START Treaties.

According to the Joint Chiefs of Staff (JCS),

The Soviets have more than 30 new strategic offensive systems in development. Projections for the next decade include new solid-propellant ICBMs, both silo-based and mobile; a liquid SS-18 follow-on; and improvements to the currently deployed ICBMs. Follow-on systems are expected to have greater accuracy and targeting flexibility. SLBM projections include continued deployment of the SS-N-20, SS-N-23, a SS-N-20 follow-on, and a new SLBM. The deployment of the Bear-H and impending deployment of the Blackjack-A intercontinental bombers will significantly increase the airbreathing threat from either the bomber itself or its standoff missiles.[4]

According to *Soviet Military Power*, "By the 1990s, assuming the continuation of the current modernization tempo, the Soviets will be in a position to field over 15,000 [strategic offensive] warheads."[5]

History of Strategic Missiles

The Soviet intercontinental-range strategic missiles first deployed in 1960 were derived from the shorter range theater missiles deployed after the Second World War (see discussion of shorter range missiles in Chapter Seven). The emphasis shifted from short-range forces to long-range forces and defensive weapons (surface-to-air missiles) in the 1950s because competition with the United States required missile forces capable of threatening each other's homeland.

Land-based Missiles

The world's first intercontinental ballistic missile (ICBM), the SS-6 Sapwood, designed by the Korolev design bureau, was flight tested for the first time on 3 August 1957 and reached operational status in the spring of 1960. The highly unstable, nonstorable liquid propellant severely limited the SS-6's reliability and effectiveness.[6] Only four missiles were operational (see Table 5.4).[7]

---

1 See DOD, FY 1981 *Annual Report*, p. 81; SAC, *Soviet Military Capabilities*, July 1981, p. 18. Heavy reliance on liquid fuel propulsion systems and problems with guidance technology kept the cost of operating the force relatively high prior to the fourth generation; throughout the 1970s only a small number of missiles were kept on full alert; Berman and Baker, *Soviet Strategic Forces*, p. 36. By the mid-1970s a higher percentage of ICBMs were in quick reaction alert; DOD, FY 1980 *Annual Report*, p. 75. One unconfirmed report notes that about one-third of the missile force is not operational at any one time for scheduled maintenance; Jonathan Marshall, "Soviet ICBMs Aren't Reliable Enough for First Strike," *San Jose Mercury*, 16 December 1982, p. 11.
2 This excludes 12 Golf II class submarines, which carry 36 SS-N-5 Serb missiles and warheads and are not part of strategic forces (see Chapter Seven).
3 Studeman, USN, Statement before HASC, March 1988, p. 33.
4 JCS, FY 1989, p. 40.
5 SMP 1988, p. 47.

6 The SS-6 had two stages: the first consisted of four RD-107 engines arranged around the missile, while the second consisted of four RD-108 engines in the main body; David Holloway, "Military Technology," in Ronald Amann, Julian Cooper, and R.W. Davies, *The Technological Level of Soviet Industry* (New Haven, CT: Yale University Press, 1977), p. 458.
7 The first reconnaissance satellites sent back photographs in August 1961 showing that no more than four SS-6s had been deployed; Jeffrey T. Richelson, "U.S. Intelligence and Soviet Star Wars," *Bulletin of the Atomic Scientists*, May 1986, p. 13. All SS-6s were retired by 1968. USAF, *Summary Review*, 1975, p. B-1; Desmond Ball, *Politics and Force Levels: The Strategic Missile Program of the Kennedy Administration* (Berkeley: University of California Press, 1980), p. 55; David Holloway, *The Soviet Union and The Arms Race*, 2d ed. (New Haven, CT: Yale University Press, 1984), pp. 43, 66-67; Freedman, *U.S. Intelligence*, p. 73; SASC, FY 1976 DOD, Part 4, p. 1475.

5
Land-based Missiles

Table 5.1
Strategic Offensive Nuclear Forces (mid-1988)[1]

Delivery System	Number Launchers	Number Warheads	Force Loading	Yield Per Warhead (Kt)	Total Megatonnage
Intercontinental Ballistic Missiles					
SS-11 Mod 2/3	420	3 MRV	420	1100[2]	462
SS-13 Mod 2	60	1	60	750	45
SS-17 Mod 3	130	4 MIRV	520	750	390
SS-18 Mod 4	308	10 MIRV	3080	550	1694
SS-19 Mod 3	350	6 MIRV	2100	550	1155
SS-24 Mod 1	20	10 MIRV	200	550	1100
SS-25	126	1	126	550	69
Subtotal	**1414**		**6500**		**4900**
Submarine-launched Ballistic Missiles					
SS-N-6 Mod 3	256	2 MRV	256	1000	256
SS-N-8	286	1	286	1500	429
SS-N-17	12	1	12	1000	6
SS-N-18 Mod 3	224	7 MIRV	1568	500	784
SS-N-20	100[3]	10 MIRV	1000	200	100
SS-N-23	64	4 MIRV	256	100	26
Subtotal	**942**		**3400**		**1600**
Bombers					
Tu-95 Bear					
Bear A	(20)	2	(40)	1000	40
Bear B/C	(30)	4	(120)	1000	120
Bear G	(45)	6	(270)	1000	270
Tu-142 Bear					
Bear H	(60)	8	(520)	250	130
Subtotal	**160**		**950**		**560**
Total	**2516**		**10800**		**7100**

1 MRVs on SS-11 and SS-N-6 are counted as one warhead in terms of force loading. The subtotal, total force loadings, and megatonnage figures are rounded.
2 Average yield of SS-11 missile—either of 210 SS-11 Mod 2 with one 1100 Kt warhead or of 210 Mod 3 with three 350 Kt warheads (total 1050 Kt).
3 An additional SS-N-20 launcher on one Golf V class submarine is not considered to be operational.

Though the SS-6 never did materialize as a viable weapon system, SS-6 technology was later used as a booster for nearly 1000 satellite launches through 1983, including the launch of the first three Sputnik satellites.[8]

The second generation of long-range missiles—the liquid-fueled SS-7 Saddler and SS-8 Sasin—began flight testing in 1961. These were the first Soviet ICBMs to be deployed in quantity. The SS-7 was first deployed in 1962 in nonprotected, aboveground launch pads.[9] A year later deployment of the SS-8 missiles began at both nonprotected and "hard" aboveground sites.[10] Neither missile was very accurate owing to reliance on command guidance (easily disrupted by electronic interference). The use of storable liquid fuel in the SS-7 significantly reduced the preparation time needed to launch the missile, but the guidance systems in both the SS-7 and SS-8 missiles led to declining operational readiness when they were kept on alert.[11]

---

8 The Soviet Union launched Sputnik I, a 184-pound satellite, into earth orbit on 4 October 1957. The SS-6 one and one-half stage booster was used for 976 launches through 1983; TRW, Space Log, 1957-1982 and 1982-1983. Over 500 boosters were produced, with 480 space launches using the boosters through 1974; ACS/I, USAF, Summary Review, 1975, p. B-1.
9 A year later the SS-7 missiles were deployed in semi-hardened horizontal shelters (described as coffin-like revetments, unlike the single dispersed silos of the U.S. Minuteman force); Hanson W. Baldwin, New York Times, 26 July 1962; as cited in Berman and Baker, Soviet Strategic Forces, p. 91.
10 DOD, FY 1965 Annual Report (class.), p. 37. Soft sites were estimated to have a hardness of 3 psi, hard sites a hardness of 300 psi; Robert McNamara, Secretary of Defense, memo to the president, draft, 23 September 1961 [declassified], p. 16. The Soviets give a figure of 25 psi for the soft-horizontal concrete coffins; cited by Stephen M. Meyer, "Soviet Nuclear Operations," in Ashton B. Carter, John D. Steinbruner and Charles A. Zraket, eds., Managing Nuclear Operations (Washington, DC: The Brookings Institution, 1987), p. 488. Other sources have given psi ranges for the "coffin" basing mode of 100-300 psi (Ball, Politics and Force Levels, op. cit., p. 57) or up to 500 psi (USAF, Trends, 1976, p. 15). Both the SS-7 and the SS-8 were displayed for the first time in the 7 November 1964 parade in Moscow; Prados, Soviet Estimate, p. 189.
11 Air Force Magazine, March 1978, p. 51. Additionally, warheads for the SS-7 were reported to have been located some distance from the missile sites; Berman and Baker, Soviet Strategic Forces, p. 18. The launch procedures for these missiles were still quite lengthy; SMP 1983, pp. 19-20.

5
Land-based Missiles

Table 5.2
Strategic Offensive Force Loadings (1956-1988)[1]

End Year	ICBMs		SLBMs		Bombers		Totals	
	Lncher	Warhead	Lncher	Warhead	Lncher	Warhead	Lncher	Warhead
1956	-	-	-	-	22	84	22	84
1957	-	-	-	-	28	102	28	102
1958	-	-	6	6	50	180	56	186
1959	-	-	33	33	75	250	108	283
1960	4	4	30	30	104	320	138	354
1961	10	10	57	57	120	356	187	423
1962	30	30	72	69	133	382	235	481
1963	80	80	72	69	150	440	302	589
1964	180	180	72	69	173	522	425	771
1965	225	225	75	72	163	532	463	829
1966	333	333	78	75	159	546	570	954
1967	701	701	87	72	159	576	947	1349
1968	909	909	138	120	159	576	1206	1605
1969	1053	1053	221	194	157	568	1431	1815
1970	1361	1361	317	287	157	568	1835	2216
1971	1511	1511	407	362	157	568	2075	2441
1972	1547	1547	503	458	157	568	2207	2573
1973	1587	1587	595	556	157	568	2339	2711
1974	1587	1587	679	640	157	568	2423	2795
1975	1587	1917	771	732	157	568	2515	3217
1976	1539	2099	849	810	157	568	2545	3477
1977	1433	2363	972	1311	157	568	2562	4242
1978	1398	3218	1002	1730	157	568	2557	5516
1979	1398	4186	993	1817	157	568	2548	6571
1980	1398	5002	990	1910	157	568	2545	7480
1981	1398	5302	1038	2426	157	568	2593	8296
1982	1398	5862	990	2474	157	568	2545	8904
1983	1398	6270	978	2462	167	568	2543	9300
1984	1398	6420	982	2646	160	560	2540	9626
1985	1398	6420	980	2872	160	720	2538	10012
1986	1398	6420	948	2888	160	800	2506	10108
1987	1418	6452	962	3130	155	860	2535	10442
1988	1414	6506	979	3378	160	950	2553	10834

1 MRVs are counted as one warhead. In order to facilitate keeping track of the counting rules used here, the total launcher and warhead numbers have not been rounded, thus giving the appearance of greater precision than is warranted.

Roughly two-thirds of the second-generation SS-7 and SS-8 missiles were deployed at soft sites (two launchers per site). While this offered the advantage of easier reload capability, the sites were highly vulnerable to attack.[12] The hardened SS-8 silos improved survivability, though their grouping in threes presented a single aim point.[13] It was more difficult to conduct refire operations.[14]

By October 1965, 222 SS-7 and SS-8 ICBMs were deployed, the vast majority of which were SS-7s. All were retired by 1979, in accordance with terms of the Interim Agreement on the Limitation of Strategic Offensive Arms (SALT I), so as to make room for new SLBM deployments.

Third-generation ICBMs included six missile types produced by several design bureaus. Three were operational (SS-9, SS-11, and SS-13), and three were cancelled

---

12 DOD, FY 1967 Annual Report (class.), p. 57; Berman and Baker, *Soviet Strategic Forces*, p. 91.
13 USAF, *Summary Review*, 1975, p. B-1.
14 DOD, FY 1967 Annual Report (class.), p. 57; Berman and Baker, *Soviet Strategic Forces*, p. 91.

5
Land-based Missiles

Table 5.3
Strategic Land-based Missiles (mid-1988)

Delivery System	Year Deployed	Number Launchers	Number Warheads	Warhead Yield (Kt)	Throwweight (1000 lbs)	Range (km)
SS-11 Mod 2	1973[1]	210	1	1100	2.5	13,000
SS-11 Mod 3	1973	210	3 MRV	350	2.5	13,000
SS-13 Mod 2	1969	60	1	750	1.1	9400
SS-17 Mod 3	1979[2]	130	4 MIRV	750	6.3	10,000
SS-18 Mod 4	1979[3]	308	10 MIRV	550	16.7	11,000
SS-19 Mod 3	1979[4]	350	6 MIRV	550	8.0	10,000
SS-24 Mod 1	1987	20	10 MIRV	550	5.0	10,000
SS-25	1985	126	1	550	2.6	10,500

1 SS-11 Mod 1 was originally deployed in 1966.
2 The SS-17 Mod 1 was originally deployed in 1975.
3 The SS-18 Mod 1 was originally deployed in 1974.
4 The SS-19 Mod 1 was originally deployed in December 1974.

The number of single warhead modifications of the SS-17, SS-18, and SS-19 deployed is unknown, but thought to be negligible.

(SS-X-10, SS-X-14, and SS-X-15).[15] The third-generation ICBMs offered improved accuracy and electronic safeguards and were more survivable owing to being housed in underground "hardened" silos in widely separated locations.[16]

The first third-generation ICBM was the liquid-fueled SS-9 Scarp—designed by the Yangel design bureau, initially tested in 1963-1964, and deployed in 1966. The SS-9 was probably intended to replace the SS-7 to attack large-area targets, but was reoriented to give the Soviets their first "hard target" capability against the U.S. Minuteman ICBM force.[17] In addition to the basic missile, two SS-9 variants (Mod 3 and Mod 4) were developed. The SS-9 Mod 3 was reportedly a depressed-trajectory fractional orbital bombardment system (FOBS) and was deployed at Tyuratam beginning in 1969.[18] The SS-9 Mod 4 three-warhead multiple reentry vehicle (MRV) was deployed in 1971.[19] Between 1966 and 1972, 288 SS-9 missiles of all types were deployed.

Starting in 1966 the Soviets began deploying the Chelomei design bureau's smaller, less expensive, liquid-fueled SS-11 Sego missile. The rate of deployment for the missile came as a surprise to U.S. intelligence analysts.[20] Between 1966 and 1974, 1030 SS-11 missiles were deployed, supplementing the force of SS-7, SS-8, and SS-9 missiles.[21] In addition to the basic missile, two SS-11 variants were developed and deployed in 1973: the SS-11 Mod 2, which was the first Soviet ICBM to carry penetration aids, and the SS-11 Mod 3, which employed a three-warhead MRV system.[22]

The SS-11 was the first of several Soviet ICBMs assigned a number of different roles. Originally, the missile

---

15 The global-range SS-X-10 Scrag was developed by the Korolev design bureau. It was tested concurrently with the SS-9 Mod 3 in a fractional orbital bombardment system (FOBS), or depressed-trajectory mode, and was cancelled by 1968 after eight test firings; USAF, *Summary Review*, 1975, pp. B-1 and B-10. See SMP 1985, p. 41, for an estimate of the cancellation date. The SS-X-15 Scrooge, a derivative of the SS-13 consisting of the first and third stages, was an attempt to build either a mobile shorter-range ICBM or a mobile, longer-range intermediate-range ballistic missile (IRBM). Coincidentally, the SS-X-15, like the SS-X-10, was cancelled after eight research, development, test and evaluation (RDT&E) test firings and never was deployed. The SS-X-15 has been variously described as a mobile ICBM (e.g., USAF, *Summary Review*, 1975, p. B-10); a test bed mobile ICBM (e.g., SAC, *Soviet Military Capabilities*, July 1981, p. 19), a mobile, shorter-range ICBM (e.g. SMP 1984, p. 25), and an IRBM (e.g., Berman and Baker, *Soviet Strategic Forces*, p. 102; Meyer, "Soviet Theatre Nuclear Forces," Part II, p. 18). The maximum range of the missile was never fully established, but the reported estimates of the range (5000-7400 km) would make the missile unsuitable as an ICBM, unless it were deployed in the far north; see, for example, DOD, FY 1972 *Annual Report* (class.), Table 6; Berman and Baker, *Soviet Strategic Forces*, pp. 102-103; Meyer, "Soviet Theatre Nuclear Forces," Part II, pp. 18 and 54. The SS-X-14 medium-range ballistic missile (MRBM), cancelled in 1970 after 19 tests (including two crew-training firings in 1969 and 1970), consisted of the second and third stages of the SS-13; DOD, FY 1972 *Annual Report* (class.), Table 6. Both the SS-X-14 and SS-X-15 missiles are also reported to have been deployed briefly with active training units along the Sino-Soviet border, and later in some areas of the European Soviet Union (see, for example, Ray Bonds, *Russian Military Power* (New York: Bonanza Books, 1982), pp. 220-221; John W. R. Taylor, "Gallery of Soviet Aerospace Weapons," *Air Force Magazine*, March 1980, p. 132; Berman and Baker, *Soviet Strategic Forces*, p. 60. SMP 1985, p. 41, indicates a deployment period of 1974-1976 for the SS-X-15.

16 USAF, *Summary Review*, 1975, p. B-1. First-generation silos were hardened to withstand 200-400 psi; Berman and Baker, *Soviet Strategic Forces*, p. 91.

17 HASC, FY 1980 DOD, Part 3, Book 1, p. 126. See also USAF, *Summary Review*, 1975, p. B-1; Berman and Baker, *Soviet Strategic Forces*, pp. 53, 117.

18 There was considerable uncertainty as to the precise capabilities and extent of deployment of the SS-9 Mod 3. See, for example, JCS, FY 1976, p. 11. In all, 22 SS-9 Mod 3 tests were conducted between 1965 and 1970 from Tyuratam, including one test in September 1969 and two tests in 1970 that were apparently for crew training; DOD, FY 1972 *Annual Report* (class.), Table 4. The utility of depressed trajectory attacks against aircraft alert bases would have been negated by the deployment of U.S. early-warning satellites beginning in 1968. Of the 18 launchers for the SS-9 Mod 3 missiles at Tyuratam, 12 were dismantled or destroyed and six were converted for testing other missiles in accordance with the SALT II Treaty (Article VII, Paragraph 2, Second Common Understanding).

19 The SS-9 Mod 4 was tested 22 times from August 1968 through November 1970; DOD, FY 1972 *Annual Report* (class.), Table 4. An additional test series was begun in 1973, after a 26-month break. The three reentry vehicles (RVs) carried in that test were of a much different design and were equipped with parachutes to insure a soft landing and recovery; other tests in the series conducted during 1973 showed some targeting flexibility; JCS, FY 1975, p. 13; JCS, FY 1974, p. 11. There was much uncertainty at first as to whether the SS-9 utilized a MIRV or MRV system. It was finally classified a MRV system because it did not have a full independent targeting capability. The accuracy of the Mod 4 was particularly poor—twice as bad as earlier SS-9 variants; HASC, FY 1980 DOD, Part 3, Book 1, p. 126. For accuracy estimates, see Berman and Baker, *Soviet Strategic Forces*, p. 105.

20 Secretary of Defense McNamara did not even mention the missile in his classified February 1966 Report to Congress; DOD, FY 1967 *Annual Report* (class.), p. 57.

21 JEC, Allocation of Resources - 1975, Part 1, p. 97.

22 A third variant, the SS-11 Mod 4, received a fairly extensive test program, which started at Sary Shagan in 1974. It carried 3-6 very small, very light warheads that had a very slow reentry and impact speed and whose impact pattern could be controlled. According to the Defense Intelligence Agency (DIA), "[i]t was not a MIRV but a MRV system," which they speculated was designed as a biological or chemical counter-city weapon. The test program was never completed and the system was not deployed. See HASC, FY 1980 DOD, Part 3, Book 1, pp. 126-127; Berman and Baker, *Soviet Strategic Forces*, pp. 104-105.

Table 5.4
Soviet ICBM Forces (1960-1988)

	End-1960	1961	1962	1963	1964	1965	1966	1967	1968	1969	1970	1971	1972
Soviet Union ICBM Launchers[1]													
SS-6 Sapwood	4	4	4	4	4	4	4	4	4	0			
SS-7 Saddler		6	26	64	153	186	186	186	186	186	186	186	186
SS-8 Sasin				12	23	23	23	23	23	23	23	23	23
SS-9 Scarp M1,M2,M3						12	30	108	156	204	252	257	238
SS-9 M4											0	25	50
SS-11 Sego M1							90	380	540	600	840	960	990
SS 11 M2 & M3													0
SS-13 Savage										40	60	60	60
SS-17 Spanker M1													
SS-17 M2													
SS-17 M3													
SS-18 Satan M1 & M3													
SS-18 M2													
SS-18 M4													
SS-19 Stiletto M1													
SS-19 M2													
SS-19 M3													
SS-24 Scalpel													
SS-25 Sickle													
Total	4	10	30	80	180	225	333	701	909	1053	1361	1511	1547
Soviet Union ICBM Warheads													
SS-6	4	4	4	4	4	4	4	4	4	0			
SS-7		6	26	64	153	186	186	186	186	186	186	186	186
SS-8				12	23	23	23	23	23	23	23	23	23
SS-9 M1,M2,M3[2]						12	30	108	156	204	252	257	238
SS-9 M4[3]											0	25	50
SS-11 M1[4]							90	380	540	600	840	960	990
SS-11 M2 & M3[5]													0
SS-13										40	60	60	60
SS-17 M1[6]													
SS-17 M2[7]													
SS-17 M3[8]													
SS-18 M1 & M3[9]													
SS-18 M2[10]													
SS-18 M4[11]													
SS-19 M1[12]													
SS-19 M2[13]													
SS-19 M3[14]													
SS-24[15]													
SS-25[16]													
Total (MRV = 1)	4	10	30	80	180	225	333	701	909	1053	1361	1511	1547
Total (MRV = 3)	4	10	30	80	180	225	333	701	909	1053	1361	1561	1647

Note: MRVs are counted as one warhead. In order to facilitate keeping track of the counting rules used here, the total launcher and warhead numbers have not been rounded, thus giving the appearance of greater precision than is warranted.

1. The initial operational capability (IOC) dates vary in different U.S. government sources. Initial deployment dates are from SMP 1985, p. 41.
2. Single reentry vehicle (RV). Mod 3 is the fractional orbital bombardment system (FOBS).
3. Up to three warheads on MRV. The MRV was a precursor to the MIRV, where the warheads could not be independently targetable. Because the area in which the warheads can be targeted is limited, many tables count the multiple RVs as one warhead. For purposes of estimating warhead production they should be counted separately.
4. Single RV. Mod 1 retired first to compensate for SS-25. All retired by end of 1987. Mod 2 uses penetration aids.
5. Up to three warheads on MRV. Assumes 210 Mod 2 and 210 Mod 3. Mod 2 is assumed to be next in line to be retired to compensate for SS-25 deployments.
6. Up to four warheads on MIRV.
7. Single RV.
8. Up to four warheads on MIRV.
9. Single RV.
10. Up to eight warheads on MIRV.
11. Up to ten warheads on MIRV.
12. Up to six warheads on MIRV.
13. Single RV.
14. Up to six warheads on MIRV.
15. Up to ten warheads on MIRV.
16. Single RV.

	1973	1974	1975	1976	1977	1978	1979	1980	1981	1982	1983	1984	1985	1986	1987	1988
	186	186	186	138	78	0										
	23	23	23	23	9	0										
	188	188	178	152	90	82	43	0								
	100	100	100	100	100	50	25	0								
	955	830	610	490	430	330	230	220	160	130	130	100	55	28	0	
	75	200	350	420	420	420	420	420	420	420	420	420	420	420	420	420
	60	60	60	60	60	60	60	60	60	60	60	60	60	60	60	60
			10	20	50	80	120	130	130	30	0					
			20	20	20	20	10	0								
										110	150	150	150	150	139	130
			10	36	36	36	36	26	26	16	0					
						40	140	154	162	162	92	0				
								50	120	120	200	308	308	308	308	308
				60	100	100	120	180	180	180	80	0				
						20	60	60	40	40	10	0				
								20	80	240	330	360	360	360	360	350
															5	20
													45	72	126	126
	1587	1587	1587	1539	1433	1398	1398	1398	1398	1398	1398	1398	1398	1398	1418	1414
	186	186	186	138	78	0										
	23	23	23	23	9	0										
	188	188	178	152	90	82	43	0								
	100	100	100	100	100	50	25	0								
	955	830	610	490	430	330	230	220	160	130	130	100	55	28	0	
	75	200	350	420	420	420	420	420	420	420	420	420	420	420	420	420
	60	60	60	60	60	60	60	60	60	60	60	60	60	60	60	60
			40	80	200	320	480	520	520	120	0					
						20	20	20	20	10	0					
										440	600	600	600	600	556	520
			10	36	36	36	36	26	26	16	0					
						320	1120	1232	1296	1296	736	0				
								500	1200	1200	2000	3080	3080	3080	3080	3080
				360	600	600	720	1080	1080	1080	480	0				
						20	60	60	40	40	10	0				
								120	480	1440	1980	2160	2160	2160	2160	2100
															50	200
													45	72	126	126
	1587	1587	1917	2099	2363	3218	4186	5002	5302	5862	6270	6420	6420	6420	6452	6506
	1862	1987	2467	2719	2983	3738	4656	5422	5722	6282	6690	6840	6840	6840	6872	6926

Sources: Authors' estimates based on DIA, Intercontinental Strategic Forces Summary - USSR, DDB-2680-253-85, August 1985; SMP 1981, 1983, 1984, 1985, 1986, 1987, 1988; USAF, *Trends*, 1976; USAF, *Summary Review*, 1975; SASC/SAC, Soviet Strategic Force Developments, 1985; Berman and Baker, *Soviet Strategic Forces*; McGwire, *Military Objectives*; Freedman, *U.S. Intelligence*; Prados, *Soviet Estimate*; Raymond L. Garthoff, "The Meaning of the Missiles," *Washington Quarterly*, Autumn 1982, pp. 76-82; Desmond Ball, *Politics and Force Levels: The Strategic Missile Program of the Kennedy Administration* (Berkeley: University of California Press, 1980); Richard K. Betts, *Nuclear Blackmail and Nuclear Balance* (Washington, D.C.: The Brookings Institution, 1987), esp. pp. 3-32, 144-172.

5

Land-based Missiles

may have been targeted at U.S. nuclear-armed aircraft carriers.[23] Later it was reoriented at land targets in the United States, and then at targets in Europe and Eurasia, as Soviet efforts to develop long-range, solid-fuel, mobile ballistic missiles proved unsuccessful. Finally, with deployment of the three-warhead Mod 3, the SS-11 was directed at countervalue-area targets and at command and control centers.[24]

The last of the third-generation missiles, the SS-13 Savage, was the first large Soviet missile to use solid fuel. First deployed in 1969, the SS-13 was slated to be a mobile missile, but difficulties with the guidance system and the rocket motors, as well as the high cost associated with mobile operations, precluded its deployment in this mode, and the missile was deployed in underground silos instead.[25] Only 60 SS-13 missiles were ever deployed.[26] A more accurate SS-13 Mod 2 version was fielded in 1973.

Design work on fourth-generation ICBMs began in 1965-1966[27] and resulted in the deployment of three large liquid-fuel missiles (SS-17, SS-18, SS-19) in 1974-1975. The new generation featured greater accuracy through the incorporation of on-board digital computers and advanced guidance calibration technologies,[28] MIRVs,[29] increased survivability,[30] and "cold" launch techniques with "an inherent refire capability."[31] A fourth ICBM, the solid-fuel, mobile SS-X-16 Sinner (Soviet designation RS-14), failed to reach operational status.

The largest of the fourth-generation missiles, the liquid-fueled SS-18 Satan, was the expected "heavy" missile replacement for the SS-9. The first test of the single-warhead SS-18 Mod 1 version occurred in 1972,[32] and the missile was introduced inlate 1974.[33] Two other fourth-generation missiles, the liquid-fueled SS-17 Spanker and the SS-19, were developed as follow-ons to the SS-11.[34] The SS-17 was first tested in 1972 in a single-warhead configuration. Initially, the SS-17 development program advanced more rapidly than that of the SS-19,[35] and it appeared that the SS-17 was the most advanced system.[36] The SS-19, however, became in April 1973 the first Soviet missile to be tested in a MIRVed configuration.[37] In December 1974 the SS-19 also became the first Soviet MIRVed missile to be deployed at a launch site,[38] surprising U.S. intelligence analysts.[39] Flight-testing of the MIRVed SS-18 Mod 2 commenced in August 1973,[40] with deployment in 1976 in converted SS-9 silos.[41]

By the end of 1975, SS-17 and SS-19 missiles had been deployed in converted SS-11 silos.[42] SS-17s with four warheads fulfilled SS-7 mission requirements, and SS-19 missiles with six warheads fulfilled SS-11 mission requirements, while also supplementing the MIRVed SS-18s. Single-warhead versions of the SS-17 and SS-19 missiles, possibly targeted against tactical and naval command and control centers, were tested in 1976 and deployed in 1977 and 1978, respectively.[43]

By 1979, 100 SS-17 missiles, nearly 200 SS-18 missiles, and more than 200 SS-19 missiles were operational (see Table 5.4). With the introduction of MIRVed missiles, the number of ICBM warheads increased significantly, despite reductions in the number of launchers from 1607 to 1398. Improved and more accurate versions of the fourth generation missiles[44]—the SS-17 Mod 3, SS-

---

23 With the exception of the SS-11 and the SS-19, the Chelomei design bureau has focused entirely on naval missiles. See Berman and Baker, *Soviet Strategic Forces*, pp. 121-122; and Fleet Admiral S.G. Gorshkov, "The Development of Soviet Naval Science," in DIA, trans., *Selected Articles from U.S.S.R. Naval Digest (Morskoy Sbornik)*, 1967, pp. 18-21, cited by Berman and Baker, *Soviet Strategic Forces*, p. 121.
24 HASC, FY 1980 DOD, Part 3, Book 1, p. 126.
25 In 1968, the U.S. estimated that about one-third of projected SS-13 deployments (100 of 250-300) would be in mobile launchers; DOD, FY 1969 *Annual Report* (class.), p. 58.
26 The SS-X-14 missile, based on the upper two stages of the SS-13, was never deployed (see Chapter Seven).
27 SMP 1985, p. 41. While the United States had clear indications of the emergence of the fourth-generation missiles, they were somewhat surprised at the pace of the development and deployment program and the quality of the missiles; HASC, FY 1980 DOD, Part 3, Book 1, p. 130; See also Prados, *Soviet Estimate*, p. 221.
28 Accuracy improvements are thought to be in part the result of a successful attempt to gain Western guidance control technology (e.g., computers and precision ball-bearing grinding machines); DIA, *Strategic Ballistic Missile Projections*, DST-1000S-267-82, 30 September 1982, pp. 30-31 (partially declassified and released under the FOIA).
29 HASC, FY 1980 DOD, Part 3, Book 1, p. 126. The accuracy of the SS-9 and SS-11 MRV guidance systems was very poor, which partly explains the move toward MIRV systems in the next generation of land-based missiles.
30 SMP 1983, p. 21. The silo conversion program began in 1970 with the upgrading of SS-9 silos to increase their survivability and to accommodate the SS-18; SMP 1984, p. 22. New, hardened launch control centers (LCCs) were also in place by 1976; USAF, *Trends*, 1976, p. 14. By the mid-1970s, one-quarter of the silos and LCCs were considered hard and the remainder soft to moderately hard; HASC, FY 1984 DOD, Part 2, p. 17.
31 USAF, *Trends*, 1976, p. 4. The SS-17 and SS-18 missiles use a cold-launch technique in which the missile is "popped out" of the silo by a gas generator before the main booster engines are fired. This technique limits damage to the silo which can therefore, in principle, be reloaded in a relatively short time; SAC, *Soviet Military Capabilities*, July 1981, p. 17.
32 Prados indicates that the first test occurred prior to the signing of the SALT I agreements; Prados, *Soviet Estimate*, p. 221. Since the first of the fourth generation missiles was tested in April 1972, at least according to Freedman, *U.S. Intelligence*, p. 215, the first SS-18 test would have taken place in April or May 1972. Freedman reports that the first SS-18 test was at the end of 1972, and that the missile carried a single warhead flown to short range; ibid., p. 217.
33 Freedman, *U.S. Intelligence*, p. 175. The SS-18 Mod 1 was deployed in 20 new silos at SS-9 complexes prior to the signing of the SALT I agreements in May 1972. These new silos, plus an additional 30 SS-11 silos deployed during 1974, brought the ICBM force to its peak deployment level of 1607 at the end of 1974, before four SS-8s were retired; USAF, *Summary Review*, 1975, p. B-2.
34 Because of the extensive test programs for these systems, U.S. intelligence analysts believed they were competing designs. The possibility that both could become operational was not ruled out; JCS, FY 1975, p. 16. It was believed that a similar competitive design and flight test program was employed prior to the decision to deploy the SS-9 (ibid.), presumably in place of the SS-X-10. The cost of just the 30 SS-17 and 27 SS-19 RDT&E firings held through 1974 was estimated by the U.S. Air Force at $461.26 million for the SS-17, and $622.69 million for the SS-19 ($15.375 million and $23.06 million average per firing, respectively). This compared to an average-per-firing RDT&E cost of $0.9 million per Minuteman III. (All figures in 1973 dollars); USAF, *Summary Review*, 1975, pp. B-10, B-13.
35 By the end of 1973, the Soviets had conducted fourteen SS-17 and eight SS-19 flight tests, with an additional 16 SS-17 and 15 SS-19 tests conducted in 1974; USAF, *Summary Review*, 1975, p. B-10.
36 JCS, FY 1976, p. 16.
37 JCS, FY 1976, p. 16; JCS, FY 1977, p. 35; JEC, Allocation of Resources - 1975, Part 1, p. 68. Prados notes that the April 1973 MIRV test was a test of a modified SS-11 Mod 3 missile and that the Soviets first tested "a real MIRV warhead" with the SS-18 Mod 2 missile in August 1973; Prados, *Soviet Estimate*, pp. 221, 235.
38 JEC, Allocation of Resources - 1975, Part 1, p. 68; Prados, *Soviet Estimate*, p. 222.
39 JCS, FY 1976, p. 16.
40 Prados, *Soviet Estimate*, p. 221.
41 The SS-18 Mod 2 was progressively reported as carrying: 5 to 8 warheads (JCS, FY 1975, p. 15); at least 6 and as many as 8 warheads (JCS, FY 1976, p. 16); 8 warheads (JCS, FY 1977, p. 33; JCS, FY 1978, p. 9); and 8 or 10 warheads (JCS, FY 1979, p. 22). The introduction of the MIRVed version created a problem for U.S. intelligence since differences between the two variants could not be distinguished. The assumption was that a few SS-18s would continue to have a single warhead; JEC, Allocation of Resources - 1977, Part 3, p. 90. This assumption was reinforced by the fact that a longer range, more accurate single-warhead SS-18 variant commenced deployment in 1976; JCS, FY 1978, p. 34.
42 JCS, FY 1977, p. 35.
43 Berman and Baker, *Soviet Strategic Forces*, p. 124.
44 R. Jeffrey Smith, "An Upheaval in U.S. Strategic Thought," *Science*, 2 April 1982, pp. 30-34; CIA, *Soviet Acquisition of Western Technology*, April 1982, p. 10; CIA, *Soviet Acquisition of Militarily Significant Western Technology: An Update*, (Washington, D.C.: September 1985), p. 9.

18 Mod 4, and SS-19 Mod 3—began flight-testing in 1977 (and were deployed beginning in 1979) even as the original versions of the missiles were beginning their operational service.[45] Most, if not all, deployed SS-17 and SS-19 missiles were reported to be Mod 3 variants by the end of 1984, and the SS-18 Mod 4 deployment program was essentially complete by the end of 1985.[46] Approximately one-half of the fourth generation missiles were deployed in "superhard" silos.[47]

The first of the fifth-generation ICBMs—the mobile, single-warhead SS-25 Sickle—entered service in the fall of 1985.[48] A second missile—the MIRVed SS-24 Scalpel—entered service sometime between September and December 1987.[49] Both fifth-generation missiles are solid-fueled, thereby offering reduced reaction times, improved efficiency, and significantly decreased handling and storage difficulties.[50] Deployment of a large force of mobile ICBMs could represent as significant a change in Soviet force structure as MIRVing did in the late 1970s. It also represents a major resource allocation decision, since mobile systems require more support infrastructure than silo-based systems and are therefore more costly to operate.[51]

The SS-24 was first flight-tested on 26 October 1982, after which the Soviet Union declared the missile to be the one new missile allowed under the SALT II Treaty. The SS-25 was first flight-tested on 8 February 1983, and again soon after on 4 May. U.S. intelligence analysts concluded that the missile appeared to be a second new missile—in violation of the provisions of the SALT II Treaty, a charge that had been formalized by January 1984 in a presidential report.[52] The Soviet Union has consistently asserted that the SS-25 is a permissible SS-13 missile modification under the treaty.

Two additional new or modified ICBMs have entered the engineering and flight testing stage of development:

- A liquid-fueled, heavy ICBM, designated the SS-X-26 and labeled the TT-09 during testing, which may replace the SS-18.[53] The first two flight tests of the missile from the Tyuratam test range failed on 2 April 1986 and sometime during August 1986.[54] The missile was successfully tested in December 1986, October 1987, and in early 1988.[55] According to *Soviet Military Power*, the missile should enter series production soon, and "preparations for deployment are already underway."[56]
- A Mod 2 version of the SS-24 is expected to begin flight-testing at Plesetsk in the next few years.[57] This missile is likely to have better accuracy and greater throwweights than the Mod 1.[58]
- A third possible development by the end of the decade is a new version of the mobile SS-25, which could possibly be MIRVed,[59] though currently there is no evidence that the Soviets are planning to deploy a MIRVed SS-25 version.
- It is reported that the United States also expects the Soviet Union to begin flight-testing an operational maneuvering reentry vehicle (MaRV) for its ballistic missiles, probably by the end of the decade.[60]

Sea-based Missiles

The first Soviet sea-based ballistic missiles were based upon the German V-2 and were called the Golem I and Golem II. Although never operational, they were prepared for launch in float containers that were towed un-

---

45. The new SS-17 and SS-18 missiles were deployed before—and the SS-19 missiles were deployed after—the signing of the SALT II Treaty. The SALT II agreement was signed by President Carter and General Secretary Brezhnev in Vienna on 18 June 1979; SAC, A Resolution to Approve the Funding for the MX Missile, 98th Cong., 1st sess, S. Con. Res. 26, p. 45. In 1979, it was reported that the United States had downgraded its estimate of the yield of the SS-18 warhead from 1.2 Mt to 600 Kt (since downgraded again), and the estimate of the yield of each SS-19 warhead from 800 to 550 Kt. In the case of the SS-18, the revision followed a review of existing test data, rather than new test data. See Walter Pincus, "U.S. Downgrades Soviet ICBM Yield," *Washington Post*, 31 May 1979, p. A1.
46. Some single-warhead SS-17 and SS-19 Mod 2 missiles were still deployed in 1984 when the deployment programs for all operational ICBMs were noted by SMP as "virtually complete," with the SS-18 force reportedly entirely comprised of Mod 4 missiles; SMP 1984, p. 24; interview with DIA analyst, April 1984. In 1985, SMP reported that the deployment programs for the ICBM force were complete (SMP 1985, p. 30), though in fact deployment of the SS-18 Mod 4 was still underway (but nearing completion). At the end of 1985 the deployment programs for the ICBM force were "essentially complete," according to SMP 1986 (preface, p. 26).
47. According to SMP 1988, p. 46, 818 silos have been rebuilt since 1972, some 700 since 1980; SMP 1984, p. 22; SMP 1985, p. 29; SMP 1986, p. 24. Hardening levels are claimed to be 6000 psi (Clarence J. Robinson, "Soviets Testing New Generation of ICBM," *Aviation Week & Space Technology*, 3 November 1980, p. 28). One report puts the figure as high as 7000 psi for the SS-18 and SS-19 force; Harold Silber, "Soviets Could Make 3rd Strike, Source Says," *Omaha World-Herald*, 4 April 1982, p. 1. In the early 1980s, nearly 50 percent of the ICBM force was considered superhard—some 40 percent hard and 10 percent soft to moderately hard (HASC, FY 1984, DOD, Part 2, p. 17)—and prepared to withstand the impact of electromagnetic interference (including electromagnetic pulse [EMP]) and to clear debris after an attack so that missiles could be fired (*Soviet Aerospace*, 12 September 1983, p. 8).
48. At the Standing Consultative Commission meeting in late April 1985, the Soviet Union informed the U. S. delegation that 20 US-11s were being removed and 18 SS-25s were being deployed; Walter Pincus, "Moscow Says It Will Honor SALT II Missile Limits," *Washington Post*, 9 May 1985, p. A22. The U.S. intelligence community did not agree that SS-25 deployments had begun by the end of the summer (Bill Gertz, "U.S. Skeptical of Soviets' Reports on SS-25 Missiles," *Washington Times*, 21 August 1985, p. 2). Secretary of Defense Weinberger officially confirmed the deployment of 27 missiles on 22 October during a speech before the Ethics and Public Policy Center in Washington; Michael Weisskopf, "Soviets Said to Deploy Missile," *Washington Post*, 23 October 1985, p. A4; see also, "New Soviet SS-25s Violate SALT II, Weinberger Says," *Baltimore Sun*, 7 December 1985, p. 2.
49. JCS, FY 1989, p. 39, states that the SS-24 was not deployed as of 30 September 1987.
50. See Berman and Baker, *Soviet Strategic Forces*, p. 87. There reportedly has been at least one accident relating to problems with the Soviet liquid-fueled ICBM force. Following the 1979 accident at McConnell AFB in Kansas, where the oxidizer component of a Titan II ICBM leaked fuel and exploded, SAC released a photograph of a Soviet silo where a similar accident had occurred two years before; Andrew Cockburn, *The Threat: Inside the Soviet Military Machine* (New York: Random House, 1983), p. 200.
51. SASC/SAC, Soviet Strategic Force Developments, 1985, p. 6.
52. President's Report to the Congress on Soviet Noncompliance with Arms Control Agreements (The White House: 23 January 1984), pp. 4-5.
53. SMP 1985, p. 31; SMP 1986, p. 28; SASC/SAC, Soviet Strategic Force Developments, 1985, p. 9.
54. Bill Gertz, "Soviet Test of SS-18 May Violate SALT II," *Washington Times*, 13 April 1986, p. 13; Michael R. Gordon, "U.S. Reports Failure in Recent Soviet Test of Big New Missile," *New York Times*, 15 April 1986, pp. A1, A8. The test silo at Tyuratam is reportedly larger than those holding earlier models of the SS-18.
55. SMP 1988, p. 4. Bill Gertz, "Soviets Successfully Test Missile That Will Be Largest in Arsenal," *Washington Times*, 7 January 1987, p. A3. The Soviets tested the missile again in October 1987; Bill Gertz, "Soviet Missiles Near Hawaii Ignite Outrage in Senate," *Washington Times*, 5 October 1987, p. A3.
56. SMP 1988, pp. 4, 47.
57. SMP 1988, p. 101.
58. See, for example, SMP 1985, p. 31; SMP 1986, p. 28; DOD, FY 1987 Annual Report, p. 59; ACDA, FY 1987 ACIS, p. 26.
59. SMP 1986, p. 28; SASC/SAC, Soviet Strategic Force Developments, 1985, p. 9.
60. Hugh Lucas, "Soviet MaRV to Begin Flight Tests," *Jane's Defence Weekly*, 19 January 1985, p. 96.

Table 5.5
Soviet Ballistic Missile Submarine Forces (1958-1988)

	End-1958	1959	1960	1961	1962	1963	1964	1965	1966	1967	1968	1969	1970	1971
Soviet Union Submarines														
Golf I SSB	2	4	10	19	22	22	22	22	22	18	16	15	14	7
Golf II					1	1	1	1	1	5	6	7	8	13
Golf III														
Golf IV														
Golf V														
Hotel I/II SSBN		7	0	0	1	1	1	2	3	6	8	7	7	7
Hotel III												1	1	1
Yankee I SSBN											3	8	14	20
Yankee II														
Delta I SSBN														
Delta II														
Delta III														
Delta IV														
Typhoon														
Total	2	11	10	19	24	24	24	25	26	29	33	38	44	48
Soviet Union SLBM Launchers[1]														
Golf I[2]	6	12	30	57	66	66	66	66	66	54	48	45	42	21
Golf II[3]					3	3	3	3	3	15	18	21	24	39
Golf III[4]														
Golf IV[5]														
Golf V[6]														
Hotel I/II[7]		21	0	0	3	3	3	6	9	18	24	21	21	21
Hotel III[8]												6	6	6	6
Yankee I[9]											48	128	224	320
Yankee II[10]														
Delta I[11]														
Delta II[12]														
Delta III[13]														
Delta IV[14]														
Typhoon[15]														
Total	6	33	30	57	72	72	72	75	78	87	138	221	317	407
Soviet Union SLBM Warheads														
SS-N-4	6	33	30	57	66	66	66	66	66	54	48	45	42	21
SS-N-5 Sark					6	6	6	9	12	33	42	42	45	60
SS-N-6 Serb[16]											48	128	224	320
SS-N-8 Sawfly														
SS-N-17 Snipe														
SS-N-18 Stingray[17]														
SS-N-20 Sturgeon[18]														
SS-N-23 Skiff[19]														
Total (MRV=1)	6	33	30	57	69	69	69	72	75	72	120	194	287	362
Total (MRV=2)[20]														

Note: MRVs are counted as one warhead. In order to facilitate keeping track of the counting rules used here, the total launcher and warhead numbers have not been rounded, thus giving the appearance of greater precision than is warranted.

1. The initial operational capability (IOC) dates vary in different U.S. government documents. Initial deployment dates are from SMP 1985, p. 40.
2. Carries 3 SS-N-4 SLBMs.
3. Carries 3 SS-N-5 SLBMs. These boats were originally GOLF Is with SS-N-4 SLBMs.
4. Carries 6 SS-N-8 SLBMs. This was a one-of-a-kind conversion from GOLF I, with SS-N-4 SLBMs to carry the SS-N-8 SLBMs for test purposes.
5. Carries 4 SS-N-6 SLBMs. This is a test platform for the SS-N-6.
6. Carries 1 SS-N-20 SLBM. This is a test platform for the SS-N-20.
7. Carries 3 SS-N-5 SLBMs. It is unclear whether the seven HOTEL Is (each carrying three SS-N-4) were actually operational. They were removed from service in 1960-1961 while being converted to HOTEL II so as to carry three SS-N-5. In addition one new HOTEL II was built as well.
8. Carries 6 SS-N-8 SLBMs. This boat was originally a HOTEL II and was converted as a test platform for the SS-N-8 SLBM.
9. Carries 16 SS-N-6 SLBMs.
10. Carries 12 SS-N-17 SLBMs.
11. Carries 12 SS-N-8 SLBMs.
12. Carries 16 SS-N-8 SLBMs. The DELTA II is a lengthened version of the DELTA I submarine.
13. Carries 16 SS-N-18 SLBMs.

1972	1973	1974	1975	1976	1977	1978	1979	1980	1981	1982	1983	1984	1985	1986	1987	1988
7	7	7	7	5	4	3	1	0								
13	13	13	13	13	13	13	13	13	13	13	13	13	13	13	13	12
						1	1	1	1	1	1	1	1	1	1	0
					1	1	1	1	1	0						
				1	1	1	1	1	1	0						
7	7	7	7	7	7	7	7	6	6	6	6	2	2	0		
1	1	1	1	1	1	1	1	1	1	1	1	1	1	1	1	1
26	30	32	33	34	33	31	30	29	28	24	24	23	21	18	17	16
					1	1	1	1	1	1	1	1	1	1	1	1
		1	4	9	13	18	18	18	18	18	18	18	18	18	18	18
	1	2	3	4	4	4	4	4	4	4	4	4	4	4	4	4
					4	8	9	10	13	14	14	14	14	14	14	14
													1	2	3	4
									1	1	1	2	3	3	4	5
54	**60**	**66**	**73**	**78**	**87**	**89**	**86**	**85**	**87**	**84**	**80**	**80**	**78**	**76**	**76**	**76**
21	21	21	21	15	12	9	3	0								
39	39	39	39	39	39	39	39	39	39	39	39	39	39	39	39	36
					6	6	6	6	6	6	6	6	6	6	6	0
				4	4	4	4	4	4	0						
						1	1	1	1	1	1	1	1	1	1	1
21	21	21	21	21	21	21	21	21	21	18	18	18	18	6	6	0
6	6	6	6	6	6	6	6	6	6	6	6	6	6	6	6	
416	480	512	528	544	528	496	480	464	448	384	384	368	336	288	272	256
					12	12	12	12	12	12	12	12	12	12	12	12
	12	48	108	156	216	216	216	216	216	216	216	216	216	216	216	216
	16	32	48	64	64	64	64	64	64	64	64	64	64	64	64	64
					64	128	144	160	208	224	224	224	224	224	224	224
													16	32	48	64
									20	20	20	40	60	60	80	100
503	**595**	**679**	**771**	**849**	**972**	**1002**	**993**	**990**	**1038**	**990**	**978**	**982**	**980**	**948**	**962**	**979**
21	21	21	21	15	12	9	3	0								
60	60	60	60	60	60	60	57	57	57	57	45	45	39	39	39	36
416	480	512	528	548	532	500	484	468	448	384	384	368	336	288	272	256
	34	86	162	226	286	292	292	292	292	292	292	292	292	292	286	286
						12	12	12	12	12	12	12	12	12	12	12
					448	896	1008	1120	1456	1568	1568	1568	1568	1568	1568	1568
									200	200	200	400	600	600	800	1000
													64	128	192	256
458	**556**	**640**	**732**	**810**	**1311**	**1730**	**1817**	**1910**	**2426**	**2474**	**2462**	**2646**	**2872**	**2888**	**3130**	**3378**
	688	**828**	**954**	**1503**	**1970**	**2105**	**2198**	**2714**	**2762**	**2750**	**2934**	**3160**	**3176**	**3402**	**3634**	

14 Carries 16 SS-N-23 SLBMs.
15 Carries 20 SS-N-20 SLBMs.
16 Some missiles have two warheads on MRV. The MRV was a precursor to the MIRV, where the warheads could not be independently targetable. Because the area in which the warheads can be targeted is limited, many tables count the multiple RVs as one warhead. For purposes of estimating warhead production, they should be counted separately.

17 The SS-N-18 Mod 1 carries up to three warheads on MIRV; the SS-N-18 Mod 2 carries a single reentry vehicle; the SS-N-18 Mod 3 carries up to seven warheads on MIRV. Counting assumption is seven warheads.
18 Carries up to 10 warheads on MIRV.
19 Carries up to four warheads on MIRV.
20 Assumes the SS-N-6 Mod 3 with two warheads on MRV introduced in 1974 and gradually put on 18 Yankee I submarines.

Sources: Authors estimates based on DIA, Intercontinental Strategic Forces Summary - USSR, DDB-2680-253-85, August 1985; SMP 1981, 1983, 1984, 1985, 1986, 1987, 1988; USAF, Trends, 1976; USAF, Summary Review, 1975; SASC/SAC, Soviet Strategic Force Developments, 1985; USN, Soviet Naval Developments (Rev. 1/81); USN, Soviet Naval Developments (Rev. 4/85); Polmar, Guide to the Soviet Navy, 1986; Polmar, Guide to the Soviet Navy, 1983; Berman and Baker, Soviet Strategic Forces; MccGwire, Military Objectives; Freedman, U.S. Intelligence; Prados, Soviet Estimate.

5

Sea-based Missiles

derwater behind a submarine and uprighted before launching.[61] The first Soviet SLBM prototypes based on the land-based Scud A short-range missile (itself modeled after the V-2), were tested in September 1955 from a modified Zulu class attack submarine.[62] The Zulu system may have achieved a limited operational status by early 1959, despite problems with reliability.[63]

The first ballistic missile designed exclusively for naval application was the SS-N-4 Sark.[64] The 300-350 nautical mile[65] surface-launched SS-N-4 (2-3.5- megaton yield)[66] may have been ready for submarine installation on six modified Zulu V class diesel-powered ballistic missile submarines (SSBs) (two missiles each) in 1958.[67] Full operational status was achieved in 1960 on the diesel-powered Golf class submarine and the Soviet's first nuclear-powered ballistic missile submarine (SSBN), the Hotel class. Twenty-three of the Golf I SSBs and eight of the Hotel I SSBNs were operational by 1963, with three SS-N-4 missiles each.[68] Both the Golf and Hotel classes were converted from submarines originally conceived as attack submarines.

The decision to concentrate on ICBMs as the principal means of nuclear weapons delivery caused some slowdown in submarine deployments and probably caused the cancellation of a nuclear-powered submarine specifically designed to carry the Soviet's first submerged-launch SLBM: the SS-N-5 Serb.[69] As a consequence, 13 Golf class and seven Hotel class submarines were fitted with the SS-N-5. (The first Hotel II with SS-N-5 became operational in 1963, and the first Golf II class conversion occurred in 1965.)[70]

During 1961-1962 new impetus was given to the Soviet sea-based strategic missile program, partly in response to the rapid deployment of the U.S. Polaris submarine force. The Yankee class, probably originally intended as the platform for the SS-NX-13 anti-carrier ballistic missile (tested from 1970 until November 1973, but never deployed),[71] was redirected to carry 16 SS-N-6 missiles, a design derived from the SS-11 ICBM.[72] The Yankee class, which became operational in 1968, was the first modern ballistic missile design in the Soviet Navy. A total of 34 Yankee submarines were deployed by 1974. The short range of the SS-N-6 missile required forward patrols of the Yankee class if it were to hit targets in the United States. Continuous patrols were established in the Atlantic in 1969, and in the Pacific in 1971; these patrols lasted until late 1987.[73]

The SS-N-6 was a vast improvement over the SS-N-5; it had almost twice the range, fifty percent greater accuracy, and improved reliability. Two longer range 1600-nautical mile variants of the SS-N-6 were introduced in 1974, the SS-N-6 Mod 3 armed with two warheads (MRVs).[74]

The first Delta I class submarine, which was a lengthened modification of a Yankee class hull rather than a new design,[75] entered service in July 1973[76] carry-

---

61 A number of incomplete German float containers fell into Soviet hands when they occupied German Baltic bases in 1945; John Jordan, "Soviet Ballistic Missile Submarines-Part 1," *Jane's Defence Weekly*, 21 January 1984, pp. 86, 88. See also, Siegfried Breyer and Norman Polmar, *Guide to the Soviet Navy*, 2d ed. (Annapolis, MD: Naval Institute Press, 1977), pp. 62-63, cited by Berman and Baker, *Soviet Strategic Forces*, p. 97.

62 Some 25 tests of the naval version of the Scud were conducted through 1959; USAF, *Summary Review*, 1975, pp. C-1, C-2. See also, Breyer and Polmar, *op. cit.*

63 The missile, according to an account by an emigre who was assigned to the Northern Fleet's test and evaluation base during the 1950s, carried the designation R-11FM and had a range of up to 180 km (30 km greater than the range of the Scud A). The operation of the engine was relatively unstable, and the missile often deviated from its trajectory during testing. Moreover, an inadequate seal on the engine's hydraulic system reduced the length of time—at first three months—that a fueled missile could remain on a submarine. The missile had to be launched from the surface and only in relatively calm sea conditions when the submarine was not pitching to either side. Mikhail Turetsky, *The Introduction of Missile Systems Into The Soviet Navy (1945-1962)*, (Falls Church, VA: Delphic Associates, Inc., March 1983), pp. 65-71.

64 USAF, *Summary Review*, 1975, p. C-1. Turetsky reports that the R-13 missile, which is probably the SS-N-4, was developed from an Army prototype; Turetsky, *op. cit.*, p. 75. Neither the prototype to the SS-N-4 nor its origin is known.

65 Several sources report a range of about 350 nautical miles; see, for example, DOD, FY 1965 *Annual Report* (class.), p. 38; DOD FY 1966 *Annual Report* (class.), p. 50; USN, *Soviet Naval Developments* (Rev. 1/81), p. 131. The 1985 revision of this latter document reports an estimated range of over 600 km (325 nautical miles); *Soviet Naval Developments* (Rev. 4/85), p. 94. The Air Force reported a range of 300 nautical miles; USAF, *Summary Review*, 1975, p. C-1.

66 DOD, FY 1966 *Annual Report* (class.), p. 50. Turetsky reports that a missile developed under General Designer Makayev given the Soviet classified designation R-13 and unclassified designation D-2, had a nuclear warhead that separated from the missile body in flight and had a yield in the range of 0.5 megatons; Turetsky, *op. cit.*, p. 72-73.

67 The naval version of the Scud A may have been fitted into most or all of the Zulu V class submarines before the SS-N-4 was available for submarine installation in 1958, although this would have necessitated later modification to the launch tubes since the SS-N-4 was a larger missile; Jordan, *op. cit.*, pp. 67-87.

68 One unit of the Hotel class may have been completed as a Hotel II class carrying the SS-N-5; Polmar, *Guide to the Soviet Navy*, 1983, p. 90. Turetsky reports that at least through 1961 the diesel and nuclear submarines carrying the R-13 missile, probably the SS-N-4, usually carried one or two practice missiles with dummy warheads; Turetsky, *op. cit.*, p. 79.

69 Michael MccGwire estimates that the last five units of the Hotel SSBN were reconfigured to carry long-range cruise missiles for use in the anti-carrier role. These units emerged as the Echo I nuclear powered cruise missile submarine (SSGN), and a follow-on SSBN to carry the SS-N-5 later emerged as the Echo II SSGN; MccGwire, *Military Objectives*, Appendix B "Operational Requirements and Naval Building Programs." Also, components for an additional Golf class submarine were transferred to China and assembled in 1964.

70 The eighth Hotel class SSBN was converted as a test platform for the new SS-N-8 SLBM;

USAF, *Summary Review*, 1975, p. C-1. In 1964, Golf and Hotel submarines were assigned to patrols in the open ocean (six assigned by 1966), with regular patrols commencing in 1966 in areas west of the Azores, east of Nova Scotia, and west of Hawaii, after an extensive ocean survey; Berman and Baker, *Soviet Strategic Forces*, pp. 58, 95-96. These patrols were conducted apparently to staging areas rather than to strike stations; DOD, FY 1967 *Annual Report* (class.), p. 58. The nuclear reactors on the Hotel class submarines were very noisy, making the submarines very easy to detect, and the range of both the SS-N-4 and SS-N-5 missiles required the submarines to come relatively close to the coast to launch their missiles.

71 The SS-NX-13 may have been compatible with the Yankee class submarine since it used the SS-N-6 as a booster; USAF, *Summary Review*, 1975, p. C-2; JCS, FY 1978, p. 16. Because of its parallel testing program with the SS-N-8, the Soviets may have planned to reassign the Yankee class submarines to the anti-carrier role as the Delta class SSBNs were introduced. The SS-NX-13 had a range of approximately 350 nautical miles, and a terminal maneuvering capability of some 30 nautical miles; it would have used satellite targeting at launch and terminal radar homing; Polmar, *Guide to the Soviet Navy*, 1983, p. 366. The missile, which incorporated a terminal guidance system, may also have been intended for an anti-SSBN role; see K. J. Moore, Mark Flanigan, and Robert D. Helsel, "Developments in Submarine Systems, 1956-76," in Michael MccGwire and John McDonnell, eds., *Soviet Naval Influence: Domestic and Foreign Dimensions* (New York: Praeger, 1977), pp. 170-173; Richard T. Ackley, "The Wartime Role of Soviet SSBNs," *Proceedings*, June 1978, pp. 38-39. Technical difficulties precluded the deployment of the SS-NX-13; Berman and Baker, *Soviet Strategic Forces*, p. 58.

72 The Chelomei design bureau used components from its SS-11 missile program to produce the SS-N-6; see Berman and Baker, *Soviet Strategic Forces*, pp. 82, 130.

73 HASC, FY 1982 DOD, Part 3, p. 5. The U.S. Navy also reports that Yankee patrols began in the Atlantic in 1968 and off the Pacific Coast of the United States in 1971; USN, *Soviet Naval Developments* (Rev. 1/81), p. 15. A declassified Air Force document notes that the Yankee class initiated its first patrol in 1969; USAF, *Summary Review*, 1975, p. C-2. Berman and Baker report that patrols commenced off the Atlantic coast late in 1969, one deployed north of Bermuda and another south of Bermuda, and off the Pacific coast in 1970, with one submarine stationed west of Hawaii; Berman and Baker, *Soviet Strategic Forces*, pp. 18, 58, 96; Studeman, USN, Statement before HASC, March 1988, p. 22.

74 For a period of time, it was unclear whether the SS-N-6 Mod 3 carried two or three MRVs. For example, several DOD sources note at least two and possibly three MRVs; JCS, FY 1978, pp. 14-15; JCS, FY 1979, p. 28; JEC, Allocation of Resources - 1976, Part 2, p. 68. Other DOD sources estimate three MRVs; HAC, FY 1982 DOD, Part 2, p. 6; DOD, FY 1985 RD&A, p. II-12; SAC, *Soviet Military Capabilities*, July 1981, p. 20. However, all versions of *Soviet Military Power* cite two MRVs, although it wasn't until SMP 1984 that some confusion in the documents was cleared up. For example, SMP 1981, p. 58, notes two MIRVs rather than MRVs; SMP 1983, p. 22, notes two MRVs, but reports on p. 23 that the Yankee class SSBN carries 48 RVs (i.e., 3 RVs for each of the 16 missiles). See also, SMP 1984, p. 26; SMP 1985, p. 32; SMP 1986, p. 29.

75 SAC, FY 1974 DOD, Part 1, p. 607.

76 HAC, FY 1977 DOD, Part 2, p. 7.

5
Sea-based Missiles

ing 12 two-stage SS-N-8 missiles. The increased range of the SS-N-8—4200 nautical miles—as well as its improved accuracy,[77] came somewhat as a surprise to U.S. intelligence analysts.[78] The range of the SS-N-8 enabled the Soviet submarines to establish regular patrol areas in waters contiguous to the Soviet Union, where submarines are less vulnerable to detection and operate within the range of Soviet anti-submarine forces.[79] Eighteen Delta Is were deployed by 1978. Four lengthened versions of the Delta I, designated the Delta II class, entered service from early 1976 to 1978, each carrying 16 (rather than 12) SS-N-8 missiles.[80] A longer range version of the SS-N-8 also entered service around that time.

In 1978 the Soviet Navy deployed its first MIRVed SLBM, the SS-N-18, aboard the Delta III class SSBN.[81] Fourteen Delta III submarines were completed, each carrying 16 SS-N-18 missiles. With the deployment of the fourth Delta III SSBN, the Soviets removed the first Yankee class submarines from service to keep within the numerical limits set in the SALT I agreement.[82]

The initial deployment of the first Soviet solid-fueled SLBM, the SS-N-17, took place in 1980 aboard a modified Yankee I, which was designated Yankee II. The SS-N-17, which was reportedly similar to the SS-X-16 ICBM,[83] may have been intended as a replacement for the SS-N-6, but difficulties with solid-fuel propulsion, the limited 1675 nautical mile (3100 kilometer) range, and SALT I numerical limitations precluded additional deployments.

The Typhoon submarine, the largest constructed by any nation in terms of tonnage,[84] entered service in 1983. Laid down in 1975, the Typhoon is of a unique design: it is the only ballistic missile submarine to have the missile compartment forward of the sail.[85] It is also the quietest Soviet ballistic missile submarine yet built[86] and appears to be designed for operations under the Arctic ice.[87] It is armed with 20 SS-N-20 missiles, each with ten warheads and a range of 8300 kilometers.[88] By the early 1990s, the Soviets could have as many as eight Typhoon submarines.[89]

The Soviets introduced the Delta IV class submarine, armed with 16 long-range SS-N-23 missiles, in 1985. The Delta IV hull, further enlarged from the Delta III to accommodate the improved SS-N-23 missiles, includes features for under-ice operation.[90] The large, liquid-fueled SS-N-23 is thought to carry four warheads (MIRVs) and to be more accurate than the SS-N-18, which is carried on the Delta III SSBN.[91] The SS-N-23 is also expected to be deployed on Delta III class SSBNs as a replacement for the SS-N-18.[92] The increased range of the SS-N-23 compared to the SS-N-18 makes the SS-N-23-equipped Delta III/IV SSBNs more survivable by obviating their need to travel several hundred kilometers out into the Greenland Sea to target the entire United States, enabling the submarines to operate closer to Soviet shores, where they can be better protected.[93]

Modified versions of both the SS-N-20 and SS-N-23 are under development. At-sea flight-testing of a modified version of the SS-N-20 is predicted for 1988.[94] "A modified version of the SS-N-23 missile will probably complete testing in 1988."[95] A completely new SLBM is also reported to be under development.[96] The Typhoon, Delta IV, and Delta III construction and retrofit programs and the introduction of modified missiles are expected to result in the replacement of the entire MIRVed Soviet SLBM force by the end of the 1990s.[97] In addition, a new class of submarine is reportedly under construction at Severodvinsk in the Arctic and is likely to enter the force in the early 1990s.[98]

---

77. Stellar inertial guidance systems were introduced with the SS-N-8. The SS-N-8 missile, along with the previous generation ALBMs, lacks the high-capacity digital computer necessary for advanced multiple-RV delivery systems; DIA, *Ballistic Missile Guidance and Control-USSR and PRC*, DST-1000-293-76, 15 April 1983, p. 79 (partially declassified and released under the FOIA). The accuracy of the SS-N-8 has been estimated as improved by a factor of two over that of the SS-N-6; USAF, *Trends*, 1976, p. 76.
78. SAC, FY 1974 DOD, Part l, p. 46. The SS-N-8 shared technical characteristics of the SS-N-6; Berman and Baker, *Soviet Strategic Forces*, p. 82.
79. Forward-deployed Yankee class SSBNs began to be accompanied on patrols by nuclear-powered attack-submarine protection at about the same time; William Beecher, *Boston Globe*, 19 December 1975, cited by Berman and Baker, *Soviet Strategic Forces*, p. 64. The Delta class submarines, which began to patrol in 1974, could serve as part of a strategic reserve force; USN, *Soviet Naval Developments* (Rev. 4/85), p. 13. For a discussion of the Western understanding of the development of the Soviet Navy's so-called "sanctuary" or "bastion" strategy, see Jan S. Breemer, "The Soviet Navy's SSBN Bastions: Evidence, Inference, and Alternative Scenarios," *RUSI Journal*, March 1985, pp. 18-26. The protected patrol areas for the Delta force include the northern portion of the Norwegian Sea, the Barents Sea, and the Sea of Okhotsk.
80. One Golf and one Hotel class submarine was modified to test the SS-N-8. They remain operationally deployed with the Northern Fleet.
81. The Delta III SSBNs were a follow-on to the Delta II, similar in most respects except for a higher missile compartment to accommodate the longer SS-N-18; USN, *Soviet Naval Developments* (Rev. 4/85), p. 91. The initial deployment date for the Delta III with the SS-N-18 was incorrectly revised from 1978 to 1976 by DOD in 1984; see SMP 1984, p. 26. This revision was incorrect, however; interview with DIA analyst, April 1985. The SS-N-18 is reported to have a more refined guidance system, using two celestial observations.
82. JCS, FY 1989, p. 39; SMP 1986, pp. 29-30. Since 1978, 16 Yankee I units have been removed from service as ballistic missile submarines.
83. Berman and Baker, *Soviet Strategic Forces*, p. 82. Both missiles had a post-boost vehicle; JCS, FY 1978, pp. 11, 16.
84. The Typhoon is about the same length as the U.S. Ohio class SSBN, but its 25,000 ton submerged displacement is one-third larger than the 18,750 ton submerged displacement of the Ohio class; SMP 1986, p. 29.
85. It has been suggested that Typhoon incorporates a unique twin-hull, twin-reactor, twin-turbine arrangement allowing for independent operation of the propulsion units and providing increased hull strength; John Jordan, "Leviathan of the Deep," *Jane's Defence Weekly*, 1 March 1986, pp. 377-378.
86. Admiral Wesley L. McDonald, USN, "The Growing Warsaw Pact Threat to NATO Maritime Forces," *NATO Review*, Vol. 32, June 1984, p. 5. See also, HASC, FY 1986 DOD, Part 3, p. 3.
87. SMP 1986, p. 29; SMP 1985, p. 31; SMP 1984, p. 25; USN, *Soviet Naval Developments* (Rev. 4/85), p. 12. Under-ice features of the submarine include the flat, protected sail, retractable bow-mounted diving planes, and protected propeller shafts. Tests of such a capability reportedly took place in March 1984; Craig Covault, "Soviet Ability to Fire Through Ice Creates New SLBM Basing Mode," *Aviation Week & Space Technology*, 10 December 1984, pp. 16-17.
88. HASC, FY 1985 DOD, Part 1, p. 770. The JCS has reported that the SS-N-20 carries 6-8 warheads (JCS, FY 1986, p. 23; JCS, FY 1987, p. 21). General Secretary Brezhnev informed President Ford at their 1974 meeting in Vladivostok that the Soviet Union was going to build its own giant strategic missile submarine in response to the U.S. Trident program, and that it would be called the Tayfun.
89. SMP 1986, p. 29; SMP 1985, p. 31; USN, *Soviet Naval Developments* (Rev. 4/85), p. 12. Five Typhoons have been launched as of early 1988.
90. Polmar, *Guide to the Soviet Navy*, 1986, p. 116.
91. SMP 1986, p. 30; SMP 1985, p. 32; SMP 1984, p. 25; HASC, FY 1985 DOD, Part 1, p. 770, all refer to the larger size and greater throwweight of the SS-N-23 in comparison to the SS-N-18. Prior to the Washington summit when the United States and Soviet Union agreed that the SS-N-23 would be counted with four warheads, the missile was credited by these and all other sources as carrying up to ten warheads.
92. SMP 1986, p. 30.
93. HAC, FY 1986 DOD, Part 2, p. 908.
94. SMP 1988, pp. 40, 48.
95. SMP 1988, pp. 40, 48.
96. JCS, FY 1989, p. 40; SMP 1986, pp. 30-31.
97. The modified SS-N-20 and SS-N-23 missiles could eventually provide the Soviets with a hard-target capability from its SLBMs (SMP 1986, p. 31). But even if the modifications improve the accuracy of the missiles by 100 percent, the new versions will still be only half as accurate as the U.S. Trident II missile; Jeffrey I. Sands and Robert S. Norris, "A Soviet Trident II?" *Arms Control Today*, September 1985, p. 11.
98. SASC/SAC, *Soviet Strategic Force Developments*, 1985, p. 9.

5
ICBMs

Current Strategic Force Structure (mid-1988)

Intercontinental Ballistic Missiles

As of mid-1988, the land-based missile force consisted of 1414 missiles and 6500 warheads:

- 420 SS-11 missiles armed with at least 420 warheads
- 60 SS-13 Mod 2 missiles armed with 60 warheads
- 130 SS-17 Mod 3 missiles armed with 520 warheads
- 308 SS-18 Mod 4 missiles armed with 3080 warheads
- 350 SS-19 Mod 3 missiles armed with 2100 warheads
- 126 SS-25 mobile missiles armed with 126 warheads
- 20 SS-24 Mod 1 mobile missiles armed with 200 warheads

The SS-17, SS-18, SS-19, and SS-24 missiles have MIRVs.[99] The third modification of the SS-11 carries MRVs which have a single aim point, and the remainder of the land-based missile force has single warheads. The older missiles (with the exception of the mobile SS-24 and SS-25) are deployed in hardened underground silos at 20 complexes, primarily located along or within access of the Trans-Siberian Railroad (see Figure 3.3).[100]

The SS-11 Sego is a third-generation, two-stage, liquid-fuel missile. Two modifications currently exist: the Mod 2 carrying a single 950-1100 kiloton warhead, and the Mod 3 carrying three 100-350 kiloton MRVs. The SS-11 first became operational in 1966 (Mod 1); the upgraded Mod 2 and 3 were deployed in 1973. At the peak of deployment in 1973-1974, some 1030 SS-11s were deployed. The number had dropped to 420 by the end of 1987 (210 Mod 2 and 210 Mod 3), and SS-11s continue to be withdrawn as SS-24 and SS-25 missiles are deployed.[101] The missile has a maximum range of 7000 nautical miles (13,000 kilometers), is inertially guided, and has an accuracy of about 0.5-0.72 nautical miles; it is not capable of destroying hardened targets.[102] Its minimum trajectory is thought to be about 500 nautical miles, suitable for retargeting on Europe and Asia.[103]

The SS-13 Mod 2 Savage is a third-generation, three-stage, solid-fuel, single-warhead ICBM. Originally deployed in 1969 (Mod 1), the SS-13 reached full but limited deployment at 60 missiles by 1972. As of mid-1988, the same 60 SS-13s were deployed. The missile carries a 600-750 kiloton warhead, has a maximum range of 5100 nautical miles (9400 kilometers), is inertially guided, and has an accuracy of about 0.82 nautical miles; it is not capable of destroying hardened targets.[104]

The SS-17 Mod 3 Spanker is a fourth-generation, two-stage, liquid-fuel multiple-warhead (MIRVed) missile. The SS-17 Mod 1 and Mod 2 were deployed in 1975, and the Mod 3 was deployed in 1979. About 150 missiles were deployed by 1980; the number had begun to drop to 145 by the end of 1987, and to 130 by mid-1988, as compensation for deployment of MIRVed SS-24 missiles.[105] The missile carries four 750 kiloton warheads to a maximum range of 5000 nautical miles (10,000 kilometers). The SS-17 is capable of flexible retargeting and can hit Eurasian as well as intercontinental targets.[106] The missile has inertial guidance and has an accuracy of about 0.12-0.2 nautical miles.

The SS-18 Mod 4 Satan is a fourth-generation, two-stage, liquid-fuel, multiple-warhead (MIRVed) missile. The SS-18 Mod 1 was first deployed in 1974 as a follow-on to the SS-9, which it eventually replaced. The SS-18 Mod 2 and 3 were deployed in 1976, and the SS-18 Mod 4 was deployed in 1979. The missiles carry ten 500-550 kiloton warheads to a maximum range of 5900 nautical miles (11,000 kilometers). The missile has inertial guidance and has an accuracy of 0.1-0.14 nautical miles.

The SS-19 Mod 3 Stiletto is a fourth-generation, two-stage, liquid-fuel, multiple-warhead (MIRVed) missiles. The SS-19 Mod 1 was originally deployed in December 1974 to partially replace the SS-11. The SS-19 Mod 3 was deployed in 1979-1980. The Mod 3 carries six 550 kiloton warheads. The missile reached peak deployment of 360 missiles in 1984. Ten missiles were retired by the middle of 1988 as compensation for deployment of the SS-24 missile.[107] The missile has a maximum range of 5400 nautical miles (10,000 kilometers), inertial guidance, and an accuracy of 0.14 nautical miles. Its minimum trajectory is thought to be about 500 nautical miles, suitable for retargeting on Europe and Asia.[108]

The SS-24 Mod 1 Scalpel is a fifth-generation, three-stage, solid-fuel, medium-sized multiple-warhead (MIRVed) missile. The missile began deployment about September 1987 in the rail mobile mode. In 1985 it was predicted that the SS-24 would be deployed initially in modified SS-17 silos, to be followed by rail-mobile de-

---

99 Some single-warhead SS-17, SS-18, and SS-19 missiles may still be deployed. For example, the JCS have referred to "the most accurate versions of the SS-18 and SS-19 missiles;" JCS, FY 1987, p. 21. DIA officials indicated to the authors in a May 1984 interview that the number of single-warhead SS-17 and SS-19 missiles deployed at that time was "too few to matter," and SMP 1986 notes that the SS-18 Mod 4 program was reaching completion in 1985 (preface, p. 3). SMP 1988, p. 46, states that "[T]he majority of the current [SS-18] force consists of SS-18 Mod 4s...."

100 Complexes usually consist of a main base support area and a transfer facility for moving missiles and equipment from rails. Each complex is composed of a number of launch groups, each with a separate launch control center with ten silos in the case of the SS-11, SS-13, SS-17, and the SS-18 force; SASC, Strategic Force Modernization Programs, 1981, p. 6; SMP 1981, p. 55. According to SMP, 818 silos have been rebuilt since 1972, some 700 since 1980; SMP 1988, p. 46. Almost half of the silos are rated as "superhard." The majority of the remainder are considered "hard," and roughly ten percent are "soft to moderately hard"; HASC, FY 1984 DOD, Part 2, p. 17.

101 JCS, FY 1989, p. 39.
102 SMP 1988, p. 46.
103 DOD, FY 1976 *Annual Report*, p. III-66; JCS, FY 1978, p. 85; JCS, FY 1979, p. 87.
104 SMP 1988, p. 46.
105 JCS, FY 1989, p. 39; SMP 1988, p. 15.
106 SMP 1988, p. 46.
107 JCS, FY 1989, p. 39; SMP 1988, p. 15.
108 SMP 1988, p. 46; DOD, FY 1976 *Annual Report*, P. III-66; JCS, FY 1978, p. 85; JCS, FY 1979, p. 87.

5
ICBMs

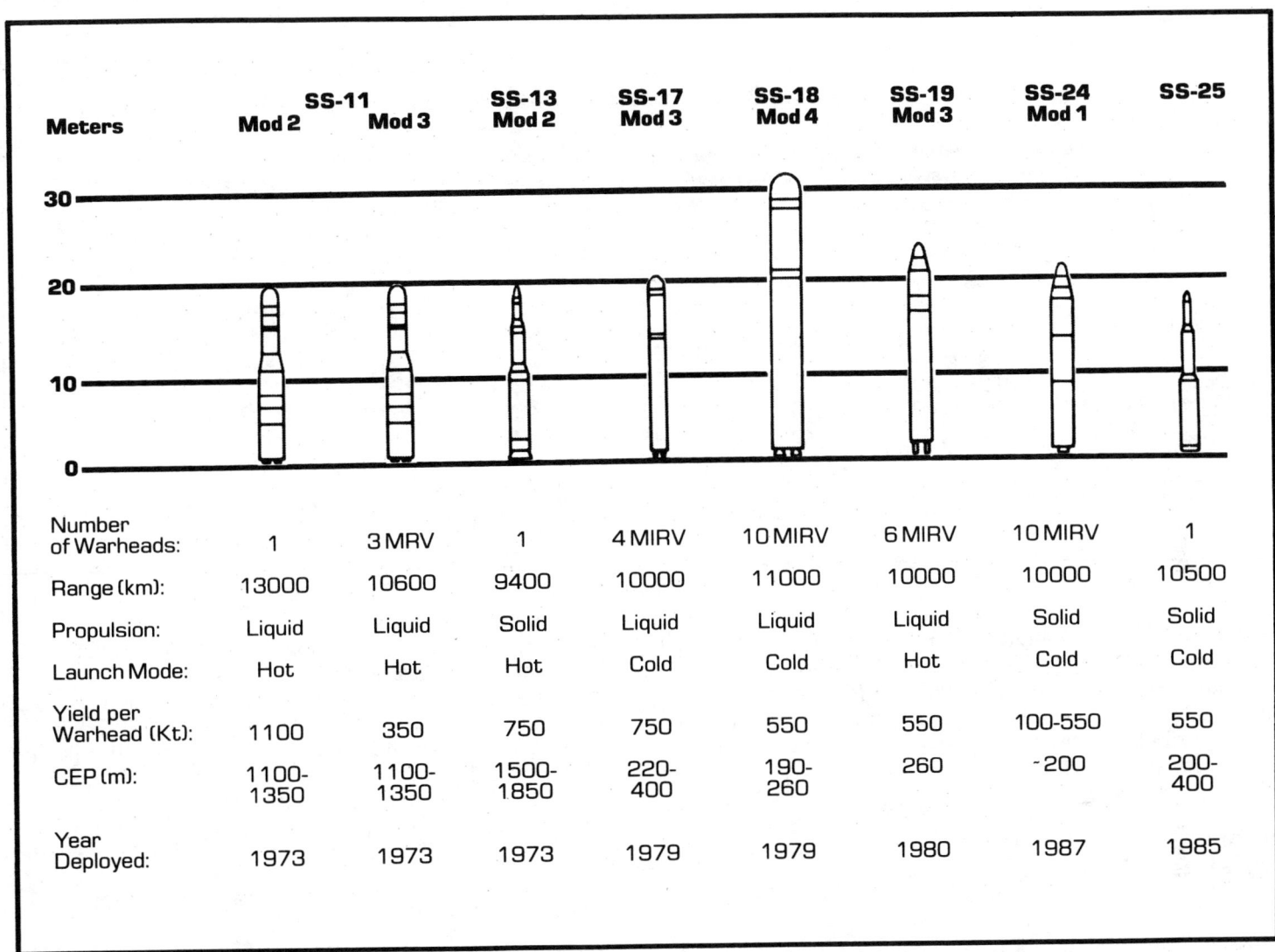

Figure 5.1 Soviet ICBMs.

ployment.[109] The missile carries up to ten 100-550 kiloton warheads to a maximum range of 5400 nautical miles (10,000 kilometers). Some reports rate the accuracy of the SS-24 as better than that of the SS-18 and SS-19. Others claim that it lacks the accuracy to threaten U.S. missile silos.[110] Some 20 were deployed by mid-1988.

The SS-25 Sickle is a fifth-generation, small, three-stage, single-warhead solid-fuel missile with a range of 5700 nautical miles (10,500 kilometers).[111] It carries a single 550 kiloton warhead. The SS-25 is deployed in a road-mobile-wheeled configuration similar to that of the SS-20 and consequently, will be highly survivable, with an inherent (though undetermined) refire capability.[112] The missile has an accuracy of 0.18 nautical miles. The Department of Defense reported that about 100 SS-25s were deployed in regiments of nine missile launchers

---

109 SMP 1984, p. 24, estimated initial operational capability in silos in 1984, with mobile deployment possibly following several years later. SMP 1985, p. 30, estimated initial silo deployment in 1986, with rail-mobile deployment possibly following by one to two years. The 1984/85 National Intelligence Estimate (NIE) estimated silo deployment in 1986 in 100 silos (50 at Kostroma in modified SS-17 silos and 50 at Plesetsk in new or converted test silos), with rail-mobile deployment in 1987 (dates are from SASC/SAC, Soviet Strategic Force Developments, 1985, p. 9; number and location of silos from Peter Samuel, "Big Soviet Buildup Foreseen," *Defense Week*, 17 June 1985, p. 15). Background briefing by senior administration official, 24 March 1986; SMP 1986, p. 27. Until the 1986 edition of SMP, it was unclear what evidence was available concerning the likelihood of a rail-mobile deployment. An illustration of a three-car train with a single rail-car transporter-erector-launcher (TEL) with the launch-canister in the raised position was presented in the 1985 edition of SMP, though the text noted that rail-mobile deployment could, not would, follow silo deployment; SMP 1985, pp. 24-25. SS-24 launchers had been observed on railroad cars at Plesetsk at least by April 1984; Walter Andrews, "Soviets Planning Mobile Missiles Force," *Washington Times*, 24 April 1984, p. 4; see also, Charles W. Corddry, "Soviets Believed Developing Giant Intercontinental Missile," *Baltimore Sun*, 13 May 1984, p. 1.

110 Michael R. Gordon, "A New Russian Missile Gets Mixed Reviews," *New York Times*, 16 August 1987, p. 2-E.

111 The SS-25 has been reported to be capable of carrying three MIRVs (see, for example, Peter Samuel, "Big Soviet Buildup Foreseen," *Defense Week*, 17 June 1985, p. 15). However, such a capability is merely inferred from estimates of the missile's throwweight, not from its test history (i.e., release or simulated release of warheads).

112 SMP 1986, p. 26; ACDA, FY 1987 ACIS, p. 26. The TEL for the SS-25 has been described as off-road capable; SMP 1984, p. 24.

5
SLBMs

Table 5.6
Strategic Submarines (mid-1988)[1]

Class	Missile System	Number Deployed	Under Construction	Fleet Assignment
Golf V	1 SS-N-20	1	—	1 Black Sea
Hotel III	6 SS-N-8	1	—	1 Northern
Yankee I	16 SS-N-6	16	—	8 Northern; 8 Pacific
Yankee II	12 SS-N-17	1	—	1 Northern
Delta I	12 SS-N-8	18	—	9 Northern; 9 Pacific
Delta II	16 SS-N-8	4	—	4 Northern
Delta III	16 SS-N-18	14	—	7 Northern; 7 Pacific
Delta IV	16 SS-N-23	4	2-3	4 Northern[2]
Typhoon	20 SS-N-20	5	2-3	5 Northern
Total		**64**	**4-6**	

1 Excludes nonstrategic Golf II class submarines (see Chapter Seven) and one Golf III class retired in 1987. Yankee class submarines are being retired at the rate of about one to three annually.

2 The Delta IV submarines are expected to be transferred to the Pacific Fleet.

each by early 1988,[113] with a compensating reduction of other missiles.[114] By mid-1988 some 126 SS-25s were estimated to be deployed. While at least three SS-25s have been tested from a modified SS-13 silo, it apparently is no longer believed that the SS-25 is replacing the SS-13, as previously reported.[115]

Submarine-launched Ballistic Missile Systems

The Soviet ballistic missile submarine force as of mid-1988 consisted of 64 submarines of nine different classes. The submarines were loaded with 942 missiles that carry approximately 3400 nuclear warheads. The ballistic missile submarines can carry from one to 20 missiles. All of the submarines have 21-inch torpedo tubes and are capable of firing nuclear torpedoes.

The Golf V is a one-of-a-kind diesel-powered submarine (not considered part of "strategic" force), which functions as a test and training platform for the SS-N-20 SLBM. One older Hotel III submarine with six launch tubes was the test platform for the SS-N-8 missile. The 12 Golf II class boats, which carry the shorter range SS-N-5 missile, have regional strike missions and are not included in strategic accountings (see Chapter Seven).[116]

The remaining 62 submarines are nuclear-powered and under SALT treaty definitions are referred to as "modern" strategic submarines. They are homeported either in the Northern or Pacific Fleets.

Seven SSBN classes make up the strategic force as of mid-1988:

- 16 Yankee I, equipped with 256 SS-N-6 missiles
- 1 Yankee II, equipped with 12 SS-N-17 missiles
- 18 Delta I, equipped with 216 SS-N-8 missiles
- 4 Delta II, equipped with 64 SS-N-8 missiles
- 14 Delta III, equipped with 224 SS-N-18 missiles
- 4 Delta IV, equipped with 64 SS-N-23 missiles
- 5 Typhoon, equipped with 100 SS-N-20 missiles

The 23 Delta IIIs, Delta IVs, and Typhoons built and deployed since 1977 are fitted with 388 multiple-warhead (MIRVed) SLBMs. Forty-six submarines fitted with long-range (SS-N-8, SS-N-18, SS-N-20, SS-N-23) SLBMs enable them to patrol in waters close to the Soviet Union and still strike targets in the United States.

As of mid-1988 there were 16 Yankee I class submarines, each of which carries 16 SS-N-6 missiles with two MRVs, for a total of 512 warheads. As newer submarines are deployed, the Soviets have been retiring Yankee I class submarines under provisions of the SALT treaties. Since 1978, 16 Yankee Is have been removed from strategic service. Two have been converted to an attack-submarine configuration, with one of these to launch the SS-N-21 sea-launched cruise missile (SLCM). A third has been

---

113 SMP 1988, p. 15; JCS, FY 1989, p. 39.
114 SMP 1986, p. 8; interview with DIA analyst, 11 April 1986. It has been reported that the U.S. intelligence community believes that 10 SS-25 launchers are deployed with each regiment, one of which is always in the field; Samuel, op. cit., p. 15, and Peter Samuel, "What You'll Hear on the Threat," Defense Week, 24 June 1985, p. 16. A DIA analyst confirmed, however, that this view is incorrect and that there is a consensus within the intelligence community that each regiment has nine launchers; interview with DIA analyst, 11 April 1986.
115 See Samuel, "Soviet Buildup," p. 15. The tests from a modified SS-13 silo took place by the summer of 1984.
116 USN, Soviet Naval Developments (Rev. 4/85), p. 13.

Table 5.7
Strategic Submarine Forces (mid-1988)

Delivery System	Year Deployed	Number Launchers	Number Warheads	Warhead Yield (Kt)	Throwweight (1000 lbs)	Range (km)
SS-N-6 Mod 3	1973[1]	256	2 MRV	1000	1.5	3000
SS-N-8	1973	286	1	1500	8.0	9100
SS-N-17	1977	12	1	1000	2.5	3900
SS-N-18 Mod 3	1977	224	7 MIRV	500	2.9	6500
SS-N-20	1983	100	10 MIRV	200	5.0?	8300
SS-N-23	1985	64	4 MIRV	100	3.0?	8300

1 The SS-N-6 Mod 1 was originally operational in 1968.

converted to a test platform for the SS-NX-24 sea-launched cruise missile. Others are likely to be converted as well. Yankee I submarines are now assigned predominantly to theater attack missions.[117]

There are 40 Delta class boats of four types. Eighteen Delta I submarines carry 12 SS-N-8 missiles each, for a total of 216 warheads. Four Delta II submarines carry 16 SS-N-8 missiles, for a total of 64 warheads. Fourteen Delta IIIs carry 16 multiple warhead SS-N-18 missiles, for a total 1,568 warheads. Four of the new Delta IV submarines, first deployed in 1985, were operational as of mid-1988. The Delta IVs carry 16 multiple warhead SS-N-23 missiles, for a total of 256 warheads. The SS-N-23, which became operational in 1986, reportedly has greater range and accuracy than the SS-N-18 deployed on Delta III class submarines. The missile is experiencing "reliability problems" and it was disclosed in early 1988 that Delta IV submarines have never gone on patrol.[118] The missile will likely be backfit into some Delta IIIs.[119] Delta IV hull five was launched in early 1988.

An even larger submarine type than the Delta boats, the Typhoon class, was deployed in 1983. The five operational Typhoons, each with 20 SS-N-20s—the Soviet's first solid-fueled MIRVed SLBM—carry 100 multiple-warhead SS-N-20 missiles, for a total of 1000 warheads. Special 26-inch tubes in the pressure hull are capable of firing the SS-N-15 nuclear depth bomb or the SS-N-16 anti-submarine warfare (ASW) missile. Two or three more Typhoon submarines are expected to be built.[120] The appearance of the Typhoon and Delta IV submarines indicates a clear intention to maintain a significant portion of the Soviet strategic strike forces at sea.[121]

Submarine-launched Ballistic Missiles

The Soviet Navy had six different types of strategic SLBMs on 63 SSBNs as of mid-1988. The 942 missiles are estimated to be armed with 3400 nuclear warheads, broken down as follows:
- 256 SS-N-6 with 512 warheads
- 286 SS-N-8 with 286 warheads
- 12 SS-N-17 with 12 warheads
- 224 SS-N-18 with 1568 warheads
- 100 SS-N-20 with 1000 warheads
- 64 SS-N-23 with 256 warheads

The typical Soviet SLBM is relatively simple, rugged, and reliable.[122] Although the yield of individual warheads has decreased (with minor exceptions) with each succeeding missile generation, the combined yield on an individual MIRVed SLBM, and on the entire sea-based missile force, has increased.

The SS-N-6 Serb is a single-stage, liquid-fueled missile currently deployed on 16 Yankee I class SSBNs. The SS-N-6 first became operational in 1968. The current modification of the missile (Mod 3) carries two MRVs (not independently targetable) and became operational in 1973. The missile has a range of 1600 nautical miles (3000 kilometers), and its two warheads have the explosive power of 375-1000 kilotons each. The missile is inertially guided and has an accuracy (circular error of probability) of about one nautical mile.

The SS-N-8 Sawfly is a single-stage, liquid-fuel single-warhead missile. It is deployed on 23 submarines: one Hotel III class, 18 Delta I class, and four Delta II class.[123] The SS-N-8 first became operational in about

---

117 Studeman, USN, Statement before HASC, March 1988, p. 21. The short range of the SS-N-6 missile originally raised fears that it would be used in strikes against the U.S. alert bomber force, but the high trajectory of the missile and the limited number available suggested that the Yankee class was not designed for this mission. Institutional resistance to a principal strategic strike role for the Navy may also have contributed to the limiting of the Yankee's role to coverage of U.S. SSBN support and communication facilities, major fleet centers and ports, and SSBN bases. See, for example, Berman and Baker, *Soviet Strategic Forces*, pp. 58, 127-130. The Yankee class submarines may have been a central portion of a strategic reserve force to be moved within range of likely targets after an initial exchange.

118 Studeman, USN, Statement before HASC, March 1988, p. 33.
119 HASC, FY 1988/1989 DOD Seapower and Strategic and Critical Materials Subcommittee, p. 9.
120 Ibid.
121 See, for example, testimony of Admiral Shapiro before HASC, 26 February 1981, p. 7, with reference to the Typhoon.
122 DIA, *Submarine-Launched Ballistic Missile Weapon Systems - USSR*, DST-1020S-418-78, 1 August 1978 p. 39 (partially declassified and released under the FOIA).
123 Neither the Golf III or Hotel III submarines were SALT accountable, but the six launchers on each submarine were SALT accountable.

5
SLBMs

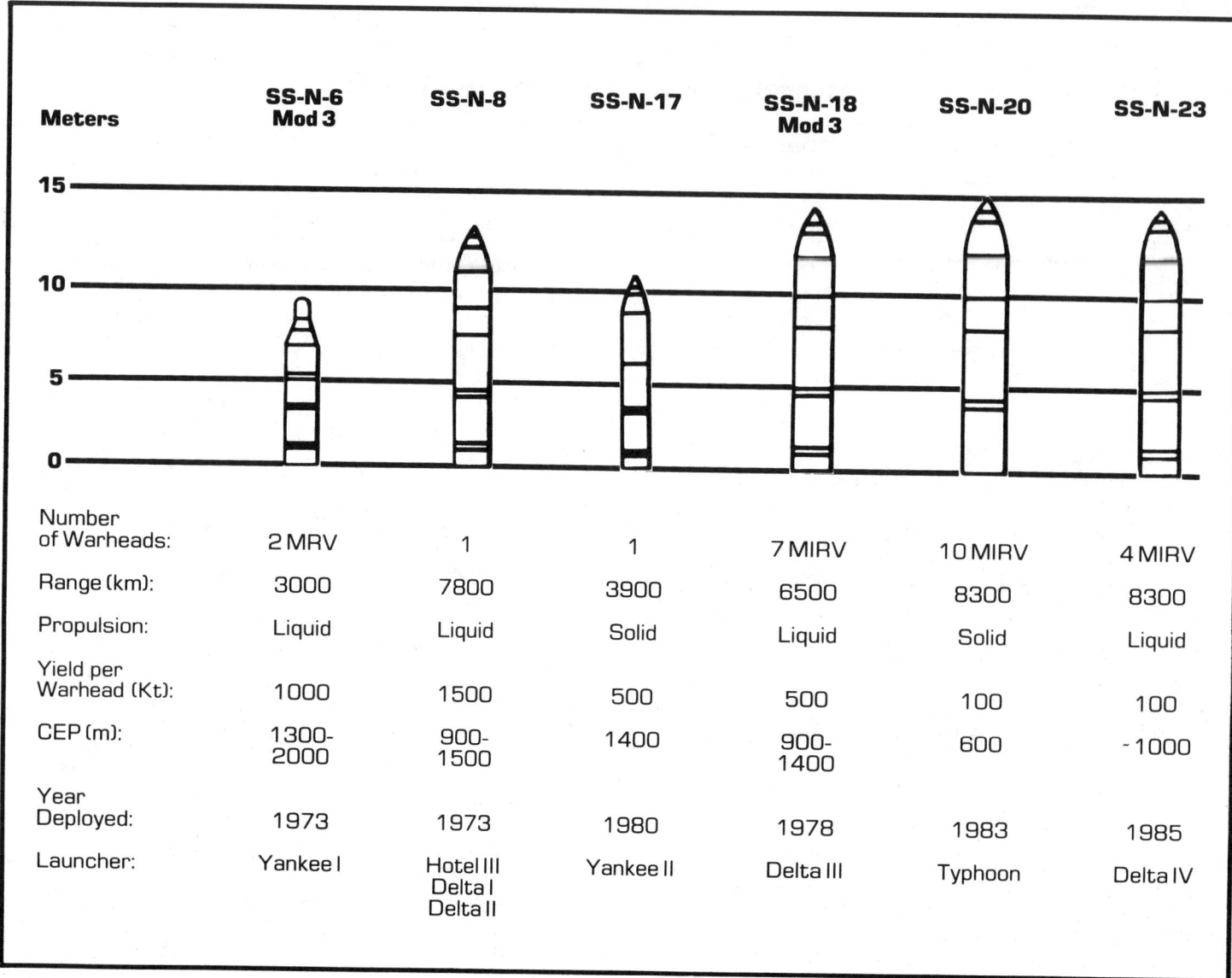

Figure 5.2 Soviet Strategic SLBMs.

1973. Each missile carries a single warhead with the explosive power of 1000-1500 kilotons. The missile has a range of 4900 nautical miles (9100 kilometers), is inertially guided, and has an accuracy (circular error of probability) of about 0.8 nautical miles.

The SS-N-17 Snipe, the first solid-fuel SLBM, is deployed on a single Yankee II class SSBN that was converted from a Yankee I in 1977 (to have four fewer launch tubes). The missile itself may not have reached operational status until 1980. Each missile carries a single 500-1000 kiloton warhead and has a range of 2100 nautical miles (3900 kilometers). The missile is inertially guided and has an accuracy (circular error of probability) of 0.75-0.8 nautical miles.

The SS-N-18 Stingray is a two-stage, liquid-fuel SLBM, the first Soviet SLBM with MIRVs. It is currently deployed on 14 Delta III class SSBNs. The SS-N-18 first became operational in 1977-1978 and is deployed in three modifications: Mod 1 with three warheads, Mod 2 with a single warhead, and Mod 3 with up to seven warheads. The average loading of SS-N-18 missiles is assumed to be seven warheads under agreed U.S. and Soviet counting rules for START negotiations.

Each SS-N-18 Mod 1 or 3 missile carries warheads with the explosive power of 200-500 kilotons each. The Mod 2 missiles carry a larger warhead with the explosive power of 450-1000 kilotons. The SS-N-18 Mod 1 and 3 missiles with MRVs have a range of 3500 nautical miles (6500 kilometers). The single-warhead Mod 2 has an extended range of 4300 nautical miles (8000 kilometers). The missile is inertially guided and has an accuracy (circular error of probability) of 0.5-0.76 nautical miles.

5
Strategic Bombers

Table 5.8
Strategic Bomber Forces (mid-1988)

Delivery System	Year Deployed	Number Launchers	Range (km)	Number Warheads
Tu-95 Bear				
Bear A	1955	20	8300	2 bombs
Bear B/C	1961	30	8300	4 bombs or 1 AS-3 Kangaroo
Bear G	1984	45	8300	4 bombs and 2 AS-4 Kitchen
Tu-142 Bear H	1984	65	8300	No bombs, 8 AS-15 Kent

AS-3 Kangaroo and AS-15 are land-attack cruise missiles. AS-4 Kitchen is an anti-ship air-to-surface missile.

The SS-N-20 Sturgeon is a three-stage, solid-fuel multiple-warhead missile deployed on five operational Typhoon class SSBNs and a single Golf V class test submarine. The SS-N-20 first became operational in 1983, and the missile is still in production. Each missile is counted as carrying 10 100-200 kiloton warheads under agreed U.S. and Soviet counting rules for START negotiations. The SS-N-20 missile is inertially guided and has an accuracy (circular error of probability) of about 0.3 nautical miles. The range of the missile is 4500 nautical miles (8300 kilometers). A modified version of the SS-N-20 is reportedly under development for deployment on Typhoon class SSBNs in the 1990s.

The SS-N-23 Skiff is the newest Soviet SLBM, a three-stage, liquid-fuel multiple-warhead missile. It is deployed on four Delta IV SSBNs and is still in production. The SS-N-23 first became operational in early 1986.[124] Each missile is counted as carrying four 100 kiloton warheads under agreed U.S. and Soviet counting rules for START negotiations. The missile is inertially guided and has a greater accuracy than the SS-N-18. The SS-N-23 may be backfit into Delta III class submarines in place of older SS-N-18s. A follow-on to the SS-N-23 is reportedly under development.

Strategic Bomber Force

The Soviet long-range heavy bomber force consists as of mid-1988 of some 160 Tu-95 Bear bombers of five types assigned to the Moscow and Irkutsk Strategic Air Armies under the direct operational control of the Supreme High Command.[125] All of the Bear bombers are capable of delivering nuclear gravity bombs; the Bear B/C bombers can carry AS-3 Kangaroo ASMs; the Bear G bombers can carry AS-4 Kitchen ASMs; and the Bear H bombers can deliver the AS-15 Kent ALCMs.[126] A total of 950 nuclear weapons are assigned to the strategic bomber force (see discussion and fact sheets on the Bear bombers in Chapter Eight).

The Soviets have taken recent steps that indicate greatly increased interest in the strategic bomber force. Two new long-range Bear variants are in production. The Bear G, a modification to older Bear B/C airframes, is configured to carry the newer, supersonic, dual-capable AS-4 missile in place of the older, much larger, subsonic, nuclear-only AS-3.[127] As of mid-1988, some 45 had been modified.[128]

The other new variant of the Bear airframe entering the inventory is the Bear H, which began production in late 1983 and became operational in November 1984.[129] The Bear H can carry at least eight, and possibly as many as twelve, of the 3000 kilometer range, nuclear-armed AS-15 Kent ALCMs internally in the bomb bay and possibly externally on pylons mounted under the wings.[130] Initial deployment of Bear H advanced more rapidly than the U.S. intelligence community had anticipated; over 70 were built by early 1988.[131] Given the roughly five fold increase in stand off missile range and average force loading and the better accuracy of the AS-15, the Bear H represents a vastly improved strike capability.

---

124 HASC, FY 1988/1989 DOD Seapower and Strategic and Critical Materials Subcommittee, p. 9.
125 Additionally, some Mya-4 Bison bombers configured as tankers (excluded from offensive force totals since 1968) could be reconverted to a bomber role. The JCS continued in their FY 1989 report (p. 39) to count 15 Bison bombers as part of the strategic forces. As of 1988, all other Bison bombers have been retired from active service.
126 Although the Backfire bomber is considered to be a "theater weapon" having "a primary mission of peripheral strike" chiefly "against Europe and Asia" (SASC, Strategic Force Modernization Programs, 1981, p. 13; JCS, FY 1981, p. 31; JCS, FY 1983, p. 107), the aircraft is often included in strategic force comparisons because of its potential capability against the United States on certain mission profiles, with either third- country post-strike recovery or inflight refueling. Because of the importance of the Backfire to theater operations, as well as downward revisions in the combat radius of the aircraft, it is not considered a strategic system. For a discussion of the Backfire's capabilities and missions, see Chapter Eight.
127 SMP 1986, p. 32; SMP 1985, p. 33; SMP 1984, p. 28.
128 SMP 1988, p. 51.
129 The Soviet Ministry of Defense announced on 13 October 1984 that new long-range cruise missiles on "strategic bombers and submarines" had begun to be deployed; Dusko Doder, "Soviets Say New Cruise Deployed," *Washington Post*, 14 October 1984, p. 1. See also, SMP 1985, pp. 7, 35; SASC/SAC, Soviet Strategic Force Developments, 1985, p. 12.
130 An illustration in SMP 1985 (pp. 6-7) shows the Bear H with four AS-15s on two wing-pylons. No official estimates of the number of AS-15s carried by the Bear H have been made, though unofficial estimates of average AS-15 loadings have included 4-6 (IISS, *Military Balance*, 1986-1987, p. 164) and eight (Collins and Cronin, *U.S./Soviet Military Balance*, 1985, p. 17). Assuming the AS-15 can be carried internally, it is believed that the Bear H could carry perhaps as many as twelve AS-15s, though average loadings would probably be less.
131 SMP 1988, p. 38; *President's Report on Continuing the Acquisition of the Peacekeeper (MX) Missile* (Washington, D.C.: March 1985), pp. 2-3.

5
Strategic Defense

Table 5.9
Soviet Strategic Bomber Forces (1956-1988)

	End-1956	1957	1958	1959	1960	1961	1962	1963	1964	1965	1966	1967	1968	1969	1970
Soviet Union Bombers (PAA)[1]															
TU-95 Bear A	2	5	10	25	48	62	75	80	85	60	45	30	30	30	30
Bear B/C								12	30	45	60	75	75	75	75
Bear G															
Bear H															
MYA-4 Bison	20	23	40	50	56	58	58	58	58	58	54	54	54	52	52
Total	**22**	**28**	**50**	**75**	**104**	**120**	**133**	**150**	**173**	**163**	**159**	**159**	**159**	**157**	**157**
Soviet Union Bomber Weapons (Force Loadings)[2]															
TU-95 Bear A[3]	4	10	20	50	96	124	150	160	170	120	90	60	60	60	60
Bear B/C[4]								48	120	180	240	300	300	300	300
Bear G[5]															
Bear H[6]															
MYA-4 Bison[7]	80	92	160	200	224	232	232	232	232	232	216	216	216	208	208
Total	**84**	**102**	**180**	**250**	**320**	**356**	**382**	**440**	**522**	**532**	**546**	**576**	**576**	**568**	**568**

Note: MRVs are counted as one warhead. In order to facilitate keeping track of the counting rules used here, the total launcher and warhead numbers have not been rounded, thus giving the appearance of greater precision than is warranted.

1. The number of bombers is assumed to be the equivalent of U.S. Primary Authorized Aircraft (PAA). This does not include aircraft in storage or inactive aircraft.
2. Force loadings for 1956-1959 are authors' estimates of bombs available for combat; for 1960-1988, the force loadings are authors' estimates based on the counting rules below.
3. Bear A bombers carry two bombs each and no air-to-surface missiles (ASMs).
4. Bear B/C bombers carry four bombs, or a single AS-3 ASM.
5. Bear G bombers carry four bombs and two AS-4 ASMs per plane. Bear B/C bombers are currently being converted to Bear G models.
6. In 1984, newly produced Bear H bombers began to be deployed. These bombers are counted as carrying eight AS-15 air-launched cruise missiles.
7. Bison bombers carried four bomber weapons each.

A heavy bomber designated Blackjack A by NATO is in development and has been undergoing flight-testing since early 1983.[132] "Blackjack can cruise subsonically over long ranges, perform high-altitude supersonic dash, and attack utilizing low-altitude, high subsonic penetration maneuvers."[133] First identified in November 1981,[134] the Blackjack was expected to enter service in 1986-1987. Eleven Blackjack A aircraft were still in flight-testing at the beginning of 1988, one having crashed in May 1987.[135] The JCS believes that the aircraft will enter series production and "probable" deployment in 1988;[136] *Soviet Military Power* states that deployment of the bomber "is about to begin."[137]

The Blackjack is expected to carry the AS-15 Kent ALCM, nuclear bombs,[138] and a new short-range attack missile, designated the AS-X-16.[139] The Blackjack will likely be based at Dolon with the Bear Hs—to augment them after the transfer of Bear Gs to theater forces—and probably will replace the much less capable Bear A bomber.[140] At that time both the Blackjack and the Bear H are expected to carry improved variants or follow-ons of the AS-15 Kent.[141]

Strategic Defense Nuclear Forces

The Aerospace Defense Forces have five nuclear weapon systems armed with some 4100 nuclear warheads for defense of the Soviet Union. This includes the anti-ballistic missile (ABM) system around Moscow and an extensive network of nuclear armed surface-to-air missiles (SAMs) protecting population centers and military facilities on Soviet territory.[142]

The Moscow ABM system is currently completing a refurbishment program to upgrade it from 64 old aboveground reloadable launchers to 100 silo-based launchers. The 100-missile system, which "should be completed around 1989,"[143] will contain a mix of 32

---

132. HASC, FY 1984 DOD, Part 5, p. 232; SMP 1984, p. 29.
133. SMP 1988, p. 50.
134. *Aviation Week & Space Technology*, 14 December 1981, p. 17.
135. SMP 1988, pp. 15, 50; *Aviation Week & Space Technology*, 25 May 1987, p. 19.
136. JCS, FY 1989, p. 41. See also SMP 1986, preface, p. 33; SAC/SASC, Soviet Strategic Force Developments, 1985, p. 12. The expected introduction date for the Blackjack was pushed back from 1986-1987 in SMP 1983 (p. 26) to 1987 in SMP 1984 (p. 29), and 1988 in SMP 1985 (p. 34).
137. SMP 1988, p. 50.
138. SASC/SAC, Soviet Strategic Force Developments, 1985, p. 12; SMP 1986, p. 33; SMP 1985, p. 34; SMP 1984, p. 29; SMP 1983, p. 26.
139. JCS, FY 1989, p. 41.
140. SMP 1988, p. 52; SMP, 1986, p. 33. SMP 1986 refers to replacement of first the Bear A and then the Bear G bombers by the Blackjack bomber, but does not mention the Bear B/C variants.
141. JCS, FY 1987, p. 22.
142. The SA-2 and SA-5 SAMs in Mongolia or with Groups of Forces in Eastern Europe are not nuclear-capable.
143. SMP 1988, preface, pp. 44, 55-56.

ABM Systems

1971	1972	1973	1974	1975	1976	1977	1978	1979	1980	1981	1982	1983	1984	1985	1986	1987	1988
30	30	30	30	30	30	30	30	30	30	30	30	30	30	30	30	30	20
75	75	75	75	75	75	75	75	75	75	75	75	75	65	55	45	30	30
													10	20	30	40	45
												10	10	25	40	55	65
52	52	52	52	52	52	52	52	52	52	52	52	52	52	45	30	15	0
157	157	157	157	157	157	157	157	157	157	157	157	157	167	160	160	155	160
60	60	60	60	60	60	60	60	60	60	60	60	60	60	60	60	60	40
300	300	300	300	300	300	300	300	300	300	300	300	300	260	220	180	120	120
													60	120	180	240	270
														200	320	440	520
208	208	208	208	208	208	208	208	208	208	208	208	208	180	120	60	0	
568	568	568	568	568	568	568	568	568	568	568	568	568	560	720	800	860	950

Sources: Authors' estimates based on DIA, Intercontinental Strategic Forces Summary - USSR, DDB-2680-253-85, August 1985; SMP 1981, 1983, 1984, 1985, 1986, 1987, 1988; USAF, Trends, June 1976; USAF, Summary Review, 1975; SASC/SAC, Soviet Strategic Force Developments, 1985; Berman and Baker, Soviet Strategic Forces; MccGwire, Military Objectives; Freedman, U.S. Intelligence; Prados, Soviet Estimate; SASC, FY 1987 DOD, Part 1, p. 125.

modified Galosh and 68 new Gazelle nuclear armed missiles.[144]

Four of five strategic SAMs are nuclear capable—the SA-1 Guild, SA-2 Guideline, SA-5 Gammon, and SA-10 Grumble.[145] There are a total of 8400 launchers at some 1200 sites in the Soviet Union, Eastern Europe and Mongolia; 7070 in the Soviet Union are for nuclear-capable missiles.[146] Nuclear warheads are probably available for all the SA-1s, some SA-2s, most SA-5s, and some SA-10s. The SA-10 is currently being deployed, replacing the nuclear-capable SA-1s and SA-2s and the non-nuclear SA-3 missiles. The SA-1 is being rapidly retired. The SA-X-12b Giant, which is thought to be nuclear-capable, "will soon become operational."[147]

ABM Systems

ABM defense research began in the Soviet Union in the mid-1950s.[148] In 1958, one or two large early-warning radars were initially observed under construction at the Soviet research and test site at Sary Shagan in Central

Figure 5.3 Some 2400 **SA-2 Guideline** surface-to-air missiles assigned to stratgic air defense missions in the Soviet Union are nuclear-capable.

---

144 The ABM system also consists of numerous early-warning, target acquisition, and battle management radar systems, as well as numerous command facilities, which are not the subject of the *Databook*. See also DOD/DOS, *Soviet Strategic Defense Programs*, October 1985.
145 The SA-3 Goa system is not nuclear-capable. The SA-12 Giant is about to be deployed.
146 DIA, Force Structure Summary, November 1987, p. 11, reported 8560 launchers. The 8560 number includes 1100 SA-3 launchers and 220 SA-2 and SA-5 launchers in Eastern Europe and Mongolia that are not nuclear-capable. Another 260 SA-1s are estimated to be retired through the middle of 1988. In SMP 1985, p. 48, it was reported that the Soviets had "nearly 10,000 SAM launchers." JCS, FY 1987, p. 28, reported nearly 9400 launchers. In SMP 1986, p. 54, and SMP 1987, p. 59, "more than 9000" were reported. JCS, FY 1988, p. 45, reported more than 9000 launchers.
147 SMP 1988, p. 81.
148 The R&D phase of the Moscow ABM system began in about 1956; SMP 1986, p. 46. See also the discussion of the history of the program in Sayre Stevens, "The Soviet BMD Program," and Raymond L. Garthoff, "BMD and East-West Relation," in Ashton B. Carter and David N. Schwartz, eds., *Ballistic Missile Defense* (Washington, D.C.: The Brookings Institution, 1984).

5
ABM Systems

SS-X-16 Sinner Mobile ICBM

Although the three-stage, solid-propellant mobile SS-X-16 was never operationally deployed, the status of the SS-X-16 missile has received considerable attention since the late 1970s. The missile, basically the same as the SS-20 with an added third stage, was designed to carry a single warhead and had a range of 5600 miles. The Soviet Union agreed in the SALT II Treaty not to produce, test, or deploy the missile, or the third-stage reentry vehicle, or the appropriate device for targeting the reentry vehicle of the missile, which would enable upgrade of the SS-20 to full intercontinental range (Article IV, Paragraph 8, Common Understanding).

The SS-X-16 was first tested in April 1972, the first of the fourth-generation missiles to be flight-tested. The missile development program, however, soon lagged behind that of the other fourth-generation liquid-fueled ICBMs because of problems with the solid-fuel propulsion. Twenty-six tests of the SS-X-16 were held through 1974, compared with 30 for the SS-X-17, 35 for the SS-X-18, and 27 for the SS-X-19. The testing program completed all its milestones in 1975, including sufficient testing for a mobile configuration from presurveyed sites on an extremely large transporter-erector-launcher (TEL).

In mid-1976, Air Force intelligence credited the missile with a likely operational status in late 1975 or early 1976, though this never occurred. There was one test of the missile in April 1976 (the last test of the missile), which was unsuccessful. Nonetheless, the DIA reported that the missile had reached operational status during the period 1975-1978. Up to 200 SS-16 missiles were produced prior to the signing of the SALT II Treaty, with as many as 60 stored at the test range at Plesetsk. Modifications to existing buildings and construction of new buildings at four suspected SS-16 sites at Plesetsk was begun prior to the last SS-16 flight test in April 1976 and completed by mid-1978. This construction—subsequent activity, such as the institution of security measures normally seen at operational ICBM sites and the erection of nuclear-warhead storage facilities, communications towers, and SS-16 missile- associated equipment—suggested to some analysts in the U.S. government probable deployment of about 50 SS-16 missiles. In 1985, however, support equipment for the missiles, such as transporters for warheads, were removed from the site. It is now widely accepted that the SS-16 missiles at Plesetsk were removed and sent into storage.

Sources: Freedman, *U.S. Intelligence*, p. 215; USAF, *Summary Review*, 1975, p. B-10; USAF, *Trends*, 1976, p. 2; SASC, FY 1978 DOD, Part 10, p. 6864; JEC, Allocation of Resources - 1979, Part 5, p. 111; JEC, Allocation of Resources - 1977, Part 3, p. 68; HASC, FY 1980 DOD, Part 3, Book 1, p. 127-128; DOD, FY 1981 *Annual Report*, p. 81; SMP 1984, p. 23; Peter Samuel, "Cheating Charges Detailed," *Defense Week*, 19 August 1985, p. 6; HAC, FY 1984 DOD, Part 1, p. 313; SFRC, The SALT II Treaty, Report No. 96-14, p. 417; ACDA, *Soviet Noncompliance*, Publication 120, March 1986, p. 9; Michael R. Gordon, "U.S. Says Soviet Complies on Some Arms Issues," *New York Times*, 24 November 1985, p. 18; SMP 1985, pp. 30, 41.

Asia, and in 1960 ABM components were photographed by U.S. Air Force U-2 reconnaissance aircraft.[149] During its 1961 nuclear test series, the Soviets conducted a number of what were thought to be ABM- related experiments and on 6 September conducted a high-altitude nuclear test over Sary Shagan.[150] Missiles also began to be launched from the missile test range at Kapustin Yar towards Sary Shagan to test the radars.[151]

Initial site preparation for the so-called Leningrad ABM system (using the Griffon missile) was identified in 1961. Construction proceeded for two years, but then ceased; the sites were dismantled in 1963.[152] As the Leningrad system was being dismantled, another system, using the SA-5 Gammon SAM and called the Tallinn Line, was observed under construction across the northwest approaches to the Soviet Union.[153] As deployment of the SA-5 missile progressed, however, the system was reassessed to be a conventional air defense network, rather than an ABM system.[154]

Construction on the Moscow ABM system was first observed in October 1962 and continued at a sporadic pace until late 1965, when it was accelerated.[155] Eight separate complexes in a ring about 45 nautical miles from the center of the city were initially prepared—four became operational in 1969-1970.[156] The Moscow system used the ABM-1 Galosh missile, which had a high-yield nuclear warhead and was deployed in 64 aboveground launchers at four complexes. An improved missile, the ABM-1B, replaced the initial Galosh in the mid-1970s.[157]

Since the early 1970s, the Soviets have been working

---

149 Freedman, *U.S. Intelligence*, pp. 81, 87; Prados, *Soviet Estimate*, p. 152; Stevens, *op. cit.*, p. 192.
150 Freedman, *U.S. Intelligence*, p. 87; Prados, *Soviet Estimate*, p. 153; Stevens, *op. cit.*, p. 193.
151 Stevens, *op. cit.*, p. 193.
152 Freedman, *U.S. Intelligence*, p. 91; Prados, *Soviet Estimate*, pp. 153-155; Stevens, *op. cit.*, pp. 192, 195.
153 DOD, FY 1966 *Annual Report* (class.), p. 52; DOD, FY 1968 *Annual Report* (class.), p. 49.
154 DOD, FY 1966 *Annual Report* (class.), p. 52, stated that the system "may well have a capability primarily against aerodynamic vehicles rather than ballistic missiles." DOD, FY 1968 *Annual Report* (class.), p. 62, stated that "this system is designed for defense against high speed aerodynamic vehicles . . .inside the atmosphere." According to Prados, the SA-5 did not have a nuclear capability at that time; Prados, *Soviet Estimate*, pp. 160-164.
155 Freedman, *U.S. Intelligence*, pp. 87-88.
156 Four of the complexes were abandoned; DOD, FY 1969 *Annual Report* (class.), p. 62.
157 JCS, FY 1976, p. 39.

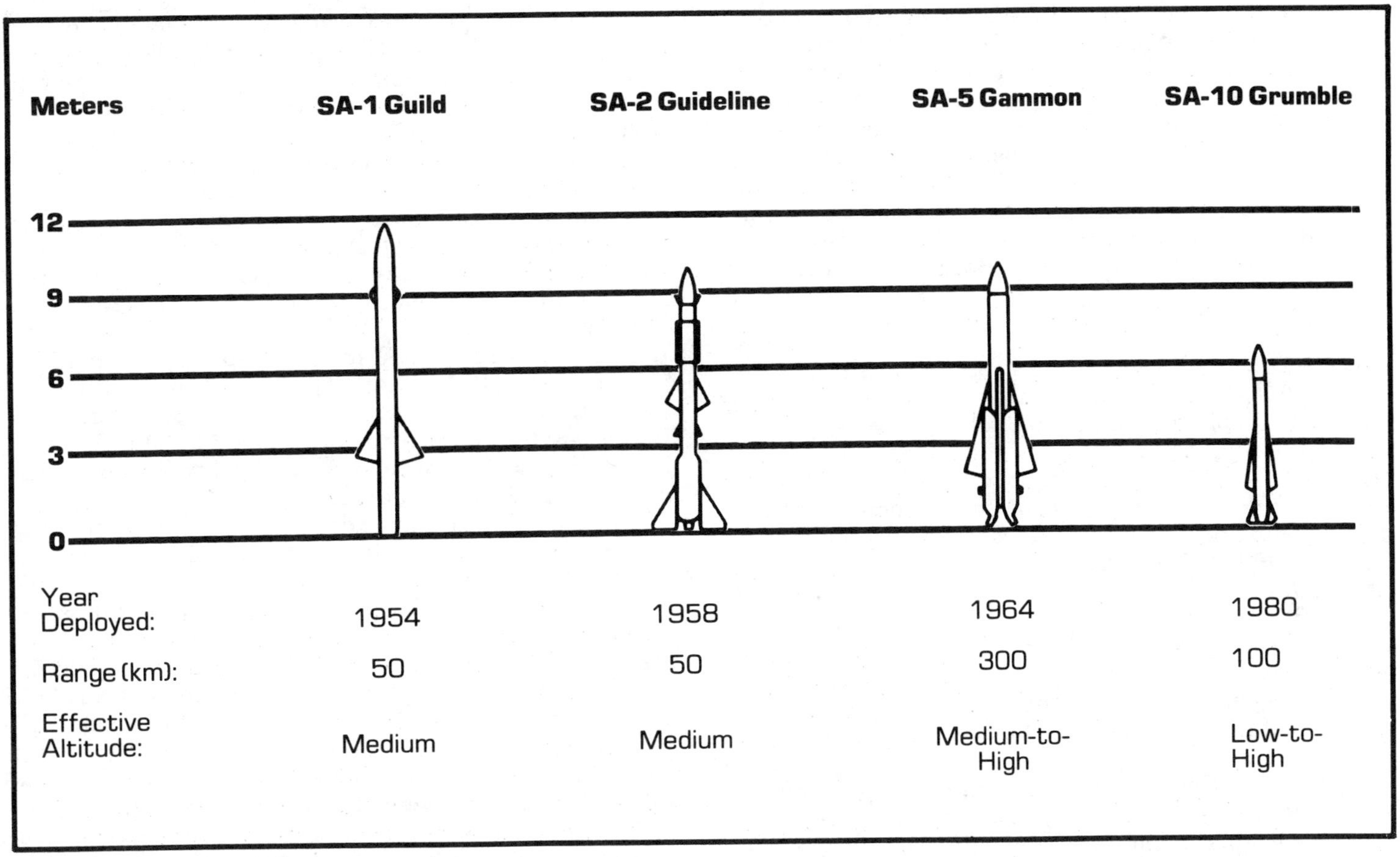

5
ABM Systems

Meters	SA-1 Guild	SA-2 Guideline	SA-5 Gammon	SA-10 Grumble
Year Deployed:	1954	1958	1964	1980
Range (km):	50	50	300	100
Effective Altitude:	Medium	Medium	Medium-to-High	Low-to-High

Figure 5.4 Nuclear Capable Surface-to-Air Missiles (1988).

to further upgrade the Moscow ABM system, including its supporting radar network and battle management systems.[158] Testing of at least one of two new missiles began in 1974 at Sary Shagan.[159] Aboveground complexes began to be dismantled starting late in 1979,[160] and construction of 100 silos began in 1981.[161]

By the end of 1985, the two new missiles were nearing deployment: a modified exoatmospheric Galosh interceptor, and the high-acceleration endoatmospheric interceptor called the Gazelle (SH-08 during development). The Gazelle reportedly became operational in mid-1986.[162] Completion of modernization of modified and new missiles, with hardened silos, should be completed around 1989.[163] The system will be armed with 100 nuclear warheads.[164]

The Reagan Administration has expressed concern that "[t]he aggregate of current Soviet ABM and ABM-

Figure 5.5 The Moscow anti-ballisitic missile system consists of 32 **ABM-1B Galosh** silo-based missiles with a multi-megaton nuclear warhead.

---

158 DOD/DOS, *Soviet Strategic Defense Programs*, op. cit., p. 13; SMP 1986, p. 42.
159 In 1974 a new missile, reportedly designated SH-04, was first tested at Sary Shagan; David R. Jones, "National Air Defense Forces," in *Soviet Armed Forces Review Annual*, 1978, Volume 2, p. 101.
160 JCS, FY 1983, p. 110.
161 DOD/DOS, *Soviet Strategic Defense Programs*, pp. 8, 13; SMP 1986, p. 46; Robert Hutchinson, "USSR Now Has 100 ABM Launchers," *Jane's Defence Weekly*, 2 November 1985, p. 959.
162 SMP 1987, p. 47.
163 SMP 1988, preface, pp. 44, 55-56.

164 There have been reports that the ABM launchers are reloadable and that the Gazelle has been tested at Sary Shagan in a rapid reload; SMP 1986, p. 43; "President's Unclassified Report on Soviet Noncompliance with Arms Control Agreements, 23 December 1985, p. 8; "Soviets Test Defense Missile Reload," *Aviation Week & Space Technology*, 29 August 1983, p. 19. The ABM Treaty prohibits "automatic or semi-automatic or other similar systems for rapid reload" of the permitted launchers (Article V[2]). It is unclear whether any such rapid reload capability exists, or that nuclear warheads are stockpiled for this purpose.

5

Surface-to-air Missiles

related activities suggest that the USSR may be preparing an ABM defense of its national territory."[165] The Soviet activities that have been noted include testing of SAMs capable of intercepting ballistic missile warheads, development of ABM components that would allow rapid construction of individual ABM sites away from Moscow, testing of the reload and refire of ABMs, and the development of new radars.[166] The ABM Treaty (under Article V[1]) expressly prohibits the development, testing, or deployment of mobile land-based ABM systems or radars.

Surface-to-air Missiles

The first Soviet SAM was the SA-1 Guild, introduced in 1954, followed by the semi-mobile SA-2 Guideline in 1958. More than 3200 high altitude SA-1 launchers were deployed at 56 operational sites in two concentric rings around Moscow, the outer one 45 nautical miles from the center of the city. As of mid-1988, some 1600 SA-1s were estimated to be operational, the missile being retired at the rate of 200-400 annually.[167]

The high-altitude SA-2 Guideline, also deployed around Moscow, as well as near other cities throughout the Soviet Union, offered improved capabilities over the SA-1, including solid fuel, longer range, better guidance, and improved electronic counter-countermeasures capability.[168] Some 4600 SA-2 launchers were deployed by 1970. As of mid-1988, some 2400 SA-2s are estimated to be operational.[169]

The SA-5 Gammon was developed in the 1950s to supplement the SA-1 and SA-2 missiles in high-altitude defenses against supersonic bombers. The missile was initially fielded in 1964-65, but was not widely deployed until 1967.[170] It has replaced some older SA-1 and SA-2 missiles. As of mid-1988, some 1950 SA-5s were deployed at 130 complexes in the Soviet Union.[171] Over the years, the Soviets have deployed numerous modifications of the SA-5, incorporating terminal maneuvering capabilities and other improvements, including the ability to interact with the newer SA-10 SAM.[172]

The SA-10 Grumble became operational in 1980 and began to replace SA-1, SA-2, and SA-3 missiles.[173] The low-to-high-altitude missile is being deployed for terminal defense of command and control facilities and key military and industrial targets.[174] The missile may have some ability to intercept cruise missiles and other small radar-cross-section targets.[175] A mobile version of the SA-10 (SA-10b) became operational in 1985-1986, possibly to support nonstrategic forces.[176] As of mid-1988, some 1100 SA-10s were estimated to be deployed at over 80 sites in the Soviet Union, with at least another 20 under construction.[177]

A new strategic SAM, the low-to-high-altitude hypersonic SA-X-12b Giant,[178] has been in development since the mid-1970s and according to *Soviet Military Power*, "will soon become operational."[179] This new missile is believed to have some capability against cruise missiles and tactical ballistic missiles.[180]

During the Reagan Administration, a controversy has been reopened over the potential ABM capability of the SA-5, SA-10, and SA-X-12 missiles.[181] The ABM Treaty (under Article VI[a]) prohibits giving missiles other than ABM interceptors "capabilities to counter strategic ballistic missiles or their elements in flight trajectory," and also prohibits "test[ing] them in an ABM mode." The potential ABM role of the SA-5 was the subject of controversy in the mid-1960s when the Tallinn Line was under construction,[182] and in 1973-1974 some 50 SA-5 flight tests were also conducted with the Square Pair radar-tracking ballistic missiles.[183] The SA-X-12 has reportedly intercepted an SS-12 Scaleboard nonstrategic missile in flight.[184] Although the SA-10 is not known to have been similarly tested, the U.S. government has raised concerns that the mobility of the system, and its widespread deployment, could provide the infrastructure for a nationwide ABM system.

---

165 DOD/DOS, *Soviet Strategic Defense Programs*, p. 45; see also, "President's Unclassified Report on Soviet Noncompliance with Arms Control Agreements," 23 December 1985, pp. 3, 8; Memorandum for the President, "Responding to Soviet Violations Policy (RSVP) Study, Part One," June 1986, p. 8, attachment to Letter, Caspar Weinberger to President Ronald Reagan, 13 November 1985.
166 ACDA, *Soviet Noncompliance*, March 1986, pp. 1-6; DOD/DOS, *Soviet Strategic Defense Programs*, October 1985; President's Unclassified Report to the Congress on Soviet Noncompliance With Arms Control Agreements, 1 February 1985, p. 11; and 23 December 1985, p. 7; "Soviets Stage Integrated Test of Weapons," *Aviation Week & Space Technology*, 28 June 1982, pp. 20-21; Stevens, op. cit., pp. 212-213; SMP 1984, p. 34; SASC, Briefing on SALT I Compliance, 96 Cong. 1st sess., 25 September 1979, p. 26.
167 DIA, *Force Structure Summary*, p. 11, reported 1860 SA-1s operational as of November 1987. IISS, *Military Balance, 1987-1988*, p. 36, reported 2200 SA-1s operational. IISS, *Military Balance, 1986-1987*, p. 38, reported 2540 SA-1s operational.
168 JCS, FY 1977, p. 45; DOD, FY 1966 Annual Report (class.), p. 52.
169 DIA, *Force Structure Summary*, p. 11. IISS, *Military Balance, 1987-1988*, p. 36, reported 2675 SA-2s operational. IISS, *Military Balance, 1986-1987*, p. 38, reported some 2730 SA-2s operational.
170 DOD, FY 1972 Annual Report (class.), p. 242; USAF, Summary Review, 1975, p. G-2.
171 DIA, *Force Structure Summary*, p. 11. IISS, *Military Balance, 1987-1988*, p. 36, reported 2030 SA-5s operational. IISS, *Military Balance, 1986-1987*, p. 38, reported 2050 SA-5s operational.
172 SMP 1986, p. 60.
173 SMP 1988, p. 81. The level of SA-1 deployment remained stable from the late 1950s until about 1980, when SA-10 deployment began.
174 SMP 1987, p. 6; DOD/DOS, *Soviet Strategic Defense Programs*, October 1985, p. 20; SMP 1986, p. 57; SMP 1985, p. 50.
175 SMP 1986, p. 57; SMP 1985, p. 48.
176 SMP 1987, p. 61.
177 DIA, *Force Structure Summary*, p. 11. Since 1981, about 150 SA-10 launch units have been deployed in defense of military industrial centers, with one-third around Moscow; SMP 1988, p. 81; see also, SMP 1987, p. 61.
178 The SA-12 Gladiator is a version of the missile assigned to Ground Forces fronts and armies replacing the SA-4; SMP 1986, p. 56; DOD/DOS, *Soviet Strategic Defense Programs*, October 1985, p. 20.
179 SMP 1988, p. 81.
180 SMP 1986, p. 57; SASC, FY 1986 DOD, Part 7, p. 3916.
181 JCS, FY 1986, p. 31; JCS, FY 1987, p. 28; DOD/DOS, *Soviet Strategic Defense Programs*, p. 48, only mentions the SA-10 and SA-X-12 missiles.
182 Prados, *Soviet Estimate*, p. 165. The "upgrading" question was questioned in DOD Annual Reports to Congress after FY 1970, and dropped after FY 1973.
183 DOD/DOS, *Soviet Strategic Defense Programs*, p. 12; SAC, hearing on SALT II Violations, 98 Cong. 2nd sess., S. Hrg. 98-665, 28 March 1984, p. 68; SASC, FY 1986 DOD, Part 7, p. 3575. After the United States raised this testing at the Standing Consultative Commission as a possible violation of the ABM Treaty, the testing ceased.
184 Michael R. Gordon, "CIA Is Skeptical the New Soviet Radar Is Part of an ABM Defense System," *National Journal*, 9 March 1985, p. 524.

Land-based Missile Systems
SS-11 SEGO

Figure 5.6 The Soviet **SS-11 Sego** ICBM was initially deployed in 1966. Over the years, it was assigned theater as well as strategic targets. Some 420 of these missiles are still operational, although they are being replaced by SS-24 and SS-25 missiles.

DESCRIPTION:	Third-generation, two-stage liquid-fuel ICBM; three modifications exist, Mod 1 and Mod 2 carrying a single warhead and Mod 3 with three MRVs; being retired as new SS-24 and SS-25 missiles are deployed
DESIGN BUREAU:	Chelomei; production facility possibly located at Plesetsk[1]
SPECIFICATIONS:	
Length:	19-20 m[2] (62-65 ft)
Diameter:	1.8 m[3] (5.9 ft); 2.4 m (7.9 ft)[4]
Stages:	2[5]
Weight at Launch:	48,000 kg[6] (106,000 lbs)
Fuel/Propulsion:	storable liquid[7]
Guidance:	inertial[8] with four gimballed chambers for control[9]
Throwweight:	Mod 1: 900 kg (2000 lbs)[10] Mod 2/3: 1100 kg (2500 lbs)[11]
Range:	Mod 1: max: 11,000 km[12] (6000 nm,[13] 6900 mi); min: 1100 km (600 nm,[14] 700 mi) Mod 2: 13,000 km[15] (7000 nm, 8000 mi) Mod 3: 10,600 km[16] (5700 nm, 6600 mi)
DUAL CAPABLE:	no
NUCLEAR WARHEADS:	
Number of warheads:	Mod 1/2: 1[17] Mod 3: 3 MRV[18]

---

1. Berman and Baker, *Soviet Strategic Forces*, p. 104.
2. A chart in SMP 1987, p. 30, indicates the length of the SS-11 Mods 1/2/3 are about 20 m. General Dynamics, *World's Missile Systems*, 1982, p. 243; *Aviation & Space Technology*, 14 March 1983, p. 153; *Jane's Weapon Systems*, 1987-1988, p. 7.
3. *Aviation Week & Space Technology*, 14 March 1983, p. 153.
4. General Dynamics, *World's Missile Systems*, 1982, p. 243.
5. SAC, *Soviet Military Capabilities*, July 1981, p. 14.
6. General Dynamics, *World's Missile Systems*, 1982, p. 243.
7. SAC, *Soviet Military Capabilities*, July 1981, p. 14.
8. Donald MacKenzie, "The Soviet Union and Strategic Missile Guidance," mimeo, Department of Sociology, University of Edinburgh, 1988, p. 21.
9. General Dynamics, *World's Missile Systems*, 1982, p. 243.
10. Paul H. Nitze, "The Balance in Numbers of Strategic Nuclear Launch Vehicles (SNLVs)," mimeo, 13 January 1981.
11. IISS, *Military Balance*, 1987-1988, p. 205; Collins and Victory, *U.S./Soviet Military Balance*, 1988, p. 13.
12. SMP 1987, p. 30.
13. SAC, *Soviet Military Capabilities*, July 1981, p. 14; DOD, FY 1972 Annual Report (class.), Table 4.
14. DOD, FY 1972 Annual Report (class.), Table 4.
15. SMP 1987, p. 30.
16. Ibid.
17. SMP 1984, pp. 21, 23.
18. Ibid.

5
SS-11 SEGO

Yield per warhead:	Mod 1/2: 950 Kt-1.1 Mt;[19] originally reported as 2-5 Mt[20] Mod 3: 100 Kt-350 Kt;[21] originally reported as 300-500 Kt[22]	First Flight Test:	Mod 1: 1965[33] Mod 2/3: 1969[34]
		Year Operation Began:	Mod 1: 1966[35] Mod 2/3: 1973[36]
DEPLOYMENT:			
Launch Platform:	underground hardened silo	Fully Deployed:	1973-1974 (at 1030 missiles)[37]
Location:	seven fields at Kozelsk, Teykovo, Perm, Gladkaya, Drovyanaya, Svobodnyy, Olovyannaya;[23] originally also deployed at Kostroma and Yedrovo (now SS-17 bases) and Tatishchevo, (now an SS-19 base);[24] Kozelsk is joint SS-11/SS-19 base[25]	**TARGETING:**	
		Types:	soft-area targets in the U.S. and Eurasia;[38] not capable of destroying hardened targets;[39] Mod 3 may be directed at countervalue targets and command and control centers;[40] some SS-11s may be intended for use against naval targets[41]
Silo Hardening:	estimated in 1976 at 751 psi; LCC at 360 psi[26]	Accuracy/CEP:	Mod 1: 0.5-0.72 nm (900-1300 m, 3000-4400 ft);[42] 0.75 nm[43] Mod 2: 0.6-0.73 nm (1100-1350 m, 3700-4400 ft)[44] Mod 3: 0.6-0.73 nm (1100-1350 m, 3700-4400 ft)[45]
Number Deployed:	420 (210 Mod 2, 210 Mod 3);[27] SS-11 Mod 1 retired by mid-1988, dropping from 100 missiles in 1985 to 28 in 1986, to 20 in March 1987, to zero by the middle of 1988;[28] 1030 SS-11s were deployed at peak in 1973-1974		
		COMMENTS:	The SS-11 was partially replaced by the SS-17. A total of 420 SS-11 Mod 2/3 missiles is assumed to have been deployed at the peak, 210 of each type.[46] Mod 2 was the first Soviet ICBM to carry penetration aids.[47] Early SS-11 deployments in Europe were probably supplements to theater nuclear forces.[48] A Mod 4 was tested, but never reached operational status.[49] 106 R&D flight tests through 1974, and 54 operational firings through 1974.[50]
Launch Mode:	hot[29]		
HISTORY:			
Design Began:	1955[30]		
R&D:	1955-1961[31]		
Engineering and Testing:	1961-1966[32]		

---

19 Berman and Baker, *Soviet Strategic Forces*, p. 105; Collins and Victory, *U.S./Soviet Military Balance*, 1988, p. 13; IISS, *Military Balance*, 1987-1988, p. 205; *Aviation Week & Space Technology*, 14 March 1983, p. 153; Paul H. Nitze, *op. cit.*
20 USAF, *Trends*, 1976, pp. 3, 13.
21 Berman and Baker, *Soviet Strategic Forces*, pp. 12, 20-21, 60, 99-100, 104-105; IISS, *Military Balance*, 1987-1988, p. 205; *Aviation Week & Space Technology*, 14 March 1983, p. 153; John W. R. Taylor, "Gallery of Soviet Aerospace Weapons," *Air Force Magazine*, March 1988, p. 87; General Dynamics, *World's Missile Systems*, 1982, p. 243; "Soviets' Nuclear Arsenal Continues to Proliferate," *Aviation Week & Space Technology*, 16 June 1980, pp. 67-69.
22 USAF, *Trends*, June 1976, pp. 3, 13.
23 SMP 1987, p. 25.
24 USAF, *Summary Review*, 1975, pp. B-3; SMP 1987, p. 25.
25 SMP 1987, p. 25.
26 USAF, *Trends*, 1976, p. 15.
27 JCS, FY 1989, p. 39; As SS-25s are deployed, SS-11s are being retired. SS-11 Mod 1s were evidently retired first and were totally eliminated in late 1987. This is probably being followed by retirements of the SS-11 Mod 2 before the SS-11 Mod 3. According to SMP 1988, p. 15, and SMP 1987, p. 30, there are 440 SS-11s.
28 JCS, FY 1989, p. 19; DIA, *Force Structure Summary*, November 1987, p. 2; SMP 1987, p. 30; SMP 1985, p. 23; JCS, FY 1988, p. 33; SMP 1986, p. 26.
29 SMP 1987, p. 30.
30 SMP 1985, p. 41.
31 Ibid.
32 Ibid.
33 Berman and Baker, *Soviet Strategic Forces*, p. 104.
34 Ibid.
35 SMP 1984, pp. 21, 23; HASC, FY 1980 DOD, Part 3, Book 1, pp. 125-126.
36 HASC, FY 1980 DOD, Part 3, Book 1, pp. 125-126; NATO, *NATO and the Warsaw Pact*, 1984, p. 27.
37 JCS, FY 1975, p.
38 SMP 1984, pp. 21, 23.
39 SMP 1988, p. 46.
40 HASC, FY 1980 DOD, Part 3, Book 1, pp. 125-126.
41 Berman and Baker, *Soviet Strategic Forces*, p. 21.
42 USAF, *Trends*, pp. 3, 13; DOD, FY 1968 *Annual Report* (class.), p. 46 stated 1.0-1.5 nm (1800-2800 m, 6100-9100 ft).
43 MacKenzie, *op. cit.*, Table 1. This is the CEP at the year of first deployment.
44 USAF, *Trends*, p. 13.
45 Ibid.
46 USAF, *Summary Review*, 1975, p. B-3.
47 Berman and Baker, *Soviet Strategic Forces*, pp. 99-100.
48 Lawrence Freedman, "The Dilemma of Theatre Nuclear Arms Control," *Survival*, January-February, 1981, p. 10n.
49 HASC, FY 1980 DOD, Part 3, Book 1, pp. 126-127.
50 USAF, *Summary Review*, 1975, p. B-8.

SS-13 Mod 2 SAVAGE (Soviet designation RS-12)

Figure 5.7 The **SS-13 Savage** ICBM, deployed in 1969, was the first large Soviet missile to use solid fuel. As of mid-1988, the same 60 SS-13 missiles that constituted full deployment in 1972 were operational.

DESCRIPTION: Third-generation, solid-fuel, single-warhead ICBM; first large Soviet missile to have solid propulsion

DESIGN BUREAU: Nadiradze; production facilities possibly located at Biysk[1]

SPECIFICATIONS:

Length: 20 m[2] (66 ft)

Diameter: First stage: 1.7 m[3] (5.6 ft)
Second stage: 1.4 m[4] (4.6 ft)
Third stage: 1.0 m[5] (3.3 ft)

Stages: 3[6]

Weight at Launch: 35,000 kg[7] (77,000 lbs)

Fuel/Propulsion: solid[8]

Guidance: inertial[9]

Throwweight: estimated to be 380-685 kg (840-1510 lbs); with best estimate reported as 500 kg (1100 lbs)[10]

Range: 9400 km[11] (5100 nm, 5800 mi)

DUAL CAPABLE: no

NUCLEAR WARHEADS:

Number of warheads: 1[12]

Yield per warhead: 600 Kt;[13] 750 Kt;[14]

DEPLOYMENT:

Launch Platform: underground hardened silo

Location: one field at Yoshkar Ola;[15] SS-13s have also been reported at the test sites at Plesetsk[16] and Ivanova (to the northeast of Moscow)[17]

Silo Hardening: estimated in 1976 at 1290 psi; LCC at 1430 psi[18]

---

1 Berman and Baker, *Soviet Strategic Forces*, p. 104.
2 A chart in SMP 1987, p. 30, indicates that the length of the SS-13 Mod 2 is about 20 m. SMP 1985, p. 29; *Jane's Weapons Systems*, 1987-1988, p. 7; John W. R. Taylor, "Gallery of Soviet Aerospace Weapons," *Air Force Magazine*, March 1988, p. 87; General Dynamics, *World's Missile Systems*, 1982, p. 211.
3 Taylor, "Gallery of Soviet Aerospace Weapons," 1988, *op. cit.*, p. 91; General Dynamics, *World's Missile Systems*, 1982, p.211.
4 *Jane's Weapons Systems*, 1987-1988, p. 7; Taylor, *Missiles of the World*, 1980, p. 97.
5 Ibid.
6 SAC, *Soviet Military Capabilities*, July 1981, p. 15.
7 General Dynamics, *World's Missile Systems*, 1982, p. 211.
8 SAC, *Soviet Military Capabilities*, July 1981, p. 15.
9 Donald MacKenzie, "The Soviet Union and Strategic Missile Guidance," mimeo, Department of Sociology, University of Edinburgh, 1988, p. 21; Berman and Baker, *Soviet Strategic Forces*, p. 104.
10 ACDA, *Soviet Noncompliance*, March 1986, pp. 7-8; Michael Weisskopf, "Soviet Said to Deploy Missile," *Washington Post*, 23 October 1985, p. A4; Peter Samuel, "Cheating Charges Detailed," *Defense Week*, 19 August 1985, p. 6, reports throwweight of SS-13 ranging approximately 380-685 kg based on NSC report entitled "Soviet Non-Compliance with Arms Control Agreements," 23 January 1984.
11 SMP 1987, p. 30. Mod 1 range was 5000 mi; DIA, *Handbook on the Soviet Armed Forces*, p. 12-10.
12 SMP 1987, p. 30.
13 Berman and Baker, *Soviet Strategic Forces*, p. 105; Collins and Victory, *U.S./Soviet Military Balance*, 1987, p. 17; "Soviets' Nuclear Arsenal Continues to Proliferate," *Aviation Week & Space Technology*, 16 June 1980, p. 69.
14 Paul H. Nitze, "The Balance in Numbers of Strategic Nuclear Launch Vehicles (SNLVs)," mimeo, 13 Jan 1981; Taylor, *op. cit.*, p. 87.
15 Taken from chart in SMP 1985, p. 26.
16 *Flight International*, 2 June 1979, p. 1822.
17 *Jane's Weapons Systems*, 1982-1983, pp. 5-6.
18 USAF, *Trends*, 1976, p. 15.

5

SS-13 SAVAGE

Number Deployed:	60 (1988)[19]	**TARGETING:** Types:	soft-area targets in the U.S. and Eurasia;[29] not capable of destroying hardened targets[30]
Launch Mode:	hot[20]	Accuracy/CEP:	0.82 nm (1500 m; 5000 ft);[31] 1.00-1.8 nm (1800-1850 m; 5900-6100 ft)[32]

HISTORY:

Design Began: 1958[21]

R&D: 1958-1964[22]

Engineering and Testing: 1904-1909[23]

First Observed: SS-13 Mod 1 was first observed at 9 May 1965 parade

First Flight Test: Mod 1: 1965[24]
Mod 2: 1970[25]

Year Operation Began: Mod 1: 1969[26]
Mod 2: 1973[27]

Fully Deployed: 1972 (at 60 missiles)[28]

COMMENTS: Originally the SS-13 may have been designed to provide a mobile, land-based strategic reserve, though guidance and motor problems were encountered in development.[33] Upper two stages thought to form the mobile theater SS-X-14, which was never operationally deployed.[34] Some SS-13s may be used as boosters for launching emergency transmitters to relay communications.[35] 44 R&D flight tests and 19 operational firings through 1974, including five operational firings in 1974.[36]

---

19 JCS, FY 1989, p. 39 and SMP 1988, p. 15.
20 SMP 1985, p. 29.
21 Ibid., p. 41.
22 Ibid.
23 Ibid.
24 Berman and Baker, *Soviet Strategic Forces*, p. 100.
25 Ibid.
26 HASC, FY 1980 DOD, Part III, Book 1, pp. 125-126; and SMP 1985, p. 41.
27 SMP 1984, p. 23.
28 DOD, FY 1973 Annual Report (class.), p. 53.
29 SMP 1984, p. 23.
30 SMP 1988, p. 46.
31 Berman and Baker, *Soviet Strategic Forces*, p. 105; "Soviets' Nuclear Arsenal Continues to Proliferate," Aviation Week & Space Technology, 16 June 1980, p. 69. Mod 1 CEP was 1.0 nm; USAF, Trends
32 IISS, Military Balance, 1987-1988, p. 205; Collins and Victory, *U.S./Soviet Military Balance*, 1988, p. 13.
33 HASC, FY 1980 DOD, Part III, Book 1, pp. 125-126; SMP 1985, p. 41.
34 Jane's Weapons Systems, 1982-1983, pp. 5-6; Taylor, *Missiles of the World*, 1980, p. 97.

SS-17 Mod 3 SPANKER (Soviet designation RS-16)

DESCRIPTION: Fourth-generation, two-stage, liquid-fuel MIRVed ICBM that partially replaced the SS-11

DESIGN BUREAU: Yangel; production facilities reportedly located at Dnepropetrovsk[1]

SPECIFICATIONS:
- Length: 24 m[2] (79 ft); approx. 20 m[3] (66 ft)
- Diameter: 2.5 m[4] (8.2 ft)
- Stages: 2[5]
- Weight at Launch: 65,000 kg[6] (143,000 lbs)
- Fuel/Propulsion: storable liquid[7]
- Guidance: inertial[8] with onboard digital computer[9]
- Throwweight: 2900 kg[10] (6300 lbs)
- Range: 10,000 km[11] (5000 nm, 6000 mi)

DUAL CAPABLE: no

NUCLEAR WARHEADS:
- Number of warheads: Mod 1: 4 MIRV
  Mod 2: 1
  Mod 3: 4 MIRV[12]
- Yield per warhead: Mod 3: 500 Kt;[13] 750 Kt[14]

DEPLOYMENT:
- Launch Platform: former SS-11 underground silos that have been modified and hardened; missile contained in a launch-canister within the silo[15]
- Location: 2 fields at Kostroma and Yedrovo[16]
- Silo Hardening: reportedly "housed in the world's hardest silos"[17]
- Number Deployed: estimated 130 (mid-1988); 138 (April 1988); 145 (end of 1987);[18] the SS-17 is undergoing retirement at Kostroma to compensate for newer deployments of SS-24 MIRVed missiles[19]
- Launch Mode: cold[20]

HISTORY:
- Design Began: 1964[21]
- R&D: 1964-1970[22]
- Engineering and Testing: 1970-1975[23]
- First Flight Test: Mod 1: September 1972 from Tyuratam to Kamchatka peninsula[24]
  Mod 2: February 1976[25]
  Mod 3: 1977[26]

---

1 Berman and Baker, *Soviet Strategic Forces*, p. 104.
2 General Dynamics, *World's Missile Systems*, 1982, p. 281; *Aviation Week & Space Technology*, 14 March 1983, p. 153.
3 A chart in SMP 1985, p. 29, indicates the length of the SS-17 is just over 20 m.
4 SMP 1988, p. 46.
5 DIA, *Handbook on the Soviet Armed Forces*, p. 12-10.
6 General Dynamics, *The World's Missile Systems*, 1982, p. 281.
7 DOD, *FY 1982 Annual Report*, p. 45.
8 Donald MacKenzie, "The Soviet Union and Strategic Missile Guidance," mimeo, Department of Sociology, University of Edinburgh, 1988, p. 22.
9 MacKenzie, "The Soviet Union and Strategic Missile Guidance," *op. cit.*, p. 30. Berman and Baker, *Soviet Strategic Forces*, p. 104.
10 USAF, *Trends*, 1976, p. 3.
11 SMP 1987, p. 30.
12 *Ibid*.
13 IISS, *Military Balance*, 1987-1988, p. 205; Collins and Victory, *U.S./Soviet Military Balance*, 1988, p. 13.
14 Berman and Baker, *Soviet Strategic Forces*, p. 105; and Paul H. Nitze, "The Balance in Numbers of Strategic Nuclear Launch Vehicles (SNLVs)," mimeo, 13 January 1981. USAF, *Trends*, 1976, p. 13, reported the SS-17 Mod 1 as having a 1.25-1.875 Mt total yield, or 300-500 Kt per warhead. The single warhead SS-17 Mod 2 had a yield variously reported as 2 Mt (John Erickson, *Soviet-Warsaw Pact Force Levels*, USSI Report 76-2, p. 29), 3.6 Mt (Berman and Baker, *Soviet Strategic Forces*, p. 105 and "Soviets' Nuclear Arsenal Continues to Proliferate," *Aviation Week & Space Technology*, 16 June 1980, p. 69), 4 Mt and 6 Mt (IISS, *Military Balance*, 1983-1984, pp. 14, 119; Collins and Victory, *U.S./Soviet Military Balance*, 1988, p. 13; John W.R. Taylor, "Gallery of Soviet Aerospace Weapons," *Air Force Magazine*, March 1983, p. 91; "Soviets' Nuclear Arsenal Continues to Proliferate," *Aviation Week & Space Technology*, 16 June 1980, p. 69).
15 SMP 1983, pp. 16-17, 19-20.
16 SMP 1985, p. 26.
17 SMP 1983, pp. 16-17, 19-20.
18 SMP 1988, p. 15. There were 145 SS-17 missiles as of the end of 1987, according to JCS, FY 1989, p. 39; retirement began in late 1987 to compensate for the deployment of the MIRVed SS-24 and for sea trials underway for Typhoon and Delta IV class submarines to maintain the 1200 MIRVed missile launcher limit set in the SALT II Treaty. The number of SS-17s was still at its peak (150 missiles) as of March, 1987 according to SMP 1987, p. 8.
19 JCS, FY 1989, p. 39; Peter Samuel, "Big Soviet Buildup Foreseen," *Defense Week*, 17 June 1985, p. 15.
20 SMP 1985, p. 29.
21 *Ibid*.
22 *Ibid*.
23 *Ibid*.
24 Berman and Baker, *Soviet Strategic Forces*, p. 104; William Beecher, "U.S. Says Soviet Improves ICBMs," *New York Times*, 21 March 1973.
25 JCS, FY 1978, p. 10.
26 Rich and Pike, *SALT*, 1984, pp. 98-99.

5

SS-17 SPANKER

Year Operation Began:	Mod 1: 1975[27] Mod 2: 1975[28] Mod 3: 1979[29]	Accuracy/CEP:	0.2 nm (400 m, 1200 ft)[33]
Fully Deployed:	1980 to late 1987 (at 150 missiles)[30]	COMMENTS:	30 R&D test firings through 1974, including 16 during 1974[34]

TARGETING:

Types: capable of destroying any unhardened targets;[31] capable of flexible targeting in Eurasia[32]

---

27 JCS, FY 1979, p. 22.
28 SMP 1985, p. 41.
29 DOD, FY 1985 RD&A, p. II-12.
30 SMP 1987, p. 8.
31 SMP 1988, p. 46.
32 Ibid.
33 Collins and Victory, *U.S./Soviet Military Balance*, 1988, p. 13; IISS, *Military Balance*, 1987-1988, p. 205. Nitze, op. cit., reported 0.2 nm (400 m, 1200 ft). Nitze deported that the Soviets provided a CEP of 0.17 nm for the SS-17 Mod 1 during the SALT II negotiations. SMP 1988, p. 46, reports that the SS-17 is less accurate than the SS-18.
34 USAF, *Summary Review*, 1975, pp. B-8, B-10.

SS-18 Mod 4 SATAN (Soviet designation RS-20)

DESCRIPTION: Fourth-generation, two-stage, liquid-fuel, heavy, MIRVed ICBM, follow-on to the SS-9

DESIGN BUREAU: Yangel; production facilities possibly located at Dnepropetrovsk[1]

SPECIFICATIONS:
- Length: approx. 32 m[2] (105 ft); 37 m (121 ft)[3]
- Diameter: 3.2 m[4]
- Stages: 2[5]
- Weight at Launch: 220,000 kg[6] (485,000 lbs)
- Fuel/Propulsion: storable liquid[7]
- Guidance: inertial[8] with onboard digital computer[9]
- Throwweight: 7600 kg[10] (16,700 lbs)
- Range: 11,000 km[11] (5900 nm, 6800 mi)

DUAL CAPABLE: no

NUCLEAR WARHEADS:
- Number of warheads: 10 MIRV[12]
- Yield per warhead: 500-550 Kt[13]

DEPLOYMENT:
- Launch Platform: former SS-9 underground silos that have been modified and hardened; missile contained in a launch-canister within the silo[14]
- Location: 6 fields at Aleysk, Dombarovskiy, Imeni Gastello, Kartaly, Uzhur (64 silos), Zhangiz Tobe[15]
- Silo Hardening: reportedly "housed in the world's hardest silos";[16] originally reported as 2500-4500 psi,[17] and some hardened to 6000-7000 psi[18]
- Number Deployed: 308 (mid-1988);[19] the majority of which are SS-18 Mod 4[20]
- Launch Mode: cold[21]

HISTORY:
- Design Began: 1964[22]

---

1. Berman and Baker, *Soviet Strategic Forces*, pp. 65, 77-84, 104-105; Commander James J. Tritten, USN, "Their Broken Promises," *Proceedings*, August 1984, pp. 56-57.
2. A chart in SMP 1987, p. 30 indicates the length of the SS-18 Mod 4 is about 32 m.
3. General Dynamics, *World's Missile Systems*, 1982, p. 283.
4. *Ibid.* (10.5 ft)
5. *Aviation Week & Space Technology*, 14 March 1983, p. 153; and *Jane's Weapons Systems, 1982-1983*, p. 6.
6. Stephen Meyer, "Verification and Risk," *International Security*, Spring 1984, Vol. 8, No. 4, p. 124.
7. DOD, FY 1982 Annual Report, p. 45.
8. Donald MacKenzie, "The Soviet Union and Strategic Missile Guidance," mimeo, Department of Sociology, University of Edinburgh, 1988, p. 22.
9. JCS, FY 1977, p. 34; MacKenzie, *op. cit.*, p. 30.
10. Collins and Victory, *U.S./Soviet Military Balance*, 1988, p. 13. The throwweight of the earlier Mods 1, 2 and 3 were reported as 7300 kg (16,000 lbs), Berman and Baker, *Soviet Strategic Forces*, p. 105; "Soviets' Nuclear Arsenal Continues to Proliferate," *Aviation Week & Space Technology*, 16 June 1980, pp. 67, 69; and IISS, *Military Balance*, 1987-1988, p. 205. Collins and Victory report throwweight for Mod 1 as 15,000 lbs, Mod 2 as 16,700 lbs, and Mod 3 as 12,000 lbs.
11. SMP 1986, p. 26. The range of the earlier Mods 1, 2, and 3 were reported as: Mod 1—12,000 km; Mod 2—11,000 km; and Mod U—16,000 km (DOD, FY 1982 Annual Report, p. 45; SMP 1983, p. 20; SMP 1981, p. 56).
12. USAF, *Trends*, 1976, p. 3; SMP 1983, pp. 16, 19-21; SMP 1985, pp. 29, 41. SMP 1986, p. 25, states "at least 10." SMP 1987, p. 30, states, "10+." Peter Samuel, "Warhead Count," *Defense Week*, 18 March 1985, p. 3, quotes Assistant Secretary of Defense Richard Perle as stating that the missile had been tested with 14 warheads. See also Prados, *Soviet Estimate*, pp. 271-273 and *Air Force Magazine*, November 1978, p. 12, which describe simulated tests of more than 10 warheads on 21 December 1978 and in early 1979. One report states the Mod 4 can carry up to 32 warheads; according to Senator Robert Dole, *Soviet Aerospace*, 8 August 1983, p. 98. Mods 1 and 3 were single-warhead variants; DOD, FY 1982 Annual Report, p. 45; SMP 1983, pp. 16, 19-21. Mod 2 was originally reported as carrying 5 to 8 warheads (JCS, FY 1975, p. 15), at least 6, and as many as 8 warheads (JCS, FY 1976, p. 16), 8 warheads (JCS, FY 1977, p. 33; JCS, FY 1978, p. 9), and 8 to 10 warheads (JCS, FY 1979, p. 22; DOD, FY 1982 Annual Report, p. 45; SMP 1983, pp. 16, 19-21).
13. Collins and Victory, *U.S./Soviet Military Balance*, 1988, p. 13; IISS, *Military Balance*, 1983-1984, pp. 14, 119; *Aviation Week & Space Technology*, 21 May 1984, p. 17. USAF, *Trends*, 1976, p. 13, reported the SS-18 Mod 1 (single-warhead variant) yield as 18-25 Mt. The SS-18 Mod 3 is presumed to have carried the same warhead. Most sources give the yield of the Mod 1 and Mod 3 as 20-24 Mt; Berman and Baker, *Soviet Strategic Forces*, p. 105; IISS, *Military Balance*, 1987-1988, p. 205; "Soviets' Nuclear Arsenal Continues to Proliferate," *Aviation Week & Space Technology*, 16 June 1980, pp. 67-69; Collins and Victory, *U.S./Soviet Military Balance*, 1988, p. 13. The 8-10 warhead SS-18 Mod 2 yield was reported as 550-900 Kt, Berman and Baker, *Soviet Strategic Forces*, p. 105; IISS, *Military Balance*, 1983-1984, pp. 14, 119); "Soviets' Nuclear Arsenal Continues to Proliferate," *Aviation Week & Space Technology*, 16 June 1980, pp. 67-69; Collins and Victory, *U.S./Soviet Military Balance*, 1988, p. 13. The 8-10 warhead SS-18 Mod 2 yield was reported as 550-900 Kt, Berman and Baker, *Soviet Strategic Forces*, p. 105; IISS, *Military Balance*, 1983-1984, pp. 14, 119); "Soviets' Nuclear Arsenal Continues to Proliferate," *Aviation Week & Space Technology*, 16 June 1980, pp. 67-69; and Collins and Victory, *U.S./Soviet Military Balance*, 1988, p. 13, or 1-2 Mt (*Jane's Weapons Systems*, 1987-88, p. 8; *Flight International*, 2 June 1979, pp. 1822-1823; Taylor, *Missiles of the World*, 1980, p. 125).
14. SMP 1983, pp. 16, 21.
15. DIA, *Force Structure Summary*, November 1987, p. 3.
16. SMP 1984, p. 21.
17. USAF, *Trends*, 1976, p. 15.
18. Howard Silber, "Soviets Could Make 3rd Strike, Source Says," *Omaha World-Herald*, 4 April 1982, p. 1; "Soviets' Nuclear Arsenal Continues to Proliferate," *Aviation Week & Space Technology*, 16 June 1980, pp. 67, 69; *Aviation Week & Space Technology*, 3 November 1980, p. 28.
19. SMP 1988, p. 15; JCS, FY 1989, p. 39.
20. SMP 1988, p. 46.
21. SMP 1986, p. 26.
22. SMP 1985, p. 41.

5
SS-18 SATAN

R&D:	1964-1969[23]
Engineering and Testing:	1969-1974[24]
First Flight Test:	Mod 1: April/May 1972[25] Mod 2: September 1973[26] Mod 3: 1975[27] Mod 4: 1977[28]
Year Operation Began:	Mod 1: 1974[29] Mod 2: 1976[30] Mod 3: 1976[31] Mod 4: 1979[32]
Fully Deployed:	1981 to present (308 missiles)[33]

TARGETING:

Types: hardened targets such as ICBM silos, air bases, command and control facilities[34]

Accuracy/CEP: 0.14 nm[35] (260 m, 850 ft); 0.1 nm[36] (190 m, 600 ft)[37]

COMMENTS: The SS-18 Mod 2 had serious problems related to the design of the post-boost vehicle.[38] A 250 m CEP, 10 warhead SS-18 Mod 5 with 550-750 Kt yield has been referred to as beginning operation in 1985, but it does not appear to have ever been deployed.[39] An improved SS-18, which may be designated the Mod 5, will soon be deployed.[40] 35 R&D test firings through 1974, including 18 during 1974.[41]

---

23 *Ibid.*
24 *Ibid.*
25 Prados, *Soviet Estimate*, p. 221; Berman and Baker, *Soviet Strategic Forces*, p. 104.
26 Prados, *Soviet Estimate*, p. 221.
27 Berman and Baker, *Soviet Strategic Forces*, p. 106.
28 Rich and Pike, *SALT*, 1984, pp. 98-99.
29 SMP 1985, pp. 29, 41; DIA, *Handbook on the Soviet Armed Forces*, p. 12-10.
30 JCS, FY 1978, pp. 9-10.
31 *Ibid.*
32 DOD, FY 1985 RD&A, p. II-12.
33 SMP 1981, p. 55.
34 SMP 1984, p. 23; SASC, *Strategic Force Modernization Programs*, 1981, p. 17.
35 Berman and Baker, *Soviet Strategic Forces*, p. 105; "Soviets' Nuclear Arsenal Continues to Proliferate," *Aviation Week & Space Technology*, 16 June 1980, pp. 67, 69; Collins and Victory, *U.S./Soviet Military Balance*, 1988, p. 13.
36 *Aviation Week & Space Technology*, 14 March 1983, p. 153.
37 The CEPs of the earlier Mods 1, 2, and 3 were reported as: Mod 1—0.31 nm; Mod 2—0.35 nm; and Mod 3—0.28 nm; USAF, *Trends*, 1976, pp. 3, 13.
38 HASC, FY 1980 DOD, Part 3, Book 1, p. 129.
39 IISS, *Military Balance*, 1987-1988, p. 205; Walter Pincus, "Soviets Believed to Have Problems with New Typhoon Missile," *Washington Post*, 18 January 1982, p. 15; Rich and Pike, *SALT*, 1984, pp. 98-99.
40 R. Jeffrey Smith, "Arms Budget Cut, Soviet Says," *Washington Post*, 27 July 1988, p. A1.
41 USAF, *Summary Review*, 1975, pp. B-8, B-10.

SS-19 Mod 3 STILETTO (Soviet designation RS-18)

DESCRIPTION:	Fourth-generation, two-stage, liquid-fuel, MIRVed ICBM that partially replaced the SS-11; being retired as SS-24 missiles are deployed	Yield per warhead:	550 Kt[16]

DESIGN BUREAU: Chelomei; production facility possibly located at Plesetsk[1]

SPECIFICATIONS:

Length: approx. 24 m[2] (79 ft); 27 m[3] (89 ft)

Diameter: 2.5-2.75 m[4] (8.2-9.0 ft)

Stages: 2[5]

Weight at Launch: 90,000 kg[6] (200,000 lbs); 78,000 kg[7] (170,000 lbs)

Fuel/Propulsion: liquid[8]

Guidance: inertial[9] with onboard digital computer[10]

Throwweight: 3600 kg[11] (8000 lbs);[12] 3400 kg (7500 lbs)[13]

Range: 10,000 km[14] (5400 nm, 6200 mi)

DUAL CAPABLE: no

NUCLEAR WARHEADS:

Number of warheads: 6 MIRV[15]

DEPLOYMENT:

Launch Platform: underground hardened silo; missile contained in a launch-canister within the silo[17]

Location: 4 fields at Derazhnya, Kozelsk, Pervomaysk and Tatishchevo;[18] 120 silos at Derazhnya and Pervomaysk are reportedly at an angle rather than vertical;[19] there are 18 additional operational SS-19 launchers at the Tyuratam missile test center[20]

Silo Hardening: reportedly "housed in the world's hardest silos;"[21] originally reported in 1974 as 2500-4000 psi;[22] some hardened to 6000-7000 psi[23]

Number Deployed: 350 (April 1988);[24] the SS-19 began retirement in 1987 to compensate for deployment of SS-24 MIRVed missiles[25]

Launch Mode: hot[26]

HISTORY:

Design Began: 1964[27]

R&D: 1964-1970[28]

---

1 Berman and Baker, *Soviet Strategic Forces*, p. 104.
2 A chart in SMP 1986, p. 26, indicates the length of the SS-19 Mod 3 is about 24 m.
3 Stephen M. Meyer, "Verification and Risk," *International Security*, Spring 1984, Vol. 8, No. 4, p. 124; Rich and Pike, *SALT*, 1984, pp. 98-99.
4 *Aviation Week & Space Technology*, 14 March 1983, p. 153; Meyer, op. cit., p. 124; *Jane's Weapons Systems*, 1987-1988, pp. 8-9; Taylor, *Missiles of the World*, 1980, p. 124.
5 *Aviation Week & Space Technology*, 14 March 1983, p. 153; *Jane's Weapons Systems*, 1987-1988, pp. 8-9.
6 SFRC, SALT II Treaty, Report No. 96-14, p. 351.
7 Meyer, op cit., p. 124.
8 DOD, FY 1982 Annual Report, p. 45.
9 Donald MacKenzie, "The Soviet Union and Strategic Missile Guidance," mimeo, Department of Sociology, University of Edinburgh, 1988, p. 22.
10 JCS, FY 1975, p. 16; JCS, FY 1976, p. 16; JCS, FY 1977, p. 35; MacKenzie, op. cit., p. 30.
11 SASC, SALT II Treaty, Part 3, p. 898.
12 IISS, *Military Balance*, 1983-1984, pp. 14, 119; Berman and Baker, *Soviet Strategic Forces*, p. 105.
13 IISS, *Military Balance*, 1987-1988, p. 205.
14 SMP 1987, p. 30.
15 SMP 1988, p. 46. The SS-19 Mod 1 was reported to have had 6 MIRVs, and Mod 2 one warhead; SMP 1983, p. 20.
16 Berman and Baker, *Soviet Strategic Forces*, p. 105; IISS, *Military Balance*, 1987-1988, p. 205; "Soviets' Nuclear Arsenal Continues to Proliferate," *Aviation Week & Space Technology*, 16 June 1980, pp. 67, 69; *Aviation Week & Space Technology*, 9 March 1981, p. 27; Collins and Victory, *U.S./Soviet Military Balance*, 1988, p. 13. USAF, Trends, 1976, p. 13; *Jane's Weapons Systems*, 1987-88, pp. 8-9 reported the SS-19 Mod 1 yield as 200 Kt per warhead. Most sources give the yield of the Mod 1 as 550 Kt per warhead; Berman and Baker, *Soviet Strategic Forces*, pp. 102-105; IISS, *Military Balance*, 1983-1984, p. 119; "Soviets' Nuclear Arsenal Continues to Proliferate," *Aviation Week & Space Technology*, 16 June 1980, pp. 67, 69; *Aviation Week & Space Technology*, 9 March 1981, p. 27; Collins and Victory, *U.S./Soviet Military Balance*, 1988, p. 13. The yield of the single-warhead Mod 2 was variously reported as 4.3 Mt (Berman and Baker, *Soviet Strategic Forces*, p. 105; "Soviets' Nuclear Arsenal Continues to Proliferate," *Aviation Week & Space Technology*, 16 June 1980, pp. 67, 69; *Aviation Week & Space Technology*, 9 March 1981, p. 27); 5 Mt (IISS, *Military Balance*, 1983-1984, p. 119); Collins and Victory, *U.S./Soviet Military Balance*, 1988, p. 13.
17 SMP 1983, p. 21.
18 SMP 1986, p. 23. SS-19s, along with SS-11s, were previously reported at Teykovo; SMP 1984, p. 21.
19 Lawrence Freedman, "The Dilemma of Theatre Nuclear Arms Control," *Survival*, January-February, 1981, p. 10n.
20 Private communications with authors.
21 SMP 1094, p. 21.
22 USAF, Trends, 1976, p. 15.
23 *Aviation Week & Space Technology*, 3 November 1980, p. 28; Howard Silber, "Soviets Could Make 3rd Strike, Source Says," *Omaha World-Herald*, 4 April 1982, p. 1.
24 JCS, FY 1989, p. 39; Ten SS-19s were retired between March and September 1987; SMP 1987, p. 8.
25 JCS, FY 1989, p. 39.
26 SMP 1986, p. 26.
27 Ibid.
28 Ibid.

5

SS-19 STILETTO

Engineering and Testing:	1970-1975[29]
First Flight Test:	Mod 1: April 1973[30] Mod 2: 1976[31] Mod 3: 1977[32]
Year Operation Began:	Mod 1: December 1974[33] Mod 2: 1977-1978[34] Mod 3: 1979-1980[35]
Fully Deployed:	1984-1987 (360 missiles)[36]

TARGETING:

Types:	hardened targets such as missile silos, air bases, and command and control facilities;[37] capable of flexible targeting;[38] some may be intended for use in Eurasia[39] and against naval command and control nodes[40]
Accuracy/CEP:	0.215 nm[41] (400 m, 1300 ft)

COMMENTS: An improved SS-19, which was never deployed, was referred to with a new RV stabilizer, improved software, a new computer system, and a new inertial guidance system that could enable the missile to have accuracy "as good as or better than anything the United States has."[42] Two tests of the Mod 3 in 1977-1978 reportedly indicated improved accuracies.[43] SS-19 had 27 R&D test firings through 1974, including 15 during 1974.[44]

---

29 *Ibid.*
30 JCS, FY 1977, p. 35; USAF, *Trends*, 1976, p. 11.
31 Rich and Pike, *SALT*, 1984, pp. 98-99.
32 *Ibid.*
33 JEC, Allocation of Resources - 1975, Part 1, p. 68.
34 Collins and Victory, *U.S./Soviet Military Balance*, 1988, p. 13; Berman and Baker, *Soviet Strategic Forces*, p. 105.
35 SMP 1984, pp. 12, 21, 23; DOD, FY 1985 RD&A, p. II-12.
36 SMP 1988, p. 46.
37 SMP 1984, p. 23; DIA, *Strategic Ballistic Missile Systems Projections — USSR*, DST-1000S-267-82, 30 September 1982, p. 3.
38 SMP 1988, p. 46.
39 SMP 1983, p. 23.
40 Berman and Baker, *Soviet Strategic Forces*, p. 124.
41 This is based upon a March 1985 NIE that lowered the accuracy of the SS-19 by over one-third; Michael R. Gordon, "CIA Downgrades Estimate of Soviet SS-19," *National Journal*, 20 July 1985, pp. 1692-1693; Bill Keller, "Imperfect Science, Important Conclusions," *New York Times*, 28 July 1985, p. E4; Jeffrey T. Richelson, "Old Surveillance, New Interpretations," *Bulletin of the Atomic Scientists*, February 1986, pp. 18-23. Berman and Baker, *Soviet Strategic Forces*, pp. 102-105; "Soviets' Nuclear Arsenal Continues to Proliferate," *Aviation Week & Space Technology*, 16 June 1980, pp. 67, 69; and *Aviation Week & Space Technology*, 9 March 1981, p. 27, all quoted prevailing DIA estimates of the time of 0.14 nm (260 m, 850 ft) for the Mod 3. The CEP of the earlier SS-19 Mod 1 was reported as 0.33 nm; USAF, *Trends*, 1976, p. 13.
42 SASC, Strategic Force Modernization Programs, 1981, p. 17; SASC, FY 1981 DOD, Part 4, p. 2422; SAC, FY 1981 DOD, Part 5, p. 1295.
43 Clarence A. Robinson, Jr., "Soviets Boost ICBM Accuracy," *Aviation Week & Space Technology*, 3 April 1978, p.14.
44 USAF, *Summary Review*, 1975, pp. B-8, B-10.

SS-24 SCALPEL[1]

Figure 5.8 The rail-mobile **SS-24 Scalpel** ICBM is one of several recently deployed (first operational about August-September 1987, 20 deployed mid-1988) fifth generation mobile missiles. Initially rail-mobile, subsequent deployment may be silo-based.

DESCRIPTION: Fifth-generation, three-stage, solid-fuel, medium-sized, MIRVed mobile ICBM; partially replacing MIRVed SS-17 and SS-19 missiles

DESIGN BUREAU: Nadiradize;[2] production facilities possibly located at Biysk; rocket motors produced at Pavlograd

SPECIFICATIONS:
- Length: approx. 21 m[3] (69 ft)
- Diameter: approx. 2.3 m[4] (7.5 ft)
- Stages: 3[5]
- Weight at Launch: approx. 95,000 kg[6] (210,000 lbs)
- Fuel/Propulsion: solid[7]
- Guidance: presumed inertial with onboard digitial computers
- Throwweight: 3200 kg (7000 lbs)[8]
- Range: 10,000 km[9] (5400 nm, 6200 mi)

DUAL CAPABLE: no

---

1. The SS-X-24 was designated PL-4 during research and development.
2. Rich and Pike, *SALT*, 1984, pp. 98-99.
3. A chart in SMP 1987, p. 30, indicates the length of the SS-24 is about 21 m.
4. George C. Wilson, "Soviets Have Trouble with MX-type Missile," *Washington Post*, 1 June 1983, p. 3; Rich and Pike, *SALT*, 1984, pp. 98-99.
5. Michael Getler, "Soviets Held Test of New Missile Three Days After Jet Downed," *Washington Post*, 16 September 1983, p. A28; Rich and Pike, *SALT*, 1984, pp. 98-99.
6. Rich and Pike, *SALT*, 1984, pp 98-99.
7. SMP 1986, p. 27.
8. Collins and Victory, *U.S./Soviet Military Balance*, 1988, p. 13. Walter Andrews, "Soviets Planning Mobile Missile Force," *Washington Times*, 24 April 1984, p. 4, and Walter Andrews, "Satellites See Soviets Violating Arms Accord," *Washington Times*, 21 May 1984, p. 1, report the throwweight of the SS-X-24 as 9600 lbs. IISS, *Military Balance*, 1987-1988, p. 05, reports the throwweight as "?8000 lbs" (3600 kg).
9. SMP 1987, p. 30.

5
SS-24 SCALPEL

NUCLEAR WARHEADS:

Number of warheads: 10 MIRV[10]

Yield per warhead: 100 Kt;[11] 300-500 Kt;[12] 500 Kt;[13] 550 Kt[14]

DEPLOYMENT:

Launch Platform: initially rail-mobile, silo deployment expected[15]

Location: Kostroma;[16] initial testing at the Plesetsk test site;[17] "an extensive network of rail support facilities continues to take shape;"[18] silo deployment could occur at Kostroma in modified SS-17 silos[19]

Number Deployed: approx. 20 (mid-1988)[20]

Launch Mode: cold[21]

HISTORY:

Design Began: 1974[22]

R&D: 1974-1980[23]

Engineering and Testing: 1980-present[24]

First Flight Test: 26 October 1982, unsuccessful due to failure of first-stage rocket motor[25]

Year Operation Began: about August-September 1987;[26] originally reported to be 1985;[27] silo deployment then predicted for 1986,[28] with rail-mobile deployment predicted for 1987 or 1988[29]

Production: Prototype production started in 1986;[30] an explosion reportedly at the main rocket motor plant for the SS-24 at Pavlograd on 12 May 1988 may have seriously affected the pace of SS-24 deployment[31]

TARGETING:

Types: hardened ICBM silos, air bases, and command and control centers

Accuracy/CEP: reportedly lacks the accuracy to threaten missile silos;[32] also reported to be 0.1 nm[33] (200 m,[34] 600 ft); reported to be more accurate than SS-18 Mod 4 and SS-19 Mod 3[35]

COMMENTS: An SS-24 Mod 2 is under development.[36] The Soviet Union provided formal notice under the SALT II Treaty that its 26 October 1982 flight test was of its one new authorized light ICBM.[37]

---

10 SMP 1988, p. 47.
11 John W. R. Taylor, "Gallery of Soviet Aerospace Weapons," *Air Force Magazine*, March 1988, p. 88.
12 *Jane's Weapon Systems*, 1987-1988, p. 10.
13 Collins and Victory, *U.S./Soviet Military Balance*, 1988, p. 13.
14 Rich and Pike, *SALT*, 1984, pp. 98-99.
15 DOD, FY 1989 Annual Report, p. 26.
16 DIA, Force Structure Summary, November 1987, p. 3.
17 SMP 1986, p. 27, 22.
18 SMP 1987, preface.
19 SASC/SAC, Soviet Strategic Force Developments, p. 9; Peter Samuel, "Big Soviet Buildup Foreseen," *Defense Week*, 17 June 1985, p. 15; *Soviet Aerospace*, 27 December 1983, Vol. 39, No. 16, p. 108.
20 SMP 1988, p. 15, reported about 10 as of April 1988.
21 SMP 1987, p. 30.
22 SMP 1985, p. 41.
23 Ibid.
24 Ibid.
25 HAC, FY 1984 DOD Part 1, p. 309; "U.S. Says Russians Successfully Tested a New Type ICBM," *New York Times*, 16 February 1983; Michael Getler and Walter Pincus, "New Soviet Missile Failed in First Flight, U.S. Officials Say," *Washington Post*, 4 December 1982, p. A3. For details of flight-test program, see Wilson, op. cit., p. 3; Getler, op. cit., p. A28; *Air Force Magazine*, January 1984, p. 17; *Aerospace Daily*, 10 January 1984, p. 44; Walter Pincus, "New Soviet Missiles Prepared," *Washington Post*, 17 March 1985, pp. A1, A17; *Soviet Aerospace*, 19 September 1983, pp. 13-14.
26 JCS, FY 1989, p. 40-41, refers to forthcoming deployment of the SS-X-24 as of 30 September 1987.
27 SMP 1984, p. 24.
28 SMP 1985, p. 30; SMP 1986, p. 27.
29 SMP 1985, p. 30; SMP 1986, p. 27.
30 SMP 1986, p. 121.
31 "Soviet Missile-Motor Plant Shut by Explosion, Pentagon Says," *Washington Post*, 18 May 1988, p. A30; "Blast Spared Nuclear Missile Facility, Soviets Assert," *Washington Post*, 19 May 1988, p. A35.
32 Michael R. Gordon, "A New Russian Missile Gets Mixed Reviews," *New York Times*, 16 August 1987, p. 2-E.
33 Collins and Victory, *U.S./Soviet Military Balance*, 1988, p. 13.
34 IISS, *Military Balance*, 1987-1988, p. 205.
35 SMP 1984, p. 24.
36 SMP 1988, p. 101.
37 HAC, FY 1984 DOD, Part 1, p. 309.

SS-25 SICKLE[1]

Figure 5.9 The road-mobile **SS-25 Sickle** missile, deployed in 1985, shown on a wheeled TEL (transporter-erector-launcher), is capable of reload/refire and off-road operations (Department of Defense artist's depiction).

DESCRIPTION: Fifth-generation, three-stage, solid-fuel, single-warhead, road-mobile, small-sized ICBM

DESIGN BUREAU: Nadiradize;[2] production facilities located at the Votkinsk Machine Building Plant (Udmurt ASSR)

SPECIFICATIONS:
Length: approx. 17.5 m[3] (57.4 ft)

Diameter: 1.7-1.9 m[4] (5.5-6.2 ft)

Stages: 3[5]

Weight at Launch: approx. 35,000 kg[6] (77,000 lbs)

---

1 The SS-25 was designated PL-5 during research and development.
2 Rich and Pike, *SALT*, 1984, pp. 98-99.
3 A chart in SMP 1987, p. 30, indicates the length of the SS-X-25 is about 17.5 m. "Approximately the same size as the U.S. Minuteman ICBM"; SMP 1984, p. 24.
4 Based on characteristics of Minuteman III; Rich and Pike, *SALT*, 1984, pp. 98-99.
5 HASC, FY 1984 DOD, Part 5, p. 233; SMP 1988, p. 47.
6 Based on characteristics of Minuteman III; SMP 1984, p. 24. See also, Rich and Pike, *SALT*, 1984, pp. 98-99.

5

SS-25 SICKLE

Figure 5.10 An **SS-25** deployment base includes garage housings with sliding roofs through which the missiles can be fired (Department of Defense artist's depiction).

Fuel/Propulsion:	solid[7]
Guidance:	presumed inertial with onboard digitial computers
Throwweight:	estimated to be 600-1200 kg[8] (1300-2600 lbs)
Range:	10,500 km[9] (5700 nm; 6500 mi)
DUAL CAPABLE:	no
NUCLEAR WARHEADS:	
Number of warheads:	1[10]
Yield per warhead:	550 Kt[11]

DEPLOYMENT:

Launch Platform:	road-mobile-wheeled TEL capable of off-road operations, and similar to the SS-20;[12] the missile can reportedly be fired from field deployment sites or through the sliding-roof garage it occupies at its base[13]
Location:	main operating bases at Yurya (former SS-7 and SS-20 base), Verkhnyaya Salda, and Yoshkar Ola;[14] 9 launchers per regiment deployed in "launcher garages equipped with sliding roofs"[15]
Number Deployed:	126 (end-1987);[16] "about 100 launchers" (March-September 1987[17] and April 1988)[18]
Launch Mode:	cold[19]

HISTORY:

Design Began:	1974[20]
R&D:	1974-1980[21]
Engineering and Testing:	1980-1985[22]
First Flight Test:	8 February 1983,[23] successful firing[24]
Year Operation Began:	1985[25]
Production:	in series production in 1986[26]

TARGETING:

Types:	unknown
Accuracy/CEP:	0.1 nm (200 m; 600 ft);[27] 0.18 nm[28] (330 m; 1100 ft); 0.2 nm (400 m;[29] 1300 ft)

---

7 SMP 1987, p. 31.
8 NSC, "Soviet Non-Compliance with Arms Control," 23 January 1984 as reported in Peter Samuel, "Cheating Charges Detailed," *Defense Week*, 19 August 1985, p. 6; see also, ACDA, Soviet Noncompliance, March 1986, pp. 7-8; Michael Weisskopf, "Soviets Said to Deploy Missile," *Washington Post*, 23 October 1985, p. A4.
9 SMP 1987, p. 30.
10 SMP 1988, p. 47. Associated Press, "U.S. Says Russians Successfully Tested a New Type ICBM," *New York Times*, 16 February 1983, p. A19, reports 4 warheads. Drew Middleton, "Soviets Said to Deploy New Missile," *New York Times*, 22 October 1984, p. A3, reports 6-9 warheads. Ted Agres, "Soviets Testing New ICBMs, CIA Reports," *Washington Times*, 19 September 1984, p. 1, and *Wall Street Journal*, 22 May 1984 report 3 warheads.
11 John W. R. Taylor, "Gallery of Soviet Aerospace Weapons," *Air Force Magazine*, March 1988, p. 88; Collins and Victory, *U.S./Soviet Military Balance*, 1988, p. 13; Rich and Pike, *SALT*, 1984, pp. 98-99.
12 SMP 1986, pp. 24, 26; SMP 1985, pp. 22, 30; SMP 1984, pp. 6, 7, 24.
13 SMP 1986, p. 47.
14 SMP 1987, p. 25.
15 SMP, 1987, p. 30; SMP 1986, p. 26; SMP 1984, pp. 6, 7, 24.

16 The SS-25 is deployed in units of nine mobile launchers, with 14 assumed deployed by end of 1987.
17 JCS, FY 1989, p. 39; SMP 1987, preface.
18 SMP 1988, p. 15.
19 SMP 1986, p. 26.
20 SMP 1985, p. 41.
21 *Ibid*.
22 *Ibid*.
23 SAC, SALT II Violations, Hearings, 99 Cong. 1st sess., S.Hrg. 98-965, p. 39; AP, "U.S. Says Russians Successfully Tested a New Type ICBM," *op. cit.*
24 *Aviation Week & Space Technology*, 21 February 1983, p. 16; AP, "U.S. Says Russians Successfully Tested a New Type ICBM, *op. cit.*
25 SMP 1988, p. 47; SMP 1986, p. 26; SMP 1985, p. 31.
26 SMP 1986, p. 121.
27 IISS, *Military Balance*, 1987-1988, p. 205, gives 200 m. Collins and Victory, *U.S./Soviet Military Balance*, 1988, p. 13, gives "0.10? nm."
28 Collins and Cronin, *U.S./Soviet Military Balance*, 1984, p. 16.
29 Jim Bussert, "The SS-25: Does It Breach SALT II?" *Jane's Defence Weekly*, 31 January 1987, p. 143.

SS-25 SICKLE

COMMENTS: The Soviet Union has been dismantling SS-11 silos to compensate for SS-25 deployments.[30] The missile has been tested at Plesetsk.[31] The Soviet Union claims this missile is an upgraded SS-13 (and not a violation of SALT II limits), but the U.S. government believes it to be a new missile, exceeding the five percent difference from the SS-13 in length, diameter, and throwweight. The SS-25 is capable of silo deployment as well as mobile deployment, although it has not been so deployed.[32] A MIRVed version of the SS-25 is possibly under development and may be deployed.[33] Capable of reload/refire operations.[34]

---

[30] SMP 1986, p. 26. The Soviet Union informed the U.S. delegation in Geneva that it intended to deploy 18 SS-25 missiles at two bases and remove 20 SS-11 missiles from operational silos; Walter Pincus, "Moscow Says It Will Honor SALT II Missile Limits," *Washington Post*, 9 May 1985, p. A22.

[31] SMP 1986, p. 26.
[32] SMP 1984, p. 24.
[33] SMP 1986, p. 28.
[34] SMP 1988, p. 47.

5
GOLF V, HOTEL III

Ballistic Missile Submarines
GOLF V, HOTEL III

	GOLF V	HOTEL III
DESCRIPTION:	Diesel-powered ballistic missile submarine (modified Golf Is) used to test the SS-N-20 SLBM	One-of-a-kind nuclear-powered ballistic missile submarine used to test the SS-N-8 SLBM
DESIGN BUREAU:	Komsomol'sk; Severodvinsk[1]	Severodvinsk[2]
SPECIFICATIONS:		
Length:	100 m[3] (328 ft)	129.5 m[4] (424.9 ft)
Beam:	8.5 m[5] (27.9 ft)	approx. 9.1 m[6] (29.9 ft)
Draft:	6.4 m[7] (21 ft)	6.7 m[8] (22 ft)
Displacement		
Surface:	2300 tons[9]	5500 tons[10]
Submerged:	2700 tons[11]	6500 tons[12]
Propulsion:	diesel-electric, 3 diesels, electric motor, 3 shafts[13]	nuclear, 1 PWR; 2 shafts; 30,000 shp[14]
Speed		
Surface:	17 kts	18 kts
Submerged	14 kts[15]	22 kts[16]
Crew:	80-85[17]	80[18]
NUCLEAR WEAPONS:		
Missile System:	1 SS-N-20 SLBM[19]	6 SS-N-8 SLBM[20]
Torpedoes:	6 21-inch (53.3 cm) (bow)[21]	6 21-inch (53.3 cm) (bow)[22]
DEPLOYMENT:		
Number Deployed:	1[23]	1[24]
Homeport:	Black Sea Fleet[25]	Northern Fleet[26]
HISTORY:		
IOC:	1978[27]	1968-1969[28]
COMMENTS:	One Golf I SSB was modified to test-fire the SS-N-20 and designated the Golf V.[29] The single Golf III with six SS-N-8 missiles was retired in 1987.[30]	One Hotel II was converted to test-fire the SS-N-8 and designated the Hotel III.[31] The Hotel III SSBN is only accountable under SALT II for its missile tubes.[32]

---

1 Polmar, *Guide to the Soviet Navy*, 1986, p. 124.
2 Ibid., p. 123.
3 DIA, *JIIKS*, Vol. XIII, 1983.
4 DIA, *ASW Handbook*, 1977, p. 6-35. Waterline length is 115 m (377.3 ft); DIA, *JIIKS*, Vol. XIII, 1983.
5 DIA, *JIIKS*, Vol. XIII, 1983; DIA, *ASW Handbook*, 1977, p. 6-47.
6 DIA, *ASW Handbook*, 1977, p. 6-35.
7 DIA, *ASW Handbook*, 1977, p. 6-47.
8 DIA, *ASW Handbook*, 1977, p. 6-35.
9 Polmar, *Guide to the Soviet Navy*, 1986, p. 124.
10 DIA, *ASW Handbook*, 1977, p. 6-35.
11 Polmar, Guide to the Soviet Navy, 1986, p. 124; Couhat, *Combat Fleets of the World*, 1988/89, p. 584.
12 DIA, *ASW Handbook*, 1977, p. 6-35.
13 DIA, *JIIKS*, Vol. XIII, 1983.
14 Polmar, *Guide to the Soviet Navy*, 1986, p. 123; Couhat, *Combat Fleets of the World*, 1988/89, p. 584.
15 DIA, *JIIKS*, Vol. XIII, 1983.
16 DIA, *ASW Handbook*, 1977, p. 6-35.
17 Polmar, *Guide to the Soviet Navy*, 1986, p. 124; Couhat, *Combat Fleets of the World*, 1988/89, p. 584.
18 Polmar, *Guide to the Soviet Navy*, 1986, p. 123; Couhat, *Combat Fleets of the World*, 1988/89, p. 584.
19 Polmar, *Guide to the Soviet Navy*, 1986, p. 124; Couhat, *Combat Fleets of the World*, 1988/89, p. 584.
20 SMP 1984, p. 22; DIA, *ASW Handbook*, 1977, p. 6-35.
21 DIA, *JIIKS*, Vol. XIII, 1983.
22 DIA, *JIIKS*, Vol. XIII, 1983.
23 DIA, *Unclassified Communist Naval Orders of Battle*, April 1986, p. 1.
24 DIA, *Unclassified Communist Naval Orders of Battle*, April 1986, p. 1; DIA, *JIIKS*, Vol. XIII, 1983.
25 DIA, *Unclassified Communist Naval Orders of Battle*, April 1986, p. 1.
26 Ibid.
27 DOD, FY 1986 Annual Report, p. 49, from chart; DOD, FY 1985 RD&A, p. II-12.
28 DOD, FY 1986 Annual Report, p. 49, from chart; Hotel III did not carry SS-N-8 SLBMs until 1973.
29 DIA, *JIIKS*, Vol. XIII, 1983.
30 JCS, FY 1989, p. 39.
31 DIA, *JIIKS*, Vol. XIII, 1983.
32 SMP 1986, p. 28.

5
YANKEE

YANKEE CLASS[1]

YANKEE II (SSBN)   YANKEE I (SSBN)

Figure 5.11 The nuclear-powered **Yankee I** was the first modern ballistic missile submarine in the Soviet Navy. Sixteen are currently (mid-1988) deployed, equipped with 256 SS-N-6 missiles. Yankee I submarines are now assigned predominantly to theater attack missions.

DESCRIPTION: Nuclear-powered, second-generation, ballistic missile submarine comprised of Yankee Is and a single, one-of-a-kind Yankee II

BUILDER: Severodvinsk 402 shipyard and Komsomol'sk;[2] with assistance at Severomorsk and Gor'kiy[3]

SPECIFICATIONS:
Length: 130 m[4] (427 ft)
Beam: 11.6 m[5] (38 ft)
Draft: 8.0 m[6] (26 ft)
Displacement
  Surface: 7800 tons
  Submerged: 9300 tons[7]
Propulsion: nuclear, 2 PWR;[8] 2 shafts, 50,000 shp[9]
Speed
  Surface: 18-20 kts;[10] 26.5 kts[11]
  Submerged: 30 kts[12]

---

1 See Chapter Nine for discussion and specifications for converted Yankee class submarines now a part of nonstrategic forces.
2 Polmar, *Guide to the Soviet Navy*, 1986, p. 121; Couhat, *Combat Fleets of the World*, 1984/85, p. 696.
3 Commander Richard T. Ackley, USN (Ret), "The Wartime Role of Soviet SSGNs," U.S. Naval Institute Proceedings, June 1978, p. 36.
4 SMP 1986, p. 28; DIA, *ASW Handbook*, 1977, p. 6-37. The waterline length is 128 m (419.9 ft); DIA, JIIKS, Vol. XIII, 1983.
5 DIA, *ASW Handbook*, 1977, p. 6-37.
6 Ibid.
7 DIA, JIIKS, Vol. XIII, 1983.
8 Polmar, *Guide to the Soviet Navy*, 1986, p. 121.
9 Polmar, *Guide to the Soviet Navy*, 1986, p. 121; Couhat, *Combat Fleets of the World*, 1988/89, pp. 583-584.
10 DIA, *ASW Handbook*, 1977, p. 6-37; DIA, JIIKS, Vol. XIII, 1983.
11 Ibid
12 DIA, JIIKS, Vol. XIII, 1983.

5
YANKEE

Figure 5.12 In 1980 the one-of-a-kind **Yankee II** (a modified Yankee I) was the initial delivery platform for the first Soviet solid-fueled SLBM, the SS-N-17.

Crew: approx. 120[13]

NUCLEAR WEAPONS:
Missile System: Yankee I: 16 SS-N-6 SLBM[14]
Yankee II: 12 SS-N-17 SLBM[15]

Torpedoes: 6 21-inch (53.3 cm) (bow);[16] 18 torpedoes[17]

DEPLOYMENT:
Number Deployed: Yankee I: 16[18]
Yankee II: 1[19]

Homeport: Yankee Is equally split between Northern and Pacific Fleet: 8 in Northern Fleet, 8 in Pacific;[20] the single Yankee II is in the Northern Fleet[21]

Operations: Yankee submarines have been conducting combat patrols within range of European and Pacific theater targets since late 1987;[22] prior to 1987, 2-3 Yankee Is typically patrolled off the U.S. Atlantic coast while 2 Yankee Is patrolled off the U.S. Pacific coast, one to the west of Hawaii and one to the northeast; 2 additional Yankee Is were regularly in transit to the U.S. Atlantic coast and 1 Yankee I was in transit to the U.S. Pacific coast; patrols off Atlantic coast began in 1968, and off Pacific coast in 1970-1971;[23] 400 m maximum operating depth, 650 m design collapse depth[24]

HISTORY:
IOC: Yankee I: 1968[25]
Yankee II: 1977;[26] SS-N-17 missile reported operational in 1980

COMMENTS: Retired Yankee I submarines are being converted to attack or cruise missile submarines (see Chapter Nine). The single Yankee II submarine may be used to launch a small communications satellite or a radio transponder for emergency communications to strategic forces.

---

13 Polmar, *Guide to the Soviet Navy*, 1986, p. 121; Couhat, *Combat Fleets of the World*, 1988/89, p. 584.
14 SMP 1986, p. 28; DIA, JIIKS, Vol. XIII, 1983.
15 Ibid.
16 DIA, JIIks, Vol. XIII, 1983.
17 Polmar, *Guide to the Soviet Navy*, 1986, p. 121.
18 SMP 1988, p. 48, indicates 17 Yankee submarines (i.e., 16 Yankee I and one Yankee II). Thirty-four Yankee Is were built from 1967 to 1974; DIA, *Intercontinental Strategic Forces Summary—USSR(U)*, DDB-2680-253-85, 1 January 1985, p. 5. One Yankee I was converted to a Yankee II in 1976-1977. In accordance with the SALT I Interim Agreement (as of end of 1987), the Soviets have, since 1978, removed 16 Yankee Is from service; SMP 1986, pp. 29-30. With the 29th Delta class submarine operational in late January 1979, the Soviets were bound by the SALT I Interim Agreement to dismantle old SLBM tubes six months after the new submarine entered sea trials. Two Yankee Is deactivated or converted by early 1979, 3 Yankee Is by June 1979, 4 by January 1980, 5 by January 1981, 7 by January 1982, 8 by November 1982, 9 by June 1983, 10 by January 1984, 12 by April 1985, 14 by March 1986, 16 by end-1987; JCS, FY 1989, p. 39; HASC, FY 1982 DOD, Part 3, pp. 5-6; SMP 1987, p. 33. The force constituted 29 total Yankees in July 1981, 28 Yankee Is in January 1981 (DOD, FY 1982, p. 46), and 26 Yankee Is by January 1982 based on Delta III deployments. Information from 1983 to 1986 from DIA's *Unclassified Communist Naval Orders of Battle* for November 1982, June 1983, November 1983, May 1984, and April 1986. One Yankee I also sank in the mid-Atlantic on 6 October 1986.
19 DIA, *Unclassified Communist Naval Orders of Battle*, April 1986, p. 1.
20 SMP 1988, p. 48.
21 DIA, *Force Structure Summary*, November 1987, p. 5; SMP 1988, p. 48.
22 Studeman, USN, Statement before HASC, March 1988, p. 22.
23 HASC, FY 1982 DOD, Part 3, pp. 5-6.
24 DIA, *ASW Handbook*, 1977, p. 6-37.
25 SMP 1981, p. 58; DOD, FY 1986 *Annual Report*, p. 49, from chart.
26 DIA, *Intercontinental Strategic Forces Summary—USSR(U)*, DDB-2680-253-85, 1 January 1985, p. 5.

5
DELTA

DELTA CLASS

DESCRIPTION: Nuclear-powered, third-generation, ballistic missile submarine in four classes

BUILDER: Delta I: Severodvinsk 402 shipyard and Komsomol'sk
Delta II/III/IV: Severodvinsk[1]

	Delta I	Delta II	Delta III	Delta IV
SPECIFICATIONS:				
Length:	140 m[2] (460ft)	155 m[3] (509 ft)	155 m[4] (509 ft)	160 m[5] (525 ft)
Beam:	12.0 m[6] (39.4 ft)	12.1 m[7] (39.7 ft)	12.1 m[8] (39.7 ft)	12.0 m[9] (39.4 ft)
Draft:	8.6 m[10] (28 ft)	8.6 m[11] (28 ft)	8.6 m[12] (28 ft)	8.6 m[13] (28 ft)
Displacement Surface:	8600 tons[14]	9600 tons[15]	11,000 tons[16]	10,750 tons[17]
Submerged:	11,750 tons[18]	11,400 tons[19]	13,250 tons[20]	13,550 tons[21]
Propulsion:	nuclear, 2 PWR;[22] 2 shafts, 50,000 shp[23]			
Speed Surface:	8 kts[24]	17 kts;[25] 20 kts[26]	17 kts;[27] 20 kts[28]	unknown
Submerged:	25 kts[29]	24.5 kts;[30] 28 kts[31]	25 kts[32]	24 kts[33]
Crew:	120[34]			

NUCLEAR WEAPONS:
Missile System: Delta I: 12 SS-N-8 SLBM[35]
Delta II: 16 SS-N-8 SLBM[36]
Delta III: 16 SS-N-18 SLBM;[37] will probably be backfit with SS-N-23[38]
Delta IV: 16 SS-N-23 SLBM[39]

Torpedoes: 6 21-inch (53.3 cm) tubes (bow)[40]

DEPLOYMENT:
Number Deployed: Delta I: 18[41]
Delta II: 4[42]
Delta III: 14[43]
Delta IV: 5 launched: 4 operational, 1 on sea trials (1988)[44]

---

1. Polmar, *Guide to the Soviet Navy*, 1986, pp. 116-120; Couhat, *Combat Fleets of the World, 1988/89*, pp. 582-583.
2. SMP 1987, p. 33. The waterline length is 136 m (446 ft); DIA, JIIKS, Vol. XIII, 1983.
3. SMP 1987, p. 33. The waterline length is 152 m (499 ft); DIA, JIIKS, Vol. XIII, 1983.
4. SMP 1987, p. 33. The waterline length is 152 m (499 ft); DIA, JIIKS, Vol. XIII, 1983.
5. SMP 1987, p. 33.
6. Polmar, *Guide to the Soviet Navy*, 1986, p. 120.
7. Ibid., p. 118.
8. Ibid.
9. Ibid., 9.116.
10. DIA, ASW Handbook, 1977, p. 6-37.
11. Ibid.
12. Ibid.
13. Polmar, *Guide to the Soviet Navy*, 1986, p. 116.
14. DIA, JIIKS, Vol. XIII, 1983.
15. Ibid.
16. Ibid.
17. Polmar, *Guide to the Soviet Navy*, 1986, p. 116.
18. DIAm HUUJSm Vol. XIII, 1983.
19. DIA, JIIKS, Vol. XIII, 1983.
20. DIA, JIIKS, Vol. XIII, 1983; DIA, ASW Handbook, 1977, p. 6-37.
21. Polmar, *Guide to the Soviet Navy*, 1986, p. 116.
22. Ibid.
23. Polmar, *Guide to the Soviet Navy*, 1986, pp. 116-120; Couhat, *Combat Fleets of the World, 1988/89*, pp. 581,583.
24. DIA, ASW Handbook, 1977, p. 6-37.
25. Ibid.
26. DIA, JIIKS, Vol. XIII, 1983.
27. DIA, *ASW Handbook*, 1977, p. 6-37.
28. DIA, JIIKS, Vol. XIII, 1983.
29. DIA, JIIKS, Vol. XIII, 1983; DIA, ASW Handbook, 1977, p. 6-37.
30. DIA, *ASW Handbook*, 1977, p. 6-37.
31. DIA, JIIKS, Vol. XIII, 1983.
32. DIA, JIIKS, Vol. XIII, 1983; DIA, ASW Handbook, 1977, p. 6-37.
33. Polmar, *Guide to the Soviet Navy*, 1986, p. 116.
34. Polmar, *Guide to the Soviet Navy*, 1986, pp. 116-120; Couhat, *Combat Fleets of the World, 1988/89*, p. 583.
35. SMP 1987, p. 33.
36. Ibid.
37. Ibid.
38. JCS, FY 1989, p. 40; "Current Naval Intelligence Issues by the Office of Naval Intelligence," March 1987, p. 5.
39. "Current Naval Intelligence Issues by the Office of Naval Intelligence," March 1987, p. 5.
40. DIA, JIIKS, Vol. XIII, 1983.
41. DIA, *Unclassified Communist Naval Orders of Battle*, April 1986, p. 1. See also, November 1982, November 1983, June 1983, May 1984, and December 1985 versions.
42. Ibid.
43. Ibid.
44. Studeman, USN, Statement before HASC, March 1988, pp. 32-33; JCS, FY 1989, p. 40. Three launched as of March 1986; SMP 1986, p. 30. Hull four was launched in early 1987; SMP 1987, pp. 31-33. SMP 1988, p. 48, reported 4 Delta submarines deployed as of April 1988.

5
DELTA

Homeport:	24 in Northern Fleet, 16 in Pacific Fleet;[45] Delta Is are evenly split between Northern and Pacific Fleets;[46] Delta IIs are assigned to Northern Fleet;[47] Delta IIIs evenly split between Northern and Pacific Fleets;[48] Delta IVs are assigned to the Northern Fleet,[49] but are expected to become part of the Pacific Fleet in 1988;[50] Gremikha in the Northern Fleet[51]		Pacific;[52] Delta IVs have not gone on patrol as of early 1988;[53] 400 m maximum operating depth, 650 m design collapse depth[54]
		HISTORY:	
		IOC:	Delta I: July 1973[55] Delta II: 1973[56] Delta III: 1977[57] Delta IV: 1985[58]
Operations:	Patrols of Delta Is began in 1974; 3-4 Deltas normally deployed in northern Atlantic waters, 2 in central Atlantic (since 1984), 2-3 in	**COMMENTS:**	Delta hull design is an enlargement and modification of the Yankee hull rather than a new design.[59] One Delta III is named *60 Let Velikyo Oktyabr*.[60]

DELTA I (SSBN)

Figure 5.13 The lengthened hull of the nuclear-powered **Delta I** class submarine (modified from the Yankee class hull) is clearly visible in this photo. Eighteen Delta Is were deployed starting in 1973, each carrying 12 two-stage SS-N-8 missiles.

DELTA II (SSBN)

Figure 5.14 Designated **Delta II** class submarines, four of these lengthened versions of the Delta I entered service between 1976 and 1978 and were assigned to the Northern Fleet.

DELTA III (SSBN)

Figure 5.15 **Delta III** SSBNs were the delivery platform for the first Soviet Navy MIRVed SLBMs, the SS-N-18. Each of the 14 Delta IIIs carry 16 SS-N-18 missiles.

Figure 5.16 First launched in 1985, **Delta IV**s are the most recent modification of this class of submarines. The hull has been further enlarged to accommodate 16 SS-N-23 SLBMs.

---

45 SMP 1988, p. 48; DIA, Force Structure Summary, November 1987, p. 5.
46 DIA, *Unclassified Communist Naval Orders of Battle*, April 1986, p. 1. See also, November 1982, November 1983, June 1983, May 1984, and December 1985 versions.
47 Ibid
48 DIA, *Unclassified Communist Naval Orders of Battle*, April 1986, p. 1.
49 Ibid.
50 Rear Admiral Hugh L. Webster, U.S. Pacific Command, Statement before the Senate Armed Services Committee, 23 March 1988, p. 2.
51 Craig Covault, "Spot Photographs Secret Base for USSR Nuclear Submarines," *Aviation Week & Space Technology*, 20 July 1987, pp. 18-21.
52 JCS, FY 1982, p. 100; Fred Hiatt, "More, Newer Soviet Subs Seen Off U.S.," *Washington Post*, 27 January 1984, p. 23; *Soviet Aerospace*, Vol. 40, No. 5, 6 February 1984, p. 34.
53 Studeman, USN, Statement before HASC, March 1988, p. 33.
54 DIA, *ASW Handbook*, 1977, p. 6-37.
55 HAC, FY 1977 DOD, Part 2, p. 7. The first Delta I was launched in 1971; USN, *Soviet Naval Developments* (Rev. 4/85), pp. 46, 90.
56 DIA, *Intercontinental Strategic Forces Summary—USSR(U)*, DDB-2680-253-85, 1 January 1985, p. 5.
57 Ibid.
58 Ibid. The first Delta IV was launched in March 1984.
59 SAC, FY 1974 DOD, Part 1, p. 607.
60 Couhat, *Combat Fleets of the World*, 1988/89, p. 583.

5
TYPHOON

TYPHOON CLASS

TYPHOON (SSBN)

Figure 5.17 The five **Typhoon** class submarines currently deployed (mid-1988) are unique in several aspects: in terms of tonnage, they are the largest submarine constructed by any nation; they are the quietest Soviet ballistic missile submarine yet built; they are designed for operation under the Arctic ice.

DESCRIPTION:	Nuclear-powered, fourth-generation, ballistic missile submarine
BUILDER:	Severodvinsk[1]
SPECIFICATIONS:	
Length:	170 m[2] (560 ft)
Beam:	25 m[3] (82 ft)
Draft:	13.0 m[4] (42.7 ft)
Displacement Surface:	18,500 tons[5]
Submerged:	25,000 tons[6]
Propulsion:	nuclear, 2 reactors, 2 shafts, approx. 100,000 shp[7]

---

1. Polmar, *Guide to the Soviet Navy*, 1986, p. 114; Couhat, *Combat Fleets of the World*, 1988/89, p. 582; Armin Wetterhahn, "The Soviet Typhoon-Class SSBN," *International Defense Review*, April 1984, pp. 417-422.
2. SMP 1987, p. 33; DIA, JIIKS, Vol. XIII, 1983.
3. SMP 1987, p. 33.
4. Polmar, *Guide to the Soviet Navy*, 1986, p. 114.
5. Couhat, *Combat Fleets of the World*, 1988/89, p. 582.
6. DIA, JIIKS, Vol. XIII, 1983; SASC, Strategic Force Modernization Programs, 1981, pp. 7, 8, 18.
7. Polmar, *Guide to the Soviet Navy*, 1986, p. 114; John Jordan, "Leviathan of the Deep," *Jane's Defence Weekly*, 1 March 1986, p. 378; Wetterhahn, *op. cit.*, pp. 417-422.

5 TYPHOON

Speed Submerged:	24-30 kts[8]
Crew:	150,[9] possibly 2 crews[10]

NUCLEAR WEAPONS:

Missile System:	20 SS-N-20 SLBM[11]
ASW Rockets:	possibly 2 26-inch (65.0 cm) tubes in pressure hull for SS-N-16 or SS-N-15[12]
Torpedoes:	6 or 8 21-inch (53.3 cm) tubes (bow)[13]

DEPLOYMENT:

Number Deployed:	5 (mid-1988)[14]
Homeport:	Northern Fleet: probably at Zapadnaya Litsa;[15] previously reported at Gremikha;[16] and Iokanga[17]
Operations:	Typhoons operated under the Arctic Ocean ice cap[18]

HISTORY:

IOC:	1983[19]
In Production:	yes

COMMENTS: Typhoon submarine has a number of noteworthy design features: missile tubes are forward of the sail structure,[20] missile tubes are entirely enclosed within a double hull casing,[21] and the submarine is configured for under-ice operations.

---

8. DIA, JIIKS, Vol. XIII, 1983 gives the speed as 24+ knots. See also Polmar, *Guide to the Soviet Navy*, 1986, p. 114; Couhat, *Combat Fleets of the World*, 1988/89, p. 582; Wetterhahn, op. cit., pp. 417-422.
9. Polmar, *Guide to the Soviet Navy*, 1986, p. 114.
10. Wetterhahn, op. cit., pp. 417-422.
11. SMP 1987, p. 33; DIA, JIIKS, Vol. XIII, 1983; JCS, FY 1985, p. 21.
12. Jordan, op. cit., p. 378.
13. Polmar, *Guide to the Soviet Navy*, 1986, p. 114; Couhat, *Combat Fleets of the World*, 1988/89, p. 582; Wetterhahn, op. cit., pp. 417-422.
14. SMP 1988, p. 48. The fifth Typhoon was launched in late 1986; one or two additional Typhoons are probably under construction as of April 1988.
15. "Soviets' New Base for Typhoon 50 km from Norway," *Jane's Defence Weekly*, 6 February 1988, pp. 192-193.
16. Craig Covault, "Spot Photographs Secret Base for USSR Nuclear Submarines," *Aviation Week & Space Technology*, 20 July 1987, pp. 18-21.
17. Ted Agres, "Soviet Navy Completing Four Tunnels to Hide Subs," *Washington Times*, 27 March 1984, p. 1.
18. Polmar, *Guide to the Soviet Navy*, 1986, p. 114; Wetterhahn, op. cit., pp. 417-422; Craig Covault, "Soviet Ability to Fire Through Ice Creates New SLBM Basing Mode," *Aviation Week & Space Technology*, 10 December 1984, pp. 16-17.
19. SMP 1983, p. 21; SMP 1984, p. 25. The first Typhoon submarine was launched in September 1980; HASC, FY 1982 DOD, Part 3, p. 7. The second Typhoon was launched in September 1982 and entered service in 1984; the third was launched in December 1983; the fourth was launched at the end of 1984, and the fifth at the end of 1986; Couhat, *Combat Fleets of the World*, 1988/89, p. 583.
20. *Soviet Aerospace*, Vol. 40, No. 6, 13 February 1984, p. 44.
21. Wetterhahn, op. cit., pp. 417-422.

5
SS-N-6 SERB

Naval Strategic Missiles
SS-N-6 SERB[1]

Figure 5.18 The **SS-N-6 Serb** is a single-stage, liquid-fueled missile with a range of 1600 nautical miles. It is estimated that 256 SS-N-6 missiles armed with 512 warheads are currently deployed (mid-1988) on 16 Yankee I class submarines.

DESCRIPTION: Third-generation, single- and multiple- warhead liquid-fuel SLBM in three modifications; Mods 1 and 2 are single-warhead and Mod 3 carries 2 MRVs, with those deployed believed to be all Mod 3s

DESIGN BUREAU: Chelomei[2]

SPECIFICATIONS:
Length: 9.65 m[3] (31.7 ft)

Diameter: 1.65 m[4] (5.40 ft)

Stages: 1[5]

Weight at Launch: 18,900 kg[6] (41,700 lbs)

Fuel/Propulsion: liquid[7]

Guidance: inertial[8]

Throwweight: 680 kg (1500lbs)[9]

Range: Mod 1: 2400 km[10] (1300 nm, 1500 mi)
Mod 2/3: 3000 km (1600 nm, 1900 mi)[11]

DUAL CAPABLE: no

NUCLEAR WARHEADS:
Number of warheads: Mod 1/2: 1[12]
Mod 3: 2 MRV[13]
Under START, all SS-N-6 misiles will be counted as carrying one warhead

---

1. The SS-N-6 is sometimes given the code name Sawfly, e.g., by Berman and Baker, IISS, and *Jane's*. Polmar, *Guide to the Soviet Navy*, 1986, p. 433 reports that the Sawfly was a competitive prototype and not the SS-N-6.
2. Berman and Baker, *Soviet Strategic Forces*, pp. 106-107.
3. A chart in SMP 1987, p. 33, indicates the length of the SS-N-6 is less than 10 m. See also, Polmar, *Guide to the Soviet Navy*, 1986, p. 433; *Jane's Weapon Systems*, 1987-88, p. 13; John Jordan, "Soviet Ballistic Missile Submarines-Part 3," *Jane's Defence Weekly*, 11 February 1984, p. 204.
4. *Jane's Weapon Systems*, 1987-88, p. 13; Jordan, *op. cit.*, p. 204.
5. SMP 1981, pp. 58-59. The SS-N-8 was the first two-stage Soviet SLBM.
6. Polmar, *Guide to the Soviet Navy*, 1986, p. 433.
7. SASC, *Strategic Force Modernization Programs*, 1981, p. 8.
8. Berman and Baker, *Soviet Strategic Forces*, pp. 106-107; Donald MacKenzie, "The Soviet Union and Strategic Missile Guidance," mimeo, Department of Sociology, University of Edinburgh, 1988, p. 42.
9. Couhat, *Combat Fleets of the World*, 1988/89, p. 563; *Aviation Week & Space Technology*, 14 March 1983, p. 153; IISS, *Military Balance*, 1987-1988, p. 206.
10. SMP 1987, p. 33.
11. *Ibid*.
12. *Ibid*.
13. SMP 1987, p. 33. JCS, FY 1979, p. 27, JCS, FY 1978, p. 14, JCS, FY 1977, p. 37, JCS, FY 1976, p. 21, and DOD, FY 1975 Annual Report (class.) reported the Mod 3 as having 2-3 MRVs. DOD, FY 1985 RD&A, p. II-12, and HAC, FY 1982 DOD, Part 2, p. 6, reported 3 MRVs.

5

SS-N-6 SERB

Yield per warhead:	Mod 1/2: approx. 0.6-1.2 Mt[14] Mod 3: approx. 0.375-1 Mt[15]	IOC:	Mod 1: 1968[24] Mod 2: 1973[25] Mod 3: 1973[26]

DEPLOYMENT:

Launch Platform: 16 Yankee I submarines, each with 16 launch tubes[16]

Number Deployed: 256 with 512 warheads (April 1988)[17]

TARGETING:

Types: soft targets such as airfields and soft C^3 sites[27]

Accuracy/CEP: 0.7 nm[28] (1300 m;[29] 4300 ft); 1 nm (2000 m; 6000 ft)[30]

HISTORY:

Design Began: 1957[18]

R&D: 1957-1963[19]

Engineering and Testing: 1963-1968[20]

First Flight Test: Mod 1: 1967[21]
Mod 2: October 1972[22]
Mod 3: 1973[23]

COMMENTS: The three Mods are thought to be relatively interchangeable.[31] The SS-N-6 can be ready for launch within 15 minutes of launch notification; all missiles could be launched within two minutes.[32]

---

14 USAF, *Trends*, 1976, p. 27.
15 Ibid.
16 JCS, FY 1989, p. 39. One Yankee I class submarine with 16 SS-N-6 missiles sank on 6 October 1986, and two others were retired in 1987.
17 SMP 1988, p. 15; JCS, FY 1989, p. 39 (as of 30 September 1987). JCS, FY 1988, p. 33, reported 304 SS-N-6s deployed as of 30 September 1986. One Yankee I class submarine with 16 SS-N-6 missiles sank on 6 October 1986, and two others were retired in 1987.
18 SMP 1985, p. 40.
19 Ibid.
20 Ibid.
21 Berman and Baker, *Soviet Strategic Forces*, pp. 106-107.
22 JCS, FY 1976, p. 22.
23 Berman and Baker, *Soviet Strategic Forces*, pp. 106-107.
24 DOD, FY 1969 *Annual Report* (class.); SMP 1985, p. 40.
25 JCS, FY 1977, p. 37.
26 Polmar, *Guide to the Soviet Navy*, 1986, p. 433.
27 SASC, FY 1980 DOD, Part 3, p. 395.
28 Collins and Victory, *U.S./Soviet Military Balance*, 1988, p. 18.
29 IISS, *Military Balance*, 1987-1988, p. 206.
30 USAF, *Trends*, 1976, p. 27.
31 JCS, FY 1976, p. 22.
32 SASC, FY 1980 DOD, Part 3, p. 395.

SS-N-8 SAWFLY

Figure 5.19 SS-N-8 Sawfly deployment is currently (mid-1988) estimated to be 286 on 23 Delta I and II class submarines. Each missile's single warhead has an explosive power of 1000-1500 kilotons.

DESCRIPTION:	Fourth-generation, single-warhead, liquid-fuel SLBM in two modifications carried on Delta I and Delta II submarines
DESIGN BUREAU:	Chelomei derivative[1]
SPECIFICATIONS:	
Length:	13 m[2] (43 ft)
Diameter:	1.8 m[3] (5.9 ft)
Stages:	2[4]
Weight at Launch:	30,000 kg[5] (66,000 lbs)
Fuel:	liquid[6]
Guidance:	stellar inertial introduced for the first time[7]
Throwweight:	Mod 1: 680 kg (1500 lbs)[8] Mod 2: 3600 kg (8000 lbs)[9]
Range:	Mod 1: 7800 km[10] (4200 nm; 4800 mi) Mod 2: 9100 km[11] (4900 nm; 5700 mi)
DUAL CAPABLE:	no

---

1. Berman and Baker, *Soviet Strategic Forces*, pp. 106-107.
2. A chart in SMP 1987, p. 33, indicates the length of the SS-N-8 is about 13 m. See also, *Jane's Weapon Systems*, 1987-88, p. 14; John Jordan, "Soviet Ballistic Missile Submarines," *Jane's Defence Weekley*, Part 3, 11 February 1984, p. 204; Part 2, January 1984, p. 122.
3. Jordan, *op. cit.*, Part 3, p. 204; Part 2, p. 122; *Aviation Week & Space Technology*, 14 March 1983, p. 153.
4. SASC, *Strategic Force Modernization Programs*, 1981, pp. 8, 18; SMP 1981, pp. 58-59. The SS-N-8 was the first Soviet two-stage SLBM.
5. Polmar, *Guide to the Soviet Navy*, 1986, p. 433.
6. SASC, *Strategic Force Modernization Programs*, 1981, pp. 8, 18; SMP 1981, pp. 58-59.
7. Donald MacKenzie, "The Soviet Union and Strategic Missile Guidance," mimeo, Department of Sociology, University of Edinburgh, 1988, p. 45; Berman and Baker, *Soviet Strategic Forces*, pp. 106-107; *Jane's Weapon Systems*, 1987-88, p. 14; Polmar, *Guide to the Soviet Navy*, 1986, p. 433.
8. IISS, *Military Balance*, 1987-1988, p. 206.
9. IISS, *Military Balance*, 1983-1984, p. 119.
10. SMP 1987, p. 33; JEC, *Allocation of Resources - 1975*, Part 1, p. 106.
11. SMP 1987, p. 33.

5

SS-N-8 SAWFLY

NUCLEAR WARHEADS:

Number of warheads: 1[12]

Yield per warhead: approx. 0.5-1.5 Mt[13]

DEPLOYMENT:

Launch Platform: Delta I and Delta II; Hotel III for testing

Number Deployed: 286 (April 1988);[14] 216 on 18 Delta Is, 64 on 4 Delta IIs, and 6 on one Hotel III test submarine[15]

HISTORY:

Design Began: 1962[16]

R&D: 1962-1968[17]

Engineering and Testing: 1968-1973[18]

First Flight Test: Mod 1: 1969[19]
Mod 2: 1976[20]

Year Operation Began: Mod 1: 1973[21]
Mod 2: 1977[22]

TARGETING:

Types: administrative centers, communications facilities, industrial complexes, population centers, and soft military targets[23]

Accuracy/CEP: Mod 1: 0.8 nm (1500 m; 5000 ft);[24] 0.5 nm (900 m; 3000 ft)[25]

---

12 *Ibid.*
13 USAF, *Trends*, 1976, p. 27; Berman and Baker, *Soviet Strategic Forces*, pp. 106-107. IISS, *Military Balance*, 1987-1988, p. 206 reports the yield of the SS-N-8 Mod 1 as 0.5-1.0 Mt, and the yield of the Mod 2 as 0.8 Mt. "Soviets' Nuclear Arsenal Continues to Proliferate," *Aviation Week & Space Technology*, 16 June 1980, p. 75, reports the yield of the SS-N-8 Mod 2 as 800 kt.
14 SMP 1988, p. 15. JCS, FY 1989, p. 39, reported the same number as of the end of 1987.
15 SMP 1986, pp. 28-29; DIA, *Intercontinental Strategic Forces Summary-USSR (U)*, DDB-2680-253-85, 1 January 1985, p. 5.
16 SMP 1985, p. 40.
17 *Ibid.*
18 *Ibid.*
19 USAF, *Summary Review*, 1975, p. C-2.
20 Berman and Baker, *Soviet Strategic Forces*, pp. 106-107.
21 USAF, *Summary Review*, 1976, p. C-2; SMP 1985, p. 40.
22 Polmar, *Guide to the Soviet Navy*, 1986, p. 433.
23 Studeman, USN, Statement before HASC, March 1988, p. 5.
24 IISS, *Military Balance*, 1987-1988, p. 206; Berman and Baker, *Soviet Strategic Forces*, pp. 106-107; Collins and Victory, *U.S./Soviet Military Balance*, 1988, p. 18.
25 *Trends*, 1976, p. 27.

146 Nuclear Weapons Databook, Volume IV

SS-N-17 SNIPE

DESCRIPTION: Fifth-generation two-stage, solid-fuel, single-warhead SLBM deployed on one Yankee II submarine. This was the first Soviet solid-fuel SLBM and first with a post-boost vehicle

DESIGN BUREAU: Chelomei derivative

SPECIFICATIONS:
- Length: 11.06 m[1] (36.29 ft)
- Diameter: 1.65 m[2] (5.41 ft)
- Stages: 1;[3] 2[4]
- Weight at Launch: 22,000 kg[5] (45,000 lbs)
- Fuel/Propulsion: solid[6]
- Guidance: inertial[7]
- Throwweight: 700 kg (1500 lbs);[8] 800 kg (2500 lbs)[9]
- Range: 3900 km[10] (2100 nm; 2400 mi)

DUAL CAPABLE: no

NUCLEAR WARHEADS:
- Number of warheads: 1[11]
- Yield per warhead: 500 Kt[12]

DEPLOYMENT:
- Launch Platform: 1 Yankee II[13]
- Number Deployed: 12 (April 1988)[14]

HISTORY:
- Design Began: 1969[15]
- R&D: 1969-1975[16]
- Engineering and Testing: 1975-1980[17]
- First Flight Test: 1975[18]
- Year Operation Began: 1980[19]

TARGETING:
- Types: administrative centers, communications facilities, industrial complexes, population centers, and soft military targets[20]
- Accuracy/CEP: 0.75 nm[21] (1400 m;[22] 4600 ft)

---

1. Jane's Weapon Systems, 1987-88, p. 14; John Jordan, "Soviet Ballistic Missile Submarines," Jane's Defence Weekly, Part 3, 11 February 1984, p. 204; Part 2, 28 January 1984, p. 125. See also, Jane's Fighting Ships, 1988-89, p. 548; Taylor, Missiles of the World, 1980, p. 129.
2. Jane's Weapon Systems, 1987-88, p. 14; Taylor, Missiles of the World, 1980, p. 129.
3. Aviation Week & Space Technology, 14 March 1983, p. 153.
4. Jane's Fighting Ships, 1988-89, p. 548.
5. Rich and Pike, SALT, 1984, pp. 104-105.
6. Berman and Baker, Soviet Strategic Forces, pp. 106-107; Collins and Glakas, U.S./Soviet Military Balance, 1983, pp. 19-22.
7. Jane's Fighting Ships, 1988-89, p. 548; Polmar, Guide to the Soviet Navy, 1986, p. 433.
8. Rich and Pike, SALT, 1984, pp. 104-105.
9. IISS, Military Balance, 1987-1988, p. 206.
10. SMP 1987, p. 33.
11. Ibid.
12. Collins and Victory, U.S./Soviet Military Balance, 1988, p. 18; IISS, Military Balance, 1987-1988, p. 206. IISS, Military Balance, 1984-1985, p. 134, reported 1 Mt.
13. JCS, FY 1989, p. 39; SMP 1987, p. 33; SMP 1983, p. 22.
14. SMP 1988, p. 15; JCS, FY 1989, p. 39; SMP 1987, p. 33.
15. SMP 1988, p. 40.
16. Ibid.
17. Ibid.
18. Polmar, Guide to the Soviet Navy, 1986, p. 433.
19. SMP 1985, p. 40.
20. Studeman, USN, Statement before HASC, March 1988, p. 5.
21. Collins and Victory, U.S./Soviet Military Balance, 1988, p. 18.
22. IISS, Military Balance, 1987-1988, p. 206.

5
SS-N-18 STINGRAY

SS-N-18 STINGRAY (Soviet designation RSM-50)[1]

DESCRIPTION: Fifth-generation, two-stage, liquid-fuel SLBM with MIRV capability, deployed in three versions, two with MIRVs and one with single warhead; first Soviet MIRVed SLBM

DESIGN BUREAU: Chelomei derivative

SPECIFICATIONS:

Length: approx. 14 m[2] (46 ft)

Diameter: 1.8 m[3] (5.9 ft)

Stages: 2[4]

Weight at Launch: approx. 34,000 kg (75,000 lbs)[5]

Fuel/Propulsion: liquid[6]

Guidance: stellar inertial[7] with the capacity for multiple star sightings[8]

Throwweight: Mod 1/3: 1300 kg (2900 lbs)[9]
Mod 1/3: 800 kg (1800 lbs)[10]

Range: Mod 1/3: 6500 km[11] (3500 nm, 4000 mi)
Mod 2: 8000 km[12] (4300 nm, 5000 mi); greater than 8000 km if PBV is used to push payload further along its trajectory[13]

DUAL CAPABLE: no

NUCLEAR WARHEADS: average loading of SS-N-18 SLBMs is assumed to be seven warheads

Number of warheads: Mod 1: 3 MIRV[14]
Mod 2: 1[15]
Mod 3: up to 7 MIRV[16]

Yield per warhead: Mod 1: 200 Kt;[17] 500 Kt[18]
Mod 2: 450 Kt;[19] 500 Kt-1 Mt[20]
Mod 3: 200 Kt;[21] 500 Kt[22]

DEPLOYMENT:

Launch Platform: 14 Delta IIIs[23]

Number Deployed: 224 (April 1988);[24] assumed average seven warheads per missile

HISTORY:

Design Began: 1964[25]

R&D: 1964-1970[26]

Engineering and Testing: 1970-1975[27]

First Flight Test: Mod 1: 1975;[28] November 1978 from submarine
Mod 2: 1977[29]
Mod 3: 1981/1982[30]

Year Operation Began: Mod 1: 1978-1979[31]
Mod 2: 1977-1978[32]
Mod 3: 1978[33]

---

1 SFRC, SALT II Treaty, Report No. 96-14, p. 345.
2 Jane's Weapon Systems, 1987-88, p. 15; John Jordan, "Soviet Ballistic Missile Submarines," Jane's Defence Weekly, Part 3, 11 February 1984, pp. 204-205; Part 2, 28 January 1984, p. 125; Taylor, Missiles of the World, 1980, p. 129.
3 Jane's Weapon Systems, 1987-88, p. 15; Taylor, Missiles of the World, 1980, p. 129.
4 SFRC, SALT II Treaty, Report No. 96-14, p. 345; SASC, Strategic Force Modernization Programs, 1981, p. 8.
5 Polmar, Guide to the Soviet Navy, 1986, p. 433.
6 SFRC, SALT II Treaty, Report No. 96-14, p. 345; SASC, Strategic Force Modernization Programs, 1981, p. 8.
7 Berman and Baker, Soviet Strategic Forces, pp. 106-107; Jordan, op. cit., Part 3, pp. 204-205; Part 2, 28 January 1984, p. 125.
8 Donald MacKenzie, "The Soviet Union and Strategic Missile Guidance," mimeo, Department of Sociology, University of Edinburgh, 1988, p. 46.
9 Rich and Pike, SALT, 1984, pp. 104-105.
10 Ibid.
11 SMP 1987, p. 33.
12 Ibid.
13 SFRC, SALT II Treaty, Report No. 96-14, p. 345; SASC, Strategic Force Modernization Programs, 1981, p. 8.
14 SMP 1987, p. 33. Polmar, Guide to the Soviet Navy, 1986, p. 433, states initially 2 MIRVs.
15 SMP 1987, p. 33.
16 Ibid. Under START, all SS-N-18 missiles will be counted as carrying seven warheads.
17 Berman and Baker, Soviet Strategic Forces, pp. 106-107; Aviation Week & Space Technology, 14 March 1983, p. 153; "Soviets' Nuclear Arsenal Continues to Proliferate," Aviation Week & Space Technology, 16 June 1980, p. 75; Aviation Week & Space Technology, 11 January 1982, p. 26.
18 Collins and Victory, U.S./Soviet Military Balance, 1988, p. 18; IISS, Military Balance, 1987-1988, p. 206.
19 Berman and Baker, Soviet Strategic Forces, pp. 106-107; "Soviets' Nuclear Arsenal Continues to Proliferate," Aviation Week & Space Technology, 16 June 1980, p. 75; Aviation Week & Space Technology, 11 January 1982, p. 26.
20 Collins and Victory, U.S./Soviet Military Balance, 1988, p. 18; IISS, Military Balance, 1987-1988, p. 206.
21 Aviation Week & Space Technology, 11 January 1982, p. 26.
22 Collins and Victory, U.S./Soviet Military Balance, 1988, p. 18; IISS, Military Balance, 1987-1988, p. 206.
23 SMP 1987, p. 33; DIA, Unclassified Communist Naval Orders of Battle, April 1986, p. 1.
24 SMP 1988, p. 15; JCS, FY 1989, p. 39; SMP 1987, p. 33; DIA, Unclassified Communist Naval Orders of Battle, April 1986, p. 1.
25 SMP 1985, p. 40.
26 Ibid.
27 Ibid.
28 Polmar, Guide to the Soviet Navy, 1986, p. 433.
29 Rich and Pike, SALT, 1984, pp. 104-105.
30 Aviation Week & Space Technology, 11 January 1982, p. 26.
31 Berman and Baker, Soviet Strategic Forces, pp. 106-107; Jane's Weapons Systems 1987-88, p. 15; Jordan, op. cit., Part 3, 11 February 1984, pp. 204-205; Part 2, 28 January 1984, p.125.
32 IISS, Military Balance, 1987-1988, p. 206; Collins and Victory, U.S./Soviet Military Balance, 1988, p. 18.
33 Collins and Victory, U.S./Soviet Military Balance, 1988, p. 18.

SS-N-18 STINGRAY

TARGETING:
Types: administrative centers, communications facilities, industrial complexes, population centers, and soft military targets[34]

Accuracy/CEP: Mod 1/2/3: 0.76 nm (1400 m; 4600 ft);[35] 0.5 nm (900 m; 3000 ft)[36]

---

[34] Studeman, USN, Statement before HASC, March 1988, p. 5.
[35] Berman and Baker, *Soviet Strategic Forces*, pp. 106-107; *Aviation Week & Space Technology*, 14 March 1983, p. 153; "Soviets' Nuclear Arsenal Continues to Proliferate," *Aviation Week & Space Technology*, 16 June 1980, 82 p. 75; *Aviation Week & Space Technology*, 11 January 1982, p. 26; Polmar, *Guide to the Soviet Navy*, 1986, p. 433.
[36] Collins and Victory, *U.S./Soviet Military Balance*, 1988, p. 18.

5
SS-N-20 STURGEON

SS-N-20 STURGEON (Soviet designation RSM-52)

DESCRIPTION:	Sixth-generation, three-stage, solid-fuel, MIRVed SLBM deployed on the Typhoon submarines	**Number Deployed:**	100 (mid-1988)[12]
DESIGN BUREAU:	Chelomei derivative	**HISTORY:**	
SPECIFICATIONS:		Design Began:	1972[13]
Length:	15 m[1] (49 ft)	R&D:	1972-1978[14]
Diameter:	2.2 m[2] (7.2 ft)	Engineering and Testing:	1978-1983[15]
Stages:	3[3]	First Flight Test:	Mod 1: 1979[16] Mod 2: possibly 1988[17]
Weight at Launch:	60,000 kg (132,000 lbs)[4]	Year Operation Began:	1983[18]
Fuel/Propulsion:	solid[5]	Production:	in March 1986, the SS-N-20 was the only Soviet SLBM in series production[19]
Guidance:	inertial[6]		
Throwweight:	presumably greater than SS-N-18	**TARGETING:**	
Range:	8300 km[7] (4500 nm;[8] 5200 mi)	Types:	administrative centers, communications facilities, industrial complexes, population centers, and soft military targets[20]
DUAL CAPABLE:	no		
NUCLEAR WARHEADS:	average loading of SS-N-20 SLBMs is assumed to be 10 warheads	Accuracy/CEP:	approx. 0.3 nm[21] (600 m, 1800 ft); a modification of the SS-N-20 may enter flight-testing before the end of the 1980s[22]
Number of warheads:	10 MIRV counted under START; previously reported as 6-9 MIRV[9]		
Yield per warhead:	100 Kt[10]	**COMMENTS:**	The SS-N-20 has had significant developmental difficulties.[23] Four flight tests in 1980 were failures;[24] two tests were successful in 1981.[25] As many as four missiles tested in October 1982 from White Sea to Kamchatka and Central Pacific, two of which were launches 20 seconds apart from the same Typhoon submarine.[26]
DEPLOYMENT:			
Launch Platform:	Typhoon submarine;[11] a single Golf V in the Black Sea is configured to test the SS-N-20, but is not nuclear armed		

---

1. A chart in SMP 1987, p. 33, indicates the length of the SS-N-20 is about 15 m.
2. John Jordan, "Soviet Ballistic Missile Submarines" *Jane's Defence Weekly*: Part 3, 11 February 1984, p. 204; Part 2, 28 January 1984, p. 125; Armin Wetterhahn, "The Soviet Typhoon-Class SSBN," *International Defense Review*, April 1984, pp. 418, 421.
3. Wetterhahn, *op. cit.*, pp. 418, 421; Polmar, *Guide to the Soviet Navy*, 1986, p. 434; Couhat, *Combat Fleets of the World*, 1988/89, p. 563.
4. Polmar, *Guide to the Soviet Navy*, 1986, p. 434.
5. SMP 1987, p. 33.
6. Polmar, *Guide to the Soviet Navy*, 1983, p. 367.
7. SMP 1987, p. 33. JCS, FY 1987, p. 21, and previous JCS reports, reported the range of the SS-N-20 as 5000 nm. The JCS, FY 1988, p. 35, reduced the range to 4500 nm, consistent with the value given in SMP 1987.
8. JCS, FY 1989, p. 40.
9. Joint communique issued at the end of the 7-10 December 1987 U.S.-Soviet summit, reprinted in *Arms Control Today*, January-February 1988, p. 16. SMP 1987, p. 33; JCS, FY 1989, p. 40 rtate 6-9 RVs. JCS, FY 1987, p. 21 and previous JCS reports, reported 6 to 8 MIRVs, consistent with the MIRV values given in SMP 1987. Studeman, USN, Statement before HASC, March 1988, p. 33, states SS-N-20 has eight warheads.
10. IISS, *Military Balance*, 1987-1988, p. 206; Collins and Victory, *U.S./Soviet Military Balance*, 1988, p. 18. IISS, *Military Balance*, 1984-1985, p. 134 reported 200 Kt.
11. SMP 1988, pp. 15, 48. As of April 1988, five Typhoons were operational. One or two additional Typhoons are probably under construction and will be operational by the early 1990s.
12. SMP 1988, pp. 15, 48.
13. SMP 1985, p. 40.
14. Ibid.
15. Ibid.
16. SMP 1981, p. 54; SASC, Strategic Force Modernization Programs, 1981, p. 5.
17. SMP 1988, p. 48.
18. HASC, FY 1985 DOD, Part 3, p. 3; SMP 1985, p. 40.
19. SMP 1986, p. 121.
20. Studeman, USN, Statement before HASC, March 1988, p. 5.
21. Collins and Victory, *U.S./Soviet Military Balance*, 1988, p. 18; Couhat, *Combat Fleets of the World*, 1988/89, p. 563.
22. SMP 1987, p. 35; SMP 1986, pp. 30-31.
23. Polmar, *Guide to the Soviet Navy*, 1986, p. 434.
24. *Jane's Weapon Systems*, 1987-88, p. 15; "Soviets' Nuclear Arsenal Continues to Proliferate," *Aviation Week & Space Technology*, 16 June 1980, p. 75.
25. *Jane's Weapon Systems*, 1987-88, p. 15.
26. Research Institute for Peace and Security, *Asian Security* (Tokyo: RIPS, 1983), p. 92; *Aviation Week & Space Technology*, 25 November 1982, p. 17; Wetterhahn, *op. cit.*, pp. 418, 421.

SS-N-23 SKIFF

DESCRIPTION:	Sixth-generation, three-stage, liquid-fuel, MIRVed SLBM deployed on Delta IV submarine; probable follow-on to SS-N-18
DESIGN BUREAU:	Chelomei[1]

SPECIFICATIONS:

Length:	approx. 14 m[2] (46 ft)
Diameter:	1.8 m[3] (5.9 ft)
Stages:	3[4]
Weight at Launch:	about 40,000 kg (88,000 lbs)[5]
Fuel/Propulsion:	liquid[6]
Guidance:	unknown
Throwweight:	reportedly greater than SS-N-18[7]
Range:	8300 km[8]

DUAL CAPABLE:	no

NUCLEAR WARHEADS:

Number of warheads:	4 MIRV counted under START; tested with, and previously reported as having, 10 MIRV[9]
Yield per warhead:	100 Kt[10]

DEPLOYMENT:

Launch Platform:	4 Delta IVs;[11] will probably be backfit into some Delta IIIs[12]
Number Deployed:	64 (April 1988)[13]

HISTORY:

Design Began:	1976[14]
R&D:	1976-1982[15]
Engineering and Testing:	1982-1987[16]
First Flight Test:	Mod 1: June 1983;[17] a modified versions of the SS-N-23 will probably complete testing in 1988[18]
Year Operation Began:	1985
Production:	in March 1986, the SS-N-23 was not in series production[19]

TARGETING:

Types:	administrative centers, communications facilities, industrial complexes, population centers, and soft military targets[20]
Accuracy/CEP:	reportedly more accurate than SS-N-18, but experiencing testing problems[21]
COMMENTS:	The SS-N-23 "apparently has suffered reliability problems. The missile is assessed to be operational, however, and work to improve its reliability continues."[22] The SS-N-23 may be retrofitted into some Delta III submarines.[23]

---

1. Rich and Pike, *SALT*, 1984, pp. 104-105.
2. A chart in SMP 1987, p. 33, indicates the length of the SS-N-23 is about 14 m.
3. Same launch type as SS-N-8 and SS-N-18.
4. Polmar, *Guide to the Soviet Navy*, 1986, p. 434.
5. Ibid.
6. SMP 1987, p. 34.
7. Ibid.
8. Ibid. (4500 nm, 5200 mi)
9. Ambassador Paul H. Nitze, Statement before SFRC, The INF Treaty, Part 2, 1-4 February 1988, p. 97; SMP 1987, p. 33.
10. Private communication with the authors.
11. SMP 1987, p. 34 reports that four Delta IVs have been launched and up to two more Delta IVs are under construction (as of April 1987).
12. "Current Naval Intelligence Issues by the Office of Naval Intelligence," March 1987, p. 5.
13. SMP 1988, p. 15; JCS, FY 1989, p. 39.
14. SMP 1985, p. 40.
15. Ibid.
16. Ibid.
17. SMP 1983, p. 23; HASC, FY 1985 DOD, Part 3, p. 3.
18. SMP 1988, p. 48.
19. SMP 1986, p. 121.
20. Studeman, USN, Statement before HASC, March 1988, p. 5.
21. SMP 1987, p. 34.
22. Studeman, USN, Statement before HASC, March 1988, p. 33.
23. JCS, FY 1988, p. 35.

ND# 6
Cruise and Anti-ship Missiles

Chapter Six
Cruise Missiles and Anti-ship Missiles

Overview

The Soviet Union has long displayed an active interest in cruise missiles and anti-ship missiles. Since 1958, it has deployed some 25 different air-, ground-, and sea-launched cruise missile types, including 17 nuclear-capable types. All but three of the nuclear-capable cruise missile types remain in service today. The 14 types currently deployed (see Table 6.1) can be launched from a variety of platforms, including aircraft, submarines, and surface warships, as well as from ground launchers. The missiles fly a variety of flight profiles and speeds and vary from short-range, anti-ship missiles to long-range, strategic, air- and sea-launched missiles.[1]

As of mid-1988 there were six nuclear-capable, air-launched cruise missile types, seven nuclear-capable, sea-launched cruise missile types, and a single ground-launched type. Four cruise missiles are known to be under development (SS-NX-24, AS-X-19, SSC-X-4, and SSC-X-5). The latter two will not be able to be deployed under terms of the INF Treaty. A total of some 2800 nuclear warheads are estimated to be deployed on Soviet cruise missiles: 2200 on air-launched versions, 500 on sea-launched versions, and 100 on ground-launched versions (see Chapter Two).

History

The postwar Soviet cruise missile program benefited greatly from exploitation of the German guided-missile program. The Soviets took operational V-1 ramjet cruise missiles, parts, launchers and assemblies, special research and production facilities, and equipment from the Germans, as well as 300-400 German missile specialists (many with experience on the V-2 missile) and complete reports of wartime developments and technical documents, including advanced studies.[2] As a result, Soviet weapon designers were able to develop a thorough familiarity with the German wartime program by 1948 and had the capability for continuing the work independently by 1950.[3] Limited numbers of a V-1 type missile were produced by 1950, and tests of this missile may have been conducted from specially configured submarines. By the end of 1952, the United States believed that the Soviets might have deployed a missile that was essentially an improved V-1,[4] though little information was actually available at the time.[5]

Several cruise missile development programs were underway in the early 1950s. A major focus was air-launched weapons. By 1952, the CIA estimated that three types of rocket-powered glide bombs were available to the Soviet military, including a V-1 type pilotless aircraft.[6] Two years later, it was estimated that by 1961 four types of ASMs would be deployed by the Soviet Union: a 20 nautical mile range subsonic missile projected to be introduced in 1955 (but which was never deployed); a 55 nautical mile range subsonic missile projected to be introduced in 1957 (but which was never deployed); a 55 nautical mile range, supersonic, anti-ship missile (to become the AS-1 Kennel), introduced in 1958; and a 100 nautical mile range supersonic missile (to become the AS-2 Kipper), introduced in 1961. Each of these missiles was predicted by the CIA to be nuclear-capable.[7]

---

1. HAC, FY 1980 DOD, Part 3, p. 508. Cruise missiles launched from aircraft are termed air-to-surface missiles and are given AS designations (for example: AS-2, AS-15). Surface-to-surface missiles launched from naval ships or submarines are given SS-N designations (for example: SS-N-3, SS-N-21). Ground-launched surface-to-surface cruise missiles are given SSC designations (for example, SSC-1). When a missile is still in research and development, an X is added to the designation, as in SS-NX-24. Soviet cruise missiles are also given NATO code names, air-launched missiles beginning with a K (for example, the AS-4 Kitchen), and sea-launched missiles beginning with an S (for example, SS-N-3 Shaddock) (See Appendix B).
2. Finished V-1 weapons and components and special machinery left in the area by U.S. forces were removed by rail from the Mittleuerkf mine in Germany to the Khimki factory complex 20 kilometers northwest of Moscow from September-October 1945 to April 1947. During 1946-1947, as many as 200 V-1s were assembled at Khimki, composed entirely of German parts; test firings of captured V-1s commenced in the summer of 1947; CIA, *A Summary of Soviet Guided Missile Intelligence*, US/UK GM-4-52, 20 July 1953 (partially declassified), pp. A-1, A-16 to A-22. See also a partially declassified CIA briefing before the Preparedness Investigating subcommittee of SASC, "Soviet Guided Missiles and Related Soviet Capabilities," 26-27 November 1957, p. 13; USAF Directorate of Intelligence and Office of Naval Intelligence, *Estimate of Soviet Air Capabilities*, 1 October 1950, Annex V, Soviet Guided Missiles, pp. 133-135, 139. According to an emigre account, the Soviets had German designers reconstruct the captured missiles, and used German assistance to help fire the captured missiles; Mikhail Turetsky, *The Introduction of Missile Systems into the Soviet Navy (1945-1962)*, (Falls Church, VA: Delphic Associates, March 1983), p. ix.
3. CIA, *Soviet Capabilities and Probable Courses of Action Through Mid-1959*, NIE 11-4-54, 28 August 1954, partially declassified, p. 57; CIA, briefing before SASC, *op. cit.*, p. 13.
4. In April 1947, then Minister of Armaments Dmitri Ustinov stated that a Soviet copy of the V-1 was being produced at Khimki. The CIA estimated that Soviet workers had taken over from German engineers in manufacturing V-1s at Khimki by January 1948, and that by 1948 an improved V-1 with longer range (400-600 km as opposed to 300 km) and improved gyroscopes (circular error probable [CEP] variously estimated as 1 nm and 2-3 nm) was in production. A smaller number of improved V-1s (30-35 missiles) were produced at Podborez'ye by April 1949. In 1948, a few Soviet submarines in the Pacific Fleet had been equipped with two V-1 launchers, and the Soviets were believed to have an operational sea-launched capability by the end of 1952. At that time the standard V-1 (175 nm), the improved V-1 (200-325 nm), and a similar, longer range, twin-pulse-jet, improved V-1 were thought to be available; CIA, *Summary, op. cit.*, pp. A-17, A-19, A-21, A-23, A-66, A-67. See also CIA, NIE 11-4-54, *op. cit.*, p. 57; Central Intelligence Group, *Soviet Capabilities for the Development and Production of Certain Types of Weapons and Equipment*, 31 October 1946 (partially declassified), pp. 2-3.
5. A May 1955 CIA intelligence estimate noted that "it is probable that the USSR now has some guided missiles in operational status, and that a growing Soviet guided missile capability will develop within the next several years'; CIA, *Soviet Capabilities and Probable Soviet Course of Action through 1960*, NIE 11-3-55, 17 May 1955 (partially declassified), p. 25. No new evidence had appeared since the publication of CIA, *Soviet Capabilities and Probable Programs in the Guided Missile Field*, NIE 11-6-54, 5 October 1954. In fact, according to the 1955 CIA report, there was "no firm current intelligence on what particular types of missiles the USSR is presently developing, or may now have in operational use"; CIA, NIE 11-3-55, *op. cit.*, p. 25.
6. The three types included a 10 mile range glide bomb with optical or radar tracking and radio command, a similar bomb that had a short, underwater terminal phase, and a 200 mile V-1 type with preset guidance plus radio command (CEP of four miles). It is believed that the Soviets exploited the German ASMs, personnel, and equipment. Production of German ASMs was accomplished in the Soviet Union by 1947-1948. These missiles were at least prepared for testing as the Soviet Naval Technical Staff had target practice devices built that were later visited by Soviet naval air school instructors; CIA, *Summary, op. cit.*, pp. C-3, C-7, C-9.
7. CIA, Briefing before SASC, *op. cit.*, pp. 30-31.

6
History

Table 6.1
Soviet Nuclear-Capable Cruise Missiles and Anti-ship Missiles

Type	Year Deployed	Status	Range (nm)	Mission Profile[1]
Air-launched				
AS-2 Kipper	1961	Being phased out	115	AS, Secondary LA/S
AS-3 Kangaroo	1960	Active	350	LA/Su
AS-4 Kitchen	1967	Active	300	AS, Secondary LA/S
AS-5 Kelt	1965	Active	120	AS/T
AS-6 Kingfish	1970	Active	250	AS, Secondary LA/S
AS-9 Kyle?	1975	Active	50	LA/S
AS-11 Kilter?	1984	Active	350	DS/S
AS-15 Kent	1984	Active	1900	LA/Su
AS-X-16	—	Under development	~300	DS, LA/S
AS-X-19	—	Under development	1600	LA/S
Sea-launched				
SS-N-1 Scrubber	1958	Retired	100	AS/Su
SS-N-3a/c Shaddock	1962	Active	250	AS, LA/T
SS-N-3b Sepal	1962	Active	150	AS, LA/T
SS-N-7 Starbright	1968	Active	35	AS/Su
SS-N-9 Siren	1970	Active	60	AS/T
SS-N-12 Sandbox	1976	Active	300	AS/S
SS-N-19 Shipwreck	1980	Active	300	AS, Secondary LA/S
SS-N-21 Sampson	1987	Active	1600	LA/Su
SS-N-22 Sunburn		Active	120	AS/S
SS-NX-24	—	Under development	1600	LA/S
Ground-launched				
SSC-1b Sepal		Active	240	AS/T
SSC-X-4	—	Eliminated under INF	1600	LA/Su
SSC-X-5	—	Eliminated under INF	1600	LA/S

1 Mission types: AS: anti-ship; DS: defense suppression; LA: land attack. Profile types: S: supersonic; Su: subsonic; T: transonic.

Nikita Khrushchev stated in 1955 that "a submarine equipped with guided missiles is the most suitable naval weapon, and its development will be emphasized by the Soviet Navy."[8] Nevertheless, the first deployed Soviet cruise missile was the air-launched AS-1 Kennel, which entered service in 1958. This missile was deployed on medium-range Badger bombers and was fitted with a conventional warhead for anti-ship strikes.[9] During the next five years, eight other nuclear-capable cruise missiles were fielded: the SS-N-1 Scrubber (1958), SS-N-3c Shaddock (1960), the AS-3 Kangaroo (1960), the AS-2 Kipper (1961), the SS-N-3a Shaddock (1962), and its ground-launched variant, the SSC-1b Sepal (1962).

Following the failed attempt to adapt the ground-launched SSC-2b conventional missile for delivery by a Sverdlov-class cruiser,[10] the first anti-ship cruise missile, the SS-N-1 Scrubber, was deployed beginning in 1958 on four Kildin class destroyers, and from 1960, on Krupnyy class destroyers. The nuclear-capable SS-N-1 had a range of 45-100 nautical miles.[11] The missile was never widely deployed because of its low reliability and poor accuracy and was retired from operational service by the late 1970s or early 1980s.[12]

All of the first-generation cruise missiles were large, short-range, relatively unsophisticated, inaccurate, and

---

8 Ibid., p.42.
9 The 1957 NIE had later mistakenly estimated that this subsonic cruise missile could carry a nuclear warhead up to about 55 nautical miles; CIA, *Main Trends in Soviet Capabilities and Policies 1957-1962*, NIE 11-4-57, 12 November 1957 (partially declassified), p. 27. The Kennel's ground-launched derivative, the SSC-2a, also carried only a conventional warhead. This 300 nautical mile-range land-attack missile was deployed at fixed or mobile sites.
10 The SSC-2b Samlet was developed between 1952 and 1958 for Soviet naval shore defenses. During 1956-1957 a launcher was installed on a Sverdlov class cruiser (the Admiral Nakhimov) and several successful launches were made. But the experiment was discontinued due to the cumbersome launcher system, the limitations of the missile itself, and the need to build special ships for the missile; Turetsky, *op. cit.*, pp. 40, 48. See also, Admiral Sergei G. Gorshkov, *The Sea Power of the State*, (Annapolis, MD; Naval Institute Press, 1979), p. 204.
11 According to one observer, "On approach to the target, a suspended warhead separated, descended several meters into the water, and was supposed to strike the underwater part of the hull while the remainder of the missile struck above water;" Turetsky, *op. cit.*, p. 50. While it is unclear whether the nuclear version as well the conventional version of the SS-N-1 missiles would use this same concept, this recollection by a former Soviet specialist assigned to a Northern Fleet test base may have some bearing on the assessment of subsequent Soviet missiles given the Soviet proclivity for improving upon existing concepts and hardware in new development efforts.
12 The Kildin class destroyers, with six missiles carried onboard for the single SS-N-1 launcher, was one of three classes of Soviet surface ships with a theoretical missile reload capability (the others being the Kynda class cruisers with SS-N-3b missiles and the Kiev class aircraft carriers with SS-N-12 missiles). Four Kildin destroyers were at one time deployed, three of which were converted to other purposes by 1973. The remaining ship is probably held in reserve in the Pacific Fleet; DIA, *Unclassified Communist Naval Orders of Battle*, May 1986, p. 3. The eight Krupnyy class destroyers carried two SS-N-1 launchers; all were retired by 1977.

6
History

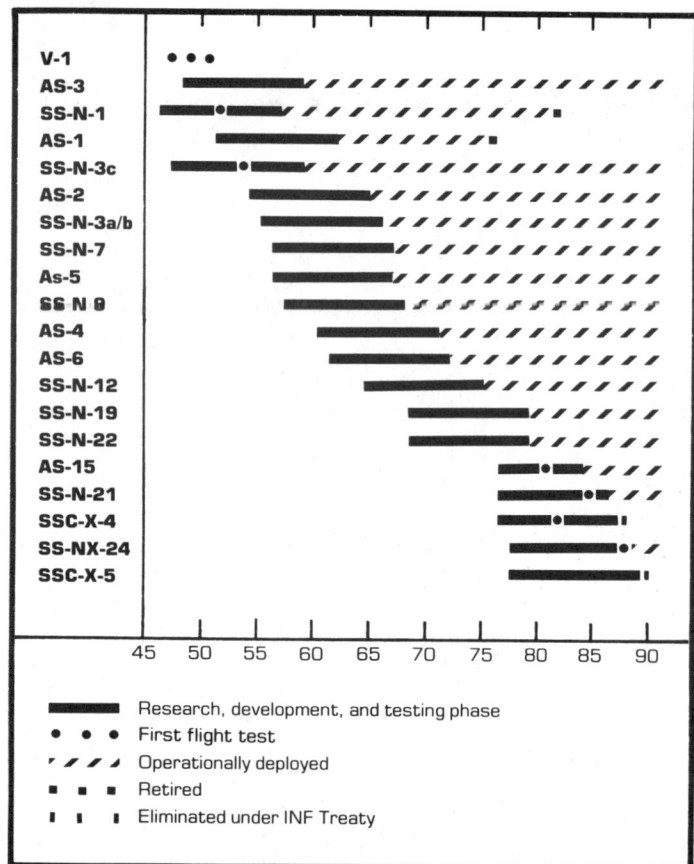

Figure 6.1 Soviet Cruise Missile and Anti-ship Missile Development.

Since January 1981, the Soviet Union has been developing a new generation of long-range, nuclear-armed, air-, sea-, and ground-launched, land-attack cruise missiles (air-launched AS-15 Kent, sea-launched SS-N-21 Sampson, and the ground-launched SSC-X-4) similar to current modern U.S. long-range missiles.[14] The AS-15 Kent was first deployed on Bear H bombers in 1984 and is being produced in large numbers. The SS-N-21 Sampson was initially deployed on a converted Yankee class platform in late 1987 and will also be produced in large numbers. The SSC-X-4 will not be deployed under the terms of the INF Treaty. A generation of supersonic, long-range cruise missiles is in the final stages of flight-testing (sea-launched SS-NX-24 and air-launched BL-10).

The vast majority of all Soviet cruise missile types have been for anti-ship missions, all of which are assessed as being nuclear-capable.[15] The capability of cruise missiles in this role was demonstrated on 25 October 1967 when two Egyptian Komar class guided-missile boats sank the Israeli destroyer Elath with conventionally armed SS-N-2 Styx missiles.[16] Nearly every large Soviet combatant and many patrol craft are armed with nuclear-capable, anti-ship cruise missiles.[17]

Land-attack cruise missiles have played a secondary role in Soviet developments.[18] By 1952, the Soviets had attempted to place launchers for improved V-1 missiles on submarines to test the feasibility of using unguided missiles with a 325 nautical mile maximum range for shore bombardment.[19] Their performance was not particularly good, however, even after the control system was upgraded. The program was abandoned after a submarine that went to sea carrying empty launch/containers sank on its return voyage.[20]

The SS-N-3c Shaddock and the AS-3 Kangaroo were the first nuclear-armed, land-attack cruise missiles.[21] Both missiles entered service in 1960, and both carried only nuclear warheads. Both missiles lacked terminal homing, and they were probably intended for attacking large-area targets. Indications of renewed Soviet interest in new land-attack missiles was not again detected until the late 1970s, almost two decades after these missiles had entered service.[22] A development program began in January 1981 on at least two different designs—one subsonic and one supersonic—and in 1984, the AS-15 Kent was deployed on the Bear H strategic bomber, the first Soviet land-attack cruise missile deployed since the 1960s.

designed primarily for anti-ship missions.[13] The second generation of nuclear-capable cruise missiles entered service from 1965 to 1976. This new generation included the air-launched AS-4 Kitchen (1967), AS-5 Kelt (1968), and AS-6 Kingfish (1968), and the sea-launched SS-N-7 (1968), SS-N-9 Siren (1969), and SS-N-12 Sandbox (1976). These missiles were still quite large and heavy, but they offered improved accuracy and reliability. In 1980 two new sea-launched anti-ship cruise missiles were deployed, the SS-N-19 and SS-N-22. While these missiles offered significantly improved anti-ship capabilities, they are primarily modern versions of a long line of relatively short-range weapons designed for surface ship attacks.

---

13 ACDA, FY 1980 ACIS, p. 34. The longer range AS-3 and SS-N-3c were designed for land-attack missions.
14 SMP 1988, p. 40.
15 See, for example, ACDA, FY 1980 ACIS, p. 187; ACDA, FY 1981 ACIS, pp. 380-381; ACDA, FY 1983 ACIS, p. 224; HAC, FY 1980 DOD, Part 2, p. 2280; USN, *Soviet Naval Developments* (Rev. 4/85), p. 144.
16 Use of a nuclear warhead for the SS-N-2 was reportedly not envisioned at the time of its development, though such a possibility was not excluded; Turetsky, op. cit., p. 52. Some Western analysts believed the missile could carry a nuclear warhead; see, e.g., Center for Strategic and International Studies, *Soviet Sea Power*, Special Report Series No. 10 (Washington, DC: CSIS, June 1969), p. 47.
17 DIA, *Sea-Launched Aerodynamic Missile Systems (Current and Projected) - USSR and PRC*, DST-1330S-205-77, 1 March 1977.
18 See discussion by Carrie Elizabeth Martin, "Soviet Naval Long-Range Land-Attack SLCM: Emerging Implications and Issues," Naval Postgraduate School thesis, Monterey, CA, March 1984 (partially declassified and released under the FOIA) pp. 16ff.

19 USAF and ONI, *Estimating Soviet Air Capabilities*, op. cit., p. 139.
20 According to an emigre report, three obsolete submarines of the Northern Fleet were involved in the test program. The first submarine had one launcher/container installed behind the conning tower, and the other two had two launcher/containers installed, one on each side of the upper deck. A two-year search for the missing submarine was unsuccessful; Turetsky, op. cit., pp. 59-61.
21 The SSC-2a Salish, derived from the AS-1 Kennel, was a 100-150 nautical mile range, conventionally armed land-attack missile launched from fixed and mobile launchers. It may have been deployed into the 1970s, though it has now been withdrawn from service; Taylor, *Missiles of the World* 1980, p. 95; Gunston, *Rockets & Missiles*, p. 28.
22 According to former Secretary of the Navy John Lehman, seven different Soviet anti-ship cruise missiles with ranges above 300 miles could be used for land-attack missions to strike targets within 150 miles of U.S. coasts; HAC, FY 1986 DOD, Part 2, p. 914. These missiles include the SS-N-2, SS-N-3, SS-N-7, SS-N-9, SS-N-12, SS-N-19, and SS-N-22. None of these missiles, however, with the exception of the SS-N-3c and the possible exceptions of the SS-N-12 and SS-N-19, carry out such missions.

6
Air-launched Missiles

Table 6.2
Soviet Air-launched Nuclear-Capable Cruise Missiles

Type	Platform	Missiles Deployed	Nuclear Warheads
AS-2 Kipper	Badger C	70	70
AS-3 Kangaroo	Bear B/C	30	30
AS-4 Kitchen	Blinder B, Backfire B/C, Bear G	760	800
AS-5 Kelt	Badger G, Badger C Modified	440	440
AS-6 Kingfish	Badger G Modified	300	300
AS-15 Kent	Bear H, (Blackjack)	480	570

Air-launched Missiles

ASMs were among the first Soviet guided weapons to be deployed in the post-war period. The first operational Soviet cruise missile to be deployed was the 50 nautical mile range conventionally armed, AS-1 Kennel missile, which entered service in 1958 aboard Tu-16 Badger B aircraft. It was soon followed by the 100 nautical mile range, nuclear-capable AS-2 Kipper, which entered service in 1961 aboard Badger C bombers. Both missiles were designed for use by Soviet Naval Aviation (SNA) against surface ships. They were powered by turbojet engines and employed mid-course radio command with active terminal homing guidance. The AS-2 could be fired from any altitude, whereas the AS-1 had to be launched from below 25,000 feet.[23] The AS-1 was removed from operation in about 1971,[24] and the AS-2 has been largely superseded by follow-on missiles, though it still can be carried by Badger C/G aircraft.

The Soviet Union currently deploys six different nuclear-capable, air-launched missile types: the AS-2 Kipper, the AS-3 Kangaroo, the AS-4 Kitchen, the AS-5 Kelt, the AS-6 Kingfish, and the AS-15 Kent. An inventory of some thousands of ASMs is estimated to exist, armed with 2200 nuclear warheads (see Table 6.2).

The AS-3 Kangaroo is a very large, nuclear-only, long-range cruise missile carried by Bear B/C bombers of the Strategic Air Armies. The subsonic missile was introduced in 1961, the first nuclear-armed, land-attack cruise missile fielded.[25] The AS-3 is the largest Soviet ASM ever deployed, being the size of an Su-7 Fitter airplane. It has a 350 nautical mile maximum range, though it has a somewhat shorter effective range. It lacks terminal homing and is probably intended for attacking large-area targets. The AS-3 was never deployed in large numbers, and it is being replaced by the dual-capable AS-4 Kitchen. (Bear B/C bombers are redesignated Bear G.)

Type	Platform	
AS-2 Kipper	Badger C	
AS-3 Kangaroo	Bear B/C	
AS-4 Kitchen	Blinder B, Backfire B, Bear G	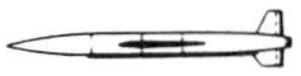
AS-5 Kelt	Badger C Modified, Badger G	
AS-6 Kingfish	Badger G Modified	not available
AS-15 Kent	Bear H (Blackjack)	not available

Figure 6.2 Air-launched Nuclear-Capable Cruise Missiles and Anti-ship Missiles (mid-1988).

The AS-4 Kitchen is a dual-capable supersonic missile powered by a liquid-propellant rocket. It was first seen in the 1961 Aviation Day carried by a Blinder B bomber, but it did not enter service until 1967. The AS-4 can conduct both land-attack and anti-ship missions. In the land-attack role, it is carried by the Blinder B, newly converted Bear Gs, and Backfire B bombers assigned to the Strategic Air Armies. It is thought to be limited in this role and mainly oriented towards naval-base attack. In the anti-ship role, it is carried by Backfire bombers assigned to SNA. Bear G bombers also increasingly have maritime anti-ship missions with AS-4s.

The AS-5 Kelt is a transonic cruise missile introduced in 1965 to replace the AS-1 and AS-2. It is deployed on Badger C/G bombers in SNA. The AS-6

---

23 Center for Strategic and International Studies, *op. cit.*, p. 51.
24 The Badger B designation associated with the AS-1 missile was eliminated at that time; Gunston, *Rockets & Missiles*, p. 134.
25 The SSC-2a Salish, derived from the AS-1 Kennel, was a 100-150 nautical mile-range, conventionally armed, land-attack missile launched from fixed and mobile launchers. It may have been deployed into the 1970s, though it has now been withdrawn from service; Taylor, *Missiles of the World*, 1980, p. 95; Gunston, *Rockets & Missiles*, p. 28.

6

Sea-launched Cruise Missiles

Kingfish entered service in 1970, also on SNA Badger C/G bombers. The AS-6 was at first thought to be a modification of the AS-4, but has since been reassessed as being a new missile with a higher flight performance and significantly improved accuracy. It has a 150-250 nautical mile range and its speed and propulsion are similar to that of the AS-4.

In 1984 the Soviet Union also deployed the AS-15 Kent, its first long-range cruise missile of a new generation. The subsonic long-range capabilities of the missile represented a major breakthrough in Soviet capabilities. The Soviets are also reported to have deployed in 1984 a new nuclear-capable ASM known as the AS-11 Kilter, which is carried by Fencer aircraft in SNA.[26] The 350 nautical mile range supersonic (Mach 3.5) missile has programmed guidance and terminal homing.

Sea-launched Cruise Missiles

The Soviet Navy has given high priority to incorporating sea-launched cruise missiles (SLCMs) into their surface ships and submarines.[27] Since the introduction of the first SLCM in 1958, there has been steady progress in technological sophistication, launcher and platform performance, and cruise missile diversity. Open-ocean naval deployments have given the Soviet Navy the capability of conducting nuclear, anti-ship missile strike operations in most of the world's oceans.[28] As a 1979 U.S. Navy briefing to the House Appropriations Committee noted, "The Soviet Navy routinely deploys anti-ship cruise missiles on surface ships and submarines with nuclear warheads."[29]

The Soviet Navy currently deploys seven different types of nuclear capable SLCMs and anti-ship missiles: the SS-N-3 Shaddock/Sepal, the SS-N-7 Starbright, the SS-N-9 Siren, the SS-N-12 Sandbox, the SS-N-19 Shipwreck, the SS-N-21 Sampson, and the SS-N-22 Sunburn. All but the SS-N-3c and the SS-N-21 are thought to be dual-capable. As of mid-1988, Soviet ships and submarines had the capacity to carry a total of 960 SLCMs, and it is estimated that the Soviet Navy possesses 400 nuclear versions (see Table 6.3).[30]

The oldest, most numerous, nuclear-armed SLCM in the Soviet Navy, the SS-N-3, was first deployed on a modified Whiskey class attack submarine in 1960. The first of the SS-N-3 family of nuclear-capable, anti-ship cruise missiles, the SS-N-3c Shaddock, was tested as early as 1954. This unguided, nuclear-armed missile (no conventional warhead was developed) reached only limited deployment on six Whiskey and five Echo I class submarines, all of which were discarded or converted to attack submarines by the mid-1970s.[31] By contrast, the dual-capable SS-N-3a Shaddock cruise missile, with a 220 nautical mile range, was widely deployed beginning in 1962 on Echo II, Juliett, and Whiskey Long Bin cruise missile submarines. From 1970 to 1975, the peak years of SS-N-3a deployments, 320 launch tubes were operational on over 50 submarines. The SS-N-3b Sepal, with a 150 nautical mile range, also entered service in 1962 on surface ships.

The SS-N-3 is currently deployed in two versions, the submarine-launched SS-N-3a/c Shaddock, and the surface-launched SS-N-3b Sepal. It is estimated that there are a total of 228 SS-N-3 missiles deployed, with 120 nuclear warheads. The SS-N-3a/c is deployed on Echo II and Juliett class cruise missile submarines, and the SS-N-3b is deployed on Kresta I and Kynda class cruisers.[32] SS-N-3s on Echo II class submarines are being replaced by SS-N-12s.

The SS-N-3 and its successor, the nuclear-capable SS-N-12 Sandbox, were developed for the capability of attacking aircraft carriers far from the Soviet Union before they reached striking position. This meant a long-range, high-speed missile with an ability to locate and track the target without exposing the launch or the reconnaissance platforms. The SS-N-3 was fitted for mid-course guidance provided by either shore-based aircraft or ship-based helicopters.[33]

The SS-N-3 was the longest range missile until the introduction of the SS-N-12 Sandbox in 1976.[34] The SS-N-12 is an advanced version of the SS-N-3a/b, with improvements in propulsion (ramjet and rocket-ramjet as opposed to turbojet engines) and guidance. It offers slightly longer range (300 nautical miles as opposed to 200 for the SS-N-3) and approximately twice the speed of its predecessor.

The SS-N-12 (along with the newer SS-N-19 Shipwreck) is currently the longest range Soviet anti-ship SLCM, arming Kiev class aircraft carriers, Slava cruisers, and modified Echo II class cruise missile submarines. Some 200 missiles are deployed, with 76 nuclear war-

---

26. Collins and Victory, *U.S./Soviet Military Balance*, 1988 p. 45; SMP 1987, p. 79. SMP 1988, p. 79, refers to the AS-11 as an anti-radiation missile used for long-range standoff attacks on NATO air defenses. Collins and Victory also report that the short-range (25 nautical mile) AS-9 Kyle missile deployed in 1975 has a nuclear warhead (p. 23). Rear Admiral Walter M. Locke, former director of the Joint Cruise Missile Project, refers to the AS-9, AS-10, and AS-11 as "nuclear-capable;" letter to the editor of the *New York Times*, 8 May 1982, p. 22.
27. ACDA, FY 1986 ACIS, p. 64.
28. HAC, FY 1980 DOD, Part 1, p. 282.
29. HAC, FY 1980 DOD, Part 2, p. 2280 (testimony of Admiral Hayward). Secretary of Defense Harold Brown stated at a press conference in June 1980, following a NATO Nuclear Planning Group meeting in Bodo, Norway, that "there has been an introduction of [Soviet] nuclear warhead cruise submarines in the Baltic Sea," and that "the cruise missile launching submarines certainly have nuclear warheads'; quoted in William M. Arkin, "Soviet Cruise Missile Programs," *Arms Control Today*, May 1983, p. 4. The U.S. intelligence community believes that the Soviets routinely deploy nuclear warheads with anti-ship cruise missiles on surface ships and submarines.
30. This is calculated based upon the following: average two nuclear-armed SLCMs per nuclear-capable surface ship, except the larger Kiev and Kirov classes, which are armed with four; average four nuclear armed SLCMs per nuclear-capable cruise missile submarine, except for the Oscar class, which is armed with 12. The number of nuclear-armed SLCMs at sea may be higher or lower, depending on operational missions. Since the SLCMs are large and all of the ships and submarines fire them from special launchers, it is assumed that there are no operational reloads.
31. Several test launches of the SS-N-3c were made in the first half of the 1960s to a range of 600-900 kilometers; SASC, SALT II Treaty, Part 2, 1979, p. 49. The aerodynamic range of the missile may thus be more than 450 nautical miles.
32. The Kynda class cruisers carry eight SS-N-3b launchers with the possibility of eight missile reloads. The ability to reload the launchers underway—or indeed, in any rapid manner—is questionable.
33. Mid-course correction would only be able to insure that the missile was following a preprogrammed flight course, unless real-time data was available from reconnaissance aircraft. The submarines would be extremely dependent on the reconnaissance aircraft at the extreme ranges of the missiles; John Jordan, "Soviet Cruise Missile Submarines" Part 2, *Jane's Defence Weekly*, 2 June 1984, pp. 883-884.
34. Echo I class cruise missile submarines began conversion to attack submarines in 1976.

6
Sea-launched Missiles

Table 6.3
Soviet Nuclear-Capable Sea-launched Cruise and Anti-ship Missiles (mid-1988)

Type	Platform	Missiles Deployed	Nuclear Warheads
SS-N-3a/c Shaddock	Juliett, Echo II	148	104
SS-N-3b Sepal	Kynda, Kresta I	80	16
SS-N-7 Starbright	Charlie I, Papa	90	44
SS-N-9 Siren	Charlie II, Papa Nanuchka, Sarancha	208	78
SS-N-12 Sandbox	Kiev, Slava, Echo II	200	76
SS-N-19 Shipwreck	Kirov, Oscar	136	56
SS-N-21 Sampson	Akula, Sierra, Victor III, Yankee Notch	16?	16?
SS-N-22 Sunburn	Sovremennyy, Tarantul III	80	24
SS-NX-24	(conv. Yankee, Oscar, new SSGN)	—	—
Total		**958**	**400**

Stockpile total is rounded.

Type	Platform	Missiles Deployed	Nuclear Warheads
SS-N-3a/c Shaddock	Juliett, Echo II	148	104
SS-N-3b Sepal	Kynda, Kresta I	80	16
SS-N-7 Starbright 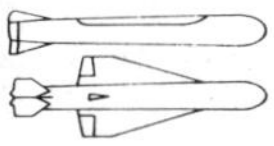	Charlie I, Papa	90	44
SS-N-9 Siren 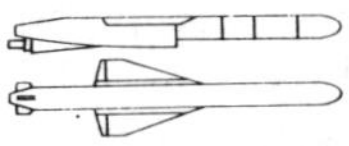	Charlie II, Papa, Nanuchka, Sarancha	208	78
SS-N-12 Sandbox 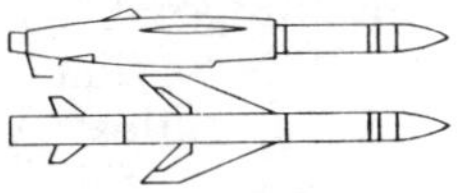	Kiev, Slava, Echo II	200	76
SS-N-19 Shipwreck 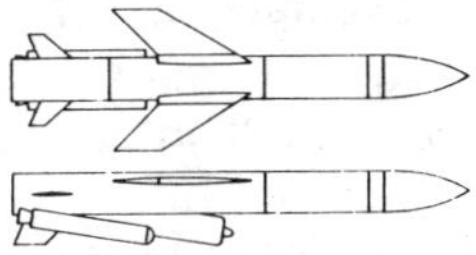	Kirov, Oscar	136	56
SS-N-21 Sampson 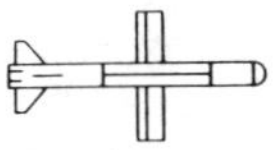	Akula, Sierra, Victor III, Yankee Notch	16?	16?
SS-N-22 Sunburn	Sovremennyy, Tarantul III	80	24
not available			
Total		**960**	**400**

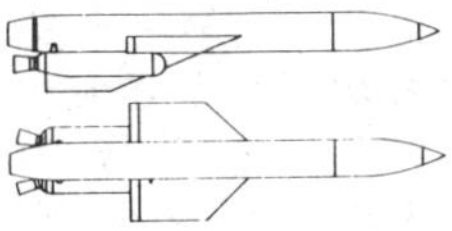

Stockpile totals are rounded. The SS-N-1 Scrubber, which was deployed on Kildin and Krupnyy class destroyers, has been retired.

Figure 6.3 Nuclear-Capable Sea-launched Cruise Missiles and Anti-ship Missiles (mid-1988).

heads. About 15 of 26 operational Echo II class submarines are reported to have been converted from the SS-N-3 to launch the SS-N-12.

The SS-N-7 Starbright was deployed in 1968 on Charlie I (and possibly Charlie II and Papa) cruise missile submarines. The SS-N-7 overcame a major limitation of the SS-N-3a: the need for the submarine to surface for perhaps 20 to 30 minutes while the missile was prepared for launching.[35] The SS-N-7 was the first sea-launched anti-ship missile able to be fired from a submerged submarine.

Some 90 of the 30 nautical mile (56 kilometer) range SS-N-7 missiles and 44 nuclear warheads are estimated to be deployed. The short-range anti-ship missile has two major limitations: it still requires precise targeting data for anti-ship strikes near maximum range; and it uses a terminal homing radar that, because of its low-altitude flight profile, may home on the first target encountered, instead of the intended target.[36]

The nuclear-capable SS-N-9 Siren was meant to overcome the disadvantages of the SS-N-7. The SS-N-9 has a range of 60 nautical miles (100 kilometers)—double that of the SS-N-7—and can be fired from submerged submarines. It has a high altitude flight profile and employs infrared and active terminal radar homing.

After the SS-N-3, the SS-N-9 Siren is the most numerous, sea-launched anti-ship missile deployed in the Soviet Navy. First deployed in 1969, the missile arms Charlie II and Papa class cruise missile submarines, Nanuchka I and III class patrol combatants, and Sarancha class patrol combatant hydrofoils. Some 208 missiles are operational, with an estimated 78 nuclear warheads.

Two new nuclear-capable anti-ship SLCMs, the SS-N-19 Shipwreck and SS-N-22 Sunburn, entered service in 1980 on new classes of ships and submarines. The SS-N-19, a derivative of the SS-N-3/12, is deployed on two of the Soviet Navy's most heavily armed ships—the Kirov cruisers (20 missiles each) and the Oscar class submarines (24 missiles each). Vertically launched from both platforms, the 300 nautical mile (550 kilometer) range missile significantly enhances the Soviet Navy's long-range, anti-ship capabilities. The missiles are "targeted primarily against NATO carrier battle groups."[37] Some 136 missiles and 56 nuclear warheads are estimated to be deployed.

The SS-N-22 has been described as "the Soviets' highest technology anti-ship missile,"[38] and is deployed on Sovremennyy class destroyers (eight missiles each) and on Tarantul III class patrol combatants. This 60 nautical mile (100 kilometer) range missile is an improved version of the SS-N-9. Some 80 missiles are deployed with an estimated 24 nuclear warheads. Both the SS-N-19 and the SS-N-22 are supersonic (about Mach 2.5) and have terminal homing capabilities.

In late 1987, the Soviets are believed to have deployed in limited number the first of their new generation of long-range subsonic SLCM: the SS-N-21 Sampson. The 1600 nautical mile (3000 kilometer) range SS-N-21 is similar to the U.S. Tomahawk.[39] Launch platforms include Akula, Sierra, and Victor III class attack submarines and converted Yankee class SSNs. The Soviet Union has a second long-range, nuclear-armed SLCM under development, which may become operational in 1988: the larger, SS-NX-24. The larger supersonic SS-NX-24 is undergoing testing on a converted, Yankee class SSGN and could be operationally deployed on those boats or the large Oscar class cruise missile submarines "in the next few years."[40]

Ground-launched Cruise Missiles

The first Soviet ground-launched cruise missiles (GLCMs) had anti-ship missions. From the end of World War II until the late 1950s, Soviet coastal artillery (the Coastal Missile-Artillery Force) consisted of captured, heavy, German ordnance and old naval guns removed from scrapped naval ships.[41] Only three GLCMs have been fielded by the Coastal Missile-Artillery Force. The first, the conventional SSC-2b Samlet missile, was deployed for Soviet shore defense out to a maximum range of 40 nautical miles. Derived from the MiG-15 aircraft and powered by turbojet engines taken from retired aircraft, the SSC-2b was reportedly deployed at fixed installations with six to nine launchers each. The fixed installations were replaced by mobile launchers in the 1960s,[42] and the SSC-2b was phased out of service.

The two other weapons are the nuclear-capable, 100 nautical mile range SSC-1a Shaddock and the nuclear-capable, 300 nautical mile range SSC-1b Sepal—ground-launched versions of the SS-N-3a Shaddock and SS-N-3b Sepal, respectively.[43] Both missiles were first deployed in 1962; the SSC-1a was retired in the 1970s.

Until the early 1970s, the Coastal Missile-Artillery Force was reported to consist of some 19 regiments.[44] Since then, all but two or three Coastal Artillery regiments have been disbanded. Today, launch sites exist in all four fleet areas.[45] Each regiment is believed to have 15-18 reloadable SSC-1b Sepal launchers.[46] The SSC-1b missiles are estimated to be armed with approximately 100 nuclear warheads.

---

35 Jordan, op. cit., Part 2, pp. 883-884.
36 Jordan, op. cit., Part 2, pp. 883-884; op. cit., Part 3, p. 107.
37 SMP 1988, p. 83.
38 SASC, FY 1986 DOD, Part 8, p. 4362.
39 HASC, FY 1988/1989 DOD Seapower and Strategic and Critical Materials Subcommittee, p. 10.
40 SMP 1988, p. 53; HAC, FY 1986 DOD, Part 2, p. 908.
41 DIA, *Naval Weapons Systems Handbook—USSR*, Vol. I (less missiles), ST-HB-08-61-73, 20 July 1973 (partially declassified and released under the FOIA), p. IB-1.
42 Turetsky, op. cit., pp. 40, 42.

43 The SSC-1az and SSC-1b, according to one analyst, may be the same missile; see Polmar, *Guide to the Soviet Navy*, 1983, p. 36.
44 The distribution of these regiments was three in the Northern Fleet, six in the Baltic Fleet, five in the Black Sea Fleet, and five in the Pacific Fleet; Polmar, *Guide to the Soviet Navy*, 1983, p. 36. At the time of the Cuban Missile Crisis, three cruise missile sites for coastal defense were identified in Cuba, with three sites considered operational; CIA, *Major Consequences of Certain U.S. Courses of Action on Cuba*, SNIE 11-9-62, 20 October 1962, p. 3.
45 SMP 1988, p. 87.
46 Polmar, *Guide to the Soviet Navy*, 1983, p. 36. The organization of the Coastal Artillery Division is unknown. If it follows the organizational structure of the Ground Forces Artillery Division, the division would consist of two or three regiments.

6
Cruise Missile Developments

For theater offensive land-attack, rather than for anti-ship or coastal defense, the Soviets began in the late 1970s to investigate new ground-launched cruise missile designs: the subsonic SSC-X-4 and the supersonic SSC-X-5. Further development of either missile is banned under the terms of the INF Treaty.

Long-Range Cruise Missile Developments

The first reports of new Soviet long-range cruise missiles date from the late 1970s.[47] By 1979, Secretary of Defense Harold Brown noted that the Soviet Union "may be developing a long-range cruise missile of their own design."[48] Development of the new cruise missiles was confirmed in February 1982 Congressional testimony,[49] and initial tests, which began in January 1981, were confirmed to be underway by General Secretary Yuri Andropov later in 1982.[50]

The Soviet program consisted of at least six new systems: the AS-15 Kent, the BL-10 (designated the AS-X-19 in flight-testing), the SS-N-21 Sampson, the SS-NX-24, the SSC-X-4 and the SSC-X-5. The AS-15, SS-NX-21, and SSC-X-4 are air-, sea-, and ground-launched variants of a small (21-inch-diameter), subsonic cruise missile similar in design to the U.S. Tomahawk sea- and ground-launched cruise missile.[51] The missiles have a range of about 3000 kilometers and use a guidance system similar to the U.S. Terrain Contour Matching (TERCOM).[52]

The air-launched version, the AS-15 Kent, reached initial operational capability with the Bear H strategic bomber in October 1984 and will likely be carried on the Blackjack bomber, now near deployment. By mid-1988, some 440 AS-15s were estimated to be deployed on Bear Hs.

The sea-based variant, the SS-N-21 Sampson, entered limited operation in late 1987 and is expected to become fully operational in 1988. The missile is small enough to be fired from standard 21-inch (533-mm) torpedo tubes. The missile was initially tested on a modified Victor III from the Northern Fleet,[53] and later on Akula submarines in the Pacific Fleet.[54] It has reportedly been deployed on Victor III—a converted, Yankee, ballistic missile submarine (designated Yankee Notch SSN)—and on Sierra and Akula class attack submarines.[55]

A larger, supersonic, SLCM, designated the SS-NX-24, was first reported to be under development in 1983. It is being tested from a newly converted, Yankee class cruise missile submarine and is "expected to be operational in the next few years."[56] The SS-NX-24 will have a slightly shorter range (less than 3000 kilometers) than the SS-N-21, but will be supersonic. It will be deployed on the converted Yankee class—possibly on the Oscar class—or on a new cruise missile submarine reported under development.[57] The air-launched cruise missile (ALCM) variant of the SS-NX-24—designated BL-10 in development and now called the AS-X-19, also with supersonic capabilities—has also been reported to be under development for the Blackjack bomber.[58] A ground-launched version of the SS-NX-24, designated the SSC-X-5 was evidently not far enough along in development to be specifically counted in the INF Treaty, is banned under its terms. A shorter range ASM, similar to a short-range attack missile (SRAM) and designated the AS-X-16, is also in development for deployment on the Blackjack bomber.[59]

---

47. According to one analyst, in the late 1970s the Soviet Union may have conducted at least eight tests of a 750 mile range cruise missile that was never deployed from a Backfire bomber; Joel Wit, "Soviet Cruise Missiles," *Survival*, November-December 1983, p. 252.
48. DOD, FY 1980 *Annual Report*, p. 73.
49. Secretary of the Air Force Verne Orr testified on 11 February 1982 that "only in recent years has evidence appeared that they are developing a small cruise missile comparable in size and performance to our ALCM'; SASC, FY 1983 DOD, Part 2, p. 1029. Later in February, Dr. Richard D. DeLauer, then Undersecretary of Defense for Research and Engineering, stated "There is strong evidence the Soviets have several [deleted] cruise missiles under development. The sea and ground launched versions could become operational [deleted];" HASC, FY 1983 DOD, Part 2, p. 209.
50. Yuri Andropov confirmed on 21 December 1982 that the testing program was underway when he noted, that "We will be compelled to counter the challenge of the American side by deploying our own long-range cruise missile, which we are already testing . . . ."; quoated in Serge Schmemann, "Soviet Warns on Long-Range Cruise Missiles," *New York Times*, 1 August 1984, p. 3.
51. The ground-launched variant, the SSC-X-4, will be eliminated under the terms of the INF Treaty.
52. According to the CIA the Soviet Union acquired U.S. documents on cruise missiles which use radar terrain maps and apparently applied the technology to their new generation of cruise missiles; CIA, *Soviet Acquisition of Militarily Significant Western Technology: An Update*, September 1985, p. 9.
53. HAC, FY 1986 DOD, Part 2, p. 908.
54. Edward Neilan, "Soviet Cruise Missile Tested in Sea of Japan," *Washington Times*, 28 December 1987, p. 1.
55. SMP 1988, p. 53.
56. Ibid.
57. HAC, FY 1986 DOD, Part 2, p. 9
58. DOD, FY 1989 *Annual Report*, p. 27; Clarence A. Robinson, Jr., "Soviets Test New Cruise Missile," *Aviation Week & Space Technology*, 2 January 1984, p. 14; John W. R. Taylor, "Gallery of Soviet Aerospace Weapons," *Air Force Magazine*, March 1987, p. 98.
59. JCS, FY 1989, p. 41.

6

AS-2 KIPPER

Air-launched
AS-2 KIPPER

DESCRIPTION:	Air-launched, supersonic, airplane-configuration, anti-ship, and land-attack cruise missile fired by Badger C bomber and assigned to Soviet Naval Aviation; being phased out and replaced by AS-5 Kelt	**DUAL CAPABLE:**	yes[11]
		NUCLEAR WARHEAD:	
		Yield:	200-600 Kt[12]
		Weight:	approx. 1000 kg (2200 lbs)[13]
SPECIFICATIONS:		**DEPLOYMENT:**	
Length:	10 m (32.9 ft);[1] 9.45 m[2] (31 ft)	Launch Platform:	Badger C; one or two missiles are carried partially embedded in the fuselage[14]
Diameter:	.9 m (3 ft)[3]		
Span:	4.9 m[4] (16 ft)	Number Deployed:	some 70 Badger C (1988); one nuclear AS-2 is thought to exist for each bomber (see Chapter Two)
Weight:	4200 kg[5] (9260 lbs)		
Fuel/Propulsion:	turbojet; possibly Lyulka AL-5[6]	**HISTORY:**	
Speed:	Mach 0.8 at launch, Mach 1.4-1.5 maximum speed above 36,000 ft, Mach 1.2 at final cruise approach to target[7]	IOC:	1961 on Badger C;[15] first observed at Tushino Airport, Moscow in July 1961 during Soviet Aviation Day display[16]
		Production:	not thought to be in production
Guidance:	inertial guidance with mid-course radio command update or programmed autopilot; active (radar/infrared) terminal homing[8]	**TARGETING:**	
		Accuracy/CEP:	0.5-1.5 km (.3-.8 nm, 2000-5000 ft)[17]
Range:	185-210 km (100-115 nm)[9]	**COMMENTS:**	AS-2 is intended to attack targets with large radar signatures.
Launch Altitude:	11,000 m (36,000 ft)[10]		

---

1. HAC, FY 1980 DOD, Part 3, p. 506.
2. General Dynamics, *World's Missile Systems*, 1982, p. 117; Polmar, *Guide to the Soviet Navy*, 1986, p. 420; *Aviation Week & Space Technology*, 8 March 1982; Taylor, *Missiles of the World*, 1980, p. 59; Malzeyev, "Soviet Air-Launched Cruise Missiles," 1978.
3. General Dynamics, *World's Missile Systems*, 1982, p. 117; Taylor, *Missiles of the World*, 1980, p. 59; Malzeyev, "Soviet Air-Launched Cruise Missiles," 1978.
4. Polmar, *Guide to the Soviet Navy*, 1986, p. 420; Taylor, *Missiles of the World*, 1980, p. 59; Malzeyev, "Soviet Air-Launched Cruise Missiles," 1978.
5. Polmar, *Guide to the Soviet Navy*, 1986, p. 420; Couhat, *Combat Fleets of the World*, 1988/89, p. 564; Taylor, *Missiles of the World*, 1980, p. 59; Malzeyev, "Soviet Air-Launched Cruise Missiles," 1978.
6. Polmar, *Guide to the Soviet Navy*, 1986, p. 420; Couhat, *Combat Fleets of the World*, 1988/89, p. 564; Taylor, *Missiles of the World*, 1980, p. 59; Gunston, *Rockets & Missiles*, 1979, p. 134.
7. *Aviation Week & Space Technology*, 24 January 1977, p. 42; William M. Arkin, "Soviet Cruise Missile Programs," *Arms Control Today*, May 1983, p. 4; Taylor, *Missiles of the World*, 1980, p. 59; Gunston, *Rockets & Missiles*, 1979, p. 134; Malzeyev, "Soviet Air-Launched Cruise Missiles," 1978.
8. Malzeyev, "Soviet Air-Launched Cruise Missiles," 1978; Taylor, *Missiles of the World*, 1980, p. 59; Arkin, op. cit., p. 4; Couhat, *Combat Fleets of the World*, 1988/89, p. 564; *Aviation Week & Space Technology*, 24 January 1977, p. 42.
9. General Dynamics, *World's Missile Systems*, 1982, p. 117; Polmar, *Guide to the Soviet Navy*, 1986, p. 420; Meyer, "Soviet Theatre Nuclear Forces," Part II, p. 54; *Aviation Week & Space Technology*, 24 January 1977, p. 42; Arkin, op. cit., p. 4; Couhat, *Combat Fleets of the World*, 1988/89, p. 564; Taylor, *Missiles of the World*, 1980, p. 59; Malzeyev, "Soviet Air-Launched Cruise Missiles," 1978.
10. Malzeyev, "Soviet Air-Launched Cruise Missiles," 1978; *Aviation Week & Space Technology*, 24 January 1977, p. 42.
11. SMP 1981, p. 47; Couhat, *Combat Fleets of the World*, 1988/89, p. 564; Malzeyev, "Soviet Air-Launched Cruise Missiles," 1978.
12. Meyer, "Soviet Theatre Nuclear Forces," Part II, p. 54.
13. Polmar, *Guide to the Soviet Navy*, 1986, p. 420; General Dynamics, *World's Missile Systems*, 1982, p. 117; Couhat, *Combat Fleets of the World*, 1988/89, p. 564; Malzeyev, "Soviet Air-Launched Cruise Missiles," 1978.
14. USN, *Soviet Naval Developments* (Rev. 4/85), p. 133; General Dynamics, *World's Missile Systems*, 1982, p. 117; Polmar, *Guide to the Soviet Navy*, 1986, p. 394.
15. DIA, *Handbook on the Soviet Armed Forces*, p. 9-23.
16. Taylor, *Missiles of the World*, 1980, p. 59; Malzeyev, "Soviet Air-Launched Cruise Missiles," 1978.
17. Meyer, "Soviet Theatre Nuclear Forces," Part II, p. 54.

AS-3 KANGAROO

DESCRIPTION: Air-launched, subsonic, long-range, nuclear-only strategic cruise missile carried by Bear B/C bombers of the Strategic Air Armies; being replaced by AS-4 Kitchen on Bear G bombers

SPECIFICATIONS:
- Length: 15.0 m (49.1 ft)[1]
- Diameter: 1.85 m² (6.07 ft)
- Span: 9.15 m (30 ft)[3]
- Weight: 11,000 kg[4] (24,000 lbs)
- Fuel/Propulsion: turbojet; possibly Tumansky R-11[5]
- Speed: subsonic[6]
- Guidance: preprogrammed autopilot control with no terminal homing[7]
- Range: 500-650 km (275-350 nm)[8]
- Launch Altitude: approx. 11,000 m (36,000 ft)[9]

DUAL CAPABLE: nuclear only[10]

NUCLEAR WARHEAD:
- Yield: 0.8-3 Mt[11]
- Weight: approx. 2300 kg (5000 lbs)[12]

DEPLOYMENT:
- Launch Platform: Bear B/C;[13] one missile is carried per plane
- Number Deployed: some 30 Bear B/C remaining (they are being converted to Bear G version with AS-4); one missile is thought to exist for each bomber; some 70 Bear B/C with AS-3 were deployed at the peak in 1980-1981.

HISTORY:
- IOC: 1962 (Bear B);[14] 1963 (Bear C);[15] first observed at Tushino Airport, Moscow, in July 1961 at Aviation Day flypast[16]
- Production: not in production

TARGETING:
- Accuracy/CEP: 0.5-1.5 km (.3-.8 nm, 2000-5000 ft)[17]

COMMENTS: Being replaced by dual-capable AS-4 Kitchen (Bear B/C aircraft are redesignated Bear G).[18] Missile is similar in size and configuration to an Su-7 Fitter A fighter.[19]

---

1. HAC, FY 1980 DOD, Part 3, pp. 506, 609.
2. Taylor, *Missiles of the World*, 1980, p. 56; Malzeyev, "Soviet Air-Launched Cruise Missiles," 1978.
3. General Dynamics, *World's Missile Systems*, 1982, p. 109; Taylor, *Missiles of the World*, 1980, p. 56; Malzeyev, "Soviet Air-Launched Cruise Missiles," 1978.
4. Ibid.
5. General Dynamics, *World's Missile Systems*, 1982, p. 109; Gunston, *Rockets & Missiles*, 1979, p. 134.
6. SMP 1987, p. 36. Numerous non-government references report the AS-3 as supersonic, although this is doubted: General Dynamics, *World's Missile Systems*, 1982, p. 109; Taylor, *Missiles of the World*, 1980, p. 56; Malzeyev, "Soviet Air-Launched Cruise Missiles," 1978; Collins and Victory, *U.S./Soviet Military Balance*, 1988, pp. 23, 78.
7. John W. R. Taylor, "Gallery of Soviet Aerospace Weapons," *Air Force Magazine*, March 1987, p. 98; *Aviation Week & Space Technology*, 24 January 1977, p. 42; Collins and Victory, *U.S./Soviet Military Balance*, 1988, pp. 23, 78.
8. SMP 1981, p. 61; DOD, FY 1972 Annual Report (class.), p. 57. There has been some disagreement within the U.S. intelligence community about the range of the AS-3; see Peter Samuel, 'Pentagon and State Department Clashing Over New Soviet Arms Curb Violations," *New York City Tribune*, 11 December 1986, p. 1.
9. Malzeyev, "Soviet Air-Launched Cruise Missiles," 1978; *Aviation Week & Space Technology*, 24 January 1977, p. 42.
10. Office of Naval Intelligence, "Current Naval Intelligence Issues by the Office of Naval Intelligence," March 1987, p. 8.
11. DOD, FY 1972 Annual Report (class.), Table 4; DOD, FY 1971 Annual Report (class.), p. 57; Collins and Victory, *U.S./Soviet Military Balance*, 1988, pp. 23, 78; ISS, *Military Balance*, 1987-1988, p. 207.
12. Malzeyev, "Soviet Air-Launched Cruise Missiles," 1978; Collins and Victory, *U.S./Soviet Military Balance*, 1988, p. 78.
13. USN, *Soviet Naval Developments* (Rev. 4/85), p. 143; DIA, *Handbook on Soviet Armed Forces*, p. 9-23.
14. USAF, *Trends*, 1976, p. 35. HAC, FY 1980 DOD, Part 3, pp. 506 and 609, states 1960.
15. USAF, *Trends*, 1976, p. 35.
16. Taylor, *Missiles of the World*, 1980, p. 56; Malzeyev, "Soviet Air-Launched Cruise Missiles," 1978.
17. Meyer, "Soviet Theatre Nuclear Forces," Part II, p. 54.
18. SMP 1987, p. 36.
19. Malzeyev, "Soviet Air-Launched Cruise Missiles," 1978.

6 AS-4 KITCHEN

AS-4a/b/c KITCHEN

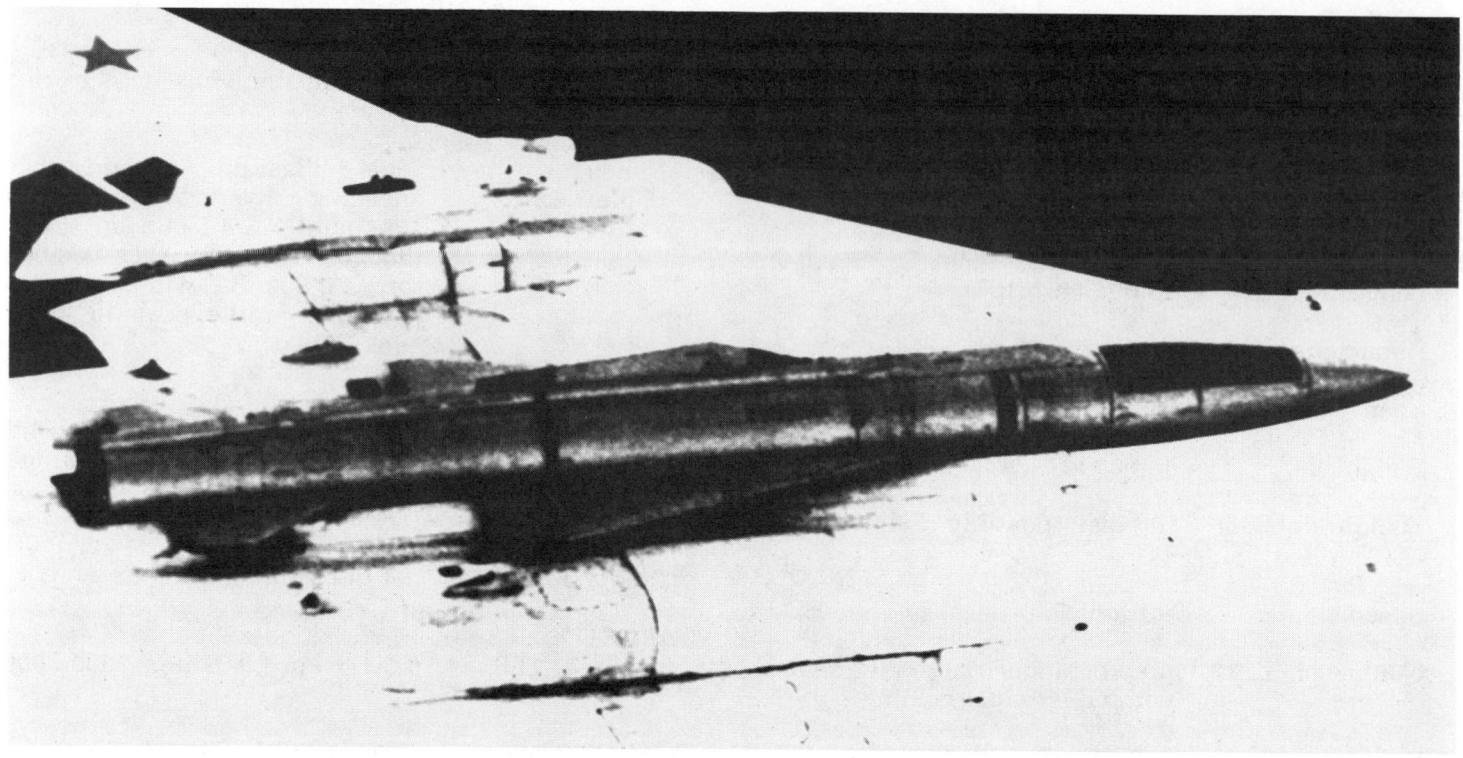

Figure 6.4 The **AS-4 Kitchen**, here shown recessed on the centerline mount of a Backfire B bomber, is a supersonic, dual-capable missile used to conduct both anti-ship and theater missions.

DESCRIPTION: Air-launched, supersonic, airplane-configuration, long-range, dual-capable, anti-ship and theater/strategic cruise missile in three modifications on Blinder, Backfire, and Bear G bombers; assigned to Strategic Air Armies and Soviet Naval Aviation (SNA)[1]

SPECIFICATIONS:

Length: 11.3 m (37.1 ft)[2]

Diameter: .9 m[3] (3 ft)

Span: 3.35 m (11 ft);[4] also variously reported as 2.45 m[5] (8 ft) and 3.0 m (9.8 ft)[6]

Weight: 6500 kg[7] (14,300 lbs); 6000 kg[8] (13,200 lbs)

Fuel/Propulsion: turbojet[9]

Speed: Mach 0.9 at launch; Mach 2.5-3.5 maximum speed at 80,000 ft, Mach 1.2 at final cruise approach to target[10]

Guidance: land-attack version has inertial guidance with no terminal homing; anti-ship version has programmed active (J-band), passive radar, or infrared terminal homing[11]

---

1. HAC, FY 1986 DOD, Part 5, p. 155.
2. HAC, FY 1980 DOD, Part 3, pp. 506, 509.
3. General Dynamics, *World's Missile Systems*, 1982, p.119; Malzeyev, "Soviet Air-Launched Cruise Missiles," 1978.
4. Polmar, *Guide to the Soviet Navy*, 1986, p. 420.
5. *Flight International*, 2 June 1979, pp. 1854-1855; Taylor, *Missiles of the World*, 1980, p. 59.
6. General Dynamics, *World's Missile Systems*, 1982, p. 119; Malzeyev, "Soviet Air-Launched Cruise Missiles," 1978.
7. Polmar, *Guide to the Soviet Navy*, 1986, p. 420; Couhat, *Combat Fleets of the World*, 1988/89, p. 564.
8. General Dynamics, *World's Missile Systems*, 1982, p. 119; Taylor, *Missiles of the World*, 1980, p. 59; Malzeyev, "Soviet Air-Launched Cruise Missiles," 1978.
9. Polmar, *Guide to the Soviet Navy*, 1986, p. 420.
10. Polmar, *Guide to the Soviet Navy*, 1983, p. 357; General Dynamics, *World's Missile Systems*, 1982, p. 119; *Aviation Week & Space Technology*, 24 January 1977, p. 2; Couhat, *Combat Fleets of the World*, 1984/85, p. 675; Malzeyev, "Soviet Air-Launched Cruise Missiles," 1978.
11. John W. R. Taylor, "Gallery of Soviet Aerospace Weapons," *Air Force Magazine*, arch 1987, p. 98; General Dynamics, *World's Missile Systems*, 1982, p. 119; Polmar, *Guide to the Soviet Navy*, 1986, p. 420; Malzeyev, "Soviet Air-Launched Cruise Missiles," 1978; *Jane's Weapon Systems*, 1987-88, p. 775.

AS-4 KITCHEN

Range: 280-560 km (150-300 nm);[12] variants may differ in range

Launch Altitude: 11,000-12,000 m (35,000-40,000 ft)[13]

DUAL CAPABLE: yes[14]

NUCLEAR WARHEAD:
Yield: 1 Mt[15]

Weight: approx. 1000 kg[16] (2200 lbs)

DEPLOYMENT:
Launch Platform: Backfire B: 1 capable on centerline mount partially submerged in fuselage or 2 on pylons under the fixed center section panel of each wing[17]

Bear G: 2 capable under each wingroot, replacing single AS-3 on former Bear B/C[18]

Blinder B: 1 semi-submerged in fuselage bomb bay[19]

Assignment: Backfires in Strategic Air Armies and SNA; Bears and Blinders in Strategic Air Armies, but not in SNA

Number Deployed: 760 (1988): 90 on 45 Bear G, 610 on 305 Backfire, 60 on 60 Blinder B; UK Defence Minister stated 1000 missiles had been produced up to 1976[20]

HISTORY:
IOC: 1967;[21] first observed at Tushino Airport, Moscow in July 1961 during Soviet Aviation Day display on Tu-22 Blinder B[22]

Figure 6.5 **AS-4 Kitchen** aboard Tu-26 Backfire bomber. Although the Backfire is credited with the capability to carry two AS-4 missiles under the fixed root of each wing, the size of the missile seems to preclude this capability for long-range missions.

Production: in production for deployment on Backfire and Bear G bombers

TARGETING:
Accuracy/CEP: unknown

COMMENTS: Three versions are thought to exist: a nuclear-armed, land-attack, strategic version; a dual-capable, anti-ship version; and a defense-suppression version. AS-4 normally has a terminal dive profile, though "it also is estimated to have a low altitude approach capability when launched at reduced range."[23]

---

12 USN, *Soviet Naval Developments* (Rev. 4/85, p. 143; HAC, FY 1980 DOD, Part 2, p. 160; DOD, FY 1969 Annual Report (class.), p. 60.
13 *Aviation Week & Space Technology*, 24 January 1977, p. 42.
14 Office of Naval Intelligence, "Current Naval Intelligence Issues by the Office of Naval Intelligence," March 1987, p. 8; ACDA, FY 1983 ACIS, March 1982, pp. 222-224.
15 Collins and Victory, *U.S./Soviet Military Balance*, 1988, p. 23; IISS, *Military Balance*, 1987-1988, p. 207; Meyer, "Soviet Theatre Nuclear Forces," Part II, p. 54. IISS, *Military Balance*, 1983-1984, p. 121, reports 200 Kt yield. Collins and Victory, *U.S./Soviet Military Balance*, 1988, p. 45, also reports a 500 Kt yield.
16 Couhat, *Combat Fleets of the World*, 1988/89, p. 564; Polmar, *Guide to the Soviet Navy*, 1986, p. 420.
17 SMP 1984, p. 29; USN, *Soviet Naval Developments* Rev. 4/85), p. 143; General Dynamics, *World's Missile Systems*, 1982, p. 119; IISS, *Military Balance*, 1987-1988, p. 207; Senator Steve Symms, quoted in *Soviet Aerospace*, 12 September 1983, p. 8.
18 SMP 1987 p. 36; General Dynamics, *World's Missile Systems*, 1982, p. 119.
19 USN, *Soviet Naval Developments* (Rev. 4/85), p. 143; General Dynamics, *World's Missile Systems*, 1982, p. 119.
20 Air Vice-Marshal R.A. Mason and John W. R. Taylor, *Soviet Air Force* (London: Jane's Publishing Co., 1986), pp. 259-260.
21 HAC, FY 1980 DOD, Part 3, pp. 506, 509; DOD, FY 1968 Annual Report (class.), p. 48.
22 Taylor, *Missiles of the World*, 1980, p. 59; General Dynamics, *World's Missile Systems*, 1982, p. 119; Malzeyev, "Soviet Air-Launched Cruise Missiles," 1978.
23 ACDA, FY 1980 ACIS, March 1979, p. 187.

6
AS-5 KELT

AS-5a/b KELT

Figure 6.6 The **AS-5 Kelt** is here carried on the starboard wing pylon of its launch platform, the Tu-16 Badger. There were 440 of these transonic, dual-capable AS-5 cruise missiles deployed by 1988.

DESCRIPTION: Air-launched, transonic, airplane-configuration, long-range, anti-ship missile in two modifications; assigned to Badger C Modified/G of Soviet Naval Aviation; superseded AS-1 Kennel and now replacing AS-2 Kipper

SPECIFICATIONS:

Length: 8.6 m (28.2 ft);[1] 9.5 m[2] (31 ft)

Diameter: .9 m[3] (3 ft)

Span: 4.6 m (15 ft)[4]

Weight: 3500 kg (7700 lbs);[5] 4700 kg[6] (10,400 lbs)

Fuel/Propulsion: liquid-fuel rocket propulsion

Speed: Mach 0.8 at launch, Mach 1.2 maximum speed at 30,000 ft, Mach 0.9 low level cruise[7]

Guidance: inertial guidance with active (J-band) or passive infrared terminal homing[8]

Range: 180-220 km (100-120 nm)[9]

Launch Altitude: approx. 9000 m (30,000 ft)[10]

DUAL CAPABLE: yes[11]

---

1. HAC, FY 1980 DOD, Part 3, pp. 506, 509.
2. General Dynamics, *World's Missile Systems*, 1982, p. 111; Malzeyev, "Soviet Air-Launched Cruise Missiles," 1978; Polmar, *Guide to the Soviet Navy*, 1986, p. 420; Taylor, *Missiles of the World*, 1980, p. 57.
3. General Dynamics, *World's Missile Systems*, 1982, p. 111; Malzeyev, "Soviet Air-Launched Cruise Missiles," 1978.
4. Polmar, *Guide to the Soviet Navy*, 1986, p. 420; General Dynamics, *World's Missile Systems*, 1982, p. 111; Taylor, *Missiles of the World*, 1980, p. 57; Malzeyev, "Soviet Air-Launched Cruise Missiles," 1978.
5. General Dynamics, *World's Missile Systems*, 1982, p. 111; Malzeyev, "Soviet Air-Launched Cruise Missiles," 1978.
6. Polmar, *Guide to the Soviet Navy*, 1986, p. 420; Couhat, *Combat Fleets of the World*, 1988/89, p. 564.
7. *Jane's Weapon Systems*, 1987-88, p. 776; *Aviation Week & Space Technology*, 24 January 1977, p. 42; Malzeyev, "Soviet Air-Launched Cruise Missiles," 1978.
8. *Jane's Weapon Systems*, 1987-88, pp. 775-776; William M. Arkin, 'Soviet Cruise Missile Programs," *Arms Control Today*, May 1983, p. 4; *Flight International*, 2 June 1979, pp. 1854-1855; Polmar, *Guide to the Soviet Navy*, 1986, p. 420; Gunston, *Rockets & Missiles*, 1979, p. 135.
9. USN, *Soviet Naval Developments* (Rev. 4/85), pp. 133, 143; DOD, FY 1970 Annual Report (class.), p. 82.
10. *Aviation Week & Space Technology*, 24 January 1977, p. 42; Gunston, *Rockets & Missiles*, 1979, p. 135.
11. SMP 1981, p. 47.

6

AS-5 KELT

NUCLEAR WARHEAD:
Yield: 1 Mt[12]

Weight: 450-900 kg (1000-2000 lbs)[13]

DEPLOYMENT:
Launch Platform: Badger C Modified/G: 2 capable on wing pylons[14]

Number Deployed: 440 (1988): 300 on 150 Badger G, 140 on 70 Badger C Modified; UK defence minister stated well over 1000 missiles delivered by the spring of 1976[15]

HISTORY:
IOC: 1965 on Badger C;[16] 1968 on Badger G[17]

Production: probably completed production as Badger bombers are being retired

TARGETING:
Accuracy/CEP: unknown

COMMENTS: Has sea-skimming trajectory for anti-shipping role.[18] About 25 AS-5s were used by Egypt during the 1973 Middle East War. Five reportedly eluded air and ground defenses.[19]

---

12 Collins and Victory, *U.S./Soviet Military Balance*, 1988, p. 23. Collins and Cronin, *U.S./Soviet Military Balance*, 1985, pp. 18, 35, and 59, reported 350-500 Kt.
13 SMP 1981, p. 47.
14 USN, *Soviet Naval Developments* (Rev. 4/85), pp. 133, 143; HAC, FY 1980 DOD, Part 2, 160; DIA, *Handbook on the Soviet Armed Forces*, p. 9-23; General Dynamics, *World's Missile Systems*, 1982, p. 111.
15 Air Vice-Marshall R. A. Mason and John W. R. Taylor, *Soviet Air Forces* (London: Jane's Publishing Co., 1986), p. 260.
16 HAC, FY 1980 DOD, Part 3, pp. 506, 509.
17 DIA, *Handbook on the Soviet Armed Forces*, p. 9-23; DOD, FY 1970 Annual Report (class.), p. 82.
18 General Dynamics, *World's Missile Systems*, 1982, p. 111.
19 John W. R. Taylor, "Gallery of Soviet Aerospace Weapons," *Air Force Magazine*, March 1987, p. 98.

AS-6a/b KINGFISH

DESCRIPTION: Air-launched, supersonic, long-range, anti-ship, and strategic cruise missile in two modifications fired from Badger G Modified bombers

SPECIFICATIONS:

Length: 10.5 m[1] (34.4 ft)

Diameter: .9 m[2] (3.0 ft)

Span: 2.5 m (8.2 ft);[3] 2.9 m (9.5 ft)[4]

Weight: approx. 4800-5000 kg (11,000 lbs)[5]

Fuel/Propulsion: turbojet;[6] solid-fuel booster;[7] liquid-propellent rocket motor[8]

Speed: Mach 0.8 at launch; Mach 2.5-3 maximum[9]

Guidance: inertial guidance with active (J-band) radar or passive infrared terminal homing[10]

Range: 280-460 km (150-250 nm)[11]

Launch Altitude: 11,000 m (36,000 ft)[12]

DUAL CAPABLE: yes[13]

NUCLEAR WARHEAD:

Yield: 350 Kt-1 Mt;[14] 100-500 Kt, most often reported as 200 Kt[15]

Weight: 450-900 kg (1000-2000 lbs)[16]

DEPLOYMENT:

Launch Platform: Badger G Modified: capable of carrying two, one under each wing;[17] Backfire theoretically capable of carrying AS-6, but the missile has only been observed on Badger C/G[18]

Number Deployed: 300 on 150 Badger G Modified bombers (1988)

HISTORY:

IOC: 1970 (on Badger);[19] first photographed by Japanese Air Self Defense Force interceptor in December 1977[20]

Production: probably completed production as Badger bombers are being retired

TARGETING:

Accuracy/CEP: unknown

---

1 Polmar, *Guide to the Soviet Navy*, 1986, p. 420; Taylor, *Missiles of the World*, 1980, p. 58.
2 Meyer, "Soviet Theatre Nuclear Forces," Part II, p. 54; Malzeyev, "Soviet Air-Launched Cruise Missiles," 1978.
3 Polmar, *Guide to the Soviet Navy*, 1986, p. 420; Taylor, *Missiles of the World*, 1980, p. 58.
4 Meyer, "Soviet Theatre Nuclear Forces," Part II, p. 54; Malzeyev, "Soviet Air-Launched Cruise Missiles," 1978.
5 Polmar, *Guide to the Soviet Navy*, 1986, p. 420; Meyer, "Soviet Theatre Nuclear Forces," Part II, p. 54; Couhat, *Combat Fleets of the World*, 1988/89, p. 564; Malzeyev, "Soviet Air-Launched Cruise Missiles," 1978.
6 Polmar, *Guide to the Soviet Navy*, 1986, p. 420; Taylor, *Missiles of the World*, 1980, p. 58.
7 *Jane's Weapon Systems*, 1987-88, p. 776; Malzeyev, "Soviet Air-Launched Cruise Missiles," 1978.
8 Air Vice-Marshall R. A. Mason and John W. R. Taylor, *Soviet Air Forces* (London: Jane's Publishing Co., 1986), p. 260.
9 *Jane's Weapon Systems*, 1987-88, p. 776; Malzeyev, "Soviet Air-Launched Cruise Missiles," 1978; Polmar, *Guide to the Soviet Navy*, 1986, p. 420; *Aviation Week & Space Technology*, 24 January 1977, p. 42.
10 Collins and Victory, *U.S./Soviet Military Balance*, 1988, p. 23; Taylor, *Missiles of the World*, 1980, p. 58; Polmar, *Guide to the Soviet Navy*, 1986, p. 420; William M. Arkin, "Soviet Cruise Missile Programs," *Arms Control Today*, May 1983, p. 4; *Jane's Weapon Systems*, 1987-88, p. 776.
11 USN, *Soviet Naval Developments* (Rev. 4/85), pp. 143. Some non-government references report longer ranges, up to 700 km (380 nm), for high-altitude launches: Meyer, "Soviet Theatre Nuclear Forces," Part II, p. 54; *Jane's Weapon Systems*, 1987-88, p. 776.
12 *Aviation Week & Space Technology*, 24 January 1977, p. 42.
13 SMP 1981, p. 47; ACDA, FY 1983 ACIS, pp. 222-224.
14 IISS, *Military Balance*, 1987-1988, p. 207. Collins and Victory, *U.S./Soviet Military Balance*, 1988, p. 23, also gives 1 Mt.
15 Meyer, "Soviet Theatre Nuclear Forces," Part II, p. 54; *Jane's Weapon Systems*, 1987-88, p. 776; IISS, *Military Balance*, 1982-1983, p. 121; *Flight International*, 2 June 1979, pp. 1854-1855; Collins and Victory, *U.S./Soviet Military Balance*, 1988, p. 45.
16 SMP 1981, p. 47.
17 John W. R. Taylor, "Gallery of Soviet Aerospace Weapons," *Air Force Magazine*, March 1987, p. 98; USN, *Soviet Naval Developments* (Rev. 4/85), pp. 133, 143; DIA, *Handbook on the Soviet Armed Forces*, pp. 9-23 states that Badger carries one AS-6.
18 Malzeyev, "Soviet Air-Launched Cruise Missiles," 1978; Meyer, "Soviet Theatre Nuclear Forces," Part II, p. 54, reported the AS-6 as being carried on Backfire, but Polmar, *Guide to the Soviet Navy*, 1986, p. 420, states that although the AS-6 was 'believed to have been developed for use from the Backfire bomber . . . up to press time of this edition the AS-6 has been observed only on Badger aircraft."
19 DIA, *Handbook on the Soviet Armed Forces*, p. 9-23; HAC, FY 1980 DOD, Part 3, p. 509.
20 Mason and Taylor, *op. cit.*, p. 260.

AS-15 KENT

Figure 6.7 AS-15 Kent cruise missiles, first deployed in late 1984, are probably mounted in the bomb bays on a rotary launcher of the Bear H. As the first Soviet subsonic, long-range, low-altitude, strategic cruise missile, it has greatly enlarged Soviet capabilities.

DESCRIPTION:	Air-launched, subsonic, low-altitude, long-range, strategic cruise missile similar in design to the U.S. Tomahawk SLCM[1] and launched by Bear H bombers of Strategic Air Armies

SPECIFICATIONS:

Length:	approx. 7 m[2] (23 ft)
Span:	3.3 m (10.7 ft)[3]
Weight:	unknown
Fuel/Propulsion:	turbojet
Speed:	subsonic;[4] Mach 0.6[5]
Guidance:	'similar in design to the U.S. Tomahawk;'[6] inertial[7]
Range:	approx. 3000 km[8] (1900 mi)
Ceiling:	unknown
DUAL CAPABLE:	no[9]

---

1 SMP 1987, pp. 37, 38.
2 Ibid., p. 38.
3 John W. R. Taylor, "Gallery of Soviet Aerospace Weapons," *Air Force Magazine*, March 1987, p. 98.
4 SMP 1987, p. 37.
5 Collins and Victory, *U.S./Soviet Military Balance*, 1988, p. 23.
6 SMP 1987, p. 37.
7 Collins and Victory, *U.S./Soviet Military Balance*, 1988, p. 23.
8 SMP 1987, pp. 37-38.
9 Ibid., p. 38.

6

AS-15 KENT

NUCLEAR WARHEAD:
  Yield: 250 Kt[10]

  Weight: unknown

DEPLOYMENT:
  Launch Platform: Bear H;[11] Blackjack

  Number Deployed: 480 (1988): 8 AS-15 each on 60 Bear H bombers

HISTORY:
  IOC: November 1984 (on Bear H)[12]

  Production: In production (1988)

TARGETING:
  Accuracy/CEP: 0.25 nm (46 m; 150 ft)[13]

COMMENTS: Flight-testing began in late 1981[14] and included launches from Backfire bombers.[15] Sea-launched version is SS-N-21 Sampson. Ground-launched version is SSC-X-4.

---

10 Collins and Victory, *U.S./Soviet Military Balance*, 1988, p. 23; *Jane's Weapon Systems*, 1987-88, p. 776.
11 SMP 1988, p. 53; SMP 1985, pp. 6, 7. The Bear H has been depicted as carrying 4 AS-15s under the wing.
12 SMP 1987, p. 35.
13 Clarence A. Robinson, Jr., "Soviets Test New Cruise Missiles,'*Aviation Week & Space Technology*, 2 January 1984, p. 14.
14 SMP 1983, preface, p. 2.
15 Taylor, "Gallery of Soviet Aerospace Weapons," 1987, *op. cit.*, p. 98.

6
SS-N-3 SHADDOCK/SEPAL

Sea-launched

SS-N-3a/c SHADDOCK (Soviet designation P-6/P-7)
SS-N-3b SEPAL

Figure 6.8 The **SS-N-3** launcher is pictured aboard the Juliett class cruise missile submarine, which must surface to launch the missile. It is estimated that there are 228 SS-N-3 missiles with 120 nuclear warheads currently (mid-1988) deployed. The SS-N-3 is fitted with mid-course guidance and was developed to attack aircraft carriers, although they may have land attack missions.

DESCRIPTION: Sea-launched, transonic, medium-range cruise missile originally developed as a strategic land-attack weapon (SS-N-3c) and currently deployed in three land-attack and anti-ship variants;[1] the SS-N-3a/c variants are submarine-launched, and the SS-N-3b is surface ship-launched

SPECIFICATIONS:

Length: SS-N-3c: 11.7 m (38.5 ft);[2] SS-N-3a/b: 10.2 m (33.6 ft)[3]

Diameter: 1 m[4] (3.3 ft)

Span: 2.1 m[5] (6.8 ft)

Weight: SS-N-3c: 5400 kg[6] (12,000 lbs); SS-N-a/b: 4500 kg (9900 lbs)[7]

---

1 Polmar, *Guide to the Soviet Navy*, 1986, p. 428; John Jordan, "Soviet Cruise Missile Submarines": Part 1, *Jane's Defence Weekly*, 26 May 1984, pp. 881-884; Part II, *Jane's Defence Weekly* 2 June 1984, pp. 841-844.
2 HAC, FY 1980 DOD, Part 3, pp. 506, 510; Polmar, *Guide to the Soviet Navy*, 1986, p. 428.
3 Polmar, *Guide to the Soviet Navy*, 1986, p. 428.
4 Ibid.
5 Polmar, *Guide to the Soviet Navy*, 1983, p. 363; Gunston, *Rockets & Missiles*, 1979, p. 80.
6 Polmar, *Guide to the Soviet Navy*, 1986, p. 428; Couhat, *Combat Fleets of the World*, 1988/89, p. 563.
7 *Jane's Fighting Ships*, 1982-1983, p. 170.

6
SS-N-3 SHADDOCK/SEPAL

Fuel/Propulsion: initial boost by two solid boosters;[8] turbojet cruise[9]

Speed: Mach 0.9-1.4[10]

Guidance: SS-N-3a/b: inertial guidance with mid-course correction provided by reconnaissance aircraft or surface ships;[11] possible radar terminal homing[12]

SS-N-3c: inertial guidance only[13]

Range: maximum effective range about 450 km (250 nm), though significantly longer (up to 450 nm) aerodynamic range;[14] a/c: 400 km (220 nm); b: 280 km (150 nm)[15]

DUAL CAPABLE: yes;[16] SS-N-3c is nuclear-only

NUCLEAR WARHEAD:
Yield: approx. 350 Kt;[17] SS-N-3c may have higher yield (800 Kt)[18]

Weight: 1000 kg (2200 lbs)[19]

DEPLOYMENT:
Launch Platform: SS-N-3a/c:[20] Echo II SSGN, 8 in 4 twin launchers;[21] (being upgraded with SS-N-12)[22] Juliett SSG, 4 in 2 twin launchers[23]

SS-N-3b: Kresta 1 CG, 2 in 1 twin launcher[24] Kynda CG, 4 in 2 quad launchers[25]

HISTORY:
IOC: SS-N-3a/b: 1962[26]
SS-N-3c: 1960[27]

Production: in series production in 1985-1986[28]

TARGETING:
Accuracy/CEP: 0.3-0.8 nm (0.5-1.5 km, 2000-5000 ft)[29]

COMMENTS: Ground-launched SSC-1 Sepal is same basic missile. Submarines must surface to launch the SS-N-3a/c.[30] An unarmed SS-N-3a crashed in Finland's Lake Inari on 28 December 1984 after being fired from a Juliett submarine in the Barents Sea. The missile overflew Norway. The Soviets attempted to change its course with radio commands, but failed.[31]

---

8 *Jane's Weapon Systems*, 1987-88, pp. 483-484.
9 *Jane's Weapon Systems*, 1987-88, p. 484; Polmar, *Guide to the Soviet Navy*, 1983, p. 363; Taylor, *Missiles of the World*, 1980, p. 109-110.
10 Charles A. Sorrels, *U.S. Cruise Missile Programs: Development, Deployment and Implications for Arms Control* (New York: McGraw-Hill, 1983), p. 126; Taylor, *Missiles of the World*, 1980, p. 109-110; *Aviation Week & Space Technology*, 24 January 1977, p.42; Jordan, *op. cit.*, Part 1, pp. 841-844; Jordan, *op cit.*, Part 2, pp. 882-884; *Flight International*, 2 June 1979, pp. 1856-1857.
11 Polmar, *Guide to the Soviet Navy*, 1986, p. 428; Gunston, *Rockets & Missiles*, 1979, p. 80; Couhat, *Combat Fleets of the World*, 1988/89, p. 563; Jordan, op cit., Part 1, pp. 841-844; Jordan, *op. cit.*, pp. 882-884.
12 Polmar, *Guide to the Soviet Navy*, 1986, p. 428; Taylor, *Missiles of the World*, 1980, pp. 109-110; *Flight International*, 2 June 1979, pp. 1856-1857.
13 HAC, FY 1980 DOD, Part 3, pp. 703-704; Couhat, *Combat Fleets of the World*, 1988/89, p. 563.
14 USN, *Soviet Naval Developments* (Rev. 4/85), pp. 38, 92, 102, 143; HAC, FY 1980 DOD, Part 2, p. 160; DIA, *Handbook on the Soviet Armed Forces*, 9-22; DOD, FY 1969 Annual Report (class.), p. 60.
15 Secretary of Defense Melvin R. Laird, statement before HAC, 4 March 1971, prepared 1 March 1971, p. 240.
16 ACDA, FY 1983 ACIS, p. 224; USN, *Soviet Naval Developments* (Rev. 4/85), pp. 38, 92, 102, 143; DIA, *Handbook on the Soviet Armed Forces*, p. 9-22.

17 IISS, *Military Balance*, 1987-1988, p. 206; Collins and Victory, *U.S./Soviet Military Balance*, 1988, p. 45; *International Defense Review*, February 1985, p. 140.
18 *Jane's Weapon Systems*, 1987-88, p. 484.
19 Couhat, *Combat Fleets of the World*, 1988/89, p. 563.
20 Earlier Whiskey Long Bin SSG and Whiskey Twin Cylinder SSG with SS-N-3 were retired in 1985; Polmar, *Guide to the Soviet Navy*, 1986, 136. See DIA, JIIKS, Vol. XIII, 1983.
21 SASC, FY 1980 DOD, Part 6, p. 2997; HAC, FY 1980 DOD, Part 2, p. 160.
22 SASC, FY 1986 DOD, Part 8, p. 4364.
23 *Ibid.*
24 Polmar, *Guide to the Soviet Navy*, 1986, p. 428.
25 USN, *Soviet Naval Developments* (Rev. 4/85), pp. 38, 92, 102, 143; Polmar, *Guide to the Soviet Navy*, 1986, p. 428.
26 HAC, FY 1980 DOD, Part 3, pp. 506, 510.
27 *Ibid.*
28 ACDA, FY 1986 ACIS, p. 64; SMP 1986, p. 121.
29 Meyer, "Soviet Theatre Nuclear Forces," Part II, p. 54.
30 Polmar, *Guide to the Soviet Navy*, 1986, p. 428; Jordan, *op. cit.*, Part 1, pp. 841-844; Jordon, *op. cit.*, Part 2, pp. 882-884.
31 *International Defense Review*, February 1985, p. 140.

SS-N-7 STARBRIGHT[1]

DESCRIPTION: Submarine-launched, short-range, anti-ship cruise missile; first Soviet sea-launched missile capable of submerged launch

SPECIFICATIONS:
- Length: 7.0 m (23 ft)[2]
- Diameter: 0.5-0.55 m[3] (1.6-1.8 ft)
- Weight: 2900 kg[4] (6400 lbs)
- Fuel/Propulsion: solid-fuel rocket[5]
- Speed: Mach 0.9[6]
- Guidance: autopilot with active radar terminal homing[7]
- Range: approx. 56 km (30 nm);[8] 65 km (35 nm)[9]

DUAL CAPABLE: yes[10]

NUCLEAR WARHEAD:
- Yield: 200 kt[11]
- Weight: 500 kg[12] (1100 lbs)

DEPLOYMENT:
- Launch Platform: Charlie I SSGN: 8 SS-N-7[13]
  Charlie II SSGN: 8 SS-N-7, later subs have been upgraded to SS-N-9[14]
  Papa: 10 SS-N-7 or SS-N-9[15]

HISTORY:
- IOC: 1968[16]
- Production: no longer in production[17]

TARGETING:
- Accuracy/CEP: unknown

COMMENTS: Being replaced by SS-N-9 in Charlie II and Papa classes.

---

1. Polmar, *Guide to the Soviet Navy*, 1986, p. 428; Couhat, *Combat Fleets of the World*, 1988/89, p. 563 refers to the SS-N-7 as Siren, which is the name for the SS-N-9.
2. HAC, FY 1980 DOD, Part 3, p. 506.
3. *Flight International*, 2 June 1979, pp. 1856-1857.
4. Polmar, *Guide to the Soviet Navy*, 1986, p. 428.
5. Polmar, *Guide to the Soviet Navy*, 1986, p. 428; William M. Arkin, "Soviet Cruise Missile Programs," *Arms Control Today*, May 1983, p. 4; *Flight International*, 2 June 1979, pp. 1856-1857.
6. *Jane's Weapon Systems*, 1987-88, p. 484; Polmar, *Guide to the Soviet Navy*, 1986, p. 428; Collins and Victory, *U.S./Soviet Military Balance*, 1988, p. 45.
7. *Aviation Week & Space Technology*, 24 January 1977, p. 42; *Flight International*, 2 June 1979, pp. 1856-1857; *Jane's Weapons Systems*, 1987-88, p. 484.
8. USN, *Soviet Naval Developments* (Rev. 4/85), p. 144; HAC, FY 1980 DOD, Part 2, p. 160.
9. *Jane's Weapon Systems*, 1987-88, p. 484; Couhat, *Combat Fleets of the World*, 1984/85, p. 674.
10. ACDA, FY 1983 ACIS, p. 224.
11. *Jane's Weapon Systems*, 1982-83, p. 57; Collins and Victory, *U.S./Soviet Military Balance*, 1988, p. 45; IISS, *Military Balance*, 1987-1988, p. 206.
12. *Jane's Weapon Systems*, 1987-88, p. 484; Polmar, *Guide to the Soviet Navy*, 1986, p. 428; Couhat, *Combat Fleets of the World*, 1988/89, p. 563; *Flight International*, 2 June 1979, pp. 1856-1857.
13. USN, *Soviet Naval Developments* (Rev. 4/85), p. 144.
14. Polmar, *Guide to the Soviet Navy*, 1986, p. 428; Couhat, *Combat Fleets of the World*, 1988/89, p. 563; *Jane's Weapon Systems*, 1987-88, p. 484.
15. DIA, JIIKS, Vol. XIII, 1983.
16. HAC, FY 1980 DOD, Part 3, p. 506; DIA, *Handbook on the Soviet Armed Forces*, p. 9-23.
17. SMP 1986, p. 121. ADCA, FY 1986 ACIS, p. 64 reported that the SS-N-7 was in production.

6

SS-N-9 SIREN

Figure 6.9 The **SS-N-9 Siren**, transonic, short-range, anti-ship missile, is contained in two triple launchers on board the Nanuchka I patrol combatant. The SS-N-9 has a range of 60 nautical miles (100 kilometers) and can also be fired from submerged submarines.

DESCRIPTION: Sea-launched, transonic, short-range, anti-ship missile

SPECIFICATIONS:

Length: 8.8 m (29 ft)[1]

Diameter: unknown

Weight: 3300 kg[2] (7300 lbs)

Fuel/Propulsion: solid-fuel rocket[3]

Speed: Mach 0.8-0.9;[4] Mach 1.4[5]

Guidance: inertial with active radar or infrared terminal homing;[6] mid-course command update required for maximum range[7]

Range: 100 km[8] (about 60 nm)[9]

DUAL CAPABLE: yes[10]

---

1. HAC, FY 1980 DOD, Part 3, pp. 506, 508; Polmar, *Guide to the Soviet Navy*, 1983, p. 364; Couhat, *Combat Fleets of the World*, 1988/89, p. 564.
2. Polmar, *Guide to the Soviet Navy*, 1986, p. 429.
3. Jane's Weapon Systems, 1987-88, p. 484; Polmar, *Guide to the Soviet Navy*, 1986, p. 429.
4. Jane's Weapon Systems, 1987-88, p. 170; Polmar, *Guide to the Soviet Navy*, 1986, p. 429; *Aviation Week & Space Technology*, 24 January 1977, p. 42.
5. Charles A. Sorrels, *U.S. Cruise Missile Programs: Development, Deployment and Implications for Arms Control* (New York: McGraw-Hill, 1983), pp. 126-127; Collins and Victory, *U.S./Soviet Military Balance*, 1988, p. 45.
6. Polmar, *Guide to the Soviet Navy*, 1986, p. 429; Jane's Weapons Systems, 1987-88, p. 484; *Aviation Week & Space Technology*, 24 January 1977, p. 42; Couhat, *Combat Fleets of the World*, 1988/89, p. 564; *Flight International*, 2 June 1979, pp. 1856-1857.
7. Polmar, *Guide to the Soviet Navy*, 1986, p. 429.
8. SMP 1981, p. 46.
9. USN, *Soviet Naval Developments* (Rev. 4/85), pp. 122, 144; HAC, FY 1980 DOD, Part 3, pp. 506, 508.
10. HAC, FY 1980 DOD, Part 3, pp. 506, 508; ACDA, FY 1983 ACIS, p. 224.

SS-N-9 SIREN

NUCLEAR WARHEAD:
- Yield: 200 Kt[11]
- Weight: 500 kg[12] (1100 lbs)

DEPLOYMENT:
- Launch Platform: Charlie II SSGN: 8 SS-N-9 or SS-N-7[13]
  Papa SSGN: 10 SS-N-9 or SS-N-7[14]
  Nanuchka PGG: 6 SS-N-9 in 2 triple launchers[15]
  Sarancha PGGH: 4 SS-N-9 in 2 twin launchers[16]

HISTORY:
- IOC: 1969 (surface ships); 1971 (submarines)[17]
- Production: in series production[18]

TARGETING:
- Accuracy/CEP: unknown

---

11 IISS, *Military Balance, 1987-1988*, p. 206; Collins and Victory, *U.S./Soviet Military Balance, 1988*, p. 45.
12 Couhat, *Combat Fleets of the World, 1988/89*, p. 564; *Flight International*, 2 June 1979, pp. 1856-1857.
13 SMP 1987, p. 81; USN, *Soviet Naval Developments* (Rev. 4/85), pp. 122, 144; DIA, JIIKS, Vol. XIII, 1983.
14 USN, *Soviet Naval Developments* (Rev. 4/85), pp. 122, 144; ACDA, FY 1983 ACIS, p. 224.
15 USN, *Soviet Naval Developments* (Rev. 4/85), pp. 122, 144.
16 Ibid.
17 HAC, FY 1980 DOD, Part 3, pp. 506, 508; Polmar, *Guide to the Soviet Navy*, 1986, p. 429.
18 SMP 1986, p. 121.

SS-N-12 SANDBOX (Soviet designation P-35)

Figure 6.10 Side-view of a Slava class cruiser armed with 16 **SS-N-12 Sandbox** long-range, anti-ship SLCMs in eight twin launchers.

DESCRIPTION: Sea-launched, supersonic, medium-range, anti-ship cruise missile in two versions; improved SS-N-3a/b missile, which it is replacing on Echo II SSGNs[1] while also being deployed on surface warships

SPECIFICATIONS:

Length: 11.7 m (38.5 ft)[2]

Diameter: unknown

Span: .25 m[3] (.8 ft)

Weight: approx. 5000 kg[4] (11,000 lbs)

Fuel/Propulsion: rocket boost with turbojet cruise[5]

Speed: Mach 2.5[6]

Guidance: inertial cruise with active radar or infrared terminal homing;[7] targeting beyond the horizon is provided by video-command mid-course correction (via Hormone helicopter or surface ship)[8]

Range: 550 km[9] (300 nm)

DUAL CAPABLE: yes[10]

NUCLEAR WARHEAD:
  Yield: 350 Kt;[11] 100-200 Kt[12]
  Weight: 1000 kg[13] (2200 lbs)

---

1 SASC, FY 1986 DOD, Part 8, p. 4364.
2 HAC, FY 1980 DOD, Part 3, p. 506; Polmar, *Guide to the Soviet Navy*, 1986, p. 429.
3 *Flight International*, 2 June 1979, pp. 1856-1857.
4 Ibid.
5 Polmar, *Guide to the Soviet Navy*, 1986, p. 429; Taylor, *Missiles of the World*, 1980, p. 128.
6 *Flight International*, 2 June 1979, pp. 1856-1857; Collins and Victory, *U.S./Soviet Military Balance*, 1988, p. 45. See also SMP 1985, pp. 97-98; SASC, FY 1986 DOD, Part 8, p. 4361.
7 ACDA, FY 1980 ACIS, p. 187; SMP 1985, pp. 97-98; SMP 1981, p. 43; Polmar, *Guide to the Soviet Navy*, 1986, p. 429; Jane's Weapons Systems, 1987-88, p. 485.
8 ACDA, FY 1980 ACIS, p. 187; SMP 1985, pp. 97-98; SMP 1981, p. 43.
9 SMP 1987, p. 85; HASC, FY 1983, DOD, Part 4, p. 2; SMP 1981, p. 43.
10 ACDA, FY 1983 ACIS, p. 224.
11 IISS, *Military Balance*, 1987-1988, p. 206; Collins and Victory, *U.S./Soviet Military Balance*, 1988, p. 45.
12 Meyer, "Soviet Theatre Nuclear Forces," Part II, p. 54.
13 *Jane's Weapon Systems*, 1987-88, p. 485; Polmar, *Guide to the Soviet Navy*, 1986, p. 4855; Couhat, *Combat Fleets of the World*, 1988/89, p. 564; *Flight International*, 2 June 1979, pp. 1856-1857.

6
SS-N-12 SANDBOX

DEPLOYMENT:
Launch Platform: Kiev CVHG: 8 SS-N-12 in 4 twin lauchers[14]
Slava CG: 16 SS-N-12 in 8 twin launchers[15]
Echo II SSGN: 8 SS-N-12[16]

HISTORY:
IOC: 1973;[17] 1976[18]

Production: in series production in 1986[19]

TARGETING:
Accuracy/CEP: unknown

Figure 6.11 Side view of **SS-N-12** launchers aboard the Minsk, a Kiev class cruiser.

---

14 SMP 1987, p. 85; USN, *Soviet Naval Developments* (Rev. 4/85), p. 144; SASC, FY 1986 DOD, Part 8, p. 4361.
15 SMP 1987, p. 86.
16 SMP 1987, p. 85; USN, *Soviet Naval Developments* (Rev. 4/85), p. 144.
17 IISS, *Military Balance*, 1987-1988, p. 206.
18 Collins and Victory, *U.S./Soviet Military Balance*, 1988, p. 45.
19 SMP 1986, p. 121; ACDA, FY 1986 ACIS, p. 64.

SS-N-19 SHIPWRECK

Figure 6.12 Kirov class cruisers carry 20 **SS-N-19** SLCMs in vertical launchers underdeck; the first Soviet ships to use such launchers. Here the Frunze is shown on its maiden voyage.

Figure 6.13 Closeup view of deck of Kirov class cruiser showing 20 hatch covers of **SS-N-19** vertical launchers and smaller covers for surface-to-air missiles.

DESCRIPTION: Sea-launched, supersonic, medium-range, anti-ship cruise missile deployed on Kirov cruisers and Oscar cruise missile submarines

SPECIFICATIONS:

Length: over 10 m[1] (33 ft)

Diameter: unknown

Weight: unknown

Fuel/Propulsion: turbojet[2]

Speed: possibly as great as Mach 2.5[3]

Guidance: inertial with active radar terminal homing;[4] possible updates by aircraft or forward observers[5]

Range: 550 km[6] (300 nm)

DUAL CAPABLE: yes[7]

NUCLEAR WARHEAD:

Yield: 500 Kt[8]

Weight: approx. 1000 kg (2200 lbs)[9]

DEPLOYMENT:

Launch Platform: Kirov CGN: 20 SS-N-19[10] Oscar SSGN: 24 SS-N-19,[11] capable of submerged launch[12]

HISTORY:

IOC: July 1980 (Kirov); 1981 (Oscar)[13]

Production: in series production in 1986[14]

TARGETING:

Accuracy/CEP: unknown

---

1 John Jordan, "Soviet Cruise Missile Submarines," Part 3, *Jane's Defence Weekly*, 30 June 1984, pp. 1077-1080.
2 Polmar, *Guide to the Soviet Navy*, 1986, p. 431.
3 *Jane's Weapon Systems*, 1987-88, p. 485; Collins and Victory, *U.S./Soviet Military Balance*, 1987, p. 50.
4 *Jane's Weapon Systems*, 1987-88, p. 485; Polmar, *Guide to the Soviet Navy*, 1986, p. 431; Collins and Victory, *U.S./Soviet Military Balance*, 1988, p. 45.
5 *Jane's Weapon Systems*, 1987-88, p. 485; Polmar, *Guide to the Soviet Navy*, 1986, p. 431; Collins and Victory, *U.S./Soviet Military Balance*, 1988, p. 45.
6 SMP 1988, p. 69; SMP 1987, p. 84; SASC, FY 1984 DOD, Part 6, pp. 2940, 2976.
7 SMP 1987, p. 84.
8 Collins and Victory, *U.S./Soviet Military Balance*, 1988, p. 45.
9 Collins and Glakas, *U.S./Soviet Military Balance*, 1983, p. 82.
10 SMP 1988, p. 83; SMP 1987, p. 86.
11 SMP 1988, p. 83; SMP 1987, pp. 81, 84.
12 SMP 1981, p. 46.
13 *Jane's Fighting Ships*, 1988-89, p. 550; JCS FY 1984, p. 28; Collins and Victory, *U.S./Soviet Military Balance*, 1988, p. 45; IISS, *Military Balance*, 1987-1988, p. 206 reports 1980.
14 SMP 1986, p. 121; ACDA, FY 1986 ACIS, p. 64.

6
SS-N-19 SHIPWRECK

Figure 6.14 Department of Defense artist's drawing of a **Kirov** class cruiser, delivery platform for the long-range, anti-ship, nuclear-capable **SS-N-19 Shipwreck** SLCM, showing its vertical launch capability and the arrangement of below deck launchers.

COMMENTS: The SS-N-19 evolved from SS-N-3/12 designs.[15] The SS-N-19 on Oscar is "targeted primarily against NATO carrier battle groups."[16]

---

15 Polmar, *Guide to the Soviet Navy*, 1986, p. 431.
16 SMP 1983, p. 43.

SS-N-21 SAMPSON

Figure 6.15 This converted Yankee-class submarine (designated **Yankee Notch**) was modified to carry the new **SS-N-21 Sampson** SLCM, which has a 1600 nautical mile (3000 kilometer) range. The SS-N-21 entered limited service in late 1987.

DESCRIPTION:	Submarine-launched, subsonic, long-range, land-attack cruise missile similar in design to the U.S. Tomahawk SLCM[1]	Speed:	Mach 0.6-0.7[4]
		Guidance:	similar to U.S. Tomahawk, presumed inertial updated by possible TERCOM radar[5]
SPECIFICATIONS:			
Length:	approx. 7 m² (23 ft)	Range:	3000 km[6] (1600 nm)
Diameter:	small enough to be fired from standard Soviet torpedo tubes[3]	**DUAL CAPABLE:**	initially believed deployed with nuclear warheads, may be made accurate enough to permit the use of conventional warheads in the future[7]
Weight:	unknown		
Fuel/Propulsion:	turbofan		

---

1. SMP 1987, pp. 37-38; SMP 1986, pp. 33-34; SMP 1985, p. 35; SMP 1984, pp. 30-31; DOD, FY 1984 Annual Report, p. 134.
2. SMP 1984, pp. 30-31; SMP 1985, p. 35.
3. SMP 1987, p. 3.
4. Collins and Victory, *U.S./Soviet Military Balance*, 1988, p. 45; Couhat, *Combat Fleets of the World*, 1988/89, p. 564. See also, SMP 1984, pp. 30-31; SASC, FY 1986 DOD, Part 8, p. 4364; HAC, FY 1986 DOD, Part 2, pp. 908, 914.
5. Collins and Victory, *U.S./Soviet Military Balance*, 1988, p. 45.
6. SMP 1984, pp. 30-31; SMP 1985, p. 35; ACDA, FY 1986 ACIS, p. 64; SMP 1983, preface, p. 23; JCS, FY 1986, pp. 23-24.
7. SMP 1984, pp. 30-31; SMP 1985, p. 35.

SS-N-21 SAMPSON

NUCLEAR WARHEAD:
- Yield: approx. 200 Kt;[8] 300 Kt[9]
- Weight: unknown

DEPLOYMENT:
- Launch Platform: Victor III SSN, a single converted Yankee (designated Yankee Notch),[10] Akula SSN, Sierra SSN[11]

HISTORY:
- Tested: first tested late 1981[12]
- IOC: late 1987 in Northern Fleet[13]
- Production: in series production (1988)

TARGETING: primary role reported as theater strike[14] secondary role likely against C^3 facilities and naval bases[15]

Accuracy/CEP: unknown

COMMENTS: The AS-15 Kent is the air-launched version of the missile, and the SSC-X-4 is the ground-launched version, which was under development but is banned under the INF Treaty.[16] The SS-N-21 will probably not be deployed on surface ships.[17]

---

8 *Defense Week*, 21 November 1983, p. 11.
9 Collins and Victory, *U.S./Soviet Military Balance*, 1988, p. 45.
10 SMP 1988, p. 85.
11 Ibid. The Mike SSN was previously reported in earlier editions of SMP to be a potential SS-N-21 launch platform.
12 Lt. General James A. Williams (Director of DIA), "The Soviet Strategic Threat," *Defense/84*, May 1984, p. 10; SMP 1983, preface, p. 23. SMP 1988, p. 40, states that development began in January 1981.
13 SMP 1987, p. 37. Initial IOC estimate was 1983; SAC, FY 1984 DOD, Part 1, p. 458. "Probably" 1984; SMP 1984, pp. 30-31. Expected mid-1980s; Polmar, *Guide to the Soviet Navy*, 1983, p. 366. Expected in 1985; SMP 1985, p. 35; ACDA, FY 1986 ACIS, p. 64.
14 HASC, FY 1985 DOD, Part 3, pp. 1,3.
15 SASC, FY 1986 DOD, Part 8, p. 4364.
16 SMP 1988, p. 53.
17 ACDA, FY 1986 ACIS, p. 64.

SS-N-22 SUNBURN

Figure 6.16 Here a Sovremenyy class destroyer serves as launch platform for eight (four on each side) supersonic, nuclear-capable **SS-N-22 Sunburn** SLCMs, described as "the Soviet's highest technology anti-ship missile."

DESCRIPTION: Sea-launched, supersonic, short-range, anti-ship cruise missile; improved SS-N-9 design carried by Sovremennyy class destroyers and Tarantul III class patrol combatants

SPECIFICATIONS:
- Length: 9.15 m (30.0 ft)[1]
- Diameter: unknown
- Weight: unknown
- Fuel/Propulsion: solid-fuel rocket[2]
- Speed: Mach 2.5[3]
- Guidance: mid-course guidance update with active radar or infrared terminal homing[4]
- Range: approx. 100 km (60 nm);[5] 220 km (120 nm) reported with mid-course update[6]

---

1. Polmar, *Guide to the Soviet Navy*, 1986, p. 431. *Jane's Defence Weekly*, 21 July 1984, p. 59, reports that the missile is carried in a 10.5 m (34.4 ft) container.
2. Polmar, *Guide to the Soviet Navy*, 1986, p. 431.
3. Couhat, *Combat Fleets of the World*, 1988/89, p. 564; Collins and Victory, *U.S./Soviet Military Balance*, 1988, p. 45. SASC, FY 1986 DOD, Part 8, p. 4362, indicates the SS-N-22 is supersonic.
4. *Jane's Defence Weekly*, 21 July 1984, p. 59; Polmar, *Guide to the Soviet Navy*, 1986, p. 431; Collins and Victory, *U.S./Soviet Military Balance*, 1988, p. 45.
5. Polmar, *Guide to the Soviet Navy*, 1986, p. 431; Collins and Victory, *U.S./Soviet Military Balance*, 1988, p. 45.
6. *Jane's Defence Weekly*, 21 July 1984, p. 59.

6
SS-N-22 SUNBURN

DUAL CAPABLE: yes;[7] nuclear only[8]

NUCLEAR WARHEAD:
  Yield: 200 Kt[9]

  Weight: unknown

DEPLOYMENT:
  Launch Platform: Sovremenyy class destroyer: 8 SS-N-22;[10] Tarantul III class patrol combatant: 4 SS-N-22

HISTORY:
  IOC: 1981[11]

  Production: in series production in 1986[12]

TARGETING:
  Accuracy/CEP: unknown

COMMENTS: The "SS-N-22 is the Soviet's highest technology anti-ship missile."[13]

---

7 Polmar, *Guide to the Soviet Navy*, 1986, p. 431; IISS, *Military Balance*, 1987-1988, p. 206.
8 Collins and Victory, *U.S./Soviet Military Balance*, 1988, p. 45.
9 Ibid.
10 SMP 1988, p. 83; SMP 1987, p. 86.
11 Polmar, *Guide to the Soviet Navy*, 1986, p. 431; Collins and Victory, *U.S./Soviet Military Balance*, 1988, p. 45.
12 SMP 1986, p. 121; ACDA, FY 1986 ACIS, p. 64.
13 SASC, FY 1986 DOD, Part 8, p. 4362.

SS-NX-24

DESCRIPTION: Submarine-launched, supersonic, long-range, land-attack cruise missile[1]

SPECIFICATIONS: larger than the SS-N-21

    Length: approx. 12 m^2 (39 ft)

    Diameter: unknown

    Weight: unknown

    Fuel/Propulsion: unknown

    Speed: supersonic; Mach 2[3]

    Guidance: unknown

    Range: 3000 km[4] (1600 nm)

DUAL CAPABLE: initially deployed with nuclear warheads, with conventional warheads possible in the future[5]

NUCLEAR WARHEAD:

    Yield: unknown

    Weight: unknown

DEPLOYMENT:

    Launch Platform: reconfigured Yankee class submarine is the test platform for the SS-NX-24;[6] a new class of SSGN or the Oscar class may also be the launch platform for the missile[7]

HISTORY:

    IOC: could become operational "in the next few years" (from April 1988)[8]

TARGETING: capability against hardened objects[9]

    Accuracy/CEP: unknown

COMMENTS: A ground-launched version (SSC-X-5) was under development, but is banned under the INF Treaty.[10] Development began before 1983.[11]

---

1. SMP 1987, pp. 37-38; SMP 1986, pp. 33-34; SMP 1985, p. 35; SMP 1984, pp. 30-31.
2. Taken from chart in SMP 1987, p. 38.
3. Polmar, *Guide to the Soviet Navy*, 1986, p. 432.
4. HAC, FY 1986 DOD, Part 2, p. 908.
5. SMP 1987, pp. 37-38; SMP 1984, pp. 30-31; Lt. General James A. Williams (Director DIA), "The Soviet Strategic Threat," *Defense/84*, May 1984, p. 11.
6. SMP 1987, pp. 37-38.
7. HAC, FY 1986 DOD, Part 2, p. 908; HASC, FY 1985 DOD, Part 3, pp. 1, 3.
8. SMP 1988, p. 53. SMP 1987, p. 38, reported in April 1987, "It could become operational by 1988." SMP 1984, pp. 30-31, reported in April 1984 that "it could be operational within the next 2 years." SMP 1985, p. 35, reported in April 1985 'The SS-NX-24 could be operational within the next two years." SMP 1986, p. 33, reported that "It could become operational by 1987."
9. SMP 1984, pp. 30-31; SMP 1985, p. 35; HASC, FY 1985 DOD, Part 3, pp. 1, 3.
10. SMP 1988, p. 53.
11. HASC, FY 1985 DOD, Part 3, pp. 1, 3.

6
SSC-1 SEPAL

Ground-launched Cruise Missiles
SSC-1b SEPAL

DESCRIPTION:	Ground-launched coastal missile under the control of the Coastal Missile Artillery Force, land-launched version of the SS-N-3c Shaddock[1]	**NUCLEAR WARHEAD:**	
		Yield:	50-200 Kt;[12] 350 Kt[13]
		Weight:	unknown
SPECIFICATIONS:		**DEPLOYMENT:**	
Length:	10.2 m (33.5 ft)[2]	Launch Platform:	8-wheel vehicle[14]
Diameter:	about 1 m[3] (3 ft)	Location:	launch sites exist in all four fleet areas[15]
Span:	2.1 m[4] (6.7 ft)		
Weight:	approx. 4500 kg[5] (9900 lbs)	**HISTORY:**	
		IOC:	1962[16]
Fuel/Propulsion:	initial boost by two rockets, turbo-jet or ramjet cruise[6]	Production:	Not thought to be in production
Speed:	Mach 0.95-1.4[7]	**TARGETING:**	
		Accuracy/CEP:	reportedly .3-.4 nm (.5-.8 km;[17] 1600-2600 ft)
Guidance:	radio command with active radar terminal homing; mid-course corrections via helicopter or aircraft is necessary for maximum range[8]	**COMMENTS:**	Each coastal missile battalion has 15-18 missiles (including reloads).[18] Sepal is supplemented by non-nuclear SSC-3 Styx.[19]
Range:	300 km (160 nm[9]); 450 km [10] (240 nm)		
DUAL CAPABLE:	yes[11]		

---

1 Polmar, *Guide to the Soviet Navy*, 1986, p. 426.
2 HAC, FY 1980 DOD, Part 3, p. 506.
3 *Jane's Weapon Systems*, 1987-88, p. 157; *Flight International*, 2 June 1979, pp. 1856-1857.
4 *Flight International*, 2 June 1979, pp. 1856-1857.
5 Ibid.
6 *Jane's Weapon Systems*, 1987-88, p. 157; *Aviation Week & Space Technology*, 8 March 1982, pp. 146-147; *Flight International*, 2 June 1979, pp. 1856-1857; Taylor, *Missiles of the World*, 1980, p. 109.
7 William M. Arkin, "Soviet Cruise Missile Programs," *Arms Control Today*, May 1983, p. 4; *Flight International*, 2 June 1979, pp. 1856-1857; Taylor, *Missiles of the World*, 1980, p. 109.
8 *Jane's Weapon Systems*, 1987-88, p. 157; "Soviet Coastal Artillery and Rocket Troops," *Jane's Defence Weekly*, 25 February 1984, p. 278; Arkin, *op. cit.*," p. 4; *Flight International*, 2 June 1979, pp. 1856-1857.
9 SMP 1988, p. 87.
10 Polmar, *Guide to the Soviet Navy*, 1986, p. 426; *Jane's Weapon Systems*, 1987-88, p. 157.
11 Polmar, *Guide to the Soviet Navy*, 1986, p. 426 reports that 'it can carry a conventional and probably a nuclear warhead."
12 *Aviation Week & Space Technology*, 8 March 1982, pp. 146-147; *Flight International*, 2 June 1979, pp. 1856-1857.
13 IISS, *Military Balance*, 1987-1988, p. 206.
14 Polmar, *Guide to the Soviet Navy*, 1986, p. 426; Meyer, "Soviet Theatre Nuclear Forces," Part II, p. 54.
15 SMP 1988, p. 87.
16 *Aviation Week & Space Technology*, 8 March 1982, pp. 146-147; IISS, *The Military Balance*, 1987-1988, p. 206.
17 *Aviation Week & Space Technology*, 8 March 1982, pp. 146-147. This reported accuracy is inconsistent with the missile reported to have a conventional capability.
18 *Jane's Weapon Systems*, 1987-88, p. 157; Meyer, "Soviet Theatre Nuclear Forces, Part II," p. 54; Gunston, *Rockets & Missiles*, 1979, p. 28.
19 SMP 1988, p. 87.

6

SSC-X-4

SSC-X-4 (Soviet designations RK-55)

Figure 6.17 The subsonic **SSC-X-4** is a ground-launched, mobile, long-range cruise missile which, under the terms of the INF Treaty, will be eliminated. Here shown on static disply, this photograph was part of the official exchange to facilitate verification of the Treaty.

DESCRIPTION: Ground-launched, mobile, long-range, subsonic cruise missile similar to the SS-N-21 and the AS-15,[1] and eliminated under the INF Treaty

SPECIFICATIONS:
- Length: 8.09 m[2] (26.5 ft)
- Diameter: 0.51 m[3] (1.67 ft)
- Weight (with fuel)
  - In canister: 2440 kg[4] (5380 lbs)
  - Without canister: 1700 kg[5] (3750 lbs)
- Fuel/Propulsion: turbojet
- Speed: subsonic[6]
- Guidance: inertial updated by possible TERCOM radar

- Range: 3000 km (1600 nm)[7]
- Ceiling: unknown

DUAL CAPABLE: not assessed to be initially, could eventually have been made accurate enough to permit the use of conventional warheads[8]

NUCLEAR WARHEAD:
- Yield: unknown
- Weight: unknown

DEPLOYMENT:
- Launch Platform: tractor-trailer vehicle, with launchers for four missiles

---

1. SMP 1987, pp. 37-38; SMP 1986, pp. 33-34; SMP 1985, p. 35; SMP 1984, pp. 30-31.
2. INF Treaty, Memorandum of Understanding, December 1987, p. 38. Chart in SMP 1987, pp. 37-38, reports 23 ft.
3. INF Treaty, Memorandum of Understanding, December 1987, p. 38.
4. Ibid.
5. Ibid.
6. Taken from chart in SMP 1987, pp. 37-38.
7. SMP 1987, p. 38; JCS, FY 1986, p. 24.
8. SMP 1986, p. 33; SMP 1984, pp. 30-31; SMP 1985, pp. 35, 40.

6
SSC-X-4

Figure 6.18 The **SSC-X-4** GLCM is shown here housed within its launch canister, which would be loaded on a truck-mounted launcher.

Figure 6.19 The tractor-trailer vehicle mounts four **SSC-X-4** launch canisters.

HISTORY:

R&D:	1976-1982[9]
Engineering and Testing:	1982-1986[10]
First Observed:	March 1983[11]
First Flight Tests:	late 1981-1982[12]
IOC:	1990; expected IOC prior to the INF Treaty[13]

TARGETING: may have been assigned targets in support of the Eurasian theater[14]

Accuracy/CEP: unknown

---

9 SMP 1985, p. 40.
10 Ibid.
11 *Aerospace Daily*, 7 April 1983, p. 217.
12 JCS, FY 1986, p. 24; SMP 1983, preface, p. 2.
13 JCS, FY 1988, p. 32. SMP 1987, p. 37, stated possible deployment in 1987. SMP 1986, p. 33, reported that "the SSC-X-4 will probably become operational this year." SMP 1985, p. 35, reported in April 1985 that it "may not be ready for operational deployment until late this year or next" (see also, p. 40). SMP 1984, pp. 30, 31, estimated deployment in 1985.
14 SMP 1987, p. 37.

Chapter Seven
Non-Strategic Missiles, Rockets, and Artillery

Overview

Non-strategic theater and battlefield missiles, rockets and artillery make up 20 percent of the Soviet nuclear arsenal, which amounts to an estimated 6700 warheads as of mid-1988. The nuclear weapons allocated for theater and battlefield use range from artillery that can fire 30 kilometers to the SS-20 missile, which has a range of some 5000 kilometers. Eight different types of missiles are deployed (including one sea-based, short-range ballistic missile). Three different calibers of artillery (152mm, 203mm, and 240mm) are thought to have some nuclear capability. The weapons include:

- two long-range "theater" ballistic missile types (SS-20 Saber and SS-4 Sandal) deployed exclusively in the Soviet Union under the control of the Strategic Rocket Forces (SRF); these missiles will be eliminated under the INF Treaty;
- one theater-range submarine-launched ballistic missile (SLBM) type (SS-N-5 Serb) deployed on Golf II class diesel-powered submarines and assigned to the Navy;[1]
- the SS-12M Scaleboard B "operational-tactical" ballistic missile assigned to front-level formations of the Ground Forces; these missiles will be eliminated under the INF Treaty;
- three missile types (Scud B, SS-21 Scarab, and SS-23 Spider) and one rocket type (FROG-7) assigned to the Ground Forces at front, army, and division levels; the SS-23 missiles will be eliminated under the INF Treaty;
- nuclear-capable artillery of three calibers (152mm, 203mm, and 240mm) assigned to the Ground Forces at front, army, division and regimental levels; and
- possible atomic demolition munitions (ADMs).

Modernization and expansion of non-strategic missiles and artillery from the mid-1970s to the mid-1980s more than doubled the number of nuclear-capable delivery systems of these types. Missiles first deployed in the late 1950s and 1960s were mostly replaced or supplemented by new missiles with greater accuracy, reliability, and range, as well as improved mobility.[2] Nuclear-capable artillery guns replaced older systems that were not nuclear-capable. The INF Treaty, however, and obsolescence of the FROG-7 and Scud-B missiles (both first deployed in 1965), will reduce the size of the missile force from some 1845 launchers at the end of 1987 to about 500 launchers in the mid-1990s.

History

The first Soviet ballistic missiles were derived from the short-range German A-4 (V-2) missiles.[3] Following the occupation of Nazi Germany, some 200 specialists from the Institute Raabe in Bleicherode and the test range at Peenemunde were deported to the Soviet Union to continue their research.[4] Existing production facilities, a stock of A-4 components, drawings, and about 50 A-4 missiles, and three to five prototypes of the G-2 (an improved A-4 missile) were sent to the Soviet Union. From August to October 1947, 15-30 German-built V-2s with a range of 320 kilometers were tested from the Soviet range at Kapustin Yar.[5]

The first Soviet serial production version of the V-2, the SS-1a Scunner, was tested in 1947,[6] and production began in early 1948.[7] The Korolev design bureau made modifications to the SS-1a to increase its range by roughly a factor of two and to improve its reliability. The resultant missile, designated the SS-2 Sibling, was first tested in 1950.[8] Neither of these V-2 modifications were

---

1. SS-N-5 SLBMs deployed on one Hotel II class submarine, and a portion of the SS-N-6 SLBMs deployed on Yankee class submarines, are also believed to be assigned theater missions.
2. HASC, FY 1984 DOD, Part 3, p. 817; DIA, *Soviet Front Fire Support*, p. 75. The Soviets have apparently had accidents with their older short-range missiles. One accident involving a warhead of a short-range missile evidently took place 24 May 1983 near Turnov, Czechoslovakia. Authorities reportedly took radiation measurements at the site of the accident; "Very Serious Accidental Explosion in CSSR," *Vienna Kurier*, 14 January 1984, p. 3, translated in FBIS-SOV-84-011, 17 January 1984, Volume III, No. 011, p. F1.
3. CIA, *A Summary of Soviet Guided Missile Intelligence*, US/UK GM-4-52, 20 July 1953 (partially declassified), pp. A-1, A-4, A-38, A-54; Directorate of Intelligence, Headquarters, U.S Air Force (USAF), and Office of Naval Intelligence (ONI), Department of the Navy, *An Estimate of Soviet Air Capabilities and Air Order of Battle*, 1 October 1950, Annex V, "Soviet Guided Missiles" (National Archives Record Group 341, Entry 267, Box 126, No. 2-17738) pp. 133-139.
4. The specialists transferred to the Soviet Union did not include many of the head specialists of the Peenemunde research force. German propulsion experts were sent to Khimki, aerodynamics, structure, and design specialists to Kaliningrad, and guidance and control experts to Leningrad, Kuibyshev, Monino, and Ilyinskaya; CIA, *A Summary, op. cit.*; HQ USAF and ONI, *op. cit.*
5. USAREUR, *Identification Handbook*, p. 273.
6. Doug Richardson, "Soviet Strategic Nuclear Rockets Guide," *Flight International*, 11 December 1976, p. 1729; Ray Bonds, ed., *The Soviet War Machine: An Encyclopedia of Russian Military Equipment and Strategy* (London: Chartwell, 1976), pp. 202-203.
7. Provisions for the pilot production lines at Kaliningrad may have been made by German technicians during 1947; HQ USAF and ONI, *op. cit.*, p. 138.
8. The Soviets released photographs in the late 1950s showing the launch of SS-2s, what the Soviets called "geophysical rockets"; Richardson, *op. cit.*, p. 1729. The range of the SS-2 was estimated at 560-740 kilometers; USAICS, *Communist Weapons and Equipment Handbook*, p. 138.

Non-strategic Long-range Missiles

Table 7.1
Soviet Non-strategic Long-range Missiles (1956-1988)

Year	SS-3	SS-4	SS-5	SS-20	Launchers	Warheads
1956	24	—	—	—	24	24
1957	48	—	—	—	48	48
1958	48	—	—	—	48	48
1959	48	—	—	—	48	48
1960	48	72	—	—	120	120
1961	48	236	—	—	284	284
1962	48	400	24	—	472	472
1963	48	564	70	—	682	682
1964	38	600	76	—	714	714
1965	28	608	97	—	733	733
1966	28	608	97	—	733	733
1967	8	604	97	—	709	709
1968	8	600	97	—	705	705
1969	—	568	97	—	665	665
1970	—	568	93	—	661	661
1971	—	568	90	—	658	658
1972	—	568	90	—	658	658
1973	—	568	90	—	658	658
1974	—	568	90	—	658	658
1975	—	568	90	—	658	658
1976	—	568	90	—	658	658
1977	—	568	90	—	658	658
1978	—	488	86	9	583	601
1979	—	428	74	72	574	718
1980	—	388	60	126	574	826
1981	—	364	35	180	579	939
1982	—	300	35	270	605	1145
1983	—	232	16	333	581	1247
1984	—	224	—	378	602	1358
1985	—	112	—	387	499	1273
1986	—	80	—	441	521	1403
1987	—	65	—	405	470	1280
1988 (mid)	—	52	—	405	457	1267

Sources: Berman and Baker, *Soviet Strategic Forces*, p.136; DOD, FY 1965 *Annual Report* (class.), pp. 36-38; DOD, FY 1966 *Annual Report* (class.), p. 49; DOD, FY 1967 *Annual Report* (class.), p. 56; DOD, FY 1968 *Annual Report* (class.), pp. 45, 47; DOD, FY 1969 *Annual Report* (class.), pp. 57, 61; DOD, FY 1970 *Annual Report* (class.), p. 83; SMP (all editions); JCS (various editions); IISS, *Military Balance* (various editions).

operationally deployed,[9] and it is believed that there was a shift in development emphasis from V-2 type missiles to surface-to-air missiles and "ultra-long-range" strategic missiles instead.[10]

The first shorter range nuclear missile to enter service was the SS-3 Shyster in 1955.[11] First shown publicly in the 7 November 1957 parade in Moscow, it was a single-stage, medium-range ballistic missile (MRBM) using a non-storable liquid propellant. Radio-guided, it had a range of 1200 kilometers (roughly twice that of the SS-2 Sibling). The SS-3 was never widely deployed, however, because newer and more reliable medium and shorter range missiles, such as the SS-4 Sandal (a version of the SS-3) and the SS-12 Scaleboard, received greater attention.

The very short range FROG (Free-Rocket-Over-Ground) series of unguided, solid-propellant rockets also began deployment in the late 1950s. The first two of the

---

[9] The SS-1 Scunner and SS-2 Sibling served only as research rockets and crew training platforms; Berman and Baker, *Soviet Strategic Forces*, pp. 96-97. A 1966 U.S. Army pamphlet noted that both the SS-1a and SS-2, while obsolete, may have been still in use, possibly with nuclear warheads; USAREUR, *Identification Handbook*, pp. 273, 281.

[10] Former V-2 specialists were dispersed after 1948, some to surface-to-air projects and others to Ostashkov to work on what U.S. intelligence expected to be a long-term project to develop an "ultra-long-range" missile; HQ USAF and ONI, *op. cit.*, pp. 138-139.

[11] The SS-3 was under the control of Long Range Aviation (LRA) until the establishment of SRF in 1959.

7

Non-strategic Missiles

family also appeared publicly in the 7 November 1957 parade in Moscow—the 70 kilometer range FROG-1 on a modified JS-3 heavy tank chassis and the 30 kilometer-range FROG-2 on a modified PT-76 amphibious tank chassis. These two missiles were followed by the 26 kilometer-range FROG-3 and the 52 kilometer-range FROG-4 and FROG-5, all of which first appeared in the 1960 May Day parade in Moscow. The FROG-3 replaced the FROG-1 and 2 by mid 1966;[12] the FROG-4 and -5 were never deployed widely.[13] The FROG-3, -4, and -5 missiles were mounted on the modified PT-76 chassis, an improvement over the FROG-2. They were the same basic two-stage rocket (the FROG-1 and -2 rockets were single-stage), differing only in the size and shape of the warhead.[14] The 14-70 kilometer-range, single-stage FROG-7 was first displayed in the 7 November 1965 parade in Moscow on a ZIL-135 wheeled vehicle, which offered greater road mobility. The missile was deployed in 1965-1966.

With the deployment of the 2000 kilometer-range SS-4 Sandal in 1958—the first Soviet missile to use storable liquid fuel— the Soviets obtained a significant theater nuclear-strike capability separate from long-range strategic forces. The SS-4 was soon supplemented by the 4100 kilometer-range SS-5 intermediate-range ballistic missile (IRBM), which entered service in 1961.[15] More than 700 SS-3, SS-4, and SS-5 launchers were operational at peak deployment in the mid-1960s, with all but 100 directed at targets in or related to Western Europe.[16]

Both the SS-4 and SS-5 required enormous time and effort to prepare to fire. The SS-4 required approximately eight hours to be readied to fire; the SS-5 could only be maintained at a state of readiness for five hours. Over 85 percent of the 600 SS-4s and half of the nearly 100 SS-5 missiles were deployed at aboveground soft sites, with the remainder in semi-hardened launchers.[17] The aboveground launching sites for both missiles could theoretically be reused within four to six hours for the SS-4, and, six to eight hours for the SS-5.[18]

Soviet efforts to deploy six SS-4 and four SS-5 groups (with four launchers each) in Cuba in 1962 led to the Cuban Missile Crisis. Each launcher was assessed by U.S. intelligence analysts as being reloadable, and a total of 48 SS-4 and 32 SS-5 missiles were thought to be planned.[19]

The 150 kilometer-range, mobile SS-1b Scud-A, first seen in 1957, was deployed around 1961. It was derived from the SS-1a Scunner, but had twice the range. Two other much larger mobile missiles were observed during 1965 parades on self-propelled transporter-erector-launchers (TELs).[20] One of these missiles, the SS-X-14 Scamp MRBM,[21] was derived from the top two stages of the SS-13 intercontinental ballistic missile (ICBM)[22] and was first tested in 1965. The other, the SS-X-15 Scrooge IRBM, consisted of the first and third stages of the SS-13 and was first tested in 1968.[23] Both the SS-X-14 and SS-X-15 had solid-fuel propellant, and both underwent operational testing until at least 1970. Test results were apparently unfavorable, and neither missile was ever widely deployed,[24] except for a small training complement of SS-14 and SS-15 missiles that may have been operational for a brief period in the Soviet Far East.[25]

While the mobile SS-14 and SS-15 were failures, the SS-12 Scaleboard, an 800 kilometer-range battlefield missile, was not. First tested around 1967, the SS-12 Mod 1 Scaleboard was deployed in 1969 on a wheeled vehicle. It offered significant mobility, reliability, and accuracy advantages over the SS-3, which it superseded along with the SS-4. The SS-12M Scaleboard B, a modified SS-12 with improved accuracy and slightly longer range, was developed in the mid-1970s and introduced with Soviet units in 1979-1980. U.S. intelligence agencies at first thought that the upgrades—such as solid fuel versus storable liquid fuel, and the addition of dual capability—im-

---

12 USAREUR, *Identification Handbook*, pp. 261, 263.
13 For example, a 1982 DIA document reports the FROG-7 is replacing the FROG-3 and FROG-5 in active divisions, with no mention made of the FROG-4; DIA, *Soviet Front Fire Support*, p. 107. Two earlier Army documents refer only to FROG-3 and FROG-7 missiles; USA, *Handbook on Soviet Ground Forces*, p. 6-39, USA, *Understanding Soviet Military Developments*, p. 69. A 1971 USAICS training document fails even to mention the FROG-5 of the series; USAICS, *Communist Weapons and Equipment Handbook*, pp. 127-133. Other documents claimed that the FROG-4 and FROG-5 were still deployed in Warsaw Pact countries in the early 1980s; see, for example, Major James Brusstar, "FROG: The Division-Level Nuclear Weapons," *Review of Soviet Ground Forces*, (DIA) December 1981, No. 4, p. 5. FROG-6 was a gunnery training rocket with a dummy warhead.
14 USAREUR, *Identification Handbook*, pp. 261-269.
15 CIA, *Major Consequences of Certain U.S. Courses of Action in Cuba*, SNIE 11-19-62, 20 October 1962 (declassified), p. 2.
16 SMP 1981, p. 26. There were 28 SS-3 missiles and 705 SS-4s and SS-5s deployed at the peak.
17 DOD, FY 1966 *Annual Report* (class.), p. 50.
18 SMP 1981, p. 26; JCS, FY 1982, p. 102.
19 Raymond L. Garthoff, *Reflections on the Cuban Missile Crisis* (Washington, DC: The Brookings Institution, 1987), p. 20. Twenty of the 24 SS-4 launchers were believed to be fully operational before the resolution of the crisis on 28 October 1962; the remaining four launchers were expected to be operational in early November. U.S. intelligence had identified 33 SS-4 missiles, but knew there might be more. Soviet leaders informed the U.S. that there were in fact 42 SS-4 missiles in Cuba. The first four SS-5 launchers were expected to be fully operational by 1 December, and the second and third SS-5 groups on 15 December 1962. The fourth SS-5 group was clearly planned, and construction of the site had begun, though the base had not yet proceeded far enough to be confirmed as a site before dismantling had begun. Delivery of the last six SS-4 and all 32 SS-5 missiles was stopped by the "quarantine" blockade. No nuclear warheads were ever identified in Cuba; Raymond L. Garthoff, *Intelligence Assessment and Policymaking: A Decision Point in the Kennedy Administration* (Washington, DC: The Brookings Institution, 1984), p. 31 and the memorandum, "The Military Significance of the Soviet Missile Bases in Cuba," October 1962, reprinted in *ibid.*, pp. 32-33. For more on the issue of nuclear warheads in Cuba see, Richard Ned Lebow, "Was Khrushchev Bluffing in Cuba?" *Bulletin of the Atomic Scientists*, April 1988, pp. 38-42; Raymond L. Garthoff, "Did Khrushev Bluff in Cuba? No", *Bulletin of the Atomic Scientists*, July/August 1988, pp. 40-43.
20 The Scamp appeared for the first time in public in the 9 May 1965 parade in Moscow and the Scrooge first appeared in the 7 November 1965 parade; USAREUR, *Identification Handbook*, pp. 285, 297; USAICS, *Communist Weapons and Equipment Handbook*, p. 148.
21 This missile has been variously reported with two different NATO code names. Scamp is reported in USAREUR, *Identification Handbook*, p. 285, and in DOD, FY 1972 *Annual Report* (class.), Table 6. Scapegoat is reported in Berman and Baker, *Soviet Strategic Forces*, p. 102.
22 The SS-X-14 Scamp IRBM was referred to as an operational-tactical missile by the Soviets; USAICS, *Communist Weapons and Equipment Handbook*, p. 148. See also, Jim Bussert, "The SS-25: Does It Breach SALT II?" *Jane's Defence Weekly*, 31 January 1987, pp. 143-144.
23 DOD, FY 1972 *Annual Report* (class.), Table 6. The Soviets claimed that the cylinder on the TEL associated with the Scrooge missile contained a solid-propellant ICBM (USAICS, *Communist Weapons and Equipment Handbook*, p. 149), and the United States has described the missile as a testbed mobile ICBM (SAC, *Soviet Military Capabilities*, July 1981, p. 19) or mobile, shorter range ICBM (SMP 1984, p. 25).
24 SMP 1984, p. 25. The SS-14 was tested a total of 19 times in 1965 and 1967-1970. It was the more successful of the two programs, with a test success rate of at least 84 percent. The SS-15 failed in three of its five 1968 tests. Three 1969 tests were successful; DOD, FY 1972 *Annual Report*(class.), Table 6.
25 Raymond L. Garthoff, "The Soviet SS-20 Decision," *Survival*, Vol. XXV, No. 3, May-June 1983, p. 110; Berman and Baker, *Soviet Strategic Forces*, p. 111.

Non-strategic Missiles

Table 7.2
Soviet INF Missiles, Launchers, and Bases (1987[1]/mid-1988[2])

	SS-20	SS-4	SS-12	SS-23	Other
Missiles					
Deployed[3]	405/405	65/60	220/85	167/127	0
Non-deployed[4]	245/249	105/89	506/633	33/112	6[5]
Subtotal	**650/654**	**170/149**	**726/718**	**200/239**	**6**
Inert Training Missiles	42/61	147/77	185/190	96/121	0
Launchers					
Deployed[6]	405/405	80/63	115/37	82/64	0
Non-deployed[7]	118/104	6/9	20/95	20/42	0
Total Launchers	523/509	85/72	135/132	102/106	0
Bases					
Soviet Union					
Bases for Deployed Missiles	48/48	13/12	6/5	5/5	0
Bases for Non-deployed Missiles	23/20	5/4	12/6	9/3	4[8]
Subtotal	**71/68**	**18/16**	**18/11**	**14/8**	**4**
East Germany					
Bases for Deployed Missiles	0/0	0/0	4/0	2/0	0
Czechoslovakia					
Bases for Deployed Missiles	0/0	0/0	1/0	0/0	0
Total Bases	**71/68**	**18/16**	**23/11**	**16/10**	**4**

1 As of 1 November 1987 as stated in the INF Treaty Memorandum of Understanding signed in December 1987.
2 INF Treaty: 1 June 1988, Data Update.
3 In the INF Treaty the terms *deployed* and *non-deployed* do not have the conventional meanings. Under Article II, "[t]he term "deployed missile" means an intermediate-range missile located within a deployment area or a shorter-range missile located at a missile operating base."
4 In the INF Treaty the terms *deployed* and *non-deployed* do not have the conventional meanings. Under Article II, "[t]he term "non-deployed missile" means an intermediate-range missile located outside a deployment area or a shorter-range missile located outside a missile operating base."
5 Non-deployed SS-5 missiles in storage.
6 In the INF Treaty the terms *deployed* and *non-deployed* do not have the conventional meanings. Under Article II, "[t]he term "deployed launcher" means a launcher of an intermediate-range missile located within a deployment area or a launcher of a shorter-range missile located at a missile operating base."
7 In the INF Treaty the terms *deployed* and *non-deployed* do not have the conventional meanings. Under Article II, "[t]he term "non-deployed launcher" means a launcher of an intermediate-range missile located outside a deployment area or a launcher of a shorter-range missile located outside a missile operating base."
8 Includes two SS-5 bases and two SSC-X-4 bases.

plied that the new missile was a completely new design, and it was designated SS-22. The Soviets also gave it a new designation, the OTR-22. By 1985, however, it was concluded that the two were modifications of the same missile, and the SS-22 was redesignated the SS-12 Mod 2, and subsequently the SS-12M Scaleboard B.[26]

The failure to develop mobile long-range missiles in the 1960s led to the use of the SS-11 ICBM in a theater role. Two former SS-4/5 missile bases in the western Soviet Union were converted for SS-11s beginning in 1968, and in 1969-1970, SS-11s replaced more SS-4/5s, which were transferred east, mostly in 1968.[27] SS-4 and SS-5 force levels remained relatively constant through the 1970s until the deployment of the mobile SS-20 in 1977.

All of the SS-5s were retired by the end of 1983,[28] and the number of SS-4s was reduced to 112 by October 1985, to 65 by the end of 1987, and, to 60 by June 1988.[29] The remaining operational SS-4s will be withdrawn under the terms of the INF Treaty.

The SS-20 was first deployed in late 1977 to replace the SS-4 MRBM and SS-5 IRBM. The new mobile solid-fuel missile represented a significant increase over its predecessors in range, accuracy, reliability, reaction and reload time, and survivability.[30] The missile was the first Soviet non-strategic weapon armed with multiple warheads. The missile reached full deployment in 1986, at 441 launchers.[31]

---

26 Until mid-1985, NATO continued to use the SS-22 designation. High-level U.S. and NATO officials continued to use the SS-22 designation up until the signing of the INF Treaty in December 1987.
27 Gregory Treverton, "Nuclear Weapons in Europe," Adelphi Paper No. 168, IISS, p. 6; SMP 1981, p. 26; DOD, FY 1972 Annual Report (class.), Table 6.
28 General Secretary Andropov claimed on 27 October 1983 that all SS-5s were taken out of service; *Pravda*, 27 October 1983, p. 1.
29 In early October 1985, 112 SS-4s were deployed; background briefing by a senior White House official, 8 October 1985. For 1987 figure see, INF Treaty, Memorandum of Understanding, December 1987. For 1988 figure see, INF Treaty: 1 June 1988 Data Update.
30 The SS-20, which is believed to have a circular error probable (CEP) of about 300 meters, is eight times as accurate as the SS-4; interview with DOD official, 27 November 1985. The DIA reportedly estimates that the SS-20 has a 95 percent launcher reliability, a 97 percent in-flight reliability, and a 97 percent warhead reliability, with an overall reliability of 89 percent; Jack Anderson, "War Game Gives a New Look at Soviet Missiles," *Washington Post*, 3 July 1984, p. C8.
31 The total SS-20 force was expected to grow to over 450 by 1987; SASC/SAC, Soviet Strategic Force Developments, 1985, p. 3. One SS-20 main operating base at Yurya was deactivated for conversion to the SS-25; Peter Samuel, "Big Soviet Buildup Foreseen," *Defense Week*, 17 June 1985, p. 15; Ted Agres, "Soviets Testing New ICBMs, CIA Reports," *Washington Times*, 18 September 1984, p. 1; Robert Roth, "U.S. Warns of New Soviet Missiles," *Philadelphia Inquirer*, 23 September 1984, p. 7.

7

Long-range Missiles

Towards the late 1970s, it appeared that not only would the SS-20 replace the SS-4 and SS-5, but that an entire new generation of short-range missiles was going to be deployed to replace the SS-12 Scaleboard, Scud, and FROG. These missiles—the SS-22, SS-23 and SS-21—never have been deployed in the form or quantities that were predicted. The SS-22 (as discussed above) proved to be just a modification of the SS-12, and will be eliminated under the INF Treaty. The SS-23, first deployed in 1985 to replace the Scud, was some six years behind schedule, and now will be eliminated under the INF Treaty as well. The SS-21, replacing the FROG since 1976, did not begin full scale fielding until 1981, and is still behind the predictions of the late 1970s in terms of schedule.

Long-range Missiles

As of the signing of the INF Treaty, the Soviet Union had 405 SS-20 operational launchers and 650 missiles (405 deployed and 245 non-deployed),[32] as well as 65 SS-4 missiles.[33] General Secretary Gorbachev had promised in October 1985 in Paris that the number of SS-20 launchers on "standby alert" targeted against Europe would be reduced to 243, but the reduction was not reflected in any official U.S. or other Western accountings prior to the INF Treaty.[34]

The SS-20 Saber (Soviet designation RSD-10) is a fourth-generation, solid-fuel mobile IRBM based on the upper two stages of the SS-X-16 mobile ICBM (see Chapter Five). Three modifications reportedly exist, two with a single warhead (Mod 1 and Mod 3), and a third (Mod 2 which is considered to be the most common type) carrying three 250 kiloton warheads (MIRVs). The SS-20 became operational in 1977, replacing the SS-5 and partially replacing the SS-4.

There has always been a dispute within the U.S. intelligence community over the exact range of the missile. Most sources report that the missile has a range of 5000 kilometers (3100 miles). This is the estimate of the Defense Intelligence Agency (DIA), but the CIA reportedly estimates the missile's range at 4400 kilometers (2750 miles).[35]

The SS-20 missile is assigned to Strategic Rocket Forces and at the time of the INF Treaty signing was deployed in the Soviet Union at 48 bases—two-thirds within range of Europe and the Middle East, and the re-

Table 7.3
SS-20 Saber Missile Deployments (1987/1988)[1]

Deployment Areas	Regiments	Launchers	Storage Facilities
Akhtyrka	2	18	
Barnaul	4	36	1
Belokorovichi	1	9	1
Brody	1	9	
Chervonograd	1	9	
Drovyanaya	5	45	1
Gezgaly	1	6	1
Glukhov	2	18	
Kansk	4	36	1
Korosten'	1	6	
Lebedin	1	9	1
Lida	1	9	
Lipniki	1	9	
Lutsk	2	18	1
Mozyr'	1	9	1
Novosibirsk	5	45	1
Petrikov	1	6	
Polotsk	1	9	
Postavy	1	9	1
Rechitsa	1	6	
Ruzhany	1	6	
Slavuta	1	9	
Slonim	1	9	
Slutsk	1	9	
Smorgon'	2	18	
Vetrino	1	9	
Vysokaya Pech'	2	12	
Zasimovichi	1	6	
Zhitkovichi	1	6	

Non-Deployed Facilities

Chita	elimination facility
Kansk	eimination facility
Kapustin Yar	training facility, test site, and elimination facility
Kolosovo	missile storage site
Krasnodar	training facility
Sarny	elimination facility
Serpukhov	training facility
Zherebkovo	missile storage site

1 As of 1 November 1987 as stated in the INF Treaty Memorandum of Understanding signed in December 1987, and as of 1 June 1988 as stated in the INF Treaty: 1 June 1988, Data Update.

---

32 Prior to the INF Treaty, most sources credited each SS-20 launcher with an operational reload missile; e.g., HASC, FY 1984 DOD, Part 1, p. 1281; SMP 1981, p. 27; SMP 1983, p. 37; SASC, Strategic Force Modernization Programs, 1981, p. 5. There were a number of unconfirmed reports of a 1983 debate in the intelligence community on whether the SS-20 launcher comes equipped with a single reload missile or two; see *Aerospace Daily*, 1 June 1983, p. 173; *Newsweek*, 6 June 1983, p. 19. One source reported that there were five to six reload missiles per regiment; John Barry, "Geneva Behind Closed Doors," *Times* (London), 31 May 1983. Steven J. Dryden, "U.S. Says Soviets Adding SS20s Despite Freeze," *Washington Post*, 18 September 1985, p. 23, reported that as of September 1985, 49 SS-20 regiments with 441 launchers were deployed at 11 main operating bases in the Soviet Union. For an update to mid-1988, see Tables 7.1 and 7.2.

33 For an update to mid-1988, see Tables 7.1 and 7.2.

34 The facilities for 36 launchers were partially dismantled, though it was unclear up to the time of the INF Treaty data exchange between the United States and Soviet Union what happened to the missiles and launchers that were removed; Walter Pincus, "Navy Picks Two Missile Subs for Possible '86 Dismantling," *Washington Post*, 27 November 1985, p. A2; Michael R. Gordon, "U.S. Arms Stance Is Firm, Aide Says," *New York Times*, 28 November 1985, p. A3.

35 This debate is reflected in the 1984 NATO publication, *NATO and the Warsaw Pact*, which cites a 4400 kilometer range for the missile. In 1980, the Air Force noted that the missile had a 4400-5000 kilometer range; HQ USAF, *Military Forces Handbook: Military Forces of the USSR and Warsaw Pact*, Air Force Pamphlet 200-11, 31 March 1980, p. 3-1. Soviet negotiator Yuri Kvitsinksy told Paul Nitze that the missile's true range is little more than 2500 miles, which reportedly is as far as it has been test-fired.

Long-range Missiles

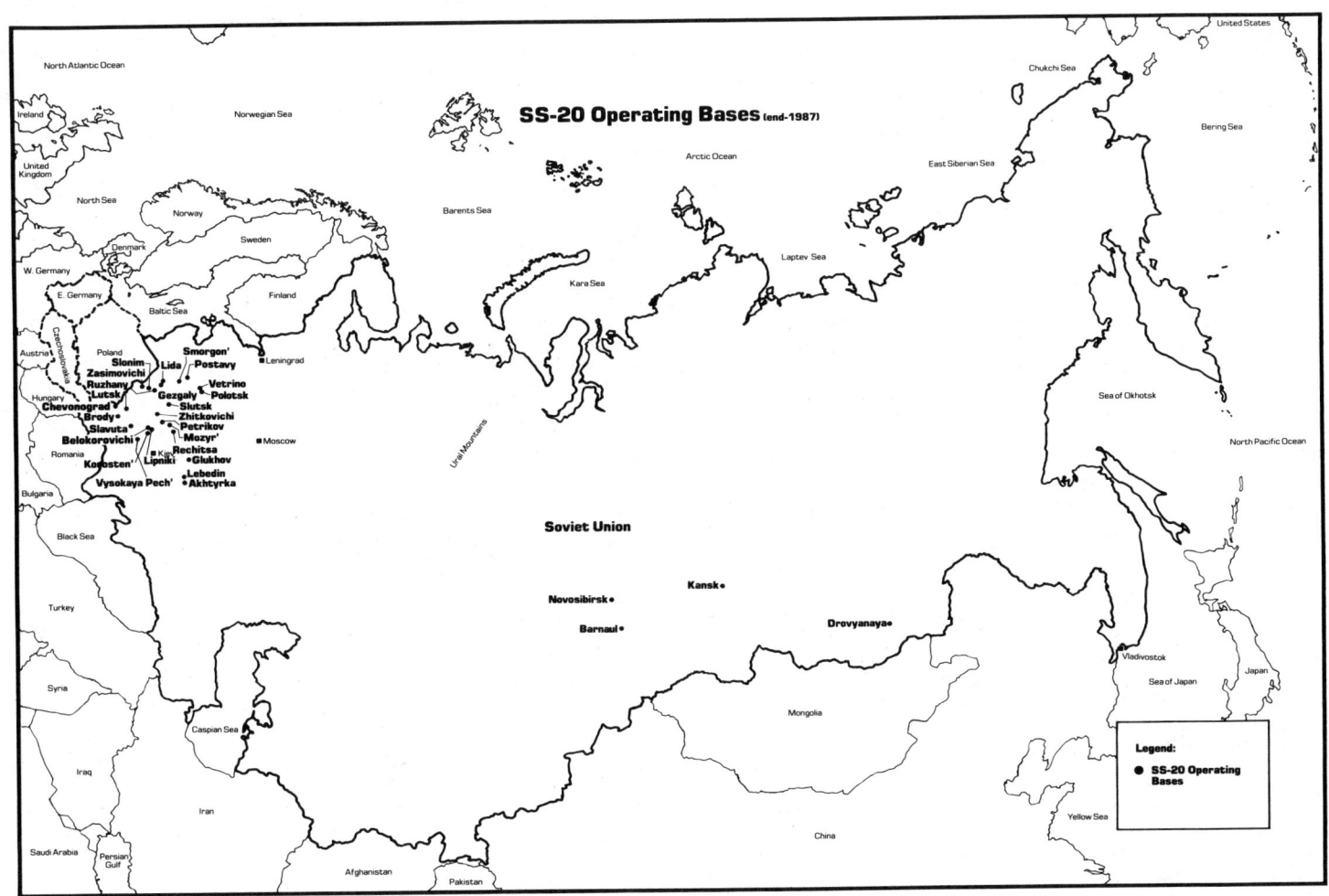

Figure 7.1 SS-20 Operating Bases (end-1987).

mainder within range of Asia (and Alaska) (see Figure 7.1). Each SS-20 regiment consists of either two or three battalions of six or nine mobile launchers. (Each battalion has two launchers.) Regiments are reportedly located at presurveyed alert sites close to main operating bases at all times. Missiles can also be fired from the missile storage buildings at main operating bases through sliding roofs or from sites that are not presurveyed,[36] though the latter would entail a degradation in accuracy. It is also believed that the SS-20 can be transported by the new AN-72 Condor heavy-lift transport aircraft.[37]

A modified SS-20, first tested in 1984 but now also banned by the INF Treaty, was reportedly intended to improve the lethality of the first-generation SS-20.[38] The missile reportedly carried the designation SS-X-28. In 1983 the DIA first reported it was under development.[39]

The SS-4 Sandal (Soviet designation R-12), which the SS-20 partially replaced, is a first-generation MRBM. Deployed in 1959, the SS-4 was the first Soviet missile to use storable liquid fuel. This large, single-stage missile has a range of 1770 kilometers (1100 miles) and carries a single one-megaton warhead. At peak deployment in 1964-1966, some 608 SS-4 missiles were operational. The number was reduced to 112 in 1985, to 65 by late 1987, and to 52 by March 1988.[40]

A final long-range Soviet theater weapon is the submarine-launched SS-N-5 Sark, a single-stage, liquid-fueled missile. It is deployed on 12 Golf II class diesel-pow-

---

36 SASC, FY 1983 DOD, Part 7, p. 4331.
37 SMP 1985 contains an artist's illustration of the Condor on-loading an SS-20 TEL; SMP 1985, p. 80.
38 SMP 1985, p. 36; SASC/SAC, Soviet Strategic Force Developments, 1985, p. 3.
39 JEC, Allocation of Resources - 1983, Part 9, p. 203.
40 SMP 1988, p. 15.

7

Tactical Missiles and Rockets

ered ballistic missile submarines (SSBs), each of which have three launch tubes. These submarines are homeported in the Baltic Sea and the Sea of Japan.[41] The SS-N-5 first became operational in 1963. Each missile carries a single warhead with an explosive power of 1200-2000 kilotons. Because the missile has a range of 750 nautical miles (1400 kilometers), it is not considered part of strategic forces and was therefore not SALT accountable. The missile is inertially guided and has an accuracy (circular error of probability) of 1-2 nautical miles.

Operational-Tactical and Tactical Missiles and Rockets

The Soviets have deployed a number of types of "operational-tactical" rockets and missiles, (*operativno-takticheskiy raket*) meaning those weapons intended to affect the preparation, course, and outcome of a battle. Currently, five types are deployed, and all are capable of firing nuclear, conventional, and chemical warheads. The five types include:

- SS-12M Scaleboard B missiles (formerly designated SS-12 Mod 2 and SS-22);
- SS-23 Spider missile, a follow-on replacing Scud-B;
- SCUD-B missiles;
- SS-21 Scarab missile, a follow-on replacing the FROG; and
- the FROG-7 rockets.

The number of tactical surface-to-surface missile (SSM) launchers is approaching 1500, an increase of 500 since 1977.[42] Each of the launchers is thought to have reload capabilities, with more than five additional missiles per launchers available for the SS-12M Scaleboard B, and more than two available for the SS-23.

The SS-12M Scaleboard B (Soviet designation OTR-22) is a mobile solid-fuel, short-range ballistic missile (SRBM) assigned to the front and theater levels in the Ground Forces. The Scaleboard B was first deployed in 1979-1980, replacing the liquid-fuel SS-12 Mod 1 Scaleboard, which was first deployed in 1969. Though capable of firing nuclear, conventional, or chemical warheads, the SS-12M Scaleboard B is thought to be primarily intended for nuclear missions.[43] The 800 kilometer (560 mile) range missile carries a 500 kiloton warhead and has an accuracy of 200-400 meters (650-1300 feet). The prelaunch time of the missile is on the order of two to four hours.[44]

As of December 1987, when the INF Treaty was

Figure 7.2 SS-4 Bases (end-1987).

signed, there were 135 SS-12 launchers, 220 deployed missiles, and 506 non-deployed missiles. The ratio of missiles to launchers is more than five to one.[45] Prior to the INF Treaty data exchange, it was assumed by the U.S. government that there was one reload missile available for each Scaleboard launcher.[46]

As of the signing of the INF Treaty, SS-12M missiles were deployed at four bases in the Soviet Union, four bases in East Germany,[47] and one base in Czechoslovakia. Forward deployment outside the Soviet Union to East Germany and Czechoslovakia began in early 1984—the first deployment of Scaleboard missiles outside of the Soviet Union.[48] Some 50 were reported to be forward

---

41 Six of the Golf II submarines were stationed in the Baltic Sea and six were in the Sea of Japan. They are continuing to be retired; Collins and Victory, *U.S./Soviet Military Balance*, 1988, p. 15, show 9 as of 1 January 1988.
42 USA, *Understanding Soviet Military Developments*, p. 32.
43 HASC, FY 1984 DOD, Part 5, pp. 1280-1281.
44 USA, *Handbook on Soviet Ground Forces*, p. 5-23.
45 For an update to mid-1988, see Table 7.2.
46 DIA, *Soviet Front Fire Support*, p. 70; JCS, FY 1986, p. 38.
47 The first missiles were withdrawn from Bischofswerda and Waren on 25 February 1988; Robert J. McCartney, "Soviet Pullout of Missiles Begins Today," *Washington Post*, 25 February 1988, p. A37.
48 The Soviets had warned of the introduction of new tactical nuclear missiles in 1983 (Dusko Doder, "Soviets Warn: Nuclear Arms in East Europe," *Washington Post*, 14 October 1983, p. A24), and announced preparatory work for deployments in East Germany and Czechoslovakia on 24 October 1983 after plans to increase nuclear deployments to Eastern Europe to counter NATO deployments had been agreed to by the two countries; Dusko Doder, "Moscow to Deploy Missiles Westward," *Washington Post*, 25 October 1983, p. 1; Serge Schmemann, "Moscow Prepares A-Arms in Europe," *New York Times*, 25 October 1983, p. 1; Moscow Domestic Television Service, 24 October 1983, in FBIS-SOV, 25 October 1983, p. AA1. The new missiles became operational first in Czechoslovakia and East Germany; *Washington Post*, 8 December 1983, p. 40. The first report of their operational status in East Germany came on 19 December 1983, (Tass report from a *Krasnaya Zvezd* correspondent, reported in the *Dallas Morning News*, 18 December 1983, p. 3-A), with confirmation by the Soviet Union in January 1984 that new "tactical" missiles of "an enhanced range" were deployed to East Germany; see, for example, John F. Burns, "Soviet Is Manning New Missiles Units," *New York Times*, 18 January 1984, p. 5.

Tactical Missiles and Rockets

Table 7.4
SS-4 Sandal Missile Deployments (1987/1988)[1]

Deployment Areas

	Missiles		Launch Stands	
	Dec 1987	June 1988	Dec 1987	June 1988
Aluksne	5	5	6	5
Gusev	5	5	7	5
Karmelava	5	5	5	5
Kolomyya	5	5	6	5
Malorita	5	5	6	6
Ostrov	5	5	8	7
Pinsk	5	5	5	5
Skala-Podol'skaya	5	*	6	*
Sovetsk	5	5	6	5
Stryy	5	5	7	5
Taurage	5	5	5	5
Ukmerge	5	5	6	5
Vyru	5	5	6	5

Non-deployed Facilities

	December 1987	June 1988
Bataysk	missile repair facility	missile repair facility
Kapustin Yar	missile repair facility and test range	*
Kolosovo	missile storage facility	missile/launcher storage facility
Lesnaya	elimination facility	elimination facility
Zherebkovo	missile storage facility	missile/launcher storage facility

* Facility not listed in the INF Treaty: 1 June 1988, Data Update.

1 As of 1 November 1987 as stated in the INF Treaty Memorandum of Understanding signed in December 1987, and as of 1 June 1988 as stated in the INF Treaty: 1 June 1988, Data Update.

deployed by the beginning of 1985, approximately two-thirds being deployed in East Germany.[49]

The SS-1c Scud-B is a mobile battlefield SSM deployed at front and army level in the Ground Forces. The missile first appeared in public in the 7 November 1961 parade in Moscow and entered service in 1965, replacing the SS-1b Scud-A, which was deployed in 1961. (The replacement was completed by 1977.) Scud-B offered almost twice the range, improved guidance, and greater reliability over the Scud-A.[50] Both Scud missiles used storable liquid fuel and were initially deployed on a modified JS-3 heavy tank chassis. Scud-Bs were subsequently upgraded to be carried by the MAZ-543 eight-wheeled vehicle, which provides the missile system with greater road mobility and reduces the number of support vehicles.[51] The 280 kilometer (170 mile) range missile is dual-capable and can deliver a 1-10 kiloton warhead. Prelaunch preparation time for the Scud-B is two to four hours.[52]

The Scud-B, which is not subject to elimination under the terms of the INF Treaty, is now being replaced by the SS-23 Spider, which will be eliminated. The SS-23 (Soviet designation OTR-23) is a mobile, solid-fuel SSM that offers almost twice the range of the Scud-B (500 as opposed to 280 kilometers),[53] as well as greater accuracy, reliability, and flexibility.

The SS-23 was believed to be ready for deployment in 1979, but was reported as still not with operational units by April 1985.[54] In March 1987, *Soviet Military Power* reported that the first operational SS-23 brigade of 12-18 launchers was activated in the Belorussian Military District in 1985.[55] The Joint Chiefs of Staff reported that approximately 36 launchers in two or three brigades were active in 1987.[56] The INF Treaty revealed that these public estimates were significantly lower than the actual level of SS-23 deployments. As of December 1987, the Soviets reported having 102 SS-23 launchers, 167 deployed missiles, and 72 non-deployed missiles.[57] The INF Treaty data exchange confirmed that the SS-23 had a reload capability, as previously indicated.[58]

The FROG-7 is an unguided, single-stage, short-range SSM assigned to divisions of the Ground Forces. The 12-70 kilometer (7-44 nautical mile)-range missile has replaced virtually all of the older FROG launchers, with the exception of some remaining FROG-3s.[59] The FROG-7B, a variant of the FROG-7 introduced in the late 1960s, is slightly longer and is thought to be the commonly deployed missile today. Three warhead yields are believed to be available for the rocket: one, ten, and twenty-five kilotons. Prelaunch times for the FROGs are approximately 30 minutes.[60] Four launchers are assigned to each missile battalion of Soviet motorized and armored divisions. Some 370 launchers were estimated to be deployed at the end of 1987; however, the SS-21 Scarab is now replacing FROG missiles in Soviet divisions.

The SS-21 Scarab, a mobile, short-range SSM was first introduced in 1976.[61] The 14-120 kilometer (9-75

---

49 ACDA, FY 1984 *Annual Report*, p. 20. The first SS-22s were reportedly spotted at Bernsdorf, East Germany in January 1984 ("SS-22 Reported in East Germany," *New York Times*, 26 January 1984, p. A4), with more forward deployed in May 1984 ("Three Threats NATO's Not Addressing," *Armed Forces Journal International*, May 1984, p. 35; *Soviet Aerospace*, 21 May 1984, p. 21; Soviet announcement on 14 May 1984), and later in September 1984; "Soviet Is Said to Put More SS-22 Missiles into Eastern Europe," *New York Times*, 30 September 1984, p. 4.
50 USAREUR, *Identification Handbook*, p. 277; USA, *Understanding Soviet Military Developments*, p. 69; USAICS, *Communist Weapons and Equipment Handbook*, p. 135.
51 USAREUR, *Identification Handbook*, p. 279.
52 USA, *Handbook on Soviet Ground Forces*, p. 5-23.
53 SMP 1983, p. 38; HASC, FY 1984 DOD, Part 3, p. 1793. The SS-23 has also been identified with a 300 km range; see, for example, HASC, FY 1984 DOD, Part 3, pp. 1037.
54 SMP 1985, pp. 38, 67; *NATO and the Warsaw Pact*, 1984, p. 36. General Bernard Rogers, Supreme Allied Commander Europe, noted, "The SS-23 is not deployed yet, or rather we don't know about that. It's that close;" Robert Hutchinson, "NATO Ministers Can't Abdicate CW Decision Says SACEUR," *Jane's Defence Weekly*, 27 April 1985, p. 723.
55 SMP 1987, p. 41.
56 JCS, FY 1988, p. 48.
57 For an update to mid-1988, see Table 7.2.
58 DIA, *Soviet Front Fire Support*, p. 70.
59 Ibid., p. 107; HASC, FY 1984 DOD, Part 3, 1036; Brusstar, op. cit., p. 5.
60 USA, *Handbook on Soviet Ground Forces*, p. 5-23.
61 The phaseout of the FROGs was slower than anticipated, with clear signs of widespread replacement, particularly of the FROG-3, evident only in 1983; HASC, FY 1984 DOD, Part 3, p. 1036.

7
Nuclear Artillery

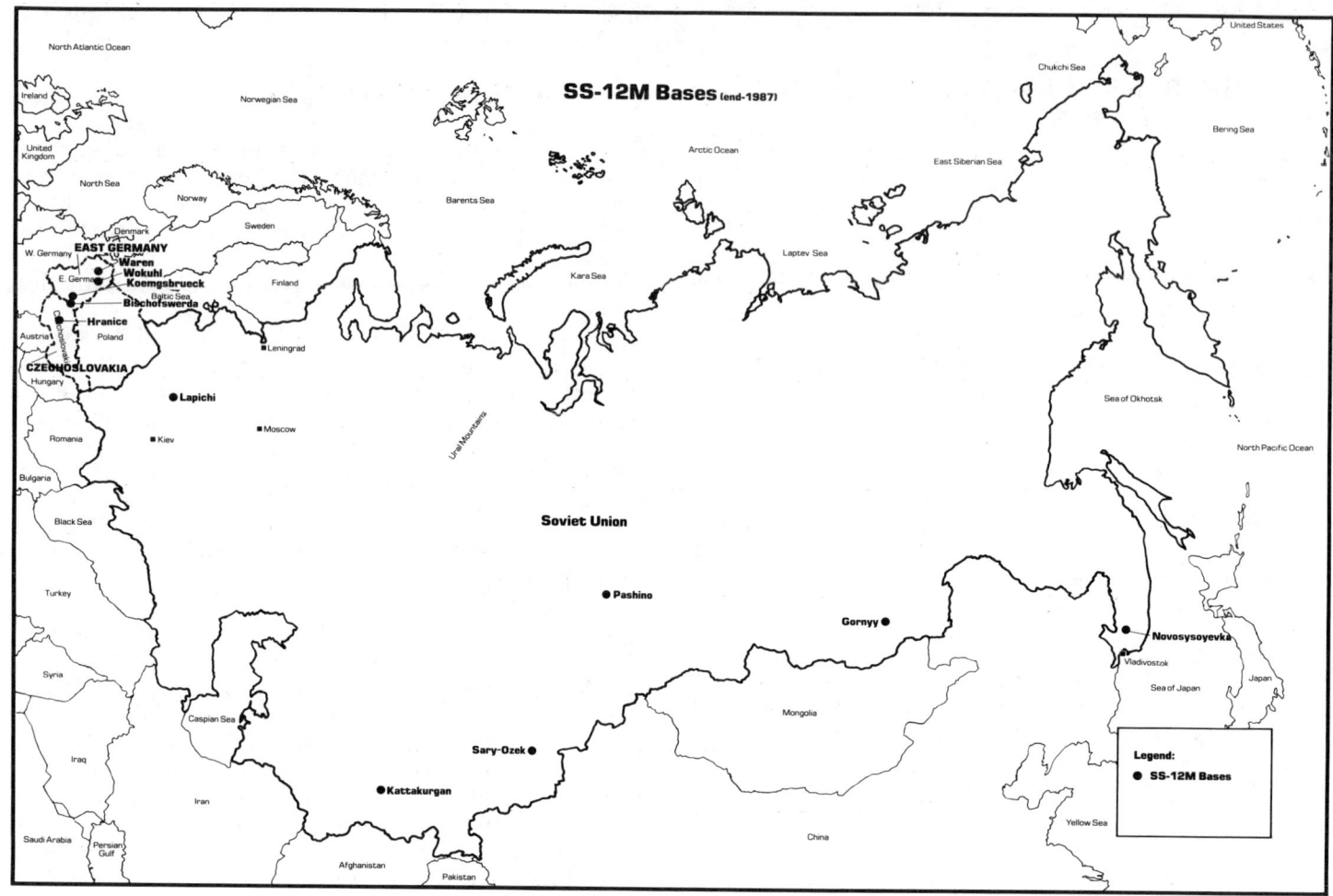

Figure 7.3 SS-12M Bases (end-1987).

mile) range missile is a guided weapon with accuracy, reaction time and refire and retargeting capability significantly enhanced over the FROG-7. It is carried on a six-wheeled amphibious TEL and can be fired vertically, whereas the FROG-7 is fired at an angle. Thus the SS-21 missile need not be launched from open areas for larger than 45-degree angle firings.[62] Two warheads are reportedly available for the SS-21, with yields of about 10 and 100 kilotons each. Both the SS-21 and FROG-7 are reloadable, and three "ready-to-fire" missiles are thought to be carried by a resupply vehicle deployed with the launchers.[63]

The SS-21 was introduced into Eastern Europe during 1979 exercises and began replacing FROGs in 1981. All Category I divisions have now been upgraded to the SS-21, including all Soviet divisions in East Germany and Czechoslovakia and most divisions opposite Western Europe.

Nuclear Artillery

An expansion and modernization program for large-caliber artillery systems in Soviet Ground Forces has been evident since the mid-1970s.[64] Nine artillery pieces of three different tube sizes—152mm, 203mm, and 240mm—are now believed to be capable of firing nuclear projectiles. Five of the guns have been introduced since the mid-1970s. As of mid-1988, some 6700 nuclear-capable guns were deployed with an estimated 2000 nuclear artillery projectiles (see Chapter Two). The nuclear warhead yields are believed to range from sub-kiloton to 20 kilotons and possibly include an enhanced radiation (ER) capability.[65]

---

62 *Ibid.*, p. 1711.
63 DIA, *Soviet Front Fire Support*, p. 72.
64 There was a 30 percent increase in the numbers of artillery pieces (including multiple rocket launchers) deployed in Europe between 1978 and 1983 alone; Chris Bellamy, *Red God of War: Soviet Artillery and Rocket Forces* (London: Brassey's Defence Publishers, 1986), p. 4.
65 According to a report by Phillip A. Karber of BDM Corporation, the 2S3 152mm gun-how- itzer has a sub-kiloton warhead, the M-1976 and 2S5 152mm guns have 2-5 kiloton warheads, the M-1975 203mm gun has a 5-20 kiloton warhead, and the M-1975 240mm mortar probably has an enhanced radiation (ER) warhead; "Three Threats NATO's Not Addressing," *op. cit.*, p. 87. The United States believes that the Soviets have the capability to build an ER weapon; SASC, FY 1979 DOE, p. 41. The Soviets have discussed in their military literature the utility of ER-type weapons, and the United States believes that this understanding could have led them to develop ER warheads; see, SASC, FY 1980 DOE, p. 225.

7
Nuclear Artillery

Table 7.5
SS-12M Scaleboard B Missile Deployments (1987/1988)[1]

Deployment Areas	Type of Base	Launchers		Missiles	
		Dec 1987	June 1988	Dec 1987	June 1988
Soviet Union					
Gornyy	brigade	14	14	36	36
Kattakurgan	battalion	5	5	9	9
Lapichi	battalion	5	*	9	*
Novosysoyevka	brigade	14	14	37	40
Pashino	battalion	4	4	0	0
Saryozek	brigade	15	0	36	0
Czechoslovakia					
Hranice	2 brigades	24	*	39	*
East Germany					
Bischofswerda	battalion	5	*	8	*
Koenigsbrueck	brigade	11	*	19	*
Waren	brigade	12	*	22	*
Wokuhl	battalion	6	*	5	*

Non-deployed Facilities

	December 1987	June 1988
Balkhash	missile storage facility	missile storage facility
Berezovka	launcher storage	*
Bronnaya Gora	missile storage facility	missile storage facility
Kamenka	training base	*
Kazan'	training base	*
Ladushkin	missile storage facility	missile storage facility
Lozovaya	missile storage facility	missile storage facility
Saratov	training base	*
Saryozek	missile elimination facility	missile elimination facility
Stan'kovo	launcher elimination facility	launcher elimination facility

* Facility not listed in the INF Treaty: 1 June 1988, Data Update.

[1] As of 1 November 1987 as stated in the INF Treaty Memorandum of Understanding signed in December 1987, and as of 1 June 1988 as stated in the INF Treaty: 1 June 1988, Data Update.

Original Soviet interest in nuclear artillery grew out of a desire to have a counterweapon to the U.S. 280mm atomic cannon, which was first deployed to Europe in October 1952.[66] As Khrushchev stated in his memoirs:

> Our military people were able to get the government to give them funds to develop a nuclear cannon of our own. We used to haul it out for military parades on Red Square. It had an enormous barrel and always made a powerful impression, but we weren't very enthusiastic about it. The thing was terribly heavy and difficult to transport; it was hard to camouflage; its range was very short; it performed badly on the testing range and required a great expense and huge quantites of raw material to make one small warhead. In short, it was good for nothing.[67]

The cannon referred to by Khrushchev was either the M-1957 310mm self-propelled gun or the M-1957 420mm self-propelled mortar, both of which were first seen in public in the 7 November 1957 parade in Moscow. An improved version of the M-1957 mortar, with extensive modifications to both the weapon and the vehicle, was displayed in the 1 May 1960 parade (and was designated the M-1960).[68] The M-1957 guns were deployed in limited numbers only for what was believed to be a short period of time.[69] The M-1960 was thought to

---

66 USAICS, *Communist Weapons and Equipment Handbook*, pp. 102, 104.
67 Nikita Khrushchev, *Khrushchev Remembers: The Last Testament*, translated and edited by Strobe Talbott (Boston: Little, Brown, 1974), p. 53.
68 USAREUR, *Identification Handbook*, pp. 397, 399, 401; USAICS, *Communist Weapons and Equipment Handbook*, pp. 102, 104.
69 DIA, *Artillery Trends and Scientific and Technical Projections*, DST-1130S-027-80, 30 September 1980, p. 205.

7

Nuclear Artillery

Figure 7.4 SS-23 Bases (end-1987).

be retired in the mid-1960s, replaced by the FROG series of rockets.

The M-240 towed 240mm heavy mortar made its first public appearance in 1955.[70] About 150 M-240 guns were produced and assigned to heavy artillery brigades at the front level; they were never deployed outside the Soviet Union.[71] The M-240 was the last of the super-heavy Soviet guns to be deployed, and attention was shifted instead to mostly smaller caliber 122mm, 130mm, and 152mm guns.

The most significant development in nuclear-capable artillery occurred in the early 1970s, when a new generation of self-propelled 122mm and 152mm artillery guns appeared. These two guns were to replace the standard D-30 122mm and D-20 152mm towed howitzers in Soviet divisions. The 2S3 (M-1973) 152mm SP howitzer (nicknamed *acacia* in Russian) is basically a copy of the U.S. M-109 155mm howitzer, but is larger. It was introduced in large numbers starting about 1978[72] and has been assigned to motorized rifle and tank divisions. (The 2S3 is nuclear-capable.)[73] In 1976, a new towed 152mm gun—the M-1976—was deployed, and began replacing the M-46 130mm gun. In 1981, a self-propelled version of the M-1976—designated 2S5 (M-1981)—was deployed. These two guns have larger barrels than the earlier 2S3 and longer ranges.[74] The 2S5 and its towed counterpart are army- and front-level weapons, as opposed to division weapons.

In 1975, a new 240mm self-propelled mortar—the 2S4 (M-1975)—and a new 203mm (8-inch) self-propelled gun—the 2S7 (M-1975)—were introduced. These were the first new large-caliber Soviet guns of any significance to be deployed since the 1950s. Although self-propelled, neither gun had an armored turret, but the armored carrier provided greater mobility and protection for the ammunition (and most of the crew) than earlier guns.[75] The 2S4 mortar tube, however, is mounted on the back of the chassis so that it can be swung down into firing position—a time-consuming task—and the gun is not thought to be any greater in range than the M-240.[76] The 2S7 has an extremely long gun barrel, enabling it to fire projectiles at least 30 kilometers without rocket assist.

U.S. intelligence analysts have long believed that larger caliber artillery guns, such as the M-1955 203mm towed gun-howitzer and the M-240 240mm towed heavy mortar, had a nuclear capability.[77] In the mid-1970s, the U.S. Department of Defense began to refer to "possibly artillery" in their discussion of Soviet theater nuclear forces.[78] In 1979, Secretary of Defense Harold Brown reported that "some of their artillery weapons are capable of delivering nuclear projectiles."[79] A year later, Secretary of Defense Brown stated that "some of their 203mm and 240mm artillery pieces, now deployed only in the USSR, have been adapted to fire nuclear projectiles."[80]

In early 1982, the Soviet government appeared to acknowledge possession of modern nuclear-capable artillery,[81] and this is believed to include 152mm, 203mm, and 240mm artillery systems.[82] Some reports in the early 1980s indicated that the older 152mm guns were not nuclear-capable.[83] As new 152mm artillery guns were deployed in Eastern Europe, *Soviet Military Power* stated that they "are nuclear capable and replace older pieces

---

70 It is unclear when it actually acquired a nuclear capability; USAICS, *Communist Weapons and Equipment Handbook*, p. 160; DIA, *Soviet Front Fire Support*, pp. 70-71, 97.
71 SMP 1984, p. 59; "Heavy Mortars and Howitzers," *Jane's Defence Weekly*, 15 September 1984, pp. 460-461.
72 See Bellamy, op. cit., pp. 142ff.
73 SMP 1988, p. 75.
74 Bellamy, op. cit., pp. 146-147.
75 Ibid., op. cit., p. 143.
76 Ibid., op. cit., pp. 144-146.
77 See, for example, SMP 1981, p. 31; USA, *Understanding Soviet Military Developments*, pp. 31, 71-72, 74; USA, *Handbook on Soviet Ground Forces*, p. 6-43; USAICS, *Communist Weapons and Equipment Handbook*, p. 56; U.S. Army Command and General Staff College, *Soviet Artillery Doctrine*, Reference Book 30-3, 19 May 1976, pp. A-2, A-6. The new self-propelled 203mm and 240mm pieces have also been described as *now* having a nuclear capability, possibly implying that earlier versions did not; HASC, FY 1984 DOD, Part 3, p. 1036.
78 JCS, FY 1975, p. 79; DOD, FY 1977 RDTE, p. IV-102.
79 DOD, FY 1980 Annual Report, p. 83.
80 DOD, FY 1981 Annual Report, p. 92.
81 USSR Ministry of Defense, *Whence the Threat to Peace* (Moscow: Military Publishing House, 1982), p. 8, makes reference to, but does not refute, the statement in SMP 1981, p. 28, about nuclear-capable 203mm and 240mm.
82 DIA, *Soviet Self-Propelled Artillery*, DDI-1130-6-76, May 1976, p. 9.
83 HASC, FY 1984 DOD, Part 3, p. 1037.

7
Nuclear Artillery

Table 7.6
SS-23 Spider Missile Deployments (1987/1988)[1]

Deployment Areas	Type of Base	Launchers		Missiles	
		Dec 1987	June 1988	Dec 1987	June 1988
Soviet Union					
Bayram-Ali	brigade	12	12	0	0
Slobudka	brigade	12	12	26	26
Stan'kovo	brigade	18	0	40	0
Tsel'	brigade	12	12	26	26
Semipalatinsk	brigade	12	12	22	22
East Germany					
Jena-Forst	brigade	12	12	47	47
Weissenfels	brigade	4	4	6	6

Non-deployed Facilities		
	December 1987	June 1988
Berezovka	launcher storage facility	*
Ladushkin	missile storage facility	missile storage facility
Kamenka	training facility	*
Kazan'	training facility	*
Saratov	training facility	*
Saryozek	missile elimination facility	missile elimination facility
Stan'kovo	launcher elimination facility	launcher elimination facility

* Facility not listed in the INF Treaty: 1 June 1988, Data Update.

1 As of 1 November 1987 as stated in the INF Treaty Memorandum of Understanding signed in December 1987, and as of 1 June 1988 as stated in the INF Treaty: 1 June 1988, Data Update.

which were not nuclear capable."[84] Nonetheless, there now seems to be unanimity in the intelligence community that the newer 2S3 (M-1973) and 2S5 (M-1981) self-propelled howitzers, as well as the M-1976 towed 152mm howitzer, are nuclear-capable.[85]

One Soviet artillery expert cautions, however, against believing that the proliferation of weapons of these calibers means that there has been a significant increase in nuclear artillery:

> The new 152mm and 203mm guns and the 240mm mortar can all fire nuclear rounds. However, the Soviets have always shown less interest than the West in atomic tube artillery, preferring rockets to deliver weapons of mass destruction. The limited range of the mortar in particular, casts doubts on whether firing nuclear rounds is one of the prime roles . . . .
> There is a tendency in Western circles to stress the nuclear capabilities of Soviet tube artillery in order to make a political point . . . . [T]he Soviets do not envisage deploying nuclear artillery as a mirror image of NATO practice. Tactical rockets, also under the command of the Soviet Ground Forces' Artillery and Rocket Troops, remain the principal means of delivering nuclear weapons, and the main significance of tube artillery and multiple rocket launchers remains their ability to deliver conventional and chemical ordnance.[86]

Currently, at least six nuclear-capable artillery guns are thought to be in production: the M-1976 towed 152mm gun, the 2S3 (M-1973) self-propelled 152mm gun/howitzer, the 2S5 (M-1981) self-propelled 152mm gun, the 2S7 (M-1975) 203mm gun, the M-1980? 203mm howitzer, and the 2S4 (M-1975) 240mm mortar.[87] Towed artillery and mortar systems continue to be replaced by self-propelled systems.[88] Production of self-propelled guns was reported in early 1988 to be at "an all-time high."[89] When the new guns are fully deployed, the DIA believes that the total number of nuclear capable artillery tubes will exceed 10,000.[90]

---

84 SMP 1983, p. 40.
85 SMP 1985, pp. 68, 80; SMP 1984, p. 59; SASC, FY 1984 DOD, Part 5, p. 2410. The Joint Chiefs of Staff now consider the older 152mm guns to be nuclear-capable as well; JCS, FY 1986, p. 40; JCS, FY 1985, p. 38. See also, DIA, *Soviet Self-Propelled Artillery, op. cit.*, p. 9; HASC, FY 1984 DOD, Part 3, pp. 1036-1037, 2379; *NATO and the Warsaw Pact*, 1984, p. 40; DIA, *Soviet Front Fire Support*, p. 72; SASC, Strategic Force Modernization Program, 1981, p. 13.
86 Bellamy, *op. cit.*, pp. 148-149, 171.
87 New deployments of the 2S4 M-1975 240mm mortar reportedly ended in 1984; DOD, FY 1986 Annual Report, p. 40. But SMP 1987, p. 41, states that they "are being added to the inventory."
88 SMP 1988, p. 68.
89 *Ibid.*, p. 38.
90 SMP 1987, p. 41; SMP 1986, p. 39.

7

Nuclear Artillery

Since the mid-1970s, there have been a number of notable changes in artillery force structure relating to nuclear-capability:[91]

- Artillery battalions in divisions are being expanded from 18 to 24 guns each, and non-divisional units are being expanded from six to eight guns per battery. A typical motorized rifle division has 72 nuclear-capable 152mm guns, compared with 18 in the early 1970s.
- Artillery batteries in motorized rifle regiments have been upgraded to battalions.
- Army-level artillery regiments are being expanded to brigade size with the addition of a fourth battalion.
- New 2S5, 2S7, and 2S4 guns are replacing older towed models in front and army artillery divisions and brigades.[92]
- New 152mm self-propelled (both the 2S3 and 2S5) and towed guns (M-1976) were first deployed to Eastern Europe in 1982,[93] followed by 203mm and 240mm guns.[94]
- New artillery units have been formed, including new artillery divisions[95] and separate heavy artillery brigades.[96]

Atomic Demolition Munitions

The Soviet Union may have developed and deployed atomic demolition munitions (ADMs) in the 1970s, though precise information on Soviet capabilities is unavailable. Partially released U.S. intelligence documents discuss Soviet ADMs. One partially declassified document refers to photographs (which were not released) of a candidate system and an emplaced ADM.[97]

---

[91] SMP 1988, p. 75; Captain John Gordon IV, "The Evolution of Soviet Fire Support, 1940-1988," *Field Artillery*, June 1988, pp. 18-21.
[92] SMP 1988, p. 75.
[93] HASC, FY 1984 DOD, Part 3, pp. 1037; *NATO and the Warsaw Pact*, 1984, p. 42.
[94] The 203mm and 240mm artillery pieces were not deployed outside the Soviet Union as of 1980; DOD, FY 1981 *Annual Report*, p. 92. Initial deployments to the Group Soviet Forces, Germany occurred in 1981; *Jane's Defence Review*, Vol. 2, No. 5, 1981, p. 390.
[95] SMP 1986, p. 66.
[96] UK Ministry of Defence, *Statement on the Defence Estimates*, 1984, p. 42.
[97] DIA, *A Guide to Foreign Nuclear Weapon Systems Under the Control of Ground Force Commanders*, DST-1040S-541-83-Chg. 1, 17 August 1984, (partially declassified and released under the FOIA), p xiii, 73. See also System Planning Corporation, *A Comparison of U.S. and Soviet Tactical Nuclear Weapon Systems*, SPC Report 245, prepared for the Assistant Director, Net Technical Assessment, DOD, Office of the Director of Defense Research and Engineering, January 1976. The discussions in both documents and the photographs in the DIA document have not been publicly released. The photographs may be of a U.S. weapon. The Joint Chiefs of Staff have also reported that the Soviets may have ADMs; JCS, FY 1975, p. 79.

Nuclear-Capable Artillery

	M-1955 (D-20)	M-1976	2S3 (M-1973)	2S5 (M-1981)
Type	Towed Howitzer	Long-range Towed Gun	SP Gun— Howitzer with Turret	SP Long-range Gun without Turret
Speed:	—	—	50 km/h	50 km/h
Weight of gun:	5720 kg	unknown	30 MT	30 MT
Crew:	7-10	unknown	4-5	unknown
Maximum range:	17.2-18.4 km	~30 km	17.2; 27 km with RAP	~30 km
Rate of fire:	4-5/min	4-5/min	4-5/min	unknown
Weight of HE projectile:	40.8 kg	unknown	unknown	unknown
Dual-capable:	possibly	yes	probably	yes
IOC:	1955	1976-1983	1973-1978	1981
Deployment:	unknown	Soviet Union; Eastern Europe	Soviet Union; Eastern Europe	Soviet Union; Eastern Europe

Note: The D-1 (M-1943) towed howitzer, introduced in 1943, is not nuclear-capable.

Sources: DIA, *Force Structure Summary*, November 1987, p. 15; *SMP* 1987, pp. 41, 64, 72; *SMP* 1986, p. 64; *SMP* 1985, p. 68; *SMP* 1984, p. 59; *SMP* 1983, p. 40; JCS, FY 1985, p. 38; JCS, FY 1983, p. 111; SASC, FY 1984 DOD, Part 5, p. 2410; USA *Understanding Soviet Military Developments*, p. 71; USAICS, *Handbook on Soviet Ground Forces*, p. 231; HASC, FY 1984 DOD, Part 3, p. 817; JEC, *Allocation of Resources*, 1977, p. 71; USA, *Handbook on Soviet Ground Forces*, p. 6-43; USA, *Organization and Equipment of the Soviet Army*, p. 4-2; USAICS, *Communist Weapons and Equipment Handbook*, p. 54, 55; DIA, *Warsaw Pact Ground Forces Equipment Identification Guide*, pp. 50, 54, 58; U.S. Army Command and General Staff College, *Soviet Artillery Doctrine*, RB 30-3, 19 May 1976, p. A-5; USAREUR, *Identification Handbook*, pp. 177, 181; *NATO and the Warsaw Pact*, 1984, p. 42.

Figure 7.5 152mm Nuclear-Capable Artillery.

Figure 7.6 The **D20 152mm** towed howitzer as used by Ground Forces in the field—one of nine artillery pieces with three different tube sizes—now believed to be nuclear-capable.

Figure 7.7 The **2S3 (M-1973) 152mm** self-propelled gun/howitzer (now thought to be nuclear-capable) was assigned to motorized rifle and tank divisions in the early 1970s. Production of self-propelled guns was reported in early 1988 to be at an "all-time high."

7
Nuclear-Capable Artillery

Figure 7.8 The large barrel, long-range, nuclear-capable **2S5 (M-1981) 152mm** was introduced in 1981 as a self-propelled gun/howitzer deployed at army and front levels. Shown here on rail-transport, artillery force structure has been rapidly expanding; for example, from 18 nuclear-capable 152mm guns in the early 1970s to 72 per typical motorized rifle division in the 1980s.

	M-1955 (M55)	2S7 (M-1975)	(M-1980?)
	not available	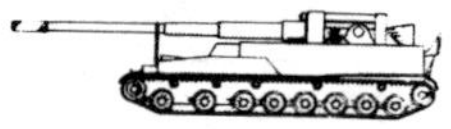	not available
Type	Towed Gun—Howitzer	Long-barreled SP Gun with Turret	SP Howitzer
Speed:	unknown	unknown	unknown
Weight of gun: (firing position)	20,400 kg	unknown	unknown
Crew:	unknown	unknown	unknown
Maximum range:	29.2 km	at least 30 km	21.3; 30 km with RAP
Rate of fire:	0.5/min	unknown	unknown
Weight of HE projectile:	unknown	102 kg	102 kg
Dual-capable:	possibly	yes	yes
IOC:	1955	1975–1977	1980
Deployment:	in small numbers in Soviet Union only	150–200 (1988); Soviet Union; Eastern Europe	small numbers only; Soviet Union; Eastern Europe

Sources: *SMP* 1987, pp. 41, 63, 72; *SMP* 1986, p. 64; *SMP* 1985, p. 68; *SMP* 1984, p. 59; *SMP* 1981, p. 31; UK *Ministry of Defense Statement of Defence Estimates*, 1984, p. 42; HASC, FY 1984 DOD, Part 3, p. 817; DOD, FY 1986 *Annual Report*, p. 16; DIA, *Warsaw Pact Ground Equipment Handbook*, pp. 56-57; USAREAUR, *Identification Handbook*, p. 189; "Heavy Mortars and Howitzers," *Jane's Defence Weekly*, 15 September 1984, p. 460.

Figure 7.9 203mm Nuclear-Capable Artillery.

7
Nuclear-Capable Artillery

Type	M-240 (M-1952?) (M-1953?)	2S4 (M-1975)
	not available	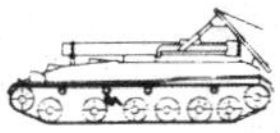
	Towed Smoothbore Mortar	SP Mortar without Turret
Speed:	—	unknown
Weight of gun: (firing position)	3610 kg	unknown
Crew:	8–9	unknown
Maximum range:	9.7 km	9.7 km
Rate of fire:	1/min	1/min
Weight of HE projectile:	100 kg	100 kg
Dual-capable:	yes; probably has been dropped	yes
IOC:	1955	1975–1976
Deployment:	in small numbers in Soviet Union only	260 (1988); Soviet Union; Eastern Europe

Sources: DIA, Force Structure Summary, November 1987, p. 15; SMP 1987, pp. 41, 72; SMP 1986, p.64; SMP 1985, p. 68; SMP 1984, p. 59; USA, Understanding Soviet Military Developments, 74; DIA, Warsaw Pact Ground Forces Equipment Identification Guide, p. 12; USAICS, Communist Weapons and Equipment Handbook, pp. 160-161; USAREUR, Identification Handbook, p. 137, DIA Handbook on the Soviet Armed Forces, p. 8-22; HASC, FY 1984 DOD, Part 3, p. 817; "Heavy Mortars and Howitzers," Jane's Defence Weekly, 15 September 1984, pp. 460-461.

Figure 7.10 240mm Nuclear-Capable Artillery.

Figure 7.11 The **2S7 (M1975)** nuclear-capable, self-propelled, eight-inch (203mm) gun has an extremely long barrel, enabling it to fire projectiles at least 30 kilometers without rocket assist.

Figure 7.12 The **M-240 240mm** towed heavy mortar is thought to be nuclear-capable, but also the last of the super-heavy Soviet guns to be deployed.

Nuclear Weapons Databook, Volume IV **205**

7
GOLF II SSB

Ballistic Missile Submarine
GOLF II SSB

Figure 7.13 Aerial view of a **Golf II** class diesel-powered ballistic missile submarine, launch platform for the **SS-N-5 Sark**, a single-stage, liquid-fueled missile with a range of 750 nautical miles (1400 kilometers). The Golf II submarines are largely obsolete and are assigned to the Baltic Sea and Sea of Japan.

DESCRIPTION:	Diesel-powered ballistic missile submarine currently assigned theater missions	Speed:	
		Surface:	17 kts
		Submerged:	14 kts[9]
DESIGN BUREAU:	Komsomol'sk; Severodvinsk[1]	Crew:	80-85[10]
SPECIFICATIONS:		**NUCLEAR WEAPONS:**	
Length:	100 m[2] (328 ft)	Missile System:	3 SS-N-5 SLBMs aft of the sail[11]
Beam:	8.5 m[3] (27.9 ft)		
Draft:	6.4 m[4] (21 ft)	Torpedoes:	Six 21-inch (53.3 cm) (bow)[12]
Displacement:		**DEPLOYMENT:**	
Surface:	2300 tons[5]	Number Deployed:	12 (mid-1988)[13]
Submerged:	2800 tons[6]		
Propulsion:	Diesel-electric, 3 diesels, electric motor, 3 shafts;[7] for operations in the patrol mode, the centerline shaft can be driven by a creep motor giving quiet operation and long endurance[8]	Home port:	6 in Baltic Fleet, 6 in Pacific Fleet[14]

---

1. Polmar, *Guide to the Soviet Navy*, 1986, p. 125.
2. USN, *Soviet Naval Developments* (Rev. 4/85), p. 94. Waterline length is 97 m (318.2 ft); DIA, JIIKS, Vol. XIII, 1983.
3. DIA, *ASW Handbook*, 1977, p. 6-47; DIA, JIIKS, Vol. XIII, 1983.
4. DIA, *ASW Handbook*, 1977, p. 6-47.
5. USN, *Soviet Naval Developments* (Rev. 4/85), p. 94; DIA, JIIKS, Vol. XIII, 1983.
6. DIA, JIIKS, Vol. XIII, 1983.
7. Ibid.
8. DIA, *ASW Handbook*, 1977, pp. 6-46, 6-47.
9. DIA, JIIKS, Vol. XIII, 1983.
10. Couhat, *Combat Fleets of the World*, 1988/89, p. 584; Polmar, *Guide to the Soviet Navy*, 1986, p. 125.
11. SMP 1984, p. 53; USN, *Soviet Naval Developments* (Rev. 4/85), p. 94; DIA, JIIKS, Vol. XIII, 1983.
12. DIA, JIIKS, Vol. XIII, 1983.
13. SMP 1988, p. 53. A single Golf II was retired from the Baltic Fleet in 1987. See also, USN, *Soviet Naval Developments* (Rev. 4/85), p. 94; DIA, JIIKS, Vol. XIII, 1983. The submarines are continuing to be retired; Collins and Victory, *U.S./Soviet Military Balance*, 1988, p. 15, show nine as of 1 January 1988.
14. SMP 1988, p. 53; SMP 1987, p. 17; DIA, *Unclassified Communist Naval Orders of Battle*, DDB-1200-124-84, April 1986, p. 1.

GOLF II SSB

Figure 7.14 Golf II class SSB (front view) - Twelve are currently (mid-1988) deployed in the Baltic Sea and the Sea of Japan where they have regional targeting missions.

HISTORY:
IOC: 1965[15]

COMMENTS: 23 Golf Is were built from 1958 to 1962, 13 of these were modified to Golf II starting in 1965.[16] 13 Golf II submarines were included in SALT II accountability, but not the 39 SS-N-5 missiles they carry.[17]

While the submarines have gone on patrol in the Baltic Sea and the Sea of Japan,[18] at least in the Baltic "they do not, in order not to cause concern in the Nordic countries, perform armed patrols with nuclear weapons on board."[19]

---

15 DOD, FY 1986 Annual Report, p. 49, from chart.
16 DIA, JIIKS, Vol. XIII, 1983.
17 IISS, Military Balance, 1987-1988, p. 33.
18 USN, Soviet Naval Developments (Rev. 4/85), p. 94. See also, DIA, ASW Handbook, 1977, pp. 6-46, 6-47.
19 Soviet General Gelij Batenin, quoted in Igor Pavlov, "Soviet Baltic-Missiles Not Removed," (Novosti) (translation from Danish), Pressebureauet APN, 31 December 1987.

7
SS-N-5 SARK

Naval Non-strategic Missiles
SS-N-5 SARK

DESCRIPTION:	Second-generation, single-warhead, liquid-fuel SLBM	**DEPLOYMENT:** Launch Platform:	12 Golf IIs[13]
DESIGN BUREAU:	Yangel[1]	Number Deployed:	36 (mid-1988)[14]
SPECIFICATIONS:		**HISTORY:**	
Length:	12.9 m[2] (42.3 ft); 10.7 m[3] (35.1 ft)	Design Began:	1952[15]
Diameter:	1.2-1.5 m[4] (3.9 ft-4.9 ft)	R&D:	1952-1958[16]
Stages:	1[5]	Engineering and Testing:	1958-1963[17]
Weight at Launch:	approx. 16,500 kg[6] (36,400 lbs)	First Flight Test:	1962[18]
Fuel/Propulsion:	liquid[7]	Year Operation Began:	1963[19]
Guidance:	inertial[8]	**TARGETING:**	
Throwweight:	approx. 1000 kg[9] (2200 lbs)	Types:	area targets
Range:	1400 km[10] (750 nm; 870 mi)	Accuracy/CEP:	1-2 nm[20] (2-4 km; 6000-12,000 ft)
DUAL CAPABLE:	no	**COMMENTS:**	The SS-N-5 may have been originally intended for Echo class submarines and retrofitted to Golf IIs and Hotel IIs in place of the SS-N-4 Sark.[21]
NUCLEAR WARHEADS:			
Number of warheads:	1[11]		
Yield per warhead:	1-2 Mt[12]		

---

1. Berman and Baker, *Soviet Strategic Forces*, pp. 106-107.
2. SMP 1983, p. 22, from chart; *Jane's Weapon Systems*, 1987-88, p. 12; Polmar, *Guide to the Soviet Navy*, 1986, p. 433; John Jordan, "Soviet Ballistic Missile Submarines" *Jane's Defence Weekly: Part I*, 21 January 1984, p. 88; Part 3, 11 February 1984, pp. 203-204.
3. Jordan, *op. cit.*, Part I, p. 88; Jordon, *op. cit.*, Part 3, 11 February 1984, pp. 203-204; General Dynamics, *World's Missile Systems*, 1982, p. 245; Taylor, *Missiles of the World*, 1980, p. 109.
4. Polmar, *Guide to the Soviet Navy*, 1986, p. 433; Jordan, op. cit., Part I, p. 88; Jordon, *op. cit.*, Part 3, 11 February 1984, pp. 203-204; General Dynamics, *World's Missile Systems*, 1982, p. 245; Taylor, *Missiles of the World*, 1980, p. 109; *Jane's Weapon Systems*, 1987-88, pp. 12-13.
5. SMP 1981, p. 59, indicates that the SS-N-8 was the first two-stage Soviet SLBM. See also p. 58.
6. Polmar, *Guide to the Soviet Navy*, 1986, p. 433; General Dynamics, *The World's Missile Systems*, 1982, p. 245; *Jane's Weapon Systems*, 1987-88, p. 12.
7. Berman and Baker, *Soviet Strategic Forces*, pp. 106-107; Collins and Victory, *U.S./Soviet Military Balance*, 1987, p. 22.
8. Berman and Baker, *Soviet Strategic Forces*, pp. 106-107.
9. Rich and Pike, *SALT*, 1984, pp. 104-105.
10. SMP 1983, p. 22.
11. Ibid.
12. USAF, *Summary Review*, 1975, p. C-1. *Jane's Weapon Systems*, 1987-88, p. 12; Polmar, *Guide to the Soviet Navy*, 1986, p. 433; Couhat, *Combat Fleets of the World*, 1988/89, p. 563; and Rich and Pike, *SALT*, 1984, pp. 104-105, report the yield of the SS-N-5 as 0.8 Mt. *Aviation Week & Space Technology*, 14 March 1983, p. 153; IISS, *Military Balance*, 1987-1988, p. 206; and General Dynamics, *World's Missile Systems*, 1982, p. 245 report 1.0 Mt. Collins and Victory, *U.S./Soviet Military Balance*, 1988, p. 18, reports 1.0-2.0 Mt. Berman and Baker, *Soviet Strategic Forces*, pp. 106-107, reports 4.0 Mt.
13. SMP 1987, p. 17.
14. SMP 1988, p. 15. A single Golf II class submarine with three SS-N-5 was retired in 1987. The submarines are continuing to be retired; Collins and Victory, *U.S./Soviet Military Balance*, 1988, p. 15, reports 27 SLBMs (i.e. nine submarines) as of 1 January 1988.
15. SMP 1985, p. 40.
16. Ibid.
17. Ibid.
18. *Jane's Weapon Systems*, 1982-83, pp. 7-8.
19. SMP 1985, p. 40; USAF, *Summary Review*, 1975, p. 27.
20. USAF, *Summary Review*, 1975, p. 27.
21. *Jane's Weapon Systems*, 1982-83, pp. 7-8.

SS-20 SABER

Missile Systems
SS-20 SABER (Soviet designation RSD-10 Pioner)

Figure 7.15 The 54.10 ft (16.49 m) **SS-20 Saber** was first deployed in 1977. This static display photograph (without warhead section) was part of the official data exchange in the INF Treaty to facilitate verification.

DESCRIPTION: Fourth-generation, mobile IRBM assigned to Strategic Rocket Forces; two or three modifications reportedly exist[1] (reportedly Mod 1, Mod 2, Mod 3); the SS-20 is to be eliminated under the INF Treaty

DESIGN BUREAU: A.D. Nadiraze, Biysk;[2] missile production at Votkinsk Machine Building Plant, Votkinsk (Udmurt ASSR), and launcher production at Barrikady Plant, Volgograd;[3] launcher repair at Bataysk

SPECIFICATIONS:
- Length: 16.49 m[4] (54.10 ft)
  - First Stage: 8.58 m (28.15 ft)
  - Second Stage: 4.60 m (15.09 ft)
- Diameter:
  - First Stage: 1.79 m[5] (5.87 ft)
  - Second Stage: 1.47 m (4.82 ft)
- Stages: 2
- Weight (missile in canister): 42,700 kg[6] (94,140 lbs)
  - First Stage: 26,630 kg (58,710 lbs)
  - Second Stage: 8,630 kg (19,030 lbs)
- Fuel: solid
- Guidance: inertial

Figure 7.16 The arrangement of three reentry vehicles of the **SS-20** is seen as part of the official data exchange in the INF Treaty. The U.S. government requested a picture of the "front end" of the missile in a subsequent data exchange in order to measure the size of the missile with its warheads. The SS-20 was the first Soviet non-strategic weapon armed with multiple warheads.

- Throughweight: unknown
- Range: 5000 km[7] (3100 mi); CIA reportedly estimates the range to be 2750 mi (4400 km) while DIA reportedly estimates 3100 mi (5000 km); range of possible single-warhead version (Mod 3) or reduced payload is reported as 7500 km[8]

DUAL CAPABLE: no

NUCLEAR WARHEADS:
- Number: 3 MIRV (Mod 2)[9]; so-called Mod 1 and 3 missiles are reported to have one warhead[10]

---

1. IISS, *Military Balance*, 1987-1988, p. 205; David Baker, "European Theatre Nuclear Weapons," *Jane's Defence Review*, Vol. 4, No. 4, 1983, pp. 317, 320.
2. Berman and Baker, *Soviet Strategic Forces*, pp. 102-103.
3. INF Treaty, Memorandum of Understanding, December 1987.
4. Ibid.
5. Ibid.
6. Ibid.
7. JCS, FY 1986, p. 35; SMP 1984, pp. 12, 50-52.
8. General Dynamics, *World's Missile Systems*, 1982, p. 287.
9. INF Treaty, Memorandum of Understanding. SASC, FY 1980 DOD, Part 6, p. 2786, reported a four-MIRV version of the SS-20.
10. SMP 1984, pp. 12, 50-52; IISS, *Military Balance*, 1987-1988, p. 205; Baker, op. cit., pp. 317 and 320.

7
SS-20 SABER

Figure 7.17 Canister housing for the **SS-20** missile seen on static display as part of the INF Treaty data exchange.

Figure 7.18 **SS-20** missile transport vehicle. SS-20s were located at 48 bases within the Soviet Union at the time of the INF Treaty signing.

Yield per Warhead:	250 Kt rather than 150 Kt;[11] selectable yield warheads on Mod 2 with yields reported as 75, 250, and 600 Kt; single-warhead Mod 1 reported at 1.5 Mt,[12] and Mod 3 at 50-75 Kt[13]

DEPLOYMENT:

Launch Platform:	TEL on 12-wheeled truck[14]
Location:	Soviet Union only: 29 deployed areas, 48 operating bases, 12 with storage sites; 270 missiles west of the Urals, 171 east of the Urals at full deployment (see Table 7.3)[15]
Number Deployed:	405 operational systems (end-1987/mid-1988); 650 missiles (405 deployed, 245 non-deployed); 42 inert training missiles; 527 launchers (405 deployed, 122 non-deployed)[16]
Reload Capability:	theoretically yes[17]

HISTORY:

Year Design Began:	1965-1968[18]
First Flight Test:	Fall 1974[19]
Site Preparation Begun:	1976[20]
IOC:	1977

---

11 Numerous sources continue to refer to a 150 Kt warhead. See Collins and Victory, *U.S./Soviet Military Balance*, 198, p. 40; IISS, *Military Balance*, 1987-1988, p. 205; Baker, *op. cit.*, pp. 317, 320.
12 IISS, *Military Balance*, 1987-1988, p. 205; Baker, *op. cit.*, pp. 317 and 320.
13 Baker, *op. cit.*, pp. 317, 320; General Dynamics, *World's Missile Systems*, 1982, p. 287.
14 INF Treaty, Memorandum of Understanding.
15 DOD, FY 1986 *Annual Report*, p. 16; SMP 1985, p. 37.
16 At full deployment, some 441 operational launchers were deployed (attained September 1985), up from approximately 250 in 1950; SMP 1988, p. 53.
17 "The Soviets have the capability to reload and refire SS-20;" *ibid.*; SMP 1981, pp. 26-27. See further discussion of reloads in Chapter Two.
18 Berman and Baker, *Soviet Strategic Forces*, pp. 102-103.
19 JCS, FY 1978, p. 85.
20 Raymond L. Garthoff, "The Soviet SS-20 Decision," *Survival*, May-June 1983, p. 113.

SS-20 Saber

Figure 7.19 SS-20 transporter-erector-launcher (TEL). Each SS-20 regiment consists of either two or three battalions of six to nine mobile launchers.

Production: 36 missiles in production up to late 1987[21]

TARGETING:

Types: nuclear weapons storage sites, airbases, C³ facilities

Accuracy/CEP: accuracy of newer missiles (probably with guidance system upgrades) has improved at presurveyed sites from 762 m (2500 ft) to 285 m (935 ft);[22] the accuracy is less from sites that are not presurveyed; a more accurate version of the SS-20 began testing in 1984[23]

Retargeting: reaction time (max.) is 1 hour plus;[24] reload time is several hours[25]

COMMENTS: The SS-20 is the lower two stages of the SS-X-16 and appeared as a backup application for the failed missile.[26] Some believe that the IRBM role was given to the first two stages of the SS-16 by design.[27] A follow-on missile has been reported to be under development.[28] SS-20 regiments consist of 6 or 9 launchers in 2 or 3 battalions with groups of 3-5 regiments

Figure 7.20 SS-20 launcher garage as seen as part of the data exchange in the INF Treaty.

at larger main operating bases. 5 or 6 trucks with reload missiles exist per regiment. One regiment is at a presurveyed firing site close to the command and control location for the main operating base at all times.

Reported DIA estimates of 95 percent launcher reliability, 97 percent in-flight reliability, and 97 percent warhead reliability, with an overall reliability of 89 percent.[29] Some 150 test launches of the SS-20 took place from 1974 to 1987.[30]

---

21 A. Gorokhov, "Reportage from Plants Named in the Treaty on Intermediate- and Shorter-range Missiles," *Pravda*, 27 January 1988, p. 3.
22 Jack Anderson, "War Game Gives a New Look at Soviet Missiles," *Washington Post*, 3 July 1984, p. C8; Berman and Baker, *Soviet Strategic Forces*, pp. 102-103; General Dynamics, *World's Missile Systems*, 1982, p. 287. IISS, *Military Balance*, 1987-1988, p. 205, and Baker, *op. cit.*, pp. 317, 320, report accuracy of Mod 2 to be 400 m.
23 SMP 1987, preface, p. 4.
24 SMP 1981, p. 27.
25 HASC, FY 1984 DOD, Part 5, p. 1287.
26 DOD, FY 1977 *Annual Report*, p. 102; JCS, FY 1978, p. 85.
27 Baker, *op. cit.*, pp. 317, 320.
28 SMP 1984, pp. 12, 50-52.
29 Anderson, *op. cit.*, p. C8.
30 Private communications with the authors.

7
SS-4 SANDAL

SS-4 SANDAL (Soviet designation R-12)

Figure 7.21 The **SS-4 Sandal** has a 2000 kilometer range, but the missile requires approximately eight hours preparation before it is ready to fire. This was the missile involved in the 1962 Cuban Missile Crisis.

Figure 7.22 The **SS-4** was the first Soviet missile to use liquid storable fuel (liquid nitric acid and kerosene). The size of this fuel truck indicates the amount of fuel stored for each 74.7 foot (22.77 meter) single-stage SS-4 missile.

DESCRIPTION: First-generation, fixed MRBM deployed at both soft and hard sites and assigned to Strategic Rocket Forces; the SS-4 was partially retired as the SS-20 was deployed, although withdrawals ended in 1985, presumably resuming again in 1987; the SS-4 is to be eliminated under the INF Treaty.

DESIGN BUREAU: Yangel[1]

SPECIFICATIONS:

Length:	22.77 m[2] (74.70 ft)
Diameter:	1.65 m[3] (65 in)
Stages:	1
Weight (empty):	3,350 kg[4] (7390 lbs)
(at launch):	27,000-28,000 kg[5] (60,000-62,000 lbs)

---

1 Berman and Baker, *Soviet Strategic Forces*, pp. 102-103.
2 INF Treaty, Memorandum of Understanding, December 1987.
3 Ibid.
4 Ibid.
5 Taylor, *Missiles of the World*, 1980, pp. 96-97; *Jane's Weapon Systems*, 1982-83, pp. 3-4; General Dynamics, *World's Missile Systems*, 1982, p. 205.

SS-4 SANDAL

Figure 7.23 SS-4 missile launcher as seen as part of the data exchange for the INF Treaty. SS-4s are maintained at fixed sites; 85 percent at aboveground soft sites, the remainder in semi-hardened launchers.

Fuel:	originally cryogenic LOX/kerosene; later storable liquid nitric acid and kerosene[6]
Propulsion:	RD-214 rocket engine (or close relative thereof), also used as a first stage for satellite launchers[7]
Speed:	6900 km/h (4300 mph)[8]
Guidance:	inertial guidance with jet vane steering;[9] missiles were converted from radio command guidance by 1962[10]
Throwweight:	1300-1400 kg (2800-3000 lbs)[11]
Range:	1770 km[12] (1100 mi); 2000 km[13] (1240 mi)
DUAL CAPABLE:	no[14]
NUCLEAR WARHEADS: Number:	1
Yield:	while most authors give 1 Mt,[15] yields from 500 Kt to 3 Mt have been cited[16]
DEPLOYMENT: Launch Platform:	fixed sites, both aboveground (soft) and protected (hard);[17] each site has at least 5 launchers[18]
Location:	13 operational bases in the western Soviet Union;[19] 79 launch stands; formerly deployed in central Asia[20] (see Table 7.4)
Number Deployed:	52 operational (April 1988);[21] 170 missiles (65 deployed, 105 non-deployed); 147 inert training missiles;[22] number has been reduced from 608 in 1964-1966, although 112 were deployed from late 1985 to 1987; 81 launchers (79 deployed, 2 non-deployed)
Reload Capability:	soft launchers reportedly have a refire capability;[23] hard sites have no reload capability

---

6 DIA, *Handbook on the Soviet Armed Forces*, p. 12-7; DOD, FY 1972 Annual Report (class.), Table 6; Berman and Baker, *Soviet Strategic Forces*, pp. 102-103.
7 Gunston, *Rockets & Missiles*, 1979, pp. 9, 50.
8 Taylor, *Missiles of the World*, 1980, pp. 96-97.
9 Berman and Baker, *Soviet Strategic Forces*, pp. 102-103; Gunston, *Rockets & Missiles*, 1979, pp. 9, 50; General Dynamics, *The World's Missile Systems*, 1982, p. 205.
10 Gunston, *Rockets & Missiles*, 1979, pp. 9, 50; General Dynamics, *The World's Missile Systems*, 1982, p. 205; *Jane's Weapon Systems*, 1982-83, pp. 3-4.
11 IISS, *Military Balance*, 1987-1988, p. 205; Gunston, *Rockets & Missiles*, 1979, pp. 9, 50.
12 DIA, *Handbook on the Soviet Armed Forces*, p. 12-7.
13 SMP 1983, p. 35; SMP 1981, p. 26; *NATO and the Warsaw Pact*, 1982, p. 49; JCS, FY 1986, p. 35; CIA, *Major Consequences of Certain U.S. Courses of Action in Cuba*, SNIE 11-19-62, 20 October 1962, p. 2.
14 Taylor, *Missiles of the World*, 1980, pp. 96-97. *Jane's Weapon Systems*, 1987-88, p. 6, incorrectly states that the SS-4 is dual-capable.
15 IISS, *Military Balance*, 1987-1988, p. 205; Collins and Victory, *U.S./Soviet Military Balance*, 1988, p. 40; *Jane's Weapon Systems*, 1987-88, p. 6; David Baker, "European Theater Nuclear Weapons," *Jane's Defence Review*, Vol. 4, No. 4, 1983, p. 319.
16 Berman and Baker, *Soviet Strategic Forces*, pp. 102-103; Meyer, "Soviet Theatre Nuclear Forces," Part II, p. 54.
17 *NATO and the Warsaw Pact*, 1982, p. 49; Berman and Baker, *Soviet Strategic Forces*, pp. 102-103.
18 INF Treaty, Memorandum of Understanding, December 1987; JCS, FY 1982, pp. 31-32; Berman and Baker, *Soviet Strategic Forces*, pp. 102-103.
19 SMP 1983, pp. 8, 36-37; SMP 1984, pp. 12, 51-52.
20 *Jane's Weapon Systems*, 1982-83, pp. 3-4.
21 SMP 1988, p. 15.
22 JCS, FY 1987, p. 31, and SMP 1987, p. 8, reported 112 SS-4 missiles deployed.
23 JCS, FY 1982, p. 102.

7

SS-4 SANDAL

Figure 7.24 The **SS-4** fixed launch platform—each site has at least five launchers.

HISTORY:

Year Design Began:	1949-1950[24]
Prototype:	1953-1955[25]
First Flight Test:	1957[26]

IOC:	1958[27]
Production:	some 2300 missiles produced[28]

TARGETING:

Types:	military targets are primarily nuclear storage sites, command and control installations, and airbases in Western Europe
Accuracy/CEP:	approx. 2300 m (7400 ft; 1.24 nm)

COMMENTS: The SS-4 was developed as a version of the SS-3 and was the first operational Soviet missile to use storable liquid fuel. It was the missile involved in the 1962 Cuban Missile Crisis. Prior to the INF Treaty, the missile was projected to be retired by 1990.[29] With an upper stage added, SS-4s without explosive warheads have been used to launch satellites from Plesetsk and Kapustin Yar.

---

24 Berman and Baker, *Soviet Strategic Forces*, pp. 102-103.
25 Meyer, "Soviet Theatre Nuclear Forces," Part II, p. 56.
26 Berman and Baker, *Soviet Strategic Forces*, pp. 102-103.
27 JCS, FY 1987, p. 31; DIA, *Handbook on the Soviet Armed Forces*, p. 12-7; and JCS, FY 1984, p. 41, give the IOC as 1959. JCS, FY 1983, p. 29, gives the IOC as 1960.
28 Private communications with authors.
29 JCS, FY 1987, p. 32.

SS-12M[1] SCALEBOARD B (Soviet designation OTR-22)

Figure 7.25 The **SS-12M Scaleboard B** missile, though capable of firing nuclear, conventional or chemical warheads, is thought to be intended primarily for nuclear missions. It has an 800 kilometer (500 mile) range and will be eliminated under the INF Treaty.

DESCRIPTION:	Mobile short- to medium-range ballistic missile deployed primarily at front level in the Ground Forces; the SS-12 Mod 1 was replaced by the SS-12M Scaleboard B; the SS-12 is to be eliminated under the INF Treaty
DESIGN BUREAU:	Missile production at Votkinsk Machine Building Plant, Votkinsk (Udmurt ASSR), and launcher production at Barrikady Plant, Volgograd

SPECIFICATIONS (SS-12M):

Length:	12.38 m[2] (40.62 ft);
First Stage:	4.38 m[3] (14.37 ft)
Second Stage:	5.37 m[4] (17.62 ft)
Diameter: First and Second Stages:	1.01 m[5] (3.31 ft)
Stages:	2[6]
Weight:	approx. 9700 kg[7] (21,000 lbs); without front section: 8800 kg[8] (19,400 lbs)
Fuel:	SS-12M: solid;[9] SS-12: reportedly storable liquid fuel[10]
Guidance:	inertial[11]
Throwweight:	unknown
Range:	maximum 900 km[12] (560 mi); 800 km effective range[13]
DUAL CAPABLE:	SS-12M: yes, nuclear-conventional- and chemical-capable;[14] SS-12: no[15]

NUCLEAR WARHEADS:

Number:	1
Yield:	SS-12M: 0.5 Mt[16] SS-12: 1.0 Mt[17]

---

1 The SS-12M Scaleboard B was formerly referred to as the SS-12 Mod 2 and the SS-22.
2 INF Treaty, Memorandum of Understanding, December 1987.
3 Ibid.
4 Ibid.
5 Ibid.
6 Ibid.
7 Ibid.
8 Collins and Victory, U.S./Soviet Military Balance, 1988, p. 40.
9 Ibid.
10 DOD, FY 1986 Annual Report, p. 16; Taylor, Missiles of the World, 1980, p. 125; Jane's Defence Weekly, 2 June 1984, p. 867; David Fairhall, "New Soviet N-Missile Targeted in W. Europe," Guardian, 27 January 1984; Baltimore Sun, 26 January 1984, p. 1; USAICS, Handbook on the Soviet Ground Forces, p. 232; Gunston, Rockets & Missiles, 1979, p. 27; General Dynamics, World's Missile Systems, 1982, p. 217.
11 USAICS, Handbook on the Soviet Ground Forces, p. 232.
12 DIA, Force Structure Summary, November 1987, p. 14. SS-12M "significantly improved the missile's accuracy while maintaining its 900 kilometer range"; SMP 1988, p. 54; SMP 1987, p. 41; USA, Understanding Soviet Military Developments, pp. 32, 69. DIA, Warsaw Pact Ground Force Equipment Identification Guide, p. 118, states "less than 1000 km."
13 USAICS, Handbook on the Soviet Ground Forces, p. 232; USA, Handbook on Soviet Ground Forces, pp. 5-23, 6-39.
14 SMP 1987, p. 74; HASC, FY 1984 DOD, Part 5, pp. 1280-1281.
15 DIA, Warsaw Pact Ground Forces Equipment Identification Guide, p. 118; USA, Understanding Soviet Military Developments, pp. 32, 69; USAICS, Handbook on the Soviet Ground Forces, p. 232.
16 IISS, Military Balance, 1987-1988, p. 206; Collins and Victory, U.S./Soviet Military Balance, 1988, p. 40.
17 USA, Understanding Soviet Military Developments, p. 69 states, "submegaton range," and USA, Handbook on Soviet Ground Forces, pp. 5-23, 6-39, states, "megaton range."

7

SS-12M SCALEBOARD B

Figure 7.26 The **SS-12** transport vehicle, as seen as part of the INF Treaty data exhange.

Figure 7.27 As of December 1987 when the INF Treaty was signed, there were 135 of these **SS-12** eight-wheeled mobile launchers, 220 deployed missiles and 506 non-deployed missiles. The ratio of missiles to launchers is five to one.

DEPLOYMENT:

Launch Platform: TEL on eight-wheeled MAZ-543P (SS-12) and MAZ-7310 (SS-12M) chassis[18]

Location: some six brigade and four battalion operational bases (see Table 7.5);[19] brigade of 12-18 launchers at Fronts;[20] two brigades deployed in East Germany and Czechoslovakia during 1984, the first permanent deployment of such missiles outside the Soviet Union;[21] initial deployment of SS-12s was concentrated in the Soviet Far East[22]

Number Deployed: 726 missiles (220 deployed, 506 non-deployed); 233 inert training missiles; 135 launchers (115 deployed, 20 non-deployed); 72 facing Europe, and 40 facing Far East; one battalion (4-6 launchers) opposite eastern Turkey, and one battalion (4-6 launchers) in strategic reserve[23]

Reload capability: SS-12M: no;[24] SS-12: yes; up to 60 minute reaction time at pre-surveyed sites; reload time varied; the refueling process was reported to take 15 minutes[25]

HISTORY:

First Seen: November 1967

IOC: SS-12M: 1979-1980;[26] 1984[27]

SS-12: 1969

---

18 Supplied by MAZ in Minsk; "Scaleboard: Victim of the INF Treaty," *Jane's Defence Weekly*, 20 February 1988, pp. 324-325.
19 SMP 1987, p. 41.
20 SMP 1988, p. 54; SMP 1987, p. 41.
21 SMP 1988, p. 54; SMP 1987, p. 41.
22 DOD, FY 1972 Annual Report (class.), Table 4.
23 SMP 1987, p. 41; SMP 1984, p. 53. The SS-12 Scaleboard was replaced by the SS-12M Scaleboard B.
24 JCS, FY 1988, p. 48.
25 DIA, *Warsaw Pact Ground Forces Equipment Identification Guide*, p. 118.
26 JCS, FY 1982, p. 103; SMP 1981, p. 28.
27 Collins and Victory, *U.S./Soviet Military Balance*, 1988, p. 40.

SS-12M SCALEBOARD B

Production: SS-12 was in production from about 1969 to at least 1977; the SS-12M was then placed in production[28]

TARGETING:
Accuracy/CEP: SS-12M: 300-370 m (1000-1200 ft)[29]

SS-12: 700-900 m (2300-3000 ft)[30]

COMMENTS: The original SS-12 was replaced by a new modification (designated SS-12M Scaleboard B), even though the new missile was originally designated SS-22, and then SS-12 Mod 2.[31] Associated with END TRAY radar.[32]

Figure 7.28 The **SS-12** missile erected "on location" at a field firing site. The SS-22 was deployed primarily at the front level in the Ground Forces, but will be eliminated under the INF Treaty.

---

28 General Dynamics, *World's Missile Systems*, 1982, p. 217.
29 Collins and Victory, *U.S./Soviet Military Balance*, 1988, p. 40; IISS, *Military Balance*, 1987-1988, p. 206.
30 IISS, *Military Balance*, 1983-1984, p. 119; Collins and Glakas, *U.S./Soviet Military Balance*, 1983, p. 36, reports 0.4 nm. Collins and Victory, *U.S./Soviet Military Balance*, 1988, p. 40 reports 0.25 nm.
31 SMP 1984, p. 53.
32 USAICS, *Handbook on the Soviet Ground Forces*, p. 232.

7 SS-23 SPIDER

SS-23 SPIDER (Soviet designation OTR-23)

Figure 7.29 SS-23 Spider mobile solid-fuel SSM was deployed by the Ground Forces at seven bases in the Soviet Union and Eastern Europe at the time of the signing of the INF Treaty.

DESCRIPTION: Mobile, battlefield, surface-to-surface ballistic missile being introduced at army/front level in the Soviet Army and replacing the SCUD missile; the SS-23 is to be eliminated under the INF Treaty

DESIGN BUREAU: Missile production at the Votkinsk Machine Building Plant, Votkinsk (Udmurt ASSR), and launcher production at the V. I. Lenin Petropavlovsk Heavy Machine Building Plant, Petropavlovsk

SPECIFICATIONS:
Length (with
Front Section): 7.52 m[1] (24.67 ft)
First Stage only: 4.56 m[2] (14.96 ft)

Diameter: 0.97 m[3] (3.18 ft)

Weight (without
Front Section): 3990 kg[4] (8800 lbs)

Fuel: solid[5]

Guidance: inertial

Range: 500 km[6] (300 mi)

DUAL CAPABLE: yes; nuclear-, chemical-, and conventional-capable[7]

NUCLEAR WARHEADS:
Number: 1[8]

Yield: 100 Kt[9]

DEPLOYMENT:
Launch Platform: eight-wheeled TEL[10]

Location: six brigades and one battalion at seven bases in the Soviet Union and Eastern Europe (see Table 7.6); first operational brigade (12-18 launchers) in Belorussian Military District (Western TVD)[11]

Number
Deployed: 239 missiles (167 deployed, 72 non-deployed); 64 inert training missiles; 102 launchers (82

---

1 INF Treaty, Memorandum of Understanding, December 1987.
2 INF Treaty: 1 June 1988, Data Update, p. 61.
3 INF Treaty, Memorandum of Understanding, December 1987.
4 Ibid.
5 No evidence of liquid fuel in INF Treaty Memorandum of Understanding, December 1987; Collins and Victory, *U.S./Soviet Military Balance*, 1988, p. 40.
6 DIA, *Force Structure Summary*, November 1987, p. 14; SMP 1987, p. 42; SMP 1985, p. 67.
7 SMP 1987, p. 74.
8 INF Treaty, Memorandum of Understanding, December 1987.
9 Collins and Victory, *U.S./Soviet Military Balance*, 1988, p. 40.
10 SMP 1985, p. 67; INF Treaty, Memorandum of Understanding, December 1987.
11 SMP 1987, p. 41.

SS-23 SPIDER

Figure 7.30 The **SS-23** missile transport vehicle.

Figure 7.31 INF Treaty data exchange revealed that as of December 1987 there were 102 of these eight-wheeled **SS-23** missile launchers, a higher number than had been previously estimated by U.S. sources.

	deployed, 20 non-deployed); approximately 36 launchers in two or three brigades;[12] deployed in "limited" numbers as of 1987[13]	Production:	some 250 SS-23 missiles were produced[17]
Reload capability:	probably with reduced reaction and refire times over SCUD	**TARGETING:** Accuracy/CEP:	"improved accuracy" over SCUD and similar to the SS-21;[18] 370 m (0.20 nm)[19]
HISTORY: Development:	prototype reported in 1974-1976[14]	COMMENTS:	Designed as the successor to the 1960s-vintage SCUD.[20]
IOC:	1985;[15] IOC is reported by various sources to be 1979-1982[16]		

---

12 JCS, FY 1988, p. 48.
13 SMP 1987, p. 74.
14 Meyer, "Soviet Theatre Nuclear Forces," Part II, p. 56.
15 SMP 1988, p. 55; SMP 1987, pp. 41, 74
16 IISS, *Military Balance, 1987-1988*, p. 206 reports 1979/80; Collins and Victory, *U.S./Soviet Military Balance, 1988*, p. 40; Meyer, "Soviet Theatre Nuclear Forces," Part II, p. 54.

17 Private communications with the authors.
18 SMP 1987, p. 64; SMP 1985, p. 67.
19 Collins and Victory, *U.S./Soviet Military Balance*, 1988, p. 40.
20 SMP 1987, p. 54.

7 SS-1 SCUD-B

SS-1c SCUD-B (Soviet designation T-7B)

Figure 7.32 The **SS-1c SCUD B** aboard its transporter on parade in Moscow. This nuclear-, chemical-, and conventional-capable mobile SSM is deployed at front and army levels in the Ground Forces in Eastern Europe and throughout the Soviet Union.

DESCRIPTION:	Mobile, battlefield, surface-to-surface ballistic missile deployed at front and army levels in the Ground Forces; "the ground force's primary nuclear fire support means"[1]
DESIGN BUREAU:	unknown
SPECIFICATIONS:	
Length:	11.50 m[2] (37.70 ft); 11.4 m[3] (37.40 ft)
Diameter:	90 cm (35 in);[4] 84 cm (33 in);[5]
Stages:	1
Weight:	approx. 6370 kg[6] (14,000 lbs)
Fuel:	storable liquid
Guidance:	inertial[7]
Throwweight:	unknown
Range:	280 km[8] (170 mi); 300 km[9] (190 mi)
DUAL CAPABLE:	yes; nuclear-, chemical-, and HE-capable[10]
NUCLEAR WARHEADS:	
Number:	1
Yield:	1-10 Kt
Weight:	770-860 kg[11] (1700-1900 lbs)
DEPLOYMENT:	
Launch Platform:	TEL in both wheeled and tracked versions; SCUD-A tracked vehicle (now obsolete) based on JS-3 tank; wheeled vehicle based on MAZ-543[12]

---

1 SMP 1988, p. 55.
2 DIA, *Warsaw Pact Ground Forces Equipment Identification Guide*, p. 114.
3 USA, *Organization and Equipment of the Soviet Army*, pp. 4-5.
4 DIA, *Warsaw Pact Ground Forces Equipment Identification Guide*, p. 114.
5 USA, *Organization and Equipment of the Soviet Army*, pp. 4-5.
6 *Ibid.*
7 USAICS, *Handbook on the Soviet Ground Forces*, p. 232.
8 *Ibid.*; USA, *Organization and Equipment of the Soviet Army*, pp. 4-5; USA, *Handbook on Soviet Ground Forces*, pp. 5-23, 6-39; USA, *Understanding Soviet Military Developments*, pp. 32, 69.
9 DIA, *Force Structure Summary*, November 1987, p. 14; SMP 1987, p. 41.
10 DIA, *Warsaw Pact Ground Forces Equipment Identification Guide*, p. 114; USA, *Understanding Soviet Military Developments*, pp. 32, 69; DIA, *Handbook on the Soviet Armed Forces*, p. 8-24; USA, *Organization and Equipment of the Soviet Army*, pp. 4-5; USA, *Handbook on Soviet Ground Forces*, pp. 5-23, 6-39.
11 USA, *Organization and Equipment of the Soviet Army*, pp. 4-5.
12 USA, *Understanding Soviet Military Developments*, pp. 32, 69; USAICS, *Handbook on the Soviet Ground Forces*, p. 232; USA, *Handbook on Soviet Ground Forces*, pp. 5-23, 6-39; DIA, *Handbook on the Soviet Armed Forces*, p. 8-24.

7
SS-1 SCUD-B

Figure 7.33 Top view of the eight-wheeled **SCUD B** transporter vehicle providing road mobility for this dual-capable missile and its 1-10 kiloton warhead.

Figure 7.34 SCUD B TEL, erected on site. Pre-launch preparation time is thought to be 2-4 hours.

Location:	Eastern Europe; throughout the Soviet Union
Number Deployed:	620 launchers (November 1987);[13] some 500 facing Europe, 100 facing Far East, 75 opposite eastern Turkey and southwest Asia, and 25 in the strategic reserve;[14] some 2500 missiles thought to be deployed; being replaced by SS-23
Reload Capacity:	yes; prelaunch preparation time is 2-4 hours; up to 60 minute reaction time after arrival at presurveyed sites[15]

HISTORY:

First Observed:	7 November 1957 (SCUD A)
	7 November 1965 (SCUD B)
IOC:	1965[16]
Retired:	SS-1b SCUD A retired by 1977
Production:	not in production (1986); circa 1965-1980

TARGETING:

Accuracy/CEP:	930 m (0.50 nm)[17]

---

13 DIA, *Force Structure Summary*, November 1987, p. 14; SMP 1988, p. 55; ACDA, "Nuclear Forces," Fact Sheet, 24 April 1987, in *NATO's Sixteen Nations*, June 1987 (p. 103), incorrectly reported over 725 launchers operational.
14 This distribution is roughly based on a 700 launcher force. SMP 1987, p. 41; SMP 1985, p. 38. IISS, *Military Balance*, 1982-1983, reported approximately 540 launchers: 450 facing Europe and 90 facing the Far East.
15 DIA, *Warsaw Pact Ground Forces Equipment Identification Guide*, p. 114; USA, *Handbook on Soviet Ground Forces*, p. 5-23.
16 Collins and Victory, *U.S./Soviet Military Balance*, 1988, p. 40.
17 *Ibid.*

7
SS-1 SCUD-B

COMMENTS: SCUD missile is based on German V-2. The SCUD-A was introduced in 1957 and was replaced by SCUD-B beginning in 1965. By 1977, all SCUD-As were retired. The SS-23 was scheduled to replace the SCUD missile. A SCUD-C with longer range and lower CEP has been referenced but was not deployed.

SCUD brigades exist at army and front levels and consist of three battalions with four or six launchers each and a reload capability.[18] The missile is also in service in Bulgaria, Czechoslovakia, East Germany, Egypt, Hungary, Iraq, Libya, Poland, Syria, and Romania.

---

18 SMP 1987, p. 41.

SS-21 SCARAB (Soviet name Tochka)

Figure 7.35 The **SS-21 Scarab** (Soviet name Tochka), a mobile, short-range, battlefield SSM, was photographed in Red Square in Moscow on 9 May 1985 on its TEL vehicle. This 14-120 kilometer (9-75 mile) range missile is a guided weapon with better accuracy, reaction time and refire/retargeting capability than the FROG-7, which it replaces.

DESCRIPTION:	Mobile, battlefield, surface-to-surface missile deployed at division level in Ground Forces, and replacing FROG missiles
DESIGN BUREAU:	unknown
SPECIFICATIONS:	
Length:	6.2 m[1] (20 ft)
Diameter:	65 cm[2] (26 in)
Stages:	1
Weight:	1.5 Mt[3]
Fuel:	solid[4]
Guidance:	unknown, probably inertial[5]
Throwweight:	250 kg[6]
Range:	minimum: 14 km (8.7 mi) maximum: 120 km[7] (75 mi)
DUAL CAPABLE:	yes; nuclear-, conventional- and chemical-capable[8]

---

1. "Scarab: An Exercise in Soviet Modernization," *Jane's Defence Weekly*, 11 July 1987, p. 51; *Jane's Weapon Systems*, 1982-1983, p. 40 (based on unconfirmed reports), reported 9.44 m (31 ft).
2. "Scarab: An Exercise in Soviet Modernization," *op. cit.*, p. 51; *Jane's Weapon Systems*, 1982-1983, p. 40 (based on unconfirmed reports), reported 46 cm (14.4 in).
3. "Scarab: An Exercise in Soviet Modernization," *op. cit.*, p. 51.
4. Collins and Victory, *U.S./Soviet Military Balance*, 1988, p. 40.
5. Chris Bellamy, *Red God of War: Soviet Artillery and Rocket Forces* (London: Brassey's Defense Publishers, 1986), p. 156.
6. "Scarab: An Exercise in Soviet Modernization," *op. cit.*, p. 51.
7. DIA, Force Structure Summary, November 1987, p. 14; *Ground International*, July 1980, p. 35. SMP 1987, p. 42, and SMP 1984, pp. 52-53, report 100 km.
8. SMP 1987, p. 74; HASC, FY 1984 DOD, Part 3, pp. 1280-1281, 1711; SMP 1981, p. 31.

7
SS-21 SCARAB

NUCLEAR WARHEADS:
- Number: 1
- Yield: two yield ranges, approx. 10 and 100 Kt

DEPLOYMENT:
- Launch Platform: six-wheeled, cross-country amphibious-capable Zil-375 TEL similar to the SA-8 SAM
- Location: so far deployed only opposite NATO;[9] the SS-21 has been deployed to Czechoslovakia and East Germany;[10] all Soviet divisions in Eastern Europe have been reequipped from FROG-7s to SS-21s;[11] "division-level SS-21 battalions are being consolidated into brigades in Soviet armies in East Germany"[12]
- Number Deployed: 140 launchers (April 1988);[13] 130 launchers (September 1987);[14] some 780 missiles are thought to be deployed. SS-21 is replacing FROG-7, reportedly at a rate of 4 launchers per month; SS-21 launchers (including non-Soviet Warsaw Pact) are deployed: 100 in Eastern Europe (Czechoslovakia and East Germany), the remainder almost all in the Western TVD[15]
- Reload Capacity: yes, presumably similar to FROG-7; the SS-21 is vertically launched, thus decreasing launch time in open areas[16]

Figure 7.36 The **SS-21** is carried on this six-wheeled, cross-country, amphibious TEL and can be fired vertically, thus decreasing launch time because it does not need as much set up area as the FROG missiles which it is replacing. Some 140 launchers and 780 missiles are thought to be deployed (April 1988).

HISTORY:
- Development: early 1970s
- First Seen: 9 May 1985 Victory Day Parade, Moscow
- IOC: 1976;[17] full deployment apparently did not begin until 1981[18]
- Production: 1975-present; production and deployment continues (1986)[19]

TARGETING:
- Accuracy/CEP: approx. 300 m (1000 ft);[20] more accurate than FROG-7[21]

COMMENTS: One tactical missile battalion (OTRB) with four launchers is deployed per tank and motorized rifle division. Four transporter/transloader vehicles are also assigned to the battalion.

---

9 SMP 1987, p. 74.
10 *Ibid.*; *Aviation Week & Space Technology*, 21 May 1984; *Jane's Defence Weekly*, 2 June 1984, p. 867; and Richard Burt, quoted in *Jane's Defence Weekly*, 7 April 1984, p. 507, following a NATO meeting.
11 "Scarab: An Exercise in Soviet Modernization," *op. cit.*, pp. 51-53.
12 SMP 1988, p. 55.
13 *Ibid.*
14 DIA, *Force Structure Summary*, November 1987, p. 14.
15 SMP 1987, p. 66.
16 HASC, FY 1984 DOD, Part 3, p. 1711.
17 JCS, FY 1982, p. 103; SMP 1981, p. 31; "Scarab: An Exercise in Soviet Modernization," *op. cit.*, pp. 51-53.
18 SMP 1981, p. 31; JCS, FY 1982, p. 103.
19 DOD, FY 1986, *Annual Report*, p. 16.
20 IISS, *Military Balance*, 1987-1988, p. 206; Collins and Victory, U.S./Soviet Military Balance, 1988, p. 40; Meyer, "Soviet Theater Nuclear Forces," Part II, p. 54.
21 SMP 1984, pp. 52-53; JCS, FY 1982, p. 103.

FROG-7 (Soviet designation R-70 Luna-M or T-5E)

Figure 7.37 The **FROG-7** (aboard its TEL) is an unguided, single-stage, short-range SSM deployed at division level in the Ground Forces. It is being replaced by the more accurate SS-21 Scarab.

DESCRIPTION:	Mobile, battlefield, surface-to-surface ballistic rocket (Free Rocket Over Ground) deployed at division level in the Ground Forces. Two modifications exist, the FROG-7 and FROG-7B[1]
DESIGN BUREAU:	unknown
SPECIFICATIONS:	
Length:	FROG-7: 9.00 m[2] (29.5 ft); FROG-7B: 9.50 m[3] (31.2 ft)
Diameter:	55 cm[4] (21.7 in); span is reportedly 1.8 m (5.9 ft);[5] warhead diameter same as rocket body[6]
Stages:	1
Weight:	2300-2500 kg[7] (5100-5500 lbs)
Fuel:	solid
Guidance:	spin stabilized unguided ballistic trajectory[8]
Throwweight:	unknown
Range:	minimum 12 km (7.5 mi); maximum 70 km[9] (43.5 mi)
DUAL CAPABLE:	yes; nuclear-, chemical- and HE-capable[10]
NUCLEAR WARHEADS:	
Number:	1
Yield:	3-200 Kt; 25 Kt class[11]
Weight:	450 kg[12] (990 lbs)

---

1 DIA, *Warsaw Pact Ground Forces Equipment Identification Guide*, p. 102.
2 Ibid., p. 102; USA, *Organization and Equipment of the Soviet Army*, pp. 4-5.
3 DIA, *Warsaw Pact Ground Forces Equipment Identification Guide*, pp. 97-102.
4 Ibid., p. 102; USA, *Organization and Equipment of the Soviet Army*, pp. 4-5.
5 General Dynamics, *World's Missile Systems*, 1982, p. 65.
6 DIA, *Warsaw Pact Ground Forces Equipment Identification Guide*, p. 97.
7 Ibid., p. 102; USA, *Organization and Equipment of the Soviet Army*, pp. 4-5.
8 Taylor, *Missiles of the World*, 1980, p. 36; *Jane's Weapon Systems*, 1982-1983, pp. 39-40; General Dynamics, *World's Missile Systems*, 1982, p. 65. USAICS, *Handbook on the Soviet Ground Forces*, p. 232 reports inertial guidance.
9 DIA, *Force Structure Summary*, November 1987, p. 14; SMP 1987, p. 42; SMP 1984, p. 52; DIA, *Warsaw Pact Ground Forces Equipment Identification Guide*, p. 102; USA, *Handbook on Soviet Ground Forces*, p. 5-23.
10 DIA, *Warsaw Pact Ground Forces Equipment Identification Guide*, p. 102; USAICS, *Handbook on the Soviet Ground Forces*, p. 232; DIA, *Handbook on the Soviet Armed Forces*, p. 8-24; USA, *Organization and Equipment of the Soviet Army*, pp. 4-5; USA, *Handbook on Soviet Ground Forces*, p. 5-23.
11 USA, *Handbook on Soviet Ground Forces*, p. 5-23.
12 USA, *Organization and Equipment of the Soviet Army*, pp. 4-5.

7
FROG-7

Figure 7.38 The **FROG-7** is carried and launched from an eight-wheeled TEL fired at an angle, with reported reload capability of one rocket every 20 minutes.

Figure 7.39 **FROG-7** being lifted onto its TEL.

DEPLOYMENT:
Launch Platform: eight-wheeled ZIL-135 TEL with on board crane for reloading (lack of amphibious capability)[13]

Location: throughout the Soviet Union, Eastern Europe, Mongolia, and Afghanistan in motorized rifle and tank divisions

Eastern European deployments include Czechoslovakia: 50 km west of Turnov, Zvolen, Turnov, 50 km north of Plzen, between Milovice and Pardubice; Hungary: 25 km northwest of Veszprem, 25 km southeast of Szekesfehervor, Kecskemet, 35 km west of Budapest; Poland: Borne, Swiebodzin

Number Deployed: about 660;[14] total FROG-7/SS-21 launcher inventory is approximately 900: about 500 FROG-7 and SS-21 launchers (140 SS-21, 370 FROG-7) opposite Europe; 215 FROGs in Far East, some 100 in southern Soviet Union opposite eastern Turkey and southwest Asia, and 75 in strategic reserve[15]

Reload Capability: yes; each FROG battalion of four launchers has reload vehicles that carry three rockets (all types);[16] 15-30 minute reaction time after arrival at presurveyed sites; reload capability reportedly one rocket every 20 minutes[17]

HISTORY:
First Seen: 7 November 1967

IOC: 1965;[18] late 1960s (FROG-7B)

Production: 1965-1972

TARGETING:
Accuracy/CEP: 500-700 m (1600-2300 ft)

COMMENTS:
The FROG-7 is currently being replaced by the SS-21. FROG missiles are also in service in Bulgaria, Czechoslovakia, Egypt, Hungary, Libya, Iraq, North Korea, Poland, Rumania, and Syria.[19]

---

13 DIA, *Soviet Front Fire Support*, p. 107; Gunston, *Rockets & Missiles*, p. 25; *Jane's Weapon Systems, 1982-1983*, pp. 39-40.
14 SMP 1988, p. 55.
15 SMP 1988, p. 41, 66.
16 DIA, *Warsaw Pact Ground Forces Equipment Identification Guide*, pp. 99 and 102.
17 Ibid., p. 102; USA, *Handbook on Soviet Ground Forces*, p. 5-23.
18 DIA, *Soviet Front Fire Support*, p. 107.
19 Taylor, *Missiles of the World*, 1980, p. 36; General Dynamics, *The World's Missile Systems*, 1982, p. 65.

8

Nuclear-Capable Aviation

Chapter Eight
Nuclear-Capable Aviation

Overview

The Soviet Air Forces and Navy have some 5800 aircraft of 15 types that are thought to be capable of delivering nuclear weapons.[1] These aircraft are classified into four major categories: strategic bombers assigned to Strategic Air Armies (SAAs); medium-range bombers and longer range fighters in the SAAs or Soviet Naval Aviation (SNA); tactical fighters assigned to the Air Forces of the Military Districts and Groups of Forces (AFMD/GOF), and to SNA; and anti-submarine maritime patrol aircraft assigned to SNA. The medium-range bombers constitute the predominant, non-strategic, nuclear-capable aircraft of the Soviet Union (strategic bombers are further discussed in Chapter Five).[2]

The nuclear-capable aircraft can deliver air-to-surface missiles and nuclear bombs (air-launched missiles are discussed in greater detail in Chapter Six). Some 700 nuclear-armed, air-launched missiles are estimated to be assigned to strategic bombers, some 1500 are assigned to non-strategic aircraft, and some 5200 gravity bombs are estimated to be available for aircraft delivery. Though little is known about the nuclear bomb stockpile, a 2000 pound nuclear bomb, with a yield of about 350 kilotons, is thought to be the standard weapon. In the early 1980s, this bomb was reportedly supplemented with a new, lighter weight, 250 kiloton bomb.[3]

History

The development of bombers by the Soviet Union began in the early 1930s. By 1940 the Soviets had the largest force of four-engine bombers in the world.[4] During World War II, however, Soviet bombing strikes behind enemy lines were rare and generally ineffective. This was partly due to significant reductions in the bomber force in 1940 and to priority emphasis being placed on air operations in close support of ground forces.[5] In 1944, three U.S. B-29 bombers were forced to land at Vladivostok (on 29 July, 20 August, and 21 November) after bombing missions over Japan. They were interned and copied by aircraft designer Andrei Tupolev.[6] The Soviet copy of the B-29, designated the Tu-4 Bull, began production in March 1945[7] and was first seen in the 3 August 1947 air show near Moscow.[8]

Although U.S. intelligence agencies assessed the Tu-4 as having the capability to deliver nuclear bombs immediately after the first Soviet atomic test in August 1949,[9] nuclear weapons did not become available for operational use until at least 1953. By then, one or two Tu-4

---

1 According to the U.S. Department of Defense, any aircraft that can carry weapons could be equipped for a nuclear role given the availability of nuclear weapons and pilots trained for nuclear weapons delivery; SASC, FY 1980 DOD, Part 3, p. 846. The aircraft counted and discussed here are those assessed to have a primary mission of nuclear delivery. Some fighters, interceptors, and reconnaissance and tanker aircraft could be converted for nuclear weapons delivery. For instance, according to NATO, the types of Soviet aircraft facing Europe that are technically capable of delivering nuclear weapons include all interceptor, reconnaissance, fighter-bombers/ground-attack aircraft, and bombers in both combat and non-combat units; *NATO and the Warsaw Pact*, 1984, pp. 10-11, and 1982, pp. 15, 17, 46. Additionally, non-Soviet Warsaw Pact countries have as many as 1060 aircraft that in theory could deliver nuclear weapons (figures attributed to DOD analyst Phillip A. Petersen, by Benjamin Schemmer, "U.S. Unveils Multi-Source Evidence of New Soviet Threats in German Forum," *Armed Forces Journal International*, August 1984, p. 52).
2 DIA, *Soviet Air Forces, Strategic Bombers*, 1981, p. 4.
3 Private communications with the authors.
4 USAF, *Summary Review*, 1975, p. D-1. Under chief designer Andrei N. Tupolev, the Central Institute for Aerodynamics and Hydrodynamics (TsAGI), turned out the four-engine ANT-6, or TB-3 (*tsazhelyy bombardirovshchik*, "heavy bomber"), first flown on 22 December 1929, with a production run of over 800 beginning in 1932; the two-engine ANT-40, or SB-2 (*skorostnoy bombardirovshchik*, "fast bomber"), tested in mid-1935 with immediate series production; and under Tupolev's management but designed by Vladimir M. Petlyakov (1891-1942), the four-engine ANT-42, or TB-7 (later called the Pe-8), first flown in December 1936, with series production from 1939 and service entry in 1941. Ilyushin's two-engine long-range bomber (*dal'nyy bombardirovshchik*), the Il-4, was also an important development since it became the backbone of the long-range bomber force during World War II, with some 5250 produced between 1940 and 1944; Whiting, *Soviet Air Power*, pp. 7, 10-11; Gunston, *Aircraft of the Soviet Union*, 1983, pp. 290-292, 309-312, 224-226, 104-106.
5 The Soviet long-range aviation force was scrapped in 1940 following a disastrous campaign in the war with Finland. Reconstituted in 1942, the force did very little strategic bombing in World War II. Only 7 percent of all the sorties flown by all components of Soviet aviation were attacks more than a few miles beyond the forward edge of the battle area; Whiting, *Soviet Air Power*, pp.17, 50. See also, V. D. Sokolovskiy, ed., *Military Strat-

egy*, 3 ed. translated by the Air Force Systems Command, Foreign Technology Division, FTD-HT-23-555-68, 1968, pp. 165-166.
6 Gunston, *Aircraft of the Soviet Union*, 1983, p. 323. The engines were also successfully duplicated by Arkadiya D. Shvetsov; Whiting, *Soviet Air Power*, pp. 18-19. Seventeen engines for 13 aircraft—including the Il-28 Beagle and Tu-16 Badger and the first effective jet interceptor, the MiG-15—were developed from captured German engine designs and purchased British designs, the latter including Rolls-Royce Nene and Derwent V turbojets purchased in 1947. Robert P. Berman, *Soviet Air Power in Transition* (Washington, DC: The Brookings Institution, 1978), pp. 8-9; Colin Munro, *Soviet Air Forces* (New York: Sports Car Press, 1982), p. 55. See also, USAF, Directorate of Intelligence, *Significant Developments in Soviet Air Power—1948-1953*, National Archives, Record Group 341, Entry 214, 23 December 1952, pp. 5-6.
7 USAF, *Soviet Aerospace Handbook*, 1978, p. 35.
8 USAF, *Operational Capabilities of USSR in Certain Areas*, Air Intelligence Division Study No. 146/11, National Archives Record Group 341, Entry 267, 6 January 1948, p. 5. The first five aircraft were delivered to units in March 1947; Paul C. Droz, Office of the Director of Intelligence, HQ, USAFE, 1 August 1949, memorandum to Director of Intelligence, USAF, OINB 350.05, National Archives Record Group 341, Entry 267, Box 105, File Number 2-8580. Sufficient numbers were delivered in 1948 for operational testing; HQ, USAF, Directorate of Intelligence, and Department of the Navy, Office of Naval Intelligence, *An Estimate of Soviet Air Capabilities and Air Order of Battle*, National Archives Record Group 341, Entry 267, Box 127, File Number 2-18347, 1 October 1950, p. 25.
9 Deputy Chief of Staff, Operations, Department of the Air Force, *A Report to the National Security Council*, 14 April 1950, p. 28. By the beginning of 1950, nine Tu-4 regiments were believed to have been formed, with an authorized strength of 32 aircraft per regiment. However, the actual strengths of the Tu-4 regiments was an average of 67 percent of authorized strength; USAF, Directorate of Intelligence, and Department of the Navy, Office of Naval Intelligence, *op. cit.*, October 1950, p. 66; HQ, USAF, Directorate of Intelligence, and Department of the Navy, Office of Naval Intelligence, *An Estimate of Soviet Air Capabilities and Air Order of Battle*, National Archives Record Group 341, Entry 267, Box 127, File Number 2-18347, 1 December 1950, p. 11; USAF, *Estimate of Soviet Air Capabilities*, Air Intelligence Report No. 100-146/18-34, National Archives Record Group 341, Entry 267, Box 109, 1 October 1949, Appendix A, 12 December 1949, p. 43.

History

squadrons may have been specially trained and certified for nuclear delivery missions.[10]

The first Soviet turbojet bomber was the Il-28 Beagle, which was designed by Sergei V. Ilyushin (1894-1977) and first flown on 8 July 1948.[11] It entered service in Long Range Aviation of the Air Force and SNA in 1950-1951.[12] Given the small size of the nuclear bomb stockpile in the early 1950s, nuclear delivery missions probably remained the responsibility of the Tu-4 bombers, which had the range to strike European NATO targets without forward basing in Eastern Europe.[13] The Il-28's main mission was conventional bombing on the battlefield; nuclear delivery was a secondary mission.[14]

The Tu-16 Badger, the first Soviet aircraft specifically designed for long-range missions, entered Air Force service in 1954. (The following year it was deployed with SNA.)[15] The Tu-16 allowed the Soviets to retire the older piston-engine Tu-4 Bulls. The Badger initially carried only gravity bombs, including nuclear bombs, but was then subsequently fitted, starting in 1961 to carry nuclear-capable ASMs.[16] About half of the Air Force's Badger strike variants and virtually all in SNA were armed with ASMs by the early 1970s.[17] None of these planes ever figured prominently in Soviet strategic plans vis-a-vis the continental United States. In the beginning of the 1960s, the United States believed that almost 20 percent of the Badger force (approximately 150 aircraft) could attack North American targets on two-way nuclear bombing missions. But by the end of the 1960s, Badgers were reassessed as not having a two-way intercontinental capability.[18]

The first indication of Soviet development of a long-range bomber came in July 1951 when a single four-engine aircraft, considerably larger than the Tu-4, was observed in flight at the Moscow Air Show.[19] Considered a heavy bomber prototype rather than an operational type,[20] this Type-31 aircraft[21] was soon followed by the first flight of the prototype four-engine turbojet Mya-4 Bison in late 1953,[22] and the prototype four-engine turboprop Tu-95 Bear, completed in 1953[23] and first flown in the late summer of 1954.[24] Both aircraft initially entered operational service in 1955 to provide a capability of delivering large, first-generation nuclear weapons at intercontinental distances, a capability not available with the medium-range bombers then in service.[25]

The Bison and Bear designs were optimized for high-altitude long-range cruise, and their development coincided with the growing number of nuclear weapons available to the Soviet military.[26] The bombers were estimated by the United States as being able to carry up to four eight megaton bombs.[27] Only about 100 Bear and 50 Bison strike variants were deployed: the slow-moving Bear was vulnerable to air defenses, and the Bison could only reach the United States on one-way missions and apparently did not perform very well.[28] Soviet nuclear-strike capabilities were improved somewhat with the modification of 69 Bear aircraft to carry a single, nuclear-only AS-3 kangaroo missile. These ASM strike variants,

---

10. Meyer, "Soviet Theatre Nuclear Forces," Part II, p. 5. The Air Force noted in September 1952 that the Soviet Union "has now and will have for the next several years sufficient aircraft, trained crews, and base facilities to enable them to attempt to deliver in the United States the entire atomic bomb stockpile that is and will become available to them;" HQ USAF, Directorate of Intelligence, *A Summary of Soviet Air Capabilities Against North America*, National Archives Record Group 341, Entry 214, Box 68, File 2-35242, 18 September 1952, p. 2. The USAF reported a few months later that they "have moved from a point in 1945 where they neither possessed an atomic weapon nor had the capability to deliver it, to a present capability to attempt the delivery in the United States the full stockpile of atomic weapons which is, or may become, available;" HQ USAF, Directorate of Intelligence, *Significant Developments in Soviet Air Power*, op. cit., p. 5.
11. The flight is often incorrectly reported as occurring on 8 August; Gunston, *Aircraft of the Soviet Union*, 1983, p. 115.
12. Gunston, *Aircraft of the Soviet Union*, 1983, p. 115; USAF,*Soviet Aerospace Handbook*, 1978, p. 44; Alexander Boyd, *The Soviet Air Force Since 1918* (New York: Stein and Day, 1977),pp. 116-118; Whiting, *Soviet Air Power*, p. 19. In SNA, the Il-28 delivered torpedoes. As many as 700 Beagles were in SNA in the early 1950s; Whiting, *Soviet Air Power*, p. 74. This number was reduced to about 50 by the late 1960s; the Beagle was retired by 1978.
13. Meyer, "Soviet Theatre Nuclear Forces," Part II, pp. 5-7.
14. DIA, *Guide to Nuclear Weapon Systems Available to the Soviet Front Commander*, ST-CS-02-18-73, March 1973 (partially declassified and released under the FOIA), p. xii.
15. A competing prototype to the Tu-16, called the Il-46, was developed by the Ilyushin design bureau, but was rejected for series production; Matthew Evangelista, *Innovation and the Arms Race* (Ithaca, NY: Cornell University Press, 1988), pp. 171-172.
16. The conventional AS-1 ASM was first deployed on Badger B aircraft in 1958. Also deployed on some Tu-4 Bull bombers, the AS-1 was judged no longer operational in 1971 when the Badger B designation was eliminated; see Gunston, *Rockets & Missiles*, p. 134.
17. DOD, FY 1974 *Annual Report* (class.), p. 24 (declassified and released under the FOIA).
18. In 1964 and 1965, Secretary of Defense Robert S. McNamara stated that up to 150 Badgers could strike North American targets on two-way missions (DOD, FY 1965 *Annual Report* [class.],p.56; DOD, FY 1966 *Annual Report* [class.], p. 51), and repeated his belief that "a limited force" could carry out such missions in subsequent years; DOD, FY 1967 *Annual Report* (class.), pp. 56, 59; DOD, FY 1968 *Annual Report* (class.), p. 48; DOD, FY 1969 *Annual Report* (class.), p. 60. Secretary of Defense Clark M. Clifford also supported this contention in 1969 (DOD, FY 1970 *Annual Report* [class.], p. 83), as did Melvin R. Laird the following year; DOD, FY 1971 *Annual Report* (class.), p. A-11. In McNamara's FY 1968 statement, no Badgers were noted as having a capability to strike the continental United States on two-way missions, and Badgers were excluded in Soviet strategic nuclear forces totals: DOD, FY 1968 *Annual Report* (class.), p. 45.
19. CIA, *Soviet Capabilities for Attack on the U.S. Through 1957*, SNIE-11-2-54, 24 February 1954, p. 3; HQ USAF, *Estimate Soviet-Bloc Air Strength in Operational Units, Mid-1954*, n.d. (classified on 19 November 1952), p. 2.
20. HQ USAF, *Estimate Soviet-Bloc Air Strength*, op. cit., p. 2.
21. The Type-31 was possibly the Tu-85 design bureau designation. The Tu-85 was developed in prototype from the basic Tu-4 via intermediate stages but was never deployed; Gunston, *Guide to the Modern Soviet Air Force*, 1982, p. 122; Gunston, *Aircraft of the Soviet Union*, 1983, p. 326.
22. Vladimair M. Myasishchev, (1902-1978) formerly a designer in the Tupolev design bureau, was charged by Stalin in late 1949 to develop a jet bomber to fly intercontinental missions; Gunston, *Aircraft of the Soviet Union*, 1983, p. 209.
23. DIA, *Soviet Air Force, Strategic Bombers*, 1981, p. 14.
24. Norman Polmar, "The Ubiquitous 'Bear,' " *Proceedings*, December 1985, p. 55; Gunston, *Aircraft of the Soviet Union*, 1983, p. 333.
25. DIA, *Soviet Air Force, Strategic Bombers*, op. cit., pp. 1-2, 13-14. See also, CIA, *Soviet Guided Missiles and Related Soviet Capabilities*, briefing for Preparedness Investigating Subcommittee of the Armed Services Committee of the Senate, 26 and 27 November 1957, p. 35, and DIA, *Bison Weapon System*, DST-1310S-003-79, 31 August 1979, p. xi. The Soviets attempted what proved to be a deceptive flyover of Bison bombers at the 13 July 1955 Tushino parade in Moscow. First ten and then two flights of nine Bisons flew past the reviewing stand, almost double the number of Bisons seen in the 1955 May Day air parade. Although only ten aircraft had flown in the parades, the appearance of so many aircraft reinforced the latest trends in U.S. estimates of Soviet bomber strength, helping to create what became known as the "bomber gap." Evidence that the U.S. intelligence community had overestimated the Soviet Bison strength in testimony before Congress became available by August 1956, with revised estimates being made by the spring of 1957; see Prados, *Soviet Estimate*, pp. 38-50; Freedman, *U.S. Intelligence*, pp. 65-67.
26. USAF, *Summary Review*, 1975, p. D-1.
27. *Damage Limiting, A Rationale for the Allocation of Resources by the US and the USSR*, prepared for the Director of Defense Research and Engineering, 21 January 1964, p. 12. In the late 1960s, the average force loading of the strategic bomber force was estimated at one to two warheads per bomber. For example, McNamara's DOD, FY 1969 *Annual Report* (class.), p. 57, estimates that as of 1 October 1967 there were 155 bombers carrying 227-237 warheads. Clifford's DOD, FY 1970 *Annual Report* (class.), p. 76, estimates the force as of 1 September 1968 as comprising 150 bombers carrying 258 warheads, and Laird's DOD, FY 1971 *Annual Report* (class.), p. A-3, estimates the force as of 1 October 1968 as comprising 150 bombers carrying 171-181 warheads. These figures, Laird notes in his DOD, FY 1973 *Annual Report* (class.), p. 55, "should not create an impression of precise intelligence which would be quite unjustifiable in light of available information."
28. Nikita Khrushchev, edited and translated by Strobe Talbott, *Khrushchev Remembers: The Last Testament* (Boston: Little, Brown, 1974), p. 40. Khrushchev reports that they were not sure if the Bison could fly through anti-aircraft fire, and that the aircraft did not perform well in its flight tests; a number of test pilots were killed. It is believed that one of the operational Bison strike aircraft was destroyed in a crash. Bear production facilities were turned to the civilian transport version, the Tu-114 Cleat, and Bison production was cancelled.

designated Bear B/C and introduced in 1962 and 1963-1964 respectively, were also fitted with an aerial refueling capability.[29]

The Il-28 remained the only nuclear-capable, ground-attack fighter-bomber until the late 1950s.[30] The first-generation jet fighters, designed as high-altitude interceptors, were not well suited to the ground-attack mission because of limited combat radii and restricted maneuverability at low altitudes.[31] The Yak-28 Brewer, a follow-on to the Il-28, introduced supersonic speed to the ground-attack mission, but the plane had a smaller payload than the Il-28.[32] The Brewer was considered to be nuclear-capable,[33] with some 200 of the strike variants (A/B/C) deployed before the aircraft's partial retirement and modification to special-purpose missions (electronic warfare and reconnaissance) during the 1970s.

The first second-generation ground-attack fighters, the Su-7 Fitter and several variants of the MiG-21 Fishbed, entered service in the late 1950s.[34] Though neither plane was primarily a nuclear delivery platform, their introduction gave tactical aviation an extensive potential capability. Although the Su-7 Fitter A was easy to handle, it was limited by a very short combat radius, minimal endurance, and a small ordnance load. The Su-7 was designed for close-air support, with a secondary nuclear mission.[35] The MiG-21 Fishbed became the standard fighter in the Soviet military. Between 1958 and 1984, some 2500 MiG-21s were introduced.

The Tu-22 Blinder, which entered service in 1962, was the first Soviet bomber capable of a short supersonic dash.[36] Because of the aircraft's limited range and payload capabilities, less than 200 strike variants were produced before the program ended in 1969 and attention was turned to the development of a new, more capable, medium-range bomber. Beginning in 1967, some of the aircraft were modified to carry the AS-4 ASM.[37]

Development of the Backfire bomber began about the time the Blinder B became operational. In mid-1969, the first two Backfire A prototypes were observed by U.S. intelligence. Some 12 Backfire As were produced, and by the beginning of 1974 an operational squadron for crew training was activated.[38] Later that year the first Backfire B entered service. By using more powerful engines and a streamlined fuselage, the Backfire B's range was greater than that of the Backfire A. By further streamlining the fuselage, the Backfire C achieved an even greater increase in range.[39] It was under development by 1978[40] and entered service by mid-1983.[41]

A full-scale modernization of Soviet tactical air forces began in 1969 with the introduction of the late-model MiG-21 Fishbed aircraft.[42] This new third-generation fighter featured increased range and payload, improved avionics, and all-weather and night capabilities.[43] The late-model MiG-21 was joined by the new Su-17 Fitter C, which became operational in 1972.[44] According to the DIA, the Fitter C "represents a quantum advance in ground attack capability over earlier Fitter designs dating from the early 1960's."[45] Designed for partial use in the ground-attack role,[46] the Fitter C's improved avionics and more powerful engine provided double the external load capacity from shorter airfields, a 30 percent increase in range, and greater weapons delivery accuracy over the Su-7 Fitter A.[47]

The introduction of third-generation tactical aircraft shifted the emphasis from primarily defensive air-superiority missions to offensive air-to-surface missions.[48] The new aircraft significantly increased the payload that now could be delivered to a far greater range. This was particularly true for a 300-550 nautical mile combat radius, where the total bombing capabilities of Soviet tactical ground attack aircraft increased from 100 metric tons in 1975 to 1900 metric tons in the mid-1980s.[49]

The most capable third-generation nuclear attack plane is the Su-24 Fencer, first introduced in December 1974. The Fencer was the first modern Soviet aircraft to have a weapon system officer, and the first to be specifi-

---

29 USAF, *Soviet Aerospace Handbook*, 1978, p. 47.
30 Thomas W. Wolfe, *Soviet Power and Europe, 1945-1970* (Baltimore, MD: Johns Hopkins University Press, 1970), p. 40, as cited in Berman, op. cit., p. 30.
31 See the discussion and notes in Matthew Evangelista, "The Evolution of Soviet Tactical Air Forces," *Soviet Armed Forces Review Annual*, 1982-1983, Vol. 7, p. 455.
32 USAF, *Soviet Aerospace Handbook*, p. 45. The normal payload of the Il-28 was 2200 lbs (Gunston, *Guide to the Modern Soviet Air Force*, 1982, p. 46) with a maximum of 6000 lbs; USAF, *Soviet Aerospace Handbook*, p. 44. The Yak-28 Brewer C could carry 4400 lbs of ordnance; Gunston, *Guide to the Modern Soviet Air Force*, 1982, p. 146.
33 DIA, *Guide to Nuclear Weapon Systems*, op. cit., p. xii; DIA, *A Guide to Foreign Theater Nuclear Weapon Systems Under the Control of Ground Force Commanders*, DST-1040S-541-83-Chg.-1, 17 August 1984, p. xii.
34 A prototype of the Su-7 was flown in 1956, and production models appeared in 1959; Evangelista, op. cit., p. 266.
35 Soviet engineers reportedly indicated to an Egyptian general that the Su-7 was capable of carrying a nuclear weapon on each of its two weapon pylons; John W. R. Taylor, "The Next Generation of Soviet Air Power," *Jane's Defence Weekly*, 14 January 1984, p. 37; See also, John W. R. Taylor, "Gallery of Soviet Aerospace Weapons," *Air Force Magazine*, March 1981, p. 106.
36 DOD, FY 1965 *Annual Report* (class.), p. 56. A follow-on to the Bison, the Mya-50 Bounder, was flight-tested in 1957, but cancelled, probably because of the new emphasis on land-based missiles for strategic nuclear delivery. See William Green and Gordon Swanborough, *The Observer's Soviet Aircraft Directory* (London: Frederick Warne, 1975), p. 29.
37 One of the ten Blinders participating in the 1961 Aviation Day flyby at Tushino Airport was carrying what was apparently a dummy AS-4 missile; DOD, FY 1965 *Annual Report* (class.), p. 38. But the AS-4 variant of the Blinder, the Blinder B, did not actually become operational until 1967, when most of the Blinders in the Aviation Day flyby were equipped with the missile; *Jane's All the World's Aircraft*, 1984-1985, p. 245; DOD, FY 1968 *Annual Report* (class.), p. 48; DOD, FY 1969 *Annual Report* (class.), p. 60.
38 DOD, FY 1975 *Annual Report* (class.), p. 79. All twelve, plus at least two prototypes, were available for development testing by the beginning of 1973; John W. R. Taylor, "Jane's All the World's Aircraft Supplement," *Air Force Magazine*, February 1979, p. 66.
39 *Aviation Week & Space Technology*, 23 July 1984, p. 16.
40 Bonner Day, "Soviet Bombers: A Growing Threat," *Air Force Magazine*, November 1978, pp. 84-87.
41 JEC, Allocation of Resources - 1983, Part 9, p. 198.
42 The Fishbed L and N variants incorporate significant advances in construction standards over their predecessors; W.R. Taylor, "Gallery of Soviet Aerospace Weapons," 1981, op. cit., p. 103.
43 The new MiG-21 Fishbed, for instance, had an improved radar and an improved bomb sight; USAF, Air Force Systems Command, *Have Point: Appendix A, Volume II, Threat*, October 1974 (partially declassified and released under the FOIA), pp. A-22, A-23.
44 Whiting, *Soviet Air Power*, p. 47; Taylor, "Gallery of Soviet Aerospace Weapons," 1981, op. cit., p. 106.
45 Testimony by Lt. General Samuel V. Wilson, Director, DIA, in JEC, Allocation of Resources - 1976, Part 2, p. 87.
46 JEC, Allocation of Resources - 1983, Part 9, p. 198. Only the Su-24 Fencer was designed exclusively for a ground-attack role; see, for example, SMP 1981, p. 34.
47 Taylor, "Gallery of Soviet Aerospace Weapons," op. cit., 1981, p. 106.
48 JEC, Allocation of Resources - 1976, Part 2, pp. 67-68; SASC, FY 1981 DOD, Part 4, p. 1939; HQ USAF, *Military Forces Handbook, Military Forces of the USSR and Warsaw Pact*, AFP 200-11, 31 March 1980, p. 3-5; USAF, *Soviet Aerospace Handbook*, p. 40; SASC, FY 1980 DOD, Part 3, p. 840; SMP 1981, p. 32. One analyst believes that Frontal Aviation never had a defensive orientation. Rather, it lacked the hardware to successfully implement its offensive doctrine; L. M. Hansen, 'Front Aviation in Combined Arms Warfare," in *Soviet Combined Arms: Past and Present*, College Station Papers No. 1 (College Station, TX: Texas A & M University, 1981), pp. 58-59.
49 SMP 1981, p. 34; SMP 1985, p. 87.

8
Strategic Bombers

cally designed for a long-range ground-attack role. The Fencer largely fulfills the theater missions previously assigned to Badger bombers, and its fighter designation is an anomaly.[50] The Fencer's range allows it to strike most targets in NATO Europe from bases in the Soviet Union, whereas its tactical predecessor, the Yak-28 Brewer, had to be forward deployed.[51] Fencer deployments in the Far East in 1979 extended tactical aircraft range to almost all of the Japanese islands.[52] Its permanent deployment to Eastern Europe, beginning with an August 1981 move to the Debrecen air base in Hungary, marked what is thought to be the first permanent storage of nuclear warheads outside of the Soviet Union.[53] The conversion from the Su-7 Fitter to the Su-24 Fencer in regiments in East Germany began in January 1982 and was completed by the mid-1980s.

Another nuclear-capable ground-attack fighter, the MiG-27 Flogger D, was introduced in 1975.[54] At the time of its introduction, the Flogger D was capable of carrying a greater bomb load further than any other fighter.[55] An improved version, the Flogger J, was introduced in 1981. The limited MiG-27 production indicates the shift from simple but numerous aircraft to fewer, more sophisticated ones: Frontal Aviation aircraft inventory doubled from 1968 to 1976.[56]

Concurrent with equipment upgrades and the introduction of new fighters in the late 1970s and early 1980s, changes in tactics and operational training were also initiated.[57] New training programs stressed pilot independence and initiative to improve penetration and overall capabilities.[58] However, preplanned attacks and ground-control intercepts continue to characterize Soviet operations.[59] Soviet pilots fly as little as five hours a month, except during the summer, when flying time increases to about 20 hours a month.[60] Annually, they fly between 80 and 120 hours a year, though combat-related pilots fly at a higher rate.[61]

Over time, the Soviet Air Forces tactical force structure has shifted from interceptor to ground-attack roles. According to *Soviet Military Power*, "[t]he number of theater and front-level ground attack regiments opposite NATO has increased from 26 to 43 since 1978, while the number of fighter-interceptor units has declined by 14 percent."[62] In the Far East, "[t]he number of ground-attack regiments has increased from 15 to 21 since 1978."[63]

As the fourth generation of fighters started to be introduced in 1983—MiG-29 Fulcrum, Su-27 Flanker A, MiG-31 Foxhound, and Su-25 Frogfoot—Air Force and Air Defense units experienced only modest growth, being focused instead on improved air defense capabilities.[64] None of the newer planes appear to have air-to-surface bombing missions. (The Frogfoot is a close-air support plane similar to the U.S. non-nuclear A-10.) The primary mission of the Flanker, for instance, is to escort and protect ground-attack aircraft conducting deep strikes.[65]

Current Nuclear-Capable Aircraft (mid-1988)

Strategic Bombers

Some 160 nuclear-capable Bear bombers in five versions are assigned to the intercontinental Moscow Air Army and the regional Irkutsk Air Army.[66] These are the only true intercontinental aircraft in the Soviet military, with an unrefueled combat radius of 8300 kilometers (5200 miles). All but the Bear A can be refueled in air.

As of mid-1988, the bombers carry some 1380 nuclear weapons, including bombs, short-range ASMs, and long-range cruise missiles. The three older variants, now some 50 Bear A/B/C aircraft, are slowly being phased out as newer Bear G/H bombers, introduced in 1984, are produced and enter the force. As of mid-1988, there were some 110 Bear G/H bombers. Bear G bombers can carry two or three dual-capable AS-4 Kitchen ASMs in place of a single, nuclear-only AS-3 Kangaroo missile carried on the older Bear B/C. As of mid-1988, an estimated 45 Bear Gs were deployed, with about 10 per year being modified. Bear H bombers can carry up to eight AS-15 Kent long-range air-launched cruise missiles (ALCMs). Some 65 were deployed as of mid-1988; the bomber is being produced at a rate of about 20 per year.

---

50 USAF, *Soviet Aerospace Handbook*, p. 40; SMP 1981, p. 34; HQ USAF, *Military Forces Handbook*, op. cit., p. 3-5. The Fencer was at first identified as a fighter and given the fighter odd-numbered designation of Su-19 and a fighter code name (beginning with F).
51 SMP 1981, p. 34.
52 SASC, FY 1981 DOD, Part 4, p. 1918.
53 A Fencer regiment was temporarily deployed to Templin, East Germany, in July 1979, the first deployment of the aircraft outside of the Soviet Union.
54 One or two preproduction squadrons of the MiG-23 Flogger A were first displayed during the 1967 Aviation Day flyby at Domodedovo Airport. The prototype squadrons entered service in 1971 for evaluation. The U.S. Air Force notes that the MiG-23 was first available in 1970 and deployed in accelerated numbers in 1973 (HQ USAF, *Military Forces Handbook*, op. cit., p. 3-5), the date of initial deployments to East Germany; Whiting, *Soviet Air Power*, p. 22. The production version Flogger B was first available in 1972. In 1973, it was deployed to the Group of Soviet Forces, Germany. The MiG-23 Flogger B/G was the first Soviet interceptor to be credited with a look-down/shoot-down (though limited) capability; SMP 1984, p. 39. All Flogger A/B/G versions are air-superiority fighters with little ground-attack capability. The Flogger D was such a radical change from the MiG-23 Flogger A/B/G that it was given a separate designator (MiG-27) by the Soviets. JEC, Allocation of Resources - 1983, Part 9, p. 198; Georg Panyalev, "The MiG-23 Flogger--A Versatile Family of Soviet Combat Aircraft," *International Defense Review*, Vol. 10, No. 1, February 1977, p. 53.
55 JEC, Allocation of Resources - 1983, Part 9, p. 198.
56 DOD, FY 1976 Annual Report, p. 126.
57 Capt. Rana J. Pennington, USAF, "Closing the Tactics Gap," *Air Force Magazine*, March 1984, p. 83.
58 *Ibid.*, pp. 84-88; SMP 1983, p. 43.
59 SMP 1985, p. 86; see also, HQ USAF, *Military Forces Handbook*, op. cit., p. 3-5.
60 Berman, op. cit., p. 57; "Air Power of the Pact," *Flight International*, 5 June 1976, p. 1513.
61 Combat-related pilots fly about 180 sorties a year; SMP 1985, p. 86. Overall, tactical pilots fly about half as much, and combat-related pilots about 80 percent as much, as their U.S. counterparts; Michael Gordon, "Must Reading," *National Journal*, 13 April 1985, p. 831. Soviet training flights are quite removed from realistic combat flight training, and a considerable portion of non-flying time is spent in cross-training for maintenance activities and political indoctrination; Joshua M. Epstein, *Measuring Military Power: The Soviet Air Threat to Europe* (Princeton, NJ: Princeton University Press, 1984), pp. 106-108.
62 SMP 1987, p. 67.
63 *Ibid.*, p. 69.
64 The Fulcrum and Flanker interceptors incorporate true look-down/shoot-down radars, enabling them to engage low-flying aircraft or cruise missiles; *Ibid.*, p. 78.
65 *Ibid.*, p. 67.
66 SMP 1988, p. 79.

8

Non-strategic Bombers

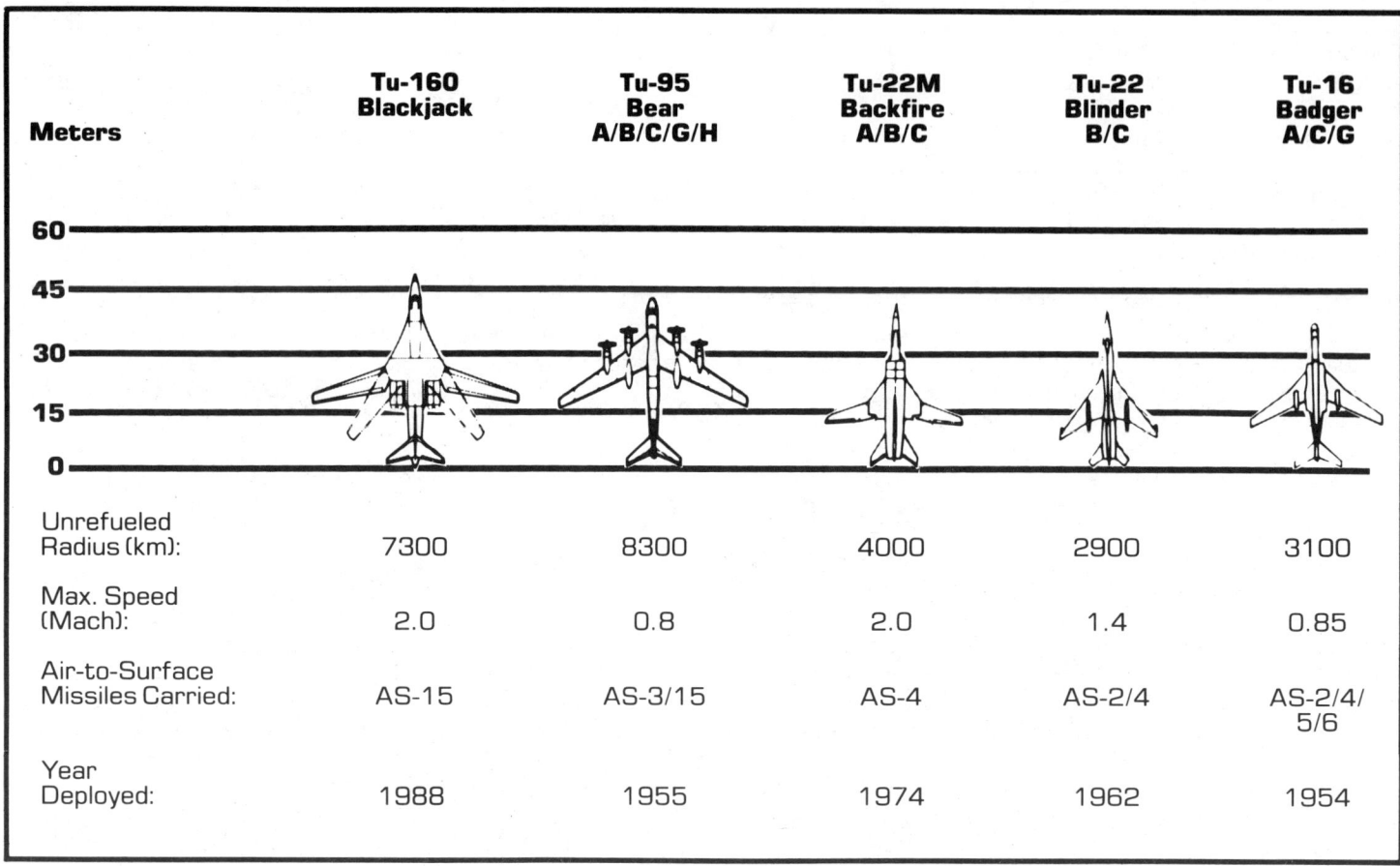

Figure 8.1 Soviet Bombers.

The Tu-160 Blackjack A bomber continues in flight-testing as of mid-1988.[67] The variable-geometry-wing, supersonic strategic bomber has been undergoing flight-testing since at least November 1981, when it was first observed. The bomber will be capable of carrying a combination of gravity bombs, AS-15 long-range ALCMs, and shorter range ASMs.[68] In addition to the AS-15, a new short-range attack missile, similar to the U.S. SRAM and designated AS-X-16, is expected to be carried by the Blackjack.[69] The Blackjack began operational service in mid-1988.[70] According to one source, a long-range "supercruise, cruise missile-carrying platform derived from the Tu-144 transport" is under development and could carry the AS-X-19 as well.[71]

Non-strategic Bombers

Some 1000 medium-range, nuclear-capable bombers of three types are assigned to the SAAs and to SNA as of mid-1988: 320 Backfires, 440 Badgers, and 150 Blinders. Of the three bomber types, only the Backfire is still in production. About half of the annual production of up to 30 aircraft enters service with the SAAs, with the other half going to SNA.[72] The overall medium-range bomber inventory has been decreasing, mostly due to attrition.

The Tu-16 Badger, introduced in 1954, is still widely deployed in the SAAs and in SNA, but it is being retired and replaced by the Backfire bomber. The A, C, and G variants are nuclear-capable (the C and G each come in two modifications).[73] The Badger A, the basic bomber version, is primarily used today for training or mine laying. Badger As can carry only nuclear bombs in internal bomb bays, whereas the Badger C and G can carry three different ASMs: the AS-2 Kipper, AS-5 Kelt, or AS-6 Kingfish. The Badger C cannot deliver bombs and carries the AS-2. The modified Badger C has been upgraded to carry the AS-5. The Badger G carries the AS-5. The modi-

---

67 Eleven bombers are deployed at the Soviet Flight Research Institute at Ramenskoye as of early 1988; *Ibid.*, p. 50.
68 SMP 1987, p. 37.
69 JCS, FY 1989, p. 41.
70 *Aviation Week & Space Technology*, 8 August 1988, p. 14.
71 *Aviation Week & Space Technology*, 28 March 1988, p. 15.
72 While nearly 325 Backfires have been produced through the middle of 1988, including one squadron of 15-30 developmental Backfire A aircraft, only about 40 percent of the force has been operationally assigned to combat units of the SAAs and 35 percent assigned to combat units of Naval Aviation. The remaining aircraft are probably used for testing and crew training; private communications with authors.
73 The Badger B version, originally deployed with the AS-1 Kennel ASM (now retired), is considered to be a conventional only bomber.

8
Non-strategic Bombers

Table 8.1
Nuclear Capable Aircraft (1988)

Type	Function	Service[1]	Number Deployed
Be-12 Mail	Short-range maritime patrol	SNA	95
Il-38 May	Medium-range maritime patrol	SNA	45
Ka-25 Hormone	Short-range ASW helicopter	SNA	115
Ka-27 Helix	Short-range ASW helicopter	SNA	60
MiG-21bis Fishbed L	Short-range fighter	AF	500
MiG-23 Flogger B/G	Short-range fighter	AF	1140-1570
MiG-27 Flogger D/J	Short-to medium-range attack	AF	830
Su-7 Fitter A	Short-range attack	AF	45-80
Su-17 Fitter C/D/H	Short-to medium-range attack	AF, SNA	870
Su-24 Fencer	Medium-range attack	SAA	850
Tu-16 Badger A/C/G	Medium-range bomber	SAA/SNA	440
Tu-22 Blinder A/B	Medium-range bomber	SAA/SNA	150
Tu-26 Backfire A/B/C	Medium-range bomber	SAA/SNA	321
Tu-142 Bear F	Long-range maritime patrol	SNA	60
Tu-95/-142 Bear A/B/C/G/H	Long-range strategic bomber	SAA	160
Tu-160 Blackjack A	Long-range strategic bomber	SAA	10

1 Soviet Naval Aviation (SNA); Strategic Air Armies (SAA); Air Forces of the Military Districts and Groups of Forces (AFMD/GOF or AF).

fied Badger G (replacing non-nuclear Badger Bs) has been upgraded to carry the AS-6. All the Badger C and G versions can also deliver nuclear bombs.

Of the 2000 Badger bombers produced from 1953 to 1983, some 440 nuclear-capable strike versions remain in operation as of mid-1988. About 250 Badger A/G versions are deployed in the SAAs, and some 190 Badger A/C/G versions are assigned to SNA.[74] A Badger squadron with nuclear-capable bombers deployed to Cam Ranh Bay, Vietnam, in mid-November 1983, and SNA Badger Cs have been reported to have operated in Afghanistan in the spring of 1983.[75] An additional 200 or so Badger bombers have been modified into reconnaissance, maritime patrol, electronic warfare, and tanker configurations.

The Tu-22 Blinder, first introduced in 1962, was the first Soviet bomber capable of supersonic performance. The bomber carries the highly versatile AS-4 Kitchen ASM, which was designed specifically for the airplane.[76] The Blinder, however, was never deployed in large numbers. Some 185 Blinder bombers of all types are deployed with the SAA and with SNA, including 150 strike versions and 35 support planes: some 30 Blinder A gravity bombers assigned to SNA, and about 120 Blinder A/B gravity- and ASM-equipped bombers in the SAAs. About half of the Blinder bombers in the SAAs are believed to be Blinder Bs equipped to carry the AS-4 ASM,[77] and the other half are Blinder A gravity bomb variants. Some 15 Blinder C reconnaissance versions are deployed in the SAAs, and about 20 Blinder C/D reconnaissance and training versions are deployed in SNA.

The Tu-26 Backfire bomber, first introduced in 1974, provided significantly enhanced deep-strike capabilities compared with the Badger and Blinder. The Backfire's improved capabilities provide significant flexibility in the aircraft's primary missions of theater and anti-ship strikes, missions for which the United States believes the Backfire is "ideally suited."[78] As of mid-1988, some 320 Backfire bombers of three types (A/B/C) were deployed: 180 in the SAAs and 145 assigned to SNA.

The newest version of the Backfire, introduced in 1986, is the Backfire C. Despite improvements in aircraft performance, the new Backfire bomber has essentially the same weapons carrying load as the earlier Backfire B: internally carried nuclear bombs or dual-capable AS-4 ASMs carried under the fixed center section panel of each wing.[79]

The Backfire C also does not appear to have an aerial refueling probe, unlike the Backfire B. Considerable de-

---

74 SMP 1987, pp 8, 35.
75 "Soviet Naval Aviation Bomber Force Modernization," *Jane's Defence Review*, Vol. 4, No. 7, 1983, p. 619.
76 Air Vice-Marshal R. A. Mason and John W. R. Taylor, *Soviet Air Force* (London: Jane's Publishing Company, 1986), p. 159.
77 DOD, FY 1974 *Annual Report* (class.), p. 24.
78 JEC, Allocation of Resources - 1976, Part 2, p. 71.
79 A third AS-4 could be carried on a centerline mount under the fuselage. No bombs could be carried internally in this configuration; see "Jane's All the World's Aircraft Supplement," *Air Force Magazine*, February 1988, p. 89. NATO reported that longer range INF aircraft carry two or three nuclear warheads; *NATO and the Warsaw Pact*, 1984, p. 36. Secretary of Defense Harold Brown presented an illustrative force loading of four warheads for the Backfire bomber and two warheads for the Badger and Blinder bombers; DOD, FY 1982 *Annual Report*, p. 66. The Backfire has also been attributed by some analysts with the capability to carry the AS-6 Kingfish and AS-15 Kent cruise missiles, which they carried for flight-testing, but the missiles are not expected to become operational with the Backfire bombers; John W. R. Taylor, "Gallery of Soviet Aerospace Weapons," *Air Force Magazine*, March 1987, p. 86.

8

Tactical Aircraft

bate has been focused on whether the Backfire bomber has an intercontinental strike capability. The Soviet Union has consistently claimed that the aircraft is a theater weapon, while some U.S. intelligence analysts believe that it has the capability to strike the continental United States. This could be achieved either by one-way missions with recovery in third countries (such as Cuba) or by two-way missions using Arctic staging bases and in-flight refueling.[80] All deployed Backfires currently lack the probes for aerial refueling, and given the limited number of aerial tankers in the Soviet inventory, the Soviet Union could not easily utilize the Backfire for strategic attacks on the United States.[81]

Tactical Aircraft

Nuclear-capable tactical aircraft in the Soviet inventory include more than 1700 Su-24 Fencer, Su-17 Fitter C/D, MiG-27 Flogger D/J, and Su-7 Fitter types. Additionally, a portion of the MiG-21bis Fishbed L and MiG-23 Flogger B/G fighter interceptors have a secondary nuclear-capable role.[82] In a nuclear mission, these aircraft primarily deliver nuclear bombs; only the Su-24 Fencer is thought to be capable of carrying a nuclear-capable ASM.

The Su-24 Fencer, introduced into squadron service in December 1974, has the longest range and is "the best deep-interdiction aircraft" in the tactical air forces.[83] The Fencer is an all-weather, low-altitude penetrator and is highly capable in attacking fixed targets.[84] The plane has twice the combat radius of the Fitter, which it is replacing, while carrying a comparable payload.[85] By mid-1988, some 850 Su-24 Fencers were deployed: 450 assigned to the SAAs, 365 assigned to the AFMD/GOF, and some 35 assigned to SNA.[86] The Fencer (along with the Su-17 Fitter) has almost completely replaced the Su-7 Fitter A.

The Su-17 Fitter C/D variable geometry wing fighter, first operational in 1972-1973, is assigned to the Air Forces of the Military Districts and Groups of Forces and to SNA. At the end of 1987, some 875 nuclear-capable versions were fielded. Fitter C/Ds can carry conventional AS-7, conventional bombs, or nuclear bombs.[87] Fitter performance is judged as "generally not as good as the ground attack versions of [MiG-27] Flogger [D/J]."[88] The Fitter C/D and other non-nuclear Fitter versions have almost completely replaced the Su-7 Fitter A, which was first deployed in 1959 (and was completely different from the later Fitter C/Ds).

The MiG-27 Flogger D/J, first introduced in 1975, is the most numerous nuclear-capable airplane in the tactical air forces. It is also the aircraft most often used in military exercises in the nuclear delivery role, particularly in Eastern Europe. Some 730-810 aircraft were deployed as of 1987. Flogger D/Js are designed for low-level attacks at transonic speeds. They carry either AS-7 Kerry, AS-10 Karen, AS-12 Kegler, or AS-14 Kedge conventional ASMs or bombs (including nuclear bombs).[89]

Certain variants of the MiG-23 Flogger and MiG-21 Fishbed fighter force are thought to have secondary roles of nuclear delivery, even though the aircraft are primarily air-superiority fighters. The most likely candidates are MiG-23 Flogger B/G (MiG-23M and MiG-23MF) aircraft, although the same versions are also assigned to interceptor units of the Air Defense Forces (PVO). The most likely nuclear-capable variant of the MiG-21 Fishbed is the third-generation MiG-21bis Fishbed L which has improved avionics and longer range; the slightly older MiG-21MF/PFMA Fishbed J and MiG-21SMB Fishbed K are thought to be primarily concentrated on air-superiority missions.[90]

The MiG-23 Flogger, first introduced in 1972, forms the backbone of the Air Defense Forces; some 1750 are assigned to the AFMD/GOF. The MiG-21 Fishbed is one of the most commonly flown aircraft in the world, and since its introduction in 1958, it has been upgraded with over a dozen variants. Almost 1700 late-model Fishbeds of these types are operational in the Air Forces of the Military Districts.[91]

Soviet Naval Aviation

SNA[92] is a central part of the offensive nuclear-strike capabilities of the Soviet Navy. Some 1600 fixed-wing aircraft and helicopters comprise the SNA force. Some

---

80 The DIA has always considered the Backfire "a theater weapon" (SASC, Strategic Force Modernization Programs, 1981, p. 13), and the JCS has stated that the bomber has "a primary mission of peripheral strike"; JCS, FY 1981, p. 13; see also, JCS, FY 1983, p. 107. Up to 1986, the DIA also assessed, however, that the Backfire could reach the United States on two-way missions if staged from Arctic bases, even if it was not refueled in flight; SMP 1985, p. 15 (see also the first three editions of SMP). See also SFRC, SALT II Hearings, Part 2, pp. 247-248; SAC, Soviet Military Capabilities, July 1981, p. 29 DIA, Soviet Air Force, Strategic Bombers, 1981, pp. 2-3. The DIA estimate of the range of the Backfire was at variance with that of the CIA, which was more than one-third lower. In SMP 1986, p. 33, the maximum unrefueled combat radius for the bomber was revised downward from 5500 kilometers (3400 miles) to 4000 kilometers (2485 miles); see also, SMP 1987, p. 36. At the same time, SMP 1986 noted that "Backfire can be equipped with a probe to permit in-flight refueling to increase its range. This would improve its capabilities against the contiguous United States" (p. 32). With the revision, the DIA's estimate has moved substantially towards that of the CIA; see Michael R. Gordon, "Pentagon Reassesses Soviet Bomber," New York Times, 1 October 1985, p. A8. One of several factors leading to the revised estimate, Gordon reports, was new information about the Backfire's fuel consumption rate.
81 Initially, some, but not all, Backfire Bs were equipped with refueling probes; JCS, FY 1980, p. 50; HASC, FY 1984 DOD, Part 5, p. 247. All probes were removed by July 1980, following SALT II assurances that the bomber would not be used for intercontinental missions.
82 SASC, FY 1981 DOD, Part 4, p. 1939; Berman, op. cit., pp. 71-72. Many other interceptors could also be used for ground-attack missions, though their use in nuclear missions would be highly unlikely. Interceptor aircraft and fighter types believed by NATO to be capable of conversion to nuclear delivery include the Tu-28P Fiddler, MiG-21 Fishbed, Su-15 Flagon, MiG-23 Flogger B/G, MiG-25 Foxbat A/E, MiG-29 Fulcrum, and the MiG-31 Foxhound A; NATO and the Warsaw Pact, 1984, pp. 11, 21; see also, USA, Understanding Soviet Military Developments, p. 43. The DIA believes that at least the Fitter C, Flogger D, and Fishbed N are nuclear-capable; DIA, A Guide to Foreign Theater Nuclear Weapon Systems, op. cit., p. xii.
83 SMP 1987, p. 79.
84 JEC, Allocation of Resources - 1983, Part 9, p. 198.
85 SMP 1987, p. 79.
86 Ibid., pp. 35, 79; SMP 1986, p. 78; SMP 1985, p. 33.
87 The U.S. Navy notes that the AS-7 Kerry can be carried by Fitter Cs; USN, Soviet Naval Developments (Rev. 4/85), p. 143.
88 JEC, Allocation of Resources - 1983, p. 198.
89 Taylor, "Gallery of Soviet Aerospace Weapons," 1987, op. cit., p. 90; see also Taylor, "Gallery of Soviet Aerospace Weapons," 1981, op. cit., p. 105.
90 NATO believes that a nuclear-capable model Fishbed entered service in 1965 (NATO and the Warsaw Pact, 1984, p. 32), but it is more likely that the first true nuclear-capable model was the MiG-21MF/PFMA Fishbed J, entering service in 1969 with additional wing pylons to carry four air-to-air Atoll missiles, fuel tanks, or bombs. The Fishbed J was the first of four dual-purpose Fishbed variants (J/K/L/N) designed for both ground-attack and air combat roles; see also, Taylor, "Gallery of Soviet Aerospace Weapons," 1987, op. cit., p. 87.
91 SMP 1987, p. 78.
92 The Russian name for the Naval Aviation force is Aviatsiya Voyenno-Morskovo Flota (AVMF); USN, Soviet Naval Developments (Rev. 4/85), p. 131.

8
Soviet Naval Aviation

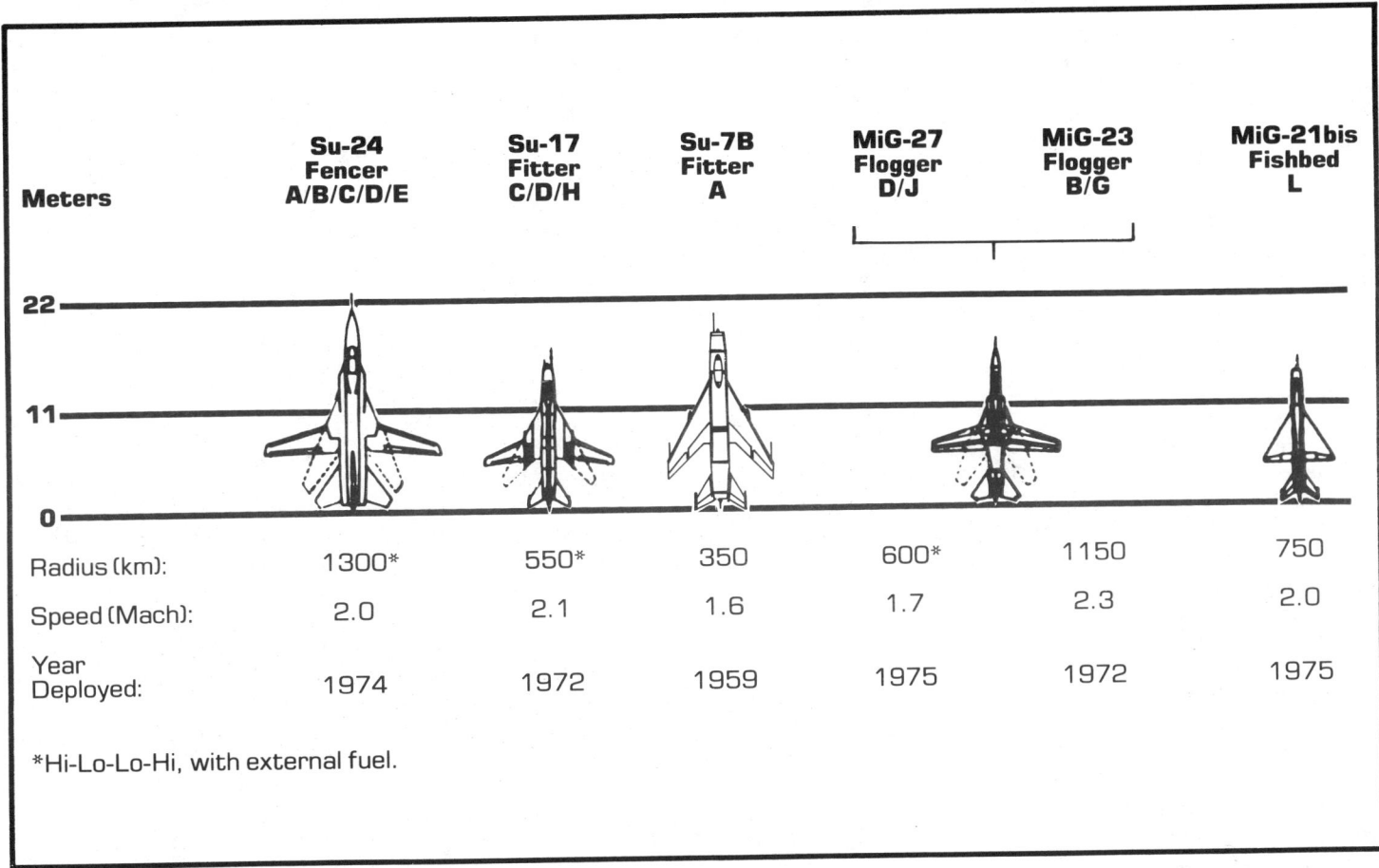

Figure 8.2 Soviet Nuclear-Capable Fighters.

850 aircraft of nine types are believed to be nuclear-capable. SNA nuclear missions include anti-ship strikes, anti-submarine warfare, and support of ground and amphibious operations.[93]

Until the establishment of the PVO in 1948, SNA had primary responsibility for air defense of coastal areas. But in 1955 Khrushchev initiated cut backs on Soviet naval programs, and fighters, fighter-bombers and some Il-28 medium bombers were transferred to PVO reducing SNA strength by more than half.[94] Since the main task of the Soviet Navy was defending the homeland from carrier-based aviation, Badger bombers with anti-ship missions were transferred to SNA beginning in 1955.[95] Initial overflights by Badgers of U.S. carriers began in 1963,[96] and the mission of SNA was expanded to include limited nuclear strikes.[97] The shift of ASM-armed Badgers to SNA, however, did not change Naval Aviation's basic defensive orientation, although in mid-November 1983, the first Soviet deployment of strike aircraft outside the Warsaw Pact since 1972 occurred with a group of SNA Badger bombers deploying to Cam Ranh Bay, Vietnam.[98]

Since the mid-1960s, the capability of SNA has expanded from pure defense of home waters to limited interdiction of enemy warships and defense of the Soviet fleet in waters close to land bases. Long-range anti-ship capabilities were significantly expanded with the initial deployment of the Backfire bomber with SNA in 1975.[99]

---

93 With initial deployments of Su-17 Fitter Cs in 1982, the SNA has enhanced its mission of close-air support of naval infantry and ground forces, at least in the Baltic and Pacific Fleets; USN, *Soviet Naval Developments* (Rev. 4/85), p. 49. SNA Backfires have also been used in support of Warsaw Pact amphibious operations during the Zapad 1981 exercise in the Baltic; David R. Griffiths, "Backfires Spotted in New Role," *Aviation Week & Space Technology*, 8 June 1981, p. 57.
94 Whiting, *Soviet Air Power*, p. 75.
95 About 45 Badgers were in SNA in mid-1957; CIA, *Main Trends in Soviet Capabilities and Policies 1957-62*, NIE 11-4-57, 12 November 1957, p. 57; Senate Committee on Commerce and National Ocean Policy Studies, Hearings on Soviet Ocean Development, October 1976, p. 60. Transfers to SNA increased substantially in 1959.
96 Berman, op. cit., p. 21.

97 General-lieutenant Gulyayev, former chief of Naval Aviation for the Baltic Fleet, noted in 1965, "In the event of war, naval aircraft armed with nuclear warhead missiles could strike outside the range of anti-aircraft missiles and almost beyond potential fighter-interceptor range, thereby permitting Naval Aviation to effectively carry out the mission of destroying enemy warships and transports at sea"; see Paul J. Murphy, *Naval Power in Soviet Policy*, Studies in Communist Affairs, Vol. 2 (Washington, DC: GPO, 1978), p. 182.
98 HASC, FY 1984 DOD, Part 4, p. 43; CINCPAC, "Pacific Area Update," P4048.1P1-4, 17 February 1984, p. 14. Six Badger Gs and 10 other Badger types now operate from Cam Ranh Bay.
99 The first few Backfire Bs appeared at an operational SNA base by 1973; DOD, FY 1974 Annual Report (class.), pp. 21-22.

8
Soviet Naval Aviation

In the fall of 1982 Backfires demonstrated the increased reach of their anti-ship striking power, simulating an attack against two U.S. aircraft carriers operating in the northwest Pacific. This was the first use of Backfires against aircraft carriers, and the first use of the aircraft over the open ocean in the Pacific.[100] Longer range anti-submarine warfare (ASW) and maritime reconnaissance aircraft have also been introduced, including the Be-12 Mail seaplane in 1966-1967, the Il-38 May in 1968, and the Tu-142 Bear F long-range bomber in 1973.

The primary SNA strike aircraft are 145 Backfire and 190 Badger C/G bombers carrying four types of nuclear-capable ASMs.[101] Backfires are supplanting older Badgers on a less than one-for-one basis.[102] Thirty-five Blinder A bombers and 70 Su-17 Fitter C fighter-bombers transferred from the Air Force in the 1960s and 1970s, respectively, could also provide anti-ship strikes. In addition to the SNA aircraft, ASM-equipped Backfire, Bear G/H, Blinder and Badger bombers of the SAAs could also be used for anti-ship missions. Such aircraft regularly participate in SNA exercises.

About 60 Tu-142 Bear F, 45 Il-38 May, and 95 Be-12 Mail fixed-wing aircraft conduct anti-submarine patrol and strike missions at long, medium, and short ranges, respectively. These aircraft are armed with depth bombs and torpedoes, both of which could be nuclear-armed, and carry a variety of ASW detection equipment. Additionally, Ka-25 Hormone A and Ka-27 Helix A helicopters, which operate from a variety of Soviet warships and from land bases, are capable of delivering nuclear depth bombs.[103]

The Be-12 Mail provides coastal coverage. First deployed in 1966, it has a radius of 230 miles and carries bombs, depth charges, mines, or torpedoes. The Il-38 May, first deployed in 1968, is a derivative of the Il-18 commercial airliner[104] in much the same way as the U.S. P-3 Orion was derived from the Lockheed Electra transport. The May, the standard open-ocean maritime patrol craft, has a patrol radius twice that of the Mail, with similar weapons loads. The May has operated from airfields in Libya, Ethiopia, South Yemen, Mozambique, and Syria.[105] The Tu-142 Bear F, first identified in 1973, serves in the long-range maritime patrol role. Only a small number of Bear F aircraft were originally built as ASW aircraft,[106] with the remainder coming from modified Bear bombers. Bear Fs deploy to Cam Ranh Bay, Vietnam, and San Antonio de los Banos, Cuba.[107]

SNA will undergo a major transformation over the next decade with the deployment of its Tbilisi class nuclear-powered aircraft carriers. The final flight deck configuration for the carrier will include a conventional take off system with catapults and arresting gear. An active test and evaluation program at the Saki naval airfield on the Crimean peninsula has been underway to test catapult designs and capabilities. Aircraft that have been associated with the program include a modified MiG-27 Flogger D and the Su-25 Frogfoot ground-attack aircraft, and the Su-27 Flanker and the MiG-29 Fulcrum fighter-interceptors. These aircraft are either candidates for the carrier air-wing or test aircraft for particular aspects of sea-based aviation.[108]

---

100 SNA Backfires flew two separate simulated strikes on the night of 30 September and early morning hours of 1 October 1982, coming within 105 and 94 nautical miles, respectively, of the dual carrier battle group; HASC, FY 1984 DOD, Part 1, p. 1253; HASC, FY 1984 DOD, Part 4, p. 43.
101 The majority of the Badger Gs in the Soviet inventory serve with SNA; Taylor, "Gallery of Soviet Aerospace Weapons," 1981, op. cit., p. 102.
102 USN, Soviet Naval Developments (Rev. 4/85), p. 30.
103 Nuclear depth bombs could also be carried by the nearly 100 land-based Mi-14 Haze helicopters, which are too large to fit the elevators of the Moskva class cruisers and Kiev class carriers. For a description of the Haze helicopters, see Polmar, Guide to the Soviet Navy, 1983, pp. 343-344, and Taylor, "Gallery of Soviet Aerospace Weapons," 1987, op. cit., p. 96.
104 Gunston, Aircraft of the Soviet Union, 1983, p. 121.
105 HFAC, The Soviet Role in Asia, 97 Cong. 2nd sess., July 1982, p. 8; Taylor, "Gallery of Soviet Aerospace Weapons," 1987, op. cit., p. 85.
106 JEC, Allocation of Resources - 1976, Part 2, p. 69. According to this source, all aircraft built as Bear Fs were completed by 1971, two years before the Bear F entered service.
107 There was a five fold increase in overseas SNA deployments from 1979 to 1985. Bear Ds and Fs began operating out of Vietnam in April 1979. The Bear Ds have operated primarily over the South China Sea, and the Bear Fs over the South China Sea and the western Philippine Sea. Bear Ds also deploy to Angola; JEC, Allocation of Resources - 1983, Part 6, pp. 58-59. Periodic deployments to Cuba of Tu-95 Bear D non-nuclear reconnaissance versions have taken place since November 1981 and of Tu-142 Bear Fs since early 1983. USN, Soviet Naval Developments (Rev. 4/85), pp. 10-11; JEC, Allocation of Resources - 1983, Part 6, pp. 58-59; Taylor, "Gallery of Soviet Aerospace Weapons," 1987, op. cit., p. 87.
108 SMP 1985, p. 101.

8
Tu-95/Tu-142 BEAR

Strategic Bombers
Tu-95 BEAR A/B/C/G[1]
Tu-142 BEAR H

Figure 8.3 As of mid-1988, some 65 **Bear H** bombers were deployed, each believed capable of carrying up to eight AS-15 Kent long-range air-launched cruise missiles.

DESCRIPTION: Swept-wing, four-engine, long-range, turboprop strategic bomber deployed in five variants;[2] the upgraded Bear G is a modified B/C capable of delivering the supersonic AS-4; the newly produced Tu-142 Bear H carries the long-range AS-15; the naval variant (Tu-142 Bear F) is discussed later

DESIGN BUREAU: Tupolev; Bear H manufactured at Taganrug[3] and Kuybyshev[4]

SPECIFICATIONS (Tu-95):[5]
Dimensions:
- Length: approx. 45 m[6] (148 ft)
- Height: 12.1 m[7] (39.95 ft)
- Wingspan: 48.5 m[8] (159 ft)
- Takeoff Weight: 154,000 kg[9] (340,000 lbs)
- Powerplant: 4 Kuznetsov NK-12MV turboprop engines[10]
- Ceiling: 12,500 m-13,700 m[11] (41,000-45,000 ft)

---

1. Tu-20 is the Soviet military design bureau designation. Western authorities use Tu-95 because the military designation was not known until after the prototype aircraft was first flown. For background, see Gunston, *Aircraft of the Soviet Union*, 1983, pp. 333-336.
2. DIA, *Soviet Air Force, Strategic Bombers*, 1981, p. 14.
3. SMP 1984, pp. 12, 27, 28, 96.
4. SMP 1986, pp. 120.
5. For specifications of the Tu-142, see Tu-142 Bear F discussed below.
6. Figure taken from chart in SMP 1987, p. 36; USN, *Soviet Naval Developments* (Rev. 4/85), p. 135.
7. John W. R. Taylor, "Gallery of Soviet Aerospace Weapons," *Air Force Magazine*, March 1983, p. 91; *Jane's All the World's Aircraft*, 1987-88, p. 282.
8. Taylor, "Gallery of Soviet Aerospace Weapons," 1983, *op. cit.*, p. 91; *Aviation Week & Space Technology*, 14 March 1983, p. 123.
9. Taylor, "Gallery of Soviet Aerospace Weapons," 1983, *op. cit.*, p. 91.
10. Ibid.; *Jane's All the World's Aircraft*, 1987-88, p. 282. NK are the initials of engine designer Nikolai Kuznetsov.
11. *Aviation Week & Space Technology*, 14 March 1983, p. 123; Polmar, *Guide to the Soviet Navy*, 1986, pp. 390-393.

8

Tu-95/Tu-142 BEAR

Figure 8.4 **Bear G** bomber, intercontinental in range, and capable of being refueled, can carry four bombs in internal bays and two AS-4s on pylons under each wingroot. The bombers are increasingly being assigned maritime missions.

Unrefueled combat radius:	8300 km[12] (4500 nm, 5200 mi)
Aerial Refueling Capability:	all variants but Bear A;[13] Bear H is air-refuelable by the long-range Midas, which became operational in 1987[14]
Speed (max):	Mach 0.74 (425 kts) at 41,000 ft;[15] Mach 0.8[16] (500 kts)
Crew:	5
NUCLEAR WEAPONS:	Gravity bombs or air-launched missiles; Bear A: 2 bombs in internal bays[17] Bear B/C: 4 bombs in internal bays normal force loading or 1 AS-3 ASM under fuselage Bear G: 4 bombs in internal bays; normal force loading and 2 AS-4 on pylon under each wingroot;[18] Bear H: 8 AS-15, probably in rotary launcher in bomb bay[19] (possibly only 4 AS-15 internally);[20] 8 AS-15; possible future capability on two wing pylons

Figure 8.5 Close-up of the new **Bear H** bomber, an intercontinental aircraft with unrefueled combat radius of 8300 kilometers (5200 miles). The bombers are based at Dolon in central Asia and conduct long-range patrols over the Arctic.

DEPLOYMENT:

Number:	160 operational Bear bombers (April 1988);[21] reportedly some 20 Bear A; about 30 Bear B/C;[22] more than 45 Bear G;[23] just over 60 Bear H[24]

---

12 DIA, *Force Structure Summary*, November 1987, p. 21; SMP 1987, p. 36.
13 SMP 1981, pp. 60-61.
14 SMP 1988, pp. 21.
15 Lionel A. Boudreaux, *Meeting the Soviet Bomber Threat*, Air University Research Study, Air Command and Staff College, May 1978, pp. 21, 22.
16 SMP 1987, p. 36; DIA, November 1987, p. 21; SMP 1985, p. 34.
17 John W. R. Taylor, "Gallery of Soviet Aerospace Weapons," *Air Force Magazine*, March 1988, p. 77.
18 SMP 1987, p. 36; Taylor, "Gallery of Soviet Aerospace Weapons," 1988, *op. cit.*, p. 77.
19 SMP 1988, p. 50; Collins and Victory, *U.S./Soviet Military Balance*, 1988, p. 21; Taylor, "Gallery of Soviet Aerospace Weapons," 1988, *op. cit.*, p. 77.
20 SMP 1985, pp. 6, 8, 33.
21 SMP 1988, p. 15; JCS, FY 1989, p. 39. JCS, FY 1988, p. 33, and SMP 1987, p. 35, reported 155 deployed.
22 SMP 1987, p. 36; JCS, FY 1985, p. 21.
23 SMP 1988, p. 51.
24 DIA, *Force Structure Summary*, November 1987, p. 8. SMP 1988, pp. 15, 50, reports 160 Bear, of which about 100 are other than Bear H; consequently, there are about 60 Bear H.

8
Tu-95/Tu-142 BEAR

Location: about 90 (Bear A and Bear H) assigned to the Moscow Air Army;[25] about 70 (all Bear B/Cs and Bear Gs) assigned to Irkutsk Air Army;[26] Bear H bombers stationed at Dolon in Central Asia[27]

HISTORY:

Prototype completed: 1953[28]

First Flight Test: 1954[29]

IOC:
- Bear A: 1955[30]
- Bear B: 1961-1962[31]
- Bear C: 1963[32]
- Bear G: 1984[33]
- Bear H: November 1984

Production: some 20 Bear H bombers were produced each year in 1984, 1985 and 1986[34]

COMMENTS: Bear A does not carry ASMs. Bear B/Cs are being converted to Bear Gs. Some Bear Bs operate in maritime reconnaissance role. Bear D, first seen in 1965, is unarmed electronic warfare, reconnaissance, and targeting variant; about 15 are deployed. Bear E is a strategic reconnaissance variant. Bear F (Tu-142) is a naval maritime patrol/ASW variant with major changes in design (discussed separately). Bear H and J are based on the Tu-142 Bear F airframe. Bear J, first deployed in 1985, is Soviet equivalent of U.S. VLF radio relay TACAMO aircraft.

---

25 SMP 1987, p. 35; SMP 1988, p. 79. According to one report, Bear H bombers may be assigned to the Irkutsk Air Army; "Bear-H Mission Details Reported," *Jane's Defence Weekly*, 16 April 1988, p. 756.
26 SMP 1988, p. 79.
27 Ibid., p. 52.
28 DIA, *Soviet Air Force, Strategic Bombers*, 1981, p. 14.
29 Taylor, "Gallery of Soviet Aerospace Weapons," 1983, op. cit., p. 91; Polmar, *Guide to the Soviet Navy*, 1986, pp. 390-393.
30 DIA, *Soviet Air Force, Strategic Bombers*, 1981, p. 14; USAF, *Trends*, 1976, p. 35.
31 USAF, *Trends*, 1976, p. 35.
32 Ibid.
33 SMP 1984, p. 28.
34 SMP 1986, p. 120; SMP 1987, p. 122.

8

Tu-160 BLACKJACK A[1]

Figure 8.6 The **Tu-160 Blackjack A** bomber, with a MiG-29 Fulcrum in the foreground, is shown at the Kubinka Air Base where it was inspected by U.S. Secretary of Defense, Frank C. Carlucci on 2 August 1988. This variable-geometry-wing, supersonic strategic bomber is similar to but larger than the U.S. B-1 bomber.

DESCRIPTION: Long-range, variable-geometry-wing, four-engine, supersonic strategic bomber similar to but larger than the U.S. B-1[2]

DESIGN BUREAU: Tupolev; manufactured at Kazan Airframe Plant[3]

SPECIFICATIONS:
Dimensions:

Length: 53.9 m (177 ft);[4] approx. 51 m[5] (170 ft)

Height: 13 m[6] (42 ft)

Wingspan

Swept: 33.5 m[7] (110 ft)

Spread: 55.70 m[8] (182.7 ft)

Takeoff Weight: approx. 260,000-270,000 kg[9] (580,000-590,000 lbs)

---

1. JCS, FY 1988, p. 36, refers to this bomber as the Blackjack A. Known as RAM-P during development; "Blackjack: Soviet B-1 or Better?" *Flight International*, 11 December 1982, pp. 1700-1704.
2. SMP 1983, pp. 7, 13, 23, 26.
3. SMP 1986, p. 120.
4. *Aviation Week & Space Technology*, 8 August 1988, p. 15.
5. Taken from chart in SMP 1987, p. 36.
6. "Blackjack: Soviet B-1 or Better?," *op. cit.*, pp. 1700-1704 reported about 14 m (45 ft) based on the single *Aviation Week & Space Technology* photograph in the 14 December 1981 issue at p. 17. Clarence A. Robinson, Jr., "Soviets Deploying New Fighters," *Aviation Week & Space Technology*, 28 November 1983, pp. 19-20.
7. John W. R. Taylor, "Gallery of Soviet Aerospace Weapons," *Air Force Magazine*, March 1987, p. 87. Bill Sweetman, "Blackjack, the Biggest Bomber by Far," *International Defense Review*, No. 5/84, pp. 539-542, reported 36.7 m (120 ft).
8. *Jane's All the World's Aircraft*, 1987-88, pp. 284-285.
9. *Flight International*, 1 August 1987, p. 69; "Blackjack: Soviet B-1 or Better?," *op. cit.*, pp. 1700-1704; Robinson, *op. cit.*, pp. 19-20. The weight is apportioned 260,000 lbs empty, 290,000 lbs fuel capacity, and 36,000 lbs for the bomb load.

Tu-160 BLACKJACK A

Powerplant:	4 Koliesov or Kuznetsov NK-144 turbofan;[10] 50,000 lbs thrust each	HISTORY: First Observed:	at Ramenskoye test center on 25 November 1981[25]
Ceiling:	approx. 20,000 m[11] (70,000 ft)	First Flight Test:	1983[26]
Unrefueled combat radius:	7300 km[12] (3900 nm, 4500 mi)	IOC:	mid-1988;[27] "[C]ould be operational as early as 1988";[28] "probable deployment beginning in 1988";[29] the first Blackjack regiment should begin forming in 1988[30]
Aerial Refueling Capability:	unknown; alluded to by Soviets[13]		
Speed (max):	Mach 2.0;[14] 1200 kts[15]		
Crew:	unknown	COMMENTS:	Blackjack will replace Bear A and Bison bombers. It may have a maritime attack role.[31] The Blackjack is the world's largest and heaviest bomber.[32]
NUCLEAR WEAPONS:	Gravity bombs, 12 AS-15 Kent cruise missiles and short-range ASMs (including the SRAM-like missile under development, the AS-X-16),[16] or a combination of each;[17] up to 36,000 lbs;[18] possible delivery platform for future supersonic cruise missile, the AS-X-19[19]		
DEPLOYMENT: Number:	11 Blackjacks produced (as of April 1988);[20] seven in advanced flight-testing as of March 1987;[21] a Blackjack bomber crashed during flight-testing in May 1987;[22] at least 100 are expected to be built[23]		
Location:	operational base possibly under construction near Murmansk[24]		

---

10 HASC, FY 1984 DOD, Part 5, pp. 429-430; Taylor, "Gallery of Soviet Aerospace Weapons," 1987, op. cit., p. 87; "Blackjack: Soviet B-1 or Better?," op. cit, pp. 1700-1704. NK are the initials of engine designer Nikolai Kuznetsov.
11 *Aviation Week & Space Technology*, 14 March 1983, p. 123.
12 DIA, *Force Structure Summary*, November 1987, p. 8; SMP 1988, p. 50.
13 JCS, FY 1983, p. 51.
14 DIA, *Force Structure Summary*, November 1987, p. 8; SMP 1988, p. 50.
15 SMP 1985, p. 334.
16 JCS, FY 1989, p. 41.
17 SMP 1987, p. 37.
18 *Aviation Week & Space Technology*, 8 August 1988, p. 15.
19 The AS-X-19 was previously known as the BL-10 during early testing; DOD, FY 1989 Annual Report, p. 27.
20 SMP 1988, p. 50.
21 SMP 1987, p. 25.
22 "Blackjack Bomber Crashes in USSR," *Aviation Week & Space Technology*," 25 May 1987, p. 19.
23 *Aviation Week & Space Technology*, 8 August 1988, p. 15.
24 Taylor, "Gallery of Soviet Aerospace Weapons," 1987, op. cit., p. 87.
25 See photograph in *Aviation Week & Space Technology*, 14 December 1981, p. 17.
26 HASC, FY 1984 DOD, Part 5, p. 232; SMP 1983, p. 13.
27 In early August Gen.-Col. Boris F. Korolkov, first deputy commander-in-chief of the Soviet air force, said that the bomber recently became operational; *Aviation Week & Space Technology*, 8 August 1988, p. 14.
28 SMP 1987, p. 37.
29 JCS, FY 1989, p. 41.
30 SMP 1988, p. 50.
31 Studeman, USN, Statement before HASC, March 1988, p. 39.
32 SMP 1988, p. 50.

8
Tu-26 BACKFIRE

Bombers
Tu-26 BACKFIRE A/B/C (Tu-22M)[1]

Figure 8.7 There have been three versions of the **Tu-26 Backfire** (A/B/C), each an improvement on the last. Their primary missions are theater and anti-ship strikes. Initially some Backfires were equipped with aerial refueling probes, but these were removed by July 1980 following SALT assurances.

DESCRIPTION:	Medium-range, variable-geometry-wing, twin-engine bomber assigned to Strategic Air Armies (SAAs) and Soviet Naval Aviation (SNA), replacing the Badger
DESIGN BUREAU:	Tupolev; manufactured at Kazan, Central Asia
SPECIFICATIONS:	
Dimensions:	
Length:	42 m[2] (140 ft)
Height:	10 m[3] (33 ft); 9 m[4] (30 ft)
Wingspan:	
Fully extended:	(20°): 34.5 m[5] (113 ft)
Fully swept:	(65°): 23.4 m[6] (76.9 ft)
Takeoff Weight (max):	143,770 kg[7] (294,180 lbs); 130,000 kg[8] (290,000 lbs)
Powerplant:	2 unidentified upgraded versions of the Kuznetsov NK-144 turbofans[9]

---

1. Tu-22M is reportedly the Soviet designation and was used in the SALT II talks. USN, *Soviet Naval Developments* (Rev. 4/85), p. 132. The original design bureau designation for the prototype is unknown, though Tu-136 has been suggested; see Gunston, *Aircraft of the Soviet Union*, 1983, p. 350. Backfire B is believed to have the service designation Tu-26, though Soviet negotiators used the designation Tu-22M (or Tu-22 modified) during the SALT II talks. However, the Tu-22 Blinder is a completely different aircraft, and the various explanations for this designation—the Backfire perhaps was originally designed as a fixed-wing aircraft (Georges Lafon, "A New Look at the Tupolev Tu-26 'Backfire,'" *Interavia*, January 1982, p. 78) or modified from a Tu-22 (Gunston, *Guide to the Modern Soviet Air Force*, 1982, p. 127)—remain unconvincing. It has also been suggested that the Backfires in the SAAs are designated Tu-26, with those in the SNA designated Tu-22M.
2. USN, *Soviet Naval Developments* (Rev. 4/85), p. 132; Polmar, *Guide to the Soviet Navy*, 1986, p. 390. Previously estimated to be 40 m; see Bonner Day, "Soviet Bombers: A Growing Threat," *Air Force Magazine*, November 1978, pp. 84-87; Polmar, *Guide to the Soviet Navy*, 1983, pp. 330-331.
3. Polmar, *Guide to the Soviet Navy*, 1986, p. 390; John W. R. Taylor, "Gallery of Soviet Aerospace Weapons," *Air Force Magazine*, March 1983, pp. 80-81; Gunston, *Guide to the Modern Soviet Air Force*, 1982, p. 128.
4. *Soviet Aerospace*, Vol. 39, No. 2, 19 September 1983, p. 9; *Soviet Aerospace*, Vol. 39, No. 13, 5 December 1983, p. 85; Polmar, *Guide to the Soviet Navy*, 1983, pp. 330-331; Bill Sweetman, "Blackjack: The Biggest Bomber by Far," *International Defense Review*, No. 5/1984, p. 552.
5. "In Soviet Service-20: Tupolev Backfire," *Air Internationa*, June 1988, p. 272. *Flight International*, 1 August 1987, p. 69; Day, *op cit.*, pp. 84-87.
6. "Jane's All the World's Aircraft Supplement," *Air Force Magazine*, February 1988, p. 90.
7. USAF, *Trends*, 1976, p. 37.
8. *Flight International*, 1 August 1987, p. 69; *Jane's All the World's Aircraft*, 1987-88, pp. 283-284.
9. Taylor, "Gallery of Soviet Aerospace Weapons," 1983, *op. cit.*, pp. 80-81; Gunston, *Guide to the Modern Soviet Air Force*, 1982, pp. 128-131; Polmar, *Guide to the Soviet Navy*, 1986, pp. 388-390; *Aviation Week and Space Technology*, 14 March 1983, p. 123. NK are the initials of engine designer Nikolai Kuznetsov.

Tu-26 BACKFIRE

Figure 8.8 The **Tu-26 Backfire** bomber is shown being escorted by F-16. Backfires are assigned to both the Air Forces and Soviet Naval Aviation.

Ceiling:	17,000 m[10] (55,000 ft); 19,000 m[11] (62,300 ft) with afterburner
Unrefueled loaded combat radius:	approx. 4000 km[12] (2100 nm, 2500 mi); U.S. intelligence estimates vary with date and intelligence agency;[13] CIA combat radius is 1824-2150 nm, with range at 3525-4150 nm; DIA radius is 5500 km[14] (2900 nm), and range is 5600 nm;[15] Backfire C version has a greater range capability than B version[16]
Aerial Refueling Capability:	capable, but not currently equipped with refueling probes; refueling probes removed by July 1980 in relation to SALT II assurances, but reinstallation on Backfire B could occur in a short period, assuming no internal changes were made in the aircraft.[17] Backfire C does not appear to have a flight refueling probe[18]
Speed:	can operate at high altitude and subsonic speed, or dash at supersonic speeds at low altitudes during penetration of air defenses; Maximum: Mach 2.0;[19] 1100 kts;[20] High cruise: 900 km/h (560 mph) at 33,000 ft;[21] Low penetration: 800 km/h (500 mph)[22]
Crew:	4 (pilot, co-pilot, navigator and defense-systems operator)
NUCLEAR WEAPONS:	Two weapons; normally carries one AS-4 Kitchen ASM on centerline mount, or two under the fixed center section panel of each wing;[23] may also carry the AS-6 Kingfish;[24] internal bomb bay (which can theoretically carry two bombs) cannot be used when a missile is carried on centerline mount (which is semi-recessed);[25] although AS-15 ALCM has been tested from Backfire, it is not likely to arm the bomber[26]
Payload:	9430 kg (20,800 lbs);[27] 7940 kg (17,500 lbs);[28] 12,000 kg (26,000 lbs)[29]
DEPLOYMENT: Number:	321 (April 1988);[30] Backfire bombers are almost evenly divided between SAAs and SNA: 178 in SAAs and 143 in SNA;[31] 15-30 Backfire A produced

---

10 Gunston, *Guide to the Modern Soviet Air Force*, 1982, p. 130; *Soviet Aerospace*, Vol. 39, No. 2, 19 September 1983, p. 9; *Soviet Aerospace*, Vol. 39, No. 13, 5 December 1983, p. 85; Polmar, *Guide to the Soviet Navy*, 1986, p. 390.
11 Gunston, *Guide to the Modern Soviet Air Force*, 1982, p. 130.
12 DIA, *Force Structure Summary*, November 1987, p. 8; SMP 1987, p. 36. Unrefueled loaded combat radius is reported by most sources previously as about 5500 km (3000 nm; 3400 mi); USN, *Soviet Naval Developments* (Rev. 4/85), p. 132; SMP 1985, pp. 34, 85; DOD, FY 1978 Annual Report (class.), p. 66; SMP 1981, p. 60; SMP 1983, pp. 12, 27; SMP 1984, pp. 14, 15, 23, 24; *Jane's All the World's Aircraft*, 1987-88, pp. 283-284; USAF, *Soviet Aerospace Handbook*, 1978, pp. 48-49.
13 USAF, *Trends*, 1976, p. 37 states 4300-4500 nm; USAF, *Soviet Aerospace Handbook*, pp. 48-49; Day, op. cit., pp. 84-87; and *Soviet Aerospace* Vol. 39, No. 2, 19 September 1983, p. 9, estimate 5400 nm.
14 DIA, *Force Structure Summary*, November 1987, p. 21.
15 "Soviets' Nuclear Arsenal Continues to Proliferate," *Aviation Week & Space Technology*, 16 June 1980, p. 76.
16 SMP 1987, p. 67; *Aviation Week & Space Technology*, 23 July 1984, p. 16.
17 SMP 1985, pp. 34, 85.
18 "Jane's All the World's Aircraft Supplement," op. cit., p. 90.
19 DIA, *Force Structure Summary*, November 1987, p. 8; DOD, FY 1971 Annual Report (class.), p. 58; DOD, FY 1972 Annual Report (class.), p. 61.
20 DIA, *Force Structure Summary*, November 1987, p. 21; SMP 1985, pp. 34, 85; DOD, FY 1978 Annual Report (class.), p. 66; SMP 1981, p. 60; USN, *Soviet Naval Developments* (Rev. 4/85), p. 132; SMP 1982, pp. 14, 15, 23, 24; Michael R. Gordon, "Pentagon Reassesses Soviet Bomber," *New York Times*, 1 October 1985, p. A8.
21 Gunston, *Guide to the Modern Soviet Air Force*, 1982, p. 130; *Soviet Aerospace*, Vol. 39, No. 2, 19 September 1983, p. 9; *Soviet Aerospace*, Vol. 39, No. 13, 5 December 1983, p. 85.
22 Polmar, *Guide to the Soviet Navy*, 1986, pp. 388-390; *Soviet Aerospace*, Vol. 39, No. 2, 19 September 1983, p. 9; *Soviet Aerospace*, Vol. 39, No. 13, 5 December 1983, p. 85.
23 USN, *Soviet Naval Developments* (Rev. 4/85), p. 132; SMP, FY 1982, pp. 100-101. SMP 1984, p. 29, states that the Backfire can "carry two wing mounted AS-4s on pylons."
24 SMP 1988, p. 123.
25 Polmar, *Guide to the Soviet Navy*, 1986, p. 389; IISS, *Military Balance*, 1987-1988, p. 207. The weapons bay is some 23 ft (7.0 m) in length and 5.5 ft (1.7 m) in width; "In Soviet Service-20: Tupolev Backfire," op. cit., p. 273.
26 John W. R. Taylor, "Gallery of Soviet Aerospace Weapons," *Air Force Magazine*, March 1988, p. 76.
27 USAF, *Trends*, 1976, p. 37.
28 IISS, *Military Balance*, 1987-1988, p. 207.
29 "In Soviet Service-20: Tupolev Backfire," op. cit., p. 273; Day, op. cit., pp. 84-87; *Soviet Aerospace*, Vol. 39, No. 2, 19 September 1983, p. 9; *Soviet Aerospace*, Vol. 39, No. 13, 5 December 1983, p. 85; DOD, FY 1985 Annual Report, pp. 21, 134.
30 SMP 1988, p. 15, and JCS, FY 1989, p. 39 reported 305. SMP 1987, p. 8, reported 290 Backfires (as of March 1987). Polmar, *Guide to the Soviet Navy*, 1986, p. 389, reported 260 Backfires. JCS, FY 1986, p. 19, reported 230 Backfires.
31 SMP 1988, p. 15; *Force Structure Summary*, November 1987, pp. 8, 21.

8

Tu-26 BACKFIRE

Location:	SAAs: assigned to the Smolensk and Irkutsk Air Armies;[32] Belaya, (Transbaikal MD); possible Backfire bases at Sol'tsy and Voronezh; over 40 SAA in the Far East;[33] SNA: over 40 at Alekseyevka, Pacific Fleet;[34] Byhkov, Baltic Sea Fleet; Oktyabirskoye, Black Sea Fleet;[35] Backfire C regiment replaced Badger regiment in Black Sea Fleet during 1986;[36] and are replacing Badgers in the Far East[37]	COMMENTS:	Backfire A was the developmental and initial production version; Backfire B was the serial-production version with increased range (new wings) and fuel capacity and reduced drag with incorporation of new forward-folding landing gear; Backfire C further increased range and incorporated wedge-type air intakes.[45] Backfire has nuclear-strike, conventional-strike, anti-shipping, mining, and reconnaissance missions. Its primary mission is "to perform peripheral [non-strategic] attack and naval missions."[46]
HISTORY:			
Year Design Began:	mid-1960s		
First Seen:	1969;[38] Backfire A prototype first observed near Kazan manufacturing plant in Central Asia in July 1970[39]		
First Flight:	1969 (Backfire A);[40] 1972 (Backfire B);[41] 1986 (Backfire C)[42]		
IOC:	1974;[43] first few observed in 1973[44]		
Production:	limited to an annual rate of 30 aircraft, by letter agreement accompanying the SALT II Treaty		

---

32 SMP 1988, p. 79.
33 SMP 1987, p. 67; *Aviation Week & Space Technology*, 24 September 1984, p. 23.
34 SMP 1984, pp. 12, 157; *Aviation Week & Space Technology*, 24 September 1984, p. 23. SMP 1988, p. 123, reported that over 90 Backfire and Badger bombers were assigned to the Pacific Fleet Air Force.
35 SMP 1984, pp. 14-15, 23-24; CINCPAC, "Pacific Area Update," P4048.IPI-4, 17 February 1984, p. 22.
36 SMP 1987, p. 67. SMP 1988, p. 86, reported that the first Backfire Cs were deployed in the Black Sea Fleet in 1985.
37 DOD, FY 1989 Annual Report, p. 34.
38 Gunston, *Aircraft of the Soviet Union*, 1983, p. 350; *Soviet Aerospace*, Vol. 39, No. 2, 19 September 1983, p. 9; *Soviet Aerospace*, Vol. 39, No. 13, 5 December 1983, p. 85.
39 Day, op. cit., pp. 84-87; *Jane's All the World's Aircraft*, 1987-88, pp. 283-284.
40 USAF, *Summary Review*, 1975, pp. D-2, D-3.
41 HASC, FY 1982 DOD, Part 3, p. 21.
42 SMP 1987, p. 87.
43 HASC, FY 1984 DOD, Part 5, pp. 429-430; JCS, FY 1984, p. 15; DOD, FY 1983 RDA, pp. II-8.
44 DOD, FY 1974 Annual Report (class.), pp. 21-22, II-38.
45 Day, op. cit., pp. 84-87; *Jane's All the World's Aircraft*, 1987-88, pp. 283-284.
46 DOD, FY 1980 Annual Report (class.), p. 69; USN, *Soviet Naval Developments* (Rev. 4/85), p. 132.

Tu-22 BLINDER A/B (Tu-105)[1]

Figure 8.9 The **Blinder B (Tu-22)**, introduced in 1962, was the first Soviet supersonic bomber. Some 185 of all types (A/B/C/D) are deployed, including 150 strike versions and 35 support planes.

DESCRIPTION:	Medium-range twin-engine bomber, the first supersonic bomber to enter Soviet service; assigned to SAAs (Blinder A/B) and SNA (Blinder A)
DESIGN BUREAU:	Tupolev; manufactured at Kazan[2]
SPECIFICATIONS:	
Dimensions:	
Length:	40.5 m[3] (133 ft)
Height:	10.67 m[4] (35 ft)
Wingspan:	23.75 m[5] (78 ft)
Takeoff Weight (max):	83,900 kg[6] (185,000 lbs)
Powerplant:	2 Koliesov VD-7 or VD-7F turbojets[7]
Ceiling:	18,000 m[8] (60,000 ft)
Range (max):	6500 km (4000 mi)[9]
Unrefueled combat radius:	2900-3300 km[10] (1800-2050 mi);
Aerial Refueling Capability:	yes[11]
Speed (max):	Mach 1.4;[12] 800 kts;[13] high cruise: 900 kmh (560 mph) at 11,000 m (36,000 ft); Mach 0.85[14]
Crew:	3 in tandem[15]
NUCLEAR WEAPONS:	Blinder A: two weapons bays with probable capability to carry 4 nuclear bombs; Blinder B: 4 weapons, including nuclear bombs and one AS-4 Kitchen ASM;[16] Blinder D: possible weapons capability[17]

---

1 Gunston, *Aircraft of the Soviet Union*, 1983, p. 340; Polmar, *Guide to the Soviet Navy*, 1986, p. 390. Tu-105 is the Soviet design bureau designation.
2 Gunston, *Aircraft of the Soviet Union*, 1983, p. 341.
3 USN, *Soviet Naval Developments* (Rev. 4/85), p. 135.
4 Jane's All the World's Aircraft, 1987-88, p. 283.
5 Ibid.
6 USN, *Soviet Naval Developments* (Rev. 4/85), p. 135; Jane's All the World's Aircraft, 1987-88, p. 283.
7 USN, *Soviet Naval Developments* (Rev. 4/85), p. 135; Polmar, *Guide to the Soviet Navy*, 1986, p. 390; Gunston, *Aircraft of the Soviet Union*, 1983, p. 342. VD are the initials of engine designer Vladimir Dobrynin. Koliesov was a Dobrynin successor.
8 Jane's All the World's Aircraft, 1987-88, p. 283; Polmar, *Guide to the Soviet Navy*, 1986, p. 390.
9 Gunston, *Guide to the Modern Soviet Air Force*, 1982, p. 125.
10 DIA, *Force Structure Summary*, November 1987, p. 8; SMP 1987, p. 36; DOD, FY 1971 Annual Report (class.), p. 58.
11 SMP 1985, pp. 85-86.
12 DIA, *Force Structure Summary*, November 1987, p. 8; SMP 1987, p. 36; SMP 1986, p. 33; USAICS, *Handbook on the Soviet Ground Forces*, p. 243; USN, *Soviet Naval Developments* (Rev. 4/85), p. 135.
13 DIA, *Force Structure Summary*, November 1987, p. 21.
14 Polmar, *Guide to the Soviet Navy*, 1986, p. 390.
15 John W. R. Taylor, "Gallery of Soviet Aerospace Weapons," *Air Force Magazine*, March 1988, p. 76.
16 USAF, *Soviet Aerospace Handbook*, 1978, pp. 47-48, 50; USN, *Soviet Naval Developments* (Rev. 4/85), p. 135; Polmar, *Guide to the Soviet Navy*, 1986, p. 390.
17 Polmar, *Guide to the Soviet Navy*, 1986, p. 390.

8

Tu-22 BLINDER

Figure 8.10 The **Tu-22 Blinder** has an unrefueled combat radius of 2900-3300 km (1800-2050 miles) and aerial refueling ability.

Payload: 5400 kg (12,000 lbs);[18]
8000 kg (17,600 lbs)[19]

DEPLOYMENT:
Number: some 150 strike versions (Blinder A/B);[20] about 90 Blinder A (30 in SNA, 60 in SAA), 60 Blinder B (all in SAA) (1988);[21] some 35 additional reconnaissance (Blinder C) and training (Blinder D) versions are deployed

Location: SAA bombers assigned to the Smolensk and Irkutsk Air Armies;[22] SNA deployments in the southern Ukraine and Estonia;[23] bases possibly include Chernyakhovsk and Saki

HISTORY:
Year Design Began: 1950s

First Flight: 1959 (Tu-105)[24]

First Seen: 1961[25]

IOC: 1962;[26] 1967 (Blinder B)[27]

Production: ended production in 1969[28]

COMMENTS: Blinder A version is a gravity bomber. Blinder B version assigned to SAAs can carry AS-4 ASMs. Blinder C is a photo-reconnaissance/maritime patrol version. Blinder D is a trainer.

Also in service in Libyan and Iraqi air forces.

---

18 IISS, *Military Balance, 1987-1988*, p. 207; Collins and Victory, *U.S./Soviet Military Balance, 1988*, p. 76.
19 Gunston, *Guide to the Modern Soviet Air Force*, 1982, p. 125; Polmar, *Guide to the Soviet Navy*, 1986, p. 390.
20 SMP 1988, p. 15, reports 135 Blinder bombers, although it does not specify which types have been retired.
21 DIA, *Force Structure Summary*, November 1987, pp. 8, 21. SMP 1988, p. 15, and SMP 1987, pp. 8, 35, 79 reported 135 Blinders; see also, IISS, *Military Balance, 1987-1988*, p. 206; John W. R. Taylor, "Gallery of Soviet Aerospace Weapons," *Air Force Magazine*, March 1987, p. 86; Collins and Victory, *U.S./Soviet Military Balance*, 1988, p. 35; USAF, *Soviet Aerospace Handbook*, pp. 47-48, 50; USN, *Soviet Naval Developments* (Rev. 4/85), p. 135; Polmar, *Guide to the Soviet Navy*, 1986, p. 390.
22 SMP 1988, p. 79.
23 Taylor, "Gallery of Soviet Aerospace Weapons," 1987, op. cit., p. 86.
24 Gunston, *Guide to the Modern Soviet Air Force*, 1982, p. 126.
25 USAF, *Soviet Aerospace Handbook*, pp. 47-48.
26 DOD, FY 1971 Annual Report (class.), p. A-11; USAF, *Soviet Aerospace Handbook*, pp. 47-48.
27 Polmar, *Guide to the Soviet Navy*, 1986, p. 390.
28 USAF, *Soviet Aerospace Handbook*, pp. 47-48.

Tu-16 BADGER A/C/G[1]

Figure 8.11 A U.S. Navy A-6E Intruder is here shown escorting a **Tu-16 Badger G**, one of four modifications of this medium-range, nuclear-capable bomber. The Badger G can carry two AS-5 Kelt ASMs on wing pylons as well as bombs in internal bays.

DESCRIPTION: Medium-range, twin-engine bomber; nuclear-capable in four modifications and assigned to SAAs and SNA; being replaced by Backfire

DESIGN BUREAU: Tupolev; possibly manufactured at Kharkov or Kazan[2]

SPECIFICATIONS:
Dimensions:

Length: 34.8 m[3] (114 ft)

Height: 10.8 m[4] (35.5 ft)

Wingspan: 33 m[5] (110 ft)

Takeoff Weight (max): 77,000 kg[6] (170,000 lbs)

Powerplant: 2 Mikulin RD-3M turbojets[7]

Ceiling: 12,000-14,000 m[8] (40,000-46,000 ft)

Unrefueled combat radius: 3100 km[9] (1700 nm)

Aerial Refueling Capability: yes;[10] uses a unique wingtip-to-wingtip transfer

Speed (max): Mach 0.85;[11] 500 kts;[12] high cruise: Mach 0.8[13] (850 kmh; 530 mph); low penetration: unknown

Crew: 6-7[14]

---

1. Original designation was Type 39 aircraft and the Tu-88 Samolet. Tupolev design bureau designation was Tu-88; CIA, Soviet Capabilities and Probable Soviet Courses of Action Through 1960, NIE 11-3-55, 17 May 1955, p. 62. Two versions of the Badger C exist: one which carries the AS-2 ASM, and one which carries the AS-5 (designated Badger C Modified). Two versions of the Badger G exist: one which carries the AS-5 ASM and one which carries the AS-6 (designated Badger G Modified).
2. Gunston, *Aircraft of the Soviet Union*, 1983, p. 331.
3. Dimensions for A; *ibid.*, p. 332; Polmar, *Guide to the Soviet Navy*, 1986, p. 394.
4. Polmar, *Guide to the Soviet Navy*, 1986, p. 394; Dimensions for A; Gunston, *Guide to the Modern Soviet Air Force*, 1982, p. 116.
5. USN, *Soviet Naval Developments* (Rev. 4/85), p. 133; Polmar, *Guide to the Soviet Navy*, 1986, p. 394; Gunston, *Aircraft of the Soviet Union*, 1983, p. 332.
6. USN, *Soviet Naval Developments* (Rev. 4/85), p. 133; Gunston, *Aircraft of the Soviet Union*, 1983, p. 332.
7. Gunston, *Aircraft of the Soviet Union*, 1983, p. 332; USN, *Soviet Naval Developments* (Rev. 4/85), p. 133. RD-3M engines have replaced AM-3 and AM-3M engines. RD stands for *Reaktivnyi Dvigatyel* (reaction engine or turbojet), from the Alexsandr A. Mikulin design bureau.
8. Polmar, *Guide to the Soviet Navy*, 1986, p. 394. Performance with AM-3M engines.
9. DIA, *Force Structure Summary*, November 1987, pp. 8, 21; SMP 1987, p. 36.
10. DOD, FY 1971 Annual Report (class.), A-11.
11. DIA, *Force Structure Summary*, November 1987, p. 8; SMP 1987, p. 36.
12. DIA, *Force Structure Summary*, November 1987, p. 21.
13. Polmar, *Guide to the Soviet Navy*, 1986, p. 394.
14. John W. R. Taylor, "Gallery of Soviet Aerospace Weapons," *Air Force Magazine*, March 1984, pp. 111-112; Polmar, *Guide to the Soviet Navy*, 1986, p. 394; *Jane's All the World's Aircraft*, 1987-88, p. 280.

8
Tu-16 BADGER

Figure 8.12 Bottom view of the **Tu-16 Badger C**, which has two variations—one carries two AS-2 ASMs under the fuselage, while the Badger C Modified carries the AS-5 Kelt on wing pylons. All Badger bombers are gradually being retired, and are being replaced by the Backfire.

Figure 8.13 The **Badger** has a unique aerial refueling capability using wingtip-to-wingtip transfer as illustrated in this photograph.

NUCLEAR WEAPONS:	Average four weapons per Badger;[15] Badger A: bombs in internal bays;[16] Badger C: two AS-2 Kipper or AS-5 Kelt, two AS-2 under fuselage or AS-5 on wing pylons;[17] no bombs on C version (AS-5-capable versions are called Badger C Modified);[18] Badger G: bombs and AS-5 Kelt, two AS-5 on wing pylons with bombs in internal bays;[19]
	Badger G Modified: bombs and AS-6 Kingfish
Payload:	9000 kg (20,000 lbs);[20] 8000 kg (18,000 lbs) in weapons bay of A version[21]

DEPLOYMENT:

Number:	some 440 strike versions (Badger A/C/G): some 250 Badger A/G in SAA, 190 Badger A/C/G in SNA (1988);[22] estimated 70 Badger A (50 SAA, 20 SNA); 70 Badger C/C Modified (all SNA); 300 Badger G (200 SAA, 100 SNA); half considered Badger G Modified; some 90-100 tanker versions and some 170 electronic warfare/reconnaissance versions, as well as a few training versions; Badger bombers are being retired;[23] and replaced by Backfire, most likely in the coming decade[24]
Location:	SAA bombers assigned to the Smolensk and Irkutsk Air Armies;[25] SNA bombers assigned to Northern, Baltic, Black Sea, and Pacific Fleets;[26] Bobruysk (140 km SE of Minsk);[27] deployed to Cam Ranh Bay, Vietnam, in mid-November 1983;[28] some 10 strike variants are part of a composite squadron as of early 1988[29]

---

15 DIA, *Force Structure Summary*, November 1987, p. 8.
16 USN, *Soviet Naval Developments* (Rev. 4/85), p. 133; Taylor, "Gallery of Soviet Aerospace Weapons," 1984, *op. cit.*, pp. 111-112; Polmar, *Guide to the Soviet Navy*, 1983, pp. 331-332.
17 USN, *Soviet Naval Developments* (Rev. 4/85), p. 133; IISS, *Military Balance*, 1987-1988, p. 207; Polmar, *Guide to the Soviet Navy*, 1986, p. 394.
18 *Jane's All the World's Aircraft*, 1987-88, p. 279.
19 USN, *Soviet Naval Developments* (Rev. 4/85), p. 133; *Jane's All the World's Aircraft*, 1987-1988, p. 279.
20 Polmar *Guide to the Soviet Navy*, 1986, p. 394; Collins and Victory, *U.S./Soviet Military Balance*, 1987, p. 82.
21 Polmar *Guide to the Soviet Navy*, 1986, p. 394.
22 DIA, *Force Structure Summary*, November 1987, pp. 8, 21; Collins and Victory, *U.S./Soviet Military Balance*, 1988, p. 35; SMP 1987, pp. 8, 35; Polmar, *Guide to the Soviet Navy*, 1986, p. 394. John W. R. Taylor, "Gallery of Soviet Aerospace Weapons," *Air Force Magazine*, March 1988, p. 75, says 260 in SAAs and 190 in SNA. Some of these strike versions are non-nuclear-capable Badger B bombers, but the number is unknown.
23 SMP 1988, p. 15, reported 272 Badgers in the SAAs and 120 Badgers in SNA, although no explanation was given for the increased number in SAAs, and the data did not correspond with DIA, *Force Structure Summary*, November 1987, pp. 8, 21.
24 SMP 1988, p. 79.
25 *Ibid.*
26 Taylor, "Gallery of Soviet Aerospace Weapons," 1988, *op. cit.*, p. 76. During the summer of 1985, Fencer E aircraft replaced Badger bombers in the Black Sea Fleet; SMP 1988, p. 86.
27 *Jane's Defence Weekly*, 18 August 1984, p. 211. An explosion at the air base on 14 May 1984 caused by a Badger crash (while reportedly returning from operations in Afghanistan) destroyed a number of Badger aircraft.
28 CINCPAC, "Pacific Area Update," P4048.IPI-4, 17 February 1984, p 14; SMP 1987, p. 69.
29 Studeman, USN, Statement before HASC, March 1988, p. 40; SMP 1988, pp. 27-28.

8
Tu-16 BADGER

HISTORY:

Year Design Began: unknown

First Flight: prototype first flown in late 1952[30]

First Seen: 1954[31]

IOC: 1954;[32] 1955(SNA)[33]

Production: production ended in 1983 after about 2000 Badgers were produced[34]

COMMENTS: Badger A version, the basic bomber, is used primarily for tanker training and mine-laying missions and can carry only bombs in internal bays. Badger B versions originally deployed with AS-1 Kennel (now retired) are conventional-only bombers. Badger C carries AS-2 ASMs. Badger C Modified and Badger G versions carry AS-5 ASMs. Badger G Modified versions are replacing B versions and carry newer AS-6 ASMs and bombs.

Badger D/E/F/K versions are reconnaissance or maritime patrol aircraft. Badger H/J are electronic countermeasures (ECM) aircraft. As many as 80 Badger As are configured as aerial tankers.

Also in service in the Chinese (Xian H-6), Egyptian, Indonesian, Iraqi, and Libyan militaries.

---

30 *Jane's All the World's Aircraft*, 1987-88, p. 278; Polmar, *Duide to the Soviet Navy*, 1986, p. 394.
31 DOD, FY 1971 Annual Report (class.), p. A-11.
32 *Ibid.*; DOD, FY 1970 Annual Report, p. 82.
33 Senate Committee on Commerce and National Ocean Policy Studies, Hearings on Soviet Ocean Development, October 1976, p. 60.
34 Taylor, "Gallery of Soviet Aerospace Weapons," 1988, *op. cit.*, p. 75.

8
Su-24 FENCER

Tactical Aircraft
Su-24 FENCER A/B/C/D/E[1]

Figure 8.14 Beginning in August 1981 **Su-24 Fencer** fighter-bombers permanently deployed to Eastern Europe. This is thought to mark the first permanent storage of nuclear warheads outside the Soviet Union. Today the Fencer is the centerpiece of Soviet Air Forces non-strategic ground attack capabilities.

DESCRIPTION: All-weather, variable-geometry-wing, twin-engine, medium-range fighter-bomber used by the Air Force; superseded Yak-28 Brewer and is replacing Su-7 Fitter A and Su-17 Fitter D

DESIGN BUREAU: Sukhoi

SPECIFICATIONS:
Dimensions:
- Length: 21.3 m[2] (69.9 ft)
- Height: 5.5 m[3] (18.0 ft)

Wingspan:
- Swept: 10.2 m[4] (33.5 ft)
- Spread: 17.2 m[5] (56.3 ft)

Takeoff Weight (max): approx. 39,000 kg[6] (86,000 lbs)

Powerplant: 2 turbojets, reported to be Lyulka AL-21F[7] or Tumansky R-29B-300,[8] or versions of these engines

Ceiling: 17,500 m[9] (57,400 ft)

Range (max): approx. 6400 km[10] (3500 nm)

---

1. The Su-24 was originally designated Su-19, but was changed to Su-24 due to a reassessment of its mission as a fighter-bomber rather than a fighter. (Odd numbers are used for fighter designations.)
2. *Flight International*, 1 August 1987, p. 69; *Jane's All the World's Aircraft*, 1987-88, p. 275; Graham Warwick, "Military Aircraft of the World," *Flight International*, 1 March 1980, pp. 672-673.
3. *Jane's All the World's Aircraft*, 1987-88, p. 275; Warwick, *op. cit.*, pp. 672-673.
4. SMP 1981, p. 34.
5. *Jane's All the World's Aircraft*, 1987-88, p. 275; Warwick, *op. cit.*, pp. 672-673; Gunston, *Aircraft of the Soviet Union*, 1983, p. 278.
6. SAC, FY 1981 DOD, Part 4, p. 896; *Jane's All the World's Aircraft*, 1987-88, p. 233; Gunston, *Aircraft of the Soviet Union*, 1983, p. 278.
7. *Jane's All the World's Aircraft*, 1987-88, p. 275; Warwick, *op. cit.*, pp. 672-673. AL are the initials of engine designer Arkhip Lyulka.
8. *Jane's Defence Review*, Vol. 2, No. 5, 1981, p. 387; Georg Panyalev, "Su-24 Fencer: A Closer Look," *International Defense Review*, May 1981, p. 11. The Sergei K. Tumansky design bureau uses R (*Reaktivnyi*) rather than the designer's initials.
9. SMP 1981, p. 34.
10. Gunston, *Aircraft of the Soviet Union*, 1983, p. 280.

Su-24 FENCER

Figure 8.15 The **Su-24 Fencer**, introduced in December 1974, was the Soviet Union's first long-range fighter to concentrate on ground attack roles. It was the first non-bomber aircraft to have a second seat for a weapons systems officer.

Figure 8.16 The **Fencer** can carry two nuclear bombs and has the capability of carrying a 3000 kg (5500 lb) payload. Its rear center fuselage pylon is reportedly designed specifically for a nuclear bomb.

Unrefueled combat radius:	1300 km[11] (700 nm); 900 nm[12]
Aerial Refueling Capability:	Fencer D has aerial refueling capability; others do not[13]
Speed (max):	1250 kts;[14] Mach 2.0;[15] Mach 2.2[16]
Crew:	2 (side-by-side seating)

NUCLEAR WEAPONS: 2 nuclear bombs; can carry a nuclear bomb on any of eight pylons;[17] rear center-fuselage pylon is reportedly specifically for nuclear bomb;[18] can carry the AS-11 Kilter, which may have a nuclear capability;[19] 3000 kg[20] (5500 lb) payload

DEPLOYMENT:
Number: about 850 of all types;[21] more than 500 in the SAAs;[22] some 315 in Air Forces of the Military Districts; some 65 Fencer E, 35 of them in SNA[23]

Location: SAA bombers assigned to the Legnica and Vinnitsa Air Armies;[24] some 250 Fencers in the Far East;[25] based in the Western, Southwestern and Far Eastern TVDs, and Eastern Europe: Tukums (Riga, Latvia) (two regiments), Chernyakhovsk (Kaliningrad) (two regiments), Lusatia, Starokonstantinov (Ukraine) (two regiments), Gorodok (Ukraine), Samtredia, Iliysk; Debrecen, Hungary; Zagan and Szprotaeea, Poland; Brand/Briesen, East Germany;[26] Fencer E in Baltic Fleet;[27] deployment began to Eastern Europe in August 1981 with the equipping of Debrecen AB, Hungary, followed by the two bases in Poland; in January 1982, Fencer began arriving in East Germany, replacing SU-7s

HISTORY:
First Flight: 1970 (prototype); 1973 (Su-24)[28]

IOC: December 1974 (Fencer A); 1981 (Fencer C);[29] 1983 (Fencer D)[30]

Production: in series production (1988)[31]

---

11. Hi-Lo-Lo-Hi, with external fuel; DIA, *Force Structure Summary*, November 1987, p. 18; SMP 1987, p. 78.
12. SASC, FY 1982 DOD, Part 3, p. 1084.
13. John W. R. Taylor, "Gallery of Soviet Aerospace Weapons," *Air Force Magazine*, March 1987, p. 91; SASC, FY 1980 DOD, Part 3, p. 843.
14. SMP 1985, p. 82; SMP 1984, pp. 28, 55, 57; SMP 1983, p. 43.
15. DIA, *Force Structure Summary*, November 1987, p. 18; SMP 1987, p. 78.
16. *Jane's All the World's Aircraft*, 1987-88, p. 275; Panyalev, *op. cit.*, p. 11; Collins and Cronin, *U.S./Soviet Military Balance*, 1985, p. 58.
17. SMP 1984, pp. 28, 55, 57; DOD, FY 1979 Annual Report, p. 69; *Jane's All the World's Aircraft*, 1987-88, p. 275.
18. Panyalev, *op. cit.*, p. 11.
19. SMP 1987, p. 79.
20. DIA, *Force Structure Summary*, November 1987, p. 18; SMP 1987, p. 79.
21. SMP 1988, p. 79; SMP 1987, p. 79.
22. SMP 1988, p. 79; SMP 1987, pp. 35, 77; SMP 1984, pp. 28, 55, 57.
23. John W. R. Taylor, "Gallery of Soviet Aerospace Weapons," *Air Force Magazine*, March 1988, p. 81.
24. SMP 1988, p. 79.
25. *Ibid.*, p. 123.
26. Deployment began to Eastern Europe in August 1981 with the equipping of Debrecen AB, Hungary, followed by two bases in Poland: Zagan AB and Szprotaeea AB. In January 1982 Fencers began arriving at Brand/Briesen AB in East Germany to replace 40 Su-7s presently deployed there; Taylor, "Gallery of Soviet Aerospace Weapons," 1987, *op. cit.*, p. 91. *Jane's All the World's Aircraft*, 1987-88, p. 275; Martin Streetly, "Su-24 Fencer-C: Major Equipment Changes," *Jane's Defence Weekly*, 22 June 1985, p. 1226.
27. The Fencer E was assigned to the Baltic Fleet during the summer of 1985, replacing Badger bombers; SMP 1988, p. 86.
28. Streetly, *op. cit.*, p. 1226.
29. SMP 1984, pp. 28, 55, 57; NATO and the Warsaw Pact, 1984, p. 32.
30. Taylor, "Gallery of Soviet Aerospace Weapons," 1987, *op. cit.*, p. 91.
31. SMP 1987, pp. 64-65.

8
Su-24 FENCER

COMMENTS: Somewhat comparable to the U.S. F-111, but smaller and with a smaller mission radius, and inferior in avionics and overall performance.[32] Comparable to the U.S. Navy A-6 attack aircraft.[33] Fencer was the first Soviet fighter aircraft designed specifically for ground attack—and the first to carry a weapons system officer.[34]

Fencer A/B are basic versions with minor modifications. Fencer C has major equipment upgrades, including enhanced ECM. Fencer D incorporated in-flight refueling and numerous upgrades and is primarily assigned to the SAAs.[35] In early 1986, a squadron of Fencer E fighter-bomber/reconnaissance variants entered service in the Baltic Fleet Air Force of SNA.[36] The planes can be armed "with a variety of air-to-surface ordnance."[37]

---

32 DOD, FY 1986 *Annual Report*, p. 18; SMP 1984, pp. 28, 55, 57; SAC, FY 1981 DOD, Part 4, p. 896.
33 JCS, FY 1989, p. 60.
34 SMP 1981, p. 34.
35 SMP 1986, p. 78.
36 SMP 1987, p. 88.
37 *Ibid.*, p. 66.

MiG-27 FLOGGER D/J

Figure 8.17 The **MiG-27 Flogger D** shown here landing with wings extended, is designed for low-level attacks at transonic speeds. At the time it was introduced in 1975, the nuclear-capable ground attack fighter had the ability to carry a greater bomb load than any other Soviet fighter.

DESCRIPTION: All-weather, variable-geometry, ground-attack aircraft assigned to AFMD/GOF, being replaced by the Su-27 Flanker

DESIGN BUREAU: Mikoyan-Gurevich

SPECIFICATIONS:
Dimensions:
- Length: 16 m[1] (53 ft)
- Height: 4.5 m[2] (14.8 ft)

Wingspan:
- Swept: 8.1-8.2 m[3] (26.6-26.9 ft)
- Spread: 14.25 m[4] (46.75 ft)

Takeoff Weight (max): 18,000 kg[5] (40,000 lbs)

Powerplant: Tumansky R-29-300 turbojet[6]

Ceiling: 16,000 m[7] (52,500 ft)

Range (max): 2500 km[8] (1350 nm)

---

1 *Jane's All the World's Aircraft*, 1987-88, pp. 258-260. Specifications for Flogger D; Gunston, *Guide to the Modern Soviet Air Force*, 1982, p. 84.
2 *Jane's All the World's Aircraft*, 1987-88, pp. 258-260. Specifications for Flogger D.
3 SMP 1981, pp. 32, 34; *Jane's All the World's Aircraft*, 1987-88, pp. 258-260. Specifications for Flogger D; Gunston, *Aircraft of the Soviet Union*, 1983, p. 189.
4 *Jane's All the World's Aircraft*, 1987-88, pp. 258-260. Specifications for Flogger D.
5 *Jane's All the World's Aircraft*, 1987-88, pp. 258-260. Specifications for Flogger D; Graham Warwick, "Military Aircraft of the World," *Flight International*, 1 March 1980, pp. 672-673.
6 John W. R. Taylor, "Gallery of Soviet Aerospace Weapons," *Air Force Magazine*, March 1987, p. 90. The Sergei Tumansky design bureau uses R (*Reaktivnyi*) rather than the designer's initials.
7 SMP 1981, pp. 32, 34.
8 *Jane's All the World's Aircraft*, 1987-88, pp. 258-260. Specifications for Flogger D; Gunston, *Guide to the Modern Soviet Air Force*, 1982, p. 84; Gunston, *Aircraft of the Soviet Union*, 1983, p. 190.

8

MiG-27 FLOGGER

Unrefueled Combat Radius:	600 km[9] (325 nm); 1200 km[10] (650 nm); 550-800 km[11] (300-400 nm)	**HISTORY:** First Flight:	1970[19]
Aerial Refueling Capability:	unknown	IOC:	1975 (Flogger D);[20] 1981 (Flogger J)[21]
Speed (max):	980 kts;[12] Mach 1.7[13]	Production:	ended in the mid-1980s[22]
Crew:	1	**COMMENTS:**	The MiG-27 has many features in common with the MiG-23, but differs in mission and characteristics enough to have received a different designation.
NUCLEAR WEAPONS:	One weapon; can carry at least one nuclear bomb under rear fuselage or on five underwing pylons;[14] 3000 kg[15] (6600 lb) payload		
DEPLOYMENT: Number:	730-830 (1988)[16]		At least one squadron active in East German Air Force.[23] First Indian Flogger J squadron declared operational during 1986.[24]
Location:	Western, Far Eastern, and Southwestern TVDs;[17] stationed at Finsterwalde and Mirow/Rechlin-Larz in East Germany; deployed on the Kola peninsula[18]		

---

9 Hi-Lo-Lo-Hi, with external fuel; DIA, *Force Structure Summary*, November 1987, p. 18; SMP 1987, p. 78.
10 SMP 1984, pp. 55, 57, 96; SMP 1981, pp. 32, 34.
11 SMP 1981, pp. 32, 34; Christopher Bellamy, "Conventional Quick Kill," *Jane's Defence Weekly*, 19 May 1984, p. 784.
12 SMP 1985, p. 82; SMP 1984, pp.55, 57, 96; SMP 1983, p. 43.
13 DIA, *Force Structure Summary*, November 1987, p. 18; SMP 1987, p. 78.
14 SMP 1984, pp. 55, 57, 96; John W. R. Taylor, "Gallery of Soviet Aerospace Weapons," *Air Force Magazine*, March 1988, p. 80.
15 DIA, *Force Structure Summary*, November 1987, p. 18; SMP 1987, p. 78; SMP 1985, p. 82.
16 Air Vice-Marshal R. A. Mason and John W. R. Taylor, *Soviet Air Force* (London: Jane's Publishing Company, 1986), p. 210; Taylor, "Gallery of Soviet Aerospace Weapons," 1988, op. cit., p. 80.
17 SMP 1984, pp. 55, 57, 96.
18 "Soviets' Buildup in North Exceeds Production Level," *Aviation Week & Space Technology*, 15 May 1981, p. 102.
19 Gunston, *Guide to the Modern Soviet Air Force*, 1982, p. 85.
20 HASC, FY 1980 DOD, Part 3, Book 2, p. 2115; JEC, Allocation of Resources - 1977, Part 3, p. 68.
21 *Jane's All the World's Aircraft*, 1987-88, pp. 258-260.
22 SMP 1988, p. 39.
23 Taylor, "Gallery of Soviet Aerospace Weapons," 1987, p. 90.
24 *Flight International*, 1 August 1987, p. 64.

MiG-23 FLOGGER B/G

Figure 8.18 The **MiG-23 Flogger G** with AA7 and AA8 air-to-air missiles incorporated new radar and infrared sensors under the cockpit.

DESCRIPTION: All-weather, variable-geometry-wing interceptor and ground-attack aircraft assigned to AFMD/GOF, being replaced by MiG-29 Fulcrums and Su-27 Flankers

DESIGN BUREAU: Mikoyan-Gurevich

SPECIFICATIONS:
Dimensions:

Length: 16.8 m[1] (55.1 ft)

Height: 4.5 m[2] (14.8 ft); 4.35 m[3] (14.3 ft)

Wingspan:

Swept: 8.17 m[4] (26.8 ft)

Spread: 14.25 m[5] (46.75 ft)

Takeoff Weight (max): 12,700-20,000 kg[6] (28,000-44,100 lbs)

Powerplant: MiG-23M Flogger B: Tumansky R-27 turbojet[7]; MiG-23MF Flogger B and MiG-23 Flogger G: Tumansky R-29B turbojet[8]

Ceiling: 18,000 m[9] (60,000 ft)

---

1. Gunston, *Guide to the Modern Soviet Air Force*, 1982, p. 70.
2. "Extensive Developments to MiG-23," *Jane's Defence Weekly*, 27 July 1985, p. 168.
3. Gunston, *Guide to the Modern Soviet Air Force*, 1982, p. 70.
4. SMP 1981, pp. 32, 34; SMP 1985, p. 82.
5. "Extensive Developments to MiG-23," *op. cit.*, p. 168.
6. *Ibid.*; Gunston, *Guide to the Modern Soviet Air Force*, 1982, p. 70.
7. "Extensive Developments to MiG-23," *op. cit.*, p. 168; Tim Wrixon, "Air Defence Equipment - World Review," *Jane's Defence Weekly*, 17 March 1984, p. 405. The Sergei Tumansky design bureau uses R (*Reaaktivnyi*) rather than the designer's initials.
8. John W. R. Taylor, "Gallery of Soviet Aerospace Weapons," *Air Force Magazine*, March 1987, p. 88.
9. SMP 1981, p. 32; *Jane's All the World's Aircraft*, 1983-1984, pp. 216-218.

8
MiG-23 FLOGGER

Figure 8.19 The **MiG-23 Flogger B** and its variants form the backbone of the Soviet Air Forces and Air Defense Forces; some 1750 aircraft are assigned to the Air Forces of the Military Districts/Groups of Soviet Forces.

Range (max):	2600-2800 km[10] (1400-1500 nm)	Location:	some are assigned to Legnica and Vinnitsa Air Armies to act as escorts for SU-24 Fencers;[16] air defense units at Kursk, Smolensk, Yaroslav-Tunoshnoye, Yefremov, Kubinka;[17] Etorofu Island, Kuriles[18]
Unrefueled combat radius:	1150 km[11] (620 nm)		
Aerial Refueling Capability:	No		
Speed (max):	1350 kts;[12] Mach 2.3-2.5[13]	**HISTORY:**	
Crew:	1	First Seen:	prototype observed at Domodedovo Airport on 9 July 1967[19]
NUCLEAR WEAPONS:	Probably can carry a single nuclear bomb on pylon under center fuselage[14]	First Flight:	1966[20]
		IOC:	1972 (MiG-23M Flogger B);[21] 1975 (MiG-23MF Flogger B); 1978 (MiG-23MF Flogger G)[22]
DEPLOYMENT:			
Number:	1140-1570 total in AFMD/GOF, plus 420 non-nuclear versions in Air Defense Forces[15]	Production:	ended in the mid-1980s[23]

---

10 USAICS, *Handbook on the Soviet Ground Forces*, pp. 243-244; Gunston, *Guide to the Modern Soviet Air Force*, 1982, p. 71.
11 DIA, *Force Structure Summary*, November 1987, pp. 10, 18; SMP 1987, p. 78. SMP 1985, p. 82, gives 1300 km. SMP 1981, p. 32, gives 900-1200 km, and at p. 34 gives 1300 km.
12 SMP 1985, p. 82.
13 USAICS, *Handbook on the Soviet Ground Forces*, pp. 243-244. DIA, *Force Structure Summary*, November 1987, pp. 10, 18, and SMP 1987, p. 78, give Mach 2.3.
14 SMP 1987, p. 66; DOD, FY 1979 Annual Report, p. 69; USAICS, *Handbook on the Soviet Ground Forces*, pp. 243-244.
15 IISS, *Military Balance*, 1987-1988, p. 36; John W. R. Taylor, "Gallery of Soviet Aerospace Weapons," *Air Force Magazine*, March 1988, p. 78.
16 SMP 1988, p. 79.
17 Taylor, "Gallery of Soviet Aerospace Weapons," 1988, op. cit., p. 78; *Jane's Defence Weekly*, 18 February 1984, p. 231.
18 Clyde Haberman, "Japan Warns of a Soviet Military Buildup in Asia," *New York Times*, 15 September 1984, p. 4.
19 Gunston, *Aircraft of the Soviet Union*, 1983, p. 187.
20 Gunston, *Guide to the Modern Soviet Air Force*, 1982, p. 71.
21 IOC of Flogger B; DOD, FY 1983 RDA, P. II-11. Prototype Flogger A aircraft reached IOC in 1971.
22 "Extensive developments to MiG-23," op. cit., p. 168.
23 SMP 1988, p. 39.

8
MiG-23 FLOGGER

COMMENTS: First series-production aircraft was MiG-23M Flogger B (Flogger A was prototype). MiG-23MF Flogger B had upgraded turbojet, which was incorporated into later-production MiG-23 Flogger Gs as well. Flogger G also incorporated new radar and infrared sensor under cockpit.[24] MiG-23 Flogger C is non-nuclear, tandem-seat training plane.[25] MiG-23 Flogger K is air-superiority fighter.

---

[24] "Extensive developments to MiG-23," op. cit., p. 168; Wrixon, op. cit., p. 405.

[25] Jane's All the World's Aircraft, 1983-1984, pp. 216-218.

8
Su-17 FITTER

Su-17 FITTER C/D/H

Figure 8.20 Right side view of two Soviet **Su-17 Fitter C** aircraft in flight. These aircraft, when introduced in 1972, represented powerful advances in the Soviet Union's air-to-surface tactical force. Improved avionics and more powerful engines increased range, load capability, and weapons delivery accuracy.

DESCRIPTION: All-weather, variable-geometry-wing, fighter/ground-attack aircraft used by Air Forces (Fitter D/H) and SNA (Fitter C); replaced Su-7 Fitter A

DESIGN BUREAU: Sukhoi

SPECIFICATIONS:
- Dimensions:
  - Length: 18.75 m[1] (61.52 ft) including probes
  - Height: 4.75 m[2] (15.6 ft)
  - Wingspan:
    - Swept: 9.9 m[3] (32.5 ft)
    - Spread: 14.0 m[4] (45.9 ft)
- Takeoff Weight (gross): Fitter C: 17,700 kg[5] (39,000 lbs)

  Fitter H: 19,200 kg[6] (42,330 lbs)
- Powerplant: Lyulka AL-21F-3 turbojet[7]
- Ceiling: 18,000 m[8] (59,000 ft)
- Range (max): 2250 km[9] (1200 nm)
- Unrefueled combat radius: Fitter C: 630 km[10] (340 nm)

  Fitter D/H: 550 km[11] (300 nm); 700 km[12] (380 nm)
- Aerial Refueling Capability: unknown
- Speed (max): Fitter D/H: Mach 2.1;[13] 1200 kts[14]
- Crew: 1

NUCLEAR WEAPONS: Can carry at least one nuclear bomb on one of six to eight weapon pylons;[15] Fitter C: 3100 kg[16] (6800 lbs); Fitter D/H: 3000 kg[17] (6600 lb) bomb payload

DEPLOYMENT:
- Number: about 870; 800 Air Forces, 70 SNA[18]

---

1. Specifications for Fitter C; USN, *Soviet Naval Developments* (Rev. 4/85), p. 136; *Jane's All the World's Aircraft*, 1987-88, p. 274.
2. Specifications for Fitter C; *Jane's All the World's Aircraft*, 1987-88, p. 274.
3. SMP 1981, pp. 33, 34; SMP 1983, p. 43; SMP 1984, pp. 55, 57 SMP 1985, p. 82.
4. Specifications for Fitter C; *Jane's All the World's Aircraft*, 1987-88, p. 274; Polmar, *Guide to the Soviet Navy*, 1986, p. 398.
5. Specifications for Fitter C; USN, *Soviet Naval Developments* (Rev. 4/85), p. 136; *Jane's All the World's Aircraft*, 1987-88, p. 274; Graham Warwick, "Military Aircraft of the World," *Flight International*, 1 March 1980, pp. 672-673.
6. Gunston, *Guide to the Modern Soviet Air Force*, 1982, p. 106.
7. Specifications for Fitter C; *Jane's All the World's Aircraft*, 1987-88, p. 273; Polmar, *Guide to the Soviet Navy*, 1986, p. 398; Gunston, *Aircraft of the Soviet Union*, 1983, p. 278. AL are the initials of engine designer Arkhip Lyulka.
8. SMP 1981, p. 33, 34; Gunston, *Aircraft of the Soviet Union*, 1983, p. 278.
9. "In Soviet Service-4: Sukhoi Su-17," *Air International*, May 1979, pp. 223-224; Gunston, *Guide to the Modern Soviet Air Force*, 1982, p. 108.
10. Specifications for Fitter C; *Jane's All the World's Aircraft*, 1987-88, p. 274; Gunston, *Guide to the Modern Soviet Air Force*, 1982, pp. 107-108.
11. DIA, *Force Structure Summary*, November 1987, p. 18; SMP 1987, p. 78.
12. SMP 1984, p. 55; SMP 1983, p. 43; SMP 1981, pp. 33, 34. SMP 1981, p. 33, gives 550-900 km for the Fitter C/D/H.
13. DIA, *Force Structure Summary*, November 1987, p. 18; SMP 1987, p. 78.
14. SMP 1984, pp. 55, 57; SMP 1983, p. 43; SMP 1985, p. 82.
15. SMP 1984, pp. 55, 57; DOD, FY 1979 Annual Report, p. 69; *Jane's All the World's Aircraft*, 1987-88, p. 274.
16. SMP 1987, p. 87.
17. DIA, *Force Structure Summary*, November 1987, p. 18; SMP 1987, p. 78; SMP 1984, pp. 55, 57.
18. Some 1060 Fitters of all types (Fitter C/D/E/F/G/H/J/K) are deployed, and some 875 are thought to be nuclear-capable versions; DIA, *Force Structure Summary*, November 1987, p. 21; John W. R. Taylor, "Gallery of Soviet Aerospace Weapons," *Air Force Magazine*, March 1988, p. 81; SMP 1988, p. 86.

8
Su-17 FITTER

Location: assigned to MDs/Groups of Soviet Forces in Eastern Europe: at least Belorussian, Baltic, and Carpathian MDs; East Germany (Grossenhain, Neuruppin, and Templin/Gross-Delln); Baltic and Pacific Fleets[19]

HISTORY:

First Flight: 1966 (Su-22I prototype); 1970 (production version)[20]

First Seen: July 1967 Soviet Aviation Day at Domodedovo (Su-22I prototype, also known as Fitter B)[21]

IOC: 1972-1973 (Fitter C);[22] 1976 (Fitter D)[23]

Production: in production but "cut drastically over the past several years"[24]

COMMENTS: Comparable to the U.S. A-7A/D Corsair II.[25] Fitter C is the basic version, serving with SNA and Air Forces. It is land-based and is assigned to ground-attack/close-air-support missions, including support of Naval Infantry.[26] Su-17M Fitter D is assigned to Air Forces and has improved avionics, an electro-optical or laser weapon-guidance system, and a terrain avoidance radar.[27] Su-17UM Fitter E is a non-nuclear two-seat trainer. Fitter G is a non-nuclear two-seat trainer with combat capability. Fitter H/K are later reconnaissance versions of Fitter D and may carry armaments. Some 165 are deployed.[28]

Flown by air forces of Algeria, Angola, Czechoslovakia, Egypt, Iraq, Libya, North Yemen, Peru, Poland, South Yemen, Syria, and Vietnam.

---

19 SMP 1987, p. 88; "In Soviet Service-4: Sukhoi Su-17," op. cit., pp. 223-224; Polmar, Guide to the Soviet Navy, 1986, p. 398.
20 Polmar, Guide to the Soviet Navy, 1986, p. 398; Gunston, Guide to the Modern Soviet Air Force, 1982, p. 108.
21 Jane's All the World's Aircraft, 1984-85, pp. 238-239; Polmar, Guide to the Soviet Navy, 1986, p. 398.
22 HASC, FY 1980 DOD, Part 3, Book 2, p. 2115; USN, Soviet Naval Developments (Rev. 4/85), p. 135.
23 HASC, FY 1980 DOD, Part 3, Book 2, p. 2115.
24 SMP 1988, p. 39.
25 SMP 1984, p. 55.
26 USN, Soviet Naval Developments (Rev. 4/85), p. 135.
27 Jane's All the World's Aircraft, 1983-84, pp. 231-233; Polmar, Guide to the Soviet Navy, 1986, p. 398.
28 SMP 1987, pp. 66, 78; NATO and the Warsaw Pact, 1984, p. 32. Some 200 Fitter H/K are deployed; Taylor, "Gallery of Soviet Aerospace Weapons," 1988, op. cit., p. 81.

MiG-21bis FISHBED L

Figure 8.21 **MiG-21 Fishbed** is one of the most commonly flown aircraft in the world. Since its introduction in 1958, over 2500 MiG-21s have entered service. Almost 1700 of the later-model variants are operational in the Air Forces of the Military Districts (AFMD).

DESCRIPTION:	All weather, improved fighter/interceptors assigned to AFMD/GOF and currently being replaced by MiG-29 Fulcrums and Su-27 Flankers
DESIGN BUREAU:	Mikoyan-Gurevich
SPECIFICATIONS:	
Dimensions:	
Length:	15.76 m[1] (51.85 ft) including boom
Height:	4.5 m[2] (14.9 ft)
Wingspan:	7.2 m[3] (23.6 ft)
Takeoff Weight (max.):	9400 kg[4] (20,725 lbs)
Powerplant:	Tumansky R-25 turbojet[5]
Ceiling:	18,000 m[6] (50,000 ft)
Range (max):	1800 km[7] (970 nm)
Unrefueled combat radius:	approx. 750 km[8] (400 nm)
Aerial Refueling Capability:	yes
Speed (max):	1205 kts;[9] Mach 2.0[10]
Crew:	1
NUCLEAR WEAPONS:	One nuclear bomb; two 500 kg bombs maximum can be carried under wings; Fishbed L may not be able to carry bombs[11]

---

1. Performance and specifications for MiG-21MF Fishbed J; *Jane's All the World's Aircraft*, 1987-88, pp. 254-255; Gunston, *Aircraft of the Soviet Union*, 1983, p. 184.
2. *Jane's All the World's Aircraft*, 1987-88, pp. 254-255.
3. Specifications for L/N; SMP 1981, pp. 33, 34.
4. John W. R. Taylor, "Gallery of Soviet Aerospace Weapons," *Air force Magazine*, March 1987, p. 87.
5. Replaced Tumansky R-11 and Tumansky R-13-300 turbojet engines on earlier MiG-21 versions; Taylor, "Gallery of Soviet Aerospace Weapons," 1987, *op. cit.*, p. 87; Gunston, *Aircraft of the Soviet Union*, 1983, p. 183. The Sergei Tumansky design bureau uses R (*Reaktivnyi*) rather than the designer's initials.
6. Specifications for L/N; SMP 1981, pp. 33, 34. See also Taylor, "Gallery of Soviet Aerospace Weapons," 1987, *op. cit.*, p. 87.
7. USAICS, *Handbook on the Soviet Ground Forces*, pp. 243-244.
8. DIA, *Force Structure Summary*, November 1987, p. 18; SMP 1987, p. 78. Specifications for L; SMP 1985, p. 82 gives 500 km.
9. SMP 1985, p. 82, SMP 1983, p. 43; SMP 1984, p. 96; SMP 1981, pp. 33, 34.
10. DIA, *Force Structure Summary*, November 1987, p. 18; SMP 1987, p. 78.
11. SMP 1984, p. 75, and later DOD documents dropped bomb carrying as a mission of the Fishbed L.

8
MiG-21bis FISHBED L

Figure 8.22 The venerable **MiG-21 Fishbed** is an all-weather, improved fighter/interceptor with multi-role variants. The later Fishbed J, K, L, and N versions have both nuclear nuclear and non-nuclear roles).

DEPLOYMENT:

Number: almost 500 late-model Fishbeds are operational;[12] some 135 Fishbed L;[13] 65 non-nuclear Fishbed H[14]

Location: some are assigned to the Legnica and Vinnitsa Air Armies to act as escorts for Su-24 Fencers[15]

HISTORY:

First Flight: 16 June 1956 (MiG-21 prototype)[16]

First Seen: June 1956 Soviet Aviation display at Tushino Airport, Moscow[17]

IOC: 1958 (MiG-21)
1967 (MiG-21PFMA Fishbed J)[18]
1969-1970 (MiG-21MF Fishbed J)[19]
1971 (MiG-21SMB Fishbed K)[20]
1975-1976 (MiG-21bis Fishbed L)
1978 (MiG-21bis Fishbed N)

Production: not in production; MiG-21bis Fishbed N believed to be produced 1978-1984[21]

COMMENTS: MiG-21PFMA/MF Fishbed J and MiG-21MB Fishbed K multirole fighters are limited-range, theoretically nuclear-capable, versions with two extra pylons for air-to-air missiles (AAMs), but are thought to concentrate mostly on air-superiority tasks.

---

12 SMP 1987, p. 78.
13 IISS, *Military Balance*, 1987-88, p. 207
14 John W. R. Taylor, "Gallery of Soviet Aerospace Weapons," *Air Force Magazine*, March 1988, p. 77.
15 SMP 1988, p. 79.
16 *Jane's All the World's Aircraft*, 1987-88, pp. 254-255.
17 Ibid.
18 Gunston, *Guide to the Modern Soviet Air Force*, 1982, p. 68.
19 Taylor, "Gallery of Soviet Aerospace Weapons," 1987, op. cit., p. 87; *Jane's All the World's Aircraft*, 1987-88, pp. 254-255; Gunston, *Aircraft of the Soviet Union*, 1983, p. 183.
20 Gunston, *Aircraft of the Soviet Union*, 1983, p. 183.
21 SMP 1984, p. 96; *Jane's All the World's Aircraft*, 1987-88, pp. 254-255.

8

Su-7B FITTER A

Su-7B FITTER A (BMK FITTER A)

DESCRIPTION: Daylight, swept-wing, ground-attack aircraft being replaced by Su-17 Fitter and Su-24 Fencer

DESIGN BUREAU: Sukhoi; manufactured at Novosibirsk

SPECIFICATIONS:
  Dimensions:
  Length: 17.37 m[1] (57.0 ft) including probe
  Height: 4.57 m[2] (15.0 ft)
  Wingspan: 8.93 m[3] (29.3 ft)

  Takeoff Weight (gross): 13,500 kg[4] (30,000 lbs)

  Powerplant: Lyulka AL-7F-1 turbojet[5]

  Ceiling: 15,00 m[6] (49,000 ft)

  Range (max): 1450 km[7] (780 nm)

  Unrefueled combat radius: 250-350 km[8] (130-190 nm)

  Aerial Refueling Capability: unknown

  Speed (max): Mach 1.6;[9] Mach 1.2[10] with four loaded pylons

Crew: 1 (two-seat training version)

NUCLEAR WEAPONS: Probably can carry one nuclear bomb under fuselage;[11] 2000 kg[12] (4400 lb) payload

DEPLOYMENT:
  Number: about 45-80 remaining, but being phased out of service[13]
  Location: Su-7 Fitter As at Brand-Briesen, East Germany converted to Su-24 Fencer in 1982

HISTORY:
  Year Design Began: 1954[14]
  First Flight: S-1 prototype in 1955; production version in 1958[15]
  First Seen: 1956 Soviet Aviation Day[16]
  IOC: 1959;[17] 1960[18]
  Production: not in production, being retired at a rapid rate

---

1 Jane's All the World's Aircraft, 1984-85, pp. 236-237; Gunston, Aircraft of the Soviet Union, 1983, p. 272.
2 Jane's All the World's Aircraft, 1984-85, pp. 236-237.
3 Ibid.; Gunston, Aircraft of the Soviet Union, 1983, p. 272.
4 Jane's All the World's Aircraft, 1984-85, pp. 236-237.
5 Ibid.; Gunston, Aircraft of the Soviet Union, 1983, p. 272. AL are the initials of engine designer Arkhip Lyulka.
6 SMP 1981, p. 33.
7 Jane's All the World's Aircraft, 1984-85, pp. 236-237; Gunston, Aircraft of the Soviet Union, 1983, p. 272.
8 SMP 1981, p. 33.
9 Jane's All the World's Aircraft, 1984-85, pp. 236-237; Gunston, Aircraft of the Soviet Military Balance, 1985, p. 58.
10 Jane's All the World's Aircraft, 1984-85, pp. 236-237; Collins and Cronin, U.S./Soviet Military Balance, 1985, p. 58.
11 Jane's All the World's Aircraft, 1984-85, pp. 236-237.
12 SMP 1981, p. 33.
13 IISS, Military Balance, 1987-88, p. 207; John W. R. Taylor, "Gallery of Soviet Aerospace Weapons," Air Force Magazine, March 1988, p. 81.
14 Gunston, Guide to the Modern Soviet Air Force, 1982, p. 94.
15 Jane's All the World's Aircraft, 1984-85, pp. 236-237; Gunston, Aircraft of the Soviet Union, 1983, p. 271.
16 Jane's All the World's Aircraft, 1984-85, pp. 236-237.
17 DIA, Handbook on the Soviet Armed Forces, pp. 10-11; NATO and the Warsaw Pact, 1984, p. 32.
18 USAF, Soviet Aerospace Handbook, 1978, p. 42.

8
Tu-142 BEAR F

Naval Aviation
Tu-142 BEAR F

DESCRIPTION:	Four-turboprop, long-range, maritime reconnaissance/ASW aircraft in at least four modifications assigned to SNA (the strategic Bear bombers are described above)	**NUCLEAR WEAPONS:**	Capable of carrying nuclear torpedoes and depth bombs in two internal bays;[13] payload is more than 8000 kg (17,600 lbs)[14]

DESIGN BUREAU: Tupolev

SPECIFICATIONS:

Dimensions:

- Length: 49.5 m[1] (162.4 ft)
- Height: 12.1 m[2] (39.8 ft)
- Wingspan: 51.1 m[3] (167.7 ft)

Takeoff Weight (max): 188,000 kg[4] (414,000 lbs)

Powerplant: 4 Kuznetsov NK-12MV turboprop engines[5]

Ceiling: 13,500 m[6] (44,000 ft)

Range (max): approx. 11,000-13,000 km[7] (6000-7000 nm)

Unrefueled combat radius: 8300 km[8] (4500 nm, 5200 mi)

Aerial Refueling Capability: yes[9]

Speed (max): 500 kts;[10] 450 kts;[11] 800-890 km/h[12] (430-480 mph)

Crew: 5

DEPLOYMENT:

Number: 60 (1988)[15]

Location: assigned to the Northern and Pacific Fleets;[16] temporary deployments are regularly made to Cuba and Vietnam;[17] over 20 Bear F deployments to Cuba since 1981;[18] four Bear F stage from Vietnam[19]

HISTORY:

IOC: 1970;[20] 1971-1972 (Bear F)[21]

Production: Bear F Mod 3/4 in production[22]

COMMENTS: Bear F has been modified several times, with one modification providing nearly 20 percent enlargement of the aft weapons bay. Of the 20 Bear F aircraft identified by 12 February 1980, 5 were standard version, 4 were Mod 1, 7 were Mod 2, and 4 were Mod 3 (the last with the enlarged aft weapons bay).[23] Bear F Mod 3 has enlarged weapons bay (27 x 14 m).[24] Patrol endurance is about 28 hours at economical cruising speed of 400 mph (650 km/h).[25] Bear H and J variants (described above) are based on Tu-142 Bear airframe.

---

1. Polmar, *Guide to the Soviet Navy*, 1986, p. 393; *Jane's All the World's Aircraft*, 1987-88, p. 282; Gunston, *Aircraft of the Soviet Union*, 1983, p. 335.
2. Polmar, *Guide to the Soviet Navy*, 1986, p.393; *Jane's All the World's Aircraft*, 1987-88, p. 282; Gunston, *Guide to the Modern Soviet Air Force*, 1982, pp. 120-123.
3. Polmar, *Guide to the Soviet Navy*, 1986, p. 93; *Jane's All the World's Aircraft*, 1987-88, p. 282; Gunston, *Aircraft of the Soviet Union*, 1983, p. 335.
4. *Jane's All the World's Aircraft*, 1987-88, p. 281; Gunston, *Aircraft of the Soviet Union*, 1983, p. 335.
5. Polmar, *Guide to the Soviet Navy*, 1986, p. 393; Collins and Victory, *U.S./Soviet Military Balance*, 1988, p. 84; *Jane's All the World's Aircraft*, 1987-88, p. 282. Gunston, *Aircraft of the Soviet Union*, 1983, p. 335, says four NK-12M or MA. NK are the initials of engine designer Nikolai Kuznetsov.
6. Gunston, *Guide to the Modern Soviet Air Force*, 1982, p. 121.
7. *Jane's All the World's Aircraft*, 1987-88, p. 282; Gunston, *Guide to the Modern Soviet Air Force*, 1982, p. 121.
8. DIA, *Force Structure Summary*, November 1987, p. 21; SMP 1987, p. 36.
9. Polmar, *Guide to the Soviet Navy*, 1986, p. 390.
10. DIA, *Force Structure Summary*, November 1987, p. 21; SMP 1987, p. 36.
11. USN, *Soviet Naval Developments* (Rev. 4/85), p. 135.
12. Polmar, *Guide to the Soviet Navy*, 1986, pp. 390-393; Collins and Victory, *U.S./Soviet Military Balance*, 1988, p. 44; Gunston, *Guide to the Modern Soviet Air Force*, 1982, pp. 121.
13. USN, *Soviet Naval Developments* (Rev. 4/85), p. 135.
14. Polmar, *Guide to the Soviet Navy*, 1986, p. 393; Gunston, *Guide to the Modern Soviet Air Force*, 1982, p. 121.
15. DIA, *Force Structure Summary*, November 1987, p. 21; Polmar, *Guide to the Soviet Navy*, 1986, p. 393; Collins and Victory, *U.S./Soviet Military Balance*, 1988, p. 44. Most are Mod 3 or Mod 4; *Air Force Magazine*, August 1988, p. 90.
16. The Bear F Mod 4 entered service with the Northern Fleet in 1985; SMP 1988, p. 86.
17. SMP 1987, p. 69; USN, *Soviet Naval Developments* (Rev. 4/85), p. 135.
18. SMP 1988, p. 29.
19. Studeman, USN, Statement before HASC, March 1988, p. 40.
20. SMP 1987, p. 88.
21. USN, *Soviet Naval Developments* (Rev. 4/85), p. 135. The Bear A entered service with Strategic Aviation in 1955.
22. SMP 1988, p. 86. The Tu-142 airframe reentered production in the mid-1980s; John W. R. Taylor, "Gallery of Soviet Aerospace Weapons," *Air Force Magazine*, March 1987, p. 87; USN, *Soviet Naval Developments* (Rev. 4/85), p. 135; Polmar, *Guide to the Soviet Navy*, 1986, p. 390.
23. DIA, *Bear Weapon System*, DST-1310S-004-79, 12 February 1980, Appendix D, p. 124.
24. Ibid.
25. Gunston, *Guide to the Modern Soviet Air Force*, 1982, pp. 121.

Il-38 MAY

Figure 8.23 The Il-38 May, first deployed in 1968, and essentially a copy of the U.S. P-3, conducts medium-range, anti-submarine patrol and strike missions with depth bombs and torpedoes, both of which could be nuclear-armed.

DESCRIPTION: Four-turboprop, medium-range maritime reconnaissance/ASW aircraft assigned to SNA

DESIGN BUREAU: Ilyushin

SPECIFICATIONS:
  Dimensions:

  Length: 36 m[1] (118 ft); about 39.6 m[2] (130 ft) with magnetic anomaly detection (MAD) boom

  Height: 10.2 m[3] (33.3 ft)

  Wingspan: 37.4 m[4] (122.7 ft)

  Takeoff Weight (max): approx. 64,000 kg[5] (141,000 lbs)

  Powerplant: 4 Ivchyenko AI-20M turboprop engines[6]

Ceiling: 11,250 m[7] (37,000 ft)

Range (max): 7240-8300 km[8] (3900-4500 nm)

Unrefueled combat radius: 2540 km[9] (1370 nm), including 3-hour loiter

Aerial Refueling Capability: unknown

Speed (max): 630 km/h[10] (390 mph); Patrol: 135 kts[11] (250 km/h, 155 mph) at 50-100 m

Crew: 12

NUCLEAR WEAPONS: Capable of carrying nuclear torpedoes, bombs, or depth bombs in two internal weapons bays[12]

---

1. USN, *Soviet Naval Developments* (Rev. 4/85), p. 141.
2. Polmar, *Guide to the Soviet Navy*, 1986, p. 400; *Jane's All the World's Aircraft*, 1987-88, p. 245; Graham Warwick, "Military Aircraft of the World," *Flight International*, 1 march 1980, pp. 672-673; Gunston, *Aircraft of the Soviet Union*, 1983, p. 121.
3. Polmar, *Guide to the Soviet Navy*, 1986, p. 400; *Jane's All the World's Aircraft*, 1987-88, p. 245; Warwick, *op. cit.*, pp. 672-673.
4. USN, *Soviet Naval Developments* (Rev. 4/85), p. 141; Polmar, *Guide to the Soviet Navy*, 1986, p. 400; *Jane's All the World's Aircraft*, 1987-88, p. 245; Gunston, *Aircraft of the Soviet Union*, 1983, p. 121.
5. USN, *Soviet Naval Developments* (Rev. 4/85), p. 141.
6. Ibid.; *Jane's All the World's Aircraft*, 1987-88, p. 245; Gunston, *Guide to the Modern Soviet Air Force*, 1982, p. 48. AI are the initials of engine designer Aleksandr Ivchyenko.
7. DIA, *ASW Handbook*, 1977, p. 6-56.
8. Polmar, *Guide to the Soviet Navy*, 1986, p. 400; Warwick, *op. cit.*, pp. 672-673; Gunston, *Aircraft of the Soviet Union*, 1983, p. 121.
9. DIA, *ASW Handbook*, 1977, p. 6-56.
10. USN, *Soviet Naval Developments* (Rev. 4/85), p. 141.
11. DIA, *ASW Handbook*, 1977, p. 6-56.
12. USN, *Soviet Naval Developments* (Rev. 4/85), p. 141; Collins and Victory, *U.S./Sovite Military Balance*, 1988, pp. 44, 84.

8
IL-38 MAY

DEPLOYMENT:

Number: 45 (1988)[13]

Location: Baltic Fleet; Northern Fleet; temporary patrols have been made from Aden, South Yemen, Libya, Tiyas in Syria, Mozambique, and Ethiopia[14]

HISTORY:

First Flight: 1967-1968 (prototype)[15]

IOC: 1968[16]

Production: not in production[17]

COMMENTS: Adapted from a commercial aircraft design (the Il-18 Coot airliner).[18] Patrol endurance is about 12 hours at cruising speed of 250 mph.[19] Flown by Indian Navy (Dabolim, Goa).

Figure 8.24 Underside of the **Il-38 May** depicting its ASW magnetic anomaly detection (MAD) boom at the rear and a surface search radar below the cockpit area. Falling sonobuoy is visible below open bomb bay doors.

---

13 DIA, *Force Structure Summary*, November 1987, p. 21.
14 USN, *Soviet Naval Developments* (Rev. 4/85), p. 141; John W. R. Taylor, "Gallery of Soviet Aerospace Weapons," *Air Force Magazine*, March 1987, p. 85.
15 Polmar, *Guide to the Soviet Navy*, 1986, p. 400.
16 USN, *Soviet Naval Developments* (Rev. 4/85), p. 141.
17 Ibid.
18 Ibid.
19 Ibid.

8

Be-12 MAIL

Be-12 MAIL (Soviet name Tchaika; "Seagull")[1]

Figure 8.25 The **Be-12 Mail** is a short-range maritime patrol sea plane providing coastal coverage. It is land-based, has a radius of 230 miles, and carries bombs, depth charges, mines, or torpedoes.

DESCRIPTION:	Twin-turboprop, coastal maritime reconnaissance seaplane assigned to SNA	Takeoff Weight (max):	29,500 kg[5] (65,000 lbs)
DESIGN BUREAU:	Beriev design bureau at Taganrog	Powerplant:	two Ivchyenko AI-20D turboprop engines[6]
SPECIFICATIONS: Dimensions:		Ceiling:	11,300 m[7] (37,000 ft)
Length:	30 m[2] (99 ft) with MAD boom	Range (max):	4000 km[8] (2200 nm); 230 mi radius of shore bases[9]
Height:	7 m[3] (23 ft)	Aerial Refueling Capability:	no
Wingspan:	29.7 m[4] (97.4 ft)		

---

1. Polmar, *Guide to the Soviet Navy*, 1986, pp. 400-401. The name is unofficial; Gunston, *Aircraft of the Soviet Union*, 1983, p. 69.
2. USN, *Soviet Naval Developments* (Rev. 4/85), p. 140; Gunston, *Aircraft of the Soviet Union*, 1983, p. 69.
3. *Jane's All the World's Aircraft*, 1987-88, p. 244; Polmar, *Guide to the Soviet Navy*, 1986, pp. 400-401; Gunston, *Guide to the Modern Soviet Air Force*, 1982, p. 40.
4. USN, *Soviet Naval Developments* (Rev. 4/85), p. 140; *Jane's All the World's Aircraft*, 1987-88, p. 244; Gunston, *Aircraft of the Soviet Union*, 1983, p. 69.
5. USN, *Soviet Naval Developments* (Rev. 4/85), p. 140.
6. Ibid.; Polmar, *Guide to the Soviet Navy*, 1986, pp. 400-401; Gunston, *Aircraft of the Soviet Union*, 1983, p. 69. AI are the initials of engine designer Aleksandr Ivchyenko.
7. *Jane's All the World's Aircraft*, 1987-88, p. 244; Polmar, *Guide to the Soviet Navy*, 1986, pp. 400-401; Gunston, *Aircraft of the Soviet Union*, 1983, p. 69.
8. *Jane's All the World's Aircraft*, 1987-88, p. 244; Polmar, *Guide to the Soviet Navy*, 1986, pp. 400-401; Gunston, *Aircraft of the Soviet Union*, 1983, p. 69.
9. John W. R. Taylor, "Gallery of Soviet Aerospace Weapons," *Air Force Magazine*, March 1987, p. 85.

Be-12 MAIL

Speed (max):	330 kts[10] (610 km/h; 380 mph); Patrol: 320 km/h[11] (200 mph)	**HISTORY:** First Flight:	1960[16]
Crew:	5[12]	First Seen:	1961 Aviation Day at Tushino Airport[17]
NUCLEAR WEAPONS:	Capable of carrying torpedoes and depth bombs in internal weapons bay and possibly on two large or two smaller external pylons[13]	IOC:	1966-1967[18]
		Production:	not in production
DEPLOYMENT: Number:	95 (1988)[14]	**COMMENTS:**	ASW and reconnaissance coverage out to some 370 km (200 nm) from shore.[19] Equipped with magnetic anomaly detection (MAD) system, radar, and sonobuoys.[20]
Location:	land-based in the Northern and Black Sea Fleets[15]		A new seaplane, designated TAG-D, with a possible ASW role, is under development, and may replace the Be-12 Mail.[21]

---

10 USN, *Soviet Naval Developments* (Rev. 4/85), p. 140; *Jane's All the World's Aircraft*, 1987-88, p. 244.
11 *Jane's All the World's Aircraft*, 1987-88, p. 244; Collins and Victory, *U.S./Soviet Military Balance*, 1988, p. 44; Polmar, *Guide to the Soviet Navy*, 1986, pp. 400-401; Gunston, *Guide to the Modern Soviet Air Force*, 1982, p. 40.
12 John W. R. Taylor, "Gallery of Soviet Aerospace Weapons," *Air Force Magazine*, March 1988, p. 75.
13 USN, *Soviet Naval Developments* (Rev. 4/85), p. 140; *Jane's All the World's Aircraft*, 1987-88, p. 244; Polmar, *Guide to the Soviet Navy*, 1986, pp. 400-401.
14 About 100 were built; DIA, *Force Structure Summary*, November 1987, p. 21; Polmar, *Guide to the Soviet Navy*, 1986, pp. 400-401; Taylor, "Gallery of Soviet Aerospace Weapons," 1988, op. cit., p. 75.
15 *Jane's All the World's Aircraft*, 1987-88, p. 244; Taylor, "Gallery of Soviet Aerospace Weapons," 1988, op. cit., p. 75.
16 Polmar, *Guide to the Soviet Navy*, 1986, p. 400; Gunston, *Aircraft of the Soviet Union*, 1983, p. 69.
17 *Jane's All the World's Aircraft*, 1987-88, p. 244.
18 DIA, *ASW Handbook*, 1977, p. 2-3; USAF, *Soviet Aerospace Handbook*, 1978, p. 76; *Jane's All the World's Aircraft*, 1987-88, p. 244; William Green and Gordon Swanborough, *The Observer's Soviet Aircraft Directory* (London: Frederick Warne, 1975), p. 91; Gunston, *Guide to the Modern Soviet Air Force*, 1982, pp. 40-41.
19 *Jane's All the World's Aircraft*, 1987-88, p. 244.
20 DIA, *ASW Handbook*, 1977, p. 2-3.
21 Studeman, USN, Statement before HASC, March 1988, p. 38.

8

Ka-27 HELIX A and Ka-25 HORMONE A

Nuclear Capable ASW Helicopters
Ka-27 HELIX A and Ka-25 HORMONE A

Figure 8.26 The **Ka-27 Helix** is a short-range ASW helicopter. There are approximately 60 Ka-27s deployed on Kiev, Kirov and Sovremennyy class ships.

Figure 8.27 There are some 115 **Ka-25 Hormone A** short-range anti-submarine helicopters currently deployed on Kiev, Kirov and Sovremennyy class ships.

	Ka-27 Helix A	Ka-25 Hormone A[1]
DESIGN BUREAU:	Kamov	Kamov
SPECIFICATIONS:		
Length (fuselage):	11 m[2] (36 ft)	9.8 m[3] (32 ft)
Rotor Diameter:	16 m[4] (52 ft)	16 m[5] (52 ft)
Height:	5.5 m[6] (18 ft)	5.37 m[7] (17.6 ft)
Weight (max):	8800 kg[8] (19,400 lbs)	7300 kg[9] (16,000 lbs)
Powerplant:	2 Isotov TV-3-117V turboshaft engines[10]	2 Glushyenkov GTD-3F/BM turboshaft engines[11]
	Ka-27 Helix A	Ka-25 Hormone A
Ceiling:	6000 m[12] (20,000 ft)	3500 m[13] (11,500 ft)
Range (max):	unknown	650 km[14] (350 nm) / 400 km[15] (215 nm)
Unrefueled combat radius:	300 km[16] (160 nm)	250 km (135 nm);[17]
Speed (max):	140 kts (260 km/h;[18] 161 mph)	120 kts (220 km/h;[19] 140 mph)
Crew:	3-5[20]	4-5[21]

---

1. NATO changed the Ka-20 Harp code name to Ka-25 Hormone for production versions; *Jane's All the World's Aircraft*, 1987-88, p. 251; Gunston, *Aircraft of the Soviet Union*, 1983, p. 135.
2. USN, *Soviet Naval Developments* (Rev. 4/85), p. 139; *Jane's All the World's Aircraft*, 1987-88, pp. 253-255. Data for Ka-32; "Jane's All the World's Aircraft Supplement," *Air Force Magazine*, October 1985, pp. 111-113.
3. USN, *Soviet Naval Developments* (Rev. 4/85), p. 138; *Jane's All the World's Aircraft*, 1987-88, pp. 251-252; Gunston, *Aircraft of the Soviet Union*, 1983, p. 136.
4. USN, *Soviet Naval Developments* (Rev. 4/85), p. 139.
5. Ibid., p. 138.
6. *Jane's All the World's Aircraft*, 1987-88, pp. 253-255.
7. Ibid., pp. 251-252; Gunston, *Aircraft of the Soviet Union*, 1983, p. 136.
8. USN, *Soviet Naval Developments* (Rev. 4/85), p. 139; Gunston, *Aircraft of the Soviet Union*, 1983, p. 136.
9. USN, *Soviet Naval Developments* (Rev. 4/85), p. 138.
10. Ibid., p. 139; Polmar, *Guide to the Soviet Navy*, 1986, p. 404; *Jane's All the World's Aircraft*, 1987-88, pp. 253-255; "Jane's All the World's Aircraft Supplement," op. cit., pp. 111-113. According to *Flight International*, 1 August 1987, p. 61 the engine provides 2200 shp.
11. USN, *Soviet Naval Developments* (Rev. 4/85), p. 138; Polmar, *Guide to the Soviet Navy*, 1986, p. 406; *Jane's All the World's Aircraft*, 1987-88, p. 251. GTD stands for Gelikopter Turbo-Dvigatyel. The engine provides 990 shp; Gunston, *Aircraft of the Soviet Union*, 1983, p. 136.
12. "Jane's All the World's Aircraft Supplement," op. cit., pp. 111-113.
13. *Jane's All the World's Aircraft*, 1987-88, p. 252.
14. Polmar, *Guide to the Soviet Navy*, 1983, p. 346.
15. Gunston, *Aircraft of the Soviet Union*, 1983, p. 136.
16. DIA, *Force Structure Summary*, November 1987, p. 21.
17. Ibid.
18. Ibid.
19. Ibid.
20. Ibid.
21. *Jane's All the World's Aircraft*, 1987-88, pp. 253-255; Polmar, *Guide to the Soviet Navy*, 1986, p. 404.

Ka-27 HELIX A and Ka-25 HORMONE A

Figure 8.28 Close-up of the **Ka-27 Helix**.

Figure 8.29 **Ka-25 Hormone A**s can carry nuclear depth bombs and possibly nuclear torpedoes in an internal weapons bay.

	Ka-27 Helix A	Ka-25 Hormone A
NUCLEAR WEAPONS:	Nuclear depth bombs and possibly nuclear torpedoes carried in internal weapons bay[22]	Nuclear depth bomb and possibly nuclear torpedoes carried in internal weapons bay[23]
DEPLOYMENT:		
Number:	about 60 Helix A[24]	about 115[25]
Platform:	Kiev CVHG, Kirov CGN, and Sovremennyy DDG class ships[26]	Kara, Kresta I/II, Kirov CGN, Moskva CHG, Kiev CVHG, Ivan Rogov, Berezina[27]
HISTORY:		
First Seen:	on Udaloy destroyer in September 1981[28]	prototype Ka-20 Harp observed in July 1961[29]
IOC:	1982[30]	1967[31]
Production:	in production	not in production
COMMENTS:	Helix A is basic ASW version. Helix B is a sea-based, missile target acquisition, and precision-guided weapons anti-tank version.[32] Helix C is military search/rescue version. Ka-32 is civilian variant of Ka-27.[33] Being replaced by Ka-27 Helix A.	Hormone A is basic ASW version. Hormone B is a missile target acquisition and mid-course guidance version supporting SS-N-3, SS-N-12, and SS-N-19 SLCMs. Hormone C is utility version.[34]

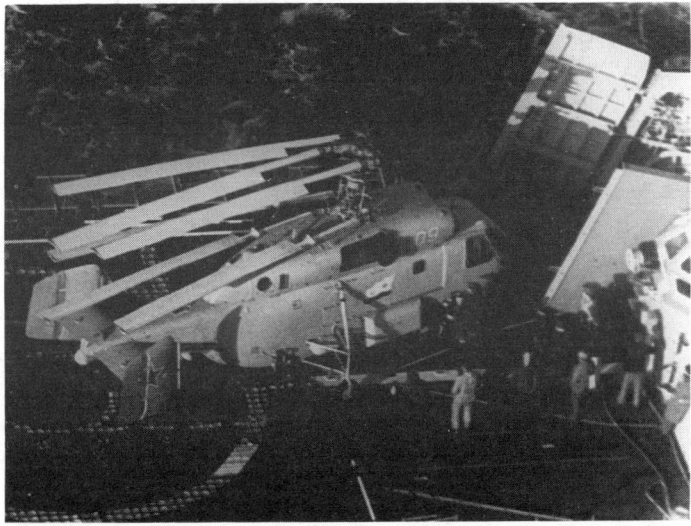

Figure 8.30 Aerial view of the **Ka-27 Helix A** helicopter with rotor blades folded at hanger entrance aboard the Soviet guided-missile destroyer Udaloy.

---

22 John W. R. Taylor, "Ka-27/32 Helix Helicopters in Close Up," *Jane's Defence Weekly*, 21 December 1985, pp. 1356-1358.
23 USN, *Soviet Naval Developments* (Rev. 4/85), pp. 138; Polmar, *Guide to the Soviet Navy*, 1986, p. 406; *Jane's All the World's Aircraft*, 1987-88, pp. 251-252; "Jane's All the World's Aircraft Supplement," *op. cit.*, pp. 111-113.
24 DIA, *Force Structure Summary*, November 1987, p. 21.
25 DIA, *Ibid*. Some 460 Ka-25s were built from 1967-1975; John W. R. Taylor, "Gallery of Soviet Aerospace Weapons," *Air Force Magazine*, March 1987, p. 95.
26 Taylor, "Ka-27/32 Helix Helicopters in Close Up," *op. cit.*, pp. 1356-1358.
27 USN, *Soviet Naval Developments* (Rev. 4/85), p. 138.
28 During the Zapad-81 series of exercises in the Baltic; *Jane's All the World's Aircraft*, 1987-88, pp. 253-255. See also, *Flight International*, 1 August 1987, p. 63.
29 *Jane's All the World's Aircraft*, 1987-88, pp. 251; Polmar, *Guide to the Soviet Navy*, 1986, p. 406.
30 Taylor, "Ka-27/32 Helix Helicopters in Close Up, *op. cit.*, pp. 1356-1358.
31 USAF, *Soviet Aerospace Handbook*, 1978, p. 77.
32 SMP 1987, p. 69.
33 Taylor, "Ka-27/32 Helix Helicopters in Close Up," *op. cit.*, pp. 1356-1358.
34 *Jane's All the World's Aircraft*, 1987-88, p. 251; Polmar, *Guide to the Soviet Navy*, 1986, p. 404.

9
Naval Nuclear Weapons

Chapter Nine
Naval Nuclear Weapons

Overview

The Soviet Navy consists of about 1000 ships and 370 submarines as of mid-1988. In terms of numbers of vessels, this is the largest navy in the world. Some 280 ships and 340 submarines are principal combat ships; the remainder are minor patrol vessels and training and support ships that are not capable of open-ocean operations. About 276 surface warships and 338 submarines can carry a nuclear-capable weapon system.[1] According to the U.S. Department of Defense (DOD), Soviet naval forces "routinely" carry nuclear warheads.[2]

As of mid-1988, the non-strategic nuclear-capable ships consist of six aviation ships (aircraft carriers), 34 cruisers, 52 destroyers, 119 frigates, and 65 patrol combatants. There are some 76 ballistic missile submarines—of which 64 are strategic (discussed in Chapter Five)—and 12 older Golf II submarines, which have non-strategic missions and are not SALT- or START-accountable (discussed in Chapter Seven). There are, in addition, 60 cruise missile attack submarines, and 202 attack submarines.

Soviet non-strategic naval nuclear weapons include one type of submarine-launched ballistic missile (SLBM), seven sea-launched cruise missiles (SLCMs) and anti-ship missiles, four air-to-surface missiles (ASMs), three anti-submarine warfare (ASW) missiles, three different types of surface-to-air missiles (SAMs), nuclear depth bombs, two types of nuclear torpedoes, nuclear artillery projectiles, one coastal missile, and possibly nuclear mines.[3] A total of about 400 cruise and anti-ship missiles and 1400 nuclear ASW, 260 anti-air, 100 artillery projectile, and 100 coastal missile warheads are deployed as of mid-1988.

With only six "aircraft carriers" (none capable of handling conventional takeoff and landing aircraft) and a limited number of ships carrying ASW helicopters, Soviet Naval Aviation (SNA) is mostly land-based. SNA, in which is invested a considerable portion of the Soviet Navy's nuclear capability, operates ten types of nuclear-capable aircraft and helicopters, which are able to deliver nuclear bombs, depth bombs, and ASMs.

Since 1980, 11 new and two modified classes of Soviet nuclear-capable submarines and surface combatants have been introduced, with six different new nuclear-capable weapon systems.[4] Nine nuclear-capable ship and seven submarine classes are thought to be currently in production; a large-deck aircraft carrier will enter the operational force in the mid-1990s, and a wing-in-ground-effect vehicle, the new eight-engine Utka class, will be deployed with six SS-N-22 SLCMs.[5] New, longer range anti-ship cruise missiles with increased standoff range and an ability to penetrate defenses are reported in development.[6]

The quality, sophistication and versatility of individual ships and submarines and the capabilities of the new nuclear-capable weapon systems have vastly increased. The increase in the number of nuclear-capable ships and submarines and the improvements in weapons have been accompanied by a generally higher peacetime operating tempo, longer range deployments, and exercises practicing naval nuclear capabilities.[7] Since 1984, however, the trend has generally reversed. Soviet naval deployments overseas are declining, most major exercises are being conducted in waters close to the Soviet mainland, and construction is significantly declining.[8]

History

Soviet naval expansion since the Second World War—incremental expansion of capabilities and missions, areas of operation, and overall power—has taken place in four general phases.[9] From the late 1940s to the late 1950s, the main concentration was defense of the

---

1 SMP 1987, p. 43, states that "Some 288 surface warships, 340 submarines, and about 30 other combatant ships carry at least one of these systems." JCS, FY 1989, p. 54, states, "Almost all major surface combatants (about 290), all submarines (about 340), as well as a few other combatants (some 31) are armed with at least one, or a mix of nuclear weapons systems."
2 HAC, FY 1980 DOD, Part 1, p. 282.
3 According to the U.S. Joint Chiefs of Staff, "The Soviet Navy maintains an extensive sea-based non-strategic nuclear force comprising both anti-surface warfare (ASUW) and anti-submarine warfare (ASW) systems. The Soviets maintain an inventory of nuclear armed torpedoes as well as ASW depth bombs;" JCS, FY 1988, p. 49. The Department of Defense report, Soviet Military Power 1987, states, that "the newest versions of both [nuclear torpedo and depth bomb] entered service in the early 1980s'; SMP 1987, p. 43. See also, JCS, FY 1982, p. 32. Mines delivered by aircraft, ships, or submarines may have a nuclear capability.
4 The seven new classes of submarines are Typhoon and Delta IV SSBNs, Oscar SSGN, and Akula, Kilo, Mike, and Sierra SSNs. The four classes of surface combatants are Kirov and Slava cruisers and Sovremennyy and Udaloy destroyers. One modified submarine (Yankee SSN/Notch/SSN/SSGN) and one modified patrol combatant (Tarantul II) have also been introduced. The new nuclear-capable weapon systems are the SS-N-20 and SS-N-23 SLBMs, SS-N-19, SS-N-21, and SS-N-22 cruise missiles, and the SA-N-6 SAMs.
5 SMP 1988, pp. 131, 134; Studeman, USN, Statement before HASC, March 1988, p. 37. The submarine classes are Oscar I, Yankee (conversions), Akula, Sierra, Victor III, Kilo, and Tango. The ship classes are Tbilisi, Utka, Kirov, Slava, Sovremennyy, Udaloy, Grisha V, Nanuchka III, and Tarantul.
6 SMP 1985, p. 110.
7 HASC, FY 1985 DOD, Part 3, p. 5; SASC, FY 1986 DOD, Part 8, p. 4361.
8 Studeman, USN, Statement before HASC, March 1988, p. 39.
9 For further discussion, See, Donald W. Mitchell, A History of Russian and Soviet Sea Power (New York: Macmillan Publishing Co., Inc.: 1974; Michael MccGwire, ed., Soviet Naval Developments: Capability and Context (New York: Praeger Publishers, 1973); Michael MccGwire, Ken Booth, John McDonnell, eds., Soviet Naval Policy: Objectives and Constraints (New York: Praeger Publishers, 1975); Michael MccGwire, John McDonnell, eds., Soviet Naval Influence: Domestic and Foreign Dimensions (New York: Preger Publishers, 1977); DIA, Sea-Launched Aerodynamic Missile Systems (Current and Projected)—USSR and PRC, DST-1330S-205-77, 1 March 1977 (partially declassified and released under the FOIA); DIA, Soviet Naval Shipbuilding, DDI-1922-10-76, July 1976, p. 5 (partially declassified and released under the FOIA); Myron J. Smith, Jr., The Soviet Navy, 1941-1978: A Guide to Sources in English (Santa Barbara, CA: ABC-Clio, 1980).

coastal areas of the Soviet Union. More than 50 percent of the submarines and more than 70 percent of the surface ships and patrol craft were designed for this purpose. By 1958, Soviet naval forces consisted of nearly 900 surface ships and craft and 550 diesel-powered submarines. Some 250 diesel-powered Whiskey and Zulu class submarines could conduct combat operations on the open seas.[10] None of the principal surface warships (cruisers, destroyers, and frigates) were armed with SSMs or SAMs. A decade later, all were either discarded, retrofitted or placed in the reserves.

The second phase of development began in about 1958 when programs initiated in the 1953-1954 period began to reach fruition. The objective was naval capabilities to increase the maritime defense perimeter around the Soviet Union. Nuclear-capable submarines and surface ships capable of delivering cruise missiles and anti-ship missiles, torpedoes, and possibly SAMs were introduced. First-generation nuclear-powered submarines—the Hotel ballistic missile, Echo I and II class cruise missile and November class attack submarines—were built in smaller numbers but with greatly improved capabilities. Diesel-powered Juliett and Whiskey class cruise missiles and Foxtrot and Romeo class attack submarines were also built. Nuclear-capable surface ships introduced during this period were Kildin and Krupnyy class destroyers with SS-N-1 Scrubber cruise missiles, as well as Kanin and Kashin class destroyers and Kynda class cruisers with SA-N-1 and SA-N-3 SAMs.

The primary mission of the Navy during the second phase remained defense of the sea approaches to the Soviet Union, particularly anti-carrier activities.[11] A rudimentary sea-denial capability in certain ocean areas was developed,[12] and the first forward deployments of attack and ballistic missile submarines took place.[13] Deployments of attack submarines armed with nuclear torpedoes began around 1958, and deployments of cruise missile-armed submarines began in 1960. The first Soviet ballistic-missile-submarine forward deployment may have taken place in the spring of 1959.[14] Eight diesel attack submarines were based in Albania from 1958 until they were evicted in 1961.[15]

The first significant Soviet open-ocean naval exercise occurred in July 1961 in the Norwegian Sea.[16] By 1964, ships armed with nuclear-capable cruise missiles participated in open-ocean maneuvers, and in 1964 these ships formed part of the first continual naval presence—in the Mediterranean Sea[17]—outside Soviet coastal waters.

The third phase commenced in 1967 and lasted until the late 1970s. New ships and submarines increased capabilities for open-ocean ASW operations.[18] Surface combatants with dedicated nuclear-capable ASW weapon systems introduced during this period include the Kiev and Moskva aircraft carriers, the Kresta II and Kara class cruisers, and the Krivak frigates. Second-generation nuclear-powered Charlie I and Charlie II submarines with nuclear-capable cruise missiles were introduced, as were Alfa and Victor attack submarines. The Alfa and Victor are able to carry nuclear torpedoes, and SS-N-15 Starfish rocket delivered nuclear depth bombs (introduced in 1973).

During this period, the Soviet Navy experienced an eightfold increase in out-of-area ship days[19] and conducted the 1970 and 1975 worldwide "Okean" exercises. Naval presence in the Mediterranean Sea and Pacific and Atlantic Oceans increased significantly. Operations in the Caribbean began in July 1969, and the establishment of a periodic presence off the West African coast followed in November 1970.

Ships introduced during the third phase were more than one-third larger in tonnage and included better capabilities for sustained operations.[20] They were given an improved armament suite with greater anti-ship and anti-air capability, even while nuclear-capable ASW systems received emphasis.[21] As the Soviet ballistic missile submarine force grew, a new anti-Western (or pro-Soviet) ASW mission was introduced as strategic submarines began patrolling in waters protected by Soviet naval forces and land-based aviation.[22]

The fourth phase of development, which began in the late 1970s and continues today, is characterized by well-equipped combatants designed to fulfill multiple roles in worldwide operations. Individual ships and sub-

---

10 *Jane's Fighting Ships*, 1958-59 (Raymond V. B. Blackman, ed.). All of the submarines designed exclusively for coastal defense were removed from service by 1966.
11 Effective anti-carrier operations were not possible due primarily to the lack of air cover for the anti-ship missile ships. The requirement that Echo class submarines remain on the surface in order to prepare and fire the nuclear-capable SS-N-3 cruise missiles, and the inability of diesel-powered submarines to conduct sustained out-of-area operations, also hampered anti-carrier operations.
12 HASC, FY 1980 DOD, Part 4, p. 2.
13 DIA, *ASW Handbook*, 1977, pp. 1-2, 2-1, 2-2. This period also witnessed a shift away from, and then a recommitment to, sea-based nuclear delivery systems as a result of Khrushchev's decision to concentrate on the ICBM, the need to counter Western nuclear-strike aircraft carriers, and the sharply increased U.S. defense budget and rapid buildup of Polaris ballistic missile submarines in 1959-1960; Michael MccGwire, 'The Rationale for the Development of Soviet Seapower,' *Proceedings*, May 1980, pp. 157-159.
14 On 29 May 1959, a submerged Zulu class submarine converted to carry ballistic missiles was tracked by the USS Grenadier, a Guppy II class attack submarine, in the Norwegian Sea. This was the first submerged Soviet strategic missile submarine to be tracked by U.S. forces; USN, Commander Submarine Development Group Two, *Report of Operations of USS Grenadier During Atlantic Barrier Operations in the Greenland-Iceland-United Kingdom Area and in Tracking Soviet Submarine 29-30 May in Norwegian Sea Area*, 6 July 1959, pp. 1-3.
15 The first four Whiskey class attack submarines transited from the Baltic to Ulone Bay, Albania, in August 1958; U.S. Naval Forces, Eastern Atlantic and Mediterranean, Head-

quarters of the Commander-in-Chief, *Report of Operations and Condition of Command, 1 July 1958 to 21 March 1959*, 31 March 1959, p. 1. Their wartime mission was most likely preventing U.S. ships from entering the Aegean Sea, where they could threaten Soviet contingency operations designed to seize the Turkish Straits.
16 A slightly larger exercise occurred in 1962, and a pattern of biennial (spring and summer or fall) major open-ocean exercises in the Norwegian Sea was established in 1963; Donald C. Daniel, "Trends and Patterns in Major Soviet Naval Exercises," *Naval War College Review*, Spring 1978, pp. 35-36.
17 DIA, *Handbook on the Soviet Armed Forces*, p. 9-1; Daniel, op. cit., p. 36.
18 From 1964 to 1979, 34.3 percent of all delivered Soviet surface tonnage and 11.3 percent of all submarines (including SSBNs) were dedicated to ASW; Gary Charbonneau, "The Soviet Navy and Forward Deployment," *Proceedings*, March 1979, p. 37.
19 Soviet ship-days out-of-area doubled in 1967 from the previous year and increased more than eightfold by 1974 before levelling off.
20 The Soviet Navy still lacked sea- or shore-based air cover, and new ships therefore emphasized capabilities for operations outside the range of shore-based air cover and logistic support.
21 DIA, *ASW Handbook*, 1977, p. 2-2.
22 ACDA, FY 1979 ACIS, p. 178. Western analysts refer to these protected areas as submarine "bastions." With the introduction of longer range SS-N-8, SS-N-18, and SS-N-20 missiles, Soviet submarines were able to cover all targets from homeports or home waters in the Norwegian and Barents Seas; HAC, FY 1986 DOD, Part 2, p. 908.

9
ASW Systems

Table 9.1
Soviet Nuclear-Capable Ships and Submarines (1988)

Type	Number	Nuclear Weapons
Submarines		
Ballistic Missile	76	SS-N-5, 6, 8, 17, 18, 20, 23, SS-N-15/16, torpedoes
Cruise Missile	60	SS-N-3, 7, 9, 12, 19, SS-N-15/16, torpedoes
Attack	202	SS-N-15/16, SS-N-21, torpedoes
Surface Ships		
Aircraft Carriers	6	FRAS-1, SS-N-12, ASW hel, SA-N-3, torpedoes
Cruisers	34	SS-N-3, SS-N-12, SS-N-19, SA-N-1, SA-N-3, SA-N-6, torpedoes, naval artillery, ASW helicopters
Destroyers	52	SS-N-22, SA-N-1, torpedoes, ASW helicopters
Frigates	119	torpedoes
Patrol Combatants	65	SS-N-9, SS-N-22,65 SS-N-9, SS-N-22, torpedoes
TOTAL	**614**	

marines are better able to conduct nuclear anti-surface, anti-air, and anti-submarine missions. This phase includes increasingly complicated naval exercises, a more than 30 percent increase in out-of-area ship days, and a further expansion of the Soviet Navy's areas of operations. Forward deployments include a continuous naval presence established in the South China Sea since February 1979, supported by the naval and air base at Cam Ranh Bay, Vietnam.[23] The lack of sea-based air cover continues to be a deficiency of Soviet naval operations.[24]

Naval Nuclear Weapon Systems (mid-1988)

The nuclear-capable naval weapon systems deployed with the Soviet Navy include seven anti-ship missiles launched from surface combatants (discussed further in Chapter Six), patrol combatants and submarines, four air-launched anti-ship missiles, four anti-submarine rockets and missiles (two surface- and two submarine-launched), depth bombs, torpedoes, and possibly as many as three different SAMs. Attack submarines can also deliver mines—which some analysts believe may be nuclear-capable—and five aging Sverdlov class cruisers are believed capable of firing nuclear 152mm artillery shells.[25]

Anti-Submarine Nuclear Weapon Systems

The Soviet Navy has a total of about 1400 nuclear ASW warheads on five different kinds of weapons: nuclear torpedoes, a submarine rocket nuclear depth bomb, a dual-capable submarine launched ASW missile, a ballistic rocket, and air-delivered nuclear depth bombs.

A nuclear-tipped torpedo deployed on diesel submarines beginning in 1958 was the first nuclear weapon deployed with the Soviet Navy. Today, 575 of the standard 21-inch (533mm) nuclear torpedoes of at least two types are estimated to be deployed on virtually all nuclear-capable Soviet surface ships and submarines.[26] The older type—Type 65—was presumably introduced in the mid-1960s; a new type—ET-80—was introduced in the early 1980s.[27]

Two incidents involving Soviet attack submarines indicate the routine carriage of nuclear torpedoes. The first reportedly occurred in December 1972, when a nuclear-powered submarine from the Northern Fleet suffered an accident while on patrol off the east coast of North America. The accident occurred in the forward section of the submarine and was caused, according to CIA intelligence reports, by a radiation leak from a nuclear-armed torpedo.[28] The second occurred in October 1981 when a Whiskey class attack submarine ran aground near the Karlskrona naval base in Sweden. Swedish Defense Ministry authorities detected the presence of Uranium-238, leading them to conclude that the submarine probably had "one or more nuclear weapons aboard."[29]

The Soviet Union also deploys three types of nuclear-armed missiles and rockets for anti-submarine missions: the FRAS-1 rocket, the SS-N-15 Starfish nuclear

---

23. U.S. Pacific Command, "Pacific Area Update," P4048.1P1-4, 17 February 1984, pp. 11-13; SMP 1985, pp. 130-131.
24. Ships outside the range of land-based air cover (roughly 300 miles from a base) are particularly vulnerable to interdiction strikes by U.S. carriers; HAC, FY 1986 DOD, Part 2, p. 916.
25. 'Soviet Sea Mines," *Jane's Defence Review*, Vol. 4, No. 2, 1983, p. 105; Collins and Victory, *U.S./Soviet Military Balance*, 1988, p. 42.
26. This estimate is based upon an approximate average of one nuclear torpedo per ship and submarine capable of carrying 21-inch torpedoes. More than one per deployed ship or submarine is possible.
27. JCS, FY 1989, p. 54; SMP 1987, p. 43.
28. CIA, "Soviet Submarine Accidents (DOI: 1971-1973),' intelligence report (partially declassified under the FOIA), p. 2.
29. Frank J. Prial, "Sweden to Release Soviet Sub: Finds Signs of Nuclear Arms," *New York Times*, 6 November 1981, p. 1; Leonard Downie, Jr., "Soviet Sub 'Probably' Has A-Arms, Sweden Says,' *Washington Post*, 6 November 1981, p. 1. Details of the measurements were reported in Olle Sunstrom, "U137 och U238—en faststalld kombination," *FOA Tidningen* Swedish Defense Research Institute, Stockholm, December 1982.

9
Non-strategic Submarines

depth bomb, and the SS-N-16 Stallion ASW missile.[30] Twin-rail SUW-N-1 launchers with FRAS-1 (Free Rocket Anti-Submarine) rockets are deployed on Kiev and Moskva class surface ships. The missile is a nuclear-only variant of the Soviet Army's FROG-7 short-range rocket. It is estimated that 25 missiles with nuclear warheads are deployed.

The submarine-launched SS-N-15 Starfish rocket-propelled nuclear depth bomb was deployed in 1973 and is similar to the U.S. Navy's SUBROC.[31] It is fired from either 21- or 26-inch torpedo tubes and is carried on Typhoon, Charlie I/II, Oscar I, Victor I/II, Alfa, Sierra, Mike, and Akula class submarines. Romeo and Tango class diesel attack submarines may also be capable of firing the SS-N-15. The SS-N-16 Stallion ASW missile is also launched from torpedo tubes and is longer range than the SS-N-15 (120 versus 37 kilometers). It is dual-capable—able to carry a nuclear or conventional torpedo. First deployed in 1979-1981, it is thought to be deployed on the Typhoon, Oscar I, Victor II/III, Sierra, Mike, and Akula classes. There is an estimated total of 400 nuclear warheads in the Soviet stockpile for SS-N-15s and SS-N-16s. It is estimated that each submarine is allocated an average of four rocket-propelled ASW nuclear weapons.

The Soviet Navy also deploys at least two types of ASW nuclear depth bombs, which are deliverable by three types of land-based fixed-wing aircraft and two ship-based helicopters. There are 200 land-based aircraft: about 95 Be-12 Mail, 60 Tu-142 Bear F, and 45 Il-38 May patrol planes and 175 Hormone A and Helix A helicopters. It is estimated that there are about 400 nuclear depth bombs—roughly one per nuclear-capable airplane and helicopter. These aircraft may also be capable of delivering nuclear torpedoes and mines.

Anti-Air Warfare (AAW)

The Soviet Navy operates three types of nuclear-capable SAMs: the SA-N-1 Goa, the SA-N-3 Goblet, and the SA-N-6 Grumble.[32] A total of 260 nuclear versions are estimated to exist: four per ship on six aircraft carriers and some 60 cruisers and destroyers. The 12 nautical mile (22 kilometer)-range SA-N-1 Goa is deployed on Kresta I, Kynda, Kanin, Kashin, and SAM Kotlin class cruisers and destroyers. The 20 nautical mile (37 kilometer)-range SA-N-3 Goblet is deployed on the Moskva and Kiev class carriers and the Kresta II and Kara class cruisers.[33] The 35 nautical mile (65 kilometer)-range SA-N-6 Grumble, which is a derivative of the land-based SA-10 SAM missile deployed in strategic defense forces, is deployed on one ship of the Kara class and on newer Kirov and Slava class cruisers.

Non-Strategic Submarines

The Soviet non-strategic submarine force consists of about 300 submarines, including some 20 different cruise missile and torpedo attack classes. Nearly three-quarters of the cruise missile and one-third of the torpedo attack submarines are nuclear-powered, and some 90 percent are capable of firing nuclear torpedoes or other nuclear weapons.

Cruise Missile Submarines

There are currently 60 cruise missile submarines (SSG/SSGNs) in seven different classes, carrying an estimated 500 nuclear-capable sea-launched cruise missiles (SLCMs) and anti-ship missiles of five different types.[34] The newer Oscar I and Charlie II class cruise missile submarines are assigned to the Northern Fleet. Some Charlie I, Echo II, and Juliett class submarines are assigned to the Pacific Fleet, and Juliett class submarines are also assigned to the Baltic and Black Sea Fleets. One class of boats—the Juliett class—is diesel-powered and the remainder are nuclear-powered.

All of the cruise missile submarines are capable of firing nuclear torpedoes from their standard 21-inch torpedo tubes, as well as launching anti-ship missiles from separate launchers. Charlie I, Charlie II, and Papa class submarines can also fire the SS-N-15 nuclear depth bomb. The Oscar I class can fire both the SS-N-15 nuclear depth bomb and the SS-N-16 ASW missile.

The Juliett and Echo II class submarines, introduced in 1961-1962, carry the SS-N-3a/c. Juliett boats can carry four missiles, and Echo IIs can carry eight. Modification of the Echo II class submarines to carry eight SS-N-12s in place of the SS-N-3s is continuing. Fifteen had reportedly been refitted to fire the SS-N-12 by 1986, and the rest will presumably be upgraded.[35]

The Charlie I class submarines and the single submarine of the Papa class submarine carry SS-N-7 missiles, although the Papa submarine may also be capable of carrying the SS-N-9. Six submarines of the Charlie II class carry eight SS-N-9 missiles each. The Papa SSGN can fire ten missiles.

Oscar I class submarines, which first entered service in 1981, are capable of firing 24 SS-N-19 long-range cruise missiles. This represents the most capable and

---

30. Some reports credit the SS-N-14 Silex anti-submarine and anti-ship missile (once called the SS-N-10) with a nuclear depth bomb payload. The weapon, however, is not believed to be nuclear-armed.
31. The Soviets reportedly benefitted by copying the design of the SUBROC; CIA, *Soviet Acquisition of Militarily Significant Western Technology: An Update*, September 1985, p. 31.
32. According to U.S. Naval Intelligence, "a wide variety of naval weapons... have nuclear capability, including... certain anti-aircraft weapons"; SASC, FY 1984 DOD, Part 6, pp. 2971-2972. The SA-N-2 Guideline and the SA-N-7 Gadfly could be nuclear-capable as well.
33. This missile is thought to be nuclear-capable. However, it is derived from the non-nuclear, land-based SA-6 Gainful.
34. Akula, Sierra, Victor III, and Yankee attack submarines (SSNs) can also fire the SS-N-21 Sampson SLCM.
35. Six had been modified by 1984; Couhat, *Combat Fleets of the World*, 1984/85, p. 701; Couhat, *Combat Fleets of the World*, 1988/89, p. 587. Modification results in a bulge on either side of the sail and a bulge at the forward ends of the missile tubes abreast of the sail.

9

Attack Submarines

Table 9.2
Soviet Navy Deployments by Fleet (mid-1988)

Ship Type	Northern Fleet	Baltic Fleet	Black Sea Fleet	Caspian Flotilla	Pacific Fleet	Total
Submarines	175	47	27	—	122	371
Ballistic Missile	39	6	1	—	30	76
Attack	87	38	25	—	85	235[1]
Cruise Missile	46	3	1	—	10	60
Major Surface Combatants	74	50	74	5	77	280
Aircraft Carriers	1	—	3	—	2	6
Cruisers	11	4	8	—	11	34
Destroyers/Frigates	62	46	63	5	64	240[2]
Other Surface Combatants	84	96	70	32	128	410[3]
Auxiliaries	99	46	64	5	97	311

1. There are some 202 nuclear-capable submarines. Some 30 other non-nuclear-capable submarines include Beluga, Echo, Golf, Hotel, India, Lima, Uniform, Whiskey, X-ray, Yankee, and Zulu boats designated auxiliary submarine (SSA/SSAN), auxiliary communications submarine, (SSQ/SSQN), submarine (principal military capability unknown) (SSUN), and training submarine (SST).
2. There are 171 nuclear-capable destroyers and frigates accounted for in the *Databook*. Some 60 additional minor frigates (1 Koni, 12 Grisha II, 29 Petya, and 18 Mirka), as well as some ships held in reserve, are not nuclear-capable.
3. Some 67 patrol combants of the Turya, Nanuchka I/III, Sarancha, and Tarantul III class are nuclear-capable. All other ships of this class are not nuclear capable.

Sources: Authors' estimates based upon SMP 1988, pp. 14-15; DIA, *Force Structure Summary*, November 1987, pp. 12-13, 19; DIA, *Unclassified Communist Naval Orders of Battle*, May 1984 and April 1986; private communications with the authors.

---

heavily armed Soviet anti-ship platform. The Oscar submarine continues in production;[36] the third was launched in 1987;[37] the fourth began sea trials in 1986.[38] A single Yankee ballistic missile submarine has been converted to fire cruise missiles and is the test platform for the yet to be deployed SS-NX-24 long-range SLCM.[39] The Yankee SSGN will likely carry 12 SS-NX-24 missiles. A new nuclear-powered submarine specifically designed to carry the SS-NX-24 is believed to be under construction.[40]

Attack Submarines

The Soviet Navy currently operates 76 nuclear-powered and 126 diesel-powered nuclear-capable attack submarines.[41] All of these attack submarines have 21-inch torpedo tubes and can therefore fire standard nuclear torpedoes. In addition, Victor I, Victor II, Victor III, Alfa, Sierra, Mike, and Akula class submarines carry either the SS-N-15 nuclear depth bomb or the SS-N-16 dual-capable ASW missile.[42] Carriage of these weapons may require a 26-inch torpedo tube and special fire control systems. Victor III, Sierra, Akula, and converted Yankee classes can also carry the SS-N-21 Sampson, which was deployed in late 1987.[43]

Three new attack submarine classes have become operational since 1987: Akula, Mike, and Sierra. These new submarines incorporate substantial advances in sound-quieting and warfighting potential. Akula hull number one, first launched in 1984, was still undergoing sea trials as of March 1988.[44] Second boats of the Sierra and Akula classes, first introduced in 1986-1987, were launched in 1986, and a third Akula was launched in 1987.[45] Both submarine classes are in production.[46] The Mike class submarine, which was launched in 1983, is a one-of-a-kind experimental testbed.[47]

According to the U.S. Navy, the Victor III class nuclear-powered and the Kilo class diesel-powered submarines remain in production—the Kilo class in "large numbers" at three shipyards.[48] In addition, Yankee class ballistic missile submarines are being converted to attack submarines. The first conversion, which took place in 1983, included installation of updated fire control and

---

36 SMP 1988, p. 38.
37 Studeman, USN, Statement before HASC, March 1988, p. 34.
38 SMP 1987, p. 67.
39 SMP 1985, p. 35.
40 Studeman, USN, Statement before HASC, March 1988, p. 34. See also, SASC/SAC Soviet Strategic Force Developments, 1985, Chart II; and HAC, FY 1986 DOD, Part 2, p. 908. SMP 1988, p. 83, refers to the current Oscar as the Oscar I class, indicating that the new submarine may be designated Oscar II.
41 According to SMP 1988, p. 129, a significant number of diesel submarines were retired during the 1980s.
42 The Tango class diesel-powered attack submarines also may carry the SS-N-15 or SS-N-16 missile.

43 HAC, FY 1986 DOD, Part 2, p. 914. The missile was initially tested on a modified Victor III from the Northern Fleet and was test-fired during 1987 from the submarine for the first time.
44 Studeman, USN, Statement before HASC, March 1988, p. 30.
45 Studeman, USN, Statement before HASC, March 1988, p. 34; SMP 1987, p. 67; HASC, FY 1988/1989 DOD Seapower and Strategic and Critical Materials Subcommittee, p. 10.
46 SMP 1988, p. 38.
47 *Ibid.*, p. 85.
48 *Ibid.*, p. 38; Studeman, USN, Statement before HASC, March 1988, pp. 30, 34; SMP 1987, p. 67; HASC, FY 1988/1989 DOD Seapower and Strategic and Critical Materials Subcommittee, p. 10. In 1987, four Kilos were launched, only one of which was built for the Soviet Navy.

Table 9.3
Major Soviet Submarine and Naval Accidents

Year	Event
1961	A nuclear submarine assigned to practice a salvo-firing of two R-13 missiles during Northern Fleet exercises suffers a nuclear power plant accident caused by a break in a cooling pipe.
1966-1968	In a sudden catastrophic accident, one of three nuclear reactors of the Soviet icebreaker Lenin suffers meltdown caused by a leakage of radiation-contaminated water. There are 27-30 fatalities, with many others suffering radiation sickness. Lenin is out of commission for about three years. The damaged reactor is never replaced.
1966	Rumors around 1966 of a radiation leakage from a submarine in the reactor shielding at base in Polyarnyy in the Northern Fleet. Several reportedly die from radiation sickness.
1967	November class SSN has mishap in Mediterranean believed related to propulsion system. The submarine is towed.
1968	Entire crew of 90 men perish when Northern Fleet nuclear submarine fails to return from patrol to homeport of Severomorsk. The submarine is later found on bottom of estuary to Kolskiy Zaliv.
1967-1968	A Golf I class SSB is lost at sea in 1968 in the mid-Pacific with the entire crew. Portions of the submarine were later raised in 1974 by the CIA ship Glomar Explorer.
1970	November class SSN participating in exercise "OKEAN 1970" catches on fire on 11 April approximately 300 nautical miles northwest of Spain. The submarine is scuttled, with a great loss of life, to prevent fire from reaching the nuclear reactor.
1972	Hotel II class SSBN surfaces in late February in the North Atlantic off the coast of Newfoundland due to a loss of power caused by a propulsion casualty. Deaths believed to have occurred. The submarine is towed back to the Soviet Union on the surface.
1974	Kashin class DDG is lost in Black Sea on 31 August.
1977	About 12 officers serving on a nuclear submarine in the Atlantic return to Leningrad via Aeroflot from Canada suffering from radiation exposure. Cause of accident is unknown.
1977	Fire of undetermined origin occurs on a nuclear submarine on patrol in the Indian Ocean. Submarine may be one of first nuclear-powered submarines using liquid sodium as a heat transfer agent. The submarine is towed back to the Soviet Union.
1978	An Echo II SSGN is observed dead in water in August near Rockall Bank north of Scotland following loss of power due to a propulsion system casualty. The submarine is towed back to the Soviet Union.
1980	An Echo class SSN suffers a serious propulsion casualty off coast of Okinawa. All power is lost, and at least nine men are believed to have died following a fire in the propulsion spaces. The submarine is towed to Vladivostok.
1981	A nuclear submarine operating in the Baltic in early September has an accident. Crew members are reportedly sealed in the reactor compartment and suffer severe radiation poisoning. The submarine is towed back to the Soviet Union.
1983	A Charlie I class SSGN armed with cruise missiles sinks east of the tip of Kamchatka peninsula in June. The submarine had about 90 people aboard. The accident was probably due to mechanical failure unrelated to the nuclear power plant, and there was no evidence of radioactive contamination. It was raised in early August.
1983	Victor class SSN is involved in an accident with the USS McCloy in November.
1984	A Golf II class SSBN is crippled in the Sea of Japan in September and is towed back to its base at Vladivostok.
1986	On 3 October a liquid-fuel SS-N-6 SLBM in the third port launch tube on a Yankee I class SSBN explodes while the submarine is on patrol 880 kilometers east of Bermuda. The submarine sinks on October 6 after being taken in tow. At least three crewmen are killed in the explosion.

Note: The Soviets have had considerable problems in operating their submarines. Since 1975, they have had over 200 submarine accidents, some of which have resulted in lost submarines, serious damage, and fatalities. Reactor shielding in Soviet submarines was initially very poor, and while there have been improvements, shielding is not believed up to Western standards.

Sources: Polmar, *Guide to the Soviet Navy*, 1983 and 1986; HASC, Naval Nuclear Propulsion Program—1982, 29 April 1982, pp. 18-19; CIA summaries of nuclear incidents, released under the FOIA; Frederic N. Smith, "USSR: Nuclear Submarine Problems Continue," *Defense & Foreign Affairs Daily*, 23 January 1985, p. 2; *Soviet Aerospace*, 15 August 1983, pp. 104-105; "Soviet N-sub Sinking in Pacific Reported," *Washington Times*, 11 August 1983, p. 1; Mikhail Turetsky, *The Introduction of Missile Systems into the Soviet Navy*, p. 79; USN, *Soviet Naval Developments* (Rev. 4/85), p. 94; *New York Times*, 23 September 1984, p. 9.

9
Surface Ships

sonar systems, to "enable the Yankee SSN to launch a wider variety of weapons."[49] A second conversion, which took place in 1985, resulted in a second variant that is designated Yankee SSN and is equipped to fire the SS-N-21 Sampson SLCM.[50]

Surface Ships

Aircraft Carriers

The Soviet Navy has six aircraft carriers, four Kiev class guided-missile Vertical Short Takeoff and Landing (V/STOL) aircraft carriers (CVHGs), and two Moskva class aviation cruisers (CHGs).[51] The ships are much smaller than U.S. aircraft carriers, and only the Kiev class can launch fixed-wing aircraft. What is more, the aircraft are only capable of short takeoff and landing operations. Conventional takeoff jet aircraft are still unable to operate off of Soviet aircraft carriers.

The four Kiev class ships each carry a number of nuclear weapons: eight SS-N-12 SLCMs (with eight reloads), one twin SUW-N-1 launcher with FRAS-1 ballistic rockets, 72 SA-N-3 SAMs, and 10 21-inch torpedo tubes. In addition, the Kiev class ships with their angled flight deck can embark about 30 aircraft: 12 Yak-36 Forger short takeoff and landing (STOL) fighters and up to 24 Ka-25 Hormone A/B or Ka-27 Helix A helicopters. These Forger aircraft may be capable of delivering nuclear bombs, and the Ka-25 Hormone A and Ka-27 Helix A helicopters can deliver nuclear depth bombs. Two Moskva class ships were introduced in 1967 and are homeported in the Black Sea. They are not capable of launching cruise missiles or embarking fixed-wing aircraft, but carry one twin SUW-N-1 launcher with FRAS-1 ballistic rockets and 44 SA-N-3 SAMs. In addition, the Moskva class ships embark about 14 Ka-25 Hormone A helicopters capable of delivering nuclear depth bombs.

The Soviets have at least two large-deck (65,000-70,000 ton) Tbilisi (formerly Brezhnev) class aircraft carriers under construction at the Nikolayev Shipyard in the Black Sea. The keel of the first of the aircraft carriers, called the Tbilisi, was laid in January 1983, is expected to commence sea trials in 1989, and will be deployed in about 1995.[52] These aircraft carriers will ultimately be able to accommodate some 35-60 aircraft. The aircraft carrier is now being described as being "designed for ramp-assisted aircraft launch."[53] Initially it appears that it will be restricted to STOL fighters (including a new fighter-attack aircraft—Yak-41) and Ka-27 Helix helicopters.[54] This is due to problems the Soviets have evidently experienced with "catapult design, manufacturing, installation, and maintenance." According to the U.S. Navy, "there is thus a possibility the first unit may initially appear similar to an enlarged Kiev with a vertical short take off and landing (V/STOL)/helo or short take off arrested landing (STOAL) airwing. Once catapult problems are solved, retrofit and upgrade of the older unit(s) could be accomplished."[55]

Cruisers

The Soviet Navy operates 34 cruisers, all nuclear-armed. The Kirov class is nuclear-powered; the remainder are diesel-powered. The cruisers can deliver SLCMs and anti-ship missiles, nuclear torpedoes, and SAMs, as well as embark ASW helicopters.

The newest cruiser is the Kirov class, of which two are operational, a third is fitting out, and a fourth is under construction in the Baltic.[56] The Kirov was the first surface combatant to deploy with the Soviet Navy's longest range SAM system—the SA-N-6—and with the medium-range SLCM, the SS-N-19. The ships carry 20 SS-N-19s in vertical launchers, as well as 96 SA-N-6 SAMs. They also have eight 21-inch torpedo tubes. The Kirov is also capable of carrying up to three Ka-25 Hormone or Ka-27 Helix helicopters, which can deliver nuclear depth bombs.

The second cruiser production program is the conventionally powered Slava, which became operational in 1982.[57] Two Slava class cruisers are currently operational, a third is fitting out, and unit four is under construction at Nikolayev.[58] The Slava can launch 16 SS-N-12 SLCMs, 64 SA-N-6 SAMs from vertical launchers, and has 10 21-inch torpedo tubes.

Besides the two classes of cruisers that are under construction, there are five other nuclear-capable classes: Kara, Kresta I, Kresta II, Kynda, and Sverdlov. Seven Kara class cruisers deployed between 1973 and 1980 mount 72 SA-N-3 SAMs and 10 21-inch torpedo tubes, as well as carry a single Ka-25 Hormone A, which can deliver nuclear depth bombs. The four Kresta I class cruisers, deployed from 1967 to 1969, can launch four SS-N-3b SLCMs and 44 SA-N-1 SAMs, and have 10 21-inch torpedo tubes. One Ka-25 Hormone A can be carried. The ten Kresta II cruisers, operational from 1969 to 1978, can fire 10 21-inch torpedo tubes and 72 SA-N-3 SAMs, as well as carry a single nuclear-capable Ka-25 Hormone A. Four Kynda class, deployed from 1962 to 1965, can launch 16 SS-N-3b SLCMs (eight are reloads), and 24 SA-N-1 SAMs and have six 21-inch torpedo tubes. Finally, five older Sverdlov class cruisers deployed from 1951 to 1955 may be nuclear-capable with their 12 152mm artillery guns.[59]

---

49 SMP 1988, p. 85.
50 Ibid., p. 85.
51 The fourth Kiev class carrier became operational in 1987; Studeman, USN, Statement before HASC, March 1988, p. 35.
52 Ibid.
53 SMP 1988, preface, p. 5.
54 Carrier aircraft trials and testing is taking place at the Saki naval airfield on the Crimean peninsula. The Su-27, MiG-29, and Su-25 are being evaluated at the test center; SMP 1985, pp. 99-101; Studeman, USN, Statement before HASC, March 1988, p. 35.
55 HASC, FY 1988/1989 DOD Seapower and Strategic and Critical Materials Subcommittee, p. 12. See also, Studeman, USN, Statement before HASC, March 1988, p. 35.
56 HASC, FY 1988/1989 DOD Seapower and Strategic and Critical Materials Subcommittee, p. 12; Studeman, USN, Statement before HASC, March 1988, p. 36.
57 SMP 1988, p. 84.
58 HASC, FY 1988/1989 DOD Seapower and Strategic and Critical Materials Subcommittee, p. 13; Studeman, USN, Statement before HASC, March 1988, p. 36.
59 Instead of the standard 12 the Admiral Senyavin has six guns and the Zhdanov has nine guns.

9
Surface Ships

Geographic Constraints

Despite having the world's longest coastline (primarily along the Arctic Ocean), the Soviet Union is severely constrained by ports that lack open access to the high seas. In winter, ice impedes almost every port except for those at bases on the Black, Baltic, and Barents Seas. Even in favorable weather, Soviet naval forces in all four fleets must funnel through natural "choke points" to reach open waters. Access to the open Atlantic Ocean for the Northern Fleet can be gained only by passing through NATO's Greenland-Iceland-Norway (GIN) Gap. Ships from the Baltic Fleet must pass through the Kattegat (only 40 miles wide) at the mouth of the Baltic through waters bordered by Norway on the north and Denmark on the south. Access to the Mediterranean for the Black Sea Fleet can only be gained through the Turkish Straits which are governed by the Montreaux Convention of 1936.[1] The Straits comprise the Bosporus (18 miles long and as narrow as 800 yards wide) the Dardanelles (47 miles long and three to four miles wide) and the Sea of Marmara in between. Egress from the Mediterranean is constrained by the Strait of Gibraltar (10 miles wide). Finally, access to the Sea of Japan, the South China Sea, and the Indian and Pacific Oceans from Pacific Fleet headquarters at Vladivostok (the only major naval port in the Pacific that can be logistically supported overland) and other ports in the region is hindered by the Soya Strait (La Perouse) (25 miles wide), the Tsugaru Strait (10 miles wide), and the Korea Strait (30 miles wide between Korea and Tsushima Island). Even the Tatar Strait between Sakhalin Island and the Soviet mainland, the access point to the Sea of Okhotsk, tapers to 10 to 20 miles wide and would be relatively easy to mine or cut off. Only Petropavlovsk on the Bering Sea has open access to the ocean.

---

1 The Montreaux Convention imposes restrictions on the passage of Soviet combatants—eight days notice of the transit of naval combatants, with the exception of oilers and distilling ships—and prohibits the passage of submarines (except in route to other ports for repairs). See Charles Maechling, Jr. 'Crisis at the Turkish Straits, Proceedings, August 1988, pp. 63-71. The Convention has forced the Soviet Union to provide submarines from the Northern Fleet for operations in the Mediterranean Sea.

Destroyers

The Soviet Navy has 52 nuclear-capable destroyers of 11 classes. The destroyers carry 21-inch torpedo tubes, some of the older ships carry SAMs, and some carry SLCMs. The newest Udaloy class can carry two Ka-27 Helix A anti-submarine helicopters.

Two classes of destroyers, both initially deployed in 1981, are currently under construction—the Sovremennyy class and the Udaloy class. Eight Sovremennyy ships are active or on sea trials, unit eleven has been launched and six more are under construction.[60] The Sovremennyy boats carry eight SS-N-22 SLCMs and four 21-inch torpedo tubes. Nine Udaloy class ships are active or on sea trials, and three more are under construction.[61] The Udaloy class carries eight "long-range cruise missile-delivered ASW weapons,"[62] and has eight 21-inch torpedo tubes.

The nine older classes of destroyer are all fitted with 21-inch torpedo tubes. The single ship of the Kildin class can fire the SS-N-1 SLCM. Five Kanin class and seven SAM Kotlin class ships can carry 16 SA-N-1 SAMs each. Twelve Kashin class and six Modified Kashin class can deliver 36 SA-N-1s.

Frigates/Patrol Combatants

One hundred and nineteen frigates and 67 patrol combatants of the Soviet Navy are nuclear-capable. The 119 frigates of four classes and 30 guided-missile patrol combatants of the Turya class all carry 21-inch torpedo tubes. A new class of frigate, probably a follow-on to the Krivak class, is under construction at Kalingrad Shipyard in the Baltic and could begin sea trials by mid-1989.[63] Seventeen Nanuchka I class and 11 Nanuchka III class guided-missile patrol combatants carry nine SS-N-9 SLCMs. Eight Tarantul III class patrol combatants carry four SS-N-22 SLCMs, and a single Sarancha class guided-missile patrol combatant (hydrofoil) carries four SS-N-9 SLCMs.

Nuclear Weapon Support Ships

The Soviet Union has only about 30 auxiliary naval ships that are capable of nuclear weapons support—either transportation, maintenance, or supply.[64] Sixteen ships are missile tenders (AEMs) which transport ballistic and cruise missiles to Soviet bases, ships, and submarines. A single large replenishment oiler (Berezina class) can provide underway weapons support to submarines. Twelve submarine tenders (AS) also provide underway and moored transport and supply for attack submarines. These Ugra and Don class ASs can support as many as 12 submarines at sea with supplies, fuel, water, and spare torpedoes. No Soviet amphibious ships or landing craft are thought capable of transporting nuclear weapons. (There are no ground-launched nuclear weapons assigned to Naval Infantry).

---

60 SMP 1988, p. 85; Studeman, USN, Statement before HASC, March 1988, p. 37.
61 Ibid.
62 SMP 1986, p. 84. A photograph in SMP 1987, p. 87, shows two quad deck-mounted launchers.
63 Studeman, USN, Statement before HASC, March 1988, p. 37.
64 An additional 12 ships are Special Liquids Tankers (AOSs) capable of transporting radioactive waste and SLBM fuel, and two are repair ships (ARs) that transport nuclear materials supporting nuclear reactors on ships and submarines.

9
OSCAR I (SSGN)

Cruise Missile Submarines
OSCAR I[1] (SSGN)

OSCAR (SSGN)

Figure 9.1 Close-up of **Oscar I** class nuclear-powered cruise missile attack submarine. Called the Soviet Union's most capable and heavily armed anti-ship platform, it is capable of submerged launch firing of 24 SS-N-19 long-range cruise missiles.

DESCRIPTION:	Nuclear-powered cruise missile submarine capable of submerged launch
BUILDER:	Severodvinsk
SPECIFICATIONS:	
Length:	150 m[2] (490 ft)
Beam:	17.5 m[3] (57.4 ft)
Displacement:	
Surface:	10,000-11,500 tons[4]
Submerged:	16,000 MT[5]
Draft:	11 m[6] (36 ft)
Propulsion:	nuclear; 2 PWRs; 90,000 shp[7]

---

1. SMP 1988, p. 83, refers to the Oscar class as the Oscar I class.
2. SMP 1987, p. 81. Couhat, *Combat Fleets of the World*, 1988/89, p. 585, reports, 146.0 m and for the third and later submarines, 156.0 m.
3. Polmar, *Guide to the Soviet Navy*, 1986, p. 128; John Jordan, 'Soviet Cruise Missile Submarines,'' Part 3, *Jane's Defence Weekly*, 30 June 1984, p. 1080.
4. Polmar, *Guide to the Soviet Navy*, 1986, p. 128; Jordan, op. cit., p. 1080. Couhat, *Combat Fleets of the World*, 1988/89, p. 585, reports 13,000 tons for the third submarine and later.
5. SMP 1987, p. 81. Previous editions of SMP reported 14,000 MT.
6. *Jane's Fighting Ships*, 1988-89, p. 550; Couhat, *Combat Fleets of the World*, 1988/89, p. 585; *Jane's Defence Review*, Vol. 2, No. 2, 1981, pp. 163-164.
7. *Jane's Fighting Ships*, 1988-89, p. 550.

OSCAR I (SSGN)

Figure 9.2 The **Oscar I** class submarine first entered service in 1981 and continues in production; four operational, five launched (1988). The fifth submarine may be a new type—designated Oscar II—to carry either the SS-N-21 or SS-N-24 sea-launched cruise missiles.

Speed:
   Surface: unknown

   Submerged: 30-35 kts[8]

Crew: approx. 130[9]

NUCLEAR WEAPONS:
   Cruise: 24 SS-N-19,[10] mounted in banks of 12 on either side and external to the pressure hull;[11] probably platform for SS-NX-24 when deployed[12]

   ASW Rockets: SS-N-15 nuclear depth bombs and SS-N-16 ASW missiles[13]

   Torpedoes: six 21-inch (53.3 cm) or 26-inch (65.0 cm) tubes in the bow;[14] possibly two additional in the stern

DEPLOYMENT:
   Number Deployed: 4 operational, 5 launched (1988)[15]

   Homeport: Northern Fleet[16]

HISTORY:
   IOC: 1981[17]

   Production: in production (1988)[18]

COMMENTS: SS-N-19 on Oscar "targeted primarily against NATO carrier battle groups."[19]

---

8 Ibid.; Polmar, *Guide to the Soviet Navy*, 1986, p. 128. Couhat, *Combat Fleets of the World*, 1988/89, p. 585.
9 *Jane's Fighting Ships*, 1988-89, p. 550.
10 SMP 1988, p. 83.
11 *Jane's Fighting Ships*, 1988-89, p. 550.
12 HAC, FY 1986 DOD, Part 2, p. 908.
13 Couhat, *Combat Fleets of the World*, 1988/89, p. 585; Collins and Victory, *U.S./Soviet Military Balance*, 1988, pp. 43, 107.
14 *Jane's Defence Review*, Vol. 2, No. 2, 1981, pp. 163-164; Couhat, *Combat Fleets of the World*, 1988/89, p. 585; Collins and Victory, *U.S./Soviet Military Balance*, 1988, pp. 43, 107. Polmar, *Guide to the Soviet Navy*, 1986, p. 128.
15 DIA, *Unclassified Communist Naval Orders of Battle*, DDB-1200-124-86, April 1986, p. 1. The fourth unit began sea trials in 1986 (SMP 1987, p. 67) and was deployed in 1987. The third unit was launched in 1987; Studeman, USN, Statement before HASC, March 1988, p. 34; *Jane's Fighting Ships*, 1988-89, p.550.
16 SASC, FY 1986 DOD, Part 8, p. 4364.
17 JCS, FY 1984, p. 28; HASC, FY 1983 DOD, Part 4, p. 3; SMP 1985, pp. 94, 96, 97.
18 Studeman, USN, Statement before HASC, March 1988, p. 34.
19 SMP 1988, p. 83.

9
CHARLIE I/II (SSGN)

CHARLIE I/II (SSGN)

Figure 9.3 Nine **Charlie I** cruise missile submarines are currently (1988) deployed, including this one leased to India in May 1988.

DESCRIPTION:	Nuclear-powered, second-generation cruise missile submarine in two versions; capable of submerged launch
BUILDER:	Gor'kiy
SPECIFICATIONS:	
Length:	Charlie I: 93.9 m[1] (308 ft) Charlie II: 102.9 m[2] (337 ft)
Beam:	Charlie I/II: 10 m[3] (32.8 ft)
Displacement:	
Surface:	Charlie I: 3960 MT[4] Charlie II: 4420 MT[5]
Submerged:	Charlie I: 4775 MT[6] Charlie II: 5385 MT[7]
Draft:	Charlie I/II: 7.6 m[8] (25 ft)
Propulsion:	nuclear, 1 PWR, 15,000 shp[9]
Speed:	
Surface:	16 kts
Submerged	28 kts[10]

---

1. DIA, *ASW Handbook*, 1977, p. 6-41; *Jane's Fighting Ships*, 1988-89, p. 551.
2. DIA, *ASW Handbook*, p. 6-41; SMP 1985, p. 96; DIA, *Soviet Naval Shipbuilding*, DDI-1922-10-76, July 1976 (partially declassified and released under the FOIA), p. 4.
3. DIA, JIIKS, Vol. XIII, 1983.
4. DIA, *ASW Handbook*, 1977, p. 6-41.
5. Ibid.
6. Ibid.
7. Ibid.
8. Ibid.
9. Polmar, *Guide to the Soviet Navy*, 1986, pp. 131-133. Couhat, *Combat Fleets of the World*, 1988/89, p. 586, reports 30,000 hp for the Charlie II.
10. DIA, JIIKS, Vol. XIII, 1983; Polmar, *Guide to the Soviet Navy*, 1986, pp 131-133.

CHARLIE I/II (SSGN)

Figure 9.4 There are six **Charlie II** class cruise missile submarines, all capable of carrying eight SS-N-9 missiles each, and all currently (1988) assigned to the Northern Fleet.

Figure 9.5 Elevated stern view of **Charlie I** class submarine underway.

Crew: 85-100[11]

NUCLEAR WEAPONS:
Cruise: Charlie I: eight SS-N-7[12]
Charlie II: eight SS-N-9;[13] early reports indicated probable SS-N-7 capability[14]

ASW Rockets: SS-N-15 nuclear depth bomb[15]

Torpedoes: six 21-inch (53.3 cm) torpedo tubes in the bow;[16] 12-14 torpedo tube-launched weapons[17]

DEPLOYMENT:
Number Deployed: 15 (1988); nine Charlie I (one additional leased to India 1 May 1988),[18] six Charlie II;[19] one Charlie I sank in June 1983 east of the tip of Kamchatka peninsula; the submarine was raised in early August 1983;[20] it did not reenter service

Homeport: approx. eight Charlie Is in Northern Fleet, one in Pacific Fleet; six Charlie IIs in Northern Fleet;[21] Charlies patrol in the Mediterranean[22]

HISTORY:
IOC: Charlie I: 1968[23]
Charlie II: 1974;[24] 1973[25]

Production: last boat to enter service was in 1982-1983; construction was halted in favor of Oscar class

COMMENTS: Reactor plant same used in Victor SSN and similar to that in Yankee-Delta SSBN classes.[26] 400 meter normal diving depth, 600 meter maximum

---

11 Polmar, *Guide to the Soviet Navy*, 1986, pp. 131-133; Couhat, *Combat Fleets of the World*, 1988/89, p. 586; *Jane's Fighting Ships*, 1988-89, pp. 551-553.
12 Statement of Admiral Sumner Shapiro before the HASC, 14 February 1979, (mimeo) p. 8, on the Soviet naval threat; DIA, JIIKS, Vol. XIII, 1983; *Jane's Fighting Ships*, 1988-89, p. 550.
13 SMP 1985, p. 96; DIA, JIIKS, Vol. XIII, 1983.
14 Polmar, *Guide to the Soviet Navy*, 1983, pp. 97-98; Couhat, *Combat Fleets of the World*, 1984/85, pp. 699-700. Later editions of Polmar and Couhat dropped any reference to the SS-N-7 on the Charlie II.
15 Polmar, *Guide to the Soviet Navy*, 1986, pp. 131-133; *Jane's Fighting Ships*, 1988-89, p. 551; Couhat, *Combat Fleets of the World*, 1988/89, p. 586.
16 DIA, JIIKS, Vol. XIII, 1983; Polmar, *Guide to the Soviet Navy*, 1986, pp. 131-133; Couhat, *Combat Fleets of the World*, 1988/89, p. 586; *Jane's Fighting Ships*, 1988-89, p. 551.
17 *Jane's Fighting Ships*, 1988-89, p. 551; Polmar, *Guide to the Soviet Navy*, pp. 131-133; Couhat, *Combat Fleets of the World*, 1988/89, p. 585.
18 Twelve submarines were reportedly built; one sank in 1983, the others' disposition is unknown. DIA, *Unclassified Communist Naval Orders of Battle*, DDB-1200-124-86, April 1986, p. 1, reports 16 Charlie I/IIs, which would mean 10 Charlie I and 6 Charlie II. See also Polmar, *Guide to the Soviet Navy*, 1986, pp. 131-133; Studeman, USN, Statement before HASC, March 1988, p.51.
19 DIA, JIIKS, Vol. XIII, 1983, reports five Charlie IIs constructed as of 15 April 1983. Polmar, *Guide to the Soviet Navy*, 1986, p. 131; Couhat, *Combat Fleets of the World*, 1988/89, p. 586; and Collins and Victory, *U.S./Soviet Military Balance*, 1988, p. 105 report a sixth Charlie II deployed in 1982-1983.
20 Couhat, *Combat Fleets of the World*, 1988/89, p. 586; *Soviet Aerospace*, 15 August 1983, pp. 104-105; "Soviet N-sub Sinking in Pacific Reported," *Washington Times* 11 August 1983, p. 1.
21 Couhat, *Combat Fleets of the World*, 1988/89, p. 586.
22 *Jane's Fighting Ships*, 1988-89, p. 552.
23 SMP 1981, p. 46; DIA, JIIKS, Vol. XIII, 1983.
24 SMP 1987, p. 81.
25 DIA, JIIKS, Vol. XIII, 1983.
26 Polmar, *Guide to the Soviet Navy*, 1983, p. 98.

9

PAPA, ECHO II, JULIETT

Cruise Missile Submarines (SSG/N)
PAPA, ECHO II, JULIETT

Figure 9.6 This **Papa** class cruise missile submarine is a one-of-a-kind ship, nuclear-propelled but not likely nuclear-armed or currently part of the front-line operational force.

Figure 9.7 The Soviet **Echo II** class submarine entered service in 1962 and carries eight SS-N-3a/c cruise missiles. Of the 26 Echos currently (1988) deployed, some 15 have been modified to carry eight SS-N-12 missiles.

	Papa	**Echo II**	**Juliett**
DESCRIPTION:	One-of-a kind, nuclear-propelled cruise missile submarine; not likely nuclear-armed or operational	Nuclear-propelled cruise missile submarine deployed between 1962 and 1967	Diesel-powered cruise missile submarine produced between 1962 and 1967; only diesel-powered unit still active as front-line submarine
BUILDER:	Gor'kiy	Komsomol'sk; Severodvinsk	Gor'kiy
SPECIFICATIONS:			
Length:	109.7 m[1] (360.7 ft)	115.8 m[2] (379.9 ft)	86.9 m[3] (285.8 ft)
Beam:	12.2 m[4] (40 ft)	9.8 m[5] (32 ft)	10.1 m[6] (33.1 ft)
Displacement:			
Surface:	6400 MT;[7] 5500 tons[8]	5050 MT[9]	3000 tons[10]
Submerged:	8000 MT;[11] 6500 tons[12]	6350 MT;[13] 5800 tons[14]	3700 tons[15]

---

1. DIA, *ASW Handbook*, 1977, p. 6-43.
2. *Ibid.*, p. 6-35.
3. *Ibid.*, 1977, p. 6-45.
4. DIA, JIIKS, Vo. XIII, 1983; DIA *ASW Handbook*, 1977, p. 6-43.
5. DIA, *ASW Handbook*, 1977, p. 6-35.
6. *Ibid.*, p. 6-45.
7. *Ibid.*, p. 6-43.
8. DIA, JIIKS, VOL XIII, 1983.
9. DIA, *ASW Handbook*, p. 6-35.
10. DIA, JIIKS, Vol. XIII, 1983.
11. DIA, *ASW Handbook*, 1977, p. 6-43.
12. DIA, JIIKS, Vol. XIII, 1983.
13. DIA, *ASW Handbook*, 1977, p. 6-35.
14. DIA, JIIKS, Vol. XIII, 1983.
15. DIA, JIIKS, Vol. XIII, 1983.

9
PAPA, ECHO II, JULIETT

	Papa	**Echo II**	**Juliett**
Propulsion:	2 nuclear reactors; twin shafts;[16] 60-75,000 hp[17]	2 nuclear reactors;[18] twin shafts; 30,000 hp[19]	diesel-electric twin shafts; 5000 hp[20]
Speed:			
Surface:	16 kts	20 kts[21]	19 kts[22]
Submerged:	30 kts[23]	25 kts[24]	17 kts[25]
Crew:	85-90	90	80
NUCLEAR WEAPONS:			
Cruise:	10 SS-N-7/9[26]	8 SS-N-3a/c or SS-N-12[27]	4 SS-N-3a[28]
ASW Rockets:	SS-N-15[29]	none	none
Torpedoes (tubes):	6 21-inch (53.3 cm) bow[30]	6 21-inch (53.3 cm) bow; 2 16-inch (40.6 cm) stern;[31] carries 20 torpedoes[32]	6 21-inch (53.3 cm) bow;[33] carries 18 torpedoes[34]
DEPLOYMENT:			
Number Deployed:	1 (1988)[35]	26 (1988); 29 built[36]	15 (1988)[37]
Homeport:	Northern Fleet	some 21 in Northern Fleet and 5 in Pacific Fleet	some 11 Northern Fleet, 4 Pacific Fleet, 3 Baltic Fleet since 1981, 1 Black Sea Fleet
HISTORY:			
IOC:	1973-1975[38]	1962	1962
Production:	not in production	not in production	not in production
COMMENTS:	Must surface to launch its missiles.[39] The submarine has never patrolled beyond the local area.		

---

16. Polmar, *Guide to the Soviet Navy*, 1986, p. 130; Couhat, *Combat Fleets of the World*, 1988/89, p. 585; *Jane's Fighting Ships*, 1988-89, p. 551.
17. Polmar, *Guide to the Soviet Navy*, 1986, p. 130; *Jane's Fighting Ships*, 1988-89, p. 552.
18. Polmar, *Guide to the Soviet Navy*, 1986, p. 134; *Jane's Fighting Ships*, 1988-89, p. 552.
19. Polmar, *Guide to the Soviet Navy*, 1986, pp. 134; Couhat, *Combat Fleets of the World*, 1988/89, p. 587.
20. Polmar, *Guide to the Soviet Navy*, 1986, p. 136; Couhat, *Combat Fleets of the World*, 1988/89, p. 587; *Jane's Fighting Ships*, 1988-89, p. 553.
21. DIA, *ASW Handbook*, 1977, p. 6-35.
22. DIA, JIIKS, Vol. XIII, 1983. Polmar reports 16 knots; Polmar, *Guide to the Soviet Navy*, 1986, p. 136. Jane's reports 12 knots; *Jane's Fighting Ships*, 1988-89, p. 553.
23. DIA, JIIKS, Vol. XIII, 1983. Polmar reports 39 knots; Polmar, *Guide to the Soviet Navy*, 1986, p. 130. Jane's also reports 39 knots; *Jane's Fighting Ships*, 1988-89, p. 551.
24. DIA, JIIKS, Vol. XIII, 1983.
25. *Ibid*. Polmar reports 14 knots; Polmar, *Guide to the Soviet Navy*, 1986, p. 136. Jane's reports 12 knots; *Jane's Fighting Ships*, 1988-89, p. 553.
26. DIA, JIIKS, Vol. XIII, 1983.
27. SMP 1987, p. 85, states, "The Soviets are proceeding gradually with a program to convert the older 1960s-era SS-N-3-equipped Echo II SSGNs to carry the improved, 550-kilometer-range supersonic SS-N-12 antiship cruise missle"; DIA, JIIKS. Vol. XIII, 1983; USN *Soviet Naval Developments* (Rev. 4/85), p. 92; DIA, *The Soviet Submarine Force*, DDI-1200-56-57. December 1976, p. V.B.14.
28. DIA, JIIKS, Vol. XIII, 1983.
29. Polmar, *Guide to the Soviet Navy*, 1986, p. 130; *Jane's Fighting Ships*, 1988-89, p. 551; Collins and Cronin, *U.S./Soviet Military Balance*, 1985, pp. 81-82.
30. DIA, JIIKS, Vol. XIII, 1983.
31. DIA, JIIKS, Vol. XIII, 1983.
32. *Ibid*.
33. *Ibid*.
34. *Jane's Fighting Ships*, 1988-89, p. 553.
35. DIA, JIIKS, Vol. XIII, 1983.
36. DIA, JIIKS, Vol. XIII, 1983. One Echo-II class SSGN was modified in 1980 for special operations; Polmar, *Guide to the Soviet Navy*, 1986, p. 160.
37. Sixteen submarines were built. One was decommissioned in 1984-1985; see Polmar, *Guide to the Soviet Navy*, 1986, p. 136; and DIA, JIIKS, Vol. XIII, 1983.
38. Collins and Victory, *U.S./Soviet Military Balance*, 1988, p. 106.
39. DIA, JIIKS, Vol. XIII, 1983.

9

PAPA, ECHO II, JULIETT

JULIETT (SSG)

Figure 9.8 The **Juliett** is the Soviet Union's only diesel-powered cruise missile submarine. Produced between 1962 and 1967, there are currently 15 active (1988).

YANKEE NOTCH

Yankee Conversions (SSN/SSGN)
YANKEE NOTCH

DESCRIPTION: Nuclear-powered, former ballistic missile submarines converted into three types of attack and cruise missile platforms

BUILDER: Severodvinsk and Komsomol'sk

SPECIFICATIONS:

Length: 130 m[1] (427 ft)

Beam: 11.6 m[2] (38 ft)

Displacement:
Surface: unknown
Submerged: 10,000 MT[3]

Propulsion: nuclear, 2 PWR;[4] 2 shafts, 50,000 shp[5]

Speed:
Surface: 18-20 kts;[6] 26.5 kts[7]
Submerged: 30 kts[8]

Crew: unknown

NUCLEAR WEAPONS:
Cruise: Yankee Notch SSN is launch platform for SS-N-21;[9] SS-NX-24 large cruise missile has been tested from one Yankee converted SSGN;[10] hull could be fitted with 12 SS-NX-24s[11]

ASW Rockets: unknown

Torpedoes: six 21-inch (53.3 cm) bow;[12] carries 18 torpedoes[13]

DEPLOYMENT:
Number Deployed: 1 Yankee Notch SSN;[14] 1 standard SSN; 1 SSGN is being used in the Northern Fleet as a test vehicle for the SS-NX-24[15]

HISTORY:
IOC: conversion completed: 1984 (SSN);[16] 1984-1985[17]

Production: "The Soviets are beginning series conversion on the reconfigured class of Yankee SSN."[18]

COMMENTS: Yankee SSN has had extensive modifications made and probably has been equipped with updated fire-control and sonar systems that will enable it to launch a wider variety of weapons.[19] The Yankee SSGN began launch tests of the SS-NX-24 in 1985.[20]

---

1. Polmar, *Guide to the Soviet Navy*, 1986, p. 128; SMP 1987, p. 81. Reportedly, a 10 meter increase in length occurred during the modification process of the SS-N-21 capable Yankee Notch boats; Tonne Huitfeldt, "Soviet SS-N-21 Equipped Yankee in Norwegian Sea," *Jane's Defence Weekly*, 16 Januar 1988, pp. 44-45; *Aviation Week & Space Technology*, 22 February 1988, p. 29.
2. Commander Richard T. Ackley, USN (Ret), "The Wartime Role of Soviet SSGNs," *Proceedings*, June 1978, p. 36.
3. SMP 1987, p. 81. Polmar, *Guide to the Soviet Navy*, 1986, p. 128, gives 13,650 tons for the submerged displacement of the Yankee SSGN.
4. DIA, *ASW Handbook*, 1977, p. 6-37.
5. Polmar, *Guide to the Soviet Navy*, 1986, p. 128.
6. DIA, *ASW Handbook*, 1977, p. 6-37.
7. Ibid.
8. DIA, JIIKS, Vol. XIII, 1983.
9. Studeman, USN, Statement before HASC, March 1988, p. 33.
10. SMP 1987, p. 37.
11. Polmar, *Guide to the Soviet Navy*, 1986, p. 128.
12. Ibid.
13. Ibid.
14. SMP 1988, p. 53.
15. Ibid., p. 85; SMP 1987, pp. 37, 67, 82.
16. SMP 1987, p. 81.
17. Polmar, *Guide to the Soviet Navy*, 1986, p. 128.
18. SMP 1987, p. 67.
19. SMP 1988, p. 85; SMP 1987, pp. 82-83; HASC, FY 1985 DOD, Part 3, p. 3.
20. Polmar, *Guide to the Soviet Navy*, 1986, p. 128.

9
AKULA (SSN)

Attack Submarines
AKULA (SSN)[1]

Figure 9.9 The **Akula** class nuclear-powered attack submarine is one of three new classes of submarines, recently introduced, with superior sound-quieting and warfighting potential. The first Akula was, as of March 1988, still undergoing sea trials. All the Akulas are assigned to the Pacific Fleet.

DESCRIPTION:	Nuclear-powered attack submarine (SSN) similar to Victor II and Sierra SSNs; is a follow-on to the Victor III[1]	Beam:	12 m[5] (39.3 ft)
		Displacement:	
		Surface:	6800 tons[6]
BUILDER:	Komsomol'sk	Submerged:	8000 MT;[7] 8300 tons[8]
SPECIFICATIONS:	comparable in size to Sierra[2]	Propulsion:	nuclear, 2 PWR; 1 shaft[9]
Length:	107 m[3] (351 ft)	Speed:	
		Surface:	unknown

---

1 SMP 1988, p. 85.
2 SASC, FY 1986 DOD, Part 8, p. 4364.
3 SMP 1987, p. 81.
4 Polmar, *Guide to the Soviet Navy*, 1986, p. 139.
5 Ibid.
6 SMP 1987, p. 81.
7 Polmar, *Guide to the Soviet Navy*, 1986, p. 139.
8 Ibid.

AKULA (SSN)

Submerged:	30+ kts[10]	Homeport:	Pacific Fleet
Crew:	unknown	**HISTORY:**	
NUCLEAR WEAPONS:		Launched:	July 1984[15]
Cruise Missile:	SS-N-21[10]	Sea Trials:	April 1985[16]
ASW Rockets:	SS-N-15 nuclear depth bomb and the SS-N-16 ASW missile[11]	IOC:	1987 (limited operation)
Torpedoes:	six 21-inch or 26-inch (53.3 cm or 65 cm) tubes[12]	COMMENTS:	Akula incorporates substantial advances in sound-quieting and warfighting capability.[17] It has performance characteristics that are probably similar to Sierra.[18]
DEPLOYMENT:			
Number Deployed:	3 (1988); Akula hull one was still undergoing sea trials as of March 1988;[13] a third Akula was launched in 1987;[14] another is under construction		

---

9 *Ibid.*
10 Studeman, USN, Statement before HASC, March 1988, p. 33; SMP 1988, p. 53. The Akula was used to test-fire SS-N-21 missiles from the northern part of the Sea of Japan in late 1987; Edward Neilan, "Soviet Cruise Missile Tested in Sea of Japan," *Washington Times*, 28 December 1987, p. 11.
11 SMP 1987, p. 81. Polmar, *Guide to the Soviet Navy*, 1986, p. 139, reports SS-N-16.
12 Polmar, *Guide to the Soviet Navy*, 1986, p. 139; *Jane's Fighting Ships*, 1988-89, p. 554.
13 Studeman, USN, Statement before HASC, March 1988, p. 30; SMP 1987, p. 81.
14 Studeman, USN, Statement before HASC, March 1988, p. 34.
15 SASC, FY 1986 DOD, Part 8, p. 4364.
16 SMP 1985, pp. 96-97.
17 Studeman, USN, Statement before HASC, March 1988, p. 30.
18 SASC, FY 1986 DOD, Part 8, p. 4364.

9

MIKE (SSN)

MIKE (SSN)

Figure 9.10 The **Mike** class attack submarine, which was launched in 1983, is a one-of-a-kind experimental ship. Though thought to be the most modern quiet Soviet nuclear submarine, it does not seem to be headed for series production.

DESCRIPTION:	One-of-a-kind, titanium-hulled, nuclear-powered attack submarine (SSN); most modern of Soviet attack submarines	Submerged:	9700 MT[3]
		Propulsion:	2 advanced liquid-metal-cooled reactor;[4] 60,000 shp
BUILDER:	Severodvinsk	Speed:	
SPECIFICATIONS:		Surface:	unknown
Length:	110 m[1] (360 ft)	Submerged:	26+ kts;[5] 36-38 kts[6]
Beam:	approx. 12.0 m[2] (39.3 ft)	Crew:	95[7]
Displacement: Surface:	7800 tons		

---

1 SMP 1987, p. 81; *Soviet Aerospace*, Vol. 40, No. 7, 21 February 1984, pp. 45-46.
2 Polmar, *Guide to the Soviet Navy*, 1986, p. 140.
3 HAC, FY 1986 DOD, Part 2, p. 909; SMP 1985, pp. 95-96; SASC, FY 1986 DOD, Part 8, p. 4363. SMP 1987, p. 81, reports 6400 MT as the submerged displacement.
4 Polmar, *Guide to the Soviet Navy*, 1986, p. 140.
5 Collins and Victory, *U.S./Soviet Military Balance*, 1988, p. 106.
6 Polmar, *Guide to the Soviet Navy*, 1986, p. 140. *Jane's Fighting Ships*, 1988-89, p. 554, reports 38 knots.
7 Polmar, *Guide to the Soviet Navy*, 1986, p. 140.

MIKE (SSN)

NUCLEAR WEAPONS:	early reports stated that the Mike SSN was a candidate platform for the SS-N-21, although it no longer has this mission[8]	Sea Trials:	completed by February 1985[14]
		IOC:	1986;[15] 1985[16]
ASW Rockets:	SS-N-15 nuclear depth bomb or SS-N-16 ASW missile[9]	Production:	originally thought to be a follow-on to the Alfa;[17] but a second submarine was not launched, and it does not appear that the Mike will enter series production[18]
Torpedoes:	six 21-inch (53.3 cm) tubes;[10] possible 26-inch (65 cm) tubes[11]		
DEPLOYMENT:			
Number Deployed:	1[12]	**COMMENTS:**	Mike is reportedly quieter than most other Soviet nuclear submarines and "may have some performance capabilities superior to those of U.S. submarines"[19]
Home Port:	Northern Fleet		
HISTORY:			
Launched:	May 1983[13]		

---

[8] HASC, FY 1988/1989 DOD Seapower and Strategic and Critical Material Subcommittee, p. 10; SMP 1987, p. 37; SMP 1984, p. 31; HASC, FY 1985 DOD, Part 3, p. 3; SMP 1985, pp. 95-96.
[9] SMP 1987, p. 81; SMP 1985, pp. 95-96.
[10] *Soviet Aerospace*, Vol. 40, No. 7, 21 February 1984, pp. 45-46; Collins and Victory, *U.S./Soviet Military Balance*, 1988, p. 107.
[11] Polmar, *Guide to the Soviet Navy*, 1986, p. 140.
[12] DIA, *Unclassified Communist Naval Orders of Battle*, DDB-1200-124-86, April 1986, p. 1.
[13] Nick Childs and Antony Preston, "Submarine Developments and Worldwide Review," *Jane's Defence Weekly*, 18 August 1984, p. 233.
[14] SASC, FY 1986 DOD, Part 8, p. 4363.
[15] SMP 1987, p. 81.
[16] SASC, FY 1986 DOD, Part 8, p. 4363.
[17] SMP 1984, p. 31.
[18] HAC, FY 1986 DOD, Part 2, p. 909; SMP 1986, p. 81; Office of Naval Intelligence, "Current Naval Intelligence Issues," March 1987, p. 5.
[19] SASC, FY 1986 DOD, Part 8, p. 4363.

9 SIERRA (SSN)

SIERRA (SSN)

Figure 9.11 Sierra class nuclear-powered attack submarine underway. A follow-on to the Victor III class, the Sierra has improved depth and sensor capabilities.

DESCRIPTION:	Nuclear-powered attack submarine (SSN); follow-on to the Victor III class[1]	**SPECIFICATIONS:**	about 20 percent larger than Victor III[2]
BUILDER:	Gor'kiy	Length:	110 m³ (360 ft)
		Beam:	larger than Victor III[4]

---

1. SMP 1988, p. 85.
2. SMP 1987, p. 82.
3. *Ibid.*, p. 81.
4. HASC, FY 1985 DOD, Part 3, p. 23.

SIERRA (SSN)

Displacement:
- Surface: 6000 MT[5]
- Submerged: 7600 MT[6]

Propulsion: 2 PWR; 40,000 shp[7]

Speed:
- Submerged: 35 kts;[8] slightly faster than Victor III[9]

Crew: 100[10]

NUCLEAR WEAPONS:
- Cruise Missile: SS-N-21[11]
- ASW Rockets: ASW missile, including the SS-N-15 nuclear depth bomb and the SS-N-16 ASW conventional and nuclear missiles[12]
- Torpedoes: six 21-inch (53.3 cm) and/or 26-inch (65.0 cm) tubes (bow);[13] reportedly carries 18 torpedoes[14]

DEPLOYMENT:
- Number Deployed: 2 (1988);[15] only two launched by March 1987, another is under construction
- Homeport: Northern Fleet[16]

HISTORY:
- Launched: July 1983[17]
- IOC: 1986[18]
- Production: in series production (1988);[19] production rate will be slower than the Akula;[20]

Figure 9.12 Close-up aerial bow view of Sierra class submarine.

COMMENTS: Differs little in hull form from Victor III.[21] Somewhat quieter,[22] with improved depth and sensor capabilities.[23]

---

5 Polmar, *Guide to the Soviet Navy*, 1986, p. 141.
6 SMP 1987, p. 81. SMP 1986, p. 84, reported 8200 MT. SMP 1985, p. 96, reported 8000 MT.
7 Jane's Fighting Ships, 1988-89, p. 555.
8 Polmar, *Guide to the Soviet Navy*, 1986, p. 141; Jane's Fighting Ships, 1988-89, p. 555.
9 HASC, FY 1985 DOD, Part 3, p. 23; SASC, FY 1986 DOD, Part 8, p. 4363.
10 Jane's Fighting Ships, 1988-89, p. 555.
11 Studeman, USN, Statement before HASC, March 1988, p. 33; SMP 1988, p. 53.
12 SMP 1987, pp. 81-82.
13 Polmar, *Guide to the Soviet Navy*, 1986, p. 141.
14 *Aviation Week & Space Technology*, 24 September 1984, p. 87.
15 HASC, FY 1988/1989 DOD Seapower and Strategic and Critical Material Subcommittee, p. 10.
16 SASC, FY 1986 DOD, Part 8, p. 4363.
17 HASC, FY 1985 DOD, Part 3, p. 23.
18 SMP 1987, p. 81.
19 SMP 1988, p. 85.
20 HAC, FY 1986 DOD, Part 2, p. 909.
21 SMP 1985, pp. 96-97.
22 HASC, FY 1985 DOD, Part 3, p. 23; SASC, FY 1986 DOD, Part 8, p. 4363.
23 SASC, FY 1986 DOD, Part 8, p. 4363.

9
ALFA (SSN)

ALFA[1] (SSN)

Figure 9.13 The **Alfa** is considered the world's fastest and deepest diving nuclear-powered attack submarine. However, after producing seven ships (six are currently deployed), production was halted because the Alfas were unreliable and too noisy and therefore vulnerable to detection during high speed operation.

DESCRIPTION:[1]	World's fastest and deepest diving nuclear-propelled attack submarine (SSN) and only submarine that uses a titanium alloy for the pressure hull
BUILDER:	Sudomekh Shipyard, Leningrad
SPECIFICATIONS:	
Length:	79 m[2] (259 ft); 81.5 m[3] (267 ft)
Beam:	9.5 m[4] (31 ft)
Displacement:	
Surface:	3500 tons[5]
Submerged:	4200 tons[6]
Propulsion:	one liquid-metal-cooled nuclear reactor;[7] 45,000 shp[8]
Speed:	
Surface:	20 kts[9]
Submerged:	43-45 kts[10]
Crew:	40-45
NUCLEAR WEAPONS:	"doesn't carry much firepower"[11]

---

1 The Soviets refer to it as *zolotaya ryba* (golden fish) apparently because of the high unit cost; Polmar, *Guide to the Soviet Navy*, 1986, p. 142.
2 SMP 1987, p. 81.
3 DIA, *ASW Handbook*, 1977, p. 6-43.
4 *Ibid*.
5 DIA, JIIKS, Vol. XIII, 1983.
6 *Ibid*. SMP 1987, p. 81, reported submerged displacement of 3700 MT. Polmar, *Guide to the Soviet Navy*, 1986, p. 142, and *Jane's Fighting Ships*, 1988-89, p. 556, report 3700 tons.
7 Polmar, *Guide to the Soviet Navy*, 1986, p. 142; Milan Vego, "Soviet Alfa-Class SSN," *NAVY International*, March 1984, p. 139. *Jane's Fighting Ships*, 1988-89, p. 556, reports two reactors.
8 Polmar, *Guide to the Soviet Navy*, 1986, p. 142.
9 Vego, *op. cit.*, p. 139.
10 HAC, FY 1986 DOD, Part 2, p. 926; Polmar, *Guide to the Soviet Navy*, 1986, p. 142; *Jane's Fighting Ships*, 1988-89, p. 4556; Vego, *op. cit.*, p. 139.
11 HAC, FY 1986 DOD, Part 2, p. 926.

ALFA (SSN)

ASW Rockets:	SS-N-15[12] fired from two tubes[13] with four possible reload missiles[14]	First Observed:	April 1969 (fitting out)[19]
		Sea Trials Began:	1971[20]
Torpedoes:	six 21-inch (53.3 cm) tubes (bow);[15] 18 torpedoes or 36 mines	IOC:	1978[21]
		Production:	Alfa production terminated after seven because it was too noisy and more vulnerable to detection and attack

DEPLOYMENT:

Number Deployed: 6 (1988);[16] 7 built, one was scrapped in 1974 at the Sudomekh Shipyard after a brief operating period[17]

Homeport: Northern Fleet[18]

COMMENTS: Operating depth is at least 600 m (2000 ft) to over 900 m (3000 ft) with crushing depth at 1350 m (4400 ft).[22]

HISTORY:

Keel Laid: 1967

---

12 SMP 1987, p. 81.
13 Polmar, *Guide to the Soviet Navy*, 1986, p. 142; Vego, *op. cit.*, p. 139.
14 Vego, *op. cit.*, p. 139.
15 DIA, JIIKS, Vol. XIII, 1983.
16 DIA, *Unclassified Communist Naval Orders of Battle*, DDB-1200-124-86, April 1986, p. 1.
17 DIA, *Soviet Naval Shipbuilding*, DDI-1922-10-76, July 1976 (partially declassified and released under the FOIA), p. 4; *Jane's Fighting Ships*, 1988-89, p. 556; Vego, *op. cit.*, p. 139.
18 HASC, FY 1983 DOD, Part 4, p. 3.
19 DIA, *Soviet Naval Shipbuilding*, *op cit.*, p. 4.
20 HAC, FY 1981 DOD, Part 3, p. 206.
21 SMP 1987, p. 81; SMP 1985, p. 96; HAC, FY 1981 DOD, Part 3, p. 206.
22 Polmar, *Guide to the Soviet Navy*, 1986, p. 142; Couhat, *Combat Fleets of the World*, 1988/89, p. 589; Vego, *op. cit.*, p. 139.

9

VICTOR (SSN)

VICTOR (SSN)

VICTOR I (SSN)

Figure 9.14 Though no longer in production, there are 16 **Victor I** class nuclear-powered high-speed attack submarines currently deployed (1988), each capable of firing SS-N-15 ASW rocket-thrown nuclear depth charges and up to 18 torpedoes.

	Victor I	Victor II	Victor III
DESCRIPTION:	Nuclear-powered, high-speed attack submarine	Nuclear-powered, high-speed attack submarine	Nuclear-powered, high-speed attack submarine
BUILDER:	Admiralty, Leningrad	Admiralty, Leningrad	Admiralty, Leningrad; Komsomol'sk
SPECIFICATIONS:			
Length:	93.0 m[1] (305 ft)	101.8 m[2] (334.0 ft)	104.0 m[3] (341 ft)
Beam:	10.5 m[4] (34.4 ft) 10.5 m[5] (34.4 ft) 10.5 m (34.4 ft)		
Displacement:			
Surface:	4300 tons[6]	4600 tons[7]	4900 tons[8]
Submerged:	5100 tons[9]	5680 tons[10]	6200 tons[11]
Propulsion:	nuclear, 2 PWR; 1 shaft; 30,000 shp[12]	nuclear, 2 PWR; 1 shaft; 30,000 shp[13]	nuclear, 2 PWR; 1 shaft; 30,000 shp[14]

---

1 DIA, *ASW Handbook*, 1977, p. 6-41.
2 *Ibid.*
3 SMP 1985, p. 96; DIA, *Soviet Naval Shipbuilding*, DDI-1922-10-76, July 1976 (partially declassified and released under the FOIA), p. 4.
4 DIA, *ASW Handbook*, 1977, p. 6-41.
5 *Ibid.*
6 DIA, JIIKS, Vol. XIII, 1983.
7 *Ibid.*
8 *Ibid.*
9 *Ibid.*
10 *Ibid.*
11 *Ibid.*
12 Polmar, *Guide to the Soviet Navy*, 1986, p. 146; Couhat, *Combat Fleets of the World*, 1988/89, p. 590.
13 Polmar, *Guide to the Soviet Navy*, 1986, p. 145; Couhat, *Combat Fleets of the World*, 1988/89, p. 590.
14 Polmar, *Guide to the Soviet Navy*, 1986, p. 144; Couhat, *Combat Fleets of the World*, 1988/85, p. 589.

9
VICTOR (SSN)

Figure 9.15 Close-up view of the **Victor II** class submarine which is an enlarged (29 feet longer) version of the Victor I.

Figure 9.16 Rear view of the **Victor III** class submarine, improved version of Victor II, 19-20 currently deployed. The Victor III remains in production (1988).

	Victor	**Victor II**	**Victor III**
Speed:			
Surface:	unknown	unknown	unknown
Submerged:	32 kts[15]	31 kts[16]	31 kts[17]
Crew:	90	100	100
NUCLEAR WEAPONS:			
Cruise:	none	none	SS-N-21[18]
ASW Rockets:	SS-N-15[19]	SS-N-15 and/or SS-N-16 in two tubes[20]	SS-N-15 and/or SS-N-16 in two tubes[21]
Torpedoes:	6 21-inch (53.3 cm) tubes (bow);[22] carries 18 torpedoes[23]	6 21-inch (53.3 cm) tubes (bow);[24] carries 21 torpedoes[25]	2 or 6 21-inch (53.3 cm) tubes (bow);[26] carries 18 torpedoes[27]

---

15 DIA, JIIKS, Vol. XIII, 1983.
16 Ibid.
17 Ibid.
18 SMP 1988, p. 53. A modified Victor III in the Northern Fleet was one of the original test platforms for the SS-N-21; HAC, FY 1986 DOD, Part 2, p. 914; SMP 1984, pp. 30-31.
19 Polmar, Guide to the Soviet Navy, 1986, p. 146.
20 Polmar, Guide to the Soviet Navy, 1986, p. 145; Collins and Victory, U.S./Soviet Military Balance, 1988, p. 43.
21 SMP 1987, p. 81; SMP 1985, p. 96; Polmar, Guide to the Soviet Navy, 1986, p. 144; Couhat, Combat Fleets of the World, 1988/89, p. 589; Jane's Fighting Ships, 1988-89, p. 557.
22 DIA, JIIKS, Vol. XIII, 1983.
23 Jane's Fighting Ships, 1988-89, p. 558.
24 DIA, JIIKS, Vol. XIII, 1983.
25 Jane's Fighting Ships, 1988-89, p. 558.
26 DIA, JIIKS, Vol. XIII, 1983. Polmar, Guide to the Soviet Navy, 1986, p. 144, reports two 21-inch (53.3 cm) torpedo tubes and four 26-inch (65 cm) torpedo tubes.
27 Jane's Fighting Ships, 1988-89, p. 557.

9

VICTOR (SSN)

	Victor I	Victor II	Victor III
DEPLOYMENT:			
Number Deployed:	16 (1988)[28]	7 (1988)[29]	19-20 (1988);[30] 22nd Victor III launched in 1987[31]
Homeport:	unknown	Pacific Fleet, others unknown	Northern and Pacific Fleets (assigned 1983)
HISTORY:			
IOC:	1967[32]	1972[33]	1979[34]
Production:	not in production	not in production	in series production (1988)[35]
COMMENTS:	First Soviet submarine with an Albacore-type hull. Victor I is follow-on to the November class SSN. Diving depth is 400 m.	Enlarged (29 ft/9 m longer) version of the Victor I.	Improved version of Victor II. Victor IIIs accompany Soviet ballistic missile submarines when at sea.[36]

---

28 DIA, *Unclassified Communist Naval Orders of Battle*, DDB-1200-124-86, April 1986, p. 1.
29 Ibid.
30 Ibid., p. 2, reports 17 Victor III.
31 Studeman, USN, Statement before HASC, March 1988, p. 34.
32 DIA, JIIKS, Vol. XIII, 1983.
33 Ibid.
34 Ibid.; SMP 1985, p. 96.
35 Studeman, USN, Statement before HASC, March 1988, pp. 30, 34.
36 HAC, FY 1986 DOD, Part 2, p. 913.

ECHO I, NOVEMBER, HOTEL II

ECHO I (SSN)

Figure 9.17 Conversion of **Echo I** cruise missile submarines to Echo I nuclear-powered attack submarines fulfilled part of the Soviet Union's objective of increasing its maritime defense perimeter.

NOVEMBER (SSN)

Figure 9.18 The **November** class attack submarine, first deployed in 1958, was the Soviet Union's first nuclear-powered submarine. Twelve are reported to be currently deployed (1988).

	Echo I	November	Hotel II
DESCRIPTION:	Nuclear-powered attack submarine converted from cruise missile submarine	Nuclear-powered attack submarine; first Soviet nuclear-powered submarine	Nuclear-powered attack submarine converted from ballistic missile submarines in the early 1980s
BUILDER:	Komsomol'sk	Severodvinsk	Komosol'sk; Severodvinsk 402
SPECIFICATIONS:			
Length:	111.8 m[1] (366.8 ft)	109.8 m[2] (360.2 ft)	115 m (377.3 ft)[3]
Beam:	9.8 m[4] (32.2 ft)	9.1 m[5] (29.8 ft)	9 m (29.5 ft)[6]

1. SMP 1985, pp. 96-97.
2. DIA, ASW Handbook, p. 6-35.
3. DIA, JIIKS, Vol. XIII, 1983.
4. SMP 1985, pp. 96-97.
5. Ibid.
6. DIA, JIIKS, Vol. XIII, 1983.

9
ECHO I, NOVEMBER, HOTEL II

Figure 9.19 Four **Hotel II** class attack submarines were converted from ballistic missile submarines in the early 1980s.

	Echo I	November	Hotel II
Displacement:			
Surface:	4500 tons[7]	4200 tons[8]	4750 tons[9]
Submerged:	5200 tons[10]	5000 tons[11]	5600 tons[12]
Propulsion:	nuclear, 2 PWR; two shafts; 25,000 shp[13]	nuclear, 2 PWR; two shafts; 30,000 shp[14]	nuclear, 2 PWR; two shafts; 30,000 shp[15]
Speed:			
Surface:	20 kts[16]	16 kts[17]	20 kts[18]
Submerged:	27-28 kts[19]	28-30 kts[20]	26 kts[21]
Crew:	75;[22] 92[23]	80-86[24]	approx. 80[25]
NUCLEAR WEAPONS:			
Cruise:	none	none	none
ASW Rockets:	none[26]	none	none

7. Ibid.
8. Ibid.
9. Ibid.
10. Ibid.
11. Ibid.
12. Ibid.
13. Polmar, *Guide to the Soviet Navy*, 1986, p. 147; Couhat, *Combat Fleets of the World*, 1988/89, p. 591; *Jane's Fighting Ships*, 1988-89, p. 559.
14. Polmar, *Guide to the Soviet Navy*, 1986, p. 148; Couhat, *Combat Fleets of the World*, 1988/89, p. 591; *Jane's Fighting Ships*, 1988-89, p. 559.
15. *Jane's Fighting Ships*, 1988-89, p. 549; Polmar, *Guide to the Soviet Navy*, 1986, p. 149.
16. Polmar, *Guide to the Soviey Navy*, 1986, p. 147.
17. Ibid., p. 148.
18. Ibid., p. 149.
19. DIA, JIIKS, Vol. XIII, 1983.
20. Ibid.
21. Ibid.
22. Polmar, *Guide to the Soviet Navy*, 1986, p. 147; Couhat, *Combat Fleets of the World*, 1988/89, p. 591.
23. *Jane's Fighting Ships*, 1988-89, p. 559.
24. Polmar, *Guide to the Soviet Navy*, 1986, p. 148; Couhat, *Combat Fleets of the World*, 1988/89, p. 591; *Jane's Fighting Ships*, 1988-89, p. 559.
25. Polmar, *Guide to the Soviet Navy*, 1986, p. 149.
26. Polmar, *Guide to the Soviet Navy*, 1983, p. 109, reported possible SS-N-15.

ECHO I, NOVEMBER, HOTEL II

	Echo I	**November**	**Hotel II**
Torpedoes:	6 21-inch (53.3 cm) tubes (bow); 2 16-inch (40.6 cm) tubes (stern);[27] carries 20 torpedoes or 40 mines[28]	6 21-inch (53.3 cm) tubes (bow); 2 16-inch (40.6 cm) tubes (stern);[29] carries 28 torpedoes[30]	6 21-inch (53.3 cm) tubes (bow)[31]
DEPLOYMENT:			
Number Deployed:	3 (1988)[32]	12 (1988);[33] 14 reported built between 1958 and 1963; one sank in 1970; one or two have been retired[34]	4 (1988)[35]
HISTORY:			
IOC:	1970	April 1958[36]	Early 1980s
Production:	not in production	not in production	not in production
COMMENTS:	Five Echo I SSGNs with 6 SS-N-3 tubes were converted to Echo SSNs between 1970 and 1974.[37]	November SSN sank off the Atlantic coast of Spain in April 1970.	

---

27. DIA, JIIKS, Vol. XIII, 1983.
28. *Jane's Fighting Ships*, 1988-89, p. 559.
29. DIA, JIIKS, Vol. XIII, 1983. Polmar, *Guide to the Soviet Navy*, 1986, p. 148, reports eight 21-inch torpedo tubes forward.
30. *Jane's Fighting Ships*, 1988-89, p. 559.
31. *Jane's Fighting Ships*, 1988-89, p. 549; Polmar, *Guide to the Soviet Navy*, 1986, p. 149.
32. DIA, *Unclassified Communist Naval Orders of Battle*, DDB-1200-124-86, April 1986, p. 1; DIA, JIIKS, Vol. XIII, 1983, reports five deployed.
33. DIA, *Unclassified Communist Naval Orders of Battle*, op. cit., p. 1.
34. DIA, JIIKS, Vol. XIII, 1983. See also, Polmar, *Guide to the Soviet Navy*, 1986, p. 148.
35. The original eight Hotel I class submarines were constructed between 1958 and 1962 and fitted with SS-N-4 missiles. When they were converted to carry the SS-N-5 misile, between 1963 and 1970, they were designated Hotel II. One was further converted as an SS-N-8 test platform and designated Hotel III. Four Hotel II have been converted to attack submarines. The remaining three are either communications/auxiliary submarines or in reserve.
36. Polmar, *Guide to the Soviet Navy*, 1986, p. 148, reports the first unit was commissioned on 8 April 1958. Couhat, *Combat Fleets of the World*, 1988/89, p. 591, reports, the first unit was completed in August 1958.
37. Polmar, *Guide to the Soviet Navy*, 1986, p. 147.

9

DIESEL-POWERED ATTACK SUBMARINES

Diesel-Powered Attack Submarines (SS)

KILO (SS)

Figure 9.20 The **Kilo** class diesel-powered attack submarine, capable of carrying 12 torpedoes, is thought to be in production in large numbers. It is primarily for coastal protection and has been exported to a number of countries.

TANGO (SS)

Figure 9.21 The **Tango** diesel-powered attack submarine has been in production since 1973. There are currently 20 Tangos in service (1988). This class ship is often deployed to the Mediterranean.

	Kilo	Tango	Foxtrot	Romeo	Whiskey	Zulu
DESCRIPTION:	Diesel-powered, medium-range attack submarine	Diesel-powered, long-range attack submarine	Diesel-powered, long-range attack submarine	Diesel-powered, medium-range attack submarine	Diesel-powered attack submarine	Diesel-powered, long-range attack submarine
BUILDER:	Komsomol'sk	Gor'kiy	Leningrad	Gor'kiy	Leningrad; Gor'kiy; Komsomol'sk; Marti (Nikolayev Shipyard)	Severodvinsk; Sudomekh (Leningrad)
SPECIFICATIONS:						
Length:	67.1 m[1] (220 ft)	91.3 m[2] (300 ft)	97.3 m[3] (319 ft)	76.8 m[4] (252 ft)	76.0 m[5] (249 ft)	90.0 m[6] (295 ft)
Beam:	9.0 m[7] (29.5 ft)	9.0 m[8] (29.5 ft)	7.5 m[9] (24.6 ft)	7.0 m[10] (23 ft)	6.3 m[11] (20.7 ft)	7.5 m[12] (24.6 ft)
Displacement:						
Surface:	2500 tons[13]	3000 tons[14]	1950 tons[15]	1400 tons[16]	1080 tons[17]	1950 tons[18]
Submerged:	3000 MT[19]	3900 MT[20]	2500 MT[21]	1800 MT[22]	1350 tons[23]	2300 tons[24]

1. Polmar, *Guide to the Soviet Navy*, 1986, p. 150.
2. DIA, *ASW Handbook*, 1977, p. 6-53.
3. *Ibid.*, p. 6-49.
4. *Ibid.*, p. 6-71. "Displacement length and speed vary among units"; DIA, JIIKS, Vol. XIII, 1983.
5. DIA, *ASW Handbook*, 1977, p. 6-51; "Displacement length and speed vary among units"; DIA, JIIKS, Vol. XIII, 1983.
6. USN, *Soviet Naval Developments* (Rev. 4/85), p. 103.
7. Polmar, *Guide to the Soviet Navy*, 1986, p. 150.
8. DIA, *ASW Handbook*, 1977, p. 6-53.
9. *Ibid.*, p. 6-49.
10. *Ibid.*, p. 6-51.
11. *Ibid.*
12. Polmar, *Guide to the Soviet Navy*, 1986, p. 155; Couhat, *Combat Fleets of the World*, 1988/89, p. 595.
13. Polmar, *Guide to the Soviet Navy*, 1986, p. 150; Couhat, *Combat Fleets of the World*, 1988/89, p. 592.
14. USN, *Soviet Naval Developments* (Rev. 4/85), p. 100; DIA, JIIKS, Vol. XIII, 1983.
15. USN, *Soviet Naval Developments* (Rev. 4/85), p. 93; DIA, JIIKS, Vol. XIII, 1983.
16. USN, *Soviet Naval Developments* (Rev. 4/85), p. 99; DIA, JIIKS, Vol. XIII, 1983.
17. DIA, JIIKS, Vol. XIII, 1983.
18. USN, *Soviet Naval Developments* (Rev. 4/85), p. 103; DIA, JIIKS, Vol. XIII, 1983.
19. SMP 1987, p. 81.
20. *Ibid.* DIA, JIIKS, Vol. XIII, 1983 reports 3700 MT.
21. DIA, *ASW Handbook*, 1977, p. 6-49; DIA, JIIKS, Vol. XIII, 1983.
22. DIA, *ASW Handbook*, 1977, p. 6-51; DIA, JIIKS, Vol. XIII, 1983.
23. DIA, JIIKS, Vol. XIII, 1983.
24. *Ibid.*

9

DIESEL-POWERED ATTACK SUBMARINES

Figure 9.22 The **Foxtrot**, though no longer in production, is one of the longer (319 feet) Soviet submarines and one of the most frequently used for long-range patrols, often deploying to the Indian Ocean, the Mediterranean, or the Caribbean.

Figure 9.23 There are currently (1988) four **Romeo** diesel-powered attack submarines in the Soviet Navy, each armed with eight 21-inch torpedo tubes, six in the bow, two in the stern.

Figure 9.24 The **Zulu** class diesel-powered attack submarine is a long-range version of the Whiskey, fitted with six more torpedo tubes (total of 10, six bow, four stern).

Figure 9.25 The Soviet Union's first post-war submarine (1950 deployment) was the diesel-powered attack submarine called **Whiskey** class. It has had many subsequent modifications. A submarine of this class (No. 137) went aground inside Swedish territorial waters on 27 October 1981, near Karlskrona naval base. After measuring ionizing radiation from the submarine, the Swedish Prime Minister announced on 5 November that the Government believed the submarine "is in all probability armed with nuclear warheads," presumably torpedoes.

	Kilo	Tango	Foxtrot	Romeo	Whiskey	Zulu
Propulsion:	diesel-electric; twin shafts[25]	diesel-electric; 3 shafts[26]	diesel-electric; 3 shafts[27]	diesel-electric; twin shafts[28]	diesel-electric; twin shafts[29]	diesel-electric; 3 shafts[30]
Speed: Surface:	12 kts[31]	20 kts[32]	18 kts[33]	17 kts[34]	18 kts[35]	18 kts[36]

---

25. SMP 1985, pp. 96-97; Polmar, *Guide to the Soviet Navy*, 1986, p. 150.
26. DIA JIIKS, Vol. XIII, 1983.
27. *Ibid.*
28. *Ibid.*
29. *Ibid.*
30. *Ibid.*
31. Polmar, *Guide to the Soviet Navy*, 1986, p. 150.
32. DIA JIIKS, Vol. XIII, 1983.
33. *Ibid.*
34. *Ibid.*
35. *Ibid.*
36. *Ibid.*

9

DIESEL-POWERED ATTACK SUBMARINES

	Kilo	**Tango**	**Foxtrot**	**Romeo**	**Whiskey**	**Zulu**
Submerged:	17 kts[37]	16 kts[38]	16 kts[39]	14 kts[40]	14 kts[41]	16 kts[42]
Crew:	approx. 60[43]	70-72[44]	75-80[45]	approx. 55[46]	50-55[47]	approx. 70[48]
NUCLEAR WEAPONS:						
ASW Rockets:	none	possible[49]	none	none	none	none
Torpedoes:	6-8 21-inch (53.3 cm) tubes (bow) (12 torpedoes)[50]	8 21-inch (53.3 cm) tubes[51]	6 21-inch (53.3 cm) tubes (bow); 4 16-inch (40.6 cm) tubes (stern)[52]	8 21-inch (53.3 cm) tubes (6 bow, 2 stern)[53]	4 21-inch (53.3 cm) tubes (bow); 2 16-inch (40.6 cm) tubes (stern)[54]	10 21-inch (53.3 cm) tubes (6 bow, 4 stern)[55]
DEPLOYMENT:						
Number Deployed:	11 (1988)	20 (1988)	45 (1988)	4 (1988)	45 (1988)	1 (1988)
HISTORY:						
IOC:	1980[56]	1973[57]	1958[58]	1958[59]	1950[60]	1952[61]
Production:	at least two in production; 1 launched in 1987[62]	in production[63]	not in production	not in production	not in production	not in production
COMMENTS:	Replacement for Whiskey and Romeo classes.[64] First extended patrol to South China Sea in 1984.[65] Joined Northern Fleet in 1986.[66] Joined Pacific Fleet in 1987 or 1988.[67]	Replacement for Foxtrot.[68] Frequently deploys to Mediterranean.[69]	Replacement for Zulu.[70] Used more frequently than any other Soviet sub, deploying to Indian Ocean, Mediterranean, and Carribean.[71]		First post-war submarine. 236 built, with many modifications[72]	26 built between 1952 and 1955. Long-range version of Whiskey fitted with more torpedo tubes.[73]

---

37. Collins and Victory, *U.S./Soviet Military Balance*, 1988, p. 106.
38. DIA JIIKS, Vol. XIII, 1983.
39. Ibid.
40. Ibid.
41. Ibid.
42. Ibid.
43. Polmar, *Guide to the Soviet Navy*, 1986, p. 150; Couhat, *Combat Fleets of the World*, 1988/89, p. 592.
44. Polmar, *Guide to the Soviet Navy*, 1986, p. 151; Couhat, *Combat Fleets of the World*, 1988/89, p. 592.
45. Polmar, *Guide to the Soviet Navy*, 1986, p. 152; Couhat, *Combat Fleets of the World*, 1988/89, p. 593.
46. Polmar, *Guide to the Soviet Navy*, 1986, p. 154.
47. Polmar, *Guide to the Soviet Navy*, 1986, p. 156; Couhat, *Combat Fleets of the World*, 1988/89, p. 593.
48. Polmar, *Guide to the Soviet Navy*, 1986, p. 155.
49. SMP 1987, p. 81; USN, *Soviet Naval Developments* (Rev. 4/85), p. 100; Polmar, *Guide to the Soviet Navy*, 1986, p. 151.
50. Polmar, *Guide to the Soviet Navy*, 1986, p. 150; Collins and Victory, *U.S./Soviet Military Balance*, 1988, p. 43; Couhat, *Combat Fleets of the World*, 1988/89, p. 592.
51. DIA, JIIKS, Vol. XIII, 1983.
52. Ibid.
53. Ibid.
54. Ibid.
55. Ibid.
56. SMP 1987, p. 81.
57. Ibid.; Navy, *Soviet Naval Developments* (Rev. 4/85), p. 100.
58. DIA, JIIKS, Vol. XIII, 1983.
59. Ibid.
60. Collins and Victory, *U.S./Soviet Military Balance*, 1988, p. 106.
61. USN, *Soviet Naval Developments* (Rev. 4/85), p. 103; DIA, JIIKS, Vol. XIII, 1983.
62. Four Kilo class submarines were launched in 1987, only one of which was built for the Soviet Navy; Studeman, USN, Statement before HASC, March 1988, p. 34.
63. Studeman, USN, Statement before HASC, March 1988, p. 34.
64. Polmar, *Guide to the Soviet Navy*, 1986, p. 154.
65. SMP 1985, pp. 96-97.
66. SMP 1986, p. 67.
67. SMP 1987, p. 69.
68. DIA, JIIKS, Vol. XIII, 1983.
69. USN, *Soviet Naval Developments* (Rev. 4/85), p. 100.
70. Polmar, *Guide to the Soviet Navy*, 1986, p. 152.
71. USN, *Soviet Naval Developments* (Rev. 4/85), p. 93; DIA, *ASW Handbook*, 1977, p. 6-48; Polmar, *Guide to the Soviet Navy*, 1986, p. 152.
72. Polmar, *Guide to the Soviet Navy*, 1986, p. 156.
73. DIA, JIIKS, Vol. XIII, 1983.

Aircraft Carriers
TBILISI[1]

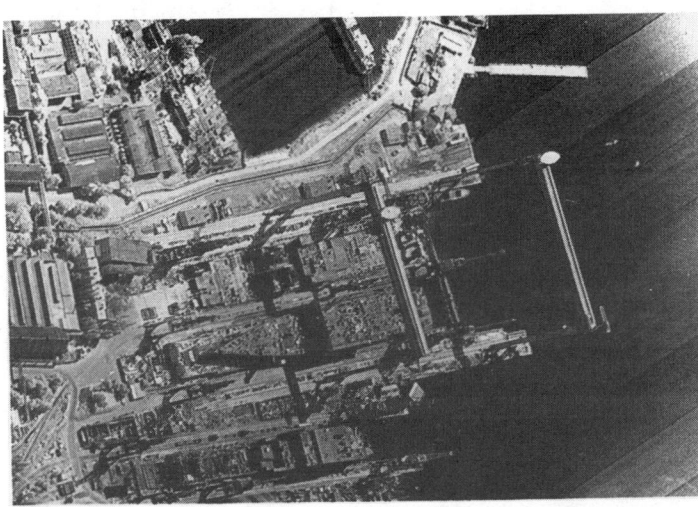

Figure 9.26 Computer enhanced reconnaissance satellite photo of the Soviet Navy's first nuclear-powered aircraft carrier, **Tbilisi**, under construction in two sections at the Nikolayev 444 shipyard on the Black Sea. (AP/Wide World Photos, Inc.)

Figure 9.27 Twin gantry cranes hover over the unusual two-part construction of the **Tbilisi**, expected to become operational in the mid-1990s. The aircraft carrier may be capable of accommodating some 35-60 aircraft, but it is unlikely that it will carry conventional take-off and landing jets when it is initially deployed. (AP/Wide World Photos, Inc.)

DESCRIPTION:	Large-deck, nuclear-powered aircraft carrier
BUILDER:	Nikolayev Shipyard, Black Sea[2]
SPECIFICATIONS:	
Length:	300 m[3] (980 ft); 335 m[4] (1100 ft)
Draft:	unknown
Displacement:	65,000 MT;[5] 65,000-75,000 tons[6]
Propulsion:	combined nuclear and steam (CONAS);[7] nuclear-powered;[8] propulsion system will probably be based on that of the Kirov CGN[9]
Speed:	unknown
Crew:	unknown
NUCLEAR WEAPONS:	presumably nuclear bombs and ASW nuclear depth bombs; first unit will initially appear with V/STOL aircraft, Ka-27 Helix helicopters, and ramp-launched/arrested landing, conventional take-off and landing (CTOL) aircraft,[10] including possible Su-27 Flanker and MiG-29 Fulcrum; a new aircraft—Yak-41—will be specifically deployed for sea-based operations on the carrier;[11] about 60-70 aircraft (approx. half fighter-attack) could eventually be carried[12]
DEPLOYMENT:	
Number Deployed:	at least two under construction; several could be built by the end of the century;[13] reportedly 4-8 planned[14]
Homeport:	first carrier will probably serve in the Pacific Fleet[15]

---

1 The aircraft carrier was designated by NATO as Black-Com 2 (Black Sea Combatant No. 2) during development and later was called the Kremlin class and the Brezhnev class; JCS, FY 1989, p. 31; *Jane's Defence Weekly*, 11 August 1984, pp. 171-173.
2 Studeman, USN, Statement before HASC, March 1988, p. 35.
3 SMP 1987, p. 83; *Jane's Fighting Ships*, 1988-89, p. 567.
4 SMP 1987, p. 83; *Jane's Defence Weekly*, 29 July 1984, p. 91.
5 SMP 1988, p. 84; SMP 1987, p. 83; HASC, FY 1985 DOD, Part 3, pp. 1-2.
6 SASC, FY 1986 DOD, Part 8, p. 4361.
7 Norman Polmar, "The New Carrier," *Proceedings*, August 1988, p. 67.
8 DOD, FY 1985 *Annual Report*, pp. 24, 134; SASC, FY 1986 DOD, Part 8, p. 4361.
9 SMP 1985, pp. 99-101. The CONAS plant in the Kirov cruisers has two PWRs (for normal cruising) and two oil-fired boilers (for higher speeds), which provide 150,000 shp. The Tbilisi will be twice as large as the Kirovs, which could mean four PWRs and four boilers. See Polmar, *op. cit.*
10 Studeman, USN, Statement before HASC, March 1988, p. 35.
11 SMP 1985, pp. 99-101. The Yak-36 Forger A/B, now flying from Kievs are expected onboad the Tbilisi; Polmar, *op. cit.*
12 HASC, FY 1985 DOD, Part 3, pp. 1-2; USN, *Soviet Naval Developments* (Rev. 4/85), p. 37; Polmar, *op. cit.*

9
TBILISI

HISTORY:

Laid: groundwork was laid in 1982;[16] first keel in January 1983;[17] second on 10 December 1985[18]

Launch: 5 December 1985[19]

Sea Trials: expected to commence sea trials in 1989[20]

IOC: mid-1990s;[21] limited operations with Su-27 Flanker-B variant 2 possible by 1992[22]

COMMENTS: Long-lead time items such as the nuclear power plant, were in production as of 1983.[23] Flight deck and aircraft systems testing continues at Saki airfield in the Crimea.[24] Building rate, one per four or five years.[25]

---

13 JCS, FY 1985, p. 38.
14 *Jane's Defence Weekly*, 28 July 1984, p. 91; *Jane's Defence Weekly*, 11 August 1984, pp. 171-173.
15 SASC, FY 1984 DOD, Part 6, p. 2931.
16 HASC, FY 1985 DOD, Part 3, pp. 1-2.
17 *Ibid.*; SASC, FY 1986 DOD, Part 8, p. 4361; *Jane's Defence Weekly*, 28 July 1984, p. 91; *Jane's Defence Weekly*, 11 August 1984, pp. 171-173.
18 Polmar, *op. cit.*
19 SMP 1987, p. 86.
20 Studeman, USN, Statement before HASC, March 1988, p. 35; SMP 1988, p. 84.
21 SASC, FY 1986 DOD, Part 8, p. 4361.
22 Studeman, USN, Statement before HASC, March 1988, p. 36.
23 SASC, FY 1984 DOD, Part 6, p. 2931.
24 Studeman, USN, Statement before HASC, March 1988, p. 35.
25 Polmar, *op. cit.*

9
KIEV (CVHG), MOSKVA (CHG)

Aviation Ships
KIEV (CVHG), MOSKVA (CHG)

KIEV CVHG

Figure 9.28 Side view of the **Kiev** aircraft carrier assigned to the Northern Fleet. At 896 feet in length and 36,000 tons displacement, the Kiev is much smaller than U.S. aircraft carriers.

	Kiev (CVHG)	**Moskva (CHG)**
DESCRIPTION:	V/STOL aircraft carrier	Guided-missile aviation cruiser[1]
BUILDER:	Nikolayev	Nikolayev
SPECIFICATIONS:		
Length:	273 m[2] (896 ft)	189 m[3] (620 ft)
Beam:	50 m[4] (164 ft)	34.2 m[5] (112)
Draft:	10 m[6] (33 ft)	9.4 m[7] (31 ft)
Displacement		
Standard:	36,000 tons[8]	14,500-15,500 tons[9]
Combat load:	43,000 tons[10]	17,000 MT[11]

---

1. Essentially an ASW helicopter carrier with the appearance of a cruiser forward and a helicopter carrier aft.
2. SMP 1987, p. 83. DIA, *ASW Handbook*, 1977, p. 6-3, reports 274 m (890 ft). For an early assessment see Captain J. W. Kehoe, Herbert A. Meier, Major Larry J. Kennedy, and LtC Don C. East, "U.S. Observations of the Kiev," *Proceedings*, July 1977, pp. 105-111; and Lt. Ulrich Schulz-Torge, "The Kiev: A German View," *Proceedings*, July 1977, pp. 111-115.
3. DIA, *ASW Handbook*, 1977, p. 6-5.
4. *Ibid.*, p. 6-3.
5. *Ibid.*, p. 6-5.
6. *Ibid.*, p. 6-3.
7. *Ibid.*, p. 6-5.
8. Polmar, *Guide to the Soviet Navy*, 1986, p. 165.
9. *Ibid.*, p. 168; Couhat, *Combat Fleets of the World*, 1988/89, p. 576.
10. Polmar, *Guide to the Soviet Navy*, 1986, p. 165.
11. DIA, *ASW Handbook*, 1977, p. 6-5.

9

KIEV (CVHG), MOSKVA (CHG)

Figure 9.29 Front view of the **Kiev** class V/STOL aircraft carrier. The design of the ship essentially shows a large cruiser with a flight deck appended.

Figure 9.30 The four **Kiev** class guided-missile V/STOL aircraft carriers each carry a number of nuclear-capable systems, including ASW rockets and cruise missiles. Approximately 30 aircraft and helicopters may also be capable of delivering nuclear weapons.

Figure 9.31 The **Kiev** class aircraft carrier during at sea maneuvers. Flight deck is shown with Yak-36 Forger STOL aircraft to right and three Ka-25 Hormone helicopters in the foreground.

	Kiev (CVHG)	**MOSKVA (CHG)**
Propulsion:	4 steam turbines;[12] 4 shafts;[13] 200,000 shp[14]	steam turbines;[15] 2 shafts;[16] 100,000 shp[17]
Speed:	32 kts[18]	29 kts[19]
Crew:	1200 (including air group)[20]	approx. 850 (plus air group)[21]
NUCLEAR WEAPONS:		
Cruise Missiles:	8 SS-N-12 in 4 twin launchers with 16 total missiles[22]	none

---

12. Polmar, *Guide to the Soviet Navy*, 1986, p. 165; *Jane's Fighting Ships*, 1988-89, p. 567.
13. Ibid.
14. Polmar, *Guide to the Soviet Navy*, 1986, p. 165.
15. Polmar, *Guide to the Soviet Navy*, 1986, p. 168; USN, *Soviet Naval Developments* (Rev. 4/85), p. 104.
16. Polmar, *Guide to the Soviet Navy*, 1986, p. 168.
17. Ibid., p. 168.
18. DIA, *ASW Handbook*, 1977, p. 6-3.
19. Ibid., p. 6-5.
20. Polmar, *Guide to the Soviet Navy*, 1986, p. 165.
21. Ibid., p. 168; *Jane's Fighting Ships*, 1988-89, p. 570.
22. Polmar, *Guide to the Soviet Navy*, 1986, p. 165; USN, *Soviet Naval Developments* (Rev. 4/85), p. 104; *Jane's Fighting Ships*, 1988-89, p. 567. The SS-N-12 launchers on the Baku appear to be in one bank towards the bow, rather than four twin-launchers; *Jane's Defence Weekly*, 25 July 1988, p. 1269.

9
KIEV (CVHG), MOSKVA (CHG)

Figure 9.32 The **Moskva** class aviation ship, sometimes credited as being an "aircraft carrier," is very small by U.S. standards (620 feet in length, about 15,000 tons displacement). Ka-25 Hormone helicopters are positioned on the aft deck.

	Kiev (CVHG)	**MOSKVA (CHG)**
ASW Rockets:	1 twin SUW-N-1 with FRAS-1 rockets[23]	1 twin SUW-N-1 with FRAS-1 rockets[24]
Torpedoes:	10 21-inch torpedo tubes	none

---

23. DIA, *ASW Handbook*, 1977, p. 6-3.
24. Ibid., p. 6-5.

9
KIEV (CVHG), MOSKVA (CHG)

Figure 9.33 The **Moskva** class ships are guided-missile aviation cruisers, originally introduced in 1967. The ships do not launch cruise missiles but do carry ASW rockets, SAM missiles, and Ka-25 Hormone A helicopters capable of delivering nuclear depth bombs.

	Kiev (CVHG)	**Moskva (CHG)**
Surface-to-air Missiles:	2 twin SA-N-3 with 72 missiles[25]	2 twin SA-N-3 with 44 missiles[26]
Aircraft:	approx. 30,[27] composed of 12 Yak-36 Forger STOL aircraft[28] and up to 24 helicopters, either Ka-25 Hormone A/Bs or Ka-27 Helix As;[29] presumably nuclear bombs and ASW nuclear depth bombs	14 Ka-25 Hormone helicopters;[30] presumably ASW nuclear depth bombs
DEPLOYMENT:		
Number Deployed:	4 (1988)	2 (1988)
Homeport:	Kiev and Baku in Northern Fleet; Minsk and Novorossiysk in Pacific Fleet	Moskva and Leningrad in Black Sea Fleet
HISTORY:		
IOC:	1987 (Baku);[31] July 1976 (Kiev);[32] 1979 (Minsk);[33] March 1982 (Novorossiysk)[34]	July 1967 (Moskva);[35] 1968 (Leningrad)[36]
COMMENTS:	Baku has enhanced communications and surveillance systems[37]	

---

25. Polmar, *Guide to the Soviet Navy*, 1986, p. 165. Collins and Victory, *U.S./Soviet Military Balance*, 1988, p. 89, also gives 2 SA-N-4 (twin).
26. Polmar, *Guide to the Soviet Navy*, 1986, p. 168; Collins and Victory, *U.S./Soviet Military Balance*, 1987, p. 96.
27. Polmar, *Guide to the Soviet Navy*, 1986, p. 165.
28. HASC, FY 1985 DOD, Part 3, pp. 1, 4; Polmar, *Guide to the Soviet Navy*, 1986, p. 168; Collins and Victory, *U.S./Soviet Military Balance*, 1988, p. 88.
29. HASC, FY 1985 DOD, Part 3, pp. 1, 4; Polmar, *Guide to the Soviet Navy*, 1986, p. 165; Collins and Victory, *U.S./Soviet Military Balance*, 1988, p. 88; *Jane's Fighting Ships*, 1988-89, p. 567.
30. Polmar, *Guide to the Soviet Navy*, 1986, p. 168; Collins and Victory, *U.S./Soviet Military Balance*, 1988, p. 88.
31. Studeman, USN, Statement before HASC, March 1988, p. 16. The Baku was reportedly launched on 17 April 1982 and passed through the Turkish Straits for the first time in June 1988; *Jane's Defence Weekly*, 25 June 1988, p. 1269.
32. Polmar, *Guide to the Soviet Navy*, 1986, p. 166.
33. SASC, FY 1982 DOD, Part 4, p. 1644; Polmar, *Guide to the Soviet Navy*, 1986, p. 166.
34. HASC, FY 1983 DOD, Part 4, p. 2.
35. Polmar, *Guide to the Soviet Navy*, 1986, p. 168; Couhat, *Combat Fleets of the World*, 1988/89, p. 575.
36. SMP 1981, pp. 39, 43.
37. Studeman, USN, Statement before HASC, March 1988, p. 16.

Cruisers
KIROV (CGN)

Figure 9.34 The **Kirov** class is the newest class Soviet cruiser and its first nuclear-powered surface ship.

DESCRIPTION:	Nuclear-powered guided-missile cruiser, Soviet ARKR;[1] used as command ship in Northern and Pacific Fleets
BUILDER:	Baltic Shipyard 189, Leningrad

SPECIFICATIONS:
Length: 248 m[2] (814 ft)

Displacement:
Standard: 22,000-23,000 tons[3]
Combat load: 23,000-24,000 MT;[4] 27,900 tons[5]

Draft: 8.8 m[6] (29 ft)

---

1 Jane's Fighting Ships, 1988-89, p. 569. In Russian ARKR (atomny raketnyy kreyser) means nuclear-powered missile cruiser.
2 SMP 1987, p. 83; CIA, Characteristics of the Kirov Nuclear-Powered Guided Missile Cruiser, SW 81-10058, June 1981, p. 111.
3 HASC, FY 1982 DOD, Part 3, pp. 15, 22, 25; SMP 1981, pp. 39, 43.
4 CIA, op cit., p. 111.
5 JCS, FY 1983, p. 45; SMP 1987, p. 83.
6 Polmar, Guide to the Soviet Navy, 1986, p. 172.

9
KIROV (CGN)

Figure 9.35 The *Kirov* class cruiser is a powerful combatant with ability to carry 20 SS-N-19 SLCMs in vertical launchers, 96 SA-N-6 SAMs (eight missiles in each of 12 vertical launchers), eight 21-inch torpedo tubes, and up to three Ka-25 Hormone or Ka-27 Helix helicopters which can deliver nuclear depth bombs.

Propulsion:	combined nuclear and steam (CONAS); 2 PWRs, with oil-fired boilers for superheat;[7] 2 shafts;[8] 150,000-160,000 shp[9]
Speed:	32-33 kts with superheater (29 nuclear-powered only)[10]
Crew:	800-900[11]
NUCLEAR WEAPONS:	
Cruise Missiles:	20 SS-N-19 in non-reloadable 45 degree angled vertical launchers[12]
Torpedoes:	8 21-inch (53.3 cm) torpedo tubes[13]
Surface-to-air Missiles:	96 SA-N-6 SAMs;[14] 12 vertical launchers, with 8 missiles per launcher
Aircraft:	3 Ka-25 Hormone or Ka-27 Helix helicopters;[15] presumably ASW nuclear depth bombs
DEPLOYMENT:	
Number Deployed:	2 (Kirov and Frunze) (1988)[16]
Homeport:	Kirov: Northern Fleet; Frunze: Pacific Fleet (arrived in November 1985)
HISTORY:	
IOC:	July 1980 (Kirov);[17] 1984 (Frunze)[18]
Production:	third unit (Kalinin) is being fitted out and six more are under construction[19]
COMMENTS:	Kirov is the Soviet Union's first nuclear-powered surface warship, and first ship with reloadable SS-N-14 Silex non-nuclear missile system.

---

7 CIA, op cit., p. 111.
8 Polmar, *Guide to the Soviet Navy*, 1986, p. 172.
9 CIA, op. cit., p. 111; Polmar, *Guide to the Soviet Navy*, 1986, p. 172; *Jane's Fighting Ships*, 1988-89, p. 569. Couhat, *Combat Fleets of the World*, 1988/89, p. 597, reports, 90,000 shp on reactors alone.
10 CIA, op. cit., p. 111.
11 Polmar, *Guide to the Soviet Navy*, 1986, p. 172; Couhat, *Combat Fleets of the World*, 1988/89, p. 595; *Jane's Fighting Ships*, 1988-89, p. 569.
12 SMP 1987, p. 86; CIA, op. cit., p. 111; HASC, FY 1985 DOD, Part 4, p. 2; *Jane's Fighting Ships*, 1988-89, p. 569.
13 Polmar, *Guide to the Soviet Navy*, 1986, p. 172; *Jane's Fighting Ships*, 1988-89, p. 569; Collins and Victory, *U.S./Soviet Military Balance*, 1988, p. 93.
14 SMP 1987, p. 86; SASC, FY 1984 DOD, Part 6, p. 2937; HASC, FY 1982 DOD, Part 3, pp. 15, 21-23, 25; Polmar, *Guide to the Soviet Navy*, 1986, p. 172; Couhat, *Combat Fleets of the World*, 1988/89, p. 595.
15 SMP 1988, p. 83; Polmar, *Guide to the Soviet Navy*, 1986, p. 172; Couhat, *Combat Fleets of the World*, 1988/89, p. 595; *Jane's Fighting Ships*, 1988-89, p. 569.
16 Studeman, USN, Statement before HASC, March 1988, p. 36.
17 *Jane's Fighting Ships*, 1988-89, p. 569.
18 SMP 1985, p. 99.
19 Studeman, USN, Statement before HASC, March 1988, p. 36; SMP 1988, p. 83.

SLAVA (CG)[1]

Figure 9.36 The new **Slava** class cruiser, though conventionally powered and smaller than the Kirov class, is a formidable combatant with its anti-submarine, anti-ship, and air-defense systems.

DESCRIPTION:[1] Multipurpose guided-missile cruiser with anti-submarine, anti-ship and air-defense systems; a heavily armed smaller version of the Kirov

BUILDER: 61 Kommuna Shipyard, Nikolayev (north), Black Sea

SPECIFICATIONS:
- Length: 187 m[2] (614 ft)
- Displacement: 12,000 MT[3]
- Draft: 8 m[4] (26 ft)
- Propulsion: gas turbines; 2 shafts; 120,000 shp[5]
- Speed: 32-34 kts[6]
- Crew: about 600[7]

NUCLEAR WEAPONS:
- Cruise Missiles: 16 SS-N-12 in 8 twin launchers;[8] possible SS-N-22[9]
- Torpedoes: 10 21-inch (53.3 cm) torpedo tubes[10]
- Surface-to-air Missiles: 8 SA-N-6 vertical launchers with 64 missiles[11]

DEPLOYMENT:
- Number Deployed: 2 (1988)[12]
- Homeport: Black Sea Fleet; Northern Fleet

HISTORY:
- IOC: 1982 (entered inventory);[13] 1984[14]
- Production: third unit (Chervona Ukraina) is fitting out, and unit four is under construction[15]

---

1 SMP 1981, p. 44; Polmar, *Guide to the Soviet Navy*, 1986, p. 176; SASC, FY 1984 DOD, Part 6, p. 2938. NATO designation was previously Black-Com-1 (Black Sea Combatant No. 1) pending knowledge of the lead ship name. Krasina was subsequently assigned by NATO. Slava is Russian for "glory."
2 SMP 1987, p. 83.
3 Ibid.; SMP 1985, p. 100, reported 12,500 MT.
4 *Jane's Fighting Ships*, 1988-89, p. 571; Armin Wetterhahn, "The Soviet Guided Missile Cruiser Slava," *International Defense Review*, January 1984, pp. 21-26.
5 SMP 1987, p. 86; Polmar, *Guide to the Soviet Navy*, 1986, p. 1762; Wetterhahn, op. cit., pp. 21-26.
6 Wetterhahn, op. cit., pp. 21-26; Couhat, *Combat Fleets of the World*, 1988/89, p. 598; *Jane's Defence Review*, Vol. 2, No. 5, 1981, p. 387.
7 Wetterhahn, op. cit., pp. 21-26.
8 SMP 1988, p. 84; SMP 1987, p. 86; HASC, FY 1985 DOD, Part 3, pp. 1-2; HASC, FY 1983 DOD, Part 4, p. 2; Collins and Victory, *U.S./Soviet Military Balance*, 1988, p. 93.
9 *International Defense Review*, October 1983, p. 1375.
10 Polmar, *Guide to the Soviet Navy*, 1986, p. 176; Wetterhahn, op. cit., pp. 21-26; *Jane's Fighting Ships*, 1988-89. p. 571. Collins and Victory, *U.S./Soviet Military Balance*, 1988, p. 93, reports six torpedo tubes.
11 SMP 1988, p. 84; SMP 1987, p. 86; HASC, FY 1985 DOD, Part 3, pp. 1-2; SMP 1985, pp. 98-99; Polmar, *Guide to the Soviet Navy*, 1986, p. 176; Wetterhahn, op. cit., pp. 21-26; *Jane's Fighting Ships*, 1988-89, p. 571.
12 Studeman, USN, Statement before HASC, March 1988, p. 36. The second ship is called the Marshal Ustinov.
13 SMP 1988, p. 84; SMP 1987, p. 86.
14 SASC, FY 1986 DOD, Part 8, p. 4362.
15 Studeman, USN, Statement before HASC, March 1988, p. 36; SMP 1988, p. 84.

9

KARA (CG)

KARA (CG)

KARA CG

Figure 9.37 Designated a BPK (large anti-submarine ship) by the Soviets, the **Kara** class is also well outfitted with guided missile and anti-air capabilities including 72 SA-N-3 SAMs and ten 21-inch torpedo tubes. It also may carry a single Ka-25 Hormone A helicopter which can deliver nuclear depth bombs.

DESCRIPTION:	Guided-missile cruiser with major anti-submarine and anti-air capabilities; Soviet BPK class, considered to be more in the destroyer than cruiser category[1]	**BUILDER:**	61 Kommuna Shipyard, Nikolayev (north)
		SPECIFICATIONS:	
		Length:	173.1 m² (568 ft)
		Beam:	18.6 m³ (61 ft)

---

1 Polmar, *Guide to the Soviet Navy*, 1986, pp. 179-180; Couhat, *Combat Fleets of the World*, 1988/89, p. 601; *Jane's Fighting Ships*, 1988-89, p. 572; SASC, FY 1984 DOD, Part 6, p. 2938. BPK (*bol'shoy protivolodochnyy korabl'*) means large anti-submarine ship.

2 DIA, *ASW Handbook*, 1977, p. 6-7; JEC, *Allocation of Resources—1976*, Part 2, p. 90.
3 Ibid.

KARA (CG)

Displacement: Standard:	8200 tons[4]	Aircraft:	one Ka-25 Hormone A helicopter[15] possible Ka-27 Helix[16]
Combat load:	9700 MT[5]	**DEPLOYMENT:**	
Draft:	6.7 m[6] (22 ft)	Number Deployed:	7 (1988):[17] Nikolayev (September 1971), Ochakov (March 1973), Kerch (September 1974), Azov (November 1975), Petropavlovsk (November 1976), Tashkent (November 1977), and Tallinn (April 1980)[18]
Propulsion:	4 gas turbines, 2 shafts;[7] 120,000 shp[8]		
Speed:	32-34 kts[9]		
Crew:	520-540[10]	Homeport:	numbers 1-4, Black Sea; numbers 5-7, Pacific Fleet[19]
NUCLEAR WEAPONS:		**HISTORY:**	
Cruise Missiles:	none	IOC:	1973[20]
Torpedoes:	ten 21-inch (53.3 cm) torpedo tubes in two 5-tube mounts[11]	Production:	not in production
Surface-to-air Missiles:	2 twin SA-N-3 launchers,[12] with 72 missiles;[13] Azov (no. 4 ship of class) is a test ship for missile systems and also has 8 SA-N-6 launchers and has had torpedo tubes removed[14]		

---

4 Polmar, *Guide to the Soviet Navy*, 1986, p. 179; Couhat, *Combat Fleets of the World*, 1988/89, p. 601; Armin Wetterhahn, "The Soviet Guided Missile Cruiser Slava," *International Defense Review*, January 1984, p. 22; *Jane's Fighting Ships*, 1988-89, p. 572.
5 DIA, *ASW Handbook*, 1977, p. 6-7.
6 *Ibid.*
7 Polmar, *Guide to the Soviet Navy*, 1986, p. 179; Wetterhahn, *op. cit.*, p. 22; Collins and Victory, *U.S./Soviet Military Balance*, 1988, p. 91.
8 Polmar, *Guide to the Soviet Navy*, 1986, p. 179; Couhat, *Combat Fleets of the World*, 1988/89, p. 601; *Jane's Fighting Ships*, 1988-89, p. 572.
9 DIA, *ASW Handbook*, 1977, pp. 6-7; USN, *Soviet Naval Developments* (Rev. 4/85), p. 108; Polmar, *Guide to the Soviet Navy*, 1986, p. 179; *Jane's Fighting Ships*, 1988-89, p. 572.
10 Polmar, *Guide to the Soviet Navy*, 1986, p. 179; Couhat, *Combat Fleets of the World*, 1988/89, p. 601; Wetterhahn, *op. cit.*, p. 22; *Jane's Fighting Ships*, 1988-89, p. 572.
11 DIA, *ASW Handbook*, 1977, p. 6-7; JEC, *Allocation of Resources*—1976, Part 2, p. 90.
12 JEC, *Allocation of Resources*—Part 2, 1976, p. 90; DIA, *Soviet Naval Shipbuilding*, DDI-1922-10-76, July 1976 (partially declassified and released under the FOIA), p. 10.
13 Polmar, *Guide to the Soviet Navy*, 1986, p. 179. The Azov has one launcher with 36 missiles.
14 *Ibid.*, p. 179; Wetterhahn, *op. cit.*, p. 22; *Jane's Fighting Ships*, 1988-89, p. 572.
15 JEC, *Allocation of Resources*—1976, Part 2, p. 90; Polmar, *Guide to the Soviet Navy*, 1986, p. 179; USN, *Soviet Naval Developments* (Rev. 4/85), p. 108; Wetterhahn, *op. cit.*, p. 22; IISS, *Military Balance*, 1987-1988, p. 37; SASC, FY 1984 DOD, Part 6, p. 2938.
16 USN, *Soviet Naval Developments* (Rev. 4/85), p. 108.
17 HASC, FY 1982 DOD, Part 3, p. 17; Polmar, *Guide to the Soviet Navy*, 1986, p. 179; Couhat, *Combat Fleets of the World*, 1988/89, p. 600.
18 Commissioning dates; *Jane's Fighting Ships*, 1988-89, p. 572.
19 Polmar, *Guide to the Soviet Navy*, 1986, p. 180.
20 DIA, *Handbook on the Soviet Armed Forces*, p. 9-15.

9

KRESTA, KYNDA, SVERDLOV Cruisers

KRESTA I/II (CG), KYNDA (CG), SVERDLOV (CL)

Figure 9.39 A slightly modified version of the Kresta I, the ten **Kresta II** cruisers are a bit longer, have no cruise missile launchers, but can fire torpedoes and carry 72 SA-N-3 SAMs.

Figure 9.38 The four **Kresta I** cruisers were the first Soviet surface ships to have a helicopter hanger. Each can carry one Ka-25 Hormone A and has the capability to launch four SS-N-3b SLCMs and 44 SA-N-1 SAMs.

	Kresta I/II CG	Kynda CG	Sverdlov CL
DESCRIPTION:	Guided-missile cruiser; first Soviet surface ship with helicopter hanger; being replaced by Udaloy and Sovremennyy	Guided-missile cruiser	Guided-missile light cruiser and command ship
BUILDER:	Zhdanov Shipyard, Leningrad	Zhdanov Shipyard, Leningrad	Marti, Nikolayev (south); Baltic Works, Leningrad; Severodvinsk
SPECIFICATIONS:			
Length:	I: 155.5 m[1] (510 ft); II: 159.0 m[2] (522 ft)	141.7 m[3] (465 ft)	210.0 m[4] (690 ft)
Beam:	17 m[5] (56 ft)	15.8 m[6] (52 ft) 22 m[7] (72 ft)	
Draft:	7.5 m[8] (25 ft)	6.5 m[9] (21 ft)	7.2 m (24 ft)[10]
Displacement: Standard:	I: 6200 tons[11]	4400 tons;[12]	12,900 tons[13]

---

1. DIA, *ASW Handbook*, 1977 p. 6-9.
2. Ibid.
3. Ibid., p. 6-11.
4. Polmar, *Guide to the Soviet Navy*, 1986, p. 192; Couhat, *Combat Fleets of the World*, 1988/89, p. 607.
5. DIA, *ASW Handbook*, 1977, p. 6-9.
6. Ibid., p. 6-11.
7. Polmar, *Guide to the Soviet Navy*, 1986, p. 192; Couhat, *Combat Fleets of the World*, 1988/89, p. 607.
8. DIA, *ASW Handbook*, 1977, p. 6-9.
9. Ibid., p. 6-11.
10. Polmar, *Guide to the Soviet Navy*, 1986, p. 192; Couhat, *Combat Fleets of the World*, 1988/89, p. 607.
11. Polmar, *Guide to the Soviet Navy*, 1986, p. 185; Couhat, *Combat Fleets of the World*, 1988/89, p. 603.
12. Polmar, *Guide to the Soviet Navy*, 1986, p. 188; *Jane's Fighting Ships*, 1988-89, p. 575. Couhat, *Combat Fleets of the World*, 1988/89, p. 604, reports, 4600 tons.
13. Polmar, *Guide to the Soviet Navy*, 1986, p. 192; Couhat, *Combat Fleets of the World*, 1988/89, p. 607.

KRESTA, KYNDA, SVERDLOV Cruisers

Figure 9.40 The four **Kynda** class guided missile cruisers can launch their share of firepower. Each carries eight SS-N-3b SLCMs in two quad launchers with eight reloads, 24 SA-N-1 SAMs, and has six 21-inch torpedo tubes.

	Kresta I/II CG	**Kynda CG**	**Sverdlov CL**
Combat:	I: 7600 MT;[14] II: 7700 MT[15]	5550 MT[16]	17,200 tons[17]
Propulsion:	steam turbine; 2 shafts; 100,000 shp[18]	steam turbine; 2 shafts; 100,000 shp[19]	steam turbine; 2 shafts; 110,000 shp[20]
Speed:	32-25 kts[21]	34 kts[22]	32 kts[23]
Crew:	380-400[24]	375-390[25]	approx. 1000[26]
NUCLEAR WEAPONS:			
Cruise Missiles:	I: 4 SS-N-3b in 2 twin launchers, no reloads.[27] II: none	8 SS-N-3b in 2 quad launchers with 8 reloads[28]	none
Torpedoes:	10 21-inch (53.3 cm) torpedo tubes in two 5-tube mounts[29]	6 21-inch (53.3 cm) torpedo tubes in 2 triple mounts[30]	none

---

14 DIA, *ASW Handbook*, 1977, p. 6-9; USN, *Soviet Naval Developments* (Rev. 4/85), p. 109.
15 DIA, *ASW Handbook*, 1977, p. 6-9; USN, *Soviet Naval Developments* (Rev. 4/85), p. 110.
16 DIA, *ASW Handbook*, 1977, p. 6-11.
17 Polmar, *Guide to the Soviet Navy*, 1986, p. 192; USN, *Soviet Naval Developments* (Rev. 4/85), p. 111.
18 Polmar, *Guide to the Soviet Navy*, 1986, pp. 182,184; Couhat, *Combat Fleets of the World*, 1988/89, pp. 602-603; *Jane's Fighting Ships*, 1988-89, pp. 573-574; Collins and Victory, *U.S./Soviet Military Balance*, 1988, p. 91.
19 Polmar, *Guide to the Soviet Navy*, 1986, p. 188; USN, *Soviet Naval Developments* (Rev. 4/85), p. 110; Couhat, *Combat Fleets of the World*, 1984/85, p. 724; Collins and Victory, *U.S./Soviet Military Balance*, 1988, p. 91.
20 Polmar, *Guide to the Soviet Navy*, 1986, p. 192; USN, *Soviet Naval Developments* (Rev. 4/85), p. 111.
21 Polmar, *Guide to the Soviet Navy*, 1986, pp. 182, 184; Couhat, *Combat Fleets of the World*, 1988/89, pp. 602-603; Collins and Victory, *U.S./Soviet Military Balance*, 1988, p. 91.
22 DIA, *ASW Handbook*, 1977, p. 6-11.
23 Polmar, *Guide to the Soviet Navy*, 1986, p. 192; USN, *Soviet Naval Developments* (Rev. 4/85), p. 111; Couhat, *Combat Fleets of the World*, 1988/89, p. 607.
24 Polmar, *Guide to the Soviet Navy*, 1986, p. 188; Couhat, *Combat Fleets of the World*, 1988/89, pp. 602-603; *Jane's Fighting Ships*, 1988-89, pp. 573-574.
25 Polmar, *Guide to the Soviet Navy*, 1986, p. 188; Couhat, *Combat Fleets of the World*, 1988/89, p. 604; *Jane's Fighting Ships*, 1988-89, p. 575.
26 Polmar, *Guide to the Soviet Navy*, 1986, p. 192; Couhat, *Combat Fleets of the World*, 1988/89, p. 607.
27 Polmar, *Guide to the Soviet Navy*, 1986, pp. 182, 184; USN, *Soviet Naval Developments* (Rev. 4/85), pp. 109-110; Collins and Victory, *U.S./Soviet Military Balance*, 1988, p. 93; 'Update on the 'Kresta I,'" *Jane's Defence Weekly*, 30 June 1984, pp. 1064-1065.
28 USN, *Soviet Naval Developments* (Rev. 4/85), p. 110; Polmar, *Guide to the Soviet Navy*, 1986, p. 188; Collins and Victory, *U.S./Soviet Military Balance*, 1988, p. 93.
29 DIA, *ASW Handbook*, 1977, p. 6-9.
30 *Ibid.*, p. 6-11.

9

KRESTA, KYNDA, SVERDLOV Cruisers

Figure 9.41 Close-up composite of the **Sverdlov** class cruisers, originally deployed in 1952. Although primarily used as flag ships for afloat commands, the ships may be nuclear-capable with their 12 152mm guns.

	Kresta I/II CG	**Kynda CG**	**Sverdlov CL**
Surface-to-air Missiles:	I: 2 twin SA-N-1 with 44 missiles.[31] II: 2 twin SA-N-3 with 72 missiles[32]	1 twin SA-N-1 with 24 missiles[33]	none
Aircraft:	Kresta I: none. Kresta II: 1 Ka-25 Hormone A helicopter	none	none
Artillery:	none	none	12 152mm guns[34]
DEPLOYMENT:			
Number Deployed:	4 Kresta I; 10 Kresta II (1988)[35]	4 (1988)[36]	5 (1988)[37]
Homeport:	Kresta I: 1 Northern Fleet, 1 Baltic Fleet. Kresta II: 6 Northern Fleet, 1 Baltic Fleet, 3 Pacific Fleet	1 Baltic Fleet; 1 Black Sea Fleet; 2 Pacific Fleet	2 Northern Fleet; 1 Baltic Fleet; 2 Black Sea Fleet
HISTORY:			
IOC:	I: 1967[38] II: 1970[39]	June 1962[40]	1952[41]
Production:	not in production	not in production	not in production
COMMENTS:			Some seven ships of this class are in reserve.

---

31. Polmar, *Guide to the Soviet Navy*, 1986, pp. 182, 184; Collins and Victory, *U.S./Soviet Military Balance*, 1988, p. 93; 'Update on the 'Kresta I,'' op. cit., pp. 1064-1065.
32. Polmar, *Guide to the Soviet Navy*, 1986, pp. 182, 184; Collins and Victory, *U.S./Soviet Military Balance*, 1988, p. 93.
33. Collins and Victory, *U.S./Soviet Military Balance*, 1988, p. 93.
34. The gun is reportedly called the MK-5-5YC model; Captain Michael P. Ley, "Naval Gunfire Support: What We Need to Understand," *Field Artillery*, February 1988, p. 41. Polmar, *Guide to the Soviet Navy*, 1986, p. 192; USN, *Soviet Naval Developments* (Rev. 4/85) p. 111; Couhat, *Combat Fleets of the World*, 1988/89, p. 607. One command ship (Admiral Senyavin) has six 152mm guns, the other (Zhdanov) has nine 152mm guns.
35. Polmar, *Guide to the Soviet Navy*, 1986, pp. 182, 184.
36. DIA, *ASW Handbook*, 1977, p. 6-11.
37. DIA, *Unclassified Communist Naval Orders of Battle*, DDB-1200-124-86, April 1986, p. 3, lists 10 Sverdlov class. One additional Sverdlov class cruiser is a gunnery training ship; Polmar, *Guide to the Soviet Navy*, 1986, p. 192.
38. Polmar, *Guide to the Soviet Navy*, 1986, p. 185; Collins and Victory, *U.S./Soviet Military Balance*, 1988, p. 91.
39. USN, *Soviet Naval Developments* (Rev. 4/85), p. 110; Collins and Victory, *U.S./Soviet Military Balance*, 1988, p. 91.
40. For the lead ship Groznyy. The other in service dates are: Admiral Fokin (August 1963), Admiral Golovko (July 1964), Varyag (February 1965); Couhat, *Combat Fleets of the World*, 1988/89, p. 604. Jane's Fighting Ships, 1988-89, p. 575 reports commissioning dates.
41. Collins and Victory, *U.S./Soviet Military Balance*, 1988, p. 91.

9
SOVREMENNYY (DDG)

Destroyers
SOVREMENNYY (DDG)[1]

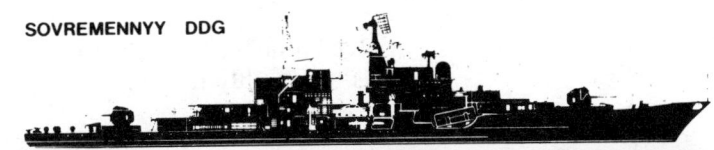

Figure 9.42 The **Sovremennyy** is a guided-missile destroyer, one of two classes of destroyers currently under construction in the Soviet Union. These are principally anti-surface ships carrying SLCMs, ASW rockets, torpedoes, and SAMs.

DESCRIPTION:[1]	Guided-missile destroyer; principally an anti-surface ship weapons platform	Propulsion:	steam turbine,[5] 2 shafts; 100,000 shp[6]
BUILDER:	Zhdanov Shipyard, Leningrad	Speed:	32-34 kts[7]
SPECIFICATIONS:		Crew:	350-380[8]
Length:	156 m[2] (512 ft)	**NUCLEAR WEAPONS:**	
Beam:	17 m (56 ft)	Cruise Missiles:	8 SS-N-22 in two quad launchers[9]
Draft:	6.0-6.5 m[3] (20-21 ft)	ASW Rockets:	120 anti-submarine rockets of unknown type[10]
Displacement:	7300 MT (combat)[4]		

---

1 Originally designated Bal-Com-2 (Baltic Combatant No.2) by NATO intelligence; Polmar, *Guide to the Soviet Navy*, 1986, p. 199; Couhat, *Combat Fleets of the World*, 1988/89, pp. 610-611; *Jane's Fighting Ships*, 1988-89, p. 577. Sovremennyy means ''Modern'' in Russian.
2 SMP 1987, p. 83.
3 Polmar, *Guide to the Soviet Navy*, 1986, p. 199; Couhat, *Combat Fleets of the World*, 1988/89, p. 611; *Jane's Fighting Ships*, 1988-89, p. 577.
4 SMP 1987, p. 83; *Jane's Fighting Ships*, 1988-89, p. 577. SMP 1985, p. 100, Polmar, *Guide to the Soviet Navy*, 1986, p. 199, and HASC, FY 1984 DOD, Part 3, p. 2, report 7900 MT.
5 *Jane's Fighting Ships*, 1988-89, p. 577; Polmar, *Guide to the Soviet Navy*, 1986, p. 199.
6 Polmar, *Guide to the Soviet Navy*, 1986, p. 199; Couhat, *Combat Fleets of the World*, 1988/89, p. 611; *Jane's Fighting Ships*, 1988-89, p. 577.
7 USN, *Soviet Naval Developments* (Rev. 4/85), p. 113; Polmar, *Guide to the Soviet Navy*, 1986, p. 199; Couhat, *Combat Fleets of the World*, 1988/89, p. 611; *Jane's Fighting Ships*, 1988-89, p. 577.
8 Polmar, *Guide to the Soviet Navy*, 1986, p. 199; Couhat, *Combat Fleets of the World*, 1988/89, p. 611; *Jane's Fighting Ships*, 1988-89, p. 577.
9 SMP 1987, p. 86; HASC, FY 1985 DOD, Part 3, p. 2; SMP 1985, pp. 98-99; SASC, FY 1986 DOD, Part 8, p. 4362; DIA, *Unclassified Naval Orders of Battle*, DDB-1200-124-86, April 1986, p. 2; *Jane's Fighting Ships*, 1988-89, p. 577.
10 SMP 1987, p. 86.

9

SOVREMENNYY (DDG)

Torpedoes:	four 21-inch (53.3 cm) torpedo tubes[11]	Homeport:	Northern, Baltic, Pacific Fleets
Surface-to-air Missiles:	2 SA-N-7 launchers[12] with 40-44 missiles[13] (possibly nuclear)	**HISTORY:** IOC:	1981[16]
Aircraft:	1 Ka-27 Helix A or Ka-25 Hormone helicopter in amidships landing area[14]	Production:	unit 11 launched and six more under construction[17]

DEPLOYMENT:
Number Deployed: 7 (number 8 fitting out) (1988)[15]

---

11 SMP 1985, p. 99; Polmar, *Guide to the Soviet Navy*, 1986, p. 199; Couhat, *Combat Fleets of the World*, 1988/89, p. 611; *Jane's Fighting Ships*, 1988-89, p. 577; Collins and Victory, *U.S./Soviet Military Balance*, 1988, p. 101.
12 Polmar, *Guide to the Soviet Navy*, 1986, p. 199; *Jane's Fighting Ships*, 1988-89, p. 577; Collins and Victory, *U.S./Soviet Military Balance*, 1988, p. 101.
13 SMP 1987, p. 86; SMP 1985, p. 99.
14 SMP 1988, p. 83; SMP 1987, p. 86; SMP 1985, p. 99.
15 SMP 1987, p. 86.

16 For the lead ship, Sovremennyy; USN, *Soviet Naval Developments*(Rev. 4/85), p. 113; Couhat, *Combat Fleets of the World*, 1988/89, p. 610; Collins and Victory, *U.S./Soviet Military Balance*, 1988, p. 99. *Jane's Fighting Ships*, 1988-89, p. 577, reports commissioning dates for the other ships in the class: Otchayannyy, "Merciless" (May 1982), Otlichnyy, "Perfect" (May 1983), Osmotritel'nyy, "Circumspect" (June 1984), Bezuprechnyy, "Irreproachable" (June 1985), Boyevoy, 'Militant" (June 1986), Stoykiy, "Steadfast" (September 1986), Okrylenny, (September 1987).
17 Studeman, USN, Statement before HASC, March 1988, p. 37.

UDALOY (DDG)[1]

UDALOY DDG

Figure 9.43 Eight **Udaloy** destroyers are currently deployed (1988). Unit 9 has been launched and at least three more are under construction.

DESCRIPTION:[1] Large guided-missile destroyer, dedicated primarily to anti-submarine warfare

BUILDER: Yantar, Kaliningrad 820; Zhdanov Shipyard, Leningrad 190

SPECIFICATIONS:
Length: 162 m[2] (531 ft)
Beam: 19.3 m (63.3 ft)
Draft: 6.2 m[3] (20 ft)
Displacement:
Standard: 6200-6700 tons[4]
Combat: 8000 MT[5]

Propulsion: 4 gas turbines;[6] 110,000-120,000 shp[7]
Speed: 30-35 kts[8]
Crew: 300-310[9]

NUCLEAR WEAPONS:
Torpedoes: eight 21-inch (53.3 cm) torpedo tubes in 2 quad mounts[10]
Surface-to-air Missiles: none nuclear capable
Aircraft: 2 Ka-27 Helix A helicopters[11]

---

1 Initially designated Bal-Com-3 (Baltic Combatant No. 3) by NATO intelligence; Polmar, *Guide to the Soviet Navy*, 1986, pp. 196-197; Couhat, *Combat Fleets of the World*, 1988/89, p. 608; *Jane's Fighting Ships*, 1988-89, p. 578. Udaloy means 'Daring'' in Russian.
2 SMP 1987, p. 83; USN, *Soviet Naval Developments* (Rev. 4/85), p. 112.
3 Polmar, *Guide to the Soviet Navy*, 1986, p. 196; Couhat, *Combat Fleets of the World*, 1988/89, p. 608; *Jane's Fighting Ships*, 1988-89, p. 578.
4 Polmar, *Guide to the Soviet Navy*, 1986, p. 196; Couhat, *Combat Fleets of the World*, 1988/89, p. 608.
5 SMP 1987, p. 83; USN, *Soviet Naval Developments* (Rev. 4/85), p. 112.
6 Polmar, *Guide to the Soviet Navy*, 1986, p. 196; *Jane's Fighting Ships*, 1988-89, p. 578; Collins and Victory, *U.S./Soviet Military Balance*, 1988, p. 99.
7 Polmar, *Guide to the Soviet Navy*, 1986, p. 196; Couhat, *Combat Fleets of the World*, 1988/89, p. 608; *Jane's Fighting Ships*, 1988-89, p. 578.
8 Ibid.
9 Ibid.
10 Polmar, *Guide to the Soviet Navy*, 1986, p. 196; *Jane's Fighting Ships*, 1988-89, p. 578.
11 SMP 1988, p. 83; USN, *Soviet Naval Developments* (Rev. 4/85), p. 112; IISS, *Military Balance*, 1987-1988, p. 37; *Jane's Fighting Ships*, 1988-89, p. 578; SASC, FY 1984 DOD, Part 6, pp. 2931, 2938-2939.

9

UDALOY (DDG)

Figure 9.44 A forward aerial view of the **Udaloy** guided-missile destroyer. The ship can carry two Ka-27 Helix A helicopters equipped for anti-submarine warfare, plus it has eight 21-inch torpedo tubes in two quad mounts and eight SA-N-8 vertical launchers capable of firing 48-64 missiles (6-8 missiles per launcher).

DEPLOYMENT:

Number Deployed: 8 (1988)[12]

Homeport: about evenly split between Northern and Baltic Fleets

HISTORY:

IOC: 1981[13]

Production: unit 9 launched and three more under construction (1988)[14]

COMMENTS: First Soviet destroyer design to carry two ASW helicopters.[15]

---

12 Studeman, USN, Statement before HASC, March 1988, p. 37.
13 HASC, FY 1982 DOD, Part 3, p. 17. *Jane's Fighting Ships*, 1988-89, p. 578 reports commissioning dates for successive ships: Vitse-Admiral Kulakov (September 1981), Marshal Vasilevsky (June 1983), Admiral Zakharov (October 1983), Admiral Spiridonov (September 1984), Admiral Tributs (August 1985), Marshal Shaposhnikov (October 1985), Simferopol (December 1986).
14 Studeman, USN, Statement before HASC, March 1988, p. 37.
15 Couhat, *Combat Fleets of the World*, 1988/89, p. 608.

9

KILDIN, KANIN, KASHIN, KOTLIN Destroyers

KILDIN/MOD KILDIN (DDG), KANIN (DDG), KASHIN/MOD KASHIN (DDG), KOTLIN/MOD KOTLIN/SAM KOTLIN (DDG)

Figure 9.45 This **Kildin** is the single ship in its guided missile destroyer class, though there are three modified Kildins currently deployed (1988).

Figure 9.46 The **Kanin** class destroyer is depicted after a missile launch. It has one twin SA-N-1 launcher with 16 missiles.

	Kildin/Mod Kildin	Kanin	Kashin/Mod Kashin	Kotlin/Mod Kotlin/ SAM Kotlin
DESCRIPTION:	Guided-missile destroyer	Guided-missile destroyer	Guided-missile destroyer; first Soviet all-gas turbine propulsion ship in two modifications	Guided-missile destroyer
BUILDER:	Komsomol'sk	61 Kommuna Shipyard, Nikolayev; Severodvinsk; Zhdanov Shipyard, Leningrad	61 Kommuna Shipyard, Nikolayev; Zhdanov Shipyard, Leningrad	Komsomol'sk; 61 Kommuna Shipyard, Nikolayev; Zhdanov Shipyard, Leningrad
SPECIFICATIONS:				
Length:	126.5 m[1] (415.0 ft)	139.0 m[2] (456.0 ft)	147.0 m[3] (482.3 ft)	126.5 m[4] (415.0 ft)
Beam:	13.0 m[5] (42.7 ft)	15.0 m[6] (49.2 ft)	15.8 m[7] (51.8 ft)	13.0 m[8] (42.7 ft)

---

1 DIA, *ASW Handbook*, 1977, p. 6-19; Polmar, *Guide to the Soviet Navy*, 1986, p. 210.
2 DIA, *ASW Handbook*, 1977, p. 6-15.
3 *Ibid.*, p. 6-13. Specifications are for the MOD Kashin, which is one meter longer than the Kashin.
4 DIA, *ASW Handbook*, 1977, p. 6-23; Polmar, *Guide to the Soviet Navy*, 1986, p. 212.
5 DIA, *ASW Handbook*, 1977, p. 6-19; Polmar, *Guide to the Soviet Navy*, 1986, p. 210.
6 DIA, *ASW Handbook*, 1977, p. 6-15.
7 *Ibid.*, p. 6-13; Polmar, *Guide to the Soviet Navy*, 1986, p. 204.
8 DIA, *ASW Handbook*, 1977, p. 6-23.

9

KILDIN, KANIN, KASHIN, KOTLIN Destroyers

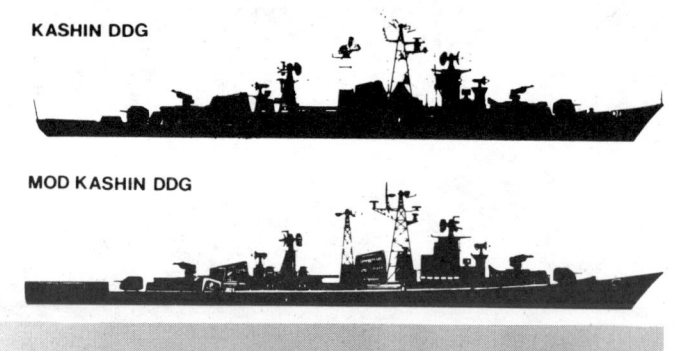

Figure 9.47 The **Kashin** and **Mod Kashin** were the first Soviet guided-missile destroyers with all gas turbine propulsion. The photo is a Mod Kashin of which there are currently six deployed (1988).

Figure 9.48 The **Kotlin** nuclear-powered destroyers have three versions; the Kotlin, Mod Kotlin, and SAM Kotlin, each with variations in the number and kinds of torpedoes and SAMs they carry.

	Kildin/Mod Kildin	**Kanin**	**Kashin/Mod Kashin**	**Kotlin/Mod Kotlin/ SAM Kotlin**
Draft:	5.6 m[9] (18 ft)	7.0 m[10] (23 ft) (includes sonar)	6.0 m[11] (20 ft) Mod: 6.7 m[12] (22 ft)	5.5 m[13] (18 ft)
Displacement:	3500 MT[14]	4750 MT[15]	4520 MT[16] Mod: 4575 MT[17]	3500 MT[18]
Propulsion:	steam turbine; 2 shafts; 72,000 shp[19]	steam turbine; 2 shafts; 72,000-80,000 shp[20]	gas turbine; 2 shafts; 96,000 shp[21]	steam turbine; 2 shafts; 72,000 shp[22]
Speed:	34 kts[23]	35 kts[24]	36 kts[25]	34 kts[26]

---

9 DIA, *ASW Handbook*, 1977, p. 6-19; Polmar, *Guide to the Soviet Navy*, 1986, p. 210.
10 DIA, *ASW Handbook*, 1977, p. 6-15.
11 Ibid., p. 6-13.
12 Ibid.
13 Ibid., p. 6-23.
14 Ibid., p. 6-19.
15 Ibid., p. 6-15.
16 Ibid., p. 6-13.
17 Ibid.
18 Ibid., p. 6-23.

19 Polmar, *Guide to the Soviet Navy*, 1986, p. 210; Couhat, *Combat Fleets of the World*, 1988/89, p. 614.
20 Polmar, *Guide to the Soviet Navy*, 1986, p. 208; Couhat, *Combat Fleets of the World*, 1988/89, p. 614.
21 Polmar, *Guide to the Soviet Navy*, 1986, pp. 204, 206.
22 DIA, *ASW Handbook*, 1977, p. 6-23; Polmar, *Guide to the Soviet Navy*, 1986, p. 212; *Jane's Fighting Ships*, 1988-89, p. 581.
23 DIA, *ASW Handbook*, 1977, p. 6-19; Polmar, *Guide to the Soviet Navy*, 1986, p. 210.
24 DIA, *ASW Handbook*, 1977, p. 6-15.
25 USN, *Soviet Naval Developments* (Rev. 4/85), p. 114.
26 DIA, *ASW Handbook*, 1977, p. 6-23; Polmar, *Guide to the Soviet Navy*, 1986, p. 212.

9

KILDIN, KANIN, KASHIN, KOTLIN Destroyers

	Kildin/Mod Kildin	Kanin	Kashin/Mod Kashin	Kotlin/Mod Kotlin/ SAM Kotlin
Crew:	285-300[27]	300-350[28]	280-300[29]	300-335[30]
NUCLEAR WEAPONS:				
Cruise Missiles:	Kildin only: (1 SS-N-1 launcher with 9 missiles)[31]	none	none	none
Torpedoes:	4 21-inch (53.3 cm) torpedo tubes in twin mounts[32]	10 21-inch (53.3 cm) torpedo tubes in 2 5-tube mounts[33]	5 21-inch (53.3 cm) torpedo tubes[34]	Kotlin: 10 21-inch (53.3 cm) torpedo tubes; 2 5-tube mounts[35] Mod Katlin/SAM Kotlin: 5 21-inch (53.3 cm) tubes
Surface-to-air Missiles:	none	1 twin SA-N-1 launcher with 16 missiles[36]	2 twin SA-N-1 launcher with 36 missiles;[37] SA-N-7 in one ship[38] (Prevornyy)	SAM Kotlin: 1 twin SA-N-1 launcher with 16 missiles[39]
DEPLOYMENT:				
Number Deployed:	4 (1988);[40] 1 Kildin, 3 Mod Kildin	5 (1988)[41]	12 Kashin; 6 Mod Kashin (1988)	2 Kotlin; 5 Mod Kotlin, 6 SAM Kotlin[42]
HISTORY:				
IOC:	1958[43]	1968[44]	1963[45]	1955 (Kotlin); 1962 (SAM Kotlin)[46]
COMMENTS:	Four Kildin ships were originally built based on the Kotlin hull plan. Three were converted to carry the non-nuclear SS-N-2 Styx.[47]	Converted Krypnyy DDG ships based on Kotlin design.[48]	Twenty ships built; one lost in Black Sea 31 August 1974.[49] Six Kashin Mods have improved electronics and 4 non-nuclear SS-N-2c Styx SSMs.[50] Provornyy is SA-N-7 test ship.[51]	First SAM Kotlin was used as SA-N-1 trial ship.[52]

---

27 Polmar, *Guide to the Soviet Navy,* 1986, p. 210; Couhat, *Combat Fleets of the World,* 1988/89, p. 614.
28 Polmar, *Guide to the Soviet Navy,* 1986, p. 208; Couhat, *Combat Fleets of the World,* 1988/89, p. 614; *Jane's Fighting Ships,* 1988-89, p. 582.
29 Polmar, *Guide to the Soviet Navy,* 1986, p. 204; Couhat, *Combat Fleets of the World,* 1988/89, p. 613; *Jane's Fighting Ships,* 1988-89, p. 579.
30 Polmar, *Guide to the Soviet Navy,* 1986, p. 212; Couhat, *Combat Fleets of the World,* 1988/89, pp. 615-616; *Jane's Fighting Ships,* 1988-89, p. 581.
31 These missiles are probably retired.
32 Collins and Cronin, *U.S./Soviet Military Balance,* 1985, pp. 33; Polmar, *Guide to the Soviet Navy,* 1986, p. 210
33 *Jane's Fighting Ships,* 1988-89, p. 582.
34 DIA, *ASW Handbook,* 1977, p. 6-23.
35 *Ibid.,* p. 6-13.
36 Polmar, *Guide to the Soviet Navy,* 1986, p. 208; USN, *Soviet Naval Developments* (Rev. 4/85), p. 114.
37 Polmar, *Guide to the Soviet Navy,* 1986, pp. 204, 206; USN, *Soviet Naval Developments* (Rev. 4/85), p. 114; Collins and Victory, *U.S./Soviet Military Balance,* 1988, p. 101.
38 Polmar, *Guide to the Soviet Navy,* 1986, p. 206; USN, *Soviet Naval Developments* (Rev. 4/85), p. 114.
39 Polmar, *Guide to the Soviet Navy,* 1986, p. 212; USN, *Soviet Naval Developments* (Rev. 4/85), p. 116; Collins and Victory, *U.S./Soviet Military Balance,* 1988, p. 101.
40 *Jane's Fighting Ships,* 1988-89, p. 581. The Mod Kildin has four non-nuclear SS-N-2 Styx missiles instead of SS-N-1.
41 *Jane's Fighting Ships,* 1988-89, p. 582.
42 Another four Kotlin, six Mod Kotlin, and one SAM Kotlin are held in reserve; *Jane's Fighting Ships,* 1988-89, p. 583.
43 Polmar, *Guide to the Soviet Navy,* 1986, p. 210; Couhat, *Combat Fleets of the World,* 1988/89, p. 614.
44 Polmar, *Guide to the Soviet Navy,* 1986, p. 208; Collins and Victory, *U.S./Soviet Military Balance,* 1988, p. 99.
45 Polmar, *Guide to the Soviet Navy,* 1986, p. 206; Collins and Victory, *U.S./Soviet Military Balance,* 1988, p. 998; Couhat, *Combat Fleets of the World,* 1988/89, p. 612.
46 Collins and Cronin, *U.S./Soviet Military Balance,* 1985, p. 33.
47 Polmar, *Guide to the Soviet Navy,* 1986, p. 210; USN, *Soviet Naval Developments* (Rev. 4/85), p. 115.
48 Polmar, *Guide to the Soviet Navy,* 1986, p. 208.
49 *Ibid.,* pp. 204, 206.
50 *Ibid.*
51 *Ibid.*
52 *Ibid.,* p. 212.

9
KRIVAK I/II (FFG)

Frigates
KRIVAK I/II (FFG)

Figure 9.49 The **Krivak** class is a nuclear-capable frigate configured with eight 21-inch torpedo tubes. There are currently 32 deployed throughout the Soviet fleets.

DESCRIPTION:	Large ASW and escort frigate	Crew:	200-220[7]
BUILDER:	Kalingrad; Kamysh-Burun Shipyard, Kerch; Zhdanov Shipyard, Leningrad	**NUCLEAR WEAPONS:**	8 21-inch (53.3 cm) torpedo tubes in 2 quad mounts[8]
SPECIFICATIONS:		**DEPLOYMENT:**	
Length:	123.5 m[1] (405.2 ft)	Number Deployed:	32 (21 Krivak I, 11 Krivak II) (1988)[9]
Beam:	14.3 m[2] (47 ft)	Homeport:	Krivak I: 8 Northern Fleet, 11 Pacific Fleet, 6 Baltic Fleet, 7 Black Sea Fleet
Draft:	4.6 m[3] (15 ft)		
Displacement:	3860 MT[4]	**HISTORY:**	
Propulsion:	gas turbine; 2 shafts; 48,000 shp[5]	IOC:	1970 (Krivak I);[10] 1975 (Krivak II)[11]
Speed:	32 kts[6]	Production:	not in production[12]

---

1. DIA, *ASW Handbook*, 1977, p. 6-17.
2. Ibid.; Polmar, *Guide to the Soviet Navy*, 1986, p. 219.
3. Polmar, *Guide to the Soviet Navy*, 1986, p. 219; *Jane's Fighting Ships*, 1988-89, p. 584.
4. DIA, *ASW Handbook*, 1977, p. 6-17.
5. Polmar, *Guide to the Soviet Navy*, 1986, p. 219; USN, *Soviet Naval Developments* (Rev. 4/85), p. 118; *Jane's Fighting Ships*, 1988-89, p. 584; Collins and Victory, *U.S./Soviet Military Balance*, 1988, p. 99.
6. HASC, FY 1985 DOD, Part 3, p. 2.
7. Polmar, *Guide to the Soviet Navy*, 1986, p. 219; Couhat, *Combat Fleets of the World*, 1988/89, p. 619; *Jane's Fighting Ships*, 1988-89, pp. 584.
8. DIA, *ASW Handbook*, 1977, p. 6-17; *Jane's Fighting Ships*, 1988-89, p. 585; Collins and Victory, *U.S./Soviet Military Balance*, 1988, p. 101.
9. Polmar, *Guide to the Soviet Navy*, 1986, p. 219; Couhat, *Combat Fleets of the World*, 1988/89, p. 619; *Jane's Fighting Ships*, 1988-89, p. 584.
10. Polmar, *Guide to the Soviet Navy*, 1986, p. 219; USN, *Soviet Naval Developments* (Rev. 4/85), p. 118; *Jane's Fighting Ships*, 1988-89, p. 585.
11. Couhat, *Combat Fleets of the World*, 1988/89, p. 618.
12. Ibid.

9
Nuclear-Capable Patrol Craft

Nuclear-Capable Patrol Craft (PGG/PGGH)
NANUCHKA I/III (PGG), SARANCHA (PGGH), TARANTUL III (PGG)

Figure 9.50 The **Nanuchka** class of ships are nuclear-capable patrol combatants. There are currently 28 (17 Nanuchka I and 11 Nanuchka III) deployed (1988). This is the Nanuchka I.

Figure 9.51 There are currently (1988) eight **Tarantul** class nuclear-capable patrol craft deployed, each capable of carrying four SS-N-22 SLCMs.

	Nanuchka I/III	Sarancha	Tarantul III
DESCRIPTION:	Patrol craft (PGG)	Patrol hydrofoil (PGGH)	Patrol craft (PGG)
BUILDER:	Petrovskiy Shipyard, Leningrad	Petrovskiy Shipyard, Leningrad	Petrovskiy Shipyard, Leningrad
SPECIFICATIONS:			
Length:	59.3 m[1] (195 ft)	45 m[2] (148 ft)	56.6 m[3] (185 ft)
Beam:	12.6 m (41.3 ft)[4]	11 m (36 ft)[5]	10.5 m (34.5 ft)[6]
Draft:	2.4 m[7] (7.9 ft)	2.6 m[8] (8.5 ft)	2.5 m[9] (8.2 ft)
Displacement:	800 tons[10]	320 tons[11]	600 tons (combat)[12]
Propulsion:	3 diesels; 3 shafts; 30,000 shp[13]	2 gas turbines; 30,000 shp[14]	2 gas turbines and 2 diesels; 2 shafts[15]
Speed:	32 kts[16]	45 kts;[17] 60 kts[18]	36-43 kts[19]

---

1 Polmar, *Guide to the Soviet Navy*, 1986, p. 233; *Jane's Fighting Ships*, 1988-89, p. 592.
2 Polmar, *Guide to the Soviet Navy*, 1986, p. 242; *Jane's Fighting Ships*, 1988-89, p. 593.
3 Roy McLeavy, *Jane's Defence Weekly*, 24 March 1984, p. 427; *Jane's Fighting Ships*, 1988-89, p. 593; Polmar, *Guide to the Soviet Navy*, 1986, p. 232.
4 Polmar, *Guide to the Soviet Navy*, 1986, p. 233.
5 *Ibid.*, p. 242.
6 *Ibid.*, p. 232.
7 *Ibid.*, p. 233; *Jane's Fighting Ships*, 1988-89, p. 592.
8 Polmar, *Guide to the Soviet Navy*, 1986, p. 242.
9 McLeavy, *op. cit.*, p. 427; *Jane's Fighting Ships*, 1988-89, p. 593.
10 USN, *Soviet Naval Developments* (Rev. 4/85), p. 122.
11 Polmar, *Guide to the Soviet Navy*, 1986, p. 242; *Jane's Fighting Ships*, 1988-89, p. 593; Collins and Victory, *U.S./Soviet Military Balance*, 1988, p. 103.
12 McLeavy, *op. cit.*, p. 427; *Jane's Fighting Ships*, 1988-89, p. 593.
13 Polmar, *Guide to the Soviet Navy*, 1986, p. 233; Couhat, *Combat Fleets of the World*, 1988/89, p. 627; *Jane's Fighting Ships*, 1988-89, p. 592.
14 Polmar, *Guide to the Soviet Navy*, 1986, p. 242; Couhat, *Fleets of the World*, 1988/89, p. 630; *Jane's Fighting Ships*, 1988-89, p. 593; Collins and Victory, *U.S./Soviet Military Balance*, 1988, p. 103.
15 Collins and Victory, *U.S./Soviet Military Balance*, 1988, p. 103; *Jane's Fighting Ships*, 1988-89, p. 593.
16 Polmar, *Guide to the Soviet Navy*, 1986, p. 233; *Jane's Fighting Ships*, 1988-89, p. 592; Collins and Victory, *U.S./Soviet Military Balance*, 1988, p. 103.
17 *Jane's Fighting Ships*, 1988-89, p. 593.
18 Polmar, *Guide to the Soviet Navy*, 1986, p. 242; Collins and Victory, *U.S./Soviet Military Balance*, 1988, p. 103.
19 *Jane's Fighting Ships*, 1988-88, p. 593; McLeavy, *op. cit.*, p. 427; Collins and Victory, *U.S./Soviet Military Balance*, 1988, p. 103.

9

Nuclear-Capable Patrol Craft

Figure 9.52 An aerial view of a **Nanuchka III** clearly depicting one of its two triple launchers, holding three of its six SS-N-9 SLCMs.

	Nanuchka I/III	**Sarancha**	**Tarantul III**
Crew:	60-70[20]	35[21]	unknown
NUCLEAR WEAPONS:	6 SS-N-9 in 2 triple launchers[22]	4 SS-N-9 in 2 twin launchers[23]	4 SS-N-22[24]
DEPLOYMENT: Number Deployed:	28 (17 Nanuchka I; 11 Nanuchka III) (1988)[25]	1 (1988)[26]	8 (1988)[27]
HISTORY: IOC:	1969 (Nanuchka I);[28] 1977-1978 (Nanuchka III)[29]	1977[30]	1981[31]
Production:	Nanuchka III in production	not in production	in production
COMMENTS:			Tarantul I/II carry the non-nuclear SS-N-2c Styx anti-ship cruise missile.

---

20 Polmar, *Guide to the Soviet Navy*, 1986, p. 233; *Jane's Fighting Ships*, 1988-894, p. 233.
21 *Jane's Fighting Ships*, 1988-89, p. 593.
22 Polmar, *Guide to the Soviet Navy*, 1986, p. 233; USN, *Soviet Naval Developments* (Rev. 4/85), p. 122; Collins and Victory, *U.S./Soviet Military Balance*, 1988, p. 103.
23 Polmar, *Guide to the Soviet Navy*, 1986, p. 242; *Jane's Fighting Ships*, 1988-89, p. 593; Collins and Victory, *U.S./Soviet Military Balance*, 1988, p. 103.
24 McLeavy, op. cit., p. 427; *Jane's Fighting Ships*, 1988-89, p. 593.
25 Polmar, *Guide to the Soviet Navy*, 1986, p. 233; *Jane's Fighting Ships*, 1988-89, p. 592.
26 Polmar, *Guide to the Soviet Navy*, 1986, p. 242; *Jane's Fighting Ships*, 1988-89, p. 593.
27 *Jane's Fighting Ships*, 1988-89, p. 593.
28 Polmar, *Guide to the Soviet Navy*, 1986, p. 233; USN, *Soviet Naval Developments* (Rev. 4/85), p. 122; Collins and Victory, *U.S./Soviet Military Balance*, 1988, p. 103.
29 Polmar, *Guide to the Soviet Navy*, 1986, p. 233; *Jane's Fighting Ships*, 1988-89, p. 592.
30 Polmar, *Guide to the Soviet Navy*, 1986, p. 242; Collins and Victory, *U.S./Soviet Military Balance*, 1988, p. 103.
31 IISS, *Military Balance*, 1983-1984, p. 17; *Jane's Defence Weekly*, 21 July 1984, p. 59.

9

Minor Surface Combatants

Minor Surface Combatants with 21-inch Torpedo Tubes

SKORYY (DD), GRISHA (FFL), RIGA (FF), TURYA (PTH)

Figure 9.53 An artist's drawing of the **Skoryy** depicts its ten torpedo tubes in two 5-tube mounts. Most of these anti-sub and anti-surface destroyers are currently laid up in reserve.

Figure 9.54 The **Riga** is an anti-sub frigate with two or three torpedo tubes in twin or triple mounts.

	Skoryy DD	Grisha FFL	Riga FF	Turya PTH
DESCRIPTION:	Anti-submarine and anti-surface destroyer	Anti-submarine frigates	Anti-submarine frigates	High-speed coastal ASW and torpedo attack craft
TORPEDO TUBES: (21-inch) (53.3 cm)	10 in two 5-tube mounts: Mod: 5 in one 5-tube mount	4 in twin mounts	2 or 3 in twin or triple mounts	4 single tubes
NUMBER DEPLOYED:	2	55 (1988):[1] 15 Grisha I; 32 Grisha III; 8 Grisha V	32 (10 more in reserve)	30
IOC:	1949	1968	1955	1974
COMMENTS:	Most laid up in the reserve.	Grisha V in production.		

Sources: Polmar, *Guide to the Soviet Navy*, 1986, pp. 216-217, 223, 229, 245-246; DIA, *Unclassified Communist Naval Orders of Battle*, DDB-1200-124-86, April 1986; *Jane's Fighting Ships*, 1988-89, pp. 586-587, 594-595.

1. Some 12 Grisha II assigned to the KGB are not thought to be nuclear capable.

Chapter Ten
Soviet Nuclear Testing
by Lynn R. Sykes and Steven Ruggi[1]

Overview

Like other areas of the military, the Soviet Union has imposed great secrecy on its nuclear testing program. It has not publicly released yield information on any of its underground weapons tests and has released only fragmentary information on a small number of atmospheric and peaceful nuclear explosions (PNEs). The following analysis of Soviet nuclear testing thus includes information on explosions announced by the United States, explosions not announced by the United States but detected by seismic means and reported by other scientific institutions, and a few explosions made public in recently declassified U.S. government documents.

The field of seismology provides the main data by which underground nuclear tests are detected and identified and their yields calculated. Even though the Soviet Union has not made available seismic data on its weapons tests,[2] a major topic of this chapter is the use of independent seismic data for the estimation of yields of known Soviet underground explosions. Since yields have been announced for such a small number of Soviet explosions, yields of weapons tests must be estimated using calibration data mainly from tests of announced yields in other countries. As a result there has been a long-standing controversy about the yields of Soviet explosions.[3]

The first Soviet test of a nuclear device occurred on 29 August 1949 on a tower variously reported to be at or near the Kazakh Test Site (KTS), near Semipalatinsk, in the vicinity of the Aral Sea in the Ustyurt Plateau, or on the northeast shore of the Caspian Sea. From 29 August 1949 to 31 December 1987 the Soviets have conducted 618 known nuclear explosions, 80 percent of which are presumed to have been for military purposes (see tables at end of chapter). Through 1985, the United States had announced 363 Soviet nuclear events by date or test series. (Some dates are the dates of announcement, not necessarily shot dates.) An additional 22 tests are known by month or year from declassified U.S. government documents. This leaves some 35 percent of the known Soviet explosions unannounced or unreported by the United States, but reported by other scientific institutions.

The Soviets twice have stopped testing for an extended period. During a bilateral moratorium, they refrained from testing for the 34-month period from 3 November 1958 until 1 September 1961. During a unilateral moratorium, they stopped for 19 months—from 26 July 1985 until 26 February 1987. After resuming testing in February 1987, the Soviets have been announcing their tests, presumably all of them. Twenty-three tests were conducted in 1987, including six PNEs, one test at Novaya Zemlya, and the remainder at the KTS in eastern Kazakhstan, southwest of Semipalatinsk.

Almost 30 percent of the known explosions (179) were conducted in the atmosphere or from above-ground towers. At least three tests were conducted underwater: one in September 1955 in the Barents Sea, another probably in September 1957 off the coast of Novaya Zemlya,[4] and the third in October 1961, also off the coast of Novaya Zemlya. The remainder of the tests (at least 436) have been conducted underground. The first Soviet underground test occurred in October 1961. The first Soviet underground test announced by the United States occurred on 2 February 1962 at the KTS.[5] The most tests in

---

1. Lynn Sykes and Steven Ruggi prepared the sections and tables on underground testing and yield estimation. The sections and tables on atmospheric testing were prepared by the *Databook* staff.

    Lynn Sykes is affiliated with the Lamont-Doherty Geological Observatory and Department of Geological Sciences of Columbia University. Steven Ruggi was affiliated with the Department of Political Science, Columbia University at the time this chapter was written and now works in documentary film making. Sykes and Ruggi wish to thank Dan Davis and Paul Richards for critically reading their manuscript, and the MacArthur Faculty Research Program in Conflict, Peace, and Security of Columbia University for financial support.

    An earlier version of this chapter was published as a Nuclear Weapons Databook Working Paper, "Soviet Underground Nuclear Testing: Inferences from Seismic Observations and Historical Perspective," NWD 86-4, November 1986.

2. This includes the unavailability of seismograms from the standard Soviet seismograph network for dates of known nuclear explosions and a failure to publish standard seismic information, such as arrival times and amplitudes of their explosions from their standard stations, as is done for earthquakes. In contrast, much more is known about U.S. nuclear testing. Yields of many U.S. explosions have been published, especially for explosions before 1973, and most tests are announced; see Robert S. Norris, Thomas B. Cochran, and William M. Arkin, "Known U.S. Nuclear Tests, July 1945 to December 1987," Nuclear Weapons Databook Working Paper, NWD 86-2 (Rev. 2A), January 1988.

3. The announcement in the *New York Times* of 2 April 1986 that the United States changed its procedure for estimating yields of Soviet nuclear tests seems to resolve some of these issues; see Michael R. Gordon, "CIA Changes Way it Measures Soviet Atom Tests," *New York Times*, 2 April 1986, pp. A1, A10. See also, Lynn R. Sykes and Dan M. Davis, "The Yields of Soviet Strategic Weapons," *Scientific American*, January 1987, pp. 29-37. This reevaluation, and another one in about 1979, leads to a lowering of the calculated yields of explosions that register given seismic amplitudes. The recognition that yields of past Soviet explosions have been seriously overestimated understandably necessitates a recalculation and reassessment of yields of past Soviet underground explosions. Sykes and Ruggi have recalculated yields in a manner that is consistent with current understanding of factors that must be taken into account in making more accurate estimates, such as variations in attenuation of short-period seismic waves among test sites and the effect of tectonic release on seismic surface waves generated by underground nuclear explosions. See also, U. S. Congress, Office of Technology Assessment, *Seismic Verification of Nuclear Testing Treaties*, OTA-ISC-361 (Washington, GPO, 1988).

4. A 1958 intelligence document notes that three tests were associated with naval applications—two underwater and one surface burst; CIA, Office of Scientific Intelligence, *Impact of a September 1958 Nuclear Test Moratorium on Soviet Nuclear Weapons Capabilities*, Prepared for the Ad Hoc Panel on Nuclear Test Limitations, Appendix E, 18 March 1958, p. 7. A September 1957 test off the coast of Novaya Zemlya could be the second underwater burst noted in this document.

5. The French Ministry of Defense estimates that 182 Soviet tests were conducted before 1963, 174 of which were conducted in the atmosphere and eight underground; Minister de la Defence, Direction de Centre d'Experimentations Nucleaire, *Organization et Functionnement de Centre d'Experimentation Nucleaire*, Dossier No. 1, "Essais Nucleaires, Tableau Recapitulatif des Explosions Annoncees et Presumees," Piece No. 7/41, 31 January 1985. Three of these underground tests are assumed to have been conducted underwater.

10
Testing Areas

Effects of Various Treaties Limiting Nuclear Testing

The Limited Test Ban Treaty (LTBT) of 1963, which has now been ratified by more than 125 countries, including the United States and the Soviet Union, prohibits nuclear explosions by the signatories in the atmosphere, space, and underwater. While the LTBT did not prohibit underground testing, it did prohibit underground tests if they cause radioactive materials to be present outside the borders of the state with jurisdiction or control over the test. There is no indication that either the Soviet Union or the United States has violated the main provision of the LTBT; neither has tested in the atmosphere, space, or underwater since 1963. However, both countries have conducted underground tests that have vented into the atmosphere, including tests that vented radioactive materials that were detected beyond their borders. Hence, both countries are, strictly speaking, in violation of that provision of the LTBT.

The Soviet Union and the United States signed the bilateral Threshold Test Ban Treaty (TTBT) in July 1974. The TTBT took effect after 31 March 1976. It sets a limit of 150 kilotons on the size of nuclear weapons tests that can be conducted by either of the two parties. This treaty also specifies that nuclear weapons tests will be conducted only at designated sites and that certain geophysical and geological information on distinct subareas of test sites will be exchanged upon ratification of the treaty. It also calls for the exchange of yield and other information on certain calibration explosions for distinct testing areas.

A companion treaty, the Peaceful Nuclear Explosions Treaty (PNET), was signed by the two countries in 1976. It prohibits individual explosions with yields exceeding 150 kilotons. It also specifies verification procedures and on-site inspection procedures for groups of explosions having aggregate yields exceeding 150 kilotons.

The U.S. Senate has not ratified either the TTBT or the PNET. Both the United States and the Soviet Union have stated that they would abide by the terms of each treaty, and both claim that they have complied with those limits.

There have been several past attempts to negotiate a full or comprehensive test ban treaty (CTBT). The latest negotiations took place from 1977 to 1980 between the Soviet Union, the United States and the United Kingdom. A comprehensive treaty still does not exist, and negotiations toward it were halted between 1980 and 1987. On 17 September 1987 the United States and the Soviet Union announced that the two sides had reached agreement to resume talks on nuclear testing by 1 December 1987. The first step under these negotiations has been to try to reach agreement on effective measures for verifying the 150-kiloton yield threshold under the TTBT. The two parties would then proceed to negotiate further intermediate limitations on nuclear testing (that is, limiting the size and/or frequency of tests), which could lead to the ultimate objective of a complete cessation of nuclear testing, as part of an effective disarmament process. Under a low-yield threshold test ban treaty (LYTBT), in which testing would be forbidden above some low yield, the precise value would be based on verification capabilities.

The 150-kiloton limits of the TTBT and PNET were not set by seismological detection and identification capabilities for underground explosions, but by other considerations. It is clear that, since they took effect in 1976, the two treaties have had an impact on the sizes or yields of nuclear weapons that could be tested at full yield. By 1976 both the Soviet Union and the United States had conducted several tests of one megaton (1000 kilotons) or larger. Both countries have tested repeatedly near the 150-kiloton limit of the TTBT since 31 March 1976, but as argued here, neither has tested significantly in excess of that limit.

one year was 50 in 1961 (see Table 10.3). The annual average of known tests in the 1950s was nine; in the 1960s, 17; in the 1970s, 19; and thus far in the 1980s, 20. The average for 38 years is a test every 22 days.

For all known Soviet explosions the combined yield is estimated to be 470 megatons, the equivalent of 30,000 Hiroshima bombs and over two and one-half times the U.S. total. Approximately 450 megatons of the total was detonated in the atmosphere prior to 1963, most in a 16-month period between September 1961 and December 1962. Since the unratified Threshold Test Ban Treaty (TTBT) took effect on 31 March 1976, the annual average yield has been about 570 kilotons, just slightly higher than the U.S. average.

Approximately two-thirds of the known Soviet nuclear explosions have occurred at the two main test sites: at the KTS (49 percent) and on the island of Novaya Zemlya in the Arctic (19 percent).

Main Areas of Testing in the Soviet Union

The Soviet Union has done repeated testing of underground nuclear explosions in six main areas (see Figure 10.1): the KTS in eastern Kazakhstan, in western Kazakhstan at sites near Azgir and Astrakhan, near Orenburg between the Volga River and the Ural Mountains, and at two sites on Novaya Zemlya Island (herein cited as northern and southern sites). In addition, the So-

10

Testing Areas

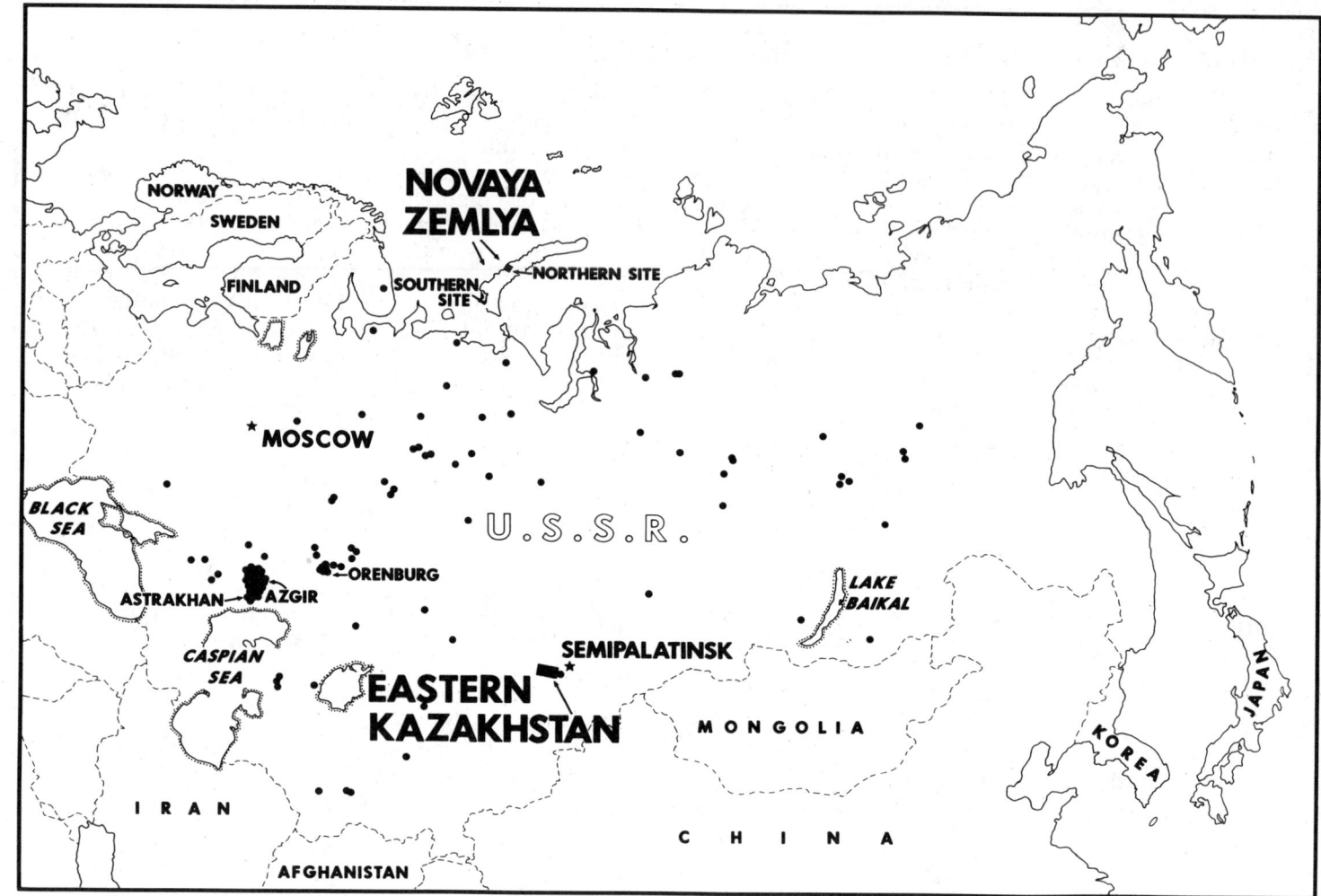

Figure 10.1 Soviet underground atomic weapons testing areas, 1963-1987 (solid boxes), and sites of underground explosions for peaceful purposes (dots).

viet Union has conducted a number of other underground nuclear tests at a wide variety of sites throughout the country. Many of these involve either one or a few explosions at a given site. A few of these explosions have been described as being used for peaceful purposes, but the actual program of PNEs is probably much larger and includes many explosions for various applications away from areas of repeated testing.

The greatest number of Soviet underground nuclear explosions have been conducted at the KTS (see Table 10.5). Atmospheric testing was conducted at that site prior to the Limited Test Ban Treaty (LTBT) of 1963.[6] The largest underground tests conducted there had a yield of about 180 kilotons. All larger underground tests were detonated in the Arctic at Novaya Zemlya. The first Soviet underground explosion announced by the United States was conducted on 2 February 1962 at the KTS. An earlier, smaller underground test on 11 October 1961 was detonated in Central Asia, possibly also at the KTS.

Tests at eastern Kazakhstan on the KTS have occurred in three distinct areas—Shagan River, Degelen Mountain, and Konyastan[7]—the farthest point of each area being approximately 100 kilometers from the next. With a few exceptions, just over 300 tests have been exploded within a rectangle of about 2000 square miles (49.700° to 50.125° North by 77.700° to 79.100° East). Most of the Soviet tests at the KTS in the 1960s occurred at Degelen Mountain and were confined to yields less than a few tens of kilotons. After 1968 most of the larger tests at the KTS, those of 50 kilotons or larger, were detonated at Shagan River. Since 1979 the Soviet Union has detonated its largest explosions at Shagan River. The So-

---

[6] The Treaty Banning Nuclear Weapon Tests in the Atmosphere, in Outer Space and Under Water, signed at Moscow on 5 August 1963, entered into force on 10 October 1963.

[7] P. D. Marshall, T. C. Bache, and R. C. Lilwall, "Body Wave Magnitudes and Locations of Soviet Underground Explosions at the Semipalatinsk Test Site," U.K. Atomic Weapons Research Establishment Report No. 0 16/84, 1984.

viet Union also tested its largest PNE at Shagan River on 15 January 1965.[8]

The second current test site is located on the island of Novaya Zemlya, which from 1958 through 1963 was the main Soviet test site. Of the 118 known tests that were held there through 1987, approximately 70 percent were atmospheric tests conducted during those early years. Included in these test series were the largest thermonuclear bombs ever exploded by any nation. Since the LTBT came into force in 1963, the Soviets have conducted underground tests on Novaya Zemlya at two sites. The northern site, where 28 tests were conducted through 1987, is a 100-square mile area (73.300° to 73.400° North by 54.500° to 55.160° East) on the Matochkin Shar Strait (Proliv). Devices are probably transported by ship from the Kola peninsula to a small dock at 73.385° North, 54.735° East, on the channel. Tests at the northern Novaya Zemlya site included two small underground explosions in 1964, and one large underground explosion per year at that site from 1966 through 1974.[9] In addition, explosions with yields of about 500 kilotons were detonated in August and October 1975.

In the fall of 1973, the Soviet Union opened a new testing area in southern Novaya Zemlya, where it tested a relatively small explosion of about 70 kilotons on 27 September. This test was followed by the largest underground explosion ever detonated by the Soviet Union—a test of 3450 ± 610 kilotons on 27 October 1973. Two additional megaton-size tests were conducted at the southern test site in the fall of 1974 and the fall of 1975.

Since the TTBT took effect in March 1976, the Soviet Union has continued to use the northern test site, with several tests in the 50-100 kiloton range. The southern Novaya Zemlya test site is not known to have been used since 1975.

The Soviet Union has conducted repeated underground nuclear explosions at two sites to the north of the Caspian Sea in western Kazakhstan, and at a site farther north near Orenburg. The Azgir area, near 47.8° North, 48.1° East was the site of at least 16 underground tests from 1966 to 1979. Eight of those from 1968 through 1979 had yields of 20 to 60 kilotons. That area is characterized regionally by thick salt deposits and large salt domes.[10] The Soviet Union has announced one PNE, conducted in salt, with a yield of 25 kilotons.[11] The date and location of the event was not announced by the Soviet Union, but it is reasonably and unambiguously associated with the Azgir explosion of 1 July 1968.[12] Another explosion in salt with a yield of 1.1 kilotons appears to be the event of 22 April 1966. The size and frequency of testing at Azgir would argue that at least some of those explosions may have been for weapons testing. Many and perhaps all of

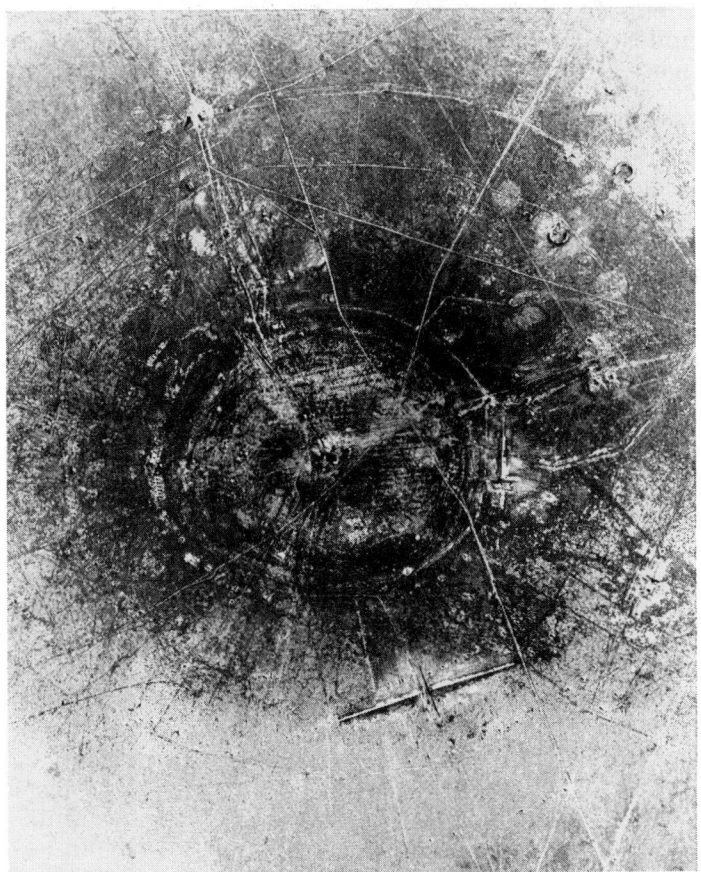

Figure 10.2 U-2 photograph of a crater from a nuclear test at the Kazakh Test Site.

them, however, may have been tests of the technology for detonating PNEs in salt, especially for creating cavities for the storage of petroleum and radioactive waste products. No known explosions occurred at Azgir from 1980 through 1985.

About 25 underground nuclear explosions were detonated to the north of Astrakhan, near 46.8° North, 48.2° East from 1980 through 1984. (The Astrakhan site is about 200 kilometers to the south of the Azgir area.) The calculated yields of several of those events are in the 5-15 kiloton range, while a number of others are smaller than five kilotons. Two explosions having yields near 15 kilotons were detonated near 51.6° North, 54.5° East, in 1971 and 1973, and six nuclear explosions with calculated yields of 5-27 kilotons were set off on two dates in July 1984 at 51.4° North, 53.3° East, in the vicinity of Orenburg. The underground explosions near Astrakhan and

---

8 This test produced a large crater that is readily visible on satellite photographs. The location of that crater has been used as the so-called master event for locating nearby underground explosions, since it and surrounding underground explosions have all been recorded by seismograph stations.
9 The calculated yields of those explosions range from about 90 to 2000 kilotons.
10 Lynn R. Sykes, Jack F. Evernden, and Ines Cifuentes, "Seismic Methods for Verifying Nuclear Test Bans," *Physics, Technology and the Nuclear Arms Race*, American Institute of Physics Conference Proceedings No. 104, 1983, pp. 85-133.
11 Ola Dahlman and Hans Israelson, *Monitoring Underground Nuclear Explosions* (Amsterdam: Elsevier Scientific Publishing Co., 1977).
12 P. D. Marshall, D. L. Springer, and H. C. Rodean, "Magnitude Corrections for Attenuation in the Upper Mantle," *Geophysical Journal of the Royal Astronomical Society*, Vol. 57, 1979, pp. 609-638.

10
Atmospheric Testing

Orenburg appear to be part of major programs to create underground storage facilities for gas condensates near major gas-producing fields in the Soviet Union.[13]

Tests have occurred in every month of the year at the KTS, though the concentration is in the second half of the year (64 percent versus 36 percent) (see Table 10.7). Because of the extreme climate at Novaya Zemlya (the sites are over 600 kilometers above the Arctic Circle), most of the underground tests there are conducted in September and October, with only a handful held during August, November, and December. Historically, the Soviets have tested at the Kazakh and Novaya Zemlya test sites nearly three times as often in the second half of the year as in the first half.

Atmospheric Testing and Nuclear Weapons Design[14]

From the limited amount of information available, it is possible to partially reconstruct the evolution of early Soviet warhead design through certain milestones in tests. The first atmospheric Soviet test was on 29 August 1949. Joe 1 (named after Joseph Stalin) was a plutonium bomb similar in design to the Nagasaki-type FAT MAN bomb, with a comparable yield of approximately 10-20 kilotons.[15] Uranium-238 (U-238) was in close proximity to the fissile material, indicative of a natural uranium tamper.[16] The second test, Joe 2, took place two years later on 24 September 1951. This test was also of a plutonium bomb, exploded on the ground, or slightly underground. The efficiency of utilization of the plutonium was greater than that of Joe 1 and its yield was at least 25 kilotons.[17]

The Joe 3 test took place on 18 October 1951. Analysis of the debris indicated that detonation was most likely close to the ground (the data were most consistent with an air burst), and that both plutonium and U-235 were used as fissionable materials.[18] Joe 3 was the first test by the Soviet Union of the more efficient composite core design. The efficiency of utilization of the plutonium in the explosion was determined to be about 35 percent, but that of uranium-235 was not determined.[19] Assuming a core of 3.5 kilograms of plutonium and 7 kilograms of uranium-235 (a ratio of uranium to plutonium lower than that employed in U.S. warheads at the time), the United States estimated the yield at about 50 kilotons.[20]

The Soviet Union did not test again until 12 August 1953 when the test named Joe 4, the first test of a Soviet thermonuclear device, took place. It was a tower shot with a yield of 200-300 kilotons. The Joe 4 device appears to have been a single-stage, boosted, fission-type configuration using U-235 as a fissile component and lithium deuteride as a fusion material.[21]

Tests named Joe 5, 6, and 7 also occurred in August 1953, all possibly of low-yield fission weapons. According to a 28 August 1954 U.S. National Intelligence Estimate:

> By the end of 1953, the USSR had tested small, medium, and large-yield nuclear weapons, and had employed thermonuclear boosting principles to produce energy yields in the range of the equivalent of a few thousand to at least one million tons of TNT. By the end of 1953, moreover, the USSR had reached a point in weapon technology at which it was capable of producing a wide variety of weapon types, and nuclear warheads for weapons other than bombs.[22]

Little is known about the design of the devices used in the seven tests in the September-October 1954 test series. More is known about the five tests of the 1955 test series. The first two tests, Joe 15 and 16, were atmospheric bursts of fission devices using plutonium with yields of 5 and 25 kilotons, respectively. Joe 17 was an underwater test (the first conducted by the Soviets) of a plutonium device with a yield on the order of 20 kilotons. The Joe 18 test took place on 6 November 1955 and had a yield of 215 kilotons. The presence of a thermonuclear component was evident from the debris,[23] and it is believed to have been a weaponized version of the Joe 4 device, a boosted configuration reduced to a more easily

---

13 Iris Y. P. Borg, "Peaceful Nuclear Explosions in Soviet Gas Condensate Fields," *Energy and Technology Review* (Lawrence Livermore National Laboratory), May 1983, pp. 30-37.
14 This section on atmospheric testing and nuclear weapons design and Table 10.1 were developed from Jeffrey I. Sands, Robert S. Norris, and Thomas B. Cochran, "Known Soviet Nuclear Explosions, 1949-1985, Revised Preliminary List," Nuclear Weapons Databook Working Paper, NWD 86-3, 2 June 1986.
15 Two reports from the Joint Atomic Energy Intelligence Committee (JAEIC), *Status of the Soviet Atomic Energy Program*, National Scientific Intelligence Estimate, 27 December 1950 and NSIE-1, CIA/SI 13-52, 8 January 1953, provide yield estimates of Joe 1 assuming a bomb model containing six kilograms of plutonium. The earlier report provides an estimate of 20 kilotons, and the latter 10-20 kilotons. All explosion times and dates are Greenwich Mean Time (GMT) unless otherwise noted.
16 See Doyle L. Northrup, Director AFOAT-1, Memorandum for Major-General Nelson, 19 September 1949.
17 JAEIC, 8 January 1953., *op. cit.*, p. 11.
18 *Ibid.* Production of highly enriched uranium by the gaseous diffusion method began in the Soviet Union in 1951.
19 *Ibid.*
20 *Ibid.* This assumes the efficiency of uranium utilization was 23 percent.
21 Although the Joe 4 device utilized solid lithium-deuteride (Li-D) fuel, it was not a two-stage thermonuclear device using an approach comparable to the Teller-Ulam design. York argues that "[i]t evidently involved one of several possible straightforward configurations for igniting relative small amounts of thermonuclear material (as compared to the U.S. Mike and Bravo devices) with a relative large amount of fissile material'; Herbert F. York, *The Advisors: Oppenheimer, Teller and the Superbomb* (San Francisco: W.H. Freeman and Co., 1976), p. 95. York elsewhere notes that Joe 4 was "a development step the United States bypassed in its successful search for a configuration that would make it possible to produce an arbitrarily large explosion with a relatively small quantity of fissionable material;" Herbert York, "The Debate Over the Hydrogen Bomb," *Scientific American*, October 1975, p. 111. Thus the lithium-deuteride was probably contained within, or proximate to, the fissile core. Li-D is less effective than deuterium-tritium (D-T) in a boosted fission device because neutrons that otherwise would be used to increase the fission efficiency are required to breed tritium from the lithium. The Joe 4 device may have been designed to confirm that solid Li-D could be used as a fusion material, rather than deuterium or deuterium and tritium in liquid or gaseous form. This was not confirmed in the U.S. program until the 28 February 1954 Bravo test. Holloway argues that since the Joe 18 device was believed to be a "weaponized version" of Joe 4, the Joe 4 design was not merely a step in the development of a staged thermonuclear device but a third type of thermonuclear bomb; David Holloway, "Soviet Thermonuclear Development," *International Security*, Vol. 4, No. 3, Winter 1979-1980, p. 194.
22 CIA, *Soviet Capabilities and Probable Courses of Action Through Mid-1959*, NIE 11-4-54, 28 August 1954 (partially declassified), p. 52. Actually, the highest yield achieved by the end of 1953 was 200-300 kilotons, although yields up to one megaton were feasible using the thermonuclear boosting principle tested with Joe 4.
23 Joint Intelligence Committee (JIC), *The JIC Semi-Annual Review of Trends in Communist Bloc Policy Including Communist China (1 October 1955 - 29 February 1956)*, JIC 133/3(56), 16 May 1956, p. 6.

10
Underground Testing

deliverable size. Finally, the Joe 19 test of 22 November 1955, was the first test of a Soviet two-stage thermonuclear device employing something like the Teller-Ulam idea, the so-called superbomb. Its yield was about 1.6 megatons. This thermonuclear weapon was the first superbomb to be delivered by aircraft. It was exploded at an altitude of several thousand feet.

Eleven high-yield thermonuclear tests were conducted from 1956 through 28 February 1958. The first five of these, through 16 April 1957, had rather low yield-to-weight ratios. Evidence of an improvement in yield-to-weight occurred beginning with the sixth high-yield thermonuclear test on 22 August 1957.[24] York claims that it took the Soviets "several more years following their 1955 test before they were able to match the explosions in [the U.S.] 1952 and 1954 tests."[25]

As of March 1958, the United States had determined that "at least three Soviet tests were associated with naval applications (two [deleted] underwater and one [deleted] surface burst), one test was conducted in conjunction with Army maneuvers, and two tests probably involved warheads in a surface-to-surface missile (SSM) and in an air-to-surface missile (ASM), respectively."[26] Although certain of the test configurations were compatible with available air-defense missiles, there was no evidence at that time that the Soviet Union had conducted either environmental effects tests using warheads compatible with air-defense applications or very high or ultrahigh altitude tests for anti-ballistic missile applications.[27]

The Soviets tested a 58 megaton multistage thermonuclear device on 30 October 1961, the largest yield device ever exploded. There is no evidence that such a high-yield device was ever weaponized,[28] though the United States believed that the device could have been delivered by the Bear long-range bomber.[29]

Underground Testing

In several ways Soviet underground testing since the LTBT of 1963 represents a continuation of its programs of testing in the atmosphere prior to 1963. For example, testing continued at two of the main areas used for atmospheric tests. Nevertheless, for a number of years the LTBT did have a decided impact on the maximum sizes of tests that the Soviet Union conducted underground: it did not conduct a megaton-size test until 1970.

Techniques have been developed over the last three decades that allow reliable discrimination between seismic signals from underground nuclear explosions and those from small earthquakes.[30] The United States, the United Kingdom, France, Sweden, and other governments maintain ongoing monitoring programs for the detection and identification of underground nuclear testing. The U.S. government has announced about 200 past Soviet underground tests, about half of all Soviet underground tests to date. The National Defense Research Institute of Sweden publishes an updated list of underground nuclear explosions by various countries.[31]

Calculation of Yields of Soviet Underground Explosions

Since the Soviet Union has not publicly released yield estimates for any of its nuclear weapons tests and has released yield information (but not precise times and places) for only a small number of PNEs, methods for the calculation of yields of most Soviet explosions must of necessity be indirect. There is enough variation in the attenuation of different types of seismic waves throughout the earth that those variations must be taken into account, or their effects calibrated, if yields are to be estimated with an accuracy better than about a factor of three.

Three main types of seismic waves can be used for yield calibration: short-period body waves (P-waves) that travel through the deep part of the earth to receiving stations, long-period surface waves, and short-period surface waves called L_g waves.[32]

Body waves have a great advantage for yield estimation in that they are recorded from explosions for the widest range of yields whereas surface waves are often not recorded from very small nuclear explosions. Body waves have the disadvantage that their attenuation varies considerably beneath various test sites. Thus, accurate yield estimates using P-waves must include a careful calibration for attenuation beneath each test site.

The attenuation of short-period P-waves is governed very much by the temperature structure of the upper mantle of the earth at depths from about 30 to 150 kilometers. This is illustrated in Figure 10.3: seismic waves

---

24 CIA, *Impact of a September 1958 Nuclear Test Moratorium, op. cit.*, p. 1.
25 York, *The Advisors, op. cit.*, p. 93.
26 CIA, *Impact of a September 1958 Nuclear Test Moratorium, op. cit.*, p. 7.
27 Ibid., pp. 7-8. On 6 September 1961, the Soviets conducted a high-altitude burst over an experimental radar at Sary Shagan, presumably to test electromagnetic pulse (EMP) effects on the radar. There were widespread but unconfirmed reports that this test was a live firing of an ABM warhead against a target; Prados, *Soviet Estimate*, p. 153. Harold Brown, then director of defense research and engineering at the Pentagon, argued that the Soviet Union had not conducted a test of a live ABM interceptor; see Freedman, *US Intelligence*, p. 87, referencing Edward Randolph Jayne, *The ABM Debate: Strategic Defense and National Security*, MIT Center for International Studies, June 1969.
28 York, *Advisors, op. cit.*, p. 93.
29 Minutes of meeting of the Status of U.S. and Soviet Nuclear Tests, 2 February 1962, presented to the President by representatives of the AEC, CIA, and DOD.
30 Sykes, Evernden, and Cifuentes, *op. cit.*, pp. 85-133; Lynn R. Sykes and Jack F. Evernden, "The Verification of a Comprehensive Nuclear Test Ban," *Scientific American*, October 1982, pp. 47-55.
31 National Defense Research Institute of Sweden (*Forsvarets Forskningsanstalt*, or FOA), *Nuclear Explosions 1945 - 29 November 1987* (printout), December 1987. We have not performed an independent analysis of seismic identification or discrimination for many of the small explosions listed in Table 10.2. In various papers Sykes and his colleagues, and others, have examined the spectral character of many Soviet explosions and have shown that their seismic signals can be discriminated from those of earthquakes. See Sykes, Evernden, and Cifuentes, *op. cit.*; Sykes and Evernden, *op. cit.*; Lynn R. Sykes and Ines Cifuentes, "Yields of Soviet Underground Nuclear Explosions from Seismic Surface Waves: Compliance with the Threshold Test Ban Treaty," *Proceedings of the National Academy of Sciences U.S.A.*, Vol. 81, 1984, pp. 1922-1925; Lynn R. Sykes and Graham C. Wiggins, "Yields of Soviet Underground Nuclear Explosions at Novaya Zemlya, 1964-1976, from Seismic Body and Surface Waves," *Proceedings of the National Academy of Sciences U.S.A.*, Vol. 83, 1986, pp. 201-205. See also, Dahlman and Israelson, *op. cit.*; Marshall, Bache and Lilwall, *op. cit.*; and P. W. Basham and P. D. Marshall, "Discrimination Between Earthquakes and Underground Explosions Employing an Improved M_S Scale: Supplementary Magnitude Data on Eurasian Events," *Seismolical Series Earth Physics Branch*, Vol. 63, Department of Energy, Mines and Resources, Earth Physics Branch, Ottawa, Canada, 1972.
32 The first two methods have been used for a longer time and are the main wave types used for estimation of yield in this chapter.

10

Underground Testing

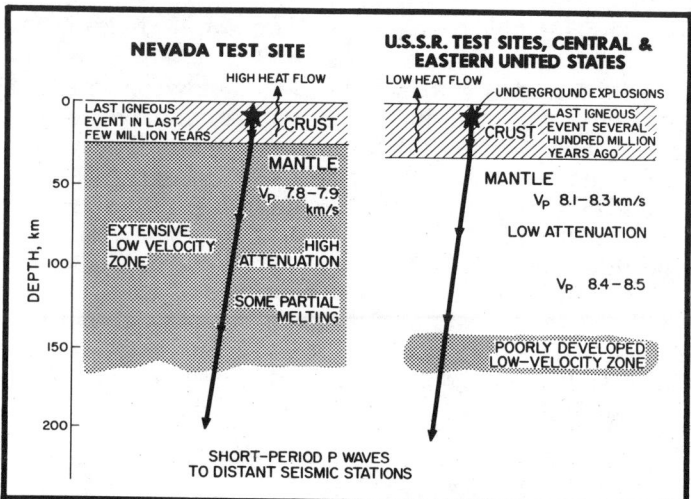

Figure 10.3 Schematic diagram of the seismic velocity and seismic attenuation structure of the outer 200 kilometers of the earth beneath the Nevada Test Site (left) and test sites in older, stable regions, such as the central and eastern United States and the main Soviet test sites (right). Variations in seismic velocity and attenuation are mainly related to variations in temperature. Temperatures are much higher at a given depth beneath Nevada than they are beneath the test sites shown on the right. Short-period P-waves leaving an explosion at the Nevada Test Site are smaller, by a factor or about two or three, than those leaving an explosion of the same yield at the test sites on the right.

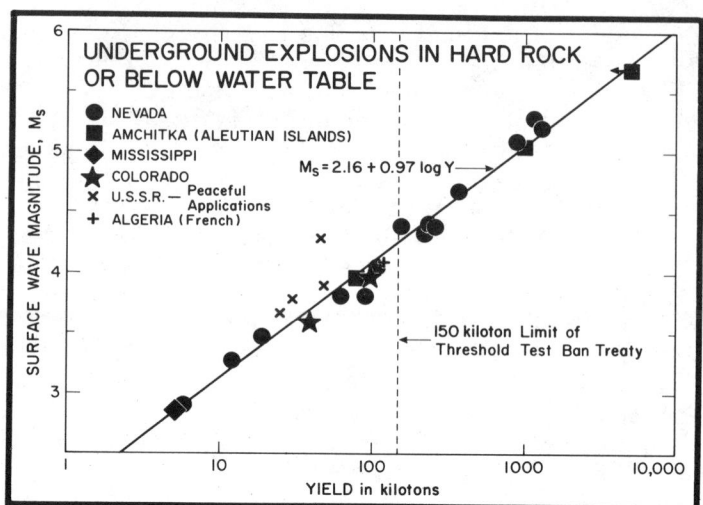

Figure 10.4 Calibration curve for the magnitude of seismic surface waves (M_s) as a function of yield for explosions of known yield at various test sites throughout the world.

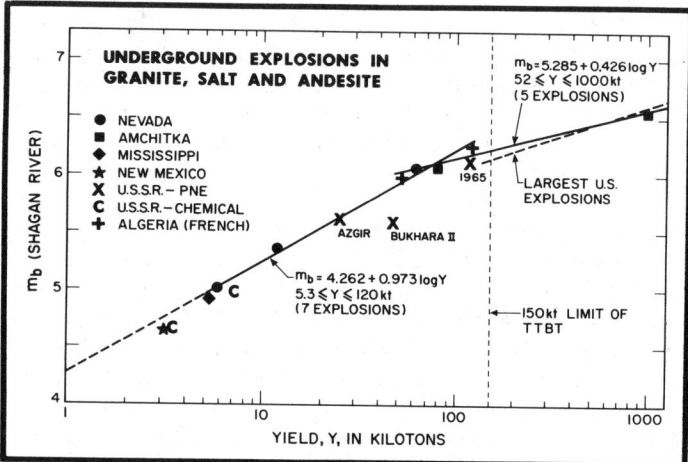

Figure 10.5 Calibration curve for magnitudes (m_b) of short-period P-waves as normalized to the Shagan River area of the Kazakh Test Site as a function of yield for contained underground nuclear explosions and two large chemical explosions in the Soviet Union. Various symbols denote data on explosions of known yield from various test sites normalized (that is, calibrated) for differences in attenuation beneath its site and Shagan River. In determining best-fitting linear relationships, Soviet data and that for Gnome explosion in New Mexico were not used. The m_b value of the 1965 explosion at the KTS, which produced a larger crater, was increased by 0.22 m_b units to account for the differences between the cratering and contained tests. Note that yields released by the Soviet Union for large chemical explosions in Central Asia and two of three PNEs fall close to predicted curve. The Bukhara II nuclear explosion was detonated at a depth close to a major geological boundary, which may account for its deviation from the predicted curve. Most of the m_b measurements are from Marshall, Bache, and Lilwall, *op. cit.*

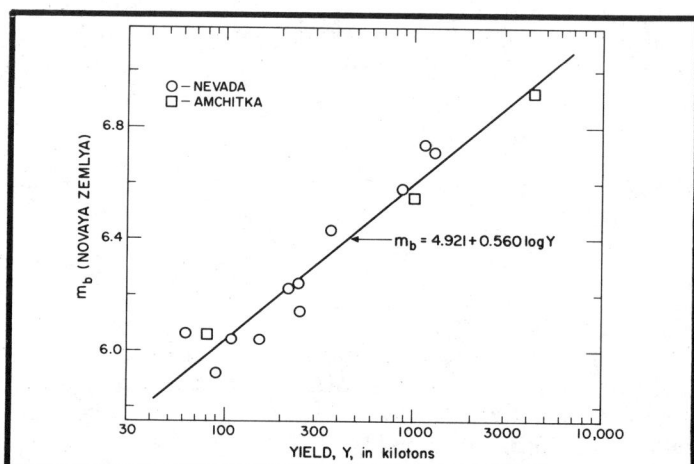

Figure 10.6 Magnitude (m_b) as a function of announced yields of very large explosions at the Nevada Test Site and Amchitka normalized to Novaya Zemlya.

10
Underground Testing

passing beneath the Nevada Test Site are highly attenuated compared to those leaving test sites in regions of older geology, such as the central and eastern United States and the main testing areas of the Soviet Union. High seismic attenuation and high temperatures at a given depth are highly correlated with low seismic velocities in that depth range, high electrical conductivity, greater heat flow from the lower crust and upper mantle, low shear velocities, and a variety of other geophysically observable parameters.[33]

Seismologists determine the seismic magnitude of an event by taking the logarithm of a measured amplitude at a given station and making a correction factor for distance so that observations at various distances give the same magnitude. The magnitude m_b is determined for short-period seismic waves and M_s for long-period surface waves.

Surface waves have the advantages of being of longer wavelength and of not being sensitive to shorter wavelength variations in attenuation and to scattering in the earth. They have a disadvantage in that underground nuclear tests typically trigger the release of natural stresses in the earth. The effect of tectonic release mainly affects longer period waves such as surface waves. Tectonic release varies from being negligible for some explosions to being very large for others. When Sykes and his colleagues have determined yields using surface waves, they have tried to do so only for those explosions for which tectonic release is small-to-moderate, or in cases in which the mechanism of the release is such as to average nearly zero for observations made over a range of azimuths. Sophisticated analyses of longer period surface waves now permit the contaminating effect of tectonic release to be separated from the effect of the pure explosion itself.

Figure 10.4 shows M_s as a function of yield for explosions of announced yield in various places. It shows that a straight-line relationship—in which the slope is nearly one between M_s and the logarithm of the yield—fits the data with relatively little scatter over a wide range of yields from 5 to 5000 kilotons. The relationship $M_s = 2.16 + 0.97 \log Y$ is used in this study in deriving yields from surface wave observations.

In contrast, a straight-line relationship does not fit the data very well for m_b as a function of yield for the same large range of yields. This is because the narrow passband used in making measurements of m_b passes from one side to the other of a parameter called the "corner frequency." The excitation of seismic waves differs considerably for frequencies much lower or much higher than the corner frequency. The corner frequency for an explosion of about 100 kilotons is within or close to the passband in which m_b is measured. Thus, it is expected that the slope of the m_b-log (yield) curve will be smaller for explosions larger than about 100 kilotons than it is for smaller explosions. This can be seen in Figure 10.5: m_b values from explosions of known yield at other test sites in very competent rock such as granite, salt, or andesite are corrected to the Shagan River testing area of the KTS using the relative attenuation values (m_b biases) of Der, et al.[34] One linear relationship with a slope close to one (solid circles) fits the data well for yields between about 5 and 75 kilotons. A smaller slope (0.426) is needed to fit the data for yields between 75 and 1000 kilotons. The two expressions shown in that figure were used in deriving yields from m_b estimates for explosions at the KTS.

Figure 10.6 shows m_b (as normalized to Novaya Zemlya) as a function of yield for very large U.S. explosions at Nevada and Amchitka Island in the Aleutians. The m_b scale in that figure can be normalized to the Nevada Test Site by subtracting 0.351 m_b units, a value derived from the relative attenuation of P-waves beneath those test sites.[35] Compared to Figure 10.5, Figure 10.6 used very large explosions in a greater variety of rock types. The scatter in m_b values for a given yield is smaller for explosions of very high yield. The upper equation in Figure 10.6 was used in deriving yields for large Soviet explosions at Novaya Zemlya.[36]

While variations in the magnitude-yield relationship do occur for different rock types, they are most extreme when seismic coupling in hard rocks is compared with that for dry alluvium. Unlike Nevada, thicknesses of dry alluvium are very limited in the Soviet Union, and the water table is at a relatively shallow depth within the main testing areas. Thus, the assumption of a magnitude-yield relationship appropriate to explosions in either hard rock or below the water table is justified for explosions larger than a few kilotons at the main Soviet testing areas.

It is reasonable to assume that most of the explosions at the KTS were fired in granite (which is shown outcropping on available geological maps within the testing area) or in hard rocks of comparable seismic coupling.[37] The relationship used to calculate yields for large explosions at Novaya Zemlya is not very sensitive to seismic coupling for contained explosions of large yield. The same magnitude-yield relationship that was used for explosions outside of the main Soviet testing areas (which assumes somewhat poorer coupling than for explosions in granite, salt, or andesite) was used for Novaya Zemlya ex-

---

33. Zoltan A. Der, Thomas McElfresh, Robert Wagner, and James Burnetti, "Spectral Character of P-waves from Nuclear Explosions and Yield Estimation," *Bulletin of the Seismological Society of America*, Vol. 75, 1985, pp. 379-390, 1222-1223. Der, et al., and other researchers have used the decay of the seismic spectrum from frequencies of about 1 to 8 Hertz (Hz) to make independent estimates of the relative attenuation of P-waves beneath various testing areas. The following testing areas are found to be associated with low seismic attenuation: Mississippi (where two U.S. tests were detonated in the 1960s), Amchitka Island in the Aleutians, and the main Soviet testing areas in eastern and western Kazakhstan and Novaya Zemlya. Regions of higher seismic attenuation include the Nevada Test Site, central Nevada, sites of U.S. peaceful explosions on the Colorado plateau in the western United States, and the former French test site in southern Algeria. These differences in attenuation of short-period seismic waves were taken into account in calibrating the yields of Soviet explosions using measured short-period seismic waves from those tests.
34. Der, et al., *op. cit.*, pp. 379-390, 1222-1223.
35. *Ibid.*
36. Sykes and Wiggins, *op. cit.*
37. Dahlman and Israelson, *op. cit.*; R. W. Alewine and T. C. Bache, *Monitoring a Threshold Test Ban Treaty*, presentation at the Symposium on Verification of Nuclear Test Ban Treaties, American Geophysical Union, Baltimore, Maryland, 2 June 1983.

10

Underground Testing

plosions with yields smaller than about 150 kilotons. If the seismic coupling is better, those yields have been overestimated.

Salt is taken to be the testing medium at the two sites in western Kazakhstan.[38] Numerous authors assumed that the 25 kiloton explosion in salt described by the Soviets was the explosion at Azgir of 1 July 1968.[39] That event falls almost exactly on the regression line shown in Figure 10.5. Thus, that relationship between m_b and yield was used in calculating yields of explosions in western Kazakhstan, after making a correction for differences in attenuation of .027 m_b units between the KTS and Azgir (or 0.378 between the Nevada Test Site and Azgir).

In calculating yields for small explosions, that is, for those smaller than about five kilotons, regression relationships determined for higher yields are used with extrapolations to smaller yields. The resulting calculated yields probably represent minimum estimates for yields smaller than about 5-10 kilotons. Smaller seismic magnitudes could result if the explosions were, in fact, detonated in materials of lower competence and poorer seismic coupling than were assumed by Sykes and Ruggi, a situation that is possible for small explosions detonated at shallow depth. Obviously, much more work needs to be done in calculating accurate yields for small explosions. In addition, the seismic magnitudes of very small explosions in the Soviet Union that Sykes and Ruggi have used to calculate yields come mainly from single large seismic arrays. The uncertainty of such individual m_b determinations is much larger than it is when m_b is taken as an average over many stations. In addition, it is assumed that station corrections derived from larger explosions for those large arrays can be applied to smaller events. Thus, while there is no question that the Soviet Union has conducted tests of a few kilotons and tests in the sub-kiloton range, estimates of yield in those ranges should be taken as very approximate. For that reason the histograms are shown as dashed lines for yields less than five kilotons.

Soviet Underground Nuclear Explosions

Table 10.2 contains a summary list of known and presumed underground nuclear explosions in the Soviet Union. Prior to 1987, the Soviet Union announced only a small number of their PNEs and none of their underground weapons tests. The accuracy of the locations of the events reported varies considerably depending upon the number of seismic stations recording them and the location procedures that were used.[40] The origin time or detonation time of underground explosions is computed using standard travel-time tables for short-period P-waves. The travel times to distant seismic stations are very much influenced by the velocity structure of the outer 150 kilometers of the earth beneath both the test site and the receiving station. Table 10.2 lists the actual computed times using standard tables.[41]

The list of Soviet explosions undoubtedly does not include many very small tests, that is, those in the 1960s of yields less than five kilotons, and more recent explosions with yields less than about one or two kilotons.[42] The Norwegian and Swedish seismic arrays locate explosions with yields of a few kilotons as well as those in the sub-kiloton range that are not located routinely by standard seismological reporting services. The Norwegian arrays have good detection capabilities for well-coupled explosions down to the sub-kiloton range for underground tests in the western one-third of the Soviet Union.

Most of the underground explosions that have been positively identified by various seismic criteria as being underground explosions and not earthquakes are confined to known testing areas and occur exactly at specific hours or minutes of the day. The main Soviet sites are characterized by very little seismic activity. Hence, a seismic event located in or near one of those areas, especially if it occurs exactly on a minute or hour, is readily suspected to be an underground explosion.[43]

Table 10.4 lists 18 small events that have not been positively identified as underground explosions, large chemical explosions, or earthquakes. About half of them were detected and located by the LASA seismic array in Montana.[44]

---

38 Sykes, et al., op. cit.; Borg, op. cit.
39 Marshall, Bache, and Lilwall, op. cit.
40 The most accurate locations are those of Marshall, Bache, and Lilwall, op. cit., in which large numbers of explosions at eastern Kazakhstan were located by the "joint epicentral determination" technique, using the cratering event of January 1965 as an absolute standard that can be located by satellite photography. Marshall, Bache, and Lilwall state that the 95 percent confidence limits are such that with few exceptions locations are accurate to three kilometers or better.

For other events that have been recorded by tens to hundreds of seismograph stations, we used the locations published by standard seismological reporting services, such as the U.S. Geological Survey and the International Seismological Centre. The absolute locations of nearly all those events are probably better than 20 kilometers. The relative locations of explosions at given test sites can be improved considerably using the joint epicentral determination technique, but we have not attempted to do that here. A number of the smallest explosions reported in Table 10.2 have been located using some of the large seismic arrays, such as the large aperture seismic array (LASA) in Montana, the Hagfors array in Sweden, and the Norwegian Seismic Array (NORSAR) in Norway. Locations made by large arrays for distant events may have uncertainties as large as 100 kilometers.

41 In most cases, the origin times come out a few seconds earlier than an even hour or minute. The relatively early (or late) computed origin times can be taken as an indication of relatively high (or low) velocity structure beneath given test sites.
H. C. Rodean, "ISC Origin Times for Announced and Presumed Underground Nuclear Explosions at Several Test Sites," Lawrence Livermore Laboratory, USRL-52882, 3 December 1979, argues that early mean times (and hence high average velocities) are associated with Soviet test sites, and later times with the U.S. test site in Nevada and the former French test site in southern Algeria. Small corrections for velocity structure and for the standard travel-time tables would indicate that those events occurred exactly on the hour and minute. Likewise, most tests by the United States have been detonated in the first 0.0-0.2 seconds of a given minute. In most cases, that minute is the start of a given hour or half-hour.

42 At the sub-kiloton level it is not clear if all of the events in Table 10.2 are, in fact, nuclear explosions or if some are large chemical explosions for industrial and other purposes. Chemical explosions with yields of one to a few kilotons are very rare and typically occur less than or about once per year in the United States and the Soviet Union. Chemical explosions with yields of about 0.1 kilotons occur many times per year at a few specific locations in the United States; those with yields of .01 kilotons are very common at many places.

43 That this is not always the case can be seen from an event that occurred near but not on the eastern Kazakhstan test site on 20 March 1976. Various seismic discriminants—including a focal mechanism and wave-form matching of P-waves, as well as its location near a major fault—all indicate that the event was an earthquake and not an underground explosion; Marshall, Bache, and Lilwall, op. cit.; Sykes, Evernden, and Cifuentes, op. cit.; C. F. Pooley, A. Douglas, and R. G. Pierce, "The Seismic Disturbances of 20 March 1976, East Kazakhstan: Earthquake or Explosions?," Geophysical Journal of the Royal Astronomical Society, Vol. 74, 1983, pp. 621-631.

44 While there is no doubt that all or most of them can be identified positively, using well-developed seismic discriminants and satellite photography, as being either underground explosions, large chemical explosions, or earthquakes, we have not sought to do that here.

10
Underground Testing

Distribution of Soviet Underground Nuclear Tests by Time and Yield

The precise number and characteristics of Soviet underground nuclear tests are unknown, although various estimates of yield and location have been made using seismic methods (see Table 10.2).[45] The Soviet Union conducted its first two known underground tests in 1961 and 1962 and did not test again underground until 1964. The Soviet Union detonated its largest underground test—3.5 megatons—on 27 October 1973. In 1965 the Soviet Union detonated a PNE that produced a large crater at the KTS for which the announced yield was 125 kilotons. Between July 1974, when the TTBT was signed, and 31 March 1976, when the TTBT took effect, the Soviet Union detonated five explosions with yields larger than 200 kilotons.

From 1 January 1980 to 31 December 1984, there were an estimated 129 Soviet nuclear tests. For that same five-year period, there were an estimated 45 Soviet tests with yields of 20 kilotons or greater. Of these 45, nine occurred at scattered locations around the Soviet Union, some or all of which may have been for peaceful purposes. The remaining 36 events were all detonated at two sites, the KTS and northern Novaya Zemlya, and were undoubtedly for military purposes. None of the tests in western Kazakhstan during that period had yields in excess of 20 kilotons.

On 29 July 1985 the Soviet Union announced a moratorium on nuclear testing, to begin 6 August 1985. There does not appear to be any indication that the Soviets tested during the time the moratorium was in effect—6 August 1985 until 25 February 1987. Soon after the Soviet Union announced its moratorium, statements were made by National Security Advisor, Robert C. McFarlane and other U.S. officials that the Soviet Union had rushed to carry out a major series of tests and that they had conducted a particularly large number of tests earlier in 1985.[46] The available evidence, including that provided by the National Defense Research Institute of Sweden, does not support those contentions.[47] In 1985 there were nine Soviet explosions, compared with 21 to 31 in each of the preceding seven years. Two of these explosions were announced by the Soviets as PNEs.[48] The Soviet Union carried out five tests of the same yield range in 1985, all of which took place at the KTS (Table 10.2).

Histograms of Soviet Underground Testing as a Function of Yield

There are a number of uncertainties and pitfalls in the estimation of yields of Soviet explosions. These difficulties arise from the fact that the Soviets have not publicly released yields for any of their underground weapon tests and have released yield information for only a few of their peaceful explosions. Even in those cases, the Soviet Union did not directly associate particular explosions with announced yields or with a specific place and date. In many cases the association with a specific explosion of known location, date, and seismic magnitude is fairly obvious, but in other cases assumptions must be made about which yield is associated with which explosion.

The more accurate yield estimates are believed to be associated with explosions of the last 15 years at the Shagan River testing area at the KTS with yields in excess of about 50 kilotons, and with those at Novaya Zemlya with yields in excess of about 80 kilotons.[49] This is because the yields of explosions away from these main testing areas have been derived using a *single* magnitude-yield relationship. It is very likely, however, that a variety of relationships must apply, given the likely geographical variations in attenuation of short-period P-waves in the mantle beneath those explosion sites and in rock type (and hence seismic coupling) near the explosion points.

The Soviet Union conducted its largest underground nuclear weapons tests at two Arctic test sites in Novaya Zemlya between October 1966 and October 1975 (see Figure 10.13). Eleven of those tests had calculated yields of 420 to 3450 kilotons. Six of these events constitute a very prominent peak at 500 kilotons in the histogram for Novaya Zemlya (Figure 10.8, top).[50] The large number of tests near 500 kilotons, especially in the interval between the signing of the TTBT in 1974 and the date it took effect in 1976, as well as the high yield of that peak, strongly suggest the testing of one or more weapons at full yield.

The Soviet SS-17 Mod 3, SS-18 Mod 4, and SS-19 Mod 3 ICBMs, all MIRVed, became operational about 1979; earlier Mods became operatonal a few years earlier. Correct determinations of the yields of the weapons on those three systems and of estimates of the megatonnage of current strategic systems could be derived from seismic data presented in Figures 10.7-10.12 and 10.13.

---

45 Dahlman and Israelson, *op. cit.*, list 190 Soviet explosions for 5 August 1963 to 31 December 1976, as compared to 198 in our list. For the period 5 August 1963 through 1985, we report 411 Soviet explosions, whereas the list furnished by the National Defense Research Institute of Sweden, *op. cit.*, contains 397.
46 Gerald M. Boyd, "U.S. and Russians Make New Offers on Nuclear Tests," *New York Times*, 30 July 1985, pp. A1, A6; Leslie Gelb, "U.S. Summit Stance: Nuclear Testing Will Go On," *New York Times*, 4 October 1985, P. A14.
47 National Defense Research Institute, *op. cit.*
48 Interview with Gen. Col. Chervov of the Soviet General Staff on Moscow Television Service, 2 April 1986; see Foreign Broadcast Information Service, FBIS-SOV-86-065, Vol. III, No. 065, 4 April 1986, p. AA8.
49 More accurate seismic magnitudes have been recalculated using station corrections for those explosions at test sites for which a non-zero value of the standard deviation in magnitude (either dm_b or dM_s) is given in Table 10.2. Yields estimated from other seismic magnitudes are generally less precise since uniform station corrections were not used, magnitudes were computed to only two significant figures, and fewer stations were often used in calculating that magnitude. Table 10.2 should be regarded as the first step in an ongoing process aimed at calculating more accurate yields.
50 The yields shown in the figures for Novaya Zemlya were calculated as an average from m_b estimates and from the M_s determinations of Sykes and Wiggins; Sykes and Wiggins, *op. cit.*, pp. 201-205.

10
Underground Testing

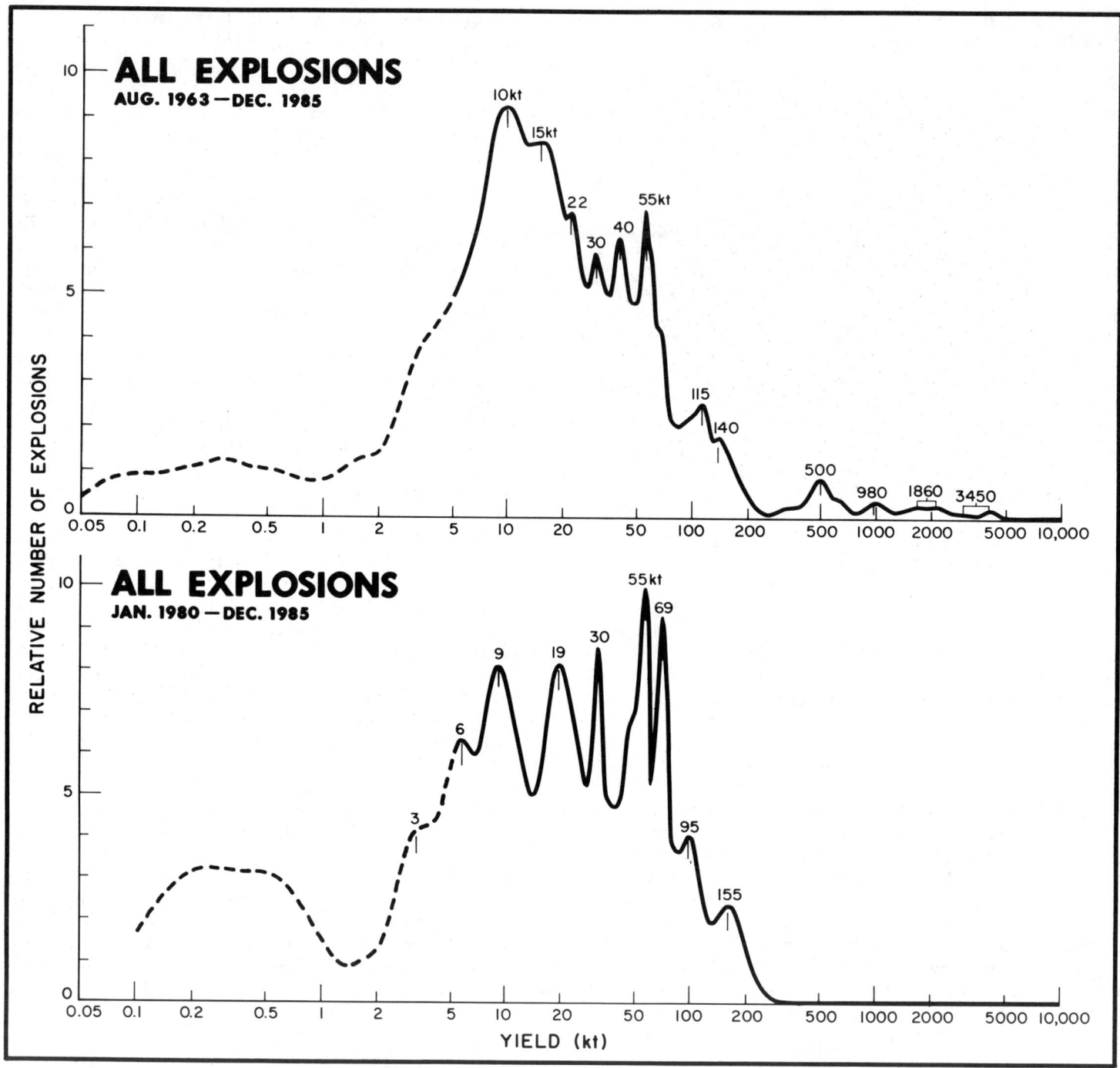

Figure 10.7 Histograms of yields for all underground nuclear explosions detonated by the Soviet Union for two time intervals. Approximate yields are indicated for prominent peaks in each histogram. Yield estimates are only approximate for yields less than about five kilotons (dashed lines).

From the histogram of larger Novaya Zemlya explosions (Figure 10.8, top), 500 kilotons seems appropriate for all three systems. Many other sources give higher yields, which may be based at least in part on incorrect calibration of yields from seismic data.

A pronounced minimum in various histograms for larger Soviet explosions that were detonated before the TTBT took effect in 1976 can be seen for the yield range of 150-500 kilotons. In 1968 and 1969 the Soviet Union tested two underground explosions at Novaya Zemlya, with yields of about 140 kilotons. In 1972 and 1973 they tested two additional times at the KTS with yields of about 100 and 180 kilotons. It seems reasonable to conclude that one or more nuclear weapons of yields near 150 kilotons were tested at full yield in those tests.

The Soviet Union does not appear to have tested un-

10 Underground Testing

Concentration of Soviet Testing into Particular Yields

The various histograms in Figures 10.7 through 10.12 are shown as questionable (dashed lines) for yields less than 5 kilotons. A variety of circumstances lead to a much greater uncertainty in calculated yields for explosions smaller than about five kilotons. These include a much greater variation in the magnitude-yield relationships resulting from more likely variations in rock type and in seismic coupling; the fact that reported seismic magnitudes for small events often come from only one or a few seismograph stations (perhaps one large seismic array); and poorly calibrated magnitude-yield relationships.

Figure 10.7 is a histogram of all Soviet underground nuclear explosions for two time intervals: one from the start of the LTBT in 1963 through 1985, another for the six-year period 1980-1985. In both time intervals, the bulk of Soviet testing has been concentrated in the yield range of several kilotons to about 100 kilotons.

One feature that is common to all of the various histograms in Figures 10.7 to 10.12 is the presence of very pronounced peaks at a few specific yields. Most of the prominent peaks have been identified on the figures, and their approximate yields indicated. A broad maximum in the histogram is evident in the top part of Figure 10.7 for yields between about 7 and 25 kilotons.[51]

The histograms in Figures 10.7 through 10.11 represent summations of Gaussian distributions for each of the explosions in the figure. The Gaussian distribution for each explosion has a unit area under it.[52] Each distribution is centered at the yield computed from its seismic magnitude, and its width is derived from the standard deviation of its seismic magnitude. Since uncertainties in magnitudes differ for various explosions, the height of the peaks in the histogram is not directly proportional to the numbers of explosions.

Figure 10.12 smooths the Soviet data using Gaussian distributions for which the uncertainty in each of the seismic magnitudes was taken to be ± 0.1 units. In this case the vertical axis is proportional to the frequency of occurrence of explosions. As expected, the smoothed versions do not show all of the pronounced peaks that are evident in Figures 10.7 through 10.11. Figure 10.12 shows prominent peaks near 9, 22 and 60 kilotons.

Neither the unsmoothed or the smoothed histograms of tests at the KTS from 1980 to 1985 (bottom part of Figures 10.9 and 10.12) indicate a prominent peak near 10 kilotons, as is seen in the testing profile for the entire period of Soviet underground testing. Most of the explosions that make up the nearly nine kiloton peak of all Soviet underground nuclear explosions from 1980 through 1985 occurred either near Astrakhan or away from the areas of repeated underground testing. Thus, that peak may consist mainly of PNEs. The yields of explosions at Astrakhan may not be estimated accurately since none of their magnitudes have been recomputed and the attenuation of P-waves beneath that site has not been studied.

The broad peak near 11-14 kilotons in tests at the KTS from 1963 to 1985 (Figure 10.9, top) consists of many explosions from the Degelen Mountain subarea. In calculating the yields of those events we used the m_b-yield relationship for the Shagan River subarea, which is better established. Small differences in seismic coupling or in attenuation of P-waves beneath the two subareas may result in a small bias in the calculated yields of the two sets of explosions.

---

51 Kidder has published a diagram of the frequency of occurrence of yields of U.S. tests from 1980 to 1984; Ray E. Kidder, *Federation of American Scientists Public Interest Report*, September 1985. His most pronounced peak in U.S. testing occurs at nearly the same range of yields as that for all Soviet explosions in the top portion of Figure 10.7.

52 Sykes and Wiggins, *op. cit.*

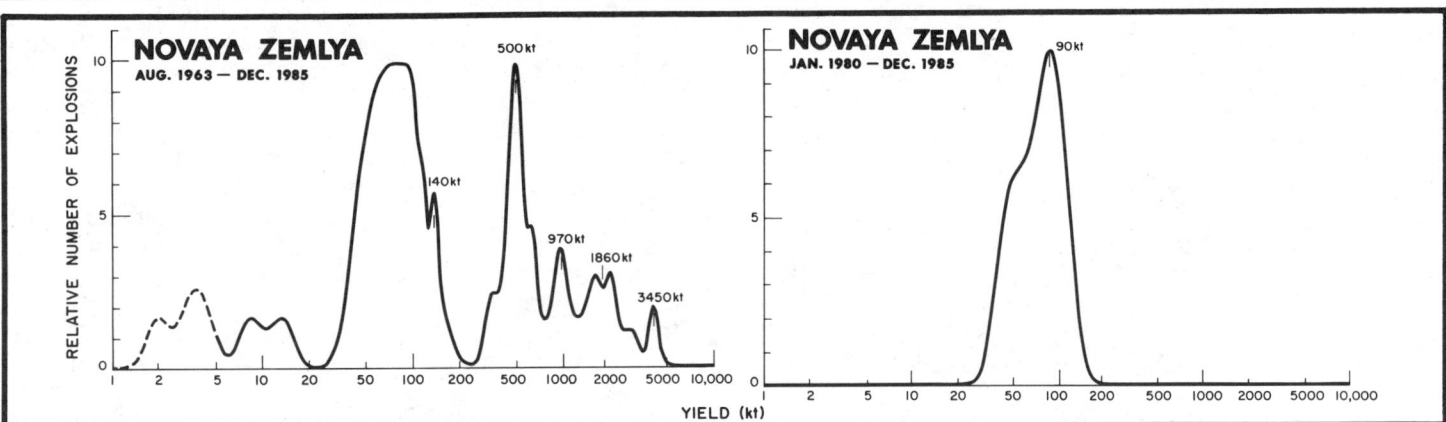

Figure 10.8 Histograms of underground explosions detonated by the Soviet Union at Novaya Zemlya test sites for two time intervals. Approximate yields are indicated for prominent peaks in each histogram. Yield estimates are only approximate for yields less than about five kilotons (dashed lines).

10
Underground Testing

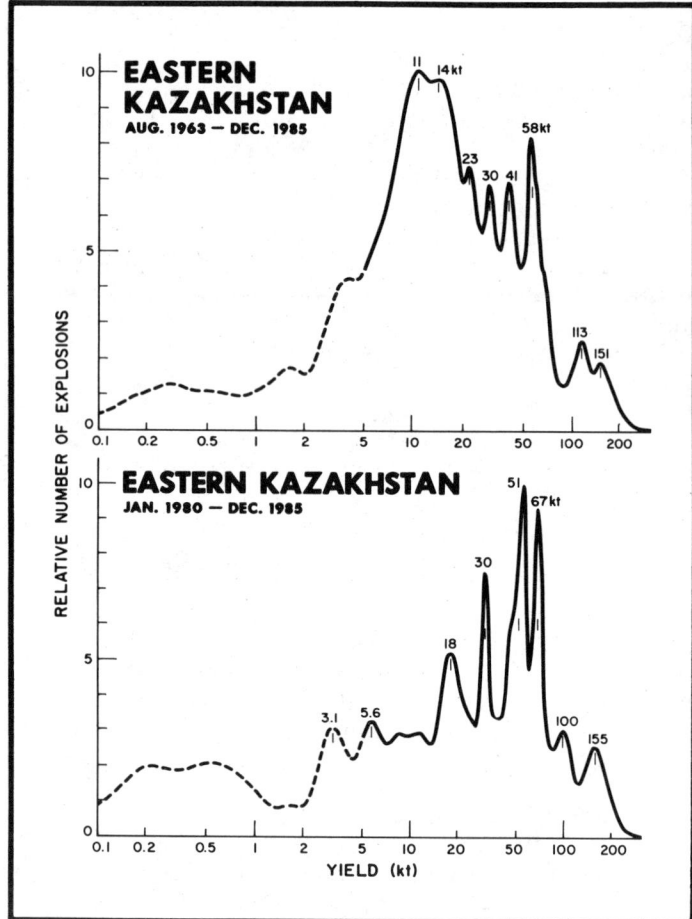

Figure 10.9 Histograms of underground nuclear explosions detonated by the Soviet Union at the Kazakhstan Test Site for two time intervals. Approximate yields are indicated for prominent peaks in each histogram. Yield estimates are only approximate for yields less than about five kilotons (dashed lines).

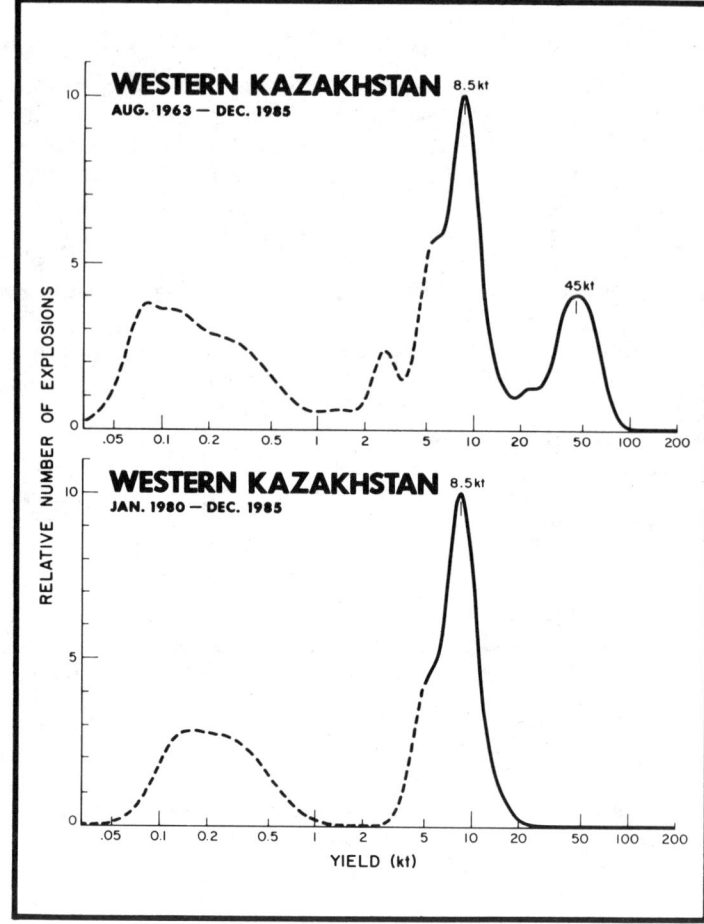

Figure 10.10 Histograms of underground nuclear explosions detonated by the Soviet Union at western Kazakhstan test sites for two time intervals. Approximate yields are indicated for prominent peaks in each histogram. Yield estimates are only approximate for yields less than about five kilotons (dashed lines).

derground at yields between about 180 and 420 kilotons.[53] The large numbers of tests at a few specific yields in the various histograms argue that the Soviet Union performed two or more full-yield nuclear tests of weapons that were deployed on their nuclear systems. Using this reasoning, it seems unlikely that the Soviet Union developed and deployed nuclear weapons systems with yields between 150 and 400 kilotons between 1963 and, at the earliest, 1979.

From June 1979 through 1984 the Soviet Union tested a number of nuclear explosions at the KTS with yields very close to 150 kilotons. In testimony before the House Foreign Affairs Committee on 8 May 1985, Dr. Donald M. Kerr, director at that time of the Los Alamos National Laboratories, stated: "[I]t's our belief that one can reasonably safely extrapolate in yield by about a factor of two. To that end, with [a] 150 kiloton limitation, we

look to something like 300 [kilotons]. If you could test at 300, it would open [up] a much higher yield range ... [which] the United States would not be able to develop new weapons in."[54] Thus, the large number of Soviet explosions since 1979 with yields near 150 kilotons could represent either full-yield tests of weapons with that yield or the partial-yield testing of weapons with yields up to about 300 kilotons.

The Soviet Union tested two weapons at Novaya Zemlya with yields near 1000 kilotons in 1970 and 1975. Various seismic evidence indicates that the latter explosion may, in fact, have been two nearby explosions with yields near 500 kilotons, closely spaced in time. If so, the interpretation that the testing and deployment of one or more weapons of yields near 500 kilotons was of the highest priority to the Soviet Union in the 1970s is strengthened. Between the signing of the TTBT in July

---

53 See Sykes and Ruggi's calculations (NWD 86-4, Appendix 2).
54 HFAC, Hearings on Proposals to Ban Nuclear Testing, 99th Cong. 1st sess., pp. 125-126.

10
Underground Testing

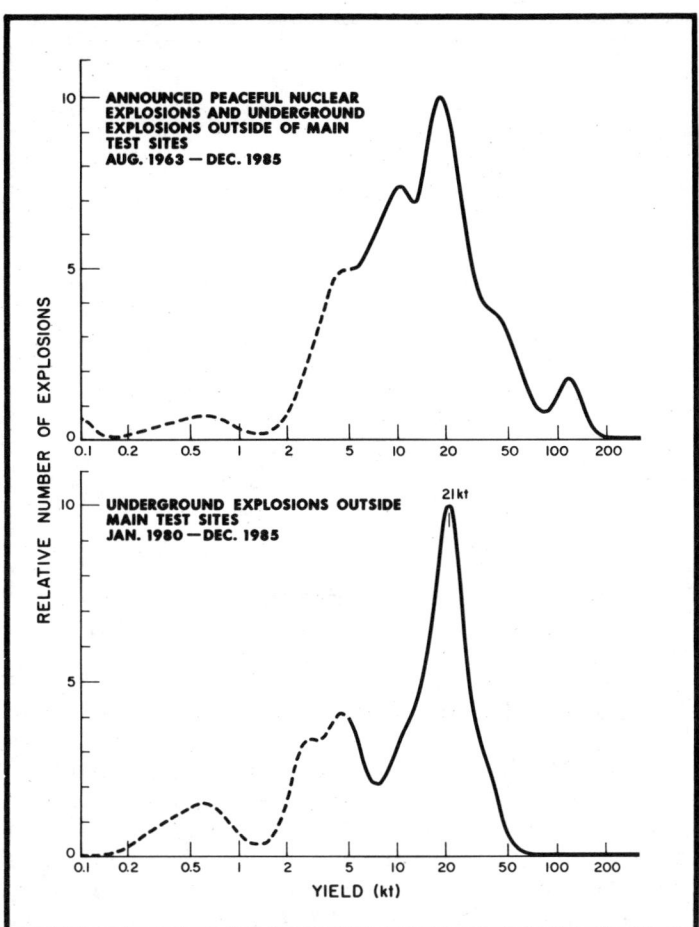

Figure 10.11 Histograms of underground nuclear explosions announced by the Soviet Union as peaceful explosions or underground explosions away from main testing areas for two time intervals. Approximate yields are indicated for prominent peaks in each histogram. Yield estimates are only approximate for yields less than about five kilotons (dashed lines).

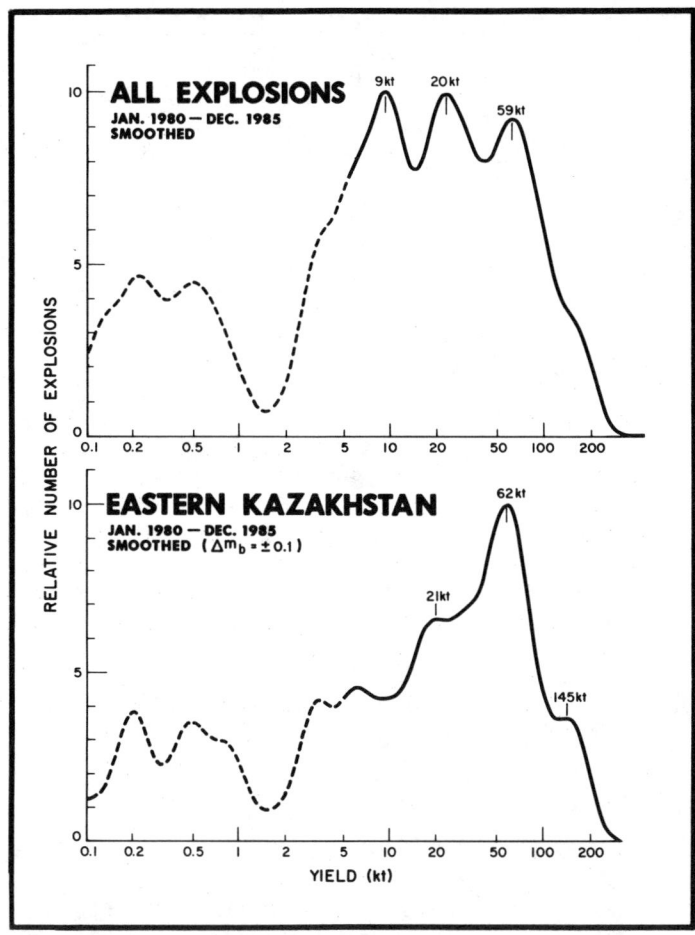

Figure 10.12 Histograms of underground nuclear explosions by the Soviet Union for time period 1980 through 1985 smoothed using standard deviation of ± 0.1 m_b units. Upper diagram shows all Soviet underground explosions; lower diagram shows explosions at the KTS.

1974 and the date it came into effect in 1976, the Soviet Union did not conduct any nuclear tests at any of its test sites with yields between 30 and 500 kilotons, a fact that also attests to the importance the Soviets were attaching to tests with yields of 500 kilotons or larger. During that 21-month interval the Soviet Union conducted three 500 kiloton tests (five, if the explosion of 18 October 1975 was in fact two explosions of 500 kilotons each).

In examining the peaks in various histograms for the period before 1976, especially for tests at Novaya Zemlya and the KTS, many of the calculated yields are close to the round numbered figures of 10, 20, 30, 40, 60, 150, 500, 1000, 2000, and 3500 kilotons. Tests at the KTS since 1980 have prominent peaks near 20, 30, 50, 70, 100, and 150 kilotons. This is perhaps not too surprising for a country in which, being on the metric system, the use of round numbers in various weights and measures is more common than it is in a country like the United States. While those "metric" yields figure prominently in Soviet testing practice, there are undoubtedly explosions that are not of those yields. Such explosions may represent the testing of either other deployed weapons or weapons whose yields deviated in practice from design yields.

Several sources estimate that warheads on some Soviet strategic systems have yields of 200 to 350 kilotons. The pronounced testing gap between yields of 180 and 420 kilotons (and perhaps between 150 and 500 kilotons) argues that warheads in that size range probably were not deployed by the Soviet Union between 1963 and 1979.

From September 1973 through November 1974 the Soviet Union tested its largest underground explosion, with a yield near 3500 kilotons, as well as two explosions with yields near 2000 kilotons. Explosions with yields near 1000 kilotons were tested in 1970 and 1975. The smaller number of tests near 1000 kilotons, compared to those near 500 kilotons, argues for the greater importance in Soviet thinking in the 1970s of one or more weapons of yields near 500 kilotons. That argument is strengthened if the explosion of 18 October 1975 was in fact two 500 kiloton tests. The one or two underground explosions near 1000 kilotons could represent either the proof testing of weapons that were previously tested in the atmos-

10
Test Ban Treaty

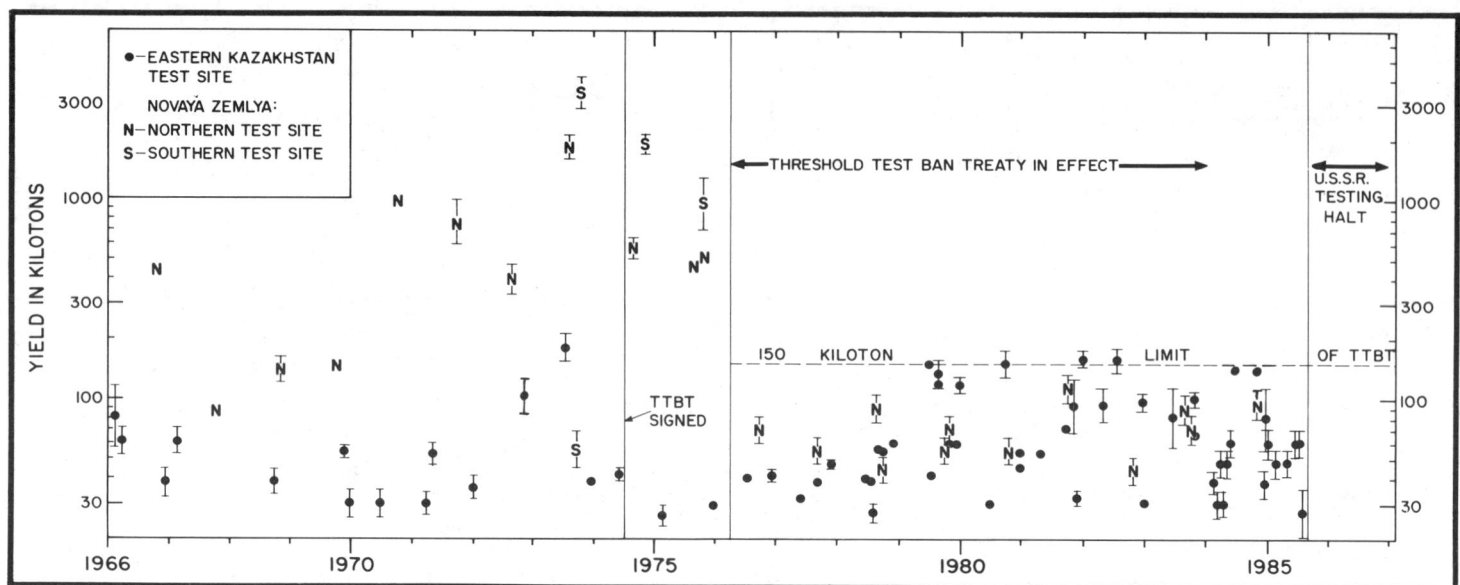

Figure 10.13 Calculated yields of all recorded Soviet nuclear weapons tests of yields greater than 25 kilotons from 1963 through 1987.

phere before 1963 or tests of new weapons for single-warhead missiles or bombers.

Soviet Compliance with the Threshold Test Ban Treaty

All of the largest Soviet tests since the TTBT became effective in 1976 have been conducted near the Shagan River area of the KTS. A great deal of U.S. effort has gone into ascertaining the attenuation of short-period P-waves beneath that test site; calibrating the bias for short-period P-waves (that is, the bias in m_b) with respect to U.S. tests in Nevada and to sites of other explosions of known yield; and thus deriving yield estimates.[55]

Nine explosions at the KTS from 1976 through 1985 had at least one yield estimate (that is, one made from either m_b or M_s) that was 125 kilotons or larger (see Table 10.13). The mean of the individual average estimates of yield is 139 ± 7 kilotons, less than the 150-kiloton limit of the TTBT.[56] While the yield calculated by one method exceeds 150 kilotons in four cases, that determined from another method is less than 150 kilotons. For three of those events the average yield is below 150 kilotons; for one event it is 161 kilotons. For one event surface waves could not be used, and the yield calculated from body waves instead is 158 kilotons.[57] In conclusion, one to a few tests may have had yields that were slightly above 150 kilotons.[58]

Uncertainties in seismological data need to be taken into account and appreciated in ascertaining if the Soviet Union has violated the TTBT. The seismological data are consistent with the Soviet Union having tested repeatedly since 1976 with yields close to the 150-kiloton limit of the TTBT, and consistent with the scatter in calculated yields being solely a function of uncertainties in the magnitudes or in the procedures for calculating yields from

---

55 Sykes and Cifuentes, op. cit., pp. 1922-1925, derived surface wave magnitudes (M_s) for a number of large eastern Kazakhstan explosions from 1978 through 1982. They obtained a maximum value (M_s [max]) that would give a maximum estimate of yield assuming that the tectonic release associated with the explosions they studied was one involving pure thrust faulting, the type of mechanism that would lead to the largest computed values of M_s for the explosion itself. They only determined maximum values of M_s for explosions that were characterized by small to moderate values of tectonic release, i.e., the release of natural stresses in the earth at or soon after large underground explosions. Table 10.8 gives yield estimates derived from m_b and those calculated from maximum values of M_s. The magnitude-yield relationships used are indicated in Appendix B of Sykes and Ruggi, op. cit.

56 If the smallest explosion of the nine, that of 18 October 1981, is eliminated, the average is 145 ± 5 kilotons. Three explosions have a yield estimate from m_b in excess of 150 kilotons: 152, 158, and 176 kilotons. Two explosions have calculated yields based on M_s (which represents a maximum value of yield) in excess of 150 kilotons: 157 kilotons and a questionable value of 173 kilotons. (Accurate estimates of M_s for explosions since 1986 have not been made.) Of the five explosions in question, four have yields determined from both m_b and M_s.

57 All of the above data are consistent with the hypothesis that the yields of the eight largest explosions mentioned above (the event of 18 October 1981 is significantly smaller, about 100 kilotons) are nearly the same. Considering the various uncertainties that enter into the estimate of yield from m_b and M_s, we estimate the accuracy of an individual estimate of yield from either m_b or M_s to be about 30 percent at one standard deviation. Thus, if the Soviet Union did in fact test eight explosions of nearly identical yield close to 150 kilotons, the scatter in the above determinations, both above and below 150 kilotons, is to be expected.

58 The document Arms Control and Disarmament Agreements published in 1982 by the Arms Control and Disarmament Agency, in describing the TTBT states:

The technical problems associated with a yield threshold were recognized by the sides in the spring of 1974 during the negotiation of the TTB Treaty. In this context the U.S.S.R. mentioned the idea of some kind of a 'mistakes' understanding concerning occasional, minor, unintended breaches. Discussions on the subject of such an understanding took place in the autumn of 1974 and in the spring of 1976. The U.S.S.R. was informed by the United States that the understanding reached would be included as part of the public record associated with submitting the TTB Treaty to the Senate for advice and consent to ratification. The entire understanding is as follows:

Both Parties will make every effort to comply fully with all the provisions of the TTB Treaty. However, there are technical uncertainties associated with predicting the precise yields of nuclear weapon tests. These uncertainties may result in slight, unintended breaches of the 150-kiloton threshold. Therefore, the two sides have discussed this problem and agreed that: (1) One or two slight, unintended breaches per year would not be considered a violation of the Treaty; (2) such breaches would be a cause for concern, however, and, at the request of either Party, would be subject for consultations. The U.S.S.R. was also informed that while the United States would not consider such a slight, unintentional breach a violation, the United States would carefully review each such breach to insure that it is not part of a general attempt to exceed the confines of the Treaty.

10
Peaceful Nuclear Explosions

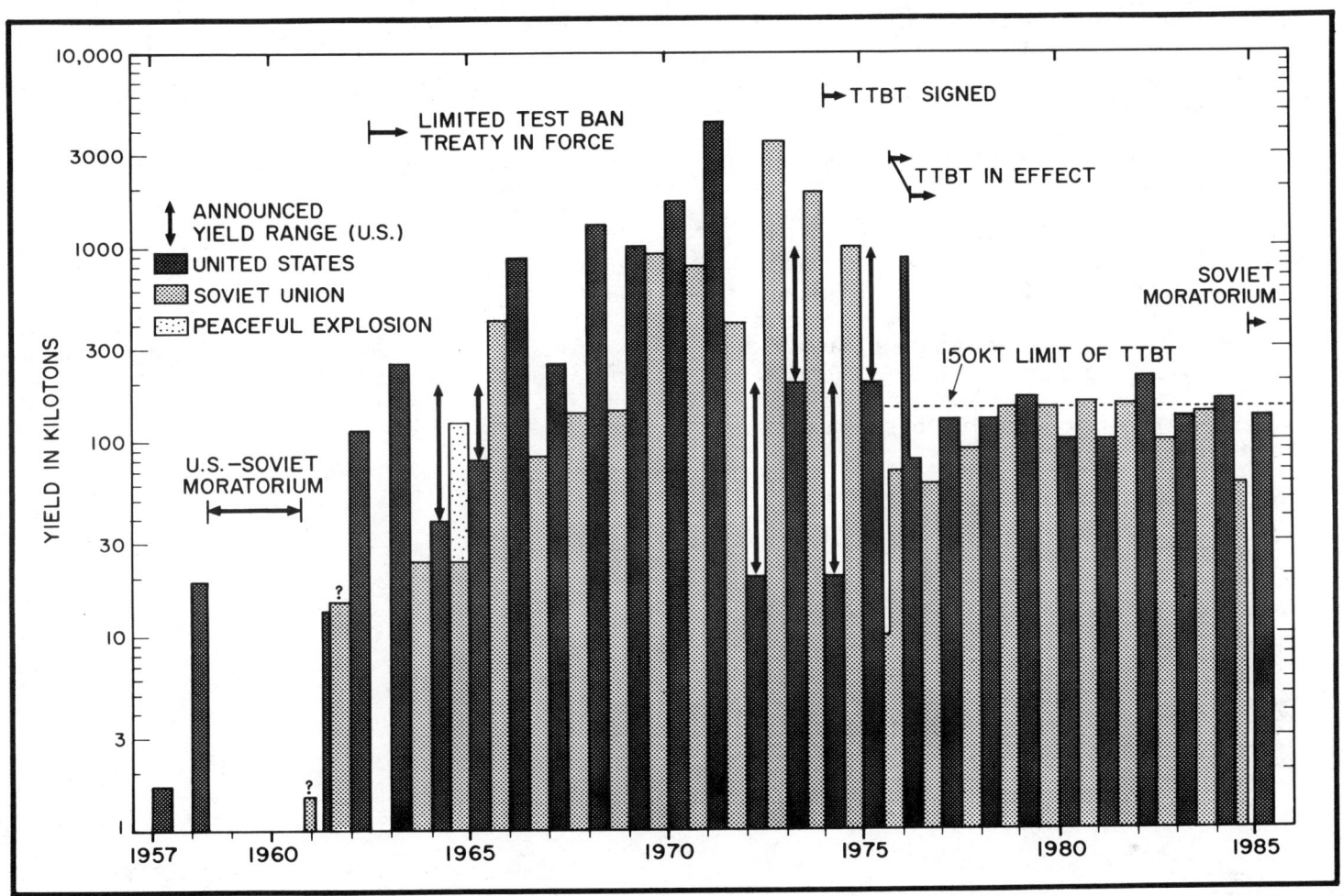

Figure 10.14 Yields of the largest Soviet and U.S. underground nuclear explosions detonated in any calendar year since the start of underground testing in 1957. Yields were determined from seismic magnitudes unless a specific yield or yield range was announced. The largest Soviet explosion in 1965 was announced as a peaceful nuclear test and is shown along with the largest weapons test that year. Yields of U.S. tests since 1976 are only approximate and are determined from magnitudes reported by the U.S. Geological Survey and International Seismological Center. Yields of Soviet tests of 1961 and 1962 are very approximate, since their seismic magnitudes have not been published. For ease of portrayal, Soviet tests in a given year are shown to the left of U.S. explosions.

magnitudes.[59] Yields of underground explosions at all other places in the Soviet Union were well below the 150-kiloton limit of the Peaceful Nuclear Explosions Treaty (PNET) (see Table 10.2). Calculated yields for events of that type during the period March 1976-1985 do not exceed 57 kilotons.

Peaceful Nuclear Explosions

The Soviet Union has carried out a major program involving nuclear explosions for peaceful purposes for more than 20 years.[60] The Soviet Union has not released enough information to permit its PNE program to be fully evaluated. More or less incomplete descriptions have been published or reported for thirteen PNEs in the Soviet Union. In each case, the date and exact place were excluded. A number of authors have made associations between the yields reported and specific seismic events in the Soviet Union.[61] Several of the explosions reported by the Soviet Union had yields smaller than two kilotons and have not been positively associated with specific seismic events. The reported Soviet nuclear explosions for peaceful purposes include cratering experiments (such as tests of earth-moving explosions for a proposed Pechora-Kama Canal); the formation of cavities in salt for underground storage of liquid gas condensates; gas stim-

---

59 See also, U.S. Congress, Office of Technology Assessment, *Seismic Verification of Nuclear Testing Treaties*, OTA-ISC-361 (Washington, DC: GPO, May 1988), p. 19 and Chapter 7, which concludes that the "Soviets are observing a yield limit consistent with compliance with the 150 Kt limit of the Threshold Test Ban Treaty."

60 For a more detailed discussion, see Dahlman and Israelson, *op. cit.*; Borg, *op. cit.*; M. D. Nordyke, "A Review of Soviet Data on the Peaceful Uses of Nuclear Explosions," *Annals Nuclear Energy* 2, 1975, pp. 657-673; "The Test Ban Treaties: Verifying Compliance," *Energy and Technology Review* (LLNL), May 1983, pp. 1-9; J. F. Scheimer and I. Y. P. Borg, "Deep Seismic Sounding with Nuclear Explosives in the Soviet Union," *Science* 226, 1984, pp. 787-792.

61 Dahlman and Israelson, *op. cit.*; Marshall, Springer, and Rodean, *op. cit.*; Borg, *op. cit.*; Nordyke, *op. cit.*; and *Energy and Technology Review* (LLNL), May 1983, *op. cit.*

10
Peaceful Nuclear Explosions

ulation; and the control of runaway oil wells.[62] In addition, it appears that the Soviet Union has used nuclear explosions for seismic sounding of the deep crust and upper mantle. Several of the Soviet nuclear explosions thought to have been used for that purpose fall along straight lines several hundreds of kilometers in length.

Table 10.11 lists explosions that were located outside of the areas where many nuclear explosions have been detonated. Those events are scattered throughout a large area of the Soviet Union. Since only one or two explosions have been detonated at many of those sites, it is reasonable to conclude that the main use of many of those explosions was for purposes other than weapons testing. In addition, the explosions since 1980 in western Kazakhstan occurred near Astrakhan, and they appear to have been used to construct cavities for storage of natural gas condensates.[63]

Yields calculated for explosions outside of the main testing areas are likely to be the most poorly estimated. The formula used for calculating yields does not take into account variations in seismic wave propagation through the upper mantle of the earth beneath various test sites, or variations in seismic coupling. In estimating yields for explosions outside the main testing areas, the assumption is that seismic coupling is not as good as it is for explosions in granite, salt or andesite, and that it is more like that for U.S. explosions in Nevada in tuff, or for U.S. and Soviet explosions in other less competent rocks.

That the Soviet Union has an ongoing interest in the use of nuclear explosions for peaceful purposes can be judged from the fact that the Soviets detonated six explosions in 1987 at localities remote from their main test sites.

---

62 Iris Y. P. Borg, "Nuclear Explosions for Peaceful Purposes," in Jozef Goldblat and David Cox, eds., *Nuclear Weapon Tests: Prohibition or Limitation?* (New York: Oxford University Press, 1988), pp. 67-68.

Table 10.1
Known Soviet Nuclear Explosions 1949-1962[a]

Date (GMT)	Time h: m: secs	Location	Lat(N)	Long(E)	Yield Range	Type
08-29-49	—	—	—		10-20 Kt (1); ~20 Kt (2)	A

Joe 1 was announced by President Truman on 09-23-49 (3). At least until mid-1953, the United States believed the test took place on or about 08-27-49 (3,4,5,6). Various locations are given for the test, including at or near the Kazakh Test Site (KTS) in Asia. According to (5), the apparent location was in the general vicinity of the Aral Sea, with the possibility that it was within a radius of a few hundred miles of 48°N and 76°E (5,7). An earlier estimate (4) put it in an area roughly centered on the northeast shore of the Caspian Sea. Time of the test reported as 1700 local time (5). Test used plutonium as the fissionable material (1) and was a tower shot (7).

09-24-51	—	—		—	at least 25 Kt (1)	A

Joe 2, announced by AEC on 10-03-51 (3); near 48°N, 76°E (5). Test used plutonium as the fissionable material and occurred on or slightly under the surface of the ground (1). Time of the test reported as 1500 local time (5), and as 1515 local time (9). Intensity of the acoustic signal was approximately of the same order of magnitude as those associated with April-May 1951 U.S. tests at Enewetak (Greenhouse) when measured at comparable distances (9).

10-18-51	—	—		—	about 50 Kt (1)	A

Joe 3, announced by AEC on 10-22-51 (3); near 48°N, 76°E. Time of test reported as 1200 local time (5). Airburst (1). Announcement made "prematurely" and without full evaluation due to leak (3). Test was a composite design using both plutonium and U-235 as the fissionable materials, with the efficiency of utilization of the plutonium about 35 percent (1).

08-12-53	—	—		—	200-300 Kt (10)	A

Joe 4, announced by AEC on 08-19-53 (3). Tower test (7). First Soviet thermonuclear test, a fusion reaction with a boosted configuration involving use of lithium deuteride (10); rainwater samples contained tritium (10). It is not known whether or not the device was a deliverable weapon (11); test reported to have taken place in Siberia (8).

08-23-53	—	—	—			A

Joe 5, 6, or 7 (12). A series of four atmospheric tests — Joe 4 through 7 — took place in 1953 (13,14), one of which was a fission explosion on 08-23-53 (12) with a yield equivalent to that of the type detonated at the Nevada Test Site (NTS). Interpretations of Joe 5, 6, and 7 are speculative, including designs for the conversion of large bombs to a large number of air-defense missiles (13). Joe 5 is the least clear of the series, especially in its motivation; it was probably an air drop, but a shot on a wooden tower cannot be excluded (14). One of the four tests, possibly Joe 4, was at first thought to have a force of one megaton (15).

09-14-54	05:36:00.0	Urals	64.000	55.000	—	A

A series of tests that began at intervals in mid-September was announced by the AEC on 10-26-54. This series presumably included test numbers 8 thru 14.

07-29-55	—	—		—	5 Kt (10)	A

Soviet test number 15, probably involving the use of plutonium (10).

08-02-55	—	—		—	25 Kt (10)	A

Soviet test number 16, probably involving the use of plutonium (10). A series of tests was announced by the AEC on 08-04-55.

09-21-55	—	Barents Sea (10)		—	order of 20 Kt (10)	UW

Soviet test number 17; the device, which probably used plutonium, was most likely moored at a depth of 100 feet or more (10). The test was announced by the AEC on 09-24-55.

11-06-55	—	KTS (16)		—	215 Kt (10)	A

Soviet test number 18 (10); airburst (16). This test has been described as a "weaponized version of the 1953 boosted configuration [i.e., 08-12-53 test] reduced to a more easily deliverable size" and it is believed to have been a boosted fission weapon using a U-235 core, as well as U-238 and lithium deuteride (10). The device was believed to have been delivered by aircraft (16). Reported to take place at about 0450 GMT somewhere between the KTS and a point 400 nautical miles to the East (17). The test was announced by the AEC on 11-10-55.

11-22-55	—	KTS (10,16)		—	1600 Kt (10)	A

Soviet test number 19 (10). A two-stage thermonuclear weapon employing both U-235 and U-233, as well as U-238 and lithium deuteride, was carried by an aircraft and set off at an elevation of several thousand feet (10). This thermonuclear weapon (18) was the Soviet Union's first high-yield thermonuclear test (19). It had a yield in the megaton range and was announced by the AEC on 11-23-55.

Table 10.1
Known Soviet Nuclear Explosions 1949-1962[a] (continued)

Date (GMT)	Time h: m: secs	Location	Lat(N)	Long(E)	Yield Range	Type
Jan-Feb 1956	—	—	—	—	—	A
		Atmospheric tests possibly in northeastern Siberian area. Some relatively short-lived artificial radioactivity was detected in February 1956, suggesting further tests in the Soviet Union. This test series was still in progress at the end of February (17).				
03-20-56?	—	—	—	—	—	A
		A series of atmospheric tests announced by the AEC on 03-21-56 took place in the few days preceding the announcement.				
03-30 to 04-01-56	—	—	—	—	—	A
		A series of atmospheric tests announced by the AEC on 04-02-56 took place in the few days preceding the announcement.				
08-24-56	—	Siberia	—	—	less than a Mt	A
		Part of a series of atmospheric tests.				
08-30-56	—	Siberia	—	—	large	A
		Part of a series of atmospheric tests. Probably one of three high-yield thermonuclear tests conducted from January 1956 through 4-15-57.				
09-02-56	—	—	—	—	—	A
		Part of a series of atmospheric tests.				
09-10-56	—	—	—	—	—	A
		Part of a series of atmospheric tests announced by the Soviet Union on 09-10-56.				
11-17-56	—	—	—	—	—	A
		Part of a series of atmospheric tests.				
01-19-57	—	—	—	—	—	A
		Part of a series of atmospheric tests.				
03-08-57	—	—	—	—	—	A
		Part of a series of atmospheric tests.				
04-03-57	—	—	—	—	—	A
		Part of a series of atmospheric tests.				
04-06-57	—	—	—	—	—	A
		Part of a series of atmospheric tests.				
04-10-57	—	—	—	—	large	A
		Probably one of three high-yield thermonuclear tests conducted from January 1956 through 4-15-57.				
04-12-57	—	—	—	—	—	A
		Part of a series of atmospheric tests.				
04-16-57	—	Siberia	—	—	large	A
		Fifth high-yield thermonuclear device (18). One additional high-yield thermonuclear test conducted between January 1956 and this date. Largest of test series.				
08-22-57	—	Siberia	—	—	substantial	A
		Test may have evidenced an improved yield-to-weight ratio for high-yield thermonuclear device; test was the sixth of such a device (18).				
September 1957		Siberia	—	—	moderate	A
		Test within preceding two days of 09-09-57 announcement by AEC.				
09-24-57	09:00:00.0	Novaya Zemlya (NZ)	73.000	55.000	Mt range	A
		Seventh high-yield thermonuclear test, possibly evidencing an improved yield-to-weight ratio for such devices (18).				
09-26-57	05:00:00.0	KTS (19)	—	—	7 to 70 Kt (19)	A
		Announced by JAEIC (19). Twelfth test of current test series, four of this series in September 1957 (two at KTS and two off the east coast of NZ) (19). It is probable that this is the twelfth test conducted in 1957. The two tests conducted off the east coast of NZ were probably two of the three tests of devices for naval applications reported to have taken place by 03-18-58; if so, one of the September 1957 tests was conducted underwater and the other was a surface burst (19).				

Table 10.1
Known Soviet Nuclear Explosions 1949-1962[a] (continued)

Date (GMT)	Time h: m: secs	Location	Lat(N)	Long(E)	Yield Range	Type
10-06-57	08:58:00.0	Novaya Zemlya	73.000	55.000	substantial	A
		Announced by the USSR as a hydrogen device. Eighth test of a high-yield thermonuclear device, possibly evidencing an improved yield-to-weight ratio for such devices (18).				
10-10-57	06:55:00.0	Arctic (NZ)	—		small	A
		"Of the 42 Soviet nuclear tests detected between August 1949 and 10 October 1957, a total of 23 have been detected since January 1956, including six thermonuclear tests" (25).				
12-28-57	—	Siberia	—	—	—	A
02-23-58		Novaya Zemlya	73.000	55.000	Mt range	A
02-27-58	07:59:00.0	Novaya Zemlya	73.000	55.000	Mt range	A
02-27-58	10:24:00.0	Novaya Zemlya	73.000	55.000	large	A
		CIA concludes that 11 thermonuclear tests were conducted overall by 02-28-58, including first device of 11-22-55 amd three (numbers nine through eleven) occurred in the last week of February, 1958 (18).				
03-14-58	—	Novaya Zemlya	73.000	55.000	below Mt range	A
03-14-58	—	Arctic	—		below Mt range	A
03-15-58	—	Arctic	—		below Mt range	A
03-20-58	—	Novaya Zemlya	73.000	55.000	small	A
03-21-58	—	Siberia	—		larger than 03-20-58 test	A
03-22-58	—	Novaya Zemlya	73.000	55.000	medium range	A
09-20-58	—	Novaya Zemlya	73.000	55.000	—	A?
09-30-58	07:50:00.0	Novaya Zemlya	73.000	55.000	moderate to high	A
09-30-58	09:55:00.0	Novaya Zemlya	73.000	55.000	moderate to high	A
10-02-58	08:00:00.0	Novaya Zemlya	73.000	55.000	moderate	A
10-02-58	09:01:00.0	Novaya Zemlya	73.000	55.000	moderate	A
10-05-58	06:00:00.0	Novaya Zemlya	73.000	55.000	—	A
10-10-58	07:51:00.0	Novaya Zemlya	73.000	55.000	relatively large	A
10-12-58	07:53:00.0	Novaya Zemlya	73.000	55.000	probably Mt range	A
10-15-58	07:51:00.0	Novaya Zemlya	73.000	55.000	probably Mt range	A
10-18-58	09:51:00.0	Novaya Zemlya	73.000	55.000	probably Mt range	A
10-19-58	07:27:00.0	Novaya Zemlya	73.000	55.000	small	A
10-20-58	08:20:00.0	Novaya Zemlya	73.000	55.000	probably Mt range	A
10-22-58	08:21:00.0	Novaya Zemlya	73.000	55.000	probably Mt range	A
10-24-58	08:03:00.0	Novaya Zemlya	73.000	55.000	probably Mt range	A
10-25-58	08:20:00.0	Novaya Zemlya	73.000	55.000	relatively large	A
11-01-58	—	Siberia	—		relatively low	A
11-03-58	—	Siberia	—		relatively low	A
		Eleven tests occurred between 09-30-58 and 10-17-58 (20), leaving three unaccounted for.				
09-01-61	—	KTS	50.000	78.000	intermediate range; 150 Kt (21)	A
09-04-61	—	KTS	50.000	78.000	low kt range; 10-80 Kt (21)	A
09-05-61	—	KTS	50.000	78.000	low to intermediate	A
09-06-61	—	East of Stalingrad	48.450	44.300	low to intermediate	A
		High-altitude burst over experimental ABM radar at Sary Shagan, probably to test EMP effects on the radar (22).				
09-10-61	09:00:00.0	Novaya Zemlya	73.000	55.000	several Mt	A
09-10-61	—	Novaya Zemlya	73.000	55.000	low to intermediate Kt	A
09-12-61	10:08:00.0	Novaya Zemlya	73.000	55.000	several Mt	A
09-13-61	—	Novaya Zemlya	73.000	55.000	low to intermediate	A
09-13-61	—	KTS	50.000	78.000	low to intermediate	A

Table 10.1
Known Soviet Nuclear Explosions 1949-1962[a] (continued)

Date (GMT)	Time h: m: secs	Location	Lat(N)	Long(E)	Yield Range	Type
09-14-61	09:56:16.7	Novaya Zemlya	74.600	51.100	several Mt	A
09-16-61	09:08:00.0	Novaya Zemlya	73.000	55.000	order of a Mt	A
09-17-61	—	KTS	50.000	78.000	intermediate	A
09-18-61	07:59:36.8	Novaya Zemlya	74.000	52.000	order of a Mt	A
09-20-61	08:12:00.0	Novaya Zemlya	73.000	55.000	order of a Mt	A
09-22-61	08:01:00.0	Novaya Zemlya	73.000	55.000	order of a Mt	A
10-02-61	10:31:00.0	Novaya Zemlya	73.000	55.000	order of a Mt	A
10-04-61	07:30:54.8	Novaya Zemlya	73.700	53.800	order of several Mt	A
10-06-61	07:00:00.0	Novaya Zemlya	73.000	55.000	several Mt	A
10-08-61	—	Novaya Zemlya	73.000	55.000	low yield range	A
10-11-61	07:40:00.0	Central Asia (maybe KTS)	—		1 to a few kilotons	UG
10-12-61	—	KTS	50.000	78.000	low to intermediate	A
10-20-61	—	Novaya Zemlya	73.000	55.000	several Mt	A
10-23-61	08:31:22.1	Novaya Zemlya	73.900	53.800	about 25 Mt	A
10-23-61	10:30:48.8	South of Novaya Zemlya At least the third underwater test	70.700	53.500	low yield	UW
10-25-61	08:33:00.0	Novaya Zemlya	73.000	55.000	intermediate to high, probably less than a Mt	A
10-27-61	08:30:26.6	Novaya Zemlya	70.700	53.500	low to intermedite	A
10-30-61	08:33:00.0	Novaya Zemlya	73.000	55.000	58 Mt	A
		Test was an airburst in the vicinity of 1200 ft. The Bear bomber was believed capable of delivering a weaponized version of the device (23).				
10-31-61	08:29:00.0	Novaya Zemlya	73.000	55.000	several Mt	A
10-31-61	08:38:00.0	Novaya Zemlya	73.000	55.000	intermediate to high, probably below a Mt	A
11-02-61	08:41:00.0	Novaya Zemlya	73.000	55.000	low to intermediate	A
11-02-61	—	Novaya Zemlya	73.000	55.000	low to intermediate	A
11-04-61	07:20:00.0	Novaya Zemlya	73.000	55.000	several Mt	A
		The AEC announced 12-09-61 in a preliminary analysis that U.S.S.R. conducted approximately 50 atmospheric tests in recent test series (31 tests announced in 1961, leaving ~19 unannounced and ~18 unaccounted for). The total yield of the 50 tests reportedly exceeded the cumulative total of all previous tests of all nations (22). This test series included a number of systems tests and at least four atmospheric effects tests (including 6 September and 6 October), and several were very advanced in yield-to-weight ratios and efficiency (23).				
02-02-62	08:00:00.00	KTS	49.700	78.100	about 10 to 20 kilotons	UG
		First underground nuclear explosion reported by the U.S. (24).				
August 1962		—	—	—	—	A
		AEC announces on 08-06-62 that tests in the low kiloton range had been conducted a few days prior to the 08-05-62 test.				
08-05-62	09:09:00.0	Novaya Zemlya	73.000	55.000	30 Mt	A
08-07-62	09:30:00.0	KTS	50.000	78.000	low kiloton	A
08-10-62	09:00:00.0	Novaya Zemlya	73.000	55.000	less than 1 Mt	A
08-20-62	09:02:14.1	Novaya Zemlya	74.300	51.500	order of several Mt	A
08-22-62	09:00:00.0	Novaya Zemlya	73.000	55.000	low Mt	A
08-25-62	05:40:00.0	KTS	50.000	78.000	low	A
08-25-62	09:00:00.0	Novaya Zemlya	73.000	55.000	order of several Mt	A
08-27-62	09:00:00.0	Novaya Zemlya	73.000	55.000	several Mt	A
09-01-62	12:40:00.0	Novaya Zemlya	73.000	55.000	—	A

Table 10.1
Known Soviet Nuclear Explosions 1949-1962[a] (continued)

Date (GMT)	Time h: m: secs	Location	Lat(N)	Long(E)	Yield Range	Type
09-02-62	—	Novaya Zemlya	73.000	55.000	intermediate	A
09-08-62	10:18:00.0	Novaya Zemlya	73.000	55.000	Mt range	A
		The AEC announced this as the tenth in current series with all detected tests are not specifically announced and a number of additional tests had been conducted.				
09-15-62	08:02:13.9	Novaya Zemlya	74.400	51.500	several Mt	A
09-16-62	10:59:00.0	Novaya Zemlya	73.000	55.000	several Mt	A
09-18-62	08:29:02.7	Novaya Zemlya	73.200	54.700	a few Mt	A
09-19-62	11:00:56.4	Novaya Zemlya	73.800	53.800	multimegaton (approx. 20 Mt)	A
		Second largest atmospheric test in current series, and fourth multimegaton test in past five days.				
09-21-62	08:01:00.0	Novaya Zemlya	73.000	55.000	a few Mt	A
09-25-62	13:03:00.0	Novaya Zemlya	73.000	55.000	multimegaton; slightly larger than 09-19-62 test (approx 25 Mt)	A
09-27-62	08:03:16.4	Novaya Zemlya	74.300	52.400	less than 30 Mt	A
10-07-62	16:32:00.0	Novaya Zemlya	73.000	55.000	intermediate	A
10-14-62	—	KTS	50.000	78.000	low yield range	A
10-22-62	03:41:00.0	KTS	50.000	78.000	a few hundred Kt	A
		High-altitude test.				
10-22-62	09:06:00.0	Novaya Zemlya	73.000	55.000	several Mt	A
10-27-62	07:35:00.0	Novaya Zemlya	73.000	55.000	intermediate	A
10-28-62	—	KTS	50.000	78.000	intermediate	A
10-28-62	04:41:00.0	KTS	50.000	78.000	low	A
		The AEC announced that one of the two tests on 10-28-62 (time unknown) was a high-altitude test; it is more likely that the intermediate yield range was the high-altitude test.				
10-29-62	07:35:00.0	Novaya Zemlya	73.000	55.000	intermediate	A
10-30-62	—	Novaya Zemlya	73.000	55.000	intermediate	A
11-01-62	06:30:00.0	Novaya Zemlya	73.000	55.000	intermediate	A
11-01-62	09:20:00.0	KTS	50.000	78.000	intermediate	A
		Altitude test.				
1-03-62	08:31:00.0	Novaya Zemlya	73.000	55.000	intermediate	A
11-03-62	—	Novaya Zemlya	73.000	55.000	intermediate	A
11-04-62	—	KTS	50.000	78.000	intermediate	A
11-17-62	—	KTS	50.000	78.000	low	A
12-18-62	—	Novaya Zemlya	73.000	55.000	intermediate	A
12-18-62	—	Novaya Zemlya	73.000	55.000	intermediate	A
12-20-62	—	Novaya Zemlya	73.000	55.000	intermediate	A
12-22-62	—	Novaya Zemlya	73.000	55.000	intermediate	A
12-23-62	11:15:00.0	Novaya Zemlya	73.000	55.000	low to a few Mt	A
		The AEC announced on 12-26-62 a number of atmospheric tests conducted between 12-23-62 and 12-25-62—the largest about 20 Mt, with the others low to a few Mts.				
12-24-62	10:44:21.9	Novaya Zemlya	74.200	52.300	—	A
12-24-62	11:11:42.0	Novaya Zemlya	73.600	57.500	about 20 Mt	A
12-25-62	13:35:57.2	Novaya Zemlya	73.400	56.500	low to a few Mt	A

Table 10.1
Known Soviet Nuclear Explosions 1949-1962[a] (continued)

Notes

a. Most of the information is from Department of Energy (DOE), *Summary of Foreign Nuclear Detonations Through December 31, 1984*, 22 May 1985; Atomic Energy Commission and DOE press announcements and releases; and the National Defence Research Institute of Sweden (Forsvarets Forskningsanstalt, or FOA), *Nuclear Explosions 1945-29 November 1987* (printout).
1. Joint Atomic Energy Intelligence Committee (JAEIC), *Status of the Soviet Atomic Energy Program*, National Scientific Intelligence Estimate, NSIE-1, CIA/SI 13-52, 8 January 1953.
2. JAEIC, *Status of the Soviet Atomic Energy Program*, Scientific Intelligence Report, 27 December 1950.
3. Atomic Energy Commission (AEC), Meeting No. 907, 20 August 1953.
4. CIA, *Status of the Soviet Atomic Energy Program*, Scientific Intelligence Report, CIA/SI 113-51, 28 July 1951.
5. CIA, *Status of the Soviet Atomic Energy Program*, Scientific Intelligence Report, CIA/SI 118-51, 6 March 1952.
6. CIA, *USSR*, National Intelligence Survey 26, "Atomic Energy, Army—October 1949," Section 73, p. 73-1.
7. Herbert F. York, *The Advisors: Oppenheimer, Teller and the Superbomb* (San Francisco: W.H. Freeman and Co., 1976).
8. Bruce A. Bolt, *Nuclear Explosions and Earthquakes: The Parted Veil* (San Francisco: W.H. Freeman and Co., 1976).
9. H. Marshall Chadwell, Assistant Director of Scientific Intelligence, CIA, memorandum for the acting director of Central Intelligence, on atomic explosions in the USSR, Harry S. Truman Library, President's Secretary's files, 1 October 1957.
10. David Holloway, "Soviet Thermonuclear Development," *International Security*, Vol. 4, NO. 3, Winter 1979-1980, pp. 192-197, quoting in its entirety Records of the U.S. Joint Chief of Staff, 1954-56, National Archives, Modern Military Branch, Record Group 318, CCS 334 JIC (12-28-55), Section 3.
11. Lewis L. Strauss, Chairman, Atomic Energy Commission, letter to Hon. Sterling Cole, Chairman, Joint Committee on Atomic Energy, 27 October 1953.
12. AEC Press Release, 31 August 1953.
13. Minutes of the 37th meeting of the General Advisory Committee to the U.S. Atomic Energy Committee Commission, 4-6 November 1953, Washington, DC.
14. Summary of preliminary findings of the Committee on Evaluating Foreign Tests, 26 February 1953.
15. Chairman, Joint Chiefs of Staff, "Continental Defense," memorandum for the Secretary of Defense, CJCS 381 , 23 June 1954.
16. Joint Intelligence Committee, *The JIC Semi-Annual Review of Trends in Communist Bloc Policy Including Communist China (1 October 1955-29 February 1956)*, JIC 133/3(56), 16 May 1956.
17. Joint Chiefs of Staff, statement from the Joint Atomic Energy Intelligence Committee, signed by Rear Admiral, USN, Edwin T. Layton, Deputy Director for Intelligence, the Joint Staff, 7 November 1955.
18. CIA, Office of Scientific Intelligence, *Impact of a September 1958 Nuclear Test Moratorium on Soviet Nuclear Weapons Capabilities*, prepared for the Ad Hoc Panel on Nuclear Test Limitations, Appendix E, 18 March 1958.
19. JAEIC, Dwight David Eisenhower Library (DDEL), Staff Secretary, Subject Series, Alphabetical Subseries, Box 7, Folder CIA Vol. I(5), 26 September 1957.
20. DDEL (Ann Whiteman File), Summary of State Department and CIA Reports—18-23 Nuclear Test Suspension, 23 October 1958.
21. Glenn T. Seaborg, *Kennedy, Khrushchev, and the Test Ban*, (Berkeley: University of California Press, 1981), p. 90.
22. Prados, *Soviet Estimate*, p. 153.
23. Lyndon Baines Johnson Library, Minutes of meeting of the Status of U.S. and Soviet Nuclear Tests, 2 February 1962, presented to the President by representatives of the AEC, CIA, and DOD.
24. DOE, *Foreign Nuclear Detonations*, 22 May 1985.
25. CIA, *Main Trends in Soviet Capabilities and Policies 1957-1962*, NIE 11-4-57, 12 November 1957.

Table 10.2
Known Soviet Underground Nuclear Explosions 1961-1987

Date (GMT)	Time h: m: secs	Location	Lat(N)	Long(E)	m_b / M_s	#sta / #sta	$Y(m_b)$ / $Y(M_s)$	$\pm dY_b$ / $\pm dY_s$	Type
10-11-61	07:40:00.0	Central Asia (maybe KTS)	—	—	—	—	1 to a few Kt		UG
02-02-62	08:00:00.00	KTS	49.700	78.100	—	—	about 10-20 Kt		UG
03-15-64	07:59:58.20	KTS	49.800	78.060	5.600	70	23	± 4	UG
05-16-64	06:00:57.80	KTS	49.820	78.120	5.600	83	23	± 4	UG
07-19-64	05:59:58.60	KTS	49.870	78.180	5.400	71	14	± 2	UG
09-18-64	07:59:57.20	Novaya Zemlya (northern site)	73.200	54.400	4.300	19	2.0	± .4	UG
		First known underground explosion at test site.							
10-25-64	07:59:58.30	Novaya Zemlya (northern site)	73.390	53.900	4.900	48	8.4	± 1.5	UG
11-16-64	05:59:58.00	KTS	49.800	78.170	—	88	—	—	UG
01-15-65	05:59:58.40	KTS	49.880	78.960	5.905 / 3.900	18 / —	125	—	UG
		Soviet-announced explosion for peaceful purposes.							
03-03-65	06:14:56.80	KTS	49.810	78.130	5.500	54	18	± 3	UG
05-11-65	06:39:57.30	KTS	49.790	78.120	4.900	19	4.5	± 0.8	UG
06-17-65	03:44:57.61	KTS	49.821	78.061	5.200	36	9.2	± 1.6	UG
07-29-65	03:05:02.10	KTS	50.400	77.900	4.500	28	1.8	± 0.3	UG
09-17-65	03:59:57.52	KTS	49.804	78.176	5.200	36	9.2	± 1.6	UG
10-08-65	05:59:58.20	KTS	49.920	78.170	5.400	55	14	± 2	UG
11-21-65	04:57:58.20	KTS	49.860	78.040	5.600	116	23	± 4	UG
12-24-65	04:59:58.22	KTS	49.871	78.135	5.000	47	5.7	± 1.0	UG
02-13-66	04:57:57.50	KTS	49.840	78.158	6.100	197	81	± 34	UG
03-20-66	05:49:57.80	KTS	49.720	78.070	6.000	160	61	± 10	UG
04-21-66	03:57:57.57	KTS	49.809	78.135	5.300	103	11	± 2	UG
04-22-66	02:58:04.00	Western Kazakhstan	47.930	47.690	4.700	38	1.1	—	UG
		Soviet-announced explosion for peaceful purposes. First known explosion in test area.							
05-07-66	03:57:58.07	KTS	49.774	78.149	4.800	33	3.6	± 0.6	UG
06-29-66	06:57:57.65	KTS	49.847	78.101	5.600	104	23	± 4	UG
07-21-66	03:57:57.50	KTS	49.738	78.140	5.300	103	11	± 2	UG
08-05-66	03:57:57.90	KTS	49.830	78.050	5.400	102	14	± 2	UG

Table 10.2
Known Soviet Underground Nuclear Explosions 1961-1987 (continued)

Date (GMT)	Time h: m: secs	Location	Lat(N)	Long(E)	Seismic Data m_b / M_s	#sta / #sta	Yield (Kt) $Y(m_b)$ / $Y(M_s)$	±dYb / ±dYs	Type
08-19-66	03:53:01.40	KTS	50.500	77.860	5.100 / —	29 / —	7.3 / —	± 1.3 / —	UG
09-07-66	03:51:58.10	KTS	49.940	77.920	4.800 / —	28 / —	3.6 / —	± 0.6 / —	UG
09-30-66	05:59:52.80	Outside main test areas	38.950	64.540	5.100 / —	90 / —	30 / —	— / —	UG
		Soviet-announced explosion for peaceful purposes.							
10-19-66	03:57:57.80	KTS	49.770	78.030	5.600 / —	138 / —	23 / —	± 4 / —	UG
10-27-66	05:57:57.90	Novaya Zemlya (northern site)	73.400	54.570	6.390 / 4.700	23 / 5	422 / 415	± 59 / ± 107	UG
12-03-66	05:02:03.50	KTS	49.720	77.900	4.800 / —	17 / —	3.6 / —	± 0.6 / —	UG
12-18-66	04:57:57.48	KTS	49.922	77.766	5.800 / —	175 / —	38 / —	± 6 / —	UG
01-30-67	04:01:57.90	KTS	49.900	78.000	4.800 / —	43 / —	3.6 / —	± 0.6 / —	UG
02-26-67	03:57:57.37	KTS	49.750	78.125	6.000 / —	207 / —	61 / —	± 10 / —	UG
03-25-67	05:57:58.90	KTS	49.780	78.060	5.300 / —	103 / —	11 / —	± 2 / —	UG
04-20-67	04:07:57.66	KTS	49.731	78.148	5.500 / —	106 / —	18 / —	± 3 / —	UG
05-28-67	04:07:57.70	KTS	49.810	78.110	5.400 / —	131 / —	14 / —	± 2 / —	UG
06-03-67	09:20:59.00	KTS	50.000	77.000	4.500 / —	4 / —	1.5 / —	± 0.3 / —	UG
06-29-67	02:56:57.80	KTS	49.870	78.100	5.300 / —	97 / —	11 / —	± 2 / —	UG
07-15-67	03:26:57.60	KTS	49.880	78.160	5.400 / —	114 / —	14 / —	± 2 / —	UG
08-04-67	06:57:58.00	KTS	49.820	78.050	5.300 / —	97 / —	11 / —	± 2 / —	UG
09-16-67	04:03:57.89	KTS	49.953	77.756	5.300 / —	110 / —	11 / —	± 2 / —	UG
09-22-67	05:03:57.43	KTS	49.972	77.726	5.200 / —	88 / —	9.2 / —	± 1.6 / —	UG
10-06-67	07:00:02.50	Outside main test areas	57.710	65.220	4.700 / —	43 / —	5.2 / —	± 0.9 / —	UG
10-17-67	05:03:58.00	KTS	49.800	78.030	5.600 / —	138 / —	23 / —	± 4 / —	UG
10-21-67	04:59:58.40	Novaya Zemlya (northern site)	73.400	54.420	5.920 / 3.990	12 / 5	93 / 77	± 12 / ± 16	UG
10-30-67	06:03:57.90	KTS	49.810	78.020	5.300 / —	114 / —	11 / —	± 2 / —	UG
11-22-67	04:03:57.62	KTS	49.980	77.777	4.800 / —	14 / —	3.6 / —	± 0.6 / —	UG
12-08-67	06:03:57.40	KTS	49.880	78.210	5.400 / —	91 / —	14 / —	± 2 / —	UG
01-07-68	03:46:57.60	KTS	49.740	78.020	5.100 / —	78 / —	7.3 / —	± 1.3 / —	UG
04-24-68	10:35:57.30	KTS	49.840	78.070	5.000 / —	60 / —	5.7 / —	± 1.0 / —	UG

Table 10.2
Known Soviet Underground Nuclear Explosions 1961-1987 (continued)

Date (GMT)	Time h: m: secs	Location	Lat(N)	Long(E)	Seismic Data m_b / M_S	#sta / #sta	Yield (Kt) $Y(m_b)$ / $Y(M_S)$	$\pm dY_b$ / $\pm dY_S$	Type
05-21-68	03:59:10.00	Outside main test areas	38.890	65.100	5.400 / —	135 / —	47 / —	— / —	UG
		Soviet-announced explosion for peaceful purposes. Multiple explosion.							
06-11-68	03:05:57.70	KTS	49.800	78.130	5.200 / —	96 / —	9.2 / —	± 1.6 / —	UG
06-19-68	05:05:57.31	KTS	49.982	79.003	5.350 / —	25 / —	13 / —	± 2 / —	UG
07-01-68	04:02:00.90	Western Kazakhstan	47.850	47.720	5.500 / —	166 / —	25 / —	— / —	UG
		Soviet-announced explosion for peaceful purposes.							
07-12-68	12:07:57.55	KTS	49.766	78.139	5.300 / —	90 / —	11 / —	± 2 / —	UG
08-20-68	04:05:57.45	KTS	49.820	78.078	4.800 / —	43 / —	3.6 / —	± 0.6 / —	UG
09-05-68	04:05:57.50	KTS	49.750	78.150	5.400 / 3.720	119 / —	14 / —	± 2 / —	UG
09-29-68	03:42:57.44	KTS	49.813	78.175	5.800 / —	168 / —	38 / —	± 6 / —	UG
11-07-68	10:02:05.40	Novaya Zemlya (northern site)	73.390	54.580	6.020 / 4.300	27 / 6	119 / 160	± 7 / ± 29	UG
11-09-68	02:53:57.70	KTS	49.760	78.060	4.900 / —	41 / —	4.5 / —	± 0.8 / —	UG
12-18-68	05:01:57.10	KTS	49.720	78.120	5.000 / —	79 / —	5.7 / —	± 1.0 / —	UG
03-07-69	08:26:57.60	KTS	49.840	78.150	5.600 / 3.560	162 / —	23 / —	±4 / —	UG
05-16-69	04:02:57.30	KTS	49.780	78.160	5.200 / —	108 / —	9.2 / —	± 1.6 / —	UG
05-31-69	05:01:56.86	KTS	49.967	77.728	5.300 / —	98 / —	11 / —	± 2 / —	UG
07-04-69	02:46:57.30	KTS	49.760	78.200	5.200 / —	112 / —	9.2 / —	± 1.6 / —	UG
07-23-69	02:46:57.66	KTS	49.817	78.170	5.400 / —	135 / —	14 / —	± 2 / —	UG
09-02-69	05:00:00.00	Outside main test areas	57.500	54.700	4.900 / —	66 / —	8 / —	— / —	UG
		Soviet-announced explosion for peaceful purposes.							
09-08-69	04:59:55.00	Outside main test areas	57.300	56.000	4.900 / —	75 / —	8 / —	— / —	UG
		Soviet-announced explosion for peaceful purposes. Double explosion.							
09-11-69	04:01:57.50	KTS	49.770	78.030	5.000 / —	65 / —	5.7 / —	± 1.0 / —	UG
09-26-69	07:00:00.00	Outside main test areas	46.000	42.400	5.640 / 3.420	173 / 10	— / —	— / —	UG
10-01-69	04:02:57.70	KTS	49.810	78.180	5.200 / —	99 / —	9.2 / —	± 1.6 / —	UG
10-14-69	07:00:06.40	Novaya Zemlya (northern site)	73.390	54.500	6.090 / 4.270	28 / 6	140 / 149	± 6 / ± 20	UG
10-20-69	09:09:02.00	Western Kazakhstan	48.100	47.800	3.700 / —	1 / —	0.09 / —	±0.03 / —	UG
11-30-69	03:32:57.07	KTS	49.913	78.961	5.954 / 4.100	38 / —	54 / —	± 4 / —	UG

Table 10.2

Known Soviet Underground Nuclear Explosions 1961-1987 (continued)

Date (GMT)	Time h: m: secs	Location	Lat(N)	Long(E)	Seismic Data m_b / M_s	#sta / #sta	Yield (Kt) $Y(m_b)$ / $Y(M_s)$	±dYb / ±dYs	Type
12-06-69	07:02:57.50	Outside main test areas	43.790	54.750	5.800 / —	180 / —	70 / —	± 12 / —	UG
12-28-69	03:46:57.65	KTS	49.954	77.748	5.700 / —	181 / —	30 / —	± 5 / —	UG
12-29-69	04:01:58.10	KTS	49.790	78.000	5.100 / —	12 / —	7.3 / —	± 1.3 / —	UG
01-29-70	07:02:57.56	KTS	49.813	78.185	5.500 / 3.680	146 / —	18 / —	± 3 / —	UG
03-27-70	05:02:57.00	KTS	49.770	78.110	5.000 / —	58 / —	5.7 / —	± 1.0 / —	UG
05-23-70	05:32:59.00	Western Kazakhstan	48.100	47.800	3.500 / —	1 / —	0.06 / —	±0.02 / —	UG
05-23-70	09:57:07.00	Western Kazakhstan	48.100	47.800	3.700 / —	1 / —	0.09 / —	±0.03 / —	UG
05-24-70	12:41:47.00	Western Kazakhstan	48.100	47.800	3.600 / —	2 / —	0.07 / —	±0.01 / —	UG
05-27-70	04:02:57.00	KTS	48.300	78.200	3.800 / —	2 / —	0.29 / —	±0.05 / —	UG
05-29-70	03:17:35.00	Western Kazakhstan	48.100	47.800	3.600 / —	1 / —	0.07 / —	±0.03 / —	UG
06-25-70	04:59:52.40	Outside main test areas Double explosion.	52.200	55.700	4.900 / —	— / —	8.4 / —	± 3.0 / —	UG
06-28-70	01:57:57.70	KTS	49.830	78.220	5.700 / —	176 / —	30 / —	± 5 / —	UG
07-21-70	03:02:57.20	KTS	49.953	77.701	5.400 / —	124 / —	14 / —	± 2 / —	UG
07-24-70	03:56:57.60	KTS	49.820	78.180	5.300 / —	105 / —	11 / —	± 2 / —	UG
09-06-70	04:02:57.56	KTS	49.780	78.046	5.400 / —	141 / —	14 / —	± 2 / —	UG
10-14-70	05:59:57.30	Novaya Zemlya (northern site)	73.310	54.890	6.600 / 5.020	33 / 7	1001 / 888	± 103 / ± 139	UG
11-04-70	06:02:57.22	KTS	50.007	77.798	5.400 / —	149 / —	14 / —	± 2 / —	UG
12-17-70	07:00:57.70	KTS	49.730	78.170	5.400 / —	139 / —	14 / —	± 2 / —	UG
12-12-70	07:00:57.40	Outside main test areas Double explosion.	43.870	54.780	6.000 / —	246 / —	113 / —	± 20 / —	UG
12-23-70	07:00:57.30	Outside main test areas	43.810	54.820	6.000 / —	254 / —	113 / —	± 20 / —	UG
03-22-71	04:32:57.80	KTS	49.791	78.142	5.700 / —	54 / —	30 / —	± 4 / —	UG
03-23-71	06:59:56.44	Outside main test areas Soviet-announced explosion for peaceful purposes.	61.390	56.220	5.500 / —	203 / —	45 / —	— / —	UG
04-25-71	03:32:57.54	KTS	49.774	78.074	5.940 / —	60 / —	53 / —	± 7 / —	UG
05-25-71	04:02:58.02	KTS	49.815	78.197	5.020 / —	20 / —	6.0 / —	± 1.2 / —	UG
06-06-71	04:02:57.23	KTS	49.988	77.720	5.480 / —	43 / —	17 / —	± 3 / —	UG
06-19-71	04:03:57.74	KTS	49.992	77.705	5.410 / —	50 / —	15 / —	± 2 / —	UG

Table 10.2
Known Soviet Underground Nuclear Explosions 1961-1987 (continued)

Date (GMT)	Time h: m: secs	Location	Lat(N)	Long(E)	m_b / M_s	#sta / #sta	$Y(m_b)$ / $Y(M_s)$	±dYb / ±dYs	Type
06-30-71	03:56:57.37	KTS	49.949	78.986	5.290 / —	22 / —	11 / —	± 2 / —	UG
07-02-71	17:00:01.94	Outside main test areas	67.660	62.000	4.700 / —	29 / —	5.2 / —	± 0.9 / —	UG
07-10-71	16:59:59.62	Outside main test areas. Double explosion.	64.200	54.770	5.200 / —	104 / —	17 / —	± 3 / —	UG
09-19-71	11:00:06.89	Outside main test areas	57.760	41.440	4.500 / —	6 / —	3.3 / —	± 0.6 / —	UG
09-27-71	05:59:55.43	Novaya Zemlya (northern site)	73.390	54.910	6.470 / 5.060	25 / 8	586 / 976	± 55 / ± 88	UG
10-04-71	10:00:02.02	Outside main test areas	61.610	47.220	4.600 / —	46 / —	4.1 / —	± 0.7 / —	UG
10-09-71	06:02:57.42	KTS	49.996	77.653	5.320 / —	44 / —	12 / —	± 2 / —	UG
10-21-71	06:02:57.41	KTS	50.001	77.629	5.510 / —	46 / —	19 / —	± 3 / —	UG
10-22-71	05:00:00.66	Outside main test areas	51.610	54.450	5.200 / —	116 / —	17 / —	± 3 / —	UG
11-29-71	06:02:57.55	KTS	49.758	78.132	5.440 / —	40 / —	16 / —	± 2 / —	UG
12-15-71	07:52:58.96	KTS	50.031	77.972	4.900 / —	31 / —	4.5 / —	± 0.8 / —	UG
12-22-71	06:59:56.51	Western Kazakhstan. Double explosion.	47.900	48.070	6.000 / —	230 / —	57 / —	± 10 / —	UG
12-30-71	06:20:57.80	KTS	49.772	78.093	5.780 / —	51 / —	36 / —	± 5 / —	UG
02-10-72	05:02:57.52	KTS	50.014	78.878	5.370 / —	35 / —	13 / —	± 2 / —	UG
03-10-72	04:56:57.42	KTS	49.752	78.142	5.410 / —	52 / —	15 / —	± 2 / —	UG
03-28-72	04:21:57.60	KTS	49.740	78.130	5.140 / —	34 / —	8.0 / —	± 1.3 / —	UG
04-11-72	06:00:02.92	Outside main test areas	37.360	62.070	4.900 / —	50 / —	8.4 / —	± 1.5 / —	UG
06-07-72	01:27:57.43	KTS	49.808	78.121	5.400 / —	39 / —	14 / —	± 2 / —	UG
07-06-72	01:02:59.91	KTS	49.781	78.093	4.420 / —	6 / —	1.5 / —	± 0.5 / —	UG
07-09-72	06:59:57.92	Outside main test areas	49.780	35.450	4.800 / 2.800	62 / —	6.6 / —	± 1.2 / —	UG
07-14-72	14:59:49.01	Outside main test areas	49.990	46.400	3.600 / —	6 / —	0.10 / —	±0.02 / —	UG
08-16-72	03:16:57.53	KTS	49.770	78.113	5.130 / —	29 / —	7.8 / —	± 1.4 / —	UG
08-20-72	02:59:57.80	Outside main test areas	49.400	48.060	5.700 / 3.400	209 / —	55 / —	± 9 / —	UG
08-26-72	03:46:57.20	KTS	49.993	77.773	5.370 / —	35 / —	13 / —	± 2 / —	UG
08-28-72	05:59:56.75	Novaya Zemlya (northern site)	73.390	54.650	6.330 / 4.760	28 / 8	329 / 479	± 28 / ± 42	UG
09-02-72	08:56:57.55	KTS	49.950	77.660	4.880 / —	9 / —	4.3 / —	± 1.2 / —	UG

Table 10.2
Known Soviet Underground Nuclear Explosions 1961-1987 (continued)

Date (GMT)	Time h: m: secs	Location	Lat(N)	Long(E)	Seismic Data m_b / M_s	#sta / #sta	Yield (Kt) $Y(m_b)$ / $Y(M_s)$	±dYb / ±dYs	Type
09-04-72	07:00:04.45	Outside main test areas	67.730	33.090	4.600 / —	47 / —	4.1 / —	± 0.7 / —	UG
09-21-72	09:00:01.41	Outside main test areas	52.190	51.940	5.000 / —	83 / —	10 / —	± 1 / —	UG
10-03-72	08:59:57.80	Outside main test areas	46.860	44.870	5.600 / —	51 / —	44 / —	± 7 / —	UG
11-02-72	01:26:57.62	KTS	49.923	78.815	6.181 / 3.903	42 / 5	126 / 78	± 20 / ± 24	UG
11-24-72	09:00:02.87	Outside main test areas	52.140	51.830	4.500 / —	40 / —	3.3 / —	± 0.6 / —	UG
11-24-72	09:59:58.04	Outside main test areas	51.850	64.180	5.200 / —	104 / —	17 / —	± 3 / —	UG
12-10-72	04:26:57.66	KTS	49.837	78.102	5.600 / —	245 / —	23 / —	± 4 / —	UG
12-10-72	04:27:07.31	KTS	50.001	78.973	5.989 / —	8 / —	59 / —	± 12 / —	UG
12-28-72	04:27:00.00	KTS	51.700	77.200	4.900 / —	1 / —	0.39 / —	±0.14 / —	UG
02-16-73	05:02:57.59	KTS	49.822	78.158	5.460 / —	46 / —	17 / —	± 2 / —	UG
04-19-73	04:32:57.51	KTS	49.995	77.647	5.320 / —	40 / —	12 / —	± 2 / —	UG
07-10-73	01:26:57.73	KTS	49.798	78.087	5.300 / —	38 / —	11 / —	± 1 / —	UG
07-23-73	01:22:57.64	KTS	49.962	78.812	6.247 / 4.700	35 / —	181 / —	± 28 / —	UG
08-15-73	01:59:57.78	Outside main test areas	42.690	67.410	5.300 / 3.400	151 / —	21 / —	± 3 / —	UG
08-28-73	02:59:57.95	Outside main test areas	50.580	68.400	5.200 / 3.400	82 / —	17 / —	± 3 / —	UG
09-12-73	06:59:54.58	Novaya Zemlya (northern site)	73.320	54.970	6.780 / 5.260	26 / 9	2099 / 1569	± 268 / ± 171	UG
09-19-73	02:59:57.63	Outside main test areas	45.680	67.800	5.100 / 3.300	98 / —	13 / —	± 2 / —	UG
09-27-73	06:59:58.45	Novaya Zemlya (southern site)	70.800	53.420	5.950 / 3.740	7 / 3	100 / 42	± 8 / ± 10	UG

First known underground explosion at test site.

Date (GMT)	Time h: m: secs	Location	Lat(N)	Long(E)	m_b / M_s	#sta / #sta	$Y(m_b)$ / $Y(M_s)$	±dYb / ±dYs	Type
09-30-73	04:59:57.76	Outside main test areas	51.660	54.540	5.200 / 3.300	134 / —	17 / —	± 3 / —	UG
10-26-73	04:26:57.74	KTS	49.759	78.164	5.240 / 4.400	38 / —	10 / —	±1 / —	UG
10-26-73	05:59:57.22	Outside main test areas	53.630	55.380	4.800 / —	65 / —	6.6 / —	± 1.2 / —	UG
10-27-73	06:59:57.65	Novaya Zemlya (southern site)	70.800	53.920	6.940 / 5.510	13 / 6	4055 / 2841	± 300 / ± 351	UG
12-14-73	07:46:57.15	KTS	50.044	78.987	5.803 / 4.400	41 / —	38 / —	± 2 / —	UG
01-30-74	04:56:57.80	KTS	49.837	78.049	4.900 / —	56 / —	4.5 / —	± 0.8 / —	UG
01-30-74	04:57:02.22	KTS	49.853	78.087	5.400 / —	135 / —	14 / —	± 2 / —	UG

Only one test on 01-30-74 at KTS announced by the AEC. It is not known which test was announced.

Table 10.2
Known Soviet Underground Nuclear Explosions 1961-1987 (continued)

Date (GMT)	Time h: m: secs	Location	Lat(N)	Long(E)	Seismic Data m_b / M_s	#sta / #sta	Yield (Kt) $Y(m_b)$ / $Y(M_s)$	± dY_b / ± dY_s	Type
04-16-74	05:52:57.40	KTS	50.041	78.943	4.440 / —	10 / —	1.5 / —	± 0.5 / —	UG
05-16-74	03:02:57.65	KTS	49.752	78.093	5.250 / —	46 / —	10 / —	± 1 / —	UG
05-31-74	03:26:57.47	KTS	49.950	78.852	5.849 / —	42 / —	42 / —	± 3 / —	UG
06-25-74	03:56:57.70	KTS	49.840	78.166	4.500 / —	8 / —	1.8 / —	± 0.6 / —	UG
07-08-74	05:59:59.75	Outside main test areas	53.680	55.080	4.600 / —	41 / —	4.1 / —	± 0.7 / —	UG
07-10-74	02:56:57.60	KTS	49.783	78.130	5.160 / —	44 / —	8.4 / —	± 1.2 / —	UG
08-14-74	14:59:58.56	Outside main test areas	68.940	75.830	5.400 / —	162 / —	27 / —	± 4 / —	UG
08-29-74	09:59:55.77	Novaya Zemlya (northern site)	73.410	54.930	6.430 / 4.880	26 / 10	497 / 636	± 43 / ± 40	UG
08-29-74	14:59:58.99	Outside main test areas	67.230	62.140	5.000 / —	78 / —	10 / —	± 1 / —	UG
09-13-74	03:02:57.61	KTS	49.778	78.081	5.170 / —	39 / —	8.6 / —	± 1.3 / —	UG
10-16-74	06:32:57.58	KTS	49.979	78.898	5.470 / —	57 / —	17 / —	± 2 / —	UG
11-02-74	04:59:56.87	Novaya Zemlya (southern site)	70.810	53.910	6.780 / 5.290	13 / 5	2099 / 1685	± 172 / ± 160	UG
12-07-74	05:59:57.65	KTS	49.933	77.636	4.500 / —	4 / —	1.8 / —	± 0.7 / —	UG
12-16-74	06:22:57.73	KTS	49.793	78.133	5.000 / —	70 / —	5.7 / —	± 1.0 / —	UG
12-16-74	06:40:57.96	KTS	49.867	78.087	4.800 / —	71 / —	3.6 / —	± 0.6 / —	UG
12-27-74	05:46:56.87	KTS	49.943	79.011	5.500 / 4.700	50 / —	18 / —	± 2 / —	UG
02-20-75	05:32:57.63	KTS	49.789	78.062	5.650 / —	64 / —	26 / —	± 3 / —	UG
03-11-75	05:42:57.64	KTS	49.747	78.146	5.380 / —	53 / —	14 / —	± 1 / —	UG
04-25-75	05:00:02.52	Western Kazakhstan	48.080	47.200	4.700 / —	24 / —	2.6 / —	± 0.5 / —	UG
04-27-75	05:36:57.25	KTS	49.949	78.926	5.560 / —	60 / —	21 / —	± 3 / —	UG
06-08-75	03:26:57.55	KTS	49.762	78.050	5.500 / —	59 / —	18 / —	± 2 / —	UG
06-30-75	03:26:57.58	KTS	50.004	78.957	4.630 / —	13 / —	2.4 / —	± 0.7 / —	UG
08-07-75	03:56:57.66	KTS	49.812	78.161	5.150 / —	39 / —	8.2 / —	± 1.2 / —	UG
08-23-75	08:59:57.93	Novaya Zemlya (northern site)	73.340	54.500	6.420 / 4.720	29 / 8	477 / 435	± 47 / ± 50	UG
09-29-75	10:59:58.31	Outside main test areas	69.600	90.460	4.800 / —	55 / —	6.6 / —	± 1.2 / —	UG
10-05-75	04:27:43.90	KTS	55.800	75.100	4.600 / —	1 / —	0.19 / —	±0.07 / —	UG

Table 10.2

Known Soviet Underground Nuclear Explosions 1961-1987 (continued)

Date (GMT)	Time h: m: secs	Location	Lat(N)	Long(E)	m_b / M_S	#sta / #sta	$Y(m_b)$ / $Y(M_S)$	± dYb / ± dYs	Type
10-18-75	08:59:56.50	Novaya Zemlya (southern site)	70.840	53.530	6.660 / 4.920	11 / 6	1281 / 700	± 147 / ± 108	UG
		Possibly two nearby explosions of yields near 500 Kt, closely spaced in time.							
10-21-75	11:59:57.74	Novaya Zemlya (northern site)	73.320	54.930	6.430 / 4.780	22 / 10	497 / 502	± 57 / ± 35	UG
10-29-75	04:46:57.33	KTS	49.946	78.878	5.616 / —	24 / —	24 / —	± 1 / —	UG
12-13-75	04:56:57.58	KTS	49.810	78.157	5.020 / —	42 / —	6.0 / —	± 0.9 / —	UG
12-25-75	05:16:57.16	KTS	50.044	78.814	5.690 / 5.200	31 / —	29 / —	± 2 / —	UG
01-15-76	04:46:57.57	KTS	49.824	78.201	5.250 / —	48 / —	10 / —	± 1 / —	UG
04-21-76	04:57:57.75	KTS	49.776	78.146	5.100 / —	42 / —	7.3 / —	± 1.3 / —	UG
04-21-76	05:02:57.19	KTS	49.890	78.827	5.280 / —	52 / —	11 / —	± 1 / —	UG
		Only one test announced by Energy Research and Development Administration (ERDA) on 04-21-76 at the KTS. It is not known which test was announced.							
05-19-76	02:56:57.81	KTS	49.796	78.058	4.820 / —	27 / —	3.7 / —	± 0.7 / —	UG
06-09-76	03:02:57.23	KTS	49.989	79.022	5.120 / —	39 / —	7.6 / —	± 1.3 / —	UG
07-04-76	02:56:57.46	KTS	49.909	78.911	5.825 / —	35 / —	40 / —	± 2 / —	UG
07-23-76	02:32:57.79	KTS	49.779	78.085	5.040 / —	49 / —	6.3 / —	± 0.9 / —	UG
07-29-76	04:59:57.96	Western Kazakhstan	47.810	48.100	5.900 / 4.400	41 / —	45 / —	± 8 / —	UG
08-04-76	02:56:58.00	KTS	49.900	77.700	4.100 / —	1 / —	0.06 / —	±0.02 / —	UG
08-28-76	02:56:57.48	KTS	49.969	78.930	5.710 / —	32 / —	30 / —	± 2 / —	UG
09-29-76	02:59:57.66	Novaya Zemlya (northern site)	73.410	54.500	5.800 / 4.500	42 / —	70 / —	± 12 / —	UG
10-20-76	07:59:57.82	Novaya Zemlya (northern site)	73.400	54.470	5.100 / 3.400	115 / —	13 / —	± 2 / —	UG
10-30-76	04:57:02.51	KTS	49.821	78.029	4.900 / —	33 / —	4.5 / —	± 0.8 / —	UG
11-05-76	03:59:56.89	Outside main test areas	61.520	112.730	5.300 / —	107 / —	21 / —	± 3 / —	UG
11-23-76	05:02:57.28	KTS	50.008	78.963	5.757 / —	43 / —	34 / —	± 1 / —	UG
12-07-76	04:56:57.38	KTS	49.922	78.846	5.834 / —	33 / —	41 / —	± 3 / —	UG
12-30-76	03:56:57.91	KTS	49.802	78.069	5.130 / 4.200	41 / —	7.8 / —	± 1.1 / —	UG
03-29-77	03:56:57.56	KTS	49.970	78.086	5.400 / —	172 / —	14 / —	± 2 / —	UG
04-25-77	04:06:57.74	KTS	49.813	78.150	5.060 / —	46 / —	6.6 / —	± 0.9 / —	UG
05-29-77	02:56:57.58	KTS	49.937	78.770	5.737 / 5.200	43 / —	32 / —	± 1 / —	UG

Table 10.2
Known Soviet Underground Nuclear Explosions 1961-1987 (continued)

Date (GMT)	Time h: m: secs	Location	Lat(N)	Long(E)	Seismic Data m_b / M_s	#sta / #sta	Yield (Kt) $Y(m_b)$ / $Y(M_s)$	±dYb / ±dYs	Type
06-29-77	03:06:57.76	KTS	50.006	78.869	5.220 / 5.000	59 / —	9.6 / —	± 1.4 / —	UG
07-26-77	16:59:57.75	Outside main test areas	69.540	90.510	5.000 / —	112 / —	10 / —	± 1 / —	UG
07-30-77	01:56:57.72	KTS	49.759	78.097	5.090 / —	55 / —	7.1 / —	± 0.9 / —	UG
08-10-77	22:00:02.00	Outside main test areas	50.950	110.780	5.000 / —	37 / —	10 / —	± 1 / —	UG
08-17-77	04:26:57.57	KTS	49.825	78.170	4.990 / —	35 / —	5.6 / —	± 0.9 / —	UG
08-20-77	21:59:58.34	Outside main test areas	64.130	99.620	5.000 / —	133 / —	10 / —	± 1 / —	UG
09-01-77	02:59:57.77	Novaya Zemlya (northern site)	73.370	54.410	5.700 / 3.700	57 / —	55 / —	± 9 / —	UG
09-05-77	03:02:57.34	KTS	50.035	78.921	5.790 / —	38 / —	37 / —	± 2 / —	UG
09-10-77	16:00:03.30	Outside main test areas	57.290	106.230	4.800 / —	30 / —	6.6 / —	± 1.2 / —	UG
09-30-77	06:59:55.90	Western Kazakstan	47.850	48.130	5.000 / 3.600	136 / —	5.4 / —	± 1.0 / —	UG
10-09-77	10:59:58.84	Novaya Zemlya (northern site)	73.470	53.980	4.600 / —	69 / —	4.1 / —	± 0.7 / —	UG
10-29-77	03:06:57.57	KTS	49.833	78.131	5.600 / —	68 / —	23 / —	± 4 / —	UG
10-29-77	03:07:02.47	KTS	50.069	78.975	5.540 / —	40 / —	20 / —	± 2 / —	UG
11-30-77	04:06:57.36	KTS	49.958	78.885	5.893 / 3.500	52 / —	47 / —	± 2 / —	UG
12-26-77	04:02:57.84	KTS	49.853	78.115	4.880 / —	38 / —	4.3 / —	± 0.7 / —	UG
03-19-78	03:46:57.41	KTS	49.959	77.746	5.210 / —	52 / —	9.4 / —	± 1.6 / —	UG
03-26-78	03:56:57.55	KTS	49.768	78.044	5.610 / 4.800	90 / —	24 / —	± 2 / —	UG
04-22-78	03:06:57.57	KTS	49.761	78.186	5.280 / 3.600	81 / —	11 / —	± 1 / —	UG
05-29-78	04:56:57.42	KTS	49.772	78.141	4.660 / —	35 / —	2.6 / —	± 0.4 / —	UG
06-11-78	02:56:57.57	KTS	49.898	78.797	5.837 / 4.400	59 / —	41 / —	± 1 / —	UG
07-05-78	02:46:57.47	KTS	49.887	78.871	5.808 / 3.700	68 / —	38 / —	± 1 / —	UG
07-28-78	02:46:57.48	KTS	49.756	78.140	5.660 / —	88 / —	27 / —	± 3 / —	UG
08-09-78	17:59:58.14	Outside main test areas	63.650	125.340	5.600 / 3.800	239 / —	44 / —	± 7 / —	UG
08-10-78	07:59:57.71	Novaya Zemlya (northern site)	73.310	54.700	5.900 / 4.300	72 / —	89 / —	± 15 / —	UG
08-24-78	18:00:03.86	Outside main test areas	65.870	112.560	5.100 / 3.700	147 / —	13 / —	± 2 / —	UG
08-29-78	02:36:57.57	KTS	49.812	78.142	5.200 / —	61 / —	9.2 / —	± 1.6 / —	UG

Table 10.2

Table 10.2
Known Soviet Underground Nuclear Explosions 1961-1987 (continued)

Date (GMT)	Time h: m: secs	Location	Lat(N)	Long(E)	Seismic Data m_b / M_s	#sta / #sta	Yield (Kt) $Y(m_b)$ / $Y(M_s)$	±dYb / ±dYs	Type
08-29-78	02:37:06.25	KTS	50.000	78.978	5.967 / 3.673	50 / 2	56 / —	± 1 / —	UG
		Only one test announced by DOE on 08-29-78 at KTS. It is not known which test was announced.							
09-15-78	02:36:57.42	KTS	49.916	78.879	5.963 / 3.831	62 / 3	55 / —	± 1 / —	UG
09-20-78	05:02:56.85	KTS	49.835	78.416	4.300 / —	20 / —	1.1 / —	± 0.2 / —	UG
09-21-78	14:59:57.65	Outside main test areas	66.530	86.260	5.200 / —	168 / —	17 / —	± 3 / —	UG
09-27-78	02:04:58.43	Novaya Zemlya (northern site)	73.380	54.440	5.600 / 4.500	17 / —	44 / —	± 7 / —	UG
10-07-78	23:59:57.00	Outside main test areas	61.530	112.870	5.200 / 3.590	57 / —	17 / —	± 3 / —	UG
10-15-78	05:36:57.72	KTS	49.753	78.165	5.120 / —	69 / —	7.6 / —	± 0.9 / —	UG
10-17-78	04:59:56.65	Western Kazakhstan	47.810	48.090	5.800 / 4.500	74 / —	35 / —	± 6 / —	UG
10-17-78	13:59:58.04	Outside main test areas	63.210	63.260	5.500 / 3.700	10 / —	34 / —	± 6 / —	UG
10-31-78	04:16:57.77	KTS	49.806	78.143	5.220 / —	80 / —	9.6 / —	± 1.1 / —	UG
11-04-78	05:05:57.32	KTS	50.034	78.943	5.576 / 3.582	76 / 4	22 / —	— / —	UG
11-29-78	04:32:57.73	KTS	49.810	78.042	5.300 / —	— / —	11 / —	± 4 / —	UG
11-29-78	04:33:02.49	KTS	49.949	78.798	5.996 / 4.300	48 / —	60 / —	± 2 / —	UG
12-14-78	04:42:57.62	KTS	49.813	78.144	4.710 / —	18 / —	2.9 / —	± 0.6 / —	UG
12-18-78	07:59:56.34	Western Kazakhstan	47.780	48.140	5.900 / 5.200	90 / —	45 / —	± 8 / —	UG
01-20-78	04:32:57.63	KTS	49.858	78.089	4.670 / —	28 / —	2.6 / —	± 0.5 / —	UG
01-10-79	08:00:00.00	Western Kazakhstan	47.000	48.000	5.000 / —	1 / —	1.4 / —	± 0.5 / —	UG
01-17-79	07:59:55.79	Western Kazakhstan	47.870	48.060	6.000 / 4.600	45 / —	57 / —	± 10 / —	UG
02-01-79	04:12:57.64	KTS	50.090	78.870	5.380 / 3.320	79 / —	14 / —	± 1 / —	UG
02-16-79	04:03:58.10	KTS	49.990	77.712	5.420 / —	68 / —	15 / —	± 2 / —	UG
05-06-79	03:16:57.65	KTS	49.774	78.049	5.190 / —	76 / —	9.0 / —	± 1.0 / —	UG
05-24-79	04:07:00.00	KTS	50.000	78.000	4.900 / —	— / —	0.39 / —	±0.14 / —	UG
05-31-79	05:54:57.65	KTS	49.835	78.127	5.240 / —	71 / —	10 / —	± 1 / —	UG
06-23-79	02:56:57.52	KTS	49.903	78.855	6.215 / 3.991	89 / 5	152 / 146	± 10 / —	UG
07-07-79	03:46:57.33	KTS	50.026	78.991	5.839 / 4.027	76 / 5	41 / —	± 1 / —	UG

Table 10.2
Known Soviet Underground Nuclear Explosions 1961-1987 (continued)

Date (GMT)	Time h: m: secs	Location	Lat(N)	Long(E)	Seismic Data m_b / M_s	#sta / #sta	Yield (Kt) $Y(m_b)$ / $Y(M_s)$	±dYb / ±dYs	Type
07-14-79	04:59:55.20	Western Kazakhstan	47.810	48.070	5.600 / 5.300	42 / —	22 / —	± 3 / —	UG
07-18-79	03:17:02.53	KTS	49.937	77.850	5.200 / 4.200	57 / —	9.2 / —	± 1.6 / —	UG
08-04-79	03:56:57.09	KTS	49.894	78.904	6.161 / 4.052	97 / 6	113 / 157	± 8 / —	UG
08-12-79	17:59:57.49	Outside main test areas	61.860	122.220	4.900 / 3.800	119 / —	8.4 / —	± 1.5 / —	UG
08-18-79	02:51:57.13	KTS	49.943	78.938	6.170 / 3.743	93 / 7	119 / —	± 9 / —	UG
09-14-79	07:33:00.00	KTS	50.000	78.000	5.200 / —	— / —	0.79 / —	±0.28 / —	UG
09-06-79	17:59:57.74	Outside main test areas	64.060	99.620	4.900 / —	115 / —	8.4 / —	± 1.5 / —	UG
09-15-79	04:07:00.00	KTS	50.000	78.000	4.600 / —	— / —	0.19 / —	±0.07 / —	UG
09-24-79	03:29:58.36	Novaya Zemlya (northern site)	73.370	54.580	5.700 / 4.500	66 / —	55 / 55	± 9 / ± 9	UG
09-27-79	04:12:57.67	KTS	49.767	78.120	4.400 / —	19 / —	1.4 / —	± 0.3 / —	UG
10-04-79	15:59:58.05	Outside main test areas	60.660	71.440	5.400 / 3.800	206 / —	27 / —	± 4 / —	UG
10-07-79	20:59:57.08	Outside main test areas	61.850	113.120	5.000 / —	110 / —	10 / —	± 1 / —	UG
10-18-79	04:16:57.70	KTS	49.837	78.148	5.190 / —	59 / —	9.0 / —	± 1.2 / —	UG
10-18-79	07:09:58.50	Novaya Zemlya (northern site)	73.340	54.730	5.800 / 4.200	47 / —	70 / —	± 12 / —	UG
10-24-79	05:59:56.66	Western Kazakhstan	47.790	48.110	5.800 / 5.200	59 / —	35 / —	± 6 / —	UG
10-28-79	03:16:56.94	KTS	49.973	78.997	5.990 / 3.974	91 / 4	59 / 127	± 2 / —	UG
11-30-79	04:52:58.18	KTS	49.789	78.144	4.470 / 3.080	20 / —	1.6 / —	± 0.3 / —	UG
12-02-79	04:36:57.45	KTS	49.891	78.796	5.998 / 4.080	78 / 5	60 / —	± 1 / —	UG
12-21-79	04:41:57.66	KTS	49.801	78.173	4.680 / —	20 / —	2.7 / —	± 0.6 / —	UG
12-23-79	04:56:57.44	KTS	49.916	78.755	6.170 / 3.772	81 / 3	119 / —	± 10 / —	UG
04-04-80	05:32:57.44	KTS	50.012	77.856	5.020 / —	25 / —	6.0 / —	± 1.3 / —	UG
04-10-80	04:06:57.81	KTS	49.805	78.108	4.980 / —	46 / —	5.5 / —	± 0.8 / —	UG
04-25-80	03:56:57.53	KTS	49.973	78.755	5.500 / —	89 / —	18 / —	± 2 / —	UG
05-22-80	03:56:57.71	KTS	49.784	78.082	5.490 / —	73 / —	18 / —	± 2 / —	UG
06-12-80	03:26:57.62	KTS	49.980	79.001	5.590 / —	74 / —	23 / —	± 2 / —	UG
06-29-80	02:32:57.69	KTS	49.939	78.815	5.707 / 3.400	69 / 2	30 / —	± 1 / —	UG

Table 10.2
Known Soviet Underground Nuclear Explosions 1961-1987 (continued)

Date (GMT)	Time h: m: secs	Location	Lat(N)	Long(E)	m_b / M_s	#sta / #sta	$Y(m_b)$ / $Y(M_s)$	±dYb / ±dYs	Type
07-13-80	08:10:00.00	KTS	50.000	78.000	5.000 / —	— / —	0.49 / —	±0.18 / —	UG
07-31-80	03:32:57.65	KTS	49.807	78.148	5.300 / —	76 / —	11 / —	± 1 / —	UG
09-14-80	02:42:39.13	KTS	49.921	78.802	6.213 / 4.043	62 / 6	150 / —	± 24 / —	UG
09-20-80	10:40:00.00	KTS	50.000	78.000	4.900 / —	— / —	0.39 / —	±0.14 / —	UG
09-25-80	06:21:10.65	KTS	49.835	78.118	4.770 / —	32 / —	3.3 / —	± 0.5 / —	UG
09-30-80	05:57:00.00	KTS	50.000	78.000	4.600 / —	1 / —	0.19 / —	±0.07 / —	UG
09-30-80	05:57:00.00	KTS	50.000	78.000	5.200 / —	1 / —	0.79 / —	±0.28 / —	UG
10-08-80	05:59:57.31	Western Kazakhstan	46.790	48.290	5.200 / 3.700	142 / —	8.6 / —	± 1.5 / —	UG
10-11-80	07:09:57.17	Novaya Zemlya (northern site) Double explosion.	73.360	54.820	5.700 / 4.000	41 / —	55 / —	± 9 / —	UG
10-12-80	03:34:14.10	KTS	49.961	79.028	5.918 / 4.094	80 / 5	50 / —	± 2 / —	UG
11-01-80	12:59:58.02	Outside main test areas	60.790	97.570	5.200 / —	153 / —	17 / —	± 3 / —	UG
12-10-80	06:59:57.66	Outside main test areas	61.730	66.760	4.600 / 3.700	47 / —	4.1 / —	± 0.7 / —	UG
12-14-80	03:47:06.40	KTS	49.899	78.938	5.953 / 3.934	64 / 6	54 / —	± 2 / —	UG
12-26-80	04:07:07.27	KTS	49.941	78.183	4.250 / —	5 / —	0.97 / —	±0.40 / —	UG
12-27-80	04:09:08.08	KTS	50.057	78.981	5.872 / 3.758	58 / 5	45 / —	± 2 / —	UG
03-29-81	04:03:50.03	KTS	50.007	78.982	5.610 / 3.700	83 / —	24 / —	± 2 / —	UG
03-31-81	07:51:56.00	KTS	50.000	79.000	3.600 / —	— / —	0.09 / —	±0.03 / —	UG
04-22-81	01:17:11.34	KTS	49.885	78.810	5.954 / 4.070	78 / 5	54 / —	± 1 / —	UG
05-25-81	04:59:57.59	Outside main test areas	68.210	53.500	5.500 / 4.200	249 / —	34 / —	± 6 / —	UG
05-27-81	03:58:12.34	KTS	49.985	78.980	5.460 / 3.400	75 / —	17 / —	± 2 / —	UG
06-05-81	03:22:00.00	KTS	50.000	78.000	4.700 / —	— / —	0.24 / —	±0.09 / —	UG
06-30-81	01:57:12.92	KTS	49.768	78.119	5.250 / —	58 / —	10 / —	± 1 / —	UG
07-05-81	03:59:00.00	KTS	50.000	78.000	4.600 / —	— / —	0.19 / —	±0.07 / —	UG
07-17-81	02:37:15.76	KTS	49.810	78.160	5.160 / —	62 / —	8.4 / —	± 1.1 / —	UG
08-14-81	02:27:12.84	KTS	49.791	78.121	4.990 / —	43 / —	5.6 / —	± 0.8 / —	UG
09-02-81	04:00:03.92	Outside main test areas	60.590	55.700	4.400 / —	30 / —	2.6 / —	± 0.5 / —	UG

Table 10.2
Known Soviet Underground Nuclear Explosions 1961-1987 (continued)

Date (GMT)	Time h: m: secs	Location	Lat(N)	Long(E)	Seismic Data m_b / M_s	#sta / #sta	Yield (Kt) $Y(m_b)$ / $Y(M_s)$	± dYb / ± dYs	Type
09-13-81	02:17:18.25	KTS	49.910	78.915	6.064 / 4.206	72 / 3	71 / —	± 2 / —	UG
09-26-81	04:59:57.45	Western Kazakhstan	46.820	48.280	5.200 / —	171 / —	8.6 / —	± 1.5 / —	UG
09-26-81	05:03:57.03	Western Kazakhstan	46.790	48.270	5.300 / —	152 / —	10 / —	± 1 / —	UG
09-30-81	12:55:00.00	KTS	50.000	78.000	4.600 / —	— / —	0.19 / —	±0.07 / —	UG
10-01-81	12:14:56.91	Novaya Zemlya (northern site)	73.320	54.550	6.000 / 3.800	75 / —	113 / —	± 20 / —	UG
10-18-81	03:57:02.64	KTS	49.923	78.859	6.033 / 4.094	54 / 3	66 / 127	± 2 / —	UG
10-22-81	13:59:57.47	Outside main test areas	63.790	97.540	5.100 / —	115 / —	13 / —	± 2 / —	UG
11-20-81	04:57:02.63	KTS	49.740	78.160	5.150 / —	44 / —	8.2 / —	± 1.2 / —	UG
11-29-81	03:35:08.60	KTS	49.887	78.860	5.730 / 4.100	82 / —	32 / —	± 3 / —	UG
12-22-81	04:31:02.88	KTS	49.831	78.147	5.060 / —	32 / —	6.6 / —	± 1.1 / —	UG
12-27-81	03:43:14.13	KTS	49.923	78.795	6.242 / 4.106	72 / 4	176 / 146	± 26 / —	UG
02-19-82	03:56:11.07	KTS	49.824	78.069	5.400 / —	147 / —	14 / —	± 2 / —	UG
04-25-82	03:23:05.27	KTS	49.903	78.913	6.089 / 4.026	70 / 5	77 / 113	± 8 / —	UG
06-11-82	10:59:00.00	KTS	50.000	78.000	4.700 / —	1 / —	0.24 / —	±0.09 / —	UG
06-25-82	02:03:04.76	KTS	49.810	78.132	4.800 / —	66 / —	3.6 / —	± 0.6 / —	UG
07-04-82	01:17:14.20	KTS	49.960	78.807	6.222 / —	62 / —	158 / —	± 22 / —	UG
07-12-82	10:29:00.00	KTS	50.000	78.000	4.600 / —	1 / —	0.19 / —	±0.07 / —	UG
07-30-82	21:00:02.94	Outside main test areas	53.800	104.140	5.000 / 4.000	104 / —	10 / —	± 1 / —	UG
07-31-82	07:08:00.00	Western Kazakhstan	47.000	48.000	4.000 / —	1 / —	0.13 / —	±0.05 / —	UG
08-23-82	02:43:04.28	KTS	49.788	78.092	4.700 / —	53 / —	2.8 / —	± 0.5 / —	UG
08-28-82	09:09:00.00	Western Kazakhstan	47.000	48.000	4.000 / —	1 / —	0.13 / —	±0.05 / —	UG
08-31-82	01:31:00.70	KTS	49.924	78.761	5.300 / 3.600	182 / —	11 / —	± 2 / —	UG
08-31-82	08:40:00.00	Western Kazakhstan	47.000	48.000	4.600 / —	1 / —	0.53 / —	±0.19 / —	UG
09-04-82	05:47:00.00	KTS	50.000	78.000	4.100 / —	— / —	0.06 / —	±0.02 / —	UG
09-04-82	17:59:58.55	Outside main test areas	69.210	81.640	5.300 / 3.500	192 / —	21 / —	± 3 / —	UG
09-15-82	04:33:00.00	KTS	50.000	78.000	5.100 / —	— / —	0.62 / —	±0.22 / —	UG

Table 10.2

Known Soviet Underground Nuclear Explosions 1961-1987 (continued)

Date (GMT)	Time h: m: secs	Location	Lat(N)	Long(E)	m_b / M_S	#sta / #sta	$Y(m_b)$ / $Y(M_S)$	±dYb / ±dYs	Type
09-21-82	02:57:00.83	KTS	49.801	78.151	5.200 / —	144 / —	9.2 / —	± 1.6 / —	UG
09-25-82	17:59:57.37	Outside main test areas	64.330	91.800	5.200 / 3.500	117 / —	17 / —	± 3 / —	UG
10-01-82	13:10:00.00	Western Kazakhstan	47.000	48.000	4.000 / —	1 / —	0.13 / —	±0.05 / —	UG
10-10-82	04:59:56.88	Outside main test areas	61.530	112.860	5.300 / —	147 / —	21 / —	± 3 / —	UG
10-11-82	07:14:58.39	Novaya Zemlya (northern site)	73.370	54.340	5.600 / 4.200	279 / —	44 / —	± 7 / —	UG
10-16-82	05:59:57.38	Western Kazakhstan	46.770	48.220	5.200 / 3.300	183 / —	8.6 / —	± 1.5 / —	UG
10-16-82	06:04:57.44	Western Kazakhstan	46.770	48.240	5.200 / 3.300	178 / —	8.6 / —	± 1.5 / —	UG
10-16-82	06:09:57.39	Western Kazakhstan	46.770	48.220	5.200 / 3.400	185 / —	8.6 / —	± 1.5 / —	UG
10-16-82	06:14:57.52	Western Kazakhstan	46.750	48.200	5.400 / 3.600	219 / —	13 / —	± 2 / —	UG
10-27-82	07:28:00.00	Western Kazakhstan	47.000	48.000	4.000 / —	1 / —	0.13 / —	±0.13 / —	UG
11-21-82	06:10:00.00	Outside main test areas	55.000	50.000	4.400 / —	1 / —	0.65 / —	±0.24 / —	UG
11-29-82	19:19:00.00	Outside main test areas	55.000	50.000	4.100 / —	1 / —	0.32 / —	±0.12 / —	UG
11-30-82	09:49:00.00	Western Kazakhstan	47.000	48.000	4.500 / —	1 / —	0.42 / —	±0.15 / —	UG
12-05-82	03:37:12.55	KTS	49.919	78.813	6.132 / 4.400	91 / —	97 / —	± 10 / —	UG
12-25-82	04:23:05.29	KTS	49.807	78.068	4.800 / 3.400	34 / —	3.6 / —	± 0.6 / —	UG
12-26-82	03:35:14.20	KTS	50.071	78.988	5.703 / —	85 / —	30 / —	± 1 / —	UG
02-01-83	13:55:00.00	Western Kazakhstan	47.000	48.000	4.300 / —	1 / —	0.26 / —	±0.09 / —	UG
02-24-83	14:11:00.00	Western Kazakhstan	47.000	48.000	4.300 / —	1 / —	0.26 / —	±0.09 / —	UG
02-25-83	06:53:00.00	Western Kazakhstan	47.000	48.000	4.200 / —	1 / —	0.21 / —	±0.07 / —	UG
03-02-83	08:45:30.00	Western Kazakhstan	48.000	49.000	3.800 / —	— / —	0.31 / —	±0.11 / —	UG
03-30-83	04:17:00.00	KTS	49.000	79.000	5.000 / —	— / —	0.49 / —	±0.18 / —	UG
04-12-83	03:41:05.20	KTS	49.810	78.220	4.900 / —	— / —	0.39 / —	±0.14 / —	UG
05-30-83	03:33:44.80	KTS	49.740	78.190	5.500 / 3.600	105 / 1	18 / —	± 3 / —	UG
06-12-83	02:36:43.70	KTS	49.910	78.970	6.100 / 4.800	104 / 5	81 / —	± 34 / —	UG
06-24-83	02:56:11.20	KTS	49.820	78.120	4.700 / —	30 / —	2.8 / —	± 0.5 / —	UG
07-10-83	03:59:57.30	Outside main test areas	51.330	53.290	5.300 / —	79 / —	21 / —	± 3 / —	UG

Table 10.2
Known Soviet Underground Nuclear Explosions 1961-1987 (continued)

Date (GMT)	Time h: m: secs	Location	Lat(N)	Long(E)	m_b / M_s	#sta / #sta	$Y(m_b)$ / $Y(M_s)$	±dYb / ±dYs	Type
07-10-83	04:04:57.20	Outside main test areas	51.340	53.290	5.300 / —	75 / —	21 / —	± 3 / —	UG
07-10-83	04:09:57.10	Outside main test areas	51.370	53.300	5.300 / —	71 / —	21 / —	± 3 / —	UG
07-28-83	03:41:00.00	KTS	49.000	79.000	5.000 / —	— / —	0.49 / —	±0.18 / —	UG
08-18-83	16:09:58.60	Novaya Zemlya (northern site)	73.380	54.870	5.900 / 4.100	108 / 3	89 / —	± 15 / —	UG
09-11-83	06:33:10.50	KTS	49.890	78.210	4.900 / —	14 / —	4.5 / —	± 0.6 / —	UG
09-24-83	04:59:57.10	Western Kazakhstan	46.820	48.290	5.100 / —	122 / —	6.8 / —	± 1.2 / —	UG
09-24-83	05:04:57.20	Western Kazakhstan	46.820	48.280	5.000 / —	115 / —	5.4 / —	± 1.0 / —	UG
09-24-83	05:09:57.50	Western Kazakhstan	46.860	48.270	4.900 / —	108 / —	4.2 / —	± 0.8 / —	UG
09-24-83	05:14:57.10	Western Kazakhstan	46.780	48.300	5.200 / —	119 / —	8.6 / —	± 1.5 / —	UG
09-24-83	05:19:57.10	Western Kazakhstan	46.800	48.300	5.200 / —	125 / —	8.6 / —	± 1.5 / —	UG
09-24-83	05:24:57.40	Western Kazakhstan	46.840	48.230	5.200 / —	118 / —	8.6 / —	± 1.5 / —	UG
09-25-83	13:09:57.90	Novaya Zemlya (northern site)	73.350	54.380	5.800 / —	110 / —	70 / —	± 12 / —	UG
10-06-83	01:47:06.80	KTS	49.930	78.840	6.040 / —	76 / —	67 / —	± 2 / —	UG
10-26-83	01:55:05.00	KTS	49.890	78.900	6.139 / 4.800	96 / 4	101 / —	± 9 / —	UG
11-20-83	03:27:04.60	KTS	50.060	79.020	5.500 / —	103 / —	18 / —	± 3 / —	UG
11-29-83	02:19:06.70	KTS	49.770	79.020	5.400 / —	93 / —	14 / —	± 2 / —	UG
12-26-83	04:29:06.80	KTS	49.840	78.220	5.500 / —	166 / —	18 / —	± 3 / —	UG
02-19-84	03:57:03.40	KTS	49.910	78.810	5.800 / 4.300	251 / —	38 / —	± 6 / —	UG
03-07-84	02:39:06.40	KTS	50.060	79.000	5.700 / —	249 / —	30 / —	± 5 / —	UG
03-29-84	05:19:08.20	KTS	49.940	79.020	5.900 / 4.300	268 / —	48 / —	± 8 / —	UG
04-15-84	03:17:09.10	KTS	49.740	78.160	5.700 / —	244 / —	30 / —	± 5 / —	UG
04-25-84	01:09:03.50	KTS	49.950	78.940	5.900 / 4.700	291 / —	48 / —	± 8 / —	UG
05-26-84	03:13:12.40	KTS	49.980	79.060	6.000 / —	325 / —	61 / —	± 10 / —	UG
06-23-84	02:57:00.00	KTS	50.000	79.000	4.400 / —	1 / —	0.12 / —	±0.04 / —	UG
07-14-84	01:09:10.50	KTS	49.890	78.960	6.200 / 4.250	316 / 7	140 / 143	± 58 / ± 21	UG
07-21-84	02:59:57.10	Outside main test areas	51.356	53.249	5.400 / 4.000	— / —	27 / —	± 9 / —	UG

Table 10.2
Known Soviet Underground Nuclear Explosions 1961-1987 (continued)

Date (GMT)	Time h: m: secs	Location	Lat(N)	Long(E)	Seismic Data m_b / M_s	#sta / #sta	Yield (Kt) $Y(m_b)$ / $Y(M_s)$	±dYb / ±dYs	Type
07-21-84	03:04:57.00	Outside main test areas	51.374	53.257	5.300 / —	1 / —	5.5 / —	± 2.0 / —	UG
07-21-84	03:09:57.00	Outside main test areas	51.353	53.271	5.300 / —	— / —	21 / —	± 7 / —	UG
07-21-84	07:41:06:00	Outside main test areas	48.000	59.000	3.800 / —	1 / —	0.62 / —	±0.23 / —	UG
08-11-84	18:59:57.40	Outside main test areas	65.079	55.287	5.100 / —	1 / —	3.4 / —	± 1.2 / —	UG
08-25-84	18:59:58.60	Outside main test areas	61.876	72.092	5.400 / —	— / —	27 / —	± 9 / —	UG
08-27-84	05:59:57.00	Outside main test areas	66.770	33.680	4.500 / —	— / —	3.2 / —	± 1.2 / —	UG
08-28-84	02:59:55.50	Outside main test areas	60.826	57.472	4.400 / —	— / —	2.6 / —	± 2.6 / —	UG
08-28-84	03:04:59.00	Outside main test areas	61.000	58.000	4.500 / —	— / —	3.3 / —	± 1.2 / —	UG
09-09-84	02:59:06.40	KTS	49.870	78.180	5.000 / —	79 / —	5.7 / —	± 1.0 / —	UG
09-15-84	06:15:00.00	KTS	50.000	79.000	5.200 / —	1 / —	0.79 / —	±0.28 / —	UG
09-17-84	20:59:57.40	Outside main test areas	55.835	87.408	4.900 / —	— / —	8.4 / —	± 3.0 / —	UG
10-18-84	04:57:05.70	KTS	49.800	78.140	4.500 / —	22 / —	1.8 / —	± 0.3 / —	UG
10-25-84	06:29:57.70	Novaya Zemlya (northern site)	73.370	54.960	5.900 / 4.700	269 / —	89 / —	± 15 / —	UG
10-27-84	01:50:10.60	KTS	49.950	78.830	6.200 / 4.246	376 / 6	140 / 141	± 58 / ± 22	UG
10-27-84	05:59:57.10	Western Kazakhstan	46.860	48.100	5.000 / —	107 / —	5.4 / —	± 1.0 / —	UG
10-27-84	06:04:56.70	Western Kazakhstan	46.840	48.080	5.000 / —	100 / —	5.4 / —	± 1.0 / —	UG
11-23-84	03:55:04.80	KTS	49.900	78.130	4.700 / —	30 / —	2.8 / —	± 0.5 / —	UG
12-02-84	03:19:06.30	KTS	49.990	79.070	5.800 / 4.600	283 / —	38 / —	± 6 / —	UG
12-16-84	03:55:02.70	KTS	49.960	78.860	6.100 / 4.600	312 / —	81 / —	± 34 / —	UG
12-28-84	03:50:10.70	KTS	49.860	78.750	6.000 / 4.100	306 / —	61 / —	± 10 / —	UG
02-10-85	03:27:07.60	KTS	49.880	78.820	5.900 / 4.400	273 / —	48 / —	± 8 / —	UG
04-19-85	13:53:58.70	Outside main test areas	44.440	57.930	4.700 / —	7 / —	5.2 / —	± 0.9 / —	UG
04-25-85	00:57:06.50	KTS	49.920	78.970	5.900 / 5.000	311 / —	48 / —	± 8 / —	UG
06-15-85	00:57:00.70	KTS	49.890	78.880	6.000 / 4.400	413 / —	61 / —	± 10 / —	UG
06-30-85	02:39:02.70	KTS	49.860	78.700	6.000 / 4.200	344 / —	61 / —	± 10 / —	UG
07-11-85	02:27:00.00	KTS	50.000	78.000	4.000 / —	1 / —	0.05 / —	±0.02 / —	UG

Table 10.2
Known Soviet Underground Nuclear Explosions 1961-1987 (continued)

Date (GMT)	Time h: m: secs	Location	Lat(N)	Long(E)	Seismic Data m_b / M_S	#sta / #sta	Yield (Kt) $Y(m_b)$ / $Y(M_S)$	±dYb / ±dYs	Type
07-18-85	21:14:57.50	Outside main test areas	65.965	40.754	5.000 / 3.600	— / —	10 / —	± 3 / —	UG
07-20-85	00:53:00.00	KTS	50.000	79.000	6.700 / —	1 / —	27 / —	± 9 / —	UG
07-25-85	03:11:00.00	KTS	50.000	79.000	5.300 / —	1 / —	1.00 / —	±0.36 / —	UG
02-26-87	04:58:24.00	KTS	49.840	78.120	5.400 / —		14 / —	± 2 / —	UG
03-12-87	01:57:18.00	KTS	49.940	78.820	5.500 / —		18 / —	± 3 / —	UG
04-03-87	01:17:09.00	KTS	49.900	78.810	6.200 / 4.700		140 / —	± 58 / —	UG
04-17-87	01:03:04.70	KTS	49.851	78.690	6.000 / 4.300		61 / —	± 10 / —	UG
04-19-87	04:00:01.80	Outside main test areas	60.781	56.220	4.500 / —		3.3 / —	± 0.6 / —	UG
04-19-87	04:05:01.20	Outside main test areas	60.674	56.295	4.400 / —		2.6 / —	± 0.5 / —	UG
05-06-87	04:02:05.6	KTS	49.830	78.125	5.600 / —		23 / —	± 1 / —	UG
06-06-87	02:37:06.9	KTS	49.865	78.143	5.300 / —		12 / —	± 1 / —	UG
06-20-87	00:53:04.8	KTS	49.901	78.726	6.100 / —		81 / —	± 34 / —	UG
07-06-87	23:59:56.6	Outside main test areas	62.110	112.770	5.100 / —		13 / —	± 2 / —	UG
07-17-87	01:17:07.0	KTS	49.779	78.128	5.800 / 4.200		38 / —	± 6 / —	UG
07-24-87	01:59:56.7	Outside main test areas	61.470	112.700	5.100 / —		13 / —	± 2 / —	UG
08-02-87	00:58:06.7	KTS	49.828	78.898	5.900 / —		48 / —	± 8 / —	UG
08-02-87	01:59:59.5	Novaya Zemlya (northern site)	73.289	54.713	5.800 / —		70 / —	± 12 / —	UG
08-12-87	01:29:56.8	Outside main test areas	61.426	112.708	5.000 / —		10 / —	± 1 / —	UG
09-16-87	07:30:01.0	KTS	49.000	78.000	5.000 / —		6 / —	± 4 / —	UG
09-18-87	02:31:57.0	KTS	49.000	78.000	4.300 / —		1.1 / —	± 0.2 / —	UG
10-03-87	15:14:57.5	Outside main test areas	47.630	56.220	5.200 / —		17 / —	± 3 / —	UG
10-16-87	06:06:00.0	KTS	49.000	78.000	4.600 / —		2.2 / —	± 0.4 / —	UG
11-15-87	03:31:06.7	KTS	49.879	78.790	6.000 / 4.400		61 / —	± 10 / —	UG
12-13-87	03:21:04.7	KTS	49.970	78.880	6.100 / 4.400		81 / —	± 34 / —	UG
12-20-87	02:55:12.0	KTS	50.100	77.500	4.800 / —		3.6 / —	± 0.6 / —	UG
12-27-87	03:05:08.0	KTS	49.900	78.590	6.100 / —		81 / —	± 34 / —	UG

Table 10.2
Known Soviet Underground Nuclear Explosions 1961-1987 (continued)

Sources.

National Defence Research Institute of Sweden (FOA), *Nuclear Explosions 1945-29 November 1987* (printout), December 1987; Ola Dahlman and Hans Israelson, *Monitoring Underground Nuclear Explosions* (Amsterdam: Elsevier Scientific Publishing Co., 1977); Bruce A. Bolt, *Nuclear Explosions and Earthquakes: The Parted Veil* (San Francisco: W.H. Freeman and Co., 1976); P. D. Marshall, T. C. Bache, and R. C. Lilwall, "Body Wave Magnitudes and Locations of Soviet Underground Explosions at the Semipalatinsk Test Site," U.K. Atomic Weapons Research Establishment Report No. O 16/84, 1984; J. I. Sands, R. S. Norris and T. B. Cochran, "Known Soviet Nuclear Explosions, 1949-1985, Revised Preliminary List," Nuclear Weapons Databook Working Paper, NWD 86-3, June 1986; various publications and lists by staff members of the Lawrence Livermore National Laboratory (LLNL), such as M. D. Nordyke, "A Review of Soviet Data on the Peaceful Uses of Nuclear Explosions," Annals Nuclear Energy, Vol. 2, 1975, pp. 657-673; "The Test Ban Treaties: Verifying Compliance," *Energy and Technology Review*, Lawrence Livermore National Laboratory, May 1983, pp. 1-9; LLNL, "Presumed Nuclear Events in the Soviet Union Occurring Away from Normal Test Sites (1965-1985)," unpublished document, 18 February 1986); and semi-annual technical reports and lists of events located by the Norwegian Seismic Array (NORSAR). In addition to these sources, we searched the lists of seismological events published by the U.S. Geological Survey in their Earthquake Data Report and those of the International Seismological Center, the International Seismological Service, and other standard seismological catalogs for areas including the main Soviet test sites. The Geological Survey of Canada also provided information on additional events. Information on double explosions was provided by Dr. Roger Clark of the University of Leeds. For a detailed listing of the sources used in this table, see Lynn R. Sykes and Steven Ruggi, "Soviet Underground Nuclear Testing: Inferences from Seismic Observations and Historical Perspective," Nuclear Weapons Databook Working Paper, NWD 86-4, November 1986.

Table 10.3
Summary of Known Soviet Nuclear Explosions, 1949-1987

Year	Number	Military	Peaceful	Location KTS	Novaya Zemlya	W. Kazakh	Other[1]	Cumulative Total	Announced by U.S. Government	Annual Yield in Kilotons[2]
1949	1	1	0	0	0	0	1	1	1	15
1950	0	0	0	0	0	0	0	1	0	0
1951	2	2	0	2	0	0	0	3	2	75
1952	0	0	0	0	0	0	0	3	0	0
1953	4	4	0	4	0	0	0	7	2	360
1954	7	7	0	0	0	0	7	14	1	260
1955	5	5	0	2	0	0	3	19	4	1865
1956	9 }+18[3]	9 }+18[3]	0	0	0	0	9	28	7	6135
1957	15	15	0	2	4	0	9	43	13	10,500
1958	29	29	0	0	26	0	3	90[3]	25	31,500
1959	0	0	0	0	0	0	0	90	0	0
1960	0	0	0	0	0	0	0	90	0	0
1961	50	50	0	6	24	0	20	140	50	200,000
1962	44	44	0	10	32	0	2	184	40	201,500
1963	0	0	0	0	0	0	0	184	0	0
1964	6	6	0	4	2	0	0	190	3	90
1965	9	8	1	8	0	0	1	199	4	210
1966	15	13	2	12	1	1	1	214	7	690
1967	17	16	1	15	1	0	1	231	4	305
1968	13	11	2	10	1	1	1	244	7	185
1969	16	12	4	10	1	1	4	260	12	430
1970	17	14	3	9	1	4	3	277	10	1110
1971	19	13	6	11	1	1	6	296	14	885
1972	22	13	9	12	1	0	9	318	14	840
1973	14	9	5	6	3	0	5	332	14	5695
1974	18	15	3	13	2	0	3	350	8	2637
1975	15	14	1	10	3	1	1	365	10	2100
1976	17	16	1	13	2	1	1	382	10	350
1977	18	14	4	11	2	1	4	401[4]	11	305
1978	27	22	5	18	2	2	5	427	20	728
1979	29	25	4	19	2	4	4	456	15	820
1980	21	18	3	17	1	1	2	477	10	500
1981	22[5]	17	5	16	1	2	3	499	9	660
1982	31	15	16	14	1	10	6	530	6	675
1983	27[5]	14	13	12	2	10	3	557	9	590
1984	29	17	12	16	1	2	10	586	17	928
1985	9	7	2	7	0	0	2	595	4	260
1986	0	0	0	0	0	0	0	595	0	0
1987	23	17	6	16	1	0	6	618	22[6]	800
TOTALS	**618**	**510**	**108**	**305**	**118**	**42**	**135**	**618**	**385**	**474,000**

---

1. Includes tests outside the main test areas and explosions whose locations are unknown. For purposes of counting numbers of military and peaceful explosions, 15 explosions of unknown purpose at Azgir in western Kazakhstan were counted as military.
2. Yield information for most atmospheric tests is unavailable. The estimates for 1949 through 1962 are based on the following:
   a. Yields of individual tests as given in Table 10.1.
   b. The following estimates for fission yield from 1949 through 1958 were presented to Congress in 1958: 1949-51, 60 Kt; 1952-1954, 500 Kt; 1955-1956, 4 Mt; 1957-1958, 21 Mt; Joint Committee on Atomic Energy, Hearings, Fallout from Nuclear Weapons Tests, Vol. I, 5-8 May 1959, p. 23.
   c. Former Chairman of the AEC, Glenn T. Seaborg has estimated that the cumulative yield of the 1961 test series was nearly 200 megatons; *Kennedy, Khrushchev, and the Test Ban* (Berkeley: University of California Press, 1981), p. 90.
   d. The French Ministry of Defense (MoD) has estimated 452 megatons for atmospheric tests through 1962; Minister de la Defence, Direction de Centre d'Experimentations Nucleaire, *Organization et Functionnement de Centre d'Experimentation Nucleaire, Dossier No. 1*, "Essais Nucleaires, Tableau Recapitulatif des Explosions Annoncees et Presumees," Piece No. 7/41, 31 January 1985.

   The annual totals for 1949, 1951, 1953, and 1955 are derived from specific yield estimates for individual tests. The estimate for 1954 is derived by taking the estimated cumulative fission yield for 1952-1954 (500 Kt) and subtracting the annual yield value for 1953. It was assumed that half of the total yield of the thermonuclear device on 8-12-53 was fission yield. The same methodology is used to derive the estimates for 1956, 1957, and 1958. For example, the 1956 yield was determined by subtracting from the estimated 1955-1956 cumulative yied (4 Mt) the known yields of the 1955 test series. For the 1957-1958 period, it was also assumed that the annual cumulative yields are at a ratio of one to three, which is the approximate ratio of high yield tests during the two years. The estimate for 1961 is that provided by Seaborg, and the estimate for 1962 is the remaining amount needed to reach the French MoD estimate for the cumulative total through 1962 (ignoring the presumed relatively small cumulative total from the three underwater and two to five underground tests conducted before 1963). Yield estimates from 1964-1987 are from Table 10.2.
3. The Stockholm International Peace Research Institute (SIPRI) and the Swedish National Defence Research Institute list 57 Soviet explosions from 1949 through 1958, and SIPRI notes that an additional 33 tests, whose dates are unknown, took place during this period; see SIPRI, *World Armaments and Disarmament*, SIPRI Yearbook: 1975, pp. 510-511, and 1976, pp. 416-417; National Defence Research Institute, *Appendix III, Nuclear Explosions 1945 - August 1985*. These additional tests are apparently included in a classified Swedish list. Table 10.1 lists 72 tests during this period, leaving at least 18 of the 33 tests unaccounted for. All of these tests presumably took place in 1956-1958 since the tests through 1955 are numbered. The locations and dates of these additional tests are unknown. Hence, the cumulative totals reflect an additional 18 weapons-related tests from 1958 on. The French MoD estimates that 182 Soviet tests were conducted before 1963, 174 of which were conducted in the atmosphere and eight of which were conducted underground (some of these were presumably conducted underwater); Minister de la Defence, *op. cit.*
4. The French MoD reports an additional 12 tests from 1963 through 1977; *ibid*. Since additional data are not available on these tests, they are excluded from the overall totals.
5. The French MoD reports 23 tests in both 1981 and 1983; *ibid*.
6. The Soviets began announcing their nuclear tests in 1987.

Table 10.4
Soviet Seismic Events That Have Not Been Identified as Being Earthquakes, Large Chemical Explosions, or Nuclear Explosions

Date (GMT)	Time h: m: secs	Location Lat(N)	Long(E)	Seismic Data m_b	#station
06-14-68	06:01:31.00	45.000	55.300	4.300	3
05-15-70	04:36:33.00	44.600	46.400	3.800	1
05-17-70	01:01:09.00	45.100	46.200	4.000	1
05-17-70	06:58:56.00	45.100	47.100	4.100	1
05-17-70	08:46:10.00	44.100	48.300	—	6
05-17-70	10:06:50.00	48.100	47.800	3.700	2
08-09-70	02:24:02.00	48.600	55.600	4.000	2
10-28-70	08:50:13.00	44.600	47.100	4.200	1
07-07-71	01:05:52.00	72.200	54.400	—	—
12-06-71	12:51:46.70	45.000	54.800	—	—
03-04-74	14:04:41.00	51.000	79.000	—	—
06-16-74	12:23:39.46	49.420	49.080	3.600	5
09-03-74	13:55:42.93	47.570	47.160	4.100	8
09-28-74	10:21:31.00	49.410	47.600	3.900	4
12-12-74	21:19:25.00	70.000	53.000	4.100	—
11-15-78	08:30:04.88	72.570	52.840	4.300	6
03-13-79	02:23:33.00	49.000	80.000	4.600	—
07-19-82	09:00:06.10	62.530	47.810	4.400	—

Sources: Large Aperture Seismic Array (LASA); International Seismological Center; Hagfors Observatory; Norwegian Seismic Array (NORSAR); Geological Survey of Canada.

Table 10.5
Known Nuclear Explosions in Eastern Kazakhstan (KTS) by Month

Year	Jan	Feb	Mar	Apr	May	Jun	Jul	Aug	Sep	Oct	Nov	Dec	Total
1949													0
1950													0
1951									1	1			2
1952													0
1953								4					4
1954													?
1955											2		2
1956													0
1957									2				2
1958													0
1959													0
1960													0
1961									5	1			6
1962		1						2		4	3		10
1963													0
1964			1		1		1				1		4
1965	*		1		1	1	1		1	1	1	1	8
1966		1	1	1	1	1	1	2	1	1		2	12
1967	1	1	1	1	1	2	1	1	2	2	1	1	15
1968	1			1		2	1	1	2		1	1	10
1969			1		2		2		1	1	1	2	10
1970	1		1		1	1	2		1		1	1	9
1971			1	1	1	3				2	1	2	11
1972		1	2			1	1	2	1		1	3	12
1973		1		1			2			1		1	6
1974	2			1	2	1	1		1	1		4	13
1975		1	1	1		2		1		2		2	10
1976	1			2	1	1	2	2		1	1	2	13
1977			1	1	1	1	1	1	1	2	1	1	11
1978			2	1	1	1	2	2	2	2	3	2	18
1979		2			3	1	2	2	3	2	1	3	19
1980				3	1	2	2		5	1		3	17
1981			2	1	1	2	2	1	2	1	2	2	16
1982		1		1		2	2	2	3			3	14
1983			1	1	1	2	1		1	2	2	1	12
1984		1	2	2	1	1	1		2	2	1	3	16
1985		1		1	2	3							7
1986													0
1987		1	1	2	1	2	1	1	2	1	1	3	16
Total	6	12	19	22	21	31	32	24	39	31	25	43	305

* Does not include peaceful nuclear explosion of 15 January 1965 used for creating a large crater on test site.

Table 10.6
Known Nuclear Explosions in Novaya Zemlya by Month

Year	Jan	Feb	Mar	Apr	May	Jun	Jul	Aug	Sep	Oct	Nov	Dec	Total
1949													0
1950													0
1951													0
1952													0
1953													0
1954													0
1955													0
1956													0
1957									2	2			4
1958		3	5						3	15			26
1959													0
1960													0
1961									9	12	3		24
1962								6	10	5	3	8	32
1963													0
1964									1	1			2
1965													0
1966										1			1
1967										1			1
1968											1		1
1969										1			1
1970										1			1
1971									1				1
1972								1					1
1973									2	1			3
1974								1			1		2
1975								1		2			3
1976										1			2
1977									1	1			2
1978								1	1				2
1979									1	1			2
1980										1			1
1981										1			1
1982										1			1
1983									1	1			2
1984										1			1
1985													0
1986													0
1987								1					1
Total		3	5					12	33	49	8	8	118

Table 10.7
Summary of Explosions in Eastern Kazakhstan (KTS) and Novaya Zemlya (NZ) by Month

	1949-1987						1964-1987					
	Number			Percentage			Number			Percentage		
Month	KTS	NZ	Total	KTS	NZ	Total	KTS	NZ	Total	KTS	NZ	Total
January	6	0	6	2.0	0.0	1.4	6	0	6	2.3	0.0	2.0
February	12	3	15	3.9	2.5	3.5	11	0	11	3.9	0.0	3.5
March	19	5	24	6.2	4.2	5.7	19	0	19	6.8	0.0	6.1
April	22	0	22	7.2	0.0	5.2	22	0	22	7.9	0.0	7.1
May	21	0	21	6.9	0.0	5.0	21	0	21	7.5	0.0	6.7
June	31	0	31	10.2	0.0	7.3	31	0	31	11.1	0.0	9.9
July	32	0	32	10.5	0.0	7.8	32	0	32	11.5	0.0	10.6
August	24	12	36	7.9	10.0	8.5	18	6	24	6.1	5.2	7.7
September	39	33	72	12.8	27.1	7.0	31	9	40	11.2	7.2	12.8
October	31	49	80	10.2	41.1	8.9	25	15	40	9.4	5.5	12.8
November	25	8	33	8.2	6.7	7.8	20	2	22	7.2	6.1	7.1
December	43	8	51	14.1	6.1	2.0	43	0	43	15.4	0.0	13.8
Total	**305**	**118**	**423**	**72.0**	**28.0**	**100.0**	**279**	**32**	**311**	**89.7**	**10.3**	**100.0**

Table 10.8
Underground Nuclear Explosions in Eastern Kazakhstan (KTS) by Yield Range (1962-1985)

Year	No Yield	<1 Kt	1-5 Kt	5-20 Kt	20-200 Kt	200-1 Mt	>1 Mt	Total
1962	1	0	0	0	0	0	0	1
1963	0	0	0	0	0	0	0	0
1964	1	0	0	1	2	0	0	4
1965	0	0	2	5	1	0	0	8
1966	0	0	3	4	5	0	0	12
1967	0	0	3	10	2	0	0	15
1968	0	0	2	7	1	0	0	10
1969	0	0	0	7	3	0	0	10
1970	0	1	0	7	1	0	0	9
1971	0	0	1	7	3	0	0	11
1972	0	1	2	6	3	0	0	12
1973	0	0	0	4	2	0	0	6
1974	0	0	5	7	1	0	0	13
1975	0	1	1	4	4	0	0	10
1976	0	1	2	6	4	0	0	13
1977	0	0	1	5	5	0	0	11
1978	0	0	4	6	8	0	0	18
1979	0	3	3	6	7	0	0	19
1980	0	5	1	5	6	0	0	17
1981	0	4	0	6	6	0	0	16
1982	0	4	3	3	4	0	0	14
1983	0	3	2	4	3	0	0	12
1984	0	2	2	1	11	0	0	16
1985	0	1	1	0	5	0	0	7
Total	**2**	**26**	**38**	**111**	**87**	**0**	**0**	**264**

		1962-1985	1980-1984
Cumulative percentage of events with yields	< 1 Kt	9	24
Cumulative percentage of events with yields	< 5 Kt	24	34
Cumulative percentage of events with yields	<20 Kt	66	60

Table 10.9
Underground Nuclear Explosions in Novaya Zemlya by Yield Range (1962-1985)

Year	No Yield	<1 Kt	1-5 Kt	5-20 Kt	20-200 Kt	200-1 Mt	>1 Mt	Total
1962	0	0	0	0	0	0	0	0
1963	0	0	0	0	0	0	0	0
1964	0	0	1	1	0	0	0	2
1965	0	0	0	0	0	0	0	0
1966	0	0	0	0	0	1	0	1
1967	0	0	0	0	1	0	0	1
1968	0	0	0	0	1	0	0	1
1969	0	0	0	0	1	0	0	1
1970	0	0	0	0	0	0	1	1
1971	0	0	0	0	0	1	0	1
1972	0	0	0	0	0	1	0	1
1973	0	0	0	0	1	0	2	3
1974	0	0	0	0	0	1	1	2
1975	0	0	0	0	0	2	1*	3
1976	0	0	0	1	1	0	0	2
1977	0	0	1	0	1	0	0	2
1978	0	0	0	0	2	0	0	2
1979	0	0	0	0	2	0	0	2
1980	0	0	0	0	1*	0	0	1
1981	0	0	0	0	1	0	0	1
1982	0	0	0	0	1	0	0	1
1983	0	0	0	0	2	0	0	2
1984	0	0	0	0	1	0	0	1
1985	0	0	0	0	0	0	0	0
Total	**0**	**0**	**2**	**2**	**16**	**6**	**5**	**31**

		1963-1985	1980-1984
Cumulative percentage of events with yields	< 1 Kt	0	0
Cumulative percentage of events with yields	< 5 Kt	6	0
Cumulative percentage of events with yields	<20 Kt	13	0

* Known double explosions counted as a single event.

Table 10.10

Underground Nuclear Explosions in Western Kazakhstan By Yield Range (1962-1985)

Year	No Yield	≤1 Kt	1-5 Kt	5-20 Kt	20-200 Kt	200-1 Mt	>1Mt	Total
1962	0	0	0	0	0	0	0	0
1963	0	0	0	0	0	0	0	0
1964	0	0	0	0	0	0	0	0
1965	0	0	0	0	0	0	0	0
1966	0	0	1	0	0	0	0	1
1967	0	0	0	0	0	0	0	0
1968	0	0	0	0	1	0	0	1
1969	0	1	0	0	0	0	0	1
1970	0	4	0	0	0	0	0	4
1971	0	0	0	0	1	0	0	1
1972	0	0	0	0	0	0	0	0
1973	0	0	0	0	0	0	0	0
1974	0	0	0	0	0	0	0	0
1975	0	0	1	0	0	0	0	1
1976	0	0	0	0	1	0	0	1
1977	0	0	0	1	0	0	0	1
1978	0	0	0	0	2	0	0	2
1979	0	0	1	0	3	0	0	4
1980	0	0	0	1	0	0	0	1
1981	0	0	0	2	0	0	0	2
1982	0	6	0	4	0	0	0	10
1983	0	4	1	5	0	0	0	10
1984	0	0	0	2	0	0	0	2
1985	0	0	0	0	0	0	0	0
Total	**0**	**15**	**4**	**15**	**8**	**0**	**0**	**42**

		1963-1985	1980-1984
Cumulative percentage of events with yields	< 1 Kt	36	40
Cumulative percentage of events with yields	< 5 Kt	45	44
Cumulative percentage of events with yields	<20 Kt	81	100

Table 10.11

Table 10.11
Underground Nuclear Explosions Outside Main Test Areas or Announced as Explosions for Peaceful Purposes by Yield Range (1962-1985)*

Year	No Yield	<1 Kt	1-5 Kt	5-20 Kt	20-200 Kt	200-1 Mt	>1 Mt	Total
1962	0	0	0	0	0	0	0	0
1963	0	0	0	0	0	0	0	0
1964	0	0	0	0	0	0	0	0
1965	0	0	0	0	1	0	0	1
1966	0	0	1	0	1	0	0	2
1967	0	0	0	1	0	0	0	1
1968	0	0	0	0	2	0	0	2
1969	1	0	0	2	1	0	0	4
1970	0	0	0	1	2	0	0	3
1971	0	0	2	3	1	0	0	6
1972	0	1	2	4	2	0	0	9
1973	0	0	0	4	1	0	0	5
1974	0	0	1	1	1	0	0	3
1975	0	0	0	1	0	0	0	1
1976	0	0	0	0	1	0	0	1
1977	0	0	0	4	0	0	0	4
1978	0	0	0	3	2	0	0	5
1979	0	0	0	3	1	0	0	4
1980	0	0	1	1	0	0	0	2
1981	0	0	1	1	1	0	0	3
1982	0	2	0	2	2	0	0	6
1983	0	0	0	0	3	0	0	3
1984	0	1	3	3	3	0	0	10
1985	0	0	0	2	0	0	0	2
Total	1	4	11	36	25	0	0	77

		1963-1985	1980-1984
Cumulative percentage of events with yields	< 1 Kt	5	12
Cumulative percentage of events with yields	< 5 Kt	19	33
Cumulative percentage of events with yields	<20 Kt	66	62

* Does not include Azgir and Astrakhan sites in western Kazakhstan unless those events are described by U.S.S.R. sources as PNEs. Multiple or double explosions cited in text counted as one event.

Table 10.12

Known Soviet Underground Nuclear Explosions by Yield Range (1961-1985)

Year	No Yield	≤1 Kt	1-5 Kt	5-20 Kt	20-200 Kt	200-1 Mt	>1 Mt	Total
1961	1	0	0	0	0	0	0	1
1962	1	0	0	0	0	0	0	1
1963	0	0	0	0	0	0	0	0
1964	1	0	1	2	2	0	0	6
1965	0	0	2	5	2	0	0	9
1966	0	0	4	4	6	1	0	15
1967	0	0	3	11	3	0	0	17
1968	0	0	2	7	4	0	0	13
1969	1	1	0	9	5	0	0	16
1970	0	5	0	8	3	0	1	17
1971	0	0	3	10	5	1	0	19
1972	0	2	4	10	5	1	0	22
1973	0	0	0	8	4	0	2	14
1974	0	0	6	8	2	1	1	18
1975	0	1	2	5	4	2	1	15
1976	0	1	2	7	7	0	0	17
1977	0	0	2	10	6	0	0	18
1978	0	0	4	9	14	0	0	27
1979	0	3	4	9	13	0	0	29
1980	0	5	2	7	7	0	0	21
1981	0	4	1	9	8	0	0	22
1982	0	12	3	9	7	0	0	31
1983	0	7	3	9	8	0	0	27
1984	0	3	6	5	15	0	0	29
1985	0	1	1	2	5	0	0	9
Total	4	45	55	163	135	6	5	413

		1961-1985	1980-1984
Cumulative percentage of events with yields	< 1 Kt	11	24
Cumulative percentage of events with yields	< 5 Kt	24	35
Cumulative percentage of events with yields	<20 Kt	64	65

Table 10.13
Large Underground Nuclear Explosions at Eastern Kazakhstan (KTS), April 1976–December 1985

Date	Y_{m_b} (Kt)	M_s(max)	YM_s (Kt)	Y_{AVE} (Kt)
Explosions with One or More Yield Estimates >125				
23 Jun 1979	152	4.26	146	149
4 Aug 1979	113	4.29	157	135
14 Sep 1980	150	large tectonic release	—	150*
13 Sep 1981	71	(4.33)	(173)	(122)
18 Oct 1981	66	4.20	127	97
27 Dec 1981	176	4.26	146	161
4 Jul 1982	158	surface waves masked by earthquake	—	158*
14 Jul 1984	140		143	141
27 Oct 1984	140		141	140
Average and standard error of mean of above nine explosions				139 ± 7
Other Large Explosions				
18 Aug 1979	119	large tectonic release	—	119*
23 Dec 1979	119	(3.87)	(58)	(88)
25 Apr 1982	77	4.15	113	95
5 Dec 1982	97			97*
6 Oct 1983	67			67*
26 Oct 1983	101			101*
16 Dec 1984	81			81*

Parentheses indicate poor determination based on three or fewer stations used for for M_S calculation.
* Yield average = Y_{AVE} based on m_b reading alone
Ym_b = Yield from m_b
YM_s = Yield from M_s

APPENDICES

Short Titles

Appendix A
Short Titles of Frequently Cited References

ACDA, FY 19xx ACIS. U.S. Congress, for the use of the Senate Foreign Relations Committee and House Foreign Affairs Committee, Fiscal Year 19xx Arms Control Impact Statements, prepared by the Arms Control and Disarmament Agency, Joint Committee Print (Washington, DC: Government Printing Office, 19xx).

Berman and Baker, *Soviet Strategic Forces*. Robert C. Berman and John C. Baker, *Soviet Strategic Forces* (Washington, DC: The Brookings Institution, 1982).

CIA, *Soviet Weapons Industry*, 1986. Central Intelligence Agency, Directorate of Intelligence, *The Soviet Weapons Industry: An Overview*, DI 86-10016, September 1986.

Collins and Cronin, *U.S./Soviet Military Balance*, 1985. John M. Collins and Patrick M. Cronin, *U.S./Soviet Military Balance: Statistical Trends, 1975-1984 (As of January 1, 1985)*, Congressional Research Service Report 85-83-F (Washington, DC: Library of Congress, 15 April 1985).

Collins and Glakas, *U.S./Soviet Military Balance*, 1983. John M. Collins and Thomas Peter Glakas, *U.S./Soviet Military Balance: Statistical Trends, 1970-1982 (As of January 1, 1983)*, Congressional Research Service Report 83-153-S (Washington, DC: Library of Congress, updated 1 August 1983).

Collins and Victory, *U.S./Soviet Military Balance*, 1987. John M. Collins and Bernard C. Victory, *U.S./Soviet Military Balance: Statistical Trends, 1977-1986 (As of January 1, 1987)*, Congressional Research Service Report 87-745-S (Washington, DC: Library of Congress, 1 September 1987).

Collins and Victory, *U.S./Soviet Military Balance*, 1988. John M. Collins and Bernard C. Victory, *U.S./Soviet Military Balance: Statistical Trends, 1980-1987 (As of January 1, 1988)*, Congressional Research Service Report 88-425-S (Washington, DC: Library of Congress, 15 April 1988).

Couhat, *Combat Fleets of the World*, 1984/85. John Labayle Couhat, ed., *Combat Fleets of the World, 1984/85: Their Ships, Aircraft, and Armament* (Annapolis, MD: Naval Institute Press, 1984).

Couhat, *Combat Fleets of the World*, 1988/89. John Labayle Couhat and Bernard Prézelin, eds., *Combat Fleets of the World, 1988/89: Their Ships, Aircraft, and Armament* (Annapolis, MD: Naval Institute Press, 1988).

DIA, *ASW Handbook*, 1977. Defense Intelligence Agency, *Soviet Antisubmarine Warfare Capabilities Handbook*, DDI-1230-1-77, August 1977; Change 1: pen and ink changes and page substitutions; information cut-off date 1 September 1978.

DIA, *Force Structure Summary*, November 1987. Defense Intelligence Agency, *Force Structure Summary-USSR, Eastern Europe, Mongolia, and Afghanistan*, DDB-2680-170-87, November 1987.

DIA, *Handbook on the Soviet Armed Forces*. Defense Intelligence Agency, *Handbook on the Soviet Armed Forces*, DDB-2680-40-78, February 1978.

DIA, *JIIKS, Vol. XIII*, 1983. Defense Intelligence Agency, Joint Imagery Interpretation Keys Structure (JIIKS), Manual 57-7, Vol. XIII (Submarines), prepared by Naval Intelligence Support Center, 15 April 1983 (not paginated).

DIA, *Soviet Front Fire Support*. Defense Intelligence Agency, *Soviet Front Fire Support*, DDB-1130-8-82, September 1982.

DIA, *Soviet Air Force, Strategic Bombers*, 1981. Defense Intelligence Agency, *Soviet Air Force, Strategic Bombers*, Air Force Intelligence Study (AFIS), DDB-1300-95-81, October 1981.

DIA, *Warsaw Pact Ground Forces Equipment Identification Guide*. Defense Intelligence Agency, *Warsaw Pact Ground Forces Equipment Identification Guide:Artillery, Rockets, and Missiles*, DDB-1100-313-82, February 1982.

DOD, FY 19xx Annual Report. Classified versions with deletions obtained under the Freedom of Information Act are cited as **DOD, FY 19xx Annual Report** (class.). Department of Defense, *Annual Report to the Congress by the Secretary of Defense*, Fiscal Year 19xx (Washington, DC: Government Printing Office, 19xx).

DOD, FY 19xx RDA. Department of Defense, *Program for Research, Development and Acquisition*, Fiscal Year 19xx (Washington, DC: Government Printing Office, 19xx).

Freedman, *U.S. Intelligence*. Lawrence Freedman, *U.S. Intelligence and the Soviet Strategic Threat*, 2d Ed. (Princeton, NJ: Princeton University Press, 1986).

General Dynamics, *World's Missile Systems*, 1982. General Dynamics, *The World's Missile Systems*, 7th ed. (Pomona, CA: April 1982).

Short Titles

Gunston, *Aircraft of the Soviet Union,* 1983. Bill Gunston, *Aircraft of the Soviet Union* (London: Osprey Publishing, 1983).

Gunston, *Guide to the Modern Soviet Air Force,* 1982. Bill Gunston, *An Illustrated Guide to the Modern Soviet Air Force* (New York: Arco Publishing, 1982).

Gunston, *Rockets & Missiles,* 1979. Bill Gunston, *The Illustrated Encyclopedia of the World's Rockets & Missiles,* (New York: Crescent Books, 1979).

HAC, FY 19xx DOD, Part x. U.S. Congress, House, Department of Defense Subcommittee of the Committee of Appropriations, Department of Defense Appropriations for 19xx (Washington, DC: Government Printing Office, 19xx).

HAC, FY 19xx EWDA, Part x. U.S. Congress, House, Energy and Water Development Subcommittee of the Committee of Appropriations, Energy and Water Development Appropriations for 19xx (Washington, DC: Government Printing Office, 19xx).

HASC, FY 19xx DOD, Part x. U.S. Congress, House, Committee on Armed Services, Defense Department Authorization and Oversight for Fiscal Year 19xx (Washington, DC: Government Printing Office, 19xx).

HASC, FY 19xx DOE. U.S. Congress, House, Committee on Armed Services, Department of Energy National Security Programs Authorization Act for Fiscal Year 19xx (Washington, DC: Government Printing Office, 19xx).

Holloway, *The Soviet Union and the Arms Race,* 1984. David Holloway, *The Soviet Union and the Arms Race,* 2d ed. (New Haven, CT: Yale University Press, 1984).

IISS, *Military Balance,* 19xx-19xx. The International Institute for Strategic Studies, *The Military Balance,* 19xx-19xx (London: IISS, 19xx).

Jane's All the World's Aircraft, 1987-88. John W.R. Taylor, ed., *Jane's All the World's Aircraft,* 1987-88 (London: Jane's Publishing Company, 1987).

Jane's Fighting Ships, 1988-89. Captain Richard Sharpe, ed., *Jane's Fighting Ships,* 1988-89 (London: Jane's Publishing Company, 1988).

Jane's Weapon Systems, 1987-88. Bernard Blake, ed., *Jane's Weapon Systems,* 1987-88 (London: Jane's Publishing Company, 1987).

JCS, FY 19xx. Joint Chiefs of Staff, *United States Military Posture,* FY 19xx, prepared by the Joint Staff.

JEC, Allocation of Resources - Year. Joint Economic Committee, Allocation of Resources in the Soviet Union and China - 1985, Part 11; 1984, Part 10; 1983, Part 9; 1982, Part 8; 1981, Part 7; 1980, Part 6; 1979, Part 5; 1978, Part 4 (Soviet Union); 1977, Part 3; 1976, Part 2; 1975, Part 1; 1974.

MccGwire, *Military Objectives.* Michael MccGwire, *Military Objectives in Soviet Foreign Policy* (Washington, DC: The Brookings Institution, 1987).

Malzeyev, "Soviet Air-Launched Cruise Missiles," 1978. Alexander Malzeyev, "Soviet Air-Launched Cruise Missiles,' *International Defense Review,* January 1978 (reprinted in International Defense Review, *Soviet Armed Forces and Their Equipment,* Special Series No. 16, 1982, pp. 54-56).

Meyer, "Soviet Theatre Nuclear Forces," Part I or II. Stephen M. Meyer, "Soviet Theatre Nuclear Forces': Part I, 'Development of Doctrine and Objectives'; Part II, "Capabilities and Implications," Adelphi Papers Nos. 187 and 188 (London: International Institute for Strategic Studies, Winter 1983-1984).

NATO and the Warsaw Pact, 1984. NATO, *NATO and the Warsaw Pact: Force Comparisons* (Brussels: NATO Information Service, 1984).

NATO and the Warsaw Pact, 1982. NATO, *NATO and the Warsaw Pact: Force Comparisons* (Brussels: NATO Information Service, 1982).

Polmar, *Guide to the Soviet Navy,* 1983. Norman Polmar, *Guide to the Soviet Navy,* 3d ed. (Annapolis, MD: Naval Institute Press, 1983).

Polmar, *Guide to the Soviet Navy,* 1986. Norman Polmar, *Guide to the Soviet Navy,* 4th ed. (Annapolis, MD: Naval Institute Press, 1986).

Prados, *Soviet Estimate.* John Prados, *The Soviet Estimate: U.S. Intelligence Analysis & Russian Military Strength* (New York: Dial Press), 1982).

Rich and Pike, *SALT,* 1984. Jonathan Rich and John Pike, *SALT: The Case for Continued Adherence* (Washington, DC: Federation of American Scientists, October 1984).

SAC, *Soviet Military Capabilities,* July 1981. Strategic Air Command, DCS/Intelligence, *Soviet Military Capabilities,* Commander's Distinguished Visitors Program (unclassified intelligence briefing), July 1981.

SAC, FY 19xx DOD, Part x. U. S. Congress, Senate, Department of Defense Subcommittee of the Committee of Appropriations, Department of Defense Appropriations for Fiscal Year 19xx (Washington, DC: Government Printing Office, 19xx).

SAC, FY 19xx EWDA, Part x. U. S. Congress, Senate, Energy and Water Development Subcommittee of the Committee of Appropriations, Energy and Water Development Appropriations for 19xx (Washington, DC: Government Printing Office, 19xx).

SASC, FY 19xx DOD, Part x. U. S. Congress, Senate, Committee on Armed Services, Department of Defense Authorization for Appropriations for Fiscal Year 19xx (Washington, DC: Government Printing Office, 19xx).

SASC, FY 19xx DOE. U. S. Congress, Senate, Committee on Armed Services, Department of Energy National Security Programs Authorization Act for Fiscal Year 19xx (Washington, DC: Government Printing Office, 19xx).

Short Titles

SASC, SALT II Treaty, Part x. U. S. Congress, Senate, Committee on Armed Services, Military Implications on the Limitation of Strategic Offensive Arms and Protocol Thereto (SALT II Treaty) (Washington, DC: Government Printing Office, 1979).

SASC/SAC, Soviet Strategic Force Developments, 1985. U. S. Congress, Senate, Committee on Armed Services and the Subcommittee on Defense of the Committee on Appropriations, Soviet Strategic Force Developments, 26 June 1985 (Washington, DC: Government Printing Office, 1986).

SASC, Strategic Force Modernization Programs, 1981. U.S. Congress, Senate, Committee on Armed Services, Strategic Force Modernization Programs (Washington, DC: Government Printing Office, 1981).

SFRC, SALT II Treaty, Part x. U. S. Congress, Senate, Committee on Foreign Relations, The SALT II Treaty (Washington, DC: Government Printing Office, 1979).

SMP [Year]. Department of Defense, *Soviet Military Power*, 1st ed., September 1981; 2d ed., March 1982; 3d ed., April 1984; 4th ed., April 1985; 5th ed., March 1986; 6th ed., March 1987; 7th ed., April 1988.

Soviet Armed Forces Review Annual, 19xx, Vol. x. David R. Jones, ed., *Soviet Armed Forces Review Annual* (Gulf Breeze, FL; Academic International Press, 19xx): 1977, Vol. 1; 1978, Vol. 2; 1979, Vol. 3; 1980, Vol. 4; 1981, Vol. 5; 1982, Vol. 6; 1982-1983 Vol. 7; 1983-1984, Vol. 8; 1984-1985, Vol. 9.

Studeman, USN, Statement before HASC, March 1988. Rear Admiral William O. Studeman, U.S. Navy, Director of Naval Intelligence, statement on intellignce issues, before the Seapower and Strategic and Critical Material Subcommittee of the House Armed Services Committee, 1 March 1988.

Taylor, *Missiles of the World*, 1980. Michael J. H. Taylor, *Missiles of the World* (New York: Charles Scribner's Sons, 1980).

USA, *Handbook on Soviet Ground Forces*. Department of the Army, *Handbook on Soviet Ground Forces*, Field Manual 30-40, 30 June 1975.

USA, *Organization and Equipment of the Soviet Army*. Department of the Army, Threats Division, Concepts and Force Design Directorate, *Handbook: Organization and Equipment of the Soviet Army*, 1 December 1976, DA Pam 550-2.

USA, *Understanding Soviet Military Developments*. Department of the Army, Office of the Assistant Chief of Staff for Intelligence, *Understanding Soviet Military Developments*, AST-11005-100-77, April 1977.

USAICS, *Communist Weapons and Equipment Handbook*. U.S. Army Intelligence Center and School (Fort Huachuca, AZ), *Communist Weapons and Equipment Handbook*, Supplemental Reading 66152, June 1971.

USAICS, *Handbook on the Soviet Ground Forces*. U.S. Army Intelligence Center and School (Fort Huachuca, AZ), *Handbook on the Soviet Ground Forces*, Supplemental Reading 69720, August 1976.

USAF, *Soviet Aerospace Handbook*, 1978. Department of the Air Force, *Soviet Aerospace Handbook*, Air Force Pamphlet 200-21, May 1978.

USAF, *Summary Review*, 1975. Assistant Chief of Staff, Intelligence, Headquarters U.S. Air Force, *Summary Review of Selected U.S. & Soviet Military Forces* (declassified 17 October 1984), 15 April 1975.

USAF, *Trends*, 1976. Assistant Chief of Staff, Intelligence, Headquarters U.S. Air Force, *Trends in U.S. & Soviet Military Forces* (declassified 17 October 1984), June 1976.

USAREUR, *Identification Handbook*. Headquarters U. S. Army, Europe, *Identification Handbook: Soviet and Satellite Ordnance Equipment*, 6th ed., Part 1, USAREUR Pam No. 30-60-1, 30 June 1966.

USN, *Soviet Naval Developments* (Rev. 1/81). Office of the Chief of Naval Operations, Department of the Navy, *Understanding Soviet Naval Developments*, 4th ed. (Washington, DC: Government Printing Office, January 1981).

USN, *Soviet Naval Developments* (Rev. 4/85). Office of the Chief of Naval Operations, Department of the Navy, *Understanding Soviet Naval Developments*, 5th ed. (Washington, DC: Government Printing Office, April 1985).

Whiting, *Soviet Air Power*. Kenneth R. Whiting, *Soviet Air Power*, AU-21 (Maxwell AFB, AL: Air University, 1985).

Appendix B
Soviet Weapons Designations[1]

Aircraft

Two designation schemes for aircraft are used. The first was adopted in 1954. The NATO Air Standards Co-ordinating Committee assigns a name when the aircraft is detected. Names beginning with following letters indicate the aircraft type:

- B = Bomber and reconnaisance aircraft
- C = Cargo
- F = Fighter
- H = Helicopter
- M = Miscellaneous fixed-wing, including maritime patrol aircraft

Jet aircraft are given multisyllabic names (for example, Flogger), and propeller-driven aircraft one-syllable names (for example, Bear). With helicopters, the number of syllables is arbitrary. Variants of a basic aircraft are indicated by a suffix letter appended to the NATO name of the aircraft: for example, Fishbed L, to correspond with the Soviet suffix provided to the aircraft to designate a change in basic performance or characteristics, for example, MiG-21bis.

The second scheme of designating aircraft is the Soviet method, adopted in 1940, which uses the names of the founders of the design bureau:

- Be = G. M. Beriev
- Il = S. V. Ilyushin
- Ka = N. I. Kamov
- La = S. A. Lavochkin
- Mi = M. L. Mil'
- MiG = A. I. Mikoyan/M. I. Gurevich
- Mya = V. M. Myasishchyev
- Pe = V. M. Petlyakov
- Su = P. O. Sukhoi
- Tu = A. N. Tupolev (designated ANT for Andrei N. Tupolev until 1947)
- Yak = A. S. Yakovlev

Each aircraft in each design bureau is assigned a number designating its sequence in development. Fighters get odd numbers (MiG-21), while all other types get even numbers. Variations on the basic types are designated by letter suffixes:

- A for aerodynamic refinement
- B for attack version
- bis for later variants
- F for *forsirovannyy* (boosted) (normally meaning the engine is equipped with an afterburner)
- M for *modifikatsirovanny* (modified) or *modifitsirovannyy* (modified for export)
- MF for progressive development
- P for *perekhvatchik* (interceptor)
- R for *razvedyvatel'nyy* (reconnaissance)
- U for *uchebnyy samolet* (trainer)
- UTI for *uchebnyy trenivrovochnyy* (fighter-trainer)

Missiles

In the early 1960s NATO adopted a system for identifying Soviet missiles based on Air Standards Co-ordinating Committee procedures. Standard abbreviations used to indicate missile types are; A, for air-to-air missiles; G, for surface-to-air missiles, K, for air-to-surface missiles, S, for surface-to-surface missiles. The missiles are numbered as they are identified, not necessarily by range or date of actual operational introduction. For example, the SA-2 Guideline was the second SAM identified, and the SS-3 Shyster was the third SSM identified. Before the system enters service an X is added, for example, SS-X-26.

Weapons Designations During Research and Development

Temporary designations are assigned to weapons based on their observation at flight-test ranges:

	Test Range	Example	Weapon
BL =	Barnaul Test Range	BL-10	AS-X-19 ALCM
EM =	Emba Test Range		Tactical SAMs
KY =	Kapustin Yar Range	KY-3	Improved Scud
		KY-12	SS-23 SLBM
NE =	Nenoska Test Range	NE-04	SS-N-20 SLBM
PL =	Plesetsk Test Range	PL-4	SS-24 ICBM
		PL-5	SS-25 ICBM
RAM =	Ramenskoye Airfield	RAM-P	Blackjack bomber
SH =	Sary Shagan Range	SH-08	ABM-3 Gazelle ABM

Ships and submarines

Since the mid-1950s, Soviet surface warships have been given code names beginning with the letter K, with roman numerals indicating principal variants (Kara,

---

[1] This appendix was prepared by Jacquelyn Walsh. The main sources were Collins and Victory, *U.S./Soviet Military Balance*, 1988; Gunston, *Aircraft of the Soviet Union*, 1983; Polmar, *Guide to the Soviet Navy*, 1986; Whiting, *Soviet Air Power*; Steven J. Zaloga, "Soviet Weapon Designations," *Jane's Defence Weekly*, 2 May 1987, pp. 835-837; and private communications with the authors.

Weapons Designations

Kresta). Since the late 1960s, most new Soviet combatant classes have been identified by their Soviet names (Kiev, Udaloy). Lesser Soviet ships have been assigned names according to where they were built (Polnocny) or first observed. Smaller ships are named for locations, insects (Osa [wasp], Komar [mosquito]), and children's nicknames (Nanuchka, Yurka).

Submarines are assigned code letter designations by Western intelligence; generally the phonetic word for the letter is used, for example, Alfa, Bravo, Charlie, Delta, etc. All 26 letters of the alphabet have been used (U, or Uniform has been used twice: initially for the Victor II class SSN, and then for a one-of-a-kind auxiliary submarine). The exceptions are the use of the Soviet terms Typhoon (*Tayfun*) and *Akula* (the Russian word for shark). Major variations within the class are indicated by roman numerals (Victor I, Victor II, and Victor III).

List of Weapons by Type[2]

Aircraft

An-2	Colt light transport
An-8	Camp transport
An-10	Cat short/medium range transport
An-12	Cub short/medium range transport
An-12	Cub-B ELINT aircraft
An-12	Cub-C ECM aircraft
An-14	Clod light transport
An-22	Cock long-range heavy transport
An-24	Coke short/medium range transport
An-26	Curl medium transport
An-28	Cash turboprop transport
An-30	Clank (survey version of An-24/26 transport)
An-32	Cline medium transport
An-72/74	Coaler medium jet transport
An-124	Condor transport
Be-6	Madge patrol aircraft
Be-8	Mole patrol aircraft
Be-10	Mallow patrol aircraft
* Be-12	Mail ASW
Be-30	Cuff short-range transport
Il-2	Bark bomber
Il-4	Bob bomber
Il-10	(no name) bomber
Il-12	Coach transport
Il-14	Crate short-range transport/ELINT aircraft
Il-18	Coot-A/Clam medium/long-range transport
Il-20	Beast fighter
* Il-28	Beagle bomber/EW aircraft
Il-28U	Mascot trainer
* Il-38	May ASW
Il-40	Brawny fighter
Il-54	Blowlamp experimental bomber
Il-62	Classic long-range transport
Il-76	Candid heavy transport
Il-76	Mainstay AEW/AWACs
Il-76	Midas aerial tanker
Il-86	Camber jet transport
Ka-10	Hat helicopter
Ka-15	Hen helicopter
Ka-18	Hog (developmental version of Ka-15)
Ka-22	Hoop experimental helicopter
Ka-25	Hormone/Harp (prototype) multipurpose helicopter
* Ka-25	Hormone-A ASW helicopter
Ka-25	Hormone-B targeting helicopter
Ka-25	Hormone-C utility helicopter
Ka-26	Hoodlum multi-purpose helicopter
* Ka-27	Helix-A ASW helicopter
Ka-27	Helix-B naval infantry helicopter
Ka-27	Helix-D SAR/utility helicopter
Ka-32	Helix-C civilian helicopter
La-7	Fin fighter
La-9	Fritz fighter
La-11	Fang fighter
La-15	Fantail fighter
La-168	Fantail prototype fighter
Li-2	(DC-3) Cab transport
* M-4	(Mya-4) Bison bomber/maritime reconnaissance
* M-12	(Be-12) Mail ASW amphibious
M-50/52	Bounder bomber
Mi-1	Hare helicopter
Mi-2	Hoplite helicopter
Mi-4	Hound helicopter
Mi-6	Hook helicopter
Mi-8	Hip helicopter
Mi-10	Harke helicopter
Mi-12	Homer helicopter
Mi-14	Haze-A ASW helicopter
Mi-14	Haze-B mine countermeasures helicopter
Mi-14	Haze-C SAR/utility helicopter
Mi-24/25	Hind attack helicopter
Mi-24	Hind-G nuclear-biological-chemical sampling helicopter
Mi-26	Halo helicopter
Mi-28	Havoc helicopter
Mi-34	Hermit trainer
MiG Ye-2A	Faceplate fighter
MiG Ye-23	Faithless fighter
MiG Ye-152M	Flipper fighter
MiG-9	Fargo/Farmer fighter
MiG-15	Fagot fighter
MiG-15UTI	Midget trainer
MiG-17	Fresco fighter
* MiG-19	Farmer fighter
MiG-21U	Mongol-A trainer
MiG-21UM	Mongol-B trainer
MiG-21F	Fishbed-C interceptor
MiG-21PF	Fishbed-D fighter
MiG-21PFM	Fishbed-F fighter
MiG-21R	Fishbed-G reconnaissance fighter
MiG-21RF	Fishbed-H reconnaissance aircraft
* MiG-21MF	Fishbed-J fighter-bomber
MiG-21SMT	Fishbed-K fighter/fighter-bomber
* MiG-21bis	Fishbed-L/N fighter-bomber
MiG-23	Flogger-A/K fighter
* MiG-23S	Flogger-B/E/G fighter-bomber
MiG-23U	Flogger-C trainer

---

[2] This list is limited to weapons that have been operating since World War II, and to classes of weapons that include at least one nuclear-capable system. The nuclear-capable systems are designated with an asterisk.

Weapons Designations

MiG-23MB	Flogger-F/H fighter-bomber (hybrid for export)
MiG-25	Foxbat-A fighter
MiG-25R	Foxbat-B/D reconnaissance
MiG-25U	Foxbat-C trainer
MiG-25	Foxbat-F anti-radiation missile capable
* MiG-27	Flogger-D/J fighter-bomber
MiG-29	Fulcrum fighter
MiG-31	Foxhound fighter
MiG-?	Fearless fighter
MiG-?	Faithless STOL fighter
Pe-2	Buck fighter-bomber
Su-7U	Movjik trainer
* Su-7BM	Fitter-A interceptor/fighter
Su-7	Fitter-B interceptor
Su-9	Fishpot-B fighter
Su-9V	Maiden trainer
Su-11	Fishpot-C fighter
Su-15(11?)	Flagon-A fighter
Su-15	Flagon-B experimental STOL fighter
Su-15	Flagon-C trainer
Su-15	Flagon-D/E/F fighter
* Su-17	Fitter-B/C/D/H fighter/fighter-bomber
* Su-20/22	Fitter fighter/interceptor
* Su-24	Fencer-A/B/C/D fighter-bomber
* Su-24	Fencer-E reconnaissance
Su-25	Frogfoot fighter
Su-27	Flanker fighter
Tu-2	Bat bomber
* Tu-4	Bull bomber
Tu-14	Bosun bomber
* Tu-16	Badger bomber/reconnaissance
Tu-20	Bear bomber
* Tu-22	Blinder bomber
* Tu-22M/26	Backfire bomber
Tu-28P	Fiddler fighter/reconnaissance
Tu-70	Cart (experimental Tu-4)
Tu-82	Butcher bomber
Tu-85	Barge bomber
Tu-91	Boot bomber/fighter
* Tu-95	Bear A/B/C/D/E/G bomber
Tu-98	Backfin bomber
Tu-104	Camel (civil version of Badger)
* Tu-105	Blinder bomber
Tu-110	Cooker (experimental Tu-104)
Tu-114	Cleat long-range transport
Tu-124	Cookpot short/medium-range transport
Tu-126	Moss AWACS
Tu-128	Fiddler fighter
Tu-134	Crusty short/medium-range transport
* Tu-142	Bear-F ASW
* Tu-142	Bear-H air-launched cruise missile bomber
Tu-144	Charger supersonic transport
Tu-154	Careless medium-range transport
* Tu-160	Blackjack bomber
Yak-8	Crib liaison aircraft
Yak-9	Frank fighter
Yak-11	Moose trainer
Yak-12	Creek light aircraft
Yak-12	Crow light/liaison aircraft
Yak-14	Mare transport
Yak-16	Cork transport
Yak-17	Feather fighter
Yak-17	Magnet trainer
Yak-18	Max trainer
Yak-18	Mouse fighter
Yak-23	Flora fighter
Yak-24	Horse helicopter
Yak-25	Flashlight-A interceptor
Yak-25	Flashlight-B fighter/reconnaissance
Yak-26	Mangrove tactical reconnaissance
Yak-27	Flashlight-C interceptor
Yak-27RU	Mandrake jet reconnaissance
* Yak-28	Brewer-C light bomber/reconnaissance
* Yak-28	Brewer-D light bomber/reconnaissance
Yak-28	Brewer-E ECM variant
* Yak-28P	Firebar-B fighter
Yak-28R	Firebar reconnaissance
Yak-28U	Maestro trainer
Yak-30	Magnum fighter
Yak-32	Mantis fighter
Yak-36MP	Forger-A VSTOL fighter
Yak-36UV	Forger-B VSTOL trainer
Yak-38	Forger V/STOL fighter
Yak-40	Codling short-range transport
Yak-42	Clobber A transport
Yak UT-2	Mink (Air-20) trainer

Missiles

Air-to-air missiles

AA-1	Alkali
AA-2	Atoll
AA-3	Anab
AA-4	Awl
AA-5	Ash
AA-6	Acrid
AA-7	Apex
AA-8	Aphid
AA-9	Amos
AA-10	Alamo
AA-11	Archer

Air-to-surface missiles

* AS-1	Kennel
* AS-2	Kipper
* AS-3	Kangaroo
* AS-4	Kitchen
* AS-5	Kelt
* AS-6	Kingfish
AS-7	Kerry
AS-8	(replaced by AT-6 Spiral)
AS-9	Kyle
AS-10	Karen
AS-11	Kilter
AS-12	Kegler
AS-14	Kedge
* AS-15	Kent ALCM
* AS-X-16	(no name) SRAM
* AS-X-19	(no name) ALCM

Anti-ballistic missiles

(SA-5)	Griffon
* ABM-1/1B	Galosh
* ABM-3	Gazelle

Anti-tank missiles

AT-1	Snapper

Weapons Designations

AT-2	Swatter A
AT-2	Swatter B (helicopter missile on Mi-24)
AT-3	Sagger manpack/ mounted on armored vehicle
AT-4	Spigot
AT-5	Spandrel
AT-6	Spiral
AT-7	Saxhorn
AT-8	Songster

Surface-to-air missiles

* SA-1	Guild
* SA-2	Guideline
SA-3	Goa
SA-4	Ganef
* SA-5	Gammon
SA-6	Gainful
SA-7	Grail
SA-8	Gecko
SA-9	Gaskin
* SA-10	Grumble
SA-12A	Gladiator
SA-X-12B	Giant
SA-13	Gopher
SA-14	Gremlin
SA-16	(no name)

Surface-to-air missiles, naval

* SA-N-1	Goa
* SA-N-2	Guideline
* SA-N-3	Goblet
SA-N-4	Gecko
SA-N-5	Grail
* SA-N-6	Grumble
SA-N-7	Gadfly
SA-N-8	(Gremlin)
SA-NX-9	(no name)

Surface-to-surface missiles

* FROG-1/2/3/4/5/7	SRBM
* SS-1a	Scunner SRBM
* SS-1b/a	Scud A/B SRBM
SS-2	Sibling SRBM
* SS-3	Shyster MRBM
* SS-4	Sandal IRBM
* SS-5	Skean IRBM
SS-6	Sapwood rocket booster
* SS-7	Saddler ICBM
* SS-8	Sasin ICBM
* SS-9	Scarp ICBM
SS-X-10	Scrag ICBM
* SS-11	Sego ICBM
* SS-12	Scaleboard A SRBM
* SS-12M	Scaleboard B SRBM
* SS-13	Savage ICBM
SS-X-14	Scamp ICBM
SS-X-15	Scrooge ICBM
SS-X-16	Sinner ICBM
* SS-17	Spanker ICBM
* SS-18	Satan ICBM
* SS-19	Stiletto ICBM
* SS-20	Saber IRBM
* SS-21	Scarab SRBM
SS-22	(designation no longer used; see SS-12M)
* SS-23	Spider SRBM
* SS-24	Scalpel ICBM
* SS-25	Sickle ICBM
* SS-X-26	(no name) ICBM

Surface-to-surface, coastal

SSC-1	Shaddock
* SSC-1b	Sepal
SSC-2a	Salish
SSC-2b	Samlet
SSC-3	Styx
SSC-X-4	
SSC-X-5	

Subsurface/sea-to-surface/ship missile

* FRAS-1	
* SS-N-1	Scrubber
SS-N-2A/2B	Styx
* SS-N-3a/c	Shaddock
* SS-N-3b	Sepal
* SS-N-4	Sark SLBM
* SS-N-5	Serb SLBM
* SS-N-6	SLBM
* SS-N-7	Starbright SLCM
* SS-N-8	Sawfly SLBM
* SS-N-9	Siren
* SS-N-12	Sandbox naval
SS-N-14	Silex naval
* SS-N-15	Starfish ASW
* SS-N-16	Stallion ASW
* SS-N-17	Snipe SLBM
* SS-N-18	Stingray SLBM
* SS-N-19	Shipwreck SSM
* SS-N-20	Sturgeon SLBM
* SS-N-21	Sampson SLCM
* SS-N-22	Sunburn SSM
* SS-N-23	Skiff SLBM
* SS-NX-24	(no name) SLCM

Alphabetical Listing

A series: NATO nicknames beginning with A used to identify Soviet air-to-air missiles

B series: NATO nicknames beginning with B used to identify Soviet bomber aircraft

C series: NATO nicknames beginning with C used to identify Soviet cargo aircraft

F series: NATO nicknames beginning with F used to identify fighter-type aircraft

G series: NATO nicknames beginning with G used to identify surface-to-air missiles

H series: NATO nicknames beginning with H used to identify Soviet helicopters

K series: NATO nicknames beginning with K used to identify Soviet air-to-surface missiles

M series: NATO nicknames beginning with M used to identify Soviet multipurpose aircraft, trainers, utility, etc.

Weapons Designations

S series: NATO nicknames beginning with S used to identify Soviet surface-to-surface missiles

Acrid	AA-6	Coke	An-24/26
Alamo	AA-10	Colt	An-2
Alkali	AA-1	Condor	An-124
Amos	AA-9	Cooker	Tu-110
Anab	AA-3	Cookpot	Tu-124
Apex	AA-7	Coot	Il-18
Aphid	AA-8	Cork	Yak-16
Archer	AA-11	Crate	Il-14
Ash	AA-5	Creek	Yak-12
Atoll	AA-2	Crib	Yak-8
Awl	AA-4	Crow	Yak-12
Backfin	Tu-98	Crusty	Tu-134
Backfire	Tu-22M/26	Cub	An-12
Badger	Tu-16	Cuff	Be-30
Barge	Tu-85	Curl	An-26
Bark	Il-2	Faceplate	MiG Ye-2A
Bat	Tu-2	Fagot	MiG-15
Beagle	Il-28	Faithless	MiG Ye-23
Bear	Tu-20/95/142	Fang	La-11
Beast	Il-20	Fantail	La-168
Bison	M-4 (Mya-4)	Fantail	La-15
Blackjack	Tu-160	Fargo	MiG-9
Blinder	Tu-22/105	Farmer	MiG-9/19
Blowlamp	Il-54	Feather	Yak-17
Bob	Il-4	Fencer	Su-24
Boot	Tu-91	Fiddler	Tu-28P/128
Bosun	Tu-14	Fin	La-7
Bounder	M-50/52	Firebar-B	Yak-28P
Brawny	Il-40	Fishbed	MiG-21
Brewer	Yak-28	Fishpot-B	Su-9
Buck	Pe-2	Fishpot-C	Su-11
Bull	Tu-4	Fitter-A	Su-7
Butcher	Tu-82	Fitter-B/C/D	Su-17/20
Cab	Li-2 (DC-3)	Flagon	Su-15
Camber	Il-86	Flanker	Su-27
Camel	Tu-104	Flashlight	Yak-25
Camp	An-8	Flashlight-C	Yak-27
Candid	Il-76	Flipper	MiG Ye-152M
Careless	Tu-154	Flogger	MiG-23
Cart	Tu-70	Flogger-D/J	MiG-27
Cash	An-28	Flora	Yak-23
Cat	An-10	Forger	Yak-36/38
Charger	Tu-144	Foxbat	MiG-25
Clam	Il-18	Foxhound	MiG-31
Clank	An-30	Frank	Yak-9
Classic	Il-62	Fresco	MiG-17
Cleat	Tu-114	Fritz	La-9
Cline	An-32	Frogfoot	Su-25
Clobber	Yak-42	Fulcrum	MiG-29
Clod	An-14	Gadfly	SA-N-7
Coach	Il-12	Gainful	SA-6
Coaler	An-72/74	Galosh	ABM-1/1B
Cock	An-22	Gammon	SA-5
Codling	Yak-40	Ganef	SA-4
		Gaskin	SA-9
		Gazelle	ABM-3?
		Gecko	SA-8
		Gecko	SA-N-4

Nuclear Weapons Databook, Volume IV   **391**

Weapons Designations

Giant	SA-X-12B	Mandrake	Yak-27RU
Gladiator	SA-12A	Mangrove	Yak-26
Goa	SA-N-1	Mantis	Yak-32
Goa	SA-3	Mare	Yak-14
Goblet	SA-N-3	Mark	Yak-7V
Gopher	SA-13	Mascot	Il-28U
Grail	SA-N-5	Max	Yak-18
Grail	SA-7	May	Il-38
Gremlin	SA-14	Midas	Il-76
Griffon	(SA-5)	Midget	MiG-15UTI
Grumble	SA-N-6	Mink	Yak UT-2
Grumble	SA-10	Mole	Be-8
Guideline	SA-N-2	Mongol	MiG-21U/UM
Guideline	SA-2	Moose	Yak-11
Guild	SA-1	Moss	Tu-114/126
Halo	Mi-26	Mouse	Yak-18
Hare	Mi-1	Movjik	Su-7U
Harke	Mi-10	Saber	SS-20
Harp	Ka-25	Saddler	SS-7
Hat	Ka-10	Sagger	AT-3
Havoc	Mi-28	Salish	SSC-2a
Haze	Mi-14	Samlet	SSC-2b
Helix	Ka-27	Sampson	SS-N-21
Helix-C	Ka-32	Sandal	SS-4
Hen	Ka-15	Sandbox	SS-N-12
Hermit	Mi-34	Sapwood	SS-6
Hind	Mi-24/25	Sark	SS-N-4/5
Hip	Mi-8	Sasin	SS-8
Hog	Ka-18	Satan	SS-18
Homer	Mi-12	Savage	SS-13
Hoodlum	Ka-26	Sawfly	SS-N-8
Hook	Mi-6	Saxhorn	AT-7
Hoop	Ka-22	Scaleboard	SS-12
Hoplite	Mi-2	Scalpel	SS-24
Hormone	Ka-25	Scamp	SS-X-14
Horse	Yak-24	Scarab	SS-21
Hound	Mi-4	Scarp	SS-9
Kangaroo	AS-3	Scrag	SS-X-10
Karen	AS-10	Scrooge	SS-X-15
Kedge	AS-14	Scrubber	SS-N-1
Kegler	AS-12	Scunner	SS-1a
Kelt	AS-5	Sego	SS-11
Kennel	AS-1	Sepal	SSC-1b
Kent	AS-15	Sepal	SS-N-3b
Kerry	AS-7	Serb	SS-N-5
Kilter	AS-11	Shaddock	SS-N-3a/c
Kingfish	AS-6	Shaddock	SSC-1a
Kipper	AS-2	Shipwreck	SS-N-19
Kitchen	AS-4	Shyster	SS-3
Kyle	AS-9	Sibling	SS-2
Madge	Be-6	Sickle	SS-25
Maestro	Yak-28U	Silex	SS-N-14
Magnet	Yak-17UTI	Sinner	SS-X-16
Magnum	Yak-30	Siren	SS-N-9
Maiden	Su-9U	Skean	SS-5
Mail	M-12 (Be-12)	Skiff	SS-N-23
Mainstay	Il-76	Snapper	AT-1
Mallow	Be-10	Snipe	SS-N-17

Weapons Designations

Songster	AT-8	Starfish	SS-N-15
Spandrel	AT-5	Stiletto	SS-19
Spanker	SS-17	Stingray	SS-N-18
Spider	SS-23	Sturgeon	SS-N-20
Spigot	AT-4	Styx	SS-N-2
Spiral	AT-6	Sunburn	SS-N-22
Stallion	SS-N-16	Swatter	AT-2
Starbright	SS-N-7		

Appendix C
Gazetteer

Name	Feature	Coordinates
Achinsk	ppl	56 15N 090 30E
Adler AF	possible bomber base	43 26N 035 58E
Akhtyrka	SS-20 base	50 16N 034 50E
Akhtyrka	SS-20 base	50 22N 034 57E
Aktask (at Kerch')	VVER	45 20N 035 44E
Alekseyevka AF	Backfire (SNA) base	49 14N 140 11E
Aleksandrovsk-Sakhalinskiy	ppl (NB)	50 54N 142 10E
Aleysk	ppl (SS-18 base)	52 28N 082 45E
Aluksne	SS-4 base	57 25N 026 50E
Anadyr'	ppl (NB)	64 45N 177 29E
Anadyr' AF	Backfire staging	64 44N 177 44E
Arkhangel'sk	ppl (NB)	50 13N 066 50E
Armenian (at Oktemberyan)	VVER	40 08N 044 07E
Arsen'yev	ppl (AP)	44 10N 133 15E
Arzamas	ppl	55 23N 043 50E
Astrakhan	ppl (NT nearby)	46 21N 048 03E
Azgir	ppl (NT nearby)	47 51N 047 56E
Balakovo	ppl	52 02N 047 47E
Balakovo	VVER	50 02N 047 35E
Balkhash	SS-12 base	52 37N 075 36E
Baltiysk	ppl (NB)	54 39N 019 55E
Bakakovo	ppl	52 02N 047 47E
Barnaul	SS-20 base	53 46N 083 57E
Barnaul	SS-20 base	53 18N 084 09E
Barnaul	SS-20 base	53 13N 084 40E
Barnaul	SS-20 base	53 19N 084 31E
Barrikady Plant (at Volgograd)	SS-12, -20, LP	48 47N 044 36E
Bataysk	SS-4 RF	47 08N 039 47E
Batumi	ppl (NB)	41 38N 041 38E
Baykonur	ppl	47 50N 066 03E
Baykonur Cosmodrome	(Soviet name for Tyuratam Missile Test Center)	
Bayram-Ali	SS-23 base	37 36N 062 11E
Belaya	ppl	57 59N 051 42E
Belaya AF	Backfire (SNA) base	52 56N 103 34E
Belokorovichi	SS-20 base	51 11N 028 03E
Beloyarskiy	ppl	56 46N 061 23E
Beloyarskiy	LGR,BN-600	56 45N 061 20E
Berezovka	SS-12,-23 LSF	50 20N 028 26E
Bilibino	ppl	68 03N 166 20E
Bilibino LGR (see Magadan LGR)		
Bischofswerda, East Germany	SS-12 base	51 09N 014 12E
Biysk	ppl (MP)	52 34N 085 15E
Bobruysk	ppl	53 09N 029 14E
Bobruysk AF	Badger base	53 08N 029 12E
Brody	SS-20 base	50 06N 025 12E
Bronnaya Gora	SS-12 base	52 37N 025 04E
Buy	ppl (Kostroma RBMK)	58 29N 041 30E
Bykhov	ppl	53 30N 030 15E
Bykhov AF	Backfire (SNA) base	53 31N 030 13E

Gazetteer

Bykovo	Moscow ABM site	55 38N 037 54E
Chelyabinsk	ppl (DB)	55 10N 061 24E
Chelyabinsk-40	(possibly same as Kyshtym Complex)	
Chernobyl	ppl	51 16N 030 14E
Chernobyl (at Pripyat)	RBMK	51 10N 030 30E
Chernyakhovsk	ppl	53 38N 021 49E
Chernyakhovsk AF	bomber base	54 36N 021 48E
Chervonograd	SS-20 base	50 23N 024 18E
Chita	SS-20 base	52 22N 113 17E
Chukotka	ppl (Magadan LGR)	68 03N 166 25E
Degelen Mountain (at the Kazakh Test Site)		49 48N 078 04E
Derazhnya	ppl (SS-19 base)	49 26N 027 16E
Desnogors	ppl (Smolensk RBMK)	54 06N 033 20E
Dimitrovgrad	ppl (VK-50, BOR-60)	54 14N 049 33E
Dnepropetrovsk	ppl (DB, MP)	48 27N 034 59E
Dodonovo	ppl (LGPR)	56 17N 093 26E
Dolon	ppl	42 42N 078 27E
Dolon AF	Bear H (SAA) base	50 32N 079 11E
Dombarovskiy	ppl (SS-18 base)	50 46N 059 32E
Drovyanaya	ppl (SS-11 base)	51 53N 113 02E
Drovyanaya	SS-20 base	51 27N 113 04E
Drovyanaya	SS-20 base	51 26N 113 03E
Drovyanaya	SS-20 base	51 23N 112 50E
Drovyanaya	SS-20 base	51 20N 113 01E
Drovyanaya	SS-20 base	51 24N 112 52E
Dubna	ppl (MP)	56 44N 037 10E
Energodar	ppl (Zaporozh'ye VVER)	47 30N 034 28E
Engel's	ppl	51 30N 046 07E
Engel's AF	bomber base	51 29N 046 12E
Fedosiya	ppl (NB)	45 02N 035 23E
Gezgaly	SS-20 base	53 33N 025 17E
Gladkaya	SS-11 base	56 22N 092 26E
Glukhov	SS-20 base	51 41N 033 31E
Glukhov	SS-20 base	51 37N 033 29E
Gor'kiy	AST	56 20N 044 00E
Gor'kiy	ppl (AP, MP, NP)	56 20N 044 00E
Gorlovka	ppl	41 48N 044 07E
Gornyy	SS-12 base	51 33N 113 02E
Gremikha	NB	68 03N 039 38E
Gusev	SS-4 base	54 44N 022 03E
Hranice, Czechoslovakia	SS-12 base	49 33N 017 45E
Ignalina	ppl	55 21N 026 10E
Ignalino	RBMK	55 21N 026 10E
Il'men (?)	MP	50 50N 044 24E
Imeni Gastello	SS-18 base	51 09N 066 21E
Iokanga	ppl (NB)	68 00N 039 41E
Irkutsk	ppl (AP, MP)	52 16N 104 20E
Ivanovo	ppl	57 00N 040 59E
Izhevsk (now Ustinov)	ppl (MP)	56 51N 053 14E
Jelgava	msl	56 40N 024 06E
Jena-Forst, East Germany	SS-23 base	50 55N 011 32E
Kalinin	ppl (MP)	56 52N 035 55E
Kalinin (at Udomlya)	VVER	57 53N 035 01E
Kalinin Machine Building Plant (at Sverdlovsk)	SSC-X-4 LP	56 47N 060 47E
Kaliningrad	ppl (DB, NP, NB)	54 43N 020 30E
Kaluga	ppl	52 05N 041 00E
Kamenka	SS-12 TF	53 11N 044 04E

Gazetteer

Kansk	ppl	56 13N 095 41E
Kansk	SS-20 base	56 23N 095 29E
Kansk	SS-20 base	56 20N 095 17E
Kansk	SS-20 base	56 11N 096 03E
Kansk	SS-20 base	56 02N 096 05E
Kansk	SS-20 EF	56 20N 095 06E
Kapustin Yar	ppl	48 34N 045 45E
Kapustin Yar Test Range:	SS-4 missile testing	48 35N 046 18E
	SS-20 missile testing	48 37N 046 18E
	SS-20 training center	48 38N 046 10E
	SS-20 EF	48 46N 045 59E
Karmelava	SS-4 base	55 01N 024 14E
Kartaly	ppl (SS-18 base)	53 03N 060 40E
Kasli	ppl	55 54N 060 45E
Kattakurgan	SS-12 base	39 38N 065 59E
Kazakh [nuclear] Test Site:		49 52N to 50 08N, 77 42E to 79 06E
Degelen Mountain		49 48N 078 04E
Shagan River		49 53N 078 58E
Konystan		49 56N 078 31E
Kazan'	ppl (DB, AP, MP)	55 45N 049 08E
Kazan'	SS-12,-23 TF	55 58N 049 11E
Kerch'	ppl (NB, NP, VVER)	45 21N 036 28E
Khabarovsk	ppl (NB)	48 30N 135 06E
Khar'kov	ppl (DB, AP)	50 00N 036 15E
Khimki	ppl (DB, MP)	55 54N 037 26E
Khmel'nitskiy	ppl	49 25N 027 00E
Khmel'nitskiy (at Slavuta)	VVER	50 18N 026 52E
Kiev	ppl (DB,AP,MP,NP)	50 26N 030 31E
Kirov	ppl (MP)	58 33N 049 42E
Kirovakan	ppl	40 48N 044 30E
Klaipeda	ppl (NB)	55 43N 021 07E
Klin	Moscow ABM Site	56 33N 036 75E
Koenigsbrueck, East Germany	SS-12 base	51 17N 013 53E
Kola (at Polyarnyya Zori)	VVER	67 35N 032 30E
Kolomyya	SS-4 base	48 40N 024 48E
Kolosovo	SS-4, -20 SF	53 31N 026 55E
Kama	ppl (Tatar VVER)	56 08N 054 10E
Komsomol'sk-na-Amure	ppl (AP, NP)	50 35N 137 02E
Konstantinovka	ppl (Nikolaev VVER)	47 50N 031 09E
Konyastan (at the Kazakh Test Site)		49 56N 078 31E
Korosten'	SS-20 base	50 52N 028 31E
Korsakov	ppl (NB)	46 38N 142 46E
Kostroma	ppl(SS-17,-24 bases)	57 46N 040 55E
Kostroma (at Buy)	RBMK	58 29N 041 30E
Kovel'	ppl	51 14N 024 41E
Kovrov	ppl (MP)	56 25N 041 18E
Kozel'sk	ppl(SS-11,-19 bases)	54 02N 035 48E
Krasnodar	SS-20 TF	45 03N 038 58E
Krasnoyarsk	ppl (MP)	56 01N 092 50E
Krasnoyarsk Radar Site		57 54N 093 05E
Kronshtadt (Kotlin Island)	ppl (NB)	60 00N 029 45E
Kurchatov	ppl (Kursk RBMK)	51 39N 035 40E
Kursk	ppl	51 42N 036 12E
Kursk	RBMK	51 40N 035 45E
Kuznetsovsk	ppl (Rovno VVER)	51 41N 025 52E
Kuybyshev	ppl (DB, AP, MP)	53 12N 050 09E
Kyshtym	ppl	55 42N 060 34E

Gazetteer

Kyshtym Complex	LGPR	55 44N 060 54E
Ladushkin	SS-12, -23 SF	54 35N 020 12E
Lapichi	SS-12 base	53 26N 028 30E
Lebedin	SS-20 base	50 33N 034 26E
Leningrad	ppl (DB, MP, NP)	59 55N 030 15E
Leningrad (at Sosnovyy Bor)	RBMK	59 54N 029 07E
Lesnaya	missile EF	52 59N 025 46E
Lida	SS-20 base	53 48N 025 20E
Liepaja	ppl (NB)	56 31N 021 01E
Lipniki	SS-20 base	51 12N 028 27E
Litsa Guba	ppl (NB)	68 38N 037 48E
Lozovaya	SS-12 SF	48 55N 036 22E
Lutsk	SS-20 base	50 56N 025 36E
Lutsk	SS-20 base	50 50N 025 04E
L'vov	ppl	49 50N 023 58E
L'vov/Sknilov AF	possoble bomber base	49 49N 023 58E
Magadan	ppl (NB)	59 34N 150 48E
Magadan (at Bilibino)	LGR	68 03N 166 25E
Malorita	SS-4 base	51 52N 024 02E
Merseberg, East Germany	ppl	51 47N 024 05E
Metsamor, Armenia	ppl (Armenian VVER)	40 04N 044 17E
Minsk	ATET	53 54N 027 34E
Minsk	ppl (DB)	53 54N 027 34E
Moscow	ppl (DB,AP,MP)	55 45N 037 35E
Motovskij Gult	ppl (NB)	69 07N 031 48E
Movopetrovskoye	Moscow ABM Site	55 98N 036 47E
Mozyr'	SS-20 base	52 02N 029 11E
Murmansk	ppl (NB)	68 58N 033 05E
Murmansk Northeast AF	Backfire staging	69 00N 033 20E
Mys-Shmidta	ppl	68 56N 179 27W
Mys-Shmidta AF	Backfire staging	68 53N 179 25E
Nakhodka	ppl (NB)	42 48N 132 52E
Neftekamsk	ppl	56 05N 054 16E
Nenoksa	ppl (NB)	64 38N 039 11E
Nikolayev	ppl (NP)	46 58N 032 00E
Nikolayev (at Konstantinovka)	VVER	47 50N 031 09E
Nizhnekamsk	ppl	55 36N 051 47E
Nizhnekamsk	VVER	55 37N 051 35E
Novaya Zemlya nuclear test site		
Northern site		73 18N to 73 24N, 54 30E to 55 10E
Southern site		70 48N to 70 50N, 54 25E to 54 55E
Novosibirsk	ppl (AP, MP)	55 02N 082 55E
Novosibirsk	SS-20 base	55 22N 083 14E
Novosibirsk	SS-20 base	55 23N 082 55E
Novosibirsk	SS-20 base	55 20N 082 56E
Novosibirsk	SS-20 base	55 19N 083 02E
Novosibirsk	SS-20 base	55 19N 083 10E
Novosysoyevka	SS-12 base	44 12N 133 26E
Novovoronezhskiy	ppl	51 19N 039 13E
Novovoronezhskiy	VVER	51 14N 039 12E
Obninsk	ppl	55 05N 036 37E
Obninsk (APS-1)	LGR	55 05N 036 40E
Ochamchire	ppl (NB)	42 43N 041 28E
Odessa	ppl (ATET)	46 28N 030 44E
Oktemberyan	ppl (Armenian VVER)	40 08N 044 02E
Oktyabr'skoye AF	Backfire (SNA) base	45 19N 034 07E

Gazetteer

Olenegorsk	ppl (NB)	68 09N 033 18E
Olenegorsk AF	Backfire staging	68 09N 033 29E
Olenyaguba	ppl (NB)	68 09N 033 18E
Ol'ga	ppl (NB)	43 45N 135 18E
Olovyannaya	ppl (SS-11 base)	50 56N 115 35E
Omsk	ppl (MP)	55 00N 073 24E
Oranienbaum	ppl (NB)	59 55N 029 46E
Orenburg	ppl (MP, NT nearby)	51 45N 055 06E
Ostrov	SS-4 base	57 32N 028 12E
Paldisk	ppl (NB)	59 20N 024 06E
Pashino	SS-12 base	55 17N 082 60E
Pavlograd	ppl (MP)	47 00N 035 03E
Pechanga	ppl (NB)	69 30N 031 12E
Perm'	ppl (SS-11 base, DB)	58 00N 056 15E
Pervomaysk	ppl (SS-19 base)	48 03N 030 52E
Petrikov	SS-20 base	52 10N 028 35E
Petropavlovsk	ppl	54 52N 069 06E
Petropavlovsk Heavy Building Plant	SS-23 LP	54 54N 069 10E
Petropavlovsk-Kamchatskiy	ppl (NB, NP)	53 01N 158 39E
Pilyugino	oilfield	53 23N 052 18E
Pinsk	SS-4 base	52 11N 025 41E
Plesetsk	ppl	62 43N 040 17E
Plesetsk Missile Test Base	missile launch site	62 72N 040 28E
Podporozh'ye	ppl	60 55N 034 06E
Polotsk	SS-20 base	55 23N 028 44E
Poltava	ppl	49 35N 034 34E
Polyarnyy, Murmansk	ppl (NB)	69 14N 033 30E
Polyarnyye Zori	ppl (Kola VVER)	67 28N 032 25E
Postavy	SS-20 base	55 10N 026 54E
Poti	ppl (NB)	42 09N 041 40E
Pripyat	ppl (Chernobyl RBMK)	51 10N 030 30E
Pushkino	Moscow ABM site	56 11N 037 44E
Ramenskoye AF	bomber test center	55 33N 038 10E
Rechitsa	SS-20 base	52 12N 030 07E
Riga	ppl (NB, MP)	56 57N 024 06E
Rostov	ppl (AP, MP)	47 11N 039 25E
Rostov (at Rostov-na-Donu)	VVER	47 32N 042 09E
Rostov-na-Donu	ppl (Rostov VVER)	47 14N 039 42E
Rovno	ppl	50 37N 026 15E
Rovno (at Kuznetsovsk)	VVER	51 23N 025 52E
Ruzhany	SS-20 base	52 49N 024 46E
Saki	ppl	45 08N 033 36E
Saki AF	bomber base	45 06N 033 37E
Saratov	ppl (AP)	51 34N 046 02E
Saratov	SS-12,-23 TF	51 34N 046 01E
Sarny ppl	(Rovno VVER)	51 20N 026 36E
Sarny	SS-20 EF	51 21N 026 35E
Saryozek	SS-12 base, SS-12, -23 EF	44 32N 077 46E
Sarova	ppl	54 55N 043 19E
Sasovo	ppl	54 20N 041 55E
Semipalatinsk	ppl	50 28N 080 13E
Semipalatinsk	SS-23 base	50 23N 080 10E
Semipalatinsk nuclear test site (see Kazakh [nuclear] Test Site)		
Serpukhov	SS-20 TF	54 54N 037 28E
Sevastopol'	ppl (NB)	44 36N 033 32E
Severodvinsk	ppl (NB, NP)	64 34N 039 50E
Severomorsk	ppl (NB)	69 05N 033 27E

Gazetteer

Location	Description	Coordinates
Shagan River (at the Kazakh [nuclear] Test Site)		50 00N 079 00E
Shchelkovo	Moscow ABM site	55 54N 037 48E
Shermetyevo	Moscow ABM site	55 54N 037 20E
Shevchenko	ppl	43 39N 051 12E
Siberian Plant	LGPR/LGR	reportedly near Troitsk
Skala-Podol'skaya	SS-4 base	48 51N 026 09E
Slavuta	ppl (Khmelinitskiy VVER)	50 18N 026 52E
Slavuta	SS-20 base	50 17N 026 42E
Slobudka	SS-23 base	52 30N 024 32E
Slonim	SS-20 base	52 56N 025 22E
Slutsk	SS-20 base	53 14N 027 42E
Smolensk	ppl (MP, AP)	54 47N 032 03E
Smolensk (at Desnogorsk)	RBMK	54 06N 033 20E
Smorgon'	SS-20 base	54 36N 026 23E
Smorgon'	SS-20 base	54 32N 026 17E
Sokolka	ppl	55 39N 051 30E
Sol-Tsio	ppl	near Leningrad
Sol'tsy	ppl	58 08N 030 20E
Sol'tsy AF	bomber base	58 09N 030 20E
Sosnovyy Bor	ppl (Leningrad RBMK)	59 54N 029 07E
Sovetsk	SS-4 base	54 59N 021 37E
Sovetskaya Gavan'	ppl (NB)	49 01N 140 18E
Stan'kovo	SS-23 base, SS-12, -23 LEF	53 38N 027 13E
Stryy	SS-4 base	49 25N 023 35E
Sukhumi	ppl	43 00N 041 02E
Sungul Radiological Institute	warhead design	56 05N 060 44E
Sverdlovsk	ppl (DB, MP)	56 51N 060 36E
Svobodnyy	ppl (SS-11 base)	51 24N 128 08E
Taganrog	ppl (DB, AP)	47 12N 038 56E
Tallinn	ppl (NB)	59 25N 024 45E
Tartu	ppl	58 23N 026 43E
Tartu AF	bomber base	58 25N 026 50E
Tatar (at Koma)	VVER	56 08N 054 10E
Tashkent	ppl (AP)	41 10N 058 50E
Tatishchevo	ppl (SS-19 base)	51 42N 045 36E
Taurage	SS-4 base	55 05N 022 20E
Tbilisi	ppl (AP)	41 42N 044 45E
Teykovo	ppl (SS-11 base)	56 52N 040 33E
Tiksi	ppl	71 36N 128 48E
Tiksi AF	Backfire staging	71 40N 128 55E
Tomsk	ppl (MP, LGPR?)	56 30N 084 58E
Troitsk	ppl (LGPR?)	54 05N 060 40E
Tsel'	SS-23 base	53 24N 028 28E
Tuapse	ppl (NB)	44 05N 039 06E
Tula	ppl (MP)	54 12N 037 37E
Tyumen'	ppl (MP)	52 04N 143 09E
Tyuratam	ppl	45 38N 063 16E
Tyuratam Missile Test Center	missile launch	45 36N 063 24E
Udomlya	ppl (Kalinin VVER)	57 53N 035 01E
Ufa	ppl (MP)	54 44N 055 56E
Ukmerge	SS-4 base	55 08N 024 39E
Ukraina AF	bomber base	51 10N 128 28E
Ulan-Ude	ppl (AP)	51 50N 107 37E
Ul'yanovsk	ppl (AP)	54 20N 048 24E
Ustinov (formerly Izhersk)	ppl (MP)	56 51N 053 14E
Uzhur	ppl (SS-18 base)	55 18N 089 50E

Gazetteer

Ventspils	ppl (NB)	57 24N 021 31E
Vereyva	Moscow ABM site	55 20N 036 25E
Verkhniy-Neyvinskiy	ppl (uranium enrichment)	57 15N 060 15E
Verknyaya Salda	ppl (SS-25 base)	58 02N 060 33E
Vetrino	SS-20 base	55 24N 028 33N
Vinnitsa	ppl	49 14N 028 29E
Vladimirovka AF	bomber test center	48 19N 046 13E
Vladivostok	ppl (NB, NP)	43 08N 131 54E
Vnukovo	Moscow ABM site	55 37N 037 18E
Volgodonsk	ppl (Rostov VVER)	47 32N 042 09E
Volgograd	ppl (see Barrikady Plant)	48 45N 044 25E
Vorkuta	ppl	67 30N 064 00E
Vorkuta AF	Backfire staging	67 30N 063 55E
Voronezh	ppl (AP, AST)	51 38N 039 12E
Voronezh Southwest AF	bomber base	51 37N 039 08E
Votkinsk	ppl (MP)	57 03N 053 59E
Votkinsk Machine Building Plant	SS-12,-20,-23,-25 production	57 02N 054 08E
Vyru	SS-4 base	57 46N 026 47E
Vysokaya Pech'	SS-20 base	50 10N 028 16E
Vysokaya Pech'	SS-20 base	50 06N 028 22E
Waren, East Germany	SS-12 base	53 33N 012 38E
Weissenfels, East Germany	SS-23 base	51 12N 012 00E
Wokuhl, East Germany	SS-12 base	53 16N 013 16E
Yedrovo	ppl (SS-17 base)	57 53N 033 42E
Yur'ya	ppl (SS-25 base)	59 03N 049 17E
Yoshkar-Ola	ppl (SS-13,-25 bases)	56 40N 047 55E
Zagorsk	Moscow ABM site	56 18N 038 22E
Zapadnaya Litsa	NB	69 25N 032 30E
Zaporozh'ye	ppl (DB, AP)	47 53N 035 05E
Zaporozh'ye (at Energodar)	VVER	47 28N 034 50E
Zarechnyy	ppl (Beloyarskiy LGR, BN-600)	56 48N 061 19E
Zasimovichi	SS-20 base	52 31N 024 09E
Zelenodol'sk	ppl (NP)	55 51N 048 33E
Zhangiz Tobe	ppl (SS-18 base)	49 13N 081 12E
Zhdanov	ppl	47 06N 037 33E
Zherebkovo	SS-4, -20 SF	47 51N 029 54E
Zhitkovichi	SS-20 base	52 12N 027 48E
Zhitomir	ppl	50 15N 028 40E
Zhitomir/Skomorokhi AF	possible bomber base	50 10N 028 45E
Zlatoust	ppl (MP, NP)	55 10N 059 40E

Abbreviations:

AF	airfield
AP	aircraft production
AST	boiling water reactor for district heating
ATET	dual-purpose VVER producing electricity and steam for district heating
DB	design bureau
EF	elimination facility
LEF	launcher elimination facility
LGPR	light water-cooled graphite-moderated plutonium production reactor
LGR	light water-cooled graphite-moderated power reactor (channel type)
LP	launcher production
LSF	launcher storage facility
MP	missile production
NB	naval base
NP	naval production
NT	nuclear testing

Gazetteer

ppl	population center (i.e., cities and towns)
RBMK	light water-cooled graphite-moderated pressurized-type power reactor (channel type)
RF	repair facility
SAA	Strategic Air Armies
SF	storage facility
SNA	Soviet Naval Aviation
TF	training facility
VVER	pressurized water power reactor

Appendix D
Conversion Factors

Length

1 in	= 2.54 cm*	1 cm	= 0.3937 in
1 ft	= 30.48 cm*		
	= 0.3048 m*	1 m	= 3.2808398 ft
1 mi (stat)	= 5280 ft*		
	= 1609.344 m*		
	= 1.609344 km*	1 km	= 0.6213711 mi (stat)
	= 0.8689762 nm		= 0.5399568 nm
1 nm	= 1852 m*		
	= 1.852 km*		
	= 6076.11549 ft		
	= 1.150779448 mi (stat)		

Speed

1 knot = 1 nm/h*
Mach 1 = speed of sound
Mach x = x times the speed of sound

Speed of Sound in U.S. Standard Atmosphere

Sea-level:	340.29 m/s;	1116.4 ft/s;	661.47 kts;	761.2 mph
3000 m:	328.58 m/s;	1078.0 ft/s;	638.71 kts;	735.0 mph
5000 m:	320.55 m/s;	1051.7 ft/s;	623.10 kts;	717.0 mph
10,000 m:	299.53 m/s;	982.7 ft/s;	582.24 kts;	670.0 mph
11,500-20,000 m:	295.07 m/s;	968.0 ft/s;	573.57 kts;	660.1 mph

Mass/Weight

1 lb (avoirdupois)	= 0.45359237 kg*	1 kg	= 2.2046226 lb
1 ton (short)	= 2000 lb*	1 MT	= 1000 kg*
	= 0.90718474 MT*		= 2204.6226 lb
			= 1.10231 ton (short)
1 ton (long)	= 2240 lb*		= 0.98421 ton (long)
	= 1.0160469 MT		

Force

1 Newton = 10^5 dyne*
1 kg weight = 2.2046226 lb weight
= 9.80665 Newton*

* Exact value

BIBLIOGRAPHY

Bibliography

Bibliography of Declassified and Partially Declassified Documents Obtained under the Freedom of Information Act

Arms Control and Disarmament Agency, *An Analysis of Civil Defense in Nuclear War*, December 1978.

Air Force, Aeronautical Systems Division (Deputy for Reconnaissance/Strike/Electronic Warfare), *Have Point, Appendix A, Volume II, Threat*, ASD/RW HP 74-1, October 1974.

_____, Air Force Intelligence Service, Intelligence Research Division (Jack Sullivan and Maj. Tom Symonds), *Soviet Theaters, High Commands and Commanders*, 14 March 1986.

_____, Air Force Systems Command/Foreign Technology Division (AFSC/FTD), *Backfire B*, RFB-22/5004/79, June 1979.

_____, AFSC/FTD, *Soviet Aircraft Design and Acquisition*, FTD-1300R-479-80, June 1980.

_____, AFSC/FTD, *Soviet Development of Radioisotope Generators*, PHS-137-68-3, September 1968, and PHS-137-69-4, August 1969.

_____, AFSC/FTD (V. Nemecek and J. Moravec), *The MIG-19*, FTD-HC-23-0655-72, 23 June 1972.

_____, AFSC/FTD (K. Susumu), *Soviet Fighters: Concepts and Technical Analysis*, FTD-HC-23-0405-73, 25 May 1973.

_____, AFSC/FTD (D. B. Van Winkle), *Cost Effective Soviet Hardware Development*, Air Force Foreign Technology Bulletin, 26 May 1981.

_____, Air University, *Mission Area Analysis, Annex B: Threat*, 31 December 1981.

_____, Air University, Air Command and Staff College (Maj. Lionel A. Boudreaux), *Meeting the Soviet Bomber Threat*, May 1978.

_____, Air University, Air Command and Staff College (Maj. Serge A. Chernay), *Salt on the Tail of the Backfire*, May 1977.

_____, Air University, Air Command and Staff College (Maj. Frederick C. Engelman, Jr.), *Trends in the Modernization of U.S.S.R. Strategic Air Defense Command and Control*, May 1979.

_____, Air University, Air Command and Staff College (Maj. Charles R. Kuhnell), *The Role of the Long-Range Bomber: A Soviet View*, May 1977.

_____, Air University, Airpower Research Institute (Kenneth R. Whiting), *Soviet Air Power*, AU-21, 1985.

_____, Air University, Air War College (Lt. Col. John W. McDermott), *The Soviet Naval Air Force and Anti-Submarine Warfare*, Report No. 410, April 1978.

_____, Air University, Air War College (Dennis McManus Ring, DIA), *Soviet Wartime Command and Control: Evolution of the State Defense Committee, the Stavka, Theaters of War, and Theaters of Military Operations*, Professional Study No. 6043, May 1976.

_____, Assistant Chief of Staff, Intelligence, *The Soviet/Warsaw Pact Threat*, Unclassified Briefing, October 1983.

_____, Assistant Chief of Staff, Intelligence, *Trends in U.S. and Soviet Military Forces*, June 1976.

_____, Assistant Chief of Staff, Intelligence, *Summary Review of Selected U.S. and Soviet Military Forces*, 15 April 1975.

_____, Assistant Chief of Staff, Studies and Analysis (Lt. Col. Richard Shearer), *The Need for Strategic Endurance*, Briefing, September 1980.

_____, Doctrine and Concepts Division, Deputy Directorate for Long Range Planning (Lt. Col. Wolfgang W. E. Samuel), *Soviet Armored Attack in Central Europe—A Concept with a Fatal Flaw*, Concept Issue Paper 80-01, January 1980.

_____, Doctrine and Concepts Division, *Factors for Calculating Equivalent Megatons of Nuclear Weapons of Various Yields and Delivery Accuracies Against Soviet Economic Targets*, 1 September 1978.

_____, Doctrine and Concepts Division, *Briefing—Soviet Military Power*, 22 February 1982.

_____, Doctrine and Concepts Division, *A History of Strategic Arms Competition, 1945-1972*, Executive Summary Report, June 1976.

Bibliography

_____, Strategic Air Command (Maj. D. Goodman), *Life at Strategic Rocket Force Sites*, SAC Intelligence Quarterly, October 1978.

_____, Tactical Air Command (Capt. Martin E. Miller), *The Artillery Threat*, 1980.

_____, Tactical Air Command (Capt. S.S. Rehrig), *Soviet Short Range Ballistic Missiles (SRBMs)—New Generation*, TAC Intelligence Briefing 79-10, TACOPS/INO, 10 April 1979.

_____, Tactical Air Command (Capt. Robert E. Young), *The Soviet Tactical Air Defense System: An Introduction*, October 1980.

_____, U.S. Air Force Europe/INOA, *The Soviet Chemical Warfare Threat*, January 1983.

Army, Foreign Science and Technology Center (FSTC), "Recent Soviet Developments in Field Artillery," *Army Scientific and Technical Intelligence Bulletin*, AST-2660R-011-81, September 1981.

_____, FSTC, "Soviet SA-14 Missile System," *Army Scientific and Technical Intelligence Bulletin*, AST-2660R-018-82, April 1982.

_____, Intelligence and Security Command (Intelligence and Threat Analysis Center), *Soviet Tactical Nuclear Study (STANS)*, ITAD-14-SNF-77 (preliminary report), 1 July 1977, and ATC-PD-1510-032-82 (final report), November 1981.

_____, Intelligence Center and School (USAICS), *USAICS Handbook on the Soviet Ground Forces*, Fort Huachuca, AZ, Supplemental Reading 69720, August 1976.

_____, U.S. Army, Europe and Seventh Army (USAREUR), *Identification Guide (Tactical Rockets and Missiles): Warsaw Pact Countries*, USAREUR Pam 30-60-3, 1 June 1972.

BDM Corporation, (R. O. Welander et al.), *The Soviet Navy Declaratory Doctrine for Theatre Nuclear Warfare*, prepared for the Defense Nuclear Agency, DNA 4434T, 23 September 1977.

_____, (R.O. Welander et al.), *Assessment of Soviet Navy Doctrine for Theatre Nuclear Warfare, Phase I*, prepared for the Defense Nuclear Agency, DNA 4122F, 7 October 1977.

Center for Naval Analyses (James M. McConnell, Institute of Naval Studies), *A Briefing: Soviet Military Doctrine and the Navy*, prepared for the Department of the Navy, CNA 80-0318.00, 12 March 1980.

Central Intelligence Agency, *A Summary of Soviet Guided Missile Intelligence*, US/UK GM 4-52, 20 July 1953.

_____, *Accidents Aboard Soviet Submarines*, 23 November 1977; plus miscellaneous intelligence reports dated early 1970s.

_____ (National Foreign Assessment Center), *Characterisitics of the Kirov Nuclear-Powered Guided-Missile Cruiser*, SW 81-10058, June 1981.

_____ (National Foreign Assessment Center), *Estimated Soviet Defense Spending: Trends and Prospects*, SR 78-10121, June 1978.

_____ (National Foreign Assessment Center), *Soviet Spending for Defense: Trends Since 1965 and the Outlook for the 1980s*, SR 79-10147, October 1979.

_____ (Office of Scientific Intelligence), *Soviet Nuclear Research Reactors*, OSI-SR/64-41, Scientific Intelligence Report No. 114, 22 September 1964.

Defense Intelligence Agency, *Aircraft Production Capability—USSR*, ST-CS-01-209-74, 30 April 1974.

_____, *Air Forces Intelligence Study (AFIS): USSR Air Defense Forces*, DDB-1300-217-82, August 1982.

_____, *Ballistic Missile Guidance and Control—USSR and China*, DST-1000S-291-83, 15 April 1983; DST-1000S-293-76, 12 March 1976.

_____, *Backfire Weapons System*, DST-1310S-054-80, 7 July 1980; DST-1310S-054-77, 29 July 1977.

_____, *Badger Weapon System, Executive Summary*, DST-1310E-017-80, 23 January 1981.

_____, *Bear Weapon System*, DST-1310S-004-79, 12 February 1980.

_____, *Bibliography of Soviet Laser Developments, May-June 1985*, DST-2700Z-005-86, September 1986.

_____, *Bison Weapon System*, DST-1310S-003-79, 31 August 1979.

_____ *Bomber Aircraft (Trends)—Eurasian Communist Countries*, DST-1310S-010-79-Chg 1, 22 January 1979; DST-1310S-010-76, 27 August 1976.

_____, *Defense Intelligence Projections for Planning (DIPP), Soviet Military Forces, Section II, Long Range Aviation*, DDE-1311-11-78, April 1978.

_____, *Defensive Missile Systems Handbook—ECC*, DST-1000H-250-77, 30 June 1977.

_____, *Defensive Missile Systems (Trends)—USSR*, DST-1000S-288-77, June 1977.

_____, *Delta Class Ballistic Missile Launching Nuclear Submarine (Weapon System)—USSR*, ST-CS-08-357-75, 28 February 1975.

_____, *Estimated Expenditures for Research and Development by the Soviet Ministry of Aviation Industry (MAP)*, DIA-450-2-6-71-INT, July 1971.

_____, *Fencer Weapon System*, DST-1320S-228-76, 13 September 1976.

_____, *Fighter Launched Missiles (Current and Projected)—ECC*, DST-1360S-020-75, 31 July 1975.

_____, *Fishbed J, K, and L Weapon System*, DST-1320S-027-76, 9 April 1976.

Bibliography

———, *Guide to Nuclear Weapon Systems Available to the Soviet Front Commanders*, ST-CS-82-18-73, March 1973.

———, *Handbook on the Soviet Armed Forces*, DDB-2680-40-78, February 1978.

———, *Human Factors R&D—USSR*, DST-1810S-596-77, February 1977.

———, *Land Launched Ballistic Missile Systems (Trends)—USSR*, DST-1000S-267-76, 20 September 1976.

———, *Missile Industry Design and Development Resources—USSR*, DST-1830S-289-80, 15 April 1980.

———, *Naval Weapons System Handbook—U.S.S.R*, Volume 1 (Less Missiles), ST-HB-08-61-73, 20 July 1973.

———, *New Soviet Long Range Strategic Aircraft: Executive Summary*, DST-1310E-010-82, 26 February 1982.

———, *November Class Nuclear-Powered Attack Submarine (Weapon System) U.S.S.R.*, ST-CS-08-49-73, 29 June 1973.

———, *Over-The-Horizon Radars for Air Defense*, DST-1710-D-929-79-RPT-7, 5 December 1979.

———, *Overview Perspective of Key USSR Research and Test Facilities Supporting Aerospace System Development*, DST-1830S-271-76, 23 January 1976.

———, *Papa Class Cruise Missile-Launching Nuclear Submarine (Weapon System)—U.S.S.R.*, DST-1222-193-77, 30 September 1977.

———, *Projected Space Programs—USSR*, DST-1400S-022-82, 30 July 1982.

———, *Scud B Study*, ST-CS-10-399-75, August 1974.

———, *Sea-Launched Aerodynamic Missile Systems (Current and Projected)—U.S.S.R. and PRC*, DST-1330S-205-77, 1 March 1977.

———, *Soviet Alfa Class SSN Study*, DST-1223S-220-79, 1 December 1979.

———, *Soviet Airborne Warning and Control System (AWACS)*, DST-1350S-025-82, 14 May 1982.

———, *Soviet Antisubmarine Warfare Capabilities Handbook*, DDI-1230-1-77, August 1977; and Change 1, 1 January 1979.

———, *Soviet Artillery Trends and Scientific and Technical Projections*, DST-1130S-027-80, 30 September 1980.

———, *Soviet AS-11 Tactical Air-to-Surface Missile System*, DST-1330S-151-83, 16 June 1983.

———, *Soviet Aviation Industry Design and Development Resources—USSR*, DST-1830S-104-81, 9 July 1981.

———, *Soviet Ballistic Missile Physical Characteristics and Functional Description*, DST-1000Z-464-77, 21 September 1977.

———, *Soviet Command and Control: A Bibliography*, DDB-2610-39-81, March 1981.

———, *Soviet Front Fire Support*, DDB-1130-8-82, September 1982.

———, *Soviet Military Materiel Production, 1960-1985*, 14 July 1986.

———, *Soviet Military Product Research and Development—An Overview*, DST-1800E-342-78, July 1978.

———, *Soviet Naval Shipbuilding*, DST-1922-10-76, July 1976.

———, *Soviet Navy Surface Ship Identification Guide*, DST-1210-13-82, September 1982.

———, *Soviet Nuclear Power Technology*, ST-CR-02-152-72, December 1971.

———, *Soviet Nuclear Powered Ballistic Missile Submarines*, DST-1221S-357-79, August 1979.

———, *Soviet Self-Propelled Artillery*, DDI-1130-6-76, May 1976.

———, *Speed Capabilities and Propulsion System Characteristics of Soviet Nuclear and Diesel Submarines*, SI-CS-08-153-72, 15 March 1972.

———, *SS-17 ICBM System*, DST-1010S-305-82, 3 March 1982.

———, *SS-18 ICBM System*, DST-1010S-341-79, 26 February 1979.

———, *SS-N-4 and SS-N-5 SLBM Systems—U.S.S.R.*, DST-1020S-204-75, 1 October 1975.

———, *Strategic Ballistic Missile Systems Projections—USSR*, DST-1000S-267-82, 30 September 1982.

———, *The Share of the Soviet Defense Effort Atributable to Meeting the PRC Threat*, SDIE SOV 1-77, 26 May 1977.

———, *The Soviet Naval Threat Circa 2000*, DST-1200F-597-82, October 1982; DST-1200F-597-84, June 1984; DST-1200F-597-85, September 1985.

———, *The Soviet Naval Threat Circa 2010*, DST-1200F-597-86, September 1986.

———, *The Soviet Nuclear Energy Program*, SAO/ST-SS-02-11-70, July 1970.

———, *The Soviet Submarine Force*, DDI-1200-56-76, December 1976.

———, *The Soviet Weapon-Acquisition Process, with Special Emphasis on the Ground Forces*, DST-1830S-336-80, 12 September 1980.

———, *Submarine Trends—USSR*, DST-1220S-604-85, December 1985.

———, *The SS-11 Mod 4 ICBM Preliminary Assessment of Characteristics and Employment Options*, DST-1010D-906-77-RPT 4, 23 May 1977.

_____, *Trends and Developments: ICBM Time On Target Capability*, DST-2660P-107-81-SPR 1, 6 April 1981.

_____, *Threat to the Non-European Defense Communications System*, DST-2610F-002-82, Vol. 1, 15 August 1982; and Vol. 2 (Appendices), October 1982.

_____, *Unclassified Communist Naval Orders of Battle*, DDB-1200-124-85, December 1985; DDB-1200-124-86, April 1986.

_____, *U.S. and Soviet Weapon System Design Practices: Volume 5—Missiles*, DST-1830S-505-80 Vol. 5, March 1980.

_____ (Ory S. Adler and Capt. Michael W. Summers), *ICBM Targeting Capability (SS-19)—USSR*, DST-1010S-325-78, 5 February 1979.

_____ (Lt. Col. William P. Baxter), *Comparative Dictionary of U.S.—Soviet Terms*, DDI-2200-33-77, August 1977.

_____ (Keywood C. Cheves), *A Guide to Foreign Tactical Nuclear Weapon Systems Under the Control of Ground Force Commanders*, DST-1040S-541-83, 9 September 1983, through DST-1040S-541-87, 4 September 1987.

_____ (Dennis Cwiak and Edison Williams, et al.), *Submarine-Launched Ballistic Missile Weapon Systems—U.S.S.R.*, DST-1020S-418-78-CHG-3, 30 July 1982.

_____ (G. E. Fedoroff, et al.), *Yankee Class Ballistic Missile-Launching Nuclear Submarine (Weapon System)—U.S.S.R.*, DST-1221S-058-76, 29 June 1976.

_____ (Robert A. Jones), *Advanced Weapons Forecasting (Techniques and Applications)-Foreign, Report No. 3, Selected Soviet Weapon Trends*, ST-CW-01-155-72, May 1974.

_____ (Karren E. Scott and Capt. Raymond D. Denzer), *Air Forces Intelligence Study (AFIS): Soviet Air Force, Strategic Bombers*, DDB-1300-95-81, October 1981.

_____ (Lee J. Stocker), *Free Rocket Over Ground (FROG-7) System*, DST-1130S-444-75, December 1975.

_____ Dr. Wallace C. Magathan, Jr, *The Soviet Role in Asia*, statement before the House Foreign Affairs Committee, July 1982.

_____ (Interagency Steering Group), *Reassessment: Soviet Armed Forces Personnel Strengths*, DDI-2680-21-75, July 1975.

_____, Defense Intelligence School (Steven R. Lucas), *Soviet Strategic Rocket Forces: An Analysis*, Intelligence Research Paper, June 1977.

Department of Defense/Department of State, *Soviet Strategic Defense Programs*, 1986.

Marine Corps, Marine Corps Development and Education Command (MCDEC), Intelligence Instruction Department, *Soviet Ground Forces Presentation*, 28 March 1984.

_____, MCDEC, Education Center, "The Threat," *MCDEC Newsletter*, No. 1-83, January-June 1983.

Navy, Admiral S. R. Foley, Jr., Commander in Chief U.S. Pacific Fleet, Navy, briefing to the Current Strategy Forum, Naval War College, 23 June 1983.

_____, Naval Postgraduate School (NPGS) (Elena W. Brown), *Soviet Naval Use of Vietnamese Military Facilities: The Military and Political Implications*, September 1980.

_____, NPGS (Michael P. Campbell), *A Perspective on Soviet Limited Nuclear Options*, March 1979.

_____, NPGS (Thom W. Ford), *Ballistic Missile Submarines of the United States and the Soviet Union: A Comparison of Systems and Doctrine*, December 1982.

_____, NPGS (Douglas E. May), *The Existence, Direction, and Extent of Bias in United States Intelligence Projections of Soviet General-Purpose Naval Forces*, September 1975.

_____, NPGS (John B. Mitchell, Jr, and Timothy A. French), *A Study of Soviet Surface ASW Forces and Missions*, March 1976.

_____, NPGS (Richard C. Myers), *Soviet Long Range ASW Aircraft: A Reassessment Study*, March 1980.

_____, NPGS (Roy E. Randolph), *Forecast of a Soviet Navy Long-Range Surface-to-Surface Cruise Missile*, March 1980.

_____, NPGS (Thomas N. Sampson II), *Trends in Soviet Frontal Aviation, 1970-1978*, March 1979.

_____, Office of the Chief of Naval Operations, Recognition Guide to Naval Ships—Major Combatants," NWP-12-7-1, April 1977.

_____, Office of Naval Intelligence, *Victor Class Nuclear Powered Attacked Submarine (Weapon System) USSR*, ST-CS-08-57-74, 10 June 1974.

North American Air Defense Command, *Soviet Land-Based Strategic Missile Capabilities Against North America*, NORAD Intelligence Planning Summary (NIPS), 28 June 1982.

RAND (Michael Checinski), *A Comparison of the Polish and Soviet Armaments Decisionmaking Systems*, prepared for the HQ USAF, R-2662-AF, January 1981.

_____ (Simon Kassel and Cathleen Campbell), *The Soviet Academy of Sciences and Technological Development*, prepared for the Defense Advanced Research Projects Agency (DARPA), R-2533-ARPA, December 1980.

_____ (Frederick M. Sallagar), *An Overview of the Soviet Threat*, prepared for the HQ USAF, R-2580-AF, February 1980.

Pacific Command, "Pacific Area Update," Brief No. P4048.1P1-4, 17 February 1984.

Bibliography

———, "The CINCPAC View," Brief, 1 March 1984.

Santa Fe Corporation (Herbert Hoppe, et al.), *Measures and Trends, US and USSR Strategic Force Effectiveness*, prepared for the Defense Nuclear Agency, DNA 4602Z, March 1978.

System Planning Corporation, *A Comparison of U.S. and Soviet Tactical Nuclear Weapons Systems*, prepared for Net Technical Assessment branch of the DOD's Office of the Director of Defense Research and Engineering (ODDR&E), SPC Report 245, January 1976.

Turetsky, Mikhail, *The Introduction of Missile Systems into the Soviet Navy (1945-1962)* (Falls Church, VA: Delphic Associates, March 1983).

Yevsikov, Victor, *Re-Entry Technology and the Soviet Space Program: Some Personal Observations* (Falls Church, VA: Delphic Associates, December 1982).

GLOSSARY

Glossary of Abbreviations and Acronyms

AAM	Air-to-Air Missile
AAW	Anti-Air Warfare
AB	Airbase
ABM	Anti-Ballistic Missile
ACDA	Arms Control and Disarmament Agency (U.S.)
ACIS	Arms Control Impact Statement
ACW	Anti-Carrier Warfare
ADD	Air Defense District
ADM	Atomic Demolition Munition
AEC	Atomic Energy Commission (U.S.)
AEM	Missile tenders
AF	Air Forces (*Voyenno-vozdushnyye sili*, VVS)
AFCENT	Allied Forces Central Europe (NATO)
AFMD	Air Forces of the Military District (Soviet Union)
AFNORTH	Allied Forces Northern Europe (NATO)
AGI	Intelligence collection ship
AI	Initials of aircraft engine designer Aleksandr Ivchyenko
AL	Initials of aircraft engine designer Arkhip Lyulka
ALCM	Air-Launched Cruise Missile
AS-	Air-to-Surface
ASAT	Anti-Satellite
ASM	Air-to-Surface Missile
AST	Boiling water reactor for district heating
ASUW	Anti-Surface Warfare
ASW	Anti-Submarine Warfare
ATET	Dual-purpose VVER producing electricity and steam for district heating
AVMF	*Aviatsiya voyenno-morskogo flota* (Soviet Naval Aviation, SNA)
AWACS	Airborne Warning And Control System
AW&ST	*Aviation Week & Space Technology*
Be-	The designation for the Beriev design bureau
BMD	Ballistic Missile Defense
BMEW	Ballistic Missile Early Warning
BPK	*Bol'shoy Protivolodochnyy Korabl'*, Large Anti-Submarine Ship (Kiev, Kara, Kresta II, Udaloy, Kashin, Kanin)
BRK	*Bol'shoy Raketnyy Korabl'*, Large Missile Ship (Kildin)
BWR	Boiling Water Reactor
C^3	Command, Control, and Communication
CENTAG	Central Army Group (NATO)
CEP	Circular Error Probable
CG	Guided missile cruiser
CGF	Central Group of Forces (Czechoslovakia)
CGN	Nuclear-powered guided missile cruiser
CHG	Guided missile aviation cruiser
CIA	Central Intelligence Agency (U.S.)
CINC	Commander-in-Chief
CL	Light cruiser
cm	Centimeter
CONAS	Combined Nuclear And Steam turbine
CONUS	Continental United States
CPSU	Communist Party of the Soviet Union
CTBT	Comprehensive Test Ban Treaty
CTOL	Conventional Takeoff/Landing aircraft
CV	Aircraft carrier
CVHG	Guided missile V/STOL aircraft carrier
D	Deuterium

Glossary

DA	*Dalnaya aviatsiya* (Long-Range Aviation, LRA)	GDR	German Democratic Republic (East Germany)
DD	Destroyer	GF	Ground Forces (*Sukhoputniye Voyska*, SV)
DDEL	Dwight David Eisenhower Library	GIN	Greenland-Iceland-Norway
DDG	Guided missile destroyer	GKES	(Russian), State Committee for Foreign Economic Relations
DEW	Directed Energy Weapons	GKNT	State Committee for Science and Technology
DIA	Defense Intelligence Agency (U.S.)	GKO	*Gosudarstvennyy komitet oborony* (State Defense Committee)
DOD	Department of Defense (U.S.)		
DODI	Department of Defense Industry (Soviet Union)	GLCM	Ground-Launched Cruise Missile
DOE	Department of Energy (U.S.)	GMT	Greenwich Mean Time
DOS	Department of State (U.S.)	GOF	Groups of Forces (Soviet Union)
E	East	Gosplan	*Soyuzno-respublikanskiy gosudarstvennyy planovyy komitet SSSR* (State Planning Committee of the USSR)
ECM	Electronic Countermeasures		
ehp	Equivalent Horsepower		
ELINT	Electronic Intelligence	GPO	Government Printing Office (U.S.)
EMP	Electromagnetic Pulse	GRU	*Glavnoye razvedyratelnoye upravleniye* (Chief Intelligence Directorate of the General Staff)
ER	Enhanced Radiation ('neutron bomb')		
EM	*Eskadrennyy Minonosets*, Destroyer (Kotlin, Skoryy)	GSF	Groups of Soviet Forces
EW	Early Warning	GSFG	Group of Soviet Forces, East Germany
EWDA	Energy and Water Development Appropriations (U.S.)	Gwd	Gigawatt-days
		h	Hour
F	Fluorine	HAC	House Appropriations Committee (U.S.)
FA	*Frontovaya aviatsiya* (Frontal Aviation)	HASC	House Armed Services Committee (U.S.)
FBIS	Foreign Broadcast Information Service (U.S.)	HCOF	High Command of Forces (Soviet Union)
FEBA	Forward Edge of the Battle Area	HE	High Explosive round
FF	Frigate	Helo	Helicopter
FFG	Guided missile frigate	HEU	Highly Enriched Uranium
FOBS	Fractional Orbital Bombardment System	hp	Horsepower
FOIA	Freedom of Information Act (U.S.)	HQ	Headquarters
FRAS	Free Rocket Anti-Submarine	HUMINT	Human Intelligence
FROD	Functionally Related Observable Differences	Hz	Hertz
		IA	*Istrebitelnaya aviatsiya* (Fighter Aviation)
FROG	Free Rocket Over Ground		
ft	Foot	IAE	*Institut atomnoy energii* (Institute of Atomic Energy)
FY	Fiscal Year		

Glossary

ICBM	Intercontinental Ballistic Missile
IISS	International Institute for Strategic Studies (U.K.)
Il-	The designation for the Ilyushin design bureau
in	Inch
INF	Intermediate-Range Nuclear Force
IOC	Initial Operational Capability
IR	Isotope Reactor
IRBM	Intermediate-Range Ballistic Missile
JCAE	Joint Committee on Atomic Energy (U.S.)
JCS	Joint Chiefs of Staff (U.S.)
JEC	Joint Economic Committee (U.S.)
Ka-	The designation for the Kamov design bureau
KB	*Konstruktorskoye byuro* (design bureau)
KEW	Kinetic Energy Weapons
kg	Kilogram
KGB	*Komitet gosudarstennoy bezopasnosti SSSR* (Committee of State Security of the USSR)
km	Kilometer
km/h	Kilometer per Hour
KR	*Kreyser*, Cruiser (Sverdlov)
Kr	Krypton
Kt	Kiloton
KTS	Kazakh Test Site (Soviet Union)
kts	Knot
LANL	Los Alamos National Laboratory (U.S.)
LASA	Large Aperture Seismic Array
lb	Pound
LCC	Launch Control Center
LGPR	Light water-cooled Graphite-moderated Plutonium production Reactor
LGR	Light water-cooled Graphite-moderated Reactor (channel-type power reactor)
Li	Lithium
LLNL	Lawrence Livermore National Laboratory (U.S.)
LMFBR	Liquid-Metal Fast-Breeder Reactor
LPAR	Large phased array radar
LRA	Long-Range Aviation (*Dalnaya aviatsiya*, DA)
LRINF	Long-Range Intermediate-Range Nuclear Forces
LTBT	Limited Test Ban Treaty
LYTBT	Low-Yield Threshold Test Ban Treaty
M	1) *Modernizirovannyy* (modernized); 2) *Modifikatsirovanny* (modification); 3) Model
m	1) Meter; 2) minute
MAD	Magnetic Anomaly Detection
MAP	*Minaviaprom* (Ministry of Aviation Industry)
MaRV	Maneuvering Reentry Vehicle
MD	Military District (Soviet Union)
Mi-	The designation for the Mil design bureau
mi	Statute mile
MiG-	The designation for the Mikoyan-Gurevich design bureau
min	Minute
MIRV	Multiple Independently targeted Reentry Vehicle
mm	Millimeter
MOD	Ministry of Defense (Soviet Union)
Mod	Modification
MOP	*Minoboronprom* (Ministry of Defense Industry)
MOU	Memorandum of Understanding
MPA	Main Political Administration (Soviet Union)
mph	Miles per Hour
MPK	*Malyy Protivolodochnyy Korabl'*, Small Anti-Submarine Ship (Grisha III)
MRBM	Medium-Range Ballistic Missile
MRK	*Malyy Raketnyy Korabl'*, Small Missile Ship (Nanuchka I, III)

Glossary

MRV	Multiple Reentry Vehicle	PBV	Post-Boost Vehicle
MT	Metric Ton	PGG	Guided missile patrol combatant
Mt	Megaton	PGGH	Guided missile patrol combatant, hydrofoil
MVD	Ministry of Internal Affairs (Soviet Union)	PKO	*Protivokosmicheskaya oborona* (anti-space defense)
Mw_e	Megawatt (electric energy)	PKR	*Protivolodochnyy Kreyser*, Anti-Submarine Cruiser, (Moskva)
Mw_t	Megawatt (thermal energy)		
N	1) Navy (*Voyenno-morskoy flot*, VMF); 2) North	PL	*Podvodnaya lodka* (attack submarine [diesel], SS)
n.a.	Not Available	PLA	*Podvodnaya lodka atomnaya* (nuclear powered attack submarine, SSN)
NATO	North Atlantic Treaty Organization		
NCA	National Command Authority (U.S.)	PLARB	*Podvodnaya lodka atomnaya raketnaya ballisticheskaya* (nuclear-powered ballistic missile submarine, SSBN)
NGF	Northern Group of Forces (Poland)		
NIE	National Intelligence Estimate		
NII	*Nauchno-issledovatelskiye institut* (Scientific Research Institute)	PLARK	*Podvodnaya lodka atomnaya raketnaya krylataya* (nuclear-powered cruise missile attack submarine, SS-GN)
NIKIET	Scientific Research and Design Institute of Power Technology		
NK	Initials of aircraft engine designer Nikolai Kuznetsov	PLRB	*Podvodnaya lodka raketnaya ballisticheskaya* (ballistic missile submarine [diesel], SSB)
nm	Nautical Mile		
NORFLT	Northern Fleet (Soviet Union)	PLRK	*Podvodnaya lodka raketnaya krylataya* (cruise missile attack submarine [diesel], SSG)
NORSAR	Norwegian Seismic Array		
NORTHAG	Northern Army Group (NATO)	PNE	Peaceful Nuclear Explosion
NPO	*Nauchno-proizvodstvennye ob'edineniya* (Scientific Production Association)	PNET	Peaceful Nuclear Explosion Treaty
		PRO	*Protivoraketnay oborona* (anti-rocket defense)
NTS	Nevada Test Site (U.S.)	psi	Pounds per Square Inch
O	Oxygen	Pu	Plutonium
OKB	*Orytnoye konstruktirskoye byuro* (aircraft design bureau)	PVO	Air Defense; see V PVO
		PWR	Pressurized Water Reactor
OMA	Office of Military Application (U.S.)	RADM	Rear Admiral (U.S.)
OMG	Operational Maneuver Groups	RBMK	Large-capacity boiling-water (or channel) reactor; high-power version of LGR
ONI	Office of Naval Intelligence (U.S.)		
ORNL	Oak Ridge National Laboratory (U.S.)		
OTH-B	Over-The-Horizon Backscatter radar	RDA	Research, Development, and Acquisition
OTVD	*Okeanskiy teatr voyennykh deystviy* (oceanic theater of military operations)	RDT&E	Research, Development, Test, and Evaluation
PACFLT	Pacific Fleet		
PAL	Permissive Action Link	RIIA	Royal Institute of International Affairs (U.K.)
PAR	Phased Array Radar		

Glossary

RKR	*Raketnyy Kreyser*, Missile Cruiser (Kirov, Slava, Kresta I, Kynda)
RTV	*Radiotekhnicheskiye voyska*, Radio-Technical Troops
RUSI	Royal United Services Institute (U.K.)
RV	Reentry Vehicle
RVSN	*Raketnyye voyska strategicheskogo naznacheniya* (Strategic Rocket Forces, SRF)
SA-	Surface-to-Air
SAA	Strategic Air Armies (Soviet Union)
SAC	Senate Appropriations Committee (U.S.)
SAC	Strategic Air Command (U.S.)
SACEUR	Supreme Allied Commander Europe (NATO)
SALT	Strategic Arms Limitation Treaty
SAM	Surface-to-Air Missile
SA-N-	Surface-to-Air, Naval
SASC	Senate Armed Services Committee (U.S.)
SGF	Southern Group of Forces (Hungary)
shp	Shaft Horsepower
SIGINT	Signal Intelligence
SIOP	Single Integrated Operational Plan (U.S.)
SIPRI	Stockholm International Peace Research Institute (Sweden)
SKR	*Storozhevoy Korabl'*, Patrol Ship (Krivak I, II, Riga
SLBM	Submarine-Launched Ballistic Missile
SLCM	Sea-Launched Cruise Missile
SMP	*Soviet Military Power* (DOD)
SNA	Soviet Naval Aviation (*aviatsiya voyenno-morskogo flota*, AVMF)
SNDV	Strategic Nuclear Delivery Vehicle
SNF	Short-Range Nuclear Forces
SNIE	Special National Intelligence Estimate (U.S.)
SP	Self-Propelled
SRAM	Short-Ramge Attack Missile
SRBM	Short-Range Ballistic Missile
SRF	Strategic Rocket Forces (Soviet Union)
SRINF	Short-Range Intermediate-Range Nuclear Forces
SS	Attack submarine (diesel); Soviet designation PL (*Podvodnaya lodka*)
SS-	Surface-to-Surface
SSA	Auxiliary submarine
SSB	Ballistic missile submarine (diesel); Soviet designation PLRB (*Podvodnaya lodka raketnaya ballisticheskaya*)
SSBN	Nuclear-powered ballistic missile submarine; Soviet designation PLARB (*Podvodnaya lodka atomnaya raketnaya ballisticheskaya*)
SSC	Coastal submarine, ground-launched surface-to-surface cruise missile
SSCM	Surface-to-Surface Cruise Missile
SSG	Cruise (guided) missile attack submarine (diesel); Soviet designation PLRK (*Podvodnaya lodka raketnaya krylataya*)
SSGN	Nuclear-powered cruise (guided) missile attack submarine; Soviet designation PLARK (*Podvodnaya lodka atomnaya raketnaya krylataya*)
SSM	Surface-to-Surface Missile
SS-N-	Surface-to-Surface, Naval
SSN	Nuclear-powered attack submarine; Soviet designation PLA (*Podvodnaya lodka atomnaya*)
SST	Target-training submarine (diesel)
SSUN	Nuclear-powered submarine, principal military capability unknown
START	Strategic Arms Reduction Talks
STOAL	Short Takeoff/Arrested Landing
Su-	The designation for the Sukhoi design bureau.
SUW-N	Surface-to-Underwater, Naval; NATO designation for Soviet surface-to-underwater naval missile
SVE	*Sovetskaya voyennaya entsiklopediya* (Soviet Military Encyclopedia)
SWU	Separation Work Units
TACAMO	Take Charge And Move Out
TEL	Transporter-Erector-Launcher

TMO	Theater of Military Operations (see TVD)	US	United States
TNF	Theater Nuclear Forces	USA	United States Army
TNT	Trinitrotoluene	USAF	United States Air Forces
TNW	Theater Nuclear Weapons	USN	United States Navy
TP	*Tekhnicheskoye predlozheniye* (technical proposal)	USSR	Union of Soviet Socialist Republics
TsKB	*Tsentralniy konstruktorskoye byuro* (central design bureau)	VD	Initials of aircraft engine designer Vladimir Dobrynin
TSMA	Theater of Strategic Military Action (see TVD)	VGK	*Verkhovnoye glavnokomandovaniye* (Supreme High Command)
TTBT	Threshold Test Ban Treaty	VLF	Very Low Frequency
TTKhs	*Taktiko-tekhnicheskiye kharakteristicheski* (technical task characteristics)	VLS	Vertical Launching System
		VMF	*Voyenno-morskoy flot* (Navy)
TTZ	*Taktiko-tekhnicheskii zadaniye* (technical task)	VPK	*Voyenno-promyshlennaya kommissiya* (Military Industrial Commission)
TU	*Tekhnicheskiye usloviye* (technical agreement)	V PVO	*Voyska protivovozdushnoy oborony* (Troops of the Air Defense); until 1981, *V PVO strany* (Troops of the National Air Defense); also referred to as the PVO
Tu-	The designation for the Tupolev design bureau		
TV	*Teatr voyny* (theater of war)	V/STOL	Vertical Short Takeoff and Landing aircraft
TVD	*Teatr voyennykh deystviy* (theater of military operations)	VTA	Military-Transport Aviation
TVR	Heavy-water reactor	VTOL	Vertical Takeoff and Landing aircraft
Tyl	Chief of Rear Services (Soviet Union)	VVER	Pressurized water power reactor
TZ	*Tekhnicheskiye zadniya* (non-military technical task)	VVS	*Voyenno-vozdushnyye sili* (Air Forces, AF)
U	Uranium	WTO	Warsaw Treaty Organization
UDMH	Unsymmetrical Demethylhyrazine; a liquid propellant	Yak-	The designation for the Yakovlev design bureau
UF_4	Uranium tetrafluoride	YeSKD	Unified System of Design Documentation
UF_6	Uranium hexafluoride	ZRV	*Zenitnyye Raketnyye Voyska*, Zenith-Rocket Troops
unk	Unknown		

Glossary

Glossary of Terms

Air-Breathing Missile
: A missile with an engine requiring the intake of air for combustion of its fuel, as in a ramjet or turbojet. (To be contrasted with the rocket-powered missile, which carries its own oxidizer and can operate beyond the atmosphere.)

Air Defense
: Defensive measures designed to destroy attacking enemy aircraft of missiles in the earth's envelope of atmosphere, or to nullify or reduce the effectiveness of such attack.

Air-Launched Cruise Missile (ALCM)
: A cruise missile transported aloft by a carrier aircraft and launched from that aircraft in flight.

Air-to-Air Missile (AAM)
: A missile launched from an aircraft at a target above the surface.

Air-to-Surface (AS-)
: Used as part of a designator to indicate a missile launched from an airborne carrier to impact on a surface target; i.e., air-to-surface missile (e.g., AS-4).

Air-to-Surface Missile (ASM)
: A missile launched from an aircraft to impact on a surface target.

Anti-Ballistic Missile (ABM)
: A defense missile used to intercept and destroy or otherwise neutralize an attacking ballistic missile in the upper reaches of the atmosphere and beyond (endoatmosphere and exoatmosphere).

Anti-Ballistic Missile System
: A system to counter strategic ballistic missiles in flight, consisting of: 1) ABM interceptor missiles; 2) ABM launchers; 3) ABM radars, which are radars constructed and deployed for an ABM role, or of a type tested in an ABM mode. Often used interchangeably with BMD (ballistic missile defense).

Anti-Ballistic Missile (ABM) Treaty
: One of two agreements signed at Moscow on 26 May 1972 known collectively as the SALT I Agreements. The original ABM Treaty limited each side to two ABM deployment areas (one national capital area and one ICBM silo launcher area), with restrictions on the deployment of ABM launchers and interceptors (100 in each area). A 1974 protocol to the treaty further restricted each side to only one ABM deployment area.

Anti-Submarine Warfare (ASW)
: Operations conducted with the intention of denying the enemy the effective use of his submarines.

Apogee
: The point at which a missile trajectory or a satellite orbit is farthest from the center of the gravitational field of the controlling body or bodies.

Atomic Demolition Munition (ADM)
: Nuclear device designed to be detonated on or below the surface, or underwater, to block, deny, and/or canalize enemy forces.

Ballistic Missile
: Any missile designed to follow the trajectory that results when it is acted upon predominantly by gravity and aerodynamic drag after thrust is terminated. Ballistic missiles generally operate outside the atmosphere for a substantial portion of their flight path and are unpowered during most of the flight.

Ballistic Missile Defense (BMD)
: Measures for defending against an attack by ballistic missiles; for example, a system composed of anti-ballistic missiles and radar and control equipment designed to intercept and destroy attacking ballitsic missiles before they reach their targets. Often used interchangeably with ABM (anti-ballistic missile).

Ballistic Trajectory
: The trajectory traced after the propulsive force is terminated and the body is acted upon only by gravity and aerodynamic drag.

Beam
: Extreme width of hull.

Glossary

Blast	The brief and rapid movement of air vapor or fluid away from a center of outward pressure, as in an explosion or in the combustion of rocket fuel; the pressure accompanying this movement. This term is commonly used for *explosion*, but the two terms may be distinguished.	Cold Launch	The use of a gas generator to build up steam pressure inside a canister housing a ballistic missile, which forces the missile out of the canister prior to the ignition of the first-stage rocket motor. The temperature of the steam used to eject the missile from the canister is substantially less than the rocket motor exhaust, hence the term *cold launch*.

Bomber
1. Light (or medium-range): A bomber designed for a tactical operating radius of under 1000 nautical miles at design gross weight and design bomb load.

2. Medium (or intermediate-range): A bomber designed for a tactical operating radius of between 1000 and 2500 nautical miles at design gross weight and design bomb load.

3. Heavy (or long-range): A bomber designed for a tactical operating radius of over 2500 nautical miles at design gross weight and design bomb load.

Boosted Fission Weapon
A nuclear weapon in which neutrons produced by thermonuclear reactions serve to enhance the fission process. The thermonuclear energy represents only a small fraction of the total explosion energy.

Booster
An auxiliary or initial propulsion system that travels with a missile or aircraft and may or may not be separated from the parent craft when its impulse has been delivered. A booster system may contain or consist of one or more units.

Bus
The projectile of a missile, with multiple reentry vehicles (MRVs or MIRVs), including the RVs (reentry vehicles), guidance system, propellant, and thrust device for altering the ballistic flight path so that RVs can be ejected sequentially toward respective targets. Also known as post-boost vehicle (PBV).

Circular Error Probable (CEP)
A measure of the delivery accuracy of a weapon system. It is the radius of a circle around a target of such size that a weapon aimed at the center has a 50 percent probability of falling within the circle.

Collateral Damage
Physical harm inflicted by intent or otherwise on persons and property as a result of attack (specifically, nuclear attack) on a primary military target.

Combat Radius
The maximum distance that an operational aircraft characteristically armed for a combat mission can fly unrefueled from its starting point and return safely, allowing for fuel expenditure involved in combat action typical of the mission profile.

Command, Control, Communication (C^3)
The exercise of authority and direction by a properly designated commander over assigned forces in the accomplishment of a mission. Command and control functions are performed through an arrangement of personnel, equipment, communications, facilities, and procedures, which are employed by a commander in planning, directing, coordinating, and controlling forces and operations in the accomplishment of a mission.

Counterforce
The employment of strategic air and missile forces in an effort to destroy, or render impotent, military capabilities of an enemy force.

Countervalue
The employment of strategic air and missile forces to attack selected enemy population centers, industries, and resources and installations that constitute the social fabric of the nation.

Cruise Missile
A guided missile that uses aerodynamic lift to offset gravity and propulsion to counteract drag. A cruise missile's flight path remains within the earth's atmosphere.

Glossary

Delivery System
: An aerospace vehicle considered as a whole, with all associated components, and integral with launchers and other installations employed in transporting, launching, targeting, guiding, and delivering on target its nuclear weapon(s).

Deployment
: 1. The transition in a weapon system development program from production and testing to installation in operational status at a base or site.

  2. However defined, the point at which a weapon becomes accountable in arms control regimes.

Depressed Trajectory
: The trajectory of a ballistic missile fired at an angle to the ground significantly lower than the angle of a minimum energy (maximum range) trajectory. Such a trajectory causes the missile to rise above the line-of-site radar horizon at a later time and has a shorter time of flight than a missile on a minimum energy trajectory to the same range. This makes detection and tracking more difficult and reduces warning time.

Draft
: The depth of water a ship draws, especially at full load.

Dual-Capable Weapons
: Weapons, weapon systems, or vehicles capable of employing nuclear or non-nuclear munitions.

Electromagnetic Pulse (EMP)
: The electromagnetic radiation from a nuclear explosion, caused by Compton-recoil electrons and photoelectrons from photons scattered in the materials of the nuclear device, in a surrounding medium. The resulting electric and magnetic fields may couple with military systems to produce damaging current and voltage sources.

Electronic Countermeasures (ECM)
: Electronic warfare involving actions taken to prevent or reduce the effectiveness of enemy equipment and tactics employing or affected by electromagnetic radiations; to exploit the enemy's use of such radiations.

Encryption
: The encoding of communications for the purpose of concealing information. In the SALT II Treaty, encryption has been applied to a practice whereby a side alters the manner by which it transmits telemetry from a weapon being tested rending the information deliberately undecipherable.

Endoatmosphere
: The area from sea level to about 40 nautical miles altitude.

Enhanced Radiation (ER)
: The effects of, and the technology employed in, that class of controlled-effects nuclear weapons designed to intensify nuclear radiation in the target area by attenuating blast and heat.

Enrichment
: Increasing the concentration of one isotope of an element relative to the other isotopes. For example, uranium-235 relative to uranium-238 or plutonium-239 relative to plutonium-240.

Equivalent Megatonnage (EMT)
: A measure used to compare the destructive potential of differing combinations of nuclear warhead yield against relatively soft countervalue targets. EMT is computed from the expression: $EMT = NY_x$, where N = number of actual warheads of yield Y; Y = yield of the actual warheads in megatons; and x = scaling.

Exoatmosphere
: The area higher than about 40 nautical miles above sea level.

Fallout
: The precipitation to earth of radioactive particulate matter from a nuclear cloud; also applied to the particulate matter itself.

Fighter-Bomber
: Tactical aircraft configured for ground attack and interdiction as well as for air combat. As dual-capable systems, fighter-bombers (such as MiG-27s) constitute a non-central system with potential for strategic missions.

Fission
: The splitting of the nucleus of a heavy atom following absorption of a neutron into two lighter nuclei, accompanied by the release of neutrons, X-rays, gamma rays, and kinetic energy of the fission products.

Glossary

Fission Weapon
: Nuclear warhead whose material is uranium or plutonium, which is brought to a critical mass under pressure from a chemical explosive detonation to create an explosion that produces blast, thermal radiation, and nuclear radiation. The complete fission of one pound of fissionable material would have a yield equivalent to 8000 tons of TNT. Commonly known as an atomic bomb.

Free Rocket Over Ground (FROG)
: Used as part of designator for a class of Soviet unguided tactical rockets, e.g., FROG-7.

Front
: The highest strategic formation of armed forces; an operational and administrative unit usually composed of three to five maneuver armies and one or two air armies. Forces organic or attached to a front could include artillery, missiles, air defense, engineer, chemical, signal, intelligence, and rear service units, plus airborne, airmobile, and special-purpose forces.

Full load
: Ship displacement complete and ready for sea in all respects.

Fusion
: The process in which two light nuclei atoms, especially isotopes of hydrogen, combine to form a heavier nucleus, with the release of a substantial amount of energy. Extremely high temperatures, resulting in highly energetic, fast-moving nuclei, are required to initiate fusion reactions.

Fusion Weapon
: Nuclear warhead containing fusion materials (e.g., deuterium and tritium), which are brought to critical density and temperature conditions by use of a primary fission reaction (thermonuclear) in order to initiate and sustain a rapid fusion process, which in turn creates an explosion that produces blast, thermal radiation, and nuclear radiation. The complete fusion of one pound of fusion material is equivalent to 36,000 tons of TNT. Commonly known as hydrogen bomb.

Guidance
: The entire process by which target intelligence information received by the guided missile is used to effect proper flight control to cause timely direction ranges for effective target interception.

Guided Missile
: An unmanned vehicle moving above the surface of the earth, whose trajectory or flight path is capable of being altered by an external or internal mechanism.

Half-Life
: The time required for the activity of a given radioactive species to decrease to half of its initial value due to radioactive decay. The half-life is a characteristic property of each radioactive species and is independent of its amount or condition. The half-life of tritium is 12.3 years.

Hard Target
: Any weapon site, command and control facility, production center, blast shelter or other strategic target which has been hardened for protection against the effects of nuclear attack.

High Command
: A formal command, with staff structure, established between the Supreme High Command and operational-strategic or operational formations (fronts, fleets, independent armies, and flotillas) to coordinate strategic operations in either strategic directions or theaters of military action.

High Explosive (HE)
: Generally applied to the bursting charges for bombs, projectiles, grenades, mines, and demolition charges.

Homing
: The technique of tracking along a position line toward the point of origin of a radio, radar, or other navigation aid.

Howitzer
: A cannon that combines certain characteristics of guns and mortars. The howitzer delivers projectiles with medium velocities, by either low or high trajectories.

Hydrogen Bomb
: A nuclear weapon in which part of the explosive energy is obtained from nuclear fusion (or thermonuclear) reaction.

Glossary

Hypersonic — Pertaining to speeds equal to or in excess of five times the speed of sound.

Inertial Guidance — A guidance system designed to project a missile over a predetermined path, wherein the path of the missile is adjusted after launch by devices wholly within the missile and independent of outside information. The system measures and converts accelerations experienced to distance traveled in a certain direction.

Initial Operational Capability (IOC) — The first attainment of the capability to employ effectively a weapon, item of equipment, or system of approved specific characteristics, which is manned or operated by an adequately trained, equipped, and supported military unit or force.

Intercontinental Ballistic Missile (ICBM) — A land-based, fixed or mobile, rocket-propelled vehicle capable of delivering a warhead to intercontinental ranges (about 3000 to 8000 nautical miles). ICBMs fly elliptical trajectories. An ICBM consists of a booster, one or more reentry vehicles, possibly penetration aids, and in some cases, a post-boost vehicle (PBV).

Intermediate-Range Ballistic Missile (IRBM) — A ballistic missile with a range capability from about 1500 to 3000 nautical miles.

Intermediate-Range Nuclear Forces (INF) — Land-based nuclear systems (missiles or aircraft) with ranges between approximately 400 kilometers and 5500 kilometers.

Kiloton (Kt) — A unit of measure of a nuclear weapon's yield, equivalent to the explosive energy of 1000 tons of TNT.

Kiloton Weapon — A nuclear weapon, the yield of which is measured in terms of thousands of tons of TNT explosive equivalents, producing yields of one to 999 kilotons.

Kinetic Energy Weapons — Weapons that use the high-speed collision of a small mass with the target as the kill mechanism.

Launcher — That equipment that launches a missile. Land-based launchers can be either fixed or mobile and are referred to as either "soft," whereby the missile and most of its launch equipment remain unprotected against nearby nuclear blasts above ground, or "hard," whereby the missile and most of its launch equipment are contained in a hardened underground silo. In either case, fixed launchers, the equipment required to launch the missile, cannot be moved. Sea-based launchers are the cruise or ballistic missile tubes on a submarine. Launchers for cruise missiles can also be installed on aircraft.

Launch Weight — The weight of the fully loaded missile at the time of launch. This would include the aggregate post-boost vehicle (PBV) and the payload.

Long-Range Intermediate-Range Nuclear Forces (LRINF) — Missiles and aircraft with ranges up to 5500 kilometers.

Mach Number — The ratio of the velocity of a body to that of sound in the surrounding medium. The speed of sound varies from about 760 mph at sea level to 600 mph at 36,000 feet.

Maneuverable Reentry Vehicle (MaRV) — A reentry vehicle capable of performing preplanned flight maneuvers during the reentry phase.

Maximum Range — The greatest distance a weapon can fire without consideration of dispersion, or the greatest distance a weapon system can fly.

Medium-Range Ballistic Missile (MRBM) — A ballistic missile with a range capability from about 600 to 1500 nautical miles.

Megaton — A unit of measurement for nuclear yield equivalent to the energy released from one million tons of TNT.

Midcourse Guidance — The guidance applied to a missile between termination of the launching phase and the start of the terminal phase of flight.

Glossary

Mortar	A muzzle-loading, indirect fire weapon with either a rifled or smooth bore. It usually has a shorter range than a howitzer, employs a higher angle of fire, and has a tube length of 10-20 calibers.	Nuclear Weapon	A device in which the explosion results from the energy released by nuclear reactions involving atomic nuclei; either fission, fusion, or both.
Multiple Independently Targetable Reentry Vehicle (MIRV)	Multiple reentry vehicles carried by a ballistic missile, each of which can be directed to a separate target. A MIRVed missile employs a post-boost vehicle (PBV) or other warhead-dispensing mechanism. The dispensing and targeting mechanism maneuvers to achieve successive desired positions and velocities to dispense each reentry vehicle (RV) on a trajectory to attack the desired target. Alternately, the RVs might themselves maneuver toward their targets after they reenter the atmosphere.	Nuclear Yield	The energy released in the detonation of a nuclear weapon, measured in terms of kilotons or megatons of TNT explosive required to produce the same energy release. Yields are categorized as: very low--less than 1 kiloton; low--1-10 kilotons; medium--10- 50 kilotons; high--50-500 kilotons; very high--over 500 kilotons.
		Order of Battle	The identification, strength, command structure, and disposition of the personnel, units, and equipment of any military force.
Multiple Reentry Vehicle (MRV)	The reentry vehicle of a ballistic missile equipped with multiple warheads where the missile does not have the capability to independently target the reentry vehicles, as distinct from a missile equipped with MIRVs.	Payload	The load a vehicle is designed to carry under specified conditions of operation. In the case of a ballistic missile, the RV(s) and anti-ballistic missile (ABM) penetration aids placed on ballistic trajectories by the main propulsion stages of the post-boost vehicle (PBV); in the case of a bomber, those bombs, missiles, or penetration aids carried internally or attached to the wing or fuselage.
National Technical Means (NTM)	Assets which are under national control for monitoring compliance with the provisions of an agreement. NTM include photographic reconnaissance satellites and aircraft-based systems such as radars and optical systems, as well as sea- and ground-based systems such as radars and antennas for collecting telemetry.	Penetration Aids	Devices employed by offensive weapon systems, such as ballistic missiles and bombers, to increase the probability of penetrating enemy defenses. They are frequently designed to simulate or to mask an aircraft or ballistic missile warhead in order to mislead enemy radar and/or divert defensive anti-aircraft or anti-missile fire.
Nautical Mile (nm)	A measure of distance equal to one minute of arc on the earth's surface. The United States has adopted the international nautical mile equal to 1852 meters or 6076.11549 feet.		
		Perigee	The point at which a satellite orbit is the least distance from the center of the gravitational field of the controlling body or bodies.
Nuclear Radiation	Particulate and electromagnetic radiation emitted from atomic nuclei in various nuclear processes. The important nuclear radiations, from the weapons effects standpoint, are alpha and beta particles, gamma rays, and neutrons.	Permissive Action Link (PAL)	A device included in or attached to a nuclear weapon system to preclude arming and/or launching until the insertion of a prescribed discrete code or combination.

Glossary

Post-Boost Vehicle (PBV)	That part of a missile that carries the reentry and thrust devices for altering the ballistic flight path so that the reentry vehicles (RVs) can be dispensed sequentially toward different targets (MIRVs). Ballistic missiles with single RVs also might use a post-boost vehicle (PBV) to increase the accuracy of the RV by placing it more precisely into the desired trajectory.
Projectile	An object projected by an applied exterior force and continuing in motion, as an artillery shell.
Propellant	That which provides the energy required for propelling a projectile. Specifically, an explosive charge for propelling a bullet, shell, or the like; also a fuel, either solid or liquid, for propelling a rocket or missile.
Radar	"Radio Detection And Ranging" equipment that determines the distance and usually the direction of objects by transmission and return of electromagnetic energy.
Radius of Action	The maximum distance a ship, aircraft, or vehicle can travel away from its base along a given course with normal combat load and return without refueling, allowing for all safety and operating factors.
Ramjet	A jet propulsion engine containing neither compressor nor turbine that depends for its operation on the air compression accomplished by the forward motion of the engine.
Range	1. The distance between any given point and an object or target. 2. The extent or distance limiting the operation or action of something, such as the range of an aircraft, ship, or gun. 3. The distance that can be covered over a hard surface by a ground vehicle, with its rated payload, using the fuel in its tank and in cans normally carried as part of the ground vehicle equipment. 4. The area equipped for practice in shooting at targets.
Reaction Time	The time interval between detection and the actual launch; considered to be an attribute of a weapon or weapon system.
Reentry Vehicle (RV)	That part of the ballistic missile which carries the nuclear warhead, designed to reenter the earth's atmosphere in the terminal portion of its trajectory.
Rocket	A self-propelled vehicle whose trajectory or course, while in flight, cannot be controlled.
Short-Range Attack Missile (SRAM)	An air-to-surface missile (ASM), such as the AS-X-19. The missile range, speed, and accuracy allow the carrier aircraft to "stand off" from its intended targets and launch missiles outside enemy defenses.
Short-Range Ballistic Missile (SRBM)	A ballistic missile with a range up to about 600 nautical miles.
Short-Range Intermediate-Range Nuclear Forces (SRINF)	Missiles and aircraft with a range of up to 1800 kilometers.
Short-Range Nuclear Forces (SNF)	Tube artillery, missiles, and rockets of much shorter range (up to 500 kilometers) than INF
Silo	Hardened, underground facility for a fixed-site ballistic missile and its crew, designed to provide prelaunch protection and to serve as a launching platform. High-yield, precision nuclear weapons are required to destroy a silo construction.
Stockpile	Nuclear storage. Also, the total number of nuclear weapons that a nation maintains in storage at all locations and that are potentially available for deployment.
Strategic Defense	Forces and measures existing to mount a defense against enemy strategic offensive forces designed to protect one's own war-making capacity.

Glossary

Strategic Forces	Nuclear weapons and delivery systems designed for nuclear attack against strategic targets or for active defense against such an attack: bombers, missile systems, and strategic interceptors.
Strategic Offense	Forces and measures existing to mount a nuclear attack against enemy strategic targets; designed to destroy the enemy's war-making capacity.
Strategic Relocatable Targets (SRT)	Mobile strategic forces, possibly forming the backbone of a strategic reserve force.
Sub-Kiloton Weapons	A nuclear weapon producing a yield below one kiloton.
Submarine-Launched Ballistic Missile (SLBM)	A ballistic missile carried in and launched from a submarine, which affords mobility and concealment for a missile force. The SALT II Treaty says "submarine-launched ballistic missile (SLBM) launchers are launchers of ballistic missiles installed on any nuclear-powered submarine or launchers of modern ballistic missiles installed on any submarine, regardless of its type"; SALT II Treaty, Article II (2).
Supreme High Command (VGK)	The highest body of Soviet military leadership. This organ reports directly to the Defense Council, which is chaired by the Commander in Chief of the Soviet Armed Forces, the General Secretary of the Communist Party of the Soviet Union.
Surface-to-Air Missile (SAM)	A surface-launched missile designed to operate against a target above the surface.
Surface-to-Air, Naval (SA-N-)	Used as part of a designator of a series of Soviet surface-to-air naval missiles; e.g., SA-N-3.
Surface-to-Surface (SS-)	Used as part of a designator to indicate a surface-to-surface missile; e.g., SS-12.
Surface-to-Surface Missile (SSM)	A surface-launched missile designed to operate against a target on the surface.
Surface-to-Surface, Naval (SS-N-)	Used as part of a designator to indicate a surface-to-surface missile; e.g., SS-N-19.
Terminal Guidance	The guidance applied to a missile between mid-course guidance and its arrival in the vicinity of the target.
Terrain Contour Matching (TERCOM)	Guidance system, presently employed in cruise missiles, that correlates preprogramming contour map data with the terrain being overflown, in order to take periodic fixes and adjust the flight path accordingly. TERCOM improves the accuracy provided by inertial guidance alone.
Theaters of military operations (TVD)	An extensive land area of a continent and its coastal seas, or the waters of an ocean (sea), including islands and adjacent continental coastal areas, as well as the airspace and outer space above them, within the bounds of which strategic groupings of armed (ground, air, and naval) may deploy and conduct military operations on a strategic scale. The military political leadership of the states (coalitions of states) determines the borders and forces of the TVD.
Theaters of War (TV)	The land, oceans, and airspace and outer space above them, within the bounds of which the armed forces of states (coalition of states) may conduct war or military operations on a strategic scale. A TV does not have strictly defined boundaries; it usually contains one continent with its surrounding waters or one ocean with its coastal areas, archipelagoes, and islands.
Thermonuclear Weapon	A weapon in which very high temperatures are used to bring about the fusion of light nucei, such as those of hydrogen isotopes (e.g., deuterium and tritium), with the accompanying release of energy. The high temperatures required are obtained by means of an atomic (fission) explosion.

Glossary

Throwweight Ballistic missile throwweight is the useful weight that is placed on a trajectory toward the target by the boost or main propulsion stages of the missile. For the purposes of SALT II, throwweight is defined as the sum of the weight of: the RV or RVs; any post-boost vehicle (PBV) or similar device for releasing or targeting one or more RVs; and any anti-ballistic missile (ABM) penetration aids, including their release devices.

Transporter-Erector-Launcher (TEL) The vehicle designed to move a land-based mobile missile (for some system types within its shelter and to break through the overhead cover), raise the missile into firing position, and serve as a platform for the launch of the missile.

Turbojet A jet engine whose air is supplied by a turbine-driven compressor, the turbine being activated by exhaust gases.

Warhead That part of a missile, projectile, torpedo, rocket, or other munition that contains either the nuclear or thermonuclear system, high explosive system, chemical or biological agents, or inert materials, intended to inflict damage.

Weapon Systems A weapon and those components required for its operation.

Yield The energy released in an explosion. The energy released in the detonation of a nuclear weapon is generally measured in terms of the kilotons (Kt) or megatons (Mt) of TNT required to produce the same energy release.

INDEX

INDEX

ABM system, 9, 14, 15, 98, 116-20
    Expansion of, 13
    Galosh (AMB-1B), 9, 13, 32, 57, 119-20
    Gazelle (ABM-2), 13, 32, 57, 120
    Radars, 57, 73
ABM Treaty, 120
Acquisition policy, 2
Aerospace Defense Forces, 116-20
Airborne warning and control system (AWACS), 58
Aircraft carriers, 14, 272, 278, 305-6
Air Defense Districts (ADD), 57
Air Defense Forces, 2, 116
    Centralization of the strategic assets of, 13
    And the chain of command, role in, 46, 66
    Independent (PVO or PVO-S), 7, 56-58, 235
    Troops, 46, 56-58
Air Forces (VVS), 2, 7, 16, 18, 228-69
    And the chain of command, role in, 46, 58-60
    Focus on cruise missiles, 9-10
    Non-strategic forces assigned to, 32, 35-36
    Resubordination of forces within, 13
    Tu-22 Blinder, 9-10
Air Forces of the Military Districts and Groups of Forces (AFMD/GOF), 59, 234
Air-to-surface (ASM) missiles, 10, 13, 15, 36-37, 98, 157-58, 229, 231-32
    Force, size of, 32
    Non-strategic, 272
    And nuclear stockpiles, 25
    Nuclear tests involving, 337
    AS-1 Kennel, 154, 155
    AS-2 Kipper, 9, 36, 154, 157, 162, 232
    AS-3 Kangaroo, 9, 32, 155, 157, 163, 229, 231
    AS-4, 13
    AS-4 Kitchen, 32, 35, 157, 158, 164-65, 231, 233
    AS-5 Kelt, 36, 157, 166-67, 232
    AS-6 Kingfish, 36, 157, 159, 168, 232, 233
    AS-11 Kilter, 14, 158
    AS-12 Kegler, 233
    AS-14 Kegler, 233
    AS-15, 4, 13, 32, 115, 116, 157, 169-70
    AS-X-16, 13, 232
    AS-X-19, 14
Akula class submarines, 14, 39, 40, 41, 160, 276
    And the SS-N-15 Starfish, 275
    And the SS-N-21 Sampson, 161
Alaska, 18, 195
Albania, 273
Alekseyev, R. Ye., 76
Aleutian Islands, 339
Alexander Brykin (navy supply ship), 31
Alfa class submarines, 40, 41, 273, 275, 276
Allied Socialist Fleets, 63
Alluvium, 339
Amchitka Island, 339
Amga class missile tenders, 31
Andropov, Yuri, 49, 161
Anti-carrier ballistic missiles, 108

Anti-satellite systems (ASAT), 57
Anti-ship missiles, 154-ff., 162, 164, 168, 173-78, 182, 272
Anti-submarine aircraft, 228, 263-69
Anti-submarine warfare (ASW), 11, 15, 61, 236, 274-75
    Helicopters, 268-69, 272
    Operations, open-ocean, 273
Anti-submarine weapons, 39-41
    FRAS-1 rocket, 11, 39, 41, 274-75, 278
    Non-strategic, 272
    SS-N-15 Starfish rocket, 39, 40, 273, 274-76
    SS-N-16, 275-76
    SS-N-17 Stallion, 11, 275
Aral Sea, 332
Arctic Circle, 336
Armed Forces, 52-53, 63-64
Artillery, 56, 76, 190, 198-205
Astrakhan, 333, 334, 335, 348
Atlantic Ocean, 273, 279
Atomic Demolitions Munition (ADM), 2, 14, 15, 56, 190, 202
Aviation Armies, 59
Azgir, 333, 334, 340
Azores, 18

B-29 bombers (U.S.), 228
Backfire aircraft, 35, 232-34, 235-36
Badger aircraft, 11, 35-36, 232-34, 235-36
Baltic Sea, 196, 278, 279
Barents Sea, 18, 279, 332
Barmin, V.P., 75
Bases, bomber (1988), 61
Be-12 Mail, 11, 236, 266-67, 275
Bear bombers, 13, 98, 115-16, 236
    Bear A, 32, 231
    Bear B/C, 13, 32, 36, 230, 231
    Bear G, 13, 18, 32, 231
    Bear H, 13, 18, 32, 156, 231
    Bear J, 19
Bearing Sea, 279
Beloyarskiy, 81, 86
Berezina class oilers, 279
Beria, Lavrenti P., 6
Blackjack, 13, 59, 116, 161
Black Sea, 278, 279
Blinder aircraft, 11, 232-34
Bosporus, 279
Britain, 5
Brown, Harold, 30, 161, 200
Bulganin, Nikolai A., 7, 49
Bulgaria, 63, 222
Bulgarian Navy, 63

C^3 centers, 54
Cam Ranh Bay (Vietnam), 235, 236, 274
Carlucci, Frank, 41
Carlucci estimates, 41-43
Caspian Sea, 332, 335
Cat House target-tracking radars, 57
Central Aerodynamic Institute, 73

Index

Central Asia, 18
Central Committee Plenum, 10
Central Intelligence Agency (CIA), 81, 88, 154, 194, 274
Central Scientific Research Institute of Aviation Motor Building, 73
Charlie class submarines, 40, 160, 273, 275, 282-83
Chernobyl accident, 81, 86
China, 56
Chita (HCOF), 65
Civil Defense, 52
Committee for State Security (KGB), 6, 16, 50, 56, 70
Communications, 52
Comprehensive Test Ban Treaty (CTBT), 333
Communist Party of the Soviet Union (CPSU), 20, 46
    Central Committee, 46, 47, 49, 71
    And the Design cycle, 95
    General Secretary of, 49, 50, 51
    Politburo, 46
    Secretariat of, 46
Condor aircraft, 195
Congress (U.S.), 49
Council of Ministers, 46, 49
    Chairman of, 50
    Military-Industrial Commission (VPK), 68, 70, 95
Crimean peninsula, 236
Cruise missiles, 9-10, 154-61
    AS-2 Kipper, 155, 162
    AS-3 Kangaroo, 155, 156, 163
    AS-4 Kitchen, 10, 156, 164-65
    AS-6 Kingfish, 10, 156, 168
    AS-15 Kent, 169
    AS-X-19, 154
    Second-generation, 10
    SSC-1b Sepal, 155
    SSC2b, 155
    SSC-X-4, 154
    SSC-X-5, 154
    SS-N-1 Scrubber, 8, 155
    SS-N-3a/c, 171, 275
    SS-N-3a Shaddock, 155
    SS-N-3c Shaddock, 155, 156
    SS-N-7, 173, 275
    SS-N-12, 176, 275
    SS-N-19, 178, 275
    SS-N-21, 180
    SS-N-22, 182
    SS-NX-24, 154, 184, 276
Cryptography, 52
Cuba, 8, 214, 236
Cuban Missile Crisis of October 1962, 8, 192, 214
Cyclotrons, 5
Czechoslovakia, 16, 196, 198, 222

Dardanelles, 279
Declaratory policy, 2
Defense Council, 46, 50, 68
Defense industry, 47
Defense Intelligence Agency (DIA), 24, 194, 201
Defense spending, Soviet, reduction of, 4
Degelen Mountain, 334
Delta class submarines, 18, 112-15, 139-40
    Delta I, 10, 108-9
    Delta II, 12

Delta III, 12, 13, 109
Delta IV class, 13, 109
Denmark, 279
Department of Administrative Organs, 47
Department of Defense, (U.S.), 18, 51, 272
    Estimates of the size of the Soviet stockpile, 22-43
    FY 1989 *Annual Report*, 41
    Information on Soviet artillery, 200
    Information on Soviet nuclear reactions, 81, 82
    Report on Soviet ICBMs, 111-12
    Study of the PVO, 57
Department of Defense Industry (DODI), 47, 49, 68
Department of Energy (U.S.), 79, 81
    Office of Military Application (DOE-OMA), 41
Deployment policy, 2
Deputy Minister of Defense, 51
Deribin, Z.A., 76
Design Bureaus (KBs), 72, 73, 74-76, 95
Design Cycle, 95
Destroyers, 14, 279
Diesel-powered ballistic missile submarines (SSBs), 37, 61, 302-4. *See also* specific classes
Disarmament, 4
District party organizations (*Oblast*), 49
Dog House target-tracking radars, 57
Dollezhal, Nikolai, 81
Dolon, 18
Dual-capable weapons, 27

Early-warning (EW) radars, 57
Eastern Europe, 200
East Germany, 17, 65, 196, 197
    Production of heavy water in, 88
    SCUD-B missiles in, 222
Echo class submarines, 275
    Echo I, 273, 299-301
    Echo II, 158, 273, 284-86
Egypt, 222
Electronic intelligence (ELINT), 57
Employment policy, 2
Enhanced radiation (ER) capability, 198
ET-80, 14, 40, 274
Ethiopia, 236
Extremely low frequency (ELF) communications system, 19

FAT MAN bomb, 336
Fencer aircraft, 158
Fighter Aviation (IA), 57, 58
First Main Administration of the USSR Council of Ministers, 6
Fission (atomic), 2, 4-5, 80
Fitter A/D aircraft, 11
Foreign minister, 50
Foxtrot (SS), 302-4
France, 81, 337
Free Rocket Over Ground (FROG), 8, 191-92
    Deployment of, by non-Soviet Warsaw Pact forces, 17
    FROG-3, 8
    FROG-7, 14, 15, 56, 190, 198, 225-26, 275
    Reloadable launchers, 27
    Replacement of, 12
Frontal Aviation (FA), 59
Fuchs, Klaus, 88
Fursov Pile (F-1), 6

Index

General Staff, 46, 50, 51-52, 61
    Academy, 66
    And the operational chain of command, 66
    Main Intelligence Directorate (GRU), 70
    Operations Directorate, 52, 63
Gerasimov, I.A., 65
Germany
    Guided and ballistic missile programs, 6, 154
    Invasion of the Soviet Union (1941), 5
    Nuclear research in, 90, 92-94. See also East Germany
Glushko, V.P., 75
Golem I, 7, 105
Golem II, 7, 105
Golf class submarines, 8, 9, 13, 61
    Golf II, 37, 108, 190, 195, 206-7, 272
    Golf V, 112, 136
Gorbachev, Mikhail, 2-4, 50-51, 194
Gorshkov, Sergei, 19
Great Patriotic War, 7, 75
Greenland-Iceland-Norway (GIN) Gap, 279
Greenland Sea, 18, 109
Grisha, 329
Ground-attack fighters, 9
Ground Forces, 2, 7, 8, 198-202
    And the Air Forces, 58
    And the chain of command, role in, 46, 55-56
    Commander-in-chief of, post of, 10
    SSMs assigned to, 32-34
    Success of, in military operations, 9
    Survivability, 12
Ground-launched cruise missiles (GLCMs), 160-61
    SSC-1b Sepal, 37, 155, 160, 185
    SSC-X-4, 14, 154, 186
Groups of Soviet forces (GSFs), 46, 56
    Commands representing, 59
Grushin, P.D., 74

Hanford Reservation (U.S.), 86
H-bomb, Soviet, 6, 337, 349
Heavy water, 5, 88
    Moderated production reactors, 90
Helicopters, 236, 272, 275
Hen House radars, 57
High Commands of Forces (HCOFs), 63-64, 65
Hiroshima, 6, 333
Hotel class submarines, 8, 9, 13, 61, 273
    Hotel II, 108, 299-301
    Hotel III, 112, 136
Human Affairs Committee (U.S.), 344
Hungary, 17, 222

Iklé, Fred C., 24
Iklé/Wohlstetter estimates, 24-27, 41-43
Il-18, 236
Il-76, 58
Il-28 Beagle, 7, 9, 229, 230
Il-38 May, 11, 236, 264-65, 275
Ilyushin, Sergei V., 229
Indian Ocean, 279
Industrial Ministries, 69, 72-73
INF Treaty, 14, 54, 190, 194, 214
    And bomber forces, 98
    And cruise missiles, 154
    And GLCMs, 161
    Signing of, missile deployments as of, 196
    And the SCUD-B, 197
    And the SS-12M Scaleboard B, 215
    And SS-20s, 195
    And the SS-23 Spider, 218
    And SSMs, information about, 33, 34
Intercontinental Ballistic Missiles (ICBMs), 27-31, 98-105, 110-12
    Bases and Test Centers, 54
    Decision to concentrate on, 108
    Development of, 2, 7
    Firings, warnings of, 57
    Force, U.S., 10
    Fourth-generation, 11-12
    KBs for, 74
    Launchers, MIRVed, 30, 341
    Peacetime alert, level of, 16
    Production, rate of, 31
    Silos, 17
    SLBM launch-detection satellites, 57
    In the SRF, 53
    SS-6 Sapwood, 8, 98-99
    SS-7, 11, 101
    SS-7 Saddler, 9, 99
    SS-8, 11, 101
    SS-8 Sasin, 9, 99, 100
    SS-9 Scarp, 10, 11
    SS-11, 10, 11, 13, 28, 101, 108, 193
    SS-11 Sego, 10, 29, 121-23
    SS-13, 192
    SS-13 Savage, 11, 29, 123-24
    SS-17, 13, 30
    SS-17 Mod 3, 341
    SS-17 Spanker, 11, 29, 125-26
    SS-18, 13, 105
    SS-18 Mod 4, 341
    SS-18 Mod 4 Satan, 127-28
    SS-18 Satan, 11, 29, 30
    SS-19, 13, 30
    SS-19 Mod 3, 341
    SS-19 Mod 3 Stiletto, 129-30
    SS-19 Stiletto, 11, 29
    SS-24, 14, 30, 105
    SS-24 Mod 2, 13
    SS-24 Scalpel, 29, 131-32
    SS-25, 28, 105
    SS-25 Sickle, 29, 105, 133-35
    SS-X-16 Sinner Mobile, 118, 194
    SS-X-26, 13
Intermediate-range ballistic missiles (IRBMs)
    SS-5, 193
    SS-5 Skean, 9
    SS-20, 12, 25, 53-54
    SS-20 Saber, 190, 191, 193-95, 209-11
    SS-X-14, 192
    SS-X-15 Scrooge, 192
Intermediate-range Nuclear Forces (INF), 4, 190, 193
Internal security, 47
International Atomic Energy Commission (IAEA), 94
Isanin, N.N., 75-76
Isayev, A.M., 75
Isotope separation, 5

Index

I.V. Kurchatov Institute of Atomic Energy, 6
Izotov, S.P., 75

Japan, 6
Jet propulsion, 6
Joe tests, 336-37
Joint Chiefs of Staff (U.S.), 51, 52, 98, 116
Joint Committee on Atomic Energy (JCAE), 24
Joint Strategic Target Planning Staff, 52
Juliett submarines, 158, 273, 275, 284-86

Ka-25 Hormone A, 236, 268-69, 275, 278
Ka-27 Helix A, 236, 268-69, 275, 278
Kamchatka peninsula, 18, 19
Kanin class cruisers, 38, 273, 275, 279, 323-25
Kapustin Yar test site, 118, 190, 214
Kara class cruisers, 38, 273, 275, 278, 314-15
Karlskrona naval base (Sweden), 274
Kashin SAM class cruisers, 38, 273, 275, 279, 323-25
Kazakhstan, 332, 333-34, 335, 340, 348
Kazakh Test Site (KTS), 332-34, 336, 339, 341-46
Kerr, Donald M., 344
KGB. See Committee for State Security (KGB)
Khrushchev, Nikita, 8-10, 155, 199
Kiev class carriers, 38, 41, 273, 278, 307-10
Kildin class destroyers, 155, 273, 279, 323-25
Kilo class submarine, 276, 302-4
Kirov class cruiser, 14, 38, 61, 278, 311-12
Kola peninsula, 18
Komar class guided-missile boats, 156
Konyastan, 334
Korolev, S.P., 6
Kotlin class cruisers, 38, 275, 279, 323-25
Kr-85, atmospheric concentrations of, 86
Kresta class cruisers, 38, 275, 278, 316-18
Krivak frigates, 273, 326
Krupnyy class destroyers, 155, 273
Kurchatov, Igor Vasil'evich, 5, 6
Kurchatov Institute of Atomic Energy (IAE), 78
Kynda class cruisers, 38, 273, 275, 278, 316-18
Kyshtym Complex, 78, 79-81, 86

Laboratory No. 2, 6
Lama class missile tenders, 31
Lance missiles (U.S.), 27
Landsat photographs (U.S.), 81
Large phased array radars (LPARs), 57
Launch control centers (LCCs), 54
Lavochkin, S.A., 75
Legnica (Poland), 65
Leningrad, 72
Libya, 236
Limited Test Ban Treaty (LTBT), 333, 334, 337, 343
Liquid-propellant missiles, 9
Long-range air-launched cruise missiles (ALCMs), 98, 194-96
Long-Range Aviation (DA), 11, 59, 229
Los Alamos National Laboratories, 88, 344
Low-yield Threshold Test Ban Treaty (LYTBT), 333
Lyul'yev, L.V., 75

McFarlane, Robert C., 341
Main Operations Directorate, 52
Main Political Administration, 16, 47

Manhattan Project, 6, 90
Mediterranean Sea, 273, 279
Medium-range Ballistic Missiles (MRBMs), 190-94
   SS-1a Scudder (R-1), 6-7, 190
   SS-2 Sibling (R-2), 7, 190
   SS-3 Shyster, 7, 191
   SS-4, 8, 9, 25, 53-54, 193, 195
   SS-4 Sandal, 190, 191, 192, 195-97, 212-14
   SS-12M Scaleboard B, 12, 56, 190, 192, 193, 215-17; deployment of, 196; and the INF Treaty, 215
   SS-21, 14, 15, 17, 56, 194, 198
   SS-22, 12, 193, 195
   SS-23, 14, 15, 56, 194, 196, 201
Megatonnage, 24, 41-43
Middle East, 194
MiG-21 Fishbed, 9, 36, 58, 230
MiG-21 Fishbed-J, 11
MiG-21 Fishbed-L, 36
MiG-21bis Fishbed-L, 260-61
MiG-23 Flogger, 11, 36
MiG-23 Flogger B/G, 36, 234, 255-57
MiG-27 Flogger, 11, 36, 58
MiG-27 Flogger D, 231, 236
MiG-27 Flogger D/J, 253-54
MiG-29 Fulcrum, 14, 58, 231, 236
MiG-31 Foxhound, 14, 58, 231
Mike class submarines, 40, 41, 275, 276, 290-91
Military art, 20
Military districts (MDs), 16, 46, 52, 56, 59
Military doctrine, 20
Military-Industrial Commission, 70
Military intelligence (GRU), 52
Military organization, 46-67
Military-Transport Aviation (VTA), 59
Ministry of Aviation Industry (MAP), 72, 73
Ministry of Communications Equipment Industry, 73
Ministry of Defense (MOD), 46
   Administration of, 52
   Collegium, 51
   And the defense industry, 69-7
   Main Political Directorate of, 51
   And Research and Development, 68
   Senior appointments in, 50
Ministry of Defense Industry (MOP), 73
Ministry of Electronics Industry, 73
Ministry of Foreign Trade, 70
Ministry of General Machine Building, 72, 73
Ministry of Machine Building, 73, 81
Ministry of Medium Machine Building, 6, 68-69, 72-73, 81
Ministry of Power and Electrification, 81, 81
Ministry of Radio Industry, 73
Ministry of Shipbuilding Industry, 72, 73
Missile tenders (AEMs), 279
Missile test sites
   Kapustin Yar, 118, 190, 214
   Plesetsk, 118, 214
   Sary Shagan (Central Asia), 117-18, 119, 339, 341, 346
Mobilization, 52
Mongolia, 56
Montreaux Convention, 279
Mortars, 12
Moscow, 72, 73
Moscow Air Show, 229

Index

Moscow Institute of Atomic Energy, 6
Moskva class carriers, 38, 41, 273, 278, 307-10
Mozambique, 236
MP 6 class missile tenders, 31
Mya-4 Bison, 7, 9, 229
Multiple independently targetable reentry vehicle (MIRV), 11-12, 28, 30, 194
    SS-24 Scalpel, 13
    And submarine missiles, 98
Multiple reentry vehicle (MRV), 11

Nadiradze, A.D., 74
Nagasaki, 6
Nanuchka class patrol combatants, 160, 279, 327-28
National Command Authority (NCA), 50
National Defense Research Institute, 341
National Intelligence Estimate (U.S.), 336
Naval Aviation, 7, 11, 15, 61, 228-69
Naval intelligence (U.S.), 63
Navy, 2, 7, 16, 18-19, 272-310
    Baltic and Black Sea Fleets, 61-63
    Caspian Sea Flotilla, 61-62
    And the chain of command, role in, 46, 61-63, 66
    Long-range capability of, 13
    Non-strategic forces assigned to, 32, 35-36
    NORFLT, 61-62
    PACFLT, 61-62
    Stockpiles of, 37-41
Navy (U.S.), 278
Nevada Test Site (U.S.), 339, 340, 348
Nikolayev Shipyard, 14, 78, 278, 305
Nitrogen plants, 88
North Atlantic Treaty Alliance (NATO), 56, 116
    Allies, 17
    Greenland-Iceland-Norway (GIN) Gap, 279
    Strategy, "flexible response," 10
North Korea, 18
North Sea, 19
Norway, 279, 340
Norwegian Sea, 18, 19, 273
Novaya Zemlya test site, 332-36, 339-44
November, 299-301
Nuclear accidents
    Chernobyl, 81
    Kyshtym Disaster, 80-81
    Naval, 274, 277
Nuclear artillery, 12, 34-35, 203-5
Nuclear constants, 5
Nuclear depth bombs, 41, 272, 275
Nuclear mines, 272, 275
Nuclear parity, 8-12
Nuclear-powered ballistic missile submarines (SSBNs), 54, 63. See also specific classes
Nuclear reactors, 79-90
    Channel-type, 82-83
    Isotope reactor (IR), 88
    PWRs, 83
    RBMK, 83, 86
    VVER, 83
Nuclear stockpiles, 14-17, 22-43
    DOD estimates of, 22-24
    Uranium, 94
Nuclear tests, 332-82
    12 August 1953, 6, 7, 88
    29 August 1949, 332, 336
    Atmospheric, 332, 334, 335, 336-336
    Atmospheric and peaceful (PNEs), 332, 335, 337, 340, 341, 347-48
    First U.S. (1945), 5
    Identification of, 337
    Involving SSMs and ASMs, 337
    Thermonuclear, 88, 337
    Underground, 332, 334, 335, 337-46
    Underwater, 7, 332
Nuclear weapon test sites (See also Missile test sites)
    Kazakh (KTS), 332-34, 336, 339, 341-46 Nevada (U.S.), 339, 340, 348 Novaya Zemlya, 332-36, 339-44

Ogarkov, Nikolai, 13, 64, 66
Okean exercises, 273
Operational art, 20
Operational command structure, 46-67
Operational Maneuver Groups (OMGs), 13
Orenburg, 333, 335, 336
Oscar submarines, 91, 275-76
Oscar I, 280-81
Oscar II, 14, 40, 41
Over-the-horizon Backscatter radars (OTH-B), 57

Pacific Ocean, 18, 273, 279
Papa class submarines, 160, 275, 284-86
Patrol combatants, 279
Peaceful Nuclear Explosions Treaty (PNET), 333, 347
Pechora-Kama Canal, 347
Peenemunde test site, 190
Permissive action link (PAL), 16
Pill Box radars, 57
Pilyugin, N.A., 75
Plesetsk, 118, 214
Plutonium
    Bombs, 5, 336
    Production of, 6, 79, 81-87
Poland, 17, 65
Polaris submarine force (U.S.), 108
Politburo, 46
    And the Defense Council, 68
    Members, and the Defense Council, 50
Political administration chief (MPA), 53
Post-nuclear reconstitution, 53
Potsdam Conference, 5
President (Soviet), 49
Presidium of the Supreme Soviet, 46, 49, 50
Production
    Aircraft, 77
    Missile, 77
    Naval, 78
    Nuclear warhead, 78-94
    Weapons systems, 76-78

Radio-Technical Troops (RTV), 57-58
Ramenskoye Air Base, 73
Reagan administration, 120
Rear Services, 52
Research and Development, 15, 52, 68-98
Riga, 329
Rocket development, 6-7

Index

Rockets, operational-tactical and tactical, 196-98
Rocket Troops, 56
Romeo class submarines, 275, 302-4

Sakhalin Island, 279
Sakharov, Andrei, 6, 88
San Antonio de los Banos (Cuba), 236
Sarancha class patrol combatant, 279, 327-28
Sary Shagan test site (Central Asia), 117-18, 119, 339, 341, 346
Scientific research institutes (NII), 72
SCUD missiles, 8, 56
    Deployment of, 17
    Reloadable launchers, 27
    Replacement of, 12, 14
    SCUD-A, 108, 197, 222
    SCUD-B, 15, 190, 197, 220-23
Sea-based missiles, 105-9. See also specific weapons
Sea-launched cruise missiles (SLCM), 37, 158-60
    Non-strategic, 272
    SS-N-1, 278
    SS-N-3, 15
    SS-N-3a Shaddock, 38, 39
    SS-N-3a/c Shaddock, 171-72
    SS-N-3b, 278
    SS-N-3b Sepal, 171-72
    SS-N-3 Shaddock, 8
    SS-N-3 Shaddock/Sepal, 38, 39
    SS-N-7 Starbright, 10, 38, 39, 173
    SS-N-9 Siren, 10, 38, 39, 159, 174-75
    SS-N-12, 278
    SS-N-12 Sandbox, 12, 38, 39, 159, 176-77
    SS-N-19, 15, 278
    SS-N-19 Shipwreck, 12, 38, 39, 178-79
    SS-N-21, 25
    SS-N-21 Sampson, 14, 38, 39, 180-81
    SS-N-22, 272, 278
    SS-N-22 Sunburn, 12, 38, 39, 182-83
    SS-NX-24, 14, 184
Sea of Japan, 19, 196, 279
Sea of Marmara, 279
Sea of Okhotsk, 18, 19, 279
Secretary of Defense (U.S.), 24, 30, 41, 51
Seismic waves, 337-39, 340, 341, 346
Seismology, 332, 337-39, 340, 341, 346, 348
Semipalatinsk, 332
Shagan River, 334-35
Short-range attack missile (SRAM), 161, 232
Siberian Plant, 81
Sierra class submarines, 14, 39, 40, 41, 160, 276, 292-93
    And the SS-N-15 Starfish, 275
    And the SS-N-21 Sampson, 161
Single Integrated Operational Plan (SIOP) (U.S.), 52
Skoryy destroyer, 329
Slava class cruiser, 14, 38, 278, 313
Solid fuel missiles, 11, 12, 13
South China Sea, 18, 274, 279
South Yemen, 236
Soviet Academies of Sciences, 5, 68, 88
Soviet Constitution, 46
Soviet Naval Aviation (SNA), 35, 37, 41, 158, 228-69
    Nuclear-capable aircraft, 272
Sovremenny class destroyer, 14, 279, 319-20
Soya Strait, 279

Space program (Soviet), 8, 47, 49
Special forces (Spetsnaz), 56
Sputnick 1, 8
Square Pair radar-tracking ballistic missiles, 120
Stalin, Joseph, 5-6, 7, 8, 49
START negotiations, 25, 30, 98, 114, 272
State Commission for the Utilization of Atomic Energy, 81
State Committee for Foreign Economic Relations (GKES), 70
State Committee for Material-Technical Supply, 68
State Committee for Science and Technology (GKNT), 68, 70
State Committee for Standards, 68
State Defense Committee (GKO), 50
State Planning Committee (Gosplan), 49, 68, 50, 70-72
Steenbeck, Max, 92
STOL fighters, 278
Strategic Air Armies, 59, 66, 115-16, 228
Strategic Air Command (SAC), 54
Strategic Arms Limitation Treaty (SALT), 13, 272
    And nuclear stockpiles, 25
    SALT I, 101, 109
    SALT II, 30, 118
    Treaty definitions, of submarines, 112
Strategic bomber force, 98, 115-16
Strategic Rocket Forces (SRF), 2, 8, 32-34, 190-226
    And the chain of command, role in, 46, 52, 53-55
    Reload of SS-18 missile silos, 30
    Strategic importance of, 9, 16, 17-18
Su-7 Fitter, 9, 58, 234
Su-7 Fitter A, 36
Su-7B Fitter A, 262
Su-17 Fitter, 59
Su-17 Fitter C, 11
Su-17 Fitter C/D, 234
Su-17 Fitter C/D/H, 36, 258-59
Su-24 Fencer, 11, 14, 59, 234
Su-24 Fencer A/B/C/D/E, 250-52
Su-25 Frogfoot, 14, 231, 236
Su-27 Flanker, 58, 231, 236
Su-27 Flanker A, 14
Submarine-launched ballistic missiles (SLBMs), 2, 28, 31-32, 61, 98, 105-9, 112-15
    KBs for, 74
    Launchers, 106
    MIRVed, 109, 112, 113
    Non-strategic, 272
    And nuclear stockpiles, 25
    Prototypes, first, 108
    Solid-fueled, 12
    SS-N-1 Scrubber, 8
    SS-N-4 Sark, 8, 108
    SS-N-5, 10, 25, 108
    SS-N-5 Sark, 9, 108, 208
    SS-N-6, 10, 108, 113
    SS-N-6 Serb, 143-44
    SS-N-8, 12, 109, 113
    SS-N-8 Sawfly, 10, 113, 145-46
    SS-N-17, 109, 113
    SS-N-17 Snipe, 12, 114, 147
    SS-N-18, 13, 109, 113, 115
    SS-N-18 Stingray, 12, 114, 148-49
    SS-N-19, 14
    SS-N-20, 109, 113
    SS-N-20 Sturgeon, 13, 115, 120

Index

SS-N-23, 109, 113, 115
SS-N-23 Skiff, 151
Submarine tenders (AS), 279
SUBROC (U.S.), 40, 275
Supersonic dash, 9
Supreme High Command (VGK), 16, 46, 50-51, 53
   And the Armed Forces, 63
   General Headquarters of (*Stavka*), 51, 52
   And the Navy, control of, 61
   Nuclear reserve of, 63
   And operational formations, 66
   And the strategic bomber force, 115
Supreme Soviet, 49
Surface-to-air missiles (SAMs), 24, 61, 98, 116, 120, 273
   KBs for, 74-75
   Non-strategic, 272
   And nuclear stockpiles, 28
   Radars, 57
   SA-1, 57
   SA-1 Guild, 7, 14, 32, 58
   SA-2, 56, 57
   SA-2 Guideline, 7, 32, 58
   SA-5, 57
   SA-5 Gammon, 32, 58
   SA-10, 57
   SA-10 Grumble, 32, 58
   SA-N-1, 273, 278, 279
   SA-N-1 Goa, 38, 275
   SA-N-3, 273, 278
   SA-N-3 Goblet, 38, 275
   SA-N-6, 278
   SA-N-6 Grumble, 12, 38, 275
   SA-X-12B Giant, 13
Surface-to-surface missiles (SSM), 32-34, 98-105, 121-35, 197-98, 273
   Nuclear tests involving, 337
SUW-N-1 launcher, 278
Sverdlov class cruisers, 38, 61, 155, 278, 316-18
Sweden, 274, 337, 340, 341
Syria, 236

Tactics, 20
Tallinn Line, 120
Tamm, Igor, 6, 88
Tango class submarines, 275, 302-4
Tarantul III, 279, 327-28
Tatar Strait, 279
Tbilisi aircraft carrier, 14, 236, 278, 305-6
Teller-Ulam idea, 337
Terrain Contour Matching (TERCOM), 161
Theaters of military operations (TVDs), 46, 64-66
Theaters of war (TVs), 46, 63-66
   Oceanic (OTVDs), 46, 65, 66
Thermonuclear fuel, 6
Thermonuclear tests, 337
Thermonuclear weapons, 88, 336
Thiessen, Adolf, 90
Threshold Test Ban Treaty (TTBT), 333, 335, 341, 342, 346
Tomahawk (U.S.), 160, 161
Topography, 52
Transporter-erector-launchers (TELs), 56, 192, 198
Trans-Siberian Railroad, 110
Tritium production, 86, 88-90

Truman, Harry S., 5-6
Try Add radars, 57
Tsiolkovsky, Konstantin E., 6
Tsugaru Strait, 279
Tu-4 Bull, 7, 228, 229
Tu-16 Badger, 59, 229, 232
Tu-16 Badger A, 7
Tu-16 Badger A/C/G, 247-49
Tu-22 Blinder, 9-10, 59, 230, 233
Tu-22 Blinder A/B, 245-46
Tu-22M Backfire, 59
Tu-26 Backfire, 11, 14
Tu-26 Backfire A/B/C, 242-44
Tu-95/142 Bear, 59
Tu-95 Bear, 9, 229
Tu-95 Bear A, 7
Tu-95 Bear A/B/C/G, 237-39
Tu-142 Bear F, 11, 236, 263, 275
Tu-142 Bear H, 237-39
Tu-160 Blackjack A, 232, 240-41
Turkish Straits, 279
Turya, 329
Twentieth Party Congress, 8
Type-31 aircraft, 229
Type-65 aircraft, 40, 274
Typhoon class, 13, 18, 40, 112-15, 141-42
   Design of, 75, 109
   And the SS-N-16 Stallion, 275
   Under-ice operations, 19

U-235 bomb, 5
Udaloy class destroyer, 14, 279, 321-22
Unified System of Design Documentation (YeSKD), 95
United Kingdom, 337
United States, 8, 9, 13, 337
   Nuclear stockpiles, 24, 25, 26
   President of, as commander-in-chief, 46
   Program of live firings, 17
Ural Mountains, 333
Uranium, 5, 86
   —235, 336
   —238, 274, 336
   Production, 90-94
Uranium Commission, 4
U.S. Strategic Air Command (SAC), 30
Ustyurt Plateau, 332
Utka class, 272
Utkin, V.F., 74

V-1, 154
V-2, 105, 108, 154, 190
Very low frequency relay (VLF), 19
Victor class submarines, 273, 276, 296-98
   And the SS-N-21 Sampson, 161
   Victor II/III, 41
   Victor III, 14, 39, 160
Vietnam, 235, 274
Volga River, 333
Voloshin, I.M., 65

Wagner, Richard L., 22
Wagner estimates, 22-27, 41-43
"War plans," 52

Index

Warsaw Pact, 9, 235
    Allies, 17
    Forces, 51, 52
Water table, 339
Weinberger, Caspar, 24
Weinberger estimates, 24-27, 41-43
Whiskey class submarines, 158, 273, 274, 302-4
Wohlstetter, Albert, 22, 24
Wohlstetter estimates, 22-27

Yak-28 Brewer, 230
Yankee class submarines, 10, 13, 108, 112-15, 278
Yankee I, 12, 109, 137-38
Yankee II, 12, 109, 137-38
Yankee Notch, 39, 287-89
    Northern fleet, 18
    Pacific fleet, 18
    SSGN, 160, 276

Zaytsev, M.M., 65
Zenith-Rocket Troops (ZRV), 57, 58
Zossen-Wuensdorf (East Germany), 65
Zulu class submarine, 8, 108, 273, 302-4